# THE CHICAGO MANUAL OF STYLE

# The Chicago Manual of Style

EIGHTEENTH EDITION

**The University of Chicago Press**
*Chicago and London*

The University of Chicago Press, Chicago 60637
The University of Chicago Press, Ltd., London

First edition published 1906. Eighteenth edition 2024.
Printed in the United States of America

33 32 31 30 29 28 27 26 25 24 1 2 3 4 5

ISBN-13: 978-0-226-81797-2 (cloth)
DOI: https://doi.org/10.7208/cmos18

Library of Congress Cataloging-in-Publication Data

Title: The Chicago manual of style.
Description: Eighteenth edition. | Chicago ; London : The University of Chicago Press, 2024. | Includes bibliographical references and index.
Identifiers: LCCN 2024009783 | ISBN 9780226817972 (cloth)
Subjects: LCSH: Printing—Style manuals. | Authorship—Style manuals. | Authorship—Handbooks, manuals, etc. | Publishers and publishing—United States—Handbooks, manuals, etc. | Authorship. | Writing.
Classification: LCC Z253 .U69 2024 | DDC 808.02/70973—dc23/eng/20240305
LC record available at https://lccn.loc.gov/2024009783

♾ This paper meets the requirements of ANSI/NISO Z39.48-1992 (Permanence of Paper).

# Contents

# **Part II** Style and Usage

## **Part III** Source Citations and Indexes

# Preface

Rules and regulations such as these, in the nature of the case, cannot be endowed with the fixity of rock-ribbed law. They are meant for the average case, and must be applied with a certain degree of elasticity.
—*Manual of Style*, 1st ed. (1906)

The rules in *The Chicago Manual of Style* have never been carved in stone, as the preface to the first edition reminds us. Not only are they to be applied "with a certain degree of elasticity," but they are subject to periodic revision as publishing practices and cultural expectations evolve. For this edition of the *Manual*, its eighteenth, our editors have once again reconsidered the rules and recommendations established in previous editions and, with input from a team of advisers and many others both inside and outside the University of Chicago Press, updated them to meet the needs of a new era. Readers everywhere have come to expect instant access to documents from practically every period of recorded history, in a nearly endless variety of styles and genres, and "Chicago style" needs to make sense within this larger context. This edition, the most extensive revision in a generation, balances tried-and-true editorial logic with an attention to real-world usage based on evidence that is easier than ever to find and evaluate.

The challenges inherent in maintaining this balance can be illustrated with a story from the *Manual*'s history. The words *Roman* and *Arabic* have long been capitalized in the context of numerals, as they were in the first eleven editions of this manual (starting in 1906, long before *Chicago* was added to its title). But then the editors of the twelfth edition (published in 1969) decided to impose lowercase: Not only had Roman and Arabic numerals lost much of their literal association with the long-ago cultures from which they came, but lowercase would align with the similar pairing of *roman* and *italic* in the context of type (*italic* is related to the proper adjective *Italian*), where it was already the norm. This change, however, failed to catch on, as anyone can now discover from the latest dictionaries and other online sources, including searchable corpora that track how words and phrases have been used over time (even with respect to capitalization) in books and other documents. For this edition we have therefore reversed course, a rare but necessary concession to actual usage.

More significant is our support for capitalizing words like *Black*, *White*, and *Indigenous* when they refer to people (see chapter 8). Though such adjectives are not derived from proper nouns (a consideration that would normally argue for lowercase), and though some writers will prefer lowercase, capitalization adds a semantically useful distinction between these terms and their generic lowercase counterparts, one that is increasingly recognized by dictionaries and other authorities. We now also endorse the use of singular *they* as needed to refer not only to someone who is nonbinary but also to anyone whose gender is unknown or irrelevant (or concealed for reasons of privacy), a natural development in a language that lacks a dedicated gender-neutral pronoun for people—and one that increasingly reflects real-world usage. Chapter 5, in addition to covering singular *they* from the standpoints of both usage and grammar, now includes discussions of person-first versus identity-first language and related concepts in a thoroughly revised section on inclusive language developed with the oversight of our advisory board and other key reviewers.

This edition also adds some significant new content, including sections on Indigenous languages and sources (in chapters 11 and 14, respectively), which benefited from the input of reviewers who are experts in these subject areas. We also received expert oversight for the new material on Korean language and romanization (in chapter 11), which complements our existing coverage of Chinese and Japanese. This new content, like many of the updates and refinements in this edition, grew out of questions and suggestions from readers writing to us via our Q&A.

Our readers also asked for more coverage of fiction and other creative genres, though not always directly: The many questions sent to us over the years from writers and editors whose focus is more literary than academic have made it clear that these genres are important to our readers and that our coverage is long overdue. The new material (some of which was developed at *CMOS Shop Talk*, our blog in support of the *Manual*) can be found in chapter 12 (in new sections on formatting and punctuating dialogue), as well as in our expanded recommendations on the parts of a book in chapter 1 and punctuation in chapter 6. Fiction and related genres also play a role in chapter 11, where we discuss the use of italics in multilingual narratives and dialogue. These and other sections throughout the *Manual* have also been updated to consider the needs of independent authors who self-publish their work (and the editors and others who collaborate with them).

In response to evolving standards for content published in digital formats, we have expanded our coverage of accessibility. In addition to providing advice on writing alternative text (or "alt text") for images in chapter 3, we now include key terms related to accessibility in a revised and expanded glossary and a new section devoted to accessibility in our bibliography. In chapter 2, we discuss strategies for checking accessibility in ebooks and other electronic formats to ensure conformance with applicable standards. And in *CMOS Online*, we now present our numbered tables as accessible HTML-formatted text.

The chapters on source citation, a pillar of Chicago style, have been reorganized with both new and experienced researchers in mind. A detailed and thorough overview of our two systems of citation—notes and bibliography (our primary system) and the stylistically similar author-date—is the subject of chapter 13. This is followed in chapter 14 by examples organized by type of source, from books and journal articles to legal and public documents. And rather than continuing to relegate author-date examples to a separate chapter as in previous editions, we now present them alongside the examples in chapter 14 for sources that might be difficult to cite in author-date format based on examples of notes and bibliography entries alone.

We have also reconsidered our coverage of math. Though we wanted to retain our math-related content in some form, usage data from *CMOS Online* for the chapter dedicated to this subject (and the lack of questions about it directed to us over the years) suggested that this specialized content was rarely consulted by our readers. We therefore eliminated the chapter and instead cover mathematical variables and other key concepts in chapters 3, 6, 7, 9, 10, and 12, where we hope they will be more useful to general editors.

Other changes are intended to clarify existing terminology and to bring Chicago style up to date with current practices. For example, we now refer to *title case* and *sentence case* rather than *headline style* and *sentence style*. Not only are actual news headlines often capitalized like sentences, putting the term *headline style* at odds with its intended meaning, but the word *case* (from *upper-* and *lowercase*) is more usefully specific in this context than *style*. On the subject of title case, we now recommend capitalizing prepositions of more than four letters in the title of a work (*A Room with a View* but *Much Ado About Nothing*). It is increasingly rare to find longer prepositions lowercased in titles, and this change aligns Chicago more closely with contemporary usage. In another title-related update, we now advise capitalizing and italicizing an initial *The* in the title of a periodical that includes one (as in *The New Yorker*), making such titles more consistent with other types of italicized titles (though we still support dropping the initial article from periodical titles in source citations and index entries).

As the revision was nearing completion, the emerging role of AI (artificial intelligence) in writing, editing, and publishing prompted some additional changes. Chapter 4 now addresses the relationship between copyright and AI. In chapter 3 we show how to credit images created with AI. And chapter 14 now includes examples of how to cite text generated by a chatbot or similar tool. (As AI continues to move into publishing workflows, we will be taking notes for the next edition of the *Manual* while keeping our readers up to date through our Q&A and at *CMOS Shop Talk*.)

These and the many other updates for this edition (listed in more detail at *CMOS Online*) have been considered in light of the long history of this manual and the continuing debt we owe to the collective wisdom of previous generations. Publishing may forever be in a state of flux, but the principles of clarity and consistency—combined with an attention to detail—never go out of style.

On behalf of the University of Chicago Press
Russell David Harper
Spring 2024

# Acknowledgments

*The Chicago Manual of Style* strives to codify the best practices of an institution and an industry. Many voices contributed to this goal, including the readers (far too numerous to list here) who have challenged us with their questions and critiques and offered suggestions through our Q&A and other channels since the publication of the seventeenth edition in 2017. This edition also benefited from a host of publishing professionals who contributed their wisdom on matters large and small. All these recommendations were compared, vetted, and applied by this edition's principal reviser, Russell David Harper, who is grateful for the innumerable contributions and many perspectives that have brought this latest edition of the *Manual* up to date. We, in turn, are grateful for his command of all those matters large and small on this, the third revision he has led.

We began the process by assembling an advisory board whose members represent various communities of readers and areas of expertise and inviting their comments on a broad plan for updates and changes. Their subsequent guidance on our preliminary outline and the entire penultimate draft of the manuscript helped us sharpen the new and revised material as well as sections we hadn't planned to update. Many thanks to the following advisers:

Michael Clarke / Managing Partner, Clarke & Esposito

Benjamin Dreyer / Former Vice President, Executive Managing Editor and Copy Chief, Random House

Katie Dublinski / Associate Publisher, Graywolf Press

Patricia Feeney / Head of Metadata, Crossref

Jane Friedman / Owner, Jane Friedman Media; Publisher and Editor, *The Hot Sheet*

Kristen Ghodsee / Professor of Russian and East European Studies and Member of the Graduate Group in Anthropology, University of Pennsylvania

Peter Ginna / Freelance Editor

Ebonye Gussine Wilkins / Chief Executive Officer, Inclusive Media Solutions LLC

Sarah Ogilvie / Senior Research Fellow in Linguistics, University of Oxford

Peter J. Olson / Freelance Manuscript Editing Coordinator, JAMA Network

Stephanie Rosen / Director of Accessibility and Librarian for Disability Studies, University of Michigan

Carol Fisher Saller / Writer and Independent Publisher

Lourdes Venard / Lead Instructor, University of California San Diego Division of Extended Studies Copyediting Certificate Program; Education Editor, News Literacy Project

Karen Yin / Founder, *Conscious Style Guide*; Publisher, *The Conscious Language Newsletter*

Many other experts from outside the University of Chicago Press read and commented on specific sections during the development of the manuscript. We thank Rachel Chong, Amy Fountain, Lorisia MacLeod, and Bronwen McKie, who advised us on and contributed to our new coverage of Indigenous languages and sources. We are grateful to Geoffrey Pullum, who offered extensive commentary on our coverage of grammar. We are also indebted to Katie Lee, Deirdre Mullervy, Jee-Young Park, Laura Ring, Valencia Simmons, Chengzhi Wang, and Ayako Yoshimura for advice on specific languages; Stephanie Vyce on intellectual property; Angela Anderson on military terminology; Lars Vilhuber on data citation; David C. Hunter on UK public documents; Leslie Keros on legal citations; Do Mi Stauber on indexing; and Susan Karani Virtanen on a wide range of issues. And we once again owe a particular debt to Bryan A. Garner and William S. Strong for their authorship of entire chapters.

Ultimately, however, *The Chicago Manual of Style* is the collective responsibility of the University of Chicago Press staff. Mary E. Laur oversaw the revision and publication of this edition, including the process of bringing together the many people acknowledged here, and advised on the many incarnations of the manuscript. In parallel to our external advisory board, an internal group including Skye Agnew, Susan Allan, Michael Boudreau, Brendan Carrick, Fabiola Enríquez Flores, Tamara Ghattas, Caterina MacLean, Mollie McFee, David Olsen, Devon Ritter, and Christine Schwab reviewed the revision plan, outline, and draft manuscript and helped refine the recommendations. Krista Coulson, Jenni Fry, Denise Kennedy, Laura Leichum, Jill Shimabukuro, and Ashley Towne also contributed to the contents in their areas of expertise.

One unique aspect of the *Manual* is that press staff members serve as both authors and book team members, roles that sometimes overlap. Once the manuscript was complete, Jenni Fry supervised the copyediting, which was handled by Erin DeWitt, Elizabeth Ellingboe, Tamara Ghattas, Beth Ina, Caterina MacLean, Renaldo Migaldi, Mark Reschke, Lindsy Rice, Lily Sadowsky, Christine Schwab, Joel Score, Adriana Smith, McKenna Smith, and Stephen Twilley. Isaac Tobin designed both the print and online editions, and Jill Shimabukuro managed the typesetting, manufacturing, and other production tasks. Rossen Angelov and Aiping Zhang oversaw the development of the online edition, with guidance from Giovanna Roman and Wayne Willis and assistance from David Jiambalvo and Scott Mitchell. Jennifer Ringblom managed the marketing efforts along with Levi Stahl and Laura Waldron, while Brian Carroll and Lauren Keene ensured a smooth experience for our online subscribers. Alan Thomas and Garrett Kiely offered guidance throughout the process, while Andrea Blatz and Mollie McFee provided logistical support. And many other staff members contributed their knowledge and skills at various stages of the process, including Emily Dalton, Sarah Gardiner, Ed Martin, Richard Martin, Peter Milne, Richard Schoen, and Langchi Zhu. On behalf of the press, Diane Mankedick proofread the book and Do Mi Stauber prepared the index.

On a final note, we remain indebted to Margaret Mahan (1933–2018), principal reviser of the fifteenth edition and esteemed mentor to several contributors to this latest edition.

The University of Chicago Press Staff
Spring 2024

# Publishing and Editing

# 1 Books and Journals

## OVERVIEW

1.1 **Books and journals.** Books are organized according to a set of conventions that have been a focus of this manual since it was first published in 1906. Given their relative length and complexity, books can serve as a useful model for most other types of published documents. Articles published periodically in scholarly journals, which are a lot like chapters in books, have also played a role in this manual from the beginning. Since then, the advice has been expanded to apply not only to academic works but also to fiction and other genres. And though many of the recommendations herein are based on the needs of traditional publishers, they should also be useful to independent authors who self-publish their works.

1.2 **Publication format.** Many book publishers now offer their content in both print and electronic formats, though some books are made available in one format only. Many publishers also offer audiobook versions. Articles in academic journals are typically published both online and in print (often in that order), though some journals, particularly in the sciences, have moved to an online-only model. A few journals publish in print only, among them certain literary journals that feature fiction and poetry and the like, though these are sometimes also available in academic databases (e.g., as scanned pages or PDF files supplied by the publisher). All publishers, regardless of medium, depend at least in part on an electronic workflow and on detailed metadata to make their works available to the public on their own websites and through library catalogs, booksellers, and search engines. The principles that apply regardless of medium or format remain the focus of this chapter.

## THE PARTS OF A BOOK

### *Introduction*

1.3 **Divisions and parts of a book — overview.** Books are traditionally organized into three major divisions: the front matter (also called preliminary matter, or prelims), the text, and the back matter (or end matter). These divisions are generally reflected in how items are grouped in the table of contents. The front matter presents information about a book's title, publisher, and copyright; it provides a way to navigate the structure of the book; and it briefly introduces the book and sets its tone. It may also include praise from reviewers and information about related titles. The text proper comprises the narrative—including arguments, data, illustrations, and so forth—often divided into chapters and other meaningful sections (including, in some cases, an introduction and conclusion). The back matter acknowledges debts to the work of others and presents sources or source notes, appendixes, and other types of documentation supporting the text but outside its central focus or narrative. Scholarly books typically include more components than novels and other books meant for a general audience, but the basic structure is the same across genres. This section discusses the parts of a book according to the standard outline of these divisions and their components presented in 1.4.

1.4 **Divisions and parts of a book — outline.** The list that follows presents the traditional arrangement for the divisions and parts of a book, using lowercase Roman numerals for pages in the front matter and Arabic numerals for all the rest. Few books contain all these elements, and some books have components not listed here. Page numbers as well as indications of recto (right-hand page) or verso (left-hand page) may be applicable only to printed-and-bound books. Starting pages that cannot be assigned page numbers until after page makeup begin on the first available recto or, in some cases, the first available page, whether recto or verso (see also 1.5). Every page except for endpapers is normally counted in the page sequence, even those on which no number actually appears, such as the title and half-title pages, copyright page, and blank pages (see 1.6). Ebooks may omit some of these elements (e.g., the half title) and may relegate some of the front matter (e.g., the copyright page) to the back, but they typically retain the order for the main text. For endpapers, see 1.81.

| | |
|---|---|
| *Front matter* | |
| Praise page(s) | i (but see 1.17) |
| *or* | |
| Book half title | i (if no praise pages) |
| Series title, other works, frontispiece, or blank | ii |
| Title page | iii |
| Copyright page | iv |
| Dedication | v |
| Epigraph | v or vi |
| (Table of) Contents | v or vii |
| (List of) Illustrations | recto or verso |
| (List of) Tables | recto or verso |
| Foreword | recto |

| | |
|---|---|
| Preface | recto |
| Acknowledgments (if not in preface or back matter) | recto |
| Introduction (if not part of text) | recto |
| Abbreviations (if not in back matter) | recto or verso |
| Chronology (if not in back matter) | recto |
| *Text* | |
| First text page (introduction or chapter 1) | 1 |
| *or* | |
| Second half title or first part title | 1 |
| Blank | 2 |
| First text page | 3 |
| Subsequent chapters | recto or verso |
| Conclusion | recto or verso |
| Epilogue or afterword | recto or verso |
| *Back matter* | |
| Acknowledgments | recto |
| Appendix (or first appendix, if more than one) | recto |
| Subsequent appendixes | recto or verso |
| Chronology (if not in front matter) | recto |
| (List of) Abbreviations (if not in front matter) | recto |
| Glossary | recto |
| Notes (if not footnotes or chapter endnotes) | recto |
| Bibliography or references | recto |
| (List of) Contributors | recto |
| Illustration credits (if not in captions or elsewhere) | recto |
| Index(es) | recto |
| Reading group guide | recto |
| About the author (if not on back cover or elsewhere) | recto |
| Colophon (production details) | recto or verso |

## *Pages and Page Numbers*

1.5 **Book pages.** The trimmed sheets of paper in a printed-and-bound book are traditionally referred to as leaves (or, especially in older books, folios, a term that can also refer to page or leaf numbers; see 1.6, 14.54). A page is one side of a leaf. The front of the leaf, the side that lies to the right in an open book, is called the recto. The back of the leaf, the side that lies to the left when the leaf is turned, is the verso. Rectos are always odd numbered, versos always even numbered. Ebooks do not typically distinguish between recto and verso.

**1.6** **Page numbers.** Printed books are paginated consecutively, and all pages except for endpapers (see 1.81) and any blank pages at the very end of the book are counted in the pagination, whether the numbers appear or not (but see 1.17). Most books include pages on which page numbers do not appear—for example, the first few pages of front matter and any blank pages—so a page labeled with Roman numeral vi might follow five opening pages that do not carry numbers, or a page 25 might follow a page 23 (with a blank page in between). All pages, with or without a number (again, except for endpapers and any blank pages at the end of the book), are included in the total page count listed by publishers, booksellers, and libraries on their websites and elsewhere (see also 1.84). When it appears, the page number, or folio, is most commonly found at the top of the page, flush left verso, flush right recto. The folio may also be printed at the bottom of the page, and in that location it is called a drop folio. Drop folios usually appear either centered on each page or flush left verso and flush right recto. Pages inserted into printed books separately—for example, galleries featuring color illustrations or photographs printed on a different type of paper (see 1.44)—are usually unpaginated but are included in the total page count. Ebooks featuring reflowable text lack fixed page numbers, though most formats include location data to help orient readers in the text (see 14.59).

**1.7** **Roman numerals for front matter.** The front matter of a book is paginated with lowercase Roman numerals (see 1.4). This traditional practice prevents renumbering the remainder of a book when, for example, a dedication page or a foreword is added at the last moment. By convention, no folio appears on blank pages or on "display" pages (i.e., such stand-alone pages as those for the half title, title, copyright, dedication, and epigraph), and a drop folio (or no folio) is used on the opening page of each succeeding section of the front matter (e.g., table of contents, foreword, preface).

**1.8** **Arabic numerals for text and back matter.** The text, or the central part of a book, begins with Arabic page 1. If the text is introduced by a second half title or opens with a part title, the half title or part title counts as page 1, its verso counts as page 2, and the first Arabic numeral to appear is the drop folio 3 on the first page of text (see 1.52, 1.55). (Some publishers ignore the second half title in paginating their books, counting the first page of text as page 1.) Page numbers generally do not appear on part titles, but if text appears on a part-title page (see 1.54), a drop folio may be used. Arabic numbering continues for the back matter. As in the front matter, the opening page of each chapter in the text and each section in the back matter carries either a drop folio or no page number.

On pages containing only illustrations or tables, page numbers are often omitted (though still counted), except in the case of a long sequence of figures or tables. (When page numbers are retained, they are usually presented along with the running heads; see also 1.16.) Page numbers are also usually omitted from the author bio and colophon, and blank pages carry no numbers.

1.9 **Page numbers for multivolume works.** Books that run to more than one volume may be paginated independently or consecutively, a decision that depends on the index and the projected number of volumes. If an index to two volumes is to appear at the end of volume 2, consecutive pagination saves index entries from having to refer to volume as well as page number. In rare cases where back matter, such as an index, must be added to volume 1 later in the production process, lowercase Roman folios may be used for the back matter; these should continue the sequence from the front matter in that volume (counting any final blank page). For example, if the last page of the front matter is xii, the back matter would start with page xiii. Multivolume works that run into the thousands of pages are usually paginated separately to avoid unwieldy page numbers; index entries and other references to such works must include volume as well as page number. In either scenario—consecutive or separate pagination across volumes—the front matter in each volume begins anew with page i.

## *Running Heads*

1.10 **Running heads defined.** Running heads—the headings at the tops of pages—function, like page numbers, as signposts. Especially useful in scholarly books and textbooks, they are sometimes omitted for practical or aesthetic reasons—in a novel or a book of poems, for example. Running heads are occasionally placed at the bottom of the page, where they are referred to as running feet (to be avoided in a book with footnotes), or, more rarely, in the left- and right-hand margins. In endnotes and other places where the information conveyed by these signposts is essential to readers, placement at the tops of pages is preferred. In this manual, *running head* is used for this element wherever it appears. For preparation of running-head copy, see 2.81. Running heads may be supplanted in ebooks by similar navigational cues.

1.11 **Running heads for front matter.** Running heads are never used on display pages (half title, title, copyright, dedication, epigraph) or on the first page of the table of contents, preface, and so forth (see also 1.16). Any element in the front matter that runs more than one page usually carries running heads, and the same running head appears on verso and recto pages.

| *Verso* | *Recto* |
|---|---|
| Contents | Contents |
| Preface | Preface |

1.12 **Running heads for text.** Chapter openings and other display pages carry no running heads (see also 1.16). The choice of running heads for other text pages is governed chiefly by the structure and nature of the book. Among acceptable arrangements for scholarly books and other types of nonfiction are the following:

| *Verso* | *Recto* |
|---|---|
| Part title | Chapter title |
| Chapter number | Chapter title |
| Chapter title | Chapter title |
| Chapter title | Chapter subtitle |
| Chapter title | Subhead |
| Subhead | Subhead |
| Chapter author | Chapter title |

For books in creative genres, including novels and collections of stories or poems, the following arrangements are common:

| *Verso* | *Recto* |
|---|---|
| Book author | Book title |
| Book title | Book title |
| Book title | Chapter title |
| Book title | Story or poem title |
| *or, in a multiauthor book,* | |
| Story or poem author | Story or poem title |

Longer titles or heads may need to be shortened; see also 2.81. In general, the more important entity (starting with the name of the author) goes on the verso and an equal or lesser entity on the recto. Running heads that feature the book title on both verso and recto may be suitable for books without named chapters or other structural divisions, including some novels and picture books; another option for such books is to omit running heads (see also 1.16). In ebook formats, running heads may consist of a book's title generated automatically from metadata (see also 1.84).

1.13 **Subheads as running heads.** When subheads in the text are used as running heads on recto pages and more than one subhead falls on a single page, the *last* one on the page is used as the running head. When subheads are used as running heads on versos, however, the *first* subhead on the page is used as the running head. (The principle is the same as for dictionary running heads.)

1.14 **Running heads for back matter.** Running heads for back matter follow the same pattern as those for front matter and text (but see 1.15). If there is an appendix, "Appendix" (or "Appendix 1" or "Appendix A," etc.) appears verso, the appendix title recto. If there is more than one index, the running heads must differentiate them (e.g., "Index of Names," "Index of Subjects").

1.15 **Running heads for endnotes.** The running heads for a section of notes in the back of the book should give either the inclusive page numbers (preferred for extensive notes) or the chapter where the relevant note references are found in the text. If chapter numbers are used, it is essential that the running heads in the text also include chapter numbers (usually on the verso; see 1.12). Thus, two facing running heads in the endnotes might read:

| *Verso* | *Recto* |
| --- | --- |
| Notes to Pages 2–10 | Notes to Pages 11–25 |
| *or* | |
| Notes to Chapter One | Notes to Chapter Two |

For a fuller explanation, see 13.50.

1.16 **Omission of running heads.** Besides display pages in the front matter (see 1.11), running heads are omitted on part titles, chapter openings, and any page containing only illustrations or tables. (For the omission of page numbers, see 1.7, 1.8.) Some types of books may omit running heads entirely (see 1.12). Pages that include lines of text in addition to an illustration or table should include running heads. Running heads may also be included in long sequences of illustrations or tables to keep readers oriented.

## *Front Matter*

### TITLE PAGES

1.17 **Praise pages.** Some books add quoted endorsements or blurbs from reviewers at the beginning of the front matter, starting on page i in a printed book (but with the folio omitted), before the half title (see 1.18). The half title then begins on the next available recto—for example, on page iii if there are one or two pages of blurbs or on page v if the blurbs run to three or four pages. (Alternatively, praise pages may be ignored for the purpose of front-matter pagination, in which case the half title is still counted as page i.) Many publishers also use the back cover (and sometimes the front) for praise, either in addition to or instead of using the first pages of the book (see also 1.79).

1.18 **Half title.** The half title (usually page i in a printed book, no folio) normally consists only of the main title (less any subtitle) and is usually counted as the very first page in a printed-and-bound book (but see 1.17). All other information—including author name, publisher, and edition—is omitted.

1.19 **Series title.** The verso following the half-title page (usually page ii in a printed book) is usually blank. But if the book is part of a series, it may include the title and volume number of the series, the name of the general editor of the series, and sometimes the titles of previously published books in the series. If the list of titles runs to more than one page, it may be continued at the very end of the back matter. If the list is very short, the series information may be put at the top of the copyright page. (Alternatively, the series title, volume, and editor may appear on the title page.) If the book is the published proceedings of a symposium, the title of the symposium, the date(s) it was held, and other relevant details may appear on page ii. Some publishers list an author's previous publications on page ii; Chicago generally lists these on the jacket or back cover (see 1.75).

1.20 **Frontispiece or two-page title.** Some books include an illustration called a frontispiece, which traditionally appears on page ii, opposite the title page. Page ii might instead be used for a title page across pages ii and iii. If a book includes both series information and a frontispiece (see 1.19), the series info may be placed on page ii (opposite the title page) and the frontispiece either on the verso facing the table of contents (e.g., in a book that includes a dedication but no epigraph) or on the verso facing Arabic page 1.

1.21 **Title page.** The title page (usually page iii or sometimes pages ii and iii) includes the following elements:

- Full title of the book
- Subtitle, if any
- The names of the author(s), editor(s) ("Edited by"), and translator(s) ("Translated by" or "Translated from the French by" or whatever applies)
- Edition number, for a new edition (see 1.27, 1.28)
- Name and location (city or cities) of publisher

Book titles are often presented in title case on the title page (see 8.160). Book designers, however, have creative license to apply all caps, lowercase, or other capitalization styles on the title page for aesthetic reasons. Designers may likewise omit a colon or other punctuation between title and subtitle if they are differentiated by type size or style. (The title metadata that determines how a book title will appear on the publisher's website and elsewhere is normally entered in title case regardless of how it appears on the title page; see 1.84.) The author's name should appear in the form preferred by the author or by which the author is generally known (as should the name of any editor or translator); Chicago usually omits any academic degrees or affiliations (but see 1.75). A publisher's logo may appear on the title page. Some publishers include the date of publication, which should correspond to the copyright date if possible (see 1.24). Unless they publish under a company name or imprint, independent authors can omit information about the publisher (though some commercial self-publishing platforms may add their own imprints).

## COPYRIGHT PAGE

1.22 **Components of a copyright page.** The Copyright Act of 1989 does not require that published works carry a copyright notice in order to secure copyright protection; nevertheless, most publishers continue to carry the notice to discourage infringement. The copyright notice is just one of several items typically included on the copyright page (usually page iv). Books published by the University of Chicago Press include the following:

- Publisher's address
- Copublisher's address (if applicable)
- Creative Commons statement (if applicable; see also 4.72)
- Copyright notice—including, if applicable, copyright dates of previous editions

and indication of copyright renewal or other changes, and followed by the statement "All rights reserved" and related language
- Publication date, including publishing history
- Country of printing
- Impression line, indicating number and year of current printing (but see 1.31)
- International Standard Book Number (ISBN) for each available format (e.g., cloth, paper, ebook)
- For continuously published resources, the International Standard Serial Number (ISSN), one for each available format, in addition to the ISBN
- A digital object identifier (DOI), if any
- For translations, indication of original-language title, publisher, and copyright
- Acknowledgments, permissions, and other credits, including design credits and acknowledgment of grants, if applicable and space permitting
- Any disclaimers or other notices about the content of the book
- Cataloging-in-Publication (CIP) data
- Paper durability statement

For an example, see figure 1.1. Information included by other publishers may vary from this list, and books published by the University of Chicago Press sometimes include additional elements. Some publishers include a land acknowledgment, a brief statement that recognizes Indigenous groups who live or meet where the publisher operates and that acknowledges any applicable treaties. Self-published authors are encouraged to include, at a minimum, a copyright statement and a list of any assigned ISBNs, together with any other information that applies (such as an LCCN; see 1.38).

1.23 **Publisher's address.** The address of the publisher—and sometimes the addresses of overseas agents—is typically, though not always, given on the copyright page. Copublished books may include the copublisher's address. An address may be abbreviated, consisting, for example, only of a city and perhaps a postal code. The URL for the publisher's home page may also be included. Self-published authors may want to include contact information to facilitate correspondence from readers.

1.24 **Copyright notice.** The usual notice consists of three parts: the symbol ©, the first year the book is published, and the name of the copyright owner. This may be followed by the phrase "All rights reserved" (and any additional language required by the publisher) and a statement of publication date or publishing history (see 1.27, 4.42). (See fig. 1.1 for an example of Chicago's copyright notice.) The year of publication should correspond to the copyright date. If a book is physically available near the end of a year but not formally published until the beginning of the

The University of Chicago Press, Chicago 60637
The University of Chicago Press, Ltd., London
© 2023 by The University of Chicago
All rights reserved. No part of this book may be used or reproduced in any manner whatsoever without written permission, except in the case of brief quotations in critical articles and reviews. For more information, contact the University of Chicago Press, 1427 E. 60th St., Chicago, IL 60637.
Published 2023
Printed in the United States of America

32 31 30 29 28 27 26 25 24 23    1 2 3 4 5

ISBN-13: 978-0-226-82413-0 (cloth)
ISBN-13: 978-0-226-82414-7 (ebook)
DOI: https://doi.org/10.7208/chicago/9780226824147.001.0001

Publication of this book has been aided by a grant from the Bevington Fund.

Library of Congress Cataloging-in-Publication Data

Names: Muka, Samantha, author.
Title: Oceans under glass : tank craft and the sciences of the sea / Samantha Muka.
Other titles: Oceans in depth.
Description: Chicago : University of Chicago Press, 2023. | Series: Oceans in depth | Includes bibliographical references and index.
Identifiers: LCCN 2022020602 | ISBN 9780226824130 (cloth) | ISBN 9780226824147 (ebook)
Subjects: LCSH: Marine aquariums. | Coral declines. | BISAC: PETS / Fish & Aquariums | NATURE / Environmental Conservation & Protection
Classification: LCC SF457.1 .M85 2023 | DDC 597.177073—dc23/eng/20220617
LC record available at https://lccn.loc.gov/2022020602

♾ This paper meets the requirements of ANSI/NISO Z39.48-1992 (Permanence of Paper).

FIGURE 1.1. A typical copyright page, including copyright notice, impression date and number (denoting 2023 for the first impression), International Standard Book Number (ISBN) for each format, digital object identifier (DOI), acknowledgment of financial assistance, Library of Congress Cataloging-in-Publication (CIP) data, and paper durability statement. See 1.22.

The University of Chicago Press, Chicago 60637
The University of Chicago Press, Ltd., London

© 2014, 2021 by The University of Chicago
All rights reserved. First edition 2014.
Second edition 2021

Printed in the United States of America

31 30 29 28 27 26 25 24 3 4 5

FIGURE 1.2. Copyright notice of a second edition (2021), with impression line indicating that this edition was printed for the third time in 2024. See 1.25.

next, the later date is preferred as both copyright and publication date. Books published by the University of Chicago Press are usually copyrighted in the name of the university ("© 2024 by The University of Chicago"). Some authors, however, prefer to copyright their works in their own names ("© 2024 by Alison A. Author"), a preference discussed in 4.44. For information on copyright notices for journals, see 1.112; for a full discussion, see 4.40–48.

**1.25** **Copyright dates of previous editions.** Each substantially new edition of a book gets a new copyright date, and the copyright date of one or more of the most recent previous editions, subject to the publisher's discretion, may appear in the copyright notice (see fig. 1.2). (Note that this advice does not apply to a new impression, or reprinting, or to a paperback or electronic version that does not constitute a new edition; see 1.28.) If the new edition is so extensive a revision that it virtually constitutes a new publication, previous copyright dates may be omitted. See also 1.27, 4.42.

**1.26** **Copyright renewal or other changes.** The date of copyright renewal or a change in the name of the copyright owner is sometimes reflected in the copyright notice if the work is reprinted. Copyright renewal (no longer required for works published in the US after 1963; see 4.28) is shown in the following manner:

© 1963 by Maurice Sendak. © renewed 1991 by Maurice Sendak.

To indicate a change in copyright ownership (e.g., if copyright is assigned to the author or someone else after the initial copyright has been registered and printed in the first impression), the name of the new copyright owner is simply substituted for that of the previous owner. The copyright date remains the same unless the copyright has been renewed. Copyrights remain legally valid even if renewal or reassignment information cannot, for some reason, appear in a new edition or printing (see also 4.32–34).

1.27 **Publishing history.** The publishing history of a book, which usually follows the copyright notice, begins with the date (year) of original publication, followed by the number and date of any new edition. In books with a long publishing history, it is acceptable to present only the original edition and the latest edition in the publishing history. (A previous publisher's name need not be given unless the licensing agreement requires that it appear in the new edition.) Items in the publishing history may appear on separate lines; periods separate multiple items on the same line.

First edition published 1906. Eighteenth edition 2024.

Revised edition originally published 2010
University of Chicago Press edition 2019

1.28 **What constitutes a new edition?** *Edition* (as opposed to *impression*, or *printing*) is used in at least two senses. (1) A *new* edition, as in a second or other numbered edition, may be defined as one in which a substantial change has been made in one or more of the essential elements of the work (e.g., text, notes, appendixes, or illustrations). Though publishers' practices vary, for a book to call itself a new edition, a significant portion should consist of new or revised material—typically at least 20 percent, but sometimes less than that. A book whose text remains unchanged except for corrections of typographical errors is better described as a new impression or a reissue; if such a book also includes a new preface or afterword (or the like), it may be called an enlarged or expanded edition but would usually need to be revised throughout to qualify as a new edition. A traditionally published book reissued by the author independently after copyright has reverted to them does not constitute a new edition unless the content has changed significantly, even with a new title and cover; likewise, an independently published book picked up by a traditional publisher and reissued without significant changes does not constitute a new edition. (2) *Edition* may also be used to designate a reissue in a different *format* (e.g., a paperback, deluxe, or illustrated edition, or an ebook edition of a book previously available only in print) or under the imprint of a different publisher. Information about the new edition or format is usually included on the copyright page (see 1.27; see also 1.25). An edition other than the first is also designated on the title page: Second Edition, Third Edition, and so forth. (Note that some publishers may use “Revised Edition” instead of “Second Edition.”) Such phrases as “revised and expanded” are sometimes included on the title page in addition to a numbered edition statement but need not be, since the nature and extent of the revision are normally described in the prefatory material or on the cover.

1.29 **Country of printing.** The country in which a book is printed is usually identified on the copyright page (see fig. 1.1). In addition, if a book is printed in a country other than the country of publication, the jacket or cover must so state: for example, “Printed in China.” This information may be removed for publication in electronic formats but need not be. Books printed on demand may carry an additional statement added to the last page of the book (as part of the printing process and not by the publisher) that includes the country of printing when applicable.

1.30 **Impression number.** A printing of a book, or impression, traditionally consists of a set number of books, generally in the hundreds or thousands, printed at one time on an offset press. Each such impression, starting with the first, may be identified on the copyright page. (Note that a paperback edition of a hardcover book is considered a separate work with its own ISBN and would have its own impression numbering.) Chicago uses a system that comprises a series of digits listed after the publishing history. The first group of numerals, reading from right to left, represents the last two digits of succeeding years, starting with the date of the most recent impression. These are followed by a series of numbers that indicate current and possible future impressions. See figures 1.1 and 1.2. Such a system was designed to spare printers from having to generate new text. Some publishers prefer to signal each impression more explicitly (e.g., Second printing, May 2025); others omit the date. Impression lines can be useful in the case of a book in which corrections have been made to an earlier printing (but see 1.28) or to track down the source of a printing error. Because they are less meaningful for books printed on demand, some publishers omit impression numbers in favor of other versioning methods (see 1.31).

1.31 **Versions for digitally printed books and ebooks.** For books printed digitally on demand (or in smaller digital print runs) and for ebooks, the

The University of Chicago Press, Chicago 60637
The University of Chicago Press, Ltd., London
© 2022 by The University of Chicago
All rights reserved. No part of this book may be used or reproduced in any manner whatsoever without written permission, except in the case of brief quotations in critical articles and reviews. For more information, contact the University of Chicago Press, 1427 E. 60th St., Chicago, IL 60637.
Published 2022
Printed in the United States of America

31 30 29 28 27 26 25 24 23 22     1 2 3 4 5

ISBN-13: 978-0-226-68976-0 (cloth)
ISBN-13: 978-0-226-68993-7 (ebook)
DOI: https://doi.org/10.7208/chicago/9780226689937.001.0001

Originally published as *Hilma af Klint. Die Menschheit in Erstaunen versetzen* © S. Fischer Verlag GmbH Frankfurt am Main, 2020.

FIGURE 1.3. Part of the copyright page of a translation, including title and copyright of the original edition (as required by contract with the original publisher). See 1.32.

traditional system of impression numbers based on large offset print runs (as described in 1.30) will not apply. Digital printing systems can keep track of versioning by generating a date stamp and other identifiers, such as the city in which the copy was printed, to keep track of different versions of a book (information that typically appears on the final page of the book). For ebooks, a unique identifier such as the ISBN or DOI can be used in combination with a last-modified date to track revisions. An alternative approach, modeled on identifiers for software programs (and specified by some self-publishing platforms), uses version numbers. For example, 1.0 might indicate the original version; 1.0.1 might indicate a minor revision and 1.1 a more significant revision; and 2.0 would indicate a new edition. This information is included in an ebook's metadata (see 1.84); the last-modified date or version number may also be listed on the copyright page or elsewhere.

1.32 **Original-language edition of a translation.** If a book is a translation from another language, the original title, publisher, and copyright information should be recorded on the copyright page (see fig. 1.3).

1.33 **Acknowledgments, permissions, and other credits.** The copyright page, if space permits, may include acknowledgments of previously published parts of a book, illustration credits, and permission to quote from copyrighted material (fig. 1.4), unless such acknowledgments ap-

The University of Chicago Press, Chicago 60637
© 2021 by Paul Davies
The author has asserted his moral rights.
All rights reserved. No part of this book may be used or reproduced in any manner whatsoever without written permission, except in the case of brief quotations in critical articles and reviews. For more information, contact the University of Chicago Press, 1427 E. 60th St., Chicago, IL 60637.
Published 2021
Paperback edition 2022
Printed in the United States of America

31 30 29 28 27 26 25 24 23 22     1 2 3 4 5

ISBN-13: 978-0-226-81629-6 (cloth)
ISBN-13: 978-0-226-82387-4 (paper)
ISBN-13: 978-0-226-81632-6 (ebook)
DOI: https://doi.org/10.7208/chicago/9780226816326.001.0001

First published by Allen Lane, an imprint of
Penguin Random House UK, 2021.

Cover image: Cosmic microwave background, as observed by
the Planck spacecraft. © ESA and the Planck Collaboration.

Library of Congress Cataloging-in-Publication Data

Names: Davies, P. C. W., author.
Title: What's eating the universe? : and other cosmic questions / Paul Davies.
Description: Chicago : The University of Chicago Press, 2021. | Includes index.
Identifiers: LCCN 2021004010 | ISBN 9780226816296 (cloth) | ISBN 9780226816326 (ebook)
Subjects: LCSH: Cosmology—Popular works.
Classification: LCC QB982 .D383 2021 | DDC 523.1—dc23
LC record available at https://lccn.loc.gov/2021004010

♾ This paper meets the requirements of ANSI/NISO Z39.48-1992
(Permanence of Paper).

FIGURE 1.4. A copyright page acknowledging earlier publication by a different publisher and including a credit for the cover image. See 1.33, 1.82.

pear elsewhere in the book—as in an acknowledgments section (see 1.46, 1.65) or in source notes (see 2.51, 13.58). For more on illustration credits, see 3.30–38. For a full discussion of permissions, see chapter 4. Some publishers also credit the designer of the cover or interior on the copyright page (see also 1.82).

1.34 **Acknowledgment of grants and subsidies.** Publishers should acknowledge grants of financial assistance toward publication on the copyright page. Acknowledgments requiring more space or greater prominence may appear elsewhere, in a separate section in the front or back matter. Wording and placement, including the use of any logo, should be as specified (or at least approved) by the grantors. Financial assistance made to authors is usually mentioned as part of the author's acknowledgments (see 1.46, 1.65).

1.35 **Disclaimers and other content notices.** Some publishers add legal disclaimers to the copyright page—for example, a statement that the people and places represented in a work are intended to be fictional or that the contents are not a substitute for medical or legal advice. It should be noted, however, that such disclaimers offer no legal protection (see also 4.42–48). Other publishers use this space to alert readers to content that may be unsuitable for some audiences (in what is sometimes referred to as a content or trigger warning); any such notice should be worded to avoid spoilers.

1.36 **International Standard Book Number (ISBN).** An ISBN is assigned to each book by its publisher under a system set up in the late 1960s by the R. R. Bowker Company and the International Organization for Standardization (ISO). The ISBN uniquely identifies the book, thus facilitating order fulfillment and inventory tracking. In addition to appearing on the copyright page (see fig. 1.1), the ISBN should also be printed on the book jacket or cover (see 1.83). Each format or binding must have a separate ISBN (e.g., for hardcover, paperback, large print, ebook, and audiobook); if practical, the copyright page should list them all, but only if they are to be published simultaneously or nearly so. Note that self-published authors should use the same ISBN for any one format even if that format is handled by more than one distributor (e.g., IngramSpark and Amazon KDP). Additional information about the assignment and use of ISBNs may be obtained from Bowker (the ISBN Agency for the United States) or from the International ISBN Agency. These agencies also provide ISBNs and other resources to self-published authors, including information about copyright, barcodes, and related matters. Some books that are part of a monograph series may be assigned an

ISSN (International Standard Serial Number) in addition to an ISBN; for more information, contact the US ISSN Center at the Library of Congress or the ISSN International Centre. (For the use of ISSNs in journal copyright statements, see 1.112.) See also 1.84.

1.37 **Digital object identifier (DOI).** Publishers that have registered their books with Crossref or one of the other international DOI registration agencies should list the DOI that refers to the book as a whole on the copyright page (see fig. 1.1). A DOI is a permanent identifier that can be used to find a book or other resource in any of its available formats, either as a link (in the form of a URL that begins https://doi.org/) or using a metadata search tool like the one available at Crossref.org. (Crossref recommends always presenting the DOI as a link.) Like an ISBN, the DOI may also appear on the book jacket or cover and should be included as part of a book's metadata (see 1.84). DOIs may also be assigned to individual chapters; this is particularly useful when chapter authors or editors are different from those for the book or when chapters might be sold individually. See also 13.7.

1.38 **Cataloging-in-Publication (CIP) data.** Since 1971 most US publishers have printed the Library of Congress Cataloging-in-Publication (CIP) data on the copyright pages of their books. CIP data is available for most books that are made available to libraries, including simultaneously published ebook versions of printed books but excluding books published *only* electronically; also excluded are print-on-demand titles from self-published authors as well as certain other formats. An example of CIP data may be found in figure 1.1. To apply for CIP data, and for up-to-date information about the program, consult the Library of Congress's online resources for publishers. A related program through the Library of Congress called CYAC (Children's and Young Adults' Cataloging) supplements the CIP program by cataloging fiction for younger readers. Publishers who do not participate in the CIP program may still be eligible for cataloging by the Library of Congress through its Preassigned Control Number (PCN) program. Only US publishers are eligible for these programs. Similar cataloging programs are offered through Library and Archives Canada, the British Library (UK and Ireland), and the National Library of Australia. To date, books that have been self-published in the United States are not eligible for the CIP program through the Library of Congress but may be eligible for the PCN program; the PCN program assigns a Library of Congress Control Number (LCCN) to books, thereby facilitating cataloging by libraries. The CIP programs in Canada, the UK, Ireland, and Australia, on the other hand, do accept self-published works that meet certain eligibility requirements. Authors who want their works cataloged in national libraries can apply for these programs directly through the applicable library website, where they will also find any related requirements for depositing and registering their works (see also 4.49).

1.39 **Paper durability and environmental statements.** Durability standards for paper have been established by the American National Standards Institute (ANSI), which since 1984 has issued statements to be included in books and other publications meeting these standards. In 1992 the standards were revised by the National Information Standards Organization (NISO) to extend to coated paper. (The International Organization for Standardization offers a similar standard, ISO 9706, available from the ISO catalog.) Under this revision, coated and uncoated papers that meet the standards for alkalinity, tearing, and paper stock are authorized to carry the following notice, which should include the permanent paper sign (a circled infinity symbol):

> ♾ This paper meets the requirements of ANSI/NISO Z39.48-1992 (Permanence of Paper).

Some publishers are entitled to include logos or statements certifying that they meet certain requirements for recycled paper or paper that has been sourced or manufactured according to certain standards intended to minimize environmental impact. (It should be noted, however, that the goals of durability and sustainability do not always align.) For more information, contact the Forest Stewardship Council, an international organization established in the 1990s to promote sustainable forest management, or Canopy, a similar organization based in Canada. Statements related to paper durability or manufacturing standards included in a printed book may be removed for publication in electronic formats but need not be. In some cases, such statements must also be omitted from a printed book that includes paper from multiple sources, not all of which meet the applicable standards.

## DEDICATION AND EPIGRAPH

1.40 **Dedication.** Choice of dedication—including whether to include one—is up to the author. It may be suggested, however, that the word *dedicated* is superfluous; a simple “to” or “for” is usually sufficient (e.g., “To my parents”). Editors of contributed volumes do not customarily include a dedication unless it is jointly offered by all contributors. Nor do translators generally offer their own dedication unless it is made clear that the dedication is not that of the original author. The dedication usually appears by itself, preferably on page v (opposite the copyright page). A less common scenario is for the dedication to share page v with an epigraph (see 1.41).

1.41 **Epigraph and epigraph source.** An author may wish to include an epigraph—a quotation that is pertinent but not integral to the text—at the beginning of the book (but see 4.91). Some book epigraphs consist of more than one quotation, but they are usually limited to one page. If there is no dedication, the epigraph may be placed on page v (see 1.4); otherwise, Chicago usually places it on page vi, opposite the table of contents. Some publishers prefer instead to place an epigraph just before the first page of the main text—as a verso that counts as the last Roman numeral page in the front matter; as unnumbered Arabic page 2 if it follows a second half title (see 1.52); or as recto page 1 or, if it follows a second half title, page 3. If needed for reasons of space, the epigraph may instead be placed on the same page as (and beneath) the dedication (see also 1.40). Epigraphs are also occasionally used at chapter openings and, more rarely, at the beginnings of sections within chapters (see 1.55). The source of an epigraph is usually given on a line following the quotation, sometimes preceded by a dash (see 12.35). Only the author's name (in the case of a well-known author, only the last name) and, usually, the title of the work need appear; beyond this, it is customary not to annotate book epigraphs (but see 13.55). Note that some quotations may require permission before they can be used as epigraphs (see 4.91).

## TABLE OF CONTENTS AND LIST OF ILLUSTRATIONS OR TABLES

1.42 **Table of contents for printed books.** The table of contents for a printed book usually begins on page v or, if page v carries a dedication or an epigraph, page vii. It should include all preliminary material that follows it but exclude anything that precedes it. It should list the title and beginning page number of each section of the book: front matter, text divisions, and back matter, including the index (see fig. 1.5). If the book is divided into parts as well as chapters, the part titles appear in the contents, but their page numbers are omitted, unless the parts include separate introductions. Subheads within chapters are usually omitted from the table of contents, but if they provide valuable signposts for readers, they may be included (as in the print edition of this manual). In a volume consisting of chapters by different authors, the name of each author should be listed in the table of contents with the title of the

# Contents



FIGURE 1.5. Table of contents showing front matter, introductory and concluding essays, parts, chapters, back matter, and location of illustration gallery. See 1.42.

chapter (as for chapters 4 and 5 in this manual). In a book containing illustrations that are printed together in a gallery or galleries (see 3.6), it is seldom necessary to list them separately in a list of illustrations. Their location may be noted at the end of the table of contents (e.g., "Illustrations follow pages 130 and 288"). Note that for novels and children's books and other creative works, the naming and numbering of parts, chapters, and sections—or whether to include a table of contents at all—is a creative decision that is usually the responsibility of the author (but see 1.43).

1.43 **Table of contents for ebooks and audiobooks.** Although a table of contents is often omitted from printed novels and other creative works (see 1.42), most ebooks include one, and it is a required navigational element for the EPUB standard—a requirement that helps to ensure accessibility. A table of contents in an ebook may appear together with other elements in the front matter (including any lists of illustrations or tables), as in printed books; whether it appears there or not, a contents list is generally made available as a menu item in the application used to read the ebook. Unlike printed tables of contents, ebook contents typically list elements that precede the contents page or are otherwise absent from the contents page in the printed book. These may include the cover, title page, copyright page, dedication, author bio, and—as a menu item—the table of contents itself when it also appears in the front matter. Audiobooks, like ebooks, depend on tables of contents to allow readers to navigate from one chapter or section or the like to another; however, audiobook narrators do not generally narrate the table of contents. For more details related to ebooks, see the latest EPUB standard; for audiobooks, consult the audiobook specification from W3C.

1.44 **List of illustrations or tables.** In a book with very few illustrations or tables or one with very many, all tied closely to the text, it is not essential to list them in the front matter. Multiauthor books, proceedings of symposia, and the like commonly do not carry lists of illustrations or tables. Where a list is appropriate (see 3.39), the list of illustrations (usually titled Illustrations but entered in the table of contents as List of Illustrations to avoid ambiguity) should match the table of contents in type size and general style. In books containing various kinds of illustrations, the list may be divided into sections headed, for example, Figures, Tables (see fig. 1.6), or Plates, Drawings, Maps. Page numbers are given for all illustrations printed with the text and counted in the pagination, even when the numbers do not actually appear on the text page. When a gallery of illustrations is printed on different stock and

**ILLUSTRATIONS**

FIGURES



. . . . . . . . . . . . . . . . . . . . . . . . .

TABLES



FIGURE 1.6. Partial list of illustrations, with subheads. If the book contained no tables, the subhead "Figures" would be omitted. If it contained many tables, these would probably be listed on a new page under the heading "Tables." How best to list illustrations of various sorts depends as much on space as on logic. See 1.44.

not counted in the pagination, its location is indicated by "Following page 000" (or sometimes "Facing page 000") in the list of illustrations (see fig. 1.7) or, more commonly, in the table of contents (fig. 1.5). A frontispiece, because of its prominent position at the front of the book (see 1.20), is not assigned a page number; its location is simply given as frontispiece. Titles given in lists of illustrations and tables may be shortened or otherwise adjusted (see 3.41). For treatment of titles, see 8.158–69.

# *Illustrations*

Following page 46



FIGURE 1.7. Partial list of illustrations showing numbers, titles, and placement of unpaginated plates. (Compare fig. 1.5.) See 1.44.

## FOREWORD, PREFACE AND ACKNOWLEDGMENTS, AND INTRODUCTION

1.45 **Foreword.** The term *foreword* should be reserved for prefatory remarks by someone other than the author—including those of an editor or compiler, especially if a work already includes an author's preface (see 1.46). The publisher may choose to mention the foreword on the title page (e.g., "With a foreword by Imani Perry"). A foreword, which is set in the same size and style of type as the text, normally runs only a few pages, and its author's name usually appears at the end, following the text. The title or affiliation of the author of a foreword may be included along with the name, and a place and date may also be included. If a foreword runs to a substantial length, with or without a title of its own, its author's name may be given at the beginning instead of at the end. See also 1.48.

1.46 **Preface and acknowledgments.** The author's own statement about a work is usually called a preface. It is set in the same size and style of type as the text and includes reasons for undertaking the work, method of research (if this has some bearing on readers' understanding of the text), brief acknowledgments (but see 1.47, 1.65), and sometimes permissions granted for the use of previously published material. A preface need not be signed; if there might be some doubt about who wrote it, however, or if an author wishes to sign the preface (sometimes just with initials), the signature normally appears at the end (see also 1.45). When a new preface is written for a new edition or for a reprinting of a book long out of print, it should precede the original preface. The original preface is then usually retitled Preface to the First Edition, and the new preface may be titled Preface to the Second Edition, Preface to the Paperback Edition, Preface 2024, or whatever fits. (Even in the absence of a new preface, the original preface may be retitled to avoid confusion.) In a book containing both an editor's preface and an author's preface, the editor's preface, which may be titled as such or retitled Editor's Foreword, comes first and should bear the editor's name at its conclusion.

1.47 **Separate acknowledgments in front matter.** If the author's acknowledgments are long, they may be put in a separate section following the preface; if a preface consists only of acknowledgments, its title should be changed to "Acknowledgments." (Acknowledgments that apply to all volumes of a multivolume work may be presented only in the first.) Placing the acknowledgments in the front matter can make sense when it is important to acknowledge up front the contributions of people beyond those listed on the title page; such instances include certain edited volumes and works whose author consists of an organization or other group (this manual is an example of the latter). For most books, however, the acknowledgments are better placed at the back of the book, preceding other back matter—now the preferred placement for most University of Chicago Press books (see 1.65). See also 4.106–7.

1.48 **Introduction belonging to front matter.** Introductions as such rarely belong in the front matter. A short introduction by a book's author, especially if it discusses the contents or origins of the book, is usually better called a preface and placed accordingly (see 1.46). A more substantial introduction by the author—or any introduction that is integral to the text of the book—belongs not in the front matter but at the beginning of the text, paginated with Arabic numerals (see 1.53). A substantial introduction by someone other than the author, however (including a new introduction to a reprint or facsimile edition of a classic novel or other well-known work), is usually included in the front matter, just before the main text, but if it is not more than three to five pages, it may more appropriately be called a foreword (see 1.45) and placed before the preface (if any).

### OTHER FRONT MATTER

1.49 **List of abbreviations.** Not every work that includes abbreviations needs a separate list of abbreviations with the terms or names they stand for. If many are used, or if a few are used frequently, a list is useful (see fig. 1.8); its location should always be given in the table of contents. If abbreviations are used in the text or footnotes, the list may appear in the front matter. If they are used only in the back matter, the list should appear before the first element in which abbreviations are used, whether the appendixes, the endnotes, or the bibliography. A list of abbreviations is generally not a substitute for using the full form of a term at its first occurrence in the text (see 10.3). In the list, alphabetize terms by the abbreviation, not by the spelled-out form. See also 13.64.

1.50 **Publisher's, translator's, and editor's notes.** Notes on the text are usually treated typographically in the same way as a preface or foreword. A publisher's note—used rarely and only to state something that cannot be included elsewhere—should either precede or immediately follow the table of contents. A translator's note, like a foreword, should precede any element, such as a preface, that is by the original author. An explanation of an editor's method or a discussion of variant texts, often necessary in scholarly editions, may appear either in the front matter (usually as the last item there) or in the back matter (as an appendix or in place of one). Brief remarks about editorial method, however—such as noting that spelling and capitalization have been modernized—are often better incorporated into an editor's preface, if there is one.

1.51 **Accessible cover descriptions.** To make a book's cover accessible to people with visual impairments or other print disabilities, a description may be added in the front matter. If there is room on the copyright page, it may be added there. Otherwise, it is usually best to add it on its own page, under a heading such as "About the Cover." Such a statement may describe photographs and other images as well as any significant typographic features used for the title and other text. For example, "Cover description: Drawing of a black, oily beach with silhouetted pumpjacks on its shore. A large red sun in an orange sky streaked with wispy clouds looms overhead, seagulls floating aimlessly. The book's main title, *Oil Beach*, is styled in tall red capital letters shadowed in black, as on a vin-

# *Abbreviations*

| | |
|---|---|
| Abert | Hermann Abert, *W. A. Mozart,* trans. Stewart Spencer, ed. Cliff Eisen (Yale University Press, 2007 [1919–1921]) |
| *AmZ* | *Allgemeine musikalische Zeitung* (Leipzig, 1798–1848) |
| Anderson | Emily Anderson, trans. and ed., *The Letters of Mozart and His Family,* 2nd ed., prepared by A. Hyatt King and Monica Carolan (Macmillan, 1966 [1938]), 2 vols. |
| *Documents* | Otto Erich Deutsch, *Mozart: A Documentary Biography,* trans. Eric Blom, Peter Branscombe, and Jeremy Noble (Stanford University Press, 1965) |
| *Dokumente* | Otto Erich Deutsch, *Mozart: Die Dokumente seines Lebens* (Bärenreiter, 1961) |
| Edge/Black | *Mozart: New Documents,* ed. Dexter Edge and David Black, first published June 12, 2014, https://sites.google.com/site/mozartdocuments/ |
| Halliwell | Ruth Halliwell, *The Mozart Family: Four Lives in a Social Context* (Clarendon Press, 1998) |
| Köchel 6 | Ludwig Ritter von Köchel, *Chronologisch-thematisches Verzeichnis sämtlicher Tonwerke Wolfgang Amadé Mozarts,* 6th ed., ed. Franz Giegling, Alexander Weinmann, and Gerd Sievers (Breitkopf & Härtel, 1964 [1862]) |
| *MBA* | W. A. Bauer, Otto Erich Deutsch, and Joseph Heinz Eibl, eds., *Mozart: Briefe und Aufzeichnungen, Gesamtausgabe,* rev. ed. (Bärenreiter, 2005 [1962–1975]), 7 vols. [references are to letter number and line] |

FIGURE 1.8. A partial list of abbreviations that uses a mix of initialisms and other shortened forms for titles mentioned in the text. See 1.49.

tage vacation postcard." This description would complement the alt text required for the cover image in the ebook and in online catalogs and elsewhere (see 3.28). Covers that are purely ornamental or that consist entirely of text may not require a separate description in the front matter.

## *Text*

1.52 **Determining page 1.** The first page of the first chapter or the introduction (see 1.53) is usually counted as Arabic page 1. Where the front matter is extensive, however, a second half title, identical to the one on page i, may be added before the text. The second half title should be counted as page 1, the first of the pages to be counted with an Arabic page number (though the page number does not appear). The page following the second half title (its verso) is usually blank, though it may contain an illustration or an epigraph; in the absence of a second half title, an illustration or an epigraph placed on the last available recto before the main text usually counts as Arabic page 1 (but see 1.41). A second half title is also useful when the book design specifies a two-page spread for chapter openings; in such a case, chapter 1 starts on page 2 (the verso following the second half title). If a book begins with a part title, the part-title page is treated as Arabic page 1 in the same manner as a second half title (unless it is preceded by a second half title, in which case the part title would count as page 3). See also 1.5, 1.6.

### TEXT DIVISIONS

1.53 **Introduction belonging to main text.** Unlike the kind of introduction that may be included in the front matter (which is often more appropriately called a preface or, if by someone other than the author, a foreword; see 1.48), a text introduction is integral to the subject matter of the book and should not include acknowledgments or other material that belongs in the front or back matter. It is acceptable, however, to refer to the contents of the book ("In the first two chapters I discuss . . ."), though some authors and editors may prefer to limit such information to a preface. A text introduction carries Arabic page numbers. If titled simply Introduction, it does not normally carry a chapter number and is usually considerably shorter than a chapter. Authors should consider adding a descriptive subtitle even to such shorter introductions, and an author who has titled chapter 1 Introduction should be encouraged to give the chapter a more evocative title. Alternatively, some authors will use Prologue or Preamble or the like as the title, especially in novels or shorter works, and sometimes as a complement to an epilogue (see 1.60); such a title can usually stand on its own. Note that a new introduction to a well-known work is usually considered part of the front matter and numbered accordingly (see 1.48).

1.54 **Division into parts.** Some books benefit from division into parts (see fig. 1.5). Each part usually carries a number and a title and should contain at least two chapters (an exception may be made for a part that includes only an introductory or concluding chapter). Chapters are numbered consecutively throughout the book; they do not begin with 1 in each part. Parts are sometimes called sections, though *section* is more commonly used for a subdivision within a chapter. Part titles that do not include introductions usually begin recto, followed by a blank verso and a recto chapter opening. If a part includes an introduction—usually short, titled or untitled—it may begin on a new recto following the part title, or on the verso of the part title, or on the part title itself. A text introduction to a book that is divided into parts precedes the part title to part 1 and needs no part title of its own. Likewise, a conclusion needs no part title, though in a book with parts it should begin recto to avoid appearing to belong only to the final part. No part title is needed before the back matter of a book divided into parts, though one may be useful before a series of appendixes or a notes section.

1.55 **Division into chapters — general.** Most nonfiction prose works are divided into numbered chapters; such chapters are typically consistent in length but need not be. Authors should aim for short, descriptive titles, which tend to give readers a better overview of a book's contents than longer, more whimsical titles. Authors of fiction and related genres, on the other hand, may choose more creative titles—or no titles at all (see also 1.42). Each chapter normally starts on a new page, verso or recto, and its opening page should carry a drop folio (see 1.5, 1.6)—or sometimes no folio—and no running head (see 1.10–16). The first chapter ordinarily begins on a recto (but see 1.52). Chapter openings usually consist of the chapter number (*chapter* is often omitted), the chapter title, and the chapter subtitle, if any; together, these are referred to as the chapter display. Note reference numbers or symbols traditionally do not appear anywhere in the chapter display of printed books; accordingly, a note that refers to the chapter as a whole remains unnumbered and precedes the numbered notes (whether it appears on the first page of the chapter or in the endnotes). A chapter epigraph, sometimes considered part of the chapter display, may include a note reference, though traditionalists may prefer an unnumbered note. See also 13.55.

1.56 **Division into chapters — multiple authors.** In multiauthor books, the chapter author's name is usually given at the head of each chapter. An affiliation or other identifying information may be put in an unnumbered footnote on the first page of the chapter (see 13.59) or in a list of contributors (1.71). An unnumbered footnote may also be used to disclose the source of a chapter or other contribution that is being reprinted from an earlier publication. (For ebook formats that do not support footnotes as such, a source note or note about the author may need to appear immediately after, or be linked from, the chapter title or author's name.) When both the author's affiliation and the source of the contribution are given in the note, it is customary, but not essential, that the affiliation come first.

1.57 **Divisions for poetry.** In a book of previously unpublished poetry, each poem usually begins on a new page. Any part titles provided by the poet should then appear on separate pages (rectos) preceding the poems grouped under them. In a collection of previously published poems, more than one poem, or the end of one and the beginning of another, may appear on the same page.

1.58 **Divisions for letters and diaries.** Letters and diaries are usually presented in chronological order, so they are seldom amenable to division into chapters or parts. For diary entries, dates may be used as headings, and in published correspondence the names of senders or recipients of letters (or both) may serve as headings. The date of a letter may be included in the heading if it does not appear in the letter itself. Such headings in diaries and correspondence do not usually begin a new page.

1.59 **Conclusion.** The main text of a nonfiction book may end with a conclusion, in which the author typically makes some final statement about the subject presented and the implications of the study or poses questions inviting further investigation. A conclusion may assume the significance and proportions of a final chapter, with or without a chapter number; in such cases, authors should consider using a more descriptive title (see also 1.53). A conclusion may begin either recto or verso, but for a book divided into parts it must begin recto so that it does not appear to belong to the final part only.

1.60 **Epilogue or afterword.** An epilogue or an afterword is a comparatively brief section that comments on the text, sometimes obliquely, or brings a fiction or nonfiction narrative up to date. Such a section is sometimes added to a new edition of a book and may be written by a different author; in either case it is then usually called an afterword (cf. 1.45). On the other hand, an epilogue or an afterword is sometimes called a postscript, a term best reserved for comments by the book's author. An epilogue or afterword generally follows any conclusion and may begin either recto or verso, but for a book divided into parts or for an afterword added to a new edition, it should usually begin recto (see also 1.59); it is set in the same size and style of type as the rest of the text.

## TEXT SUBDIVISIONS

1.61 **Subheads — wording.** Subheads within a chapter should be short and meaningful and, like chapter titles, parallel in structure and tone. Well-organized subheads help readers navigate the text, making it more accessible. The first sentence of text following a subhead should not refer syntactically to the subhead; words should be repeated where necessary. For example:

SECONDARY SPONGIOSA
The secondary spongiosa, a vaulted structure . . .
*not*
SECONDARY SPONGIOSA
This vaulted structure . . .

1.62 **Subhead levels and placement.** Many works require only one level of subhead throughout the text. Some, particularly scientific or technical works, require further subdivision. Where more than one level is used, the subheads are sometimes referred to as the A-level subhead (the first-level heading after the chapter title), B-level, C-level, and so on (or A-head, B-head, C-head, etc.). Only the most complicated works need more than three levels. The number of subhead levels required may vary from chapter to chapter. A lower-level subhead may occasionally follow an upper-level subhead with no intervening text (a scenario that is sometimes called a "stacked head"), but when a section of text is subdivided, there should ideally be at least two subsections (e.g., two or more A-level subheads in a chapter or two or more B-level subheads under an A-level subhead). Occasionally, however, a single subdivision may be called for—for example, to emphasize a unique case or a special consideration. A single subdivision may also be needed for specialized sections like chapter endnotes (see 1.69). Subheads, which usually do not need to begin on a new page, are generally set on a line separate from the following text, the levels differentiated by type style and placement (see 2.22, 2.65). The lowest level, however, may be run in at the beginning of a paragraph, usually set in italics or boldface (as in the print edition of this manual) and followed by a period. It is then referred to as a run-in subhead (or run-in sidehead). Run-in subheads are usually capitalized in sentence case (see 8.159).

1.63 **Numbered subheads.** Unless sections in a chapter are cited in cross-references elsewhere in the text, numbers are usually unnecessary with subheads. In general, subheads are more useful to a reader than section numbers alone. In scientific and technical works, however, the numbering of sections, subsections, and sometimes sub-subsections provides easy reference. There are various ways to number sections. The most common employs double or multiple (also called multilevel) numeration. In this system, sections are numbered within chapters, subsections within sections, and sub-subsections within subsections. The number of each division is preceded by the numbers of all higher divisions, and all division numbers are separated by periods, colons, or hyphens. Thus, for example, the numbers 4.8 and 4.12 signify, respectively, the eighth section and the twelfth section of chapter 4.[1] The series 4.12.3 signifies the third subsection in the twelfth section of chapter 4, and so on. The system employed by this manual is chapter number followed by paragraph number for easy cross-referencing. A system of multiple numeration may also be used for illustrations and tables (see 3.11, 3.51).

1.64 **Ornamental or typographic breaks in text.** Where a break stronger than a paragraph but not as strong as a subhead is desired, one or more asterisks, a rule, or a type ornament of some kind (e.g., a fleuron, or ❦)—or simply a blank line—may be inserted between paragraphs, in which case the paragraph following the break typically begins flush left. In some cases, two levels of break may be specified, one intended to be stronger than the other. (Whatever the book design ultimately calls for, authors should indicate such breaks with asterisks; see 2.10.) A blank line has the disadvantage that it may be missed if the break falls at the bottom of a page. This quandary can be solved by differentiating the first few words of each paragraph that follows a break—for example, with SMALL CAPITALS. Another strategy is to insert an asterisk or similar element only where such breaks coincide with a page break, and only in print; in reflowable ebook formats, where page breaks depend on a user's device and font settings, all breaks must be visibly marked.

---

1. Multiple numeration using periods should not be confused with decimal fractions. Paragraph or section 4.9 may be followed by 4.10—quite unlike the decimal fraction system.

Moreover, such "context breaks" must be properly coded in ebooks as a matter of accessibility—for example, using the hr (horizontal rule) element in HTML in conjunction with CSS (to specify how the break will display). More details on context breaks are available from the DAISY Accessible Publishing Knowledge Base, which describes best practices for creating accessible audiobooks and digital text.

## *Back Matter*

1.65 **Acknowledgments in back matter.** Though acknowledgments may be placed in the front matter (see 1.46, 1.47), Chicago now prefers to place them in the back matter for most types of books. This placement is especially advantageous for novels and other books that depend on establishing and maintaining a certain tone that may be very different from the tone used for the acknowledgments. When the acknowledgments are placed in the back matter, any remarks intended to be read before the beginning of the book should be moved into a preface or a note on the text (see 1.50).

1.66 **Appendixes.** An appendix may include explanations and elaborations that are not essential parts of the text but are helpful to a reader seeking further clarification, texts of documents, long lists, survey questionnaires, or sometimes even charts or tables. The appendix should not, however, be a repository for odds and ends that the author could not work into the text. Relevant information that is too unwieldy or expensive to produce in print may be suitable for presentation on the publisher's website and under its aegis (a practice more common with journals). Appendixes usually follow the last book chapter, though an appendix may be included at the end of a chapter (introduced by an A-level subhead) if what it contains is essential to understanding the chapter. (In multiauthor books and in books with chapters that might be sold individually, any appendix must follow the chapter it pertains to.) When two or more appendixes are required, they should be designated by numbers (Appendix 1, Appendix 2, etc.) or letters (Appendix A, Appendix B, etc.), and each should be given a title as well. Appendixes may be set either in the same type size as the text proper or in smaller type.

1.67 **Chronology or genealogy.** A chronological list of events or a genealogy of characters may be useful in certain works. It may appear in the back matter under its own heading, but if it is essential to understanding the

# MADISON CHRONOLOGY

1787

| | |
|---|---|
| 27 May–<br>17 September | JM attends Federal Convention at Philadelphia; takes notes on the debates |
| 29 May | Virginia Plan presented |
| 6 June | JM makes first major speech, containing analysis of factions and theory of extended republic |
| 8 June | Defends "negative" (veto) on state laws |
| 19 June | Delivers critique of New Jersey Plan |
| 27 June–16 July | In debate on representation, JM advocates proportional representation for both branches of legislature |
| 16 July | Compromise on representation adopted |
| 26 July | Convention submits resolutions to Committee of Detail as basis for preparing draft constitution |
| 6 August | Report of Committee of Detail delivered |
| 7 August | JM advocates freehold suffrage |
| 7 August–<br>10 September | Convention debates, then amends, report of 6 August |
| 31 August | JM appointed to Committee on Postponed Matters |
| 8 September | Appointed to Committee of Style |
| 17 September | Signs engrossed Constitution; Convention adjourns |
| ca. 21 September | Leaves Philadelphia for New York |
| 24 September | Arrives in New York to attend Congress |
| 26 September | Awarded Doctor of Laws degree in absentia by College of New Jersey |

FIGURE 1.9. Opening page of a chronology. See 1.67. For date style, see 6.41.

narrative, it is better placed in the front matter, immediately before the text. For an example, see figure 1.9.

**1.68** **Glossary.** A glossary is a useful tool in a book containing many words from other languages or other unfamiliar terms. Words to be defined should be arranged in alphabetical order, each on a separate line and followed by its definition. (The term may be followed by a period, a colon, or an em dash, or distinguished from the definition typographically, or both.) A glossary usually precedes the notes and bibliography or reference list but may follow the notes, especially if terms listed in the glossary appear in the notes. A glossary that consists mainly of terms that do not appear in the text may be included as an appendix. See also 2.27 and, for an example, the glossary in this manual.

1.69 **Endnotes.** Endnotes, generally under the title "Notes," follow any appendix material and precede the bibliography or reference list (if there is one). Any notes to an appendix may be included with the endnotes and introduced by an appropriate subhead (Appendix); however, if the appendix consists mainly of tables or other data, it may be best to keep these notes with the appendix (see 3.77–81). The notes to each chapter are introduced by a subhead indicating the chapter number and often the chapter title. The running heads to the endnotes should identify the text pages or chapters the notes apply to (see 1.15). Endnotes are normally set smaller than the text but larger than footnotes. Notes are usually placed at the ends of chapters in multiauthor books (see 13.46); such chapter endnotes are a requirement for books with chapters that might be sold individually. For unnumbered notes and notes keyed to line or page numbers, see 13.55, 13.56, 13.57. For endnotes versus footnotes, see 13.46–51.

1.70 **Bibliography or reference list.** Bibliographies and reference lists are normally set smaller than the text and in flush-and-hang style. A bibliography usually precedes the index and follows the notes, if any. In a multiauthor book or a book with chapters that might be sold individually, a brief bibliography may be placed at the end of each chapter (see 13.66). For a discussion of the various kinds of bibliographies, see 13.68; for reference lists, see 13.111. For discographies and the like, which usually precede any bibliography or reference list but may instead be included as an appendix, see 14.162. For a full discussion and examples, see chapters 13 and 14.

1.71 **List of contributors.** A list of contributors may be appropriate for a work by many authors in which only the volume editor's name appears on the title page. The list (usually headed Contributors) may appear in the front matter, but the preferred location is in the back matter, immediately before the index. Names are arranged alphabetically by last name but not inverted ("Aiden A. Author," not "Author, Aiden A."). Brief biographical notes, affiliations, and contact information (if authorized by the contributor) may accompany the names. See figure 1.10. A work by only a handful of authors does not require a formal list of contributors if the authors' names appear on the title page and biographical data is included elsewhere in the book (see 1.56, 1.75, 13.59).

1.72 **Illustration credits.** Most books that include illustrations list any necessary credits adjacent to the illustrations themselves (a placement that may be stipulated by the owner of an illustration). In some heavily il-

## Contributors

**Danielle Allen** is the James Bryant Conant University Professor at Harvard University and the author and editor of many books of political theory, including *Education and Equality, Difference Without Domination: Pursuing Justice in Diverse Democracies,* and *Democracy in the Time of Coronavirus.*

**Yochai Benkler** is the Berkman Professor of Entrepreneurial Legal Studies at Harvard Law School. His work focuses on how institutions, particularly of law, technology, and ideology, shape power in economy and society. His books include *Network Propaganda: Manipulation, Disinformation, and Radicalization in American Politics* and *The Wealth of Networks: How Social Production Transforms Markets and Freedom.* His work can be freely accessed at benkler.org.

**Leah Downey** is a PhD candidate in government at Harvard University and a visiting academic at the Sheffield University Political Economy Research Institute (SPERI). Her research develops a political theory of economic policymaking, specifically a democratic theory of macroeconomic policy. Her work has been published in the *Journal of Political Philosophy, Foreign Policy,* and *The Guardian.*

**F. Christopher Eaglin** is a PhD candidate in strategy at the Harvard Business School and a visiting scholar in the Strategy Department the Fuqua School of Business at Duke. His research explores how to build inclusive and productive economies, focusing on the roles of entrepreneurship, corporate power, and public policy in both emerging and developed markets.

**Samantha Eddy** earned her doctorate in sociology from Boston College. She is currently teaching at the College of the Holy Cross.

FIGURE 1.10. Partial list of contributors to an edited collection. See 1.71.

lustrated books, however, it may be appropriate to create a separate list of credits and place it at the end of the book (usually before any index). Another option is to include the credits in a list of illustrations at the front of the book (see 1.44). For a full discussion of illustration credits, including format and placement, see 3.30–38.

1.73 **Index.** The index, or the first of several indexes, begins on a recto; subsequent indexes begin verso or recto. In a book with both name and subject indexes, the name index should precede the subject index. Indexes in printed books are usually set two columns to a page and in smaller type than the text. For a full discussion of indexes and indexing, see chapter 15.

1.74 **Reading group guide.** Many books, particularly in the categories of fiction and general nonfiction, now include a section (typically just before information about the author) intended to guide discussion in book clubs and similar reading groups. Such a section usually consists of a list of topics for discussion, often in the form of questions, and may run to several pages.

1.75 **Biographical note.** A brief note on the author or authors (including any editors, compilers, and translators) lists previous publications and, if relevant, academic affiliation (and may be accompanied by an author photo). When such a note does not appear in the back matter (usually as the final element; but see 1.76), it may appear in the front matter or, more commonly, on the back cover or on the inside flap of the dust jacket, according to the publisher's preference (see also 1.79, 1.80). If such biographical information appears in more than one place, the details, if not the wording, must be consistent.

1.76 **Colophon.** The last page of a book occasionally contains a colophon—an inscription including the facts of production. For an example, see the last page of the print edition of this manual. For another meaning of colophon, see 1.78.

1.77 **Errata.** In rare cases, errors severe enough to cause misunderstanding are detected in a finished book that has already been printed in significant numbers. If the copies have not yet been distributed, a separate page that lists errata may be supplied. An errata page prepared along with the rest of the text may be justified when all or part of a book consists of pages scanned from an earlier publication. It may be placed either at the end of the front matter or at the end of the book and should be listed in the table of contents. The following form may be adapted to suit the particulars:

ERRATA

| *Page* | *For* | *Read* |
|---|---|---|
| 37, line 5 | Peter W. Smith | John Q. Jones |
| 182, line 15 | is subject to | is not subject to |
| 195, line 8 | figure 3 | figure 15 |
| 23, 214 | Transpose captions of plates 2 and 51. | |

Today it is more common for publishers to list such errata online, a practice especially suited to technical manuals. Publishers who make significant corrections to electronic versions of their books can include in the corrected version a notice and description of the changes (or a link to such documentation online); any readers who received the uncorrected version may need to be notified of the update. See also 1.30, 1.31.

## *Covers and Jackets*

1.78 **Clothbound covers.** The traditional clothbound (or *casebound*) hardcover book—so called for the integument of cloth stretched over a cardboard cover—may include a paper dust jacket (see 1.80). Underneath the jacket, on the cloth itself (which these days may instead consist of a heavy paper), the spine is generally imprinted with the author's (or editor's) full name, or the last name only if space is tight; the title of the book (and any edition number); and the publisher's name. The subtitle is usually omitted. The publisher's name is often shortened or replaced by an emblem or device known as a colophon or logo. (For another meaning of colophon, see 1.76.) Considering a book as it stands upright on a shelf, spine copy on American publications is most commonly printed vertically (and read from the top down), but when space allows (as with longer books with wider spines), it may be printed horizontally (for easier reading on the shelf). The front panel may be blank, but it sometimes bears stamped or printed material, such as the title and author's name or the publisher's colophon or some other decoration. The back panel is usually blank, though a product code may be necessary for books with no jacket (see 1.83).

1.79 **Paperback covers.** The spine of paperback covers (and other flexible covers), like that of cloth covers (see 1.78), usually carries the author's or editor's name, the publisher's name or colophon or both, and the title. The front cover carries the author's or editor's name, the title and (usually) the subtitle, and, where applicable, the name of a translator, a contributor of a foreword, an edition number, or the like. (Chicago encourages publishers of translated books to include the name of the translator on the front cover in addition to the title page.) The back cover usually carries promotional copy, such as a description of the book or quotations from reviews or signed blurbs (see also 1.17, 12.38), a brief biographical statement about the author (see 1.75), the series title if the book is part of a series, and, sometimes, information about the publisher (see also 1.83). Some publishers also use the back cover to alert readers to potentially sensitive content (sometimes by providing a link to more information at the author's or publisher's website), though the copyright page may be a better place for such a notice (see 1.35). Note that some paperbacks include gatefolds, also called French flaps—extensions to the front and back covers that are folded into the book just like the dust jacket to a hardcover book (see 1.80).

1.80 **Dust jackets.** Hardcover books are often protected by a paper jacket (or dust jacket). In addition to the three parts to be found on the book cover itself, the jacket also has flaps that tuck inside the front and back covers. The front and spine carry the same kind of material as the front and spine of paperback covers (see 1.79). The material included on the back of a paperback cover is begun on the front flap of the hardcover jacket and completed on the back flap (where a biographical note on the author may appear; see 1.75). The back panel sometimes includes promotional copy from the publisher. See also 1.83. An alternative to the dust jacket is provided by the paper-over-board format known as a lithocase or PLC (printed laminated cover), which allows full-color images and type to appear directly on the hard outer case.

1.81 **Endpapers.** An endpaper is one of two folded sheets of paper appearing at the beginning and end of a hardcover book (or, more rarely, a book with a sturdy paperback or other flexible binding). Half of each sheet is glued against the inside of the cover, one to the front and one to the back; the base of each is then glued, at the fold (near the spine), to the first and last page of the book. Endpapers help secure a book within its covers. The free half of each sheet is called a flyleaf. Endpapers, sometimes colored, are usually of a heavier stock than the book pages, and they sometimes feature printed text or illustrations. Endpapers are not counted in a book's pagination.

1.82 **Credit lines for cover art.** If a credit line is required for artwork included on a jacket or cover, it normally appears on the back flap of the jacket or the back cover of a paperback or other book without a jacket. Credit for artwork on a paperback cover or on the actual cover (as opposed to the jacket) of a hardcover book may also appear inside the book, usually on the copyright page, since the cover is a permanent part of the bound book (see fig. 1.4). See 3.30–38 for styling of credit lines.

1.83 **ISBN and barcodes on book covers.** In addition to the International Standard Book Number (ISBN; see 1.36), book covers must include product and price codes (barcodes). These should appear at the foot of the back cover or dust jacket or any other protective case or wrapper. A detailed overview of the process and related resources can be found at the website of the US ISBN Agency, R. R. Bowker, or the International ISBN Agency.

## *Metadata, Abstracts, and Keywords*

1.84 **Metadata for books.** Metadata consists of the title and other details that identify and describe a book or other publication. Complete and accurate metadata allows publishers, libraries, and booksellers to share information with each other and with potential readers and to track sales and inventory. Metadata for a book is usually entered into a publisher's database (either by the publisher or by a third party) and, for content that will be shared, uses a standard syntax such as XML-based ONIX. Authors who publish their books via a commercial self-publishing platform typically supply and maintain basic metadata using the platform's publishing interface. Common metadata elements include the following:

- An ISBN or other unique identifier
- Format
- Title and subtitle
- Edition number
- Series title (if any) and number in series
- Publisher
- Publication date
- Author(s) and other contributors
- Biographical notes for contributor(s)
- Extent (e.g., page count of a printed book or the duration of an audiobook)
- Number and type of illustrations
- Subject/genre
- Description
- Blurbs/reviews
- Price
- Territory where the book is sold
- Target audience/age
- Creative Commons license (for open-access [OA] books)

Published lists of standardized codes correspond to specific metadata attributes; these are supplemented by codes and identifiers from related standards. For example, ONIX code A01 would be used to identify the author of a book whereas B01 would identify the editor—just two of more than a hundred codes that define various contributor roles. A different code, supplied by Thema, an international standard for subject codes, might identify that same book as belonging to the subject category for science fiction with a focus on time travel. Because metadata determines how a book will be displayed online by booksellers and libraries and in search results (and communicates information about rights and pricing and the like), it is important to enter it accurately and update it as needed. For more detailed information, consult EDItEUR, the international organization that maintains the ONIX for Books and Thema standards. Additional guidelines are available from the Book Industry Study Group (BISG), which maintains the BISAC subject codes used by many publishers in North America.

1.85 **Abstracts and keywords for books.** Abstracts and keywords, long a feature of journal articles, are now routinely required by publishers of academic books; commercial publishers do not generally require abstracts but do assign keywords. Unlike most of the metadata categories listed in 1.84, which are used primarily by publishers and others in the book industry to create listings, track sales, and the like, abstracts and keywords are designed to help readers find and assess a book. An abstract is a brief summary of a book's content, usually limited to a few hundred words or less; publishers may also require a summary of each chapter in addition to the abstract for the book as a whole. (Publishers of fiction and other nonacademic genres, including self-publishing platforms, usually ask for a description in lieu of an abstract.) Though they usually do not appear in the book itself (except in the sciences), abstracts may be added to the code of a book's web page to improve its visibility to search engines, and they may form the basis of a book's promotional copy or of the descriptive metadata shared with libraries and booksellers. Abstracts are generally supplemented by keywords. A keyword is a word or phrase that identifies an important concept or name in the book; as with abstracts, publishers may require keywords for individual chapters as well as for the book as a whole. See also 2.29, 2.30.

## THE PARTS OF A JOURNAL

### *Introduction*

1.86 **Publication formats for journals.** Many scholarly journals are offered in print and electronic formats simultaneously; increasingly, the trend is toward online-only publications, particularly in STEM (science, technology, engineering, and mathematics) fields. Even the few remaining print-only journals (often, but not exclusively, literary journals) generally rely on an electronic workflow (and may be made available online via academic databases). Electronically published journals usually contain all the material included in any printed counterpart except, in some cases, advertising. Most journals also make their back issues available online, including issues that predate electronic publishing. Electronic journals typically present articles and other content in one of two ways (and often both): (1) as PDF files that correspond to the pages of the journal's print issues (if any); or (2) as full-text HTML suitable for viewing in a web browser and containing features and supplementary materials not available in the print edition (see 1.87, 1.124). Some journals also offer their content in ebook and other formats.

1.87 **Noting differences between print and electronic versions.** Although a printed article should include all elements that are essential to understanding, interpreting, and documenting the text, many journals publish special materials electronically that are not available in print. These features—usually referred to collectively as supplementary data or supporting information—may include very large tables, supplemental reading lists, multimedia components, and large datasets that can be exported to third-party software for analysis; some of this material may constitute the basis of an online-only appendix (see also 1.124). In addition, some journals release unedited versions of manuscripts that have been accepted for publication. With the exception of these "in press" or "forthcoming" versions (which are similar to preprints; see 1.122), any electronic-only articles, appendixes, and other features should be acknowledged in the print version (either in the table of contents or in the applicable article). See also 3.26.

1.88 **ISSNs and DOIs.** The issues of a journal are typically identified by volume number and date. The journal as a whole is identified by an International Standard Serial Number (ISSN); electronic journals are assigned a separate ISSN distinct from any counterpart for print. A journal article is identified in three ways: (1) by a page range or article ID (see 1.91); (2) by the Copyright Clearance Center code, which includes the ISSN and other information, including an article number (see 1.112); and (3) by a digital object identifier (DOI). A DOI is a unique, persistent identification string assigned to an article, book, chapter, or other freestanding content. A DOI appended to https://doi.org/ forms the basis of a persistent link (a practice recommended by the DOI registration agency Crossref for DOIs wherever they are listed). See also 13.7.

1.89 **Journal volumes and issues.** A volume of a journal usually comprises the issues published in a calendar year, though some journals (e.g., *Modern*

*Philology*) prefer the academic year beginning in the autumn. The issues within a volume are typically numbered with Arabic numerals, each new volume beginning with issue number 1. In some journals, however, the cover month, cover date, or season (Spring, Summer, etc., usually capitalized in this context) is used in lieu of an issue number. In others, issue numbering does not start over with each volume, or the journal is numbered consecutively by issue only, with no volume number. For a journal published quarterly, a volume has four issues; for one published monthly, twelve issues. Some journals, however, publish two or more volumes in one year, depending on the frequency and length of issues.

## *Page Numbers and Running Heads*

1.90 **Page numbers for journals.** Page numbers in a printed journal usually start with 1 in the volume's first issue and run continuously to the end of the volume. An issue always begins on a right-hand page (recto) and ends on a left-hand page (verso); thus the last page of an issue is an even number (though the preceding recto may be counted as the last page of content) and the first page an odd one. If issue 1 ends with page 264 (or 263, if the content ends on the preceding recto), then issue 2 starts on page 265. To help readers identify and cite articles, electronic journals with printed counterparts should list the page ranges that correspond to the printed version alongside information for the article wherever it appears (e.g., in the table of contents, at the head of the article itself, and in the citation data for the article). See figure 1.11. This should be done even for articles that are published in an electronic format that does not feature page breaks. Articles published electronically ahead of print may need to employ placeholder folios (e.g., 000–000) until the print issue has been paginated. Articles that do not appear in the print version of a journal can use a separate page-numbering system (e.g., E1, E2, . . .), again running continuously to the end of the volume; page numbers for supplementary issues may be handled similarly (S1, S2, . . .). See also 1.91.

1.91 **Page numbers for journals that use a continuous publishing model.** To facilitate publication and citation of articles independent of print issues, many STEM journals have adopted a continuous publishing model, according to which each article is assigned a unique ID (which can be derived from the DOI for the article; see 1.88) rather than a traditional page range. PDF versions of such articles are each paginated starting with the number 1, and individual pages can be cited according to the article ID plus page number (e.g., 1234, p. 1; 1234, p. 2; etc.); such pagina-

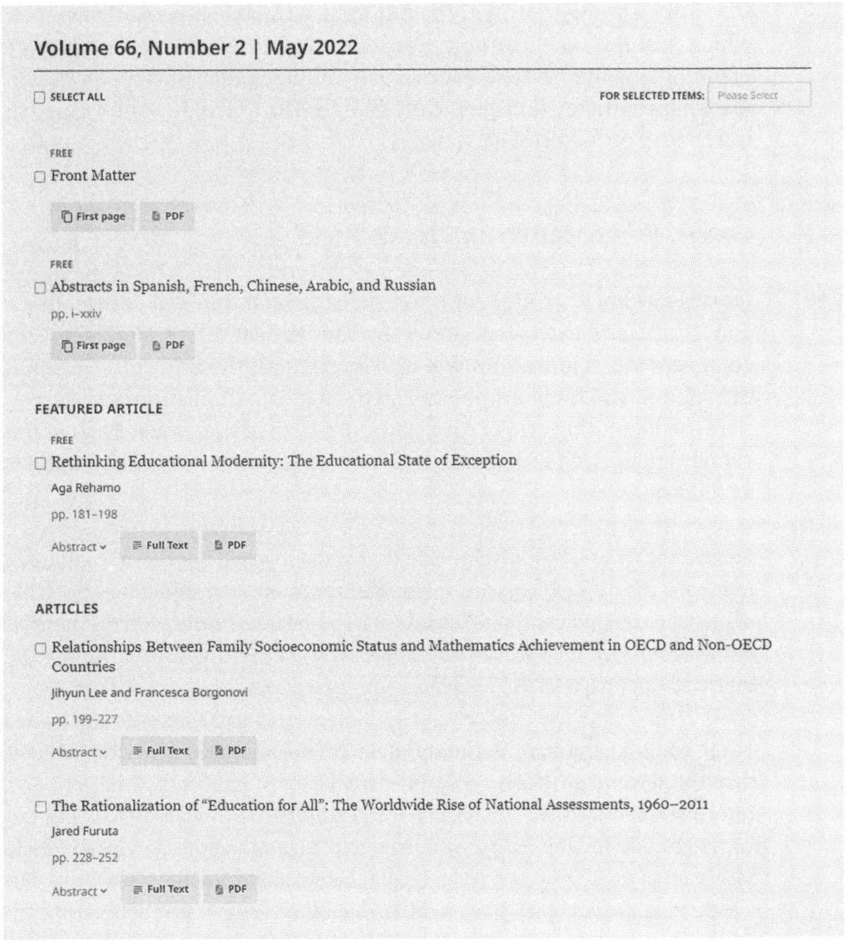
Volume 66, Number 2 | May 2022

SELECT ALL

FOR SELECTED ITEMS: Please Select

FREE

Front Matter

First page PDF

FREE

Abstracts in Spanish, French, Chinese, Arabic, and Russian

pp. i–xxiv

First page PDF

FEATURED ARTICLE

FREE

Rethinking Educational Modernity: The Educational State of Exception

Aga Rehamo

pp. 181–198

Abstract Full Text PDF

ARTICLES

Relationships Between Family Socioeconomic Status and Mathematics Achievement in OECD and Non-OECD Countries

Jihyun Lee and Francesca Borgonovi

pp. 199–227

Abstract Full Text PDF

The Rationalization of "Education for All": The Worldwide Rise of National Assessments, 1960–2011

Jared Furuta

pp. 228–252

Abstract Full Text PDF

FIGURE 1.11. Partial table of contents for an issue of an online scholarly journal. Note that the page numbers, as in many scholarly journals, are sequential throughout a volume. See 1.96.

tion is considered final and is used instead of the traditional pagination scheme in any print version of the journal. See also 14.71.

1.92 **Running heads in journals.** Journal running heads (or feet) typically bear the title of the journal (either spelled out or in abbreviated form); the author's surname or, for more than one author, a shortened version of the author list (such as Lee et al.); and the title of the article, usually shortened, or the name of the journal section (such as Brief Reports), or both. Arrangement of these pieces of information across rectos and versos varies among journals. For full-text, scrollable electronic articles, which will not have running heads per se, such information may be presented at the head of each article. Articles that have been downloaded for individual use typically show a URL and date of download in the header or footer of each page.

## *Covers, Front Matter, and Home Pages*

1.93 **Journal covers.** A printed journal is usually bound in soft covers, like a paperback, and each issue generally uses the same overall design and color scheme. A journal's spine usually contains the title of the journal, the volume and issue numbers, and the date of publication. It may also note the beginning and ending page numbers of that issue. Each of the remaining four sides of the cover also contains important information, as follows:

- *Cover 1*, the front cover, displays the title of the journal; the volume and issue numbers; the date of the issue; the publisher's name; and sometimes the table of contents or an illustration. The title of a special issue, along with the name(s) of the editor(s) of the special issue, appears on cover 1. The front cover may be offered as an image on the home page for each issue.
- *Cover 2*, the inside front cover, usually contains the masthead with the names of the editor(s) and staff, the editorial board, the journal's International Standard Serial Number (ISSN), its dates or frequency of publication, subscription information, addresses for business and editorial correspondence, and the copyright line for the entire issue (see also 1.112). Cover 2 may also include information about postage; a statement about paper durability (see also 1.39); a statement about copying beyond fair use; information about obtaining back issues; mention of a submission fee, if that is part of the journal's practice; information about indexing of the journal's articles; a statement about advertising policy; a caption for any illustration that appears on cover 1; and the URL of the journal's home page. If the journal is sponsored by a scholarly society or other organization, cover 2 may supply the name and address of the society and the names of officers. Occasionally on cover 2 but more often in the front or back matter of each issue, there may be a statement of editorial policy for the journal indicating what kind of articles the journal publishes as well as information for contributors about how and in what form to submit a manuscript.
- *Cover 3*, the inside back cover, is often given over to advertising, or it may be used for information for contributors. If the table of contents begins on the back cover, it may be completed on cover 3.
- *Cover 4*, the back cover, carries the barcode (if any) for the journal issue in the

lower right-hand corner. It may also carry the table of contents or titles of articles scheduled to appear in a forthcoming issue, or advertising. If the table of contents begins on cover 1, it may be completed on cover 4.

1.94 **Journal front matter.** Many of the elements discussed in 1.93 can equally occur in the front matter, or preliminary ("prelim") pages. Some journals, because they have a sizable staff and a large number of editors on their advisory board, have space on cover 2 only for the masthead and advisory board editors; the other items then appear in the front matter.

1.95 **Journal home pages.** Most journal home pages include all materials typically found on the covers and in the front matter of a printed journal (see 1.93, 1.94), starting with such essential information as the volume number and date of the current issue and a table of contents with links to the latest articles. A statement of copyright, frequency of publication, and ISSN (print and electronic) should also be made available from a journal's home page. In addition, journal home pages may also provide (or provide links to) some or all of the following resources:

- A fuller description of the journal and its editorial policies and information about staff members
- Information about the history of the journal and, if applicable, the sponsoring society
- More extensive information for authors about preparation and submission of electronic text, tables, math, art, and other files (e.g., video files or large datasets)
- Links to other home pages (e.g., the publisher's home page, the sponsoring society's home page, other relevant societies' home pages, and databases or other online resources associated with the journal or the field)
- Information about individual and institutional subscriptions
- Information about site license agreements and registration
- Links to tables of contents for previous issues of the journal
- Lists of articles scheduled for upcoming issues, or links to articles published online ahead of upcoming issues
- A journal-specific search engine
- Information about indexing and abstracting
- Society meeting abstracts and information about upcoming meetings
- Information about society membership
- Information about special services for subscribers (e.g., tables of contents distributed by email before publication in print)
- Links to related products or features (e.g., books, newsfeeds, blogs)
- Mail-to links for questions about manuscript submission and review, subscrip-

tions, back issues, advertising, copyright and permissions, books and new media for review, passwords and other technical issues, and other topics

These resources are generally not associated with a particular issue of the journal but are simply updated as needed (but see 1.114).

1.96 **Journal table of contents.** The table of contents, usually headed Contents, appears in the front matter or on the cover(s) of the print issue (see 1.93) and is also available from a journal's home page. The table of contents should include the title of the journal (or, for a special issue, the title of a special issue and the names of its editors); the date of publication; the volume and issue numbers; and the titles of the articles in the issue along with the authors' names and the page range for each article (or, in print, the page on which each article begins). It may contain section titles, such as Reviews, or subheads for specific content areas. Additional items listed may include review articles, book reviews, book notes, commentaries, editorials, or other substantive items, and should include a list of articles published only online or direct readers to the journal's website for a list of those articles. The electronic table of contents, in addition to providing links to each format of each item in the list, will include links to article summaries, which usually include an abstract and other information that can be viewed without a subscription. See figure 1.11. Full articles that are freely available to the public should be labeled as such. Most journals also include options for downloading citations to individual articles (see also 13.13), sometimes in the table of contents but usually with the articles themselves.

1.97 **Information for journal contributors.** Information for potential contributors can vary in length from a sentence to several pages. Some journals also include a statement of editorial policy. These components—when they do not appear on cover 2 or cover 3 in a printed journal (see 1.93)—may appear in an issue's front or back matter. In many cases, the print journal will contain a brief version of these components and direct potential authors to the journal's website for more details.

1.98 **Journal acknowledgments, announcements, and calls for papers.** Acknowledgments of reviewers, announcements of awards or conferences, and calls for papers are published periodically and may appear in the preliminary pages or at the end of a journal issue. If the issue is a supplement or special issue on a single topic, perhaps representing the proceedings of a conference or symposium, the print issue may begin with a title page that contains the title of the supplement, the name(s) of any guest editor(s), information about the source of the articles, and sponsorship information, if any.

1.99 **Journal errata.** Journals periodically publish errata, which, in print issues, may appear in the front or the back matter. Electronic journals should link from errata posted online to the articles that contain the errors; the articles themselves should be updated to link to or otherwise indicate the relevant errata. The entries in the table of contents for the original articles should also be updated to link to the errata. Small errors in online articles that are corrected after the original publication date (e.g., broken images and typographical errors) are best accompanied by a note indicating the nature of the changes and when they were made. See also 1.121.

1.100 **Journal retractions.** Occasionally a journal will issue a retraction of a previously published article that has since been identified as unacceptable (e.g., for reasons of plagiarism or data falsification). The retraction should include the title of the retracted article, the full author list, the volume and issue in which the article appeared, and a brief explanation for the retraction (usually two or three sentences). The electronic version of the retraction should include a link to the retracted article; the article itself, which remains otherwise intact, should include a link to the retraction and a notice that it has been retracted. This notice may include the words "RETRACTED ARTICLE" at the top of the scrollable HTML version and as a watermark on each page of the PDF version. For good measure, some publishers take down the HTML version. For more information, consult the website of the Committee on Publication Ethics (COPE), a nonprofit organization that publishes guidelines on retractions and related matters.

## *Metadata, Abstracts, and Keywords*

1.101 **Journal article metadata.** To make their content discoverable via search engines and in library and other bibliographic databases, journal publishers must record and maintain accurate article metadata. Metadata for a journal article includes such elements as the title and ISSN of the journal, volume and issue numbers, author(s) and author affiliation(s) (including any unique identifiers for either one, such as ORCID IDs for authors and ROR or Ringgold IDs for institutions), article title, page range or article identifier, publication date, and article DOI. Most of these data elements appear in print as well as online, though some of them function behind the scenes (e.g., author and affiliation IDs). Publishers typically share article metadata with abstracting and indexing services via a standard syntax such as the XML-based Journal Article Tag Suite (JATS), which is maintained by the US National Information Standards Organization (NISO) and used by many academic journals in the United States and elsewhere. The publisher may provide either the full text of each article in JATS markup or a truncated version containing only the article metadata and, optionally, the article references. Some services, such as Crossref and PubMed, require a custom format for article metadata. In addition to the items mentioned above, article metadata may include information about language, publication format, subject headings, access rights (including any Creative Commons license), sources of funding, and other pertinent details. See also 1.102.

1.102 **Journal article abstracts and keywords.** Most journals in the sciences and increasingly in the humanities publish abstracts along with their articles. These summaries, typically limited to a few hundred words or less, are usually supplied by the author and appear at the beginning of an article. Because abstracts are also generally made available as stand-alone items to allow subscribers and nonsubscribers alike to assess an article before they read or purchase it, they normally do not contain cited references or figure callouts or any other direct links to the article itself. Some journals have strict guidelines for what an abstract must include and how it should be structured—especially in the sciences. Abstracts are not usually required for letters, reviews, and other such materials (see 1.103). Abstracts are often supplemented by keywords—words or phrases that are intended to facilitate indexing (see 1.120). Though keywords normally repeat key terms found in the title, abstract, and text, synonyms or other variations may be added to anticipate search terms. Keyword metadata can be supplied by the author or derived (with the help of software) from a controlled vocabulary such as the Medical Subject Headings (MeSH) used by the National Library of Medicine. See also 1.101.

## *Articles and Other Components*

1.103 **Journal articles versus other components.** Journals consist principally of individual articles. Some journals also publish special kinds of articles—such as review essays, survey articles, or articles grouped as a symposium. Many articles include abstracts, which are considered part of the article (see 1.102). In addition to articles, journals may publish brief reports, letters to the editor, book reviews, book notes, announcements, calls for papers, errata, notes on contributors, and other ancillary materials.

1.104 **Journal article title, authorship, and other first-page information.** An article should include—on the first page or, in the full-text electronic version, at or near the top of the article—the title of the article, the author's or authors' name(s), and the copyright line for the particular article (see also 1.109, 1.112). Depending on the journal or on the needs of a given article, the first page may also include the affiliation of each author (and any relevant financial interests or potential conflicts of interest), an address for correspondence and reprints, dates of submission and acceptance of the article and date of electronic publication (most commonly in scientific journals), an abstract and keywords (see 1.102), an acknowledgment note, and sometimes an editor's note. A general section heading (e.g., Original Article or Review Essay) or a subject heading (e.g., Microbiology or Economics) may appear above the article title.

1.105 **Cross-references and other links in journal articles.** Full-text HTML journal articles typically include links to elements within the document (e.g., tables and illustrations, reference list entries, and notes) and often also to outside resources such as the sources cited in the reference list and subject-specific indexes or databases. They may also include links to supplementary materials not available in the print version (see 1.87). Articles are also typically accompanied by other linked items, including an article-specific contents list, links to the article in other formats (e.g., PDF), and links to the journal issue's table of contents, to the previous or next article in the issue, to the journal's home page, to search options and cited-by data, and to tools for citing and sharing the article. The display may also include thumbnail versions of the article's tables and illustrations.

1.106 **Journal article subheads.** An article, like a chapter in a book, may be divided into sections and subsections headed by subheads, sub-subheads, and so on (see 1.61–64). The number of subhead levels required may vary from article to article.

1.107 **Journal book reviews.** Many journals include a book review section. Such sections, usually headed Reviews or Book Reviews, vary greatly in length from journal to journal. Within a section, each review carries a heading that lists information about the book being reviewed. The heading includes the author's name, the title of the book, date of publication, publisher's name, number of pages (including front matter), and price. If the book is part of a series, the series title may be given.

Some journals include reviews of other journals or of films or other media. The name of the reviewer usually appears at the end of the review but occasionally follows the heading (and is more likely to follow the heading in the full-text HTML version); alternatively, reviews are given a separate title in the manner of regular articles, and the name of the reviewer follows the title at the head of the review. Book notes use the same form of headings as book reviews, but the text is much shorter and reviewers may be listed by their initials, a traditional practice that this manual discourages in favor of using full names. Some journals also publish a list of books or other materials received for review from publishers.

1.108 **Journal announcements.** Announcements include such items as notices of future conferences and symposia; calls for papers, award nominations, or research subjects; and employment opportunities.

1.109 **Journal contributors.** Journal authors and other contributors are listed at the head of an article as described in 1.104. The order in which contributors are listed is usually the responsibility of the lead author (and usually must be determined ahead of article submission), though the journal or discipline may have specific guidelines that must be followed. Basic information about contributors, such as their professional affiliations, typically appears with each article, usually at the head of the article or elsewhere on the first page. This information is also generally included as part of an article's metadata (see 1.101) and may be offered along with the abstract as part of an article's freely available online summary. Some journals offer an index of past contributors to the journal as a whole. Journals may also feature a special section with additional information about contributors, such as their publications or fields of study.

1.110 **Letters to the editor.** Letters to the editor are typically treated as a minor component of a journal, published irregularly if at all, and sometimes only online. In some scientific journals, on the other hand, letters appear as a regular, prominent feature, often with replies, and may contain equations, tables, and figures.

1.111 **Journal editorials.** An editorial is a regular feature in some academic journals and, in others, may appear on a particular occasion. When there is a change of some sort—a new editor, modifications in editorial policy or style, features added or dropped, or graphic redesign of the journal (see 1.125)—an editorial often announces and explains the change. A journal may provide an annual editorial summing up the year's activity. Some journals publish invited editorials, written by someone who is neither the journal's editor in chief nor a member of its editorial board, that comment on a particular article or group of articles. A special issue usually includes an introduction by the special issue's editor(s). The heading Editorial or Introduction is used, and the editor's name may appear at the end of the piece (a practice more common in print).

1.112 **Journal copyright lines.** In addition to the copyright line that appears on cover 2, each substantive article or element in the journal normally carries its own copyright line (or a notice that the article is in the public domain, as for works by US government employees; see also 4.72). This usually appears at the bottom of the first page of the article, below any footnotes on that page, or, for full-text articles online, at the head of the article or in some other prominent location. In journals published by the University of Chicago Press, the copyright line is usually the second of three related components: (1) information on the current issue, including the title of the journal, the volume and issue numbers, and the date of publication; (2) the copyright notice, containing the copyright symbol, the year, and the name of the copyright owner (usually either the publisher or the sponsoring society); and (3) a DOI (see 1.88) or other unique identifier.

*The Journal of Modern History*, volume 94, number 2, June 2022.
© 2022 The University of Chicago. All rights reserved. Published by The University of Chicago Press.
https://doi.org/10.1086/719491

Some journals list a Copyright Clearance Center (CCC) code containing the journal's ISSN, the year, the volume and issue numbers, the article number (assigned by the publisher), and the per copy fee for photocopying, payable through the CCC. Most but not all US journals use the CCC, which provides systems through which copyright owners can license the reproduction and distribution of materials in both print and electronic form. Its relations with equivalent agencies in other countries enable the CCC to collect fees for uses in those countries. Note that fees apply only to copyrighted material and not to articles in the public domain. See also 4.59–61, 4.110–11.

1.113 **Publication history for journal articles.** For all articles that are published online ahead of print, the date of electronic publication should appear as part of the article's history, in both the print and online versions, on the first page or otherwise near the head of the article. Some journals also include the date the article was submitted to the journal and the date it was accepted for publication. These dates provide important context for interpretation of the article; in the sciences, especially, what is known—or at least what has been reported—can change rapidly.

1.114 **Preserving the context of individual journal articles.** Publishers, libraries, and online aggregators typically offer journal content in the form of individual articles, letters, or reviews rather than in the context of the original issue as a whole. Publishers who seek to preserve the historical context of their back issues might consider making covers, front matter, and other ancillary materials from the original issue readily available along with the articles themselves. Such materials can provide important historical context about editors, sponsors, or even advertisers in the journal, all of which may be relevant in assessing the import of a work.

## *Tables and Illustrations*

1.115 **Tables in journal articles.** To ensure accessibility, tables in articles published online should be presented as HTML (see also 3.89); a link to an image of the typeset table prepared for print may also be provided. Table footnote citations can be linked to the table footnotes themselves; this is especially useful for navigation in very large tables. Links also allow readers to move freely from text to tables and back again, as well as from one table to another. Large or complex tables may be presented in a machine-readable file that allows readers to download the data and either repeat the analyses used in the article or use the data for their own analyses, perhaps in combination with data from other sources. A preview version consisting of a few lines may be offered to give readers an idea of the scope of the machine-readable file, which is in turn offered as supplementary material online (see also 1.124). For a full discussion of tables, see 3.48–89.

1.116 **Illustrations in journal articles.** An article published online might display the same illustrations available in the print version of the article, though they may be presented in the text as thumbnail versions linked to larger, higher-resolution images. These images may contain additional navigational aids like the ones described for tables (see 1.115). A greater range of illustrations can be offered in electronic journals, which can include more illustrations than would be practical in print. Color can be used freely, without the costs associated with color printing (although color accuracy can vary considerably between display devices). High-resolution images can allow readers to see more detail, and electronic illustrations may include an audio component. Videos and animations allow readers to view movement and understand processes. Any differences between the content of the print and electronic versions should be noted explicitly in both formats (see 1.87, 3.26). For a full discussion of illustrations, see 3.3–47.

## *Source Citations*

1.117 **Notes or author-date citations in journals.** One of the fundamental identifying marks of a journal is its documentation style—either notes (sometimes accompanied by a bibliography) or author-date citations. Notes, which still prevail in many humanities journals, may be footnotes or endnotes; if the latter, they appear at the end of the article, with the heading Notes. Author-date citations—used mostly by journals in science and the social sciences—consist of parenthetical text citations keyed to a reference list, which appears at the end of the article. Journals in the sciences may instead use a system of numbered references cited in the text by reference number; depending on the system, the references are listed in alphabetical order or in the order cited in the text. For a detailed overview of source citations, see chapters 13 and 14.

1.118 **Internal and external links to cited sources in journals.** In full-text electronic articles (and sometimes in enhanced PDF versions), text citations typically link to references, notes, or items in a bibliography, as the case may be, allowing readers to move from the text citation to the cited item and back to the text. Reference lists and bibliographies may in turn link to resources outside the article—for example, to cited articles or to an outside index or database (see 1.120).

## *Indexes*

1.119 **Indexes to printed journal volumes.** At the end of a volume, some journals publish an index to the articles and other pieces published in that volume. The index appears in the volume's last issue. Names of authors, titles of articles, and titles and authors of books reviewed are indexed. More detailed subject indexes, on the other hand, are now rare. In the sciences, subject indexes have been superseded by databases like PubMed (see 1.120).

1.120 **Electronic indexes and indexed searches.** Most journals have dispensed with subject indexes; readers have come to rely instead on commercial search engines or on indexed searches facilitated by the publisher or by a third-party bibliographic database like the ones from EBSCO to lead them to individual articles. In the sciences, journal subject indexes have been largely superseded by field-specific resources such as PubMed, the National Library of Medicine's bibliographic database of journal articles. PubMed allows readers to search the entire field of biomedicine for electronically indexed articles—with the help of a standard keyword vocabulary—rather than searching individual journals at a publisher's website. (Readers who reach an article through a database or search engine rather than by subscribing to the journal may need a subscription or otherwise pay to gain access to the full article.) See also 1.101, 1.102.

## *Version Control and Material Not Available in Print*

1.121 **Journal article version of record.** Most journals consider the online version of an article to be the version of record; the print version, which should contain all elements that are essential to the article, may nevertheless include only a subset of the material available online. Whenever the online version is considered the version of record, it is extremely important to document any changes to the file after the online publication date. Release of articles online before they are published in print means that errors may turn up well before the print issue has been assembled; consequently, a print issue may include an erratum that concerns an article in the same issue. In this case, the erratum should state that the article is in the current issue and should specify the date of online publication. Some journals use a system like Crossref's CrossMark to track versions and any corrections or retractions. For more information on best practices related to version control for journal articles, consult *Journal Article Versions (JAV): Recommendations of the NISO/ALPSP JAV Technical Working Group*, published by the National Information Standards Organization (bibliog. 2.8). See also 1.99, 1.100.

1.122 **Preprints.** In the sciences, many authors publish their manuscripts on preprint servers, sometimes before submitting them to peer-reviewed journals. In addition to arXiv.org, a multidisciplinary server launched in the early 1990s, servers include bioRxiv (biology), ChemRxiv (chemistry), engrXiv (engineering), medRxiv (medicine), PsyArXiv (psychology), and many others. These platforms provide an important means of sharing research and gathering feedback. Like "in press" or "forthcoming" articles accepted by journals but not yet edited, these are not to be confused with the final, edited electronic articles published ahead of a print issue (see 1.123).

1.123 **Articles published ahead of print.** Many academic journals publish fully edited, peer-reviewed articles online before they are assigned to or included in a numbered issue of the journal. Designated "ahead of print" or "first published online" or the like, these articles carry their own publication dates to facilitate citation by researchers before issue information has been finalized. PDF versions of such articles may include placeholder page numbers (e.g., 000) that are updated once the article is assigned to an issue. To formalize this process, many journals in the sciences have adopted a continuous publishing model, according to which each article is published independent of any future print issue in which it may appear; rather than eventually being paginated along with other articles in the same journal or issue, each article is typically paginated in a PDF version starting with page 1 and assigned a unique article ID (see 1.91).

1.124 **Supplemental journal content.** In addition to certain articles published ahead of print (see 1.123), journals often publish material not available in print or not applicable to print (e.g., multimedia components, large datasets); such material is usually referred to collectively as supplementary data or supporting information. Metadata for supplementary data and the like should include a DOI or other persistent identifier whenever possible (see also 1.88). Such supplemental content must be listed in any print version, and the online version must in turn make it clear that such material is available only online (see 1.87). At the same time, publishers must provide this content in a way that ensures its ongoing availability and accessibility, whether or not the online version is considered the version of record (see 1.121). By implementing standard practices for document structure and markup and for the inclusion and identification of supplemental media such as video and audio files, publishers can help ensure the permanence and accessibility of their material in libraries and other archives. Publishers can remain abreast of the latest standards for archival practices by consulting such groups as the International Organization for Standardization and the Digital Library Federation.

## *Design and Style*

1.125 **Journal design.** A journal's design—physical, visual, and editorial—is determined when the journal is founded. At that time, a designer creates a design for the cover and the overall look of a journal and specifications for all of its regular features. Because the designer designs not for a specific text but for categories of text—article title, author's name, text, heads, subheads, and so on—the design of a journal should be simple and flexible as well as visually pleasing and easy to read. The design of the online version, which may be shared across journals offered via the same parent site, will have additional considerations based on the medium. It is the job of the manuscript editor and production personnel to fit the items for a particular issue into the overall design. A long-running journal may occasionally be redesigned typographically. More rarely in print but commonly in electronic formats, minor alterations in style may be introduced to accommodate changing technologies.

1.126 **Journal editorial style.** A journal's editorial style governs such things as when to use numerals or percent signs, how to treat abbreviations or special terms, and how to organize tables. Consistency of design and style contributes to a journal's identity; readers know what to expect, and the substantive contribution of each article stands out more sharply when typographical distractions are at a minimum.

# 2 Manuscript Preparation, Manuscript Editing, and Proofreading

## OVERVIEW AND PROCESS OUTLINE

2.1 **Overview — authors, manuscript editors, and proofreaders.** This chapter is divided into three parts. The first part (2.4–52) is addressed primarily to authors, conceived broadly to include compilers, translators, volume editors, editors of journals, and contributors to journals or books. It provides guidelines for preparing manuscripts that have been accepted for publication. It also includes information that is relevant specifically to self-published authors. The second part of the chapter (2.53–104) gives a detailed look at what happens to a manuscript once it has been submitted to a publisher or, in the case of self-published authors, once it is ready to be prepared for publication. Specifically, the role of manuscript editors (also called copyeditors) is discussed. (Manuscripts typically go through several rounds of revising and editing before they are ready for copyediting. Aside from the overview in 2.53, these earlier stages are not covered here.) The third part (2.105–44) deals with proofreading—essentially, the steps authors and publishers must take to ensure that their publications are ready to be presented to the public. The chapter uses the book as a model, though considerations for journals are included where applicable. (Journals usually post specific requirements and instructions that journal authors will need to consult.) Many of the recommendations will also apply to other types of publications.

2.2 **Process outline — from approved manuscript to published work.** The following outline highlights the basic steps of the publication process from approved manuscript to published work. These steps are broadly modeled on a typical manuscript editing and proofreading schedule for a book-length work; the procedures for journals will vary. For a more detailed look at manuscript preparation, editing, and proofreading, see the discussions in the remainder of this chapter. For sample timetables for producing a book and a journal, see figures 2.1 and 2.2. For some additional steps taken by self-published authors, see 2.3.

1. **Manuscript submission.** In addition to the final manuscript, the author submits to the publisher all artwork and any necessary permissions to reproduce illustrations or previously published material or to cite unpublished data or personal communications. See 2.4–7.
2. **Manuscript editing (copyediting).** The manuscript editor suggests changes to the manuscript (and, where necessary, queries the author) and demarcates or checks the order and structure of the elements (e.g., illustrations, headings, text extracts). See 2.63–73, 2.75. For other stages of editing, see 2.53.

| | Business days | Dates | |
|---|---|---|---|
| Launch | n/a | 05/11/2023 | |
| Contract OK | n/a | 05/11/2023 | |
| Begin MS edit | 5 | 05/18/2023 | |
| MS to author | 45 | 07/20/2023 | **In editing three months** |
| MS design in | 15 | 08/10/2023 | |
| MS from author | 5 | 08/17/2023 | |
| MS design OK | 5 | 08/24/2023 | |
| Final MS to design | 5 | 08/31/2023 | |
| Final MS to production | 5 | 09/07/2023 | |
| Sample pages in | 10 | 09/21/2023 | |
| Sample pages OK | 3 | 09/26/2023 | |
| Pages in/to author | 9 | 10/09/2023 | |
| Pages and index MS from author | 20 | 11/06/2023 | |
| Pages and index MS to design | 5 | 11/13/2023 | |
| Pages to production | 5 | 11/20/2023 | |
| Pages to typesetter | 1 | 11/21/2023 | |
| Index MS to typesetter | | 11/21/2023 | |
| Revised pages in | 9 | 12/04/2023 | |
| Index pages in | | 12/04/2023 | |
| Mfg quotes requested | | 12/04/2023 | |
| Mfg quotes received | 5 | 12/11/2023 | |
| Revised pages to typesetter | | 12/11/2023 | |
| Index pages to typesetter | | 12/11/2023 | **In production six months** |
| Estimate and release routing | 2 | 12/13/2023 | |
| Page revisions completed | 10 | 12/27/2023 | |
| Final lasers requested | 5 | 01/03/2024 | |
| Final lasers in | 5 | 01/10/2024 | |
| Final lasers OK | 5 | 01/17/2024 | |
| Estimate and release approved | | 12/18/2023 | |
| Cover/jacket copy in/OK | | 01/03/2024 | |
| Cover/jacket design in | | 08/03/2023 | |
| Cover/jacket design OK | | 08/17/2023 | |
| Cover/jacket mechanical in | | 01/12/2024 | |
| Cover/jacket mechanical OK | | 01/17/2024 | |
| Order date text/cover/jacket | | 01/24/2024 | |
| Advances in | | 03/20/2024 | |
| Books in warehouse | 5 | 03/27/2024 | |

FIGURE 2.1. Sample design and production schedule for a book.

| | Business days | JANUARY v1n1 | APRIL v1n2 | JULY v1n3 | OCTOBER v1n4 |
|---|---|---|---|---|---|
| MSS, running order, signed publication agreements, covers, prelim updates due in production | | 9/21 | 12/21 | 3/22 | 6/22 |
| MSS converted / art processed / MSS to editors | 5 | 9/28 | 12/29 | 3/29 | 6/29 |
| Editing complete / MSS to typesetter | 15 | 10/19 | 1/22 | 4/19 | 7/23 |
| Page proofs typeset / proofs to authors | 5 | 10/26 | 1/29 | 4/26 | 7/30 |
| Corrections received from authors | 3 | 10/31 | 2/1 | 5/1 | 8/2 |
| PDFs annotated with editorial corrections, returned to typesetter for revised pages | 10 | 11/14 | 2/15 | 5/15 | 8/16 |
| Ahead-of-print articles posted / issue approved for pagination | 5 | 11/21 | 2/22 | 5/22 | 8/23 |
| Paginated issue from typesetter | 5 | 11/30 | 3/1 | 5/30 | 8/30 |
| Issue approved by editorial for print and post | 5 | 12/7 | 3/8 | 6/6 | 9/7 |
| Final issue materials delivered: print-ready PDFs from typesetter due to printer | 1 | 12/8 | 3/9 | 6/7 | 9/10 |
| Electronic deliverables due | 5 | 12/15 | 3/16 | 6/14 | 9/17 |
| Post electronic version and ebook | 2 | 12/19 | 3/20 | 6/18 | 9/19 |
| Mail print edition | 10 | 12/22 | 3/23 | 6/21 | 9/24 |

FIGURE 2.2. Sample production schedule for a quarterly journal.

3. **Author review.** The author reviews the edited manuscript and answers any queries. All remaining changes and adjustments to the manuscript need to be indicated by the author at this stage. See 2.77, 2.93.
4. **Final manuscript.** The manuscript editor produces a final manuscript, incorporating the results of the author's review of the edited manuscript and, among other things, double-checking each element in the manuscript against a design template for completeness, consistency, and proper markup. See 2.79–82.
5. **Proofreading and indexing.** Once the final manuscript has been converted for publication—for example, as a typeset and paginated book or journal

article or the full text of an ebook or an article to be published online—it will need to be checked by the author and any additional proofreaders in at least one format (typically PDF or print, as *page proofs* or *proof*) for errors and inconsistencies. See 2.105–44. It is also at this stage that an index may be prepared and subsequently edited (see chapter 15).

6. **Final revisions.** As the publisher makes sure all necessary corrections have been made, the index, if there is one, is proofread in its final format and corrected as needed (see 2.111). Book pages, especially, may go through several rounds of revision, though publishers usually set firm limits on changes beyond the first round of revisions. See 2.110. (Though every effort should be made to prevent and fix errors and other problems, the occasional error in a published work is inevitable.)
7. **Prepress or final review.** For a printed-and-bound book, publishers usually review the typesetter's final files—either as an inexpensive printout or on-screen—before ink is committed to paper. Once the job is on the press, an initial set of folded-and-gathered signatures (or sheets, also called F&Gs) may be sent from the printer to the publisher for review before the job is finished (see 2.112). For electronic formats, a final version must be reviewed in each context in which it will be published before it is posted or distributed or otherwise made available to the public (see 2.142–44).

2.3 **Additional steps for self-publishing authors.** Most of the steps outlined in 2.2, from manuscript editing through publication, will also apply to authors who publish their books independently. But there are several steps normally handled by traditional publishers that self-publishing authors will need to do for themselves (or arrange to have done by others), as follows:

1. Decide on the final version of the title and subtitle.
2. Write an author bio and a description of the book.
3. For print books, write copy for the back cover or jacket.
4. Design the cover. For print books, this will include not only the front cover but also the back cover and spine and, for jackets, flaps.
5. For print books, design the interior text.
6. For ebooks, create EPUB files.

All but the last of these should be attended to as soon as the manuscript is ready for copyediting. Though authors will often be able to manage the first three steps themselves, many will want to seek help for anything related to design and production (steps 4–6). For detailed information on the parts of a book (including covers and jackets), see 1.3–85.

# MANUSCRIPT PREPARATION GUIDELINES FOR AUTHORS

## *Basic Manuscript Submission Requirements*

2.4 **Manuscript submission checklist.** Before manuscript editing begins (see 2.53–104), authors should provide any of the elements in the list that follows that are to be included in the work. This list is modeled on the parts of a book (see 1.3–85). Authors contributing to a journal should consult the journal's specific submission requirements.

- Title page
- Dedication
- Epigraph
- Table of contents
- List of illustrations
- List of tables
- Preface
- Any other front matter
- All text matter, including introduction and part titles
- Acknowledgments
- Appendixes
- Glossary
- Notes
- Bibliography or reference list
- Any other back matter
- All illustrations and all tables
- Illustration captions and alternative text (see 3.28)
- A list of special characters used in the manuscript
- Abstract(s) and keywords (see 1.85)
- All permissions, in writing, that may be required to reproduce illustrations or previously published material or to cite unpublished data or personal communications (see chapter 4); this includes any necessary interviewee and photo releases

All elements should be final and up to date—including any URLs cited in the work (see 13.6–12). The publisher usually furnishes the half-title page (see 1.18), the copyright page (see 1.22–39), and copy for the running heads (see 1.10–16, 2.81). Self-published authors should add these to their checklists.

2.5 **Submitting the manuscript.** Publishers usually require the latest version of the electronic file(s) for the work, and authors are advised to make a secure backup of this final manuscript and to avoid making any further changes to it. Some publishers also require hard copy or PDF as a safeguard against any glitches in the electronic files—especially for book-length works or works with complex formatting or special typographical needs. To ensure that this copy is identical to the electronic files, any last-minute changes made to the electronic files before the manuscript is submitted must be reflected in the hard copy or PDF (see also 2.6). Authors are advised to include a cover letter specifying the author's name, the title of the work, a total word count (rather than a page count), the electronic file names, and the software used. Any material (such as artwork) that cannot be included in electronic form must be noted and described. Conversely, any material that cannot be printed or supplied as PDF (such as videos, animations, or large data files that might be included in an electronic journal or web-based publication) must also be noted and described; for all such material, the software used, the number of items, their type(s), and the individual file names must be specified. For any additional instructions, authors should check with their publishers. For advice on manuscript formatting, see 2.8–30. For advice on preparing index manuscripts, see chapter 15. For paper-only manuscripts, see 2.7. For manuscripts consisting of previously published material, see 2.48.

2.6 **Making changes after a manuscript has been submitted.** Once an author has submitted a final manuscript to the publisher, the publisher is responsible for maintaining the version of record. An author who needs to make further changes after submitting the files must therefore alert the publisher immediately. Minor changes can usually be indicated later, on the edited document that the manuscript editor will send to the author for review (see 2.77, 2.93). For major changes, the author may need to send a revised manuscript to the publisher *before* editing begins. Authors should be advised, however, that many book publishers begin manuscript preparation immediately upon receipt and may not be able to accept a revised version after the original submission of the final manuscript. Self-publishing authors who send their manuscript directly to a copyeditor should avoid making further changes until they get the edited version back. For journals, major changes are rarely permitted after an article has been accepted; schedules do not allow for them. Peer-reviewed articles that require major changes may also require additional review.

2.7 **Submitting a paper-only manuscript.** In the rare case of a typewritten manuscript, authors are typically required to submit two paper copies of the manuscript; they should keep a third copy for themselves. All text must be double-spaced to leave sufficient room for pencil-editing marks between the lines. It is essential, moreover, that everything in a paper-only manuscript be legible. Anything added in handwriting before the manuscript is submitted to the publisher must be clearly written, in upper- and lowercase letters, directly above the line or in the margin. Avoid writing on the backs of pages in case the publisher photocopies or scans the manuscript. Any correction longer than a short phrase should be provided as a separate document and inserted in the manuscript following the page to which it pertains—clearly labeled in both places to show where it should be inserted. Finally, to facilitate copying or scanning, use good-quality paper in a standard size—usually 8½ × 11 inches or A4 (210 × 297 mm). See also 2.12, 2.48.

## *Manuscript Formatting*

2.8 **Publishers' manuscript preparation guidelines.** Many publishers have specific requirements or preferences regarding choice of software and typeface, as well as formats for submitting illustrations and tables along with the manuscript. These should be followed to the letter. Consistency and simplicity in all matters is essential. Authors should know that their manuscripts will almost always be converted into another software environment for publication and that, therefore, the words themselves and the order in which they are presented are more important than the style of presentation. Provided the basic structure of chapters and sections and the like is clear, a simple presentation is always preferable to an elaborately formatted manuscript. Authors who want a more explicit idea of what publishers look for in the format and structure of a manuscript would do well to consider the steps in a manuscript editor's typical cleanup routine (see 2.85).

2.9 **Font.** Unless a publisher specifies otherwise, authors should use a widely supported, legible Unicode font like Times New Roman, Calibri (or Aptos, Microsoft's newer default font), or Arial, each of which offers broad support for special characters (see also 2.19). (Many publishers prefer Times New Roman for its serifs, which can make capital letter *I* and lowercase *l* distinct, among other advantages.) For body text, use at least 10-point Arial or 11-point Calibri (or Aptos) or Times New Roman (fonts vary in how large they appear at a given point size). For chapter titles, subheads, and other display type, a slightly larger point size will help delineate the structure of the manuscript. For footnotes and table text, use the same size as the main text or slightly smaller.

2.10 **Line spacing.** Though authors may prefer to use less line spacing on the screen, publishers have customarily required that any printout be double-spaced—including all extracts and lists, footnotes or endnotes, bibliographies or reference lists, and any other material. The extra line spacing is crucial for manuscripts edited with pencil on paper; some publishers will choose to edit the paper copy and update the electronic files based on this edited copy. (Authors concerned about saving paper are encouraged to consult with their publishers about line-spacing requirements and any option for sending PDF instead of paper; see 2.5.) Avoid extra space or blank lines between paragraphs (see 2.15). If such a break is intended to appear in the printed version, indicate this explicitly with three asterisks set on a line by themselves (see also 1.64). If two levels of breaks are required, stronger breaks may be indicated with three asterisks and weaker breaks with one; include a note to the editor or publisher explaining this choice. If blank space rather than an ornament is preferred for publication (at either level), specify this in a note to the publisher (though how such breaks are treated may ultimately be up to the book designer). For stanza breaks in poetry, see 2.24.

2.11 **Space between sentences or after colons.** One space or two? Like most publishers, Chicago advises leaving a single character space, not two spaces, between sentences and after colons used within a sentence, and this recommendation applies to both the author's manuscript and the published work. In fact, a well-structured electronic document will never include more than one consecutive character space. See also 2.15, 6.127–30.

2.12 **Page size and margins.** Whether the manuscript will be printed or not, authors should use a standard page size, which most word processors will apply by default. In North America, the standard is 8½ × 11 inches (or letter size); most other regions of the world, including the United Kingdom, use 210 × 297 millimeters (or A4). To leave enough room for handwritten queries, margins of at least one inch should appear on all four sides of the hard copy. An exception may be made for page numbers, which are usually placed half an inch from the top right of the page (see also 2.20).

2.13 **Justification.** To avoid the appearance of inconsistent spacing between words and sentences, all text in an author's manuscript (except for any centered headings or the like) should be set flush left (ragged right) rather than justified. Text that is flush left is aligned along the left margin only; text that is justified (also called full justification) aligns along both margins. Though often used for the text in a published book, full justification generally requires end-of-line hyphenation and should therefore not be applied at the manuscript stage (see also 2.16).

2.14 **Tabs versus indents.** Tabs are entered with the Tab key. Indents are applied using a word processor's indentation feature. Tabs can usually be identified on-screen by the right-pointing arrows that will appear in most word-processing programs when nonprinting characters are revealed; aside from the position of the text, indents are generally signaled on a graphical ruler or by a dialog box for paragraph formatting. (In word processing, a "paragraph" is any string of text that begins on a new line and is followed by a hard return, including not only the blocks of text traditionally referred to as paragraphs but also items in a list, headings, etc.) There are three basic types of indent:

- *First-line indent.* A first-line indent (also called a paragraph indent) is normally applied to each new paragraph of regular text. As its name suggests, only the first line is indented (from the left margin). First-line indents can be applied either with tabs or by using a word processor's indentation feature (via the ruler or a menu). The latter approach is usually preferred, however, because it is easier to convert for publication. (Some word processors will apply a first-line indent rather than a tab automatically when the Tab key is pressed.)
- *Left or right indent.* A left indent applies an equal indent relative to the left margin for each line in a paragraph, including the first line and any runover lines, and can be used to set off prose and poetry extracts. Authors should never use tabs to achieve left indents. Indents from the right margin are usually not needed at the manuscript stage.
- *Hanging indent.* A hanging indent (also called flush and hang), in which every line but the first is indented from the left margin, is used for the items in a list, including a bibliography or reference list or an index. Authors should never use tabs to achieve hanging indents.

In some cases, it will be necessary to use a first-line or hanging indent in combination with a left indent (as for a new paragraph in a block quotation or for a poetry extract; see 2.23, 2.24). For the purposes of the manuscript, the typical default value for tabs or indents can normally be used (usually half an inch). Avoid using two or more consecutive tabs. With the exception of a tab at the beginning of a new paragraph or a tab after a number or symbol in a vertical list (see 2.25), tabs should never appear within a paragraph.

2.15 **Paragraph format.** Authors should format each new paragraph with a first-line indent, applied either with the Tab key or, preferably, with their word processor's indentation feature (see 2.14); do *not* use the space bar. (In published works, the first new paragraph in a chapter or section—whether following a subhead or a space break—typically begins flush left, a style that may be applied at the manuscript stage but need not be.) Never use the Enter key or the Tab key in the middle of a paragraph; let the word processor determine the breaks at the ends of lines. When a paragraph is interrupted by a prose or poetry extract, list, equation, or the like, the text after the interruption begins flush left (i.e., with no first-line indent) unless it constitutes a new paragraph. For prose extracts, see 2.23; for poetry, see 2.24; for lists, see 2.25. See also 2.28.

2.16 **Hyphenation.** Authors should make sure the hyphenation function on their word processor is turned off. The only hyphens that should appear in the manuscript are hyphens that would appear regardless of where the text falls on the page (e.g., in hyphenated compounds). Do not worry if such a hyphen happens to fall at the end of a line or if the right-hand margin is extremely ragged. By the same token, do not attempt to manually break excessively long words (including URLs, whether long or short) with a hyphen. See also 2.101.

2.17 **Dashes.** Authors should insert dashes—the ones that indicate a break in a sentence like this—by using their word processor to insert an em dash character. (Alternatively, authors may type two consecutive hyphens with no space on either side.) The 3-em dash, used in some bibliographies for a repeated author's name, is usually best left to the manuscript editor; if it must be used, insert either three consecutive em dashes or six unspaced hyphens (see also 13.72–73). (For more on the em dash, see 6.91–98, 6.99–100.) Ensuring proper use of the en dash—a shorter dash that has special significance in certain types of compounds and in number ranges—is usually considered the manuscript editor's responsibility; authors can generally use hyphens instead. (For more on the en dash, see 6.82–90.)

2.18 **Italics, underline, and boldface.** Though underlining will generally be construed by publishers to mean italics, actual italics should be used instead wherever italics are intended. (In a redlined manuscript, underlining may denote insertions; see 2.89.) An author who intends underlining rather than italics to appear in certain instances in the published work must make these instances clear in a note to the publisher (or to the manuscript editor). Use boldface only for words that must appear thus in the published version (but see 2.40).

2.19 **Special characters.** As far as their software allows, authors should insert the character they intend rather than any keyboard substitute. For example, do not type an apostrophe (') where a prime symbol (′) is needed. Current word processors enable the user to insert many more characters than those displayed on the keyboard, and an abundance of free Unicode fonts are available from sources like Google Fonts to accommodate almost any script a writer might need (see also 2.9, 11.2). Nonetheless, if you require a character that is not available to you, insert a placeholder—for example, the unaccented version of a letter with multiple accents—and add a detailed comment for the publisher or editor using your word processor's commenting feature (or in a separate document). In all cases, authors should include a list of any special characters and submit it to the publisher along with the manuscript. See tables 11.1 and 11.2, which list some special characters alongside their names and Unicode numbers. Your list should show how each character is supposed to look; if a character is unavailable to you, copy the correct character from the applicable code chart from Unicode.org or elsewhere or draw it in by hand. Before planning to use a special font that may not support Unicode, consult your publisher. For quotation marks and apostrophes, see 6.123, 6.125.

2.20 **Page numbers and tables of contents.** Authors should use the page-numbering feature in their word processor to insert page numbers in their manuscript. The preferred position is the top of the page, flush right, unless your publisher specifies otherwise. A table of contents is usually placed after any dedication or epigraph but before any list of illustrations or tables (see 1.4 and 2.4). At a minimum, the table of contents for a book should list the title of each section, including any preface or other front matter sections, chapters or other text divisions, and any sections in the back matter. Page numbers, however, may be omitted—and they should never be added manually. Instead, you may use the table of contents feature in your word processor to insert a table of contents, which will add page numbers and automatically renumber them as needed. To make this work, you may need to apply word-processing styles to chapter titles and other major divisions (see 2.87).

2.21 **Format for chapter titles and titles of other parts.** Titles for chapters and other parts of a manuscript usually begin on a new page. Authors should use upper- and lowercase letters for these titles rather than full capitals. Chicago prefers title case for chapter and other titles (see 8.160). The titles should match the entries in the table of contents. "Chapter 1," "Chapter 2," and so on should appear above the titles to numbered chapters. (For an overview of the parts of a book or a journal, see chapter 1.)

2.22 **Format for subheads.** Authors should begin each subhead on a new line, flush left. Each level of subhead must be clearly distinguished so that the different levels can be identified and carried over for publication. Levels can be distinguished by font size (e.g., larger for first-level subheads, smaller for second-level heads). A word processor's style palette can be useful in applying such distinctions and in managing subhead levels. (Authors are encouraged to consult their publishers' manuscript preparation guidelines for the preferred approach.) Use upper- and lowercase letters rather than full capitals. Subheads may be capitalized in either sentence case or title case provided they are consistent at each level (see 8.159, 8.160). With the exception of run-in subheads (see 1.62), no period follows a subhead.

2.23 **Format for prose extracts.** Authors should indent prose extracts (also called block quotations) using their word processor's indentation feature; tabs should never be used for this purpose. The first line should *not* have an additional paragraph indent. If there is more than one paragraph within the extract, however, each new paragraph should begin with an additional first-line paragraph indent, which can be applied either with the Tab key or, preferably, with your word processor's indentation feature. See 2.14. Use a hard return only at the end of the extract and after any paragraphs within the extract. Prose extracts should have the same line spacing as the surrounding text (see 2.10); they do not need to appear in a smaller font. The text that follows an extract should get a first-line indent only if it constitutes a new paragraph; if it continues the text that introduced the extract, it should start flush left (see 2.15). See also 12.22–24. For ellipses, see 12.59–69.

2.24 **Format for poetry extracts.** Authors should format poetry extracts (i.e., quotations of poetry presented within a prose manuscript) with indents; they should *not* be centered (even if they might appear centered in the printed version). Use your word processor's indentation feature to assign both a left indent and a hanging indent to each line. Let runover lines wrap to the next line normally; use a hard return at the end of each full line of poetry but never in the middle of a line, and do not use the Tab key to indent runovers. See 2.14. Runover lines must be clearly distinguished from indented lines of poetry. If certain lines of a poem are to receive a deeper indent than others, increase the left indent value accordingly. For poetry with unusual spacing or indentation, append a photocopy or scan of the original printed poem. Indicate a stanza break with an extra hard return. The source, if given after the extract, should appear in parentheses on a separate line, indented like the first line of the poem. (In the published version, the source may have a different placement; see 12.82.) Poetry extracts should have the same line spacing as the surrounding text (see 2.10); they do not need to appear in a smaller font. The text that follows a poetry extract should get a first-line indent only if it constitutes a new paragraph; if it continues the text that introduced the extract, it should start flush left (see 2.15). See also 12.25–29. For ellipses, see 12.66.

2.25 **Format for lists and outlines.** Authors should format the items in an unnumbered list using their word processor's indentation feature to assign both a left indent and a hanging indent. Let runover lines wrap to the next line normally; do not use the Tab key to indent runovers. See 2.14. In addition, in a numbered or lettered list (including a multilevel list or outline), each number or letter should normally be followed by a period or other punctuation and a tab. Bullets in a bulleted list are likewise followed by a tab. Alternatively, you may use your word processor's list and outline features, which will apply the necessary indents, tabs, and numbers, letters, punctuation, or symbols automatically. (These automatically generated numbers or letters or symbols may need to be converted to regular text to ensure compatibility with the software used for publication, a task that is normally considered to be the manuscript editor's or publisher's responsibility.) The text that follows a list should get a first-line indent only if it constitutes a new paragraph; if it continues the text that introduced the list, it should start flush left (see 2.15). See also 6.138–43.

2.26 **Format for footnotes and endnotes.** To take advantage of automatic renumbering, authors should insert notes using their word processor's footnote or endnote function. The text of the notes should have the same line spacing as the rest of the manuscript; do not insert an extra hard return between notes (see also 2.10). Unless your publisher requests otherwise, in the manuscript notes may appear either as footnotes or as chapter or book endnotes (starting over at 1 for each chapter), regardless of how they are to appear in the published version. Do not mix footnotes and endnotes unless such a system is truly necessary (see 13.52). Notes that will be published as book endnotes without any numbers in the text should be prepared in the same way as ordinary numbered notes (see also 13.56, 13.57). Avoid appending note references to chapter titles (see 1.55). Notes to tables should be numbered separately, without using your word processor's note feature (see 2.36). For note form, see 13.27–64. For some considerations related to citation management software, see 13.13.

2.27 **Format for glossaries and lists of abbreviations.** Authors should begin each entry in a glossary or list of abbreviations on a new line, capitalized only if the term is capitalized in the text. Separate each term from the definition that follows with a period, a colon, or an em dash (choose one and use it consistently; see also 1.68, 2.17). In a glossary, begin the definition with a capital letter, as if it were a new sentence; in a list of abbreviations, the expanded term should be capitalized or lowercased as it would be in the text. Unless all definitions consist of incomplete sentences, each glossary entry should end with a period. Any term or abbreviation that is consistently italicized in the text (not just on first use) should also be italicized in the glossary or list of abbreviations. (Abbreviations of consistently italicized terms should generally themselves be italicized; see also 13.64.) Entries should have the same line spacing as the rest of the manuscript (see 2.10) and may be formatted in flush-and-hang style or with ordinary first-line paragraph indents (see 2.14). Avoid multiple columns. See also 1.49 and 1.68.

2.28 **Format for bibliographies and reference lists.** Authors should begin each entry in a bibliography or reference list on a new line. Use your word processor's indentation feature to assign a hanging indent to each line. Never use the Tab key to indent runover lines. See 2.14. Use the same line spacing as in the rest of the manuscript (see 2.10). For capitalization, use of italics, and other matters of bibliographic style, see chapters 13 and 14. For some considerations related to citation management software, see 13.13.

2.29 **Format for abstracts.** Authors may be required to submit an abstract, not only for the book as a whole but for individual chapters as well. Abstracts are typically submitted as a separate file; some publishers provide a template. Authors of nonacademic books and self-publishing authors may be asked to supply a brief description in lieu of an abstract. A book abstract normally consists of a single paragraph of no more than 250 words (some publishers allow more than that), with no tables, lists, illustrations, or notes; chapter abstracts are usually somewhat shorter. (Publishers will often specify a word limit for each.) The book abstract should give a clear summary of the book's main arguments and conclusions. Chapter abstracts should give a clear overview of each chapter. Authors should take care in writing abstracts; though they usually do not appear in the book itself (except in the sciences), they often form the basis of the promotional copy or descriptive metadata shared with libraries and booksellers. See also 1.85. Journal publishers usually have their own set of requirements for abstracts that authors can consult; see also 1.102.

2.30 **Format for keywords.** Authors may be required to submit a list of keywords, typically five to ten key terms; these usually accompany the abstract, with additional sets for any chapter abstracts (see 2.29). Keywords are designed to enhance a book's visibility to search engines by repeating significant terms found in the book's abstract, though they can also include a synonym or other related term that users might be expected to enter in a search. (Keywords should not, on the other hand, consist of terms that are unrelated to the subject of the book.) Each keyword should comprise a single word (e.g., Olympics) or an accepted compound of no more than a few words (e.g., table tennis). As with abstracts, authors should take care in choosing keywords. Journal publishers usually post their own requirements for keywords that authors can consult. See also 1.85, 1.102.

## *Preparing Illustrations and Tables*

2.31 **Formatting and submitting illustrations, captions, and tables.** Publishers usually ask authors to submit illustrations as separate files rather than embedded in the manuscript. Many publishers also prefer tables in separate files, but those created using a word processor may not need to be; consult your publisher. The approximate placement of illustrations or tables submitted as separate files should be called out in the text, keeping in mind that the exact locations of figures in a manuscript will be determined during typesetting (see 2.35). Captions for all illustrations should be furnished in a separate file; any list of illustrations should follow the table of contents (see 1.44). Authors are also encouraged to supply text descriptions for any images that may require them, preferably in a separate file to facilitate copyediting. This alternative text (or "alt text") will be used in ebook and other electronic formats to enhance accessibility for readers with print and related disabilities (see 3.28). For a more detailed overview of illustrations and tables, see chapter 3.

2.32 **Submitting artwork.** Text figures that are to be supplied in digital format or reproduced by scanning a hard-copy original—such as paintings, maps, and photographic prints—should be furnished by authors according to the publisher's specifications. Glossy prints must be clearly labeled, usually on the back of the print or on a self-sticking label, in a manner that does not damage them (see 3.16). For further discussion, see 3.15–20.

2.33 **Numbering illustrations.** Authors should number their illustrations either consecutively throughout the manuscript or, in scientific and technical books, heavily illustrated books, and books with chapters by different authors, using double numeration. Double numeration consists of the chapter number, followed by a period, followed by the figure number (e.g., fig. 1.1, 1.2, 1.3, . . . , 2.1, 2.2, 2.3, . . . , etc.). In the event a figure is dropped or added, double numeration will simplify the work needed to renumber not just the illustrations but any applicable cross-references, especially in a heavily illustrated book. Illustrations are enumerated separately from tables. Plates to be grouped in a gallery are numbered separately from figures interspersed in the text (see 3.14). Even if numbers are not to appear with the illustrations in the published version, working numbers should be assigned for identification and should accompany the captions (see 3.13). For more details, see 3.8–14.

2.34 **Numbering tables.** Authors should number their tables either consecutively throughout the manuscript or, in a book with many tables or with chapters by different authors, using double numeration (e.g., table 1.1, 1.2, 1.3, . . . , 2.1, 2.2, 2.3, . . . , etc.). In a book with many tables, double numeration can simplify the task of renumbering in the event a table is dropped or added. Tables are enumerated separately from illustrations. Very simple tabular material (e.g., a two-column list) may be presented unnumbered along with the text. See also 3.51–52.

2.35 **Formatting text references and callouts to tables and illustrations.** A *text reference* is addressed to the reader ("see table 5" or "see fig. 3.2") and will appear in the published version. A *callout* is an instruction, which will not appear in the published work, telling where a table or an illustration is to appear. In the manuscript, authors should enclose callouts in angle brackets or some other delimiter and place them on a separate line following the paragraph in which the table or illustration is first referred to ("<table 5 about here>"; "<fig. 3.2 about here>") or, if a later location is preferable, where the table or illustration is to appear. Numbered tables and illustrations usually require both a text reference and a placement callout unless they are to be grouped in a section separate from the regular text (and except for any that are included in the manuscript along with the text rather than submitted as separate files; see 2.31). Illustrations that are not referred to in the text still usually require placement callouts (see 3.8–14); unnumbered tables presented in the run of text do not require callouts (see 3.52).

2.36 **Formatting table notes and source notes.** Authors should place source notes at the foot of the table before any other notes. A source note is preceded by the word *Source* followed by a colon. Other notes to the table as a whole follow any source note and may be preceded by the word *Note* followed by a colon. Specific notes follow any other notes, and the notes to each table must be enumerated separately from any notes to the text (see 3.80). For a fuller discussion of notes to tables, see 3.77–81.

## *Cross-Checking the Manuscript*

2.37 **Items to cross-check.** Before submitting a manuscript for publication, an author must cross-check each of its parts to avoid discrepancies. The following list includes major items to check:

- All titles and subtitles (introduction, parts, chapters, etc.) against table of contents
- Subheads against table of contents (if subheads are included there; see 1.42)
- Illustrations against their captions, text references, and callouts
- Illustration captions against list of illustrations
- Tables against their text references and callouts
- Table titles against list of tables
- Internal cross-references or hyperlinks against their target destinations (see also 2.40)
- URLs and other external links against their target destinations
- Quotations against their original sources
- Notes against their references in the text
- Notes against bibliography (see chapter 13)
- Parenthetical author-date text citations against reference list (see chapter 13)
- Abbreviations against list of abbreviations
- In a multiauthor work, authors' names in table of contents against chapter headings and list of contributors

2.38 **Checking quotations against original sources.** Authors should check all quoted matter against the original sources, for both content and source citations, before submitting a manuscript for publication. This authorial task is crucial because manuscript editors will not have access to all the sources that the author has used.

2.39 **Checking URLs and other external links.** Authors should double-check any URLs and other links to outside resources just before a manuscript is submitted for publication. Those that no longer point to the intended source should be updated. At the same time, source citations that include links should be checked for completeness according to the guidelines in chapter 13; in most cases, readers should be able to find the resource with or without the link. See also 13.6–12.

2.40 **Checking cross-references.** Authors should verify all cross-references, whether to a chapter, a section, an appendix, or even a sentence of text, before a manuscript is submitted for publication. A chapter number or title may have been changed, or a passage deleted, after the original reference to it. Cross-references are best made to chapter or section numbers because these are known and can be entered at the manuscript stage. (Keep in mind, however, that references to whole chapters are often gratuitous and unhelpful; it's best to avoid peppering a manuscript with "see chapter 2 above" and "see chapter 4 below.") References to page numbers are generally discouraged because the pagination of a published work will not correspond to that of the manuscript, and the correct number will have to be supplied later in the process (usually by the author). Moreover, such cross-references may become meaningless in ebook versions that lack fixed page numbers (successful linking will require page number data from the printed version). Where absolutely necessary, use three zeros, preferably in bold (e.g., "see p. **000**"), to signal the need to supply the final page number.

## *Preparing the Electronic Manuscript Files*

2.41 **Publishers' guidelines for preparing and submitting electronic files.** For book-length projects, publishers may prefer to get separate electronic files for each of the various elements—front matter through table of contents, preface, chapters, appendixes, and so on (some of which will include embedded notes). Appropriately named separate files—especially for complex works—can help publishers get a sense of and deal with a book's component parts. Many authors (and editors), however, will prefer to work in a single file to facilitate searching and to take advantage of the outline views and other navigational tools available in word processors. Authors should always consult their publisher's manuscript preparation guidelines before submitting a final manuscript, whether for a book or for a journal article. Illustrations, which publishers handle separately from the text, should always be in separate files; tables created in an author's word-processing software may not need to be (see 2.31). Self-publishing platforms have their own formatting guidelines. These guidelines, which assume a final, edited manuscript that will be converted directly for publication, may be more detailed and specific than a traditional publisher's manuscript submission guidelines. Independent authors may therefore wish to enlist the help of editors and designers in applying the required formatting.

2.42 **Naming and saving the electronic files.** Book authors who submit chapters and other components as separate files (rather than combining them in a single file; see 2.41) should name the files such that they correspond more or less to the parts of the manuscript as listed in the table of contents (see 1.4). File names that include an author name and a descriptive label will help publishers keep track of them. For books with more than a few parts, use file names that will line up in book order in an alphanumerically sorted directory. The two-digit numerals added to the beginning of each of the following file names will facilitate this:

01 Jones contents
02 Jones preface
03 Jones chap01
04 Jones chap02
. . .
12 Jones biblio

File names usually also include extensions (e.g., .docx or .odt); whether or not these are visible, they should never be changed or deleted. A separate file for illustration captions might start with "00" (e.g., "00 Jones captions"). The illustrations themselves should usually be submitted as a separate group and named accordingly (e.g., "Jones fig 1.1," "Jones fig 1.2," etc.). File names for color illustrations may include the word *color*, especially if black-and-white illustrations have also been submitted. A complete list of all submitted files, including files for captions and illustrations, should accompany the manuscript. If PDF versions are required, these files should also be listed. If a hard copy is required, the manuscript should be arranged in the order specified in the table of contents.

2.43 **Numbering manuscript pages.** Authors should number each page of their manuscript, whether electronic or hard copy (see 2.20). Manuscripts submitted as multiple files need not be numbered consecutively from page 1 through to the end of the book. Instead, to ensure that no two pages in the manuscript are numbered the same, add descriptive page headers next to the page numbers in each file (e.g., "Introduction: 1," "Introduction: 2," etc.; "chapter 1: 1," "chapter 1: 2," etc.). Arabic numerals may be used for the front matter even though these pages may take on Roman numerals in the published work. (It is typically the job of the manuscript editor to indicate where Roman numerals will apply; see 2.80.) Manuscripts submitted as one file, on the other hand, can be numbered consecutively across the book starting with page 1 (see also 2.42). In a paper-only manuscript, pages added after the initial numbering may be numbered with *a* or *b* (e.g., 55, 55a, 55b).

2.44 **Removing comments and revision marks from the final files.** Unless instructed otherwise, authors should delete any comments embedded in their manuscript *before* submitting it for publication. This includes not only any comments inserted using a word processor's commenting feature but also any text formatted as "hidden." Any outstanding queries should be addressed in a cover letter. Moreover, it is crucial that any revision marks (or "tracked changes") be removed before the manuscript is submitted—and that the final manuscript represent the very latest version. (Manuscript editors should always check for hidden text, comments, and revision marks and alert the author or publisher about any potential problems.)

2.45 **Backing up the final manuscript.** In addition to saving a separate electronic copy of each crucial stage of work on their manuscript, authors are advised to save a backup copy of the version sent to the publisher for editing and publication. Prudence dictates retaining copies in at least two separate locations (e.g., on a hard drive and on a portable drive or with a secure file-hosting service). See also 2.6.

## *Preparing a Manuscript for a Multiauthor Book or Journal*

2.46 **Volume editor's manuscript preparation responsibilities.** The specific responsibilities of the volume editor, contributors, and publisher (including the manuscript editor) must be determined before a multiauthor manuscript is submitted. If there is more than one volume editor, the responsibilities of each must be spelled out. After ensuring that the contributors furnish their chapters in a uniform style agreed to by all parties, the volume editor is usually responsible for the following:

- Getting manuscripts, including illustrations, from all contributors in a form acceptable to the publisher well before the date for submitting the volume
- Securing (or ensuring that the contributors have secured) written permission from copyright owners to reproduce material in copyrighted works published elsewhere, illustrations taken from another work, and the like (see chapter 4)
- Editing each contribution for sense and checking references and other source

citations for uniformity of style (unless the publisher agrees to allow different citation styles for separate chapters; see also 2.70), then sending edited manuscripts to the contributors for their approval before the volume is submitted to the publisher (an activity distinct from the editing that will be done by a manuscript editor after the manuscript has been submitted to the publisher)
- Providing a list of contributors with their affiliations and brief biographical notes to be included in the volume
- Providing a title page, table of contents, and any necessary prefatory material
- Sending the complete manuscript to the publisher in a form acceptable for publication (having first made sure that the manuscript includes only the latest version of each contributor's chapter)
- Adhering to the publisher's schedule and ensuring that contributors do likewise, keeping track of the contributors' whereabouts at all stages of publication, and assuming the responsibilities of any contributor who cannot fulfill them

Most if not all of these responsibilities also apply to journal editors.

2.47 **Additional responsibilities of the volume editor.** Depending on the arrangement with the publisher, the volume editor may also be responsible for the following:

- Sending a publishing agreement (provided by the publisher) to each contributor and returning the agreements, fully executed, to the publisher (see 4.62)
- Checking the edited manuscript and responding to all queries, or distributing the edited manuscript to the contributors and checking it after their review to ensure that all queries have been answered
- Proofreading the final version of the volume or delegating proofreading to the contributors and then checking their corrections
- Preparing the index

## *Compiling a Manuscript from Previously Published Material*

2.48 **Preparing previously published material.** Manuscripts for an anthology or other work comprising previously published material are said to have been *compiled*. If the compiler retypes the original sources or scans them using optical character recognition (OCR), the resulting text should be incorporated into a manuscript that follows the formatting requirements outlined in paragraphs 2.8–30. Manuscripts consisting of retyped text or text prepared with OCR must be proofread word for word against the original material *before* the final manuscript is submitted to the publisher for editing; in addition, publishers may request copies of the originals. If the original material is submitted on paper only, make sure the material is entirely legible (publishers may prefer legible single-sided photocopies or scans to pages from the original source). Unless there is ample space to insert corrections above the printed lines, any corrections should be written in the margins (see 2.124–38). See also 4.109.

2.49 **Permissible changes to previously published material.** The compiler of previously published material may make the following changes to the published material without editorial comment:

- Notes may be renumbered
- Cross-references to parts of the original work that are no longer relevant may be deleted
- Obvious typographical errors and minor grammatical slips that were clearly not intended may be silently corrected

See also 12.7–8. If wholesale changes have been made—for example, in spelling or capitalization conventions or notes style—the compiler should note such changes in a preface or elsewhere. For deletions indicated by ellipsis dots, see 12.59–69.

2.50 **Footnotes or endnotes in previously published material.** Footnotes that appear as such in the original pages may be presented as footnotes or endnotes in the published version. If a compiler's or volume editor's notes are being added along with the original footnotes or endnotes, the new notes should be intermingled with but distinguished from the original notes (see 13.54); if the original material is being submitted to the publisher on paper only, it may be preferable to produce a separate electronic document for the notes.

2.51 **Source notes for previously published material.** Each selection of previously published material should be accompanied either by a headnote (a brief introduction preceding the selection) or by an unnumbered footnote on the first page of text. The compiler should also include the source, the name of the copyright owner if the selection is in copyright (see chapter 4, esp. 4.2–54), and the original title if it has been changed. See also 13.58. If a selection has previously appeared in various places and different versions, the source note need not give the entire publishing history but must state which version is being reprinted.

2.52 **Reproducing previously published illustrations.** Compilers should contact their publisher about how to obtain illustrations from previously published material in a format suitable for printing. Photocopies of illustrations are not acceptable for reproduction. The compiler should procure glossy prints or the original publisher's scans. If these are unavailable, it may be possible to reproduce an illustration from the original publication. Compilers are also encouraged to supply alternative text descriptions for any illustrations that may require them (see also 3.28).

## MANUSCRIPT EDITING

### *Principles of Manuscript Editing*

2.53 **Levels of editing and who is responsible.** This chapter uses the general term *manuscript editing* to refer to the editing that is done after a manuscript has been accepted for publication. Manuscript editing can entail several different levels of editing and review, but this section focuses specifically on *copyediting*. Copyediting is not to be confused with either developmental editing or line editing, both of which occur earlier, or with proofreading, which occurs later.

- *Developmental editing* directly shapes the content of a work, the way material should be presented, the need for more or less documentation of sources and how such citations should be handled, and so on; unlike line editing and copyediting, it does not focus specifically on details at the sentence or word level. Developmental editing is typically undertaken by the editor who acquires the work for the publisher but may instead be handled by the author's agent or by a separate editor hired to do the work. Since it may involve total rewriting or reorganization of a work, developmental editing is always done (if needed) *before* copyediting begins.
- *Line editing* focuses on word choice, phrasing, and other matters of writing style at the sentence level. Though it frequently overlaps with copyediting, a separate line edit is best undertaken (if needed) *before* copyediting begins. Like developmental editing, it is typically handled by the author's agent or acquiring editor (after any developmental editing) but may instead be performed by a line editor hired for that purpose.
- *Copyediting* prepares an otherwise final manuscript for publication. It consists of both mechanical editing (see 2.55) and, where needed, substantive editing (see 2.56). As the final stage of editing before publication, copyediting requires attention to every word and mark of punctuation in a manuscript, a thorough knowledge of the style to be followed, and the ability to make quick, logical, and defensible decisions. It is usually undertaken by the publisher, either in house or through the services of a freelance copyeditor.
- *Proofreading* entails reviewing a work for any remaining errors after the manu-

script has been typeset for publication in print or converted for publication as an ebook or online—but before it has been published. Proofreading, which is often the responsibility of the author, is the subject of the third and last section of this chapter (2.105–44).

Each of these levels is subject to the approval of the author. Self-publishing authors may benefit from each stage of review outlined above and are encouraged at the very least to enlist the services of a professional copyeditor prior to publication. For a comprehensive overview of the editing process, see *What Editors Do: The Art, Craft, and Business of Book Editing*, edited by Peter Ginna (bibliog. 2.9). For more on developmental editing, consult Scott Norton's *Developmental Editing: A Handbook for Freelancers, Authors, and Publishers* (bibliog. 2.1).

2.54 **Sensitivity and authenticity readings.** In addition to the editing described in 2.53, some manuscripts will benefit from a separate reading to flag material that may be deemed inappropriate or harmful, particularly to underrepresented groups; others will benefit from a similar review that ensures the accuracy of period details and any other content that may be outside the author's direct personal experience. These are known as sensitivity and authenticity readings, respectively, though the concepts overlap, and the terms are sometimes used interchangeably. Though usually associated with fiction, sensitivity and authenticity readings have the potential to improve the quality of any type of book, including scholarly nonfiction. Such readings consist of reviews by an expert with special knowledge of subject areas or viewpoints that may be unfamiliar to the author. Authors are typically responsible for arranging for any such readings, though publishers may enlist sensitivity or authenticity readers for books that are likely to need them. Such readers usually provide suggestions directly to authors in the form of queries rather than edits. It is then up to the author to implement them or not. A sensitivity or authenticity reading should take place *before* the final manuscript is submitted for copyediting (but after any developmental editing); once copyediting has begun, it may be too late to make the necessary changes by the agreed-upon deadline, putting the publication schedule at risk. Copyeditors should nonetheless alert the publisher or the author to any potential problems at the earliest opportunity (and be prepared to incorporate the results of any last-minute feedback). In journal publishing, a sensitivity or authenticity reading may be included as part of peer review. For more information, see section 1.4 of the bibliography, which lists sources that cover inclusive language. See also 5.255–67.

2.55 **Mechanical editing.** Mechanical editing involves the consistent application of a particular style to a written work—including text and documentation and any tables and illustrations. The central focus of part 2 in this manual, *style* is used here to refer to rules related to capitalization, spelling, hyphenation, and abbreviations; punctuation, including ellipsis dots, parentheses, and quotation marks; and the way numbers are treated. Mechanical editing also includes attention to grammar, syntax, and usage. The rules set forth in a style manual like this one may be supplemented by a publisher's house style or the style of a particular discipline. Journal editors in particular follow a journal's established style, augmented by additional resources specific to the subject area. Books in a series or multivolume works should all follow one style consistently, as should separately authored chapters in a multiauthor book (but see 2.46). The style of any work, as well as occasional deviations from it, must be determined by the author, editor, and publisher before editing begins. For substantive editing, see 2.56. See also 2.57, 2.61.

2.56 **Substantive editing.** Substantive editing deals with the organization and presentation of existing content. It involves rewriting to improve word choice or to eliminate ambiguity, reorganizing or tightening disorganized or loosely written sections, adjusting or recasting tables, and other remedial activities. (It should not be confused with developmental editing, a more drastic process; see 2.53.) In general, no substantive editing should be undertaken without agreement between the publisher and editor, especially for book-length works; if major substantive work is needed, the author should be consulted and perhaps invited to approve a sample before the editing proceeds. A journal's manuscript editors, however, working on rigid schedules, may need to do substantive editing without prior consultation with authors if problems of organization, writing style, and presentation have not been addressed at earlier stages.

2.57 **Editorial discretion.** A light editorial hand is nearly always more effective than a heavy one, and a flexible approach is usually better than a prescriptive one for anything beyond the correction of outright errors and inconsistencies. In other words, an editor should never mindlessly enforce "the rules" without accounting for an author's style, the viewpoint of the narrator and any other voices in the manuscript (including in quoted passages and dialogue), and the conventions of the discipline or genre in which the author's work is situated. An experienced editor will recognize and not tamper with unusual figures of speech or idiomatic usage and will know when to make an editorial change and when simply to suggest it, whether to delete a repetition or an unnecessary recapitulation or simply point it out to the author, and how to suggest tactfully that an expression may be inappropriate or that an assertion might not be accurate. (Editors who discover problems that go beyond the scope of copyediting should be prepared to report these to the author or publisher at the earliest opportunity; see also 2.54, 2.62.) In general, an author's style should be respected, whether it is baroque or minimalist. On the other hand, editors should be aware of any requirements of a publisher's house style and impose these within reason, including any policies that are essential to the publisher—for example, those covering inclusive language (see 5.255–67). For communicating with the author and querying, see 2.74–78.

2.58 **Estimating editing time.** It is important to come up with a realistic estimate for how long the job of manuscript editing should take. This estimate (which is typically determined by the publisher and agreed to by the manuscript editor or, in the case of self-publishers, negotiated between author and editor) is important not only in ensuring the quality of the editor's work but in determining a reasonable fee as well as a schedule for completing the work. Most estimates start with the length of the manuscript. Because of inevitable variations in fonts and margins and the like, the length is best determined by a word count rather than a page count (a word count can be derived from a page count for paper-only manuscripts). A 100,000-word academic book manuscript, edited by an experienced editor, might take seventy-five to one hundred hours of work before being sent to the author, plus ten to twenty additional hours after the author's review. This rough estimate may need to be adjusted to factor in any complexities in the text—including any source citations, tables, and illustrations—and how much formatting and markup will be required (see 2.85). If in doubt, a copyeditor should edit a small sample for the author or publisher to serve as the basis of an estimate. An additional factor is of course the publication schedule, which may determine how many days are available for the editing stage or, in turn, may need to be adjusted depending on the estimate of editing time. Also pertinent is information about the author's availability to review the edited manuscript, amenability to being edited, propensity to revise, and so forth.

2.59 **Stages of manuscript editing.** Editors performing a copyedit will usually go through a manuscript three times—once to do the initial editing, easily the longest stage; a second time to review, refine, and sometimes correct the editing; and a third time after the author's review (see 2.78, 2.93). Editors working on electronic manuscripts may also be required to perform an initial, systematic cleanup (see 2.85), though a publisher's manuscript editing or production department may perform such a cleanup before turning a manuscript over to a copyeditor. (The publisher may likewise prefer to review and finalize the manuscript after it has been reviewed by the author rather than return it to the copyeditor.) Most editors begin the initial editing stage—sometimes in conjunction with the electronic cleanup—by looking through the entire document to assess the nature and scope of the work that will be required, to identify any matters that should be clarified with the author before editing begins, and to reduce the number of surprises that could cause delays if discovered later in the process. Then, some editors will edit the notes, bibliography, tables, figures, and other components separately from the text; others edit notes and other textual apparatus, or a part of it, along with the text. Whatever the procedure, all elements must be compared to ensure that the notes match their text references, citations correspond to the entries in the bibliography or reference list, tables correspond to any discussion of them in the text, and so on.

2.60 **Choosing a dictionary and other reference works.** A good dictionary is essential to a manuscript editor. For spelling, Chicago prefers the dictionary entries at Merriam-Webster.com (for more details, see 7.1). Editors also need reference works that furnish reliable spellings and identifications of persons, places, historical events, technical terms, and the like. For some basic reference works, see section 4 of the bibliography. For a complete discussion of names and terms, see chapter 8. If a system of source citation other than Chicago is to be used, the applicable style manual should be at hand (see bibliog. 1.1).

2.61 **Keeping an editorial style sheet.** To ensure consistency, for each manuscript the editor must keep an alphabetical list of words or terms to be capitalized, italicized, hyphenated, spelled, or otherwise treated in any way unique to the manuscript. Changes that are made simply for consistency with house style need not be noted on the style sheet. It is enough to note, for example, "In all other respects, Chicago style is followed." (For paper-only manuscripts it is useful to add the page number of the first occurrence of each item.) Special punctuation, unusual diacritics, and other items should also be noted on the style sheet. For fiction, an editor's style sheet may also include sections that list the names of characters (and their pronouns), places, and other elements of the fictional world and that keep track of the narrative timeline or chronology of events. For a book that is part of a series, the editor may need to refer to style sheets for earlier books in the series (and should request these from the publisher as needed). Not only the author but also the pub-

action plans
antiracist

child welfare workers
co-citizen
Conservative Party (Norwegian)
Convention on Human Rights

first-person singular
ghetto-like
government

jinns (plur. of jinn)
King and Queen (per author's request)

Labor government
Labor Party (Norwegian)

minister of child and family affairs
Ministry of Child and Family Affairs

non-word
north (of Norway)
northerners
Norwegian Pakistanis

Parliament
Progress Party
pro-immigrant
pro-multicultural

situation analysis
Somali, Somalis
Students' Antiracist Movement

Third World

Ungdom mot vold (rom)

Western Europe

Youth Against Violence (Ungdom mot vold)

*Mechanical matters*
(1995:47–48) colon betw. year and pp.
Ellipses: three-dot method, not three-or-four
Quoted newspaper headlines: sentence case
"emphasis mine"

FIGURE 2.3. Manuscript editor's style sheet. When prepared for a paper-only manuscript, the style sheet usually indicates the page number for the first appearance of each item. See 2.61.

lisher may need to refer to the style sheet at various stages of editing and production. See figure 2.3.

2.62 **Fact-checking.** In book publishing, the author is finally responsible for the accuracy of a work; most book publishers do not perform fact-checking in any systematic way or expect it of their manuscript editors unless specifically agreed upon up front. Nonetheless, obvious errors, including errors in mathematical calculations, should always be pointed out to the author, and questionable proper names, bibliographic references, and the like should be checked and any apparent irregularities queried. Editors need to be systematic about what they fact-check to avoid being distracted from the work at hand. It will sometimes be efficient to point out and correct obvious errors of fact that can be easily double-checked against reliable sources. Editors of fiction may need to add continuity checking to fact-checking to make sure details in one part of the book match up with details elsewhere (or in related books by the same author or in a series). For anything beyond that, however, fact-checking should be limited to what is needed to form an effective and judicious query to the author (see 2.75). For more information, consult Brooke Borel, *The Chicago Guide to Fact-Checking* (bibliog. 2.1). For sensitivity and authenticity readings, see 2.54.

## *Editing Specific Parts of a Manuscript*

2.63 **Editing front matter.** An editor should check any half title, title page, table of contents, and list of illustrations against the text and captions and against any applicable documentation included with the manuscript; discrepancies should be queried. If subheads are to be dropped from the table of contents, the author should be consulted (see also 1.42). For books, the editor should pay attention to the order of elements and may be asked to label the manuscript to ensure correct Roman numeral pagination (see 1.7; see also 2.80). Publishers generally prepare the copyright page, though editors may be expected to review any credits and other elements for accuracy and style (see 1.22).

2.64 **Editing part titles and chapter or article titles.** The editor of a book manuscript should ensure that part and chapter titles and their subtitles, if any, are consistent with the text in spelling, hyphenation, and italics. Chicago recommends that all titles be in title case unless a work is part of a series or journal that follows some other capitalization style (see 8.160). Part and chapter titles must be checked against the table of contents, and any discrepancy must be queried. Each title should be identified on the manuscript according to the publisher's requirements (for electronic manuscripts, see 2.86–88; for paper manuscripts, see 2.104). See also 1.53–60.

2.65 **Editing subheads.** Subheads should be checked for consistency with the text in spelling, hyphenation, and italics, and for parallel structure and tone. The text that immediately follows a subhead should be adjusted as needed for proper wording relative to the subhead (see 1.61). If there is more than one level of subhead, the hierarchy needs to be checked for sense and each level clearly identified (for electronic manuscripts, see 2.86–88; for paper manuscripts, see 2.104). It may be wise in an electronic manuscript to apply the appropriate markup for the different subhead levels based on the author's typographic distinctions at the outset, lest these distinctions be eliminated by any cleanup routine (see 2.85). If there are more than three levels of subhead, determine whether the lowest level can be eliminated. If subheads are to appear in the table of contents, they must be cross-checked for consistency. Subheads may be in either sentence case (see 8.159) or title case (see 8.160) provided they are capitalized consistently across each level (and unless a work is part of a series or journal that specifies a style for subhead capitalization). If in doubt about which capitalization style to apply, or if the majority of subheads consist of full sentences, choose sentence case as the more readable alternative. No period is added to the end of a subhead, even if the subhead is a complete sentence, except in the case of a run-in head (see 1.62). See also 1.61–64.

**2.66** **Editing cross-references.** All references to tables, figures, appendixes, bibliographies, or other parts of a work should be checked by the manuscript editor. If the author, for example, mentions a statistic for 2024 and refers readers to table 4, which gives statistics only through 2023, the editor must point out the discrepancy. Place-names on a contemporary map that illustrate the text must be spelled as in the text. Cross-references to specific pages—the numbering of which is subject to change in the published version—should be minimized or eliminated. See also 2.40.

**2.67** **Editing quotations and previously published material.** Aside from adjusting quotation marks and ellipsis dots and the like to conform to house style (see 12.7–8), the editor must do nothing to quoted material unless the author is translating it from another language (or modernizing it), in which case it may be lightly edited (see 11.18); transcribed interviews or field notes may also be subject to editing (see 12.56, 12.57, 12.58). Misspelled words and apparent transcription errors should be queried. An author who appears to have been careless in transcribing should be asked to recheck all quotations for accuracy, including punctuation. The editor should ensure that sources are given for all quoted material, whether following the quotation or in a note, and that the author has noted any stylistic changes in a preface or elsewhere (see 2.49). In editing previously published material, especially if it has been abridged, the editor should read for sense to ensure that nothing is out of order or has been inadvertently omitted. Discrepancies should be queried. If the previously published material has been provided on paper only, any ambiguous end-of-line hyphens should be clarified (see 2.101). See also 2.48.

**2.68** **Editing notes.** Each note must be checked against the text to ensure that its text reference is correct and in the right place and that any terms used in the note are treated the same way as in the text. When notes are to be printed as footnotes, the author may be asked to shorten an excessively long note or to incorporate some of the note into the text. Lists, tables, and figures should be placed not in footnotes but in the text or in an appendix. Manuscript editors may sometimes request an additional note to accommodate a needed source or citation. More frequently, in consultation with the author, they will combine notes or delete unneeded ones. See 13.60–64. An editor working on paper must take special care in renumbering notes. See also 2.69.

2.69 **Editing note citations, bibliographies, and reference lists.** Citations in notes, bibliographies, and reference lists must be carefully checked for documentation style (chapters 13 and 14; but see 2.70). Further, every subsequent reference to a work previously cited in the text or in a note must be given in the same form as the first reference or in the same shortened form (see 13.32–39). In a work containing a bibliography as well as notes, each citation in the notes should be checked against the bibliography and any discrepancy resolved or, if necessary, queried in both contexts so that the author can easily compare them (see 2.75). A bibliography need not include every work cited in the notes and may properly include some entries that are not cited. If author-date style is used, the editor should check all text citations against the reference list while editing the text and query or resolve any discrepancies. Bibliographies and reference lists should be checked for alphabetical order and, where applicable, for chronological order. For bibliographies, see 13.65–73; for reference lists and text citations, see 13.111–14, 13.115–28. Many editors find it helpful to edit the bibliography or reference list before the text and notes. Editors working on-screen may need to make sure that the source citations and related text are free of any underlying codes generated by the author in creating or organizing them (see 13.13).

2.70 **Flexibility in style for source citations.** Imposing house style on notes prepared in another style can be immensely time-consuming and, if the existing form is consistent and clear to the reader, is often unnecessary. This is especially true of books, many of which are intended to stand alone. Before making sweeping changes, the manuscript editor should consult with the author or the publisher or both. In journal editing, on the other hand, such flexibility is generally not allowed. For the published journal, citations are often linked to the resources themselves; the creation of such links can be facilitated by a consistent, predictable format across articles.

2.71 **Editing illustrations and captions.** Wording in diagrams, charts, maps, and the like should generally conform to the spelling and capitalization used in captions or the text. Captions in turn must conform to the style of the text. Source information should be edited in consultation with the publisher and in conformance with any letters of permission. (If permissions are outstanding, the publisher, not the editor, should take up the matter with the author.) Illustrations may be added, dropped, or renumbered during editing; it is therefore essential to make a final check of all illustrations against their text references and callouts (see 2.35) and against the captions and list of illustrations to be sure that they match and that the illustrations show what they say they do. If the author has provided alternative text, it should be checked for accuracy and style. For details on preparing illustrations and captions, see 3.3–47. For checking credits, see 3.30–38. For alternative text, see 3.28.

2.72 **Editing tables.** Tables are usually best edited together, as a group, to ensure consistent style and presentation. Tables should also be checked for consistent numbering and correspondence with the text—including text references and placement callouts (see 2.35). For specific guidelines on editing tables, see 3.82–89.

2.73 **Editing indexes.** The schedule for editing an index—which, if it depends on page number locators rather than paragraph numbers, is almost never prepared before book or journal pages have been composed—must usually correspond to the schedule for reviewing corrections to proofs. For a more detailed discussion, including an index-editing checklist, see 15.131–33.

## *Communicating with Authors*

2.74 **Contacting the author after an initial review of the manuscript.** Editors of book-length works are urged to contact their authors early on, after an initial review of the manuscript. This is especially important if an editor has questions or plans to make significant changes that, in the event the author proves not to be amenable, might take time and effort to undo. Likewise, to expedite production, a journal's manuscript editors may notify authors right away of any plans for systematic changes. Most authors are content to submit to a house style; those who are not may be willing to compromise. Unless usage is determined by journal or series style, the author's wishes should generally be respected. For a manuscript that requires extensive changes, it may be wise, if the schedule allows, to send a sample of the editing for the author's approval before proceeding (see 2.56).

2.75 **Writing author comments and queries.** Editors may generally impose a consistent style and correct errors without further comment—assuming these changes are apparent on the edited manuscript. Corrections to less obvious problems may warrant a comment. Comments should be concise, and they should avoid sounding casual, pedantic, condescending, or indignant; often, a simple "OK?" is enough. Comments that are not answerable by a yes or a no may be more specific: "Do you mean X or Y?" Examples of instances in which an editor might comment or query include the following:

- To note, on an electronic manuscript, that a particular global change has been corrected silently (i.e., without marking or tracking the change) after the first instance
- To point out a discrepancy, as between two spellings in a name, or between a source cited differently in the notes than in the bibliography
- To point out an apparent omission, such as a missing quotation mark or a missing source citation
- To point out a possible error in a quotation
- To point out repetition (e.g., "Repetition intentional?" or "Rephrased to avoid repetition; OK?")
- To ask for verification, as of a name or term whose spelling cannot be easily verified
- To ask for clarification where the text is ambiguous or garbled
- To point to the sources an editor has consulted in correcting errors of fact (but see 2.62)

For the mechanics of entering queries on a manuscript, see 2.92 (for electronic manuscripts) and 2.97 (for paper manuscripts).

2.76 **Writing a cover letter to the author.** The letter or email sent to the author with the edited manuscript, or sometimes separately, should include some or all of the following items (unless already communicated):

- An explanation of the nature and scope of the editing—for example, adjustment of spelling and punctuation to conform to house style (or to a particular style manual) and occasional rephrasing for clarity or to eliminate inadvertent repetition
- If the editing has been shown, an indication of how this has been done—that is, with change-tracking (redlining) software (see 2.89) or with pencil and paper (2.96)—and brief instructions for interpreting the marks
- Instructions as to how the author should respond to queries, veto any unwanted editing, and make any further adjustments to the edited manuscript (see 2.93, 2.96)

- A warning that the author's review of the edited manuscript constitutes the last opportunity to make any substantive changes, additions, or deletions and that quoted matter and citations should be checked if necessary
- A reminder to review the editing carefully, since even editors are fallible and the correction of any errors missed in editing and not caught until proofs may be deemed "author's alterations" and charged to the author (see 2.141)
- A reminder to retain a copy of the reviewed and corrected manuscript (to refer to at the proofreading stage)
- The deadline for return of the edited copy
- A brief discussion about the index, if any—whether the author is to prepare it, whether instructions are needed (see chapter 15), or whether a freelance indexer is to be engaged at the author's expense
- A request for confirmation of the author's contact information and availability for the rest of the publishing process

2.77 **Sending the edited manuscript to the author.** An electronically edited book manuscript—because of its length and, often, its complexity—may be sent to the author as hard copy or as a PDF file that the author is asked to print out. Alternatively, the author may be asked to review the PDF file using the commenting tools in Adobe Reader or the like (see 2.138), a common procedure for journal articles and other shorter works. The author reads and marks this printout as necessary (or adds comments in the PDF file), then returns it to the editor, who incorporates the author's marks into the word-processed manuscript. The author may instead review the manuscript using the same word-processing software that the editor has used—a procedure that saves printing and shipping costs. An editor working with an author in this manner needs to make sure the author does not make any undocumented changes—inadvertently or otherwise. For this reason, most copyeditors do not allow authors to collaborate with them by making simultaneous edits in a shared document online (e.g., using a cloud-based platform like Google Docs), preferring instead to maintain control of their own version of the document and turning it over to the author only when the editing is ready for review. For good measure, editors may choose to lock the document for editing such that any changes the author makes will be visibly tracked. A pencil-edited manuscript should be scanned or photocopied before being sent to the author; likewise, editors should advise authors to photocopy or scan paper manuscripts with their handwritten comments before returning them in case the original is lost.

2.78 **Checking the author's review of the edited manuscript.** When the manuscript comes back from the author, the editor goes through it once again to see what the author has done, checking that all queries have been answered and editing any new material. (If the author has rewritten extensively, another editing pass and author review may be needed; editors should inform the publisher of any such rewrites and get advice on how to proceed.) Except for style adjustments, the author's version should prevail; if that version is unacceptable for any reason, a compromise should be sought. As a part of this process, the editor updates the electronic files (see 2.94) or, if a manuscript is to be updated or typeset from a pencil-edited paper copy, clarifies or retypes the new material and crosses out the queries (see 2.97).

## *Preparing a Final Manuscript for Production*

2.79 **Ensuring correct markup.** Ensuring correct markup for a manuscript entails double-checking that each of its component parts has been properly identified in the final, edited manuscript, according to whatever system of markup has been used at that stage. For a book, these parts will include title and table of contents, chapters and sections and subsections, individual subheads, paragraphs of text, extracts, lists, notes, illustrations and captions, tables, and so forth. (Journal articles and other smaller documents may include fewer component parts.) Character-level markup must also be checked. This includes the markup required for any numeral, symbol, letter, word, or phrase that might be differentiated from the surrounding text—for example, a word or phrase that might be italicized for emphasis or a cross-reference (like the ones at the end of this paragraph) that might be hyperlinked online. Checking markup is usually the manuscript editor's responsibility, at least initially. Manuscript editors are closest to the content and will be able to spot any missing or incorrectly identified elements, or items that are not accounted for in the publisher's design template or style sheets. Once a manuscript is in production, however, markup generally becomes the responsibility of the publisher's production department. (Self-published authors who do not engage the services of a manuscript editor or book designer will need to pay close attention to the details described in this section and to be aware of any formatting and submission guidelines provided by their self-publishing platform.) For electronic markup options, see 2.86–88; for paper manuscripts, see 2.104. For an overview of the parts of a book or a journal, see chapter 1.

2.80 **Ensuring correct pagination.** Publishers may require editors of book manuscripts to indicate on the manuscript where Roman page numbers are to end and Arabic numbers begin—whether or not the number will actually appear (see 1.52). Furthermore, if there is a part title and the first chapter begins on page 3, "Arabic p. 3" will have to be specified at the chapter opening. The editor might also be required to specify whether subsequent elements are to begin on a recto or on a verso (see 1.4). Repagination of typeset, printed books is expensive; the editor should check that all elements—in the front matter, the text, and the back matter—are in their correct order and that the order is reflected in the table of contents. For journals, see 1.90.

2.81 **Preparing running heads.** Editors of book manuscripts may be required to provide a list of suggested copy for running heads (or feet) (see 1.10–16). The list must clearly indicate which heads are to appear on versos (left-hand pages) and which on rectos (right-hand pages). To fit on a single line, usually containing the page number as well (see 1.6), a chapter or article title may have to be shortened for a running head but must include the key terms in the title. (In some cases, the key terms will be in the chapter subtitle.) For certain languages other than English, it is important to retain any word that governs the case ending of another word in the running head. The author's approval may be needed; if possible, the editor should send the running-head copy to the author along with the edited manuscript. Running-head copy normally accompanies the manuscript to the typesetter and should be included with the other electronic files. If the running heads are to reflect the content of particular pages (rather than chapters or sections), the exact copy must be determined after (or as) the pages are typeset. For example, running heads to notes that include page ranges can be determined only from the typeset pages (see 1.15). These are typically indicated by the publisher on the first proofreading copy. To accommodate the potential for running heads in electronic formats, short forms for chapter and other titles can be specified as part of the title metadata (see 1.84); these may be used for running heads where needed or for other purposes.

2.82 **A production checklist.** Manuscripts that are ready to be typeset or converted for publication are usually accompanied by a checklist of vital statistics that includes information about the project and how it is to be produced. (This list is typically prepared by a publisher's production editor rather than by a manuscript editor.) Such a checklist, essential for book-length works, might consist of the following information:

- Name of author(s) and title of work
- A list of component parts of the project: electronic files, printout, illustrations, and so forth

- Details about the software used to prepare the final manuscript and a list of file names
- A list of any special characters or fonts (see also 2.19)
- An indication of how the electronic files have been marked up for production, a list of markup labels or styles, and any special instructions
- A list of any material that is still to come
- An indication of how notes are to be set—for example, as footnotes, as chapter endnotes, or as endnotes to the book
- A list of elements to be included in the front matter, the text, and the end matter, and an indication of which elements must start recto (see 1.4)
- For book-length manuscripts, an indication of who will be receiving page proofs, and in what format (e.g., print or PDF)

## *The Mechanics of Electronic Editing*

### PREPARATION AND CLEANUP

2.83 **Saving the manuscript files and keeping backups.** It is best to save and back up a manuscript in stages, creating separate copies of each significant version. The author's original, unedited copy should be archived (i.e., saved without further changes), as should every significant stage of the editing process. Each major stage should be saved with a different name—for example, by appending "author's original," "clean unedited," "first edit," "to author," and so forth to the file name. For complex projects, use different directories (i.e., folders) for the different stages. Exercise caution when saving files and working on new versions: Avoid saving over—or inadvertently working on—an earlier version of a file. Also take care not to inadvertently edit with change tracking turned off. During editing, open documents should be saved frequently, especially if automatic saving is unavailable. Some editors archive daily or weekly versions so that an earlier stage of the editing can be consulted if necessary. (File-hosting services may archive previous versions automatically, allowing access to these earlier versions or to deleted files—though without the benefit of the descriptive file names described above.) Each significant version should be backed up to a second location as protection against loss.

2.84 **Manuscript cleanup tools.** Many publishers provide manuscript editors with a cleaned-up version of the author's electronic file(s)—formatted and ready to edit. The publisher usually specifies the required software and may expect the editor to use or apply a certain type of markup (see 2.86–88). (Publishers may instead give editors hard copy only, updating the electronic files from the pencil-edited copy as part of the production process; for paper editing, see 2.95–104.) Some editors, however, are required to clean up and format the author's electronic files themselves. A full-featured word processor like Microsoft Word provides a number of tools that can save time by automating certain tasks. At the very least, it is important to learn about find-and-replace options, including the use of pattern matching (with wildcards or regular expressions), and about macros, which can save keystrokes by replicating and repeating repetitive tasks (including tasks that involve finding and replacing). (Consult the Help documentation in your word processor for instructions and examples.) Some editors take advantage of third-party add-ins preloaded with cleanup macros, enhanced find-and-replace options, and other editing tools.

2.85 **Manuscript cleanup checklist.** Before editing the manuscript, the editor must be certain that the files represent the author's latest version (the presence of embedded revision marks may be a sign that this is not the case; see 2.44). The next step is to get the electronic files ready to edit—if the publisher has not done this already. The following checklist suggests a set of steps that can be adapted as necessary to become part of an editor's word-processing cleanup routine. Not all manuscripts will require each step, and the suggested order need not be adhered to. Some of the steps can be automated, but most of the checklist can also be accomplished manually—that is, applied on a case-by-case basis, as part of the first read-through (see 2.59). Always review—and be prepared to undo—any global change before saving a permanent version of a file. Modify this checklist as needed to accord not only with the requirements of a specific manuscript but also with those of the publisher. Automatic redlining should usually be turned *off* during these steps (see 2.89).

1. Convert files for use in the editing software required by the publisher, if necessary.
2. To avoid having to apply this checklist more than once, consider combining separate files into a single electronic file. (Care must be taken to produce a complete manuscript, in the proper order and with no inadvertent deletions; always double-check the beginning and ending of each component and any notes thereto both when combining multiple files and when breaking a single file into smaller components.) Another option is to use macros that work across multiple files in a single directory (see 2.84).
3. If necessary, change the language settings of the manuscript and any subdocuments (e.g., from British English to American English, or vice versa). This will ensure that the spelling and grammar checker gives appropriate suggestions.

4. Scroll through the whole manuscript (preferably with nonprinting characters such as spaces, tabs, and paragraph marks showing) and look for and fix any formatting problems (e.g., hard returns in the middle of a paragraph) or conversion errors (e.g., special characters that look wrong), with reference to the original manuscript as necessary.
5. Identify any graphic elements and tables and handle appropriately—for example, moving figures or tables to separate files (see 2.31, 2.35).
6. Apply appropriate markup, as required, to any elements that are easy to identify at the outset but whose visual cues may be lost as the formatting is cleaned up. Look for chapter titles, subheads (and subhead levels), epigraphs, text and poetry extracts, extra line space (which may signal a stanza break in poetry or require an ornament or other device in text), and so forth. See also 2.86–88.
7. Delete or fix extraneous spaces and tabs, including instances of two or more consecutive spaces (between sentences or anywhere else) or spaces or tabs at the ends of paragraphs. Multiple spaces used to create first-line paragraph and other indents should be replaced either with tabs or, preferably, with software-defined indents (see also 2.14).
8. Change instances of multiple hard returns to single hard returns (but see item 6).
9. Change underlining to italics. Some underlining, however, may be intended to represent true underscore (e.g., in a manuscript that transcribes handwritten letters); this should be preserved, with a note to the publisher explaining the exception. See also 6.2.
10. Fix quotation marks and apostrophes; make sure that apostrophes at the beginning of words are correct (e.g., ’em *not* ‘em for “them”). But first determine, as applicable, that left and right single quotation marks have not been used by the author to stand in for breathing marks or other orthographic devices in transliterated languages (see chapter 11). See also 6.123, 6.125.
11. Fix commas and periods relative to quotation marks (see table 6.1).
12. Regularize em dashes and ellipses. For proper use of em dashes, see 6.91–98. For ellipses, see 12.59–69.
13. Replace hyphens between numerals with en dashes as appropriate. If you are using a macro to do this, it may be more efficient to let the macro run and to fix or add any exceptions during the first editing pass. For proper use of en dashes, see 6.82–90.
14. Convert footnotes to endnotes, or vice versa.
15. Delete any optional or conditional hyphens (i.e., software-dependent hyphens that allow words to break across the end of a line whether or not the hyphenation feature is turned on). Most word processors will allow you to search for these.
16. Find any lowercase els used as ones and any ohs (capital or lowercase) used as zeros—or vice versa—and fix. This can be done by using pattern matching

to search for two-character combinations containing either an el or an oh next to an expression that will find any numeral (see also 2.84).

17. Fix any other global inconsistencies that might be amenable to pattern-matching strategies. For example, in a bibliography in which two- or three-letter initials in names have been closed up, you can search for and evaluate capital letter combinations and replace as necessary with the same combination plus a space (e.g., changing E.B. White to E. B. White).
18. Adjust line spacing, font, and margins as desired.

As a final step—assuming these steps have been applied before editing—save a copy of the resulting clean, unedited manuscript in case it becomes necessary to refer to it later (see 2.83).

## ELECTRONIC MARKUP

2.86 **Generic markup for electronic manuscripts.** Manuscript editors are usually expected to identify each element of a manuscript, from headings to block quotations, using some form of markup. The most basic way to do this is with generic labels modeled on the descriptive identifiers used on pencil-edited manuscripts (see 2.104). Such labels are enclosed in angle brackets (< >), curly brackets ({ }), or some other delimiters that can be identified using the Find feature in a word processor. (This generic application of delimiters must not be mistaken for the ones used in HTML tags and the like; see 2.88.) However, because such identifiers must be replaced for publication and risk finding their way into the published work, this manual no longer recommends them as a markup strategy at the editing stage. Instead, and unless a publisher specifies otherwise, manuscript editors are advised to use word-processing styles (see 2.87). If necessary (e.g., if they are unable to use word-processing styles), authors may be instructed to use limited generic markup to help their editors identify the parts of a manuscript. For example, each first-level subhead could begin with "<A>" and each second-level head with "<B>," and so on. Most other elements, however—including chapter titles, prose and poetry extracts, and the like—are best identified through formatting alone (i.e., font sizes, indents, and so forth). An exception is generally made for placement callouts for figures, which authors and editors alike may insert within angle brackets for easy identification by the typesetter (see 2.35).

2.87 **Word-processing styles.** Manuscript editors are often expected to apply word-processing styles that correspond to each distinct element of the manuscript, including chapter numbers and titles, subheads, text, prose extracts, poetry, and so forth. Some publishers provide a template loaded with paragraph and character styles defined for a book or article manuscript. The advantage of using styles is that manuscript editors (and their authors) can work in a familiar software environment while facilitating the more detailed markup required for publication in electronic formats. Each word-processing style carries a unique name and, depending on the style, can be applied either to a paragraph or to one or more characters within a paragraph. (A paragraph in a word processor is any string of text followed by a hard return.) Paragraph-level style names should be descriptive, corresponding to the type of element (e.g., "chapter number" or "A-head") rather than to its format or appearance. Character-level styles, on the other hand, can usually be applied through formatting alone (e.g., italics or superscript). Appropriate font size, line spacing, italics, and other formatting attributes should be defined for each style in the word-processed manuscript to facilitate editing and author review. On the other hand, accuracy and consistency in applying styles is more important than any formatting in the manuscript. The publisher will map the styles to a design template for the printed work or to a tag set that accommodates presentation in multiple formats, including print (see 2.88). If there are any text elements that do not lend themselves easily to the styles in a given template, it may be necessary to define new styles or to query the publisher. (Authors reviewing the edited manuscript should be advised not to modify styles.) An annotated list of styles should accompany the manuscript sent to production.

2.88 **Formal markup languages.** A manuscript edited on paper or in a word processor may have to be converted and marked up at some point according to the rules defined for an XML tag set or the like, especially if it is to be published as an ebook or online. Such a conversion can be facilitated during the editing stage by applying word-processing styles (see 2.87). Styles are mapped to corresponding tags, and additional markup is added to delineate the structure of the manuscript, facilitate linking, and so forth. Each element, including each document or subdocument, is identified by a pair of opening and closing tags according to the rules of the particular markup language. Tags are nested; for example, the body of the document, enclosed between an opening and a closing tag, will include all sections and subsections of the document, and each of those parts in turn will be delimited by a pair of tags that identify the element and its place in the hierarchy. Tags are also used to delimit any element that needs to be differentiated from the surrounding text (such as an emphasized word) or that may have a special function (such as a cross-reference that will be linked to its destination). Such tagging is structural as well as semantic: Each element is identified according to what it is rather than by how it will ultimately be presented. Details about presentation, including appearance and function, are specified in a style sheet for each format of publication. If editing takes place after conversion to a formal markup language, the editor usually helps to ensure that the tags have been applied correctly (see also 2.142–44). The successful implementation of such a workflow, on the other hand, requires significant technical expertise.

## TRACKING CHANGES AND INSERTING QUERIES

2.89 **Tracking changes (redlining).** To show their work and thus facilitate the author's review, many editors use the change-tracking feature in their word processor to produce what is sometimes referred to as a *redlined* version of the manuscript (a name that invokes, in another medium, the editor's red pencil). The principle is simple: When the tracking feature is turned on, text that is added is underlined, like this; text that is deleted is struck through, ~~like this~~. (Added or deleted text can be displayed in a variety of other ways depending on software and settings.) Author queries are inserted using the word processor's commenting feature (see 2.92). For a demonstration, see figure 2.4. (Comments and changes usually appear in color by default; editors sending black-and-white printouts to their authors for review must take care that everything remains legible.) For any change that might be ambiguous or hard to interpret (e.g., a struck-through hyphenated term), it can be helpful to include an explanatory comment to the author at the first occurrence. By the same token, it is best to avoid making changes that might be missed; when in doubt, strike out the entire term and replace it with the corrected or preferred version. For example, to mark a change from "Du Bois" to "DuBois" (as when quoting a source that styles the name of the American educator and writer that way), show ~~Du Bois~~DuBois rather than Du-Bois, the latter of which may be mistaken for a hyphenated term. See also 2.90. For marking changes on PDF files, see 2.138.

2.90 **Making silent changes (not tracking).** Whether to track all editing, mechanical as well as substantive, depends on a number of factors, including the editor's and publisher's preferences. In order to avoid irritating or distracting the author, some editors will prefer to track only the first instance of a global change (such as capitalization of a certain term) and alert the author to the change in a comment (see 2.92). Certain adjustments should almost never be shown—for example, changes to margins or a global application of "smart" quotation marks and apostrophes (see

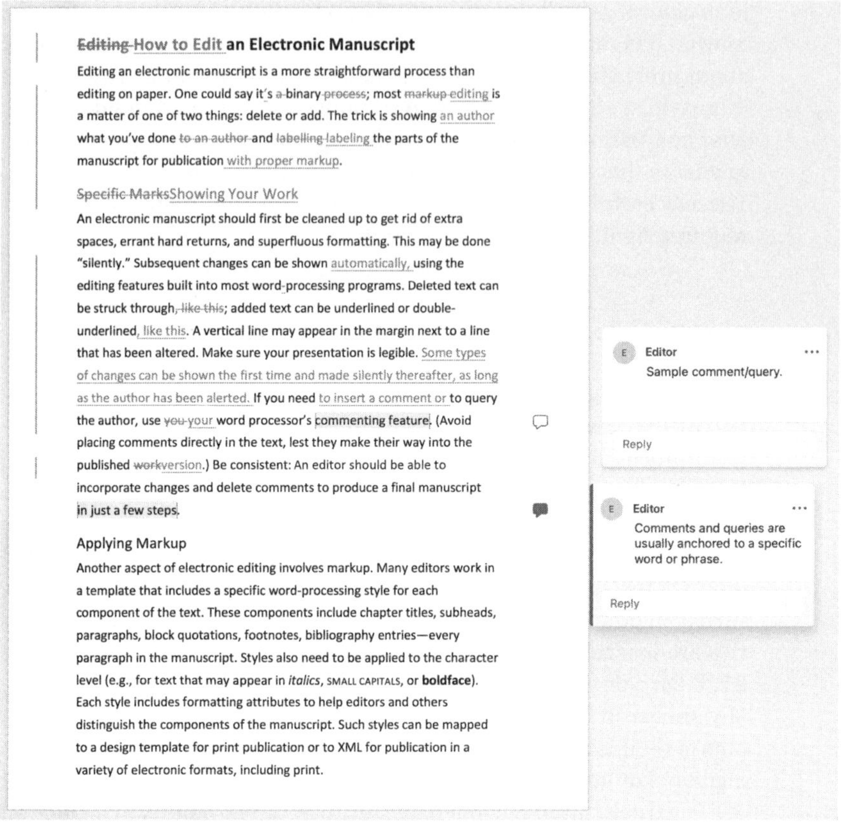

**~~Editing~~ How to Edit an Electronic Manuscript**

Editing an electronic manuscript is a more straightforward process than editing on paper. One could say it's ~~a~~ binary ~~process~~; most ~~markup~~ editing is a matter of one of two things: delete or add. The trick is showing an author what you've done ~~to an author~~ and ~~labelling~~ labeling the parts of the manuscript for publication with proper markup.

~~Specific Marks~~Showing Your Work

An electronic manuscript should first be cleaned up to get rid of extra spaces, errant hard returns, and superfluous formatting. This may be done "silently." Subsequent changes can be shown automatically, using the editing features built into most word-processing programs. Deleted text can be struck through~~, like this~~; added text can be underlined or double-underlined, like this. A vertical line may appear in the margin next to a line that has been altered. Make sure your presentation is legible. Some types of changes can be shown the first time and made silently thereafter, as long as the author has been alerted. If you need to insert a comment or to query the author, use ~~you~~ your word processor's commenting feature. (Avoid placing comments directly in the text, lest they make their way into the published ~~work~~version.) Be consistent: An editor should be able to incorporate changes and delete comments to produce a final manuscript in just a few steps.

Applying Markup

Another aspect of electronic editing involves markup. Many editors work in a template that includes a specific word-processing style for each component of the text. These components include chapter titles, subheads, paragraphs, block quotations, footnotes, bibliography entries—every paragraph in the manuscript. Styles also need to be applied to the character level (e.g., for text that may appear in *italics*, SMALL CAPITALS, or **boldface**). Each style includes formatting attributes to help editors and others distinguish the components of the manuscript. Such styles can be mapped to a design template for print publication or to XML for publication in a variety of electronic formats, including print.

E Editor
Sample comment/query.
Reply

E Editor
Comments and queries are usually anchored to a specific word or phrase.
Reply

FIGURE 2.4. A manuscript page illustrating the principles of on-screen revision marks (redlining) and author queries using Microsoft Word. Markup for headings, paragraphs, and text has been applied using Word's paragraph and character styles. See 2.87, 2.89.

6.123, 6.125). In general, most of the things listed in the cleanup checklist at 2.85 may be done silently. If a section of the manuscript such as a bibliography has been heavily edited, the editor may send a clean version of that section for the author to approve, with or without a version showing the edits for reference. But if changes have not been tracked for any reason, the editor must delineate for the author the nature of the editing either in a comment or in the cover letter with the edited manuscript (see 2.76).

2.91 **Document comparison software.** Document comparison software can highlight the differences between two versions of a document automatically. Best results are had with shorter documents in which the latest version is compared against an earlier version that has already been cleaned up and formatted (see 2.85). Comparing an edited document against the author's original manuscript may result in too many changes being reported, or worse, the results may be unintelligible. Editors should turn to document comparison software only in specific instances—for example, to make sure they are working on the latest version of a document. For communicating changes to the author, which usually requires a more predictable presentation in which some types of changes are made silently while others are spelled out as clearly as possible, editors should track their changes as they edit (see 2.89).

2.92 **Inserting comments and queries.** Editors should insert queries to the author using the commenting feature in their word processor; authors, for their part, should be asked to respond to these queries using this same feature. See figure 2.4 for an example. Avoid using footnotes or bracketed text to insert queries. As a matter of principle, it is best to avoid typing anything directly into the document that is not intended for publication. (Exceptions can be made for image callouts and similar elements intended to be incorporated into the markup for the published version; see 2.35. Another exception is made by some publishers for embedded notes, which in certain applications do not support comments; alternatively, such comments may be anchored to the text at the applicable note reference marker.) See also 2.75.

2.93 **Author's review of the redlined manuscript.** Authors who review changes and queries on-screen should be asked to use a compatible version of the software that was used to edit the manuscript. (Authors who cannot accommodate this request may have to review a printout instead or annotate a PDF file; see 2.77.) To guard against unwanted changes—inadvertent or otherwise—the editor may want to protect the manuscript with a password such that any changes the author makes will be visibly tracked. (Editors are advised to take care not to lose the password; it will be needed in order to unlock the files returned by the author and prepare the final manuscript.) Editors should include detailed instructions for making changes and adding or responding to queries. With password protection, authors can usually be asked simply to type any additions into the manuscript and delete any of the editor's changes or other unwanted text. For comments and replies to queries, however, authors should generally be advised to use the commenting feature lest any of their comments inadvertently make it into the published version (see also 2.92).

2.94 **Accepting or rejecting tracked changes and deleting queries.** After the author has returned the redlined manuscript, the editor should go through each tracked change carefully and accept it or reject it, as the case may be, using the available word-processing tools. New material inserted by the author should be edited as necessary, and any other type of change should be checked for continuity with the surrounding text. It may be wise to read through each author comment or query first in order to spot any potential problems. After all comments and queries have been read and all changes have been incorporated, any remaining comments and queries should be deleted. Because of the potential for errors introduced at this stage, a spelling and grammar check should be run again as a final step. The final manuscript should have no remaining tracked changes or comments, with the exception of any comments intended for the publisher (though it may be better to send these in a cover letter).

## *The Mechanics of Editing on Paper*

2.95 **Keeping a clean copy of paper manuscripts.** An editor working on paper should always keep a clean copy of the unedited manuscript to refer to—or as a backup in case any reediting is necessary. If the paper copy is a printout of an electronic manuscript, it is enough to archive a copy of the latter.

2.96 **Marking manuscripts on paper.** Editing a manuscript on paper—whether it is to be typeset from scratch or used to update the author's electronic manuscript—requires a technique similar to the one used for marking corrections on proofs (see 2.124–38). To allow for the more extensive changes typical of the editing stage, however, paper manuscripts are usually double-spaced so that edits can appear above the word or words they pertain to, rather than in the margin. (Manuscripts that consist of photocopies of tightly spaced previously published material are edited in the manner of page proofs.) All editorial changes should be made in a color that will reproduce clearly if the edited manuscript is photocopied or faxed, and the author should be asked to respond to the editing in a color distinct from that used by the editor. For marking queries, see 2.97. For a sample of a correctly marked manuscript, see figure 2.5.

2.97 **Marking author queries on paper manuscripts.** In manuscripts edited on paper, queries are best written in the margin. When the author has responded, they can simply be crossed out. Chicago discourages the use of sticky notes for queries: They cannot be easily photocopied or scanned, and they may have to be detached in the process of updating the electronic files or (for paper-only manuscripts) typesetting the final

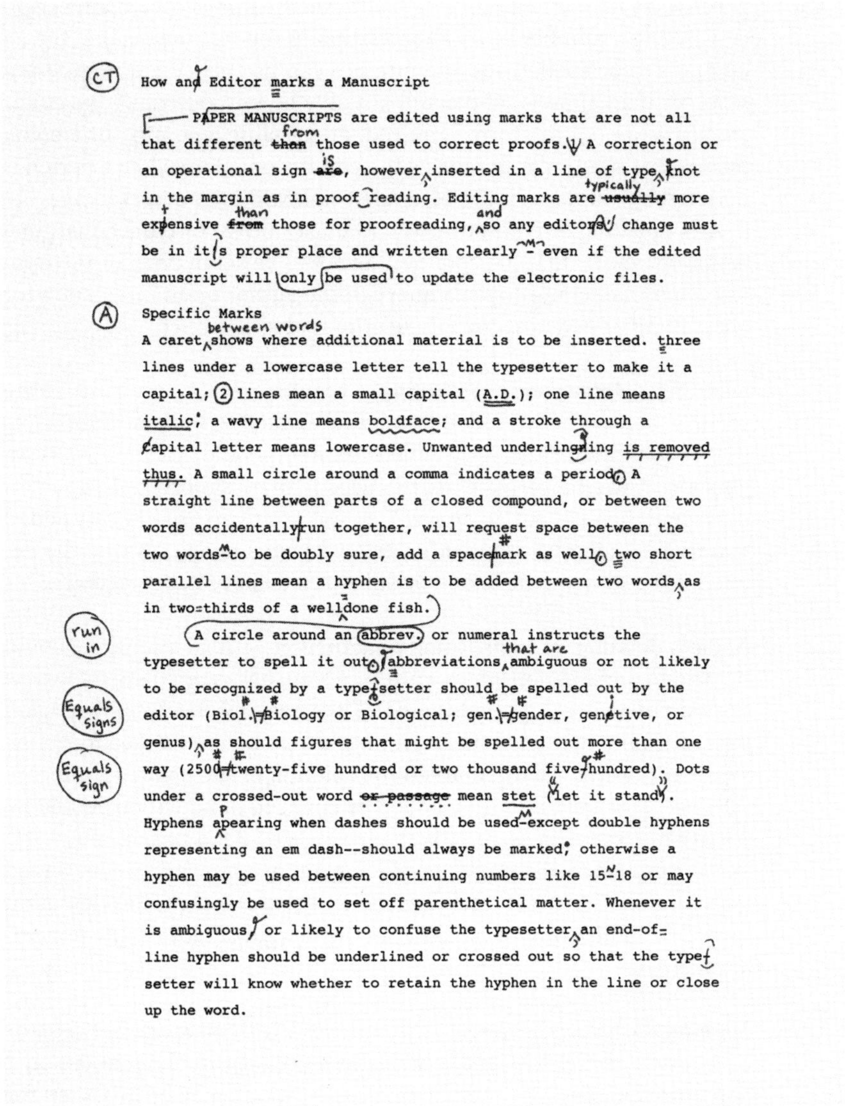

How and Editor marks a Manuscript

PAPER MANUSCRIPTS are edited using marks that are not all that different than those used to correct proofs. A correction or an operational sign are, however inserted in a line of type not in the margin as in proof reading. Editing marks are usually more expensive from those for proofreading, so any editors change must be in its proper place and written clearly - even if the edited manuscript will only be used to update the electronic files.

Specific Marks

A caret shows where additional material is to be inserted. three lines under a lowercase letter tell the typesetter to make it a capital; 2 lines mean a small capital (A.D.); one line means italic; a wavy line means boldface; and a stroke through a capital letter means lowercase. Unwanted underlingning is removed thus. A small circle around a comma indicates a period, A straight line between parts of a closed compound, or between two words accidentallyrun together, will request space between the two words-to be doubly sure, add a spacemark as well, two short parallel lines mean a hyphen is to be added between two words as in two=thirds of a welldone fish.

A circle around an abbrev. or numeral instructs the typesetter to spell it out, abbreviations ambiguous or not likely to be recognized by a type setter should be spelled out by the editor (Biol.=Biology or Biological; gen.=gender, genetive, or genus) as should figures that might be spelled out more than one way (2500=twenty-five hundred or two thousand five hundred). Dots under a crossed-out word or passage mean stet (let it stand). Hyphens apearing when dashes should be used-except double hyphens representing an em dash--should always be marked, otherwise a hyphen may be used between continuing numbers like 15-18 or may confusingly be used to set off parenthetical matter. Whenever it is ambiguous, or likely to confuse the typesetter an end-of= line hyphen should be underlined or crossed out so that the type- setter will know whether to retain the hyphen in the line or close up the word.

FIGURE 2.5. An example of a hand-marked manuscript page. See 2.96.

pages (and thus may no longer be in place when the pencil-edited manuscript is sent back to the author with the proofs). For more extensive queries that require more space than the margin affords, a separate sheet, keyed by letter or symbol to a specific place in the manuscript, may be prepared.

2.98 **Three uses for circling.** Circling has three meanings on a manuscript. (1) Circling a number or an abbreviation in the text means that the element is to be spelled out. If a number can be spelled out in different ways, or if an abbreviation could possibly be misconstrued, the editor should write out the form required. (2) Circling a comma or a colon means that a period is to replace the comma or colon; when a period is inserted by hand, it should be circled so it will not be missed by whoever is updating or typesetting the manuscript. (3) Circling a marginal comment shows that the comment is not to be set in type (or incorporated into the manuscript); a query to the author or an instruction for typesetting or updating the manuscript is always circled.

2.99 **Inserting, deleting, and substituting.** A regular caret (Λ), used to indicate an insertion point for added text but also used to indicate subscripts (and, similarly, to indicate an added comma), should be carefully distinguished from an inverted caret (V), used to mark superscripts, apostrophes, and the like. But, in general, do not use a caret to indicate added text that is being substituted for deleted text; simply cross out the deleted text and write the text to be substituted above it. See figure 2.5.

2.100 **Adding, deleting, or transposing punctuation.** Special attention should be paid to punctuation when words are transposed or deleted; the new position of commas, periods, and the like must be clearly shown. Likewise, any punctuation at the beginning or end of text marked for transposition must be clearly marked for deletion or inclusion, as the case may be. More generally, any added or changed punctuation should be clearly marked—for example, by circling an added period, placing a caret over an added comma, or placing an inverted caret under added quotation marks. If necessary, write (and circle) "colon," "exclamation point," or whatever applies, either in the margin or close to the punctuation change.

2.101 **Marking dashes and hyphens.** Two hyphens with no space between or on either side clearly signal em dashes and need not be marked on a paper-only manuscript. Actual em dashes, which may be mistaken for en dashes in some typefaces, should be marked (with a capital letter *M* written above the line); 2- or 3-em dashes, even if consistently typed, should also be marked (with *2M* or *3M*), as should en dashes (with an *N*) to prevent them from being mistaken for hyphens. Alternatively, a global instruction may be issued—for example, "all hyphens between inclusive numbers are to be set as en dashes." End-of-line hyphens should be marked to distinguish between soft (i.e., conditional or optional) and hard hyphens. Soft hyphens are those hyphens that are invoked only to break a word at the end of a line; hard hyphens are permanent (such as those in *cul-de-sac*) and must remain no matter where the hyphenated word or term appears. See also 2.16.

2.102 **Capitalizing, lowercasing, and marking for italics or boldface.** To indicate that a lowercase letter should be capitalized, triple underline it; to make it a small capital, double underline it. To lowercase a capital letter, run a slanted line through it. To mark for italics, underline the word(s) to be italicized with a straight line; for boldface, make the underlining wavy. For manuscripts that are to be typeset from scratch, there is usually no need to underline words that appear in italics in the manuscript if the typesetter is instructed to italicize them. (Italics in some fonts are difficult to distinguish at a glance; underlining may reduce the incidence of missed italics.) If an author has used both underlining and italics, special instructions are needed (see 2.18).

2.103 **Marking paragraph indents, flush left or right, and vertical spacing.** Use a three-sided rectangular mark to indicate that text or other elements should be moved to the left (⊏) or to the right (⊐). A line may be drawn from the open side of the mark to the element to be moved (see fig. 2.5). To indicate paragraph indents, use the paragraph symbol (¶). To mark vertical space, use a rectangular mark that "points" up (⊓) or down (⊔); adjust the width to accommodate the element. To indicate a blank line, write "one-line #" and circle it. (In typographic usage the sign # means space, not number.)

2.104 **Marking the components of a paper manuscript.** The components of a paper manuscript—chapter number and title, subheads, prose extracts, poetry, and so forth—are marked with labels or descriptions that are circled and placed at the beginning of the element or in the margin next to it. For example, a circled "A" may be used to indicate a first-level subhead (see fig. 2.5). The handwritten labels are similar to the ones that are sometimes used for generic markup in an electronic manuscript (see 2.86). See also 2.98.

## PROOFREADING

### *Introduction*

2.105 **What is proofreading?** Proofreading is the process of reading a document and scrutinizing all its components to find errors and mark them for correction. Each major stage of a manuscript intended for publication—

especially the final version the author submits to the publisher and, later, the copyedited version of the same—is generally reviewed in this way. Proofreading here, however, applies to the review of the manuscript *after* it has been converted to a format for publication but *before* it is published. Usually, this format consists of the typeset and paginated pages of a book or journal article (referred to as proofs or proof and read either on paper or as PDF) or the full text of a book or journal article intended for publication in one or more electronic formats other than PDF. Also subject to proofreading are covers and jackets or other packaging as well as the abstracts and other components that are published along with the work or as part of one or more electronic formats. For an illustration of how the stages described in this chapter fit into the overall publishing process for books and journals, see the outline at 2.2. For proofreaders' marks, see 2.124; for PDF markup, see 2.138. For proofing and testing electronic formats, see 2.142–44.

2.106 **Who should proofread?** For the majority of publications, authors are considered the primary proofreaders, and it is they who bear final responsibility for any errors in the published work. To help mitigate this responsibility, a professional proofreader may be hired by either the author or the publisher. (Self-publishing authors can also benefit from the services of a proofreader, whether or not they have also hired a professional editor.) Moreover, the manuscript editor and book designer and other publishing personnel are generally responsible for ensuring that the author's corrections (and those of any other proofreader) are successfully incorporated into the work before it gets published and that all related materials (promotional copy, web page listings, etc.) are free of errors and inconsistencies.

2.107 **Proofreading schedule.** Since many people are involved in the production of a book, a few days' delay in returning proofs to the publisher or typesetter can cause a major delay in publication. When the time scheduled for proofreading appears to conflict with the demands of accuracy, or if any other problem arises that might affect the schedule, the proofreader should immediately confer with the publisher. For journals, where there is little room for delays of any kind, proofreading deadlines are generally nonnegotiable. See also 2.2.

## *Stages of Proof*

2.108 **Keeping a record of each proofreading stage.** A record must be kept by the publisher of when each stage of proof has been corrected and by whom. For printed books, publishers typically rely on a primary set of proofs (also called a master set) during the first proofreading stage. This primary set is either (a) a single printout read and marked for corrections by the author and marked with additional corrections by the publisher and any others who have read or reviewed the primary set or copies thereof, or (b) a PDF version of the same. Some publishers send a duplicate set of page proofs to the author and then transfer the author's corrections to the primary set. For PDF, it is important to name the different iterations of the file appropriately and collate all corrections in the primary file. At the next stage, revised proofs are usually reviewed by the publisher, who retains the primary version of this new set or file and a record of each additional round of corrections until the work has been published. (Each new round of corrections should be reflected in the file name for the PDF—e.g., by "rev01," "rev02," etc.) At each stage, the author and other proofreaders should each be required to sign off before a corrected version is delivered for further review. Likewise, for covers and jackets or other packaging, each person assigned to proofread should be required to sign off on the proofreading copy before a corrected version is routed for further review.

2.109 **First proofs and "galley" proofs.** The author or sometimes a designated proofreader reads the first proofreading copy (*first proofs* or *first pages*), preferably against the edited manuscript (see 2.115). For books, an index may be prepared from this first set of page proofs, either by the author or by a professional indexer (see chapter 15). For some complex book-length works, first proofs are issued in the form of "galleys." Strictly speaking, the term *galley proofs* is an anachronism, dating from the era when printers would arrange type into "galleys" from which long, narrow prints were prepared to proofread or edit type before the arduous task of composing it, by hand, into the form of book pages. Today, if a complex project presents a danger of extensive corrections at the page-proof stage, a publisher might request galley proofs (loosely paginated and with or without illustrations in place), since corrections to galleys will not entail having to redo page references in an index. These galleys are generated from the same electronic files as first proofs would be. (As an alternative to the galley stage, publishers might choose to undertake a proofreading of the final electronic manuscript.) The index is prepared not from the galleys, since pagination is not final, but from the "first" proofs that are issued at the next stage.

2.110 **Revised proofs.** After corrections to the first proofs have been made, the results must be checked for accuracy. This usually involves comparing *revised proofs* (also called *second pages*) for all pages against the first pages (now known as "foul" proofs). These revised proofs should also be checked for any other differences between them and the first proofs and to make sure hyphenation errors or other page makeup problems have not been introduced. If the typesetter has circled or bracketed or otherwise indicated any changes to page makeup resulting from the corrections, the proofreader can check revised proofs more efficiently. Any corrections that have resulted in repagination may require adjustments to page references in the index. To maintain a proper record, nothing must be marked on the pages or in the PDF file for the foul proofs at this stage; any further corrections must be marked only on the revised printout or revised PDF. Any additional rounds of revision should be kept to a minimum.

2.111 **Index proofs.** Most indexes are prepared from the paginated first set of proofs (unless they reference paragraph numbers rather than page numbers, in which case they can be prepared from the final manuscript). Indexes must be proofread quickly, in the same time that the revisions to the first proofs are being checked. For the sake of efficiency, editors rather than authors usually proofread indexes. For a full discussion of indexes, see chapter 15.

2.112 **Prepress and press proofs.** For works that will be printed and bound, publishers usually review prepress proofs. Prepress proofs present an inexpensive image of what will come off the printing press—generated either from negative film or, more commonly, from electronic files. (The final typesetter's files—usually PDF—can generally be considered equivalent to prepress proofs.) These proofs—a "now or never" opportunity to look at what will be published, *before* ink is committed to paper—are normally checked for completeness of contents; page sequence; margins; and location, sizing, position, and cropping (if any) of illustrations. For reasons of press schedule and expense, publishers will generally allow only the correction of grave errors at this stage, such as an incorrect title or a misspelled author's name. One additional look—at actual press sheets, folded into signatures and gathered into the proper page sequence (and called F&Gs)—is sometimes also granted to book and journal publishers. (Press sheets that include full-color illustrations are occasionally sent to the publisher to approve before the entire work is printed.) By the time the publisher sees a complete set of F&Gs, copies of the work are off the press and may be in the bindery. Since any correction at this stage would involve reprinting an entire signature, the publisher may decide to tolerate any remaining errors (while compiling a list of corrections for any future reprint). See also 1.77.

2.113 **Book cover and jacket proofs.** Whereas most publishers (and authors) will live, if not happily, with the inevitable typo inside a book, an error on the cover is a more serious matter. Proofs of die copy—author's name, title, publisher's imprint, and any other matter to be stamped on the spine or cover of a hardbound book—should be checked with extreme care. Likewise, proofs of jacket copy and paperback cover copy should be read and checked word for word (if not letter by letter), with special attention paid as follows:

- The cover should be consistent with the interior of the work in content and style. For example, the author's name and the title of the work—everywhere they appear, including cover, spine, and jacket flaps—must match those on the title page of the book (though the subtitle may be omitted from the cover or jacket). An author's full name is sometimes shortened in the running text of flap copy.
- Biographical material on the author should be checked against any biographical material inside the book, though the wording need not be identical.
- If the work is part of a series or a multivolume set, the series title or volume number must match its counterpart inside the book.
- The price (if it is to appear), the ISBN, and any necessary credit line for a photograph of the author or for artwork used on the cover or jacket must be verified.

Jacket and cover proofs and each stage of revisions thereto should be reviewed by everyone involved in the production of the book—including editors, designers, marketing personnel, and (for at least some of the stages) authors.

2.114 **Journal cover proofs.** Although the elements that appear on the covers of academic journals vary considerably, the following suggestions should apply to most journals: The front cover (called cover 1) must be checked carefully to ensure that elements that change with each issue, such as the volume and issue numbers and the month, date, or season of publication, are accurate and up to date. The spine must be similarly checked. If the contents of the issue are listed on cover 1, they must be checked against the interior to be sure that authors' names and article titles match exactly and, for journals that publish various types of articles, that articles have been listed in the correct section of the journal. If inclusive page numbers appear on the spine, these must be verified. The inside of the front cover (cover 2) often includes subscription prices and information on how to subscribe, names of editors and members of the editorial board, or copyright information; all such information must be checked. Covers 3 (inside of back cover) and 4 (back cover) may contain advertisements, instructions to authors on submitting articles, or a list of articles to appear in future issues. They all must be verified by the proofreader.

## *How to Proofread and What to Look For*

2.115 **Proofreading against copy.** In proofreading parlance, *copy* refers to the edited manuscript. Proofs should be checked against the version of the manuscript that contains the author's final changes and responses to queries (see 2.78), though authors and dedicated proofreaders typically do a "cold read," checking against the manuscript only to resolve any questions. In the event that the page proofs were typeset from a paper-only manuscript, the proofreader must read word for word against the edited manuscript, noting all punctuation, paragraphing, capitalization, italics, and so forth and ensuring that any handwritten editing has been correctly interpreted by the typesetter. Likewise, any element in an otherwise electronic manuscript that has been set from edited hard copy (e.g., math or tables) should be proofread carefully against the hard copy. Whether type has been set from electronic files or from paper, the proofreader must mark only the proofs, never the manuscript, which at this point in the process is known as "dead" or "foul" copy. To assign responsibility for errors correctly (see 2.140), the manuscript as earlier approved by the author must be kept intact. For checking revised proofs, see 2.110.

2.116 **Proofreading for spelling errors.** The proofreader should remain alert for the kinds of errors that are often missed even by context-sensitive spelling and grammar checkers—from common typos such as *it's* where *its* is meant or *out* where *our* is meant, to more subtle errors like *lead* for *led* or *breath* for *breathe*, as well as other misspellings. The manuscript editor's style sheet (see 2.61) may be a useful reference. Note that a change to the spelling of a particular term should never be indicated globally; instead, each change must be marked throughout the proofs (if possible, the PDF should be searched to find and evaluate other instances of the term).

2.117 **Proofreading for word breaks.** End-of-line hyphenation should be checked, especially in proper names and terms in any language that may be outside the range of the dictionaries that automatically assign line breaks during typesetting. The first set of proofs is usually the first time that words have been divided, conditionally, at the ends of lines. Chicago recommends the word breaks suggested by the dots between syllables in the dictionary entries at Merriam-Webster.com (see 7.1). For words or names not listed in a dictionary, a liberal approach is advisable, since usage varies widely and any change requested may entail further breaks or create tight or loose lines (lines with too little or too much space between words). Such problems may be avoided if a list of nondictionary words and their preferred hyphenation (or an editor's style sheet if it includes this information) is submitted to the typesetter along with the manuscript. When it is a question of an intelligible but nonstandard word break for a line that would otherwise be too loose or too tight, the nonstandard break (such as the hyphenation of an already hyphenated term) may be preferred. No more than three succeeding lines should end in a hyphen (see 7.48). See also 2.16, 7.36–48. For dividing URLs at the end of a line, see 7.47.

2.118 **Proofreading for typeface and font.** Each element in proofs—for example, chapter numbers and titles, subheads, text, extracts, and figure captions—should be checked to ensure that it is presented in a consistent typeface and style in accordance with the design for the publication. Heads and subheads, in particular, should be checked for the typographic style assigned to their level (see 2.22, 2.65), and all set-off material (excerpts, poetry, equations, etc.) should be checked for font, size, and indentation. All material in italics, boldface, small capitals, or any font different from that of the surrounding text should be looked at to be sure the new font starts and stops as intended. Note that the conversion of manuscript files into other formats for publication can result in unexpected errors, such as the dropping or transmutation of a special character throughout the work or the inadvertent incorporation of a comment or other "invisible" electronic material into the text (see 2.92). For a systemic typesetting error, it may be preferable to indicate the change globally with a single instruction to avoid cluttering the proofs with corrections of each instance. When a systemic problem is identified—especially one for a printed work that will affect pagination across more than a few pages and therefore the index—the publisher should be alerted immediately in case new first proofs are needed.

2.119 **Checking and proofreading page numbers and running heads.** Page numbers and running heads must be checked to ensure that they are present where they are supposed to be and absent where they are not (see 1.5–9, 1.10–16, 2.81), that the correct page number appears following a blank page, and that the typesetter has followed instructions as to what should appear on a recto, a verso, or a two-page spread. Running heads must be both proofread and checked for placement. For running heads to endnotes, the page numbers may need to be verified or supplied by checking the pages of text that correspond to the notes (see 1.15).

2.120 **Checking and proofreading illustrations and tables.** The proofreader must verify that all illustrations appear in the right location in the text, in the right size, right side up, not "flopped" (turned over left to right, resulting in a mirror image) or distorted, and with their own captions. Captions should be read as carefully as the text, and any locators should be checked to make sure they accurately refer to the parts or location of the illustrations to which they refer (see 3.24). Tables must be proofread both for content and for alignment. Where an illustration or a table (or more than one of either) occupies a full page, no running head or page number should appear (unless the page number appears as a drop folio); but if several full pages of illustrations or tables appear in sequence, the proofreader may request that page numbers (if they are absent), and sometimes running heads as well, be added to better orient readers (see 1.16). For a table presented as a two-page broadside, the proofreader should make sure it falls on facing pages (i.e., verso and recto; see also 3.88). If there are lists of illustrations and tables, all captions and titles should be checked against the lists, and page numbers must be verified or added.

2.121 **Proofreading for overall appearance.** For printed works, each page or, better, each pair of facing pages should be checked for length (see 2.122), vertical spacing, position of running heads and page numbers, and so forth. Conformity to the design specifications must be verified. Such apparent impairments as fuzzy type, incomplete letters, and blocks of type that appear lighter or darker than the surrounding text may be due to poor photocopying or a faulty printout. If in doubt, the proofreader may query "Type OK?" or "Too dark?" More than three consecutive lines that end with a hyphen or begin or end with the same word should be pointed out and, if possible, appropriate adjustments should be suggested. A page should not end with a subhead. Nor should a page begin with the last line of a paragraph unless it is full measure; a short line in this position is sometimes called a widow. A page can, however, end with the first line of a new paragraph, or what is sometimes referred to as an orphan. The last word in any paragraph must not be hyphenated unless at least four letters (in addition to any punctuation) are carried over to the final line. A word may break across a spread (verso to recto) but usually should not break at the end of a spread (recto to verso). A blank line space between paragraphs may need an ornament or other device if it falls between pages (see 1.64). To correct any of these occurrences, page length may be adjusted.

2.122 **Checking facing pages for text alignment.** Although facing pages of text must align, it is usually acceptable for both pages to run a line long or short to avoid widows (see 2.121) or to accommodate corrections. For example, if a correction on page 68 requires an added line, the typesetter may be asked to add space above a subhead on page 69 so that the two pages wind up the same length. Type can sometimes be rerun more loosely or more tightly to add (*gain*) or eliminate (*lose*) a line.

2.123 **Proofreading for sense.** The proofreader must query—or correct, if possible—illogical, garbled, repeated, or missing text. Any rewriting, however, must be limited to the correction of fact or of gross syntactical error, since all source checking and substantive and stylistic changes should have been done at the editing stage. Changes that would alter page makeup across more than a couple of pages in printed works should be avoided, since repagination not only is expensive but, for books, can affect the index.

## *How to Mark Proofs*

2.124 **Proofreaders' marks.** The marks explained in the paragraphs in this section and illustrated in figures 2.6 and 2.7 are commonly understood by typesetters and other publishing and printing personnel working in English. They can be used to mark up any kind of paper document, and they form the basis of the tools for annotating PDF files in Adobe Reader and similar applications (see 2.138). Proofreaders who annotate the PDF version (or transfer their marks from a printout to the PDF) will therefore benefit from a thorough understanding of the principles discussed in this section.

2.125 **Where to mark proofs.** Corrections to paper proofs must always be written in the margin, left or right, next to the line concerned. A mark must also be placed in the text—a caret for an addition, a line through a letter or word to be deleted or replaced—to indicate where a correction is to be made. Never should a correction be written or marked only between the lines, where it could be missed. If a line requires two or more corrections, these should be marked in the margin in the order in which they occur, separated by vertical lines (see fig. 2.7). A guideline or an arrow should be used only when a correction cannot be written next to the line in which it occurs.

2.126 **Circling comments and instructions on proofs.** As with queries and instructions handwritten on a paper manuscript (see 2.98), verbal in-

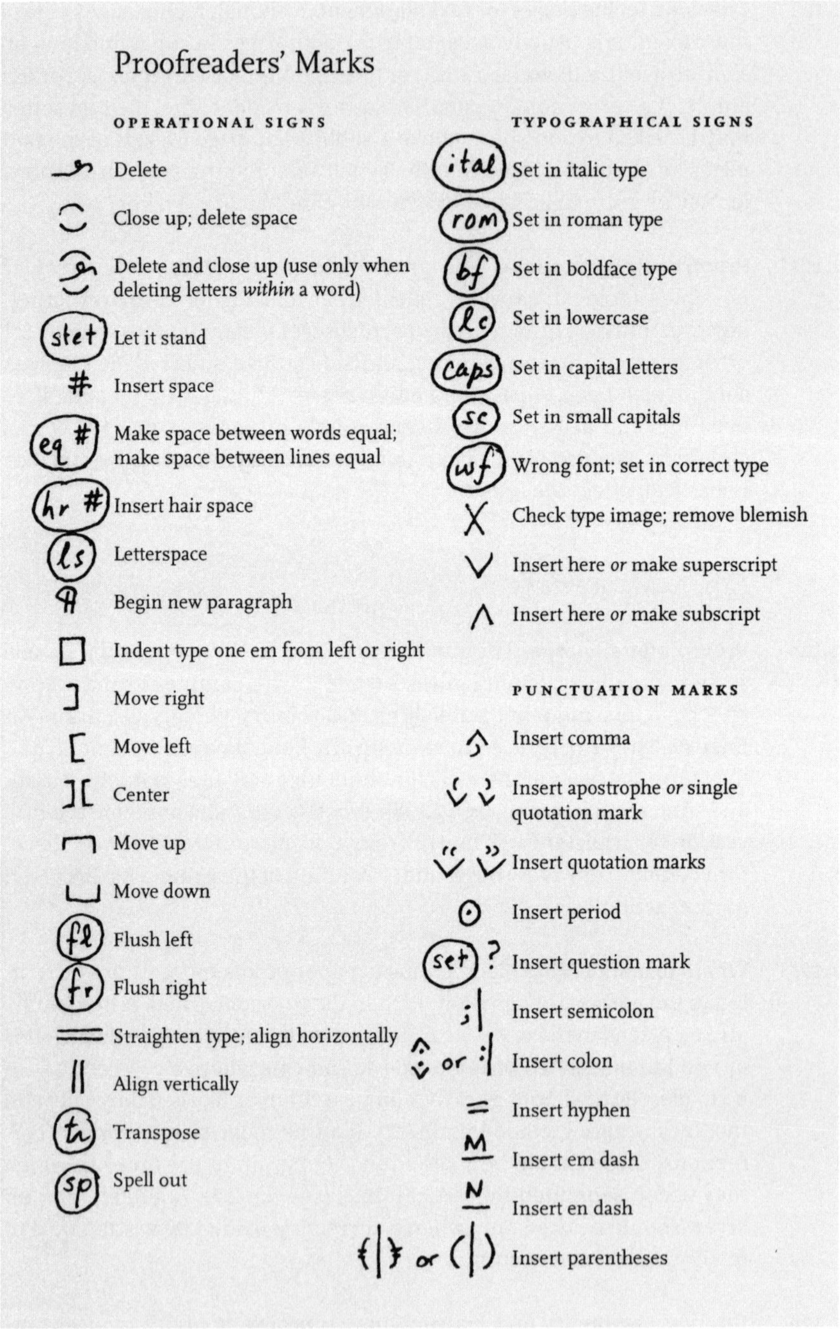
Proofreaders' Marks
OPERATIONAL SIGNS
Delete
Close up; delete space
Delete and close up (use only when deleting letters *within* a word)
Let it stand
Insert space
Make space between words equal; make space between lines equal
Insert hair space
Letterspace
Begin new paragraph
Indent type one em from left or right
Move right
Move left
Center
Move up
Move down
Flush left
Flush right
Straighten type; align horizontally
Align vertically
Transpose
Spell out
TYPOGRAPHICAL SIGNS
Set in italic type
Set in roman type
Set in boldface type
Set in lowercase
Set in capital letters
Set in small capitals
Wrong font; set in correct type
Check type image; remove blemish
Insert here *or* make superscript
Insert here *or* make subscript
PUNCTUATION MARKS
Insert comma
Insert apostrophe *or* single quotation mark
Insert quotation marks
Insert period
Insert question mark
Insert semicolon
Insert colon
Insert hyphen
Insert em dash
Insert en dash
Insert parentheses

FIGURE 2.6. Proofreaders' marks.

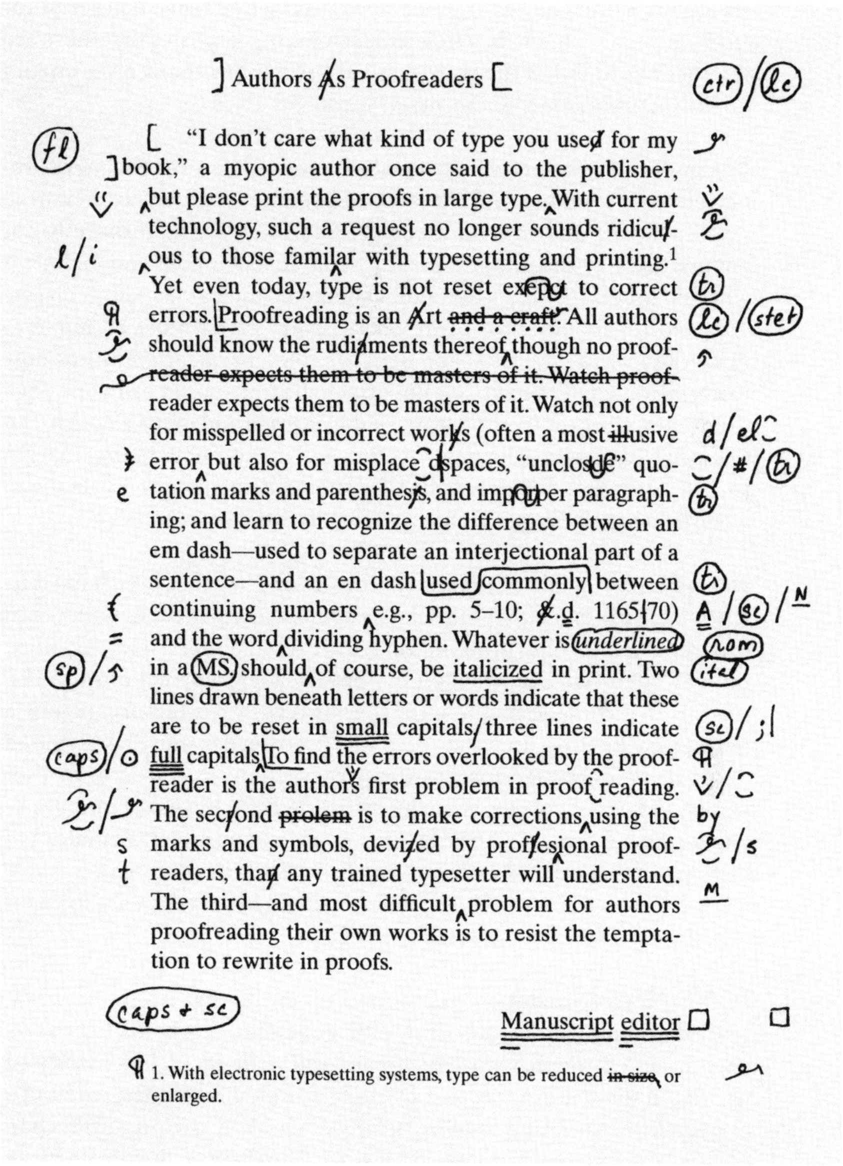

Authors As Proofreaders

"I don't care what kind of type you used for my book," a myopic author once said to the publisher, but please print the proofs in large type. With current technology, such a request no longer sounds ridicul- ous to those familar with typesetting and printing.[1] Yet even today, type is not reset exepct to correct errors. Proofreading is an Art and a craft. All authors should know the rudiiments thereof though no proof- reader expects them to be masters of it. Watch proof- reader expects them to be masters of it. Watch not only for misspelled or incorrect works (often a most illusive error but also for misplace dspaces, "unclosde" quo- tation marks and parenthesis, and imporper paragraph- ing; and learn to recognize the difference between an em dash—used to separate an interjectional part of a sentence—and an en dash used commonly between continuing numbers e.g., pp. 5–10; a.d. 1165-70) and the word dividing hyphen. Whatever is underlined in a MS. should of course, be italicized in print. Two lines drawn beneath letters or words indicate that these are to be reset in small capitals/ three lines indicate full capitals. To find the errors overlooked by the proof- reader is the authors first problem in proof reading. The secfond prolem is to make corrections using the marks and symbols, devized by proffesional proof- readers, than any trained typesetter will understand. The third—and most difficult problem for authors proofreading their own works is to resist the tempta- tion to rewrite in proofs.

Manuscript editor

1. With electronic typesetting systems, type can be reduced in size or enlarged.

FIGURE 2.7. Marked proofs.

structions written on paper proofs—such as "see attached typescript" or "ital" or "rom"—should be circled. Such circling indicates that these are instructions and that the words and abbreviations themselves should not be incorporated into the actual work.

2.127 **Communicating extensive changes on proofs.** Wherever the marks required to fix a line or two threaten to become illegible, cross out the whole passage and rewrite it correctly in the margin. If there is not enough room in the margin, make a separate document and include it with the proofs; the insertion point should be indicated in both places. To avoid repagination of print works, every effort must be made to match the word count (or, for tight fits, the character count) of new material to that of the old. For material to be transposed from one page to another, circle or otherwise mark the passage and make a note in the margin; clearly mark the new location and make a note in that margin as well. Most types of global changes should be marked individually to ensure that each change is made correctly (see also 2.118).

2.128 **Making marks legible on proofs.** All corrections to paper proofs must be written clearly (such that they can be spotted at a glance) in upper- and lowercase letters. Red proof markings are often preferred for visibility, but any color will do provided the proofreader's corrections are distinct from any made by the publisher or typesetter. Either a pen or a pencil may be used; in either case, the proofreader must be prepared to eradicate unwanted marks. Messy corrections may lead to further errors; indistinct corrections may be overlooked. If a small number of late-stage, hand-marked corrections to proofs must be transmitted to the typesetter electronically, the marks must be dark enough to show up clearly on a scan, and they must not extend to the edges of the paper lest they be cut off on the recipient's copy.

2.129 **Marking copy for deletion on proofs.** To indicate that a letter, a word, or more should be deleted, draw a diagonal line through a letter or a straight line through a word or phrase and write the delete mark (see fig. 2.6) in the margin. No part of the text should be obliterated, and a punctuation mark that is to be deleted should be circled rather than crossed through, so that it is still visible. The form of the delete mark in the margin need not be exactly as shown in figure 2.6, but it should be made in such a way as not to be confused with a *d*, an *e*, or an *l*. The delete mark is used only when something is to be removed. When something is to be substituted for the deleted matter, only the substitution is written in the margin next to the line or lines that have been struck through. The mark for "delete and close up" should be used only when a letter or a hyphen is deleted from within a word or, in the case of longer deletions, when the material that remains is to be joined with no intervening space. See figure 2.7.

2.130 **Adding or deleting spaces on proofs.** All words in the same line should be separated by the same amount of space, though the spacing will vary from line to line in justified setting (where type is aligned along both the left and the right margins). When spaces within a line are unequal, insert carets in the problem areas of the text and write the equal-space mark (eq #) in the margin. To delete space between letters or words, use the close-up mark (see fig. 2.6) in the text as well as in the margin. To call for more space between words or letters, insert a vertical line in the text where the space is to be inserted and make a space mark (#) in the margin. The space mark is also used to show where more vertical space (or *leading*, a term derived from the lead strips that were used in the era of metal type) is needed between lines. See also 2.103.

2.131 **Marking changes to paragraphing or indents on proofs.** To indicate a new paragraph, insert an L-shaped mark in the text to the left and partly under the word that is to begin a new paragraph and write the paragraph mark (¶) in the margin. To run two paragraphs together, draw a line in the text from the end of one paragraph to the beginning of the next and write "run in" in the margin. To indent a line one em space (see 6.128) from the left or right margin, draw a small square (□) to the left of the material to be indented and repeat the square in the margin. To indent two or more ems, draw a rectangle divided into two or more squares. To repeat the indents for more than one consecutive line, draw a line down from the square to the level of the baseline of the last affected line.

2.132 **Marking adjustments to position or alignment on proofs.** If a line of type, a title, an item in a table, or any other text appears too far to the left or right, use the marks for moving type right (⊐) or left (⊏). If text that is supposed to be centered appears not to be, use both marks (⊐⊏)—one on each side—to indicate centering. Use the marks for moving type up (⊓) or down (⊔) when something appears vertically out of place. All these marks must be inserted in the text and also indicated in the margin. To indicate that an indented line of type should start flush left (at the left-hand margin), insert a move-left (⊏) mark at the left of the first word in that line and write "fl" (flush left) in the margin, circled (see fig. 2.7). To indicate that an element should appear flush right—or that a line of type should be justified at the right margin—do the same thing but with the move-right (⊐) mark and marginal "fr" (flush right) or "justify." Finally, to indicate inaccurate alignment in tabular matter, use the mark for vertical alignment (‖) or horizontal alignment (=), as the case may be. To apply any of these marks to more than one consecutive line (or column), make the mark long enough to encompass each affected line.

2.133 **Marking items to be transposed on proofs.** To indicate that letters, words, or phrases should be moved from one place to another, circumscribe them in a way that precisely demarcates the items (including any punctuation) to be interchanged and write and circle "tr" (transpose) in the margin (see fig. 2.7). For transposition of larger chunks of text or other elements, it may be best to draw a bracket or other mark around each item and include a circled instruction in the margin.

2.134 **Marking items to be spelled out on proofs.** When an abbreviation or numeral is to be spelled out, circle it and write the spell-out mark (circled "sp") in the margin. If there is any ambiguity about the spelling, write the full word in the margin. See also 2.98.

2.135 **Using "stet" to revert corrections or deletions on proofs.** To undelete or restore something that has earlier been marked for deletion or correction, place a row of dots in the text under the material that is to remain, cross out the marginal mark or correction, and write "stet" ("let it stand")—or to avoid any ambiguity, "stet as set"—in the margin, circled.

2.136 **Marking changes to capitalization and font on proofs.** To indicate that a capital letter should be lowercased, draw a slash through the letter and write "lc" in the margin. To show that a lowercase letter should be capitalized, draw three lines under it and write "cap" in the margin. For small capital letters, draw two lines under the letters or words and write "sc" in the margin. For italics, draw a single line under the letter or words and write "ital" in the margin. To change italics to roman, circle the italicized letter or words and write "rom" in the margin. For boldface, draw a wavy line under the letter or words and write "bf" in the margin. To remove boldface, circle the boldface letter or words and write "not bf" in the margin. Remember to circle all marginal instructions (see 2.126). See also figures 2.6 and 2.7.

2.137 **Marking changes to punctuation and accents on proofs.** To change a punctuation mark, circle it and write the correct mark in the margin. To add a mark, insert a caret and write the mark in the margin. Lest they be missed or misinterpreted, all punctuation marks in the margin should be clarified thus: A comma should have a caret over it; an apostrophe or a quotation mark should have an inverted caret under it; a parenthesis should have two short horizontal lines through it; a period should be circled; semicolons and colons should be followed by a short vertical line; question marks and exclamation points should be accompanied by the circled word "set"; and hyphens, en dashes, and em dashes should be differentiated by their appropriate symbols (see fig. 2.6). If an accent or a diacritical mark is missing or incorrect, the entire letter should be crossed out in the text and written in the margin with its correct accent; never must the accent alone appear in the margin. For clarity, the name of any potentially ambiguous accent or diacritical mark (e.g., "macron") should also be written and circled in the margin (see 11.2).

**2.138** **Proofreading tools for PDF.** The proofreading symbols and related markup developed for paper and pencil have been adapted for PDF readers by Adobe and others. The advantages of proofreading on-screen—including searchable text and comments, typed annotations, automatic time and user stamps, no shipping costs, and quick turnaround—have influenced many publishers to incorporate PDF tools into their proofreading workflow. (Those who prefer to proofread on paper can still do so if they have access to a printer and are willing to transfer their marks to PDF later on.) With PDF proofreading tools, any annotation or other markup added to a page will automatically generate a corresponding item in a separate list that identifies the annotation by type and records the name of the reviser, the date and time the annotation was entered or last revised, the page number, and the text of the annotation, if any. Tools typically include options for striking out, inserting, or replacing text; adding highlighting or underlining; inserting notes; and drawing lines and other shapes. As on paper, any such markup overlays the text, leaving the original unchanged. Typesetters who use Adobe InDesign, however, can import proofreading markup and comments from Adobe Acrobat and incorporate insertions and deletions automatically, a process that must be coordinated in advance with the proofreader. It is important to avoid redundant markup (e.g., the use of one tool to draw a line through a word and a different tool to insert a correction in the same place); choose a single tool wherever possible, adding at most a virtual note to ensure that the intent of the markup is understood (e.g., "Correct spelling to 'felicidad' and put word in italics as shown"). All annotations should be apparent on the page, but the corresponding list generated by the software can help ensure that none are missed. Whoever is responsible for making the changes can go systematically through the document and use the available tools to mark each item in the list as corrected (or not), further annotating any of the items as needed.

## *Double-Checking Proofs and Assigning Responsibility*

2.139 **Double-checking proofs.** In addition to the tasks outlined in 2.115–23, the proofreader must perform the following checks, according to the needs of the particular work:

- Check article or chapter titles and, if necessary, subheads or other heads against the table of contents to ensure consistent wording and verify or add beginning page numbers in the table of contents. Query—or mark for deletion, if necessary—any item listed in the table of contents that does not appear in the work.
- If footnotes are used, ensure that each footnote appears, or at least begins, on the page that includes its superscript reference number or symbol.
- Check for and fill in any missing cross-references (see 2.40).
- For a book, check the half title and the title page to be sure the title is correct and the author's or volume editor's name is spelled right; verify that the information on the copyright page is accurate and complete.
- For a journal, check the covers, spine, and any front or back matter copy that is unique to the particular journal; with the previous year's volume at hand, check the elements that change with each issue, such as volume and issue numbers and date, month, or season of publication; ensure that the inclusive page numbers that appear on the spine are accurate; check front and back matter for any elements that may have changed, such as subscription prices or names of editors and members of the editorial board; ensure that copyright lines are included and accurate on all individual articles or other elements of the journal that carry them.

For additional checking required for electronic formats, see 2.142–44.

2.140 **Assigning responsibility for errors on proofs.** The proofreader may be asked to distinguish between errors introduced by the typesetting process, errors that were left uncorrected in the manuscript, and errors that were introduced during editorial cleanup after the author reviewed the editing. In such cases, corrections should be accompanied by abbreviations determined by the publisher or typesetter, such as PE (printer's error—the customary term for what is generally a typesetter's error), AA (author's alteration), EA (editor's alteration), and DA (designer's alteration). All such indications should be circled to prevent their being incorporated into the corrected proofs.

2.141 **Author's alterations (AAs) versus editor's alterations (EAs).** For books, a publisher's contract may allow an author to make, without penalty, alterations in proofs in terms of a percentage of the initial cost of the typesetting. Since the cost of corrections is very high relative to the cost of the original typesetting, an AA allowance of (for example) 5 percent does not mean that 5 percent of the proofs may be altered. An author may be asked to pay the cost of AAs beyond the AA allowance stipulated in the contract. Any rewriting or adding of new material by the author is considered an AA. Page numbers added to cross-references in proofs are also usually considered AAs. Corrections of errors uncaught or even introduced in editing are considered AAs if the author reviewed and approved the edited manuscript. Correction of an error introduced into the manuscript by the publisher after the author's review—made by the manuscript editor, for example, in entering the author's final adjustments—is an EA and not chargeable to the author. Supplying page numbers in lists of tables and illustrations and in running heads to notes constitutes an EA. For articles, consult the journal publisher.

## *Proofing and Testing Electronic Formats*

2.142 **Checklist for proofing and testing electronic formats.** Every component of a publication must be checked and tested in its final format—from PDF to ebook formats to the full text of a work to be published online—*before* it gets published. In addition, the full text of publications offered in more than one format must be proofread word for word, according to the procedures outlined earlier in this chapter, in at least one format. Elements appearing in one format and not another will also need to be proofread, and no element should be overlooked. This advice applies equally to any type of work, including self-published works. In addition to many of the tasks outlined in 2.115–23 and 2.139, a thorough check will include some or all of the following steps:

1. Look carefully at the layout to make sure that no elements are missing, that all elements are presented as intended, and that no markup added for another purpose (e.g., for a print version) adversely affects the electronic version.
2. Confirm that all special characters have been converted correctly (see 2.118; see also 11.2). Any character not available in Unicode and instead treated as an in-line image must be checked for legibility and proper appearance.
3. Verify that all internal and external links and any other features intended to be clicked, tapped, swiped, or otherwise manipulated by the reader work as intended. For web publications and apps, a site map (i.e., a list or chart of all navigable pages) may facilitate this process.
4. Make sure that any illustrations and tables or other components outside the run of text are present and function and appear as desired (see also 3.24).

**EPUB QA CHECKLIST**

GENERAL

Scroll/page through the entire book on at least one device, looking for missing content or content that is in the wrong location, missing page breaks, and other major formatting issues. Then test your EPUB file on devices for all of the retailers you will be targeting.

SPECIFIC

*Metadata:* The EPUB metadata should include, at a minimum, the title, author, language, and ISBN. Ensure that the title in the metadata matches the official title of the book as seen on the title page and front cover.

*Linking:* Check all URLs to make sure they link where intended. Check links for cross-references to chapters, figures, and the like. Check links to and from the table of contents.

*Cover image:* Ensure that the title matches the official title of the book as seen on the title page and in the metadata. Back covers are not normally included in ebooks.

*Copyright page:* Check for the correct ISBN(s) for the ebook format(s). If there is an ISBN for print, make sure it is properly labeled: for example, "978-0-226-23410-6 (cloth)." Check any links to author and publisher websites.

*Table of contents:* Check the linking of each item in the TOC to ensure it points to the correct location in both HTML and navigation views. Also check any list of figures, tables, etc. Check that the cover, table of contents, start page, and any other navigational landmarks work as specified.

*Page numbers:* Make sure page numbers have been embedded in the EPUB for books with a printed counterpart. Include the corresponding page list navigation element.

*Headings:* Check all part and chapter headings for proper size, alignment, and line spacing. Make sure hyphenation for headings has been disabled.

*Embedded fonts:* Test any embedded fonts at both small and large sizes. Glyphs should be legible on both E Ink and LCD displays. Make sure content also displays acceptably when the embedded fonts are turned off.

*Special characters and Unicode:* All special characters, including non-Latin text, symbols, and other nonstandard text, should be tested in the target reading systems, with and without embedded fonts turned on. Replace any non-Unicode fonts with Unicode text.

*Character styles:* Bold, italic, and other character styles should be checked for proper appearance. Small caps, especially, should be checked on each reading system. If you are concerned about accessibility or semantic markup, be sure to use the correct HTML and CSS code for those elements based on the context. Text colors may be used, but they should not be too light. Light text color may be unreadable on grayscale E Ink screens.

*Block quotations and lists:* Check block quotations, lists, and the like for acceptable layout. Check poetry for hanging indents and stanza breaks.

FIGURE 2.8. Sample checklist for a book prepared as an EPUB file. See also 2.142.

*Notes:* All notes should be linked in both directions. In reflowable formats, footnotes are usually converted to endnotes. If not, they should be placed after the paragraph or section, not in between words or sentences. Do notes with "ibid." appear out of context (e.g., in a pop-up)? Consider replacing with a short form of the citation.

*Bibliography:* Check for proper formatting. If long URLs are included, it is best to left-justify the text of the whole bibliography to avoid large gaps between words.

*Index:* Retain any index from a printed counterpart, including all entries. Page number references should link to the proper location in the book. This can be either the print page number anchor or an anchor specific to that reference. References to figures, images, and tables should link directly to the element, not just to the page on which it appears. "See" and "see also" references should link to their targets in the index.

IMAGES

- Check all images for quality and readability on target reading systems.
- Image resolution and file size should conform to retailer specs for each reading system.
- Images should be saved in an RGB color space, not CMYK.
- Use transparent backgrounds as applicable.
- Check captions for alignment; they should appear on the same page as the image whenever possible. Use CSS to scale images as necessary.

TABLES AND CHARTS

- Tables should be coded in HTML, if at all possible, rather than presented as images.
- Check tables for legibility and to make sure content fits well on the screen when possible.
- Wherever possible, convert simple lists and the like to regular paragraph text, especially if they were presented in tabular format only to accommodate the printed page.
- Check charts and graphs for legibility. Charts that use color in meaningful ways should include explanations where needed for readers with grayscale screens.

AUDIO AND VIDEO CONTENT

- Check retailer specs for multimedia content and encode/size as applicable.
- Include proper fallbacks (e.g., an image or an explanation that the media content is not supported in the reading system). If possible, include a link showing where the reader can access the media content online.
- Videos should always include a poster image.

FIGURE 2.8 (*continued*)

5. Make sure that the content of each format matches exactly—if that is the intent—or varies as intended, and that any intended variation is noted explicitly in both versions (see 1.87).
6. Make sure that alt text for illustrations that require them (including in-line images as well as captioned figures) is accurate and complete and that all other accessibility requirements have been met (see also 2.143).
7. Test for valid EPUB, HTML, or other markup using one of the tools offered for that purpose by W3C and others.

8. Proofread any recent changes in each format for spelling, sense, and proper integration into each new context.

Anyone responsible for proofing and testing electronic copy must look at every element of the publication systematically—preferably according to a more detailed checklist that will have been created during the development stages of the project or that applies to the latest procedures for publication in one or more formats. For a sample checklist for ebook formats, see figure 2.8.

2.143 **Checking for accessibility.** Works published in electronic formats should be checked to make sure they meet applicable accessibility requirements, including the Web Content Accessibility Guidelines from W3C, an international organization that develops and maintains standards for websites and related formats, including EPUB. A variety of tools have been designed to help publishers with this process. For ebooks, the DAISY Consortium offers Ace, a tool designed to evaluate EPUB files. For PDF files, the PDF/UA Foundation offers PAC (PDF Accessibility Checker). Premium versions of Adobe Acrobat can check PDF files for accessibility within the app. For content published online, a list of evaluation tools and related resources is available from the Web Accessibility Initiative of W3C. Any of these tools can help pinpoint accessibility problems, but human reviewers should also be involved in checking accessibility, not only to evaluate the results of automated testing but to review content and recommend any necessary fixes. Whenever possible, such reviewers should include people with print disabilities and users who are relatively inexperienced at reading online. At a minimum, users should check for clear and logical page titles, appropriate alternative text for images and captions or transcripts for audio or video, logical headings and page structure, text that resizes as needed and that has sufficient contrast and appropriate colors, and accessible keyboard navigation. For writing and editing alt text, see 3.28.

2.144 **Preparing notes for an audiobook.** In addition to proofreading, an author may be asked to prepare notes for an audiobook version, either by annotating a PDF of the final pages or by adding comments to the word-processing file of the final, edited manuscript. (Some authors may be asked to mark up a printed copy instead, or to prepare notes at an earlier stage of the manuscript.) These notes will be referred to by the audiobook narrator(s), who, in turn, may prepare their own annotated version of the script. Most such notes will clarify pronunciation (e.g., for "Wilkes-Barre" say "WILKS bare-uh"), but it can also be useful to note any special emphasis, shifts in tone of voice, and pacing (including any significant pauses). And though most audiobooks follow the text of the book word for word, the occasional adjustment might be needed for something that works on the page but not out loud (e.g., "the 'wrong' answer" might be glossed for the audiobook as "the quote-unquote wrong answer"). Experienced audiobook narrators will have their own solutions to such things, but an author's notes are usually appreciated.

# 3 Illustrations and Tables

## OVERVIEW

3.1 **Illustrations defined.** Illustrations, also called figures (and sometimes referred to as artwork or art), consist of images presented separately from the run of text. For the purposes of publication, such images usually consist of digital files optimized for specific publication formats. Illustrations can reproduce anything from paintings, photographs, and line drawings to maps, charts, and examples from musical scores. This list is sometimes extended to include multimedia files presented in electronic publication formats. For a full discussion of illustrations—including guidelines on preparation, placement, numbering, captioning, and alternative text, with examples drawn mainly from University of Chicago Press publications—see 3.3–47.

3.2 **Tables defined.** A table is a more or less complex list presented as an array of vertical columns and horizontal rows. Like illustrations, tables are presented separately from the run of text. Tables are also related to illustrations in that both can be said to constitute a visual representation of data. Because they consist of alphanumeric text, however, tables are preferably typeset along with the text rather than produced separately as images so the data can be searched and otherwise made available as text in electronic formats. For a full discussion of tables—including guidelines on preparation, placement, numbering, and editing, with examples drawn from University of Chicago Press publications—see 3.48–89.

## ILLUSTRATIONS

### *Types of Illustrations and Their Parts*

3.3 **Continuous tone versus halftone.** Continuous-tone art is any image such as a painting or a photograph that contains gradations of shading from light to dark—in black and white (grayscale) or color (see fig. 3.1). In order to duplicate continuous-tone images in offset printing, which uses one ink color (black) for black-and-white reproduction and four inks (cyan, magenta, yellow, and black—abbreviated CMYK) for color, a halftone reproduction must be produced (see fig. 3.2). A halftone breaks the image into an equally spaced array of dots that vary in size to create the illusion of continuous tone from dark to light. For both black-and-white halftone reproduction and illustrations that will be reproduced in color, authors should consult their publisher's guidelines for preparing digital artwork. (Chicago offers such guidelines on its books and journals web-

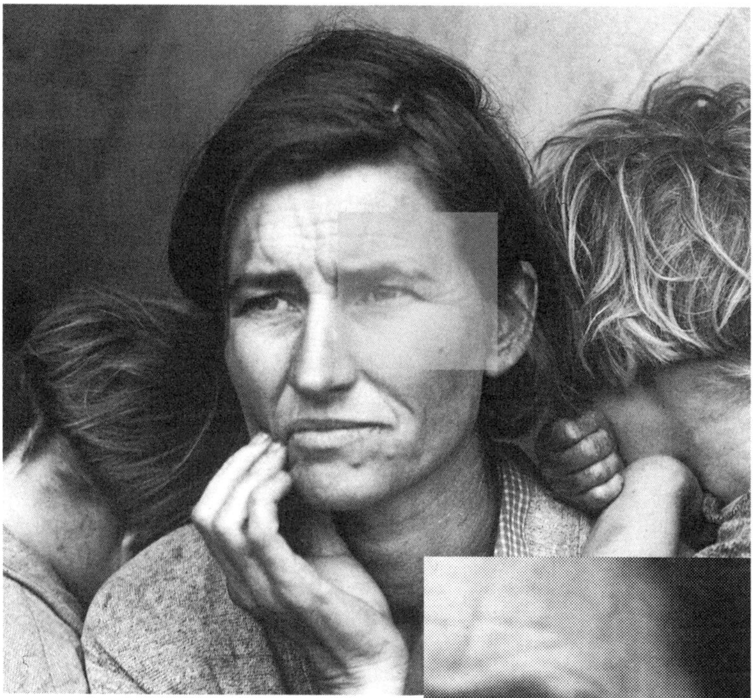

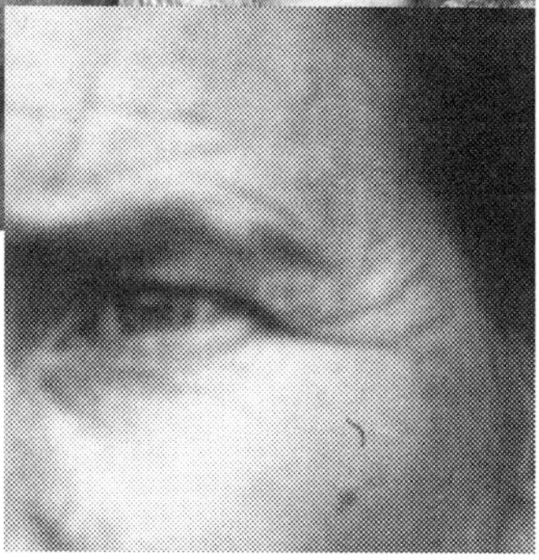

FIGURE 3.1. A halftone image of an original photo.

FIGURE 3.2. Detail of figure 3.1 showing the halftone dot pattern. See 3.3.

sites.) Color images produced digitally and intended for the screen are rendered in pixels and in RGB (red, green, and blue) mode and need to be converted to CMYK for printing.

3.4 **Line art.** Artwork consisting of solid black on a white background, with no gray screens (i.e., shading)—such as a pen-and-ink drawing—is traditionally known as line art. See figures 3.3 and 3.4. Line art may be reproduced in black and white or in color. Charts are usually created with software and rendered for publication as line art. (For more on charts, see 3.42–47.) Musical examples may be treated as line art and scanned if they are not typeset from scratch for publication—generally by specialists. See figure 3.5. Publishers can often reproduce software-generated line art without having to remake it provided it has been properly pre-

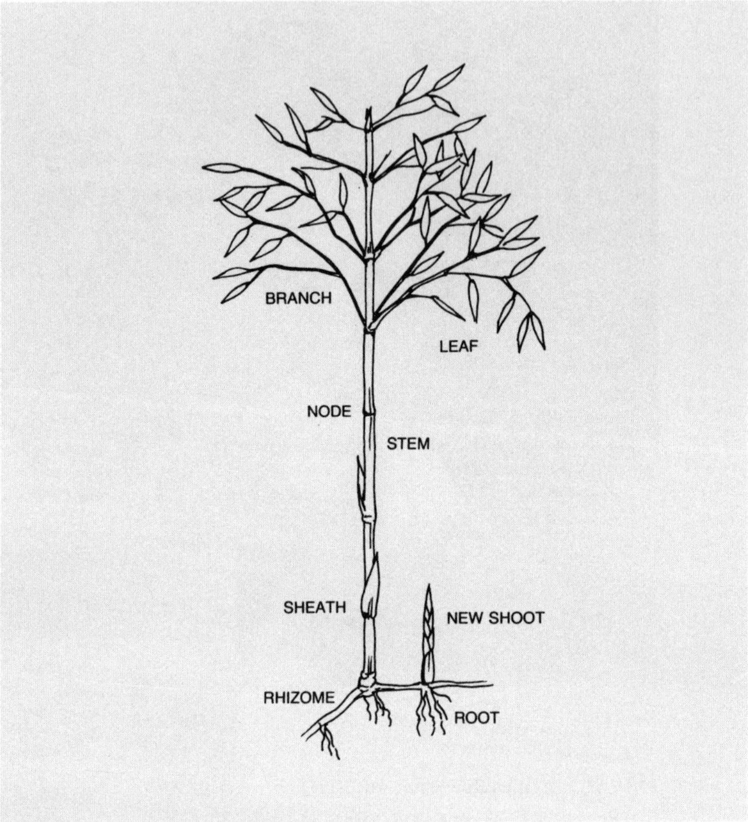


FIGURE 3.3. A line drawing with descriptive labels (see 3.4, 3.7). The surrounding text of the work from which this unnumbered and uncaptioned figure was drawn identifies the plant as a *Sinarundinaria* stem.

pared; authors should obtain guidelines from the publisher. For the use of shading in line art, see 3.19. For more on the conventions related to musical notation, see 7.75–80.

3.5 **Text figures and plates.** Illustrations—whether halftones or line art—that are interspersed in the text are referred to as text figures. (Occasionally, a special type of illustration, such as a map or a musical example, will be referred to in a work by type rather than by the generic term *figure*. See fig. 3.5.) The term *plate*, strictly speaking, refers to a full-page illustration that is printed separately, typically on coated paper; plates can appear individually between certain pages of text but are more often gathered into galleries (see 3.6). (In a work that con-

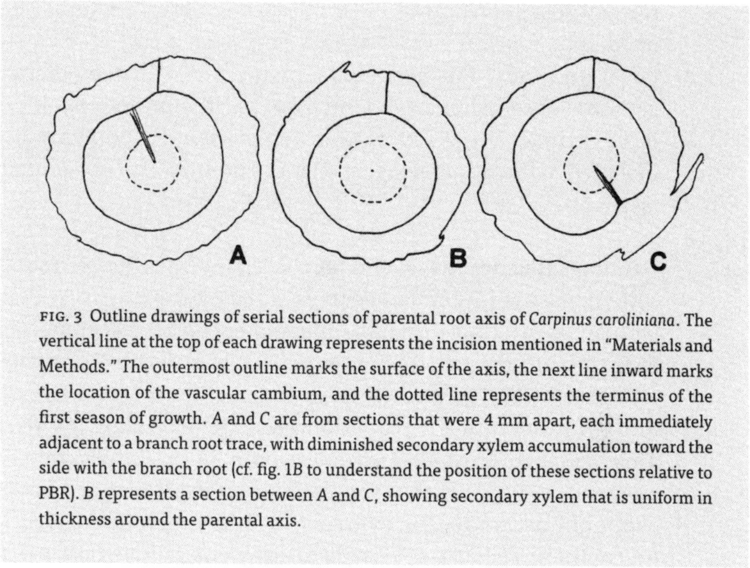
A
B
C
FIG. 3 Outline drawings of serial sections of parental root axis of *Carpinus caroliniana*. The vertical line at the top of each drawing represents the incision mentioned in "Materials and Methods." The outermost outline marks the surface of the axis, the next line inward marks the location of the vascular cambium, and the dotted line represents the terminus of the first season of growth. *A* and *C* are from sections that were 4 mm apart, each immediately adjacent to a branch root trace, with diminished secondary xylem accumulation toward the side with the branch root (cf. fig. 1*B* to understand the position of these sections relative to PBR). *B* represents a section between A and C, showing secondary xylem that is uniform in thickness around the parental axis.

FIGURE 3.4. A line drawing, including figure number and caption (see 3.4, 3.8–14, 3.21–29). The drawing's three parts, labeled with capital letters, are discussed in the caption (see 3.7).

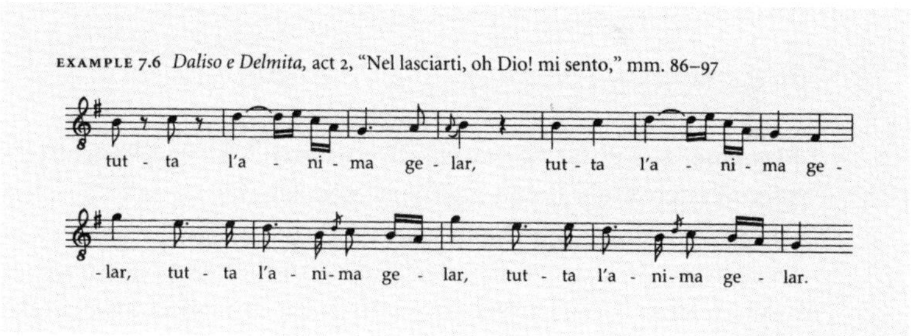


EXAMPLE 7.6 *Daliso e Delmita*, act 2, "Nel lasciarti, oh Dio! mi sento," mm. 86–97

FIGURE 3.5. Musical examples carry their captions above the illustration rather than below. Such examples can be reproduced photographically (e.g., from a published score) or typeset by specialists (see 3.4).

tains both photographs and line art, *plate* is sometimes used—a little loosely—for the former and *figure* for the latter.)

3.6 **Galleries.** A gallery (also known as an *insert*) is a section of a printed work devoted to illustrations—usually halftones. If printed on stock different from that used for the text, a gallery is not paginated; for example, an eight-page gallery could appear between pages 134 and 135. Such a gallery will typically consist of four, eight, twelve, or more pages (for purposes of printing and binding, it is always a number that can be divided by four). A gallery always begins on a recto (i.e., a right-hand page) and must fall between signatures (the groups of folded-and-gathered sheets that are bound together in a printed book). If the gallery is printed along with the text, on the same paper, its pages may be included in the numbering, even if the numbers do not actually appear (see 1.44).

3.7 **Captions, legends, keys, and labels.** The terms *caption* and *legend* are sometimes used interchangeably for the explanatory text that appears with an illustration—usually immediately below but sometimes above or to the side. (In a distinction rarely made today, the term *caption* once referred strictly to a phrasal title or a headline, whereas *legend* referred to the full-sentence explanation immediately following the caption. This manual uses *caption* to refer to both.) A *key* (also sometimes called a legend) appears within the illustration itself and not as part of the caption; it identifies the symbols used in a map or a chart. For more on captions, see 3.21–29. *Labels* are any descriptive terms that appear within an illustration. They may also be symbols (often letters) used to indicate an illustration's parts. See figures 3.3, 3.4, 3.6. See also 3.12, 3.45. For alternative text, see 3.28.

## *Placement and Numbering of Illustrations*

3.8 **Placement of illustrations relative to text.** Unless illustrations are presented separately (as in a gallery; see 3.6, 3.14), each should appear as soon as possible after the first text reference to it. In an electronic work, a captioned thumbnail image linked to its larger counterpart(s) may appear after the paragraph in which the image is first referenced. In printed works, to accommodate page makeup, the image may precede the reference only if it appears on the same page (or same two-page spread) as the reference or if the text is too short to permit placing all figures and tables after their references. For illustrations that will be interspersed in the text, the author or (if the author has not done so) the editor must provide callouts that indicate in the manuscript the preferred location for each, placed at an appropriate break between paragraphs or sentences (see 2.35). (For illustrations that are to appear together in a printed gallery, placement callouts are usually unnecessary.) Note that a *callout* (e.g., "fig. 5 about here") is an instruction for typesetting or production and will not appear in the published work (for *text references*, which are addressed to readers, see 3.9). In electronic markup, a callout points to a specific source file. In a printed work,

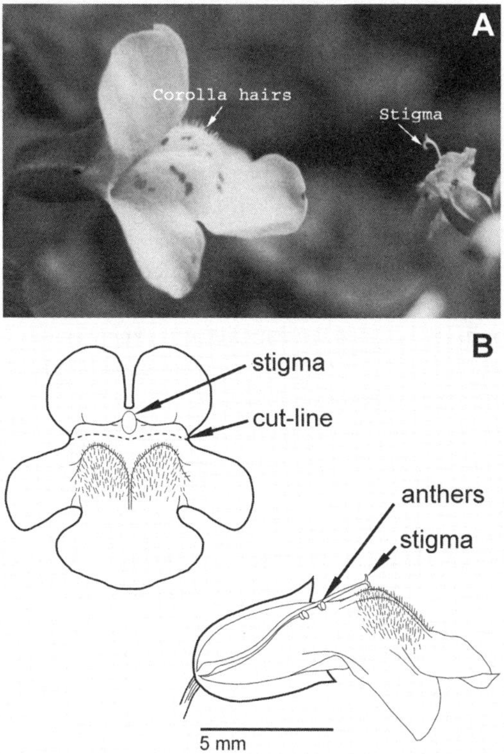


**Fig. 1** Flower of *Mimulus guttatus*. *A*, Side-view photograph of two flowers illustrating the corolla hairs and stigma. The corolla and anthers have been pulled back to reveal the stigma and style on the left-hand flower. *B*, Line drawings of a front view and a side view. The cut line used in the phenotypic manipulation is illustrated in the front view. For the side view, the upper portion of the corolla has been removed to reveal the positions of the reproductive parts relative to the corolla hairs.

FIGURE 3.6. A figure consisting of a photograph and a line drawing, each with descriptive labels and identified by the letters *A* and *B*, respectively (see 3.7, 3.12).

most illustrations will appear at either the top or the bottom of a page; in reflowable electronic formats, placement may vary with text size and other factors.

3.9 **Text references to numbered illustrations.** If there are more than a handful of illustrations in a work, they normally bear numbers (but see 3.13), and all text references to them should be by the numbers: "as figure 1 shows . . ."; "compare figures 4 and 5." If an electronic version of a work contains figures not available in a printed counterpart, any text references to these figures in the print version must make this clear (e.g., by adding "available online" after the reference; see also 1.87). An illustration should never be referred to in the text as "the photograph opposite" or "the graph on this page," for such placement may not be possible in the published version (but see 3.24). In text, the word *figure* is set in roman, lowercased, and spelled out except in parenthetical references, where the abbreviation *fig.* may be used. (In some publications, such terms are routinely capitalized whenever they appear with a number.) *Plate*, however, should not be abbreviated to *pl.* In captions, these terms are sometimes distinguished typographically from the rest of the caption (see 3.23).

3.10 **Continuous versus separate numbering of illustrations.** All types of illustrations may be numbered together in one continuous sequence throughout a work. For the convenience of the reader, a specific category of illustration may sometimes be numbered separately in book-length works (e.g., map 1, map 2, . . .); illustrations in a different medium are always numbered separately (e.g., video 1, video 2, . . .). In a work published in both print and electronic versions, illustrations should be numbered according to the same system and using the same numbers in both versions (see also 1.87, 3.9). For double numeration, see 3.11. For illustrations in a gallery, see 3.6, 3.14.

3.11 **Double numeration of illustrations.** In scientific and technical books, heavily illustrated books, and books with chapters by different authors, double numeration may be employed. Each illustration carries the number of the chapter followed by the illustration number, usually separated by a period. Thus, for example, figure 9.6 is the sixth figure in chapter 9. Should a chapter contain only one illustration, a double number would still be used (e.g., figure 10.1). Appendix figures may be numbered A.1, A.2, and so on or, if there are several appendixes and each bears a letter, A.1, A.2, B.1, B.2, and so on. Similarly, if an introduction has figures, these may be numbered I.1, I.2, I.3, and so on. At the editing stage, double numeration makes it easier to handle mul-

Fig. 8.34. *Above,* stick insect (fam. *Phasmatidae*) with details of head and legs; *center,* further details of parts of a stick insect; *below,* praying mantis (fam. *Mantidae*) with details of head and of legs, including, *right below,* details of tarsus, femur, and elongate coxa (trocaster not shown). Paris, Bibliothèque de l'Institut de France, MS 974, fol. between 112 and 113. © Photo RMN—Gérard Blot.

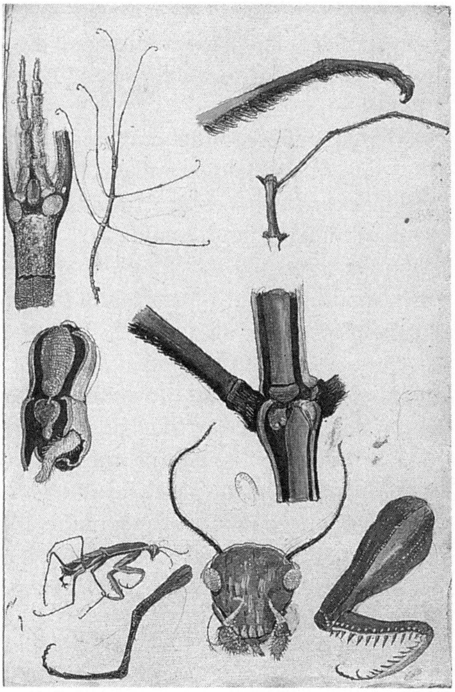

FIGURE 3.7. The relative position of each part in this composite figure is identified in the caption (see 3.24).

tiple illustrations and, should any be added or removed, involves far less renumbering. It also makes it easier for readers to find a particular illustration. This manual uses double numeration for illustrations and tables as well as for text paragraphs. See also 1.63.

3.12 **Identifying the parts of an illustration.** Chicago recommends the use of Arabic numerals for illustrations of all kinds: "figure 12," "fig. 10.7." Where a figure consists of several parts, the parts may carry letters (*A*, *B*, *C*, etc.); a single caption, keying the letters to the parts, suffices (see figs. 3.4, 3.6). Text references may then refer, for example, to "fig. 10.7C" (note that the letter, which may be italicized in the caption, is not italicized in the text reference). Parts may also be described according to their relative positions on a printed page (see fig. 3.7; see also 3.24); the relative positions must be maintained in an electronic version if the same description is to be used. (In the rare and undesirable event that a figure has to be added at a late stage to a work destined for print, when it is no longer feasible to renumber all the other figures, "fig. 10.7A" might refer to a figure inserted between figures 10.7 and 10.8.)

3.13 **Working numbers for unnumbered illustrations.** In some works where illustrations are neither integral to the text nor specifically referred to, numbers are unnecessary. In the editing and production stages, however, all illustrations should carry working numbers, as should their captions, to ensure that they are correctly placed. Such working numbers should appear in illustration file names, on any photocopies, and in any placement callouts in the text (see 3.8).

3.14 **Numbering illustrations in a gallery.** When illustrations are gathered together in a gallery, they need not be numbered unless referred to in the text, although in the editing and production stages they should carry working numbers to ensure the correct order (see 3.13). If numbers are required and the work also contains illustrations interspersed in the text, two number sequences must be adopted. For example, text illustrations may be referred to as "figure 1" and so on and gallery illustrations as "plate 1" and so on.

## *Preparation of Artwork*

3.15 **Submitting artwork to the publisher.** Authors preparing illustrations electronically must consult their publishers before submitting the files. Many publishers require hard copies or PDF along with artwork submitted in electronic form. (A still image may be required for an audiovisual file submitted as an enhancement to an electronic work.) A list of the software programs used to create the digital artwork should also be furnished, and the publisher should be made aware of any special fonts used in the construction of drawings, diagrams, maps, and so forth; the publisher may need the author to supply these fonts (usually provided they are free and not subject to end-user license agreements). See also 2.5, 2.41. Any author-supplied scans must be made in accordance with the publisher's guidelines, preferably by a professional graphic arts service; Chicago offers such guidelines on its books and journals websites. For color art intended for print, digital scans or photographs furnished by the lending institution or prepared by a professional prepress service are generally preferred. (Authors should check their contracts to ensure that illustrations are permitted and, if so, that color is also permitted.) Images obtained from the internet—unless they have been specifically optimized for print—are usually not acceptable. Authors who plan to self-publish their works in print would do well to consult Chicago's detailed guidelines in addition to any guidelines provided by their self-publishing platform to get an idea of the steps required to ensure the best possible reproduction quality. Finally, authors can help publishers make their works accessible by providing alt text with any images that may require it (see 3.28).

3.16 **Identifying artwork for the publisher.** Artwork submitted in electronic form should be saved in separate files with descriptive names that accurately identify each file (see also 2.37); these names should be included on any corresponding hard copies along with the numbers that correspond to the figure callouts in the manuscript. Original artwork submitted as hard copy (e.g., photographic prints) must be clearly identified by the author or, failing that, by the publisher, in a manner that does not harm the original. Each item should be numbered on the back in pencil, very gently, making sure no mark is visible on the other side. If the paper does not accept lead pencil, a sticky note should be used. To be avoided are ballpoint pens, grease pencils, felt-tip markers, staples, and paper clips. For numbering, see 3.8–14; for captions, see 3.21–29.

3.17 **Author's inventory of artwork.** Along with artwork, the author should supply a complete list of illustrations, noting any that are to appear in color, any sizing restrictions, any duplicates or extras, and any that are still to come. (Note, however, that for both books and journals, it is always expected and often mandatory that all illustrations be supplied at the time a manuscript is submitted; see 2.4.) If the work is to be published in print and electronic versions that will vary in the number of illustrations or in the use of color, that information must be noted in the inventory (see also 3.26).

3.18 **Publisher's inventory of artwork.** As soon as the illustrations arrive from the author, publishers should check each one against the author's inventory (see 3.17). If an illustration does not meet the publisher's resolution or file format requirements for digital art, or if a hard-copy photograph or transparent original is damaged or otherwise may not be reproducible, a replacement copy will need to be requested. (Missing illustrations will also need to be tracked down.) Each illustration should also be checked to be sure that it is properly numbered and labeled and that it corresponds correctly to its caption; the publisher should also confirm whether the author supplied alt text and for which illustrations.

(Authors should supply captions and alt text in separate files to facilitate copyediting; see 2.31.) Some publishers, particularly in STEM fields, may need to review images for any inappropriate manipulation. Finally, publishers should check for any necessary permissions (see 4.79–98, 4.99–109).

3.19 **Cropping, scaling, and shading.** To make suggestions for reframing, or cropping, an image—that is, cutting it down to remove extraneous parts—authors should either crop a digital copy or mark a printout or, for a hard-copy photograph or transparency, mark up a photocopy to avoid damaging the original. For images that need to be scaled, finished dimensions must be computed from the dimensions of the original. Authors need to be aware of this especially when preparing line art that contains labels or a key. The relations between font size, line weight (thickness, measured in points), and final printed size should be considered when drawings are created to ensure legibility. By scaling the image to its intended size and printing it out (or by using a photocopying machine), it is possible to get an idea of what the printed version will look like. Avoid hairline rules, which may disappear when printed. Likewise, avoid shading or color, which may print poorly when reduced; use stripes, spots, and other black-and-white fill patterns in charts to distinguish areas from plain black or white. In general, images that will reproduce well in black and white will be more accessible than color images. If color and shading are used, the information in the image should not depend solely on the color or shading. (Many publishers now accept shading or color within properly prepared line art submitted electronically in specific formats; consult your publisher's manuscript submission guidelines before preparing final art.) See also 3.42–47.

3.20 **Artwork to be redrawn by the publisher.** In some cases, a publisher may agree to make corrections to or redraw line art (e.g., a line drawing or a chart) submitted for publication. (Authors should check with their publishers in advance.) Authors submitting such art should clearly mark any labels (words or symbols) to be altered or added on a photocopy or scan or, if there are more than a few, in a separate document, keyed to the illustration. Where possible, wording, abbreviations, and symbols should be consistent with those used in the text. By a similar token, capitalization should be reserved for those terms that would be capitalized in running text. All names on a map that is to be redrawn should be prepared as a separate list, in which countries, provinces, cities, rivers, and so forth are divided into separate groups, each group arranged alphabetically.

## *Captions and Alternative Text*

3.21 **Format and wording for captions.** A caption—the explanatory material that appears outside (usually below) an illustration—is distinct from a key and from a label, which appear within an illustration (see 3.7; see also 3.45). A caption may consist of a word or two, an incomplete or a complete sentence, several sentences, or a combination. No punctuation is needed after a caption consisting solely of an incomplete sentence. If one or more full sentences follow it, each (including the opening phrase) should have closing punctuation. In a work in which most captions consist of full sentences, incomplete ones may be followed by a period for consistency. Captions should be capitalized in sentence case (see 8.159), but formal titles of works included in captions should be capitalized in title case (see 3.22).

Wartime visit to Australia, winter 1940

The White Garden, reduced to its bare bones in early spring. The box hedges, which are still cut by hand, have to be carefully kept in scale with the small and complex garden as well as in keeping with the plants inside the "boxes."

3.22 **Formal titles in captions.** Titles of works should be presented according to the rules set forth in chapter 8 (see 8.157–204), whether standing alone or incorporated into a caption. Accordingly, most titles in English will appear in title case (see 8.160), and many titles—including those for paintings, drawings, photographs, statues, and books—will be italicized; others will appear in roman type, enclosed in quotation marks (see 8.164). For titles in other languages, see 11.8–12. Generic titles, however (as in the last example below), are not usually capitalized.

Frontispiece of *Christian Prayers and Meditations* (London: John Daye, 1569), showing Queen Elizabeth at prayer in her private chapel. Reproduced by permission of the Archbishop of Canterbury and the Trustees of the Lambeth Palace Library.

The head of Venus—a detail from Botticelli's *Birth of Venus*.

Francis Bedford, *Stratford on Avon Church from the Avon*, 1860s. Albumen print of collodion negative, 18.8 × 28.0 cm. Rochester, International Museum of Photography at George Eastman House.

Friedrich Overbeck and Peter Cornelius, double portrait, pencil drawing, 1812. Formerly in the Collection Lehnsen, Scarsdale, New York.

3.23 **Separating illustration numbers from captions.** Illustration numbers should be distinct from the captions they introduce. A period after the number usually suffices (as in the first example below), and this is the format that authors should use in preparing their captions. Other treatments are sometimes used in the published version of a work. If the number is distinguished typographically—for example, by boldface—the period may not be necessary. Extra space may be added between the number and the caption to ensure legibility, as in the second example (which uses an em space; see 6.128). Whether *figure* is spelled out or abbreviated as *fig.* may be specified by journal style or, for books, may be up to the designer or editor or both.

Figure 3. Detailed stratigraphy and geochronology of the Dubawnt Supergroup.

**PLATE 5** Palace of the Governors, Santa Fe, New Mexico. Undated photograph, circa 1900.

The word *figure* or *plate* is occasionally omitted—for example, in a book whose illustrations consist of a long series of continuously numbered photographs.

3.24 **Using locators in captions.** Italicize such terms as *top, bottom, left, right, above, below, left to right, clockwise from left,* or *inset* to identify elements within a single illustration or parts of a composite or, in print publications, an illustration that does not appear on the same page as the caption. (Where such terms apply in print but not in the ebook, they may need to be commented out or otherwise removed from the latter before publication.) If the term precedes the element it identifies, it should be followed by a comma or, if a list follows, a colon. When it appears in mid-sentence or follows the element, it may appear in parentheses. See figure 3.7.

Fig. 4. *Above left,* William Livingston; *above right,* Henry Brockholst Livingston; *below left,* John Jay; *below right,* Sarah Livingston Jay

*Left to right:* Madeleine K. Albright, Dennis Ross, Ehud Barak, and Yasir Arafat

*Overleaf:* The tall trees of the valley, planted by Russell Page, are reflected among the water lilies, *Nymphaea,* and pickerelweed, *Pontederia cordata.*

Figure 2. Schematic block diagram showing upper plate (*top*) and lower plate (*bottom*) of the Battle Lake thrust-tear fault system.

If the various parts of a figure have been assigned letters, these are used in a similar way, usually italicized (see also 3.12). Likewise, descriptive terms used to identify parts of a figure are usually italicized.

Figure 3. DNA sequence from a small region within the *PC* gene, showing the G→T transition at nucleotide 2229. The partial sequence of intron 13 is also shown. *A*, wild-type sequence; *B*, sequence from a PC-deficient Micmac homozygous for the mutation.

Figure 2. Duration of hospital stay for 22 patients colonized or infected with extended-spectrum β-lactamase-producing *Escherichia coli* isolates belonging to clonally related groups A (*gray bars*) and B (*white bars*). The black point represents the date when the microorganism was isolated, and the asterisk indicates stay in the geriatric care hospital.

In the last example above, the letters identify the study groups and not parts of the figure and are therefore not italicized.

3.25 **Identifying symbols or patterns used in figures.** When symbols or patterns are used in a map or chart, they must be identified either in a key within the figure or in the caption. See figures 3.8, 3.9. See also 3.24.

Fig. 9.4. Photosynthetic light response. Data are presented from shade-grown (■) and open-grown (□) culms of the current year.

*or*

Fig. 9.4. Photosynthetic light response. Data are presented from shade-grown (*filled squares*) and open-grown (*open squares*) culms of the current year.

3.26 **Identifying electronic enhancements in captions.** The caption to an illustration published in both print and electronic versions should add in the print version an indication of any enhancement—such as color or video—available only online.

Figure 3. Egg candling showing embryonic development inside the egg. This figure appears in color online.

On the other hand, if the online version is the version of record (as will be the case for most journals), it is generally unnecessary to specify online when a feature available there is not available in print. See also 1.87.

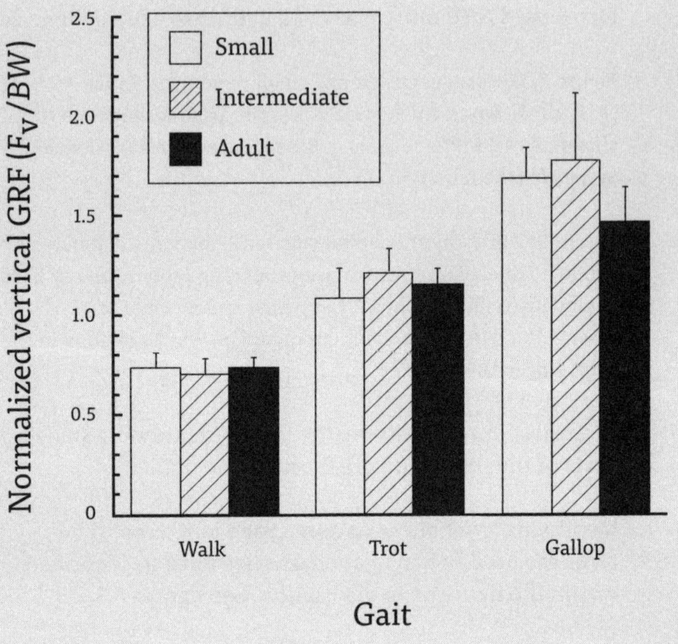


Figure 4. Normalized peak vertical forelimb GRFs versus gait. Normalized peak vertical forelimb GRFs for different gaits in the small, intermediate, and adult groups. Peak vertical forces ($F_V$) were normalized by dividing the forces by the body weight (*BW*) of the goat. Error bars represent ±1 sd.

FIGURE 3.8. A bar chart (also called a bar graph) with a key to the three types of bars (see 3.25). The caption includes the standard deviation (sd) for the T-shaped error bars. See also 3.42–47.

3.27 **Including original dimensions in captions.** When a caption provides the dimensions of an original work of art, these follow the work's medium and are listed in order of height, width, and (if applicable) depth. This information need appear only if relevant to the text, unless the rights holder requests that it be included (see 3.33).

Oil on canvas, 45 × 38 cm
Bronze, 49 × 22 × 16 in.

See also the example in 3.22. Photomicrographs, in scientific publications, may include in their captions information about the degree of magnification (e.g., original magnification, ×400; *scale bar*, 100 µm).

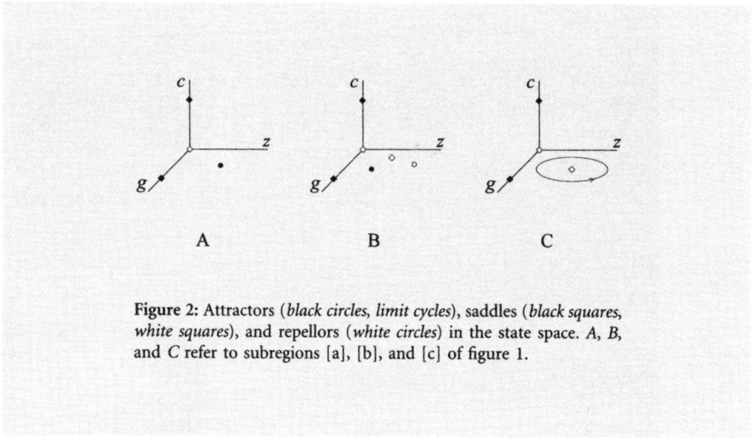

c
z
g
c
z
g
c
z
g
A
B
C
**Figure 2:** Attractors (*black circles, limit cycles*), saddles (*black squares, white squares*), and repellors (*white circles*) in the state space. *A, B,* and *C* refer to subregions [a], [b], and [c] of figure 1.


FIGURE 3.9. The symbols in this graph are identified in the caption. Compare figure 3.8 and the examples in 3.25. See also 3.42–47.

3.28 **Alternative text and descriptions.** To ensure accessibility in electronic publication formats for readers with print disabilities, publishers should include alternative text ("alt text") for any image that needs it. Whereas a caption typically describes what an image *is*, alt text describes what an image *shows* (within the context of a publication). Some captions, however, do both, and when an image is fully described in a caption or in the adjacent text, alt text may be shorter and less descriptive. If an image is purely decorative and serves no other purpose, alt text is usually unnecessary. When alt text is needed, it is added to the image markup, typically as an "alt" attribute in HTML (when alt text is unneeded, the attribute remains empty, or null, so that screen readers will ignore the image). Though there is technically no limit to how long alt text can be, it is best when it is brief (usually no more than 250 characters, including spaces, though the character limit for some screen readers will be lower than that). Alt text should be punctuated like ordinary text (but cannot contain markup for italics or paragraphs or the like). In the following example based on figure 3.10, note how the caption differs from the alt text:

*Caption*
Neil Armstrong's "double horizon" shot of Buzz Aldrin, July 20, 1969. Marshall Space Flight Center, NASA.

*Alt text*
Photograph of astronaut Buzz Aldrin standing on the surface of the moon, with Neil Armstrong visible as a tiny reflection in Aldrin's helmet visor. The lunar

FIGURE 3.10. Neil Armstrong's "double horizon" shot of Buzz Aldrin, July 20, 1969. Marshall Space Flight Center, NASA. See 3.28.

horizon behind Aldrin's head aligns with the opposite horizon reflected in his visor.

If some of these details are described in the text near the image, the alt text could be shorter:

Photograph of astronaut Buzz Aldrin standing on the surface of the moon, his back to the horizon.

Alt text, normally invisible on the screen, will be read aloud by text-to-speech tools as readers encounter an image (usually after introducing it as an image); alt text may also be incorporated into braille displays and other assistive technologies. Though publishers may write alt text in house or enlist a third party to do it, authors are usually in the best position to write it, at least initially, and are encouraged to send alt text along with any captions when they submit their manuscript for publication (see also 2.4). The alt text would then be edited along with the captions and reviewed again at the proofreading stage (see 2.142–44). In addition to alt text, some images (e.g., charts and graphs with complex data) will benefit from an extended description added to the image markup as a link; the linked-to description should be submitted either in the same document or in a separate one. For more information, consult the resources provided by the W3C Web Accessibility Initiative (WAI) and, for EPUB, the EPUB Accessibility specification.

3.29 **Alternative text for math.** Whenever possible, mathematical expressions intended for the screen should be prepared as marked-up text rather than as images. The occasional simple expression in a nontechnical context may not require any markup beyond italics for variables and the like (see 7.73). More complex expressions (and any mathematical object in a technical document) should be marked up in MathML, which can be embedded in HTML and rendered by browsers or read by screen readers. Authors can facilitate conversion to MathML by preparing their documents in LaTeX, a document authoring and markup system introduced in the 1980s that remains in wide use among STEM authors, or by using an equation editor in Microsoft Word or Google Docs (preferably a full-featured extension such as MathType from Wiris). If math must be presented as an image only (preferably as a scalable vector graphic, which will retain its clarity when enlarged), alternative text that restates the math using a combination of words and numerals will be required. Even for math that has been properly prepared, an image with alternative text can serve as a backup for devices and platforms that do not support MathML. For more information about creating accessible math, consult the MathML resources from W3C.

## *Credit Lines*

3.30 **Sources and permissions.** A brief statement of the source of an illustration, known as a credit line, is usually appropriate and sometimes required by the owner of the illustration. Illustrative material under copyright, whether published or unpublished, usually requires permission from the copyright owner before it can be reproduced. You cannot simply download a photo of your favorite Picasso from somebody's website and use it to illustrate your history of cubism; before attempting to reproduce the painting, you must write to obtain written permission, as well as a suitable copy of the work, from the museum or person who owns it. Nor may you use a photograph or other portrayal of an identifiable human subject without the consent of that person or someone acting on their behalf (e.g., by means of a model release form). Although it is the author's responsibility, not the publisher's, to obtain permissions, the publisher should be consulted about what needs permission and the best way to obtain it. For crediting works that are offered under a Creative Commons license or that are in the public domain (neither of which usually require permission), see 3.35, 3.36. For a fuller discussion of permissions, see 4.94, 4.99–109.

3.31 **Placement of credit lines.** A credit line usually appears at the end of a caption. It is sometimes placed in parentheses to differentiate it from the caption. (A photographer's name occasionally appears in small type parallel to the bottom or side of a photograph.) The examples below show a variety of treatments adapted to suit the sources. For the accession number in the last example, see 14.133.

Fig. 37. The myth that all children love dinosaurs is contradicted by this nineteenth-century scene of a visit to the monsters at Crystal Palace. (Cartoon by John Leech. "Punch's Almanack for 1855," *Punch* 28 [1855]: 8. Photo courtesy of the Newberry Library, Chicago.)

Fig. 4. Untitled photograph of a uniformed female police officer holding a child, Baltimore, Maryland, May 6, 2015. Collection of the Smithsonian National Museum of African American History and Culture, Gift of Devin Allen. © Devin Allen.

Fig. 13. Icon panel of the Buddha's footprints (*Buddhapāda*) with wheels in the central hollow, auspicious marks, and a lotus-blossom frame, perhaps 1st century BCE or CE. Palnad limestone. From the stūpa at Amarāvatī, India. Now in the British Museum, London. © The Trustees of the British Museum.

Fig. 8. *Pleasure and Wealth*. 6th century AD. Mosaic, 53 × 33 in. (134.6 × 83.8 cm). Museum of Fine Arts, Boston, 2006.848. Photo © 2020, Museum of Fine Arts, Boston.

If most or all of the illustrations in a work are from a single source, that fact may be stated in a note or, in the case of a book, in the preface or acknowledgments or on the copyright page. In a heavily illustrated book, all credits are sometimes listed together in the back matter (see

1.4) or, more rarely, in the front matter—sometimes as part of a list of illustrations (see 3.39–41). Note, however, that some permissions grantors stipulate placement of the credit with the illustration itself; others may charge a higher fee if the credit appears elsewhere.

3.32 **Crediting author as source of illustration.** Although an illustration created by the author may not require a credit line, it is generally best to include one. Use the author's full name as it is credited on the title page or elsewhere (e.g., "Photo by Teju Cole"), even if the author is the source of all illustrations in the work. Though "Photo by author" or the like may work, a credit that includes the name will be more meaningful when the illustration is viewed out of context. In works with more than one author, credit only the author who is the source of the illustration.

3.33 **Crediting material from copyrighted sources.** Unless fair use applies (see 4.88–98), or unless blanket permission has been granted by means of a Creative Commons or similar license (see 3.35), an illustration reproduced from a published work under copyright always requires formal permission, as does any copyrighted illustration found online or elsewhere. In addition to author, title, publication details, and (occasionally) copyright date, the credit line should include any page or figure number. If the work being credited is listed in the bibliography or reference list, only a shortened form need appear in the credit line (see last example below). For material acquired from a commercial agency, see 3.37. For proper citation style, see chapters 13 and 14.

Reproduced by permission from Mark Girouard, *Life in the English Country House: A Social and Architectural History* (Yale University Press, 1978), 162.

Reproduced by permission from George B. Schaller et al., *The Giant Pandas of Wolong* (University of Chicago Press, 1985), 52. © 1985 by the University of Chicago.

Rebecca Belmore, *Fringe*, 2007. Collection of the National Gallery of Canada, Ottawa. Reprinted by permission of the artist.

Reproduced by permission from Nakano et al., "Ecosystem Metabolism," fig. 3.

Some permissions grantors request specific language in the credit line. In a work with many illustrations, such language in one or two credit lines may conflict with consistent usage in the rest. Editorial discretion should then be exercised; in giving full credit to the source, an editor may follow the spirit rather than the letter. (Where the grantor is intractable, it may be simpler to use the language requested.)

3.34 **Crediting commissioned material.** Work commissioned by the author—such as maps, photographs, drawings, or charts—is usually produced under a "work made for hire" contract (see 4.9–12). Even if no credit is required under such an arrangement, professional courtesy dictates mentioning the creator (unless the illustration is legibly signed and the signature reproduced).

Map by Megan Perry
Photo by Sergio González
Drawing by Giulia Albertazzi

3.35 **Crediting material obtained free of charge.** For material that the author has asked for and obtained free and without restrictions on its use, the credit line may use the word *courtesy*.

Photograph courtesy of Ford Motor Company

Mies at the groundbreaking ceremony of the National Gallery, September 1965. Courtesy of Reinhard Friedrich.

Credits for illustrations found online and subject to a Creative Commons license should specify the license (but will not typically include the word *courtesy*).

Photo by Mehmet Karatay (Wikimedia Commons, CC BY-SA 3.0)

For more on Creative Commons licenses, see 4.72.

3.36 **Crediting material in the public domain.** Illustrations from works in the public domain (see 4.20–34) may be reproduced without permission. For readers' information, however, a credit line is appropriate.

Illustration by Joseph Pennell for Henry James, *English Hours* (Houghton, Mifflin, 1905), facing p. 82.

Engraving of Frederick Douglass by Augustus Robin, reprinted from *Life and Times of Frederick Douglass* (Hartford, CT, 1882), frontispiece.

Neil Armstrong's "double horizon" shot of Buzz Aldrin, July 20, 1969. Marshall Space Flight Center, NASA.

3.37 **Crediting agency material.** Photographs of prints, drawings, paintings, and the like obtained from a commercial agency usually require a credit line. A slash usually separates the name of the creator from the name of the agency (with a space on either side if at least one of these entities consists of an open compound, as in the examples below; see also 6.112–21). In the second example below, one person is credited for the photograph and another for the artwork. See also 3.33.

Cannupa Hanska Luger, *Mirror Shield Project*, Oceti Sakowin camp, Standing Rock, ND, December 3, 2016 (detail). Photograph by Scott Olson / Getty Images.

Kapwani Kiwanga, *Oryza*, 2021. Photograph: Marc Domage / le Crédac. © Kapwani Kiwanga / ADAGP, Paris, 2021.

3.38 **Crediting adapted material.** An author creating an illustration adjusted from, or using data from, another source should credit that source for reasons of professional courtesy and readers' information.

Figure 1.2. Weight increase of captive pandas during the first years of life. (Data from New York Zoological Park; National Zoological Park; Giron 1980.)

Fig. 7. Cut injuries (*circled*) depicted on right side of the head and right ear of the *Terme Boxer*. (Lanmas / Alamy Stock Photo; courtesy Ministero della Cultura, Museo Nazionale Romano; circles added by author.)

Adapted from DuVernay (2024, fig. 5).

If the illustration was created by or with the help of artificial intelligence (AI), that fact should be noted in the credit.

Fig. 3. Image generated by DALL·E 2, April 7, 2023, from the prompt "An ornate bookshelf with a portal into another dimension."

## *Lists of Illustrations*

3.39 **When to include a list of illustrations.** For book-length printed works, the criterion for when to include a list of illustrations is whether the illustrations are of intrinsic interest apart from the text they illustrate. Most books that feature illustrations will not require such a list. But, for example, a book on Roman architecture, illustrated by numerous photographs of ancient buildings, might benefit from a list. If included, a list of illustrations usually follows the table of contents in a book-length work. A list of illustrations may occasionally double as a list of credits if these do not appear with the illustrations themselves (see 3.31). For guidelines and examples, see 1.44 and figures 1.6, 1.7.

3.40 **Listing illustrations from a gallery.** Illustrations that are to appear in printed galleries are not always listed separately. For example, in a book containing interspersed line art and two photo galleries, a line reading "Photographs follow pages 228 and 332" might be inserted after the detailed list of figures. If all the illustrations were in galleries, that line could appear at the end of the table of contents (see fig. 1.5). (All illustrations, including those in galleries, should be listed if integral to the text.)

3.41 **Shortening captions for a list of illustrations.** In the list of illustrations, long captions should be shortened to a single line (or two at the most). The number at the end of each of the two entry examples below indicates the page on which the illustration would be found.

[*Caption*] Fig. 18. The White Garden, reduced to its bare bones in early spring. The box hedges, which are still cut by hand, have to be carefully kept in scale with the small and complex garden as well as in keeping with the plants inside the "boxes."

[*Entry in list*] 18. The White Garden in early spring 43

[*Caption*] Plate 21. The tall trees of the valley, planted by Russell Page, are reflected among the water lilies, *Nymphaea*, and pickerelweed, *Pontederia cordata*.

[*Entry in list*] 21. Page's tall trees reflected among water lilies 75

## *Charts*

3.42 **Charts defined.** A chart, also called a graph, is a device that presents data in a simple, comprehensible form—often along a set of *x*- and *y*-axes. A chart is considered line art and should be numbered and labeled as a figure (fig. 1, fig. 2, etc.). It should be used only if it summarizes the data more effectively than mere words can. While integral to the text, it should, like a table, make sense on its own terms. For guidance in chart design, consult Edward R. Tufte, *The Visual Display of Quantitative Information* (bibliog. 2.2). Charts intended for black-and-white reproduction should not be created in color, nor should charts that use color depend for their meaning on color alone (i.e., meaningful differences indicated by color should also be indicated with labels, icons, crosshatching, or similar techniques). Charts published online or in ebook formats may require alt text or an extended description to ensure accessibility (see 3.28). For an example of a typical chart, see figure 3.8. Figure 3.9—essentially a three-part graph—is a less typical example.

3.43 **Consistency among charts.** Where two or more charts are used within a work, especially if they deal with comparable material, they should follow a consistent style in graphics and typography. Whatever graphic device is used, elements of the same kind must always be represented in the same way. Different visual effects should be used only to distinguish one element from another, never just for variety.

3.44 **Axes and curves in graphs.** Both the $x$ (horizontal) and $y$ (vertical) axes should be labeled (as in fig. 3.8); the axes serve a function similar to that of column heads and stubs in a table (see 3.53). The label on the $y$-axis is read from the bottom up, though it may instead appear at the top of the axis. Curves are usually presented in graphically distinct forms—for example, one may be a continuous line, another a broken (or dashed) line. The elements in a bar chart or a pie chart that correspond to curves—the bars or the wedges—are also usually distinct. Use black and white for curves or fills rather than shading or color unless your publisher allows shading or color in appropriately prepared electronic files (see 3.19). All such elements should be labeled or else identified in a key or in the caption (see 3.7, 3.25).

3.45 **Chart titles and labels.** The title of a chart appears as part of the caption, immediately following the figure number, and is capitalized in sentence case (see 8.159). See 3.7; compare 3.55. Labels, the descriptive items within a chart, are normally lowercased (with the exception of proper nouns or other terms that would be capitalized in running text); if phrases, they may be capitalized in sentence case. Labels may be explained or discussed in a caption as needed (as in fig. 3.9).

3.46 **Abbreviations in labels.** Abbreviations and symbols may be used in labels provided they are easily recognizable or explained in a key or in the caption. (The meaning of any abbreviation taken from the text should be clear from the figure alone in case the figure is reproduced in another context, apart from the text.) A form such as "US$millions" may be more appropriate for nonspecialized (or non-English-speaking) readers than "US$M," but the shorter form is acceptable if readers will find it clear and it is used consistently. Numbers and abbreviations are covered in chapters 9 and 10.

3.47 **Genealogical and pedigree charts.** Some charts show relationships between elements in a way that cannot be conveniently arranged along axes or into rows and columns. Charts that show family or genetic structure, in particular, may require a different visual arrangement that highlights multiple relationships. A genealogical chart (often referred to as a table), for example, attempts to show important relationships within a family or several families by means of branching and connecting lines. Figure 3.11 illustrates the complicated connection of Constantine the Great to Hilderic, King of the Vandals. These charts require careful planning to illustrate relationships with minimal crossing of lines or extraneous data and, for a printed work, to remain within a reproducible shape and size. Similar to the genealogical chart is the pedigree chart, used mainly in genealogical works. These fan-shaped diagrams illustrate the ancestry of a given person, typically detailing the two parents, four grandparents, eight great-grandparents, and sixteen great-great-grandparents. They may also show several generations of offspring from a single pair of ancestors.

## TABLES

### *Introduction*

3.48 **Table preparation.** This section describes and illustrates the basic elements of a table and accepted ways of editing, arranging, and typesetting these elements. No one table in this chapter should be taken as a prototype; all merely illustrate workable patterns and may be adapted according to the data and the potential users of the tables. Though most tables can be created using the table editor in a word processor, they are nonetheless expensive (i.e., time-consuming) both to typeset and to correct in proofs and should therefore be designed and constructed with care. It is wise to consult the publisher on the appropriate number, size, and physical form of any tables to be included in a work. A table should be as simple as the material allows and understandable on its own; even a reader unfamiliar with the material presented should be able to make general sense of a table. The text may highlight the main points in a table and summarize its message but should not duplicate the details. For additional advice on table preparation, consult the *Publication Manual of the American Psychological Association* (bibliog. 1.1). For instructions on file preparation and formatting, consult your publisher. Chicago offers instructions for table preparation on its journals website.

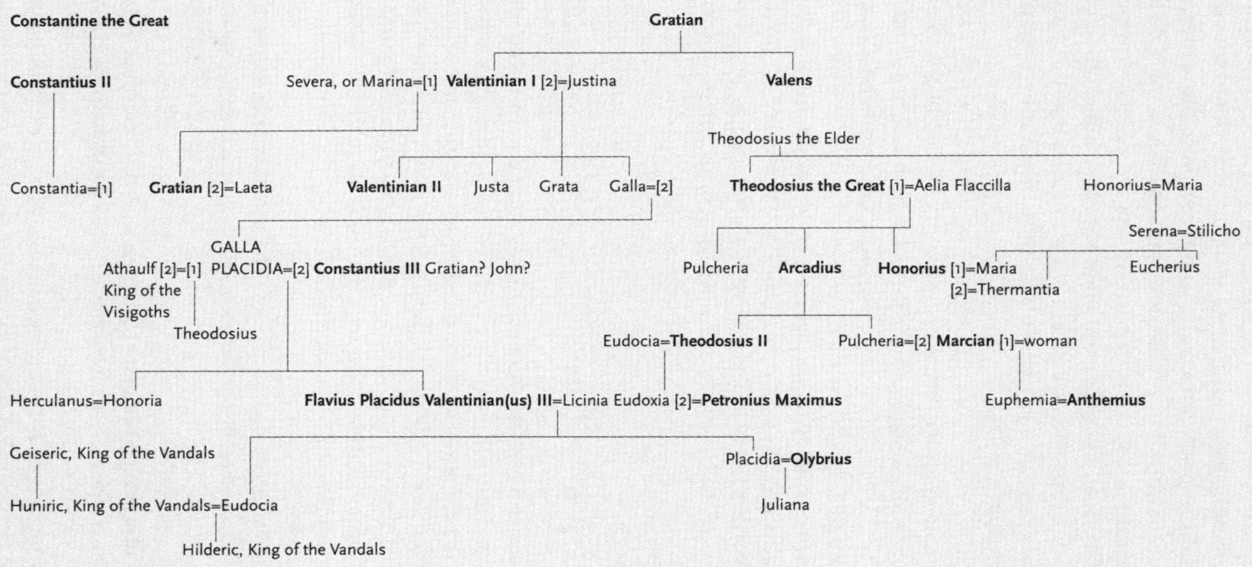


Fig. 18.5. The family of Galla Placidia Augusta. Stemmata are simplified; emperors are shown in boldface type.

FIGURE 3.11. A genealogical chart (see 3.47).

3.49 **Use of tables.** A table offers an excellent means of presenting a large number of individual, similar facts so that they are easy to scan and compare. A simple table can give information that would require several paragraphs to present textually, and it can do so more clearly. Tables published online allow for the presentation of even more data, well beyond what may be practical in print. Tables are most appropriate for scientific, statistical, financial, and other technical material. In certain contexts—if, for example, exact values are not essential to an author's argument—a graph or a bar chart (see 3.42), or plain text, may more effectively present the data.

3.50 **Consistency among tables.** Because a prime virtue of tables is easy comparison, consistency in style is indispensable both within one table and among several. A consistent style for titles, column heads, abbreviations, and the like should be followed for all tables in a single work. Similarly, choices related to line spacing, indentation, fonts, rules, and other distinguishing features in the published version of the table must be made uniformly for all tables in a work. Certain tables, however, may require rules or other devices not needed in other tables in the same work.

## *Table Numbering and Placement*

3.51 **Table numbers and text references.** Tables should be numbered separately from any illustrations (table 1, table 2, etc.). In a book with many tables, or with chapters by different authors, double numeration by chapter is often used, as it is for illustrations (table 1.1, table 1.2, . . . , table 2.2, table 2.3, . . . , etc.; see 3.11). Every table should be cited in the text by the number rather than by location relative to the text, either directly or parenthetically (but see 3.52).

> The first column of table 2 displays the results of a model predicting the age trajectory of health, controlling for differences by cohort and excluding all other predictors.

> Ethnographic observation brought to light four analytically distinct but empirically interrelated types of worker response to the new regimes (see table 5.3).

Note that the word *table* is lowercased in text references. (In some publications, such terms are routinely capitalized whenever they appear with a number.) Table numbers follow the order in which the tables are to appear in the text, and first mentions should follow that order as well. (But where context demands a reference to a table in a subsequent chapter of a book, such wording as "A different set of variables is presented in chapter 5, table 10" may be appropriate.) Each table, even in a closely related set, should be given its own number (tables 14, 15, and 16, *rather than* tables 14A–C). For table numbers and titles, see 3.55.

3.52 **Placement of tables relative to the text.** A simple list or other tabular matter that requires no more than a few columns can usually be presented in the run of text and left unnumbered and untitled (see, e.g., the two-column list at 1.4 in this manual). A numbered table should appear as soon as possible after the first text reference to it. To accommodate page makeup, tables may break over one or more pages or be presented broadside across facing pages (see 3.87, 3.88). The author or (if the author has not done so) the editor must provide callouts that indicate in the manuscript the preferred location for each numbered table (see 2.35). Note that a *callout* (e.g., "table 3 about here") is an instruction for typesetting or production and will not appear in the published work (for *text references*, which are addressed to readers, see 3.51). In print, most tables that run to less than a page will appear at either the top or the bottom of a page. In electronic formats, tables may be marked up and presented with the run of text (sometimes as a thumbnail image that links to the full table). See also 3.8.

## *The Parts of a Table*

3.53 **Table structure and use.** A table normally consists of rows and columns, which are analogous to the horizontal (*x*) and vertical (*y*) axes of a graph, respectively. The data in most tables include two sets of variables. One set of variables is defined in the top row of a table, in the column headings (see 3.57); the other set is defined along the far left-hand column of the table by the stub entries (see 3.60). If the data consist of dependent and independent variables, the independent variables are usually presented in the stub column, though this choice is sometimes limited by the physical dimensions of the table (see 3.87). The intersection between a row defined by a stub entry and a column defined by a column head is a cell (sometimes called a data cell). The anatomy of a basic table is presented in figure 3.12.

3.54 **Horizontal and vertical rules.** To produce a clear, professional-looking table, rules should be used sparingly. Many tables will require just three rules, all of them horizontal—one at the very top of the table, below the title and above the column heads; one just below the column heads; and

TABLE 1. Table title

| | Spanner head[a] | | Spanner head | |
|---|---|---|---|---|
| Stub column head | Column head | Column head | Column head | Column head |
| Stub entry | | | | |
| Stub subentry | 0.00 | 0.00 | 0.00[b] | 0.00 |
| Stub subentry | 0.00 | 0.00 | 0.00 | 0.00 |
| Stub entry[c] | | | | |
| Stub subentry | 0.00 | 0.00 | 0.00 | 0.00 |
| Stub subentry | 0.00 | 0.00 | 0.00 | 0.00 |
| Stub entry | 0.00 | 0.00 | 0.00[b] | 0.00 |

*Source:* A source note acknowledges the source of the data, if not the author's own.

*Note:* General note to table. A general note might be used to explain how to interpret the data.

[a] Note to the first spanner head.

[b] Note that applies to the data in two different data cells.

[c] Note to the second stub entry.

FIGURE 3.12. A five-column table modeling the basic parts of a table discussed in 3.53–70.

one at the bottom of the table, along the bottom of the last row, above any notes to the table. Additional horizontal rules may be required to separate spanner heads from column heads (see 3.58) or to enclose cut-in heads (see 3.59). A rule above a row of totals is traditional but not essential (unless required by a journal or series style). See also 3.64. Vertical rules should be used sparingly—for example, when a table is doubled up (see 3.87) or as an aid to comprehension in an especially long or complex table.

3.55 **Table numbers and titles.** Table titles should be as succinct as possible and should not suggest any interpretation of the data. For example, a title such as "Grammar and punctuation errors at suburban schools" is preferable to "High degree of grammar and punctuation errors at suburban schools." Titles should be in noun form, and participles are preferred to relative clauses: for example, "Households subscribing to à la carte channels," not "Households that subscribe to à la carte channels." Table titles may be capitalized in sentence case (see 8.159), as in the examples in this chapter, or in the more traditional title case (see 8.160), provided one style prevails throughout the work. The title, which appears above the table, usually follows the number on the same line, separated by punctuation or by space and typographic distinction (as in the second example below, which uses bold for the table number followed by an em space; see 6.128). (Less commonly, the number appears on a line by itself, the title starting a new line.) The number is always preceded by the word *table*.

Table 6. Ratios of parental income coefficients to SAT score coefficients

**Table 12** Fertilizer treatment effects on *Lythrum salicaria* and *Penthorum sedoides*

For table numbering and placement, see 3.51–52.

3.56 **Parenthetical information in table titles.** Important explanatory or statistical information is often included in parentheses in a title. Such material should be set in sentence case even if the main title is in title case. More detailed information should go in a note to the table (see 3.79, 3.80).

Federal employees in the Progressive Era (total plus selected agencies)
Scan statistics $S_L$ of varying lengths $L$ for sib-pair data (broad diagnosis)
Gender as a factor in successful business transactions ($N = 4{,}400$)

For the use of *N* in statistical tables, see 3.86.

3.57 **Column heads.** Space being at a premium, column heads should be as brief as possible and are best capitalized in sentence case (as in all examples in this chapter). As long as their meaning will be clear to readers, abbreviations may be used as needed. The first column (the stub) does not always require a head (see 3.60). In a work that includes multiple tables, column heads should be treated consistently. Like table titles, a column head may require an indication of the unit of measurement used or some other clarification of the data in the column. Such material, which may consist of a symbol or an abbreviation ($, %, km, *n*, and so on), should follow the column head in parentheses (see fig. 3.13). Parentheses may also be used in column heads when some of the data in the cells are in parentheses. For example, a column head might read "Children with positive results, % (no. positive/no. tested)," and a cell under this head could contain "27.3 (6/22)." If columns must be numbered for text reference, use Arabic numerals in parentheses, centered immediately below the column head, above the rule separating the head from the column (see also 3.87).

3.58 **Spanner heads.** When a table demands column heads of two or more levels—that is, when related columns require both a collective head

TABLE 2. Real-world magnitudes of the relationship between tort reform and death rates

| Tort reform | Annual death rates (%) | Number of deaths in 2019 | Deaths across all years |
|---|---|---|---|
| Cap on noneconomic damages | -3.54 | -333 | -5,242 |
| Higher evidence standard for punitive damages | -2.57 | -982 | -11,798 |
| Product liability reform | -3.83 | -1,267 | -16,841 |
| Prejudgment interest reform | -4.88 | -647 | -9,060 |
| Collateral source reform | | | |
| Offset awards | +4.71 | +938 | +14,160 |
| Admit evidence | +2.43 | +294 | +4,468 |
| Net effect | | -1,998 | -24,314 |

*Note:* Values presented are average changes. These computations are based on the coefficients from the primary regression (table 3) and the average annual populations and average annual death rates in the states that had each reform. The sums of the individual reforms differ by one from the net effects owing to rounding.

FIGURE 3.13. A four-column table with two levels of stub entries (*first column*). Note the parenthetical indication in the second column head, specifying percentages for the values in that column (see 3.57).

and individual heads—spanner heads, or spanners (sometimes called decked heads), are used. A horizontal rule, called a spanner (or straddle) rule, appears between the spanner and the column heads to show which columns the spanner applies to (see figs. 3.12, 3.14). For ease of reading, spanner heads should seldom exceed two levels.

3.59 **Cut-in heads.** Cut-in heads, spanning all columns but the first, may be used as subheads within a table. They usually appear between horizontal rules (see fig. 3.15), though extra vertical space above each head may be used instead. An exceptionally long table with one or more cut-in heads may be a candidate for division into two or more tables.

3.60 **Stub entries.** The left-hand column of a table, known as the stub, is usually a vertical listing of categories about which information is given in the corresponding columns to the right. The individual rows in the stub, referred to in this manual as *stub entries*, may also be referred to as *row headings*. If all the entries are of like kind, the stub usually carries a column head (e.g., "Tort reform" in fig. 3.13); even a general head such as "Characteristic" or "Variable" or "Year" aids readers. If the entries are self-explanatory (as in fig. 3.15), a head may be omitted from the stub; a

TABLE 3. Survey responses from patients who received intravenous (IV) prostanoids at center 1 in 2022

| Question type and characteristic | No. (%) of patients, by prostanoid received | | |
|---|---|---|---|
| | Epoprostenol (*n* = 48) | Treprostinil (*n* = 24) | *P* |
| IV catheter–related question | | | |
| Person responsible for care of IV catheter | | | |
| Patient | 22 (47) | 10 (43) | |
| Adult caregiver | 23 (49) | 13 (57) | |
| Both | 2 (4) | 0 (0) | .82 |
| Catheter type | | | |
| Groshong | 23 (50) | 12 (50) | |
| Broviac | 23 (50) | 12 (50) | 1.00 |
| Catheter-dressing type | | | |
| Occlusive | 27 (57) | 15 (63) | |
| Nonocclusive | 20 (43) | 9 (38) | .68 |
| Allowed >2 days between changes of dressing | 14 (29) | 7 (29) | 1.00 |
| Used sterile gloves when changing dressings | 38 (79) | 17 (71) | .43 |
| Used mask when changing dressings | 28 (58) | 13 (54) | .74 |
| Always washed hands before changing dressings | 46 (96) | 22 (92) | .60 |
| Medication-related question | | | |
| Person responsible for medication preparation | | | |
| Patient | 21 (45) | 12 (52) | |
| Adult caregiver | 24 (51) | 10 (43) | |
| Both | 2 (4) | 1 (4) | .82 |
| Used needleless device to access vial of medication or diluent[a] | 4 (8) | 5 (21) | .15 |
| Cleaned top of vial of medication or diluent[a] with alcohol before use | 45 (94) | 24 (100) | .55 |
| Always washed hands before medication preparation | 46 (96) | 22 (92) | .60 |
| Miscellaneous question | | | |
| Used a swimming pool or hot tub | 3 (6) | 4 (17) | .18 |

[a] Refers to the treprostinil vial for patients who received treprostinil and to the diluent vial for patients who received epoprostenol.

FIGURE 3.14. A four-column table with a spanner head across the second and third columns, separated from the column heads by a horizontal rule (see 3.58). Note the three levels of stub entries (see 3.61). Note also that the spanner head specifies two units for each column—number and, in parentheses, percentage (see 3.57).

TABLE 4. Distribution of estimated school quality

| | All schools | Rural | Urban |
|---|---|---|---|
| | | OLS estimates[a] | |
| Mean | -.120 | -.178 | -.063 |
| Minimum | -.72 | -.72 | -.30 |
| Maximum | .33 | .33 | .18 |
| | | MLE estimates[b] | |
| Mean | -.063 | -.101 | -.025 |
| Minimum | -.43 | -.43 | -.26 |
| Maximum | .40 | .40 | .17 |

*Note:* School quality is measured as proportional deviations from Taha Hussein School.

[a] School-quality estimates from col. 1, table 1.

[b] School-quality estimates from col. 3, table 1.

FIGURE 3.15. A four-column table with two cut-in heads ("OLS estimates" and "MLE estimates") across three columns, separated by horizontal rules (see 3.59); a general note (see 3.79); and two lettered footnotes (see 3.80).

head may also be omitted if the entries are too unlike (as in fig. 3.17). If the stub entries are words, they are capitalized in sentence case. Unless they are questions, they carry no end punctuation. They should be consistent in syntax: Authors, Publishers, Printers (*not* Authors, Publishing concerns, Operates print shop). Some tables do not include a stub (see 3.71).

3.61 **Stub entries with subheads.** Items in the stub may form a straight sequential list (e.g., all the US states listed alphabetically) or a classified list (e.g., the states listed by geographic region, with a subhead for each region). The first word in a subentry as well as in a main entry is capitalized, to avoid confusion with runover lines. Subentries are further distinguished from main entries by being indented (as in fig. 3.13), or italics (or bold) may be used for the main entries and roman for the subentries. A combination of italics and indents may also be used, especially if sub-subentries are required. There is generally no need for colons following main entries unless a particular journal style requires them. See also 3.62.

3.62 **Runover lines in stub columns.** If there are no subentries, runover lines in stub entries should be indented (typically by one em in typeset copy). Only if there is extra space between rows should runovers be set flush left. If there are indented subentries, any runover lines must be more deeply indented than the lowest level of subentry (see fig. 3.14). Runovers from main entries and from subentries carry the same indent from the left margin (in typeset copy, typically one em farther to the right than the indent for the lowest level of subentry). See also 6.128.

3.63 **Abbreviations in stub columns.** As in column heads (see 3.57), where space is at a premium, symbols or abbreviations ($, %, km, *n*, and so on) are acceptable in the stub. Ditto marks (" ") to indicate information that repeats from one row to the next are not, however, since they save no space and make work for readers. Any nonstandard abbreviations must be defined in a note to the table (see 3.80).

3.64 **Totals.** When the word *Total* appears at the foot of the stub, it is often indented more deeply than the greatest indent above (see fig. 3.22) or distinguished typographically (see fig. 3.16). See also 3.75, 3.76.

3.65 **Using leaders with stub entries.** Leaders—several spaced periods following a stub entry—are sometimes used in a table where the connection between the stub entries and the rows they apply to would otherwise be unclear. Some journals routinely use leaders in stubs (see fig. 3.17); books use them more rarely. Another practice—used routinely by some journals—is to apply shading to every other row.

3.66 **Table body and cells.** Strictly speaking, the table body includes all rows, columns, and heads. Nonetheless, it is often convenient to consider the body of a table as consisting of the points of intersection between the stub entries and the column headings—the real substance of the table. These intersections are called cells (or data cells). The fifth cell in the fourth column of the table in figure 3.13, for example, contains the datum "+14,160." Though cells are usually occupied by data, they may be empty (see 3.68).

3.67 **Column data.** Whenever possible, columns should carry the same kinds of information. For instance, amounts of money should appear in one column, percentages in another, and information expressed in words in another (though two types of data can share the same column, as in the table in fig. 3.14; see 3.70). No column should contain identical information in all the cells; such information is better handled in a note.

3.68 **Empty cells.** If a column head does not apply to one of the entries in the stub, the cell should either be left blank or, better, filled in by an em dash (see 6.79) or three unspaced ellipsis dots (...). If a distinction is

TABLE 5. State expansion in the Progressive Era: Number of federal employees (total plus selected agencies)

| Selected agencies | 1909 | 1917 | Increase (%) |
|---|---|---|---|
| Dept. of Agriculture | 11,279 | 20,269 | 79.7 |
| Interstate Commerce Commission | 560 | 2,370 | 323.2 |
| Dept. of Justice | 3,198 | 4,512 | 41.1 |
| Dept. of Commerce and Labor[a] | 11,999 | 14,993 | 25.0 |
| Dept. of the Navy[b] | 3,390 | 6,420 | 89.4 |
| Dept. of War[c] | 22,292 | 30,870 | 38.5 |
| Dept. of the Interior[d] | 17,900 | 22,478 | 25.6 |
| Federal Reserve Board | ... | 75 | |
| Civil Service Commission | 193 | 276 | 43.0 |
| Federal Trade Commission | ... | 244 | |
| Shipping Board | ... | 22 | |
| *Total* | | | |
| DC and non-DC | 342,159 | 497,867[e] | 45.5 |
| Excluding Post Office | 136,799 | 198,199 | 44.9 |

*Sources: Reports of the United States Civil Service Commission* (GPO): 1910, table 19; 1917, tables 9–10; 1919, p. vi; US Department of Commerce, Bureau of the Census, *Statistical Abstract of the United States, 1917* (GPO, 1918), table 392.

[a] The Departments of Commerce and Labor were combined until 1913. The Civil Service Commission continued to combine their employees in its subsequent reports through 1917. Separate employment figures for the Labor Department, taken from *The Anvil and the Plow: A History of the Department of Labor* (GPO, 1963), appendix, table 6, show an essentially stable personnel level (2,000 in 1913, 2,037 in 1917). The bulk of employees (1,740) were attached to the Bureau of Immigration and Naturalization in 1917. The Bureau of Labor Statistics was second in importance, with 104. The Children's Bureau had 103, an increase of 88 from 1913; and the Conciliation Service had only 12, taken from the secretary's personal allotment. In the next two years of wartime, given new labor-market and conciliation functions, the departments' personnel would almost triple; however, the number fell back sharply in 1920.

[b] Exclusive of trade and labor employees.

[c] Excludes "ordinance and miscellaneous" categories.

[d] Includes Land, Pension, Indian, and Reclamation Services.

[e] Excludes Panama Canal workforce.

FIGURE 3.16. A four-column table with *Total* appearing in italics, to distinguish it from the stub entries above and below. Compare figure 3.22. See also 3.64. Also note the use of ellipsis dots for cells with no data; cells for which data are not applicable are blank. See 3.68.

needed between "not applicable" and "no data available," a blank cell may be used for the former and an em dash or ellipsis dots for "no data" (see fig. 3.16). If this distinction is not clear from the text, a note may be added to the table. (Alternatively, the abbreviations *n/a* and *n.d.* may be used, with definitions given in a note.) A zero means literally that the quantity in a cell is zero (see figs. 3.14, 3.17).

TABLE 6. Decisions on submitted manuscripts

| | | | Time from receipt to decision | | | | | | | |
|---|---|---|---|---|---|---|---|---|---|---|
| | | | Less than 1 month | | 1–2 months | | 2–3 months | | More than 3 months | |
| | 2023 | 2022 | 2023 | 2022 | 2023 | 2022 | 2023 | 2022 | 2023 | 2022 |
| Accepted | | | | | | | | | | |
| Original manuscript accepted as submitted or with minor revisions | 0 | 2 | 0 | 0 | 0 | 0 | 0 | 1 | 0 | 1 |
| Conditional acceptance of original manuscript; revised version accepted | 0 | 0 | 0 | 0 | 0 | 0 | 0 | 0 | 0 | 0 |
| Acceptance of resubmission of revised manuscript | 16 | 14 | 2 | 1 | 1 | 0 | 4 | 2 | 9 | 9 |
| Rejected | | | | | | | | | | |
| Original manuscript rejected with suggestion of resubmission | 34 | 26 | 5 | 3 | 6 | 4 | 3 | 2 | 20 | 17 |
| Original manuscript rejected without suggestion of resubmission | 249 | 260 | 165 | 161 | 34 | 34 | 16 | 18 | 34 | 47 |
| Rejection of resubmission of revised manuscript | 22 | 26 | 2 | 0 | 1 | 0 | 2 | 1 | 14 | 26 |
| Total new submissions received | 283 | 288 | | | | | | | | |
| Total resubmissions received | 38 | 41 | | | | | | | | |
| Manuscripts withdrawn | 0 | 3 | | | | | | | | |
| Total submissions received | 321 | 332 | 174 | 165 | 42 | 38 | 25 | 26 | 77 | 100 |
| Percentage of total | 100 | 100 | 54 | 50 | 13 | 11 | 8 | 8 | 24 | 30 |

FIGURE 3.17. An eleven-column table with three levels of column heads, separated by spanner rules (see 3.58), and with leader dots from stub entries (see 3.65). Note also the two rows of totals; the rule above these rows is common but by no means required (see 3.64).

TABLE 7. Innovations in measures of Amgen operating performance and stock market returns: Correlation matrix for the variables

| | Revenue | Net income | Operating cash flow | Free cash flow | S&P 500 return | CRSP return |
|---|---|---|---|---|---|---|
| Revenue | 1.00 | | | | | |
| Net income | .03 | 1.00 | | | | |
| Operating cash flow | −.07 | .91 | 1.00 | | | |
| Free cash flow | .09 | .12 | .04 | 1.00 | | |
| S&P 500 return | .05 | .04 | .22 | .16 | 1.00 | |
| CRSP return | .08 | .00 | .19 | .16 | .99 | 1.00 |

*Note:* For revenue, the innovation is defined as the log-first difference. For all the other operating variables, it is the arithmetic-first difference.

FIGURE 3.18. A seven-column matrix, in which the six column heads are identical to the six stub entries. Those cells that repeat order-independent relationships from other cells are left blank. See 3.69.

TABLE 8. Average Euclidean distances between populations, calculated from morphological data

| Population | Chunliao | Lona | Yunshanchau | Tunchiu | Tenchu | Hohuanshan | Tatachia |
|---|---|---|---|---|---|---|---|
| Chunliao | ... | | | | | | |
| Lona | .57 | ... | | | | | |
| Yunshanchau | .75 | 1.25 | ... | | | | |
| Tunchiu | .71 | 1.03 | .78 | ... | | | |
| Tenchu | 1.15 | 1.10 | 1.59 | .97 | ... | | |
| Hohuanshan | 1.51 | 1.43 | 2.00 | 1.65 | 1.16 | ... | |
| Tatachia | 1.85 | 2.03 | 2.17 | 1.69 | 1.24 | 1.55 | ... |

FIGURE 3.19. An eight-column matrix. The intersections of like columns and stub entries are marked with ellipsis dots. See 3.69.

3.69 **Matrixes.** A matrix is a tabular structure designed to show reciprocal relationships within a group of individuals, concepts, or other entities. In a matrix, the stub entries are identical to the column heads; therefore, the cells present two identical sets of intersections. The cells that would contain repeated data may be left blank if the relational order is not significant (see fig. 3.18); in some matrixes, the intersection of matching heads may be left blank or marked with an em dash or ellipsis dots (as in fig. 3.19). See also 3.68.

3.70 **Presenting multiple values in a single cell.** To allow for fewer columns, a single cell may contain two values, with one appearing in parentheses (see fig. 3.14). Such cases should be clarified in the column heading (see 3.57) or in a note.

## *Cell Alignment and Formatting*

3.71 **Alignment of rows.** Each cell in a row aligns with the stub entry to which it belongs. If the stub entry occupies more than one line, the cell entry is normally aligned on the last line of the stub entry (see fig. 3.14). But if both the stub and one or more cells contain more than one line, the first lines are aligned throughout the body of the table. First lines are also aligned in a table where the content of each column is of the same sort—in other words, where the first column is not a stub as described in 3.60 (see fig. 3.20). See also 3.72.

3.72 **Alignment of column heads.** Column heads that share a row align on the baseline; if any head occupies more than one line, all the heads in that row align on the last (lowest) line. Each column head except in the stub column is normally centered on the longest (i.e., widest) cell entry. If the longest entry is unusually long, adjustment may be necessary to give an appearance of balance. If centering does not work, align column heads and cells on the left. The stub head and entries are always aligned on the left.

3.73 **Alignment of numbers within columns.** Within a column, numbers without decimal points are usually aligned on the last digit, "ranged right" (see fig. 3.17). If the numbers include decimal points, they are typically aligned on the decimal point (see fig. 3.14). For quantities less than 1.0, zeros do not need to be added before the decimal in a table unless prescribed by a journal or series style (though they would usually be required in running text). See also 9.21. Where spaces rather than commas are used to separate groups of digits (see 9.57), alignment is made on the decimal comma. In all these arrangements, the column of numerals as a whole is usually centered within the column on the longest (i.e., widest) numeral. A column including different kinds of numbers is best aligned on the ones that occur most frequently (as in the table in fig. 3.21, in which most of the values are aligned on the decimal point, but the values for *N* are centered; see also 3.86). Ellipses and em dashes are centered (see fig. 3.16). Note that the advice in this paragraph applies mainly to printed formats and by extension PDF. In tables presented in

TABLE 9. Role-style differentiae in the Lewin, Lippitt, and White "group atmosphere" studies

| Authoritarian | Democratic | Laissez-faire |
|---|---|---|
| All determination of policy by leader | All policies a matter of group discussion and decision, encouraged and assisted by the leader | Complete freedom for group or individual decision, with a minimum of leader participation |
| Techniques and activity steps dictated by the authority, one at a time, so that future steps were uncertain to a large degree | Activity perspective gained during discussion period, and general steps to group goal sketched; when advice was needed, the leader suggested two or more alternative procedures from which choice could be made | Various materials supplied by leader, who made clear a willingness to supply technical information when asked but took no other part in work discussion |
| Leader usually dictated the task and companion of each member | Members were free to work with whomever they chose, and division of tasks was left to the group | Complete nonparticipation of the leader |
| Leader tended to be "personal" in praise and criticism of each member's work; remained aloof from active group participation except when demonstrating | Leader was "objective" in praise and criticism and tried to be a regular group member in spirit without doing too much work | Leader did not comment on member activities unless questioned, did not attempt to appraise or regulate the course of events |

FIGURE 3.20. A three-column table with no stub entries (see 3.60, 3.71).

HTML, which lacks certain alignment options available for print, either left alignment or centering may be preferred for numeric data (see also 3.89).

3.74 **Alignment of columns consisting of words.** When a column consists of words, phrases, or sentences, appearance governs left-right alignment. If no runover lines are required, entries may be centered. Longer entries usually look better if they begin flush left. Runover lines may be indented or, if enough space is left between entries, aligned flush left with the first line (as in fig. 3.20).

3.75 **Format for totals, averages, and means.** Extra vertical space or short rules sometimes appear above totals at the foot of columns but may equally well be omitted. No rules, however, should appear above aver-

TABLE 10. Descriptive statistics

| Variable | Mean | Standard deviation |
|---|---|---|
| Cohort indicator | | |
| 1946 | .128 | .33 |
| 1947 | .140 | .35 |
| 1948 | .145 | .35 |
| 1949 | .148 | .35 |
| 1950 | .145 | .35 |
| 1951 | .145 | .35 |
| 1952 | .148 | .35 |
| Education indicator | | |
| Less than *baccalauréat* | .718 | .45 |
| *Baccalauréat* only | .096 | .29 |
| University diploma (*bac* + 2) | .074 | .26 |
| University degree | .111 | .31 |
| Years of higher education | 1.440 | 2.47 |
| Wage (log) | 9.170 | .49 |
| Middle-class family background | .246 | .43 |
| *N* | 26,371 | 26,371 |

*Source:* Labor Force Survey 1990, 1993, 1996, and 1999.

*Note:* Sample is male wage earners born between 1946 and 1952.

FIGURE 3.21. A three-column table in which values are aligned on the decimal point (in print only) except for *N* values (*last row*); see 3.73.

ages or means. Consistency must be maintained and, where applicable, journal or series style followed. The word *Total* in the stub is often indented. Subtotals are similarly treated. See figure 3.22. See also 3.64, 3.76.

3.76 **When to use totals.** Totals and subtotals may be included or not, according to how useful they are to the presentation. When the percentages in a column are based on different *n*'s, a final percentage based on the total *N* may be informative and, if so, should be included (see 3.86). Note that rounding often causes a percentage total to be slightly more or less than 100. In such cases the actual value (e.g., 99% or 101%) should be given—if it is given at all—and a note should explain the apparent discrepancy. See also 3.64, 3.75.

## *Notes to Tables*

3.77 **Order and placement of notes to tables.** Notes to a table are of four general kinds and, where two or more kinds are needed, should appear in

TABLE 11. Sample sizes across language versions, role groups, and years

| | Role/group | | | |
|---|---|---|---|---|
| Language/year | Undergraduates | Postgraduates | Faculty | Subtotal |
| American | | | | |
| 2021 | 38,026 | 18,330 | 13,138 | 69,494 |
| 2022 | 53,954 | 17,015 | 12,669 | 83,638 |
| 2023 | 44,132 | 18,375 | 12,169 | 74,676 |
| Subtotal | 136,112 | 53,720 | 37,976 | 227,808 |
| British | | | | |
| 2021 | 12,853 | 4,263 | 2,054 | 19,170 |
| 2023 | 26,140 | 7,774 | 1,900 | 35,814 |
| 2023 | 9,902 | 3,357 | 1,107 | 14,366 |
| Subtotal | 48,895 | 15,394 | 5,061 | 69,350 |
| Total | | | | 297,158 |

FIGURE 3.22. A five-column table with subtotals and total (see 3.64, 3.75).

this order: (1) source notes, (2) other notes applying to the whole table, (3) notes applying to specific parts of the table, and (4) notes on significance levels. Notes to a table always appear immediately below the table they belong to (i.e., as table footnotes) and must be numbered separately from the text notes. But if a multipage table contains no general notes and any specific notes pertain only to a single page, these notes may appear at the foot of the printed pages they apply to. In electronic formats without fixed pages, all notes are usually grouped at the bottom of the table (and specific notes may be linked to their references in the table).

3.78 **Acknowledging data in source notes to tables.** If data for a table are not the author's own but are taken from another source or other sources, professional courtesy requires that full acknowledgment be made in an unnumbered note. The note is introduced by *Source* or *Sources*, in italics and followed by a colon (see fig. 3.21), though other treatments are acceptable if consistently followed. A source note precedes any other notes to the table.

*Sources:* Data from Richard H. Adams Jr., "Remittances, Investment, and Rural Asset Accumulation in Pakistan," *Economic Development and Cultural Change* 47, no. 1 (1998): 155–73; David Bevan, Paul Collier, and Jan Gunning, *Peasants and Government: An Economic Analysis* (Clarendon Press, 1989), 125–28.

If the sources are listed in the bibliography or reference list, a shortened form may be used:

*Sources:* Data from Adams (1998); Bevan, Collier, and Gunning (1989).

Unless fair use applies (see 4.88–98), a table reproduced without change from a published work under copyright requires formal permission. Credit should be given in a source note. See 3.33 for more information about styling credit lines, including examples. For more on source citations, see chapters 13 and 14.

3.79 **Notes applying to the whole table.** A note applying to the table as a whole follows any source note and is introduced by the word *Note*, in italics and followed by a colon, though other treatments are acceptable if consistently followed. See figures 3.12, 3.13, 3.15, 3.18, 3.21. If the substance of a general note can be expressed as a brief phrase, it may be added parenthetically to the title (for examples, see 3.56). Some publications, especially in the sciences, use headnotes, which immediately follow the title and expand on or qualify it; such a headnote is similar to the explanatory information in a figure caption (see 3.21).

3.80 **Notes to specific parts of a table.** For notes that apply to specific parts of a table, superscript letters, numbers, or symbols may be used; one system should be used consistently across all tables. Though superscript letters are generally preferred, the choice may depend on context. Numerals may be preferred for tables whose data consist mainly of words or letters (e.g., tables 11.3, 11.4, and 11.5 in this manual), whereas symbols may be preferred for tables that include mathematical or chemical equations, where superscript letters or numerals might be mistaken for exponents. Each table should have its own series of notes—beginning with *a* (usually in roman), 1, or *—separate from the text notes and the notes to other tables. The sequence runs from left to right, top to bottom, as in text. Unlike note reference numbers in text, however, the same letter, number, or symbol is used on two or more elements if the corresponding note applies to them. (A note reference attached to a column head is assumed to apply to the items in the column below it; a reference attached to a stub entry applies to that row.) The superscript letter, number, or symbol is repeated at the foot of the table at the beginning of the corresponding note and may be followed by a space (if done so consistently) but never by a period. See figures 3.14, 3.15, 3.25. Where symbols are used, the sequence is as follows:

1. * (asterisk; but do not use if *p* values occur in the table; see 3.81)
2. † (dagger)
3. ‡ (double dagger)
4. § (section mark)
5. || (parallels)
6. # (number sign, or pound)

When more symbols are needed, these may be doubled and tripled in the samc sequence:

*, †, ‡, etc., **, ††, ‡‡, etc., ***, †††, ‡‡‡, and so on.

3.81 **Notes on significance levels.** If a table contains notes on significance levels (also called probability notes), asterisks may be used as reference marks. If two or three standard significance levels are noted, a single asterisk is used for the least significant level, two for the next higher, and three for the third. If values other than these three are given, however, letters are preferable to asterisks, to avoid misleading the reader. In the note, the letter *p* (probability) is usually lowercase and in italics. Zeros are generally omitted before the decimal point. Probability notes follow all other notes (see fig. 3.23).

* $p < .05$
** $p < .01$
*** $p < .001$

These short notes may be set on the same line; if they are spaced, no intervening punctuation is needed, but if they are run together, they should be separated by semicolons. For more on *p* values, consult the *Publication Manual of the American Psychological Association* (bibliog. 1.1). Some journals capitalize *p*, and some give probability values in regular table notes.

## *Editing Tables*

3.82 **Editing table content.** Tables should be edited for style—with special attention to matters of capitalization, spelling, punctuation, abbreviations, numbers, and use of symbols. They should be checked for internal consistency, consistency across multiple tables (e.g., to ensure

TABLE 12. Determinants of vote for McClellan in 1864

| | Coefficient | SE | Odds ratio |
|---|---|---|---|
| Church seats held by | | | |
| Pietist sects (%) | −.454** | .117 | .635 |
| Liturgical sects (%) | .356* | .183 | 1.428 |
| Labor force in manufacturing (%) | −.700** | .269 | .497 |
| Indicator = 1 if county above county mean for | | | |
| Personal property wealth | −.024 | .040 | .976 |
| Real estate wealth | −.082* | .039 | .921 |
| Free population who are slave owners (%) | .159** | .025 | 1.172 |
| Free population born in | | | |
| Ireland (%) | .009* | .004 | 1.010 |
| Britain (%) | −.025** | .006 | .975 |
| Germany (%) | .013** | .003 | 1.013 |
| Other foreign country (%) | −.011** | .004 | .989 |
| Logarithm of county population | −.053* | .026 | .948 |
| Indicator = 1 if region is | | | |
| Middle Atlantic | .506** | .062 | 1.659 |
| East north central | .304** | .074 | 1.355 |
| West north central | −.199** | .097 | .820 |
| Border | .115 | .133 | 1.122 |
| West | .110 | .126 | 1.116 |
| Constant | .374 | .269 | |

*Note:* Results are from a weighted generalized least squares regression in which the dependent variable is $\log[M_i/(100 - M_i)]$, where $M_i$ is the percentage of the vote cast for McClellan. County characteristics are county characteristics in 1860. $N = 941$ observations. Adjusted $R^2 = .223$. Our electoral data come from Clubb, Flanigan, and Zingale (2006). Our county characteristics are from Inter-university Consortium for Political and Social Research (2004), with the exception of the percentage born in a particular country, which we estimated from the 1860 census sample of Ruggles et al. (2004).

* $p < .05$

** $p < .01$

FIGURE 3.23. A four-column table with notes on significance, or probability, levels (*p*), following a general note (see 3.81).

uniform treatment of column heads and stub entries), and consistency with the style of the surrounding text. (The meaning of any abbreviation taken from the text should be clear from the table alone in case the table is reproduced in another context, apart from the text.) Any totals should be checked and discrepancies referred to the author for resolution. As in the text, note references must be checked against the notes, and the correct sequence of letters or symbols must be verified (see 3.80). Tables should be checked for relevance vis-à-vis the text, and they should be checked alongside each other for redundancy. A lay reader or a nontechnical editor should be able to make logical sense of a table, even if the material is highly technical.

3.83 **"Percent" versus "percentage."** Despite changing usage, Chicago continues to regard *percent* as an adverb ("per, or out of, each hundred," as in *10 percent of the class*)—or, less commonly, an adjective (*a 10 percent raise*)—and to use *percentage* as the noun form (*a significant percentage of her income*). The symbol %, however, may stand for either word. See also 3.85.

3.84 **Number ranges.** Anyone preparing or editing a table must ensure that number ranges do not overlap, that there are no gaps between them, and that they are as precise as the data require. It must be clear whether "up to" or "up to and including" is meant. Dollar amounts, for example, might be given as "less than $5, $5–$9, $10–$14, and $15–$19" (not "$1–$5, $5–$10," etc.). If greater precision is needed, they might be given as "$1.00–$4.99, $5.00–$9.99," and so forth. The symbols < and > must be used only to mean less than and more than. In a table including age ranges, >60 means "more than 60 years old" (i.e., "61 and up," *not* "60 and up," which would be represented by ≥60). For ≥ and ≤, insert the correct symbols (do not use underline).

3.85 **Signs and symbols in tables.** In a column consisting exclusively of, for example, dollar amounts or percentages, the signs should be omitted from the cells and included in the column head (see 3.57 and figs. 3.13, 3.14) or, occasionally, in the stub entry (see fig. 3.23). Mathematical operational signs preceding quantities in a column of numbers are not necessarily aligned with other such signs but should appear immediately to the left of the numbers they belong to (see fig. 3.13).

3.86 **"N" versus "n."** An italic capital *N* is used in many statistical tables to stand for the total number of a group from which data are drawn (see fig. 3.21). An italic lowercase *n* stands for a portion of the total group (see fig. 3.14). For example, if *N* refers to the total number of subjects in a study, a lowercase *n* might be used when specifying the number of subjects assigned to different groups.

3.87 **Adjusting and checking tables.** When preparing a table for publication, editors and compositors may need to adjust or check its format according to the following general guidelines:

1. *Adjusting long tables and wide tables.* Tables that are long and narrow with few columns but many rows, on the one hand, and very wide tables with many columns but few rows, on the other, may not work well—if at all—especially in print. The remedy for a long, skinny table is to double it up, running the table in two halves, side by side, with the column heads re-

TABLE 13. Relative contents of odd isotopes for heavy elements

| Element | Z | γ | Element | Z | γ |
|---|---|---|---|---|---|
| Sm | 62 | 1.480 | W | 74 | 0.505 |
| Gd | 64 | 0.691 | Os | 76 | 0.811 |
| Dy | 66 | 0.930 | Pt | 78 | 1.160 |
| Eb | 68 | 0.759 | Hg | 80 | 0.500 |
| Yb | 70 | 0.601 | Pb | 82 | 0.550 |
| Hf | 72 | 0.440 | | | |

FIGURE 3.24. A three-column table doubled into two columns (see 3.87).

peated over the second half. This approach can also allow a narrow but not necessarily long table to run the width of a page (see fig. 3.24). For a wide, shallow table, the remedy is to turn it around, making column heads of the stub items and stub items of the column heads; if the table turns out to be too narrow that way, it can then be doubled up. Some tables may need to be presented broadside (rotated ninety degrees counterclockwise and read left to right from the bottom to the top of a page), like figure 3.17 in the printed edition of this manual. See also 3.53. For long tables, the editor may need to specify whether and where "continued" lines and repeated column heads are allowed (see 3.88) and where notes should appear (see 3.77, 3.80).

2. *Adjusting oversize tables—other options.* If an oversize table cannot be accommodated in a printed work by the remedies suggested above, further editorial or typographic adjustments will be needed. Wording may be shortened or abbreviations used. Omitting the running head when a table takes a full page (see 1.16) allows more space for the table itself. A wide table may extend a little into the left margin if on a verso or the right margin if on a recto or, if it looks better, equally on both sides. For a particularly large table, the publisher may decide to reduce the type size or to publish the table in electronic form only, if that is an option. To reduce excessive width, two other measures (neither very convenient for readers) are worth considering: (1) numbers are used for column heads, and the text of the heads is relegated to notes, as illustrated in figure 3.25; or (2) column heads are turned on their sides so that they read up the printed page rather than across.
3. *Checking rules.* The editor should ensure that rules appear as needed and that spanner rules are the right length and are distinct from underlining (so that a rule and not italicized text appears in the typeset version). See 3.54, 3.58.
4. *Checking alignment of numbers and text.* Alignment of rows and columns must be clearly specified in the manuscript. Editors should check to make sure that numbers have been aligned properly (e.g., by decimal point) and that stub entries are aligned with and correspond to the rows to which they

TABLE 14. Timing of socialist entry into elections and of suffrage reforms

| Country | (1) | (2) | (3) | (4) | (5) | (6) | (7) |
|---|---|---|---|---|---|---|---|
| Austria | 1889 | 1897 | 1907 | — | 1919 | — | — |
| Belgium | 1885[a] | 1894 | 1894 | 45.7 | 1948 | 38.4 | 22.2 |
| Denmark | 1878[a] | 1884 | 1849 | 28.1[b] | 1915 | 24.6 | 23.9 |
| Finland | 1899 | 1907 | 1906 | 22.0 | 1906 | — | 22.0 |
| France | 1879 | 1893 | 1876 | 36.5[c] | 1946 | 33.9 | 24.9 |
| Germany | 1867 | 1871 | 1871 | 25.5 | 1919 | 34.2[d] | 34.0[d] |
| Italy | 1892[a] | — | 1913 | — | 1945 | — | — |
| Netherlands | 1878 | 1888 | 1917 | — | 1917 | — | — |
| Norway | 1887 | 1903 | 1898 | 34.1 | 1913 | 27.7 | 28.8 |
| Spain | 1879 | 1910 | 1907 | — | 1933 | — | — |
| Sweden | 1889 | 1896 | 1907 | 28.9 | 1921 | 35.0 | 37.0 |
| Switzerland | 1887 | 1897 | 1848 | — | — | — | — |
| United Kingdom | 1893[a] | 1892[e] | 1918 | — | 1928 | — | — |

*Note:* Column headings are as follows: (1) Socialist Party formed; (2) first candidates elected to Parliament; (3) universal male suffrage; (4) workers as a proportion of the electorate in the first elections after universal male suffrage; (5) universal suffrage; (6) workers as a proportion of the electorate in the last election before extension of franchise to women; and (7) workers as a proportion of the electorate in the first election after the extension.

[a] Major socialist or workers' parties existed earlier and dissolved or were repressed.

[b] In 1884, approximate.

[c] In 1902.

[d] Under different borders.

[e] Keir Hardie elected.

FIGURE 3.25. An eight-column table with numbers replacing column heads to reduce width. The heads are defined in a general note to the table. Notes to specific parts of the table are indicated by superior (superscript) letters. See 3.87.

apply. See 3.71–76. Old-style numerals (like this: 1938), though elegant as page numbers or in text that contains few numerals, should be avoided in tabular matter because they do not align horizontally as well as (and can be harder to read than) regular "lining" numerals (like this: 1938). (If old-style numerals must be used, a font that includes a fixed-width "tabular" version must be chosen to ensure that numbers will align vertically within a column.)

5. *Checking running heads on full-page tables.* The editor should be sure that running heads are omitted on full-page and multipage tables (but see 1.16, 2.120).
6. *Checking typefaces and markup.* In a book that is not part of a series, the designer will set the typographic style for tables, as for the text and other elements. Journals follow their own established style for presentation and markup. Editors should make sure tables are edited in accord with the design, and formatting and markup for electronically prepared tables should be checked to make sure they have been consistently and correctly applied

TABLE 15. Type of private capital flow (millions of US dollars)

| | 1992 | 1993 | 1994 | 1995 | 1996 |
|---|---|---|---|---|---|
| | | | Asia | | |
| *China* | | | | | |
| GDP | 469,003 | 598,765 | 546,610 | 711,315 | 834,311 |
| Current account | 6,401 | -11,609 | 6,908 | 1,618 | 7,243 |
| Capital inflows | -250 | 23,474 | 32,645 | 38,674 | 39,966 |
| Equity | 7,922 | 24,266 | 34,208 | 36,185 | 39,981 |
| Bank credits | 4,008 | 2,146 | 3,786 | 8,405 | 10,625 |
| *Indonesia* | | | | | |
| GDP | 139,116 | 158,007 | 176,892 | 202,131 | 227,370 |
| Current account | -2,780 | -2,106 | -2,792 | -6,431 | -7,663 |
| Capital inflows | 6,129 | 5,632 | 3,839 | 10,259 | 10,847 |
| Equity | 1,947 | 2,692 | 2,573 | 4,285 | 5,195 |
| Bank credits | 663 | 1,573 | 2,030 | 8,021 | 12,602 |
| | | | Latin America | | |
| *Argentina* | | | | | |
| GDP | 228,990 | 257,842 | 281,925 | 279,613 | 297,460 |
| Current account | -5,462 | -7,672 | -10,117 | -2,768 | -3,787 |
| Capital inflows | 7,373 | 9,827 | 9,279 | 574 | 7,033 |
| Equity | 4,630 | 4,038 | 3,954 | 4,589 | 7,375 |
| Bank credits | 1,152 | 9,945 | 1,139 | 2,587 | 959 |

TABLE 15 *(continued)*

| | 1992 | 1993 | 1994 | 1995 | 1996 |
|---|---|---|---|---|---|
| | | | Latin America | | |
| *Brazil* | | | | | |
| GDP | 446,580 | 438,300 | 546,230 | 704,167 | 774,868 |
| Current account | 6,089 | 20 | -1,153 | -18,136 | -23,602 |
| Capital inflows | 5,889 | 7,604 | 8,020 | 29,306 | 33,984 |
| Equity | 3,147 | 4,062 | 5,333 | 8,169 | 15,788 |
| Bank credits | 11,077 | 4,375 | 9,162 | 11,443 | 14,462 |
| *Chile* | | | | | |
| GDP | 41,882 | 44,474 | 50,920 | 65,215 | 69,218 |
| Current account | -958 | -2,554 | -1,585 | -1,398 | -3,744 |
| Capital inflows | 3,134 | 2,996 | 5,294 | 2,488 | 6,781 |
| Equity | 876 | 1,326 | 2,580 | 1,959 | 4,090 |
| Bank credits | 2,192 | 804 | 1,108 | 1,100 | 1,808 |

FIGURE 3.26. A six-column table with repeated column heads and "continued" indication following a page break (see 3.88).

(see also 3.89). For a useful discussion of table design, see Richard Eckersley et al., *Glossary of Typesetting Terms* (bibliog. 2.8).

3.88 **Tables of more than one page ("continued" tables).** For a vertical table of more than one page, the column heads are repeated on each page. For a two-page broadside table—which should be presented on facing pages if at all possible—column heads need not be repeated; for broadside tables that run beyond two pages, column heads are repeated only on each new verso (see also 2.120). Where column heads are repeated, the table number and "continued" should also appear. See figure 3.26. For any table that is likely to run to more than one page, the editor should specify whether "continued" lines and repeated column heads will be needed and where notes should appear (usually at the end of the table as a whole; but see 3.77). The editor should also be sure that running heads are omitted on full-page and multipage tables (but see 1.16).

3.89 **Ensuring accessibility for tables.** To ensure that they are accessible to all readers, including those who use text-to-speech tools, tables must be marked up properly. This means that all headers, data cells, columns, and rows must be identified in such a way that makes their relationships and logical reading order clear. Simple tables produced using the table editor in a word processor will usually convert to HTML or PDF for publication with minimal adjustments. More complex tables—for example, those with heads that span multiple columns or rows—may need additional markup to ensure that screen readers and other tools will recognize the intended relationships. Complex tables may also benefit from descriptive text (e.g., using the "summary" attribute in HTML5). Wherever possible, tables should be rendered as marked-up text rather than as images, with their layout and presentation defined by CSS (cascading style sheets) or, for PDF files, using a program like Adobe Acrobat. If desired, tables published using HTML and CSS can be accompanied by a link to the typeset version of the table to show exact presentation. If a table must be rendered as an image only, some form of alternative text will be needed (see 3.28). For more information, consult the resources provided by the Web Accessibility Initiative (WAI) and, for EPUB, the EPUB Accessibility specification.

# 4 Rights, Permissions, and Copyright Administration

*William S. Strong*

## OVERVIEW

4.1 **The scope of this chapter.** The foundation on which the entire publishing industry rests is the law of copyright, and a basic knowledge of it is essential for both authors and editors. This chapter gives readers that basic knowledge: how copyright is acquired, how it is owned, what it protects, what rights it comprises, how long it lasts, how it is transferred from one individual or entity to another. Once that foundation is laid, the key elements of publishing contracts are discussed, as well as the growing ecosystem of open access. The chapter then addresses authors' warranties and the important role that authors play in ensuring that their reuse of others' material in their manuscripts is lawful, whether by permission or by the doctrine of fair use. The chapter ends with a discussion of the licensing of rights (what publishers call the "rights and permissions" function). While every effort is made here to be accurate, copyright law is both wide and intricate, and this chapter makes no claim to be exhaustive. Also, this chapter should not be considered legal advice or substitute for a consultation with a knowledgeable attorney in any particular circumstance. (For more detailed treatment of specific issues, see the works listed in sec. 2.3 of the bibliography.)

## COPYRIGHT LAW AND THE LICENSING OF RIGHTS

4.2 **Relevant law.** For most publishing purposes the relevant law is the Copyright Act of 1976 (Public Law 94-553), which took effect on January 1, 1978, and the various amendments enacted since then. The 1976 act was a sweeping revision, superseding previous federal law and eliminating (though not retroactively) the body of state law known as common-law copyright. It did not, however, make old learning obsolete. Because prior law continues to govern most pre-1978 works in one way or another, anyone involved with publishing should understand both the old and the new regimes. Both will affect publishing for decades to come. Note that the law discussed in this chapter is that of the United States. The United States and most other countries are members of the Berne Convention, the oldest international copyright treaty. While the Berne Convention and certain other treaties have fostered significant uniformity around the world, anyone dealing with copyrights should bear in mind that, conventions aside, the laws of other countries may contain significant differences from US law.

4.3 **How copyright comes into being.** Whenever a book or article, poem or lecture, database or drama comes into the world, it is automatically covered by copyright so long as it is "fixed" in some "tangible" form and embodies a human author's original expression. The term *tangible* applies to more than paper and traditional media; it includes things such as electronic memory. A copyrightable work is "fixed" as long as it is stored in some manner that is not purely transitory. Thus, an email message that is stored in the sender's computer, an ad-libbed comedy riff that is filmed at the comedian's request, or a webinar that is recorded while in progress are all fixed and protected by copyright.

4.4 **Registration and notice not required.** Although it is advisable to register works with the United States Copyright Office, registration is not a prerequisite to legal protection. The practical reasons for registering are discussed in 4.52. Note that any work protected by US copyright can be registered. This includes not only works created or published in the United States but also those created or published in countries with which the United States has a copyright treaty. Copyright notice is no longer required but is recommended (see also 4.42–48).

4.5 **Original expression.** Copyright protects the original expression contained in a work. The term *expression* means the words, sounds, or images that an author uses to express an idea or convey information. Selection and arrangement of data or of preexisting materials—as in a database or anthology—constitutes expression, even without the addition of the compiler's own words. In any work, copyright protects the author's expression but not the underlying facts, ideas, or theories, no matter how novel those may be. (Thus, for example, simple graphs cannot be copyrighted, for that would extend protection to the data in them, and recipes cannot be copyrighted, for that would extend protection to a way of cooking food, although collections of recipes can be copyrighted as compilations.) That the expression be *original* for copyright purposes demands less than the term may suggest; the threshold is quite low. The law requires only a modicum of creativity: A simple abstract doodle may be protected. Where compilations of data are concerned, the law will not protect the labor—no matter how arduous—of gathering information, but it will protect very modest intellectual effort expended on selecting and arranging the data, so long as the result is not glaringly obvious (e.g., "name, address, and telephone number"). What counts is not quality or novelty but only that the work be original to the author and not copied, consciously or unconsciously, from some other source. When a work includes some material that is not original, only the original material is protected. Thus, copyright in a new, annotated edition of an eighteenth-century book will cover only the annotations. The requirement that a human author has created the expression has become significant as the use of generative AI (artificial intelligence) has become significant. If an AI creates expression in response to human prompts, that is not enough to support a copyright. The human in charge must contribute something that by itself will support a copyright, and the copyright will be limited to what that human author contributes.

4.6 **Author the original owner.** Whoever is the author (a term not synonymous with *creator*, as will be seen) controls copyright at the outset and automatically possesses certain rights in the work. How these rights are owned, transferred, and administered is the focus of this chapter.

## *Varieties of Authorship*

4.7 **Individual and joint authors.** For many types of works, the author is likely to be an individual. In scientific, technical, and medical publishing, especially in the realm of journals, a work will more likely than not involve the efforts of more than one author. Such works are typically joint works. As defined by the statute, a joint work is "a work prepared by two or more authors with the intention that their contributions be merged into inseparable or interdependent parts of a unitary whole."

4.8 **Collective works.** Works in which the independent contributions of two or more authors are combined are considered collective, rather than joint, works. Copyright in a collective work as such, which covers the selection and arrangement of materials, belongs to the compiler or editor and is separate from the copyright in each of the various components. Typical examples of collective works are newspapers, anthologies, journal issues, and edited volumes of contributed papers (see 4.62–63).

### WORKS MADE FOR HIRE

4.9 **Employer as author.** Another type of authorship is work made for hire. The law regards the employer or other controlling party as the "author" of any such work and hence as the initial copyright owner. Some works are considered made for hire by definition; some can be treated as such by agreement.

4.10 **The three categories of work made for hire.** Present law defines much more stringently than pre-1978 law the conditions that must be met for a work to be considered made for hire. First, the work may be prepared within the scope of a person's employment. Common examples of this type of work made for hire include a story by a staff writer, or a photograph by a staff photographer, in a newspaper or weekly magazine, or marketing copy written by a company's paid staff. Second, a creative party *not* on the payroll will in certain instances be treated as an "employee" if that person is acting as the "agent" of another party. Determining agency is a difficult and somewhat ad hoc task and involves considerations such as the control of one party over the other party's hours, assignments, and tools used in creating the work. The third type of work made for hire is the specially ordered or commissioned work that both hiring party and creator agree *in writing* to treat as such. This sort of arrangement is available for only a few narrowly defined types of work:

- Contributions to collective works, such as a chapter commissioned for a scholarly treatise
- Contributions to motion pictures or other audiovisual works
- Translations
- Instructional texts
- Tests and answer material for tests
- Atlases
- Compilations of data or existing materials, such as anthologies and directories
- "Supplementary works," which the statute defines as "prepared for publication as a secondary adjunct to a work by another author for the purpose of introducing, concluding, illustrating, explaining, revising, commenting upon, or assisting in the use of the other work." Examples include such things as illustrations, photographs, maps, charts, tables, figures, forewords, afterwords, bibliographies, indexes, and appendixes.

A work that qualifies for such treatment will not be considered made for hire unless the written agreement between the commissioning party and the creative party expressly says so. The written agreement should be signed before the work is created, although some courts have validated agreements signed after creation of the work where the agreement clearly reflected the original intention of the parties and the delay was excusable.

4.11 **Ineligible works.** It bears emphasizing that many kinds of works that could conceivably be commissioned do not qualify as works made for hire no matter what agreement may be made between writer and publisher. Monographs and novels, for example, are not eligible because they are not in any of the specific categories listed above. Thus, copyright in such a work remains with the writer unless expressly assigned.

This does not stop some aggressive buyers of copyrighted material from insisting that the author sign an agreement saying a work is made for hire when it is obviously not. Such agreements may end up being interpreted as in effect assignments. Although for most purposes an assignment of copyright from the author is indistinguishable in practical effect from a work-made-for-hire agreement, they have different implications for copyright duration (see 4.25) and termination (see 4.39).

4.12 **Joint authorship.** If any one of a group of coauthors is writing on a "for hire" basis, the resulting joint work will be treated as made for hire for copyright duration purposes (see 4.25), even though the other coauthor(s) might be independent and not writing "for hire." Thus, if an in-house researcher and an outside scholar collaborate on a paper, the copyright term given to that paper will be the work-made-for-hire term.

## *Rights of the Copyright Owner*

4.13 **Rights of reproduction, distribution, and display.** The author of a work possesses, at the beginning, a bundle of rights that collectively make up copyright. They belong originally to the author, who can sell, rent, give away, will, or transfer them in some other way, individually or as a package, to whomever the author wishes. When a work is to be published, the author normally transfers some or all of these rights to the publisher, by formal agreement. Two of these rights are basic from the publisher's point of view: the right to make copies of the work (by printing or by digital reproduction, or both) and the right to distribute such copies to the public—in sum, to publish the work. In the case of online publishing, reproduction and distribution blend into the act of transmitting the work on demand to the reader's computer or other device. A third right—the right of public display—applies to online exploitation of works. A work is publicly displayed when made viewable online; if the user downloads or prints out the material concerned, distribution of a copy also occurs.

4.14 **Derivative-work and performance rights.** A fourth and very important right is the right to make what the law terms derivative works—that is, works based on or derived from the original work, such as translations, abridgments, dramatizations, or other adaptations. A revised edition of a published work is generally different enough from the prior edition to qualify as a derivative work with a separate copyright. The fifth basic copyright right, the right of public performance, has only limited relevance for literary works as such; it applies, for example, when a poet gives a public reading of a poem. However, it has great significance for other works, such as plays, music, and motion pictures, that are created to be performed.

4.15 **Moral rights; integrity of copyright management information.** In addition to the foregoing rights, the law gives the creators of certain works of fine art a so-called moral right against mutilation and misattribution. A dozen or more states have enacted legislation to roughly the same effect as the federal law but generally broader. This moral right, however, whether federal or state, has no relevance to the publishing industry in the United States and will not be addressed further here. (Some publishers in other countries put moral rights notices on books and require US licensees to do so, but such notices have no legal effect in the United States.) Authors may also be able under state common law, even in the absence of a statute, to prevent the attribution to them of things that they did not write. In addition, federal law protects the integrity of "copyright management information." This information, for publications, consists of the following:

- The title and other information identifying the work, including the content of the copyright notice
- The name of, and other identifying information about, the author
- The name of, and other identifying information about, the copyright owner, including the content of the copyright notice
- Terms and conditions for use of the work
- Identifying numbers or symbols referring to such information or links to such information

Specifically, the law prevents intentional removal or alteration of copyright management information, or deliberate use of false copyright management information, if done with intent to induce, enable, facilitate, or conceal infringement.

4.16 **Trademark protection of titles and other elements.** Copying only the title of a work would likely not be considered a copyright infringement. But a title may acquire trademark protection under federal or state law or both. Book titles are harder to protect as trademarks than journal titles, because of judicial and administrative reluctance to give trademark protection to names that are used on only one specific product. (By contrast, "The Chicago Manual of Style" was able to be registered as a trademark because it is the title not of one book but, as revised and updated over the years, of a series of books.) Nevertheless, some single-book titles are clearly protectable, due to widespread public recognition.

*The Hobbit*, for example, had undoubtedly attained strong trademark status long before the brand was expanded to movies and merchandise. That trademark right, as applied to the book itself, expires when the copyright expires; anyone is free at that point to reproduce the book, title and all. But active franchising such as has occurred with *The Hobbit* will enable that trademark to survive indefinitely as applied to everything but the original book itself. The same principles would apply to the names of characters or imaginary locales (e.g., Middle-earth) used in a work.

4.17 **Basic versus subsidiary rights.** Whoever controls the copyright in a work, whether author or publisher, may not only exercise those rights directly but also empower or authorize others to exercise them. If, for example, the author of a book has transferred the whole bundle of rights to a publishing house, the publishing house will itself exercise the basic rights of reproducing and distributing (i.e., publishing) the book. It will also be responsible for administering subsidiary rights. These rights (discussed in 4.112 and 4.113) usually involve exploiting markets in which the publishing house is not active. For example, rights for other languages, audiobook rights, and motion-picture rights involve specialized markets and require special expertise. For this reason, subsidiary rights are likely to be exercised by third parties under license from the publisher, although, if the publisher is part of a large media conglomerate, licensing is often intramural. Part of the publisher's responsibility to the author should be to see that subsidiary rights are exploited as effectively as possible. Licensing subsidiary rights also includes granting what the publishing industry calls *permissions*, a term that refers to such things as the licensing of photocopied or scanned materials for classroom use and allowing others to reproduce an original illustration from the book in a new work.

4.18 **Author retention of subsidiary rights.** Authors represented by agents generally seek to retain some or all subsidiary rights. Retained subsidiary rights will then be licensed directly by the author (through the agent) to publishers in other countries, motion-picture producers, audiobook producers, and the like. Typically, however, permissions are still handled by the publisher rather than the agent or author.

4.19 **Retention of rights by non-US licensors.** When a non-US publisher licenses English-language rights to a US publisher, or enters into an English-language copublication arrangement with a US publisher, it will commonly seek to retain subsidiary rights that involve the creation of derivative works such as motion pictures. Sometimes—although this is rare in trade publishing—the licensor may demand that copyright ownership of any English-language translation resulting from the license pass to itself, at the beginning or on termination of the license. (The same is true in reverse, of course, where US publishers are the parties driving the arrangement.) However, the US licensee publisher should seek to have control over all subsidiary rights (such as book club, serialization, etc.) that involve publication of the text in any specialized market, and the same should apply to audiobook rights.

## *Copyright and the Public Domain*

4.20 **Copyright duration before 1978.** Until January 1, 1978, a dual system of copyright existed in the United States. Common-law copyright, created by the individual states, protected works from the time of their creation until publication, however long that might be. A personal letter written in the eighteenth century but never published was protected as effectively as a 1977 doctoral thesis in the making. In neither case could the document be copied and distributed (that is, published) without the express permission of either the creator of the work or the creator's legal heirs. Statutory, or federal, copyright protected works at the moment of publication and for twenty-eight years thereafter, provided that a proper copyright notice appeared in the published work. See 4.42–48. (It was also possible to obtain statutory copyright for certain types of unpublished works by registering them with the US Copyright Office, but this did not apply to literary works other than lectures.) Thereafter, copyright in the work could be renewed for another twenty-eight years if the original copyright claim had been registered with the US Copyright Office (a division of the Library of Congress) and if a renewal claim was filed by the appropriate party or parties during the final year of the first term of copyright. Thus, in the normal course of things federal copyright in a work was intended to last for a total of fifty-six years from the date of publication, after which time the work went into the public domain—that is, it became public property and could be reproduced freely. See 4.23.

4.21 **Lengthening of copyright duration in 1978.** To enter the public domain is of course the ultimate fate of all copyrighted works. However, the elaborate system described in 4.20 was replaced as of 1978 by a unitary federal copyright of substantially greater length. Subsequent amendments have lengthened the term yet further and eliminated a number of formalities that used to be required. All these changes have made entering the public domain almost theoretical for works currently being created. As will be discussed below, other changes to the law have given many older works, particularly those originally published outside the United States, an unexpected reprieve (see 4.30).

4.22 **US government works.** Works created by employees of the US government in the course of their official duties are in the public domain. Works created by private parties under government contract, however, are eligible for copyright, although federal contracts often impose certain limitations on such copyright. Works by employees of state governments or governments of other countries are presumptively copyrightable, although state governments rarely attempt to enforce their copyrights.

4.23 **Uses of public-domain works.** Once in the public domain, a work is free for all to use. The use may be direct and simple; for example, Mark Twain's novels have now lost their copyrights and may be republished free of royalty. Or the public-domain works may be the compost from which new works, such as adaptations or other derivative works, spring in due course. Such new works are entitled to copyright, but their copyright is limited to the new material they contain. Determining whether a work has entered the public domain requires attention to complex rules. These are discussed at 4.27–31 and 4.40–48. The rules are also summarized in table 4.1.

## DURATION OF COPYRIGHT FOR WORKS CREATED AFTER 1977

4.24 **"Life plus seventy."** Enacted in 1976 and effective on January 1, 1978, the present copyright law did away with the dual system of federal/common-law copyright. Present law is both simpler and more complex regarding copyright duration. It is simpler in that now one unified, federal system protects all works fixed in tangible form from the moment of fixation. It is more complex in that (1) terms of protection differ depending on authorship, and (2) works existing before 1978 are subject to a variety of special rules. The paradigmatic copyright term, under the new law, is "life plus seventy"—that is, life of the author plus seventy years. (In the case of joint authors, the seventy years are added to the life of the last author to die.) As will be seen below, however, there are many exceptions to this rule.

4.25 **Works made for hire.** Since the owner of the copyright in a work made for hire is not the actual creator of the work (often, indeed, the copyright owner is a corporate entity), the law specifies a fixed term of years for the duration of copyright. This term is ninety-five years from the

TABLE 4.1. Copyright duration

| Date of creation/ publication | US or non-US work | Type of authorship | Term of protection[1] |
|---|---|---|---|
| Created after 1977 | Either | Single author—individual | Life plus 70 years |
| | | Two or more individual authors | Life of last to die plus 70 years |
| | | Work made for hire | 95 years from first publication, or 120 years from creation, whichever expires first |
| | | Pseudonymous | 95 years from first publication, or 120 years from creation, unless identity is filed with Copyright Office |
| | | Anonymous | 95 years from first publication, or 120 years from creation, unless identity is filed with Copyright Office |
| Created before 1978 but not published before 2003 | Either | Same as any of above | Same as corresponding term above |
| Created before 1978 but published after 1977 and before 2003 | Either | Same as any of above | Same as corresponding term above or until December 31, 2047, whichever is later |
| Published or registered between January 1, 1964, and December 31, 1977 | Either | Same as any of above | 95 years from first publication |
| Published or registered before January 1, 1964 | US | Same as any of above | 95 years from first publication, if copyright was renewed in 28th year, otherwise now in public domain |
| Published in the US before January 1, 1964 | Non-US | Same as any of above | 95 years from first publication |
| Published abroad before January 1, 1964 | Non-US | Same as any of above | 95 years from first publication[2] |
| Published anywhere at least 95 years ago | Either | Same as any of above | Public domain[2] |

SOURCE: William S. Strong, *The Copyright Book: A Practical Guide*, 6th ed. (MIT Press, 2014). © 2014 Massachusetts Institute of Technology. Used by kind permission of the publisher.

NOTE: The following special rules apply for special media; these rules supersede all the above except as noted. *Mask works*: 10 years from registration or from first commercial exploitation, whichever occurs first. *Architectural works*: Same as in chart above unless (1) constructed or published before 1990, in which case not under copyright, or (2) created but neither constructed nor published before 1990, in which case same as in chart above but only if constructed before January 1, 2003, otherwise now in public domain. *Sound recordings published before February 15, 1972*: Not protected by copyright per se, but given equivalent protection for 95 years from publication, subject to special extensions set out in 17 U.S.C. § 1401(a)(2).

[1] All terms run through December 31 of the year in which they expire.

[2] This rule does not apply in the Ninth Circuit. There, non-US works published before 1978 do not start their US copyright term until publication in the United States.

date of publication or 120 years from the date of creation, whichever is the shorter.

4.26 **Anonymous and pseudonymous works.** The regular rule for duration of copyright cannot be applied if an author publishes anonymously or under a pseudonym. The law prescribes the same fixed term of copyright for these works as for works made for hire—ninety-five years from the date of publication or 120 years from creation, whichever is the shorter. If after publication, however, such an author's name is revealed and recorded in the documents of the Copyright Office, the regular "life plus seventy" rule takes over, unless, of course, the work is made for hire.

## DURATION OF COPYRIGHT FOR WORKS CREATED BEFORE 1978

4.27 **Pre-1978 unpublished works.** For unpublished works that were still under common-law copyright when the new law went into effect, there is a transitional rule. Such works are given the same copyright terms as post-1977 works, but in recognition of the fact that their authors might have died so long ago as to make "life plus seventy" meaningless, Congress added two provisos. First, such works were granted protection at least until December 31, 2002. Second, any such work that was ultimately published before December 31, 2002, is protected at least until December 31, 2047. Thus, these late-published works have a copyright term of not less than seventy years from the date the new law went into effect.

4.28 **Pre-1978 works published in the United States.** Works published during the years 1923 through 1963 were granted an extended copyright term of ninety-five years from the year of first publication if their copyrights had been properly renewed in the twenty-eighth year after first publication. This froze, for a while, the entry of works into the public domain. However, at the end of 2018 the ninety-five-year term expired for works published in the United States before January 1, 1924; at the end of 2019 it expired for works published before January 1, 1925; and so on. Now, every year, substantial numbers of works fall into the public domain. The importance of timely renewal (prior to 1964) cannot be overstated, because the term extension did not purport to revive copyright in works that had not been properly renewed. (The safest way to determine whether renewal was effected is to commission a search of the Copyright Office records through a copyright attorney or a reputable search firm. Several university libraries have also made Copyright Office renewal records available online, and the Copyright Office now has an online database that includes renewals, although the office disclaims that it is foolproof.) Works published from 1964 through 1977 will be protected without fail for ninety-five years from first publication, because renewal for such works is automatic. All the above assumes that these works were at all times published with proper copyright notice. For a discussion of copyright notice, see 4.40–48.

4.29 **New copyright for new editions.** When deciding whether a work may be republished without permission, bear in mind that each time a work is materially modified a new copyright comes into being, covering the new or revised material. Thus a seminal treatise published in 1920 is now in the public domain, but the author's revision published in 1934 may not be. One is free to republish the 1920 version, but that may be an empty privilege.

4.30 **Pre-1978 works published outside the United States.** The rules just described do not apply to works by non-US authors first published outside of the United States. Such works are generally protected in their own countries for the life of the author plus fifty or seventy years, depending on the country concerned. In the United States, such works automatically receive the same term of copyright as a pre-1978 US work, but without regard to whether proper copyright notice was used or whether copyright was renewed in the twenty-eighth year after publication. This is so because, effective January 1, 1996, Congress restored to copyright all such works that had forfeited copyright as a result of noncompliance with US notice and renewal requirements but that were still protected in their home country. Copyrights restored in this manner are subject to certain protections given to those who produced copies or derivative works before December 8, 1994, relying on the apparent forfeiture of copyright. Two points should be noted here, however. First, although it is generally assumed that a work published anywhere in the world at least ninety-five years ago is now in the public domain in the United States, an anomalous decision in the Ninth Circuit Court of Appeals has held that works by non-US authors published abroad may be exempt from this expiration rule if no effort was made at the time to comply with US copyright law. This is out of sync with the rest of US copyright jurisprudence, but it remains the law in California and other states in the Ninth Circuit. Second, it should be noted that the US copyright term for non-US works, even after restoration, does not necessarily synchronize with the protection of those works outside the United States. If a French author of a work published in 1922 lived until 1970, the work would now be in the public domain in the United States but would remain under copyright in France through 2040. If the same author had published another work in 1930, that work would retain copyright in the United States through 2025, still fifteen years less than in France. As this example shows, publishers who wish to reissue or otherwise make use of such public-domain works need to be aware that markets outside the United States may be foreclosed to them.

4.31 **Eligibility for restoration.** For purposes of the special restoration rules discussed in 4.30, a work is eligible if it was first published outside the United States and if at least one author was not a citizen of the US or domiciled in the US. The only substantial exception is for works published in the United States within thirty days after publication abroad, as had been done by some US publishers to get Berne Convention treatment "by the back door" before the United States became a member of Berne. Such works are not eligible for copyright restoration.

## RENEWING COPYRIGHT IN PRE-1978 WORKS

4.32 **Benefits of renewal.** Although renewal of copyright for works published between 1964 and 1977 was automatic, the law gives certain benefits to those who took the trouble to file actively for renewal of such copyrights. Filing for renewal fixed the ownership of the second-term copyright on the date of filing; automatic renewal vested ownership in whoever could have renewed on the *last day* of the first twenty-eight-year term. A renewal that was actively obtained constitutes prima facie evidence of copyright and its ownership; the evidentiary value of an automatically renewed copyright is subject to the discretion of the courts. Finally, and most importantly, if the renewal was allowed to happen automatically, existing derivative works can continue to be exploited for the second term of copyright, whereas active renewal gave the renewal-term owner the right to relicense derivative-work rights, unless a derivative-work license was already in place that explicitly covers the renewal term. Although the last renewals were filed in 2005, these issues will continue to have relevance.

4.33 **Renewal by the author.** The author, if living, was the person entitled to file for renewal. Publishers who had obtained renewal-term rights from authors could file for renewal on the author's behalf.

4.34 **Renewal if the author was deceased.** If an author had died before renewal, the law allocated the copyright to the author's surviving spouse, children, or other heirs according to complex rules that will not be parsed here. Again, a publisher that had contracted for renewal rights could carry out the renewal in the name of the renewal claimants.

## *Assigning or Licensing Copyright*

4.35 **Subdividing a copyright.** Copyright is often referred to as a "bundle" of rights. The basic components, as noted above (see 4.13, 4.14), are the right to reproduce the work, the right to distribute copies of a work to the public, the right to make derivative works, and the rights to perform and display a work publicly. Each of these rights may be separately licensed or assigned. Furthermore, each of them may be carved up into smaller rights along lines of geography, time, or medium. Thus, for example, the right to publish a novel may be carved up so that Publisher A gets North American rights while Publisher B gets United Kingdom rights. A French translation license may be given to Librairie C for a ten-year fixed term. Or Publisher A may receive hardcover rights while Publisher B receives subsequent paperback rights. There is theoretically no end to the ways of subdividing a copyright, other than the limits of human ingenuity and the marketplace.

4.36 **Exclusive versus nonexclusive licenses.** Licenses may be exclusive or nonexclusive. Typically, anyone making a substantial investment in exploiting a license will insist on exclusive rights, whereas persons making ephemeral use at low marginal cost—a typical case being classroom photocopying—need no more than nonexclusive rights. An exclusive licensee is treated in general like an owner of copyright and has standing to sue any infringer of that right. A nonexclusive licensee holds something more like a personal privilege than a property interest and cannot sue infringers or even, without the permission of the licensor, transfer the license to someone else. While most authorities believe that, by contrast, an exclusive licensee has the power to assign and sublicense the right concerned, a federal-court opinion in mid-2002 cast doubt on that presumption. As a precaution, anyone drafting an exclusive license should expressly state that the license may be assigned and sublicensed at the discretion of the licensee.

4.37 **Goals of the parties to a license.** Many issues in license negotiation are common to all contracts: payment terms, duration, allocation of risk, remedies for default, and so on. But in drafting a copyright license, the parties need to be very careful to define clearly the scope of the license, taking into account possible evolution of technologies and markets. The goal of a licensor is to define the licensed right narrowly so as to preserve flexibility for future licensing. The licensee also wants flexibility and therefore seeks to define the licensed right broadly. Both sides, though, have a common interest in seeing that the license is clear and understandable. Drafting a license demands and deserves care and skill, as well as good communication between the people who will be carrying out its terms and their lawyers or contract managers.

4.38 **Payment.** A license and the obligation to pay for that license are usually treated as reciprocal obligations, not mutually dependent ones. Thus the failure of a licensee to pay royalties does not automatically terminate the license and turn the licensee into an infringer. It gives the licensor a claim for contract damages, not a copyright infringement claim. Shrewd licensors will whenever possible reverse this presumption in their contracts, by stipulating that timely payment is a condition of the validity of the license; shrewd licensees will usually resist.

4.39 **Termination of transfers and licenses.** A copyright grant may contain express provisions for termination. It has long been common for book contracts to provide for reversion of rights if the book goes "out of print." As that concept does not properly account for ebooks or print-on-demand books, contract negotiations on reversion have tended to shift to setting benchmarks such as aggregate sales for a given time period, so that if sales fall below the benchmark a reversion of rights is triggered. In addition, the statute itself gives individual authors the right to terminate licenses and assignments of copyright under certain conditions. Authors may terminate any post-1977 copyright arrangement after thirty-five years, and a roughly comparable termination right applies to grants made before 1978. (The termination right is not applicable to works made for hire, and it does not apply to agreements stipulating that a specially ordered or commissioned work will be made for hire provided the work is one of the types eligible for such treatment. See 4.10.) The mechanics of termination, including the determination of who has the right to terminate if the author is deceased, are quite complicated, and no more will be said here (for additional resources, see bibliog. 2.3).

## *Copyright Notice*

4.40 **Changes to the rules.** No aspect of copyright has caused more grief than the rules of copyright notice. These rules have been responsible for most forfeitures of copyright. Largely a trap for the unwary, they were softened somewhat in 1978 and removed almost entirely in 1989. They were not without purpose or utility, but the rules prevented the United States from joining the Berne Convention, and in the end this and other disadvantages outweighed their usefulness.

4.41 **Three different regimes.** Congress could not easily dispense with the rules retroactively, however, and the resulting 1989 legislation means that we now operate simultaneously under three doctrines: (1) for works first published on or after March 1, 1989, no copyright notice is required; (2) for works first published in the United States between January 1, 1978, and February 28, 1989, copyright notice must have been used on all copies published before March 1, 1989, with the proviso that certain steps could be taken to redeem deficient notice (see 4.48); and (3) for US works first published before January 1, 1978, the copyright was almost certainly forfeited if the notice was not affixed to all copies—few excuses were or are available. (As noted in 4.30, non-US works have been retroactively exempted from these rules.) Notwithstanding the liberality of the new law, continued use of notice is strongly advised to deprive infringers of any possible defense of ignorance. The rules in 4.42–48 should therefore still be followed.

## CONTENT OF NOTICE

4.42 **Three elements of the notice.** Under present law, as under the old law, the notice consists of three parts: (1) either the symbol © (preferred because it also suits the requirements of the Universal Copyright Convention), or the word *Copyright*, or the abbreviation *Copr.*; (2) the year of first publication; and (3) the name of the copyright owner. Many publishers also add the phrase "All rights reserved," and there is no harm in doing so, but the putative advantages of it (which were limited to Latin America) have all but vanished. (Other admonitions—e.g., "No part of this work may be reproduced in any manner without the express written consent of the publisher"—may be useful as No Trespassing signs but have no legal necessity or effect.) The year of first publication is not needed for greeting cards, postcards, stationery, and certain other works not germane to the publishing industry. Where a work is in its renewal term of copyright, it is customary, but not required, to include the year of renewal as well as the year of first publication. See also 1.22–39.

4.43 **Copyright notices on unpublished works.** As this discussion demonstrates, the entire regime of copyright notice is geared toward published works, not unpublished works. Some copyright owners nonetheless put a truncated notice ("Copyright [no date] J. Smith") on materials that they wish to circulate under circumstances that do not qualify as publication. Such notices are harmless and may, again, serve as No Trespassing signs. Authors submitting manuscripts for consideration by publishers sometimes use such notices, but the recipients may find the notices unprofessional or even offensive, as indicating a lack of trust.

4.44 **Name used in the notice.** The name used in the notice should be the name of the author unless the author has assigned all rights to the publisher. However, it is not uncommon to see the publisher's name in the notice even when it does not own all rights. Conversely, authors are increasingly insisting on notice in their names even when they have assigned all rights, perhaps not realizing that having their name in the notice has absolutely no effect on the allocation of rights. Such vagaries are regrettable but harmless. When an author who has agreed to assign all rights to the publisher nonetheless demands to be named in the copyright notice, the publisher may wish to make clear in its contract with the author that this does not affect the allocation of rights so that the author is not operating under a misconception. Some publishers leave at least one right in the author's hands—often one that is not related to the publisher's primary commercial activities, such as performance rights to a scholarly monograph—rendering it accurate to name the author in the notice.

4.45 **Placement of notice.** The copyright notice should be placed so as to give reasonable notice to the consumer. The old law was very specific about its location: for books, on either the title page or the page immediately following; and for journals and magazines, on the title page, the first page of text, or the front cover. Present law simply states that the notice should be so placed as "to give reasonable notice of the claim of copyright," but most publishers continue to place it in the traditional locations required by the old law. See also 1.93, 1.104, 1.112.

4.46 **United States government materials.** When a work consists "preponderantly" of materials created by the federal government, this must be stated in the notice. This may be done either positively (e.g., "Copyright is claimed only in the introduction, notes, appendixes, and index of the present work") or negatively (e.g., "Copyright is not claimed in 'Forest Management,' a publication of the United States government reprinted in the present volume"). Works produced by state or local governments or by governments of other countries are not per se in the public domain and are not subject to this notice provision.

4.47 **Notice on derivative works.** The new copyright in a derivative work (see 4.14) entitles its publisher to use a new copyright notice with a new year of first publication, and nothing requires that such notice delineate what is and is not covered by the copyright. This sometimes has the unfortunate by-product (not always unintended, let it be said) of making users think that the scope of copyright extends to public-domain material embedded in the work. Where the derivative work is a revised edition of a prior work, the best practice is to include the publication years of all the various editions. See 1.25.

4.48 **Correcting mistakes.** Under pre-1978 law, no mechanism was available to cure the effects of a defective notice: Copyright was forfeited and that was that, unless the omission of notice was accidental and occurred in a very small number of copies. For publication between January 1, 1978, and March 1, 1989 (when the notice requirement was finally dropped altogether), a more lenient regime prevailed. A mistake in the owner's name, or a mistake by no more than a year in the date element of the notice, was largely excused. Any more serious mistake was treated as an omission of notice. Any omission of one or more of the necessary three elements would be excused if the omission was from a "relatively small" number of copies. If more extensive omission occurred, the copyright owner could still save the copyright from forfeiture by registering it (see 4.49–54) within five years after the defective publication and making a "reasonable effort" to add the notice to all copies distributed to the public after the omission was discovered. Very few cases have discussed what a "reasonable effort" is, and their explanations, being somewhat ad hoc, give limited guidance to anyone trying to determine whether a work in this category is still protected by copyright.

## *Deposit and Registration*

4.49 **Deposit requirements.** In the United States until recently, the law required copyright owners to send copies of works published in print form to the Copyright Office for deposit and use in the Library of Congress. (Only works published exclusively online were generally exempt from mandatory deposit.) Although failure to make the required deposit did not forfeit the copyright, the copyright owner was subject to a fine for noncompliance if a specific request from the Library of Congress was ignored. However, in 2023 the requirement that physical copies be deposited in the Library of Congress was found unconstitutional by the DC Circuit Court of Appeals. Whether and to what effect that ruling will be appealed to the Supreme Court is unknown at press time, but the decision seems likely to stand. The ruling explicitly did not address whether it would be unconstitutional to demand electronic deposit—for example, where a book is available in both print and ebook formats—and the Copyright Office may seek to go down that path. Deposit of one or more copies remains mandatory where the copyright owner is seeking to *register* copyright, and the ruling made clear that that requirement is legitimate.

4.50 **Registration forms and fees.** To register a work the author or other claimant should ordinarily go online to the Copyright Office's interactive application form, available (with a reasonably good tutorial) at Copyright.gov/registration. Paper forms can still be used, and they must be used for certain group registrations, but they slow the registration process to a crawl. The Copyright Office offers all these forms and intelligible explanations of its registration rules, including its complex deposit requirements, on its website. The fees for registration vary depending on which process one uses. Publishers with large lists tend to keep funds on deposit at the Copyright Office and to charge their registration fees against their deposit accounts. Group registration is available for up to 750 photographs, up to ten unpublished works, short literary works published only online, and contributions to periodicals by a single author, as well as for certain serial publications. A single fee covers all items in the group being registered. The terms and conditions of these group registration options are available at Copyright.gov.

4.51 **Need for accuracy and candor.** It is important to answer all questions on the application accurately. Copyright owners have been sanctioned by courts, or had their cases thrown out of court, for misleading the Copyright Office by, for example, failing to disclose that a work is based on preexisting materials. Statements on the application do not need to be exhaustive, but they must be correct and not evasive. However, in contrast to patent applications, there is no requirement for disclosure of adverse claims or any other information not specifically called for on the form. In the case of works for which AI has been used in the creative process, the Copyright Office requires disclosure, at least in general terms, of what expression was created by the AI and what by the human using the AI. The Copyright Office's detailed guidance on this issue may be found at Copyright.gov/ai/.

4.52 **Benefits of registration.** Registration is not necessary to *obtain* a copyright (which exists in the work from the moment it is fixed in tangible form; see 4.3) or to ensure its validity. However, the prudent course is to register copyright because of the added protection registration affords. In cases of infringement, registration is a prerequisite to bringing suit unless the work was written by a non-US author and first published abroad. Registering at the time of publication avoids a scramble to register later if infringement is discovered. Moreover, if registration has been made within three months of publication, or before an infringement begins, the copyright owner, instead of going through the difficulties of proving actual damages, can sue for "statutory damages" (in effect, an award of damages based on equity rather than on proof of loss) and, most significantly, is eligible to be reimbursed for attorney's fees. Registration as a prerequisite to these remedies applies equally to works of US origin and works authored or published outside the US. Publishers fearing prepublication piracy of books in development should also consider the "preregistration" procedure on the website of the Copyright Office.

4.53 **Registering successive editions.** If a work is substantially revised, a new registration may be advisable to protect the new material that has been added. If, however, it would be difficult to infringe the new edition without infringing the originally registered edition, a new registration may be unnecessary. A new registration is not needed when ownership of the copyright changes, such as when rights revert to an author. Rather, the assignment of the copyright, including of the registration, should be recorded in the Copyright Office. The mechanics of this are explained at Copyright.gov/recordation/.

4.54 **Correcting or amplifying a registration.** If a registration contains errors or is missing information (e.g., the name of a coauthor or co-owner), a "Supplementary Registration" can be filed to fix these problems. In general, this must be done by filing a new registration online, repeating any accurate information and adding new information. More details about supplementary registration can be found at Copyright.gov.

## THE PUBLISHING AGREEMENT

4.55 **Basic rights.** No publishing house may legally publish a copyrighted work unless it first acquires the basic rights to copy the work and distribute it to the public. Although in theory a publisher could proceed with no more than a nonexclusive license of these rights—and this is done in rare circumstances—for obvious reasons publishers generally insist on exclusive rights. In most instances these rights are acquired from the author (or other copyright owner) by means of a contract called the publishing agreement.

## *New Books*

4.56 **Basic book-contract provisions.** In book publishing the publisher typically draws up the contract for a new book, to be signed by both the publisher and the author or, in the case of a joint work, by all authors. In this contract the publisher and author agree to certain terms. The publisher undertakes to publish the book after acceptance of the manuscript and to pay the author for the rights conveyed. Usually, publishers pay book authors a stipulated royalty out of the proceeds, but in some cases a publisher will instead pay a lump-sum fee. The author, in addition to granting rights to the publisher, typically also gives certain warranties, including that the book does not infringe anyone else's copyright (see 4.76). The author usually agrees to correct and return the edited manuscript and proofs within fairly tight deadlines. Book-publishing agreements are generally lengthy and detailed documents and include many other points of agreement. Common areas of negotiation include the following:

*Basic royalties*

- Royalty rates (often different for hardcover and paperback editions), including the points at which a royalty will rise, or escalate (e.g., X percent on the first 10,000 copies, Y percent on the next 20,000 copies, and Z percent thereafter); whether royalties are paid on list price or on net receipts; and the royalty (usually a fixed percentage) on electronic editions
- Royalty advances and (for certain types of books, such as textbooks) expense allowances

*Mechanics of the publishing process*

- The standards for acceptance of the manuscript, with the publisher wanting to be able to terminate the agreement if the final submitted manuscript is not "satisfactory," and the author wanting to limit this discretion to editorial rather than business considerations, with an opportunity to cure editorial defects
- Whether the author will prepare or pay for the cost of preparation of an index
- What say the author will have over the title, cover and interior design, and marketing copy
- The period following acceptance within which the publisher must issue the work

*Subsidiary rights*

- What rights, beyond print rights in the publisher's home territory (usually defined as either the US or North America) and digital rights, are granted to the publisher, and what share the author receives of the publisher's receipts from licensing those rights
- If audiobook rights are granted to the publisher, whether the author has a veto over the choice of narrator
- What say the author will have over the exercise of other rights granted to the publisher, especially where the integrity of the text is a concern, as in abridgment and condensation

*Postpublication matters*

- The nature and extent of the author's indemnification obligations should the book be accused of violating some third party's rights; where the publisher carries "media perils" insurance, these obligations are most often determined with reference to the insurance coverage
- What happens if the rights granted to the publisher are infringed, including especially how any recoveries are divided between the publisher and the author
- The scope of the author's agreement not to write a competing work, defined by subject matter and audience
- Whether the author is obligated to revise the work if asked to, and what share of royalties the author receives for revised editions to which the author does not contribute
- How rights revert to the author if the book goes out of print or ceases to sell (see 4.39)
- On what terms the author may audit the publisher's financial records to ensure full payment of royalties due

Finally, if a book is to be published under a Creative Commons license or according to an open-access arrangement—a growing sphere of publishing—the contract should specify exactly what rights the public is being given. These alternative publishing models are discussed in more detail at 4.65–74.

4.57 **Option clauses.** In former years publishing agreements routinely contained legally binding options on "the author's next book." These are no longer universal, but they are still common, especially where a book is or might be part of a series or a set of related titles: for example, options for "the author's next book on the subject of X" or "the author's next book involving the character John Smith." Some publishers insist on a right of first review or first refusal, or a right to match outstanding offers on the author's next book.

4.58 **Other contracts.** In addition to contracts with the authors of new books, several other types of agreement are used in scholarly publishing for special kinds of works. Two of the common ones cover contributions to scholarly journals (see 4.59, 4.60) and to edited compilations (see 4.62–63).

## *Journal Articles*

4.59 **Transfers of rights.** Contributors to a journal possess at the beginning exactly the same rights in their work as authors of books. Consequently, when an article has been accepted for publication in a scholarly journal, the publisher usually asks the author to sign a formal agreement governing the allocation of rights in the contribution. Where an article has multiple authors, many publishers now for the sake of simplicity ask only the lead author to sign, but require a representation that the lead author has the authority to bind all coauthors. In the absence of a written copyright transfer agreement, all that the publisher acquires is the privilege of distributing the contribution in the context of that journal. Contributors frequently do not know this and do not understand that without broad rights the publisher cannot license inclusion in anthologies, databases, or college and university online course materials, or other uses that spread the author's message. Explaining this will often overcome the author's reluctance to sign a transfer of rights to the publisher. In the agreement currently in use at the University of Chicago Press, the publisher returns to the contributor the right to reprint the article in other scholarly works. Such a provision is fair to both sides and is to be encouraged. See also 4.65–74 regarding open-access policies applicable to certain journals and journal articles.

4.60 **Less than full rights.** In the sciences, some publishers now limit the author's transfer of right to an exclusive publishing license. Other journal publishers, when an author refuses to transfer copyright in toto, will sometimes agree to a license more closely tailored to their specific needs. Care must be taken in such cases to ensure that the contract covers all the subsidiary rights that the publisher may want to exercise or sublicense and that the publisher's rights are exclusive where they need to be. This is especially important for foreign-language and electronic-database rights. In general, the trend toward narrowing or customizing licenses from journal authors to their publishers imposes on publishers a need to keep careful records of what rights they have obtained in each article, so they do not grant subsidiary rights that they do not in fact control. See also 4.65.

4.61 **Journal editors.** The role of the journal editor must not be forgotten. The process of selecting and arranging the contents of a journal issue will generally qualify as authorship of the compilation—and other editorial apparatus may also qualify as authorship. The resulting copyrights belong to the editor, unless the editor is an employee of the company or society that owns the journal, so that the editorial output would be considered work made for hire. Where the editor is an outside contractor, journal publishers should make sure that ownership of that separate copyright is clearly agreed on.

## *Edited Compilations*

4.62 **Edited books.** The agreement described for books in 4.56 is intended for books with one or a few authors. Another type of book, common in scholarly but not in trade publishing, is one in which the chapters are contributed by various authors commissioned by an editor. The editor, by selecting and arranging the contributions included in the work, adds another layer of authorship in the same way that a journal editor does. As author of the collective work (the book as a whole), the editor should sign an agreement similar to the standard author agreement described in 4.56. A publisher may in some circumstances use an agreement of the same type for chapter contributors, especially if the contributors are to receive royalty shares. All such agreements, though, need to be modified to reflect the particular allocation of responsibilities between editor and contributors. Alternatively, in appropriate circumstances, publishers can use simpler forms for chapter authors, closer in style to journal author forms. Finally, it is possible to use work-made-for-hire agreements for all these persons, although that is the least common solution. For symposia, see 4.63.

4.63 **Symposium proceedings.** Symposium proceedings, made up of papers by different authors, are sometimes published as special issues of journals and sometimes as stand-alone books. The editor of the proceedings, in either case, has a separate status as author because the proceedings, as a whole, are a collective work; hence, this editor should be contracted with in the same way as a book editor (see 4.62). If the proceedings are being published as a journal issue, the publisher needs to clarify who owns copyright in the editor's work and to secure from every contributor a contract more or less identical to that used for authors of articles published in regular issues of the journal concerned. If the proceedings are being published as a book, the editor should sign a standard book author agreement, modified as appropriate, and the contributors should sign separate forms covering their own papers.

## *Theses and Dissertations*

4.64 **Copyright and graduate student work.** Most higher education institutions require that dissertations and some theses be submitted to an electronic repository, either institutional or commercial. Once the full text of a dissertation or thesis is published in such a repository, others may have access to the work. Authors of dissertations and theses usually retain the copyright to their work, however, and can register it with the Copyright Office. Depending on institutional policies, authors may have the option to limit access to the work or to make it available freely online according to an open-access or Creative Commons model (see 4.65, 4.72). Papers published without open access are typically obtainable only through a commercial database or a library and sometimes are made available for sale in print form. Some institutions will waive the requirement to submit to a repository in certain circumstances or will allow authors to embargo their work, delaying public access for a specified period of time; typically, though, an abstract of an embargoed thesis or dissertation will still be publicly available through the repository. It is essential that authors of dissertations and theses understand the requirements of their institutions and also the implications of any publishing options available to them, as the ability for an author to reuse some or all of the work in subsequent books or journal articles may be limited by the terms under which the thesis or dissertation is made available. Regardless of how it is published, if a thesis or dissertation includes copyrighted material beyond the conventions of fair use (including in some cases material previously published by the author), the author must secure written permission from the copyright holder and should be prepared to submit permissions documentation. For more information, see *Copyright and Your Dissertation or Thesis: Ownership, Fair Use, and Your Rights and Responsibilities*, by Kenneth D. Crews (bibliog. 2.3).

## *Open Access*

4.65 **Open-access publishing models.** The trend in academic publishing has been toward increasing public access to copyrighted works by providing the full text of digital content for free. Although open access, as this is called, is primarily found in journal publishing, especially in the sciences, a number of academic book publishers have also been experimenting with open access. For an overview of the subject, see *Open Access*, by Peter Suber (bibliog. 2.3). "Open access" does not mean that there is no publishing agreement; it means that the copyright provisions of the publishing agreement must be explicit about the nature of open access that will be applied to the work at issue and thus different from the standard traditional copyright language.

4.66 **Green open access.** There are two main types of open access. The first is "green" open access, whereby an author retains or secures the right to deposit a version of the work in a repository that is open to the public for reading and downloading. Many authors, particularly in the STEM fields, post original manuscripts (so-called preprints) of their research articles in an institutional or other repository before they have been peer reviewed or accepted for publication. Once an article has been peer reviewed and accepted, however, the question of which version is open to the public is determined by the publisher's policy or, in many instances, by the policy of a third party such as a foundation or governmental agency that funded the research. The National Institutes of Health Public Access Policy, for example (see 4.70), mandates deposit of the final manuscript as peer reviewed but not the publisher's typeset version of record. Green open access typically entails little or no additional cost to the publisher, which nonetheless expects to cover publishing costs in the usual way (i.e., through subscriptions or sales and licensing of the published version). Other types of open access are discussed under 4.67 and 4.68.

4.67 **Gold open access.** The second main type of open access, "gold" open access, operates on a quite different economic model. Articles are published under a Creative Commons license (see 4.72), and the publisher receives compensation through either an institutional subsidy or the author's payment of an "article processing charge." (Recently some universities have begun adapting this model to books, subsidizing the publication of books written by their faculty on the condition that they be subject to a Creative Commons license.) Some journals are entirely open access; others use a hybrid model that includes some open-access content and some subscription-only content. Another variation on the gold model relies on library sales or other sources of revenue to provide a baseline amount that allows publishers to "unlock" an article or book for public access.

4.68 **Diamond open access.** Some journals are entirely open access thanks to subvention by institutions or philanthropic organizations, and this is often referred to as "diamond" open access. Their contents are subject to Creative Commons licenses (see 4.72).

4.69 **University licenses.** Several universities have adopted policies under which they presumptively receive nonexclusive licenses of journal articles written by their faculty, with the right to post those articles on the internet and to make and license "noncommercial" uses. (Commonly, faculty are permitted but not encouraged to opt out of this arrangement on a case-by-case basis.) Where this arrangement applies, a faculty author who receives a publisher's standard contract is supposed to respond with a university-approved addendum, listing rights granted to the university. There are various forms of addenda in circulation; they can be problematic. One, for example, contains the following provision:

> Notwithstanding any terms in the Publication Agreement to the contrary, AUTHOR and PUBLISHER agree that in addition to any rights under copyright retained by Author in the Publication Agreement, Author retains: (i) the rights to reproduce, to distribute, to publicly perform, and to publicly display the Article in any medium for noncommercial purposes; (ii) the right to prepare derivative works from the Article; and (iii) the right to authorize others to make any noncommercial use of the Article so long as Author receives credit as author and the journal in which the Article has been published is cited as the source of first publication of the Article. For example, Author may make and distribute copies in the course of teaching and research and may post the Article on personal or institutional websites and in other open-access digital repositories.

Among its faults, this language (1) does not explicitly state what the author can, and cannot, do with derivative works that the author creates; (2) does not clarify whether what the author can distribute, display, and otherwise use is the author's own manuscript or the finished, published work; and (3) does not prevent the author from licensing the article to a competing journal, if the latter is "noncommercial" (a word that has no commonly accepted legal meaning). Another problem is that only the publisher as copyright owner has the ability to police compliance with whatever "noncommercial" licenses the author or university may give—yet the publisher has no control over the licensing activity. Publishers would be well advised to develop their own addenda to use when presented with author requests for nonexclusive rights. Such addenda might give the author and the author's employer unlimited rights to use the article internally, the right to post manuscript versions of the article on the author's website, and the right to post a PDF or similar file of the final published version on the author's website after a specified interval of time.

4.70 **Public-access policies.** In a similar vein to the university policies addressed in the previous paragraph (4.69), some government agencies have implemented policies to provide public access to the results of their taxpayer-funded research and related activities. In the United States, the model for such a policy is the one adopted by the National Institutes of Health in accordance with congressional mandate. This policy requires submission, for posting on the National Library of Medicine's PubMed Central, of the final manuscripts of all peer-reviewed articles derived from NIH-funded research. Manuscripts are to be submitted upon final acceptance for publication—that is, after the entire peer review and editorial process is complete and the article is ready for publication. This policy, unlike the university policies discussed in 4.69, is not subject to any opt-out and cannot be altered by any addendum. (Publishers may, however, choose to substitute their own published versions of articles for such manuscripts.) More than a dozen other US agencies or departments, including the National Science Foundation, the Centers for Disease Control and Prevention, and the Department of Energy, have since adopted similar public-access policies following government-issued directives.

4.71 **Authors' use of their own works.** Publishers traditionally allowed their authors to make unlimited photocopies for their own students. It has now become common to allow authors to post their works on campus websites, even where no university license applies (see 4.69); to post on their own personal websites; and to reuse their articles in books or anthologies that they write or edit. This should ideally be done in a manner that minimizes the risk to the publisher of lost revenue—for example, by avoiding use of a Creative Commons license or by using a NonCommercial license (see 4.74). The University of Chicago Press's policy on these matters, which it posts online, is not atypical and is recommended for consideration.

4.72 **Creative Commons licenses.** Creative Commons licenses offer a range of "open license" alternatives to standard "all rights reserved" copyright distribution. In essence, when a work is made subject to a Creative Commons license, the copyright owner has given up some degree of the control that the copyright law would otherwise provide: At the very least, the copyright owner has waived control over reproduction and distribution in all media and, in many cases, has also waived control over the making of derivative works (and thus over the quality and integrity of how the work is reused). Furthermore, unless the license specifies otherwise, anyone is free to use the content in a commercial manner, even in competition with the nominal copyright owner. Once applied to a work, a Creative Commons license is irrevocable.

This work is being made available under the
Creative Commons Attribution-NonCommercial-NoDerivs International
License (CC BY-NC-ND 4.0). To view a copy of this license, visit
https://creativecommons.org/licenses/by-nc-nd/4.0.

FIGURE 4.1. A Creative Commons statement from the copyright page of a book.

4.73 **How to apply a Creative Commons license.** The license is applied by placing it on the work when it is made available to the public, typically in the same place as the copyright notice. See figure 4.1 for an example of how this should be done for books; note the absence of the phrase "All rights reserved." In journals, space does not usually permit the same graphics, and figure 4.2 shows an alternative form.

4.74 **Types of Creative Commons licenses.** The six basic licenses, from least to most restrictive, are as follows:

Attribution (CC BY), whereby any member of the public is licensed to carry out unlimited free redistribution of copies of a work, including for commercial purposes, and to alter or otherwise create derivatives of that work. The only requirement it imposes on the licensee is that the author/copyright owner of the original work receive appropriate credit (hence the "by" in CC BY).

Attribution-ShareAlike (CC BY-SA)—similar to a CC BY license, except that any reuse must be licensed under identical terms (i.e., "shared alike," under a CC BY-SA license).

Attribution-NoDerivs (CC BY-ND)—similar to a CC BY license, except that the work cannot be altered or abridged (in other words, no derivative works may be made).

Attribution-NonCommercial (CC BY-NC)—similar to a CC BY license, except that any reuse must be noncommercial.

Attribution-NonCommercial-ShareAlike (CC BY-NC-SA)—similar to a CC BY-NC license, except that any reuse must be licensed under the same terms (i.e., under a CC BY-NC-SA license).

*International Journal of Plant Sciences*, volume 184, number 1, January 2023. © 2022 The University of Chicago. This work is licensed under a Creative Commons Attribution-NonCommercial 4.0 International License (CC BY-NC 4.0), which permits non-commercial reuse of the work with attribution. For commercial use, contact journalpermissions@press.uchicago.edu. Published by The University of Chicago Press. https://doi.org/10.1086/722593

FIGURE 4.2. A copyright statement for a scholarly journal article acknowledging a Creative Commons license.

Attribution-NonCommercial-NoDerivs (CC BY-NC-ND)—similar to a CC BY-NC license, except that no derivatives are allowed.

All these license forms may be found at CreativeCommons.org. (There is also the option of adding on to one of these basic arrangements by means of a CC+ license, in which the "+" customization is detailed on the publisher's website and made available by link.) While authors (particularly journal authors) may show enthusiasm for this model, publishers should approach it with caution. It is generally not in a publisher's interest to publish material under a license that does not include NC, because that enables possible competitors to make commercial use of the material without paying a royalty or license fee. So, where the publisher has a say in the matter, it should push for a BY-NC license for the individual articles in a journal. As for the journal itself, unless it is diamond open access (see 4.68), the publisher will be able to control how each issue as a whole is licensed. It will normally wish to include not only NC but also ND (no derivatives) in the Creative Commons license applicable to each issue as a whole.

## *Self-Publishing*

4.75 **Self-publishing agreements.** Authors who self-publish directly through a retail platform such as the ones offered by Amazon and Apple, or through a self-publishing aggregator that distributes to multiple retailers (and in some cases to libraries), are required to agree to one of the service's standard contracts. Under such contracts, the author generally retains copyright and gets to set the price of the work as long as it is within certain limits. Unlike contracts with traditional publishers, such contracts tend to be nonexclusive, allowing authors to sell their work through more than one platform (including on a personal website) and in other formats, including print, but some services offer exclusive options that promise special terms favorable to authors for specific formats. Authors usually cannot self-publish works that are under contract with a traditional publisher except in the rare case of a work for which the author has retained digital publishing rights. On the other hand, self-publishing a work does not necessarily preclude future publication of that work with a traditional publisher (authors can typically terminate a self-publishing agreement at any time), and self-publishing is always an option for works whose rights have reverted to the author.

## THE AUTHOR'S RESPONSIBILITIES

4.76 **Author's copyright warranties.** In signing a contract with a publisher, an author warrants (guarantees) that the work is original, that the author owns it, that no part of it has been previously published, that no other agreement to publish it or part of it is outstanding, and that any copyrighted material of other authors that is used in the work is used with permission. (The indemnification that backs up these and other warranties is, as noted in 4.56, often a subject of negotiation in publishing contracts.) Unless the publisher otherwise agrees, the burden falls on the author to ensure that permission is obtained, as discussed in 4.79–87, except where the author's use of the material is fair use, as discussed in 4.88–98. In light of the increasing use of AI to generate text and images, and the copyrightability issues that arise from that (see 4.51), publishers should strongly consider also asking authors to warrant that AI has not been used to create any elements of the work except as specifically disclosed to the publisher. Such disclosure will help the copyright registration process but will not of course eliminate the inherent risk of inadvertent reproduction of copyrighted material in AI-generated content.

4.77 **Other warranties.** The author should also warrant that the work does not libel anyone or infringe any person's right of privacy. If the work contains scientific formulas or practical advice, the author may also be asked to warrant that no instructions in the work will, if accurately followed, cause injury to anyone, although courts have so far balked (on First Amendment grounds) at imposing liability for injury on authors or publishers for inaccurate advice. Some publishers ask authors for a further warranty that any statement of fact in the work is indeed accurate, perhaps for fear of reputational risk more than of legal liability. Although the publisher is entitled to rely on authors' warranties, during the editorial process it behooves the publisher to be alert to possible exposure for defamation or invasion of privacy. With the caveat that these are complicated issues and beyond the scope of this book, as a generalization it may be said that defamation is the assertion of things that appear to be facts (not the assertion of opinions) about living people who can be identified from the text or context of the work, if those alleged facts would be likely to hold the subject up to scorn or ridicule in the relevant community. (There are countervailing considerations, such as whether the subject is a public figure, in which case the bar to liability is much higher than for private citizens.) With the same caveat, invasion of privacy takes several forms, but the most significant is the public disclosure of private facts about a living individual if the disclosure would be highly offensive to a reasonable person. If a publisher encounters material that appears to present risk on either count, the publisher should query the author on the matter, not merely rely on the author's warranty. Use of a person's real name may constitute, or exacerbate, an invasion of privacy; use of a public figure's real name in a fictional context is not actionable unless it is defamatory. Corporations, of course, have no right of privacy, and so cannot prevent the use of their names and trademarks in, say, a work of fiction. They do, however, have the right to sue for defamation of themselves or their products.

4.78 **The role of counsel.** Counsel versed in these areas of the law can be of help in reviewing passages about which the publisher has concern, determining, for example, whether permission is needed for the reproduction of certain material, or whether passages in a work are defamatory. It may be helpful for the publisher's counsel to have a direct line of communication with the author, so long as it is clear to all concerned that the lawyer represents the publisher, not the author. Counsel's suggestions for changes to the manuscript should be followed absent compelling considerations to the contrary.

## *Obtaining Permissions*

4.79 **General principles for obtaining permissions.** Budget permitting, an author may wish to commission illustrations on a work-made-for-hire basis, using forms supplied by the publisher. With this exception, an author must obtain permission to use any copyrighted material created by others, unless the intended use is a "fair use" (see 4.88–98). Technically, permission need not be in writing, but it would be most unwise to rely on oral permission. No permission is required to quote from works of the United States government or works for which copyright has expired. See 4.27–31 for guidelines to determine whether copyright for old material has expired. Bear in mind that although the original text of a classic reprinted in a modern edition may be in the public domain, recent translations and abridgments, as well as editorial introductions, notes, and other apparatus, are protected by copyright. But whether permission is needed or not, the author should always, as a matter of good practice (and to avoid any possible charge of plagiarism), credit any sources used. See 4.100 and 4.103.

4.80 **Author's role in obtaining permissions.** Publishing agreements generally place on the author the responsibility to request any permission needed for the use of material owned by others. In the course of writing a book or article, the author should keep a record of all copyright owners whose permission may be necessary before the work is published. For a book containing many illustrations, long prose passages, or poetry, obtaining permissions may take weeks, even months. For example, the author may find that an American publisher holds rights only for distribution in the United States and Canada, and that European, British Commonwealth (excluding Canada), and "rest of world" rights are held by one or more publishers across the Atlantic. The author, wishing worldwide distribution for the book (world rights), must then write to each of these requesting permission for use of the material. If the author of copyrighted material has died, or if the copyright owner has gone out of business, a voluminous correspondence may ensue before anyone authorized to grant permission can be found (see 4.86). The author should therefore begin requesting permissions as soon as a manuscript is accepted for publication. Most publishers wisely decline to begin the production process for a book until all the author's permissions are in hand.[1]

4.81 **Interview and photo releases.** Although the copyright ownership of interviews is somewhat murky, prudence requires that the interviewee's permission be obtained for the use of any extract that exceeds the bounds of fair use. (Such permission is best obtained by a broad release at the time the interview occurs, either in writing or on the sound recording made of the interview.) Photographs of living persons present another sort of challenge. The photographer unquestionably owns copyright in the image, but if that image is to be used on the cover of a book or in any marketing materials, the subject's release must be obtained. (Use of the image inside a book or article, to illustrate text, does not require such permission.)

1. It is possible to engage professional help in obtaining permissions for a large project. Specialists in this work are listed under "Consultants" in the annual publication *LMP* (*Literary Market Place*; see bibliog. 2.9). Note also that the allocation of responsibility described here may not apply in some cases, such as large-market college textbooks, for which the publisher may take on the clearing of permissions. See 4.108.

4.82 **Author's own work.** The author should remember that permission is sometimes needed to reuse or even to revise the author's own work. If the author has already allowed a chapter or other significant part to appear in print elsewhere—as a journal article, for example—then written permission to reprint it, or to update or revise it, will need to be obtained from the copyright owner of the other publication, unless the author secured the right of reuse in the contract with that earlier publisher, or unless the material was published under a Creative Commons license. The law does not require that the prior publication be credited in the new publication, but it is a common courtesy to give credit on the copyright page of a book, in a footnote on the first page of the reprinted material, or in a special list of acknowledgments. The author's earlier contract may also require such credit. And if the first publisher owns copyright in the material, it may make credit a condition of permission to reprint. Also, if the first publisher owns copyright, the new publisher will need to flag its files so that subsequent permissions requests for that material are referred to the original copyright owner.

4.83 **Fees and record keeping.** Most publishing agreements stipulate that any fees to be paid will be the author's responsibility. (Textbooks are a rare exception; see 4.108.) When all permissions have been received, the author should send them, or copies of them, to the publisher, who will note and comply with any special provisions they contain. The publisher will file all permissions with the publishing contract, where they may be consulted in the event of future editions or of requests for permission to reprint from the work. The copyeditor will check the permissions against the manuscript to be sure all necessary credits have been given. See also 1.33, 2.51, 4.106, 13.58.

4.84 **Permissions beyond the immediate use.** Many publishers, when giving permission to reprint material they control, will withhold the right to sublicense that material. In such a case the publisher of the later work will not be able to give third parties free and clear permission to use material in which content from the earlier work is embedded; they will have to go back to the original source. Some publishers will also limit their licenses to a single edition, sometimes even with a maximum print run stipulated, or to a specific time period such as five or seven years. Where this is so, the publisher receiving the permission will have to go back to the source for new permission, usually for an additional fee, for any new edition, paperback reprint, serialization, or the like. Alternatively, the publisher granting permission can stipulate up front what fees are to be paid for further uses and permit the new publisher to secure such permission automatically on payment of the agreed-upon fee.

4.85 **Permissions for unpublished works.** Getting permission for unpublished material presents an entirely different problem. Instead of a publishing corporation or licensing agent, one must deal with the author or author's heirs, who may not be easily identified or found. If the writer is dead, it may be especially difficult to determine who controls the copyrights.

4.86 **The missing copyright owner.** The problem presented by unpublished works whose authors are dead is, in a larger sense, just an example of the problem of the missing copyright owner. Another typical example is the publisher that has gone out of business or at least is no longer doing business under a given imprint. This has come to be known as the "orphan works" problem and has been the subject of proposed (but abandoned) legislation. The draft bills suggested practices that a publisher would do well to follow when considering use of an orphan work. The most important thing is to conduct a reasonable (and well-documented) effort to locate the copyright owner. The elements of a bona fide search will vary with the circumstances but would probably include a search of the Copyright Office records, an internet search, and queries to both private and public databases that might reasonably be expected to contain information as to the owner of the copyright. If such efforts yield no results, there is still some risk in going forward. Technically, use of the work might still be ruled an infringement of copyright should a copyright owner surface, but it is unlikely that any court would do more than require the payment of a reasonable permissions fee. Anyone proceeding with publication under these conditions should certainly be prepared to offer and pay a reasonable fee on receiving any objection from the rediscovered owner.

4.87 **Noncopyright restrictions on archives.** Authors who wish to include unpublished material in their works should be aware that private restrictions, unrelated to copyright, may limit its use. The keeper of a collection, usually a librarian or an archivist, is the best source of such information, including what permissions must be sought and from whom. Bear in mind that copyright in a manuscript is different from ownership of the paper on which it is written or typed. Most often a library or collector will own the physical object itself but not the right to reproduce it. Thus there may be two permissions required: one for access to the material and one for the right to copy. It is important not to mistake one for the other.

## FAIR USE: QUOTING WITHOUT PERMISSION

4.88 **Overview of the legal doctrine of fair use.** The doctrine of fair use, which allows limited use of copyrighted work without permission, was originally developed by courts as an equitable limit on the absolute rights of copyright. Although incorporated into the new copyright law, the doctrine still does not attempt to define the exact limits of the fair use of copyrighted work. It does state, however, that in determining whether the use of a work in any particular case is fair, the factors to be considered must include the following:

1. The purpose and character of the use, including whether such use is of a commercial nature or is for nonprofit educational purposes
2. The nature of the copyrighted work
3. The amount and substantiality of the portion used in relation to the copyrighted work as a whole
4. The effect of the use on the potential market for, or value of, the copyrighted work

Essentially, the doctrine allows copying that would otherwise be infringement. For example, it allows authors to quote from other authors' work or to reproduce small amounts of graphic or pictorial material for purposes of review or criticism or to illustrate or buttress their own points. Authors invoking fair use should transcribe accurately and give credit to their sources. They should not quote in such a way as to make the author of the quoted passage seem to be saying something opposite to, or different from, what was intended.

4.89 **Validity of "rules of thumb."** Although the law lays out no boundaries or ironclad formulas for fair use, some publishers have their own rules of thumb. Such rules, of course, have no legal force: Courts, not publishers, adjudicate fair use. The rules exist in part to give an overworked permissions department, which often cannot tell whether a proposed use of a quotation is actually fair, something to use as a yardstick. See also 4.98.

4.90 **A few general rules related to fair use.** Fair use is use that is fair—simply that. Uses that differ in purpose from the original, and uses that transform the copied material by changing its context or the way it is perceived, will always be judged more leniently than those that merely parallel or parrot the original. For example, substantial quotation of the original is acceptable in the context of a critique but may well not be acceptable if one is simply using the first author's words to reiterate the same argument or embellish one's own prose. Use of any literary work in its entirety—a poem, an essay, an article from a journal—is hardly ever acceptable. Use of less than the whole will be judged by whether the second author appears to be taking a free ride on the first author's labor, or may be usurping, or interfering with, the market for the first author's product. As a general rule, one should never quote more than a few contiguous paragraphs of prose or lines of poetry at a time or let the quotations, even if scattered, begin to overshadow the quoter's own material. Quotations or graphic reproductions should not be so substantial that they substitute for, or diminish the value of, the copyright owner's own publication. Proportion is more important than the absolute length of a quotation: Quoting five hundred words from an essay of five thousand is likely to be riskier than quoting that amount from a work of fifty thousand. But an even smaller percentage can be an infringement if it constitutes the heart of the work being quoted.

4.91 **Epigraphs and song lyrics.** Quotation in the form of an epigraph does not fit neatly into any of the usual fair use categories, and there has never been a lawsuit that could help provide fair use guidance. An epigraph typically uses a very small portion of a copyrighted work, in a manner that does not in any way displace demand for the work. If it is chosen for some resonance with the text it precedes, and if the reader's understanding is enriched or the reader's imagination is stimulated by that resonance, then the epigraph should probably be viewed as a transformative use of the original and should be fair use. If on the other hand it is largely decorative, the fair use argument is notably weaker. All of the foregoing can be said too of limited quotation of song lyrics, poetry, and the like in the context of, for example, an interior monologue or fictional narrative. Of course, this would not excuse the publication of a collection of epigraphs or lyrics without permission of the various authors being quoted.

4.92 **Fair use of unpublished works.** If the work to be quoted has never been published, the same considerations related to fair use apply. But if the author or the author's spouse or children are still living, some consideration should be given to their interest in controlling when the work is disclosed to the public.

4.93 **Paraphrasing.** Use that is not fair will not be excused by paraphrasing. Traditional copyright doctrine treats extensive paraphrase as merely disguised copying. Thus, fair use analysis will be the same for both. Paraphrase of small quantities of material, on the other hand, may be so minimal that it does not constitute copying at all, so that fair use analysis would never come into play.

4.94 **Pictorial and graphic materials.** A high level of uncertainty has historically plagued the question of fair use of pictorial and graphic materials. At the level of intuition, it seems that a monograph on Picasso should be free to reproduce details from his paintings in order, for example, to illustrate the critic's discussion of Picasso's brushwork. Reproducing the entire image in black and white may also be reasonably necessary to illustrate the author's analysis of Picasso's techniques of composition. Reproducing "thumbnail sketches" of images has been held to be a fair use since they are so small and of such poor resolution that they cannot reduce the commercial value of the original. However, justification wears thin when a painting is reproduced in vivid color occupying a full page; the result begins to compete with large-scale reproductions of artwork that have no scholarly purpose. Likewise, reproduction on the cover would in most cases count as commercial rather than scholarly use, and justification under the other fair use factors would thus have to be much more compelling. The same considerations apply, adjusted for the media concerned, to every other sort of pictorial material, including, for example, posters, street art, and film stills. An opinion from a leading federal court of appeals has provided a refreshingly generous reading of fair use where images are concerned. The case involved a book about the Grateful Dead; the court held that the reproduction of entire concert posters in full color was fair use because the posters were "historical artifacts," used to provide a "visual context" for the text, and reproduced at a size far smaller than life, indeed at the "minimal image size and quality necessary to ensure the reader's recognition of the images as historical artifacts." These criteria, properly applied, should free up many a use that would otherwise be smothered by caution. For an overview of the subject, see the *Code of Best Practices in Fair Use for the Visual Arts*, published online by the College Art Association.

4.95 **Charts, tables, and graphs.** Reproduction of charts, tables, and graphs presents a difficult judgment call. An aggressive approach would justify copying a single such item on the ground that one chart is the pictorial equivalent of a few sentences. A more conservative approach would argue that a graph is a picture worth a thousand words and that reproducing it without permission is taking a free ride on the first author's work. This latter approach has the flaw of being too absolute in practice, for it is difficult under this rationale to imagine *any* fair use of such an image. Where the item in question represents a small portion of the original work and a small portion of the second work, the harm seems minimal, outweighed by the benefits of open communication. Certainly, reproduction of a single graph, table, or chart that simply presents data in a straightforward relationship, in contrast to reproduction of a graph or chart embellished with pictorial elements, should ordinarily be considered fair use. Indeed, some graphs that merely present facts with little or no expressive input—the equivalent, in two dimensions, of a list—may even be beyond the protection of copyright.

4.96 **Importance of attribution.** With all reuse of others' materials, it is important to identify the original as the source. This not only bolsters the claim of fair use but also helps avoid any accusation of plagiarism. Nothing elaborate is required; a standard footnote will suffice, or (in the case of a graph or table, for example) a simple legend that says "Source: [author, title, and date of earlier work]." If the author is reproducing the graph or table verbatim rather than reformatting data taken from the original, it is preferable to say "Reprinted from [author, title, and date of earlier work]" rather than merely "Source." See also 3.30–38, 3.78, 13.58. In addition, if the material is going to be included in a work that will be distributed under a Creative Commons license, it is critical to include the copyright notice that appears in the original, so as to avoid any suggestion that the material is itself subject to the Creative Commons license.

4.97 **Unnecessary permissions.** Given the ad hoc nature of fair use and the absence of rules and guidelines, many authors and publishers tend to seek permission if they have the slightest doubt whether a particular use is fair. This is unfortunate. Fair use is valuable to scholarship, and it should not be allowed to decay because scholars fail to employ it boldly. Furthermore, excessive permissions processing tends to slow down the publication of worthwhile writings. Even if permission is sought and denied, that should not necessarily be treated as the end of the matter. The US Supreme Court has held that requesting permission should not be regarded as an admission that permission is needed. In other words, where permission is denied, or granted but for an unreasonable price, publishers and authors should consider whether a sound case might be made for fair use.

4.98 **Chicago's fair use guidelines.** To reduce the expense of responding to permissions requests, and to reduce the friction in scholarly publishing that permissions handling can create, the University of Chicago Press posts guidelines on its website for what it considers to be fair use of excerpts from its own publications. These guidelines are intended to be generous and fair to all parties. Other publishers are encouraged to adopt them.

## *Requesting Permission*

4.99 **The permissions process.** Publishers used to process permissions requests by hand, case by case, evaluating each request on its own merits and often tailoring a fee to the specific circumstances. Now, most of them maintain pages on their websites where permissions requests can be submitted digitally via email or an online form, or they outsource the work to Copyright Clearance Center in the United States or to PLSclear in the United Kingdom. Many have also adopted standard published fee schedules. Any publisher that has not yet implemented such a system should do so at the earliest opportunity, because it creates a highly efficient marketplace for reuse, to the benefit of both the publisher and its constituents. Authors seeking permission for use of other authors' work can obtain that permission more expeditiously and can realistically budget for permissions fees in advance. If, however, none of these technological options is available in a given instance, would-be users will have to resort to contacting the rights holder via phone, letter, or email if an email address is available. It should be added that rights administration for the lyrics of musical works is a very different animal. Such rights are typically owned by an entity called the "music publisher," which can be a very large corporation but is equally likely to be a small, almost invisible closely held company; the identity of the music publisher can be determined through the Copyright Office's online database or through ASCAP, BMI, or another performing rights society. The permission requester should expect a slow, very much unautomated process.

4.100 **Information to include when requesting permission.** The following information is typically provided in the permission request:

1. The title of the original work and exact identification, with page numbers, of what is to be reprinted. Identification should include, in the case of a table or figure, its number and the page it appears on (e.g., fig. 6 on p. 43); in the case of a poem, the title and the page on which the poem appears and the lines to be quoted; in the case of a prose passage, the opening and closing phrases in addition to the page numbers (e.g., "from 'The military genius of Frederick the Great' on p. 110 through 'until the onset of World War I' on p. 112"). The requester should be sure to cite the original source of the material, not any subsequent reuse of it.

2. Information about the publication in which the author wishes to reproduce the material: title, approximate number of printed pages, form(s) of publication (clothbound book, paperback book, ebook, journal, and/or electronic journal), publisher, probable date of publication, approximate print run, and list price (if available).
3. The kind of rights requested. The most limited rights a requester ought to accept are "nonexclusive world rights in the English language, for one edition," or words to the same effect. Ideally, though, more extensive rights should be sought: nonexclusive world rights for all editions in print and other media; the right to include the material in translation licenses; the right to grant customary permissions requests (but only where the licensed material is incorporated in the context of the requester's own work); and the right to assign the license as part of an assignment of the new work. The request for the right to license foreign-language editions, and the right to grant customary permissions, will, if granted, greatly simplify the downstream licensing of the new work. Unfortunately, such rights are not implicit in any nonexclusive license (see 4.36) and are not commonly granted, so that downstream licensees of works in which earlier material is used end up needing to get multiple layers of permission.

Downloadable permission request templates are available from the website of the University of Chicago Press. Note that it is up to the copyright owner to quote a fee for the proposed use and to stipulate what special conditions apply to the grant. However, if there are reasons why the requester believes a low fee would be appropriate—such as that the book will likely have very modest sales—there is nothing inappropriate about asking for consideration on that point.

## ILLUSTRATIONS

4.101 **Rights holders.** Copyright in charts, graphs, and the like is presumptively controlled by the same person or entity that owns copyright in the text that they accompany, unless otherwise indicated. Copyright in pictorial and sculptural works is typically owned by the artist, or the artist's estate or heirs, not by any publisher, although in many cases the copyright can be licensed through the Artists Rights Society (which has an online system for submitting permissions requests) or corresponding organizations outside the United States. Copyright ownership of artworks sold before 1978 is not always easy to determine, because before 1978 the law generally, but not always, assumed that so long as an original artwork remained unpublished, its copyright passed from hand to hand with ownership of the object itself, unless otherwise agreed at some point in the chain of title. For post-1977 works, copyright belongs to the artist unless the artist has explicitly assigned it to someone else in writing. But, even if a work is in the public domain, the person seeking permission to reproduce the artwork in a book or journal may, as a practical matter, need to deal with a museum that expects a fee for providing a high-resolution image, or allowing an author to make a photograph, of a work in its collection. (Some museums, by contrast, make high-resolution images of their public-domain holdings freely accessible.) Where the museum can deny permission to photograph the object, such a fee is the tariff one pays for physical access if nothing else. Where the museum is licensing its own reproduction or photograph of the work, it has less justification, for the law denies copyright to photographs that merely reproduce another two-dimensional image. Be that as it may, authors and publishers are generally loath to antagonize museums by challenging their positions.

4.102 **Stock agencies and image archives.** The pictorial works for which permissions are most easily obtained are photographs, at least where the rights are administered by a stock agency or other commercial image archive. Such agencies have vast inventories of images and published and easy-to-understand fee structures. There are also websites that act as clearinghouses for photographic permissions.

4.103 **Information to include when requesting permission.** A permission request for an illustration should be sent to the picture agency, museum, artist, or private individual controlling reproduction rights. Again, the request should be as specific as possible regarding the identity of what is to be reproduced, the form of publication in which it will appear, at what size the image will be reproduced (e.g., quarter page, half page), and the scope of rights requested. If the requester knows that the illustration will also be used elsewhere than in the text proper (such as on the cover or in directly related advertising and promotion), this fact should be noted. See 4.100.

4.104 **Requesting image descriptions.** In order to provide access to readers who are visually impaired, have other print disabilities, or rely on technology to read text aloud, works containing illustrations will need to contain alternative (alt) text: language describing each image (see 3.28). Many museums and licensing societies have descriptions that they would be pleased to share as part of the permissions process, if so requested.

4.105 **Fees.** Fees paid for reproducing material, especially illustrations procured from a stock-photo agency, usually cover onetime use only—in, say, the first edition of a book, or for a certain number of copies. If an illustration is also to be used on the cover or in advertising, a separate and higher fee is customary. And if a book is reprinted as a paperback or goes into a second edition, another fee is usually charged. For obvious reasons, such arrangements are not optimal from the publisher's standpoint, and authors should try wherever possible to obtain permission covering all editions of their works in all media. Whether the publisher or the author should pay whatever additional fee is charged for cover use may be a matter for negotiation.

## ACKNOWLEDGING SOURCES

4.106 **Credit lines.** Whether or not the use of others' material requires permission, an author should give the exact source of such material: in a note or internal reference in the text, in a source note to a table, or in a credit line accompanying an illustration. Where formal permission has been granted, the author should, within reason, follow any special wording stipulated by the grantor. For a text passage complete in itself, such as a poem, or for a table, details about the source may be followed by this simple acknowledgment:

Reprinted by permission of the publisher.

A credit line for an illustration may read, for example, as follows:

Courtesy of the Newberry Library, Chicago, Illinois.

For examples of various kinds of credit lines, see 3.30–38, 3.78, 13.58.

4.107 **Acknowledgments sections.** In a work that needs many permissions, acknowledgments are often grouped in a special acknowledgments section at the front or back of the work (see 1.47, 1.65). Some citation of the source should still, however, be made on the page containing the relevant material.

## FEES

4.108 **Responsibility for payment.** As noted above (4.83; see also 4.105), publishing agreements generally make the author responsible for any fees charged for use of others' material—and for any complimentary copies that the licensor of the material may request. A publisher may agree to meet these obligations and deduct the cost from the author's royalties. In rare instances the publisher will split the cost with the author, or even provide a budget to the author, depending on the bargaining power of the author. If it appears that a book would be enhanced by illustrations not provided by the author, many publishing agreements enable the publisher to find the illustrations and (with the author's consent) charge any fees involved to the author's royalty account. One exception to these generalizations is textbooks, where it is common for the publisher to provide a certain amount of its own funds to pay for illustrations.

4.109 **Anthologies.** A book made up entirely of other authors' copyrighted materials—stories, essays, poems, documents, selections from larger works—depends for its existence on permissions from the various copyright owners. The compiler of such a volume therefore should begin seeking permissions as soon as a contract for publication of the volume has been executed or a letter of intent has been received from the prospective publisher. Informal inquiries to copyright owners may be initiated before that time, but no sensible publisher of material to be anthologized is likely to grant permission for its use or to set fees without knowing the details of eventual publication. Once those details are known, the compiler must act quickly. Permission for a selection may be refused, or the fee charged may be so high that the compiler is forced to drop that selection and substitute another. And until all permissions have been received and all fees agreed on, the book's contents cannot be considered final.

## SUBSIDIARY RIGHTS AND PERMISSIONS

### *Granting Permission*

4.110 **Handling requests in house.** A publisher with a relatively large backlist of books and journals, such as the University of Chicago Press, may receive dozens of communications every day from people seeking to license material from its list. Some are for permission of the type discussed in 4.79–87 to reproduce small amounts of prose or verse, or an illustration or two, from a book or journal, and some are for permission to reproduce a chapter or article for educational use, whether by photocopying or by inclusion in a university's library e-reserves or its course management system. Other requests are for the right to use the entirety of a work in some new manner or modality, and these are the subsidiary rights discussed in 4.110–15. Most publishers have a "rights and permissions" staff to handle these requests.

4.111 **The rights database.** One prerequisite to an efficient and legally safe rights and permissions program is a complete and accurate record of what rights the publisher has. This is especially sensitive where third-party materials have themselves been used by permission in the material to be licensed. The publisher's rights database should also record any other conditions that might restrict the publisher's ability to license, such as a requirement that the author's approval be obtained.

## *Handling Subsidiary Rights*

4.112 **Categories of subsidiary rights.** Subsidiary rights are usually thought of as including the following categories, some applicable to all types of published works and others to books only:

*Original-language rights outside the original publisher's territory,* whereby a second publisher may be licensed to sell the book in its original version in the second publisher's own territory. Typically a US publisher will retain, and not license out, English-language rights in Canada or even all of North America. Licensed territories tend to be defined according to commonly recognized geographic regions (e.g., United Kingdom, British Commonwealth, Europe and the Middle East, or "rest of world," commonly abbreviated as "ROW"). Where a UK or Commonwealth publisher is granted exclusive English-language rights in its home territory, the work is often also licensed on a nonexclusive basis in the ROW. If a license includes digital as well as print media, great care must be taken to ensure that the distributor honors only orders that can be traced to the countries in its own territory. It is essential to maintain accurate and up-to-date metadata regarding the territory rights so that it is clear to all trading partners in which territories each publisher is allowed to sell its edition (see also 1.84).

*Translation rights,* whereby a publisher in another territory may be licensed to translate the work into another language and to exercise standard publisher's rights (reproduction, distribution, electronic display) in the translation. Note that copyright in the translation as a derivative work belongs as an initial matter to the translator or to the publisher of the translation, but the license can impose restrictions on the exercise of that copyright. Whether the foreign-language publisher can exercise motion-picture rights in its translation is an issue for negotiation, as is the ownership of the translation when the license term ends.

*Serial rights*, whereby a magazine or newspaper publisher may be licensed to publish the book or excerpts from it in a series of daily, weekly, or monthly installments. *First serial rights* refers to publication before the work has come out in book form, *second serial rights* to publication afterward.

*Paperback rights*, whereby a publisher is licensed to produce and sell a paperback version of the book. So-called trade paperbacks are normally sold through regular book retail channels, in the same manner as clothbound books. Mass-market paperbacks are often marketed through newsstands and supermarkets, although many now find their way into bookstores. Where the publisher of the paperback is the original publisher, paperback rights are not subsidiary but primary, usually with their own royalty scale. Some books are published only in paper, with no previous or simultaneous clothbound version; these are called original paperbacks.

*Book-club rights*, whereby a book club is given the right to distribute the book to its members for less than the regular list price. Copies generally are sold to the book club in bulk at a steep discount.

*Reprint rights*, whereby another publisher is licensed to reprint the work, in whole or in part, in an anthology or some other collection or (usually if the work has gone out of print in English) in an inexpensive reprint edition, for distribution in a specific non-US territory, or for a specially bound luxury edition. This category also includes licensing document-delivery companies to reproduce chapters of works or journal articles on demand.

*Abridgment and condensation rights.* The author may well have demanded a veto over the exercise of these rights; even if not, as a courtesy the author should be consulted on their exercise.

*Rights to produce an edition in braille or digital format that is accessible to people with disabilities.* It should be noted that under US copyright law various nonprofit organizations have the right to publish such editions without permission. However, many publishers consider proactive licensing as both a public service and a way of ensuring the quality of accessible texts, and they work collaboratively with nonprofits to that end.

*Dramatic rights*, which consist of "live stage" rights and "motion picture" (including television) rights. Because plays and musicals sometimes get remade as movies, and movies as plays or musicals, licensees of one typically want to control the other, but they can be licensed separately. A dramatic-rights license is most obviously necessary where a work of fiction is concerned, but motion-picture producers (including especially documentary filmmakers) will often license rights to biographies and other nonfiction works so as to ensure their ability to use material from the book concerned.

*Audio rights,* also called *audiobook rights,* whereby the work is licensed for download or streaming in a digital audio format or for recording on compact disc or the like. These rights are further divided into "dramatic" audio rights, whereby the book is read by actors reading different characters' roles, and "nondramatic" audio rights, which involve a solo actor reading the entire work.

*Graphic novel rights,* whereby a work of fiction or nonfiction is retold using the graphic and text conventions that were initially developed for comic books.

*Electronic rights,* whereby the work is licensed for sale in ebook format, for inclusion in a database, or for other electronic use. Where journals are concerned, the principal electronic subsidiary rights involve licensing the journal's content to aggregators and research services; see 4.113. (This sort of licensing also has some importance for scholarly books.) Where a book is concerned, if the publisher itself intends to issue the work in ebook or other electronic form, electronic rights should be considered not subsidiary rights but part of the publisher's basic publication right and subject to a primary royalty. Publishers should normally assign new ISBNs for the electronic versions of their works, just as they have always done when, for example, issuing a hardcover work in paperback form (see 1.36).

*Enhanced electronic rights,* whereby the text is enhanced with substantial hyperlinks, video data, and the like, creating a derivative work. If the originating publisher wishes to produce such a product and is for any reason not acquiring general derivative-work rights in the contract, it should make sure specifically to obtain the right to enhance the electronic version of the work with such features.

Subsidiary rights in the context of journals also include microform (including microfilm and microfiche) rights and the right to create summaries of articles in so-called abstract form. Reproduction by document-delivery services is also particularly relevant to journals.

4.113 **Electronic-rights licensing.** The term *electronic rights* covers a wide range of possibilities, and the number is constantly growing. Among the users of electronic rights are aggregators, who make available online a large number of publications in a given field or fields; research services, both current and archival, that permit access to databases of publications, often by subscription; and services that allow library users to "borrow" electronic copies of works. The decision whether to license some or all of such uses is a complex one. The economic issue is whether the availability of a work through these services will "cannibalize" the publisher's own projected sales, or will instead be additive. Might it even enhance the sales or stature of the work by increasing its visibility—or, to put it in the negative, would withholding the work from such a service diminish its visibility and stature? In entering into electronic-rights licenses, the publisher should satisfy itself that the delivery mechanism of the particular licensee has safeguards against excessive downloading or copying (as part of a strategy of what is known as digital rights management)—or that such downloading or copying is something the publisher can tolerate. Such licenses should generally be nonexclusive. The publisher will also generally want to ensure that an electronic license lasts only a few years, for the pace of change is such that all these issues need to be revisited frequently.

4.114 **Economic considerations.** The list in 4.112 by no means exhausts the various forms of subsidiary rights the publisher may handle, but it includes the major ones. Depending on the administrative structure of the publishing house and the importance and marketability of the work involved, various individuals or departments may handle different aspects of subsidiary-rights work—a special rights and permissions department, the sales or marketing department, the acquiring editor, or even the chief executive officer. When the publisher sells or licenses rights to others, money is paid, either in a lump sum or as a royalty, and these proceeds are normally split between the publisher and the author according to whatever terms are specified in the publishing contract. In a typical book-publishing agreement, the author receives at least 50 percent of such income and sometimes substantially more. Some publishers have tried to avoid paying the author so much by licensing at an artificially low royalty to a sister company or other affiliate, but such "sweetheart" arrangements are suspect and of doubtful legality. In general, licenses between related companies should be handled in the same way as those between unrelated companies unless the author agrees otherwise in advance.

4.115 **Permissions.** Finally, there is a broad catchall category generally called "permissions." Although the granting of permission is technically just another form of licensing, it is generally thought of as a separate activity. Unlike the subsidiary-rights licensing discussed in 4.112 and 4.113, it does not involve dividing up markets or conveying a right to a third party who will exploit the work as such commercially. Rather, it includes such things as granting permission to an author to quote material or reproduce an image beyond what fair use would allow, or authorizing a university to include a book chapter or other such material in a digital course pack or learning management system. As these examples suggest, permissions fees are typically modest, and transactions are typically nonrecurring and always nonexclusive.

# II

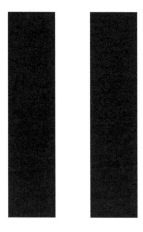

# Style and Usage

# 5 Grammar and Usage

*Bryan A. Garner*

# GRAMMAR

## *Introduction*

5.1 **The field of grammar.** In its usual sense, grammar is the set of rules (or the study of the rules) governing how words in a given language are put together to communicate ideas. Native speakers of a language learn most of the rules unconsciously—along with exceptions to the rules, which fall mostly into the category of idiom and customary usage.

5.2 **Schools of grammatical thought.** There have long been differing schools of grammatical thought—and varying vocabularies for describing grammar. So-called traditional grammar can be traced to the methods of Roman grammarians who described Latin millennia ago. Although English-language grammarians of the 1700s and 1800s sought to liberate themselves from these methods, the old nomenclature continued to channel their thinking. The twentieth century saw the rise of structuralists and transformational grammarians, and of a new language for describing language that rendered the field increasingly inaccessible to generalists. By the first quarter of the twenty-first century, a reader consulting an English grammar might encounter references to such arcane phenomena as catenatives, factives, and zero allomorphs. While recognizing the competing demands of the specialist and the generalist, this chapter avoids largely unfamiliar vocabulary in favor of older terminology to discuss the subject in a way that might helpfully inform writers and editors.

5.3 **Prescriptive versus descriptive grammar.** One axis on which grammar is often discussed has to do with prescription (how people *should* speak and write) versus description (how people *do* speak and write). Prescriptivists concern themselves with Standard English (see 5.4) and how to achieve it. Descriptivists, on the other hand, aim to depict what happens when people use language; their work thus avoids "recommended" wordings and grammatical constructions. For decades, prescriptivists accused descriptivists of adopting an "anything goes" attitude, while descriptivists attacked prescriptivists as simplistic rulemongers who ignored linguistic realities. With the recent widespread availability of empirical evidence, the better prescriptivists have acknowledged that their recommendations are merely descriptions of Standard English as evidenced in published works. Meanwhile, descriptivists, who have done much to encourage respect for dialectal language and to discourage condescension toward nonstandard varieties of English, have increasingly acknowledged that Standard English requires certain norms.

5.4 **"Standard" English.** In this chapter, the term *Standard English* (which includes speech) or *Standard Written English* (which doesn't) refers to the form of English traditionally taught in schools and most widely used for communication among English users outside their dialectal communities. Learning and using Standard English does not mean rejecting one's origins or one's native dialect; most people shift between differing varieties of language according to social context. But it does expand one's ability to communicate clearly across communities. Because there are hundreds of English dialects, each with its own rules for grammar, punctuation, and pronunciation, this chapter is limited to Standard English. When a usage is judged here to be not preferred or nonstandard or the like, it means only that the usage does not comport with Standard English.

5.5 **Parts of speech.** As traditionally understood, grammar is both a science and an art. Often it has focused—as it does here—on parts of speech and their syntax. Each part of speech performs a particular function in a sentence or phrase. Traditional grammar has held that there are eight parts of speech: nouns, pronouns, adjectives, verbs, adverbs, prepositions, conjunctions, and interjections.[1] Somewhat surprisingly, modern grammarians cannot agree on precisely how many parts of speech there are in English. At least one grammarian says there are as few as three.[2] Another insists that there are "about fifteen," noting that "the precise number is still being debated."[3] Still another puts the number at nine—combining nouns and pronouns but adding "determinatives" and subdividing conjunctions into "subordinators" and "coordinators."[4] This section deals with the traditional eight, each being treated in turn. The purpose here is to sketch the main lines of English grammar using the most widely known and accepted terminology.

## *Nouns*

### TRADITIONAL CLASSIFICATIONS

5.6 **Nouns generally.** A noun is a word that names something, whether abstract (intangible) or concrete (tangible). It may be a common noun (the

---

1. See Bryan A. Garner, *Taming the Tongue in the Heyday of English Grammar (1711–1851)* (Grolier Club, 2021), 183–87 (describing the complicated history of the subject).
2. Ernest W. Gray, *A Brief Grammar of Modern Written English* (World, 1967), 70.
3. R. L. Trask, *Language: The Basics* (Routledge, 1995), 37.
4. Rodney Huddleston et al., *A Student's Introduction to English Grammar* (Cambridge University Press, 2022), 22 (preferring the term *lexical category* to *part of speech*).

name of a generic class or type of person, place, thing, process, activity, or condition) or a proper noun (the name of a specific person, place, or thing—hence capitalized). A concrete noun may be a count noun (if what it names can be counted—as with *horses* or *cars*) or a mass noun (if what it names is uncountable or collective—as with *information* or *salt*).

5.7 **Common nouns.** A common noun is the generic name of one item in a class or group {a chemical} {a river} {a pineapple}. It is not capitalized unless it begins a sentence or appears in a title. A common noun is usually used with a determiner—that is, an article or other word (e.g., *some*, *few*) that indicates the number and definiteness of the noun element {a loaf} {the day} {some person}. Common nouns may be analyzed into three subcategories: concrete nouns, abstract nouns, and collective nouns. A concrete noun denotes something solid or real; it indicates something perceptible to the physical senses {a building} {the wind} {honey}. An abstract noun denotes something you cannot physically see, touch, taste, hear, or smell {joy} {expectation} {neurosis}. A collective noun—which can be viewed as a concrete noun but is often separately categorized—refers to a group or collection of people or things {a crowd of people} {a flock of birds} {a herd of rhinos}.

5.8 **Proper nouns.** A proper noun is the name of a specific person, place, or thing {Michelle Obama} {Moscow} {the Hope Diamond}, or the title of a work {*Citizen Kane*}. Proper nouns may be singular {Mary} {London} or plural {the Great Lakes} {the Twin Cities}. A proper noun is always capitalized, regardless of how it is used—unless someone is purposely flouting the rules {k.d. lang}. A common noun may become a proper noun {Old Hickory} {the Big Easy}, and sometimes a proper noun may be used figuratively and informally, as if it were a common noun {like Moriarty, he is a Napoleon of crime [*Napoleon* here connotes an ingenious mastermind who is ambitious beyond limits]}. Proper nouns may be compounded when used as a unit to name something {the Chatwal Hotel} {*The Saturday Evening Post*}. Over time, some proper nouns (called *eponyms*) have developed common-noun counterparts in extended senses, such as *sandwich* (from the Earl of Sandwich) and *china* (the porcelain, from the nation China). Articles and other determiners are used with proper nouns only when part of the noun is a common noun or the determiner provides emphasis {the Savoy Hotel} {Sam? I knew a Sam Hill once}.

5.9 **Mass nouns.** A mass noun (sometimes called a *noncount noun*) is one that denotes something uncountable, either because it is abstract {cowardice} {evidence} or because it refers to an aggregation of people or things taken as an indeterminate whole {luggage} {the bourgeoisie}. The key difference between mass nouns and collective nouns is that unlike collective nouns (which are count nouns), mass nouns almost never take indefinite articles and typically do not have plural forms (*a team*, but not *an evidence*; *two groups*, but not *two luggages*). A mass noun can stand alone {**music is** more popular than ever} or with a determiner other than an indefinite article (*some* music or *the* music but generally not *a* music). As the subject of a sentence, a mass noun typically takes a singular verb and pronoun {the **litigation is** so varied that **it** defies simple explanation}. Some mass nouns, however, are plural in form but are treated as grammatically singular {politics} {ethics} {physics} {news}. Others are always grammatically plural {manners} {scissors} {clothes}. But just as singular mass nouns don't take an indefinite article, plural mass nouns don't combine with numbers: You'd never say *three scissors* or *six manners*. Some that refer to concrete objects, such as *scissors* or *sunglasses*, can be enumerated by adding *pair of* {**a pair of** scissors} {**three pairs of** sunglasses}. Likewise, singular concrete mass nouns can usually be enumerated by adding a unit noun such as *piece* (with *of*) {**a piece of** cutlery} {**seven pieces of** stationery}. Both singular and plural mass nouns can take indefinite adjectives such as *any*, *less*, *much*, and *some* that express general quantity {what you need is **some courage**} {he doesn't have **any manners**}.

## PROPERTIES OF NOUNS

5.10 **Properties of nouns.** Nouns have properties of case and number. Some traditional grammarians also consider gender and person to be properties of nouns.

5.11 **Noun case.** In English, only nouns and pronouns have case. *Case* denotes the relationship between a noun (or pronoun) and other words in a sentence. Grammarians disagree about the number of cases English nouns possess. Those who consider inflection (word form) the defining characteristic tend to say that there are two: common, which is the uninflected form, and genitive (or *possessive*), which is formed by adding -*'s* or just an apostrophe. But others argue that it's useful to distinguish how the common-case noun is being used in the sentence, whether it is playing a nominative role {the doctor is in} or an objective role {go see the doctor}. They also argue that the label we put on nouns according to their function should match those we use for *who* and for personal pronouns, most of which do change form in the nominative and objective cases (*who/whom*, *she/her*, etc.). See also 5.19–25.

5.12 **Noun number.** Number shows whether one object or more than one object is referred to, as with *clock* (singular) and *clocks* (plural).

5.13 **Noun gender.** English nouns have no true gender, as that property is understood in linguistics. For example, whether a noun refers to a masculine or feminine person or thing does not determine the form of the accompanying article as it does in French, German, Spanish, and many other languages. Some English words—almost exclusively nouns denoting people or animals—are inherently masculine {uncle} {rooster} {lad} or feminine {aunt} {hen} {lass} and take the corresponding pronouns, which do have grammatical gender (see 5.46). But most English nouns are common in gender and may refer to either sex {relative} {chicken} {child}. Many words once considered strictly masculine—especially words associated with jobs and professions—have been accepted as common (or *indefinite*) in gender over time {author} {executor} {proprietor}. Similarly, many forms made feminine by the addition of a suffix {aviatrix} {poetess} have been essentially abandoned. See 5.255–67.

5.14 **Noun person.** A few grammarians attribute the property of person to nouns, distinguishing first person {I, Dan Walls, do swear that . . .}, second person {you, the professor, are key}, and third person {she, the arbiter, decides}. While those examples all use nouns in apposition to pronouns, that's not closely relevant to the question whether the nouns themselves have the property of person in any grammatical sense. But using that property in analyzing nouns does help to point out three things. First, as with grammatical case, one argument for the property of person is to keep the properties of nouns parallel to those of pronouns, even though English nouns do not change form in first, second, or third person as personal pronouns do. Second, person determines what form other words will take—here, the verbs. Third, the examples illustrate why attributing person to nouns requires a stretch of logic—if the pronouns were not present in the first two examples, the verb would be in the third person, even if Dan Walls were talking about himself and even if the speaker were addressing the professor.

## PLURALS

5.15 **Plurals generally.** Because exceptions abound, a good dictionary or usage guide is essential for checking the standard plural form of a noun. But there are some basic rules for forming plurals, some of which are covered in chapter 7 (see 7.5–15). A few matters of agreement are treated in the paragraphs that follow.

5.16 **Plural form with singular sense.** Some nouns are plural in form but singular in use and meaning {good **news is** always welcome} {**economics is** a challenging subject} {**measles is** potentially deadly}. Also, a plural word used as a word is treated as a singular {**"mice" is** the plural of "mouse"} {**"sistren" is** an archaic plural}. Some traditional plurals, such as *data* and (to a lesser extent) *media*, have gradually acquired a mass-noun sense and are increasingly treated as singular. Although traditionalists often stick to the plural uses {the **data are** inconclusive} {the **media are** largely misreporting the event}, the new singular uses—using the terms in a collective sense rather than as count nouns—exist alongside the older ones {the **data shows** the hypothesis to be correct} {the **media isn't** infallible}. (In the sciences, *data* is always plural.) In formal contexts, the most reliable approach is to retain the plural uses unless doing so makes you feel as if you're being artificial, stuffy, and pedantic. Consider using alternative words, such as *information* and *journalists*, or simply choose the newer usage. But make your play and be consistent.

5.17 **Plural-form proper nouns.** A plural geographic name is often treated as singular when the name refers to a single entity {the **United States is** a relatively young nation} {the **United Arab Emirates** favors the measures}. But there are many exceptions {the **Alps have** never been totally impassable}. Names of companies, institutions, and similar entities are generally treated as collective nouns—and hence singular in American English, even when they are plural in form {**General Motors reports** that it will earn a profit} {**American Airlines has** moved its headquarters}. In British English, however, singular nouns that refer to teams or other groups of individuals acting in concert typically take plural verbs {**Manchester United have** won the FA Cup} {**England are** now leading in World Cup standings}.

5.18 **Anomalies of the plural.** Not all English nouns show the usual singular-plural dichotomy. For example, mass nouns such as *furniture*, *spaghetti*, and *wheat* have only a singular form, and *oats*, *scissors*, and *slacks* (= pants) exist only as plurals. Some nouns look singular but are invariably plural {the **police were** just around the corner} {the **vermin seem** impossible to eradicate}. Many collective nouns that are normally singular in American English are treated in British English as plural {the **committee are** discussing the report they received} {the **government are** certain they need to encourage educational improvement} (see 5.7). Others look plural but are invariably singular {the **news is** good} {**linguistics is** my major}. Strangely enough, *person* forms two plurals—*persons* and *people*—but *people* also forms the plural *peoples* {the **peoples** of the world}.

CASE

5.19 **Function of case.** *Case* denotes the relationship between a noun or pronoun and other words in a sentence.

5.20 **Common case, nominative function.** The nominative (sometimes called the *subjective*) function denotes the person, place, or thing about which an assertion in a clause is made {the **governor** delivered a speech [*governor* is the subject]} {the **shops** are crowded because the holiday **season** has begun [*shops* and *season* are the subjects of their respective clauses]}. A noun serving a nominative function controls the verb and usually precedes it {the **troops** retreated in winter [*troops* is the subject]}, but through inversion it can appear almost anywhere in the sentence {high up in the tree sat a **leopard** [*leopard* is the subject]}. A noun or pronoun that follows a *be*-verb and refers to the same thing as the subject is called a *predicate nominative* {my show dogs are **Australian shepherds** [*Australian shepherds* is a predicate nominative]}. Generally, a sentence's predicate is the part that contains a verb and makes an assertion about the subject.

5.21 **Common case, objective function.** The objective (sometimes called the *accusative*) function denotes either (1) the person or thing acted on by a transitive verb in the active voice {the balloon carried a **pilot** and a **passenger** [*pilot* and *passenger* are objective: the direct objects of the verb *carried*]} or (2) the person or thing related to another element by a connective, such as a preposition {place the slide **under** the **microscope** [*microscope* is objective: the object of the preposition *under*]}. A noun in an objective function usually follows the verb {the queen consulted the **prime minister** [*queen* is nominative and *prime minister* is objective]}. But with an inverted construction, the object can appear elsewhere in the sentence {everything else was returned; the **jewelry** the **thieves** had already sold [*jewelry* is objective and *thieves* is nominative]}. A noun serving an objective function is never the subject of a following verb and usually does not control the number of the verb {an assembly of **strangers** was outside [the plural noun *strangers* is the object of the preposition *of*; the singular noun *assembly* is the subject of the sentence, so the verb *was* must also be singular]}.

5.22 **Genitive case.** The genitive case denotes (1) ownership, possession, or occupancy {the **architect's** drawing board} {**Arnie's** room}; (2) a relationship {the **philanthropist's** secretary}; (3) agency {the **company's** representative}; (4) description {a **summer's** day}; (5) the role of a subject {the **boy's** application [the boy applied]}; (6) the role of an object {the

**prisoner's** release [someone released the prisoner]}; or (7) an idiomatic shorthand form of an *of*-phrase {**one hour's** delay [equal to *a delay of one hour*]}. The genitive case is also called the *possessive case*, but *possessive* is a misleadingly narrow term, given the seven different functions of this case—true possession, as ordinarily understood, being only one. For instance, the fourth function above is often called the descriptive possessive. This is a misnomer, however, because the form doesn't express actual possession but instead indicates that the noun is functioning as a descriptive adjective. The genitive is formed in different ways, depending on the noun or nouns and their use in a sentence. The genitive of a singular noun is formed by adding *-'s* {**driver's** seat} {**engineer's** opinion}. The genitive of a plural noun that ends in *-s* or *-es* is formed by adding an apostrophe {**parents'** house} {**foxes'** den}. The genitive of an irregular plural noun is formed by adding *-'s* {**women's** rights} {**mice's** cage}. The genitive of a compound noun is formed by adding the appropriate ending to the last word in the compound {**parents-in-law's** message}. All these *-'s* and *-s'* endings are called *inflected genitives*. See also 7.16–29.

5.23 **The "of"-genitive.** The preposition *of* may precede a noun or proper name to express relationship, agency, or possession. The choice between an inflected genitive and an *of*-construction depends mostly on style. Proper nouns and nouns denoting people or things of higher status usually take the inflected genitive {**Hilda's** adventures} {the **lion's** paw}. Nouns denoting inanimate things can often readily take either the inflected form or the *of*-genitive {the **theater's** name} {the name **of the theater**}, but some sound right only in the *of*-genitive {the end **of everything**}. The *of*-genitive is also useful when a double genitive is called for—using both *of* and a possessive form {an idea **of Hill's**} {a friend **of my grandfather's**} (see also 7.26).

5.24 **Joint and separate genitives.** If two or more nouns share possession, the last noun takes the genitive ending. (This is called *joint* or *group possession*.) For example, *Peter and Harriet's correspondence* refers to the correspondence between Peter and Harriet. If two or more nouns possess something separately, each noun takes its own genitive ending. For example, *Peter's and Harriet's correspondence* refers to Peter's correspondence and also to Harriet's correspondence, presumably with other people. Joint possession is shown by a single apostrophe plus *-s* only when two nouns are used. If a noun and a pronoun are used to express joint possession, both the noun and the pronoun must show possession. For example, *Hilda and Eddie's vacation* becomes (when Eddie has already been mentioned) *Hilda's and his vacation* or (if Eddie is speaking in first person) *Hilda's and my vacation*.

5.25 **Distributive possessives.** When the individuals comprised in a plural noun each possess something, the object is generally also plural {**my parents** bobbed **their heads** in time with the music}. When the plural subject possesses one or more items jointly, then the object is singular {**the coauthors** discussed **their plan** for a second book}. If using a plural object might cause ambiguity, make the object singular instead. Compare *participants had to wear their watches during the test* (did each participant need more than one?) with *participants had to wear a watch during the test* (each participant needed one watch). Use a singular object when it is something that all or most of the individuals in the plural subject would collectively own or experience {**the students** expressed **their relief** after the test}.

## APPOSITIVES

5.26 **Appositives—definition and use.** An appositive is a noun element that immediately follows another noun element in order to define or further identify it {George Washington, **the first US president**, was born in Virginia [*the first US president* is an appositive of the proper noun *George Washington*]}. An appositive is said to be "in apposition" with the word or phrase to which it refers. Commas frame an appositive unless it is restrictive {Robert Burns, **the poet**, wrote many songs about women named Mary [here, *poet* is a nonrestrictive appositive noun]} {the poet **Robert Burns** wrote many songs about women named Mary [*Robert Burns* restricts *poet* by precisely identifying which poet]}. A restrictive appositive cannot be removed from a sentence without obscuring the identity of the word or phrase that the appositive relates to. See also 6.30.

## FUNCTIONAL VARIATIONS

5.27 **Nouns as adjectives.** Words that are ordinarily nouns sometimes function as other parts of speech, such as adjectives or verbs. A noun-to-adjective transition takes place when a noun modifies another noun {the **morning** newspaper} {a **state** legislature} {a **varsity** sport} (*morning, state,* and *varsity* function as adjectives). These are also termed *attributive nouns*. Note that they are typically singular in form (*car dealership,* not *cars dealership*). Occasionally the use of a noun as an adjective can produce ambiguity. For example, the phrase *fast results* can be read as meaning either "rapid results" or (less probably but possibly) "the outcome of a fast." Sometimes a noun and its adjectival form can be used interchangeably—e.g., *prostate cancer* and *prostatic cancer* both refer to cancer of the prostate gland. But sometimes the use of the noun instead of the adjective may alter the meaning—e.g., *a study group* is not necessarily *a studious group*. A preposition may be needed to indicate a noun's relationship to other sentence elements. But if the noun functions as an adjective, the preposition must be omitted; at times this can result in a vague phrase—e.g., *voter awareness* (awareness *of* voters or *by* them?). Context might suggest what preposition is implied, but a reader may have to deduce the writer's meaning.

5.28 **Nouns as verbs.** English nouns commonly pass into use as verbs; it has always been so. (Thc resulting verbs are called *denominal verbs*.) For example, in 1220 the noun *husband* meant "one who tills and cultivates the earth" {**the husband** has worked hard to produce this crop}. It became a verb meaning "to till, cultivate, and tend crops" around 1420 {you **must husband** your land thoughtfully}. New noun-to-verb transitions often occur in dialect or jargon. For example, the noun *mainstream* is used as a verb in passages such as *more school districts are mainstreaming pupils with special needs*. In formal prose, such recently transformed words should be used cautiously if at all.

5.29 **Adverbial functions.** Terms that are ordinarily nouns or noun phrases occasionally function as adverbs {we rode **single file**} {Sam walked **home**}. This shift usually happens when a preposition is omitted {we rode **in a single file**} {Sam walked **to his home**}. Traditional grammarians have typically called such nouns-as-adverbs *adverbial objectives*. An adverbial objective often modifies an adjective rather than a verb {the team is **four members** strong}.

## *Pronouns*

### DEFINITION AND USES

5.30 **Pronouns defined.** A pronoun is a word used as a substitute for a noun or, sometimes, another pronoun. It is used in one of two ways. (1) A pronoun may substitute for an expressed noun or pronoun, especially to avoid needless repetition. For example, most of the nouns in the sentence *The father told the father's daughter that the father wanted the father's daughter to walk the dog* can be replaced with pronouns (*his*, *he*, and *her*): *The father told his daughter that he wanted her to walk the dog*. (2) A pronoun may also stand in the place of an understood noun. For example, if the person addressed has been identified elsewhere, the question

*Susan, are you bringing your boots?* can be more simply stated as *Are you bringing your boots?* And in the sentence *It is too hot*, the indefinite *it* is understood to mean *the temperature* (*of something*). There are also a few word pairs, such as *each other*, *one another*, and *no one*, that function as pronouns. These are called *phrasal pronouns*.

5.31 **Antecedents of pronouns.** A pronoun typically refers to an antecedent—that is, an earlier noun, pronoun, phrase, or clause in the same or in a previous sentence. Pronouns with antecedents are called *anaphoric pronouns*. (*Anaphora* is the use of a word or phrase to refer to or replace one used earlier.) An antecedent may be explicit or implicit, but it should be clear. Miscues and ambiguity commonly arise from (1) a missing antecedent (as in *The clown's act with his dog made it a pleasure to watch*, where *it* is intended to refer to the circus, which is not explicitly mentioned in the context); (2) multiple possible antecedents (as in *Scott visited Eric after his discharge from the army*, where it is unclear who was discharged—Eric or Scott); and (3) multiple pronouns and antecedents in the same sentence (e.g., *When the bottle is empty or the baby stops drinking, it must be sterilized with hot water or it could become ill*—where one hopes that the hot-water sterilization is for the bottle).

5.32 **Adjective as antecedent.** A pronoun normally requires a noun or another pronoun as its antecedent. Because possessives function as adjectives, some writers have argued that possessives should not serve as antecedents of pronouns used in the nominative or objective case. But compare *Mr. Blain's background qualified him for the job* with *Mr. Blain had a background that qualified him for the job*. Not only is the identity of "him" perfectly clear in either construction, but the possessive in the first—a usage blessed by respected authorities—makes for a more economical sentence.

5.33 **Pronouns without antecedents.** Some pronouns do not require antecedents. The first-person pronouns *I* and *we* (as well as *me* and *us*) stand for the speaker or a group that includes the speaker, so they almost never have an antecedent. Similarly, the second-person pronoun *you* usually needs no antecedent {are **you** leaving?}, although one is sometimes supplied in direct address {Katrina, do **you** need something?}. Expletives such as *there* and *it* (some of which are pronouns) have no antecedents {**it** is time to go} {**this** is a fine mess} (see 5.246–48). And the relative pronoun *what* and the interrogative pronouns (*who*, *which*, *what*) never take an antecedent {**who** cares what I think?}. In colloquial usage, *they* often appears without an antecedent {**they** say she's a good golfer}, though skeptical listeners and readers may want to know who "they" are.

## PROPERTIES OF PRONOUNS

5.34 **Four properties of pronouns.** A pronoun has four properties: number, person, gender, and case (see 5.19–25). A pronoun must agree with its antecedent in number, person, and gender. (This is called *pronoun–antecedent agreement.*) But only the third-person singular *he, she,* and *it* are capable of indicating all three. Some pronouns can show only number—the first-person singular and plural (*I, we*). The second-person pronoun (*you*) indicates person only: It is no longer capable, without context, of showing singular or plural, since the form is the same for both in Modern English. The same has come to be true of *they* and *them.* When *they* refers to an individual, from context it indicates third-person singular. But when *they* refers to more than one person, it functions as the traditional third-person plural. (For more on *they,* see 5.51, 5.52.) First- and third-person personal pronouns (except *it*) can show nominative and objective case (*I, me*; *we, us*; *he, him*; *she, her*; *they, them*), as can *who* and *whoever* (*who, whom*; *whoever, whomever*); possessive pronouns represent the genitive case.

5.35 **Pronoun number and antecedent.** A pronoun's number is guided by that of its antecedent or referent—that is, a singular antecedent takes a singular pronoun of the same person as the antecedent, and a plural antecedent takes a plural pronoun of the same person as the antecedent {a **book** and **its** cover} {the **dogs** and **their** owner}. A collective noun takes a singular pronoun if the members are treated as a unit {the **audience** showed **its** appreciation} but a plural if they act individually {the **audience** rushed back to **their** seats}. A singular noun that is modified by two or more adjectives to denote different varieties, uses, or aspects of the object may take a plural pronoun {**British and American writing** differ in more ways than just **their** spelling [here, *writing* may be thought of as an elided noun after *British*]}. Two or more singular nouns or pronouns that are joined by *and* are taken jointly and referred to by a plural pronoun {the **boy and girl** left **their** bicycles outside}.

5.36 **Exceptions regarding pronoun number and antecedent.** There are several refinements to the rules stated in 5.35: (1) When two or more singular antecedents denote the same thing and are connected by *and,* the pronoun referring to the antecedents is singular {a **lawyer and role model** received **her** richly deserved recognition today}. (2) When two or more singular antecedents are connected by *and* and modified by *each, every,* or *no,* the pronoun referring to the antecedents is singular {**every college and university** encourages **its** students to succeed}. (3) When two or more singular antecedents are connected by *or, nor,* *either–or*, or *neither–nor*, they are treated separately and referred to by a singular pronoun {**neither the orange nor the peach** smells as sweet as **it** should}. (4) When two or more antecedents of different numbers are connected by *or* or *nor*, the pronoun's number agrees with that of the nearest (usually the last) antecedent. If possible, cast the sentence so that the plural antecedent comes last {neither the singer nor the **dancers** have asked for **their** paychecks}. (5) When two or more antecedents of different numbers are connected by *and*, they are referred to by a plural pronoun regardless of the antecedents' order {**the horses and the mule** kicked over **their** water trough}.

5.37 **Pronoun with multiple antecedents.** When a pronoun has two or more antecedents that differ from the pronoun in person, and the antecedents are connected by *and*, *or*, or *nor*, the pronoun must take the person of only one antecedent. The first person is preferred to the second, and the second person to the third. For example, if the antecedents are in the second and first person, the pronoun that follows is in the first person {**you or I** should get to work on **our** experiment [*our* is in the first person, as is the antecedent *I*]}. If the antecedents are in the second and third person, the pronoun that follows takes the second person {**you and she** can settle **your** dispute}. If the pronoun refers to only one of the connected nouns or pronouns, it takes the person of that noun {**you and Marian** have discussed **her** trip report}. At times the pronoun may refer to an antecedent that is not expressed in the same sentence; it takes the number of that antecedent, not of any connected noun or pronoun that precedes it {**neither they nor I** could do **his** work [*his* is referring to someone named in a preceding sentence]}.

5.38 **Pronoun case.** Sets of word forms by which a language differentiates the functions that a word performs in a sentence are called the word's *cases*. A pronoun that functions as the subject of a finite verb is in the nominative case {**they** went to town}. A personal pronoun in the possessive case is governed by the gender of the possessor {President Barack Obama took **his** advisers with him to Hawaii}. A pronoun that functions as the object of a verb or preposition is in the objective case {they gave **her** a farewell party} {they gave it to **him**}. A pronoun put after an intransitive verb or participle agrees in case with the preceding noun or pronoun referring to the same thing {it is **I**} (see 5.48). A pronoun used in an absolute construction is in the nominative: Its case depends on no other word {**she** being disqualified, our best hope is gone}.

5.39 **Pronouns in apposition.** The case of a pronoun used in an appositive construction is determined by the function (subject or object) of the words with which it is in apposition {**we** three—Bruce, Felipe, and **I**—traveled to Augusta} {she asked **us**—Barbara, Sarah, and **me**—to move our cars}.

5.40 **Nominative case misused for objective.** The objective case governs personal pronouns used as direct objects of verbs {call **me** tomorrow}, indirect objects of verbs {write **me** a letter}, or objects of prepositions {makes sense to **me**}. One of the most persistent departures from Standard English is to misuse the nominative case of a personal pronoun in a compound object:

NONSTANDARD: The test would be simple for **you or I**.
STANDARD: The test would be simple for **you or me**.

NONSTANDARD: Read this and tell **Laura and I** what you think.
STANDARD: Read this and tell **Laura and me** what you think.

The mistake may arise from overcorrecting another common error—using the objective case for a personal pronoun in a compound subject, as in *Jim and me want to go swimming*. A foolproof way to check for such problems is to eliminate the compound and read the sentence with the personal pronoun alone: *Read this and tell I what you think* and *Me want to go swimming* are more obviously incorrect.

## CLASSES OF PRONOUNS

5.41 **Seven classes of pronouns.** There are seven classes of pronouns (the examples listed here do not include all forms of each):

personal (*I*, *you*, *he*, *she*, *it*, *we*, and *they*);
demonstrative (*that* and *this*);
reciprocal (*each other* and *one another*);
interrogative (*what*, *which*, and *who*);
relative (*that*, *what*, *which*, and *who*);
indefinite (*another*, *any*, *each*, *either*, and *none*); and
adjective (*any*, *each*, *that*, *this*, *what*, and *which*).

Many pronouns, except personal pronouns, may function as more than one type—e.g., *that* may be a demonstrative, relative, or adjective pronoun—depending on its use in a particular sentence.

PERSONAL PRONOUNS

5.42 **Form of personal pronouns.** A personal pronoun shows by its form whether it is referring to the speaker (first person), the person or thing spoken to (second person), or the person or thing spoken of (third person). Personal pronouns, in other words, convey the source, goal, and topic of an utterance. By their form they also display number, gender, and case.

5.43 **Identification of personal pronouns.** The first person is the speaker or speakers {**I** need some tea} {**we** heard the news}. The second person shows who is spoken to {**you** should write that essay tonight}. And the third person shows who or what is spoken of {**she** is at work} {**it** is in the glove compartment} {**they** are the teacher of my first-year class} (on this singular use of *they*, see 5.34, 5.52). The first-person-singular pronoun *I* is always capitalized no matter where it appears in the sentence {if possible, **I** will send you an answer today}. All other pronouns are capitalized only at the beginning of a sentence, unless they are part of an honorific title {**His** Majesty, the King of England}.

5.44 **Changes in form of personal pronouns.** Personal pronouns change form (or *decline*) according to person, number, and case. Most personal pronouns show number by taking a singular or plural form. Although the second-person *you* and third-person *they* can be singular as well as plural in sense, these pronouns always take a plural verb, even if only a single person or thing is addressed.

THE FORMS OF PERSONAL PRONOUNS

*Singular pronouns*

| | *Nominative* | *Objective* | *Genitive* | *Reflexive* |
|---|---|---|---|---|
| *First person* | I | me | my, mine | myself |
| *Second person* | you | you | your, yours | yourself |
| *Third person* | he | him | his | himself |
| | she | her | her, hers | herself |
| | it | it | its | itself |
| | they[5] | them | their, theirs | themself, themselves |

5. Now used to refer to a nonbinary person or, in some circumstances, someone whose gender is unknown or unimportant (see 5.51, 5.52).

*Plural pronouns*

| | *Nominative* | *Objective* | *Genitive* | *Reflexive* |
|---|---|---|---|---|
| *First person* | we | us | our, ours | ourselves |
| *Second person* | you | you | your, yours | yourselves |
| *Third person* | they | them | their, theirs | themselves |

There are four essential rules about the nominative and objective cases. (1) If the pronoun is the subject of a clause, it is in the nominative case {**he** is vice president}. (2) If the pronoun is the object of a verb, it is objective {she thanked **him**}. (3) If a pronoun is the object of a preposition, it is objective {please keep this between **you** and **me**}. (4) If the pronoun is the subject of an infinitive, it is objective {Jim wanted **them** to sing}.

5.45 **Agreement of personal pronoun with noun.** When a noun has both gender and number, a personal pronoun agrees with the gender and number of the noun for which it stands {**John** writes, and **he** will soon write well} {**Sheila** was there, but **she** couldn't hear what was said} {**the pilot** was highly skilled; **they** flew the jet safely despite a storm} {**the dog** growled; **it** wouldn't come when called}. See also 5.51, 5.52.

5.46 **Personal pronouns and gender.** Only the third-person-singular pronouns *he*, *she*, and *it* directly express gender (masculine, feminine, or neuter). In the nominative or objective case, the pronoun takes the antecedent noun's gender {the president is not in **her** office today; **she's** at a seminar}. In the genitive case, the pronoun always takes the gender of the possessor, not of the person or thing possessed {the woman loves **her** spouse} {Thomas is visiting **his** sister} {the kitten pounced on **its** mother}. The singular *they* formerly referred only to a human whose gender was unknown or unimportant {**they** left **their** test paper on the desk}—and even then was often regarded as nonstandard. Today it is commonly used in reference to a nonbinary person {despite being the sole proponent, **they** stood by **their** idea}. See 5.51, 5.52. Some nouns may acquire gender through personification, a figure of speech that refers to a nonliving thing as if it were a person. Pronouns enhance personification when a gendered pronoun is used as if the antecedent represented a female or male person (as was traditionally done, for example, when a ship or other vessel was referred to with the pronoun *she* or *her*).

5.47 **Personal pronoun case.** Some special rules apply to personal pronouns. (1) If a pronoun is the subject of a clause, or follows a conjunction but precedes the verb, it must be in the nominative case {**she** owns a tan briefcase} {although Delia would like to travel, **she** can't afford to}. (2) If a pronoun is the object of a verb or preposition, it must be in the objective case {the rustic setting helped **him** relax} {that's a matter between **him** and **her**}. (3) If a prepositional phrase contains more than one object, all the objects must be in the objective case {will you send an invitation to **him** and **me**?}. (4) If a pronoun is the subject of an infinitive, it must be in the objective case {does Tina want **me** to leave?}.

5.48 **Personal pronoun after linking verb.** Strictly speaking, a pronoun serving as the complement of a *be*-verb or other linking verb should be in the nominative case {it was **she** who asked for a meeting}. When a pronoun functions as a predicate nominative, as in that example, it is termed an *attribute pronoun*. The same construction occurs when someone who answers a telephone call is asked, "May I speak to [answerer's name]?" The refined response is *This is he*, not *This is him*.

5.49 **Personal pronoun after "than" or "as – as."** The case of a pronoun following a comparative construction, typically at the end of a sentence, can depend on who or what is being compared. In *My sister looks more like our father than I* [or *me*], for example, the proper pronoun depends on the meaning. If the question is whether the sister or the speaker looks more like their father, the pronoun should be nominative because it is the subject of an understood verb {my sister looks more like our father **than I do**}. But if the question is whether the father or the speaker looks more like the sister, the pronoun should be objective because it is the object of a preposition in an understood clause {my sister looks more like my father **than she looks like me**}. Whatever the writer's intent with the original sentence, and regardless of the pronoun used, the listener or reader can't be entirely certain about the meaning. It would be better to reword the sentence and avoid the elliptical construction. With an *as . . . as* construction, such a dual meaning doesn't typically arise. Instead, it's a matter of register—formal {you're just as nervous **as I** [**am**]} or informal {you're just as nervous **as me**}. The same issue arises with *than*.

5.50 **Special uses of personal pronouns.** Some personal pronouns have special uses. (1) *He, him,* and *his* have traditionally been used as pronouns of indeterminate gender equally applicable to a male or female person {if the finder returns my watch, **he** will receive a reward}. Because these pronouns are also masculine-specific, they have been criticized as sexist when used generically, and such uses are declining (see 5.255–67). (2) The neuter *it* eliminates gender considerations even if the noun's sex could be identified. Using *it* does not mean that the noun has no sex—only that the sex is unknown or unimportant {the baby is smiling at

**its** mother} {the mockingbird is building **its** nest}. (3) *We*, *you*, and *they* can be used indefinitely—that is, without an antecedent—in the sense of "persons," "one," or "people in general." *We* is sometimes used by an individual who is speaking for a group {the council's representative declared, "**We** appreciate your concern"} {the magazine's editor wrote, "In our last issue, **we** covered the archaeological survey of Peru"}. This latter use is called "the editorial *we*." Some writers also use *we* to make their prose appear less personal and to draw in the reader or listener {from these results **we** can draw only one conclusion}. *We* and *you* can also be used before nouns in the manner of articles or limiting adjectives {**we socialists** reject that} {they look down on **us students**} {it's all right for **you rich people**}. *You* can apply indefinitely to any person or all persons {if **you** read this book, **you** will learn how to influence people}. The same is true of *they* {**they** say that Stonehenge may have been a primitive calendar [those denoted by *they* are unidentified and perhaps unimportant to the point]}. (4) *It* also has several uses as an indefinite pronoun: (a) *it* may refer to a phrase, clause, sentence, or implied thought {he said that the website is down, but I don't believe **it** [that is, *I don't believe what he said*]}; (b) *it* can be the subject of a verb (usually a *be*-verb) without an antecedent noun {**it** was too far}, or an introductory word or expletive for a phrase or clause that follows the verb {**it** is possible that Jerry Paul is on vacation}; (c) *it* can be the grammatical subject in an expression about time, weather, distance, or the like {**it** is almost midnight} {**it** is beginning to snow}; and (d) *it* may be an expletive that anticipates the true grammatical subject or object {I find **it** hard to accept this situation}.

5.51 **Generic singular "they."** Traditionally, a singular antecedent requires a singular pronoun. But even before the movement away from *he*, *him*, *his*, and *himself* as generic pronouns referring to a person of unspecified gender, people had long substituted the third-person-plural pronouns *they*, *them*, *their*, and *themselves* (or possibly *themself*) as generic singular forms—especially in speech and informal prose {somebody forgot **their** coat}. In recent years this usage has become accepted in more formal contexts (see also 5.266), and Chicago now endorses it. See also 5.52.

5.52 **Referential singular "they."** *They* and its forms have emerged as the most common alternatives to *he* and *she* for referring to people who do not identify with gender-specific pronouns. *They* has followed the pattern of *you*, which is well established as both a singular and a plural. Singular *they* is construed with a plural verb even when denoting one person {**they** have a certificate in culinary arts}. And *themself* (like *yourself*) may be used to signal the singular antecedent when it appears to be the logical choice (though some people will prefer *themselves*) {they blamed **themself** [or *themselves*]}. If an individual is known to use *they* and its forms as their personal pronouns rather than the gendered *he* or *she*, this usage should be respected. Some people use neopronouns such as *ze/zir/zirs/zirself*; unlike singular *they*, such pronouns generally take singular verbs.

## POSSESSIVE PRONOUNS

5.53 **Uses and forms of possessive pronouns.** The possessive pronouns, *my, our, your, his, her, its,* and *their*, are used as limiting adjectives to qualify nouns {**my** dictionary} {**your** cabin} {**his** diploma}. Despite their name, possessive pronouns function in a much broader series of relationships than mere possession {my professor} {your argument}. Each form has a corresponding absolute possessive pronoun (also called an *independent possessive*) that can stand alone without a noun: *mine, ours, yours, his, hers, its,* and *theirs*. The independent form does not require an explicit object: The thing possessed may be either an antecedent or something understood {this dictionary is **mine**} {this cabin of **yours** is nice} {where is **hers**?}. An independent possessive pronoun can also stand alone and be treated as a noun: It can be the subject or object of a verb {**hers** is on the table} {pass me **yours**}, or the object of a preposition {put your coat with **theirs**}. When it is used with the preposition *of*, a double possessive is produced: *That letter of Sheila's* becomes *that letter of hers*. Such a construction is unobjectionable. Note that none of the possessive personal pronouns is spelled with an apostrophe.

5.54 **Possessive pronouns versus contractions.** The possessive forms of personal pronouns are *my, mine, our, ours, your, yours, his, her, hers, its,* and *their, theirs*. Again, none of them takes an apostrophe. Nor does the possessive form of *who* (*whose*). Apart from these exceptions, the apostrophe is a universal signal of the possessive in English, so it is a natural tendency (and a common error) to overlook the exceptions and insert an apostrophe in the pronoun forms that end in *-s* (or the sibilant *-se*). Aggravating that tendency is the fact that some of the words have homophones that are contractions—another form that is signaled by apostrophes. The pronouns that don't sound like legitimate contractions seldom present problems, even if they do end in *-s* (*hers, yours, ours*). But several do require special attention, specifically *its* (the possessive of *it*) and *it's* ("it is"); *your* (the possessive of *you*) and *you're* ("you are"); *whose* (the possessive of *who*) and *who's* ("who is"); and the three homophones *their* (the possessive of *they*), *there* ("in that place" or "in that way"), and *they're* ("they are").

### REFLEXIVE AND INTENSIVE PRONOUNS

5.55 **Basic uses of reflexive and intensive pronouns.** The words *myself, ourselves, yourself, yourselves, himself, herself, themselves, themself,* and *itself* are used in two ways, and it's useful to distinguish between their functions as reflexive and intensive personal pronouns. Compare the intensive pronoun in *I burned the papers myself* (in which the object of *burned* is *papers*) with the reflexive pronoun in *I burned myself* (in which the object of *burned* is *myself*). Reflexive pronouns serve as objects that usually look back to the subject of a sentence or clause {the cat **scared itself**} {Gayla took it **on herself** to make the first move} {Haru cooked **for themself** today} {don't **repeat yourself** [the subject of this imperative sentence is understood to be *you*]}. Intensive pronouns are appositives that repeat the antecedent noun or pronoun to add emphasis {**I myself** don't care} {did you speak with the **manager herself**?} {**Kate herself** has won several writing awards} {did **you** knit that **yourself**?}. A common problem occurs when the *-self* form does not serve either of those functions. For example, the first-person pronoun in a compound might be used as a subject:

NONSTANDARD: **The staff and myself** thank you for your contribution.
STANDARD: **The staff and I** thank you for your contribution.

Or it might be used as an object that does not refer to the subject:

NONSTANDARD: Deliver the equipment to **my partner or myself**.
STANDARD: Deliver the equipment to **my partner or me**.

### DEMONSTRATIVE PRONOUNS

5.56 **Demonstrative pronouns defined.** A demonstrative pronoun (or, as it is sometimes called, a *deictic pronoun*) is one that points directly to its antecedent in the text: *this* or *that* for a singular antecedent {**this** is your desk} {**that** is my office}, and *these* or *those* for a plural antecedent {**these** have just arrived} {**those** need to be answered}. *This* and *these* point to objects that are near in space, time, or thought, while *that* and *those* point to objects that are somewhat remote in space, time, or thought. The antecedent of a demonstrative pronoun can be a noun, phrase, clause, sentence, or implied thought, as long as the antecedent is clear. *Kind* and *sort*, each referring to "one class," are often used with an adjectival *this* or *that* {**this kind** of magazine} {**that sort** of school}. The plural forms *kinds* and *sorts* are usually preferred with the plural demonstratives {**these kinds** of magazines} {**those sorts** of schools}. A demonstrative pronoun standing alone cannot refer to a human antecedent; it must be followed by a word denoting a person. For example: *I heard Mike's son playing. That child is talented.* In the second sentence, it would be erroneous to omit *child* or some such noun after *that*.

### RECIPROCAL PRONOUNS

5.57 **Reciprocal pronouns generally.** *Each other* and *one another* are called *reciprocal pronouns* because they express a mutual relationship between elements {after much discussion, the two finally understood each other} {all of us here love one another}. Compare the nuances of meaning that a reciprocal or plural reflexive pronoun creates in the same sentence: {after our hike, we all checked ourselves for ticks [each person inspected themself]} {after our hike, we checked one another for ticks [each person inspected one or more of the others]}. Reciprocal pronouns can also take the inflected genitive *-'s* to express possession {we all admired one another's watches}. Although the distinction has never been universally observed, careful writers and editors tend to reserve *each other* for two {she and I protected each other} and *one another* for more than two {all five of us watched out for one another}.

### INTERROGATIVE PRONOUNS

5.58 **Interrogative pronouns defined.** An interrogative pronoun asks a question. The three interrogatives are *who, what,* and *which*. Only one, *who*, declines: *who* (nominative), *whom* (objective), *whose* (possessive) {**who** starred in *Casablanca*?} {to **whom** am I speaking?} {**whose** cologne smells so nice?}. In the nominative case, *who* is used in two ways: (1) as the subject of a verb {**who** washed the dishes today?} and (2) as a predicate nominative after a linking verb {it was **who**?}. In the objective case, *whom* is used in two ways: (1) as the object of a verb {**whom** did you see?} and (2) as the object of a preposition {for **whom** is this building named?}. See 5.70.

5.59 **Referent of interrogative pronouns.** To refer to a person, *who, what,* or *which* can be used. But they are not interchangeable. *Who* is universal or general: It asks for any one or more persons among a universe of people. The answer may potentially include any person, living or dead, present or absent {**who** wants to see that movie?} {**who** were your greatest inspirations?}. *Who* also asks for a particular person's identity {**who** is that person standing near the Emerald Buddha?}. *Which* and *what,* when followed by a noun denoting a person or persons, are usually selective or limited; they ask for a particular member of a group, and the answer is limited to the group addressed or referred to {**which** explorers visited China in the sixteenth century?} {**what** ice-skater is your favorite?}. To refer to a person, animal, or thing, either *which* or *what* may be used {**which** one of you did this?} {**what** kind of bird is that?}. When applied to a person, *what* often asks for the person's character, occupation, qualities, and the like {**what** do you think of aged cheddar?}. When applied to a thing, *what* is broad and asks for any one thing, especially of a set {**what** is your quest?} {**what** is your favorite color?}.

## RELATIVE PRONOUNS

5.60 **Relative pronouns defined.** A relative pronoun is one that introduces a dependent (or *relative*) clause and relates it to the independent clause. Relative pronouns in common use are *who, which, what,* and *that. Who* is the only relative pronoun that declines: *who* (nominative), *whom* (objective), *whose* (possessive) {the woman **who** presented the award} {a source **whom** he declined to name} {the writer **whose** book was a best seller}. *Who* normally refers to a human being, and it can be used in the first, second, or third person. *Which* refers only to an animal or a thing. *What* refers only to a nonliving thing. *Which* and *what* are used only in the second and third person. *That* refers to a human, animal, or thing, and it can be used in the first, second, or third person. When a relative pronoun qualifies a noun element in the clause it introduces, it is sometimes called a *relative adjective*. See also 5.68, 5.233.

5.61 **Relative pronouns with personal pronouns.** A relative pronoun agrees with its antecedent in gender, person, and number. If a personal pronoun follows a relative pronoun, and both refer to the same antecedent in the independent clause, the personal pronoun takes the gender and number of that antecedent {Grady thanked the baker, **who** brought **her** signature cinnamon bread to **her** neighbors' party} (*who* and *her* refer to the baker) {we waved to Aliyah, **who** was training **their** dog to carry **their** groceries} (*who* and *their* refer to Aliyah). If the personal pronoun refers to a different antecedent from that of the relative pronoun, it takes the gender and number of that antecedent {I saw the boy and also the girl **who** pushed **him** down} {Hakeem posted a good review for the woman **who** sold **him** his new car}. A personal pronoun does not govern the case of a relative pronoun. Hence an objective pronoun such as *me* may be the antecedent of the nominative pronoun *who*, although a construction formed in this way sounds increasingly archaic or even incorrect {she was referring to me, **who** never graduated from college} {it was we **whom** they objected to}. When a construction may be technically correct but sounds awkward or artificial {I, **who** am wronged, have a grievance}, the best course may be to use preventive grammar and find a different construction {I have been wronged; I have a grievance} {having been wronged, I have a grievance}.

5.62 **Positional nuances of relative pronouns.** A relative pronoun is in the nominative case when no subject comes between it and the verb {the professor **who** lectured was brilliant}. When one or more words intervene between the relative pronoun and the verb, the relative pronoun may be governed by the following verb or by a verb or a preposition within the intervening clause {the person **whom** I called is no longer there [*whom* is the object of *called*]} {it was John **who** they thought was in the bleachers [*who* is the subject of *was*]}. When a relative pronoun is interrogative, it refers to the word or phrase containing the answer to the question for its consequent, which agrees in case with the interrogative {**whose** book is that? Joseph's}.

5.63 **Antecedent of relative pronouns.** Usually a relative pronoun's antecedent is a noun or pronoun in the independent clause on which the relative clause depends. For clarity, it should immediately precede the pronoun {the diadem **that** I told you about is in this gallery}. The antecedent may also be a noun phrase or a clause, but the result can sometimes be ambiguous: In *the bedroom of the villa, which was painted pink*, does the *which*-clause refer to the bedroom or to the villa? See 5.64.

5.64 **Remote relative clauses.** For clarity, pronouns must have unambiguous antecedents. A common problem with the relative pronouns *that*, *which*, and *who* arises if you separate the relative clause from the noun to which it refers. The longer the separation, the more pronounced the problem—especially when one or more unrelated nouns fall between the true antecedent and the clause. Consider *the guy down the street that runs through our neighborhood*: If the intent is for *that runs through our neighborhood* to refer to *the guy* rather than *the street*, the writer should reword the phrase to make that instantly clear to the reader.

AMBIGUOUS: Stress caused her to lose the **freedom** from fear, **which she once enjoyed**.

CLEAR: Stress caused her to lose **what she once enjoyed: freedom** from fear.

AMBIGUOUS: After the news came out, the CEO fired **the aide**, a friend of the president, **who was the target** of the investigation.

CLEAR: After the news came out, the CEO fired **the aide, who was the target** of the investigation and also a friend of the president.

5.65 **Omitted antecedent of relative pronoun.** If no antecedent noun is expressed, *what* can be used to mean *that which* {is this **what** you were looking for?}. But if there is an antecedent, use a different relative pronoun: *who* {where is the man **who** spoke?}, *that* (if the relative clause is restrictive, i.e., essential to the sentence's basic meaning) {where are the books **that** Jones told us about?}, or *which* (if the relative clause is nonrestrictive, i.e., could be deleted without affecting the sentence's basic meaning) {the sun, **which** is shining brightly, feels warm on my face}. See also 6.29.

5.66 **Relative pronoun and the antecedent "one."** A relative pronoun takes its number from its antecedent. That's easy enough when the antecedent is simply *one* {Lily is one who cares deeply}. But if *one* is part of a noun phrase with a plural noun such as *one of the few* or *one of those*, the relative pronoun following takes the plural word as its antecedent—not *one* {Lily is one of those people who care deeply}. Treat the pronoun as a plural and use a plural verb. The reason becomes apparent if we alter the syntax without changing the basic construction {of those people who care deeply, Lily is one}.

5.67 **Genitive forms for relative pronouns.** The forms *of whom* and *of which* are genitives {the child, the mother **of whom** we talked about, is in kindergarten} {this foal, the sire **of which** Belle owns, will be trained as a hunter-jumper}. These forms have an old-fashioned sound and can often be rephrased more naturally {the child **whose** mother we talked about is in kindergarten}. The relative *what* forms the genitive *of what* {a list **of what** we need}. The relative *that* forms the genitive *of that* (the preposition being placed at the end of the phrase) {no legend **that** we know **of**} or *of which* {no legend **of which** we know}.

5.68 **"Whose" and "of which."** The relatives *who* and *which* can both take *whose* as a possessive form (*whose* substitutes for *of which*) {a movie the conclusion **of which** is unforgettable} {a movie **whose** conclusion is unforgettable}. Some writers object to using *whose* as a replacement for *of which*, especially when the subject is not human, but the usage is centuries old and is widely accepted as preventing unnecessary awkwardness. Compare *the company whose stock rose faster* with *the company the stock of which rose faster*. Either form is acceptable, but the possessive *whose* is smoother.

5.69 **Compound relative pronouns.** *Who, whom, what,* and *which* form compound relative pronouns by adding the suffix *-ever*. The compound relatives *whoever, whomever, whichever,* and *whatever* apply universally to any or all persons or things {**whatever** you do, let me know} {**whoever** needs to write a report about this book may borrow it}.

5.70 **"Who" versus "whom."** *Who* and *whoever* are nominative pronouns. Each can be used as a subject {**whoever** said that?} or as a predicate nominative {it was **who**?}. *Whom* and *whomever* are the objective forms, used as the object of a verb {you called **whom**?} or of a preposition {to **whom** are you referring?}. Three problems arise with determining the correct case. First, because the words are so often found in the inverted syntax of an interrogative sentence, their true function in the sentence can be hard to see without sorting the words into standard subject–verb–object syntax.

NONSTANDARD: **Whom** should I say is calling?
STANDARD: **Who** should I say is calling? (*Who* is the subject of *is*.)

Rearranging the first sentence (*I should say whom is calling*) makes it easier to determine that the case is incorrect. Second, determining the proper case can be confusing when the pronoun serves a function (say, nominative) in a clause that itself serves a different function (say, objective) in the main sentence. The pronoun's function in its clause determines its case.

NONSTANDARD: I'll talk to **whomever will listen**.
STANDARD: I'll talk to **whoever will listen**.

INFORMAL: **Whoever you choose** will suit me.
FORMAL: **Whomever you choose** will suit me.

In the first example, the entire clause *whoever will listen* is the object of the preposition *to*. But in the clause itself, *whoever* serves as the subject, and that function determines its case. Similarly, in the second example *whomever* is the object of *choose* in the clause, so it technically ought to be in the objective case even though the clause itself serves as the subject of the sentence. Third, as the second example above shows, a further distraction can arise when the *who*-clause itself contains a nested clause, typically of attribution or identification (here, *you choose*). Except in the most formal prose, *whom* is more likely to appear as the object of a preposition {for **whom** is it intended} rather than as the object of a verb {you intended **whom** as the recipient?}. For more than a century, commentators have sometimes announced the demise of *whom*. But it is firmly rooted in formal English. In dialogue, though, and less formal prose, *who* is likely to displace *whom*—except after a preposition {for **whom** the bell tolls}.

### INDEFINITE PRONOUNS

5.71 **Indefinite pronouns generally.** An indefinite pronoun is one that generally or indefinitely represents an object, usually one that has already been identified or doesn't need exact identification. The most common examples are *another, any, both, each, either, neither, none, one, other, some,* and *such*. There are also compound indefinite pronouns such as *anybody, anyone, anything, everybody, everyone, everything, nobody, no one, oneself, somebody,* and *someone*. *Each, either,* and *neither* are also called *distributive pronouns* because they separate the objects referred to from others referred to nearby. Indefinite pronouns have number. When an indefinite pronoun is the subject of a verb, it is usually singular {**everyone** is enjoying the dinner} {**everybody** takes notes during the first week}. But sometimes an indefinite pronoun carries a plural sense in informal prose {**nobody** could describe the music; they hadn't been listening to it} {**everyone** understood the risk, but they were lured by promises of big returns}. The forms of indefinite pronouns are not affected by gender or person, and the nominative and objective forms are the same. To form the possessive, the indefinite pronoun may take *-'s* {that is **no one's** fault} {is this **anyone's** jacket?} or the adverb *else* plus *-'s* {don't interfere with **anybody else's** business} {**no one else's** cups were broken}.

## *Adjectives*

### TYPES OF ADJECTIVES

5.72 **Adjectives defined.** An adjective is a word (of a type sometimes called an *adjunct*) that modifies a noun or pronoun; it is often called a *de-*

*scribing word*. An adjective tells you what sort, how many, how large or small, whose, etc. It may modify an understood as well as an expressed noun {he is a **good** as well as a **wise** man [*man* is understood after *good*]}. An adjective may add a new idea to a noun or pronoun by describing it more definitely or fully {**red** wagon} {**human** error}. Or it may be limiting {**three** pigs} {**this** time}. Most adjectives derive from nouns, as *plentiful* derives from *plenty* or as *stylish* derives from *style*; some derive from verbs, roots, or other adjectives. Often a suffix creates the adjective. Among the suffixes that often distinguish adjectives are *-able* {manageable}, *-al* {mystical}, *-ary* {elementary}, *-ed* {hammered}, *-en* {wooden}, *-esque* {statuesque}, *-ful* {harmful}, *-ible* {inaccessible}, *-ic* {artistic}, *-ish* {foolish}, *-ive* {demonstrative}, *-less* {helpless}, *-like* {childlike}, *-ly* {ghostly}, *-ous* {perilous}, *-some* {lonesome}, and *-y* {sunny}. But many adjectives do not have distinctive endings and are recognizable only by their function {old} {tall} {brilliant}.

5.73 **Proper adjectives.** A proper adjective is one that, being or deriving from a proper name, always begins with a capital letter {a **New York** minute} {a **Cuban** cigar} {a **Canadian** dollar}. (But see 8.62.) A proper name used attributively is still capitalized, but it does not cause the noun it modifies to be capitalized. A place-name containing a comma—such as *Moscow, Idaho*; *New Delhi, India*; or *Washington, DC*—should generally be avoided as an adjective because a second comma may be considered obligatory {we met in a **Moscow, Idaho,** restaurant}. Substituting a prepositional phrase for the proper adjective may make the text less awkward and more readable {we met in a restaurant in **Moscow, Idaho**}. Or, if the place is well known or has already been introduced, a shorter form of the name may suffice: *a New Delhi marketplace* or *a DC office*.

## ARTICLES AS LIMITING ADJECTIVES

5.74 **Articles defined.** An article is a limiting adjective that precedes a noun or noun phrase and determines its use to indicate something definite (*the*) or indefinite (*a* or *an*). An article might stand alone or be used with other adjectives {**a** road} {**an** elaborate design} {**the** yellow-brick road}.

5.75 **Definite article.** A definite article points to a definite object that (1) is so well understood that it does not need description (e.g., *the package is here* is a shortened form of *the package that you expected is here*); (2) is a thing that is about to be described {**the** sights of Chicago}; or (3) is important {**the** grand prize}. The definite article belongs to nouns in the singular {**the** star} or the plural number {**the** stars}.

5.76 **Indefinite article.** An indefinite article points to a nonspecific object, thing, or person that is not distinguished from the other members of a class. The thing may be singular {**a** student at Princeton}, or uncountable {**a** multitude}, or generalized {**an** idea inspired by Milton's *Paradise Lost*}.

5.77 **Indefinite article in specific reference.** In a few usages, the indefinite article provides a specific reference {I saw **a great movie** last night} and the definite article a generic reference {**the Scots** are talking about independence [generalizing by nationality]}.

5.78 **Choosing "a" or "an."** With the indefinite article, the choice of *a* or *an* depends on the sound of the word it precedes. *A* precedes words with a consonant sound, including /y/, /h/, and /w/, no matter how the word is spelled {**a** eulogy} {**a** historic occasion} {**a** onetime pass}. *An* comes before words with a vowel sound {**an** insurance agent} {**an** *X-Files* episode} {**an** hour ago}. The same is true for abbreviations. If the first letter or syllable is sounded as a consonant, use *a* {**a** BTU calculation} {**a** PDF file}. If the first sound is a vowel, use *an* {**an** MBA degree} {**an** ATM}. See also 7.32–33, 10.10.

5.79 **Articles with coordinate nouns.** In a series of coordinate nouns, an article may appear before each noun, but it is not necessary when the same type of article (definite or indefinite) applies to each noun {**the rosebush and hedge** need trimming}. If the things named make up a single idea, it's especially unnecessary to repeat the article {in the highest degree of dressage, **the horse and rider** appear to be one entity}. And if the named things are covered by one plural noun, the definite article should not be repeated {in the first and second years of college}. But if you want to distinguish concepts or add emphasis, then do repeat the article {**the time**, **the money**, and **the effort** were all wasted}. For indefinite articles, you may use or omit the article before each subsequent noun {fruit salad needs an orange, a mango, and a banana} {bring a raincoat, hat, and umbrella}. In the last example, the first two items would take *a* while the last would take *an*, but only the first item need be matched with *a* or *an* {bring an umbrella, raincoat, and hat}.

5.80 **Effect of article on meaning.** Because articles have a demonstrative value, the meaning of a phrase may shift depending on the article used. For example, *an officer and gentleman escorted Princess Grace to her car* suggests (though ambiguously) that the escort was one man with two descriptive characteristics. But *an officer and a friend escorted Princess Grace to her car* suggests that two people acted as escorts. Similarly, *do* *you like the red and blue cloth?* suggests that the cloth contains both red and blue threads. But *do you like the red and the blue cloth?* suggests that two different fabrics are being discussed. The clearest way to express the idea that the cloth contains both red and blue is to hyphenate the phrase as a compound modifier: *red-and-blue cloth*; and with two kinds of cloth, the clear expression is either to repeat the word *cloth* (*the red cloth and the blue cloth*) or to use *cloth* with the first adjective rather than the second (*the red cloth and the blue*).

5.81 **Omitted article and zero article.** The absence of an article may alter a sentence's meaning—e.g., the meaning of *the news brought us little comfort* (we weren't comforted) changes if *a* is inserted before *little*: *the news brought us a little comfort* (we felt somewhat comforted). An article that is implied but omitted is called a *zero article*, common in idiomatic usage. For example, in the morning you may *make the bed*, but at night you *go to bed* (not *the bed*)—and notice *in the morning* versus *at night*. The zero article often occurs in idiomatic references to time, illness, transportation, personal routines, and meals {by sunset} {has cancer} {travel by train} {go to bed} {make breakfast}.

5.82 **Article as pronoun substitute.** An article may sometimes substitute for a pronoun. For example, the blanks in *a patient who develops the described rash on ___ hands should inform ___ doctor* may be filled in with either a possessive pronoun or the definite article (*the*). (If a possessive pronoun is used, singular "their" would now usually be preferable to "his or her"; see 5.266.)

## POSITION OF ADJECTIVES

5.83 **Basic rules for position of adjectives.** An adjective that modifies a noun element usually precedes it {perfect storm} {spectacular view} {a good bowl of soup}. Such an adjective is called an *attributive adjective*. An adjective may follow the noun element if the adjective (1) expresses special emphasis {reasons **innumerable**} {captains **courageous**}; (2) occurs in this position in standard usage {court-**martial**} {notary **public**}; (3) is a predicate adjective following a linking verb {I am **ready**}; (4) functions as an appositive set off by commas or dashes {the man, **tall and thin**, stood in the corner}; or (5) modifies a pronoun of a type usually followed by an adjective {anything good} {everything yellow} {nothing important} {something wicked}. (An adjective that follows its noun is termed a *postpositive adjective*.) Some adjectives are always in the predicate and never appear before what they modify {the city is **asleep**} {the door was **ajar**}. Others appear uniformly before the nouns they modify {**utter** nonsense} {a **mere** child}. Phrasal adjectives (see 5.96) may precede or follow what they modify. When a modifying phrase follows the noun element it modifies, it is traditionally called an *adjective phrase*.

5.84 **Adjective after possessive.** When a noun phrase includes a possessive noun, as in *children's shoes* or *the company's president*, the adjective follows the possessive {children's **athletic** shoes} {the company's **former** president} (unless the reference is to athletic children or a former company). The same is true of possessive pronouns {her **red** dress}.

5.85 **Adjective modifying pronoun.** An adjective modifying a pronoun usually follows the pronoun {the searchers found him **unconscious**} {some like it **hot**}, sometimes as a predicate adjective {it was **insensitive**} {who was so **jealous**?}. Occasionally, however, an adjective precedes the pronoun it modifies {**flustered**, he sat down} {they offered her the director position but, **uncertain**, she demurred}.

5.86 **Predicate adjective.** A predicate adjective is an adjective that follows a linking verb (see 5.105) but modifies the subject {the child is **afraid**} {the night became **colder**} {this tastes **delicious**} {I feel **bad**}. If an adjective in the predicate modifies a noun or pronoun in the predicate, it is not a predicate adjective. For example, in *the train will be late*, the adjective *late* modifies the subject *train*. But in *the train will be here at a late hour*, the adjective *late* modifies the noun *hour*, not the subject *train*. So even though it occurs in the predicate, it is not known as a *predicate adjective*, which by definition follows a linking verb.

5.87 **Date as adjective.** Dates are often used as descriptive adjectives, more often today than in years past. If a month-year or month-day date is used as an adjective, no hyphen or comma is needed {October 31 festivities} {December 2022 financial statement}. If a full month-day-year date is used, then a comma is sometimes considered necessary both before and after the year {the May 27, 2024, ceremonies}. This awkward construction is best avoided {commencement ceremonies on May 27, 2024}.

## DEGREES OF ADJECTIVES

5.88 **Three degrees of adjectives.** An adjective is gradable into three degrees: the positive or absolute {hard}, the comparative {harder}, and the superlative {hardest}. A positive adjective simply expresses an object's quality without reference to any other thing {a big balloon} {bad news}.

5.89 **Comparative adjectives.** A comparative adjective expresses the relationship between a specified quality shared by two things, often to determine which has more or less of that quality {a cheaper ticket} {a happier ending}. The suffix *-er* usually signals the comparative form of a common adjective having one or two syllables {light–lighter} {merry–merrier}. These forms are called *synthetic comparatives.* A positive adjective with three or more syllables typically takes *more* or *less* instead of a suffix to form the comparative {intelligent–more intelligent} {purposeful–less purposeful}. These forms are called *periphrastic comparatives.* As noted, some adjectives with two syllables take the *-er* suffix {lazy–lazier} {narrow–narrower}, but most two-syllable adjectives take *more* or *less* {more hostile} {less fearful}. A two-syllable adjective ending in *-er, -le, -ow, -ure,* or *-y* can often use either *more* or the *-er* suffix {maturer–more mature} {mellower–more mellow}.

5.90 **Superlative adjectives.** A superlative adjective expresses the relationship between at least three things and denotes an extreme of intensity or amount in a particular shared quality {the biggest house on the block} {the bitterest pill of all}. The suffix *-est* usually signals the superlative form of a common adjective having one or two syllables {light–lightest}. These forms are called *synthetic superlatives.* An adjective with three or more syllables takes *most* or *least* instead of a suffix to form the superlative {quarrelsome–most quarrelsome} {humorous–least humorous}. These forms are called *periphrastic superlatives.* Some adjectives with two syllables take the *-est* suffix {holy–holiest} {noble–noblest}, but most two-syllable adjectives take *most* or *least* {most fruitful} {least reckless}.

5.91 **Forming comparatives and superlatives.** A few rules govern the forming of a short regular adjective's comparative and superlative forms. (1) If the adjective is a monosyllable ending in a single vowel followed by a single consonant, the final consonant is doubled before the suffix is attached {red–redder–reddest}. (2) If the adjective ends in a silent *-e,* the *-e* is dropped before the suffix is added {polite–politer–politest}. (3) A participle used as an adjective requires *more* or *most* before the participle; no suffix is added to form the comparative or the superlative {this teleplay is **more boring** than the first one} {I am **most tired** on Fridays}. (4) A few one-syllable adjectives—*real, right,* and *wrong*—can take only *more* and *most.* Even then, these combinations occur only in informal contexts. (5) *Eager, proper,* and *somber,* unlike many other two-syllable adjectives, also take only *more* and *most;* none can take a suffix. (6) A two-syllable adjective to which the negative prefix *un-* has been added can usually take either a suffix or *more* or *most,* even if the total number of syllables is three {unhappiest} {most unhappy}. (7) Many adjectives are irregular—there is no rule that guides their comparative and superlative forms {good–better–best} {less–lesser–least}. A good dictionary will show the forms of an irregular adjective. (8) An adjective can never take both a suffix and *more* or *most* (or *less* or *least*). This grammatical fault, known as a *double comparative* (e.g., *more greener*) or *double superlative* (e.g., *least greenest*), is regarded as nonstandard.

5.92 **Equal and unequal comparisons.** A higher degree of comparison is signaled by a suffix (*-er* or *-est*) or by *more* or *most*. A lower degree is shown by *less* (comparative) or *least* (superlative) {cold–less cold} {less cold–least cold}. (See 5.89, 5.90.) Equivalence is shown by the use of the *as–as* construction {this is as old as that} and sometimes by *so*, but usually in the negative, where it signals a lower degree {that test was not so hard as the last one}.

5.93 **Noncomparable adjectives.** An adjective that by definition describes an absolute state or condition—e.g., *entire, impossible, pregnant, unique*—is called *noncomparable*. It cannot take a comparative suffix and cannot be coupled with a comparative term (*more, most, less, least*). Nor can it be intensified by a word such as *very, largely*, or *quite*. But on the rare occasion when a particular emphasis is needed, a good writer may depart from this rule and use a phrase such as *more perfect*, as the framers of the United States Constitution did in composing its preamble {We the People of the United States, in order to form a **more perfect** Union . . .}.

## SPECIAL TYPES OF ADJECTIVES

5.94 **Participial adjectives.** A participial adjective is simply a verb's participle that modifies a noun or pronoun. It can be a present participle (verb ending in *-ing*) {the dining room} {a walking stick} {a rising star} or a past participle (usually a verb ending in *-ed*) {an endangered species} {a completed assignment} {a proven need}. Some past-participial forms have only this adjectival function, the past-participial verb having taken a different form {a shaven face} {a graven image}. A past participle functioning as an adjective may itself be modified with an adverb such as *quite* {a quite fatigued traveler}, *barely* {a barely concealed wince}, *little* {a little-known fact}, or an adverbial phrase such as *very much* {a very much distrusted public official}. If the past participle has gained a strong adjectival quality, *very* will suffice without the quantitative *much* {very tired} {very drunk}. But if the participial form seems more like a verb, *very* needs *much* {very much appreciated} {very much delayed}. A few past participles (such as *bored, interested, pleased, satisfied*) are in the middle of the spectrum between those having mostly adjectival qualities and those having mostly verbal qualities. With these, the quantitative *much* is normally omitted. See also 5.114.

5.95 **Coordinate adjectives.** A coordinate adjective is one that appears in a sequence with one or more related adjectives to modify the same noun. Coordinate adjectives should be separated by commas or by *and* {skilled, experienced chess player} {nurturing and loving parent}. If one adjective modifies the noun and another adjective modifies the idea expressed by the combination of the first adjective and the noun, the adjectives are not considered coordinate and should not be separated by a comma. For example, *a lethargic soccer player* describes a soccer player who is lethargic. Likewise, phrases such as *white brick house* and *wrinkled canvas jacket* are unpunctuated because the adjectives are not coordinate: They have no logical connection in sense (a white house could be made of many different materials; so could a wrinkled jacket). The most useful test is this: If *and* would fit between the two adjectives, a comma is necessary.

5.96 **Phrasal adjectives.** A phrasal adjective (also called a *compound modifier*) is a phrase that functions as a unit to modify a noun. A phrasal adjective follows these basic rules: (1) Generally, if placed before a noun, the phrase should be hyphenated to avoid misdirecting the reader {dog-eat-dog competition}. There may be a considerable difference between the hyphenated and the unhyphenated forms: Compare *small animal hospital* with *small-animal hospital*. (2) If a compound noun is an element of a phrasal adjective, the entire compound noun must be hyphenated to clarify the relationship among the words {time-clock-punching employees}. (3) If more than one phrasal adjective modifies a single noun, hyphenation becomes especially important {nineteenth-century song-and-dance numbers} {state-inspected assisted-living facility}. (4) If two phrasal adjectives end in a common element, the ending element should appear only with the second phrase, and a suspended hyphen should follow the unattached words to show that they are related to the ending element {middle- and upper-class operagoers}. (5) If the phrasal adjective denotes an amount or a duration, the plural should be dropped. For instance, *a truck weighing 3,000 pounds* is *a 3,000-pound truck*, and a shop *open 24 hours a day* has *a 24-hour-a-day schedule*. The plural is retained only for fractions {a two-thirds majority}. (6) If a phrasal adjective becomes awkward, the sentence should probably be recast. For example, *The news about the lower-than-expected third-quarter earnings disappointed investors* could become *The news about the third-quarter earnings, which were lower than expected, disappointed investors*.

Or perhaps this: *Investors were disappointed by the third-quarter earnings, which were lower than expected.* See also 7.87–96.

5.97 **Exceptions for hyphenating phrasal adjectives.** There are exceptions to hyphenating phrasal adjectives: (1) If a phrasal adjective follows a linking verb, it is often unhyphenated—e.g., compare *a well-trained athlete* with *an athlete who is well trained.* (2) When a proper name begins a phrasal adjective, the name is not hyphenated {the Monty Python school of comedy}. (3) A two-word phrasal adjective that begins with an adverb ending in *-ly* is not hyphenated {a sharply worded reprimand} (but *a not-so-sharply-worded reprimand*). See also 7.90, 7.91, 7.92.

5.98 **Adjectives as nouns.** An adjective-to-noun shift (sometimes called an *adnoun*) is relatively common in English. Some adjectives are well established as nouns and are perfectly suitable for most contexts. For example, *a postmortem examination* is often called *a postmortem; collectible objects* are *collectibles*; and *French people* are *the French*. Any but the most established among such nouns should be used only after careful consideration. If there's an alternative, it will almost certainly be better. For example, there is probably no good reason to use the adjective *collaborative* as a noun (i.e., as a shortened form of *collaborative enterprise*) when the perfectly good *collaboration* is available. See also 5.27–29.

5.99 **Adjectives as verbs.** Adjective-to-verb shifts are uncommon in English but occur once in a while, usually as jargon or slang {the cargo tanks were **inerted** by introducing carbon dioxide into them} {it would be silly to **low-key** the credit for this achievement}. They generally don't fit comfortably into formal prose.

5.100 **Other parts of speech functioning as adjectives.** Words that ordinarily function as other parts of speech, but sometimes as adjectives, include nouns (see 5.27), pronouns (see 5.53), and verbs (see 5.111).

## *Verbs*

### DEFINITIONS

5.101 **Verbs generally.** A verb shows the performance or occurrence of an action or the existence of a condition or a state of being, such as an emotion. It's the main word in a predicate, which makes an assertion about the subject {the dancers stepped back and forth on the stage}, and it may be the only word in the predicate {the engine hummed}. More often than any other part of speech, a verb (usually in the imperative voice) can express a full thought by itself, the subject being understood {Run!} {Enjoy!} {Think!}. (One-word sentences such as *Why?* or *Yes* alone can express complete thoughts as well, but these are in fact elliptical sentences omitting a clause implied by context {Why [did she do that]?} {Yes[, you may borrow that book].}.)

5.102 **Transitive and intransitive verbs.** Depending on the presence or absence of an object, a verb is classified as transitive or intransitive. A transitive verb requires an object to express a complete thought; the verb indicates what action the subject exerts on the object. For example, *the cyclist hit a curb* states what the subject *cyclist* did to the object *curb*. (A few transitive verbs have what are called *cognate objects*, which are closely related etymologically to the verb {drink a drink} {build a building} {see the sights}.) An intransitive verb does not require an object to express a complete thought {the rescuer **jumped**}, although it may be followed by a prepositional phrase serving an adverbial function {the rescuer **jumped to the ground**}. Many verbs may be either transitive or intransitive, the different usages often distinguishing their meanings. For example, when used transitively, as in *the king's heir will succeed him*, the verb *succeed* means "to follow and take the place of"; when used intransitively, as in *the chemist will succeed in identifying the toxin*, it means "to accomplish a task." With some verbs, no such distinction is possible. For example, in *I will walk; you ride*, the verb *ride* is intransitive. In *I will walk; you ride your bike*, the verb *ride* is transitive, but its meaning is unchanged. A verb that is normally used transitively may sometimes be used intransitively to emphasize the verb and leave the object undefined or unknown {the patient eats poorly [*how well* the patient eats is more important than *what* the patient eats]}. The test for whether a given verb is transitive is to try it with various possible objects. For each sentence in which an object is plausible, the verb is being used transitively. If an object doesn't work idiomatically, the verb is being used intransitively.

5.103 **Ergative verbs.** Some verbs, called *ergative* or *ambitransitive verbs*, can be used transitively or intransitively {the impact **shattered** the windshield} {the windshield **shattered**}. The noun that serves as the object when the verb's use is transitive becomes the subject when the verb's use is intransitive. For example, with the noun *door* and the verb *open*, one can say *I opened the door* (transitive) or *the door opened* (intransitive). Many verbs can undergo ergative shifts {the torpedo **sank the boat**} {the **boat sank**}. For example, the verb *ship* was once exclusively transitive {the company **shipped the books** on January 16}, but in commercial usage it is now often intransitive {**the books shipped** on January 16}. Likewise, *grow* (generally an intransitive verb) was transitive only in horticultural contexts {the family **grew** several types of **crops**}, but commercial usage now makes it transitive in many other contexts {how to **grow your business**}. Careful writers and editors employ such usages cautiously if at all, preferring well-established idioms.

5.104 **Regular and irregular verbs.** The past-tense and past-participial forms of most English words are formed by appending *-ed* to the basic form {draft–drafted–drafted}. (Sometimes a final consonant is doubled.) If the verb ends in *-e*, only a *-d* is appended {charge–charged–charged}. These verbs are classified as *regular*, or *weak* (the latter is a term used in philology to classify forms of conjugation). But nearly two hundred common verbs have maintained forms derived mostly from Old English roots {begin–began–begun} {bet–bet–bet} {bind–bound–bound} {bite–bit–bitten}. These verbs are called *irregular*, or *strong*. The various inflections of strong verbs defy simple classifications, but many past-tense and past-participial forms (1) change the vowel in the base verb (as *begin*), (2) keep the same form as the base verb (as *bet*), (3) share an irregular form (as *bind*), or (4) change endings (as *bite*). (The vowel change between cognate forms in category 1 is called an *ablaut*.) The verb *be* is highly irregular, with eight forms (*is*, *are*, *was*, *were*, *been*, *being*, *be*, and *am*). Because no system of useful classification is possible for irregular verbs, a reliable memory and a general dictionary are essential tools for using the correct forms consistently. Further complicating the spelling of irregular verbs is the fact that the form may vary according to the sense of the word. When used to mean "to offer a price," for example, *bid* keeps the same form in the past tense and past participle, but when it means "to offer a greeting," it forms *bade* (traditionally rhyming with *glad*) and *bidden*. The form may also depend on whether the verb is being used literally {wove a rug} or figuratively {weaved in traffic}. Finally, a few verbs that are considered regular have an alternative past tense and past participle that is formed by adding *-t* to the simple verb form {dream–dreamed} {dream–dreamt}. When these alternatives are available, American English tends to prefer the forms ending in *-ed* (e.g., *dreamed*, *learned*, *spelled*), while British English often prefers the forms ending in *-t* (*dreamt*, *learnt*, *spelt*).

5.105 **Linking verbs.** A linking verb (also called a *copula* or *connecting verb*) is one that links the subject to a closely related word in the predicate—a subjective complement. The linking verb itself does not take an object, because it expresses a state of being instead of an action {Mr. Block **is the chief executive officer**} {that snake **is venomous**} {his heart's desire **is to see his sister again**}. There are two kinds of linking verbs: *be*-verbs and intransitive verbs that are used in a weakened sense, such as *appear, become, feel, look, seem, smell,* and *taste.* The weakened intransitive verbs often have a figurative sense akin to that of *become,* as in *He fell heir to a large fortune* (he didn't physically fall on or into anything) or *The river ran dry* (a waterless river doesn't run—it has dried up). (See also 5.175.) Some verbs only occasionally function as linking verbs—among them *act* {act weird}, *get* {get fat}, *go* {go bald}, *grow* {grow weary}, *lie* {lie fallow}, *prove* {prove untenable}, *remain* {remain quiet}, *sit* {sit still}, *stay* {stay trim}, *turn* {turn gray}, and *wax* {wax eloquent}. Also, some passive-voice constructions contain linking verbs {this band **was judged** best in the contest} {she **was made** sales-force manager}. If a verb doesn't have a subjective complement, then it doesn't qualify as a linking verb in that particular construction. For instance, when a *be*-verb conveys the sense "to be situated" or "to exist," it is not a linking verb {Kansas City, Kansas, **is** across the river} {there **is** an unfilled receptionist position}. Likewise, if a verb such as *appear, feel, smell, sound,* or *taste* is followed by an adverbial modifier instead of a subjective complement {he **appeared in court**} or a direct object {the dog **smelled the scent**}, it isn't a linking verb.

5.106 **Phrasal verbs.** A phrasal verb is usually a verb plus a preposition (or particle), which serves as an adverb {settle down} {act up} {phase out}. A phrasal verb is not hyphenated, even though its equivalent noun or phrasal adjective might be—e.g., compare *to flare up* with *a flare-up,* and compare *to step up the pace* with *a stepped-up pace.* Several rules apply: (1) if the phrasal verb has a sense distinct from the component words, use the entire phrase—e.g., *hold up* means "to rob" or "to delay," and *get rid of* and *do away with* mean "to eliminate"; (2) avoid the phrasal verb if the verb alone conveys essentially the same meaning—e.g., *rest up* is equivalent to *rest;* (3) don't compress the phrase into a one-word verb, especially if it has a corresponding one-word noun form—e.g., one *burns out* (phrasal verb) and suffers *burnout* (noun); and (4) if a phrasal verb ending with *in* or *on* is followed by *to,* the *to* is normally kept separate {papers should be turned in to the teacher} {we held on to the railing} (see also 5.254, under *onto*).

5.107 **Principal and auxiliary verbs.** Depending on its uses, a verb is classified as principal or auxiliary. A principal verb is one that can stand alone to express an act or state {he **jogs**} {I **dreamed** about Xanadu}. An auxiliary verb is used with a principal verb to form a verb phrase that indicates mood, tense, or voice {you **must study** for the exam!} {I **will go** to the store} {the show **was interrupted**}. The most commonly used auxiliaries are *be, can, do, have, may, must, ought, shall,* and *will.* For more on auxiliary verbs, see 5.149–58.

5.108 **Verb phrases.** The combination of an auxiliary verb with a principal verb is a verb phrase, such as *could happen, must go,* or *will be leaving.* When a verb phrase is modified by an adverb, the modifier typically goes directly after the first auxiliary verb, as in *could certainly happen, must always go,* and *will soon be leaving.* The idea that verb phrases should not be "split" in this way is quite mistaken (see 5.176). A verb phrase is negated when the negative adverb *not* is placed after the first auxiliary {we **have not** called him}. In an interrogative sentence, the first auxiliary begins the sentence and is followed by the subject {**must I** repeat that?} {**do you** want more?}. An interrogative can be negated by placement of *not* after the subject {**do you not** want more?}, but a contraction is often more natural {**don't you** want more?}. Most negative forms can be contracted {we do not–we don't} {I will not–I won't} {he has not–he hasn't} {she does not–she doesn't}, but *I am not* is contracted to *I'm not* (never *I amn't*). The corresponding interrogative form is *aren't I?* Sometimes the negative is emphasized if the auxiliary is contracted with the pronoun and the negative is left standing alone {he is not–he isn't–he's not} {we are not–we aren't–we're not} {they have not–they haven't–they've not}.

5.109 **Contractions.** Most types of writing benefit from the use of contractions. If used thoughtfully, contractions in prose sound natural and relaxed and make reading more enjoyable. *Be*-verbs and most of the auxiliary verbs are contracted when followed by *not*: *are not–aren't, was not–wasn't, cannot–can't, could not–couldn't, do not–don't,* and so on. A few, such as *ought not–oughtn't,* look or sound awkward and are best avoided. Pronouns can be contracted with auxiliaries, with forms of *have,* and with some *be*-verbs. Think before using one of the less common contractions, which often don't work well in prose, except perhaps in dialogue or quotations. Some examples are *I'd've* (I would have), *she'd've* (she would have), *it'd* (it would), *should've* (should have), *there're* (there are), *who're* (who are), and *would've* (would have). Also, some contracted forms can have more than one meaning. For instance, *there's* may be *there is* or *there has,* and *I'd* may be *I had* or *I would.* The particular meaning may not always be clear from the context.

## INFINITIVES

5.110 **Infinitives defined.** An infinitive verb, also called the verb's *root* or *stem,* is a verb that in its principal uninflected form may be preceded by *to* {to dance} {to dive}. It is the basic form of the verb, the one listed in dictionary entries. The preposition *to* is sometimes called the *sign* of the infinitive {he tried **to open** the door}, and it is sometimes classed as an adverb. In the active voice, *to* is generally dropped when the infinitive follows an auxiliary verb {you must **flee**} and can be dropped after several verbs, such as *bid, dare, feel, hear, help, let, make, need,* and *see* {you dare **say** that to me?}. But when the infinitive follows one of these verbs in the passive voice, *to* should be retained {he cannot be heard **to deny** it} {they can be made **to listen**}. The *to* should also be retained after *ought* and *ought not* (see 5.154).

5.111 **Uses of the infinitive.** The infinitive has great versatility. It is sometimes called a *verbal noun* because it can function as part of a verb phrase {someone **has to tell** her} or as a noun element {**to walk** away now seems rash}. The infinitive also has limited uses as an adjective or an adverb. As a verb, it can take (1) a subject {we wanted **the lesson to end**}, (2) an object {try **to throw the javelin** higher}, (3) a predicate complement {want **to race home**?}, or (4) an adverbial modifier {you need **to think quickly** in chess}. As a noun, the infinitive can perform as (1) the subject of a finite verb {**to fly** is a lofty goal} or (2) the object of a transitive verb or participle {I want **to hire** a new assistant}. An infinitive may be governed by a verb {**cease to do** evil}, a noun {we all have **talents to be improved**}, an adjective {she is **eager to learn**}, a participle {they are **preparing to go**}, or a pronoun {let **him do** it}.

5.112 **Split infinitive.** Although from about 1850 to 1925 many grammarians stated otherwise, it is now widely acknowledged that adverbs sometimes justifiably separate the *to* from the principal verb {they expect **to more than double** their income next year}. See also 5.176.

5.113 **Dangling infinitive.** An infinitive phrase can be used, often loosely, to modify a verb—in which case the sentence must have a grammatical subject (or an unexpressed subject of an imperative) that could logically perform the action of the infinitive. If there is none, then the sentence may be confusing. For example, in *To repair your car properly, it must be sent to a mechanic,* the infinitive *repair* does not have a logical subject; the infinitive phrase *to repair your car* is left dangling. But if the sentence is rewritten as *To repair your car properly, you must take it to a mechanic,* the logical subject is *you.*

## PARTICIPLES AND GERUNDS

5.114 **Participles generally.** A participle is a nonfinite verb that is not limited by person, number, or mood but does have tense. Two participles are formed from the verb stem: The present participle invariably ends in

-*ing*, and the past participle usually ends in -*ed*. The present participle denotes the verb's action as being in progress or incomplete at the time expressed by the sentence's principal verb {**watching** intently for a mouse, the cat settled in to wait} {**hearing** his name, Jon turned to answer}. The past participle denotes the verb's action as being completed {**planted** in the spring} {**written** last year}.

5.115 **Participial phrases.** A participial phrase is made up of a participle plus any closely associated word or words, such as modifiers or complements. It can be used (1) as an adjective to modify a noun or pronoun {**nailed to the roof**, the slate stopped the leaks} {she pointed to the clerk **drooping behind the counter**} or (2) as an absolute phrase {**generally speaking**, I prefer spicy dishes} {**they having arrived**, we went out on the lawn for our picnic}. For more on participial adjectives, see 5.94, 5.119.

5.116 **Gerunds.** A gerund is a present participle used as a noun. It is not limited by person, number, or mood. Being a noun, the gerund can be used as (1) the subject of a verb {**complaining** about it won't help}; (2) the object of a verb {I don't like your **cooking**}; (3) a predicate nominative or complement {his favorite pastime is **sleeping**}; or (4) the object of a preposition {reduce erosion by **terracing** the fields}. In some sentences, a gerund may substitute for an infinitive. Compare the use of the infinitive *to lie* as a noun {**to lie** is wrong} with the gerund *lying* {**lying** is wrong}.

5.117 **Distinguishing between participles and gerunds.** Because participles and gerunds both derive from verbs, the difference between them depends on their function. A participle is used as a modifier {the **running** water} or as part of a verb phrase {the meter **is running**}; it can be modified only by an adverb {the **swiftly** running water}. A gerund is used as a noun {**running is** great exercise}; it is modified by an adjective {**sporadic running and walking** makes for a great workout}.

5.118 **Fused participles.** As nouns, gerunds are traditionally modified by adjectives {**double-parking** is prohibited}, including possessive nouns and pronouns {**Critt's parking** can be hazardous to pedestrians}. By contrast, when a present participle is modified, it is always modified by an adverb, whether the participle serves as a verb {the dog **is barking now**}, an adjective {I'll be looking for **a loudly barking dog**}, or an adverb {the dog charged the cat, **barking the whole time**}. It is traditionally considered a linguistic fault (a *fused participle*) to use a nonpossessive noun or pronoun with a gerund:

INFORMAL: **Me painting** your fence depends on **you paying** me first.
FORMAL: **My painting** your fence depends on **your paying** me first.

In the informal example, *me* looks like the subject of the sentence, but it doesn't agree with the verb *depends*. Instead, the subject is *painting*—a gerund, here seeming to be "modified" by *me*, a pronoun. In the predicate, *you* looks like the object of the preposition *on*, but the true object is the gerund *paying*. At times, the possessive is unidiomatic. You usually have no choice but to use a fused participle with a nonpersonal noun {we're not responsible for the jewelry having been mislaid}, a nonpersonal pronoun {we all insisted on something being done}, or a group of pronouns {the settlement depends on some of them agreeing to compromise}.

5.119 **Dangling participles.** Both participles and gerunds are subject to dangling. A participle that has no syntactic relationship with the nearest subject is called a *dangling participle* or just a *dangler*. In effect, the participle ceases to function as a modifier and functions as a kind of preposition. Often the sentence is illogical, ambiguous, or even incoherent, as in *Frequently used in early America, experts suggest that shaming is an effective punishment* (*used* does not modify the closest noun, *experts*; it modifies *shaming*), or *Being a thoughtful mother, I believe Meg gives her children good advice* (the writer at first seems to be engaging in self-praise instead of praising Meg). Recasting the sentence so that the misplaced modifier is associated with the correct noun is the only effective cure {**experts suggest that shaming**, often used in early America, is an effective punishment}. But rewording to avoid the participle or gerund may be preferable {I believe that **because Meg is a thoughtful mother, she** gives her children good advice}. Using passive voice in an independent clause can also produce a dangler. In *Finding that the questions were not ambiguous, the exam grades were not changed*, the participle *finding* "dangles" because there is no logical subject to do the finding. The sentence can be corrected by using active voice instead of passive, so that the participle precedes the noun it modifies {**finding that the questions were not ambiguous**, the **teacher** did not change the exam grades}. Quite often writers will use *it* or *there* as the subject of the independent clause after a participial phrase, thereby producing a dangler without a logical subject, as in *Reviewing the suggestions, it is clear that no consensus exists.* (A possible revision: *Our review of the suggestions shows that no consensus exists.*) Compare 5.120. See also 5.181.

5.120 **Dangling gerunds.** A dangling gerund can occur when a participle is the object of a preposition, where it functions as a noun rather than as a modifier. For example, *After finishing the research, the screenplay was easy to write* (who did the research and who wrote the screenplay?). The best way to correct a dangling gerund is to revise the sentence. The example above could be revised as *After Gero finished the research, the screenplay was easy to write*, or *After finishing the research, Gero found the screenplay easy to write*. Dangling gerunds can result in improbable statements. Consider *While driving to San Antonio, my phone ran out of power*. The phone wasn't at the wheel, so *driving* is a dangling gerund. Clarifying the subject of the gerund improves the sentence {**while I was driving to San Antonio**, my phone ran out of power}. Compare 5.119.

## VOICE, MOOD, TENSE, PERSON, AND NUMBER

5.121 **Five properties of verbs.** A verb has five properties: voice, mood, tense, person, and number. Verbs are conjugated (inflected) to show these properties.

5.122 **Active and passive voice.** Voice shows whether the subject acts (active voice) or is acted on (passive voice)—that is, whether the subject performs or receives the action of the verb. Only transitive verbs are said to have voice. The clause *the judge levied a $50 fine* is in the active voice because the subject *judge* is acting. But *the tree's branch was broken by the storm* is in the passive voice because the subject *branch* does not break itself—it is acted on by the prepositional object *storm*. The passive voice is always formed by joining an inflected form of *to be* (or, in colloquial usage, *get*) with the verb's past participle. Compare *the ox pulls the cart* (active voice) with *the cart is pulled by the ox* (passive voice). As a matter of style, passive voice {the matter **will be given** careful consideration} is often inferior to active voice {**we will consider** the matter carefully}. The choice between active and passive voice may depend on which point of view is desired. For instance, *the mouse was caught by the cat* describes the mouse's experience, whereas *the cat caught the mouse* describes the cat's. The important first step is to be able to identify passive voice reliably. Remember that the mere presence of a *be*-verb does not necessarily signal passive voice. For example, *he is thinking about his finances* isn't in the passive voice; it's just a *be*-verb plus a present participle.

5.123 **Progressive conjugation and voice.** If an inflected form of *be* is joined with a verb's present participle, a progressive conjugation results {the ox **is pulling** the cart}. If the verb is transitive, the progressive conjugation is in active voice because the subject is performing the action, not being acted on. But if both the principal verb and the auxiliary are *be*-verbs followed by a past participle {the cart **is being pulled**}, the result is a passive-voice construction.

5.124 **Verb mood.** Mood (or *mode*) indicates the manner in which the verb expresses an action or state of being. The three moods are indicative, imperative, and subjunctive.

5.125 **Indicative mood.** The indicative mood is the most common in English. It is used to express facts and opinions and to ask questions {amethysts cost very little} {the botanist lives in a garden cottage} {does that bush produce yellow roses?}.

5.126 **Imperative mood.** The imperative mood uses the verb's stem to express a command {**go** away!}, a direct request {**bring** the tray in here}, an exclamation {**help**!}, or the like, and sometimes to grant permission {**come** in!}. The subject of the verb, *you*, is understood even though the sentence might include a direct address {**give** me the magazine} {Cindy, **take** good care of yourself [*Cindy* is a direct address, not the subject]}. Use the imperative mood cautiously: In some contexts it could be too blunt or unintentionally rude. You can soften the imperative by using a word such as *please* {please **stop** at the store}. If that isn't satisfactory, you might recast the sentence in the indicative {**will you stop** at the store, please?}.

5.127 **Subjunctive mood.** Although the subjunctive mood no longer appears with much frequency, it is useful when you want to express an action or a state not as a reality but as a mental conception. Typically, the subjunctive expresses an action or state as doubtful, imagined, desired, conditional, hypothetical, or otherwise contrary to fact. Despite its decline, the subjunctive mood persists in stock expressions such as *perish the thought*, *heaven help us*, and *be that as it may*.

5.128 **Subjunctive versus indicative mood.** The subjunctive mood signals a statement contrary to fact {if I **were you**}, including wishes {if **I were** a rich man}, conjectures {oh, **were it** so}, demands {the landlord insists that **the dog go**}, and suggestions {I recommend that **she take** a vacation}. Three issues often arise with these constructions. First, writers sometimes use an indicative verb form when the subjunctive form would be called for in literary English:

INFORMAL: If it **wasn't** for your help, I wouldn't have a chance of finding the place.

FORMAL: If it **weren't** for your help, I wouldn't have a chance of finding the place.

Second, indicative-mood sentences sometimes resemble these subjunctive constructions but aren't statements contrary to fact:

NONSTANDARD: I called to see **whether she were in**.
STANDARD: I called to see **whether she was in**.

Third, one often sees *If I would have gone, I would . . .*, with two conditionals, instead of *If I had gone, I would . . .* (the better choice). Although the subjunctive mood is often signaled by *if*, not every *if* takes a subjunctive verb. When the action or state might be true but the writer doesn't know, the indicative is called for instead of the subjunctive {**if I am** right about this, please call} {**if Napoleon was** in fact poisoned with arsenic, historians will need to reevaluate his associates}.

5.129 **Present subjunctive mood.** The present-tense subjunctive mood is formed by using the base form of the verb, such as *be*. This form of subjunctive often appears in suggestions or requirements {he recommended **that we be ready** at a moment's notice} {we insist **that he retain control** of the accounting department}. The present-tense subjunctive is also expressed by using either *be* plus the simple-past form of the verb or a past-form auxiliary plus an infinitive {the chair proposed **that the company be acquired** by the employees through a stock-ownership plan} {today **would be convenient for me to search** for that missing file} {**might he take down** the decorations this afternoon?}. See also 5.127.

5.130 **Past subjunctive mood.** Despite its label, the past-tense subjunctive mood refers to something in the present or future but contrary to fact. It is formed using the verb's simple-past tense, except in the case of *be*, which becomes *were* regardless of the subject's number. For example, the declaration *if only I had a chance* expresses that the speaker has little or no chance. Similarly, *I wish I were safe at home* almost certainly means that the speaker is not at home and perhaps not safe—though it could also mean that the speaker is at home but quite unsafe. This past-tense-but-present-sense subjunctive typically appears in the form *if I* (*he, she, they, it*) *were* {if I were king} {if she were any different}. That is, the subjunctive mood ordinarily uses a past-tense verb (e.g., *were*) to connote uncertainty, impossibility, or unreality where the present or future indicative would otherwise be used. Compare *If I am threatened, I will quit* (indicative) with *If I were threatened, I would quit* (subjunctive), or *If the canary sings, I smile* (indicative) with *If the canary sang* (or *should sing*, or *were to sing*), *I would smile* (subjunctive).

5.131 **Past-perfect subjunctive mood.** Just as the past subjunctive uses a verb's simple-past-tense form to refer to the present or future, the past-perfect subjunctive uses a verb's past-perfect form to refer to the past. The past-perfect subjunctive typically appears in the form *if I* (*he, she, they, it*) *had* {if he had been there} {if I had gone}. That is, the subjunctive mood ordinarily uses a past-perfect verb (e.g., *had been*) to connote uncertainty or impossibility where the past or past-perfect indicative would otherwise be used. Compare *If it arrived, it was not properly filed* (indicative) with *If it had arrived, it could have changed the course of history* (subjunctive).

5.132 **Verb tense.** Tense shows the time in which an act, state, or condition occurs or occurred. The three major divisions of time are present, past, and future (but see 5.135). Each division of time breaks down further into a perfect tense denoting a comparatively more remote time by indicating that the action has been completed: present perfect, past perfect, and future perfect. And all six of these tenses can be further divided to include a progressive tense (also called *imperfect* or *continuous*), in which the action continues.

5.133 **Present tense.** The present tense is the infinitive verb's stem, also called the *present indicative* {walk} {drink}. It primarily denotes acts, conditions, or states that occur in the present {the dog **howls**} {the air **is** cold} {the water **runs**}. It is also used (1) to express a habitual action or general truth {cats **prowl** nightly} {polluted water **is** a health threat}; (2) to refer to timeless facts, such as memorable persons and works of the past that are still extant or enduring {Julius Caesar **describes** his strategies in *The Gallic War*} {the Pompeiian mosaics **are** exquisite}; and (3) to narrate a fictional work's plot {the scene **takes** place aboard the *Titanic*}. The latter two uses are collectively referred to as the *historical-present tense,* and the third is especially important for those who write about literature. Characters in books, plays, and films *do* things—not *did* them. If you want to distinguish between present action and past action in literature, the present-perfect tense is helpful {Hamlet, who **has spoken** with his father's ghost, **reveals what he has learned** to no one but Horatio}. See also 5.136.

5.134 **Past-indicative tense.** The past indicative denotes an act, state, or condition that occurred or existed at some explicit or implicit point in the past {the auction ended yesterday} {we returned the shawl}. For a regular verb, it is formed by adding *-ed* to its base form {jump–jumped} {spill–spilled}. If the verb ends in a silent *-e,* only a *-d* is added to form both the past tense and the past participle {bounce–bounced–bounced}.

If it ends in *-y* preceded by a consonant, the *-y* changes to an *-i* before forming the past tense and past participle with *-ed* {hurry–hurried–hurried}. If it ends in a double consonant {block}, two vowels and a consonant {cook}, or a vowel other than *-e* {veto}, a regular verb forms the past tense and past participle by adding *-ed* to its simple form {block–blocked–blocked} {cook–cooked–cooked} {veto–vetoed–vetoed}. If the verb ends in a single vowel before a consonant, several rules apply in determining whether the consonant is doubled. It is typically doubled in one-syllable words {pat–patted–patted}—though words ending in *-x* are a major exception {fixed} {hexed}. In words of more than one syllable, the final consonant is doubled if it is part of the syllable that is stressed both before and after the inflection {prefer–preferred–preferred}, but not otherwise {travel–traveled–traveled}. In British English there is no such distinction: All such consonants are doubled. Irregular verbs form the past tense and past participle in various ways {give–gave–given} {stride–strode–stridden} {read–read–read}. See also 5.104.

5.135 **Future tense.** What is traditionally known as the *future tense* is formed by using *will* with a verb's stem form {will walk} {will drink}. It refers to an expected act, state, or condition {the artist **will design** a mural} {the restaurant **will open** soon}. *Shall* may be used instead of *will*, but in American English it typically appears only in first-person questions {**shall** we **go**?} and in statements of legal requirements {the debtor **shall pay** within 30 days}. In most contexts, *will* is preferred—or *must* with legal requirements. Most linguists are now convinced that, technically speaking, English has no future tense—that *will* is simply a modal verb that should be treated with all the others.[6] Yet the future tense remains a part of traditional grammar and is discussed here in the familiar way.

5.136 **Present-perfect tense.** The present-perfect tense is formed by using *have* or *has* with the principal verb's past participle {have walked} {has drunk}. It denotes an act, state, or condition that is now completed or continues up to the present {I **have put** away the clothes} {it **has been** a long day} {I will apologize, even if I **have done** nothing wrong}. The present perfect is distinguished from the past tense because it refers to (1) a time in the indefinite past {I **have played** golf there before} or (2) a past action that comes up to and touches the present {I **have played** cards for the last eighteen hours}. The past tense, by contrast, indicates a more specific or a more remote time in the past.

---

6. See, e.g., R. L. Trask, *Language: The Basics* (Routledge, 1995), 58.

5.137 **Past-perfect tense.** The past-perfect (or *pluperfect*) tense is formed by using *had* with the principal verb's past participle {had walked} {had drunk}. It refers to an act, state, or condition that was completed before another specified or implicit past time or past action {the engineer **had driven** the train to the roundhouse before we arrived} {by the time we stopped to check the map, the rain **had begun** falling} {the movie **had** already **ended**}.

5.138 **Future-perfect tense.** The future-perfect tense is formed by using *will have* with the verb's past participle {will have walked} {will have drunk}. It refers to an act, state, or condition that is expected to be completed before some other future act or time {the entomologist **will have collected** sixty more specimens before the semester ends} {the court **will have adjourned** by five o'clock}.

5.139 **Progressive tenses.** The progressive tenses, also known as *continuous tenses,* show action that progresses or continues. With active-voice verbs, all six basic tenses can be made progressive by using the appropriate *be*-verb and the present participle of the main verb, as so:

present progressive (*he is playing tennis*);
present-perfect progressive (*he has been playing tennis*);
past progressive (*he was playing tennis*);
past-perfect progressive (*he had been playing tennis*);
future progressive (*he will be playing tennis*); and
future-perfect progressive (*he will have been playing tennis*).

With the passive voice, the present- and past-progressive tenses are made by using the appropriate *be*-verb with the present participle *being,* plus the past participle of the main verb, as so:

present (*I am being dealt the cards*); and
past (*I was being dealt the cards*).

5.140 **Mixing different tenses.** A single passage may refer to related events occurring at different times. Choose the tense that best shows when for each one. For example, *Because the students **passed** their final exams* (past-indicative tense), *they **are gathering** for the graduation ceremonies* (present-progressive tense) *and **will soon file** into the auditorium* (future tense).

5.141 **Verb person.** A verb's person shows whether the act, state, or condition is that of (1) the person speaking (first person), (2) the person spoken to (second person), or (3) the person or thing spoken of (third person).

5.142 **Verb number.** The number of a verb must agree with the number of the noun or pronoun used with it. In other words, the verb must be singular or plural. Only the third-person present-indicative singular changes form to indicate number and person {I sketch} {you sketch} {she sketches} {they sketch}. The second-person verb is always plural in form, whether one person or more than one person is spoken to {**you are** a wonderful person} {**you are** wonderful people}. Similarly, the third-person *they* takes a plural verb, whether referring to one person or more than one (see 5.51, 5.52).

5.143 **Agreement in person and number.** A finite verb agrees with its subject in person and number—which is to say that a singular subject takes a singular verb {the **solution works**}, while a plural subject takes a plural verb {the **solutions work**}. When a verb has two or more subjects connected by *and*, it agrees with them jointly and is plural {**Socrates and Plato were** wise}. When a verb has two or more subjects connected by *or* or *nor*, the verb agrees with the last-named subject {**Bob or his friends have** your key} {neither the **twins nor Jon is** prepared to leave}. When the subject is a collective noun conveying the idea of unity or multitude, the verb is singular {the **nation is** powerful}. When the subject is a collective noun conveying the idea of plurality, the verb is plural {the **faculty were** divided in their sentiments}. See also 5.17.

5.144 **Agreement of indefinite pronouns.** An indefinite pronoun such as *anybody, anyone, everybody, everyone, nobody, no one, somebody,* or *someone* routinely takes a singular verb {**everyone receives** credits for this course} {**somebody knows** where the car is}.

5.145 **Relative pronouns as subjects.** A relative pronoun used as the subject of a clause can be either singular or plural, depending on the pronoun's antecedent {a woman **who likes** skydiving} {people **who collect** books}. One of the trickiest constructions involves *one of those who* or *one of those that*:

NONSTANDARD: She is one of those **employees who works** tirelessly.
STANDARD: She is one of those **employees who work** tirelessly.

In this construction, the subject of the verb *work* is *who*, and the antecedent of *who* is *employees*, not *one*. You can see this easily if you reorder the syntax (without adding or subtracting a word): *Of those employees who work tirelessly, she is one*. See also 5.66.

5.146 **False attraction to predicate noun.** When the subject and a predicate noun differ in number, the subject governs the number of the verb {**mediocrity and complacency are the source** of his ire} {**the source** of his ire **is mediocrity and complacency**}. A plural predicate noun after a singular subject may mislead a writer into error by suggesting a plural verb. When this occurs, the simple correction of changing the number of the verb may make the sentence awkward, and the better approach then is to rework the sentence:

NONSTANDARD: My **downfall are** sweets.
STANDARD: My **downfall is** sweets.
STANDARD (AND BETTER): **Sweets are** my downfall.

5.147 **Misleading connectives—"as well as," "along with," "together with," and the like.** Adding to a singular subject by using a phrasal connective such as *along with*, *as well as*, *in addition to*, *together with*, and the like does not make the subject plural. This type of distraction can be doubly misleading because the intervening material seems to create a compound subject, and the modifying prepositional phrase may itself contain one or more plural objects. If the singular verb sounds awkward in such a sentence, try the conjunction *and* instead:

NONSTANDARD: The **bride** as well as her bridesmaids **were** dressed in mauve.
STANDARD: The **bride** as well as her bridesmaids **was** dressed in mauve.
STANDARD (AND BETTER): The **bride and her bridesmaids were** dressed in mauve.

5.148 **Agreement in first and second person.** A personal pronoun used as a subject requires the appropriate verb form according to the person of the pronoun:

| | | | |
|---|---|---|---|
| I am | he is | I go | he goes |
| you are | she is | you go | she goes |
| we are | it is | we go | it goes |
| they are | | they go | |

Here comes the tricky point: Pronouns joined by *or*, *either–or*, or *neither–nor* are traditionally said to take the verb form that agrees with the nearer subject {**either he or I am** in for a surprise} {**either you or**

**he is** right} {**neither you nor I am** a plumber}. Because these constructions are admittedly awkward, speakers and writers typically find another way to express the thought {one of us is in for a surprise} {one of you is right} {neither of us is a plumber}.

## AUXILIARY VERBS

5.149 **Auxiliary verbs generally.** An auxiliary verb (sometimes termed a *helping verb*) is a highly irregular verb used with one or more other verbs to form voice, tense, and mood. It always precedes the principal verb. The most common auxiliary verbs are explained in the following sections. See also 5.107.

5.150 **Modal auxiliaries.** A subset of auxiliary verbs, called *modal auxiliaries* or *modals,* are used to express ability, necessity, possibility, willingness, obligation, and the like {they **might** be there} {she **could be** leaving at this very moment}. They are so called because they indicate the principal verb's mood. All the verbs described below are modal auxiliaries except the last two: *do* and *have.*

5.151 **"Can" and "could."** *Can* uses only its stem form in the present indicative {I can} {it can} {they can}. In the past indicative, *can* becomes *could* for all persons {he **could see** better with glasses}. *Can* does not have an infinitive form (*to be able to* is substituted) or a present or past participle. (Such words lacking one or more inflected forms normal for their word class are traditionally called *defective*. All modal auxiliaries are defective verbs.) When it denotes ability, capacity, or permission, *can* is always followed by an explicit or implicit bare infinitive as the principal verb {you **can carry** this trunk}. When used in the sense of permission, *can* is colloquial for *may* {**can** I **go** to the movies?}. *Can* also connotes actual possibility or common experience {storms **can be** severe in spring} {days **can pass** before a decision is announced}. *Could* is often used to talk about the past {she **could** hum a tune at six months of age} or to discuss someone's general ability at a given time {when he was eleven, he **could** drive a golf ball 250 yards}. But *could* is also used as a softer, less definite equivalent of *can* in reference to future events {we could travel to Cancun if you wanted to}. In this use, the meaning is close to "would be able to" {you could be promoted within six months if you'd just apply yourself!}.

5.152 **"May" and "might."** *May* denotes either permission {you may go to the movies} or possibility {I may go to the movies}. In negating permission, *may not* is sometimes displaced by the more intensive *must not*. Compare *You may not climb that tree* with *You must not climb that tree*. *May* most commonly connotes an uncertain possibility {you **may find** that assignment too difficult}, and it often becomes *might* {you **might find** that assignment too difficult}. Is there a connotative difference? Yes: *May* tends to express likelihood {we **may** get there on time}, while *might* expresses a stronger sense of doubt {we **might** get there on time—if the traffic clears}. *Might* can also express a contrary-to-fact hypothetical {we might have been able to make it if the traffic had been better}.

5.153 **"Must."** *Must* denotes a necessity that arises from someone's will {we **must obey** the rules}, from circumstances {you **must ask** what the next step is}, or from rule or obligation {all applications **must be** received by May 31 to be valid}. *Must* also connotes a logical conclusion {that **must be** the right answer} {that **must be** the house we're looking for} {it **must have been** Donna who phoned}. This auxiliary verb does not vary its form in either the present or past indicative. It does not have an infinitive form (*to have to* is substituted) or a present or past participle. Denoting obligation, necessity, or inference, *must* is always used with a bare infinitive {we **must finish** this design} {everyone **must eat**} {the movie **must be** over by now}.

5.154 **"Ought."** *Ought* denotes either what is reasonably expected of a person as a matter of duty {they **ought to fix** the fence} or what we guess or conclude is probable {they left at dawn, so they **ought to be** here soon}. It is more emphatic than *should* but less strong than *must*. This verb does not vary its form in either the present or past indicative. It has no infinitive form, or present or past participle. Denoting a duty or obligation, *ought* is always used with an infinitive, even in the negative {we **ought to invite** some friends} {the driver **ought not to have ignored** the signal}. *To* is occasionally omitted after *not* {you **ought not worry**}, but the better usage is to include it {you **ought not to worry**}. See also 5.110.

5.155 **"Should."** *Should*, the past-indicative form of *shall*, is used for all persons, and always with a principal verb {they **should be** at home} {**should** you **read** that newspaper?}. *Should* does not have an infinitive form or a present or past participle. *Should* often carries a sense of duty, compulsion, or expectation {I **should review** those financial-planning tips} {you **should clean** the garage today} {it **should be** ready by now}. Sometimes it carries a sense of inference {the package **should have been delivered** today}. And sometimes it conveys the speaker's attitude {how **should** I **know**?} {you **shouldn't have to deal** with that}. *Should* and *ought* are quite similar and often interchangeable in discussions of what is required, what is advisable, or what we think is right for people either to do or to have done. *Should* is slightly less emphatic than *ought*, but it appears with greater frequency.

5.156 **"Will" and "would."** In its auxiliary uses, *will* uses only its stem form in the present indicative {she will} {they will}. In the past indicative, the only form for all persons is *would* {we **would go** fishing on Saturdays} {she **would say** that!}. *Will* often carries a sense of the future {she **will be** at her desk tomorrow} or, in the past form *would*, expresses a conditional statement {I **would recognize** the house **if** I saw it again}. It can also express certainty {I'm sure you will understand}; decisions and other types of volition {I really will work out more}; requests, orders, and offers {will you stop that!} {will you take $5 for it?}; or typical behavior {she will read for hours on end}.

5.157 **"Do."** The auxiliary verb *do* frequently creates emphatic verbs. It has two forms in the present indicative: *does* for the third-person singular (except for singular *they*) and *do* for all other persons. In the past indicative, the only form for all persons is *did*. The past participle is *done*. As an auxiliary verb, *do* is used only in the present indicative {we **do plan** some charity work} and past indicative {**did** you **speak**?}. When the verb in an imperative statement is coupled with *not*, *do* also appears {**do not touch**!} {**don't be** late!}. When denoting performance, *do* can also act as a principal verb {he **does** well in school} {they **do** good work}. *Do* can sometimes substitute for a verb, thereby avoiding repetition {Marion **dances** well, and **so do you**} {he **caught** fewer mistakes **than you did**}.

5.158 **"Have."** This verb has two forms in the present indicative: *has* for the third-person singular (except for singular *they*) and *have* for all other persons. In the past indicative, the only form for all persons is *had*; the past participle is also *had*. When *have* functions as an auxiliary verb, the present or past indicative of *have* precedes the past participle of a verb to form that verb's present-perfect or past-perfect indicative mood {I **have looked** everywhere} {he **had looked** for a better rate}. When preceding an infinitive, *have* denotes obligation or necessity {I **have to finish** this paper tonight!}. *Had* plus *to* and an infinitive expresses the past form of *must* {I **had to leave** yesterday afternoon}. When denoting possession, action, or experience, *have* functions as a sentence's principal verb {she **has** a car and a boat} {you **have** a mosquito on your neck} {we'll **have** a party next week}. *Have* may also be used with *do* to express actual or figurative possession {**do** you **have** the time?} {**do** we **have** room?} {Vicky **did not have** her coat}.

### "BE"-VERBS

5.159 **Forms of "be"-verbs.** The verb *be* has eight forms (*be, is, are, was, were, been, being,* and *am*) and has several special uses. First, it is sometimes a sentence's principal verb meaning "exist" {I think, therefore I **am**}. Second, it is more often used as an auxiliary verb {I **was** born in Lubbock}. When joined with a verb's present participle, it denotes continuing or progressive action {the train **is** coming} {the passenger **was** waiting}. When joined with a past participle, the verb becomes passive {a signal **was** given} {an earring **was** dropped} (see 5.122). Often this type of construction can be advantageously changed to active voice {he gave the signal} {she dropped her earring}. Third, *be* is the most common linking verb that connects the subject with something affirmed of the subject {truth **is** beauty} {we **are** the champions}. Occasionally a *be*-verb is used as part of an adjective {a rock star **wannabe** [want to be]} {a **would-be** hero} or noun {a **has-been**}.

5.160 **Conjugation of "be"-verbs.** *Be* is conjugated differently from other verbs. (1) The stem is not used in the present-indicative form. Instead, *be* has three forms: for the first-person singular, *am*; for the third-person singular (except singular *they*), *is*; and for all other persons, *are*. (2) The present participle is formed by adding *-ing* to the root *be* {being}. It is the same for all persons, but the present progressive requires also using *am, is,* or *are* {I **am being** stalked} {it **is being** reviewed} {you **are being** photographed}. (3) The past indicative has two forms: The first- and third-person singular (except for singular *they*) use *was*; all other persons use *were* {she **was**} {we **were**}. (4) The past participle for all persons is *been* {I **have been**} {they **have been**}. (5) The imperative is the verb's stem {**be** yourself!}.

## *Adverbs*

### DEFINITION AND FORMATION

5.161 **Adverbs generally.** An adverb is a word (more particularly, an *adjunct*) that qualifies, limits, describes, or modifies a verb, an adjective, or another adverb {she studied **constantly** [*constantly* qualifies the verb *studied*]} {the juggler's act was **really** unusual [*really* qualifies the adjective *unusual*]} {the cyclist pedaled **very** swiftly [*very* qualifies the adverb *swiftly*]}. An adverb may also qualify a preposition, a conjunction, or an entire independent clause {the birds flew **right** over the lake [*right* qualifies the preposition *over*]} {this is **exactly** where I found it [*exactly* qualifies the conjunction *where*]} {**apparently** you forgot to check your references [*apparently* qualifies the rest of the clause]}. Some adverbs may modify an adjective {the bids differ by a **very** small amount} or an adverb {he moved along **very** quickly} but not a verb. (You can't say *He spoke very* or *She played very*.) Other adverbs of this sort—often called *intensifiers*—are *quite, rather, really, somewhat,* and *too* (see also 5.93). Grammarians have also traditionally used the term *adverb* as a catchall to sweep in words that aren't readily put into other categories (such as *not, please,* and the infinitival *to* and the particle in a phrasal verb).

5.162 **Sentence adverbs.** An adverb that modifies an entire sentence is called a *sentence adverb* {**fortunately**, we've had rain this week} {**undoubtedly** he drove his car to the depot}. Sentence adverbs commonly indicate doubt or emphasize a statement's certainty. Some common examples are *clearly, maybe, possibly,* and *undoubtedly*.

5.163 **Adverbial suffixes.** Many adjectives have corresponding adverbs distinguished by the suffix *-ly* or, after most words ending in *-ic*, *-ally* {slow–slowly} {careful–carefully} {public–publicly} {pedantic–pedantically}. Most adjectives ending in *-y* preceded by a consonant change the *-y* to *-i* when the suffix is added, but some don't {happy–happily} {shy–shyly}. A few adjectives ending in *-e* drop the vowel {true–truly} {whole–wholly}. If an adjective ends in an *-le* that is sounded as part of a syllable, *-le* is replaced with *-ly* {terrible–terribly} {simple–simply}. An adjective that ends in a double *-l* takes only a *-y* suffix {dull–dully}. Many adjectives ending in *-le* or *-ly* do not make appealing adverbs {juvenile–juvenilely} {silly–sillily}. If an *-ly* adverb looks clumsy (e.g., *ghastlily, uglily*), either rephrase the sentence or use a phrase {in a ghastly manner} {in an ugly way}. A few other suffixes are used for adverbs, especially in speech {he rides cowboy-style} {park your cars curbside}. A few nouns form adverbs by taking the ending *-ways* {side–sideways}, *-ward* {sky–skyward}, or *-wise* {clock–clockwise}. And adverbial suffixes are sometimes added to phrases {she replied matter-of-factly}. Finally, not every word ending in *-ly* is an adverb—some are adjectives {lovely} {curly}.

5.164 **Adverbs without suffixes.** Many common adverbs don't have an identifying suffix {almost} {never} {here} {now} {just} {seldom} {late} {near} {too}.

## SIMPLE VERSUS COMPOUND ADVERBS

5.165 **Simple and flat adverbs.** A simple adverb is a single word that qualifies a single part of speech {hardly} {now} {deep}. A flat or bare adverb is one that has an *-ly* form but whose adjectival form may work equally well or even better, especially when used with an imperative in an informal context {drive slow} {hold on tight} {tell me quick}. Some flat adverbs are always used in their adjectival form {work fast} because the *-ly* form has become obsolete (although it may linger in related words—e.g., *steadfast* and *steadfastly*). And the flat adverb may have a different meaning from the *-ly* adverb. Compare *I am working hard* with *I am hardly working*.

5.166 **Phrasal and compound adverbs.** A phrasal adverb consists of two or more words that function together as an adverb {in the meantime} {for a while} {here and there}. A compound adverb appears to be a single word but is a compound of several words {notwithstanding} {heretofore} {thereupon}. Compound adverbs should be used cautiously and sparingly because they tend to make the tone stuffy.

## ADVERBIAL DEGREES

5.167 **Positive adverbs.** Like adjectives (see 5.88), adverbs have three degrees: the positive, the comparative, and the superlative. A positive adverb simply expresses a quality without reference to any other thing {the nurse spoke **softly**} {the choir sang **merrily**}.

5.168 **Comparative adverbs.** A comparative adverb compares the quality of a specified action done by two persons, groups, or things {Bitey worked **longer than Arachne**} {Rachel studied **more industriously than Edith**}. Most one-syllable adverbs that do not end in *-ly* form the comparative by taking the suffix *-er* {sooner} {harder}. These forms are called *synthetic comparatives*. Multisyllable adverbs usually form the comparative with *more* or *less* {the Shakespearean villain fenced **more ineptly** than the hero} {the patient is walking **less haltingly** today}. These forms are called *periphrastic comparatives*. But there are exceptions for adverbs that end in *-ly* if the *-ly* is not a suffix {early–earlier}.

5.169 **Superlative adverbs.** A superlative adverb compares the quality of a specified action done by at least three persons, groups, or things {Sullie bowled **fastest** of all the cricketers} {of the three doctoral candidates, Dunya defended her dissertation the **most adamantly**}. In a loose sense, the superlative is sometimes used for emphasis rather than comparison {the pianist played **most skillfully**}. Most one-syllable adverbs that do not end in *-ly* form the superlative by taking the suffix *-est* {soonest} {hardest}. These forms are called *synthetic superlatives*. Multisyllable adverbs usually form the superlative with *most* or *least* {everyone's eyesight was acute, but I could see **most acutely**} {of all the people making choices, he chose **least wisely**}. These forms are called *periphrastic superlatives*. There are exceptions for adverbs that end in *-ly* if the *-ly* is not a suffix {early–earliest}.

5.170 **Irregular adverbs.** A few adverbs have irregular comparative and superlative forms {badly–worse–worst} {little–less–least}. A good dictionary is the best resource for finding an irregular adverb's forms of comparison.

5.171 **Noncomparable adverbs.** Many adverbs are noncomparable. Some, by their definitions, are absolute and cannot be compared {eternally} {never} {singly} {uniquely} {universally}. Most adverbs indicating time {now} {then}, position {on}, number {first} {finally}, or place {here} are also noncomparable.

## POSITION OF ADVERBS

5.172 **Placement of adverbs.** To avoid miscues, an adverb should generally be placed as near as possible to the word it is intended to modify. For example, in *the marathoners submitted their applications to compete immediately*, what does *immediately* modify—*compete* or *submitted*? Placing the adverb with the word it modifies makes the meaning clear—e.g., *the marathoners immediately submitted their applications to compete*. A misplaced adverb can completely change a sentence's meaning. For example, *we nearly lost all our camping equipment* states that the equipment was saved; *we lost nearly all our camping equipment* states that almost everything was lost. An adverb's placement is also important because adverbs show time {we'll meet **again**}, place or source {put the flowers **here**} {**where** did you get that idea?}, manner {speak **softly**}, degree or extent {sales are **very** good} {**how** far is it to the pub?}, reason {I don't know **why** Pat couldn't find the right answer}, consequence {we should **therefore** hasten to support her candidacy}, and number {**first**, we need to get our facts straight}. Adverbs can also express comments or observations {Vic was **undoubtedly** late} {Imani **clearly** recalled everything}.

5.173 **Adverbs that modify words other than verbs.** If an adverb qualifies an adjective, an adverb, a preposition, or a conjunction, it should immediately precede the word qualified {our vacation was **very short**} {the flight took **too long**} {your fence is **partly over** the property line} {leave **only when** the bell rings}. The adverb or adverbs modifying a single adjective, grouped with that adjective, are called an *adjective cluster* {a **classically trained** pianist}.

5.174 **Adverbs that modify intransitive verbs.** If an adverb qualifies an intransitive verb, it generally follows the verb {the students **sighed gloomily** when homework was assigned} {the owl **perched precariously** on a thin branch}. Some exceptions are *always*, *generally*, *never*, *often*, *rarely*, and *seldom*, which may precede the verb {mountaineers **seldom succeed** in climbing K2}.

5.175 **Adverbs and linking verbs.** Adverbs do not generally follow linking verbs (see 5.105), such as *be*-verbs, *appear*, *become*, *feel*, *hear*, *look*, *seem*, *smell*, and *taste*. These verbs connect a descriptive word with the clause's subject; the descriptive word after the verb applies to the subject, not the verb {he **seems** honest}. To determine whether a verb is a linking verb, consider whether the descriptive word describes the action or condition, or the subject. For example, *the sculptor feels badly* literally describes an impaired tactile sense (though that couldn't conceivably be the intended meaning). But *the sculptor feels bad* describes the sculptor as unwell or perhaps experiencing guilt (*bad* being not an adverb but a predicate adjective). Those adverbs that typically precede intransitive verbs (see 5.174), however, may modify linking verbs {she **quickly** became uncomfortable} {he **sometimes** seems dishonest}.

5.176 **Adverb within a verb phrase or infinitive.** Some adverbs that qualify a verb phrase may follow the principal verb {you must **go quietly**} {are you **asking rhetorically**?}. But the normal place for the adverb is between the auxiliary verb and the principal verb {the administration **has consistently repudiated** this view} {the reports **will soon generate** controversy} {public opinion **is sharply divided**}. There has never been a rule against such placement, and in fact it's often preferable. (See 5.108.) It is also perfectly acceptable to split an infinitive with an adverb to add emphasis, clarify meaning, or produce a natural sound. (See 5.112.) A verb's infinitive, or *to* form, is split when an intervening word immediately follows *to*. If the adverb bears the emphasis in a phrase {to boldly go} {to strongly favor}, the split infinitive is justified and often even necessary. Recasting a sentence just to eliminate a split infinitive or to avoid splitting the infinitive can alter the nuance or meaning of the sentence (compare *it's best to always get up early* [*always* modifies *get up*] with *it's always best to get up early* [*always* modifies *best*]), or it can make the phrasing sound unnatural—e.g., *it's best to get up early always*.

5.177 **Use and misuse of "only."** *Only* functions as an adjective, an adverb, and a conjunction, and it can modify any part of speech. It is probably poorly placed in sentences more often than any other word. *Only* emphasizes the word or phrase that immediately follows it. When *only* appears too early in the sentence, it has a de-emphasizing effect; it can also alter the meaning of the sentence or produce ambiguity. Compare *I bought only tomatoes at the market* (I bought nothing else) with *I bought tomatoes only at the market* (I bought nothing other than tomatoes or I didn't buy tomatoes from any other place?) and *I bought tomatoes at the market only* (I didn't buy them from any other place). In idiomatic spoken English, *only* is placed before the verb, regardless of what it modifies: *I only bought tomatoes at the market*. This may be acceptable in speech because the speaker can use intonation to make the meaning clear. But since in writing there is no guidance from intonation, rigorous placement of *only* aids reader comprehension.

## *Prepositions*

### DEFINITION AND TYPES

5.178 **Prepositions generally.** A preposition is an uninflected function word or phrase linking a noun element (the preposition's object) with another part of the sentence to show the relationship between them. Prepositions express such notions as position (*about, above, below, on, under*), direction (*in, into, to, toward*), time (*after, before, during, until*), and source (*from, of, out of*). A preposition's object (sometimes termed an *oblique object*) is usually a noun, or else a pronoun in the objective case {**between** me and them}. Usually a preposition comes before its object, but there are exceptions. For example, a preposition used with the relative pronoun *that* (or with *that* understood) always follows the object {this is the moment (that) I've been waiting **for**}. It also frequently, but not always, follows the pronouns *which* {which alternative is your decision based **on**?} {this is the alternative **on which** my decision is based} and *whom* {there is a banker (whom) I must speak with} {I can't tell you **to whom** you should apply}. See also 5.186.

5.179 **Simple and compound prepositions.** Many prepositions are relatively straightforward. A simple preposition consists of a single monosyllabic word {as} {at} {by}. A compound preposition has two or more syllables and is made from two or more words {into} {outside} {upon}.

5.180 **Phrasal prepositions.** A phrasal preposition, sometimes called a *complex preposition*, is two or more separate words used as a prepositional unit. These include *according to, because of, by means of, by reason of, by way of, contrary to, for the sake of, in accordance with, in addition to, in apposition with, in case of, in consideration of, in front of, in regard to, in respect to,* *in spite of, instead of, on account of, out of, with reference to, with regard to,* and *with respect to.* Many of these phrasal prepositions are symptoms of officialese, bureaucratese, or other types of verbose style. If a single-word preposition will do in context, use it. For example, if *about* will replace *with regard to* or *in connection with,* a judicious editor will inevitably prefer to use the simpler expression.

5.181 **Participial prepositions.** A participial preposition is a participial form that functions as a preposition (or sometimes as a subordinating conjunction). Examples are *assuming, barring, concerning, considering, during, notwithstanding, owing to, provided, regarding, respecting,* and *speaking of.* Unlike other participles, these words do not create danglers when they have no subject {**considering** the road conditions, the trip went quickly} {**regarding** Watergate, he had nothing to say}. See 5.119.

PREPOSITIONAL PHRASES

5.182 **Prepositional phrases generally.** A prepositional phrase consists of a preposition, its object, and any words that modify the object. A prepositional phrase can be used as a noun {**for James to change his mind** would be a miracle}, an adverb (also called an *adverbial phrase*) {we strolled **through the glade**}, or an adjective (also called an *adjectival phrase*) {we'd love to see the cathedrals **of Paris**}.

5.183 **Prepositional function.** Prepositions signal many kinds of relationships. For example, a preposition may express a spatial relationship {to} {from} {out of} {into}, time {at} {for} {throughout} {until}, cause {because of} {on account of}, means {like} {with} {by}, possession {without} {of}, exceptions {but for} {besides} {except}, support {with} {for}, opposition {against}, or concession {despite} {for all} {notwithstanding}.

5.184 **Placement of prepositional phrases.** A prepositional phrase with an adverbial or adjectival function should be as close as possible to the word it modifies to avoid awkwardness, ambiguity, or unintended meanings. Compare *Is there a person with a small dog named Sandy here?* (is the person or the dog named Sandy?) with *Is there a person named Sandy here with a small dog?* Or compare *The woman with the Popular Front circulates petitions* with *The woman circulates petitions with the Popular Front.*

5.185 **Refinements on placement.** If a prepositional phrase equally modifies all the elements of a compound construction, the phrase follows the last element in the compound {the date, the place, and the budget **for the**

**wedding** have been decided}. If the subject is singular and followed by a plural prepositional phrase, the predicate is singular—e.g., compare the predicate in *the man and his two daughters have arrived* with that in *the man with two daughters has arrived* and in *the man has arrived with his two daughters*.

5.186 **Ending a sentence with a preposition.** The traditional caveat of yesteryear against ending sentences or clauses with prepositions is an unnecessary and pedantic restriction. And it is wrong. As Winston Churchill is said to have put it sarcastically, "That is the type of arrant pedantry up with which I shall not put." A sentence that ends in a preposition may sound more natural than a sentence carefully constructed to avoid a final preposition. Compare *This is the case I told you about* with *This is the case about which I told you*. The "rule" prohibiting terminal prepositions was an ill-founded superstition based on a false analogy to Latin grammar.

5.187 **Clashing prepositions.** If a phrasal verb {give in} precedes a prepositional phrase {in every argument}, the back-to-back prepositions, if they are the same, will clash {he gives in in every argument}. Recast the sentence when possible to avoid such juxtaposed prepositions—e.g., *rather than continue arguing, he always gives in*, or *in every argument, he gives in*. See also 6.59. For more on phrasal verbs, see 5.106.

5.188 **Elliptical prepositional phrases.** Sometimes a prepositional phrase is elliptical, being an independent expression without an antecedent. It often starts a clause and is normally detachable from the statement without affecting the meaning. Elliptical prepositional phrases include *for example, for instance, in any event, in a word, in the last analysis*, and *in the long run* {**in any event**, call me when you arrive}.

5.189 **Pronoun case in prepositional phrases.** If a pronoun appears in a prepositional phrase, the pronoun is usually in the objective case {with me} {alongside her} {between them} (see also 5.20, 5.38). Note that *than* may function as either a conjunction {he's taller **than I** [**am**]} or a preposition {he's taller **than me**}. In formal and literary use, *than* (like *as*) has long been considered a conjunction. That is, *taller than I* has predominated in edited American English from its very beginnings, and in British English until the 1990s, and *than me, than her*, etc. have been regarded as less polished (to say the least) than *than I, than she*, etc. But in spoken English, *than* and *as* are often treated as prepositions that take a pronoun in the objective case {you're better **than me**} {you're as well known **as me**}. A possessive pronoun may be used before the preposition's object {to **my house**}.

OTHER PREPOSITIONAL ISSUES

5.190 **Prepositions and functional variation.** Some words that function as prepositions may also function as other parts of speech. The distinguishing feature of a preposition is that it always has an object. A word such as *above, behind, below, by, down, in, off, on,* or *up* can be used as either an adverb or a preposition. When used as a preposition, it takes an object {let's slide **down the hill**}. When used as an adverb, it does not {we sat **down**}. Some conjunctions may serve as prepositions (e.g., *than* and *but*). Compare the prepositional *but* in *everyone but Fuzzy traveled abroad last summer* (*but* is used to mean "except") with the conjunctive *but* in *I like the cut but not the color* (*but* introduces a clause containing an implied separate action: *I don't like the color*).

5.191 **Use and misuse of "like."** The traditional function of *like* is as an adjective {teens often see themselves as star-crossed lovers **like Romeo and Juliet**}. Though the use of *like* as a conjunction has been considered nonstandard since the seventeenth century, it is common in dialectal and colloquial usage {he ran **like** he was really scared}, increasingly displacing *as* or *as if* in ordinary speech (in *it happened just like I said it would,* traditional grammarians would replace the conjunctive *like* with *as*; and in *you're looking around like you've misplaced something, like* with *as if*). Because *as* and *as if* are conjunctions, they are followed by pronouns in the nominative case {do you work too hard, **as I** do?}. As a preposition, *like* is followed by a noun or by a pronoun in the objective case {the person in that old portrait looks **like me**}.

5.192 **"Of" phrase and verb agreement.** When a noun expressing an indefinite quantity, such as *group* or *amount,* is followed by the preposition *of* and a plural noun, the verb should usually agree with the number of the noun before the *of*-phrase {a **group** of cyclists **is** waiting to start} {the **amount** of herbs **depends** on how much flavor you want}. Certain nouns such as *percentage, majority,* and *number* are exceptions. *Percentage* is a singular noun {a small **percentage is** acceptable} but when followed by *of* plus a plural noun (whether the phrase is actual or clearly implied) is construed as plural {a small **percentage of seeds are** unlikely to germinate}. *Majority* takes a singular verb when used as a collective noun {the **majority is** wheat, but some rye is mixed in} but a plural verb when the plural *of*-phrase is spelled out {the **majority of wild animals never attack** people}. With *number of,* the choice of verb depends on whether a definite or indefinite article is used {**the number** of options **keeps** changing} {**a number** of people **have** changed their minds}. For *one of,* see 5.66.

## LIMITING PREPOSITIONAL PHRASES

5.193 **Avoiding overuse of prepositions.** Prepositions can easily be overused. Stylistically, a good ratio to strive for is one preposition for every ten to fifteen words. Five editorial methods can reduce the number of prepositions in a sentence.

5.194 **Cutting prepositional phrases.** If context permits, a prepositional phrase can be eliminated—e.g., *the most important ingredient in this recipe* could be reduced to *the most important ingredient* when it appears within a passage focused on a particular recipe.

5.195 **Cutting unnecessary prepositions.** A noun ending in *-ance, -ence, -ity, -ment, -sion,* or *-tion* is often formed from a verb {qualification–qualify} {performance–perform}. These nouns are sometimes called *nominalizations* or *zombie nouns,* and they often require additional words, especially prepositions (that is, *during her performance of the concerto* is essentially equivalent to *while she performed the concerto,* but it is somewhat more abstract and requires more words). Using a verb instead of a nominalization often eliminates one or two prepositions. For example, *our efforts toward maximization of profits failed* might be edited down to *our efforts to maximize profits failed.*

5.196 **Replacing prepositional phrases with adverbs.** A strong adverb may replace a weaker prepositional phrase. For example, *the president spoke with force* is weak compared with *the president spoke forcefully.*

5.197 **Replacing prepositional phrases with genitives.** A genitive may replace a prepositional phrase, especially an *of*-genitive. For example, *I was dismayed by the complexity of the street map* essentially equals *The street map's complexity dismayed me*. See 5.22.

5.198 **Using active voice to eliminate prepositions.** Changing from the long passive voice (with *by* after the verb) to an active-voice construction always eliminates a preposition. For example, *the ship was sailed by an experienced crew* equals *an experienced crew sailed the ship.*

## PREPOSITIONAL IDIOMS

5.199 **Idiomatic uses of prepositions.** Among the most persistent word-choice issues are those concerning prepositions. Which prepositions go with which words? You *fill* A *with* B but *instill* B *into* A; you *replace* A *with* B but *substitute* B *for* A; you *prefix* A *to* B but *preface* B *with* A; you *force* A *into* B but *enforce* B *on* A; finally, A *implies* B, so you *infer* B *from* A. And that's only the beginning of it.

5.200 **Shifts in prepositional idiom.** While prepositional idioms often give nonnative speakers of English nightmares, even native speakers of English may need to double-check them from time to time. Language shifts. There may be a difference between traditional literary usage (*oblivious of*) and prevailing contemporary usage (*oblivious to*). A writer may choose one or another preposition for reasons of euphony. (Is it better, in a given context, to *ruminate on*, *about*, or *over* a specified problem?) Sometimes, too, the denotative and connotative differences can be striking: It's one thing to be *smitten with* another and quite a different thing to be *smitten by* another.

5.201 **List of words and the prepositions construed with them.** The list below contains words that often give writers trouble. Note that some of the words included here—such as verbs that can be used transitively {the tire abutted the curb} or words that can be used without further qualification {she refused to acquiesce} {his words were considered blasphemy}—do not always take prepositions.

**abide** (*vb.*): with ("stay"); by ("obey"); *none* (transitive)
**abound** (*vb.*): in, with [resources]
**absolve** (*vb.*): from [guilt]; of [obligation]
**abut** (*vb.*): on, against [land]; *none* (transitive)
**accompanied** (*adj.*): by (not *with*) [something *or* someone else]
**accord** (*vb.*): in, with [an opinion]; to [a person]
**acquiesce** (*vb.*): in [a decision]; to [pressure]
**acquit** (*vb.*): of (not *from*) [a charge]; *none* (transitive)
**adept** (*adj.*): at [an activity]; in [an art]
**admit** (*vb.*) ("acknowledge"): *none* (not *to*) (transitive)
**admit** (*vb.*) ("let in"): to, into
**admit** (*vb.*) ("allow"): of
**anxious** (*adj.*): about, over (preferably not *to*) [a concern]
**badger** (*vb.*): into [doing something]; about [a situation]
**ban** (*vb.*): from [a place]
**ban** (*n.*): on [a thing; an activity]
**based** (*adj.*): on (preferably not *upon*) [a premise]; in [a place; a field of study]; at (preferably not *out of*) [a place]
**becoming** (*adj.*): on, to [a person]; of [an office or position]
**bestow** (*vb.*): on (preferably not *upon*) [an honoree]
**binding** (*adj.*): on (preferably not *upon*) [a person]

**blasphemy** (*n.*): against [a religious tenet]
**build** (*vb.*): on (not *off of*)
**center** (*vb.*): on, upon (not *around*) [a primary issue]
**chafe** (*vb.*): at [doing something]; under [an irritating authority]
**coerce** (*vb.*): into [doing something]
**cohesion** (*n.*): between, among [things; groups]
**collude** (*vb.*): with [a person to defraud another]
**commiserate** (*vb.*): with [a person]
**compare** (*vb.*): with (literal comparison); to (poetic or metaphorical comparison)
**comply** (*vb.*): with (not *to*) [a rule; an order]
**confide** (*vb.*): to, in [a person]
**congruence** (*n.*): with [a standard]
**connive** (*vb.*): at [a bad act]; with [another person]
**consider** (*vb.*): *none* (transitive); as [one of several possible aspects (*not* as a substitute for "to be")]; for [a position]
**consist** (*vb.*): of [components (said of concrete things)]; in [qualities (said of abstract things)]
**contemporary** (*adj.*): with [another event]
**contemporary** (*n.*): of [another person]
**contiguous** (*adj.*): with, to [another place]
**contingent** (*adj.*): on (preferably not *upon*)
**contrast** (*vb.*): to, with [a person or thing]
**conversant** (*adj.*): with, in [a field of study]
**convict** (*vb.*): of, for (not *in*)
**depend** (*vb.*): on (preferably not *upon*)
**differ** (*vb.*): from [a thing or quality]; with [a person]; about, over, on [an issue]
**different** (*adj.*): from (but when a dependent clause follows *different*, the conjunction *than* is a defensible substitute for *from what*: "movies today are different than they were in the fifties")
**dissent** (*n. & vb.*): from, against (preferably not *to* or *with*)
**dissimilar** (*adj.*): to (not *from*)
**dissociate** (*vb.*): from
**enamored** (*adj.*): of (not *with*)
**equivalent** (*adj.*): to, in (preferably not *with*)
**excerpt** (*n.*): from (not *of*)
**forbid** (*vb.*): to (formal); from (informal)
**foreclose** (*vb.*): on [mortgaged property]
**hale** (*vb.*): to, into [a place]; before [a magistrate]
**hegemony** (*n.*): over [rivals]; in [a region]
**identical** (*adj.*): with (preferred by purists), to [something else]
**impatience** (*n.*): with [a person]; with, at, about [a situation]
**impose** (*vb.*): on (preferably not *upon*) [a person]

**inaugurate** (*vb.*): as [an officer]; into [an office]
**inculcate** (*vb.*): into, in [a person]
**independent** (*adj.*): of (not *from*) [something else]
**infringe** (*vb.*): *none* (transitive); on (preferably not *upon*) [a right]
**inhere** (*vb.*): in (not *within*) [a person; a thing]
**inquire** (*vb.*): into [situations]; of [people]; after [people]
**instill** (*vb.*): in, into (not *with*) [a person]
**juxtapose** (*vb.*): to (not *with*)
**mastery** (*n.*): of [a skill or knowledge]; over [people]
**militate** (*vb.*): against [a harsher outcome]
**mitigate** (*vb.*): *none* (transitive)
**oblivious** (*adj.*): of (traditional), to [a danger; an opportunity]
**off** (*prep. & adv.*): *none* (not *of*)
**predilection** (*n.*): for [a preferred thing]
**predominate** (*vb.*) (not transitive): in, on, over [a field; rivals]
**preferable** (*adj.*): to (not *than*), over [an alternative]
**pretext** (*n.*): for [a true intention]
**reconcile** (*vb.*): with [a person]; to [a situation]
**reticent** (*adj.*): about [speaking; a topic]
**sanction** (*n.*): for [misbehavior]; of [a sponsoring body]; to [a person; an event]
**shiver** (*vb.*): from [cold]; at [something frightening]
**stigmatize** (*vb.*): *none* (transitive); as [dishonorable]
**subscribe** (*vb.*): to [a periodical or an opinion]; for [stock]
**trade** (*vb.*): for ("swap"); in ("sell"); with ("do business with"); at ("patronize"); in [certain goods]; on ("buy and sell at")
**trust** (*n.*): in [faith]; for ("beneficial trust")
**undaunted** (*adj.*): in [a task]; by [obstacles]
**unequal** (*adj.*): to [a challenge]; in [attributes]
**used** (*adj.*): to ("accustomed"); for ("applied to")
**vexed** (*adj.*): with [someone]; about, at [something]

If you're uncertain about a preposition, the Google Books Ngram Viewer can show you, based on millions of texts, which phrasings are most common, as well as something about the historical frequency of competing forms. For example, if you want to know whether *oblivious of* or *oblivious to* is the more usual phrasing, a Google *n*-gram can tell you within seconds, with quantified support.

## *Conjunctions*

5.202 **Conjunctions defined.** A conjunction is a function word that connects sentences, clauses, or words within a clause {my daughter graduated from college in December, **and** my son will graduate from high school in May [*and* connects two sentences]} {I said hello, **but** no one answered [*but* connects two clauses]} {we're making progress slowly **but** surely [*but* joins two adverbs within a clause]}. In Standard English, conjunctions connect pronouns in the same case {he **and** she are colleagues} {the teacher encouraged her **and** me}. A pronoun following the conjunction *than* or *as* is normally in the nominative case even when the clause that follows is understood {you are wiser **than I** [am]} {you seem as pleased **as she** [does]}—except in informal or colloquial English {you are wiser than me}. In the latter instance, *than* can be read as a preposition (see 5.189).

5.203 **Simple versus compound conjunctions.** A conjunction may be simple, a single word such as *and, but, if, or,* or *though*. Most are derived from prepositions. Compound conjunctions are single words formed by combining two or more words. Most are relatively modern formations; they include words such as *although, because, nevertheless, notwithstanding,* and *unless*. Phrasal conjunctions are connectives made up of two or more separate words. Examples are *as though, inasmuch as, in case, provided that, so that,* and *supposing that*. The two main classes of conjunctions are coordinating and subordinating.

5.204 **Coordinating conjunctions.** Coordinating conjunctions join words or groups of words of equal grammatical rank, such as two nouns, two verbs, two phrases, or two clauses {are you speaking to him **or** to me?} {the results are disappointing **but** not discouraging}. A coordinating conjunction may be either a single word or a correlative conjunction.

5.205 **Correlative conjunctions.** Correlative conjunctions are conjunctions used in pairs, often to join successive clauses that depend on each other to form a complete thought. Some examples of correlative conjunctions are *as–as, if–then, either–or, neither–nor, both–and, where–there, so–as,* and *not only–but also*. Correlative conjunctions must frame structurally identical or matching sentence parts {she wanted **both** to win the gold medal **and** to set a new record}; in other words, each member of the pair should immediately precede the same part of speech {they **not only read** the book **but also saw** the movie} {**if** the first **claim** is true, **then** the second **claim** must be false}.

5.206 **Subordinating conjunctions.** A subordinating conjunction connects clauses of unequal grammatical rank. The conjunction introduces a clause that is dependent on the independent clause {follow this road

**until** you reach the highway} {that squirrel is friendly **because** people feed it} {Marcus promised **that** he would help}.

5.207 **Special uses of subordinating conjunctions.** Subordinating conjunctions or conjunctive phrases often denote the following relationships: (1) *Comparison or degree*—e.g., *than* (if it follows comparative adverbs or adjectives, or if it follows *else, rather, other,* or *otherwise*), *as, else, otherwise, rather, as much as, as far as,* and *as well as* {is a raven less clever **than** a magpie?} {these amateur musicians play **as well as** professionals} {it's not true **as far as** I can discover}. (2) *Time*—e.g., *since, until, as long as, as soon as, before, after, when, as,* and *while* {**while** we waited, it began to snow} {the tire went flat **as** we were turning the corner} {we'll start the game **as soon as** everyone understands the rules} {the audience returned to the auditorium **after** the concert's resumption was announced}. (3) *Condition or assumption*—e.g., *if, though, unless, except, without,* and *once* {**once** you sign the agreement, we can begin remodeling the house} {your thesis must be presented next week **unless** you have a good reason to postpone it} {I'll go on this business trip **if** I can fly first class}. (4) *Reason or concession*—e.g., *as, inasmuch as, why, because, for, since, though, although,* and *albeit* {**since** you won't share the information, I can't help you} {Sir John decided to purchase the painting **although** it was very expensive} {she deserves credit **because** it was her idea}. (5) *Purpose or result*—e.g., *that, so that, in order that,* and *such that* {we dug up the yard **so that** a new water garden could be laid out} {he sang **so loudly that** he became hoarse}. (6) *Place*—e.g., *where* {I found a great restaurant **where** I didn't expect one to be}. (7) *Manner*—e.g., *as if* and *as though* {he swaggers around the office **as if** he were an executive}. (8) *Appositions*—e.g., *and, or, what,* and *that* {the buffalo, **or** American bison, was once nearly extinct}. (9) *Indirect questions*—e.g., *whether, why,* and *when* {he could not say **whether** we were going the right way}.

5.208 **Adverbial conjunctions.** An adverbial conjunction connects two clauses and also qualifies a verb {the valet has forgotten **where** Alvaro's car is parked [*where* qualifies the verb *is parked*]}. There are two types of adverbial conjunctions: relative and interrogative. A relative adverbial conjunction does the same job as any other adverbial conjunction, but it has an antecedent {do you recall that café **where** we first met? [*café* is the antecedent of *where*]}. An interrogative adverbial conjunction indirectly states a question {Barbara asked **when** we are supposed to leave [*when* poses the indirect question]}. Some common examples of conjunctive relative adverbs are *after, as, before, now, since, so, until, when,* and *where*. Interrogative adverbs are used to ask direct and indirect questions; the most common are *why, how, when, where,* and *what* {I don't see **how** you reached that conclusion}.

5.209 **Beginning a sentence with a conjunction.** There is a widespread belief—one with no historical or grammatical foundation—that it is an error to begin a sentence with a conjunction such as *and, but,* or *so.* In fact, a substantial percentage (often as many as 10 percent) of the sentences in first-rate writing begin with conjunctions. It has been so for centuries, and even the most conservative grammarians have followed this practice. Charles Allen Lloyd's words from 1938 fairly sum up the situation as it stands even today:

> Next to the groundless notion that it is incorrect to end an English sentence with a preposition, perhaps the most widespread of the many false beliefs about the use of our language is the equally groundless notion that it is incorrect to begin one with "but" or "and." As in the case of the superstition about the prepositional ending, no textbook supports it, but apparently about half of our teachers of English go out of their way to handicap their pupils by inculcating it. One cannot help wondering whether those who teach such a monstrous doctrine ever read any English themselves.[7]

Still, *but* as an adversative conjunction can occasionally be unclear at the beginning of a sentence. Evaluate the contrasting force of the *but* in question and see whether the needed word is really *and*; if *and* can be substituted, then *but* is almost certainly the wrong word. Consider this example: *He went to school this morning. But he left his lunch box on the kitchen table.* Between those sentences is an elliptical idea, since the two actions are in no way contradictory. What is implied is something like this: *He went to school, intending to have lunch there, but he left his lunch behind.* Because *and* would have made sense in the passage as originally stated, *but* is not the right word—the idea for the contrastive *but* should be explicit. To sum up, then, *but* is a perfectly proper way to open a sentence, but only if the idea it introduces truly contrasts with what precedes. For that matter, *but* is often an effective way of introducing a paragraph that develops an idea contrary to the one preceding it.

5.210 **Beginning a sentence with "however."** *However* has been used as a conjunctive adverb since the fourteenth century. Like other adverbs, it can be used at the beginning of a sentence. But *however* is more ponderous

7. Charles Allen Lloyd, *We Who Speak English: And Our Ignorance of Our Mother Tongue* (Thomas Y. Crowell, 1938), 19.

and has less impact than the simple *but*. As a matter of style, *however* is more effectively used within a sentence to emphasize the word or phrase that precedes it {The job seemed exciting at first. Soon, **however**, it turned out to be exceedingly dull.}. For purposes of euphony and flow, not of grammar, many highly accomplished writers shun the sentence-starting *however* as a contrasting word. Yet the word is fine in that position in the sense "in whatever way" (not followed by a comma) {however that may be, we've now made our decision}.

5.211 **Conjunctions and the number of a verb.** Coordinating and disjunctive conjunctions affect whether a verb should be plural or singular. Conjunctions such as *and* and *through* indicate that grouped sentence elements impart plurality, so a plural verb is correct {the best vacation **and** the worst vacation of my life **were** on cruises} {the first **through** seventh innings **were** scoreless}. But conjunctions such as *or* and *either–or* distinguish the elements and do not impart plurality, so the singular verb is used if the elements are singular {a squirrel **or** a chipmunk **raids** the bird feeder every day} {either William **or** Henry **dances** with Lady Hill}. Other types of conjunctions have no effect on the verb's number; for example, if *and* is used as a copulative conjunction, the verb that follows may be singular {Andrés's bicycle was new, **and** so **was** his helmet}. See also 7.8.

5.212 **Omitting "that."** When *that* is a conjunction, omitting it may result in a miscue or ambiguity, however slight {the plaintiff charged the expenses were recorded as $5,000 instead of $500 [the expenses weren't charged; insert *that* before *the expenses*]}. Although the word *that* may often be safely omitted after the verbs *say* and *think* {we said the budget needs to be accurate} {Hank thought the tire was flat}, it should be retained after other verbs, including near-synonyms {we declared **that** the budget needs to be accurate [is *needs* a noun or a verb?]} {Hank believed **that** the brochure was outdated}, to make it clear that what follows is a clause and not a complement. But when the subordinate clause begins with a pronoun, the conjunction *that* can often be safely omitted {Jane assured us she could do it} {Hank believed his tire was flat}.

## *Interjections*

5.213 **Interjections defined.** An interjection is a word or short phrase used as an exclamation with no literal meaning and having no grammatical connection with anything around it {never again!} {you don't say!}.

Because they stand outside the normal syntactic relations within a sentence, interjections are said to be used absolutely {**really**, I can't understand why you put up with the situation} {**oh no**, how am I going to fix the damage?} {**hey**, it's my turn next!}. They are often allowed to stand alone as sentences, often verbless ones {**Oh**! I've lost my wallet!} {**Ouch**! I think my ankle is sprained!} {**Get out**!} {**Whoa**!}. Introductory words like *well* and *why* may also act as interjections when they are extraneous utterances {**well**, I tried my best} {**why**, I would never do that}. The punctuation offsetting an interjection helps mark it. Compare the different meanings of *Well, I didn't know him* with *I didn't know him well*, and *Why, here you are!* with *I have no idea why you are here* and *Why? I have no idea*. See also 6.37, 6.38.

5.214 **Use of interjections.** Interjections are natural in speech {your order should be shipped, **oh**, in eight to ten days} and frequently used in dialogue (and formerly in poetry). As a mid-sentence interrupter, an interjection may direct attention to one's phrasing or reflect the writer's or speaker's attitude toward the subject, especially if the tone is informal or colloquial {because our business proposal was, **ahem**, poorly presented, our budget will not be increased this year}.

5.215 **Interjections and functional variation.** Because interjections are usually grammatically independent of the rest of the sentence, all other parts of speech may be used as interjections. A word that is classified as some other part of speech but used with the force of an interjection is called an *exclamatory noun*, *exclamatory adjective*, etc. Some examples are *good!* (adjective); *idiot!* (noun); *help!* (verb); *indeed!* (adverb); *me!* (pronoun); *and!* (conjunction); *quickly!* (adverb).

5.216 **Words that are exclusively interjections.** Some words are used only as interjections—for example, *ouch*, *whew*, *ugh*, *psst*, and *oops*.

## SYNTAX

5.217 **Syntax defined.** *Syntax* is the collective term we use to denote all the rules governing how words are arranged into sentences. In an analytic language like English—one that uses word order to show word relations—syntax is particularly important in expressing meaning.

5.218 **Statements.** Most sentences are statements having a declarative structure in which (1) the clause contains a subject and (2) the subject precedes the verb. Sometimes in speech and informal writing, the subject is merely implied {[he] missed the ball} {[I] think I'll go to the store}. In a few negative idioms, the subject may follow part of the verb phrase {scarcely had we arrived when we had to return}.

5.219 **Questions.** Sentences that seek to elicit information are known as *questions*. They have an interrogative structure, which typically begins with a question word. There are three main types: (1) yes–no questions, which are intended to prompt an affirmative or negative response {will we be gone long?}; (2) *wh-* questions, so called because they characteristically start with *who, what, when, where, why, which,* or *how* (not quite a *wh-* word, but it counts) {which apples do you want?}; and (3) alternative questions, which prompt a response relating to options mentioned in the sentence {would you rather play golf or tennis?}.

5.220 **Some exceptional types of questions.** Four types of interrogative utterances aren't classifiable under the three categories given in 5.219. Two are special types of yes–no questions. The first is the spoken sentence with a declarative structure in which one's pitch rises at the end, in a questioning way {he's going to Corpus Christi?}. To show vexation in such a question, the question mark may be paired with an exclamation point {she's going to Padre Island?!}. The second special type of yes–no question is the tag question, in which the interrogative inversion appears at the end of a statement {he has arrived, hasn't he?} {it's good, isn't it?}. A few tag questions are signaled by particular words without the interrogative inversion {it's raining, right?} {you're tired, eh?} {you want to go, yes?}. A third special type is the exclamatory question, in which the interrogative structure appears but when the statement is spoken, one's tone normally falls at the end {isn't it nice out here!} {how great is this!}. Finally, a rhetorical question is phrased in the interrogative structure but is meant as an emphatic or evocative statement, without the expectation of an answer {why should I care?} {who knows how long it might take?}. A rhetorical question can become more insistent when the question mark is omitted {you've lost the car keys; that's a problem, isn't it}. See also 6.72.

5.221 **Directives.** A directive or imperative is a sentence that instructs somebody to do or not to do something. The word *command* is sometimes used as a synonym, but most grammarians consider the term *command* more appropriate for one of eight main types of directives, all of which are in the imperative mood of the verb: (1) command {come here now!}; (2) prohibition {don't do that!}; (3) invitation {join us for dinner!};

(4) warning {watch out for rattlesnakes!}; (5) plea {stay here} {help!}; (6) request {put your book away}; (7) well-wishing {play well} {have a good time!}; and (8) advice {put on some insect repellent}.

5.222 **Exceptional directives.** Several directives depart from these common patterns, as when the subject is expressed {sit you down} {you stay there}; when they begin with *let* {let's have a picnic} {let us wait}; or when they begin with *do* {do help yourself}.

5.223 **Exclamations.** An exclamation expresses the extent to which a speaker is moved, aroused, impressed, or disgusted by something. It can take the form of a simple interjection {oh my!} {pishposh!}. Or it can follow a sentence structure consisting of *what* or *how* followed by a subject and verb {what an extraordinary novel this is!} {how well she writes!}. Exclamations are sometimes elliptically expressed {what finery!} {how pretty!} {how ugly!}. In formal, literary English, exclamations can be signaled by inverted word order {little did I expect such unfair treatment}. In the casual writing found in social media, email, and text messages, an exclamation point might signal enthusiasm or sincerity {thank you!} {that's a great idea!}, but it might sometimes be perceived as sarcastic. As a rule, exclamation points should be used with restraint. See also 6.75.

## *The Four Traditional Types of Sentence Structures*

5.224 **Simple sentence.** A simple sentence consists of a single independent clause with no dependent clause {no man is an island}. A sentence can be simple despite having internal compound constructions serving as subjects, main verbs, objects of prepositions, and others {time and tide wait for no man}.

5.225 **Compound sentence.** A compound sentence contains two independent clauses (called *coordinate clauses*) with no dependent clause {the rain was heavy, and my umbrella was not much help}. Grammarians are divided on the question whether one type of sentence should be labeled compound or simple: *She arrived early and stayed late*. Traditional grammarians have tended to call this a simple sentence with a compound predicate (where *arrived* and *stayed* are coordinate verbs). Transformational grammarians have tended to call it a compound sentence with an elided subject in the second clause {she arrived early[,] and [she] stayed late}.

5.226 **Complex sentence.** A complex sentence contains a single independent clause with one or more dependent clauses {I'll be home after I finish work}. Such a sentence may have only one dependent clause {she won **because she practiced so hard**}, or it may contain a variety of dependent clauses {the books **that were nominated** argued **that most behavioral differences among people aren't genetic in origin** [*that were nominated* is an adjective clause; *that most behavioral differences among people aren't genetic in origin* is a noun clause]}.

5.227 **Compound-complex sentence.** A compound-complex sentence contains multiple independent clauses and at least one dependent clause {it was a beautiful evening, so after we left work we went for a walk [*after we left work* is a dependent clause between two independent clauses]}. It differs from a complex sentence only in containing more than one independent clause. Like the independent clauses of a compound sentence, those of a compound-complex sentence are called *coordinate clauses*.

## *English Sentence Patterns*

5.228 **Importance of word order.** English is known as an *analytic language*—one that depends largely on word order. (A *synthetic language*, such as Latin, depends largely on inflectional forms of words.) In the transition from Old English (AD 450–1100) to Middle English (1100–1500), the language lost most of its inflected forms—except those for pronouns (*I–me–mine* etc.). Nouns no longer have nominative and accusative cases. Instead, word order governs meaning. Consider this example: *Chris sees Pat. Chris* is the subject, *sees* the verb, and *Pat* the object. It's the basic subject-verb-object (SVO) pattern. We deduce the meaning from the position of the words: Someone named Chris notices someone named Pat. If we change it to *Pat sees Chris*, the meaning is transformed because of the SVO order. We now infer that someone named Pat notices someone named Chris. The SVO pattern is highly significant: It governs the meaning of most English statements. Departures from it typically signal either unusual emphasis or the posing of a question (as opposed to the making of a statement).

5.229 **The basic SVO pattern.** Despite repeating the same fundamental word order in sentence after sentence, English offers enough variety—in vocabulary and in what can function as subjects, verbs, and objects—to keep things interesting. Consider these examples, all of which use the pattern but with interesting levels of sophistication:

| Mary | likes | pomegranates. |
|---|---|---|
| S | V | O |

| The umpire we were talking about | rejected | our arguments. |
|---|---|---|
| S | V | O |

| The woman down the street | is selling | loaves of bread. |
|---|---|---|
| S | V | O |

| The obstacles that we face | create | opportunities. |
|---|---|---|
| S | V | O |

| How you think of yourself | affects | both | the way you approach |
|---|---|---|---|
| S | V | | O |

| the problems of everyday life | and | the degree to which you're |
|---|---|---|
| O | | O |

| perceived as being well adjusted. |
|---|
| O |

5.230 **All seven syntactic patterns.** Syntactic patterns other than the SVO pattern are available, but they are limited to specific types that include two to four of these elements: subject (S), verb (V), [direct] object (O), indirect object (IO), complement (C), adverbial (A). Here are all seven basic clause patterns:

S + V: Sandy smiled.
S + V + O: Sandy hit the ball.
S + V + C: Sandy is eager.
S + V + A: Sandy plays well.
S + V + IO + O: Sandy gave Jerry the ball.
S + V + O + C: Sandy got her bag wet.
S + V + O + A: Sandy wrote her score on the card.

5.231 **Variations on syntactic order.** When clause elements appear in a different order, the inversion may indicate either a question {is Sandy all right? [V–S–C]} or a special kind of emphasis:

| Yoda | my name | is! |
|---|---|---|
| C | S | V |

| "Finished," | John | mumbled. |
|---|---|---|
| O | S | V |

| "Help!" | cried | the child. |
|---|---|---|
| O | V | S |

Inversions of this type achieve a special emphasis precisely because they depart from the normal sequence of sentence elements.

## *Clauses*

5.232 **Clauses.** A *clause* is a grammatical unit that contains a subject, a finite verb, and any complements that the verb requires. An *independent clause* can stand alone as a sentence {José saw a squirrel}, while a *dependent clause* cannot stand alone because of the presence of a word by which it would normally be linked to an independent clause {**because he was hungry**, he sat down for a meal}. A dependent clause is usually introduced either by a relative pronoun (making it a relative clause) or by a subordinating conjunction, which establishes the semantic relationship between the independent clause and the dependent one. Combining related ideas by linking one or more dependent clauses to an independent one is called *subordination*; the result is a complex sentence. Because a dependent clause is always subordinate to an independent clause for contextual meaning, it is also called a *subordinate clause*. A dependent clause commonly serves one of several functions: the direct object of a verb {everyone believed **that the note was genuine** [the *that*-clause is the direct object of *believed*]}; an adjectival clause modifying a noun element {he **who hesitates** is lost [*who hesitates* adjectivally modifies *he*]}; an adverbial clause modifying a verb or verb phrase {everyone listens **when she speaks** [the *when*-clause modifies the verb *listens*]}.

5.233 **Relative clauses.** A relative clause is a subordinate clause that is introduced by a relative pronoun and modifies the noun element (or sentence or clause) it follows {the car **that you own**} {those **who follow his progress**} {they were ten minutes late to the opera, **which meant they couldn't enter until the end of the first act**}. In some relative clauses, called *contact clauses*, the relative pronoun is merely implied {all the people **you mention** have already registered [the relative pronoun *who* is implied in *people* [*whom*] *you mention*]}. Because the necessary connective is omitted, contact clauses are a type of elliptical clause—one often involving what is known as a *whiz-deletion* (so called because it often amounts to the omission of *who is*). The relative pronoun may be omitted as long as it isn't preceded by a preposition and isn't the subject of the relative clause {the professor I most admire is Dr. Cawthon (*whom* or *that* is understood after *professor*)}. But use caution: Omitting *that* when it functions as a conjunction immediately following a verb may result in a miscue or ambiguity. See 5.212.

5.234 **Appositive clauses.** A clause used in apposition to a noun element in the sentence is called an *appositive clause*. Though these are often (but not always) introduced with the same words that introduce relative clauses (*that, which, who*), the two differ in that a relative clause functions only within the sentence, while an appositive clause is self-contained: With its introductory relative pronoun removed, it could stand on its own as a grammatical sentence {we all heard the report **that the beloved broadcaster had died** [without *that*, the remaining appositive clause is grammatically complete: *the beloved broadcaster had died*]}.

5.235 **Conditional clauses.** A conditional clause (also called a *protasis*) is an adverbial clause, typically introduced by *if* or *unless* (or *should, although, though, despite,* or another subordinating conjunction), establishing the condition in a conditional sentence. Usually this is a direct condition, indicating that the main clause (also called the *apodosis*) is dependent on the condition being fulfilled. A direct condition may be open (real or factual) or hypothetical (closed or unreal). An open condition leaves unanswered the question whether the condition will be fulfilled {**if you don't finish the work on time**, we'll have to reevaluate our arrangement}. A hypothetical condition, on the other hand, assumes that the condition has not been, is not, or is unlikely to be fulfilled {**if he had only remembered to wear a raincoat**, he wouldn't have ruined his new suit} {**if I had a hammer**, I could fix this creaky stair} {the transition would be much harder **if she left without giving notice**}. Sometimes, however, the clause may express an indirect condition {**if I recall correctly**, his assistant's name is Miljana}, alternative conditions {the party will be a success **whether or not it rains**}, or an open range of possibilities {**whatever you're doing**, it's working}.

## *Ellipsis*

5.236 **Ellipsis generally.** A grammatical ellipsis (sometimes called an omission) occurs when part of a clause is left understood and the reader or listener is able to supply the missing words. (For the use of three dots to indicate text omitted from a direct quotation or for faltering or interrupted speech, see 12.59–69.) This "recovery" of omitted words is possible because of shared idiomatic knowledge, context, and what's called the *principle of recoverability* {he preferred chocolate, she vanilla [*preferred* is understood in the second clause]}. A sentence containing such an ellipsis is called an *elliptical sentence*. In colloquial speech, an ellipsis is useful to avoid repetition, shorten the message, and make it easier to understand. It's particularly appropriate for commands and exclamations, and especially when asking or answering a question whose complete answer would essentially repeat the question. For example:

Thank you. (I thank you.)
One lump or two? (Would you like one lump of sugar or two?)
Glad you like it! (I'm glad that you like it!)
Which is better? And why? (Which choice is better, and why is it better?)
[Can you tell me who built this house?] The Tucker family. (Yes, I can tell you. The Tucker family built this house.)

## *Negation*

5.237 **Negation generally.** A statement may be expressed in positive or negative terms. Negation is the grammatical process of reversing the expression in a sentence. There are four common types: (1) using the negative particle *not* or *no*; (2) using negating pronouns such as *nobody*, *none*, *no one*, or *nothing*, or negating adverbs such as *nowhere*, *never*, or *neither*; (3) using the coordinating conjunctions *neither* and *nor* (or both of them as correlative conjunctions); (4) using words that are negative in meaning and function, such as *hardly* (= almost not), *scarcely* (= almost not), *barely* (= almost not), *few* (= not many; not much), *little* (= not much), *rarely* (= almost never), and *seldom* (= almost never)—or words having negative affixes such as *a-* {atypical}, *dis-* {disrobe}, *in-* {inimitable} (together with the assimilated forms *il-*, *im-*, and *ir-*), *non-* {nonemployee}, *un-* {untidy}, *-less* {careless}, and *-free* {hassle-free}.

5.238 **The word "not."** The simplest and most common form of negation involves using the particle *not*. Used with ordinary verbs and with auxiliary verbs, *not* typically negates a verb, an object, a phrase, or a clause. *Not* typically precedes whatever sentence element is being negated. To negate an ordinary verb in the present- or past-tense indicative mood, the verb is replaced by a compound of *do* or *did* plus *not* and a bare infinitive.

They sell newspapers in the hotel.
They do not sell newspapers in the hotel.

Kerri sings at the opera today.
Kerri does not sing at the opera today.

The waiter returned with our order.
The waiter did not return with our order.

*Not* usually immediately follows the principal verb or an auxiliary. If there are two or more verbs in the negative expression, *not* always follows the first of them.

I am happy.
I am not happy.

I should leave for work.
I should not leave for work.

I should leave for work, but I cannot find my glasses.

With participles, *not* precedes the participle {not given any warning, Josué nonchalantly opened the door} {not coming to any conclusions, the jury decided to suspend deliberations} {not having heard the news, Brett innocently asked how Tara was doing in school}. The subject is normally elided from the participial phrase. *Not* doesn't have to negate everything that follows it. It may be limited to the element immediately following {I discovered not a scientific breakthrough but a monstrous development}. A sentence containing *not* may be qualified by another element that limits the extent of the negation. The word's or clause's placement may significantly alter the scope of negation. For example:

He definitely did not accept the job offer.
[It is final: He rejected the job offer.]

He did not definitely accept the job offer.
[It is uncertain: He might still reject the offer.]

We have not eaten yet.
[We have not eaten, but we expect to eat at some time.]

*Not* can be contracted to *-n't* and appended to most auxiliary verbs without changing the form of the verb (e.g., *are not* → *aren't, would not* → *wouldn't, has not* → *hasn't*). The exceptions, involving *am, can, do, will,* and *shall*, are well known to native speakers of the language:

am → am not → [no contraction with negative: use *I'm not* etc.]
can → cannot → can't
will → will not → won't
shall → shall not → shan't

*Shan't* isn't used in American English except in jest; it still sometimes appears in British English.

5.239 **The word "no."** Unlike *not*, which can negate any element of a sentence, *no* negates only adjectives and nouns. When used with an adjective phrase, it might produce ambiguity. For example, in *we found no eggs*, it's clear that the speaker found nothing. But in *we found no fresh eggs for sale*, does the speaker mean they found no eggs at all, only eggs that weren't fresh, or eggs that were fresh but not for sale?

5.240 **Using pronouns and adverbs for negation.** Pronouns such as *nobody*, *none*, *no one*, and *nothing* and adverbs such as *nowhere* and *never* also result in negation. These words make it unnecessary to use *not*. They can help reduce the number of words and improve the flow of a sentence.

We did not see anyone in the audience.
We saw no one in the audience.

The children do not have anything to do.
The children have nothing to do.

You do not ever listen!
You never listen!

I cannot put the groceries anywhere.
There's nowhere to put the groceries.

5.241 **Using "neither" and "nor."** The correlative conjunctions *neither* and *nor* negate alternatives simultaneously. Traditionally, only pairs are framed by *neither–nor*, but writers and speakers sometimes use a *neither–nor–nor* construction, as in the last example below.

The dog and the cat are not friendly.
Neither pet is friendly.
Neither the dog nor the cat is friendly.

The radiator does not leak, and the water pump also does not leak.
Neither the radiator nor the water pump leaks.

Neither John nor Sally nor Brenda can attend the meeting.

In that last example, some writers include only the last *nor*. But a simple *neither–nor* construction isn't recommended with three or more elements, the sequence *neither–nor–nor* being preferable.

5.242 **Negative interrogative and imperative statements.** In a negative interrogative statement, the first auxiliary verb may be contracted with *not*: *Aren't you doing your homework tonight?* If it is not contracted, then *not* or *no* precedes the negated element {are you not doing your homework tonight?} {is there no satisfying you?}. Questions phrased with a negating word are called (unsurprisingly) *negative questions*; those without negation are *positive questions*. In an imperative statement, the negative particle always follows the imperative verb or is contracted with it {come no closer!} {don't talk back!} or elliptically replaces it {no closer!}.

5.243 **Double negatives.** When a sentence contains two negatives, in Standard English they are usually thought to cancel each other out to make a mild positive {he didn't *not* say anything [he did say something]} {this isn't an uncommon problem [it's more or less common]}. In dialect, by contrast, the sentence is often meant to express an emphatic negative {he didn't say nothing [he said nothing at all]} {we're not going nowhere special [we're going somewhere, but it isn't special]}. Multiple negatives often lead to ambiguity. For example, in *I wouldn't be surprised if Dan doesn't find the hammer*, does the speaker expect Dan to find the hammer or not to find it? In general, though, multiple negation results in a cancellation of other negatives {we didn't say the children couldn't come along [we didn't forbid the children's coming]}.

5.244 **Other forms of negation.** A sentence can express negation even though it doesn't contain any plainly negative elements. Two common means of achieving this effect are using *but* in the sense "if not" and using *except* in the sense "but not" {what is a pampered dog *but* [= *if not*] a child in a fur suit?} {you may borrow the car *except* [= *but not*] when it is raining}.

5.245 **"Any" and "some" in negative statements.** When the negating particle is *not*, then *any-* words must be used with it, not *some-* words. *Any-* words include *any, anyone, anybody, anything*, and *anywhere*. *Some-* words include *some, someone, somebody, something*, and *somewhere*.

NOT THIS: I don't want to see somebody. [Unless the meaning is one particular person I'm not naming.]
BUT THIS: I don't want to see anybody.

NOT THIS: There aren't some seats left.
BUT THIS: There aren't any seats left.

## *Expletives*

5.246 **Expletives generally.** Though *expletive* commonly denotes a swear word {expletive deleted}, in grammar *expletive* signifies a word that has no lexical meaning but serves a merely structural role in a sentence—as a noun element. The two most common expletives are *it* {it is true!} and *there* {there must be an answer}. An expletive *it* or *there* may be in the subject position, especially when the subject of a sentence is a clause {**it** is a rule that children must raise their hands to speak during class [**the rule** is that children must raise their hands to speak during class]} {**it** is better to stay here than to go there [**to stay here** is better than to go there]}. In this position, the expletive shifts the emphasis to the predicate containing the true subject. The sentence implies a "who" or "what" question that is answered by the subject. For example, *It is foolish to ignore facts* tells the reader "what" it is foolish to ignore and emphasizes "facts." An expletive *it* may also take the position of a direct object, especially when the real object is a clause or noun phrase {some people don't like **it** that stores are open for business on Thanksgiving [some people don't like **stores being open for business** on Thanksgiving]}.

5.247 **Expletive "it."** Whereas the pronoun *it* adds meaning to a sentence because it has an antecedent or else is the formal subject of a *be*-verb in the sense of "a person" or "a thing," an expletive *it* adds no meaning and takes the subject's or object's place when the subject or object shifts to the predicate: *It is not known what happened* can be restated as *What happened is not known*. Usually readers have no difficulty intuitively understanding whether they're encountering a pronoun *it* or an expletive *it*. But when the expletive and the pronoun appear close together, they may cause the reader to stumble {The much-anticipated feast was a disappointment; **it** was poorly cooked and presented. **It** is hard to believe that such a famous chef thought **it** would be edible, let alone delight gourmands.}. Avoid having several *it*s in a passage clash in this way. Some other names for the expletive *it* are *ambient it*, *anticipatory it*, *empty it*, *introductory it*, *nonreferential it*, and *prop it*.

5.248 **Expletive "there."** The word *there* is also frequently used as an expletive with *be* or an intransitive verb (especially a linking verb) followed by the subject {there are many different viewpoints presented in the students' essays} {there were several hundred members present at the conference}. An expletive *there* shouldn't be confused with *there* as an adverb of place. Compare *There seemed to be someone* with *Someone seemed to be there.*

## *Parallel Structure*

5.249 **Parallel structure generally.** Parallel constructions—series of like sentence elements—are common in good writing. Compound structures may link words {win, lose, or draw}, phrases {government of the people, by the people, for the people}, dependent clauses {that all men are created equal; that they are endowed by their Creator with certain unalienable rights; that among these are life, liberty, and the pursuit of happiness}, or sentences {I came; I saw; I conquered}. Every element of a parallel series must be a functional match (word, phrase, clause, sentence) and serve the same grammatical function in the sentence (e.g., noun, verb, adjective, adverb). This syntactic linking of matching elements is called *coordination*. When linked items do not match, the syntax of the uncoordinated sentence breaks down:

NONPARALLEL: She did volunteer work in the community kitchen, the homeless shelter, and taught free ESL classes offered by her church.

PARALLEL: She did volunteer work in the community kitchen, the homeless shelter, and her church, where she taught free ESL classes.

NONPARALLEL: The candidate is a former county judge, state senator, and served two terms as attorney general.

PARALLEL: The candidate is a former county judge, state senator, and two-term attorney general.

In the second example, for instance, the subject, verb, and modifier (*the candidate is a former*) fit with the noun phrases *county judge* and *state senator*, but the third item in the series renders nonsense: *The candidate is a former served two terms as attorney general.* The first two elements in the series are nouns, while the third is a separate predicate. The corrected version makes each item in the series a noun element.

5.250 **Prepositions and parallel structure.** In a parallel series of prepositional phrases, repeat the preposition with every element unless they all use the same preposition. A common error occurs when a writer lets two or more of the phrases share a single preposition but inserts a different one with another element:

NONPARALLEL: I looked for my lost keys in the sock drawer, the laundry hamper, the bathroom, and under the bed.
PARALLEL: I looked for my lost keys in the sock drawer, in the laundry hamper, in the bathroom, and under the bed.

If the series had not included *under the bed,* the preposition could have been used once to apply to all the objects: *I looked for my lost keys in the sock drawer, the laundry hamper, and the bathroom.*

5.251 **Paired joining terms and parallel structure.** Correlative conjunctions such as *either–or, neither–nor, both–and,* and *not only–but also* and some adverb pairs such as *where–there, as–so,* and *if–then* must join grammatically parallel sentence elements. It is a common error to mismatch elements framed by correlatives.

NONPARALLEL: I'd like to either go into business for myself or else to write freelance travel articles.
PARALLEL: I'd like either to go into business for myself or else to write freelance travel articles.

NONPARALLEL: Our guests not only ate all the turkey and dressing but both pumpkin pies as well.
PARALLEL: Our guests ate not only all the turkey and dressing but both pumpkin pies as well.

In the second example, the verb *ate,* when placed after the first correlative, attaches grammatically to *all the turkey* but not to *both pumpkin pies as well.* When moved outside the two phrases containing its direct objects, it attaches to both—and the phrasing becomes parallel.

5.252 **Auxiliary verbs and parallel structure.** If an auxiliary verb appears before a series of verb phrases, it must apply to all of them. A common error is to include one phrase that takes a different auxiliary verb:

NONPARALLEL: The proposal would streamline the application process, speed up admission decisions, and has proved to save money when implemented by other schools.
PARALLEL: The proposal would streamline the application process, speed up admission decisions, and—as other schools have learned—save money.

PARALLEL: The proposal would streamline the application process and speed up admission decisions. It has proved to save money when implemented by other schools.

The auxiliary verb *would* in that example renders the nonsensical *would has proved* when parsed with the third element of the predicate series. The first solution resolves that grammatical conflict, while the second breaks out the third element into a separate sentence—which also avoids shifting from future tense to past tense in mid-sentence.

## WORD USAGE

5.253 **Grammar versus usage.** The great mass of linguistic issues that writers and editors wrestle with don't really concern grammar at all—they concern usage: the collective habits of a language's native speakers. It's an arbitrary fact, but an important one, that *corollary* means one thing and *correlation* something else. Yet there seems to be an irresistible law of language that two words so similar in sound will inevitably be subject to widespread confusion—a type of mistake called *catachresis*. Some misunderstandings, such as the one just cited, are relatively new. Others, such as *lay* versus *lie* and *infer* versus *imply*, are much older.

### *Good Usage Versus Common Usage*

5.254 **Glossary of problematic words and phrases.** The best dictionaries are signaled by the imprints of Merriam-Webster, Webster's New World, American Heritage, and Oxford University Press. Still, one must use care and judgment in consulting *any* dictionary. The mere presence of a word in the dictionary's pages does not mean that the word is in all respects fit for print as Standard Written English. The dictionary merely describes how speakers of English have used the language; despite occasional usage notes, lexicographers generally disclaim any intent to guide writers and editors on the thorny points of English usage—apart from collecting evidence of what others do. So *infer* is recorded as meaning, in one of its senses, *imply*; *irregardless* as meaning *regardless*; *restauranteur* as meaning *restaurateur*; and on and on. That is why, in the publishing world, it is generally necessary to consult a style or usage guide, such as *Fowler's Modern English Usage* or *Garner's Modern English Usage*.

**a; an.** Use the indefinite article *a* before any word beginning with a consonant sound {a euphonious phrase} {a utopian dream}. Use *an* before any word beginning with a vowel sound {an officer} {an honorary degree}. The word *historical* and its variations cause missteps, but if the *h* in these words is pronounced, it takes an *a* {an hour-long talk at a historical society}. Likewise, an initialism (whose letters are sounded out) may be paired with one article, while an acronym (which is pronounced as a word) beginning with the same letter is paired with the other {an HTML website for a HUD program}.

**a lot.** Two words, not one.

**ability; capability; capacity.** *Ability* refers to a person's physical or mental power or skill to do something {the ability to ride a bicycle}. *Capability* refers more generally to the power or potential ability to do something challenging {she has the capability to play soccer professionally} or to the quality of being able to use or be used in a certain way {a jet with long-distance-flight capability}. *Capacity* refers especially to a vessel's ability to hold or contain something {a high-capacity fuel tank}. Used figuratively, *capacity* refers especially to a person's physical or mental power to learn {an astounding capacity for mathematics}. It can also be used as a synonym for *ability* {capacity for love}; as a formal word for someone's job, position, or role {in an advisory capacity}; as a word denoting an amount that can be produced or dealt with {full capacity}; or as a means of denoting size or power {engine capacity}.

**abjure; adjure.** To *abjure* is to deny or renounce publicly, especially under oath {the defendant abjured the charge of murder} or to declare one's permanent abandonment of a place {abjure the realm}. To *adjure* is to charge someone to do something as if under oath {I adjure you to keep this secret} or to try earnestly to persuade {the executive committee adjured all the members to approve the plan}. Some writers misuse *adjure* for either *abhor* (= to detest) or *require* (= to mandate).

**about; approximately.** When idiomatically possible, use the adverb *about* instead of *approximately*. In the sciences, however, *approximately* is preferred {approximately 32 coding-sequence differences were identified}. Avoid coupling either word with another word of approximation, such as *guess* or *estimate*.

**abstruse.** See **obtuse**.

**accept; except.** To *accept* something is to receive it {accept this gift} or regard it as proper {accept the idea}. To *except* something is to exclude it or leave it out {club members will be excepted from the admission charge}, and to *except to* something is to object to it.

**access, *vb.*** The use of nouns as verbs has long been one of the most common ways that word-usage changes happen in English. Today, few people quibble with using *contact*, *debut*, or *host*, for example, as a verb. *Access* can be safely used as a verb when referring to computing {access a computer} {access the internet} {access a database}. Outside the digital world, though, it can be jarring and is best avoided.

**accord; accordance.** The first word means "agreement" {we are in accord on the treaty's meaning} {we have reached an accord}. The second word means "conformity" {the book was printed in accordance with modern industry standards}.

**acquiesce.** To *acquiesce* is to do what someone else wants or to passively allow something to happen. The connotation is usually acceptance without enthusiasm or even with opposition that is not acted on. The word traditionally takes the preposition *in* {the minority party acquiesced in the nomination}, although *to* is also accepted. *With* is not standard.

**actual fact, in.** Redundant. Try *actually* or *in fact*, or simply omit.

**acuity; acumen.** What is *acute* is sharp, and these two words apply to mental sharpness. *Acuity* most often refers to sharpness of perception—the ability to think, see, or hear clearly {visual acuity}. *Acumen* always refers to mental prowess, especially the ability to think quickly and make good judgments.

**adduce; deduce; induce.** To *adduce* is to give as a reason, offer as a proof, or cite as an example in order to prove that something is true {as evidence of reliability, she adduced her four years of steady volunteer work as a nurse's aide}. *Deduce* and *induce* are opposite processes. To *deduce* is to reason from general principles to specific conclusions, or to draw a specific conclusion from general knowledge {from these clues about who committed the crime, one deduces that the butler did it}. In a related logical sense, to *induce* is to form a general principle based on specific observations {after years of studying ravens, the researchers induced a few of their social habits}. In its more common uses, however, to *induce* is (1) to persuade someone to do something, especially something unwise {nothing could induce me to try that again}, or (2) to cause a particular physical response {induce labor} {induce vomiting}.

**adequate; sufficient; enough.** *Adequate* refers to the suitability of something in a particular circumstance {an adequate explanation} {adequate provisions}. *Sufficient* refers to an amount that is enough to meet a particular need (always with an abstract concept, a mass noun, or a plural) {sufficient water} {sufficient information} {sufficient cause} {sufficient resources}. *Enough*, the best word for everyday purposes, meaning "as much or as many as are needed or wanted," modifies both count nouns {enough people} and mass nouns {enough oil}.

**adherence; adhesion.** With a few exceptions, the first term is figurative, the second literal. Your *adherence* to the transportation code requires the *adhesion* of an inspection sticker to your windshield.

**adjure.** See **abjure**.

**administrator.** See **executor**.

**admission; admittance.** *Admission* is generally figurative, suggesting particularly the rights and privileges granted with permission to enter {the student won admission to a first-rate university} or the price paid for entry {admission is $10}. *Admittance* is more limited and more a matter of physical entry, but it too is tinged with the idea of permission {no admittance beyond this point}.

**adopted; adoptive.** *Adopted* applies to a child or dependent {adopted son}. It is incorrect when applied to the ones who do the adopting; instead, use *adoptive*, the more general adjective corresponding to *adopt* {adoptive parents}.

**adverse; averse.** Though etymologically related, these words have undergone differentiation. *Adverse* means either "strongly opposed" or "unfavorable" and typically refers to things (not people) {adverse relations between the nations complicated matters} {an adverse wind blew the ship off course}. *Averse* means "feeling negatively about" or "having a strong dislike or unwillingness," and it refers to people {he's averse to asking for directions}.

**affect; effect.** *Affect*, almost always a verb, means "to influence or do something that produces a change; to have an effect on" {the adverse publicity affected the election}. To *affect* can also mean "to pretend to have a particular feeling or manner" {affecting a Scottish accent}. (The noun *affect* has a specialized meaning in psychology: emotional expressiveness. Consult your dictionary.) *Effect*, usually a noun, means "an outcome, result" {the candidate's attempted explanations had no effect} or "a change caused by an event, action, occurrence, etc." {harmful effects of smoking}. But it may also be a verb meaning "to make happen, produce" {the goal had been to effect a major change in campus politics}.

**affirmative, in the; in the negative.** These are slightly pompous ways of saying *yes* and *no*. They result in part because people are unsure how to punctuate *yes* and *no*. The ordinary way is this: *he said yes* (without quotation marks around *yes*, and without a capital); *she said no* (ditto).

**afflict.** See **inflict**.

**affront.** See **effrontery**.

**after having [+ past participle].** Though common, this phrasing is redundant. Try instead *after* [+ present participle]: Change *after having passed the audition, she . . .* to *after passing the audition, she . . .* Or this: *having passed the audition, she . . .* See 5.114.

**afterward, *adv.*; afterword, *n.*** The first means "later"; the second means "an epilogue." On *afterward(s)*, see **toward**.

**aggravate.** Traditionally, *aggravate* most properly means "to intensify (something bad)" {aggravate an injury} {an aggravated crime}. If the sense is "to bother," try *annoy* or *irritate* or *exasperate* instead.

**aid; aide.** *Aid* can be a verb (= to help) or a noun (= assistance). *Aide* is a noun (= someone assigned to help a superior), as in *congressional aide*, *military aide*, *teacher's aide*.

**ain't.** This contraction is famously dialectal—a word not to be used except either in the dialogue of a nonstandard speaker or in jest.

**alibi.** Avoid this as a synonym for *excuse*. The traditional sense is "the defense of having been elsewhere when a crime was committed."

**all (of).** Delete the *of* whenever possible {all the houses} {all my children}. The most common exception occurs when *all of* precedes a nonpossessive pronoun {all of us} {all of them}.

**all ready.** See **already**.

**all right.** Two words. Avoid *alright*, which has long been regarded as nonstandard.

**all together.** See **altogether**.

**alleged.** Traditional usage applies this participial adjective to things, especially acts {alleged burglary}, not to the actors accused of doing them {alleged burglar}. That distinction is still observed by some publications, but it has largely been abandoned. Although *allegedly* /ə-**lej**-əd-lee/ has four syllables, *alleged* has only two: /ə-**lejd**/.

**allude; elude; illude.** To *allude* is to hint at something indirectly {he alluded to the war by mentioning "our recent national unpleasantness"}. It's often loosely used where *refer* or *quote* would be better—that is, where there is a direct mention or quotation. To *elude* is to avoid capture {the fox eluded the hunters}. To *illude* (quite rare) is to deceive {your imagination might illude you}.

**allusion; reference.** An *allusion* is an indirect or casual mention or suggestion of something {the cockroach in this story is an allusion to Kafka}. A *reference* is a direct or formal mention {the references in this scholarly article have been meticulously documented}. See **reference**.

**alongside.** This term, meaning "at the side of," should not be followed by *of*.

**alot.** Nonstandard; use **a lot**.

**already; all ready.** The first refers to time {the movie has already started}; the second refers to preparation {are the actors all ready?}.

**alright.** Nonstandard; use **all right**.

**altar, *n.*; alter, *vb.*** An *altar* is a table or similar object used for sacramental purposes. To *alter* is to change.

**alternate, *adj. & n.*; alternative, *adj. & n.*** *Alternate* implies (1) a substitute for another {we took the alternate route} or (2) every other or every second {alternate Saturdays}. *Alternative* implies availability as another, usually sounder choice or possibility {alternative fuel sources}. The noun uses are analogous {the awards committee named her as alternate} {we have no alternative}.

**altogether; all together.** *Altogether* means "wholly" or "entirely" {that story is altogether false}. *All together* refers to a unity of time or place {the family will be all together at Thanksgiving}.

**amend; emend.** The first is the general term, meaning "to change or add to something written or spoken" {the city amended its charter to abolish at-large council districts} or "to make better" {amend your behavior!}. The second means "to remove one or more mistakes from" (as of a text) {for the second printing, the author emended several typos that had reached print in the first}. The noun corresponding to *amend* is *amendment*; the one corresponding to *emend* is *emendation*.

**amiable; amicable.** Both mean "friendly," but *amiable* refers to people who are easy to like {an amiable waiter} and *amicable* to relationships that involve goodwill and a lack of quarreling {an amicable divorce}.

**amid; among.** See **between**.

**amount; number.** *Amount* is used with mass nouns {a decrease in the amount of pollution} {a small amount of money}. *Number* is used with count nouns {a growing number of dissidents} {the number of coins in your pocket}.

**an.** See **a**.

**and.** Popular belief to the contrary, this conjunction usefully begins sentences, typically outperforming *moreover*, *additionally*, *in addition*, *further*, and *furthermore*. Yet it does not occur as a sentence-starter as often as *but*. See **but**; see also 5.209.

**and/or.** Avoid this Janus-faced term. It can often be replaced by *and* or *or* with no loss in meaning. Where it seems needed {take an aspirin and/or a warm drink}, try . . . *or* . . . , *or both* {take an aspirin or a warm drink, or both}. But think of other possibilities {take an aspirin, perhaps with a warm drink}.

**anecdotal.** This adjective corresponds to *anecdote*, but in one sense the words have opposite connotations. An anecdote is a story that is thought (but not known) to be true. But *anecdotal evidence* refers to accounts that are not systematically gathered or rigorously verified.

**angry.** See **mad**.

**anxious.** Avoid it as a synonym for *eager*. The standard sense is "worried, nervous, distressed."

**anyone; any one.** The one-word *anyone* is a singular indefinite pronoun used in reference to no one in particular {anyone would know that}. The two-word phrase *any one* is a more emphatic form of *any*, referring to a single person or thing in a group {do you recognize any one of those boys?} {I don't know any one of those stories}.

**anyplace.** Nonstandard; see **anywhere**.

**anyway; anyways.** The former is standard; the latter, traditionally considered dialectal, has made inroads since about 1980 but remains nonstandard.

**anywhere; any place.** The first is preferred for an indefinite location {my keys could be anywhere}. But *any place* (two words) is narrower when you mean "any location" {they couldn't find any place to sit down and rest}. Avoid the informal one-word *anyplace*.

**appertain.** See **pertain**.

**appraise; apprise.** To *appraise* is to assess or put a value on something {the jeweler appraised the necklace}. To *apprise* is to inform or notify someone about something {keep me apprised of any developments}.

**appreciate.** Three senses: (1) to understand fully; (2) to increase in value; (3) to be grateful for (something). Sense 3 often results in verbose constructions, instead of *I would appreciate it if you would let me know*, try *I would appreciate your letting me know* or, more simply, *please let me know*.

**apprise.** See **appraise**.

**approve; endorse.** *Approve* implies positive thought or a positive attitude rather than action apart from consent. *Endorse* implies both a positive attitude and active support.

**approve (of).** *Approve* alone connotes official sanction or acceptance {the finance committee approved the proposed budget}. *Approve of* suggests thinking favorably about {she approved of her sister's new hairstyle}.

**approximately.** See **about**.

**apt; likely.** Both mean "fit, suitable," but *apt* is used for general tendencies or habits {the quarterback is apt to drop the football}. *Likely* expresses probability {because he didn't study, it's likely that he'll do poorly on the exam}. Although *likely* is traditional as a synonym of *probable*, many writers and editors object to its use as a synonym of *probably*. *Apt* has two other senses: (1) "exactly right for a given situation or purpose" {an apt remark} and (2) "quick to learn" {an apt pupil}.

**area.** Often a nearly meaningless filler word, as in *the area of partnering skills*. Try deleting *the area of*. When used literally, its meaning is often important and should be retained. See also **space**.

**as far as.** Almost always wordy. Avoid using *as far as* without the completing verb *is concerned* or *goes*. Even with the verb, though, this is usually a wordy construction. Compare *as far as change is concerned, it's welcome* with *as for change, it's welcome*.

**as is.** In reference to an acquisition, *as is* is framed in quotation marks and refers to the acceptance of something without guarantees or representations of quality {purchased "as is"}. The phrase *on an "as is" basis* is verbose.

**as of yet.** See **as yet**.

**as per.** This phrase, though common in the commercial world, has long been considered nonstandard. Instead of *as per your request*, write *as you requested* or (less good) *per your request*. The recent innovation *as per usual* for *as usual* is an illiteracy.

**as such.** This pronominal phrase always requires an antecedent for *such* {science is the organized search for truth and, as such, must be looked upon as an end in itself}. The phrase is now often loosely used as a synonym for *therefore*. Avoid this misusage {science seeks out truth in an organized way and, as such, must be looked upon as an end in itself}.

**as to.** This two-word preposition is best used only to begin a sentence that could begin with *on the question of* or *with regard to* {as to those checks, she didn't know where they came from}. Otherwise, use *about* or some other preposition. Yet the phrasing *so* [adj.] *as to* is entirely idiomatic and unobjectionable {so common as to seem ubiquitous}.

**as yet; as of yet.** Stilted and redundant. Use *yet, still, so far*, or some other equivalent.

**assault; battery.** These are popularly given the same meaning. But in law, *assault* refers to a threat that causes someone to reasonably fear physical violence, and *battery* refers to a violent or repugnant intentional physical contact with another person. In the strict legal sense, an assault doesn't involve touching; a battery does.

**assemblage; assembly.** An *assemblage* is an informal collection of people or things. An *assembly* is a group of people, especially decision makers, organized for a purpose {a national assembly}; a meeting {regular public assemblies}; or the process of putting together the parts of something {instructions for assembly}.

**assent; consent.** The meanings are similar, but *assent* connotes a more affirmative agreement after careful consideration; *consent* connotes mere allowance, or sometimes grudging acquiescence.

**assumption; presumption.** An *assumption* is not drawn from strong evidence; typically, it is a hypothesis that one accepts as true without definite proof {your assumption can be tested by looking at the public records}. A *presumption* implies a basis in evidence or at least experience; if uncontradicted, a *presumption* may support a decision {the legal presumption of innocence}.

**assure.** See **ensure**.

**at the present time; at this time; at present.** These are turgid substitutes for *now, today, currently*, or even *nowadays* (a word of perfectly good literary standing). Of the three phrases, *at present* is least suggestive of bureaucratese.

**at the time that; at the time when.** Use the plain and simple *when* instead.

**attain; obtain.** To *attain* something is either to accomplish it through effort (e.g., a goal) {she soon attained a position of power} or to reach a particular age, size, level, etc. {the stock market attained a new high this morning}. To *obtain* something is to get it or gain possession of it {obtaining information}. In best usage, you *attain* a degree and *obtain* a diploma. It can be a fine distinction, and in common usage the words are often treated as synonyms.

**auger; augur.** These homophones (/**aw**-gr/) have very different meanings. The tool for boring is an *auger*. *Augur* means "a clairvoyant or seer" (noun) or "to foretell" (verb). *Augurs well* is an idiomatic equivalent of *bodes well*. The related noun *augury* refers to an indication of what will happen in the future.

**avenge, *vb.*; revenge, *vb. & n.*** *Avenge* connotes an exaction for a wrong {historically, family grudges were privately avenged}. The corresponding noun is *vengeance*. *Revenge* connotes the infliction of harm on another out of anger or resentment {the team is determined to revenge its humiliating loss in last year's championship game}. *Revenge* is much more commonly a noun {they didn't want justice—they wanted revenge}.

**averse.** See **adverse**.

**avocation; vocation.** An *avocation* is a hobby or pleasant pastime {stamp collecting is my weekend avocation}. A *vocation* is one's profession or, especially in a religious sense, one's calling {she had a true vocation and became a nun}.

**awhile; a while.** The one-word version is adverbial; it means "for a short time" {let's stop here awhile}. The two-word version is a noun phrase that functions as the object of a preposition {she worked for a while before beginning graduate studies} or of a verb {it will take a while}.

**backward(s).** See **toward**.

**bale; bail.** The somewhat less common term is *bale* (= a bundle or to form into a bundle, as of hay or cotton). *Bail* is most often a verb (= to drain by scooping, as of getting water out of a boat using a pail); it is also a noun and verb regarding the posting of security to get out of jail pending further proceedings. *Bail* is also used informally to denote leaving quickly or escaping {the couple bailed from the party}. To *bail out* someone (a phrasal verb) is to get the person out of trouble.

**based on.** This phrase has two legitimate uses. It may unimpeachably have verbal force (*base* being a transitive verb, as in *they based their position on military precedent*) or, in a passive sense, adjectival force (*based* being read as a past-participial adjective, as in *a sophisticated thriller based on a John le Carré novel*). Two other uses, however, are traditionally considered slipshod. *Based on* should not have adverbial force (as in *Rates are adjusted annually, based on the 91-day Treasury bill*) or prepositional force (as a dangling participle, as in *Based on this information, we decided to stay*). Try other constructions {rates are adjusted annually on the basis of the 91-day Treasury bill} {with this information, we decided to stay}.

**basis.** Much overworked, this word most properly means "foundation; the facts, things, or ideas from which something can be developed." It often appears in the phrase *on a . . . basis* or some similar construction. When possible, substitute adverbs (*personally*, not *on a personal basis*) or simply state the time (*daily*, not *on a daily basis*). The plural is *bases* {the legislative bases are complicated}.

**bated breath.** So spelled—not *baited breath*. Someone who waits with *bated breath* is anxious or excited (literally "holding [abating] one's breath").

**battery.** See **assault**.

**begging the question.** This phrase traditionally denotes a logical fallacy of assuming as true what has yet to be proved—or adducing as proof for some proposition something that's every bit as much in need of proof as the first proposition. For example, someone might try to "prove" the validity of a certain religion by quoting from that religion's holy text. But the phrase gets misused in many ways—as (erroneously) meaning "prompting a question," "inviting an obvious question," "evading a question," and "ignoring a question."

**behalf.** *In behalf of* means "in the interest or for the benefit of" {the decision is in behalf of the patient}. *On behalf of* means "acting as agent or representative of" {on behalf of Mr. Scott, I would like to express heartfelt thanks}.

**bemused.** This word means "bewildered, distracted, or confused." It is not a synonym of *amused*.

**benevolence; beneficence.** *Benevolence* is the attribute of being disposed to kindness or capable of doing good {the priest's benevolence was plainly evident}. It applies most often to people but may also apply to things that are beneficial. *Beneficence* is a major act of kindness or the performance of good deeds generally {the villagers thanked him for his beneficence}. The first term denotes a quality, the second conduct.

**beside; besides.** *Beside* is a preposition of position, whether literal {beside the road} or figurative {beside the point}. *Besides* may be a preposition meaning "other than" {who's going besides us?} or an adverb meaning "also" or "anyway" {besides, who wants to know?}.

**between; among; amid.** *Between* indicates one-to-one relationships {between you and me}. *Among* indicates undefined or collective relationships {honor among thieves}. *Between* has long been recognized as being perfectly appropriate for more than two objects if multiple one-to-one relationships are understood from the context {trade between members of the European Union}. *Amid* is often used with mass nouns {amid talk of war}—though it can often be used with abstract nouns in the plural {resigned amid rumors of misconduct} {the investigation comes amid growing concerns}. *Among* is invariably used with plurals of count nouns {among the children}. Avoid *amidst* and *amongst*, especially in American English.

**between you and me.** This is the correct phrasing—not *between you and I*, which is a classic example of hypercorrection. Both pronouns function as objects of the preposition *between*. True, Shakespeare put the phrase *'tween you and I* in a character's mouth, but that was at a time when English grammar was much less settled than it came to be in the eighteenth century—and that usage was an outlier even in the Elizabethan era. Further, the sociolinguistic point that Shakespeare might have been making by having a character speak that phrase may well be lost in the mists of time.

**bi-; semi-.** Generally, *bi-* means "two" (*biweekly* means "every two weeks"), while *semi-* means "half" (*semiweekly* means "twice a week"). Because these prefixes are often confused with each other, writers should be explicit about the meaning.

**biannual; semiannual; biennial.** *Biannual* and *semiannual* both mean "twice a year" {these roses bloom biannually}. But *biennial* means "once every two years" or "every other year" {our legislature meets biennially}. To avoid confusion, write *semiannual* instead of *biannual*, and consider writing *once every two years* instead of *biennial*.

**billion; trillion.** The meanings can vary in different countries. In the United

States, a *billion* is 1,000,000,000. In Great Britain, Canada, and Germany, a *billion* is traditionally a thousand times more than that (a million millions, or what Americans call a *trillion*)—though the American English sense now predominates even in British English. Further, in Great Britain a *trillion* is traditionally a million million millions, what Americans would call a *quintillion* (1,000,000,000,000,000,000). Although the American definitions are gaining acceptance, writers need to remember the historical geographic distinctions. See also 9.9.

**blatant; flagrant.** An act that is *blatant* is both bad and plain for all to see {a blatant error}. One that is *flagrant* is done brazenly as well as openly, often with a stronger suggestion of shocking illegality or immorality {a flagrant violation of the law}.

**bombastic.** A *bombastic* speech or essay is pompously long-winded and self-important but essentially empty of substance. The word has nothing to do with temper or munitions.

**born; borne.** *Born* is used only as an adjective {a born ruler} or in the fixed passive-voice verb *to be born* {the child was born into poverty}. *Borne* is the general past participle of *bear* {this donkey has borne many heavy loads} {she has borne three children}. It is also used to form compound terms {foodborne} {vector-borne}.

**both–and.** These correlative conjunctions should frame matching syntactic parts. Hence don't write *She is both a writer and she skis professionally*, but instead *She is both a writer and a professional skier*. See also 5.251.

**breach, *n. & vb.*; breech, *n.*** A *breach* is a gap in or violation of something {a breach of contract} or a serious disagreement {healing the breach between the nations}. To *breach* is to break, break open, or break through {breach the castle walls}. *Breech* refers to the lower or back part of something, especially the buttocks {a breech birth} or the part of a modern firearm where bullets are inserted {the rifle's breech}.

**bring; take.** The distinction may seem obvious, but the error is common. The simple question is, Where is the action directed? If it's toward you, use *bring* {bring home the bacon}. If it's away from you, use *take* {take out the trash}. You *take* (not *bring*) your car to the mechanic.

**but.** Popular belief to the contrary, this conjunction usefully begins contrasting sentences, typically with greater strength and speed than *however*. Avoid putting a comma after it. Cf. **and**; see also 5.209.

**by means of.** Often verbose. Use *by* or *with* if either one suffices.

**by reason of.** Use *because* or *because of* unless *by reason of* is part of an established phrase {by reason of insanity}.

**cache; cachet.** *Cache*, a count noun, refers either to a quantity of goods or valuables that have been stashed away or to a storage buffer within a computer. *Cachet*, generally a mass noun, refers most commonly to prestige or fetching appeal—or else a seal on a document or a commemorative design. *Cachet* sometimes appears, incorrectly, as *caché*.

**can; could.** *Can* means "to be able to" and expresses certainty {I can be there in five minutes}. *Could* is better for a sense of uncertainty or a conditional statement {could you stop at the cleaners today?} {if you send a deposit, we could hold your reservation}. See 5.151.

**can; may.** *Can* most traditionally applies to physical or mental ability {she can do calculations in her head} {the dog can leap over a six-foot fence}. In colloquial English, *can* also expresses a request for permission {can I go to the movies?}, but this usage is not recommended in formal contexts. *May* suggests possibility {the class may have a pop quiz tomorrow} or permission {you may borrow my car}. A denial of permission is properly phrased formally with *may not* {you may not borrow my credit card} or, less formally, with *cannot* or *can't* {you can't use the computer tonight}. See 5.151, 5.152.

**cannon; canon.** A *cannon* is an artillery weapon that fires metal balls or other missiles. A *canon* is (1) a general rule or principle, (2) an established criterion, (3) the sum of a writer or composer's work, (4) the collective literature accepted by a scholastic discipline, (5) a piece of music in which a tune is started by one performer and mimicked by each of the others, or (6) a Christian priest having special duties within a church or cathedral.

**capability.** See **ability**.

**capacity.** See **ability**.

**capital; capitol.** A *capital* is a seat of government (usually a city) {Jefferson City is the capital of Missouri}. A *capitol* is a building in which a legislature meets {the legislature opened its new session in the capitol today}.

**carat; karat; caret.** *Carat* measures the weight of a gemstone; *karat* measures the purity of gold. To remember the difference, think of *24K gold*. (In British English, the spelling *carat* serves in both senses.) *Caret* is a mark on a manuscript indicating where matter is to be inserted; borrowed from Latin in the seventeenth century, it literally means "(something) is lacking."

**career; careen.** The word *career*'s career as a verb meaning "to go full speed" may be about over, except in British English (in which the two verbs contend in what is still a tight race). In American English, its duties have been assumed by *careen* (traditionally, "to tip to one side while moving"), even though nothing in that verb's time-honored definition denotes high speed. So today in American English it's typically *careened down the hill* but in British English *careered down the hill*.

**caret.** See **carat**.

**case.** This multifaceted word is often a sign of verbal inflation, especially in its uses as a near-synonym of *situation*. For example, *in case* means "if"; *in most cases* means "usually"; *in every case* means "always." The word is justifiably used in law (in which a *case* is a lawsuit or judicial opinion) and in medicine (in which the word refers to an instance of a disease or disorder). By extension, it has analogous senses in social work, criminal detection, etc. Of course, the word can also denote a box or container {briefcase}, an argument or set of reasons {state your case}, or a grammatical word form.

**cause célèbre.** This phrase most strictly denotes a legal case, especially a prosecution, that draws great public interest. By extension, it refers to a notorious episode, event, or even person. It does not properly denote a person's pet cause. Though it retains its acute and grave accents, the phrase is now considered naturalized enough not to be italicized (except when called out as a phrase, as in the next sentence). Yet the plural retains its French form: *causes célèbres*.

**censer; censor, *n.*; sensor.** A *censer* is either a person who carries a container of burning incense or the container itself. A *censor* is a person who suppresses objectionable subject matter. A *sensor* is a mechanical or electronic device for discovering light, heat, movement, etc.

**censor, *vb.*; censure, *vb.*** To *censor* is to review books, films, letters, and the like to remove objectionable material—that is, to suppress {soldiers' letters are often censored in wartime}. To *censure* is to criticize strongly or disapprove, or to officially reprimand {the House of Representatives censured the president for the invasion} {in some countries the government *censors* the press; in the United States the press often *censures* the government}.

**center around.** Although this illogical phrasing does have apologists, stylists tend to use either *center on* or *revolve around*.

**certainty; certitude.** If you are absolutely sure about something, you display both *certainty* (firm conviction) and *certitude* (assurance of being certain). That fact you are sure about, however, is a *certainty* but not a *certitude*—the latter is a trait applied to people only.

**chair; chairman; chairwoman; chairperson.** The gender-neutral *chair* is widely regarded as the best choice. Since the mid-seventeenth century, *chair* has referred to an office of authority. See also 5.255–67.

**childish; childlike.** *Childlike* is used positively to connote innocence, eagerness, and freshness {a childlike smile}. *Childish* is pejorative; it connotes immaturity, silliness, and unreasonableness {childish ranting}.

**chord; cord.** *Chord* denotes (1) a group of harmonically consonant notes {major chords} {minor chords} or (2) a straight line joining the ends of an arc (sense 2 being a technical term in mathematics and engineering). *Cord* is the word denoting a thick string or rope {spinal cord} {umbilical cord} {vocal cord}, an enclosed wire that supplies electricity to an appliance or other equipment, or a quantity of firewood.

**circumstances.** Both *in the circumstances* and *under the circumstances* are acceptable, but *under* is now much more common in American English. *In* predominates in British English.

**cite, *n.*; site.** As a noun, *cite* is colloquial for *citation*, which refers to a source of information {a cite to *Encyclopaedia Britannica*}. A *site* is a place or location used for a particular purpose {building site} {website}. Cf. **sight.**

**citizen; subject.** In a governmental sense, these are near-synonyms that should be distinguished. A *citizen* owes allegiance to a nation whose sovereignty is a collective function of the people {a citizen of Germany}. A *subject* owes allegiance to an individual sovereign because the form of government is monarchical {a subject of the queen}.

**class.** This word denotes a category or group of things that are considered together because of their similarities {the class of woodwind instruments}. Properly, a *class* is never one type {the oboe is a type of woodwind} or one kind of thing {a drum is one kind of percussion instrument}.

**classic; classical.** *Classic* means "enduring, authoritative, outstanding" {*The Naked Night* is one of Ingmar Bergman's classic films}. *Classical* applies to a traditional set of values in literature, music, design, and other fields {classical Greek} {a classical composer} or to the definitive or earliest-characterized form {classical EEC syndrome}.

**clean; cleanse.** Although various cleaning agents are called "cleansers," *clean* displaced *cleanse* long ago in most of the word's literal senses. *Cleanse* retains the Old English root meaning "pure": Its use today usually refers to spiritual or moral (or gastrointestinal) purification.

**cleave.** This verb was originally two different words, and that difference is reflected in the opposite meanings that *cleave* has: (1) to cut apart, as with a cleaver, or to split, and (2) to adhere or cling together {standing in the rain, his clothes cleaving to his body}. (When a term is its own antonym, it is known as a *contronym*.) The conjugations are (1) *cleave, cleft* (or *clove*), *cleft* (or *cloven*); and (2) *cleave, cleaved, cleaved.*

**clench; clinch.** *Clench*, which connotes a physical action, normally involves a person's hands, teeth, jaw, or stomach {he clenched his hand into a fist}. *Clinch*, the more common term, has mostly figurative uses about finally achieving something after a struggle {clinched the victory}. But there is an exception to the nonphysical uses of *clinch*: If two people *clinch*, they hold each other's arms tightly, as in boxing.

**climactic; climatic.** *Climactic* is the adjective corresponding to *climax* {during the movie's climactic scene, the projector broke}. *Climatic* corresponds to *climate* {the climatic conditions of northern New Mexico}.

**clinch.** See **clench.**

**close proximity.** Redundant. Write either *close* or *in proximity.*

**closure; cloture.** *Closure* denotes the temporary or permanent closing or final resolution of something. *Cloture* denotes the parliamentary procedure of closing debate and taking a vote on a legislative bill or other measure.

**cohabit; cohabitate.** *Cohabit* is the traditional verb for living with another person in a sexual relationship without being married. *Cohabitate*, a back-formation from *cohabitation*, is best avoided.

**collaborate; corroborate.** To *collaborate* is to cooperate on some undertaking, especially in the arts or sciences {the participants are collaborators}. To *corroborate* something is to back up its reliability with proof or evidence {the expert corroborated the witness's testimony}.

**collegial; collegiate.** *Collegial* answers to *colleague* {a healthy collegial work environment}; *collegiate* answers to *college* {collegiate sports}.

**commendable; commendatory.** What is done for a worthy cause is *commendable* {commendable dedication to helping the poor}. What expresses praise is *commendatory* {commendatory plaque}.

**common; mutual.** What is *common* is shared by two or more people {borne by different mothers but having a common father}. What is *mutual* is reciprocal or directly exchanged by and toward each other {mutual obligations}. The expression *friend in common* was traditionally thought (pace Dickens) to be better than *mutual friend* in reference to a third person who is a friend of two others. But empirically, *mutual friend* greatly predominates in frequency over *friend in common* (or the ambiguous *common friend*), so it must be accepted as standard.

**commonweal; commonwealth.** The *commonweal* is the public welfare. Traditionally, a *commonwealth* was a state established by public compact or by the consent of the people to promote the general good (commonweal), and where the people reserved supreme authority. In the United States, the word is synonymous with *state*, four of which are still called commonwealths: Kentucky, Massachusetts, Pennsylvania, and Virginia. The Commonwealth of Puerto Rico is also a US territory.

**compare.** To *compare with* is to discern both similarities and differences between things. To *compare to* is to liken things or to note primarily similarities between them, especially in the active voice {Are you comparing me to *him*? I hope not!}.

**compelled; impelled.** If you are *compelled* to do something, you have no choice in the matter {Nixon was compelled by the unanimous Supreme Court decision to turn over the tapes}. If you are *impelled* to do something, you still may not like it, but you are convinced that it must be done {the voter disliked some candidates but was impelled by the income-tax issue to vote a straight-party ticket}. Whereas *compel* connotes an outside force, *impel* connotes an inner drive.

**compendious; voluminous.** *Compendious* means "concise, abridged." *Voluminous*, literally "occupying many volumes," most commonly means "vast" or "extremely lengthy."

**complacent; complaisant; compliant.** To be *complacent* is to be content with oneself and one's life—with the suggestion that one may be smugly unwilling to improve or unprepared for future trouble. To be *complaisant* is to be easygoing and eager to please others. To be *compliant* is to be amenable to orders or to a regimen imposed by others.

**compliment; complement.** A *compliment* is a flattering or praising remark {a compliment on your skill}. A *complement* is something that completes or brings to perfection {the lace tablecloth was a complement to the antique silver}. The words are also verbs: To *compliment* is to praise, while to *complement* is to supplement adequately or to complete. In the grammatical sense, a *complement* is a word or phrase that follows the verb to complete the predicate. The corresponding adjectives are *complimentary*, meaning (1) "expressing praise" or (2) "given to someone free of charge"; and *complementary*, meaning (1) "going well together, despite differences," or (2) "consisting of two geometric angles that, added together, take up 90 degrees."

**comprise; compose.** Use with care. To *comprise* is "to consist of, to include" {the whole comprises the parts}. To *compose* is "to make up, to form the substance of something" {the parts compose the whole}. The phrase *is comprised of*, though increasingly common, remains nonstandard. Instead, try *is composed of* or *consists of*. See **include**.

**concept; conception.** Both words may refer to an abstract thought, but *conception* also means "the act of forming an abstract thought." Avoid using either word as a high-sounding equivalent of *idea*, *design*, *thought*, or *program*.

**condole, *vb.*; console, *vb.*** These are closely related but not identical. To *condole with* is to express sympathy to {community leaders condoled with the victims' families}. The corresponding noun is *condolence* {they expressed their condolences at the funeral}. To *console* is to comfort in a time of distress or disappointment {the players consoled their humiliated coach}. The corresponding noun is *consolation* {their kind words were small consolation}.

**confidant; confidante; confident.** A *confidant* is a close companion, someone (male or female) you confide in. (*Confidante*, used in reference to a female confidant, reflects the word's French origin but is fading in English use.) *Confident* is the adjective meaning "sure that something will happen in the way one wants or expects" or "sure that something is true."

**congruous; congruent.** Both terms mean "in harmony, in agreement." The first is seen most often in its negative form, *incongruous*, meaning "strange, unexpected, or unsuitable in a particular situation" {the modern house looks incongruous in this old neighborhood}. The second is used, for example, in math to describe triangles that are identical in their angles as well as in the length of their sides {congruent angles}.

**connote; denote.** To *connote* (in reference to language) is to convey a meaning beyond the basic one, especially through emotive nuance {the new gerund *parenting* and all that it connotes}. To *denote* (again in reference to language) is to specify the literal meaning of something {the phrase *freezing point* denotes, in reference to water, 32 degrees Fahrenheit or 0 degrees Celsius}. Both words have figurative uses {all the joy that parenthood connotes} {a smile may not denote happiness}.

**consent.** See **assent**.

**consequent; subsequent.** The first denotes causation; the second does not. A *consequent* event always happens after the event that caused it, as does a *subsequent* event. But a *subsequent* event does not necessarily occur as a result of the first: It could be wholly unrelated but merely later in time.

**consider.** Add *as* only when you mean "to examine or discuss for a particular purpose" {handshaking considered as a means of spreading disease}. Otherwise, omit *as* {we consider him qualified}.

**consist.** There are two distinct phrases: *consist of* and *consist in*. The first, by far the more common one, applies to the physical components that make up a tangible thing {the computer-system package consists of software, the CPU, the monitor, and a printer}. The second refers to the essence of a thing, especially in abstract terms {moral government consists in rewarding the righteous and punishing the wicked}.

**console.** See **condole.**

**contact,** ***vb.*** If you mean *write* or *call* or *email,* say so. But *contact* is undeniably a brief way of referring to communication without specifying the means.

**contagious; infectious.** Both broadly describe a disease that is communicable. But a *contagious* disease spreads by direct contact with an infected person or animal {rabies is a contagious disease}. An *infectious* disease may also be spread by germs on a contaminated object or element, such as earth or water {tetanus is infectious but not contagious}.

**contemporary; contemporaneous.** Both express coinciding time, but *contemporary* usually applies to people, and *contemporaneous* applies to things or actions. Because *contemporary* has the additional sense of referring to recent or present time, it is unsuitable for contexts involving multiple times. That is, a reference to *Roman, Byzantine, and contemporary belief systems* is ambiguous; change *contemporary* to *present-day.*

**contemptuous; contemptible.** If you are *contemptuous,* you are feeling and showing that you think someone or something deserves no respect. If you are *contemptible,* others will have that attitude toward you.

**content,** ***n.*****; contents.** *Content* applies to the ideas, facts, or opinions in a written or oral presentation {the lecture's content was offensive to some who were present}. *Contents* usually denotes physical ingredients: the things that are inside a box, bag, room, or other container {the package's contents were difficult to discern by x-ray}. If the usage suggests many items, material or nonmaterial, *contents* is correct {table of contents} {the investigative report's contents}.

**continual; continuous.** What is *continual* may go on for a long time, but always there are brief interruptions, so that it can be characterized as intermittent or frequently repeated {continual nagging}. What is *continuous* never stops—it remains constant or uninterrupted {continuous flow of water}. A line that is continuous has no gaps.

**contravene; controvert.** To *contravene* is to conflict with or violate (the law, a rule, etc.) {the higher speed limit contravenes our policy of encouraging fuel conservation}. To *controvert* is to challenge or contradict {the testimony controverts the witness's prior statement}.

**convince.** See **persuade**.

**copyright, *vb.*** This verb, meaning "to obtain the legal right to be the only producer or seller of a book, play, film, or other creative work for a specific length of time," is conjugated *copyright–copyrighted–copyrighted*. Note the spelling, which has nothing to do with *write*.

**cord.** See **chord**.

**corollary; correlation.** A *corollary* is either (1) a subsidiary proposition that follows from a proven mathematical proposition, often without requiring additional evidence to support it, or (2) a natural or incidental result of some action or occurrence. A *correlation* is a positive connection between things or phenomena. If used in the context of physics or statistics, it denotes the degree to which the observed interactions and variances are not attributable to chance alone.

**corporal; corporeal.** What is *corporal* relates in some way to the body {corporal punishment}; what is *corporeal* has a physical form that can be touched {not our spiritual but our corporeal existence}.

**corps; core.** A *corps* is a body of like workers, as in an army, with special duties and responsibilities {Marine Corps} {press corps}. It is often misspelled like its homophone, *core*, which denotes the central or most important part of something {the core of the problem} {the earth's core}.

**correlation.** See **corollary**.

**corroborate.** See **collaborate**.

**could.** See **can**.

**couldn't care less.** This is the standard phrasing. Avoid the illogical form *could care less*.

**councillor; counselor.** A *councillor* is one who sits on a council {city councillor}. A *counselor* is one whose job is to help and advise people with problems {personal counselor}. In British English, the spelling is *counsellor*.

**couple.** Using *couple* as an adjective has traditionally been regarded as nonstandard phrasing—though it is increasingly common as a casualism. Add *of* {we watched a couple of movies}. When referring to two people as a unit {married couple}, the noun *couple* takes either a singular or a plural verb {the couple is happy} {the couple are honeymooning in Ravello}. When the pronoun *they* follows *couple*—if a pronoun is used at all, it is normally plural—the plural verb is preferable {the couple were delighted by their friends' responses}.

**court-martial.** Two words joined by a hyphen, whether the phrase functions as a noun or as a verb. Because *martial* acts as an adjective meaning "military," the plural of the noun is *courts-martial*. The third-person-singular verb is *court-martials* {if the general court-martials him, he'll have much to answer for}. In American English, the inflected spellings of the verb are *court-martialed, court-martialing*; in British English, the spellings are *court-martialled, court-martialling*.

**credible; creditable; credulous.** *Credible* means "believable; deserving trust"; *creditable* means "praiseworthy; deserving approval"; *credulous* means "gullible; tending to believe whatever one is told—and therefore easily deceived." A common error involving cognate forms of these words is in the malapropism *strains credulity*. If some form of that cliché must be used, it should read *strains credibility*.

**crevice; crevasse.** Size matters. A crack in the sidewalk is a *crevice* (accent on the first syllable) because it's narrow and typically not very deep; a fissure in a glacier or a dam is a *crevasse* (accent on the second syllable) because it's a deep open crack.

**criminal.** See **unlawful**.

**criteria.** This is the plural form of *criterion* (= a standard for judging): one *criterion*, two *criteria*. The double plural *criterias* is a solecism.

**damp, *vb.*; dampen.** Both words convey the sense "to moisten." *Damp* also means "to reduce with moisture" {damp the fire} or "to diminish vibration or oscillation of" {damp the voltage}. In a figurative sense, *dampen* means "to make [a feeling, mood, activity, etc.] less intense or enjoyable" {dampen one's hopes}.

**data.** Though originally this word was a plural of *datum*, it is now commonly treated as a mass noun and coupled with a singular verb. In formal writing (and always in the sciences), use *data* as a plural. Whatever you do, though, use the term consistently within a single writing.

**deadly; deathly.** *Deadly* means "capable of causing death" {deadly snake venom} or "likely to cause as much harm as possible" {deadly enemies}. *Deathly* means "arousing thoughts of death or a dead body" {deathly silence}.

**decide whether; decide if.** See **determine whether**.

**decimate.** This word literally means "to kill every tenth person," a means of repression that goes back to Roman times. But the word has come to mean "to inflict heavy damage or destroy a large part of something," and this use has long been predominant. Avoid *decimate* when you are referring to complete destruction. That is, don't say that a city was *completely decimated*.

**deduce.** See **adduce**.

**defamation; libel; slander.** *Defamation* is the communication of a falsehood that damages someone's reputation. If it is recorded, especially in writing, it is *libel*; otherwise, it is *slander*.

**definite; definitive.** *Definite* means "clear, exact" {a definite yes}. *Definitive* means either "not subject to further revision in the near future" {we have a definitive agreement} or "of such high quality as to be unimprovable for a long time" {the definitive guide}.

**delegate.** See **relegate**.

**deliberate, *adj.*; deliberative.** As an adjective, *deliberate* means either "planned; carefully thought out" {a deliberate response} or "slow and steady" {deliberate progress}. *Deliberative* means "of, characterized by, or involving debate"; the word most often applies to an assembly {deliberative body} or a process {deliberative meetings}.

**denote.** See **connote**.

**denounce; renounce.** To *denounce* is either to criticize harshly, especially in public {they denounced the prisoner swap}, or to accuse, as by giving incriminating information about someone's illegal political activities to the authorities {denounced him to the police}. To *renounce* is either to relinquish or reject {renounced her citizenship} or to declare publicly that one no longer believes something or will no longer behave in some way {renounce violence}.

**depend on.** Although *upon* is best reduced to *on* in this phrase, no further reduction is idiomatic: *Depend* demands an *on*. Hence don't write *That depends how we approach the problem* but rather *That depends on how we approach the problem.*

**dependant, *n.*; dependent, *adj. & n.*** In British English, the first is the preferable noun {he claimed three dependants on his tax return}; the second is the adjective {the family has become dependent on welfare}. But in American English, *dependent* is the usual form as both noun and adjective.

**deprecate.** In general, to *deprecate* is to strongly disapprove or criticize. But in the phrase *self-deprecating*—which began as a mistaken form of *self-depreciating* but is now standard—the sense of *deprecate* is "to belittle." In computing, *deprecate* serves as a warning: A *deprecated* feature or function is one that may be phased out of a future release of software, so users should begin looking for alternatives.

**derisive; derisory.** What is *derisive* ridicules as stupid or silly {derisive laughter}. What is *derisory* invites or deserves ridicule {that derisory "banana" hat}, especially when a laughably small amount of money is offered or given {my derisory paychecks}.

**deserts; desserts.** The first are deserved {he got his just deserts}, the second eaten {the many desserts on the menu}. *Just desserts* is a common misspelling (unless the meaning is "only postprandial sweets").

**despite; in spite of.** For brevity, prefer *despite*.

**determine whether; determine if.** The first phrasing is irreproachable style; the second is acceptable as a colloquialism. The same is true of *decide whether* versus *decide if.*

**differ from; differ with.** *Differ from* is the usual construction denoting a contrast {the two species differ from each other in subtle ways}. *Differ with* regards differences of opinion {the state's senators differ with each other on many issues}.

**different.** The phrasing *different from* is generally considered preferable to *different than* {this company is different from that one}, but sometimes the adverbial phrase *differently than* is all but required {she described the scene differently than he did}. In British English, *different to* is not uncommon—but it is distinctively British English, whereas *different from* is standard everywhere.

**disburse; disperse.** To *disburse* is to distribute money, especially from a large sum available for some specific purpose. To *disperse* is (1) to spread in various directions over a wide area {the clouds dispersed} or (2) to cause to go away in different directions {police dispersed the unruly crowd}.

**disc.** See **disk**.

**discomfort; discomfit.** *Discomfort* is a noun meaning "ill at ease." It can also be used as a verb meaning "to put ill at ease." But doing so often invites confusion with *discomfit,* which originally meant "to defeat utterly." Today it means "to thwart, confuse, annoy, or embarrass" {the ploy discomfited the opponent}. The distinction has become a fine one, since a *discomfited* person is also uncomfortable. *Discomfiture* is the corresponding noun.

**discreet; discrete.** *Discreet* means either "careful about not divulging secrets or upsetting others" {a discreet silence} or "showing modest taste; nonostentatious" {discreet jewelry}. *Discrete* means "separate, distinct, unconnected" {six discrete parts}.

**discriminating, *adj.*; discriminatory.** The word *discrimination* can be used in either a negative or a positive sense, and these adjectives reflect that ambivalence. *Discriminatory* means "reflecting a biased, unfair treatment" {discriminatory employment policy}. *Discriminating* means "analytically refined, discerning, tasteful" {a discriminating palate}.

**disinterested.** This word should be reserved for the sense "not having a financial or personal interest at stake and therefore able to judge a situation fairly; impartial." Avoid it as a replacement for *uninterested* (which means "unconcerned, bored").

**disk; disc.** *Disk* is the usual spelling {hard disk} {disk drive}. But *disc* is preferred in a few specialized applications {compact disc} {disc brakes} {disc golf}—particularly where the object in question is circular and flat.

**disorganized; unorganized.** Both mean "not organized," but *disorganized* suggests (1) a group in disarray, either thrown into confusion or inherently unable to work together {the disorganized 1968 Democratic National Convention in Chicago}, or (2) a person who is exceedingly bad at arranging or planning things {disorganized students}.

**disperse.** See **disburse**.

**distinctive; distinguished; distinguishable.** A *distinctive* feature is something that makes a person (or place or thing) easy to recognize {U2's distinctive sound}. It does not necessarily make that person *distinguished* (respected and admired) {the distinguished professor wears a distinctive red bow tie}. It does, however, make the person *distinguishable* (easy to see as being different from something else)—a term that does not carry the positive connotation of *distinguished*.

**dive, *vb.*** The preferred conjugation has traditionally been *dive-dived-dived*. The irregular form *dove*, though, has become the slightly predominant past-tense form in American English and should be accepted as standard: *dive-dove-dived*. Traditionalists will stick to the older inflection.

**doctrinal; doctrinaire.** *Doctrinal* means "of, relating to, or constituting a doctrine"; it is neutral in connotation {doctrinal differences}. *Doctrinaire* means "dogmatic," suggesting that the person described is stubborn and narrow-minded {a doctrinaire ideologue}.

**doubt that; doubt whether; doubt if.** *Doubt that* conveys a negative sense of strong skepticism or questioning {I doubt that you'll ever get your money back}. *Doubt whether* also conveys a sense of skepticism, though less strong {the official says that he doubts whether the company could survive}. *Doubt if* is a casual phrasing for *doubt that*.

**doubtfully, *adv.*** In recent years, this term has come into use as a sentence adverb functioning as a correlative of *hopefully* and as an antonym of *undoubtedly* {Will you be attending the party? Hopefully—but doubtfully. [That is, I hope I'll be able to go, but I doubt it.]}. Should you abstain from this usage in Standard Written English? No doubt.

**doubtless, *adv.*** Use this form (it's called a *flat adverb*)—not *doubtlessly*. See also 5.165.

**drag.** Conjugated *drag-dragged-dragged*. The past form *drug* is dialectal.

**dream.** Either *dreamed* (more typical in both American English and British English) or *dreamt* is acceptable for the past-tense and past-participial forms.

**drink, *vb.*** Correctly conjugated *drink-drank-drunk* {they had not drunk any fruit juice that day}.

**drown, *vb.*** Conjugated *drown-drowned-drowned*.

**drunk, *adj.*; drunken.** *Drunk* describes a current state of intoxication {drunk driver}. (By contrast, a *drunk*—like a *drunkard*—is someone who is habitually intoxicated.) *Drunken* describes either a trait of habitual intoxication {drunken sot} or intoxicated people's behavior {a drunken brawl}.

**dual; duel.** *Dual* is an adjective meaning "having two parts or two of something" {dual exhaust}. A *duel* is a fight between two people, historically a formal and often deadly combat with pistols or swords.

**due to.** In strict traditional usage, *due to* should be interchangeable with *attributable to* {the erratic driving was due to some prescription drugs that the driver had taken} or *owed to* {thanks are due to all who helped}. When used adverbially, *due to* is often considered inferior to *because of* or *owing to*. So in the sentence *Due to the parents' negligence, the entire family suffered*, the better phrasing would be *Because of* [or *Owing to*] *the parents' negligence, the entire family suffered*.

**due to the fact that.** Use *because* instead.

**dumb.** This word means either "stupid" or "unable to speak." In the second sense, the adjective *mute* is clearer (and less offensive) for most modern readers. But on the noun use of *mute*, see **moot**.

**dying; dyeing.** *Dying* is the present participle of *die* (= to cease living); *dyeing* is the present participle of *dye* (= to color with a liquid).

**each.** As a noun serving as the subject of a clause, *each* takes a singular verb {each of them was present that day}. But when it serves as an emphatic appositive for a plural noun, the verb is plural {they each have their virtues} {the newspapers each sell for $3}.

**each other; one another.** Traditionalists use *each other* when two things or people are involved, *one another* when more than two are involved.

**eatable.** See **edible**.

**economic; economical.** *Economic* means "of, relating to, or involving finances" {federal economic policy}. *Economical* means "thrifty; financially efficient; cheap and not wasteful" {an economical purchase}.

**edible; eatable.** What is *edible* is fit for human consumption {edible flowers}. What is *eatable* is at least minimally palatable {the cake is slightly burned but still eatable}.

**effect.** See **affect**.

**effete.** Traditionally, it has meant "worn out, sterile" or "lacking power, character, or vitality." Today it is often used to mean "snobbish," "effeminate," or "unduly pampered." Because of its ambiguity, the word is best avoided altogether.

**effrontery; affront.** *Effrontery* is an act of shameless impudence or shocking audacity. An *affront* is a deliberate insult.

**e.g.** See **i.e.**

**either.** Like *neither*, this word takes a singular verb when it functions as a subject {is either of the spouses present today?}.

**elemental; elementary.** Something that is *elemental* is an essential constituent {elemental ingredients} or a power of nature {elemental force}. Something that is *elementary* is basic, introductory, or easy {an elementary math problem}.

**elicit; illicit.** To *elicit* information or a reaction is to get it from someone, especially in challenging circumstances {to elicit responses}. Something *illicit* is disallowed by law or rule and usually also condemned generally by society {an illicit scheme}.

**elude.** See **allude**.

**embarrass.** See **harass**.

**emend.** See **amend**.

**emigrate.** See **immigrate**.

**eminent; imminent.** What is *eminent* is famous, important, and respected {the eminent professor} or derives from high standing or authority {eminent domain}. What is *imminent* is looming, likely to happen soon, and almost always bad {imminent disaster}.

**emoji; emoticon.** An *emoji* (from the Japanese; pl. *emoji* or *emojis*) is a pictorial representation, or ideogram, that consists of a face, a hand gesture, or an object or symbol intended to express or suggest an emotion or attitude—or any number of ideas or things. An *emoticon* is a representation of a smiley face or other expressive gesture rendered as a combination of common keyboard characters—e.g., ;-).

**emotive; emotional.** The first means "arousing intense feeling" {emotive language calculated to persuade the jury}; the second means "of, relating to, or involving intense feelings" {an emotional response}.

**empathy; sympathy.** *Empathy* is the ability to understand other people's feelings and problems {tremendous empathy with others}. *Sympathy* is generally compassion and sorrow one feels for another's misfortunes, especially on a particular occasion {our sympathies are with you}—but it can also be support for a plan or idea {right-wing sympathies} or a mutual understanding and warmth arising from compatibility {there was no personal sympathy between them}.

**endemic.** See **epidemic**.

**endorse.** See **approve**.

**enervate; innervate.** These words are antonyms. To *enervate* is to weaken or drain of energy. To *innervate* is to stimulate or provide with energy.

**enormity; enormousness.** *Enormity* means "monstrousness, moral outrageousness, atrociousness" {the enormity of the Khmer Rouge's killings}. *Enormousness* means "hugeness" or "immensity" {the enormousness of Alaska}.

**enough.** See **adequate**.

**enquire.** See **inquire**.

**ensure; insure; assure.** *Ensure* is the general term meaning "to make sure that something will (or won't) happen." In best usage, *insure* is reserved for underwriting financial risk. So we *ensure* that we can get time off for a vacation, and we *insure* our car against an accident on the trip. We *ensure* events and *insure* things. But we *assure* people of things by telling them what's what, so that they won't worry. The important thing to remember is that we ensure occurrences and assure people.

**enthused, *adj.*** Use *enthusiastic* instead.

**enumerable; innumerable.** What's *enumerable* is countable and listable {the enumerable issues that we need on the agenda}. What's *innumerable* can't be counted, at least not practically {innumerable stars in the sky}. The second word is far more common. Because the two are pronounced so similarly, be wary of using them in speech.

**envy.** See **jealousy**.

**epidemic; endemic; pandemic.** An *epidemic* disease breaks out, spreads through a limited area (such as a state), and then subsides {an epidemic outbreak of measles}. (The word is frequently used as a noun {a measles epidemic}.) An *endemic* disease is perennially present within a region or population {malaria is endemic in parts of Africa}. (Note that *endemic* describes a disease and not a region: It is incorrect to say *this region is endemic for* [a disease].) A *pandemic* disease is prevalent over a large area, such as a nation or continent, or the entire world {the 1918–19 flu pandemic}.

**equally as.** This is typically faulty phrasing. Delete *as.*

**et al.** This is the abbreviated form of *et alii* ("and others")—the *others* being people, not things. Since *al.* is an abbreviation, the period is required—but note that no period follows the *et* (Latin for "and"). Cf. **etc.**; see also 6.20.

**etc.** This is the abbreviated form of *et cetera* ("and other things"); it should never be used in reference to people. *Etc.* implies that a list of things is too extensive to recite. But often writers seem to run out of thoughts and tack on *etc.* for no real purpose. Also, two redundancies often appear with this abbreviation: (1) *and etc.*, which is poor style because *et* means "and," and (2) *etc.* at the end of a list that begins with *for example, such as, e.g.*, and the like. Those terms properly introduce a partial list of examples. Cf. **et al.**; see also 6.20.

**event.** The phrase *in the event that* is a verbose and formal way of saying *if.*

**eventuality.** This term often needlessly displaces more specific everyday words such as *event, result,* and *possibility.*

**every day, *adv.*; everyday, *adj.*** The first is adverbial, the second adjectival. You may wear your *everyday* clothes *every day.*

**every one; everyone.** The two-word version is an emphatic way of saying "each" {every one of them was there}; the second is a pronoun equivalent to *everybody* {everyone was there}.

**evoke; invoke.** To *evoke* something is to bring it out {evoke laughter} or bring it to mind {evoke childhood memories}. *Invoke* has a number of senses, including to assert (something) as authority {invoke the Monroe Doctrine}, to appeal (to someone or a higher power) for help {invoke an ally to intervene}, and to conjure up {invoke spirits of the past}.

**exceptional; exceptionable.** What is *exceptional* is uncommon, superior, rare, or extraordinary {an exceptional talent}. What is *exceptionable* is objectionable or offensive {an exceptionable slur}.

**executor; administrator.** In a will, a person designates an *executor* to distribute the estate after death. When a person dies without a will or without specifying an executor, the court will appoint an *administrator* to do the same. The feminine forms *administratrix* and *executrix* are unnecessary and should be avoided.

**explicit; implicit.** If something is *explicit,* it is deliberately and clearly spelled out, as in the text of a well-drafted statute. If it is *implicit,* it is not specifically stated but is either suggested in the wording or necessary to effectuate the purpose. Avoid *implicit* to mean "complete, unmitigated."

**fact that, the.** This much-maligned phrase is not always avoidable. But hunt for a substitute before deciding to use it. Sometimes *that* alone suffices.

**farther; further.** The traditional distinction is to use *farther* for a physical distance {we drove farther north to see the autumn foliage} and *further* for a figurative distance {let's examine this further} {look no further}. Although it's a refinement of slight importance, connoisseurs will appreciate it.

**faze; phase, *vb.*** To *faze* is to disturb or disconcert {Jones isn't fazed by insults}. To *phase* (usually *phase in* or *phase out*) is to schedule or perform a plan, task, or the like in stages {phase in new procedures} {phase out the product lines that don't sell}. The negative adjective for "unaffected" is *unfazed,* not *unphased.*

**feel.** This verb is weak when used as a substitute for *think* or *believe.*

**feel bad.** Invariably, the needed phrase is *feel bad* (not *feel badly*). See 5.175.

**fewer.** See **less**.

**fictional; fictitious; fictive.** *Fictional* (from *fiction* as a literary genre) means "of, relating to, or involving imagination" {a fictional story}. *Fictitious* means "imaginary; counterfeit; false" {a fictitious name}. *Fictive* means "possessing the talent for imaginative creation" {fictive gift}; although it can also be a synonym for *fictional,* in that sense it is a needless variant. Also, anthropologists use *fictive* to describe relationships in which people are treated as family members despite having no bond of blood or marriage {fictive kin}.

**finalize.** Meaning "to bring to an end or finish the last part of," this word has often been associated with inflated jargon. Although its compactness may recommend it in some contexts, use *finish* when possible.

**first.** In enumerations, use *first, second, third,* and so on. Avoid the *-ly* forms.

**fit.** This verb is undergoing a shift. It has traditionally been conjugated *fit–fitted–fitted,* but today *fit–fit–fit* is prevalent in American English {when she tried on the dress, it fit quite well}. In the passive voice, however, *fitted* is still normal {the horse was fitted with a new harness}.

**flagrant.** See **blatant**.

**flair.** See **flare**.

**flammable; inflammable.** *Flammable* was invented in the early twentieth century as an alternative to the synonymous word *inflammable,* which some people misunderstood—dangerously—as meaning "not combustible." Today *flammable* is the standard term. Its antonym is *nonflammable.*

**flare; flair.** A *flare* is an unsteady and glaring light {an emergency flare} or a sudden outburst {a flare-up of fighting}. A *flair* is an outstanding talent {a flair for mathematics} or originality and stylishness {performed with flair}.

**flaunt; flout.** *Flaunt* means "to show off ostentatiously" {they flaunted their wealth}. *Flout* means "to openly disobey" {they flouted the rules}.

**flounder; founder.** Although the figurative sense of both verbs is "to go wrong," the literal senses evoke different images. To *flounder* is to struggle awkwardly, as though walking through deep mud {the professor glared while the unprepared student floundered around for an answer}. To *founder* (usually in reference to a boat or ship) is to sink or run aground {the ship foundered on the rocks}.

**flout.** See **flaunt**.

**following.** Avoid this word as an equivalent of *after*. Consider the possible miscue in *Following the presentation, there was a question-and-answer session. After* is both simpler and clearer.

**forbear, *vb.*; forebear, *n.*** The terms are unrelated, but the spellings are frequently confused. To *forbear* is to refrain {he wanted to speak but decided to forbear [the conjugation is *forbear–forbore–forborne*]}. A *forebear* is an ancestor {the house was built by Murray's distant forebears}.

**forego; forgo.** To *forego* is to go before {the foregoing paragraph}. The word appears most commonly in the phrase *foregone conclusion*. To *forgo*, by contrast, is to do without or renounce {they decided to forgo that opportunity}.

**foreword; preface.** A book's *foreword* (not *forward*) is an introductory essay written by someone other than the book's author. An introductory essay written by the book's author is called a *preface*. See 1.45, 1.46, 1.48, 1.53.

**forgo.** See **forego**.

**former; latter.** In the best usage, these words apply only to pairs. The *former* is the first of two, the *latter* the second of two.

**fortuitous; fortunate.** *Fortuitous* means "happening by chance," usually (but not always) with a good result {the rotten tree could have fallen at any time; it was just fortuitous that the victims drove by when they did}. *Fortunate* means "lucky" {we were fortunate to win the raffle}. Today, unfortunately, *fortuitous* is poaching on the semantic turf of *fortunate*.

**forward(s).** See **toward**.

**founder.** See **flounder**.

**free rein.** So written—not *free reign*.

**fulsome, *adj.*** This word does not preferably mean "very full" but "too much, excessive to the point of being repulsive." Traditionally, a "fulsome speech" is one that is so overpacked with thanks or hyperbole as to sound insincere. The word's slipshod use arises most often in the cliché *fulsome praise*, which can suggest the opposite of what the writer probably intends.

**further.** See **farther**.

**future, in the near.** See **near future, in the**.

**gauntlet; gantlet.** Lexicographers and usage critics—especially American ones—have sought since the nineteenth century to make a distinction. Etymologically, the two words have different histories: throwing down the *gauntlet* (= glove) and running the *gantlope* (= ordeal). But *gauntlet* has taken over both meanings. The standard phrases have been *run the gauntlet* and *throw down the gauntlet* since about 1800—the former phrase by a 10-to-1 margin over the competing form *run the gantlet*. Efforts to separate the terms have run their grueling course.

**gentleman.** This word is a vulgarism when used as a synonym for *man*. When used in reference to a cultured, refined man, it is susceptible to some of the same objections as those leveled against *lady*. Use it cautiously. Cf. **lady**.

**get.** Though shunned by many writers as too casual, *get* often sounds more natural than *obtain* or *procure* {get a divorce}. It can also substitute for a stuffy *become* {get hurt}. The verb is conjugated *get–got–gotten* in American English and *get–got–got* in British English. *Get* is the only verb apart from *be*-verbs that, when coupled with a past participle, can create a passive-voice construction {get stolen} {get waylaid}.

**gibe; jibe; jive.** A *gibe* is a biting insult or taunt: *Gibes* are figuratively thrown at their target {the angry crowd hurled gibes at the miscreant}. To *jibe* is to be in accord or to agree {the verdict didn't jibe with the judge's own view of the facts}. *Jive* can be either a noun (referring to swing music or to misleading talk that is transparently untrue) or a verb (meaning "to dance to such music" or "to try to mislead with lies").

**gild.** See **guild**.

**go.** This verb is conjugated *go–went–gone*. *Went* appears as a past participle only in dialect.

**gourmet; gourmand.** Both are aficionados of good food and drink. But a *gourmet* knows and appreciates the fine points of food and drink, whereas a *gourmand* tends toward gluttony.

**graduate, *vb*.** Whereas *graduate* means "to grant a diploma to or confer a degree on," *graduate from* means "to receive a diploma or degree from (a school, university, or other institution)." A school can *graduate* a student or a student can *graduate from* a school, but a student does not *graduate* a school—at least not in good usage.

**grateful; gratified.** To be *grateful* is to be thankful or appreciative. To be *gratified* is to be pleased, satisfied, or indulged.

**grisly; grizzly.** What is *grisly* is gruesome or horrible {grisly details}. What is *grizzly* is graying or sprinkled with gray, as is the fur of the North American grizzly bear {grizzly hair}.

**guild, *n*.; gild, *vb*.** A *guild* is an organization of persons with a common interest or profession {a guild of goldsmiths}. To *gild* is to put a thin layer of gold on something {gild a picture frame}, sometimes in a figurative sense {gilding the lily}.

**hail; hale.** To *hail* is to salute or greet {hail, Caesar!}, to acclaim enthusiastically {hailed as the greatest novelist of her time}, or to shout as an attention-getter {hail a taxi}. To *hale* is to compel to go {haled into court}. *Hail* is also a noun denoting ice-pellet precipitation, or something like it {a hail of insults}. *Hale* is also an adjective describing someone who is physically sound and free from infirmities.

**half (of).** Delete the *of* whenever possible {half the furniture}. When *half* is followed by a singular noun, the verb is singular {half the state is solidly

Democratic}; when it is followed by a plural noun, the verb is plural {half the people are Republicans}.

**handful.** If *handful* applies to a mass noun, use a singular verb {a handful of trouble is ahead}. But if *handful* applies to a plural count noun, use a plural verb {only a handful of walnut trees still line Main Street}.

**hangar; hanger.** One finds *hangars* (large buildings, especially those where aircraft are kept) at an airport {airplane hangars}. Everywhere else, one finds *hangers* {clothes hangers} {picture hangers}.

**hanged; hung.** *Hanged* is used as the past participle of *hang* only in its transitive form when referring to the killing (just or unjust) of a human being by suspending the person by the neck {criminals were hanged at Tyburn Hill}. But if death is not intended or likely, or if the person is suspended by a body part other than the neck, *hung* is correct {he was hung upside down as a cruel prank}. In most senses, of course, *hung* is the past form of *hang* {Abdul hung up his clothes}.

**hanger.** See **hangar**.

**harass; embarrass.** The first word has one *r*; the second has two. The pronunciation of *harass* also causes confusion. The dominant American pronunciation stresses the second syllable, while British English stresses the first.

**harebrained.** So spelled (after the timid, easily startled animal)—not *hairbrained*.

**hark back.** So written—preferably not *harken back* or *hearken back*.

**he or she.** To avoid sexist language, many writers use this alternative phrasing (in place of the generic *he*). Use it sparingly—preferably after exhausting all other, less obtrusive methods of achieving gender neutrality. In any event, *he or she* is much preferable to *he/she*, *s/he*, *(s)he*, and the like. See also 5.51, 5.265, 5.266.

**healthy; healthful.** Traditionally, a living thing that is *healthy* enjoys good health; something that is *healthful* promotes health {a healthful diet will keep you healthy}. But gradually *healthy* is taking over both senses.

**help (to).** Omit the *to* when possible {talking will help resolve the problem}.

**historic; historical.** The shorter word refers to what is momentous in history {January 16, 1991, was a historic day in Kuwait}. *Historical*, meanwhile, refers simply to anything that pertains to or occurred in history {the historical record}. On the question whether to use *a* or *an* before *historic* and *historical*, see **a**.

**hoard; horde.** A *hoard* is a supply, usually secret and sometimes valuable. *Hoard* is also a verb meaning "to amass such a supply," especially when there is no need to do so. A *horde* was originally a tribe of Asian nomads; today a *horde* is a large crowd, especially one that moves in a noisy, uncontrolled way.

**hoi polloi.** This is a mildly disparaging phrase for "common people." It does not refer to elites, though some writers and speakers misuse it in this way (perhaps from false association with *hoity-toity*). It is a plural. Although *hoi* is Greek for "the," the phrase is commonly rendered *the hoi polloi* and has been at least since it was used by John Dryden in 1668.

**holocaust.** When capitalized, this word refers to the Nazi genocide of European Jews in World War II. When not capitalized, it refers (literally or figuratively) to extensive devastation caused by fire or to the systematic and malicious killings of human beings on a vast scale. Avoid any light or hyperbolic use of this word.

**home in.** This phrase is frequently misrendered *hone in*. (*Hone* means "to sharpen.") *Home in* refers to what homing pigeons and aerial bombs do; the meaning is "to come closer and closer to a target."

**homicide.** See **murder**.

**hopefully.** The old meaning of the word ("in a hopeful manner") seems unsustainable; the newer meaning ("I hope" or "it is to be hoped that"), as a sentence adverb, spread in the 1960s and 1970s and seems here to stay. But many careful writers still avoid the new meaning.

**horde.** See **hoard**.

**humanitarian.** This word means "involving the promotion of human welfare" {humanitarian philanthropy}. Avoid using it in a phrase such as *the worst humanitarian disaster in decades*, where it really means just "human."

**hung.** See **hanged**.

**I; me.** When you need a first-person pronoun, use one. It's not immodest to do so; it's superstitious not to. But be sure you get the right one {Sally and I are planning to go} {give John or me a call} {keep this between you and me}. See **between you and me**.

**idyllic.** An *idyll* is a short pastoral poem, and by extension *idyllic* means charming or picturesque. It is not synonymous with *ideal* (perfect).

**i.e.; e.g.** The first is the abbreviation for *id est* ("that is"); the second is the abbreviation for *exempli gratia* ("for example"). The English equivalents are preferable in formal prose, though sometimes the compactness of these two-character abbreviations makes them desirable. Always put a comma after either one. See also 6.20, 6.54.

**if; whether.** While *if* is conditional, *whether* introduces an alternative, often in the context of an indirect question. Use *whether* in two circumstances: (1) to introduce a noun clause: *he asked whether his tie was straight* (the alternatives are *yes* and *no*), and (2) when using *if* produces ambiguity. In the sentence *he asked if his tie was straight*, the literal meaning is "whenever his tie was straight, he asked"; the popular meaning "he wanted someone to tell him whether his tie did or didn't need straightening" may not be understood by all readers. More tellingly, *Call to let me know if you can come* means that you should call only if you're coming. *Call to let me know whether you can come* means that you should call regardless of whether the answer is yes or no. Avoid substituting *if* for *whether* unless your tone is intentionally informal or you are quoting someone. See **determine whether**; **whether**.

**ilk.** This noun commonly means "type" or "sort" in modern usage, and unobjectionably so today {of his ilk} {of that ilk}. The Scottish phrase *of that ilk* means "of the same name or place."

**illegal.** See **unlawful.**

**illegible; unreadable.** Handwriting or printing that is *illegible* is not clear enough to be read {illegible scrawlings}. Writing that is *unreadable* is so poorly composed as to be either incomprehensible or intolerably dull.

**illicit.** See **elicit; unlawful.**

**illude.** See **allude.**

**immigrate; emigrate.** To *immigrate* is to enter a country to live permanently, leaving a past home. To *emigrate* is to leave one country to live in another one. The cognate forms also demand attention. Someone who moves from Ireland to the United States is an *immigrant* here and an *emigrant* there. An *émigré* is also an *emigrant,* but especially one in political exile.

**imminent.** See **eminent.**

**impact; impactful.** Resist using *impact* as a verb. Try *affect* or *influence* instead. Besides being hyperbolic, *impact* is still considered a solecism by traditionalists (though it is gaining ground). Avoid *impactful,* which is jargon (replacements include *influential* and *powerful*). Cf. **access.**

**impeachment.** *Impeachment* is the legislative equivalent of an indictment, not a conviction. In the US federal system, the House of Representatives votes on impeachment, and the Senate votes on removal from office.

**impelled.** See **compelled.**

**implicit.** See **explicit.**

**imply; infer.** The writer or speaker *implies* (hints, suggests); the reader or listener *infers* (deduces). Writers and speakers often use *infer* as if it were synonymous with *imply,* but careful writers always distinguish between the two words. See **inference.**

**important; importantly.** In the phrase *more important(ly)*—usually at the outset of a sentence—traditionalists prefer the shorter form as an ellipsis of *what is more important,* normally with a comma following. But *more importantly* is now established as a sentence adverb—and it's unobjectionable.

**impractical; impracticable.** The first is the more general adjective, meaning "not sensible" or "unrealistic" {impractical planning that doesn't account for travel expenses}. The second means "impossible to carry out" {landing aircraft on that hole-ridden runway proved impracticable}. See also **practicable.**

**in actual fact.** Redundant. Try *actually* or *in fact,* or simply omit.

**in behalf of.** See **behalf.**

**in connection with.** This is a vague, fuzzy phrase {she explained the financial consequences in connection with the transaction} {Ray liked everything in connection with golf} {Phipson was compensated in connection with its report}. Try replacing the phrase with *of, related to,* or *associated with* {she explained the financial consequences of the transaction}, *about* {Ray liked everything about golf}, or *for* {Phipson was compensated for its report}.

**in excess of.** Try replacing this verbose phrase with *more than* or *over*. See **over**.

**in order to; in order for.** Often these expressions can be reduced to *to* and *for*. When that is so, and rhythm and euphony are preserved or even heightened, use *to* or *for*.

**in proximity.** See **close proximity**.

**in regard to.** This is the phrase, not the nonstandard *in regards to*. But try a single-word substitute instead: *about, regarding, concerning,* etc.

**in spite of.** For brevity, prefer *despite*.

**in the affirmative.** See **affirmative, in the**.

**in the event that.** See **event**.

**in the near future.** See **near future, in the**.

**in the negative.** See **affirmative, in the**.

**inasmuch as.** *Because* or *since* is almost always a better choice. See **since**.

**incidence; incident; instance.** Be careful with the first of these words: It has to do with relative rates and ranges {the incidence of albinism within a given society}. Perhaps leave it to scientists and actuaries. An *incident* (= an event, occurrence, or happening) should be distinguished from an *instance* (= a case, example).

**include; comprise.** The basic difference between these near-synonyms is that *include* implies nonexclusivity {the collection includes 126 portraits [suggesting that there is much else in the collection]}, while *comprise* implies exclusivity {the collection comprises 126 silver spoons [suggesting that nothing else is part of the collection]}. Oddly, in patent law—and there alone—*comprise* carries a nonexclusive sense. See **comprise**.

**incredible; incredulous.** *Incredible* properly means "too strange to be believed; difficult to believe." Colloquially, it is used to mean "astonishingly good" {it was an incredible trip}. *Incredulous* means "disbelieving, skeptical" {people are incredulous about the rising gas costs}.

**inculcate; indoctrinate.** One *inculcates* values *into* a child but *indoctrinates* the child *with* values. That is, *inculcate* always takes the preposition *into* and a value or values as its object {inculcate courage into soldiers}. *Indoctrinate* takes a person as its object {indoctrinate children with the habit of telling the truth}.

**individual.** Use this word to distinguish a single person from a group. When possible, use a more specific term, such as *person, adult, child, man,* or *woman*.

**indoctrinate.** See **inculcate**.

**induce.** See **adduce**.

**infectious.** See **contagious**.

**infer.** See **imply**.

**inference.** Prefer the verb *draw* over *make* with *inference* {they drew the wrong inferences}. Some readers confuse *inference* with *implication*. See **imply.**

**inflammable.** See **flammable**.

**inflict; afflict.** Events, illnesses, punishments, etc. are *inflicted on* living things or entities {an abuser inflicts cruelty}. The sufferers are *afflicted with* or *by* disease, troubles, etc. {agricultural communities are afflicted with drought}.

**ingenious; ingenuous.** These words are similar in form but not in meaning. *Ingenious* describes what is intelligent, clever, and original {an ingenious invention}. *Ingenuous* describes a person who is candid, naive, and without dissimulation, or an action or statement with those qualities {a hurtful but ingenuous observation}.

**innate; inherent.** An *innate* characteristic is one that a living thing has from birth; it should be distinguished, then, from a talent or disposition that one acquires from training or experience. An *inherent* characteristic is also part of a thing's nature, but life is not implied. A rock, for example, has an inherent hardness.

**innervate.** See **enervate**.

**innocent; not guilty.** If you are *innocent*, you are without blame. If you are *not guilty*, you have been exonerated by a jury. Newspapers avoid the *not guilty* phrase, though, because the consequences of accidentally leaving off the *not* could be serious. See **pleaded**.

**innumerable.** See **enumerable**.

**inquire.** The normal spellings in American English and British English alike are *inquire* and *inquiry*. *Enquire* and *enquiry* are primarily British English variants.

**insidious; invidious.** What is *insidious* spreads gradually to cause damage—at first without being noticed {an insidious conspiracy}; what is *invidious* involves moral offensiveness and serious unpleasantness {invidious discrimination}.

**instance.** See **incidence**.

**insure.** See **ensure**.

**intense; intensive.** *Intense* means (1) "having a strong effect" {intense pressures}, (2) "involving a great deal of effort during a very short time" {intense concentration}, or (3) "having unduly strong feelings or a demeanor of exaggerated seriousness" {he's a bit too intense}. *Intense* is always preferred outside philosophical and scientific usages. But *intensive* should be retained in customary terms such as *labor-intensive* and *intensive care*.

**intently; intensely.** An act done *intently* is done purposefully and with concentration and determination. One that is done *intensely* is done with great power, passion, or emotion but not necessarily with deliberate intent.

**inter; intern.** *Inter* is a verb meaning "to bury (a dead person)"; the corresponding noun is *interment*. An *intern* is a student working temporarily to gain experience, especially in a profession. *Intern* is also a verb with two senses. As an intransitive verb, it means "to work as an intern" {interning at the US Senate}; the corresponding noun is *internship*. As a transitive verb, it means "to confine (a civilian) to a certain place or district without a criminal charge, especially in wartime or for political reasons"; the corresponding noun is *internment*.

**inveigh; inveigle.** To *inveigh* is to protest, usually against something {picketers inveighed against annexation}. To *inveigle* is to cajole or ensnare, especially by misleading {inveigling a friend to attend the party}.

**invidious.** See **insidious.**

**invoke.** See **evoke.**

**irregardless.** An error. Use *regardless* (or possibly *irrespective*).

**it is I; it is me.** Both are correct and acceptable. The first phrase, using the first-person predicate nominative, is strictly grammatical (and a little stuffy); the second is idiomatic (and relaxed), and it is often contracted to *it's me*. In third-person constructions, however, a greater stringency holds sway in good English {this is he} {it isn't she who has caused such misery}.

**its; it's.** *Its* is the possessive form of *it*; *it's* is the contraction for *it is* {it's a benefit for a corporation to have its headquarters near a major airport}.

**jealousy; envy.** *Jealousy* connotes feelings of resentment toward another, particularly in matters relating to an intimate relationship {sexual jealousy}. *Envy* refers to coveting another's advantages, possessions, or abilities {his transparent envy of others' successes}.

**jibe; jive.** See **gibe.**

**karat.** See **carat.**

**kudos.** Preferably pronounced /**k[y]oo**-dos/ (not /-dohz/), this word means "praise and admiration." It is singular, not plural. Hence avoid *kudo is* or *kudos are*.

**lady.** When used as a synonym for *woman*—indeed, when used anywhere but in the phrase *ladies and gentlemen*—this word will be considered objectionable by some readers who think that it refers to a patronizing stereotype. This is especially true when it is used for unprestigious jobs {cleaning lady} or as a condescending adjective {lady lawyer}. Some will insist on using it to describe a refined woman. If they've consulted this entry, they've been forewarned. Cf. **gentleman.**

**last; lastly.** As with *first*, *second*, etc., prefer *last* when introducing a final point of discussion—or (of course) *finally*.

**latter.** See **former.**

**laudable; laudatory.** *Laudable* means "praiseworthy, even if not fully successful" {a laudable effort}. *Laudatory* means "expressing praise" {laudatory phone calls}.

**lay; lie.** Admittedly, the traditional conjugations are more blurred than ever. *Lay* is a transitive verb—that is, it demands a direct object {lay your pencils down}. It is inflected *lay–laid–laid* {I laid the book there yesterday} {these rumors have been laid to rest}. (The children's prayer *Now I lay me down to sleep* is a good mnemonic device for the transitive *lay*.) *Lie* is an intransitive verb—that is, it never takes a direct object {lie down and rest}. It is inflected *lie–lay–lain* {she lay down and rested} {he hasn't yet lain down in twenty-three hours}. In a doctor's office, you should be asked to *lie back* or *lie down*.

**leach; leech.** To *leach* is to percolate or to separate out solids in solution by percolation. A *leech* is a bloodsucker (whether literal or figurative). By extension of that noun, to *leech* is either to attach oneself to another as a leech does or to drain the resources of something.

**lead.** See **led**.

**lease; let.** Many Americans seem to think that *let* is colloquial and of modern origin. In fact, the word is three hundred years older than *lease* and just as proper. One distinction between the two words is that either the owner or the tenant can be said to *lease* property, but only the owner can be said to *let* it.

**led.** This is the correct spelling of the past tense and past participle of the verb *lead*. It is often misspelled *lead*, maybe in part because of the pronunciation of the metal *lead* and the past tense and past participle *read*, both of which rhyme with *led*.

**leech.** See **leach**.

**lend, *vb.*; loan, *vb. & n.*** *Lend* is the correct term for letting someone use something with the understanding that it (or its equivalent) will be returned. The verb *loan* is standard especially when money is the subject of the transaction—but even then, *lend* appears somewhat more frequently in edited English. *Loan* is the noun corresponding to both *lend* and *loan*, vb. The past-tense and past-participial form of *lend* is *lent*.

**less; fewer.** Reserve *less* for singular mass nouns or amounts {less salt} {less soil} {less water}. Reserve *fewer* for plural count nouns {fewer calories} {fewer people} {fewer suggestions}.

**lest.** This is one of the few English words that invariably call for a verb in the subjunctive mood {he didn't want to drive lest he take a wrong turn} {he has turned down the volume lest he disturb his roommates}. The conjunction is somewhat more common in British English than in American English.

**let.** See **lease**.

**libel.** See **defamation**.

**lie.** See **lay**.

**life-and-death; life-or-death.** The problem of logic aside (life and death being mutually exclusive), the first phrase is the standard idiom {a life-and-death decision}.

**light, *vb.*** This verb can be inflected either *light–lit–lit* or *light–lighted–lighted*—and irreproachably so. The past-participial adjective tends to be *lighted* when not modified by an *-ly* adverb {a lighted building} {a well-lighted hall} but *lit* if an *-ly* adverb precedes {brightly lit sconces} {a nicely lit walkway}.

**like; as.** The use of *like* as a conjunction (as in the old jingle "tastes good like a cigarette should") has long been a contentious issue. Traditionally speaking, *like* is a preposition, not a conjunction equivalent to *as* {you're much like me [*me* is the object of the preposition *like*]} {do as I say [the conjunction *as* connects the imperative *do* with the independent clause *I say*]}. As a casualism, however, the conjunctive *like* has become especially common since the mid-twentieth century {nobody cares like I do}. In Standard Written English, a conjunctive *like* will still provoke frowns among some readers. But the objections are slowly dwindling. If you want your prose to be unimpeachable and heightened, stick to *as* and *as if* for conjunctive senses {as we've observed, *Homo sapiens* is a social animal} {it looks as if it might rain}. See also 5.191.

**likely.** See **apt**.

**literally.** This word means "actually; without exaggeration." It should not be used loosely in figurative senses, as in *they were literally glued to their seats* (unless glue had in fact been applied). Wherever guides have accepted this usage, they should be disregarded.

**loan.** See **lend**.

**loathe, *vb.*; loath, *adj.*** To *loathe* (the *th* pronounced as in *that*) something is to detest it intensely or to regard it with disgust {I loathe tabloid television}. Someone who is *loath* (the *th* pronounced as in *thing*) is reluctant or unwilling {Tracy seems loath to admit mistakes}.

**lose; loose, *vb.*; loosen.** To *lose* something is to be deprived of it. To *loose* something is to release it from fastenings or restraints. To *loosen* is to make less tight or to ease a restraint. *Loose* conveys the idea of complete release, whereas *loosen* refers to only a partial release.

**lot.** See **a lot**.

**luxuriant; luxurious.** What is *luxuriant* is lush and grows abundantly {a luxuriant head of hair}. What is *luxurious* is lavish, extravagant, and comfortable {a luxurious resort}.

**mad; angry.** Some people object to using *mad* to mean "angry" and would reserve it to mean "insane." But the first sense dates back seven hundred years and isn't likely to disappear. As common as it is in everyday use, though, it has been so stigmatized that most people avoid it in formal writing.

**majority.** This noun preferably denotes countable things {a majority of votes cast}, not uncountable ones {the majority of the time}. Use *most* whenever it fits. When referring to a preponderance of votes cast, *majority* takes a singular verb {her majority was 7 percent}. But referring to a predominant group of people or things, it can take either a singular verb {the majority in the House was soon swept away} or a plural one {the majority of the voters were against the proposal}. Typically, if a genitive with a plural object follows *majority*, the verb should be plural {a majority of music teachers prefer using the metronome}.

**malevolent; maleficent.** *Malevolent* describes an evil mind that wishes to harm others {with malevolent intent}. *Maleficent* is similar but describes desire by the miscreant for accomplishing evil {maleficent bullying}.

**malodorous.** See **odious**.

**maltreatment.** See **mistreatment**.

**mankind.** Consider *humans, human beings*, or *people* instead.

**manslaughter.** See **murder**.

**mantle; mantel.** A *mantle* is a long, loose garment like a cloak—almost always today used in a metaphorical sense {assuming the mantle of a martyr}. A *mantel* is a wood or stone structure around a fireplace {family pictures on the mantel}.

**masterful; masterly.** *Masterful* describes a person who is dominating and imperious. *Masterly* describes a person who has mastered a craft, trade, or profession, or a product of such mastery; the word often means "authoritative" {a masterly analysis}. Because *masterly* does not readily make an adverb (*masterlily* being extremely awkward), try *in a masterly way*. See also 5.163. The association of *master* with the historical slave trade has caused many to avoid the term in a wide variety of contexts.

**may; can.** See **can**.

**may; might.** *May* expresses what is possible, is factual, or could be factual {I may have turned off the stove, but I can't recall doing it}. *Might* suggests something that is uncertain, hypothetical, or contrary to fact {I might have won the marathon if I had entered}. See 5.152.

**me.** See **I**.

**medal; meddle; metal; mettle.** A *medal* is an award for merit; a *metal* is a type of substance, usually dense and malleable. To *meddle* is to interfere. And *mettle* is a person's character, courage, and determination to do something no matter how difficult.

**media; mediums.** In scientific contexts and in reference to mass communications, the plural of *medium* is predominantly *media* {some bacteria flourish in several types of media} {the media are reporting more medical news}. Although one frequently sees *media is*, the plural use is recommended. If *medium* refers to a spiritualist, the plural is *mediums* {several mediums have held séances here}.

**memoranda; memorandums.** Although both plural forms are correct, *memoranda* has predominated since the early nineteenth century. Don't use *memoranda* as if it were singular—the word is *memorandum* {this memorandum is} {these memoranda are}.

**metal; mettle.** See **medal**.

**mete out.** The phrase meaning "to distribute" or "to assign" is so spelled {mete out punishment}. *Meet out* is a common error, especially in the erroneous past tense *meeted out*.

**might.** See **may**.

**militate.** See **mitigate**.

**minuscule.** Something that is minuscule is "very small." Probably because of the spelling of the modern word *mini* (and the prefix of the same spelling, which is recorded only from 1936), it is often misspelled *miniscule*. In printing, *minuscules* are lowercase letters and *majuscules* are capital (uppercase) letters.

**mistreatment; maltreatment.** *Mistreatment* is the more general term. *Maltreatment* denotes a harsh form of mistreatment, involving abuse by rough or cruel handling.

**mitigate; militate.** To *mitigate* is to lessen or soften the effects of something unpleasant, harmful, or serious; *mitigating circumstances* lessen the seriousness of a crime. To *militate*, by contrast, is to have a marked effect on; the word is usually followed by *against* {his nearsightedness militated against his ambition to become a commercial pilot}. Avoid the mistaken phrase *mitigate against* for the correct *militate against*.

**moot; mute.** *Moot* (/moot/) means (traditionally) "debatable" {a moot point worth our attention} or (by modern extension) "having no practical significance" {a moot question that is of no account}. *Mute* (/m[y]oot/) means "silent, speechless"—and is often considered offensive when used as a noun, especially in the term *deaf-mute*, a historical phrasing to be avoided.

**more than.** See **over**.

**much; very.** *Much* generally intensifies past-participial adjectives {much obliged} {much encouraged} and some comparatives {much more} {much worse} {much too soon}. *Very* intensifies adverbs and most adjectives {very carefully} {very bad}, including past-participial adjectives that have more adjectival than verbal force {very bored}. See 5.94.

**murder; manslaughter; homicide.** All three words denote the killing of one person by another. *Murder* and *manslaughter* are both unlawful killings, but *murder* is done maliciously and intentionally. *Homicide* includes killings that are not unlawful, such as by a police officer acting properly in the line of duty. *Homicide* also refers to a person who kills another.

**mute.** See **moot**.

**mutual.** See **common**.

**myself.** Avoid using *myself* as a pronoun in place of *I* or *me*—a quirk that arises most often after an *and* or *or*. Instead, use it reflexively {I did myself a favor} or emphatically {I myself have tried to get through that book!}. See also 5.55.

**naturalist; naturist.** *Naturalist* most often denotes a person who studies natural history, especially a field biologist or an amateur who observes and usually photographs, sketches, or writes about nature. *Naturist* denotes a nature worshipper or a nudist.

**nauseous; nauseated.** Whatever is *nauseous,* traditionally speaking, induces a feeling of nausea—it makes us feel sick to our stomachs. To feel sick is to be *nauseated.* Although the use of *nauseous* to mean *nauseated* may be too common to be called an error anymore, strictly speaking it is poor usage. Because of the ambiguity in *nauseous,* the wisest course may be to stick to the participial adjectives *nauseated* and *nauseating.*

**near future, in the.** Try *soon* or *shortly* instead.

**necessary; necessitous.** *Necessary* means "required under the circumstances" {the necessary arrangements}. *Necessitous* means "impoverished" {living in necessitous circumstances}.

**neither.** Four points. First, like *either,* this word when functioning as the subject of a clause takes a singular verb {neither of the subjects was given that medicine}. Second, a *neither–nor* construction should frame grammatically parallel expressions {neither the room's being too cold nor the heater's malfunction could justify his boorish reaction} (both noun elements). Third, a simple *neither–nor* construction should have only two elements {neither bricks nor stones}—though it's perfectly permissible to multiply *nor*s for emphasis {neither snow nor rain nor heat nor gloom of night}. Fourth, the word is acceptably pronounced either /**nee**-thər/ or /**nɪ**-thər/.

**no.** See **affirmative, in the.**

**noisome.** This word shares a root with *annoy,* not with *noise.* It means noxious, offensive, or foul-smelling {a noisome landfill}.

**none.** This word may take either a singular or a plural verb. A guideline: If it is followed by a singular noun, treat it as a singular {none of the building was painted}; if by a plural noun, treat it as a plural {none of the guests were here when I arrived}. But for special emphasis, it is quite proper (though possibly stilted) to use a singular verb when a plural noun follows {none of my suggestions was accepted}.

**nonplussed.** Traditionally meaning "surprised and confused" {she was nonplussed when he took off the mask}, this word is now frequently misused to mean "unfazed"—almost the opposite of its literal sense. Avoid this newer usage, and avoid the variant spelling *nonplused.* See **faze.**

**not guilty.** See **innocent.**

**notable; noticeable; noteworthy.** *Notable* (= readily noticed) applies both to physical things and to qualities {notable sense of humor}. *Noticeable* means "detectable with the physical senses" {a noticeable limp}. *Noteworthy* means "remarkable; deserving attention" {a noteworthy act of kindness}.

**notwithstanding.** One word. Less formal alternatives include *despite, although,* and *in spite of.* The word *notwithstanding* may precede or follow a noun {notwithstanding her bad health, she decided to run for office} {her bad health notwithstanding, she decided to run for office}.

**number.** See **amount.**

**observance; observation.** *Observance* means "obedience to a rule or custom" {the family's observance of Passover}. *Observation* means either "the watching of something" or "a remark based on watching or studying something" {a keen observation about the defense strategy}. Each term is sometimes used when the other would be the better word.

**obtain.** See **attain.**

**obtuse; abstruse.** *Obtuse* describes a person who can't understand; *abstruse* describes an idea that is hard to understand. A person who is *obtuse* is dull and, by extension, dull-witted. What is *abstruse* is incomprehensible or nearly so.

**odious; odorous; odoriferous; malodorous.** *Odious* means "hateful" or "extremely unpleasant" {odious Jim Crow laws}. It is not related to the other terms, but it is sometimes misused as if it were. *Odorous* means "detectable by smell (for better or worse)" {odorous gases}. *Odoriferous* means essentially the same thing: It has meant "fragrant" as often as it has meant "foul." *Malodorous* means "smelling quite bad." The mistaken form *odiferous* is often used as a jocular equivalent of *smelly*—but many dictionaries don't record it.

**of.** Avoid using this word needlessly after *all, off, inside,* and *outside*. Also, prefer *June 2022* over *June of 2022*. To improve your style, try removing every *of*-phrase that you reasonably can.

**off.** Never put *of* after this word {we got off the bus}.

**officious.** A person who is *officious* is aggressively nosy and meddlesome—and overeager to tell people what to do. In its modern sense, the word has nothing to do with *officer* and should not be confused with *official*.

**on; upon.** Prefer *on* to *upon* unless introducing an event or condition {put that on the shelf, please} {upon the job's completion, you'll get paid}. For more about *on*, see **onto.**

**on behalf of.** See **behalf.**

**one another.** See **each other.**

**oneself.** One word—not *one's self*.

**onto; on to; on.** When is *on* a preposition, and when an adverb? The sense of the sentence should tell, but the distinction can be subtle. *Onto* implies a movement, so it has an adverbial flavor even though it is a preposition {the gymnast jumped onto the bars}. When *on* is part of the verb phrase, it is an adverb and *to* is the preposition {the gymnast held on to the bars}. One trick is to mentally say "up" before *on*: If the sentence still makes sense, then *onto* is probably the right choice {she leaped onto the capstone}. Alone, *on* does not imply motion {the gymnast is good on the parallel bars}.

**oppress; repress.** *Oppress*, meaning "to persecute or tyrannize," is more negative than *repress*, meaning "to restrain or subordinate."

**or.** If this conjunction joins singular nouns functioning as subjects, the verb should be singular {cash or online payment is acceptable}.

**oral.** See **verbal.**

**oration.** See **peroration**.

**ordinance; ordnance.** An *ordinance* is a municipal regulation or an authoritative decree. *Ordnance* is military armament, especially artillery but also weapons and ammunition generally.

**orient; orientate.** To *orient* is to get one's bearings (literally, "to find east") {it took the new employee a few days to get oriented to the firm's suite}. Unless used in the sense "to face or turn to the east," *orientate* is a poor variation to be avoided.

**ought; should.** Both express a sense of duty, but *ought* is stronger. Unlike *should*, *ought* requires a fully expressed infinitive, even in the negative {you ought not to see the movie}. Don't omit the *to*. See 5.154, 5.155.

**outside.** In spatial references, no *of* is necessary—or desirable—after this word unless it is used as a noun {outside the shop} {the outside of the building}. But *outside of* is acceptable as a colloquialism meaning "except for" or "aside from."

**over.** As an equivalent of *more than*, this word is perfectly good idiomatic English.

**overly.** Once frowned on by sticklers, this term is now unexceptionable (as in the phrase *overly tired*).

**pair.** This is a singular form, the plural being *pairs* {three pairs of shoes}. Yet *pair* may take either a singular verb {this pair of sunglasses was on the table} or a plural one {the pair were inseparable from the moment they met}.

**palette; palate; pallet.** An artist's *palette* is either the board that an artist uses for mixing colors or (collectively) the colors used by a particular artist or in a particular work. Your *palate* is the roof of your mouth specifically or your taste in food generally. A *pallet* is a low, usually wooden platform for storing and transporting goods in commerce, or a crude bed.

**pandemic.** See **epidemic**.

**parameters.** Though it may sound elegant or scientific, this word is usually just pretentious when it is used in nontechnical contexts. Stick to *boundaries*, *limits*, *guidelines*, *grounds*, *elements*, or some other word.

**partake in; partake of.** To *partake in* is to participate in {the new student refused to partake in class discussions}. To *partake of* is either to get a part of {partake of the banquet} or to have a quality, at least to some extent {this assault partakes of revenge}.

**partly; partially.** Both words convey the sense "to some extent; in part" {partly responsible}. *Partly* is preferred in that sense. But *partially* has the additional senses of "incompletely" {partially cooked} and "unfairly; in a way that shows bias toward one side" {he treats his friends partially}.

**past; passed.** *Past* can be an adjective {past events} (often postpositive {times past}), a noun {remember the past}, a preposition {go past the school}, or an adverb {time flew past}. *Passed* is the past tense and past participle of the verb *pass* {we passed the school} {as time passed}.

**pastime.** This word combines *pass* (not *past*) and *time*. It is spelled with a single *s* and a single *t*.

**peaceable; peaceful.** A *peaceable* person or nation is inclined to avoid strife {peaceable kingdom}. A *peaceful* person, place, or event is serene, tranquil, and calm {a peaceful day free from demands}.

**peak; peek; pique.** A *peak* is an apex, a *peek* is a quick or illicit glance, and a fit of *pique* is an episode of peevishness and wounded vanity. To *pique* is to annoy or arouse: An article *piques* (not *peaks*) one's interest.

**pedal; peddle.** *Pedal* is a noun, verb, or adjective relating to the pedal extremity, or foot. As a noun, it denotes a device that is operated by the foot and does some work, such as powering a bicycle or changing the sound of a piano. As a verb, it means to use such a device. As an adjective, it means "of or concerning such a device or its use." *Peddle* is a verb meaning either "to try to sell goods to people by traveling from place to place" or "to sell questionable goods to people"—questionable because they may be illegal, harmful, or low quality {peddling magazine subscriptions door to door}.

**peek.** See **peak.**

**pendant, *n.*; pendent, *adj.*** A *pendant* is an item of dangling jewelry, especially one worn around the neck. What is *pendent* is hanging or suspended from something.

**penultimate.** This adjective means "next to last" {the penultimate paragraph in the précis}. Many people have started misusing it as a fancy equivalent of *ultimate*. The word *antepenultimate* means "the next to the next-to-last."

**people; persons.** The traditional view is that *persons* is used for smaller numbers {three persons} and *people* with larger ones {millions of people}. But today most people use *people* even for small groups {only three people were there}.

**peroration; oration.** A *peroration*, strictly speaking, is the conclusion of an *oration* (speech). Careful writers avoid using *peroration* to refer to a rousing speech or piece of writing.

**perpetuate; perpetrate.** To *perpetuate* something is to sustain it or prolong it indefinitely {perpetuate the species}. To *perpetrate* is to commit or perform an act, especially one that is illegal or morally wrong {perpetrate a crime}.

**personally.** Three points. First, use this word only when someone does something that would normally be done through an agent {the president personally signed this invitation} or to limit other considerations {Jean was affected by the decision but was not personally involved in it}. Second, *personally* is redundant when it modifies a verb that necessarily requires the person's presence, as in *The senator personally shook hands with the constituents*. Third, *personally* shouldn't appear with *I* when one is stating an opinion; it weakens the statement and doesn't reduce the speaker's liability for the opinion. The only exception arises if a person is required to advance someone else's view but holds a different personal opinion {in the chamber I voted to lower taxes because of the constituencies I represented, but I personally believed that taxes should have been increased}.

**persons.** See **people**.

**persuade; convince.** *Persuade* is associated with actions {persuade him to buy a suit}. *Convince* is associated with beliefs or understandings {she convinced the auditor of her honesty}. The phrase *persuade to (do)* has traditionally been considered better than *convince to (do)*—the latter having become common in American English in the 1950s. But either verb will take a *that*-clause {the committee was persuaded that an all-night session was necessary} {my three-year-old is convinced that Santa Claus exists}.

**pertain; appertain.** *Pertain to,* the more common term, means "to relate directly to" {the clause pertains to assignment of risk}. *Appertain to* means "to belong to or concern something as a matter of form or function" {the defendant's rights appertain to the Fifth Amendment}.

**peruse.** This term, which means "to read with great care" (*not* "to read quickly" or "to scan"), should not be used as a fancy substitute for *read.*

**phase.** See **faze**.

**phenomenon.** This is the singular {the phenomenon of texting}, the plural being *phenomena* {cultural phenomena}.

**pique.** See **peak**.

**pitiable; pitiful.** To be *pitiable* is to be worthy of pity. To be *pitiful* is either to be very poor in quality or to be so sad or unfortunate as to make people feel sympathy.

**pleaded; pled.** The first is the traditional past-tense and past-participial form {he pleaded guilty} {they have pleaded with their families}. But *pled* is increasingly common in American English in legal contexts.

**plethora.** This noun denotes an excess, surfeit, or overabundance. Avoid it as a mere equivalent of "abundance."

**populace; populous.** The *populace* is the population of a country, state, city, etc. A *populous* place is densely populated.

**pore.** To *pore over* something written is to read it intently {they pored over every word in the report}. Some writers confuse this word with *pour*.

**practicable; possible; practical.** These terms differ in shading. What is *practicable* is capable of being done; it's feasible. What is *possible* might be capable of happening or being done, but there is some doubt. What is *practical* is fit for actual use or in a particular situation. See also **impractical**.

**precede; proceed.** To *precede* is to happen before or to go before in some sequence, usually time. It also means "to outrank" or "to surpass" in some measure such as importance, but this sense is usually conveyed with the noun *precedence* {the board's vote takes precedence over the staff's recommendation}. The word is often misspelled *preceed*. To *proceed* is to go on, whether beginning, continuing, or resuming.

**precipitate, *adj.*; precipitous.** What is *precipitate* occurs suddenly or rashly, without proper consideration; it describes demands, actions, or movements. What is *precipitous* is dangerously steep; it describes cliffs and inclines.

**precondition.** Try *condition* or *prerequisite* instead.

**predominant, *adj.*; predominate, *vb.*** Like *dominant, predominant* is an adjective {a predominant point of view}. Like *dominate, predominate* is a verb {a point of view that predominates throughout the state}. Using *predominate* as an adjective is nonstandard.

**preface.** See **foreword**.

**prejudice, *vb.*** Although *prejudice* is a perfectly normal English noun to denote an all-too-common trait, the corresponding verb is a legalism. For a plain-English equivalent, use *harm* or *hurt*. But the past-participial adjective *prejudiced* is perfectly normal in the sense of "biased; harboring strong and often unfair feelings against."

**preliminary to.** Make it *before, in preparing for*, or some other natural phrasing.

**prescribe.** See **proscribe**.

**presently.** This word is ambiguous. Write *now* or *soon*, whichever you really mean.

**presumption.** See **assumption**.

**preventive.** Although the corrupt form *preventative* is fairly common, the strictly correct form is *preventive*.

**previous to.** Make it *before*.

**principle; principal.** A *principle* is a natural, moral, or legal rule {the principle of free speech}. The corresponding adjective is *principled* {a principled decision}. A *principal* is a person of high authority or prominence {a school principal} or an initial deposit of money {principal and interest}. *Principal* is also an adjective meaning "most important." Hence a *principal* role is a primary one.

**prior to.** Make it *before* or *until*.

**proceed.** See **precede**.

**process of, in the.** You can almost always delete this phrase without affecting the meaning.

**propaganda.** This is a singular noun denoting information or images, usually including false or misleading elements or manipulated perspectives, that are used by a government or political group to influence people {propaganda was everywhere}. The plural is *propagandas*.

**prophesy; prophecy.** *Prophesy* is the verb meaning "to say what will happen in the future, especially by using supernatural or magical knowledge" {the doomsayers prophesied a market collapse despite the good news}. *Prophecy* is the noun denoting a prediction, especially one made by someone claiming to have supernatural or magical powers {their prophecies did not materialize}. *Prophesize* is an erroneous form.

**proscribe; prescribe.** To *proscribe* something is to prohibit it {legislation that proscribes drinking while driving}. To *prescribe* is to say officially what must be done in a particular situation {Henry VIII prescribed the order of succession to include three of his children} or to specify a medical remedy {the doctor prescribed anti-inflammatory pills and certain exercises}.

**protuberance.** So spelled. Perhaps because *protrude* means "to stick out," writers want to spell *protuberance* (= something that bulges out) with an extra *r* (after the *t*). But the words are from different roots.

**proved; proven.** *Proved* is the preferred past participle for the verb *prove* {it was proved to be true}. Use *proven* only as an adjective {a proven success}.

**proximity.** See **close proximity**.

**purposely; purposefully.** What is done *purposely* is done deliberately or intentionally—"on purpose." What is done *purposefully* is done with a certain goal or a clear aim in mind. An action may be done *purposely* without any particular interest in a specific result—that is, not *purposefully*.

**question whether; question of whether; question as to whether.** The first phrasing is traditionally considered best. The others, though common, have been considered phraseologically inferior. Today, however, *question of whether* has become the predominant phrasing. See also **as to**.

**quick(ly).** *Quickly* is the general adverb. But *quick* is properly used as an adverb in the idiomatic phrases *get rich quick* and *come quick*. See also 5.165.

**quote; quotation.** Traditionally a verb, *quote* is often used as an equivalent of *quotation* in speech and informal writing. Also, there is a tendency for writers (especially journalists) to think of *quotes* as contemporary remarks usable in their writing and of *quotations* as being wisdom of the ages expressed pithily.

**rack; wrack.** The spelling *rack* is complex: It accounts for nine different nouns and seven different verbs. Indeed, it is standard in all familiar senses {racking his brain} {racked with guilt} {nerve-racking} {rack and ruin}. *Wrack* is the standard spelling only for the noun meaning "seaweed, kelp."

**raise; raze.** To *raise* is to elevate, move upward, enhance, bring up, etc. {we raised some money}. To *raze* is to demolish, level to the ground, remove, etc. {they razed the building}.

**reason.** Two points. First, as to *reason why*, although some object to the supposed redundancy of this phrase, it is centuries old and perfectly acceptable English. *Reason that* is not always an adequate substitute {can you give reasons why *that* is preferable to *which* as a restrictive relative pronoun?}. Second, *reason . . . is because* is not good usage—*reason . . . is that* being preferred {the reason we returned on July 2 is that we wanted to avoid hordes of tourists}.

**recur; reoccur.** To *recur* is to happen again and again {his knee problems recurred throughout the rest of the year}, to return to in one's attention or memory {she recurred to her war experiences throughout our visit}, or to come back to one's attention or memory {the idea recurred to him throughout the night}. To *reoccur* is merely to happen again {the leak reoccurred during the second big rain}.

**reek.** See **wreak**.

**reference; referral.** A *reference* is a source of information, a person to provide information, an authority for some assertion, or a strong allusion to something. It's also an attributive adjective {reference book}. It's not universally accepted as a transitive verb. *Referral* is a narrower term denoting the practice or an instance of (1) directing someone to another person who can help, especially a professional or a specialist, or (2) relegating some matter to another body for a recommendation or resolution.

**refrain; restrain.** To *refrain* is to restrain yourself or to keep from doing something; it is typically an act of self-discipline. Other people *restrain* you by stopping you from doing something, especially by using physical force {if you don't refrain from the disorderly conduct, the police will restrain you}. Yet it is possible to restrain oneself by controlling one's own emotions or behavior—and doing so is known as *self-restraint*.

**refute, *vb.*** To *refute* is to prove that a statement or an idea is wrong—not merely to deny or rebut.

**regardless.** Use this term. Avoid **irregardless**.

**regrettable; regretful.** What is *regrettable* is unfortunate or unpleasant enough to make one wish that things were otherwise. A person who is *regretful* feels sorry or disappointed about something done or lost. The adverb *regrettably*, not *regretfully*, is a synonym of *unfortunately*.

**rein; reign.** A *rein* (usually plural) controls a horse; it is the right word in idioms such as *take the reins*, *give free rein*, and, as a verb, *rein in*. A *reign* is a state of or term of dominion, especially that of a monarch but by extension also dominance in some field. This is the right word in idioms such as *reign of terror* and, as a verb, *reign supreme*.

**relegate; delegate.** To *relegate* is to assign a lesser position than before {the officer was relegated to desk duty pending an investigation}. To *delegate* is to authorize a subordinate to act in one's behalf {Congress delegated environmental regulation to the EPA} or to choose someone to do a particular job or to represent an organization or group {she was delegated to find a suitable hotel for the event}.

**reluctant.** See **reticent**.

**renounce.** See **denounce**.

**reoccur.** See **recur**.

**repellent; repulsive.** *Repellent* and *repulsive* both denote the character of driving others away. But *repulsive* has strong connotations of being so disgusting as to make one feel sick.

**repetitive; repetitious.** Both mean "occurring over and over." But whereas *repetitive* is fairly neutral in connotation, *repetitious* has taken on the nuance of tediousness that induces boredom.

**repress.** See **oppress.**

**repulsive.** See **repellent.**

**restive; restful.** *Restive* means "so dissatisfied or bored with a situation as to be impatient for change." *Restful* means "peaceful, quiet, and conducive to relaxation."

**restrain.** See **refrain.**

**reticent.** Avoid using this word as a synonym for *reluctant*. It means "unwilling to talk about what one feels or knows; taciturn" {when asked about the incident, the congressional representative became uncharacteristically reticent}.

**revenge.** See **avenge.**

**rob; steal.** Both verbs mean "to wrongfully take [something from another person]." But *rob* usually also includes a threat or act of harming, usually but not always to the person being robbed.

**role; roll.** A *role* is an acting part {the role of Hamlet} or the way in which someone or something is involved in an activity or situation, especially in reference to influence {the role that money plays as an incentive}. *Roll* has many meanings, including a roster {guest roll}; something made or done by rolling {roll of the dice}; and something in the shape of a cylinder or sphere, whether literally {dinner roll} or figuratively {bankroll}. *Roll* can also be a verb meaning to rotate {roll over!}, to wrap [something] {roll up the leftovers}, or to move on wheels {the cart rolled down the hill}.

**run the gauntlet.** See **gauntlet.**

**sacrilegious.** This is the correct spelling. There is a tendency by some to switch the *i* and *e* on either side of the *l*, but in fact the word is related to *sacrilege*, not *religion* or *religious*.

**seasonal; seasonable.** *Seasonal* means either "happening as expected or needed during a particular time of year" {snow skiing is a seasonal hobby} or "relating to the seasons or a season" {the seasonal aisle stays stocked most of the year, starting with Valentine's Day gifts in January}. *Seasonable* means "timely" {seasonable motions for continuance} or "fitting the time of year" {it was unseasonably cold for July}.

**self-deprecating.** See **deprecate.**

**semi-.** See **bi-.**

**semiannual.** See **biannual.**

**sensor.** See **censer.**

**sensual; sensuous.** What is *sensual* involves indulgence of the physical senses—especially sexual gratification. What is *sensuous* usually applies to aesthetic enjoyment; it is primarily hack writers who imbue the word with salacious connotations.

**sewer; sewage; sewerage.** *Sewer* denotes a wastewater pipe or passage. *Sewage* denotes the waste carried through such a pipe or passage. *Sewerage* denotes the sewer system as a whole, including treatment plants and other facilities, and the function of the disposal of sewage and wastewater in general.

**shall.** This word is complicated. The reality is that *shall* is little used in everyday contexts outside British English—not in North America but also not in Australia, Ireland, or Scotland. In legal contexts, it frequently appears in statutes, rules, and contracts, supposedly in a mandatory sense but actually quite ambiguously. It is perhaps the most widely litigated word in the law—with wildly varying results in its multifarious interpretations. Legal drafters are therefore often advised to avoid it altogether in favor of *must*, *is*, *will*, *may*, and other words or phrases among which *shall*'s various meanings can be allocated.[8] See also 5.135.

**shear; sheer.** *Shear* is the noun or verb relating to (1) the cutting tool or (2) a force affecting movement, such as a crosswind or the slipping of plates in an earthquake. *Sheer* is most often an adjective meaning (1) "semitransparent" {a sheer curtain}, (2) "nothing but" {sheer madness}, or (3) "almost vertical" {a sheer cliff}.

**shine.** When this verb is intransitive, it means "to give or make light"; the past tense is *shone* {the stars shone dimly}. When it is transitive, it means "to cause to shine"; the past tense is *shined* {the caterer shined the silver}.

**should.** See **ought**.

**sight; site.** A *sight* may be something worth seeing {the sights of London} or a device to aid the eye {the sight of a gun}, among other things. A *site* is a place, whether physical {a mall will be built on this site} or electronic {website}. The figurative expression meaning "to focus on a goal" is *to set one's sights*. Cf. **cite**.

**simplistic.** This word, meaning "oversimplified," has derogatory connotations. Don't confuse it with *simple*.

**since.** This word may relate either to time {since last winter} or to causation {since I'm a golfer, I know what "double bogey" means}. Some writers erroneously believe that the word relates exclusively to time. But the causal *since* was a part of the English language before Chaucer wrote in the fourteenth century, and it is useful as a slightly milder way of expressing causation than *because*. Still, if there is any possibility of confusion with the temporal sense, use *because*.

**sink.** Inflected *sink–sank–sunk*. Avoid using *sunk* as a simple past, as in *the ship sunk*.

**site.** See **cite**; **sight**.

---

8. See Garner, *Legal Writing in Plain English*, 3rd ed. (University of Chicago Press, 2023), 181–91; *Garner's Dictionary of Legal Usage*, 3rd ed. (Oxford University Press, 2011), 952–55 (collecting many authorities).

**slander.** See **defamation.**

**slew; slough; slue.** As a noun, *slew* (/sloo/) is an informal word equivalent to *many* or *lots* {you have a slew of cattle}. It is sometimes misspelled *slough* (a legitimate noun meaning "a grimy swamp," pronounced either /sloo/ or /slow/). The phrase *slough of despond* (from Bunyan's *Pilgrim's Progress* [1678]) means "a state of depression or sadness from which one cannot easily lift oneself." This term is etymologically different from *slough* (/sləf/), meaning "to discard" {slough off dry skin}. As a present-tense verb, to *slew* is to turn or slide violently or suddenly in a different direction—or to make a vehicle do so {the car keeps slewing sideways}. In American English, a variant spelling of this verb is *slue*. As a past-tense verb, *slew* corresponds to the present-tense *slay* {Cain slew Abel}.

**slow.** This word, like *slowly*, may be an adverb. Generally, prefer *slowly* {go slowly}. But in colloquial usage *slow* is often used after the verb in a pithy statement, especially an injunction {go slow!} {take it slow}. See also 5.165.

**slue.** See **slew.**

**sneak.** This verb is conjugated as a regular verb: *sneak–sneaked–sneaked*. Reserve *snuck* for dialect and tongue-in-cheek usages.

**space.** As a figurative noun, this word has become a voguish equivalent of *area* {though not initially interested in journalism, he has decided to move into that space}. Although (or perhaps because) this usage is au courant, avoid it. See also **area.**

**spit.** If used to mean "to expectorate," the verb is popularly inflected *spit–spat–spat* {he spat a curse} {he has spat many a curse}. But if used to mean "to skewer," it's *spit–spitted–spitted* {the hens have been spitted for broiling}.

**stanch.** See **staunch.**

**stationary; stationery.** *Stationary* describes a state of immobility or of staying in one place {if it's stationary, paint it}. *Stationery* denotes writing materials, especially paper for writing letters, usually with matching envelopes {love letters written on perfumed stationery}. To remember the two, try associating the *-er* in *stationery* with the *-er* in *paper*; or remember that a *stationer* is someone who sells the stuff.

**staunch; stanch.** *Staunch* is an adjective meaning "ardent and faithful" {a staunch Red Sox supporter}. *Stanch* is the American English verb meaning "to stop the flow"; it is almost always used in regard to bleeding, literally or metaphorically {after New Hampshire the campaign hemorrhaged; only a big win in South Carolina could stanch the bleeding}. In British English, however, *staunching the flow* is the standard wording.

**steal.** See **rob.**

**strait; straight.** A *strait* (often pl.) is (1), literally, a narrow channel connecting two large bodies of water separated by two areas of land {Strait of Magellan} or (2), figuratively, a difficult position {dire straits}. This is the word used in compound terms with the sense of constriction {straitlaced} {straitjacket}.

*Straight* is most often an adjective meaning unbent, steady, sober, candid, honest, or heterosexual.

**strata, *n*.** This is the plural for *stratum*. Keep it plural {Fussell identified nine discrete strata in American society}. Avoid the double plural *stratas*.

**strategy; tactics.** A *strategy* is a long-term plan for achieving a goal. A *tactic* is a shorter-term method for achieving an immediate but limited success. A strategy might involve several tactics. By the way, although *strategy* is so spelled, *stratagem* has an *a* in the middle syllable.

**subject.** See **citizen**.

**subsequent.** See **consequent**.

**such.** This word, when used to replace *this* or *that*—as in "such building was later condemned"—is symptomatic of legalese. *Such* is actually no more precise than *the*, *this*, *that*, *these*, or *those*. It's perfectly acceptable, however, to use *such* with a mass noun or plural noun when the meaning is "of that type" or "of this kind" {such impudence galled the rest of the family} {such vitriolic exchanges became commonplace in the following years}. See also **as such**.

**sufficient.** See **adequate**.

**supersede.** The root of this word derives from *sedeo*, the Latin word for "to sit, to be established," not *cedo*, meaning "to yield." Hence the spelling varies from the root in words such as *concede*, *recede*, and *secede*. Avoid the variant *supercede*.

**sympathy.** See **empathy**.

**systematic; systemic.** *Systematic* means "according to a plan or system, organized methodically, or arranged in a system." *Systemic*, meaning "affecting the whole of something," is limited in use to physiological systems {a systemic disease affecting several organs} or, by extension, other systems that may be likened to the body {systemic problems within the corporate hierarchy}.

**tactics.** See **strategy**.

**take.** See **bring**.

**tantalizing; titillating.** A *tantalizing* thing torments us because we want it badly yet it is always just out of reach. A *titillating* thing tickles us pleasantly, literally or figuratively, and the word often carries sexual connotations.

**that; which.** These are both relative pronouns (see 5.60–70). In edited American prose, *that* is used restrictively to narrow a category or identify a particular item being talked about {any building that is taller must be outside the state}; *which* is used nonrestrictively—not to narrow a class or identify a particular item but to add something about an item already identified {alongside the officer trotted a toy poodle, which is hardly a typical police dog}. *Which* is best used restrictively only when it is preceded by a preposition {the situation in which we find ourselves}. Nonrestrictively, it is almost always preceded by a comma, a parenthesis, or a dash. (In British English, writers and editors seldom observe the distinction between the two words.) Is it a useful distinction? Yes. The language inarguably benefits from having a terminological as well as a punctuational means of telling a restrictive from a nonrestrictive relative pronoun, punctuation often being ill-heeded. Is it acceptable to use *that* in reference to people? Is *friends that arrive early* an acceptable alternative to *friends who arrive early*? The answer is yes. *Person that* has long been considered good idiomatic English. Even so, *person who* is nearly three times as common as *person that* in edited English. See also 6.29.

**there; their; they're.** *There* denotes a place or direction {stay there}. *Their* is the possessive pronoun {all their good wishes}. *They're* is a contraction of *they are* {they're calling now}.

**therefore; therefor.** The words have different senses. *Therefore*, the common word, means "as a result; for that reason" {the evidence of guilt was slight; therefore, the jury acquitted the defendant}. *Therefor*, a legalism, means "for it" or "for them" {he took the unworn shirt back to the store and received a refund therefor}.

**thus.** This is the adverb—not *thusly*. Use *thus* (it's called a *flat adverb*). See 5.165.

**till.** This is a perfectly good preposition and conjunction {open till 10 p.m.}. It is not a contraction of *until* and should not be written *'til*.

**timbre; timber.** *Timbre* is a musical term meaning "tonal quality of the sound made by a particular musical instrument or voice." *Timber* is the correct spelling in all other uses, which relate to trees or wood.

**titillating.** See **tantalizing**.

**tolerance; toleration.** *Tolerance* is the habitual quality of being *tolerant*—that is, willing to allow people to say, believe, or do what they want without criticism or punishment. *Toleration* is a particular instance of being *tolerant*.

**torpid.** See **turbid**.

**tortious; tortuous; torturous.** What is *tortious* relates to torts (civil wrongs) or to acts that give rise to legal claims for torts {tortious interference with a contract}. What is *tortuous* is full of twists and turns and therefore makes travel difficult {a tortuous path through the woods}. What is *torturous* involves severe physical and mental suffering {a torturous exam}.

**toward; towards.** The preferred form in American English is *toward*: This has been so since about 1900. In British English, *towards* predominates. The same is true for other directional words, such as *upward, downward, forward,* and *backward,* as well as *afterward*. The use of *afterwards* and *backwards* as adverbs is neither rare nor incorrect (and is preferred in British English). For the sake of consistency, many American editors prefer the shorter forms without the final *s*.

**transcript; transcription.** A *transcript* is either a written record, as of a trial or a radio program, or an official record of a student's classes and grades. *Transcription* is the act or process of creating a transcript.

**transpire,** ***vb.*** Although its traditional sense is "to come to be known" {it transpired that he had paid bribes}, *transpire* more commonly today means "happen" or "occur" {what transpired when I was away?}. In that newer sense, *transpire* still carries a vague odor of jargon and pretentiousness. But that is disappearing.

**trillion.** See **billion.**

**triumphal; triumphant.** Things are *triumphal* (done or made to celebrate a victory) {a triumphal arch}. But only people feel *triumphant* (displaying pleasure and pride as a result of a victory or success) {a triumphant Caesar returned to Rome}.

**turbid; turgid; torpid.** *Turbid* water or liquid is thick and opaque from churned-up mud or detritus {a turbid pond}; by extension, *turbid* means "unclear, confused, or disturbed" {a turbid argument}. *Turgid* means "swollen," and by extension "pompous and bombastic" {turgid prose}. *Torpid* means "idle, lazy, and sleepy" {a torpid economy}.

**ultimate.** See **penultimate.**

**unexceptional; unexceptionable.** The first means "not very good; no better than average." The second means "not open to objection."

**uninterested.** See **disinterested.**

**unique.** Reserve this word for the sense "one of a kind." Avoid it in the sense "special, unusual." Phrases such as *very unique, more unique, somewhat unique,* and so on—in which a degree is attributed to *unique*—aren't the best usage. See also 5.93.

**unlawful; illegal; illicit; criminal.** This list is in ascending order of negative connotation. An *unlawful* act may even be morally innocent (for example, letting a parking meter expire). But an *illegal* act is something that society formally condemns, and an *illicit* act calls to mind moral degeneracy {illicit drug use}. Unlike *criminal,* the first three terms can apply to civil wrongs.

**unorganized.** See **disorganized.**

**unreadable.** See **illegible.**

**upon.** See **on.**

**upward(s).** See **toward.**

**use; utilize.** *Use* is usually the best choice for simplicity. *Utilize* is most often an overblown alternative of *use,* but it is occasionally the better choice when the distinct sense is "to use to best effect" {how to utilize our staff most productively}.

**venal; venial.** A person who is *venal* is mercenary or open to bribery—willing to use power and influence dishonestly in return for money {a venal government official}; a thing that is *venal* is purchasable {venal livestock}. A *venial* fault or sin is trivial enough to be pardonable or excusable {a venial offense} {a venial error}.

**verbal; oral.** If something is put into words, it is *verbal.* Technically, *verbal* covers both written and spoken utterance (in fact, all contracts are verbal). If you wish to specify that something was conveyed through speech, use *oral.*

**very.** See **much.**

**vocation.** See **avocation.**

**voluminous.** See **compendious.**

**waive; wave.** To *waive* is to relinquish claim to or not to insist on enforcing. To *wave* is to move to and fro.

**wangle.** See **wrangle.**

**whether.** Generally, use *whether* alone—not with the words *or not* tacked on {they didn't know whether to go}. The *or not* is necessary only when you mean to convey the idea "regardless of whether" {we'll finish on time whether or not it rains}. On the distinction between *whether* and *if,* see **if.**

**which.** See **that.**

**while.** *While* may substitute for *although* or *whereas,* especially if a conversational tone is desired {while many readers may disagree, the scientific community has overwhelmingly adopted the conclusions here presented}. Yet because *while* can denote either time or contrast, the word is occasionally ambiguous; when a real ambiguity exists, *although* or *whereas* is the better choice.

**who; whom.** Here are the traditional rules: *Who* is a nominative pronoun used as (1) the subject of a finite verb {it was Jim who bought the coffee today} or (2) a predicate nominative when it follows a linking verb {that's who}. *Whom* is an objective pronoun that may appear as (1) the object of a verb {I learned nothing about the man whom I saw} or (2) the object of a preposition {the woman to whom I owe my life}. Today there are two countervailing trends: First, there's a decided tendency to use *who* colloquially in most contexts; second, among those insecure about their grammar, there's a tendency to overcorrect oneself and use *whom* when *who* would be correct. Writers and editors of formal prose often resist the first of these; everyone should resist the second. See also 5.70.

**whoever; whomever.** Avoid the second unless you are certain of your grammar {give this book to whoever wants it} {I cook for whomever I love}. If you are uncertain why these examples are correct, use *anyone who* or (as in the second example) *anyone.*

**who's; whose.** The first is a contraction {who's on first?}, the second a possessive {whose life is it, anyway?}. Unlike *who* and *whom, whose* may refer to things as well as people {the Commerce Department, whose bailiwick includes intellectual property}. See 5.68.

**workers' compensation.** This is the preferred name for workplace accident-insurance plans, not *workmen's compensation.* Notice that *workers* is always plural. When used as a phrasal adjective, it is hyphenated {workers'-compensation system}.

**wrack.** See **rack.**

**wrangle; wangle.** To *wrangle* is to argue, especially angrily over a long period {still wrangling over their parents' estate}. To *wangle* is to get something or arrange for something to happen by cleverness, manipulation, or trickery {wangle a couple of last-minute tickets}.

**wreak; reek.** *Wreak* means (1) "to cause a great deal of harm or many problems" {to wreak havoc on the administration} or (2) "to punish someone in revenge" {to wreak vengeance on his erstwhile friends}. The past tense is *wreaked*, not *wrought*. (The latter is an archaic form of the past tense and past participle of *work*.) *Reek* can be a verb meaning "to stink" or a noun meaning "stench."

**wrong; wrongful.** These terms are not interchangeable. *Wrong* has two senses: (1) "immoral, unlawful" {it's wrong to bully smaller children} and (2) "improper, incorrect, unsatisfactory" {many of the math answers are wrong}. *Wrongful* likewise has two senses: (1) "unjust, unfair" {wrongful conduct} and (2) "unsanctioned by law; having no legal right" {it was a wrongful demand on the estate}.

**yes.** See **affirmative, in the**.

**your; you're.** *Your* is the possessive form of *you* {your class}. *You're* is the contraction for *you are* {you're welcome}.

## *Inclusive Language and Minimizing Bias*

5.255 **Making conscious choices.** In recent years, many writers have become more attentive to how the words they choose may reflect bias based on race, ethnicity, sex, gender, disability, and other characteristics. Sometimes such a bias is intentional, designed to examine or provoke. But often it is unintentional, rooted in unknown or unconsidered etymologies of words {master; lame} or in unexamined assumptions about what is "normal" (male; cisgender). Eliminating all bias from a piece of writing is an unrealistic goal, but making conscious choices to avoid bias and be more inclusive where possible offers important benefits to both writer and readers.[9]

5.256 **Maintaining credibility.** Biased language that is not central to the meaning of a work can distract or offend readers and therefore make the work less credible. It may cause readers to lose respect for the writer and focus not on the writer's ideas but instead on the work's political or social subtext. It may also activate their own biases in ways that prevent them from understanding what the writer is trying to say. While the topic of linguistic biases and whether and how to avoid them can be controversial, writers who are open to understanding the perspective

---

9. Here we draw on the term *conscious language* as used by Karen Yin, founder of the *Conscious Style Guide* website (see bibliog. 1.4).

they're writing from and those of any marginalized groups they're writing about are likely to make choices that more consciously and effectively represent their intended meaning.

5.257 **Evolving standards.** As awareness of the different ways in which language conveys bias evolves, so too do preferred terms and standards for inclusivity. Although some publishers recommend avoiding certain terms or specific usages in all cases, Chicago's editorial staff does not maintain a list of words or usages considered unacceptable. Rather, we adhere to the reasoning presented here, which reflects standards at the time of publication, and apply it to individual cases.

5.258 **Common areas of biased language.** Consider language choices carefully when referring to individuals or groups based on race, ethnicity, sex, gender identity, sexual orientation, disability, age, weight, appearance, nationality, religion, social standing, or similar characteristics. Avoid irrelevant references to these characteristics.

5.259 **Labels.** Characteristics are often used as labels for individuals or groups of people. Ideally, a writer will use the label preferred by the individual or group written about or for. Research what is current, as labels are sometimes rapidly adopted or discarded. More than one may be acceptable {Black; African American}. Labels sometimes considered interchangeable may in fact refer to different people {First Nations; Inuit; Métis} or may be preferred in different geographic areas or demographic cohorts {Hispanic; Latino, Latina, Latinx, Latine; Chicano, Chicana}.

5.260 **Person, not characteristic.** In general, emphasize the person, not a characteristic. When a characteristic is mentioned for meaning or vividness, it's often best to use an adjective instead of a noun, especially when referring to groups {the Vietnamese students in the library [not *the Vietnamese in the library*]}. Use care and think through the meaning of your phrasings and word choices. For instance, in the sentence *United States Supreme Court Justice Ketanji Brown Jackson is one of the most successful Black female graduates of Harvard Law School*, the phrase *Black female* may lead some readers to infer that Jackson is successful "for a female" but may be surpassed by many or all men, that she stands out only among Black graduates of Harvard Law School, or that it is abnormal for a woman or a Black person to sit on the US Supreme Court. But in *Justice Ketanji Brown Jackson, a graduate of Harvard Law School, is the first Black woman to sit on the US Supreme Court*, the purpose of the phrase *Black woman* is not likely to be misunderstood. See also 5.264.

5.261 **Person-first versus identity-first.** When someone's disability or other condition is relevant, two approaches to labeling it are possible. One is using person-first language to emphasize the person rather than the condition {an editor who is deaf}. The other is to emphasize the person's identity by putting the condition first {an autistic illustrator}. The former is often recommended because it focuses on the person. But some readers see it as stigmatizing the disability or other condition by trying to diminish its presence. Those readers may prefer identity-first language that includes the condition as an integral fact of a person's identity, as well as an element of social and political identity. The approach will depend on the audience and, when known, the person's own preference.

5.262 **Ableism.** Language that privileges physical and mental fitness and devalues disability is ubiquitous in the English language. Dealing with the issue requires sensitivity. When writing about disability, euphemisms such as *differently abled* or *special needs* can have the unfortunate result of both obscuring meaning and suggesting shame through avoidance. Word choices can subtly challenge (or reinforce) bias that favors nondisabled people by emphasizing disabled agency rather than limitations, as with *wheelchair user* (rather than *confined to a wheelchair*) or *speech impediment* (rather than *speech defect*). It's always best to use terminology that is currently accepted by the individuals or communities in question. Figurative language based on disabilities will predictably offend some readers {deaf as a post} {a lame excuse} {willfully blind} and should be avoided in favor of options that don't implicitly objectify or discredit people with disabilities {can't hear a thing} {a bogus excuse} {refuses to see}.

5.263 **Gender-neutral nouns.** The trend in American English has long been toward eliminating gender-specific suffixes. For example, *author* and *testator* are preferable to *authoress* and *testatrix*, and *actor* or *female actor* are increasingly used in place of *actress*. The suffix *-person* rarely functions well as a substitute for *-man*; *chairperson* and *anchorperson* sound more pompous and wooden than the simpler (and effective) *chair* and *anchor*. With a little thought, you can identify many gender-free choices in different contexts: *business owner* or *entrepreneur* instead of *businessman* or *businesswoman*; *crew*, *staff*, or *workers* instead of *manpower*; *humans*, *human beings*, or *people* instead of *mankind*; *supervisor*, *chief*, or *leader* (or *presiding juror* in the legal sense) instead of *foreman*; and *ancestors* instead of *forefathers*. Even *founding fathers*, while technically accurate in reference to those who participated directly in establishing the US Constitution and the American form of government, may reflect a limited perspective on whose contributions deserve credit in this effort. See also 5.264.

5.264 **Gender-specific labels as adjectives.** When gender is relevant, it may be acceptable to use a gendered noun such as *female* or *male* as a modifier {the patient requested a female doctor} {the first female president}. The adjective *nonbinary*, on the other hand, may be used to refer to someone who doesn't identify with a sex-specific modifier. When parallel references to specific sexes are required, *male* and *female* are typically the most serviceable modifiers {the vaccine-study group has 834 male and 635 female participants}; these terms are, however, often avoided as nouns in reference to humans {the females were on the right, the males on the left}. By contrast, because *man* is rarely used as a modifier, adjectival use of *woman* may unacceptably suggest that it's peculiar or exceptional for a woman to be something {a woman astronaut will lead the expedition} or may sound dismissive or derogatory {the woman plumber successfully replaced the pipe}. *Lady*, as a noun or as an adjective, is no longer normally advisable. See also 5.263.

5.265 **Options for gender neutrality in pronoun use.** Now that singular *they* is increasingly acceptable in formal prose as well as speech and informal contexts (see 5.51, 5.52), many writers use it as a gender-neutral alternative to *he*. But this option has its drawbacks, including potential confusion between referents and between singular and plural uses of *they*. In many contexts, an alternative solution might work better. The language is now in a transitional period, and no single approach to this issue will find universal favor among writers and their readers. Here are nine methods to consider, depending on context.

1. Omit the pronoun. Sometimes a personal pronoun is not really necessary. For instance, in *the programmer should update the records when data is transferred to her by the head office*, if there is only one programmer, the pronoun phrase *to her* can be omitted: *the programmer should update the records when data is transferred by the head office*. Note that the shorter sentence is tighter as well as gender-free.
2. Repeat the noun. If a noun and its pronoun are separated by many words, try repeating the noun. For instance, *a writer should be careful not to needlessly antagonize readers, because her credibility would otherwise suffer* becomes *a writer should be careful not to needlessly antagonize readers, because the writer's credibility would otherwise suffer*. Take care not to overuse this technique. Repeating a noun too frequently will irritate readers. If you have to repeat a noun more than twice in a sentence or repeat it too soon, you should probably rewrite the sentence.

3. Use a plural antecedent. By using a plural antecedent, you eliminate the need for a singular pronoun. For instance, *a contestant must conduct himself with dignity at all times* becomes *contestants must conduct themselves with dignity at all times*. The method may cause a slight change in connotation. In the example, a duty becomes a collective responsibility rather than an individual one.
4. Use an article instead of a pronoun. Try replacing the singular personal pronoun with a definite or indefinite article. Quite often you'll find that the effect on the sentence's meaning is negligible. For instance, *A student accused of cheating must actively waive his right to have his guidance counselor present* becomes *A student accused of cheating must actively waive the right to have a guidance counselor present*.
5. Use the neutral singular pronoun *one*. Try replacing the gender-specific personal pronoun with the gender-neutral singular pronoun *one*. For instance, *an actor in New York is likely to earn more than he can in Paducah* becomes *an actor in New York is likely to earn more than one in Paducah*.
6. Use the relative pronoun *who*. This technique works best when it replaces a personal pronoun that follows *if*. It also requires revising the sentence slightly. For instance, *employers presume that if an applicant can't write well, he won't be a good employee* becomes *employers presume that an applicant who can't write well won't be a good employee*. Note that the rewritten sentence is tighter as well as gender-free.
7. Use the imperative mood. The imperative eliminates the need for an explicit pronoun. Although its usefulness is limited in some types of writing, you may find that it avoids prolixity and more forcefully addresses the target audience. For instance, *a lifeguard must keep a close watch over children while he is monitoring the pool* becomes *keep a close watch over children while monitoring the pool*.
8. Use singular *they* and *their*. If you can't rewrite a sentence to improve it without using a singular personal pronoun, and if the person's gender is unimportant or unknown or must be concealed for reasons of privacy (see 5.266), consider the singular *they* (construed with a plural verb) {a student needn't have the teacher's permission if they drop the class before the third session}.
9. Revise the sentence in some other way. If no other technique produces a sentence that reads well, rewrite the sentence so that personal pronouns aren't needed at all. The amount of revision will vary depending on the audience, the purpose, and the desired level of formality. For instance, *if a student misbehaves, their privileges will be revoked* might become *misbehavior will be punished by the loss of privileges*.

5.266 **Uses of singular "they."** Singular *they* (see 5.51, 5.52) is useful primarily in three circumstances. (1) It can be used with indefinite pronouns as a substitute for feminine or masculine forms {no one in the group could remember their great-grandfather's middle name} {given the chance, anybody would try to improve their life}. When an indefinite pronoun has or could have a plural sense, *themselves* is the better reflexive choice {**everyone** buying lunch for **themselves** will need to bring cash}. But when the sense is clearly singular, *themself* is often used {**each** should serve **themself**}. (2) It can be used when the antecedent's gender is unknown or irrelevant or must remain confidential {will the **driver** of the pink sedan please move **their** car} {the **author** wants **their** privacy protected}. If an easy and unambiguous revision serves as well as or better than the version with singular *they*, you might prefer that version. (3) Some people use *they* and *them* (or some other nonbinary singular pronoun) rather than *he* and *him* or *she* and *her*; this usage, when known to apply to a specific individual, should be respected.

## A SUMMING UP

5.267 **Stability and renewal.** Although language is constantly evolving, the changes are generally slow. English usage is remarkably stable, even if it varies somewhat from generation to generation. Those who prepare work for publication should ensure that the language fits the purposes for which it is used—whatever those may be. Dialect in dialogue is one thing; purposeful dialect in an editorial is another; scholarly commentary in Standard English is quite another. People who use dictionaries and handbooks should use current ones, and use them intelligently. Effective uses of language show a satisfying balance between constraint and freedom, tradition and novelty, obedience and nonconformity. Although Standard English is unavoidably conservative, it will always be constantly renewed by the wellspring of everyday idiom—to which writers and editors must remain ever alert. Good usage in a particular context will always require wide knowledge, discerning judgment, and some degree of literary taste.

# 6 Punctuation

## OVERVIEW

6.1 **The role of punctuation and the scope of this chapter.** Punctuation should be governed by its function, which in ordinary text is to promote ease of reading by clarifying relationships within and between sentences. This function, although it allows for a degree of subjectivity, should in turn be governed by the consistent application of some basic principles lest the subjective element obscure meaning. The principles set forth in this chapter are based on a logical application of traditional practice in the United States. How strictly they are applied will depend on context and an author's writing style. A formal register may be approached differently from a conversational tone, and fiction and other creative contexts will not have the same requirements as academic prose. For punctuation in languages other than English, source citations (including bibliographies), indexes, and more, see the appropriate chapters in this manual or consult the index.

## PUNCTUATION IN RELATION TO SURROUNDING TEXT

6.2 **Punctuation and italics.** All punctuation marks should appear in the same font style—roman or italic—as the main or surrounding text, except for punctuation that belongs to a title in a different style (usually italics). For example, the word *and*, which in this sentence is in italics, is followed by a comma in roman type (also known as regular text); the comma, strictly speaking, does not belong to *and*, which is italicized because it is a word used as a word (see 7.66). Depending on the typeface, it may be difficult to tell whether a comma is in italics or not (to say nothing of periods); for other marks it will be more evident. Readers of this manual online may be able to view the HTML source code to confirm where italics begin and end, and all those who prepare manuscripts or publications using word processors and other applications will need to pay attention to this level of detail (see 2.85; see also 2.86–88). In the first four examples that follow, the punctuation marks next to italic text belong with the surrounding sentence and are therefore presented in roman. In the last two examples, the three punctuation marks that belong with the italic titles—the comma following "Hello," the exclamation point following "Dolly," and the colon following "Prose"—are in italics, whereas the comma following "Punctuation" is in roman.

For light amusement he turns to the *Principia Mathematica*!
How can they be sure that the temperature was in fact *rising*?
The letters *a*, *b*, and *c* are often invoked as being fundamental.

There are two primary audiences for *The Chicago Manual of Style*: perfectionists and humorists.

*but*

*Hello, Dolly!* premiered on Broadway in 1964.

According to *Prose: A Matter of Punctuation*, periods are usually round.

For parentheses and brackets, see 6.5; for quotation marks, see 6.6. For a different approach, see 6.4.

6.3 **Punctuation and boldface or color.** The choice of boldface (or, by extension, type in a different color), unlike that of italics (see 6.2), is sometimes an aesthetic rather than a purely logical decision. Punctuation marks following boldface or color should be dealt with case by case, depending on how the boldface is used. In the first example below, the period following "line spacing" belongs with the boldface glossary term and is therefore styled in bold; the period following "leading" is part of the surrounding sentence and is therefore *not* styled in bold. In the middle two examples, the punctuation next to the boldface terms belongs with them, like the first period in the first example. In the final example, the question mark belongs to the surrounding sentence and not to the boldface phrase (see 7.84).

**line spacing.** See **leading**.

**Figure 6.** Title page from an apocryphal *Second Poetics*.

**For sale:** a 2015 Subaru Forester and two gently used sleeping bags.

Will the installation remain stalled until I choose **I accept**?

6.4 **Punctuation and font style — aesthetic considerations.** According to a more traditional system, periods, commas, colons, and semicolons appear in the same font style as the word, letter, character, or symbol immediately preceding them if different from that of the main or surrounding text. In the third and fourth examples in 6.2, the commas following *a* and *b* and the colon following the title of this manual would be italic, as would the comma following the book title in the last example (i.e., after *Punctuation*). A question mark or exclamation point, however, would appear in the same style as the immediately preceding word only if it belonged to that word, as in the title *Hello, Dolly!* in 6.2. This system, once preferred by Chicago and still preferred by some as more aesthetically pleasing, should be reserved—if it must be used—for publications destined for print only. In electronic formats, where font style may be determined by content as well as appearance (e.g., a book title might be tagged as such, separate from any surrounding punctuation), the more logical system described in 6.2 should be preferred (but see 6.6).

6.5 **Parentheses and brackets in relation to surrounding text.** Parentheses and brackets should appear in the same style—roman or italic—as the surrounding text, not in that of the material they enclose. This system, though it may occasionally cause typefitting problems when a slanting italic letter touches an upright roman parenthesis or bracket, has two main virtues: It is easy to use, and it has long been practiced. For printed works, a thin space or a hair space may need to be added between overlapping characters (see 6.128). For electronic works, where type display may vary depending on a user's device and settings, no such adjustments should normally be made.

The Asian long-horned beetle (*Anoplophora glabripennis*) attacks maples.
The letter stated that my check had been "recieved [*sic*] with thanks."

When a phrase in parentheses or brackets appears on a line by itself, however, the parentheses or brackets are usually in the same font style as the phrase.

*[continued on page 72]*

6.6 **Quotation marks in relation to surrounding text.** Like parentheses and brackets (see 6.5), quotation marks should appear in the same style—roman or italic—as the surrounding text, which may or may not match that of the material the quotation marks enclose. In the first two examples that follow, the quotation marks are in roman; in the third example, they have been italicized as part of the italic title.

The approach to the runway was, they reported, "*extremely dangerous*" (italics in original).
"Dressing Like *Hamlet*" is the fourth article in a series on literature and fashionable existentialism.
I just finished reading *Sennacherib's "Palace Without Rival" at Nineveh*, by John Malcolm Russell.

In the relatively rare case of an italic title that ends in a quotation mark (see also 8.175), a comma or period following the title should be styled in italics—an exception to the rule that will prevent the need to switch from italics for the title to roman for the period or comma and back to italics for the closing quotation mark.

We started by reading a book called *The Return of "Twin Peaks,"* by Franck Boulègue. (The comma and closing quotation mark are both in italics.)
*but*
"Dressing Like *Hamlet*," the fourth article . . . (The comma and closing quotation mark are both in roman.)

As with parentheses and brackets, when a sentence or phrase in quotation marks appears on a line by itself, the quotation marks are usually in the same style as the sentence or phrase. See also 12.73.

6.7 **Punctuation and space — one space or two?** In typeset matter, one space, not two, should be used between two sentences—whether the first ends in a period, a question mark, an exclamation point, or a closing quotation mark or parenthesis. By the same token, one space, not two, should follow a colon. When a particular design layout calls for more space between two elements—for example, between a figure number and a caption—the design should specify the exact amount of space (e.g., em space). See also 6.127–30.

6.8 **Punctuation with URLs and email addresses.** Sentences that include an email address or a URL should be punctuated normally. Though angle brackets or other "wrappers" are standard in some applications, these are generally unnecessary in normal prose (see 6.111). Readers of print sources should assume that any punctuation at the end of an email address or URL belongs to the sentence. By the same logic, any hypertext markup for electronic formats should exclude the surrounding punctuation. For dividing an email address or a URL at the end of a line, see 7.47. See also 6.120.

You'll find the Q&A and other resources at https://www.chicagomanualofstyle .org/.
Write to me at grammar88@parsed-out.edu.

## *Punctuation in Relation to Closing Quotation Marks*

6.9 **Periods and commas in relation to closing quotation marks.** Periods and commas precede closing quotation marks, whether double or single. (An apostrophe at the end of a word should never be confused with a closing single quotation mark; see 6.126.) This is a traditional style, in use in the United States well before the first edition of this manual (1906). For an exception, see 7.84. See also table 6.1.

He described what he heard as a "short, sharp shock."
"Thus conscience does make cowards of us all," she replied.

In an alternative system, sometimes called British style (as described in the *New Oxford Style Manual*; see bibliog. 1.1), single quotation marks are used (with double reserved for quotations within quotations), and

TABLE 6.1. Punctuation relative to closing quotation marks and parentheses or brackets

| Closing mark | Double or single quotation marks* | Parentheses or brackets† |
|---|---|---|
| Period | Inside | Inside or outside; see 6.13 |
| Comma | Inside | Outside |
| Semicolon | Outside | Outside |
| Colon | Outside | Outside |
| Question mark or exclamation point | Inside or outside; see 6.10 | Inside or outside; see 6.74, 6.78 |
| Em dash | Inside or outside; see 6.93, 12.42 | Outside |

*See also 6.9, 6.74, 6.78.
†See also 6.18, 6.104, 6.107, 6.110.

only those punctuation points that appeared in the original material are included within the quotation marks; all others follow the closing quotation marks—'like this'. There are exceptions, however. For example, British publishers usually follow US style for placement of periods and commas in fictional dialogue (and whenever a grammatically complete sentence is introduced in the manner of dialogue), a style also common for quoted speech in British journalism. Conversely, many publishers follow a variation of British style but with double quotation marks. The British system (or a variation of it) may be appropriate in works of textual criticism or in computer coding and other technical or scientific settings. See also 12.7–8, 12.30–31.

6.10 **Other punctuation in relation to closing quotation marks.** Colons and semicolons—unlike periods and commas—follow closing quotation marks; question marks and exclamation points follow closing quotation marks unless they belong within the quoted matter. (This rule applies the logic that is often absent from the traditional US style described in 6.9.) See also table 6.1.

Take, for example, the first line of "Filling Station": "Oh, but it is dirty!"
We were told to read "Filling Station"; we ended up reciting Shakespeare instead.
I can't believe you don't know the poem "Filling Station"!
Which of Shakespeare's characters said, "All the world's a stage"?
"What's the rush?" she asked.
"Timber!"

6.11 **Single quotation marks next to double quotation marks.** When single quotation marks are nested within double quotation marks, and two of the marks appear next to each other, a space between the two marks, though not strictly required, aids legibility. For print publications, typesetters may place a thin space or a hair space between the two marks (as in the print edition of this manual). On the screen (including in word-processed manuscripts submitted for publication), a regular nonbreaking space can be used (or, as in the online edition of this manual, a narrow nonbreaking space); such a space will prevent the second mark from becoming stranded at the beginning of a new line (see 6.129). See also 6.128, 12.30. In the example that follows, note that the period precedes the single quotation mark (see also 6.9).

"My favorite story," I told them, "is called 'Interpreter of Maladies.' "

## PERIODS

6.12 **Use of the period.** A period marks the end of a declarative or an imperative sentence. In some contexts, a period is referred to as a dot (as in a URL) or a point (as in decimals). In British usage, a period is called a full stop. Between sentences, it is followed by a single space (see 2.11, 6.7, 6.127). A period may follow a word or phrase standing alone (as in the third example below), and it may be used in lieu of a question mark at the end of a rhetorical question (as in the fourth example; see also 6.76). For the many other uses of the period, consult the index.

The two faced each other in silence.
Wait here.
My answer? Never.
When will I ever learn.

6.13 **Periods in relation to parentheses and brackets.** When an entire independent sentence is enclosed in parentheses or square brackets, the period belongs inside the closing parenthesis or bracket. When matter in parentheses or brackets, even a grammatically complete sentence, is included within another sentence, the period belongs outside (but see also 6.104). In the third example below, two periods are required—one for the abbreviation *etc.* and one for the sentence as a whole, outside the parentheses (see also 6.14, 6.132). For periods relative to quotation marks, see 6.9.

Fiorelli insisted on rewriting the paragraph. (His newfound ability to type was both a blessing and a curse.)
Felipe had left an angry message for Isadora on the mantel (she noticed it while glancing in the mirror).
His chilly demeanor gave him an affinity for the noble gases (helium, neon, etc.).

There were many groundbreaking moments in *All in the Family*. (The one featuring "the kiss," with Sammy Davis Jr., springs to mind.)
"All the evidence pointed to the second location [the Lászlós' studio]."

Whenever possible, avoid enclosing more than one complete sentence within another sentence. Instead, either move the parenthetical sentences outside of the enclosing sentence or, if the text allows for it, combine them (e.g., by using a semicolon or by rephrasing).

6.14 **When to omit a period.** No period should follow a display line (i.e., chapter title, subhead, or similar heading), a running head, a column head in a table, a phrase used as a caption (but see 3.21), a dateline in correspondence, a signature, or an address, except when any of these end in an abbreviation. (A comma or a colon is sometimes similarly omitted for aesthetic reasons at the end of a line set in display type; see 8.167.) A run-in subhead at the beginning of a paragraph, however, is followed by a period (see 1.62). When an abbreviation or other expression that ends in a period falls at the end of a sentence, no additional period follows (see 6.132; but see also 6.13). For use or omission of the period in lists and outline style, see 6.138–43. For punctuation with URLs and email addresses, see 6.8.

6.15 **Periods in ellipses.** An ellipsis—a series of three periods, or dots (sometimes referred to as suspension points)—may be used to indicate an omission in quoted material; for a full discussion of this use, see 12.59–69. An ellipsis may also be used to indicate faltering speech or an incomplete sentence or thought (see 12.43, 12.64). For the use of ellipses in languages other than English, see 11.21, 11.35, 11.56, 11.72, 11.111. For the use of the em dash to indicate a sudden break or interruption, see 6.93.

## COMMAS

6.16 **Use of the comma.** The comma, aside from its technical uses in scientific, bibliographic, and other contexts, indicates the smallest break in sentence structure. It usually denotes a slight pause. In formal prose, however, the logical considerations that are the basis of the recommendations in this chapter come first. In less formal registers and in creative works, authors will have more leeway to use commas to control the pace of their prose and to establish a certain tone. Some authors will prefer a closely punctuated style, in which commas are used at every opportunity; others will favor an open style, in which commas are used more sparingly. Editors should be prepared to account for these differences in register, context, and authorial style. Whatever choices are made should ultimately aim to serve the reader.

6.17 **Commas in pairs.** Whenever a comma is placed before an element to set it off from the surrounding text (such as "1920" or "Minnesota" in the first two examples below), a second comma is required if the phrase or sentence continues beyond the element being set off. This principle applies to many of the uses for commas described in this section. An exception is made for commas within the title of a work (third example); such commas are considered to be independent of the surrounding sentence.

August 18, 1920, was a good day for American women.
Sledding in Duluth, Minnesota, is facilitated by that city's hills and frigid winters.
*but*
The title story in Bambara's *Gorilla, My Love* had been published in *Redbook* magazine under a different title.

6.18 **Commas relative to parentheses and brackets.** When the context calls for a comma at the end of material in parentheses or brackets, the comma should follow the closing parenthesis or bracket. A comma never precedes a closing parenthesis. (For its rare appearance before an opening parenthesis, see the examples in 6.140.) Rarely, a comma may appear inside and immediately before a closing bracket as part of an editorial interpolation (as in the last example below; see also 12.70).

After several drummers had tried out for the part (the last having destroyed the kit), the band decided that a drum machine was their steadiest option.
Her delivery, especially when she would turn to address the audience (almost as if to spot a long-lost friend), was universally praised.
"Conrad told his assistant [Martin], who was clearly exhausted, to rest."
"The contents of the vault included fennel seeds, tweezers, [straight-edged razors,] and empty Coca-Cola cans."

## *Series and the Serial Comma*

6.19 **Serial commas.** Items in a series are normally separated by commas (but see 6.64). When a conjunction joins the last two elements in a series of three or more, a comma—known as the serial or series comma or the Oxford comma—should appear before the conjunction. Chicago strongly recommends this widely practiced usage, blessed by Fowler and other authorities (see bibliog. 1.2), since it prevents ambiguity. If the last element consists of a pair joined by *and*, the pair should still be preceded by a serial comma and the first *and* (as in the last two examples below).

She posted pictures of her parents, the president, and the vice president.

Before heading out the door, he took note of the typical outlines of sweet gum, ginkgo, and elm leaves.

I want no ifs, ands, or buts.

Paul put the kettle on, Don fetched the teapot, and I made tea.

Their wartime rations included cabbage, turnips, and bread and butter.

Ahmed was configuring updates, Jean was installing new hardware, and Alan was running errands and furnishing food.

If the sentence continues beyond the series, add a comma only if one is required by the syntax of the surrounding sentence.

Apples, plums, and grapes can all be used to make wine.

*but*

Apples, plums, and grapes, available at most large grocery stores, can all be used to make wine.

In the rare case where the serial comma does not prevent ambiguity, it may be necessary to reword. In the first example below, the repetition of *and* makes it clear that Madonna is not the writer's mother (and see the examples at the end of this paragraph). In the second example, "Madonna" might be read as an appositive (see 6.30).

I thanked my mother and Madonna and Lady Gaga.

*not*

I thanked my mother, Madonna, and Lady Gaga.

Note that the phrase *as well as* cannot substitute for *and* in a series of items.

The team fielded one Mazda, two Corvettes, and three Bugattis, as well as a battered Plymouth Belvedere.

*not*

The team fielded one Mazda, two Corvettes, three Bugattis, as well as a battered Plymouth Belvedere.

In a series whose elements are all joined by conjunctions, no commas are needed unless the elements are long and delimiters would be helpful.

Would you prefer Mendelssohn or Schumann or Liszt?
You can turn left at the second fountain and right when you reach the temple, or left at the third fountain and left again at the statue of Venus, or in whatever direction Google sends you.

6.20 **Commas with "etc." and "et al."** When used as the final element in a series, the abbreviation *etc.* (*et cetera*, literally "and others of the same kind") and such equivalents as *and so forth* and *and the like* are preceded by a comma; they are followed by a comma only if required by the surrounding text. (According to a more traditional usage, such terms would be considered parenthetical and therefore set off by two commas.) In formal prose, Chicago prefers to limit the abbreviation *etc.* to parentheses, notes, and tabular matter. See also 5.254, under *etc.*

The map was far from complete (lacking many of the streets, alleys, etc. seen in earlier iterations).
The philosopher's population studies, classic textbooks, stray notes, and so forth were found in the attic.
*but*
For a discussion of periods, commas, and the like, see chapter 6.

The abbreviation *et al.* (*et alia* [neut.], *et alii* [masc.], or *et aliae* [fem.], literally "and others"), whether used in regular text or (more often) in bibliographic references, should be treated like *etc.* When *et al.* follows a single item (e.g., "Jones et al."), it requires no preceding comma. (Nor is a preceding comma required in the rare case that *etc.* follows a single item.) Note that neither *etc.* nor *et al.* is italicized in normal prose (see the first example above).

6.21 **Omitting serial commas before ampersands.** When an ampersand is used instead of the word *and* (as in company names), the serial comma is omitted.

Winken, Blinken & Nod is a purveyor of nightwear.

See also 13.90, 14.34.

## *Commas with Independent Clauses*

6.22 **Commas with independent clauses joined by a coordinating conjunction.** When independent clauses are joined by *and*, *but*, *or*, *so*, *yet*, or any other coordinating conjunction, a comma usually precedes the conjunction. If the clauses are very short and closely connected, the comma may be omitted (as in the last example below) unless the clauses are part of a series (as in the fifth example). For imperative clauses joined by a coordinating conjunction, see 6.25. For the use of a semicolon between independent clauses, see 6.60. For comma splices, see 6.23.

We activated the alarm, but the intruder was already inside.
All watches display the time, and some of them do so accurately.
Do we want to foster creativity, or are we interested only in our intellectual property?
The bus never came, so we took a taxi.
Donald cooked, Sally poured the wine, and Maddie and Cammie offered hors d'oeuvres.
*but*
Electra played the guitar and Tambora sang.

6.23 **Run-on sentences (comma splices).** When two independent clauses are joined by a comma alone—that is, without the help of a coordinating conjunction (see 6.22)—the result is a type of run-on sentence known as a comma splice (to splice is to join). In formal prose, where comma splices are usually considered an error, the remedy is either to add the appropriate conjunction or to change the comma to a more suitable mark of punctuation.

*Comma splice*
All watches display the time, some of them do so accurately.

*No comma splice*
All watches display the time, and some of them do so accurately.
All watches display the time; some of them do so accurately.
All watches display the time. Some of them do so accurately.
All watches display the time (some of them do so accurately).
All watches display the time—some of them do so accurately.

Because the occasional comma splice can be effective, especially in conversational prose and creative writing, editors should consider in each case whether a "correction" would result in a clear improvement before making or suggesting a change.

6.24 **Commas with compound predicates.** A comma is not normally required before a coordinating conjunction that joins the two parts of a compound predicate (cf. 6.22). (A compound predicate occurs when a subject that is shared by two or more clauses is not repeated after the first clause.) Note that this recommendation now extends to imperative clauses; see 6.25 for examples.

He printed out a week's worth of crossword puzzles and arranged them on his clipboard.
Kelleher tried to contact the mayor but was informed that she had stopped accepting unsolicited calls.
He stood up and opened his mouth but failed to remember his question.

A comma may occasionally be needed, however, to prevent a misreading.

She recognized the man who entered the room, and gasped.

Subject to editorial discretion, a comma may also be added when the first part of the sentence is especially long, or when the second part reads as an afterthought. Editors working with creative genres especially should consider such commas on a case-by-case basis.

Whole chapters of her novel are written in the style of a nineteenth-century travelogue, and were probably intended that way.

In sentences that use *then* as a shorthand for *and then*, a comma usually precedes the adverb. (See also 6.61.)

She filled in the last square in Sunday's puzzle, then yawned.
*but*
She filled in the last square in Sunday's puzzle and then yawned.

Compound predicates of three or more parts treated as a series are punctuated accordingly (see 6.19).

She scrubbed the floors, washed the dishes, and finished her essay on twenty-first-century labor-saving technologies.

6.25 **Imperative clauses joined by a coordinating conjunction.** When two imperative clauses are joined by a coordinating conjunction, add a comma only if the sentence would require one for other reasons (as in the fourth example below) or to prevent ambiguity (as when the clauses are especially long or complex). This departure from the advice in previous editions of this manual recognizes that the sentence can be read as having either two independent clauses (with the understood subject, *you*, omitted in both) or a single clause with a compound predicate (in which the second subject is always omitted, as described in 6.24). The first interpretation would normally require a comma, but the second—which this manual now prefers—would not.

Wait for me at the bottom of the hill on Buffalo Street or walk up to Eddy Street and meet me next to the Yield sign.
Find each instance of the word *ax* and change the spelling to *axe*.
Raise your right hand and repeat after me.
*but*
Find each instance of the word *ax*, including any in the index, and change the spelling to *axe*.

Three or more imperative clauses would be treated like any other series (see 6.19–21).

Revise the first chapter, double-check your work, and send it back to me.

## *Commas with Dependent Clauses*

6.26 **Commas with introductory dependent clauses.** When a dependent clause precedes the main, independent clause, it should be followed by a comma. A dependent clause is generally introduced by a subordinating conjunction such as *if*, *because*, or *when* (see 5.206, 5.207).

If you accept our conditions, we will agree to the proposal.
Until we have seen the light, we cannot guarantee a safe exit from the tunnel.
Whether you agree with her or not, she has a point.

Compare 6.27.

6.27 **Commas with dependent clauses following the main clause.** A dependent clause that follows a main, independent clause should *not* be preceded by a comma if it is restrictive—that is, essential to fully understanding the meaning of the main clause (see also 6.29). For instance, in the first example below, it is not necessarily true that "we will agree to the proposal"; the dependent *if* clause adds essential information.

We will agree to the proposal if you accept our conditions.
Paul sighed when he heard the news.
He wasn't running because he was afraid; he was running because he was late.

If the dependent clause is merely supplementary or parenthetical (i.e., nonrestrictive, or not essential to the meaning of the main clause), it should be preceded by a comma. Such distinctions are occasionally tenuous. In the fourth example below, the meaning—and whether the subject is running or not—depends almost entirely on the presence of the comma (compare with the third example above). If in doubt, rephrase.

I'd like the tom yum, if you don't mind.
At last she arrived, when the food was cold.
She has a point, whether you agree with her or not.
He wasn't running, because he was afraid of the dark.
*or, better,*
Because he was afraid of the dark, he wasn't running.

Where the intended meaning is not at stake, context and emphasis may also play a role. In creative genres especially, editors should pay attention to context and an author's style before imposing any change in all but the most clear-cut cases. See also 6.26.

6.28 **Commas with two consecutive conjunctions.** When a dependent clause intervenes between two other clauses joined by a coordinating conjunction, causing the coordinating and subordinating conjunctions to appear next to each other (e.g., *and if, but when*), the consecutive conjunctions need not be separated by a comma. See also 6.22, 6.26.

Burton examined the documents for over an hour, and if Smedley had not intervened, the forgery would have been revealed.
The author finally returned the manuscript, but as soon as I opened it, I could see that it was the wrong version.

By a similar logic, when a dependent clause intervenes between an independent clause and a dependent clause introduced by a subordinating conjunction, no comma is needed between the two subordinating conjunctions (e.g., *that if*).

They decided that if it rained, they would reschedule the game.

Strictly speaking, it would not be wrong to add a comma between the conjunctions in any of the examples above. Such usage, which would extend the logic of commas in pairs (see 6.17), may be preferred in certain cases for emphasis or clarity or to support an author's preference for a closely punctuated style (see 6.16). See also 6.35.

## *Commas with Relative Clauses, Appositives, and Descriptive Phrases*

6.29 **Commas with relative clauses — "that" versus "which."** A clause is said to be restrictive (or defining) if it provides information that is essential to understanding the intended meaning of the rest of the sentence. Restrictive relative clauses are usually introduced by *that* (or by *who/whom/whose*) and are never set off by commas from the rest of the sentence. The relative pronoun may occasionally be omitted (but need not be) if the sentence is just as clear without it, as in the second and fourth examples below (before "I" and "we," respectively). See also 5.212.

The manuscript that the editors submitted to the publisher was well formatted.
The book I have just finished is due back tomorrow; the others can wait.
I prefer to share the road with drivers who focus on driving rather than on what they happen to be reading.
The drivers we hire to make deliveries must have good driving records.
The author whose work I admire the most is generally the one whose books I have most recently read.

A clause is said to be nonrestrictive (or nondefining or parenthetical) if it could be omitted without obscuring the identity of the noun to which it refers or otherwise changing the intended meaning of the rest of the sentence. Nonrestrictive relative clauses are usually introduced by *which* (or *who/whom/whose*) and are set off from the rest of the sentence by commas.

The final manuscript, which was well formatted, was submitted to the publisher on time.
*Ulysses*, which I finished early this morning, is due back on June 16.
I prefer to share the road with illiterate drivers, who are unlikely to read books while driving.
Boris Pasternak, whose most famous creation was a doctor, wrote what is probably the best novel about the Russian Revolution.

Although *which* can be substituted for *that* in a restrictive clause (a common practice in British English), many writers preserve the distinction between restrictive *that* (with no commas) and nonrestrictive *which* (with commas). See also 5.254, under *that; which*.

6.30 **Commas with appositives.** A word, abbreviation, phrase, or clause that is placed in apposition to a noun (i.e., providing an explanatory equivalent) is normally set off by commas if it is nonrestrictive—that is, if it can be omitted without obscuring the identity of the noun to which it refers. (For spousal commas, see 6.31.)

The title of Miranda's first musical, *In the Heights*, refers to the Washington Heights neighborhood of Manhattan. (The word *first* tells us which musical; the title provides additional rather than essential information.)
The nation's twenty-fourth poet laureate, Ada Limón, spoke first. (Only one poet laureate can be the nation's twenty-fourth.)

If, however, the word or phrase is restrictive—that is, it provides (or may provide) essential information about the noun (or nouns) to which it refers—no commas should appear.

The movie version of Miranda's Broadway musical *Hamilton* is valuable for its subtitles. (Lin-Manuel Miranda has written more than one Broadway musical; the title identifies which one is being discussed here.)
Former poet laureate Joy Harjo took the stage. (Joy Harjo is not the world's only former poet laureate.)

See also 5.26, 6.29.

6.31 **Spousal and other relationship commas.** The rules for using commas with appositives as described in 6.30 often come up for sentences that specify the name of a spouse, partner, sibling, child, pet, or other relative or family member. When the name identifies the only one of its kind (as is generally the case with spouses but may not be the case for other types of relationships), commas would normally be required.

Desi's wife, Shondra, has a PhD. (Shondra is Desi's only wife.)
Shondra's brother, Dillon, rescued three dogs. (Dillon is Shondra's only brother.)
*but*
Dillon's dog Spot is a Dalmatian. (Dillon has more than one dog.)

Such commas may be omitted, however, when the number of spouses or siblings or dogs or whatever is either unknown or irrelevant. A comma may also be omitted when the tone is casual or conversational (as in dialogue) or to accommodate an author's creative preference for a less closely punctuated style (see 6.16).

Shondra's husband Desi is allergic to cats. (Readers will assume Shondra has only one husband, so the commas may be dropped in less formal registers.)
Desi's brother Cedric has never owned a pet. (Whether Desi has more than one brother is unknown or irrelevant.)

Commas should always be omitted to avoid an awkward possessive.

Desi's wife Shondra's cats are allergic to dogs.
*not*
Desi's wife's, Shondra's, cats are allergic to dogs.

Finally, note that there are at least two instances in which commas are always used: (1) when the generic term is preceded by an adjective that uniquely identifies it and (2) when the name comes before the generic term.

Shondra's least friendly cat, Felix, has long hair.
Shondra, Desi's wife, loves cats.

6.32 **Commas with descriptive phrases.** When a descriptive phrase that follows the noun it modifies is restrictive—that is, essential to the meaning (and often the identity) of the noun it belongs to—it should not be set off by commas. A nonrestrictive (or parenthetical) phrase, however, should be enclosed in commas (or, if it falls at the end of a sentence, preceded by a comma). In the first two examples below, the "to" phrases are parenthetical. In the third example, however, the "to" phrase is essential. See also 6.29.

Elizabeth Taylor's second marriage, to Michael Wilding, ended in divorce.
Elizabeth Taylor's fifth and sixth marriages, to Richard Burton, ended in divorce.
*but*
Elizabeth Taylor's second marriage to Richard Burton ended in divorce.

## *Commas with Participial and Adverbial Phrases*

6.33 **Commas with participial phrases.** Participial phrases begin with a past or present participle and modify a noun. An introductory participial phrase is normally set off from the rest of the sentence by a comma.

Exhilarated by her morning workout, she headed for the ocean.
Having forgotten his lines, the actor was forced to ad-lib.

When such a phrase occurs in the middle of a sentence, it should be set off by commas unless it is used restrictively, providing essential information about the main clause (see also 6.32).

The actor, having forgotten his lines, was forced to ad-lib.
*but*
Actors forgetting their lines may be forced to ad-lib. (The phrase "forgetting their lines" specifies which actors may be forced to ad-lib.)

Likewise, a comma sets off such a phrase at the end of a sentence unless the phrase is used restrictively.

She headed for the ocean, exhilarated by her morning workout.
The actor was forced to ad-lib, having forgotten his lines.
*but*
She always headed for the ocean exhilarated by her morning workout. (It is *not* true that she always headed for the ocean; it *is* true that whenever she headed for the ocean she was in a state of exhilaration from her morning workout.)

A comma should *not* be used if the participial phrase modifies the subject of a sentence by means of a linking verb (see 5.105), even if the sentence is inverted.

Running along behind the wagon was the archduke himself!

6.34 **Commas with adverbial phrases.** Adverbial phrases typically begin with a preposition; they usually modify a verb or a sentence as a whole. Although an introductory adverbial phrase can usually be followed by a comma, it need not be unless misreading is likely. Shorter adverbial phrases are less likely to merit a comma than longer ones.

On the other hand, his vices could be considered virtues.
With three consecutive swings, Jackson made history.
In 1931 Henrietta turned fifty.
*but*
Before eating, the members of the committee met in the assembly room.
To Anthony, Blake remained an enigma.

When such a phrase occurs in the middle of a sentence, it is normally set off by commas (cf. 6.32).

Jackson, with three consecutive swings, made history.
His vices, on the other hand, could be considered virtues.

At the end of a sentence, a comma is necessary only when the phrase is used in a nonrestrictive sense, providing information that is not essential to the meaning of the rest of the sentence.

Jackson made history with three consecutive swings.
Henrietta turned fifty in 1931.
*but*
Henrietta turned fifty a decade later, in 1931.

A comma should *not* be used to set off an adverbial phrase that introduces an inverted sentence.

Before the footlights stood one of the most notorious rakes of the twenty-first century.

6.35 **Commas with a participial or adverbial phrase plus a conjunction.** When a participial or adverbial phrase immediately follows a coordinating conjunction, the use of commas depends on whether the conjunction joins two independent clauses. If the conjunction is simply a part of the predicate or joins a compound predicate, the first comma follows the conjunction (see also 6.24).

We were extremely tired and, having run out of options, eager to go home.
The siblings trailed after two sets but, on the strength of Serena's serve, stormed back to win.

If the conjunction joins two independent clauses, however, the comma precedes the conjunction (see also 6.22).

We were elated, but realizing that the day was almost over, we decided to go to bed.

Strictly speaking, it would not be wrong to add (or retain) a second comma after *but* in the last example above. Such usage, which would extend the logic of commas in pairs (see 6.17), may be preferred in certain cases for emphasis or clarity or to support an author's preference for a closely punctuated style (see 6.16). See also 6.28.

## *Commas with Introductory Words and Phrases*

6.36 **Commas with introductory phrases.** Whether to use a comma to set off an introductory phrase can depend on the type of phrase, its relationship to the rest of the sentence, and its length. For participial phrases, see 6.33. For adverbial phrases, see 6.34. Some cases involving specific words are discussed below (at 6.37 and 6.38). For dependent clauses, see 6.26.

6.37 **Commas with an introductory "yes," "no," or the like.** A comma should follow an introductory *yes, no, OK, well,* or the like, except in certain instances more likely to be encountered in informal prose or dialogue.

Yes, it is true that 78 percent of the subjects ate 50 percent more than they reported.
No, neither scenario improved the subjects' accuracy.
OK, I'll try the quinoa.
Well then, we will have to take a vote.
*but*
No you will not!

6.38 **Commas with an introductory "oh" or "ah."** A comma usually follows an exclamatory *oh* or *ah* unless it is followed by an exclamation point (or a dash) or forms part of a phrase (e.g., "oh boy," "ah yes"). No comma follows a vocative *oh* or (mainly poetic) *O*. See also 7.31.

Oh, you're right!
Ah, here we are at last!
Oh no! Ah yes! Oh yeah?
My oh my!
Oh mighty king!
"O wild West Wind . . ."

## *Commas with Two or More Adjectives Preceding a Noun*

6.39 **Commas with coordinate adjectives.** As a general rule, when a noun is preceded by two or more adjectives that could, without affecting the meaning, be joined by *and*, the adjectives are separated by commas. Such adjectives, which are called coordinate adjectives, can also usually be reversed in order and still make sense. If, on the other hand, the adjectives are not coordinate—that is, if one or more of the adjectives are essential to (i.e., form a unit with) the noun being modified—no commas are used. See also 5.95.

Shelly had proved a faithful, sincere friend. (Shelly's friendship has proved faithful *and* sincere.)
It is going to be a long, hot, exhausting summer. (The summer is going to be long *and* hot *and* exhausting.)
*but*
She has many faithful friends.
He has rejected traditional religious affiliations.
She opted for an inexpensive quartz watch.

6.40 **Commas with repeated adjectives.** When an adjective is repeated before a noun, a comma normally appears between the pair.

Many, many people have enjoyed the book.

## *Commas with Dates and Addresses*

6.41 **Commas with dates.** In the month-day-year style of dates, commas must be used to set off the year—a traditional usage that not only applies the logic of commas in pairs (see 6.17) but also serves to separate the numerals for day and year. By a similar logic, when the day of the week is given, it is separated from the month and day by a comma. Commas are usually unnecessary, however, between the name for the day and the ordinal in references where the month is not expressed (see also 9.33). Commas are also unnecessary where only a month and year are given, or where a named day (such as a holiday) is given with a year. For dates used adjectivally, see 5.87. See also 9.31–38.

The performance took place on February 2, 2006, at the State Theatre in Ithaca.
The hearing was scheduled for 2:30 p.m. on Friday, August 9, 2024.
Monday, May 5, was a holiday; Tuesday the 6th was not. (See also 9.33.)
Her license expires sometime in April 2027.
On Thanksgiving Day 1998 they celebrated their seventy-fifth anniversary.

In the day-month-year system—useful in material that requires many full dates (and standard in British English)—no commas are needed to set off the year. For the year-month-day (ISO) date style, see 9.38.

The accused gradually came to accept the verdict; see his journal entries of 6 October 2022 and 4 January 2024.

6.42 **Commas with addresses.** Commas are used to set off the individual elements in addresses or place-names that are run in to the text (see also 6.17). In a mailing address, commas should be used sparingly, mainly to set off the separate lines of the address, but also to separate city and state or province (but not the postal code), apartment numbers, and the like. If in doubt about the accuracy of an address, consult the applicable postal service. (Preferred postal usage will be tailored for use on address labels and may consist of all capital letters and spare punctuation, a style that need not be emulated in regular text and related contexts.) For place-names used adjectivally, see 5.73.

A printout was sent to the author at 743 Olga Drive NE, Ashtabula, OH 44044, on May 2.
Queries can be sent to the author at 123 Main St., Apt. 10, Montreal, QC H3Z 2Y7.
Waukegan, Illinois, is not far from the Wisconsin border.
The plane landed in Kampala, Uganda, that evening.

Some institutional names include place-names set off by commas. When such a name appears in the middle of a clause, a second comma is required to set off the place-name. See also 6.87.

California State University, Northridge, has an enrollment of . . .
*but*
The University of Wisconsin–Madison has an enrollment of . . .

## *Commas with Quotations and Questions*

6.43 **Commas with quotations.** An independent clause quoted in the form of dialogue or from text and introduced with *said*, *replied*, *asked*, *wrote*, or the like (including variations of such terms) is usually introduced with a comma. This traditional usage considers the grammar and syntax of the quoted material to be separate from the text that introduces it. See also 6.69.

It was Thoreau who wrote, "One generation abandons the enterprises of another like stranded vessels."
She replied, "I hope you aren't referring to us."

Commas are required regardless of the position of the explanatory text relative to the quotation (but see 6.134).

"I hope," she replied, "you aren't referring to us."
"I hope you aren't referring to us," she replied.

If, however, such a quotation is introduced by *that*, *whether*, *if*, or a similar conjunction (see 5.206), no comma is normally needed.

Was it Stevenson who said that "the cruelest lies are often told in silence"?
He wondered whether "to think is to live."

A comma can also usually be omitted if a form of the verb *to be* intervenes between the dialogue verb and the quotation (see also 12.15).

What they said was "The apple falls far from the tree."

For the location of a comma in relation to closing quotation marks, see 6.9. For quoted titles and expressions, see 6.44; for questions, see 6.45. For words such as *yes* and *no*, see 12.47. For a more detailed discussion and illustration of the use or omission of commas before and after quoted material, including dialogue, see 12.13–17, 12.39–53, 12.59–69, and the examples throughout chapter 12.

6.44 **Commas with quoted or italicized titles and expressions.** Titles or expressions set off from the surrounding text with quotation marks or italics are usually treated like noun forms; commas are used or omitted as they would be with any other noun.

The collection *Notes of a Native Son* features an essay called "Equal in Paris."
She recites the poem "One Art" every night before bed.
Of her many favorites, "One Art" is the one she knows best.

A common mistake is to use a comma before a title or expression whenever it follows a noun that describes it (e.g., *story, novel,* or *poem*). In fact, the rule for appositives applies: The title or expression is set off by commas only if it is nonrestrictive—that is, if it can be omitted without obscuring the identity of the noun (i.e., *story, novel,* etc.) to which it refers (see 6.30). In the first example below, the quoted or italicized titles identify *which* poem by Bishop (she wrote many) and *which* novel by Weiner (she has published more than one); in the third example, the quoted words tell us *which* motto appears over the door. In the second and fourth examples, *which* essay (the second one in the collection) and *which* proverb (Tom's favorite) have already been identified.

Elizabeth Bishop's poem "One Art" was featured in Jennifer Weiner's novel *In Her Shoes* and read by Cameron Diaz in the movie adaptation of the book.
In the collection's second essay, "Everybody's Protest Novel," Baldwin critiques *Uncle Tom's Cabin.*
The motto "All for one and one for all" appears over the door.
Tom's favorite proverb, "A rolling stone gathers no moss," proved wrong.

For quotation marks versus italics for the titles of works, see 8.164. See also 7.65.

6.45 **Commas with questions.** A direct question is sometimes included within a sentence but not enclosed in quotation marks. Such a question is usually introduced by a comma (unless it comes at the beginning of a sentence) and begins with a capital letter. This usage recognizes that such a question is analogous to (and can be treated like) a direct quotation (see 6.43; see also 6.69). For the use of italics for thoughts and other unspoken discourse, see 12.49.

She wondered, What am I doing?
Legislators had to be asking themselves, Can the fund be used for the current emergency, or must it remain dedicated to its original purpose?

If the question ends before the end of the sentence, no comma is required after the question mark (see also 6.134).

What am I doing? she wondered.

If the result seems awkward, rephrase as an indirect question. An indirect question does not require a question mark, nor does it need to be set off with a comma. Indirect questions are never capitalized (except at the beginning of a sentence). See also 6.73.

She wondered what she was doing.
The question of how to tell her was on everyone's mind.
Ursula wondered why her watch had stopped ticking.
Where to find a reliable clock is the question of the hour.

## *Commas in Personal and Corporate Names*

6.46 **Commas with "Jr.," "Sr.," and the like.** Commas are not required with *Jr.* and *Sr.*, and they are never used to set off *II*, *III*, and the like when these are used as part of a name. In an inverted name, however (as in an index; see 15.49), a comma is required before such an element, which comes last.

John Doe Sr. continues to cast a shadow over his son.
Jason Deer III has turned over stewardship of the family business to his cousin.
*but*
Doe, John, Sr.
Deer, Jason, III

If a comma must be used to set off *Jr.* or *Sr.* (e.g., to conform to a particular publisher's house style), a second comma is normally required in the middle of a sentence (see 6.17); rephrase as needed to avoid the possessive.

The speech made by John Doe, Sr., ran long. (*not* John Doe, Sr.'s, speech . . .)

6.47 **Commas with "Inc.," "Ltd.," and the like.** Commas are not required with *Inc.*, *Ltd.*, and such as part of a company's name. A particular company may use such commas in its corporate documentation; articles and books about such companies, however, should follow a consistent style rather than make exceptions for particular cases.

QuartzMove Inc. was just one such company named in the suit.

If a comma must be used to set off the abbreviation, a second comma is normally required in the middle of a sentence (see 6.17); rephrase as needed to avoid the possessive. See also 6.46.

## *Commas with Antithetical Elements*

6.48 **Commas with "not" phrases.** When a phrase beginning with *not* is interjected in order to clarify a particular noun, commas should be used to set off the phrase. See also 6.49.

We hoped the mayor herself, not her assistant, would attend the meeting.
They want you, not him.

6.49 **Commas with correlative conjunctions.** In sentences that feature *not . . . but* or *not only . . . but also* and similar pairs of correlative conjunctions, whether to use commas depends on sentence structure. If the conjunctions join a compound predicate (as in the first example below; see also 6.24) or a pair of phrases (as in the second through fourth examples), commas are usually unnecessary. Note that the word *also* is sometimes omitted from *not only . . . but also* (as in the first example).

We not only camped in the woods but canoed down the river.
Works of art are created not by inspiration but by persistence.
Being almost perfectly ambidextrous, she wore not one watch but two.
They marched to Washington not only armed with petitions and determined to get their senators' attention but also hoping to demonstrate their solidarity with one another.

If the conjunctions join two independent clauses, a comma is normally used before the second one (see also 6.22). Note that the second conjunction is sometimes elided, resulting in a borderline comma splice that nonetheless can be acceptable in less formal registers (see also 6.23).

Not only did we camp in the woods, but we also canoed down the river.
*or, less formally,*
Not only did we camp in the woods, we also canoed down the river.

6.50 **Commas with "the more," "the less," and so on.** A comma is customarily used between clauses of *the more . . . the more* type. Shorter phrases of that type, however, rarely merit commas.

The more I discover about the workings of mechanical movements, the less I seem to care about the holy grail of perfectly accurate timekeeping.
*but*
The more the merrier.

## *Other Uses of the Comma*

6.51 **Commas with parenthetical elements.** If only a slight break is intended, commas may be used to set off a parenthetical element inserted into a sentence as an explanation or comment. Such elements are occasionally awkward, especially if they are inserted between an adjective and the noun it modifies; in such cases, rewording may help.

All the test participants, in spite of our initial fears, recovered.
Commas can, we are told, add nuance.
Most children fail to consider the history behind new technologies, if they think of it at all.
She was the fastest, not to mention the strongest, runner on her team.
*or, better,*
She was the fastest runner on her team, not to mention the strongest.

If a stronger break is needed or if there are commas within the parenthetical element, em dashes (6.91) or parentheses (6.101) should be used instead of commas.

6.52 **Commas with "however," "therefore," "indeed," and the like.** Commas—sometimes paired with semicolons (see 6.61)—are traditionally used to set off conjunctive adverbs such as *however*, *therefore*, and *indeed*. When the adverb is essential to the meaning of the clause, or if the emphasis is on the adverb itself, commas are usually unnecessary (as in the last two examples below).

A truly efficient gasoline-powered engine remains, however, a pipe dream.
Indeed, not one test subject accurately predicted the amount of soup in the bowl.
*but*
If you cheat and are therefore disqualified, you may also risk losing your scholarship.
That was indeed the outcome of the study.

6.53 **Commas with "such as" and "including."** The principles delineated in 6.32 apply also to phrases introduced by *such as* or *including*. If the phrase is nonrestrictive (or parenthetical), it is set off by commas. If it is restrictive (or essential), commas are not used.

The entire band, including the matutinal lead singer, overslept the noon rehearsal.
Some words, such as *matutinal* and *onomatopoetic*, are best avoided in everyday speech.
*but*
Words such as *matutinal* and *onomatopoetic* are best avoided in everyday speech.

6.54 **Commas with "that is," "namely," "for example," and the like.** Expressions of the type *that is* are usually followed by a comma. Because they apply only to what follows, they are best preceded by an em dash or (before an independent clause) a semicolon rather than a comma; alternatively, the entire phrase they introduce may be enclosed in parentheses or (in the middle of a sentence) em dashes.

There are simple alternatives to the stigmatized plastic shopping bag—namely, reusable cloth bags and foldable carts.
The committee (that is, its more influential members) wanted to drop the matter.
Luna prepared the document for editing; that is, she ran a series of macros and applied paragraph and character styles.
Bones from various small animals—for example, a squirrel, a cat, a pigeon, and a muskrat—were found in the doctor's cabinet.

Note that in formal writing, Chicago prefers to confine the abbreviations *i.e.* ("that is") and *e.g.* ("for example") to parentheses or notes, where they are followed by a comma.

The most noticeable difference between male and female ginkgo trees (i.e., the presence of berries in the latter) is also the species' most controversial feature.

6.55 **Commas for explanatory alternatives.** When an explanatory alternative introduced by *or* or the like interrupts a sentence, it is usually set off by commas. When the alternative is not explanatory, however, no commas are used.

The compass stand, or binnacle, must be situated within the helmsman's field of vision.
The slash, also known as a solidus or virgule, sits to the right of the period on a standard QWERTY keyboard.
*but*
A slash or a period can be typed without using the Shift key. (See also 7.82.)

6.56 **Commas with "too" and "either."** The adverbs *too* and *either* used in the sense of "also" generally need not be preceded by a comma. Note, however, that some authors prefer to use such commas, so editors should query before making any changes.

I had my cake and ate it too.
Rosario prefers Thelonious Monk over Duke Ellington; her brother does too.
The airport lacked charging stations; there were no comfortable chairs either.

When *too* comes in the middle of the sentence or clause, a comma is more likely to be helpful.

She, too, decided against the early showing.

See also 6.34.

6.57 **Commas with direct address (vocative commas).** Names or words used in direct address are set off by a comma (or two in the middle of a sentence); this comma is known as a vocative comma.

Ms. Jones, please come in.
Kai, your order is ready.
Hello, Ms. Philips.
Hi, Pratchi. Please sit down.
Take that, you devil.
Kiss me, you fool!
Yes, ma'am!

Are you listening, class?
It's time to go, Marta.
I am not here, my friends, to discuss personalities.

When introduced by a coordinating conjunction, the comma preceding the name is optional. It may be retained in closely punctuated prose but omitted otherwise (see also 6.16; cf. 6.35).

But Jacob, we haven't even started yet.
*or, more closely punctuated,*
But, Jacob, we haven't even started yet.

In correspondence, a comma typically follows the greeting, though a colon (or sometimes a dash) may be used instead (especially in formal correspondence; see 6.70). If the name is preceded by *Hello* or another word of greeting rather than an adjective (like *Dear*), a comma may also precede the one being addressed. However, such commas are often omitted.

Dear Lucien, . . .
Greetings, Board Members: . . .
Hi, Ketanji, . . .
*or, less formally,*
Hi Ketanji, . . .

6.58 **Commas to indicate elision.** A comma is sometimes used to indicate the omission of a word or words readily understood from the context. Note that the number of an omitted verb can be different from the number of the other verbs in the sentence (as in the third example below, where *sixth* would take the verb *has chosen*).

In Illinois there are seventeen such schools; in Ohio, twenty; in Indiana, thirteen.
Thousands rushed to serve him in victory; in defeat, none.
The first five candidates have chosen mathematics; the sixth, hermeneutics; and the seventh and eighth, volleyball.

The comma may be omitted if the elliptical construction is clear without it.

One student excels at composition, another at mathematics, and the third at sports.
Jasper missed her and she him.

6.59 **Commas between homonyms.** For ease of reading and subject to editorial discretion, two words that are spelled alike but have different functions may be separated by a comma if such clarification seems desirable.

Let us march in, in twos.
Whatever is, is good.
*but*
"It depends on what *means* means."

## SEMICOLONS

6.60 **Use of the semicolon.** In regular prose, a semicolon is most commonly used between two independent clauses not joined by a conjunction to signal a closer connection between them than a period would. (For the similar use of a colon, see 6.65.)

She spent much of her free time immersed in the ocean; no mere water-*resistant* watch would do.

Though a gifted writer, Miqueas has never bothered to master the semicolon; he insists that half a colon is no colon at all.

Note that many fiction authors consider semicolons to be unnatural in dialogue and may also object to their use in narrative; editors should resist adding any in such contexts without consulting the author. For the use of the semicolon in index entries, see 15.17, 15.104. For its use in parenthetical text citations, see 13.124. For its use with a second subtitle of a work, see 13.92.

6.61 **Semicolons with "however," "therefore," "indeed," and the like.** Certain adverbs, when they are used to join two independent clauses, should be preceded by a semicolon rather than a comma (so as to avoid a comma splice; see 6.23). These conjunctive adverbs include *however*, *thus*, *hence*, *indeed*, *accordingly*, *besides*, and *therefore* (see also 6.62). A comma usually follows the adverb but may be omitted if the sentence seems just as effective without it, as in the third example below (see also 6.34).

The accuracy of Jesse's watch was never in question; besides, he was an expert at intuiting the time of day from the position of the sun and stars. (*not* The accuracy of Jesse's watch was never in question, besides, . . .)

Kallista was determined not to miss anything on her voyage; accordingly, she made an appointment with her ophthalmologist.

The trumpet player developed a painful cold sore; thus the third show was canceled.

The adverb *then* is often seen between independent clauses as shorthand for *and then,* preceded by a comma. Though the result is a borderline comma splice (see 6.23), it is common in imperative constructions (as in the first example below) and acceptable in most contexts; some writers, however, may prefer to use a semicolon, which is strictly correct.

Touch and hold the icon, then drag it to the trash.
First we went out for shiitake burgers, then we enjoyed vegan sundaes.
*or*
First we went out for shiitake burgers; then we enjoyed vegan sundaes.
*but*
First we went out for shiitake burgers, and then we enjoyed vegan sundaes.

See also 6.22, 6.24.

6.62 **Semicolons with "that is," "for example," "namely," and the like.** A semicolon may be used before an expression such as *that is, for example,* or *namely* when it introduces an independent clause. For an example, see 6.54. See also 6.61.

6.63 **Semicolons before a conjunction.** Normally, an independent clause introduced by a coordinating conjunction is preceded by a comma (see 6.22). In formal prose, a semicolon may be used instead—either to effect a stronger separation between clauses or when the second independent clause has internal punctuation. Another option is to use a period instead of a semicolon; see 5.209.

Frobisher had always assured his grandson that the house would be his; yet there was no provision for this bequest in his will.
Garrett had insisted on remixing the track; but the engineer's demands for overtime pay, together with the band's reluctance, persuaded him to accept the original mix.
*or*
Garrett had insisted on remixing the track. But the engineer's demands . . .

6.64 **Semicolons in a complex series.** When items in a series themselves contain internal punctuation, separating the items with semicolons can aid clarity. If ambiguity seems unlikely, commas may be used instead (see 6.19). See also 6.140. Note that when a sentence continues beyond a series (as in the third example below), no additional semicolon is required.

The membership of the international commission was as follows: France, 4; Germany, 5; Great Britain, 1; Italy, 3; United States, 7.

The defendant, in an attempt to mitigate his sentence, pleaded that he had recently, on doctor's orders, gone off his medications; that his car—which, incidentally, he had won in the late 1970s on *Let's Make a Deal*—had spontaneously caught fire; and that he had not eaten for several days.

Marilynn, Sunita, and Jared, research assistants; Carlos, programming consultant; and Carol, audiovisual editor, provided support and prepared these materials for publication.

*but*

She decided to buy three watches—an atomic watch for travel within the United States, a solar-powered, water-resistant quartz for international travel, and an expensive self-winding model for special occasions.

## COLONS

6.65 **Use of the colon.** A colon introduces an element or a series of elements illustrating or amplifying what has preceded the colon. Between independent clauses it functions much like a semicolon (see 6.60); a colon, however, puts the emphasis on the clause that follows it (as in the second example below). (The colon usually conveys or reinforces the sense of "as follows"; see also 6.68.) The colon may sometimes be used instead of a period to introduce a series of related sentences (as in the third example). For capitalization following a colon, see 6.67.

The watch came with a choice of three bands: stainless steel, plastic, or leather.

They even relied on a chronological analogy: Just as the Year II had overshadowed 1789, so the October Revolution had eclipsed that of February.

Yolanda faced a conundrum: She could finish the soup, pretending not to care that what she had thought until a moment ago was a vegetable broth was in fact made from chicken. She could feign satiety and thank the host for a good meal. Or she could use this opportunity to assert her preference for a vegan diet.

For the use of colons with lists, see 6.141. For use of the em dash instead of a colon, see 6.91. For colons in ratios, see 9.60. For the use of colons with subtitles, see 13.91. For the use of colons in indexes, see 15.103. For other uses of the colon—in source citations, URLs, and other settings—consult the index or search the online edition of this manual.

6.66 **Space after colon.** In typeset matter, no more than one space should follow a colon. Further, in some settings—as in a source citation between a volume and page number with no intervening date or issue number (see 14.18, 14.74), a biblical citation (see 14.139), or a ratio (see 9.60)—*no* space should follow a colon. See also 6.7.

6.67 **Lowercase or capital letter after a colon.** When what follows the colon is *not* a complete sentence, as in the first example in 6.65, the first word following the colon is lowercased (unless it is a proper noun or other term that would normally be capitalized). When, however, a colon introduces one or more complete sentences, as in the second and third examples in 6.65, the first word that follows the colon should be capitalized. This departure from previous editions of this manual—which recommended capitalization only when a colon introduced more than one complete sentence—is intended to aid reader comprehension by signaling with a capital letter that what follows the colon should be read as a complete sentence. Also capitalized is the first word following a colon that introduces speech in dialogue or a complete-sentence quotation or question (as has always been the case; see 6.69).

6.68 **Colons with "as follows" and other introductory phrases.** A colon is normally used after *as follows*, *the following*, and similar expressions. (For lists, see 6.138–43.)

The steps are as follows: First, make grooves for the seeds; second, sprinkle the seeds; third, push the earth back over the grooves; fourth, water generously.

The following documents are required: a valid driver's license and a certified copy of your birth certificate.

On the other hand, a colon is not normally used after *namely*, *for example*, and similar expressions; these are usually followed by a comma instead (see 6.54).

6.69 **Colons to introduce quotations or questions.** A colon is often used to introduce speech in dialogue.

Axel: Somebody's knocking at the door.
Jalen: It's probably just a woodpecker.

A colon may also be used to introduce a quotation or a direct but unquoted question, especially where the introduction constitutes a grammatically complete sentence.

The author begins by challenging nature itself: "The trees were tall, but I was taller."
The question occurred to her at once: What if I can't do this?

For quotations or questions introduced with *said, replied, asked, wrote,* and the like, where a comma is normally used (see 6.43, 6.45), a colon may be used occasionally for emphasis or to set up a block quotation. See also 12.13–17.

6.70 **Colons in formal communication.** At the beginning of a speech or a formal communication, a colon usually follows the identification of those addressed. For use of a comma in direct address, see 6.57.

Honored Guests:
To Whom It May Concern:
Dear Credit and Collections Manager:

6.71 **Some common misuses of colons.** Many writers assume—wrongly—that a colon is always needed before a series or a list. In fact, if a colon intervenes in what would otherwise constitute a grammatical sentence—even if the introduction appears on a separate line, as in a list (see 6.138–43)—there is a good chance it is being used inappropriately. A colon, for example, should *not* be used before a series that serves as the object of a verb. When in doubt, apply this test: To merit a colon, the words that introduce a series or list must themselves constitute a grammatically complete sentence.

The menagerie included cats, pigeons, newts, and deer ticks.
*not*
The menagerie included: cats, pigeons, newts, and deer ticks.

An exception may be made when an introductory word or phrase is used before the colon and the verb is elided or otherwise understood. In such cases a colon (or, alternatively, a dash) is usually required.

Pros: accuracy and water resistance. Cons: cheap-looking exterior, . . . (The pros included accuracy and water resistance. Among its cons were a cheap-looking exterior, . . .)

First step: Remove the plastic tab. Second step: Insert the battery . . . (The first step is to remove the plastic tab. The second step is to insert the battery . . .)

## QUESTION MARKS

6.72 **Use of the question mark.** The question mark, as its name suggests, is used to indicate a direct question. It may also be used to indicate editorial doubt or (occasionally) to express surprise, disbelief, or uncertainty at the end of a declarative or imperative sentence. See also 6.76, 6.131, 6.133.

Who will represent the poor?
Thomas Kraftig (1610?–66) was the subject of the final essay.
This is your reply?

6.73 **Direct and indirect questions.** A question mark is used to mark the end of a direct but unquoted question within a sentence. This usage is no different from that of a directly quoted question (see 6.134). See also 6.45.

Is it worth the risk? he wondered.
*or*
He wondered, Is it worth the risk?

An indirect question never takes a question mark.

He wondered whether it was worth the risk.
How the two could be reconciled was the question on everyone's mind.

When a question within a sentence consists of a single word, such as *who, when, how,* or *why,* a question mark may be omitted, and the word is sometimes italicized (see also 12.47).

She asked herself why.
The question was no longer *how* but *when.*

A polite request disguised as a question does not always require a question mark. Such formulations can usually be reduced to the imperative.

Will the audience please rise.
Would you kindly respond by March 1.
*or*
Please respond by March 1.

*but*
Would you mind telling me your age?

6.74 **Question marks in relation to surrounding text and punctuation.** A question mark should be placed inside quotation marks, parentheses, or brackets only when it is part of (i.e., applies to) the quoted or parenthetical matter. See also 6.10, 6.134.

The ambassador asked, "Has the Marine Corps been alerted?"
"Is it worth the risk?" he asked.
Why was Farragut trembling when he said, "I'm here to open an inquiry"?
The man in the gray flannel suit (had we met before?) winked at me.
Why did she tell him only on the morning of his departure (March 18)?
"What do you suppose he had in mind," inquired Newman, "when he said, 'You are all greater fools than I thought'?"

Note that a question consisting of a fragment rather than a complete sentence can usually be capitalized.

Will there be music? Dancing?

## EXCLAMATION POINTS

6.75 **Use of the exclamation point.** An exclamation point (which should be used sparingly to be effective) marks an outcry or an emphatic or ironic comment. See also 6.131, 6.133.

Heads up!
According to one model, Miami will remain above sea level until at least 2100. We should all be so lucky!

6.76 **Exclamation rather than question.** A sentence in the form of a direct question may be marked as rhetorical by the use of an exclamation point in place of a question mark (see also 6.135). But note that a period can be equally effective in such cases (see 6.16).

How could you possibly believe that!
When will I ever learn!

6.77 **Exclamation point as editorial protest or amusement.** Writers and editors should be aware that an exclamation point added in brackets to quoted matter to indicate editorial protest or amusement risks being interpreted as contemptuous or arrogant. Unless such a sentiment is intended, this device should be avoided. Nor is it a substitute for the Latin expression *sic* (thus), which should be reserved to indicate an error in the source that might otherwise be taken as an error of transcription (see 12.72).

6.78 **Exclamation points in relation to surrounding punctuation.** An exclamation point should be placed inside quotation marks, parentheses, or brackets only when it is part of the quoted or parenthetical matter. See also 6.10, 6.134.

The performer walked off the stage amid cries of “Brava!”
I can’t believe you haven’t read “Bartleby, the Scrivener”!
Alex Ramirez (I could have had a stroke!) repeated the whole story.

## HYPHENS AND DASHES

6.79 **Hyphens and dashes compared.** Hyphens and the various dashes all have their specific appearance (shown below) and uses (discussed in the following paragraphs). The hyphen, the en dash, and the em dash are the most commonly used. Though the differences can sometimes be subtle—especially in the case of an en dash versus a hyphen—correct use of the different types is a sign of editorial precision and care. See also 2.16, 2.17, 2.101.

hyphen -
en dash –
em dash —
2-em dash ——
3-em dash ———

Note that the 2-em and 3-em dashes above consist of two and three consecutive em dashes, respectively. Though single-glyph versions of these have now been defined by Unicode, regular em dashes remain more readily available and are therefore preferred (see also 11.2). Note, however, that in some fonts a small space may appear between consecutive dashes; this may be fixed by adjusting the spacing between dashes or by using a different font.

## *Hyphens*

6.80 **Hyphens in compound words.** The use of the hyphen in compound words and names and in word division is discussed in 5.96 and in chapter 7, especially 7.36–48 and 7.87–96. See also 6.86.

6.81 **Hyphens as separators.** A hyphen is used to separate numbers that are not inclusive, such as telephone numbers (see 9.59), Social Security numbers, and ISBNs. (For hyphens with dates, see 9.38.) Hyphens are also used to separate letters when a word is spelled out letter by letter, as in dialogue or in reference to American Sign Language (see 11.135–45).

1-800-621-2376
978-0-226-15906-5 (ISBN)
"My name is Phyllis; that's p-h-y-l-l-i-s."
A proficient signer can fingerspell C-O-L-O-R-A-D-O in less than two seconds.

For hyphens in URLs and email addresses, see 7.47.

## *En Dashes*

6.82 **En dash as specialized hyphen.** Whenever an en dash is used in a number or other range or to connect compound terms (as described in 6.83, 6.84, 6.85, and 6.86), it functions as a specialized hyphen. Some other style manuals in fact call for a hyphen wherever this manual recommends an en dash. Authors, too, typically use hyphens wherever en dashes might be used instead. Editors who follow Chicago style, however, should apply en dashes as described in this section, and authors are encouraged to do the same.

6.83 **En dash as "to."** The principal use of the en dash is to connect numbers and, less often, words. With continuing numbers—such as dates, times, and page numbers—it signifies *up to and including* (or *through*). For the sake of parallel construction, the word *to* or *through* (or *until*), never the en dash, should be used if the word *from* precedes the first element in such a pair; similarly, *and* should be used if *between* precedes the first element.

The years 1993–2000 were heady ones for the computer literate.
For source citations and indexing, see chapters 13–15.
In Genesis 6:13–21 we find God's instructions to Noah.

Join us on Thursday, 11:30 a.m.–4:00 p.m., to celebrate the New Year.
I have blocked out December 2016–March 2017 to complete my manuscript.
Her articles appeared in *Postwar Journal* (3 November 1945–4 February 1946).
*but*
She was in college from 2019 to 2022. (*not* from 2019–22)
He usually naps between 11:30 a.m. and 1:30 p.m. (*not* between 11:30 a.m.–1:30 p.m.)

In other contexts, such as with scores and directions, the en dash signifies, more simply, *to*.

The London–Paris train leaves at two o'clock.
On November 20, 1966, Green Bay defeated Chicago, 13–6.
The legislature voted 101–13 to adopt the resolution.

For more on dates and times, see 9.31–38, 9.39–42. For more on number ranges, see 9.62–66. See also 6.114.

6.84 **En dash with an unfinished number range.** An en dash may be used to indicate a number range that is ongoing—for example, to indicate the dates of a serial publication or to give the birth date of a living person. No space intervenes between the en dash and any mark of punctuation that follows.

*The History of Cartography* (1987–) is a multivolume work published by Chicago.
Jack Stag (1950–) *or* Jack Stag (b. 1950)

6.85 **En dash between personal names.** When the names of two or more people are used as a compound modifier before a noun, an en dash rather than a hyphen will help to clarify that the compound name belongs to more than one person (a small departure from previous editions of this manual, which recommended a hyphen).

the Ali–Frazier match (a match between Muhammad Ali and Joe Frazier)
Epstein–Barr virus (a virus named for Anthony Epstein and Yvonne Barr)
the Mason–Dixon line (named for Charles Mason and Jeremiah Dixon)
*but*
Albers-Schönberg disease (named for Heinrich Albers-Schönberg)

Though an en dash may be appropriate in similar constructions involving common rather than proper nouns, this manual continues to recommend a hyphen unless the en dash clearly means *to* (e.g., "left-right asymmetry"; *but* "a north–south street"). See also 6.83.

6.86 **En dashes with compound adjectives.** The en dash can be used in place of a hyphen in a compound adjective when one of its elements consists of an open compound or when both elements consist of hyphenated compounds (see 7.88). Whereas a hyphen joins exactly two words, the en dash is intended to signal a link across more than two. Because this editorial nicety tends to go unnoticed by most readers, it should be used sparingly, and only when a more elegant solution is unavailable. As the first two examples below illustrate, the distinction is most helpful with proper compounds, whose limits are made clear within the larger context by capitalization. The relationship in the third example depends to some small degree on an en dash that many readers will perceive as a hyphen connecting *music* and *influenced*. The relationships in the fourth example are less awkwardly conveyed with a comma.

the post–World War II years
Chuck Berry–style lyrics
country music–influenced lyrics (*or* lyrics influenced by country music)
a quasi-public–quasi-judicial body (*or, better,* a quasi-public, quasi-judicial body)

A single word or prefix should be joined to a hyphenated compound by another hyphen rather than an en dash; if the result is awkward, reword.

non-English-speaking peoples
a two-thirds-full cup (*or, better,* a cup that is two-thirds full)

An abbreviated compound is treated as a single word, so a hyphen, not an en dash, is used in such phrases as “post-WWII.”

6.87 **En dashes with campus locations.** Some universities that have more than one campus use an en dash to link the campus location to the name of the university. Usage varies widely; where sources disagree, follow the usage of the institution to the extent it can be determined (an en dash may safely be applied, however, if the institution itself uses a hyphen to connect to an open compound). See also 6.42.

the University of Wisconsin–Madison
the University of Wisconsin–Milwaukee
*but*
the University of California, Berkeley
the State University of New York at Buffalo; the University at Buffalo; SUNY Buffalo
the University of Massachusetts Amherst; UMass Amherst

6.88 **En dashes and line breaks.** In printed publications, line breaks should generally be made after an en dash but not before, in the manner of hyphens. If possible, avoid carrying over a single character to the next line, as in a number range or score. In reflowable electronic formats, it is usually best to let the software determine such breaks. See also 7.36–48.

6.89 **En dash as em dash.** In contemporary British usage, an en dash (with space before and after) is usually preferred to the em dash as punctuation in running text – like this – a practice that is followed by some non-British publications as well. See also 6.91.

6.90 **En dash as minus sign.** The en dash is sometimes used as a minus sign, but minus signs and en dashes are distinct characters (defined by the Unicode standard as U+2212 and U+2013, respectively; see 10.70, 11.2). Both the characters themselves and the spacing around them may differ; moreover, substituting any character for another may hinder searches in electronic publications. Thus it is best to use the correct character, especially in mathematical copy.

## *Em Dashes*

6.91 **Em dashes instead of commas, parentheses, or colons.** The em dash, often simply called the dash, is the most commonly used and most versatile of the dashes. (In British usage, spaced en dashes are used in place of em dashes; see 6.89.) Em dashes are most often used to set off an amplifying or explanatory element. In that sense they can function as an alternative to parentheses (second and third examples below), commas (fourth and fifth examples), or a colon (first example)—especially when an abrupt break in thought is called for. An em dash can also be used in lieu of a period or semicolon, as in the sixth example.

It was a revival of the most potent image in modern democracy—the revolutionary idea.

The influence of three impressionists—Monet, Sisley, and Degas—is obvious in her work.

The chancellor—he had been awake half the night—came down in an angry mood.

She outlined the strategy—a strategy that would, she hoped, secure the peace.

My friends—that is, my former friends—ganged up on me.

The number of new cases has been declining—last week's daily average was the lowest since January.

To avoid confusion, the em dash should never be used within or immediately following another element set off by an em dash (or pair of em dashes); use parentheses or commas instead. (Except in dialogue—see 12.44—there should be no more than two em dashes in a sentence.)

The Whipplesworth conference—which had already been interrupted by three demonstrations (the last bordering on violence)—was adjourned promptly.

*or*

The Whipplesworth conference—which had already been interrupted by three demonstrations, the last bordering on violence—was adjourned promptly.

6.92 **Em dash between noun and pronoun.** An em dash is occasionally used to set off an introductory noun, or a series of nouns, from a pronoun that refers back to the noun or nouns and introduces the main clause.

Consensus—that was the will-o'-the-wisp he doggedly pursued.

Broken promises, petty rivalries, and false rumors—such were the obstacles she encountered.

6.93 **Em dashes for sudden breaks or interruptions.** An em dash or a pair of em dashes may indicate a sudden break in thought or sentence structure or an interruption in dialogue. (Where a faltering rather than sudden break is intended, an ellipsis may be used; see 6.15.)

"Will he—can he—obtain the necessary signatures?" asked Mill.

"Well, I don't know," I began tentatively. "I thought I might—"

"Might what?" she demanded.

For additional details and examples, see 12.42.

6.94 **Em dashes with "that is," "namely," "for example," and similar expressions.** An em dash may be used before expressions such as *that is* or *namely*. For examples, see 6.54; see also 6.62.

6.95 **Em dashes with other punctuation.** In modern usage, a question mark or an exclamation point—but never a comma, a colon, or a semicolon—may precede an em dash. A period may precede an em dash if it is part of an abbreviation (as in the third example below). A period (sometimes with a quotation mark) may also precede an em dash used before an attribution (as in the fourth example). See also 12.35, 13.54.

Without further warning—but what could we have done to dissuade her?—she left the plant, determined to stop the union in its tracks.
Only if—heaven forbid!—you lose your passport should you call home.
No one—at least not before 11:42 p.m.—could have predicted the outcome.
"We cannot all succeed when half of us are held back."—Malala Yousafzai

If the context calls for an em dash where a comma would ordinarily separate a dependent clause from an independent clause, the comma is omitted. Likewise, if an em dash is used at the end of quoted material to indicate an interruption (as in dialogue), the comma can be safely omitted before the words that identify the speaker (see also 6.93, 6.134).

Because the data had not been fully analyzed—let alone collated—the publication of the report was delayed.
"I assure you, we shall never—" Sylvia began, but Mark cut her short.

6.96 **Em dashes and line breaks.** In printed publications, line breaks should generally be made after an em dash but not before, in the manner of hyphens. Note, however, that a break should never be made between a dash and a closing quotation mark (or any other mark of punctuation) immediately following the dash (see also 6.93, 6.95). Nor should a break be made between a dash and a name or other entity that follows in an attribution. In reflowable electronic formats, however, it is usually best to let the software determine any such breaks. See also 7.36–48.

6.97 **Em dashes in lieu of quotation marks.** Em dashes are occasionally used instead of quotation marks to set off dialogue (à la writers in some European languages). Each speech starts a new paragraph. No space follows the dash.

—Will he obtain the necessary signatures?
—Of course he will!

6.98 **Em dashes in lists, indexes, and tables.** In informal settings, em dashes are sometimes used in the manner of bullet points in a vertical list (see 6.141). Such usage is best avoided in formal prose, though em dashes may sometimes be used in a similar manner to organize subentries in an index (see 15.27). In tables, an em dash may be used for an otherwise blank or empty data cell (see 3.68).

## *2-Em and 3-Em Dashes*

6.99 **2-em dash for omissions.** In a traditional usage long described in this manual, a 2-em dash (see also 6.79) represents a missing word or part of a word, either omitted to disguise a name or else missing from or illegible in quoted or reprinted material. When a whole word is missing, space appears on both sides of the dash. When only part of a word is missing, no space appears between the dash and the existing part (or parts) of the word; when the dash represents the end of a word, a space follows it (unless a period or other punctuation immediately follows). See also 7.69, 12.70.

"The region gives its —— to the language spoken there."
Admiral N—— and Lady R—— were among the guests.
David H——h [Hirsch?] voted aye.

A 2-em dash is sometimes also used in this way to avoid printing an expletive (as in quoted dialogue); asterisks, however, which can stand in for individual letters (thus making it clearer which word is meant), are generally more effective for this purpose. (Whether to disguise an expletive is usually up to the author, sometimes in consultation with a publisher. See also 12.4.)

"I don't give a f——," he answered.
*or, more precisely,*
"I don't give a f**k," he answered.

Although a 2-em dash sometimes represents material to be supplied, it should not be confused with a blank line to be filled in, which should normally appear as an underscore (e.g., ___). (In Unicode, the underscore character is known as a low line, or U+005F; see also 11.2.)

6.100 **3-em dash.** In a bibliography, a 3-em dash (see also 6.79) represents the same author(s) or editor(s) named in the preceding entry; in such usage, it is normally followed by a period (or, before *ed.* or the like, a comma).

Chaudhuri, Amit. *Odysseus Abroad*. Alfred A. Knopf, 2015.
———. *A Strange and Sublime Address*. Minerva, 1992.

It should be noted, however, that because 3-em dashes obscure important information and pose an obstacle to accessibility, this manual now recommends repeating the name(s) instead; see 13.72–73, 13.113.

## PARENTHESES

6.101 **Use of parentheses.** Parentheses—stronger than a comma and similar to the dash—are used to set off material from the surrounding text. (In British English, parentheses are also called round brackets, or brackets for short.) Like dashes but unlike commas, parentheses can set off text that has no grammatical relationship to the rest of the sentence, as in the fourth and sixth examples below.

He suspected that the noble gases (helium, neon, etc.) could produce a similar effect.

Intelligence tests (e.g., the Stanford–Binet) are no longer widely used.

Our final sample (collected under difficult conditions) contained an impurity.

Wexford's analysis (see chap. 3) is more to the point.

*Dichtung und Wahrheit* (also known as *Wahrheit und Dichtung*) has been translated as *Poetry and Truth* (or, as at least one edition has it, *Truth and Fiction*).

The disagreement between Johns and Evans (its origins have been discussed elsewhere) ultimately destroyed the organization.

For the use of parentheses as delimiters for letters or numbers in a list or outline, see 6.140, 6.143. For parenthetical references to a list of works cited, see 13.115–28. For parentheses in dialogue (where they should generally be avoided), see 12.52. For parenthetical references following quoted material, see 12.75–83. For parentheses in notes and bibliographies, see chapter 13. For parentheses in mathematics, see 6.108. For roman versus italic type, see 6.5.

6.102 **Parentheses for glosses or translations.** Parentheses are used to enclose glosses of unfamiliar terms or translations from other languages—or, if the term is given in English, to enclose the original word. In quoted matter, square brackets should be used (see 6.105). See also 7.55, 11.11.

A drop folio (a page number printed at the foot of a page) is useful on the opening page of a chapter.

The term you should use for 1,000,000,000 is *mil millones* (billion), not *billón* (trillion).

German has two terms for eating—one for the way humans eat (*essen*) and another for the way animals eat (*fressen*).

6.103 **Parentheses within parentheses.** Although the use of parentheses within parentheses (usually for bibliographic purposes) is permitted in some publications—especially in law—Chicago prefers square brackets within parentheses (see 6.107). (British style is to use parentheses within parentheses.) For parentheses in mathematics, see 6.108.

6.104 **Parentheses with other punctuation.** An opening parenthesis should be preceded by a comma or a semicolon (with a space in between) only in an enumeration (see 6.140); a closing parenthesis should never be preceded by a comma, a semicolon, or a colon. A question mark, an exclamation point, and closing quotation marks precede a closing parenthesis if they belong to the parenthetical matter; they follow it if they belong to the surrounding sentence. A period precedes the closing parenthesis if the entire sentence is in parentheses; otherwise it follows. (Avoid enclosing more than one sentence within another sentence; see 6.13.) Parentheses may appear back-to-back (with a space in between) if they enclose entirely unrelated material; sometimes, however, such material can be enclosed in a single set of parentheses, usually separated by a semicolon. See also table 6.1. For parentheses in source citations, see chapters 13 and 14.

Having entered (on tiptoe), we sat down on the nearest seats we could find.

Come on in (quietly, please!) and take a seat.

If *parenthesis* is Greek for the act of inserting, is it redundant to insert something in parentheses (i.e., in English)?

On display were the watchmakers' five latest creations (all of which Shellahan coveted).

Five new watches were on display. (Shellahan fancied the battery-powered quartz model.)

Strabo is probably referring to instruction (διδασκαλία) (Jones et al. 2024).

## BRACKETS AND BRACES

6.105 **Use of square brackets.** Square brackets (often simply called brackets) are used mainly to enclose material—usually added by someone other than the original writer—that does not form a part of the surrounding text. Specifically, in quoted matter, reprints, anthologies, and other nonoriginal material, brackets enclose editorial interpolations, explanations, translations of terms from other languages, or corrections. Sometimes the bracketed material replaces rather than amplifies the original word or words. For brackets in mathematical copy, see 6.108. See also 12.70–74.

"They [the free-silver Democrats] asserted that the ratio could be maintained."

"Many CF [cystic fibrosis] patients have been helped by the new therapy."

Satire, Jebb tells us, "is the only [form] that has a continuous development." [This was written before the discovery of the Driscoll manuscript.—Ed.]

If quoted matter already includes brackets of its own, the editor should so state in the source citation (e.g., "brackets in the original"); see 12.73 for an analogous situation with italics.

6.106 **Square brackets in translated text.** In a translated work, square brackets are sometimes used to enclose a word or phrase in the original language. (Translators should use this device sparingly.) If quoted matter already includes brackets of its own, the editor should so state in a note or elsewhere (see also 6.105).

The differences between society [*Gesellschaft*] and community [*Gemeinschaft*] will now be analyzed.

6.107 **Square brackets for parentheses within parentheses.** Chicago prefers square brackets as parentheses within parentheses, usually for bibliographic purposes. For mathematical groupings, see 6.108.

(For further discussion see Richardson's excellent analysis [1999] and Danneberger's survey [2000].)

6.108 **Parentheses and brackets in mathematics.** Parentheses and brackets are used as common delimiters in mathematical expressions. The order, which extends to braces (see 6.111), is as follows: {[( )]}. In displayed expressions, the sequence can be extended when necessary by large parentheses, brackets, and braces (in that order).

$$\Bigg\{\Bigg[\Bigg(\{[(\quad)]\}\Bigg)\Bigg]\Bigg\}$$

In running text, braces are sometimes omitted from this sequence. Mathematical angle brackets ⟨ ⟩, vertical bars | |, and double vertical bars || || carry special mathematical significance and should not be used to supplement the sequence of common delimiters.

6.109 **Square brackets in phonetics.** Square brackets may be used to enclose a phonetic transcription (e.g., using the International Phonetic Alphabet). For a similar use for slashes, see 6.119.

The verb *entretenir* [ɑ̃tʀət(ə)niʀ], like *keep*, is used in many idioms.

6.110 **Square brackets with other punctuation.** For brackets with other punctuation, most of the same principles apply as for parentheses (see 6.104).

For their use in enclosing editorial interpolations, however, the appearance of other punctuation and its position relative to the brackets may depend on the source. In the first example below, the comma after "Dear Jacob" is part of the missing greeting that the editor is interpolating (see also 12.67). In most cases, however, material added in brackets should be treated as if it were in parentheses. See also 14.44.

The original letter, the transcription of which was incomplete, probably read as follows: "[Dear Jacob,] It's been seventy years since I last set eyes on you [. . .]"

The report was unambiguous: "The scholars fled Ithaca [New York] and drove south."

*not*

The report was unambiguous: "The scholars fled Ithaca[, New York,] and drove south."

6.111 **Angle brackets and braces.** The term *angle brackets* is used here to denote the mathematical symbols for less than (<) and greater than (>) paired to work as delimiters (<. . .>). (True mathematical angle brackets, ⟨ and ⟩, not readily available in all typefaces, are reserved for mathematical notation.) Angle brackets are most often used to enclose tags in XML and related markup languages (see 2.88). By extension, some manuscript editors use angle brackets—unlikely to appear elsewhere in a typical word-processed manuscript—to enclose generic instructions for typesetting (see 2.86). Although angle brackets are sometimes used to set off URLs and email addresses (e.g., in message headers in email applications), this practice is unnecessary in regular prose. Angle brackets are also occasionally used instead of brackets in textual studies to indicate missing or illegible material (see 6.105). Braces, { }, also called curly brackets, provide yet another option for enclosing data and are used in various ways in certain programming languages. They are also used in mathematical and other specialized writing (see, e.g., 6.108). Braces are not interchangeable with parentheses or brackets. See the example phrases throughout chapter 5 for one possible use of braces.

## SLASHES

6.112 **Other names for the slash.** The slash (/)—also known as a virgule, solidus, slant, or forward slash, to distinguish it from a backward slash, or backslash (\)—has various distinct uses. For a discussion of the niceties associated with the various terms, see Richard Eckersley et al., *Glossary of Typesetting Terms* (bibliog. 2.8).

6.113 **Slashes to signify alternatives.** A slash most commonly signifies alternatives. In certain contexts it is a convenient (if somewhat informal) shorthand for *or*. It is also used for alternative spellings or names. When at least one of the terms on either side of the slash is an open compound, a space before and after the slash can make the text more legible (but may be omitted when space is tight, as in a table).

my/your
and/or
Hercules/Heracles
Margaret/Meg/Maggie
World War I / First World War

Occasionally a slash can include the sense of *and*—while still also conveying a sense of alternatives (but see 6.114). (Note that in most cases a hyphen is the better choice for *and*—e.g., "mother-daughter friendship.")

an insertion/deletion mutation (a mutation with insertions or deletions or both)
an MD/PhD program (a program that offers one or both of these degrees)
a Jekyll/Hyde personality (a personality that includes the two alternating traits)
24/7 *or* twenty-four seven (with no slash in the spelled-out form; twenty-four hours a day and seven days a week)

6.114 **Slashes with two-year spans.** A slash is sometimes used in dates instead of an en dash (see 6.83), or in some cases in combination with an en dash, to indicate the last part of one year and the first part of the next. See also 9.66.

The winter of 1966/67 was especially severe.
Enrollment increased between 2020/21 and 2023/24.
The fiscal years 2005/6–2009/10 were encouraging in one or two respects.

6.115 **Slashes with dates.** Slashes (or periods or hyphens) are used informally in all-numeral dates (e.g., 3/10/02), but this device should be avoided in formal writing and wherever clarity is essential (in the United States the month usually comes first, but elsewhere it is more common for the day to come first). If an all-numeral format must be used, use the ISO standard date format (year, month, day, in the form YYYY-MM-DD; see 9.38).

6.116 **Slashes in abbreviations.** A slash may stand as shorthand for *per*, as in "110 km/s," "$450/week," or, in certain abbreviations, in lieu of periods, as in "c/o" (in care of) or "n/a" (not applicable; see also 3.68).

**6.117** **Slashes as fraction bars.** A slash can be used to mean "divided by" when a fraction bar is inappropriate or impractical. When available, single-glyph fractions may be used (e.g., ½ *rather than* 1/2). See also 9.17.

**6.118** **Slashes to show line breaks in quoted poetry.** When two or more lines of poetry are quoted in regular text, slashes with space on each side are used to show line breaks. See also 12.29.

> "Thou hast not missed one thought that could be fit, / And all that was improper dost omit."

**6.119** **Slashes for pronunciations.** Like square brackets (see 6.109), slashes may be used to enclose a transcription representing the sound of a word or a letter. Though slashes and brackets are often used interchangeably in this role, some authors will distinguish between brackets for *phonetic* transcriptions (recording exact pronunciation in varying levels of detail) and slashes for *phonemic* transcriptions (which record sounds more generally, without accounting for contextual variations).

> The /p/ in /pet/ is not quite the same sound as the /p/ in /ˈspe-shəl/.

Note the short vertical line in /ˈspe-shəl/, which is defined by Unicode as "modifier letter vertical line" (U+02C8) and is used to mark a stressed syllable (see also 11.2).

**6.120** **Slashes in URLs and other paths.** Slashes separate directories and file names in URLs and other paths. Spaces are never used in such contexts. In publications with fixed layouts (as in print or PDF), a line break should be made before such a slash but not between two slashes (see 7.47). Some operating systems use backward slashes (or backslashes, \) or colons rather than, or in addition to, slashes. See also 13.12.

> https://www.chicagomanualofstyle.org/help.html

Note that a URL that ends in a file name (like "help.html" in the example above) will not end in a slash. A URL that does not end in a file name, on the other hand, often will include a trailing slash, especially when the URL has been copied and pasted from a browser's address bar—for example, https://www.nytimes.com/ (for the home page of *The New York Times*). Though a URL will often lead to its intended destination without this trailing slash (and will always do so for a home page), there is no need to delete it. If it is deleted for any reason, the edited URL must be checked to make sure it still works as intended.

6.121 **Slashes and line breaks.** In printed publications, where slashes are used to signify alternative terms, a line break should be made after the slash, never before. If possible, avoid carrying over a single character to the next line, as in an expression signifying a two-year span. Fractions should not be broken at the end of a line. If a slash is used to show where a line break occurs in poetry, a break can be made either after or before the slash. For URLs, a line break should be made before a slash (but after a double slash; see 7.47). In reflowable electronic formats, it is usually best to let the software determine such breaks.

## QUOTATION MARKS

6.122 **Quotation marks relative to other punctuation and text.** For the location of closing quotation marks in relation to other punctuation, see 6.9–11. For the use of quotation marks with a comma, see 6.43; with a colon, 6.69; with a question mark, 6.74; with an exclamation point, 6.78. For a full discussion of quotation marks with dialogue and quoted matter, see chapter 12. For the use of quotation marks with single words or phrases to signal some special usage, see 7.60, 7.63, 7.66. For quotation marks in French, see 11.32, 11.33; in German, 11.44; in Italian, 11.54; in Spanish, 11.70. For quotation marks with titles of certain types of works, see the examples in chapter 8.

6.123 **"Smart" quotation marks.** Published works should use directional (or "smart") quotation marks, also known as typographer's or curly quotation marks. These marks, which are available in any modern word processor, generally match the look of commas in the same typeface (but raised and, for the opening marks, inverted). For a variety of reasons, including the limitations of typewriter-based keyboards and of certain software programs, these marks are often rendered incorrectly. Care must be taken that the proper mark—left or right, as the case may be—has been used in each instance. All software includes a default quotation mark ("); in published prose this unidirectional mark, though far more portable than typographer's marks, signals a lack of typographical sophistication. Proper directional characters should also be used for single quotation marks (‘ ’). Neither the default apostrophe (') nor the grave accent character (`), the latter of which shares a key with the tilde (~) on standard US QWERTY keyboards, should be used in their place. The four directional quotation marks and their hexadecimal code points for Unicode are listed below (see also 6.125, 11.2).

| *Character* | *Unicode number* | *Description* |
|---|---|---|
| “ | 201C | left double quotation mark |
| ” | 201D | right double quotation mark |
| ‘ | 2018 | left single quotation mark |
| ’ | 2019 | right single quotation mark or apostrophe |

## APOSTROPHES

6.124 **Use of the apostrophe.** The apostrophe has three main uses: to indicate the possessive case, to stand in for missing letters or numerals, and—in rare instances—to form the plural of certain expressions. For more on the possessive case, see 5.22, 7.16–29. For contractions, see 7.30. For plurals, see 7.5–15—especially 7.15.

6.125 **“Smart” apostrophes.** Published works should use directional (or “smart”) apostrophes. In most typefaces, this mark will appear as a raised (but not inverted) comma. The apostrophe is the same character as the right single quotation mark (defined for Unicode as U+2019; see 6.123). Owing to the limitations of conventional keyboards and many software programs, the apostrophe continues to be one of the most abused marks in punctuation. There are two common pitfalls: using the “default” unidirectional mark ('), on the one hand, and using the left single quotation mark, on the other. The latter usage in particular should always be construed as an error. Some software programs automatically turn a typed apostrophe at the beginning of a word into a left single quotation mark; authors and editors need to be vigilant in overriding such automation to produce the correct mark, and typesetters need to take care not to introduce errors of their own. (If necessary, consult your software’s help documentation or special characters menu.)

We spent the ’90s (*not* ‘90s) in thrall to our gadgets.
Where’d you get ’em (*not* ‘em)?
I love rock ’n’ roll (*not* rock ‘n’ roll).

6.126 **Apostrophes relative to other punctuation.** An apostrophe (’) is considered part of the word (or number) in which it appears. An apostrophe should not be confused with a single closing quotation mark; when a word ends in an apostrophe, no period or comma should intervene between the word and the apostrophe.

The last car in the lot was the Smiths’.

## SPACES

6.127 **Use of the space.** The spaces that occur between words and other elements in running text and elsewhere are not examples of punctuation per se, but they play a supporting role. The primary use of the space is as a separator—for example, between words and between sentences (see 6.7) or between a numeral and a unit of measure (see 10.55). Spaces come in different widths (see 6.128), and nonbreaking spaces can be used to control breaks at the end of a line (see 6.129). For a list of spaces, with Unicode numbers, see table 6.2. For other uses of the space, consult the index.

6.128 **Spaces with different widths.** The regular type of space that is added to a line of text with the space bar is the one used in almost all contexts (it is the space that occurs between the words and sentences in this paragraph and almost everywhere else in this manual). This type of space (also called a word space) varies in width when a line is justified to the left and right margins. In addition, there are a number of spaces with fixed widths, based on the spaces that typesetters have been using

TABLE 6.2. Spaces, with definitions and Unicode numbers

| Name | Unicode number | Description |
|---|---|---|
| space (*or* word space) | 0020 | The space you get by pressing the space bar; varies in width in fully justified text |
| no-break space | 00A0 | The nonbreaking version of the word space |
| narrow no-break space | 202F | A narrower, fixed-width version of the no-break space |
| em space | 2003 | About the width of an em dash (—) |
| en space | 2002 | About the width of an en dash (–), or half as wide as an em space |
| three-per-em space | 2004 | A third of the width of an em space; also called a thick space |
| four-per-em space | 2005 | A fourth of the width of an em space; also called a mid space |
| thin space | 2009 | A fifth (or sometimes a sixth) of the width of an em space |
| six-per-em space | 2006 | A sixth of the width of an em space |
| hair space | 200A | Thinner than a thin space |
| zero width space | 200B | Has no width; useful for facilitating line breaks (e.g., in URLs) |
| figure space | 2007 | A nonbreaking space equal to the width of a tabular (monospaced) digit |
| punctuation space | 2008 | About the width of a period, colon, or exclamation point |

for centuries. En spaces and em spaces, which are wider than regular spaces, approximate the width of en dashes and em dashes in a particular font (see 6.79). Em spaces are sometimes used as a design element, as between a figure number and caption (see 3.23). A nonbreaking thin space or hair space may be used between contiguous single and double quotation marks (see 6.11). These fixed-width spaces are usually applied by a professional typesetter, and only for material intended for print or PDF. Though each is defined for Unicode (see 11.2), most are designed to allow breaks at the ends of lines in HTML and related formats, where they should be used with caution, if at all (cf. 6.129). For tabs and indents, see 2.14.

**6.129** **Nonbreaking spaces.** A regular nonbreaking space, readily available in word processors and page-layout programs, can be used to prevent certain elements that contain spaces from breaking over a line. These include the spaced ellipses preferred by Chicago (see 12.59) and numerals that use spaces rather than commas as separators (see 9.57, 9.58). Nonbreaking spaces can also be used to prevent a numeral from being separated from an abbreviated unit of measure (e.g., 11.5 km) or to prevent a break between initials in a name like E. B. White. The nonbreaking space is defined for Unicode (as the "no-break space," U+00A0; see also 11.2) and is widely supported in electronic publication formats. (Though authors may apply such nonbreaking spaces, they are generally the responsibility of either the manuscript editor or the publisher.) This space, like the space bar (or word) space, is designed to vary in width in HTML and related formats when a line is justified to the left and right margins; when a nonbreaking space with a fixed width is needed instead, the narrow no-break space (U+202F) may be used (as between single and double quotation marks; see 6.11). Thin spaces and other fixed-width spaces (with the exception of the figure space, U+2007, equivalent to the width of a fixed-width, or tabular, digit) are designed to allow end-of-line breaks in HTML and related formats. For print and PDF, however, any of these spaces can usually be defined as nonbreaking using a page-layout or similar program (see 6.128).

**6.130** **Spaces in mathematical expressions.** A space is normally used before and after a sign denoting a binary mathematical operation or relation, as if such signs were words. (Signs for binary operations, including plus and minus signs, act as conjunctions; signs for binary relations, including equals signs and signs for greater than and less than, act as verbs.) Spaces are also used before and after symbols denoting integration, summation, or union (as in the second example below).

$x^n + y^n = z^n$
$X \cup \emptyset = X$

However, no space precedes or follows an operation or relation sign in a subscript or superscript.

$x^{a+b}$
$y^{c-2}$

And no space follows a binary operation or relation sign when it is modifying a number or symbol (i.e., used as an adjective).

$-1$
$+\infty$
$\times 5$
$>7$

For breaking a mathematical expression at the end of a line, see 7.45. For italics for variables, see 7.73. For more detailed information, see the *ACS Guide to Scholarly Communication* or Ellen Swanson's *Mathematics into Type*, among other resources (bibliog. 2.4).

## MULTIPLE PUNCTUATION MARKS

6.131 **Likely combinations for multiple punctuation marks.** The use of more than one mark of punctuation at the same location usually involves quotation marks, em dashes, parentheses, or brackets in combination with periods, commas, colons, semicolons, question marks, or exclamation points. For quotation marks see 6.9–11, 6.43, 6.69, 6.74, 6.78. For em dashes see 6.95, 6.100. For parentheses and brackets see 6.91, 6.103, 6.104, 6.107, 6.110, 6.140. For ellipses see 12.59–69. See also table 6.1.

6.132 **Abbreviation-ending periods with other punctuation.** When an abbreviation or other expression that ends with a period occurs at the end of a sentence, no additional period follows (see 6.14). However, when any other mark of punctuation is needed immediately after the period (as after "al." in the second example below), both the period and the additional mark appear (see also 6.9, 6.13).

The study was funded by Mulvehill & Co.
Johnson et al., in *How to Survive*, describe such an ordeal.

6.133 **Periods with question marks or exclamation points.** A period (aside from an abbreviating period; see 6.132) never accompanies a question mark or an exclamation point. The latter two marks, being stronger, take precedence over the period. This principle continues to apply when the question mark or exclamation point is part of the title of a work, as in the final example below (cf. 6.134). See also 6.2.

Their first question was a hard one: "Who is willing to trade oil for water?"
What did she mean when she said, "The foot now wears a different shoe"?
We ended up watching *What Ever Happened to Baby Jane?*

6.134 **Commas with question marks or exclamation points.** When a question mark or exclamation point appears at the end of a quotation where a comma would normally appear, as in quoted speech or dialogue, the comma is omitted (as in the first example below; see also 6.45). A comma may be retained as needed, however, in two contexts: (1) after the title of a work that ends in a question mark or exclamation point (as in the second and third examples) and (2) after a quotation *not* presented as speech or dialogue (as in the fourth example). These two exceptions (the second one is new to this edition of the manual) will help to maintain clarity—especially apparent in the penultimate example, where the comma after *Help!* separates it from the following title. (The occasional awkward result may require rewording.) Compare 6.133. See also 13.98.

"Are you a doctor?" asked Mahmoud.
*but*
"Are You a Doctor?," the fifth story in *Will You Please Be Quiet, Please?*, treats modern love.
All the band's soundtrack albums—*A Hard Day's Night*, *Help!*, *Yellow Submarine*, and *Magical Mystery Tour*—were popular.
The third Smart Reply option, "Yes, please!," was clearly the best one.

6.135 **Question mark with exclamation point.** In the rare case of a question or exclamation ending with a title or quotation that ends in a question mark or exclamation point, include both marks only if they are different and the sentence punctuation seems essential (as in the first three examples below). Though it would be strictly logical to retain both marks when they are the same (as in the third through fifth examples), retaining only the first one is likely to prevent confusion.

Have you seen *Help!*?
Who shouted, "Long live the king!"?
I just love *Who's Afraid of Virginia Woolf?*!

*but*
Who starred opposite Richard Burton in *Who's Afraid of Virginia Woolf?*
Who wrote "Are You a Doctor?"
Where were you when you asked, "Why so blue?"
*not*
Who starred opposite Richard Burton in *Who's Afraid of Virginia Woolf?*?

A question mark is sometimes used in combination with an exclamation point to express excitement or disbelief (usually ?! but sometimes !?), a practice that is best avoided in formal prose; see also 6.76.

6.136 **Question mark or colon?** When a question introduces a list, a question mark usually takes precedence over a colon. A colon may be retained, however, if the list is presented as part of a sentence.

Which of the following colors do you like best?

- red
- blue
- yellow

*but*

Which color do you like best: red, blue, or yellow?

6.137 **Punctuation with emojis.** Though they are not normally appropriate in formal prose, emojis are increasingly common in fiction and other forms of creative writing. (The plural *emoji* is strictly correct, but *emojis* has become more common in English.) In general, a single emoji can be treated like a word, with a space before and after except when a comma, period, or similar mark of sentence punctuation immediately follows the emoji or when the emoji immediately follows an opening quotation mark or parenthesis or a dash. When an emoji at the end of a sentence applies to the sentence as a whole, it follows the period or other final mark of punctuation (usually with an intervening space). In the case of two or more consecutive emojis, no space appears between them. Usage varies widely, however, so editors should query before making any wholesale changes. See also 10.78.

You want me to do what now? 👀 No thanks.
I'd like to believe we were facing reality 🧐, but it was more like 🙈🙉🙊.
He gave me a big 😊 and told me to turn the page 👉. So I did.

Emoticons, which are expressed with punctuation marks and other keyboard characters, may be treated similarly. :)

## LISTS AND OUTLINE STYLE

6.138 **Lists and outlines — general principles.** Items in a list should consist of parallel elements. Unless introductory numerals or letters serve a purpose—to indicate the order in which tasks should be done, to suggest chronology or relative importance among the items, to facilitate text references, or, in a run-in list, to clearly separate the items—they may be omitted. Where similar lists are fairly close together, consistent treatment is essential. Note that the advice in this section applies primarily to lists that occur in the text. For lists of illustrations and tables, see 1.44; for lists of abbreviations, see 1.49; for glossaries, see 1.68; for indexes, see chapter 15.

6.139 **Run-in versus vertical lists.** Lists may be either run in to the text or set vertically. Short, simple lists are usually better run in, especially if the introductory text and the items in the list together form a sentence (see 6.140). Lists that require typographic prominence, that are relatively long, or that contain multiple levels (see 6.143) should be set vertically.

6.140 **Run-in lists.** If numerals or letters are used to mark the divisions in a run-in list, enclose them in parentheses. If letters are used, they are sometimes italicized (within roman parentheses; see 6.5). If the introductory material forms a grammatically complete sentence, a colon should precede the first parenthesis (see also 6.65, 6.68, 6.71). The items are separated by commas unless any of the items requires internal commas, in which case all the items will usually need to be separated by semicolons (see 6.64). When each item in a list consists of a complete sentence or several sentences, the list is best set vertically (see 6.141).

The qualifications are as follows: a doctorate in physics, five years' experience in a national laboratory, and an ability to communicate technical matter to a lay audience.

Compose three sentences to illustrate analogous uses of (1) commas, (2) em dashes, and (3) parentheses.

For the duration of the experiment, the dieters were instructed to avoid (a) meat, (b) bottled drinks, (c) packaged foods, and (d) nicotine.

Data are available on three groups of counsel: (1) the public defender of Cook County, (2) the member attorneys of the Chicago Bar Association's Defense of Prisoners Committee, and (3) all other attorneys.

You are advised to pack the following items: (*a*) warm, sturdy outer clothing and enough underwear to last ten days; (*b*) two pairs of boots, two pairs of sneakers, and plenty of socks; and (*c*) three durable paperback novels.

6.141 **Vertical lists — capitalization, punctuation, and format.** A vertical list is best introduced by a grammatically complete sentence, followed by a colon (but see 6.142). There are two basic types of lists: (1) unordered, in which the items are introduced by a bullet or other such marker or by nothing at all, and (2) ordered, in which items are introduced by numbers or letters. In unordered lists, unless the items consist of complete sentences, each item carries no end punctuation and each can usually begin lowercase (except for proper nouns and other terms that normally begin with a capital letter). For lists whose items require more prominence, capitalization may instead be preferred; choose one approach and follow it consistently. If items run over to one or more new lines, the runover lines are usually assigned a hanging indent (see 2.14). (An alternative to indenting runover lines is to insert extra space between the items.)

Your application must include the following documents:

a full résumé
three letters of recommendation
all your diplomas, from high school to graduate school
a brief essay indicating why you want the position and why you consider yourself qualified for it
two forms of identification

To avoid long, skinny lists, short items may be arranged in two or more columns.

An administrative facility can be judged by eight measures:

| | |
|---|---|
| image | quality |
| security | functional organization |
| access | design efficiency |
| flexibility | environmental systems |

Each of these measures is discussed below.

If the items are ordered with numerals (see also 6.138), a period follows the numeral. If letters are used, they are enclosed in parentheses (as described in 6.140). It is customary to capitalize items in an ordered list even if the items do not consist of complete sentences (but see 6.142). Closing punctuation is used only if items consist of complete sentences. For the use of Roman numerals and letters, see 6.143.

Compose three sentences:

1. To illustrate the use of commas in dates
2. To distinguish the use of semicolons from the use of periods
3. To illustrate the use of parentheses within dashes

In a numbered list, runover lines are aligned with the first word following the numeral; a tab, added automatically by the list feature in word-processing and page-layout programs, usually separates the number from the text of the list (see also 2.25).

To change the date display from "31" to "1" on the day following the last day of a thirty-day month, the following steps are recommended:

1. Pull the stem out past the date-setting position to the time-setting position.
2. Make a mental note of the exact minute (but see step 4).
3. Turn the stem repeatedly in a clockwise direction through twenty-four hours.
4. If you are able to consult the correct time, adjust the minute hand accordingly and press the stem all the way in on the exact second. If you are not able to consult the correct time, settle on a minute or so past the time noted in step 2.

Bulleted lists are usually formatted in the same way as numbered lists.

Use the Control Panel to make changes to your computer:

- To uninstall or repair a program or to change how it runs, go to Programs, and then choose Programs and Features.
- To adjust the resolution displayed by your monitor, go to Appearance and Personalization, and then choose Display. (Lowering the resolution will increase the size of images on the screen.)
- To add a language other than English or to change handwriting options, go to Clock, Language, and Region, and then choose Language.

If none of the items in a bulleted list consist of complete sentences, however, each item can usually begin lowercase (except for proper nouns). For bulleted lists whose items require more prominence, capitalization may instead be preferred (as throughout this manual); choose one approach and follow it consistently.

The style sheet allows for two types of lists:

- ordered lists, marked with numbers or letters
- unordered lists, marked by bullets or other ornaments (or unmarked)

Sometimes list format may not be the best choice. For example, when items in a list consist of very long sentences, or of several sentences, and the list itself does not require typographic prominence, the items may be formatted like regular paragraphs of text, each paragraph beginning with a number (and formatted with a first-line paragraph indent) and punctuated as normal prose (see also 2.15). When a list consists of a mix of complete and incomplete sentences, revise the items to make them consistent (e.g., by recasting the fragments as complete sentences); if this is not possible, consider working the items into the text instead of presenting them in a list. (If such a list must be presented as is, each item should end in a period or other final mark, whether it consists of a complete sentence or not.)

6.142 **Vertical lists punctuated as a sentence.** If the items in a vertical list complete a sentence begun in the introductory text, semicolons or commas may be used between the items, and a period should follow the final item. (If the items include internal punctuation, semicolons are preferred; see also 6.64.) Each item begins with a lowercase letter, even if the list is a numbered list (cf. 6.141). A conjunction (*and* or *or*) before the final item is optional. Such lists, often better run in to the text, should be set vertically only if the context demands that they be highlighted.

Reporting for the Development Committee, Jobson reported that

1. a fundraising campaign director was being sought;
2. the salary for this director, about $150,000 a year, would be paid out of campaign funds; and
3. the fundraising campaign would be launched in the spring of 2024.

In the case of an unnumbered or bulleted list, the punctuation and capitalization would remain the same as in the example above.

6.143 **Vertical lists with multiple levels (outlines).** Where items in a numbered list are subdivided (i.e., into a multilevel list, also called an outline), both numerals and letters may be used. Any runover lines should be aligned with the first word following the numeral or letter; a tab usually separates the number or letter from the text of the list (see also 2.25).

Applicants will be tested for their skills in the following areas:

1. Punctuation
   a. Using commas appropriately
   b. Deleting unnecessary quotation marks
   c. Distinguishing colons from semicolons
2. Spelling
   a. Using a dictionary appropriately
   b. Recognizing homonyms
   c. Hyphenating correctly
3. Syntax
   a. Matching verb to subject
   b. Recognizing and eliminating misplaced modifiers
   c. Distinguishing phrases from clauses while singing the "Conjunction Junction" song

In the following example, note that the numerals and letters denoting the top three levels are set off by periods and those for the lower four by single or double parentheses, thus distinguishing all seven levels by punctuation as well as indentation. Note also that numerals of more than one digit are aligned vertically on the last digit.

I. Historical introduction
II. Dentition in various groups of vertebrates
    A. Reptilia
        1. Histology and development of reptilian teeth
        2. Survey of forms
    B. Mammalia
        1. Histology and development of mammalian teeth
        2. Survey of forms
            a) Primates
                (1) Lemuroidea
                (2) Anthropoidea
                    (a) Platyrrhini
                    (b) Catarrhini
                        i) Cercopithecidae
                        ii) Pongidae
            b) Carnivora
                (1) Creodonta
                (2) Fissipedia
                    (a) Ailuroidea
                    (b) Arctoidea
                (3) Pinnipedia
            c) Etc. . . .

In a list with fewer levels, one might dispense with capital Roman numerals and capital letters and instead begin with Arabic numerals. What is important is that readers see at a glance the level to which each item belongs. Note that each division and subdivision should normally contain at least two items.

# 7 Spelling, Distinctive Treatment of Words, and Compounds

## OVERVIEW

7.1 **Recommended dictionaries.** For spelling, Chicago prefers the first-listed entries in the *Merriam-Webster Dictionary* at Merriam-Webster.com, referred to throughout this manual as *Merriam-Webster* (see also 7.2). That dictionary, originally based on the printed *Merriam-Webster's Collegiate Dictionary* (11th ed., 2003), carries the name *Collegiate Dictionary* on some platforms. Whenever possible, refer to the larger and more frequently updated online dictionary rather than its printed counterpart. For words not found at Merriam-Webster.com, refer to *Merriam-Webster Unabridged* (the ongoing online update to *Webster's Third New International Dictionary*). If, as occasionally happens, the dictionary at Merriam-Webster.com disagrees with *Merriam-Webster Unabridged*, the more frequently updated entries at Merriam-Webster.com should be followed. For further definitions or alternative spellings, refer to another standard dictionary such as Dictionary.com, which is based on the *Random House Unabridged Dictionary* (and supplemented by other sources). At least for spelling, one source should be used consistently throughout a single work. (For full bibliographic information on these and other English dictionaries, including Canadian, British, and Australian references, see bibliog. 3.1.)

7.2 **Variant spellings.** *Merriam-Webster* lists two main kinds of variants: equal and secondary. Equal variants are separated by *or*; secondary variants follow *also*, with multiple secondary variants joined by *or*. (Other types of variants carry specific labels, such as *or less commonly* and *chiefly British*.) For spelling, Chicago advises choosing the first-listed term, even in the case of equal variants, with two notable exceptions: First, an author's preference for a discipline-specific usage should be respected. For example, *archeology*, though it is a second-listed equal variant of *archaeology*, is the spelling preferred by certain specialists. Second, an author's stated preference for a variant spelling that reflects its origins in a language other than English should also be respected. For example, though *Hawaii* is listed first in *Merriam-Webster*, the equal variant *Hawaiʻi*—with a glottal stop known as an *ʻokina*—may be preferred by some authors for its fidelity to the Hawaiian language (see also 11.77). Note that this advice applies only to words used in English and listed in *Merriam-Webster* (or another English-language dictionary). To use another example, the spelling *crepe* is listed first in *Merriam-Webster* and would be Chicago's preference in English, but the second-listed *crêpe* (with a circumflex over the *e*, reflecting how the word is spelled in French) should be used not only when an author prefers it (assuming a publisher's house style allows for such flexibility) but also whenever the French word is needed (see also 11.40). See also 7.3.

7.3 **Non-US spelling.** In English-language works by non-US authors that are edited and produced in the United States, editors at Chicago generally change spelling used in other English-speaking countries to American spelling (e.g., *colour* to *color*, *analyse* to *analyze*). Since consistency is more easily maintained by this practice, few authors object. In quoted material, however, spelling is left unchanged (see 12.7).

7.4 **Supplementing the dictionary.** Much of this chapter is devoted to matters not easily found in most dictionaries: how to form the plural and possessive forms of certain nouns and compounds; how to break words at the end of a printed line, especially those that are not listed in the dictionary; when to use capitals, italics, or quotation marks for distinctive treatment of words and phrases; and, perhaps most important but placed at the end of the chapter for easy reference (7.96), when to use hyphens with compound words, prefixes, and suffixes.

## PLURALS

7.5 **Standard plural forms.** Most nouns form their plural by adding *s* or—if they end in *ch*, *j*, *s*, *sh*, *x*, or *z*—by adding *es*. Most English speakers will not need help with such plural forms as *thumbs*, *churches*, *fixes*, or *boys*, and these are not listed in standard dictionary entries, including those in *Merriam-Webster*. (All inflected forms are listed in *Merriam-Webster Unabridged*, and any dictionary published online will generally accommodate the correct plural forms in searches. See also 7.1.) Like most dictionaries, *Merriam-Webster* does give the plural forms of words ending in *y* that change to *ies* (*baby* etc.); words ending in *o* (*ratio*, *potato*, etc.); certain words of Latin or Greek origin, such as *crocus*, *datum*, and *alumna*; and all words with irregular plurals (*child*, *leaf*, etc.).

7.6 **Alternative plural forms.** Where *Merriam-Webster* gives two forms of the plural—whether as primary and secondary variants, like *zeros* and *zeroes*, or as equal variants, like *millennia* and *millenniums*—Chicago normally opts for the first. In some cases, however, different forms of the plural are used for different purposes. A book may have two *indexes* and a mathematical expression two *indices*, as indicated in the *Merriam-Webster* entry for *index*.

7.7 **Plurals of compound nouns.** *Merriam-Webster* gives the plural form of most compounds that are tricky (*fathers-in-law, coups d'état, courts-martial, chefs d'oeuvre*, etc.). For those not listed, common sense can usually provide the answer.

bachelors of science
masters of arts
spheres of influence
child laborers

7.8 **Plurals for centuries.** The plural is normally used to refer to more than one century when the ordinals (or other modifiers) are joined by *and*; the plural is also used for ranges expressed with *through*. For ranges expressed with *to* or for alternatives expressed with *or* or *nor*, use the singular. Also use the singular in compound modifiers (as in the last example below; see also 7.95).

the eighteenth and early nineteenth centuries
in the fifth through eighth centuries
*but*
from the twentieth to the twenty-first century
as of the fifth or sixth century
eighteenth- and nineteenth-century technologies

7.9 **Plurals of proper nouns.** Names of persons and other capitalized nouns normally form the plural by adding *s* or *es*. Exceptions, including the last example below, are generally listed in *Merriam-Webster* (whose entry for *Romani*, formerly *Romany*, now a second-listed equal variant, was updated after the last edition of this manual was published; see also 7.10).

Tom, Dick, and Harry; *pl.* Toms, Dicks, and Harrys
the Jones family, *pl.* the Joneses
the Martinez family, *pl.* the Martinezes
the Bruno family, *pl.* the Brunos
Sunday, *pl.* Sundays
Germany, *pl.* Germanys
Pakistani, *pl.* Pakistanis
*but*
Romani, *pl.* Romani

An apostrophe is never used to form the plural of a family name: "The Smiths live here" (*not* "Smith's"). For the apostrophe in the possessive form of proper nouns, see 7.17.

7.10 **Plural form for names of Indigenous groups.** For the plurals of names of Indigenous groups, including Native American groups, Chicago usually defers to the first-listed form in *Merriam-Webster*, in the absence of any overriding preference of the author or publisher. For names not found there, or for additional guidance, check an up-to-date encyclopedia or other trusted resource (such as a website sponsored by the Indigenous group in question) or, unless the author or publisher has a preference, opt for consistency with other such names mentioned in the text. Note that some groups, when referring to themselves, do not include a definite article; when in doubt, retain the *the* but follow the name with *people* or *Nation* (usually capitalized) or whatever applies. See also 8.39.

the Hopi people (*or* the Hopi) of northeastern Arizona; the Hopi Tribe (a sovereign nation)
the Iroquoian language spoken by the Cherokee people (*or* the Cherokee); the Cherokee Nation
the Māori people (*or* the Māori)
the Haudenosaunee (*also known as* the Iroquois *or* the Iroquois Confederacy); the languages of the Haudenosaunee; the nations of the Haudenosaunee; the Seneca and Cayuga Nations

7.11 **Singular form used for the plural.** Names ending in an unpronounced *s* or *x* are best left in the singular form.

the seventeen Louis of France
the two Dumas, father and son
two Charlevoix (*or, better,* two towns called Charlevoix)
The class included three Margaux. (*but* two Felixes)

Occasionally, a name ending in a pronounced *s* may also be left in the singular, subject to editorial discretion (e.g., "three Mercedes"). Compare 7.9.

7.12 **Plural form of italicized words.** If an italicized term such as the title of a newspaper or book or a word used as a word must be written in the plural, the *s* is normally set in roman. A title already in plural form, however, may be left unchanged. In case of doubt, avoid the plural by rephrasing.

two *Chicago Tribune*s and three *Milwaukee Journal Sentinels*
several *Madame Bovary*s (*or, better,* several copies of *Madame Bovary*)
too many *sic*s

*but*
four *New York Times*

The plural endings to italicized words in another language should also be set in italics.

*Blume, Blumen*
*cheval, chevaux*
*señor, señores*

7.13 **Plural form for words in quotation marks.** The plural of a word or phrase in quotation marks may be formed in the usual way (without an apostrophe). If the result is awkward, reword. Chicago discourages a plural ending following a closing quotation mark.

How many more "To be continueds" (*not* "To be continued"s) can we expect?
*or, better,*
How many more times can we expect to see "To be continued"?

7.14 **Plurals of noun coinages.** Words and hyphenated phrases that are not nouns but are used as nouns usually form the plural by adding *s* or *es*. (If in doubt, consult *Merriam-Webster Unabridged*, which indicates the preferred inflected forms for most nouns, including all of the examples below.)

ifs, ands, or buts
dos and don'ts
threes and fours
thank-yous
maybes
yeses and noes

7.15 **Plurals for letters, abbreviations, and numerals.** Numerals and abbreviations usually form the plural by adding *s*. To aid comprehension, a lowercase letter forms the plural with an apostrophe and an *s* (compare "two *a*s in *llama*" with "two *a*'s in *llama*"). And in a departure from previous editions, this manual now recommends also forming the plural of an uppercase letter with an apostrophe, primarily to avoid constructions such as *A*s, *I*s, and *U*s, which may be confused with words. For some exceptions beyond those listed in the last four examples below, see 10.48; see also 10.59 (for the International System). For the omission of periods in abbreviations like "BS," "MA," and "PhD," see 10.4.

an acronym spelled with two *A*'s (see also 7.68)
the three R's (see also 7.67)
*x*'s and *y*'s
the 1990s
IRAs
URLs
BSs, MAs, PhDs
vols.
eds.
*but*
p. (page), pp. (pages)
n. (note), nn. (notes)
MS (manuscript), MSS (manuscripts)
pj's (as listed in *Merriam-Webster*)

## POSSESSIVES

### *The General Rule*

7.16 **Possessive form of most nouns.** The possessive of most *singular* nouns is formed by adding an apostrophe and an *s*. The possessive of *plural* nouns (except for a few irregular plurals, like *children*, that do not end in *s*) is formed by adding an apostrophe only. For the few exceptions to these principles, see 7.20–22. See also 5.22.

the horse's mouth
a bass's stripes
the virus's toll
puppies' paws
children's literature
a flock of sheep's mysterious disappearance

7.17 **Possessive of proper nouns, abbreviations, and numbers.** The general rule stated at 7.16 extends to the possessives of proper nouns, including names ending in *s*, *x*, or *z*, in both their singular and plural forms, as well as abbreviations and numbers.

*Singular forms*
Kansas's legislature
Chicago's lakefront
Venus's atmosphere

Alexis's classmates
Darius's friends
Marx's theories
Jesus's adherents
Berlioz's works
Tacitus's *Histories*
Borges's library
Dickens's novels
Malraux's masterpiece
Josquin des Prez's motets

*Plural forms*
the Lincolns' marriage
the Williamses' new house (*Williamses* is the plural of *Williams*)
the Martinezes' daughter
dinner at the Browns' (i.e., at the Browns' place)

*Abbreviations and numbers*
FDR's legacy
HP Inc.'s latest offerings
Apollo 11's fiftieth anniversary

Avoid forming the possessive of an abbreviation that is followed by a spelled-out form in parentheses (or vice versa).

the long history of IBM (International Business Machines)
*not*
IBM's (International Business Machines') long history

7.18 **Possessive of words and names ending in unpronounced "s."** Words and names ending in an unpronounced *s* form the possessive in the usual way—with the addition of an apostrophe and an *s* (which, when such forms are spoken, is usually pronounced).

Descartes's three dreams
the marquis's mother
François's efforts to learn English
Vaucouleurs's assistance to Joan of Arc
Albert Camus's novels

7.19 **Possessive of names like "Euripides."** Classical proper names of two or more syllables that end in an *eez* sound form the possessive in the usual way (though when these forms are spoken, the additional *s* is generally not pronounced).

Euripides's tragedies
the Ganges's source
Xerxes's armies

## *Exceptions to the General Rule*

7.20 **Possessive of nouns plural in form, singular in meaning.** When the singular form of a noun ending in *s* is the same as the plural (i.e., the plural is uninflected), the possessives of both are formed by the addition of an apostrophe only. If ambiguity threatens, use *of* to avoid the possessive.

politics' true meaning
economics' forerunners
this species' first record (*or, better,* the first record of this species)

The same rule applies when the name of a place or an organization or a publication (or the last element in the name) is a plural form ending in *s*, such as *the United States*, even though the entity is singular. If the result is awkward, consider rewording to avoid the possessive.

the United States' role (*or, better,* the role of the United States)
Highland Hills' late mayor
Callaway Gardens' former curator
the National Academy of Sciences' new policy

7.21 **"For . . . sake" expressions.** For the sake of euphony, a few *for . . . sake* expressions used with a singular noun that ends in an *s* end in an apostrophe alone, omitting the additional *s*.

for goodness' sake
for righteousness' sake

Aside from these traditional formulations, however, the possessive in *for . . . sake* expressions may be formed in the normal way.

for expedience's sake
for appearance's sake (*or* for appearances' sake [plural possessive] *or* for the sake of appearance [*or* appearances])
for Jesus's sake

7.22 **An alternative practice for words ending in "s."** Some writers and publishers prefer the system, formerly more common, of simply omitting the possessive *s* on all words ending in *s*—hence "Dylan Thomas' poetry," "Etta James' singing," and "that business' main concern." Though easy to apply and economical, such usage, which frequently disregards pronunciation and risks appearing inconsistent relative to singular names that do not end in *s*, is not recommended by Chicago.

## *Particularities of the Possessive*

7.23 **Joint versus separate possession.** Closely linked nouns are considered a single unit in forming the possessive when the thing being "possessed" is the same for both; only the second element takes the possessive form.

my aunt and uncle's house
Gilbert and Sullivan's *Iolanthe*
Minneapolis and St. Paul's transportation system

When the things possessed are discrete, both nouns take the possessive form.

my aunt's and uncle's medical profiles
Gilbert's or Sullivan's mustache
New York's and Chicago's transportation systems

7.24 **Compound possessives.** In compound nouns and noun phrases, the final element usually takes the possessive form, even in the plural.

student assistants' responsibilities
my daughter-in-law's address
my sons-in-law's addresses

7.25 **Possessive to mean "of."** Analogous to possessives, and formed like them, are certain expressions that would otherwise include *of*. (Such usage is one of the genitive forms discussed in 5.22.) In the first example below, the literal meaning is "in a time [or period] of three days." If the result seems ambiguous or awkward, reword.

in three days' time (*or* in three days)
an hour's delay (*or* a one-hour delay)
six months' leave of absence (*or* a six-month leave of absence)

7.26 **Double possessive.** According to a usage that is sometimes referred to as the double possessive or double genitive (see 5.23), a possessive form may be preceded by *of* where *one of several* is implied. Where the meaning is not literally possessive, however, the possessive form should not be used.

a friend of Nora's (*or* a friend of hers)
a student of mine
*but*
a student of Kierkegaard (where *student* means *observer* or *follower*)

7.27 **Possessive versus attributive forms for groups.** Although terms denoting group ownership or participation sometimes appear without an apostrophe (i.e., as an attributive rather than a possessive noun), Chicago dispenses with the apostrophe only in proper names (often corporate names) that do not officially include one. In a few established cases, a singular noun can be used attributively; if in doubt, choose the plural possessive. (Irregular plurals such as *children* and *women* must always be in the possessive.)

children's rights (*or* child rights)
farmers' market
women's soccer team
boys' clubs
veterans' organizations
players' unions
taxpayers' associations (*or* taxpayer associations)
consumers' group (*or* consumer group)
*but*
*Publishers Weekly*
Diners Club
Department of Veterans Affairs

In some cases, the distinction between attributive and possessive is subtle. Of the following two examples, only the first connotes actual possession.

the Lakers' game plan (the team's game plan)
*but*
the Lakers game (the game featuring the team)

When in doubt, opt for the possessive.

7.28 **Possessive with gerund.** A noun followed by a gerund (see 5.116) may take the possessive form in some contexts. This practice, usually limited to proper names and personal pronouns, should be used with caution. For an excellent discussion, see "Possessive with Gerund," in *Fowler's Dictionary of Modern English Usage* (bibliog. 1.2). The possessive is normally used when the gerund rather than the noun that precedes it is intended as the subject or object of a clause, as in the first three examples below. In the fourth example, *Jerod* works better than *running* as the object of the verb *saw*; *running* is then functioning as a participle (verb form) rather than a gerund (noun form), so the possessive is not used.

We all agreed that Jerod's running away from the tigers had been the right thing to do.
Our finding a solution depends on the nature of the problem.
Eleanor's revealing her secret (*or* Eleanor's revelation) resulted in a lawsuit.
*but*
None of us actually saw Jerod running away from the tigers.

When the noun or pronoun follows a preposition, the possessive is usually optional.

She was worried about her daughter (*or* daughter's) going there alone.
I won't stand for him (*or* his) being denigrated.
The problem of authors (*or* authors') finding the right publisher can be solved.

For some additional considerations, see 5.118.

7.29 **Possessive with italicized or quoted terms.** As with plurals (see 7.12), when an italicized term appears in roman text, the apostrophe and *s* should be set in roman. When the last element is plural in form (if not necessarily in meaning), add only an apostrophe, in roman (see 7.20). Chicago discourages, however, attempting to form the possessive of a term enclosed in quotation marks (a practice that is seen in some periodical publications where most titles are quoted rather than italicized). See also 8.172.

*The Atlantic*'s editor in chief
*The New York Times*' new fashion editor
*The Great Gatsby*'s admirers
*but*
admirers of "Ode on a Grecian Urn"

## CONTRACTIONS AND INTERJECTIONS

7.30 **Contractions.** In contractions, an apostrophe normally replaces omitted letters. Some contractions, such as *won't* or *ain't*, are formed irregularly. Colloquialisms such as *gonna* or *wanna* take no apostrophe (there being no obvious place for one). *Merriam-Webster* lists many common contractions, along with alternative spellings and, where appropriate, plurals. Note that an apostrophe—the equivalent of a right single quotation mark (' *not* ')—is always used to form a contraction (see 6.125).

singin'     gov't     'tis (*not* 'tis)     dos and don'ts     rock 'n' roll

A contraction that ends in a period (e.g., *Dr.*) is generally referred to as an abbreviation (see 10.2).

7.31 **Interjections.** As with contractions, *Merriam-Webster* lists such interjections as *achoo*, *ugh*, *er*, *um*, and *sh*. For those not found in the dictionary—or where a different emphasis is desired—plausible spellings should be sought in literature or invented.

atchoo!     shhh!

The interjection *oh* is not to be confused with the vocative *O* (found mainly in poetry and prayer), which is always capitalized; *oh* is capitalized only at the beginning of a sentence. See also 6.38.

Where, oh where, have you been?
Oh! It's you!
*but*
"Thine arm, O Lord, in days of old . . ."

## "A" AND "AN"

7.32 **"A" and "an" before "h."** The indefinite article *a*, not *an*, is used in English before words beginning with a pronounced *h*. (British English differs from American English in not pronouncing the *h* in many cases; when in doubt, check a standard dictionary.) See also 5.78.

a hotel     a historical study
*but*
an honor     an heir

7.33 **"A" and "an" before abbreviations, symbols, and numerals.** Before an abbreviation, a symbol, or a numeral, the use of *a* or *an* depends on (or, conversely, determines) how the term is pronounced. In the first example below, "MS" would be pronounced *em ess*; in the second, it would be pronounced *manuscript*. In the sixth example, "EULA" would be pronounced *yoo luh*. In the last two examples, "007" would be pronounced *oh oh seven* and *double oh seven*, respectively.

an MS treatment (a treatment for multiple sclerosis)
a MS in the National Library
an NBC anchor
a CBS anchor
a URL
a EULA violation
an EU member
an @ sign
an 800 number
an 007 field (in a library catalog)
a 007-style agent

## LIGATURES

7.34 **When not to use ligatures.** The ligatures *æ* (*a* + *e*) and *œ* (*o* + *e*) should not be used in Latin or transliterated Greek words. Nor should they be used in words adopted into English from Latin, Greek, or French (and thus to be found in English dictionaries). Compare 7.35.

aesthetics
*Encyclopaedia Britannica* (contrary to corporate usage)
oedipal
a trompe l'oeil mural
a tray of hors d'oeuvres
Emily Dickinson's oeuvre

7.35 **When ligatures should be used.** The ligature *æ* (*a* + *e*) is needed for spelling Old English words in an Old English context. And the ligature *œ* (*o* + *e*) is needed for spelling French words in a French context. (See also 11.23.) Compare 7.34.

| | |
|---|---|
| Ælfric | le nœud gordien |
| es hæl | *Œuvres complètes* |

## WORD DIVISION

7.36 **Dictionary word division.** The advice in this section applies only to published works and mainly to print and PDF (which have fixed layouts) rather than to reflowable electronic formats; word breaks should not be applied at the manuscript stage (see 2.16). For end-of-line word breaks, as for spelling and plural forms, Chicago turns to *Merriam-Webster* as its primary guide (see also 7.1). The dots between syllables in the entries in *Merriam-Webster* indicate where breaks may be made; in words of three or more syllables, there is usually a choice of breaks. The paragraphs in this section are intended merely to supplement, not to replace, the dictionary's system of word division—for example, by suggesting preferred breaks where more than one might be possible. These recommendations are also intended to serve as a guide for determining appropriate hyphenation settings in page-layout applications. Most such programs automate hyphenation relative to a standard dictionary but allow users to define certain rules (e.g., to specify the minimum number of characters to carry to a new line or the maximum number of consecutive lines that can end in a hyphen) and to make exceptions (e.g., for specific words). For division of non-English words (other than those that are included in an English-language dictionary), see chapter 11. For end-of-line breaks relative to en and em dashes, see 6.88, 6.96; for slashes, see 6.121; for nonbreaking spaces, see 6.129.

7.37 **Word divisions that should be avoided.** Single-syllable words, including verb forms such as *aimed* and *helped*, are never divided. Since at least two letters must appear before a break, such words as *again*, *enough*, and *unite* also cannot be divided. And at least three letters must appear after a break, so divisions that carry only two letters over to the next line, even where indicated by *Merriam-Webster*, are usually also avoided (but see 6.88, 6.121).

women (*rather than* wom-en)
losses (*rather than* loss-es)
sur-prises (*rather than* surpris-es)

In languages other than English, however, it may be not only permissible but customary to carry two-letter word endings to the next line (see, e.g., 11.36, 11.37, 11.45, 11.46, 11.57, 11.58, 11.73, 11.74).

7.38 **Dividing according to pronunciation.** In the usage preferred by Chicago and reflected in *Merriam-Webster*, most words are divided according to how the break will affect pronunciation rather than according to derivation.

knowl-edge (*not* know-ledge)
democ-racy *or* de-mocracy (*not* demo-cracy)

Special attention should be paid to breaks in certain words with multiple meanings and pronunciations, such as *proj-ect* (noun) and *pro-ject* (verb), which automatic hyphenation may not properly account for.

7.39 **Dividing after a vowel.** Unless a resulting break affects pronunciation, words are best divided after a vowel. When a vowel forms a syllable in the middle of a word, it should remain on the first line if possible. Diphthongs are treated as single vowels (e.g., the *eu* in *aneurysm*).

criti-cism (*rather than* crit-icism)
liga-ture (*rather than* lig-ature)
an-tipodes *or* antipo-des (*rather than* antip-odes)
aneu-rysm (*rather than* an-eurysm)

7.40 **Dividing compounds, prefixes, and suffixes.** Hyphenated or closed compounds and words with prefixes or suffixes are best divided at the natural breaks.

poverty- / stricken (*rather than* pov- / erty-stricken)
thanks-giving (*rather than* thanksgiv-ing)
dis-pleasure (*rather than* displea-sure)
re-inforce (*rather than* rein-force)

7.41 **Dividing words ending in "ing."** Most gerunds and present participles may be divided before the *ing*. When the final consonant before the *ing* is doubled, however, the break occurs between the consonants. For words ending in *ling*, check the dictionary.

| | |
|---|---|
| certify-ing | run-ning |
| giv-ing | fiz-zling |
| dab-bing | bris-tling |

7.42 **Dividing proper nouns and personal names.** Proper nouns of more than one element, especially personal names, should be broken, if possible, between the elements rather than within any of the elements. If a break within a name is needed, consult the dictionary. Many proper nouns appear, with suggested divisions, in the listings of biographical and geographic names in *Merriam-Webster*. For fuller treatment, consult *Merriam-Webster Unabridged* (see 7.1). Those that cannot be found in a dictionary should be broken (or left unbroken) according to the guidelines elsewhere in this section. If pronunciation is not known or easily guessed, the break should usually follow a vowel.

Alek-sis
Heitor Villa- / Lobos (*or, better,* Heitor / Villa-Lobos)
Ana-stasia

A personal name that includes initials should be broken after the initials. A break before a number or *Jr.* or *Sr.* should be avoided. A nonbreaking space can prevent such breaks (see 6.129).

Susan B. / Anthony
M. F. K. / Fisher
Elizabeth II (*or, if necessary,* Eliza- / beth II)

7.43 **Dividing numerals.** Large numbers expressed as numerals are best left intact. To avoid a break, reword the sentence. If a break must be made, however, it should come only after a comma and never after a single digit. See also 7.45.

1,365,- / 000,000 *or* 1,365,000,- / 000

7.44 **Dividing numerals with abbreviated units of measure.** A numeral used with an abbreviated unit of measure is best left intact; either the numeral should be carried over to the next line or the abbreviation should be moved up. A nonbreaking space can prevent such breaks (see 6.129). (Numerals used with spelled-out units of measure, which tend to form longer expressions, may be broken across a line as needed.)

345 m (*not* 345 / m)
24 kg
55 BCE
6:35 p.m.

7.45 **Dividing mathematical expressions.** A mathematical expression run in to the text may be allowed to break at the space either before or after an operation sign (e.g., + − × ÷ ± ∪ ∩) or a relation sign (e.g., = ≠ > < ≥ ≤ → ⊃ ⊂ ∈ ≅ ≡); see also 6.130. Displayed expressions that will not fit on one line should, however, be broken *before* an operation or relation sign. Runover lines are aligned on the relation signs:

$$\begin{aligned} h(x) &= (x - \alpha)(x - \beta)(x - \gamma) \\ &= x^3 - (\alpha + \beta + \gamma)x^2 + (\alpha\beta + \alpha\gamma + \beta\gamma)x - \alpha\beta\gamma. \end{aligned}$$

If a runover line begins with an operation sign, the operation sign should be lined up with the first character to the right of the relation sign in the line above it:

$$\begin{aligned} \frac{\pi}{4} = {} & \frac{1}{2} - \frac{1}{3 \times 2^3} + \frac{1}{5 \times 2^5} - \frac{1}{7 \times 2^7} + \frac{1}{9 \times 2^9} - \frac{1}{11 \times 2^{11}} + \cdots \\ & + \frac{1}{3} - \frac{1}{3 \times 3^3} + \frac{1}{5 \times 3^5} - \frac{1}{7 \times 3^7} + \frac{1}{9 \times 3^9} - \cdots \\ & + \frac{1}{4} - \frac{1}{3 \times 4^3} + \frac{1}{5 \times 4^5} - \frac{1}{7 \times 4^7} + \cdots. \end{aligned}$$

For additional rules on breaking expressions, consult Ellen Swanson, *Mathematics into Type* (bibliog. 2.4).

7.46 **Division in run-in lists.** A number or letter, such as (3) or (c), used in a run-in list (see 6.140) should not be separated from the beginning of what follows it. If it occurs at the end of a line, it should be carried over to the next line. A nonbreaking space can prevent such breaks (see 6.129).

7.47 **Dividing URLs at the end of a line.** If a URL needs to be divided at the end of a line in a work published in print or as a PDF (or other format with fixed line breaks), the break should be made *after* an initial http:// or https:// (or, if necessary, after the initial colon); *before* a single slash (/), period, comma, colon (other than the first), hyphen, tilde (~), underscore (_), question mark, number sign, or percent symbol; or *before or after* an equals sign or an ampersand. Such breaks help to signal that the URL has been carried over to the next line. A hyphen should never be added to a URL to denote a line break, nor should a hyphen that is part of a URL appear at the end of a line (authors may, however, allow breaks at hyphens in their manuscripts; see text below). If a particularly long element must be broken to avoid a seriously loose or tight line, it can be broken between words or syllables according to the guidelines for word division offered in 7.36–48 (but without adding a hyphen). Editors, proofreaders, and typesetters should use their discretion in applying these recommendations, aiming for a balance between readability and aesthetics. See also 6.8.

https://
www.chicagomanualofstyle.org/

https://www
.chicagomanualofstyle.org/

https://www.chicago
manualofstyle.org/

https://www.jstor.org/stable
/2921689

https://time.com/6203311/james-webb
-telescope-images-stars-history/

To facilitate such breaks, typesetters can apply zero-width spaces before each slash and at other potential break points in URLs (see table 6.2). (An actual space or a hard return should not be used for this purpose.) To avoid conversion errors and other potential problems, authors should generally avoid adding breaks to URLs in their manuscripts (see 2.16). Moreover, it is generally unnecessary to specify breaks for URLs in electronic publication formats with reflowable text. Note that a trailing slash at the end of a URL copied and pasted from an address bar (as in several of the examples above) should usually be retained (see 6.120).

**7.48** **Hyphenation and appearance.** For aesthetic reasons, no more than three succeeding lines should be allowed to end in hyphens. (Such hyphens are sometimes referred to as a hyphen stack or ladder.) And though hyphens are necessary far more often in justified text, word breaks may be needed in material with a ragged right-hand margin to avoid exceedingly uneven lines. (In manuscript preparation, however, hyphenation should never be applied; see 2.16.) In reflowable electronic publication formats, end-of-line hyphenation may be applied automatically by a particular application or device; if desired, such hyphenation can be suppressed in specific contexts for aesthetic reasons (as for chapter titles and other headings).

## ITALICS, CAPITALS, AND QUOTATION MARKS

**7.49** **Setting off proper names and titles of works.** Except for the advice on styling musical and computer terminology, most of the recommendations in this section are related to the distinctive treatment of letters, words, and phrases as such. For the use of italics, capitals, and quotation marks to indicate or set off proper nouns and titles of works, see chapter 8. For the use of italics for unspoken discourse, see 12.49.

7.50 **Italics and markup.** Italics have been used for centuries as the default means of setting off text from the surrounding context, which is usually in roman (i.e., *not* in italics; the term *roman* is synonymous with *regular*). Boldface is another traditional option, though it is less common. (In the typewriter era, underlining was the usual way of indicating italics on a manuscript; underlining continues to mean italics in pencil editing and proofreading, whereas a wavy underline means bold.) Italics as such are used for emphasis, key terms or terms in another language, words used as words, titles of works, and so on. For electronic publication formats, semantic markup can be added that specifies the nature of the content (e.g., emphasized text) and not just how it will be presented on the screen. Among other advantages, such markup can make text more accessible—for example, by determining how a word will be vocalized by text-to-speech applications. See also 2.86–88.

## *Emphasis*

7.51 **Italics for emphasis.** Use *italics* for emphasis only as an occasional adjunct to efficient sentence structure. Overused, italics quickly lose their force. Seldom should as much as a sentence be italicized for emphasis, and never a whole passage. In the first example below, the last three words, though clearly emphatic, do not require italics because of their dramatic position at the end of the sentence.

> The damaging evidence was offered not by the arresting officer, not by the injured plaintiff, but by the boy's own mother.

On the other hand, the emphasis in the following example depends on the italics:

> It *was* Leo!

7.52 **Boldface or underlining for emphasis.** Occasionally, **boldface** or <u>underlining</u> (also called underscoring) is used for emphasis. In formal prose, however, italics are the traditional choice (see 7.51). Though the terms *bold* and *underline* both convey the idea of emphasis, bold text for emphasis risks appearing too emphatic in many contexts, whereas underlining may conflict with the style used for hyperlinks and, on edited manuscripts, with tracked changes, where underlining is often used to denote added text (see 2.89). Underlining also has the disadvantage of interfering with descenders on lowercase letters. See also 7.58, 7.59, 7.84.

7.53 **Asterisks for emphasis.** Some contexts (including certain social media platforms) do not support the use of bold or italic text; where that is the case, asterisks may be used for emphasis instead, *like this*. This use of asterisks is roughly equivalent to **boldface**; where it is important to specify italics literally rather than simply to show emphasis, the underscore character may be used instead, _like this_. Note that Unicode includes bold and italic letters (mainly for math); because these characters may be misinterpreted by screen readers and search engines (making them inaccessible to some readers), they should not be used as a workaround when italics and bold are unavailable.

7.54 **Capitals for emphasis.** Initial capitals, once commonly used to lend importance to certain words, are now mainly used in this way only ironically or in jest (but see 8.95).

> "OK, so I'm a Bad Role Model," admitted Mary cheerfully.

Capitalizing an entire word or phrase for emphasis is rarely appropriate in formal prose. If capitals are wanted—in dialogue or in representing newspaper headlines, for example—small caps rather than full capitals look more graceful. Note that "capitalizing" a word means setting only the initial letter as a capital. Capitalizing a whole word (or phrase), LIKE THIS, is known as "setting in full caps" (or "all caps"). Because all caps can be interpreted as shouting or angry, they should be used with discretion, if at all. Some publishers apply small capitals—or "small caps," LIKE THIS—to minimize the impact of capital letters. (For the use of small capitals in representing terms in American Sign Language, see 11.135–45.) See also 10.9.

> "Be careful—WATCH OUT!" she yelled.
> We could not believe the headline: POLAR ICE CAP RETURNS.

## *Words from Other Languages*

7.55 **Unfamiliar words and phrases from other languages.** Italics are the traditional choice for singling out non-English words and phrases in an English-language context. (Extended passages or quotations that are entirely in another language are usually *not* italicized.) This usage should be reserved for terms that do not appear in *Merriam-Webster* or that would be unfamiliar to many readers. *Merriam-Webster* now lists many non-English words and phrases that might not be considered familiar in English, so some editorial discretion will be required (see also 7.56). If a term becomes familiar through repeated use, it need be italicized only on its first occurrence. If it appears only rarely, italics may be retained. Italics should be applied only to words that use the Latin alphabet (e.g., *shiyuzheng* but not 官场失语症 in the fourth example below).

The *quatrième chant* in Bocage corresponds to book 8 in Milton's *Paradise Lost*.
Each of us received a personalized *Kaffeetasse* (coffee cup) as a gift.
They informed us that they were fans of *fútbol* (soccer).
These instances of "bureaucratic *shiyuzheng*" (官场失语症, literally translated as "bureaucratic aphasia") were documented during a trip to Shandong province.

Note that italics may not be appropriate for non-English words used as part of the vocabulary of a multilingual author, narrator, or character (as in fictional dialogue). An editor who encounters such usage in an otherwise English-language context should query the author before making any changes. Nor does this rule extend to proper nouns (e.g., Musée d'Orsay), which can generally appear in roman type (except for titles of books and other such terms that would normally be italicized). For further discussion and examples, including the treatment of translated terms, see 11.3–7. For capitalization in other languages, see 11.20.

7.56 **Roman for familiar words from other languages.** Non-English words and phrases that are likely to be familiar to readers should appear in roman (*not* italics) if used in an English context. (This will sometimes include non-English terms that would count as familiar to a multilingual author, narrator, or character; see 7.55.) Most terms listed in *Merriam-Webster* will not need italics; however, not all words listed there will be familiar to readers, so editorial discretion may be required. Note that German nouns should be capitalized unless lowercased in *Merriam-Webster*; lowercase listings that are labeled as "often capitalized" may be lowercased unless capitalization is needed for consistency with other German nouns. (This is a departure from previous editions of this manual, which recommended lowercase for any German noun listed in *Merriam-Webster*; see also 11.42.) See also 7.57.

We shared croissants in the morning and banh mi in the afternoon.
In the Ottoman Empire, a pasha would have been a soldier or an official.

The concept of Weltanschauung is important in German philosophy.
The last kaiser ruled until 1918.
We avoided any expression that we considered obscure or recherché.
Who are you calling bourgeois?
We preferred telenovelas to anime.
In Greek philosophy, eros is not incompatible with agape.
*but*
He never missed a chance to *épater le bourgeois*. (listed in *Merriam-Webster*, but as a "French phrase")

If a familiar term, such as *mise en scène* (listed in *Merriam-Webster* as a noun), should occur in the same context as a less familiar one, such as *mise en bouteille* (not in *Merriam-Webster*), either both or neither should be italicized, so as to maintain internal consistency. See also 7.55.

7.57 **Roman for Latin words and abbreviations.** Commonly used Latin words and abbreviations are not normally italicized. If in doubt, check *Merriam-Webster*. Note, however, that *Merriam-Webster* now lists many Latin terms that would not be considered common; when in doubt, apply italics.

| | | |
|---|---|---|
| a priori | in vitro | passim |
| de novo | et al. | *but* |
| ibid. | ca. | *contra bonos mores* |

Because of its special use in quoted matter, *sic* is best italicized.

"mindful of what has been done here by we [*sic*] as agents of principle"

## *Highlighting Key Terms and Expressions*

7.58 **Italics or boldface for key terms.** Key terms in a particular context are often italicized on their first occurrence. Thereafter they are best set in roman.

The two chief tactics of this group, *obstructionism* and *misinformation*, require careful analysis.

Occasionally, boldface may be used for key terms, as in a textbook or to highlight terms that also appear in a glossary; such usage should be noted in the text. See also 7.84.

7.59 **Linked text.** In electronic publication formats, hyperlinks may be added to text to facilitate cross-references within the same work or to allow readers to move to another resource online. In electronic formats, linked text is typically signaled by a change in formatting (such as underlining) as well as a change in color relative to the surrounding text. The default behavior may be modified to match the design of a particular publication (as in the online edition of this manual). In a book or other work published in both print and electronic formats, linked text is usually left unformatted in the print version (except for any italics or other formatting already applied for other reasons). There are few rules for choosing what text to use as the basis of a link, but some general principles apply:

- Linked text should be brief but descriptive.
- The text should make sense without the link.
- Punctuation at the beginning or end of the linked text is not usually included. An exception may be made for a question mark or exclamation point at the end of a title or quotation.
- An initial *a*, *an*, or *the* may be included as part of a linked phrase. But if the link is to a proper name, include the article only if it is part of the name (or if it is part of a larger phrase that includes the name).
- Avoid using a URL as the basis of linked text except as part of a source citation.
- An image used as a link should include alt text that describes the function of the link or that names its target (see also 3.28).

In the following examples, underlining shows where links would be applied:

For definitions of key terms, see <u>the glossary</u>.
The eighteenth edition of <u>*The Chicago Manual of Style*</u> was published in 2024.
For more information, see the <u>*AP Stylebook*</u> (under "a.m., p.m.").
A brief history of the Oxford comma, "<u>Oxford, Chicago, and the Serial Comma</u>," was published at *CMOS Shop Talk*.
<u>Results of this research</u> were reported on Tuesday in *Nature*.
The museum featured <u>a series of oil paintings</u> by Frida Kahlo.

For more guidance on links, including tips for making them accessible, consult the DAISY Accessible Publishing Knowledge Base.

7.60 **"Scare quotes."** Quotation marks are often used to alert readers that a term is used in a nonstandard (or slang), ironic, or other special sense. Such scare quotes imply "This is not my term" or "This is not how the term is usually applied." Like any such device, scare quotes lose their force and may irritate readers if overused. See also 7.62, 7.63.

My rotary simulation app allows me to "dial" phone numbers again.
"Child protection" sometimes fails to protect.

7.61 **Mixing single and double quotation marks.** In works of philosophy or other specialized contexts, single and double quotation marks are sometimes used to signal different things. For example, single quotation marks might be used for special terms and double quotation marks for their definitions. Chicago discourages such a practice, preferring a mix of italics, quotation marks, and parentheses instead.

7.62 **"So-called."** A word or phrase preceded by *so-called* need not be enclosed in quotation marks. The expression itself indicates irony or doubt. If, however, it is necessary to call attention to only one part of a phrase, quotation marks may be helpful.

So-called child protection sometimes fails to protect.
Her so-called mentor induced her to embezzle from the company.
*but*
These days, so-called "running" shoes are more likely to be seen on the feet of walkers.

7.63 **Common expressions and figures of speech.** Quotation marks are rarely needed for common expressions or figures of speech (including slang). They should normally be reserved for phrases borrowed verbatim from another context or terms used ironically (see 7.60).

Myths of paradise lost are common in folklore.
I grew up in a one-horse town.
Only techies will appreciate this joke.
*but*
Though she was a lifetime subscriber to the *Journal of Infectious Diseases*, she was not one to ask "for whom the bell tolls."

7.64 **Signs and notices.** Specific wording of common short signs or notices is capitalized in title case in running text (see 8.160). A longer notice is better treated as a quotation.

The door was marked Authorized Personnel Only.
She encountered the usual Thank You for Not Smoking signs.

We were disturbed by the notice "Shoes and shirt required of patrons but not of personnel."

7.65 **Mottoes.** Mottoes may be treated the same way as signs (see 7.64). If the wording is in another language, it is usually italicized and capitalized in sentence case (see 8.159). See also 6.44, 7.55.

The flag bore the motto Don't Tread on Me.
My old college has the motto *Souvent me souviens.*
The motto "All for one and one for all" appears over the door.

## *Words as Words and Letters as Letters*

7.66 **Words and phrases used as words.** When a word or phrase is not used functionally but is referred to as the word or phrase itself, it is either italicized or enclosed in quotation marks. Proper nouns used as words, as in the third example below, can usually be italicized (a slight departure from previous editions); however, names used as such usually are not (as the second "Celsius" in the fourth example). See also 7.67.

The term *critical mass* is more often used metaphorically than literally.
What is meant by *neurobotics*?
*iPhone* is spelled with a lowercase *i* and a capital *P*.
The word *Celsius* derives from the name Celsius.

Although italics are the traditional choice, quotation marks may be more appropriate in certain contexts. In the first example below, italics set off the Spanish words, and quotation marks are used for the English (see also 7.55). In the second example, quotation marks help to convey the idea of speech.

The Spanish verbs *ser* and *estar* are both rendered by "to be."
Many people say "I" even when "me" would be more correct.

Quotation marks would also be appropriate in contexts where italics are not available (as on certain social media platforms).

7.67 **Letters as letters.** Individual letters and combinations of letters of the Latin alphabet are usually italicized.

the letter *q*
a lowercase *n*

a capital *W*
The plural is usually formed in English by adding *s* or *es*.
He signed the document with an *X*.
I need a word with two *e*'s and three *s*'s.

Roman type, however, is traditionally used in several common expressions (see also 7.15).

Mind your p's and q's!
dotting the i's and crossing the t's
the three R's (traditionally capitalized; see also 7.15)

Roman type is always used for phonetic symbols. For details, consult Geoffrey K. Pullum and William A. Ladusaw, *Phonetic Symbol Guide* (bibliog. 5).

7.68 **Scholastic grades.** Letters used to denote grades are usually capitalized and set in roman type. Plural forms take an apostrophe (a departure from advice in previous editions; see 7.15).

She finished with three A's, one B, and two C's.

7.69 **Letters standing for names.** A letter used in place of a name is usually capitalized and set in roman type. If it bears no relation to an actual name, it is not followed by a period.

Let us assume that A sues B for breach of contract . . .

If a single initial is used to abbreviate an actual name, it is usually followed by a period; if used to conceal a name, it may be followed by a 2-em dash and no period (see 6.99). If no punctuation follows the dash, it must be followed by a space.

Professor D. will be making his entrance shortly.
Senator K—— and Representative L——, among others, were in attendance.

If two or more initials are used as an abbreviation for an entire name, no periods are needed. See also 8.4, 10.14.

Kennedy and Johnson soon became known as JFK and LBJ.

7.70 **Letters as shapes.** Letters that are used to represent shapes are capitalized and set in roman type (an S curve, an L-shaped room). (Using a sans serif font in a serif context, as is sometimes done, does not necessarily aid comprehension and, unless the sans serif perfectly complements the serif, tends to look clumsy.)

7.71 **Names of letters.** When legibility cannot be counted on, editors and proofreaders occasionally need to name letters ("a cue, not a gee"). The name of a letter, as distinct from the letter itself, is usually set in roman, without quotation marks. The following standard spellings are drawn from *Merriam-Webster*. With vowels, which are not named in standard dictionaries, it may be best to give an example ("*a* as in *apple*"). (For the names of special characters, see chapter 11, esp. tables 11.1 and 11.2.)

| | | | | | |
|---|---|---|---|---|---|
| *b* | bee | *k* | kay | *s* | ess |
| *c* | cee | *l* | el | *t* | tee |
| *d* | dee | *m* | em | *v* | vee |
| *f* | ef | *n* | en | *w* | double-u |
| *g* | gee | *p* | pee | *x* | ex |
| *h* | aitch | *q* | cue | *y* | wye |
| *j* | jay | *r* | ar | *z* | zee |

7.72 **Rhyme schemes.** Lowercase italic letters, with no space between, are used to indicate rhyme schemes or similar patterns.

The Shakespearean sonnet's rhyme scheme is *abab, cdcd, efef, gg.*

7.73 **Mathematical variables.** Single letters used as variables in mathematical expressions and text are generally italicized, whether used alone or in combination, a practice that extends to lowercase Greek letters. (In disciplines other than mathematics, physics, and statistics, lowercase Greek letters are typically set in roman.) Single letters representing constants are also italicized (as the base of natural logarithms *e* and the ideal gas constant *R* in the fifth and sixth examples below, respectively), though some publishers specify roman for *e* and other mathematical constants, reserving italics for physical constants. Numerals are always set in roman, as are most signs for operations and relations (+, =, etc.).

| | | |
|---|---|---|
| $a + b = c$ | $A = \pi r^2$ | $P_x$ (probability of $x$) |
| $f(x)$ | $e^{i\pi} + 1 = 0$ | $x$-axis, $y$-axis |
| $\alpha \geq \beta$ | $PV = nRT$ | $a_{2n}$ |

Abbreviations for units of measurement, common functions, geometric points, and chemical elements (see 10.69) are set in roman type, as are abbreviations and other nonvariable subscripts and superscripts (as the roman subscript "L" in the fourth example below, an abbreviation for *lung*). Abbreviations consisting of more than one letter are also set in roman, as are uppercase Greek letters.

| | |
|---|---|
| 30 kg | $V_{\mathrm{L}}$ (lung volume) |
| $e^{ix} = \cos x + \sin x$ | $\mathrm{GR}_{\mathrm{max}}$ (growth rate maximum) |
| points A and B | $\Omega = 2^N$ |

Symbols for mathematical vectors, tensors, and matrices are set in bold. For example, Newton's second law can be expressed as $\mathbf{F} = m\mathbf{a}$, where force (**F**) and acceleration (**a**) are both vector quantities and mass ($m$) is a scalar quantity. For additional coverage of mathematical expressions, see the *ACS Guide to Scholarly Communication* or Ellen Swanson's *Mathematics into Type*, among other resources (bibliog. 2.4). *The CSE Manual* also provides useful information (see bibliog. 1.1). For spaces next to mathematical operators and the like, see 6.130.

7.74 **Communication code words.** Terms used as code words in aviation and other fields that rely on radio communications are usually capitalized but not italicized. The NATO phonetic alphabet, the most widely used of these, consists of the following twenty-six words:

| | | |
|---|---|---|
| Alfa | Juliett | Sierra |
| Bravo | Kilo | Tango |
| Charlie | Lima | Uniform |
| Delta | Mike | Victor |
| Echo | November | Whiskey |
| Foxtrot | Oscar | Xray |
| Golf | Papa | Yankee |
| Hotel | Quebec | Zulu |
| India | Romeo | |

## *Music: Some Typographic Conventions*

7.75 **Suggested references for music publishing.** Music publishing is too specialized to be more than touched on here. Authors and editors requiring detailed guidelines may refer to D. Kern Holoman, *Writing About Music* (bibliog. 1.1). For an illustration of typeset music, see figure 3.5. For styling the titles of musical works, see 8.195–99. For a more general reference work, consult *The New Grove Dictionary of Music and Musicians* and the other Grove musical dictionaries, available from Oxford Music Online (bibliog. 4.1).

7.76 **Musical pitches.** Letters standing for musical pitches (which in turn are used to identify keys, chords, and so on) are usually set as roman capitals. The terms *sharp*, *flat*, and *natural*, if spelled out, are set in roman type and preceded by a hyphen. Editors unfamiliar with musicological conventions should proceed with caution. In the context of harmony, for example, some authors may regard a hyphenated "C-major triad" as being based on the note rather than the key of C. See also 7.79.

middle C
the key of G major
the D-major triad *or* D major triad
an F augmented triad (an augmented triad on the note F)
G-sharp *or* G♯
the key of B-flat minor *or* B♭ minor
Beethoven's E-flat Major Symphony (the *Eroica*)
an E string

A series of pitches are joined by en dashes.

The initial F–G–F–B♭

7.77 **Octaves.** In technical works, various systems are used to designate octave register. Those systems that group pitches by octaves begin each ascending octave on C. In one widely used system, pitches in the octave below middle C are designated by lowercase letters: c, c♯, d, . . . , a♯, b. Octaves from middle C up are designated with lowercase letters bearing superscript numbers or primes: $c^1$, $c^2$, and so on or c′, c″, and so on. Lower octaves are designated, in descending order, by capital letters and capital letters with subscript numbers: C, $C_1$, $C_2$. Because of the many systems and their variants in current use, readers should be alerted to the system employed (e.g., by an indication early in the text of the symbol used for middle C). Technical works on the modern piano usually designate all pitches with capital letters and subscripts, from $A_1$ at the bottom of the keyboard to $C_{88}$ at the top. Scientific works on music usually designate octaves by capital letters and subscripts beginning with $C_0$ (middle C = $C_4$). When pitches are otherwise specified, none of these systems is necessary.

middle C     A 440     the soprano's high C

To indicate simultaneously sounding pitches (as in chords), the pitches are listed from lowest to highest and are sometimes joined by plus signs.

C + E + G

7.78 **Chords.** In the analysis of harmony, chords are designated by Roman numerals indicating what degree of the scale the chord is based on.

V (a chord based on the fifth, or dominant, degree of the scale)
$V^7$ (dominant seventh chord)
iii (a chord based on the third, or mediant, degree of the scale)

Harmonic progressions are indicated by capital Roman numerals separated by en dashes: IV–I–V–I. While Roman numerals for all chords suffice for basic descriptions of chordal movement, in more technical writing, minor chords are distinguished by lowercase Roman numerals, and other distinctions in chord quality and content are shown by additional symbols and Arabic numerals.

7.79 **"Major" and "minor."** In some works on musical subjects where many keys are mentioned, capital letters are used for major keys and lowercase for minor. If this practice is followed, the words *major* and *minor* are usually omitted.

7.80 **Dynamics.** Terms indicating dynamics are usually given in lowercase, often italicized: *piano*, *mezzo forte*, and so on. Where space allows, the spelled-out form is preferred in both text and musical examples. Symbols for these terms are rendered in lowercase boldface italics with no periods: ***p***, ***mf***, and so on. "Editorial" dynamics—those added to a composer's original by an editor—are sometimes distinguished by another font or by parentheses or brackets.

## *Computer Terms*

7.81 **Application-specific versus generic usage.** Typographic conventions for writing the names of keys, menus, commands, and the like vary according to device, operating system, and application (also called program or app) and may also depend on a particular version of any one of those. In general, a specific reference to a named component or function should follow the usage in the device or software itself. Likewise, names for recognized standards should follow accepted usage. Generic references often require no special treatment. For more comprehensive coverage, see the style guides published by Microsoft and Apple (bibliog. 1.1) or consult a user's guide or similar documentation for a specific context. For the treatment of proper names for software and devices, see 8.156.

7.82 **Capitalization for keys, menu items, and file formats.** The basic alphabet keys as well as all named keys are capitalized even if they are lowercased on a particular keyboard. Named menu items and labels for toolbars, tabs, buttons, icons, and the like are usually spelled and capitalized as in a particular application or operating system or on a particular device. Abbreviations for file formats are rendered in full capitals unless expressed as extensions (see also 10.55). Items or actions that are not specifically labeled can usually be treated generically.

The function key F2 has no connection with the keys F and 2.
The Fn key is a common feature on laptops.
The Option (⌥) key on a Mac is similar to the Alt key on a typical PC.
The Ctrl key on a PC is like the Command (⌘) key on a Mac.
Unlike Macs, PCs include both a Delete key and a Backspace key.
One purpose of the Return key (or, on a PC, Enter) is to insert a hard return.
To activate Caps Lock, double-tap Shift (the arrow key).
To show your work in Word, use Track Changes.
Airplane Mode can be toggled on and off using the airplane icon in the Control Center.
Choosing Cut from the Edit menu is an alternative to pressing Ctrl+X.
Save the file as a PNG or a GIF, not as a JPEG.
*but*
The space bar on some ergonomic keyboards is split in two. (But see the fourth example under 7.83.)
The extensions .html and .htm are both used for HTML files.

7.83 **Keyboard combinations and shortcuts.** To indicate that different keys are to be pressed simultaneously (as in a keyboard shortcut), use the plus sign or the hyphen without a space on either side. The choice of plus or hyphen may depend on the operating system; in the examples below, the plus sign is used for examples from Microsoft Windows and the hyphen for macOS (as Apple's operating system is now known). Spell out and capitalize words like *Shift*, *Hyphen*, and *Space* and anything else that might otherwise be ambiguous. (The capital *S* in the second and third examples does *not* indicate that the Shift key should be pressed as part of the combination.)

To insert a double dagger using a Mac, press Option-Shift-7; on a PC, press Alt+0135 (on the numeric keypad).
To save, press Ctrl+S.
To save, press Command-S.
To insert a nonbreaking space in Word, type Ctrl+Shift+Space (Option-Space on a Mac).
If the screen freezes, press Ctrl+Alt+Delete.
To empty the trash without a prompt, press Option-Shift-Command-Delete.

7.84 **Setting off file names and words to be typed or selected.** In most contexts, a combination of quotation marks and capitalization will be sufficient for setting off file names and words to be typed or selected or that otherwise require user interaction or input. References to named items that use title case do not usually require quotation marks (see 8.160); items that use sentence case usually do (see 8.159). For file names or words or other strings to be typed, quotation marks can be used; any punctuation that belongs to the surrounding sentence should appear *outside* the quotation marks (an exception to the usual rule; see 6.9).

To list your music by album title, tap More, then tap Albums.
To start page numbering on the second page, choose the Layout tab from the Page Setup dialog box and select the checkbox labeled "Different first page."
If your server uses "index.html" as its default file name, the name of your own default file cannot be "index.htm".
To change the directory to your desktop, type "cd Desktop".

When a greater prominence than capitalization or quotation marks is desired, a different type treatment may be used to highlight or set off elements. A single treatment may be applied across different types of elements, or different treatments may be used to signal different things. For example, boldface or italics might be used for menu items and the like, while a fixed-width (monospaced) "code" font such as Courier could signal items to be typed and directory paths, file names, variables, and other strings. Any punctuation that follows such text should appear in the font of the surrounding text; see also 6.2, 6.3. Any quotation marks, single or double, belonging to text in a fixed-width font should be of the default, nondirectional kind (cf. 6.123).

To insert a thorn, choose **Symbol** from the **Insert** tab, then enter **00FE** in the **Character code** field.
Click **Save As**; name your file `appendix A, draft`.
To set the value, type `$var = "1"`. (*not* `“1”`)

Type `c:\KindleGen\kindlegen`, followed by a space and the file name(s) for your book content.

For additional guidance, consult the latest style guides from Microsoft and Apple (bibliog. 1.1).

7.85 **Terms like "web" and "internet."** Terms related to the internet are capitalized only if they are trademarked as such or otherwise constitute a proper name. The names of formal protocols are capitalized but may be lowercased when referred to generically (earlier editions of this manual showed only the lowercase forms). Generic terms that are capitalized as part of a proper name may be lowercased when used alone or in combination (see also 8.69). For treatment of the names of keys, menu items, and file formats, see 7.82. For terms such as *email*, see 7.96. For additional examples, see the spelled-out forms under 10.55.

Hypertext Transfer Protocol (HTTP); *but* a hypertext transfer protocol; hypertext
Internet Protocol (IP); *but* an internet protocol; the internet; net neutrality; intranet
Voice over Internet Protocol (IP); *but* voice over IP; VoIP
Wi-Fi (a trademark); wireless network; Ethernet (a trademark); cellular (or mobile) networks; NFC (near-field communication)
the World Wide Web Consortium (W3C); the World Wide Web; the web; website; web page
the Open Source Initiative (the corporation); open-source platforms

7.86 **Hashtags.** To ensure hashtags are not only sufficiently legible but also accessible to screen readers, it is best to start each word with a capital letter. Single-word hashtags may be capitalized for the sake of consistency with multiword hashtags but need not be. Words like *iPhone* may be left as is. Note that this advice does not extend to hashtags in direct quotations, which should reflect the capitalization in the source.

#AmEditing (*not* #amediting)
#ChicagoStyle
#ThrowbackThursday
#MeToo
#iPhonePhotography (*but* #MyIPhone)
#Photography (*or* #photography)
#DogsOfInstagram
#CMOSTips

## COMPOUNDS AND HYPHENATION

7.87 **To hyphenate or not to hyphenate.** Far and away the most common spelling questions for writers and editors concern compound terms—

whether to leave them open, hyphenate them, or close them up as a single word. Prefixes (and occasionally suffixes) can be similarly troublesome. The first place to look for answers is the dictionary. This section, including the hyphenation guide in 7.96, offers guidelines for spelling compounds not necessarily found in the dictionary (though some of the examples are drawn from *Merriam-Webster*) and for treatment of compounds according to their grammatical function (as nouns, adjectives, or adverbs) and their position in a sentence. See also 5.96. For en dashes, which may be used in certain compound expressions instead of hyphens, see 6.82–90.

7.88 **Compounds defined.** An open compound is spelled as two or more words (*high school*, *lowest common denominator*). A hyphenated compound is spelled with one or more hyphens (*mass-produced*, *kilowatt-hour*, *non-English-speaking*). A closed (or solid) compound is spelled as a single word (*screenshot*, *smartphone*). A permanent compound is one that has been accepted into the general vocabulary and can be found in the dictionary (like all but one of the examples in this paragraph thus far). A temporary compound is a new combination created for some specific, often onetime purpose (*dictionary-wielding*, *impeachment hound*); such compounds, though some eventually become permanent, are not normally found in the dictionary. Not strictly compounds but often discussed with them are words formed with prefixes (*antigrammarian*, *postmodern*); these are dealt with in section 4 of 7.96. (For examples of combining forms—a type of prefix in which a word like *electric* is modified to form a combination like *electromagnetic*—see section 2 of 7.96, under *combining forms*.)

7.89 **The trend toward closed compounds.** With frequent use, compounds that are open or hyphenated tend to become closed (*on line* to *on-line* to *online*). In some cases, one term will become closed (*online*) while a closely related term remains hyphenated or open (*on-screen*). When in doubt, such pairs may be made consistent (e.g., by closing both).

7.90 **Hyphens and readability.** A hyphen can make for easier reading by showing structure and, often, pronunciation. Words that might otherwise be misread, such as *re-creation* or *co-op* (as opposed to *recreation* or *coop*), should be hyphenated. Hyphens can also eliminate ambiguity. For example, the hyphen in *much-needed clothing* shows that the clothing is greatly needed rather than abundant and needed. Where no ambiguity could result, as in *public welfare administration* or *graduate student housing*, hyphenation is unnecessary (see also 7.91).

7.91 **Compound modifiers before or after a noun.** When compound modifiers (also called phrasal adjectives) such as *high-profile* or *book-length* precede a noun, hyphenation usually lends clarity. With the exception of proper nouns (such as *United States*) and compounds formed by an adverb ending in *-ly* plus an adjective (see 7.93), it is never incorrect to hyphenate adjectival compounds before a noun. When such compounds *follow* the noun they modify, hyphenation is usually unnecessary, even for adjectival compounds that are hyphenated in *Merriam-Webster* (such as *well-read* or *one-sided*). Two additional exceptions apply: First, unless ambiguity threatens, a noun in the form of an open compound can usually remain open when used as a modifier before another noun (*high school student*, *guest room access*; see also 7.90); when in doubt, check *Merriam-Webster*. Second, certain terms listed as hyphenated adjectives in *Merriam-Webster* remain hyphenated after the noun (see 7.92).

7.92 **Compound modifiers that are always hyphenated.** Compound modifiers that are hyphenated before a noun can usually remain open when they follow the noun (as described in 7.91). For example, a *well-read* student is *well read*. However, some compound modifiers are always hyphenated, even after a noun (see also 7.88). Examples include (but are not limited to) the following: *all-consuming*, *cost-effective*, *dyed-in-the-wool*, *first-rate*, *high-spirited*, *ill-advised*, *old-fashioned*, *short-lived*, *fat-free*, and *wild-eyed*. When in doubt, and if the term is not listed here or under 7.96, check *Merriam-Webster*; if the term is listed there as a hyphenated adjective, it may remain hyphenated after a noun (subject to editorial discretion).

7.93 **Adverbs ending in "-ly."** Compounds formed by an adverb ending in *-ly* plus an adjective or participle (such as *largely irrelevant* or *smartly dressed*) are not hyphenated either before or after a noun, since ambiguity is virtually impossible (*a smartly dressed couple*). (The *-ly* ending with adverbs signals to the reader that the next word will be another modifier, not a noun.) Note, however, that when such a compound consists of more than two words, hyphens may lend clarity (*a not-so-smartly-dressed couple*). Note also that some words ending in *-ly* are adjectives, not adverbs (*early*, *friendly*); hyphens should be retained as needed in compounds formed with such words (*an early-morning walk*; but see 7.94).

7.94 **Multiple hyphens.** Multiple hyphens are usually appropriate for such phrases as *an over-the-counter drug* or *a winner-take-all contest*. If, however, the compound modifier consists of an adjective that itself modifies a compound, additional hyphens may not be necessary. The expressions *late nineteenth-century literature* and *early twentieth-century growth* are clear without a second hyphen. (Similar expressions formed with *mid*—which Chicago now treats as a type of combining form—do not follow this pattern; see 7.96, section 3, under *mid*.) See also 7.96, section 3, under *century*.

7.95 **Suspended hyphens.** When the second part of a hyphenated expression is omitted, the suspended hyphen is retained, followed by a space (or, in a series, by a comma). Such a hyphen is called a suspended hyphen.

fifteen- and twenty-year mortgages
Chicago- or Milwaukee-bound passengers
five-, ten-, and twenty-dollar bills
*but*
a five-by-eight-foot rug (a single entity)
a three-to-five-year gap (a single range)

Omission of the second part of a closed compound follows the same pattern.

over- and underfed cats

Omission of the *first* part of a hyphenated compound follows a similar pattern; the first part of a closed compound, however, should usually be repeated.

state-owned and -operated hospitals
*but*
overfed and overworked mules (*not* overfed and -worked mules)

7.96 **Hyphenation guide.** In general, Chicago prefers a spare hyphenation style: If no suitable example or analogy can be found either in this section (7.87–96) or in the dictionary, hyphens should be added only if doing so will prevent a misreading or otherwise significantly aid comprehension. Each of the four sections of the following table is arranged alphabetically by category or other key term. The first section deals with compounds according to category; the second section, with compounds according to parts of speech. The third section lists examples for specific terms. The fourth section lists common prefixes, most of which join to another word to form one unhyphenated word; note especially the hyphenated exceptions. (Compounds formed with suffixes—e.g., *nationhood*, *penniless*—are almost always closed.)

## 1. COMPOUNDS ACCORDING TO CATEGORY

| | |
|---|---|
| **age terms** | |
| a *three-year-old*<br>a *five-year-old* child<br>a *fifty-five-year-old* woman<br>a test for *nine-to-ten-year-olds*<br>a group of *ten-* and *eleven-year-olds*<br>but<br>*seven years old*<br>*eighteen years of age* | Hyphenated in both noun and adjective forms (except as in the last two examples); note the space after the first hyphen in the fifth but not the fourth example (see 7.95). The examples apply equally to ages expressed as numerals. |
| **chemical compounds** | |
| *sodium chloride*<br>*sodium chloride* solution | Open in both noun and adjective forms. |
| **colors** | |
| *emerald-green* tie<br>*reddish-brown* flagstone<br>*blue-green* algae<br>*snow-white* dress<br>*black-and-white* print<br>but<br>his tie is *emerald green*<br>the stone is *reddish brown*<br>the water is *blue green*<br>the clouds are *snow white*<br>the truth isn't *black and white* | Hyphenated before but not after a noun. |
| **compass points and directions** | |
| *northeast*<br>*southwest*<br>*east-northeast*<br>a *north–south street*<br>*the street runs north–south* | Closed in noun, adjective, and adverb forms unless three directions are combined, in which case a hyphen is used after the first. When *from . . . to* is implied, an en dash is used (see 6.83). |
| **ethnic terms.** See **proper nouns and adjectives relating to geography or nationality** in section 2. | |
| **foreign phrases.** See **non-English phrases.** | |
| **fractions, compounds formed with** | |
| a *half hour*<br>a *half dozen*<br>a *half-hour* session<br>a *quarter mile*<br>a *quarter-mile* run<br>an *eighth note* | Noun forms open; adjective forms hyphenated. See also **number** entries in this section and **half** in section 3. |

| 1. COMPOUNDS ACCORDING TO CATEGORY (continued) | |
|---|---|
| **fractions, simple** | |
| *one-half*<br>*two-thirds*<br>*three-quarters*<br>*one twenty-fifth*<br>*one and three-quarters*<br>a *two-thirds* majority<br>*three-quarters* done<br>a *one twenty-fifth* share | Hyphenated in noun, adjective, and adverb forms, except when the second element is already hyphenated. See also **number + noun** and 9.15. |
| **money** | |
| a *five-cent* raise<br>*sixty-four-million-dollar* question<br>a deal worth *thirty million dollars*<br>*multimillion-dollar* deal<br>but<br>*$30 million* loan<br>a *$50–$60 million* loss | For amounts with spelled-out units, hyphenate before a noun but leave open after; where units are expressed as symbols, leave open in all positions, except between number ranges. See also **number + abbreviation** and 9.22–27, 9.62. |
| **non-English phrases** | |
| an *a priori* argument<br>a *Sturm und Drang* drama<br>*in vitro* fertilization<br>a *tête-à-tête* approach | Open unless hyphens appear in the original language. |
| **number + abbreviation** | |
| the *33 m* distance<br>a *2 kg* weight<br>a *3 ft. high* wall<br>a *7 lb., 8 oz.* baby | Always open (but see 10.64). See also **number + noun**. |
| **number + noun** | |
| a *hundred-meter* race<br>a *seven-hundred-acre* wheat farm<br>a *250-page* book<br>a *fifty-year* project<br>a *three-inch-high* statuette<br>it's *three inches high*<br>a *one-and-a-half-inch* hem<br>*one and a half inches*<br>a *seven-pound, eight-ounce* baby<br>a *six-foot-two* [or *six-foot, two-inch*] adult<br>he's *six feet two* [or *six feet, two inches tall*]<br>he's *six two*<br>*five-to-ten-minute* intervals (a single range)<br>but<br>*five- or ten-minute* intervals (two values) | Hyphenated before a noun, otherwise open. Note the space after the first number in the last example (see 7.95). See also **number + abbreviation** and 9.14. |

| 1. COMPOUNDS ACCORDING TO CATEGORY (continued) | |
|---|---|
| **number + *percent*** | |
| *50 percent*<br>a *10 percent* raise<br>a *30–40 percent* increase | Noun and adjective forms always open, except between number ranges. See also 9.20, 9.62. |
| **number, ordinal, + noun** | |
| *third-floor* apartment<br>*103rd-floor* view<br>on the *third floor*<br>*fifth-place* contestant<br>*eighth-grade* graduation<br>*twenty-first-row* seats<br>in the *twenty-first row*<br>an *eighth grader* | Hyphenated before a noun, otherwise open (but see **numbers, spelled out**). See also **century** and **first, second, third** in section 3. |
| **number, ordinal, + superlative** | |
| a *second-best* decision<br>*third-largest* town<br>*fourth-to-last* contestant<br>he arrived *fourth to last* | Hyphenated before a noun, otherwise open. |
| **numbers, spelled out** | |
| *twenty-eight*<br>*three hundred*<br>*nineteen forty-five*<br>*five hundred fifty-two* contestants<br>*twenty-eighth*<br>*three hundredth*<br>*five hundred fifty-second* contestant | Twenty-one through ninety-nine hyphenated; others open. Applies equally to cardinals and ordinals. See also **fractions, simple**. |
| **relationships.** See **foster**, **grand**, **in-law**, and **step** in section 3. | |
| **time** | |
| at *three thirty*<br>the *three-thirty* train<br>a *four o'clock* train<br>the *5:00 p.m.* news | Usually open; forms such as “three thirty,” “four twenty,” etc. are hyphenated before the noun. |

| 2. COMPOUNDS ACCORDING TO PARTS OF SPEECH | |
|---|---|
| **adjective + noun** | |
| *small-state* senators<br>a *high-quality* alkylate<br>a *middle-class* neighborhood<br>a *top-ten* school<br>the neighborhood is *middle class*<br>placed in the *top ten* | Hyphenated before but not after a noun. |

| 2. COMPOUNDS ACCORDING TO PARTS OF SPEECH (continued) | |
|---|---|
| **adjective + participle** | |
| *tight-lipped* person<br>*high-jumping* grasshoppers<br>*open-ended* question<br>a *lighthearted* inquiry<br>the question was *open ended*<br>he was *softheaded* | Hyphenated before but not after a noun. Some permanent compounds are closed; check *Merriam-Webster*. |
| **adverb ending in -*ly* + participle or adjective** | |
| a *highly paid* ragpicker<br>a *fully open* society<br>he was *mildly amusing* | Open whether before or after a noun (see also 7.93). |
| **adverb not ending in -*ly* + participle or adjective** | |
| a *much-needed* addition<br>it was *much needed*<br>a very *well-read* child<br>*little-understood* rules<br>a *too-easy* answer<br>the *best-known* author<br>the *highest-ranking* officer<br>the *worst-paid* job<br>a *lesser-paid* colleague<br>the *most efficient* method<br>a *less prolific* artist<br>a *more thorough* exam<br>a *rather boring* play<br>the *most skilled* workers (most in number)<br>but<br>the *most-skilled* workers (most in skill)<br>a *very much needed* addition | Hyphenated before but not after a noun; certain compounds, including those with *more, most, less, least,* and *very,* can usually be left open unless ambiguity threatens. When the adverb rather than the compound as a whole is modified by another adverb, the entire expression is open. |
| **combining forms** | |
| *electrocardiogram*<br>*socioeconomic*<br>a *Franco-American* alliance<br>*politico-scientific* studies<br>the *practico-inert* | Closed if listed as such in *Merriam-Webster*; otherwise hyphenated. See also **proper nouns and adjectives relating to geography or nationality**. |
| **gerund + noun** | |
| *running shoes*<br>*cooking class*<br>*running-shoe* store | Noun forms open; adjective forms hyphenated. See also **noun + gerund**. |

| 2. COMPOUNDS ACCORDING TO PARTS OF SPEECH (continued) | |
|---|---|
| **noun + adjective** | |
| *computer-literate* writers<br>*world-famous* doctor<br>*fan-friendly* stadium<br>they are *computer literate*<br>she is *world famous*<br>the stadium is *fan friendly* | Hyphenated before a noun; usually open after a noun. |
| **noun + gerund** | |
| *mountain climbing*<br>a *mountain-climbing* enthusiast<br>*time-clock-punching* employees<br>a *Nobel Prize–winning* chemist (see 6.86)<br>*decision-making*<br>*head-hunting*<br>*bookkeeping*<br>*caregiving*<br>*copyediting* | Noun forms usually open; adjective forms hyphenated before a noun. Some permanent compounds hyphenated or closed (see 7.88). |
| **noun + noun, single function (first noun modifies second noun)** | |
| *student nurse*<br>*restaurant owner*<br>*directory path*<br>*tenure track*<br>*tenure-track* position<br>*home-rule* governance<br>*shipbuilder*<br>*gunrunner*<br>*copyeditor* | Noun forms open; adjective forms hyphenated before a noun. Some permanent compounds closed (see 7.88). |
| **noun + noun, two functions (both nouns equal)** | |
| *writer-director*<br>*philosopher-king*<br>*city-state*<br>*city-state* governance | Both noun and adjective forms always hyphenated. |
| **noun + numeral or enumerator** | |
| *type A*<br>a *type A* executive<br>*type 2* diabetes<br>*size 12* slacks<br>a *page 1* headline<br>*number one* hit (or *No. 1* hit)<br>*Title IX* exemptions | Both noun and adjective forms always open. See also **adjective + noun.** |

| 2. COMPOUNDS ACCORDING TO PARTS OF SPEECH (continued) | |
|---|---|
| **noun + participle** | |
| a *Wagner-burdened* repertoire<br>*flower-filled* garden<br>*action-packed* movie<br>the garden was *flower filled*<br>the movie was *action packed*<br>but<br>the room was *air-conditioned*<br>the events were *stage-managed* | Hyphenated before a noun, otherwise open unless verb form hyphenated in *Merriam-Webster* (see also **phrases, verbal**). |
| **participle + noun** | |
| *chopped-liver* pâté<br>*cutting-edge* methods<br>their approach was *cutting edge* | Adjective forms hyphenated before but not after a noun. |
| **participle + *up*, *out*, and similar adverbs** | |
| *dressed-up* children<br>*burned-out* buildings<br>*ironed-on* decal<br>we were *dressed up*<br>that decal is *ironed on*<br>we *ironed on* the decal | Adjective forms hyphenated before but not after a noun. Verb forms always open. |
| **phrases, adjectival** | |
| an *over-the-counter* drug<br>a *matter-of-fact* reply<br>an *up-to-date* solution<br>a *touch-and-go* situation<br>her tone was *matter of fact*<br>his equipment was *up to date*<br>the situation was *touch and go* | Hyphenated before a noun; usually open after a noun. See also **phrases, adverbial**. |
| **phrases, adverbial** | |
| played each other *one-on-one*<br>collided *head-on*<br>spoke *matter-of-factly*<br>worked *part-time*<br>passed *hand to hand*<br>fought *mano a mano*<br>took things *day by day*<br>available *over the counter* | Hyphenated if listed as a hyphenated adverb in *Merriam-Webster*; otherwise open. |
| **phrases, noun** | |
| *stick-in-the-mud*<br>*jack-of-all-trades*<br>a *flash in the pan* | Hyphenated or open as listed in *Merriam-Webster*. If not in the dictionary, open. |

| 2. COMPOUNDS ACCORDING TO PARTS OF SPEECH (continued) | |
|---|---|
| **phrases, verbal** | |
| *babysit*<br>*handcraft*<br>*air-condition*<br>*fast-talk*<br>*stage-manage*<br>*strong-arm*<br>*sucker punch* | Closed, hyphenated, or open as listed in *Merriam-Webster*. If not in the dictionary, leave open. |
| **proper nouns and adjectives relating to geography or nationality** | |
| *African Americans*<br>*African American* president<br>a *Chinese American*<br>*French Canadians*<br>*South Asian Americans*<br>the *Scotch Irish*<br>the *North Central* region<br>*Middle Eastern* countries<br>but<br>*Sino-Tibetan* languages<br>*Anglo-American* cooperation<br>*Anglo-Americans*<br>the *Spanish-American* War<br>the *US-Canada* border | Open in both noun and adjective forms, unless the first term is a prefix or unless *between* is implied. See also 8.40. |

| 3. COMPOUNDS FORMED WITH SPECIFIC TERMS | |
|---|---|
| **ache** | |
| *toothache*<br>*stomachache*<br>*earache* | Always closed. |
| **all** | |
| *all out*<br>*all along*<br>*all over*<br>an *all-out* effort<br>an *all-American* player<br>the book is *all-encompassing*<br>but<br>we were *all in* [tired] | Adverbial phrases open; adjectival phrases usually hyphenated both before and after a noun. |
| **book** | |
| *reference book*<br>*coupon book*<br>*checkbook*<br>*cookbook* | Closed or open as listed in *Merriam-Webster*. If not in the dictionary, open. |

| 3. COMPOUNDS FORMED WITH SPECIFIC TERMS (continued) | |
|---|---|
| **borne** | |
| *waterborne*<br>*foodborne*<br>*mosquito-borne* | Closed if listed as such in *Merriam-Webster*. If not listed there, hyphenated. |
| **century** | |
| the *twenty-first century*<br>*fourteenth-century* monastery<br>*twenty-first-century* history<br>a *mid-eighteenth-century* poet<br>*late nineteenth-century* photographs<br>her style was *nineteenth century* | Noun forms always open; adjectival compounds hyphenated before but not after a noun. See also **old** and **mid** (below) and 7.94, 9.34. |
| **cross** | |
| a *cross section*<br>a *cross-reference*<br>*cross-referenced*<br>*cross-stitch*<br>*cross-grained*<br>*cross-country*<br>*crossbow*<br>*crossover* | Many compounds formed with *cross* are in *Merriam-Webster* (as those listed here). If not in *Merriam-Webster*, leave noun forms open; hyphenate adjective, adverb, and verb forms. |
| **e** | |
| *email*<br>*ebook*<br>*esports*<br>*e-bike*<br>*e-commerce*<br>*eBay* | Close up *email*, *ebook*, and *esports* and certain proper nouns. Hyphenate other *e*-terms. See also 8.155. |
| **elect** | |
| *president-elect*<br>*vice president–elect*<br>*mayor-elect*<br>*county assessor–elect* | Hyphenated, but use an en dash if *elect* follows an open compound (see 6.86). See also **vice**. |
| **ever** | |
| *ever-ready* help<br>*ever-recurring* problem<br>*everlasting*<br>he was *ever eager* | Usually hyphenated before but not after a noun; some permanent compounds closed. |
| **ex** | |
| *ex-partner*<br>*ex-marine*<br>*ex–corporate executive* | Hyphenated, but use en dash if *ex-* precedes an open compound (see 6.86). |

| 3. COMPOUNDS FORMED WITH SPECIFIC TERMS (continued) | |
|---|---|
| **first, second, third** | |
| *firsthand* knowledge<br>*first-* and *secondhand* knowledge (see 7.95)<br>*first-class* tickets<br>*third-rate* production<br>the tickets were *first-class*<br>the production was *third-rate*<br>upgraded to *first class*<br>learned at *first hand* | Adjective forms usually hyphenated before and after the noun, except for a few closed compounds listed in *Merriam-Webster*. Noun forms usually open. Terms with *fourth*, *fifth*, etc. follow a similar pattern. |
| **fold** | |
| *fourfold*<br>*hundredfold*<br>but<br>*twenty-five-fold*<br>*150-fold* | Hyphenated with hyphenated forms of spelled-out numbers or with numerals; otherwise closed. |
| **foster** | |
| *foster mother*<br>*foster parents*<br>a *foster-family* background | Noun forms open; adjective forms hyphenated. |
| **free** | |
| *fat-free* yogurt<br>*toll-free* number<br>*accident-free* driver<br>the yogurt is *fat-free*<br>the number is *toll-free*<br>the driver is *accident-free* | Compounds formed with *free* as second element are hyphenated both before and after a noun. |
| **full** | |
| *full-length* mirror<br>the mirror is *full length*<br>three *bags full*<br>a *suitcase full* | Hyphenated before a noun, otherwise open. Use *ful* only in such permanent compounds as *cupful*, *handful*. |
| **general** | |
| *attorney general*<br>*postmaster general*<br>*lieutenants general* | Always open; in plural forms, *general* remains singular. |
| **grand, great-grand** | |
| *grandfather*<br>*granddaughter*<br>*great-grandmother*<br>*great-great-grandchild* | *Grand* compounds closed; *great* compounds hyphenated. |

| 3. COMPOUNDS FORMED WITH SPECIFIC TERMS (continued) | |
|---|---|
| **half** | |
| a *half-finished meal*<br>it was *half finished*<br>we were *half asleep*<br>a *half sister*<br>a *half hour*<br>a *half-hour* session<br>*halfway*<br>*halftime* show (of a game)<br>*half-time* hours (of a job)<br>worked *half-time* (of a job)<br>we played *half seriously*<br>we *half expected* to fly | Adjective forms hyphenated before but not after the noun; noun, adverb, and verb forms usually open. Some permanent compounds closed (check *Merriam-Webster*). See also **fractions** in section 1 and **phrases, adverbial** in section 2. |
| **house** | |
| *schoolhouse*<br>*courthouse*<br>*safe house*<br>*rest house* | Closed or open as listed in *Merriam-Webster*. If not in the dictionary, open. |
| **ill** | |
| *ill-advised* trip<br>*ill-defined* goals<br>the trip was *ill-advised*<br>the goal was *ill-defined* | Hyphenated before and after the noun. |
| **in-law** | |
| *sister-in-law*<br>*parents-in-law* | All compounds hyphenated; only the first element takes a plural form. |
| **like** | |
| *catlike*<br>*childlike*<br>*Christlike*<br>*Zen-like*<br>*bell-like*<br>a *penitentiary-like* institution | Closed or hyphenated as in *Merriam-Webster*. If not in *Merriam-Webster*, hyphenated; compounds retain the hyphen both before and after a noun. |
| **mid** | |
| *midair*<br>*midday*<br>*midsemester*<br>*mid-sentence*<br>*mid-thirties*<br>*mid-Atlantic*<br>*mid- to late thirties* (see 7.95) | Closed or hyphenated as in *Merriam-Webster*. (Chicago now treats *mid* as an adjective combining form rather than as a prefix.) If not listed there, hyphenate. |

| 3. COMPOUNDS FORMED WITH SPECIFIC TERMS (continued) | |
|---|---|
| **near** | |
| in the *near term*<br>a *near accident*<br>a *near-term* proposal<br>a *near-dead* language | Noun forms open; adjective forms hyphenated. |
| **odd** | |
| a *hundred-odd* manuscripts<br>*350-odd* books | Always hyphenated. |
| **old** | |
| a *three-year-old*<br>a *105-year-old* woman<br>a *decade-old* union<br>a *centuries-old* debate<br>a child who is *three years old*<br>the debate is *centuries old* | Noun forms hyphenated. Adjective forms hyphenated before a noun, open after. See also **age terms** in section 1. |
| **on** | |
| *online*<br>*onstage*<br>*ongoing*<br>*on-screen*<br>*on-site* | Sometimes closed, sometimes hyphenated. Check *Merriam-Webster* and hyphenate if term is not listed. See also 7.89. |
| **percent.** See **number + *percent*** in section 1. | |
| **pseudo.** See section 4. | |
| **quasi** | |
| a *quasi corporation*<br>a *quasi-public* corporation<br>*quasi-judicial*<br>*quasiperiodic*<br>*quasicrystal* | Noun forms usually open; adjective forms usually hyphenated. A handful of permanent compounds are listed in *Merriam-Webster*. |
| **self** | |
| *self-restraint*<br>*self-realization*<br>*self-sustaining*<br>*self-conscious*<br>the behavior is *self-destructive*<br>*selfless*<br>*unselfconscious* | Both noun and adjective forms hyphenated, except where *self* is followed by a suffix or preceded by *un*. |

| 3. COMPOUNDS FORMED WITH SPECIFIC TERMS (continued) | |
|---|---|
| **step** | |
| *stepbrother*<br>*stepparent*<br>*step-granddaughter*<br>*step-great-granddaughter* | Always closed except with *grand* and *great*. |
| **style** | |
| dined *family-style*<br>*1920s-style* dancing<br>danced *1920s-style*<br>*Chicago-style* hyphenation<br>according to *Chicago style*<br>*sentence-style* capitalization<br>capitalized *sentence-style*<br>use *sentence style* | Adjective and adverb forms hyphenated; noun forms usually open. |
| **then** | |
| the country's *then-president*<br>*then-President* Bush<br>*then–Vice President* Biden<br>our *then–assistant principal* | When *then* is used in the sense of *former*, a hyphen will prevent misreading (a departure from previous editions). Use an en dash when *then* precedes an open compound (see 6.86). See also **vice**. |
| **vice** | |
| *vice-consul*<br>*vice-chancellor*<br>*vice president*<br>*vice-presidential* duties<br>a speech that was *vice presidential*<br>*vice admiral*<br>*viceroy* | Adjective forms hyphenated before the noun; noun forms sometimes hyphenated, sometimes open, occasionally closed. Check *Merriam-Webster* and hyphenate if term is not listed. See also **elect** and **then**. |
| **web (internet)** | |
| a *website*<br>a *web crawler*<br>a *web page*<br>*web-related* matters | Noun forms open or closed, as shown; if not in *Merriam-Webster*, leave open. Adjective forms hyphenated before a noun. See also 7.85. |
| **wide** | |
| *worldwide*<br>*citywide*<br>*Chicago-wide*<br>the canvass was *university-wide* | Closed if listed as such in *Merriam-Webster*. If not listed there, hyphenated; compounds retain the hyphen both before and after a noun. |

| 4. WORDS FORMED WITH PREFIXES | |
|---|---|
| Compounds formed with prefixes are normally closed, whether nouns, verbs, adjectives, or adverbs. A hyphen should be used, however, (1) before a capitalized word or a numeral, as in *un-American*, *pre-1950*; (2) before a compound term, as in *non-self-sustaining*, *pre–Vietnam War* (use an en dash before an open compound; see 6.86); (3) to separate two *i*'s, two *a*'s, and other combinations of letters or syllables that might cause misreading, as in *anti-intellectual*, *extra-alkaline*, *pre-authorize*; (4) to separate the repeated terms in a double prefix, as in *re-review*, *sub-subentry*; (5) when a prefix or combining form stands alone, as in *over- and underused*, *macro- and microeconomics*. Compounds formed with prefixes and other combining forms not listed here, such as *auto*, *tri*, and *para*, follow the same pattern. A few of the terms listed in this section depart from *Merriam-Webster*. In general, the usage outlined here takes precedence; however, the occasional hyphen not shown here may be retained or added for clarity or as a matter of authorial preference (subject to editorial discretion). | |
| **ante** | antebellum, antenatal, antediluvian |
| **anti** | antihypertensive, antihero, antifascist, antiracist, antisemitism, *but* anti-inflammatory, anti-Hitlerian, anti-antifascist |
| **bi** | binomial, bivalent, bisexual |
| **bio** | bioecology, biophysical, biosociology |
| **cis** | cisgender, cissexual, cisatlantic, *but* cis-Victorian, *cis*-2-pentene (*cis* in italics), cis male (*cis* as adjective) |
| **co** | coequal, coauthor, coeditor, coordinate, cooperation, coworker, *but* co-op, co-opt |
| **counter** | counterclockwise, counterrevolution |
| **cyber** | cyberspace, cyberbullying |
| **de** | decompress, deconstruct, deontological, *but* de-emphasize, de-stress |
| **extra** | extramural, extrafine, *but* extra-administrative |
| **hyper** | hypertension, hyperactive, hypertext |
| **infra** | infrasonic, infrastructure |
| **inter** | interorganizational, interfaith |
| **intra** | intrazonal, intramural, *but* intra-arterial |
| **macro** | macroeconomics, macromolecular |
| **mega** | megavitamin, megamall, *but* mega-annoyance |
| **meta** | metalanguage, metaethical, *but* meta-analysis (not the same as *metanalysis*) |

| 4. WORDS FORMED WITH PREFIXES (continued) | |
|---|---|
| **micro** | microeconomics, micromethodical |
| **mid** | See section 3. |
| **mini** | minivan, minimarket |
| **multi** | multiauthor, multiconductor, *but* multi-institutional |
| **neo** | neonate, neoorthodox, Neoplatonism, neo-Nazi (*neo* lowercase or capital and hyphenated as in dictionary; lowercase and hyphenate if not in dictionary) |
| **non** | nonbinary, nonviolent, nonevent, nonnegotiable, *but* non-beer-drinking |
| **over** | overmagnified, overshoes, overconscientious |
| **post** | postdoctoral, postmodernism, *but* post-traumatic, post-Vietnam, post–World War II (see 6.86) |
| **pre** | premodern, preregistration, prewar, preempt, *but* pre-authorize, pre-Columbian, Pre-Raphaelite (*pre* lowercase or capital as in dictionary; lowercase if term is not in dictionary) |
| **pro** | proactive, proindustrial, promarket, *but* pro-choice, pro-life, pro-Canadian |
| **proto** | protolanguage, protogalaxy, protomartyr |
| **pseudo** | pseudotechnocrat, pseudomodern, *but* pseudo-Tudor |
| **re** | reedit, reunify, reproposition, *but* re-cover, re-creation (as distinct from *recover*, *recreation*) |
| **semi** | semiopaque, semiconductor, *but* semi-invalid |
| **sub** | subbasement, subzero, subcutaneous |
| **super** | superannuated, supervirtuoso, superpowerful |
| **supra** | supranational, suprarenal, supraorbital, *but* supra-American |
| **trans** | transgender, transshipment, transmembrane, transcontinental, transatlantic, *but* trans-American, *trans*-2-pentene (*trans* in italics), trans fat, trans man, trans woman (*trans* as adjective) |
| **ultra** | ultrasophisticated, ultraorganized, ultraevangelical |
| **un** | unfunded, unneutered, *but* un-English, un-unionized |
| **under** | underemployed, underrate, undercount |

# 8 Names, Terms, and Titles of Works

## OVERVIEW

8.1 **Proper nouns and adjectives.** Proper nouns, which refer to specific people, places, and other named entities, are usually capitalized, as are many of the adjectives and other terms derived from or associated with them. For the latter, Chicago has traditionally preferred a sparing use of capitals (what in previous editions has been referred to as a "down" style). For example, although *Brussels* (the Belgian city) and *French* (a proper adjective derived from the word *France*) are normally capitalized, Chicago recommends lowercase *brussels sprouts* and *french fries* to signal that such sprouts are not necessarily from Brussels and such fries are not literally French. In recent years, however, many writers have maintained a preference for capitalizing words like *Brussels* and *French* however they might be used, a trend that this manual now supports for more terms than in previous editions (see 8.62). At the same time, terms like *Black* and *Indigenous*, when applied to people, have become accepted as proper adjectives despite not being derived from proper nouns, a development that Chicago also supports (see 8.39). There are many terms that can have both a proper and a generic use. For example, *President Taft* (where *President* is a title) and *the University of Chicago* (where *University* is part of the name) would be capitalized, whereas the generic nouns *president* and *university* would not be, even when they refer to a specific person or university (see 8.20–34). In general, the recommendations in this chapter are designed to recognize common usage (which may favor capitalization), supported by logic (which in turn may argue for lowercase); when in doubt, follow *Merriam-Webster* (see 7.1) or, for terms not listed there, an up-to-date encyclopedia or other reputable source. For titles of works, which in most contexts are capitalized in title case (also called headline style), see 8.158.

8.2 **Italics and quotation marks for titles and other terms.** Chicago prefers italics to set off the titles of major or freestanding works such as books, journals and other periodicals, movies and television shows, musicals and plays, and paintings. This practice extends to cover the names of ships and other craft, species names, and legal cases. Quotation marks are usually reserved for the titles of subsections of larger works—including chapters and articles, television episodes, and poems in a collection. Some titles—for example, of a book series or a website, under which any number of works or documents may be collected—are neither italicized nor placed in quotation marks. For more on the titles of works, including matters of capitalization and punctuation, see 8.157–204. For the use of italics and quotation marks to highlight or set off certain letters, words, and phrases, see 7.49–86.

## PERSONAL NAMES

8.3 **Personal names — additional resources.** For names of well-known deceased persons, Chicago generally prefers the spellings in the biographical entries in *Merriam-Webster* (see 7.1) or, for names not found there, *Encyclopaedia Britannica* (bibliog. 4.3). For living persons, consult either *Merriam-Webster* or *Britannica* or, for names not found there, *Who's Who* or *Who's Who in America*, among other resources. (See bibliog. 4.1 for these and other useful works.) For the spelling of any well-known person's name, living or otherwise, Wikipedia can also be a helpful resource. In all cases, it is imperative to double-check a name in at least one additional source. Where different spellings appear in different sources (e.g., Breugel versus Brueghel or Breughel, for the famous family of Flemish painters), the writer or editor must make a choice and stick with it. Names of known and lesser-known persons not in the standard references can usually be checked and cross-checked at any number of reputable online resources (e.g., for authors' names, library catalogs or booksellers). The name of a living person should, wherever possible, correspond to that person's preferred usage. For some caveats related to using real names (as in fiction), see 4.77.

8.4 **Capitalization of personal names.** Names and initials of persons, real or fictitious, are capitalized. A space should be used between any initials, except when initials are used alone. See also 7.69, 10.14.

| | |
|---|---|
| Jane Doe | M. F. K. Fisher |
| George S. McGovern | Malcolm X |
| P. D. James | LBJ |

Unconventional spellings strongly preferred by the bearer of the name or pen name (e.g., bell hooks) should usually be respected in appropriate contexts (library catalogs usually capitalize such names). E. E. Cummings can be safely capitalized; it was one of his publishers, not he himself, who lowercased his name. Most editors will draw the line at beginning a sentence with a lowercased name and choose either to rewrite or to capitalize the first letter for the occasion. When a personal name includes a lowercase particle, the particle is capitalized if it begins a sentence or a note (but lowercase if it begins a bibliography entry). See also 8.5, 8.6.

8.5 **Names with particles or prefixes.** Many names include particles such as *de*, *d'*, *de la*, *el*, *von*, *van*, and *ten*. Practice with regard to capitalizing and spacing the particles varies widely, and confirmation should be sought in a biographical dictionary or other authoritative source. When the surname is used alone, the particle is usually (but not always) retained, capitalized or lowercased and spaced as in the full name (though always capitalized when beginning a sentence or a note; see also 8.4). *Le*, *La*, and *L'* are usually capitalized when not preceded by *de*; *the*, which sometimes appears with the English form of a Native American name, can be lowercased unless it begins a sentence or a note. The list below illustrates a variety of usages. Conventions for styling names with particles in French and several other languages, most of which are observed in an English-language context, are covered in 8.8, 8.9, 8.10, 8.11, 8.12, 8.15, 8.35. For determining alphabetical order, see 15.79.

Alfonse D'Amato; D'Amato
Walter de la Mare; de la Mare
Paul de Man; de Man
Thomas De Quincey; De Quincey
Ellen DeGeneres; DeGeneres
W. E. B. Du Bois; Du Bois
Daphne du Maurier; du Maurier
Page duBois; duBois
Robert M. La Follette Sr.; La Follette
John le Carré; le Carré (the pen name)
Pierre-Charles L'Enfant; L'Enfant
Farouk El-Baz; El-Baz
Abraham Ten Broeck; Ten Broeck
the Prophet (Tenskwatawa)
Robert van Gulik; van Gulik
Stephen Van Rensselaer; Van Rensselaer
Wernher von Braun; von Braun
*but, at the beginning of a sentence,*
Von Braun's designs . . .

Prefixes such as *Fitz*, *Mc*, and *O'* generally stay with the surname and are usually capitalized.

Melissa McCarthy; McCarthy
Shaquille O'Neal; O'Neal

Note that lowercase letters in particles and prefixes usually get capitalized in an all-caps context.

MELISSA MCCARTHY (*not* McCARTHY)

8.6 **Screen names and other aliases.** Screen names, stage names, and other invented names and aliases often exhibit unconventional capitalization. In general, follow the usage of the bearer as far as it can be determined. This advice extends to what are technically usernames (as in the fourth example below); though usernames (unlike passwords) are not normally case sensitive, readers will expect them to match what they find online. The word *the*, normally lowercase as part of a name (see 8.5), is sometimes capitalized in a stage name or alias (as in the third example); if spelled creatively (as in the second example), capitalization is the norm. See also 8.35.

André the Giant
Megan Thee Stallion
tracks featuring The Weeknd
people who follow @JLo, @Oprah, @BarackObama, @BrunoMars, @taylor swift13, @ChicagoManual, @nytimes, and @NASA
a photo on Flickr by rvjak

An all-lowercase name usually gets an initial capital at the beginning of a sentence unless it begins with an @ sign, in which case the better option may be to reword.

Rvjak's photos included . . .
@nytimes posted that . . .
*or, better,*
*The New York Times* (@nytimes) posted that . . .

8.7 **Hyphenated and extended names.** A hyphenated last name or a last name that consists of two or more elements should usually retain each element. (In the case of someone who is generally known by a shorter form, that form may be used, but only after the fuller form has been established.) For names of prominent or historical figures, *Merriam-Webster* and other standard dictionaries usually indicate where the last name begins (as in an alphabetical listing).

Victoria Sackville-West; Sackville-West
Ralph Vaughan Williams; Vaughan Williams (*not* Williams)
Ludwig Mies van der Rohe; Mies van der Rohe (*not* van der Rohe); Mies
*but*
John Hope Franklin; Franklin
Charlotte Perkins Gilman; Gilman

For unhyphenated compound names of lesser-known persons for whom proper usage cannot be determined, use only the last element (including any particle[s]; see 8.5). For Spanish last names, see 8.12.

8.8 **French names.** The particles *de* and *d'* are lowercased (except at the beginning of a sentence). When the last name is used alone, *de* (but not *d'*) is often dropped. Its occasional retention, in *de Gaulle*, for example, is suggested by tradition rather than logic. (When a name begins with closed-up *de*, as in *Debussy*, the *d* is always capitalized.)

Jean d'Alembert; d'Alembert
Alfred de Musset; Musset

Alexis de Tocqueville; Tocqueville
*but*
Charles de Gaulle; de Gaulle

When *de la* precedes a name, *la* is usually capitalized and is always retained when the last name is used alone. The contraction *du* is usually lowercased in a full name but is retained and capitalized when the last name is used alone. (When a name begins with closed-up *du*, as in *Dupont*, the *d* is always capitalized.)

Jean de La Fontaine; La Fontaine
René-Robert Cavelier de La Salle; La Salle
Philippe du Puy de Clinchamps; Du Puy de Clinchamps

When the article *le* accompanies a name, it is capitalized with or without the first name.

Gustave Le Bon; Le Bon

Initials standing for a hyphenated given name are usually hyphenated.

Jean-Paul Sartre; J.-P. Sartre; Sartre

There is considerable variation in French usage; the guidelines and examples above merely represent the most common forms.

8.9 **German and Portuguese names.** In the original languages, particles in German and Portuguese names are lowercased and are usually dropped when the last name is used alone. Usage varies, however, so it is important to consult a biographical dictionary or other reliable resource.

Alexander von Humboldt; Humboldt
Maximilian von Spee; Spee
Heinrich Friedrich Karl vom und zum Stein; Stein
Ludwig van Beethoven; Beethoven
Jânio da Silva Quadros; Quadros
*but*
Ursula von der Leyen; von der Leyen
Vasco da Gama; da Gama

8.10 **Italian names.** Particles in Italian names are most often uppercased and retained when the last name is used alone. Usage varies, however, so it is important to check against a reliable resource.

Gabriele D'Annunzio; D'Annunzio
Lorenzo Da Ponte; Da Ponte
*but*
Luca della Robbia; della Robbia

In many older aristocratic names, the particle is traditionally lowercased and dropped when the last name is used alone.

Beatrice d'Este; Este
Lorenzo de' Medici; Medici
*but*
Leonardo da Vinci; Leonardo ("da Vinci" is an epithet, not a surname; see also 8.35)

8.11 **Dutch names.** In Dutch names, the particles *van*, *van den*, *ter*, and the like are usually lowercased when the full name is given but capitalized when only the last name is used.

Johannes van Keulen; Van Keulen
Pieter van den Keere; Van den Keere
Vincent van Gogh; Van Gogh
Gerard ter Borch; Ter Borch
Corrie ten Boom; Ten Boom
*but*
Eddie Van Halen; Van Halen

8.12 **Spanish names.** Many Spanish names are composed of both the father's and the mother's family names, usually in that order, sometimes joined by *y* (and). When the given name is omitted, persons with such names are usually referred to by both family names but sometimes by only one (usually, but not always, the first of the two family names), according to their own preference (or, sometimes, to established usage). It is never incorrect to use both.

José Ortega y Gasset; Ortega y Gasset *or* Ortega
Pascual Ortiz Rubio; Ortiz Rubio *or* Ortiz
Federico García Lorca; García Lorca (popularly known as Lorca)

Spanish family names that include an article, a preposition, or both are treated in the same way as analogous French names.

Tomás de Torquemada; Torquemada
Manuel de Falla; Falla

Bartolomé de Las Casas; Las Casas
Gonzalo Fernández de Oviedo; Fernández de Oviedo

Traditionally, a married woman replaced her mother's family name with her husband's (first) family name, sometimes preceded by *de*. If, for example, María Carmen Mendoza Salinas married Juan Alberto Peña Montalvo, she could change her legal name to María Carmen Mendoza (de) Peña or, if the husband was well known by both family names, to María Carmen Mendoza (de) Peña Montalvo. Many women in Spanish-speaking countries, however, no longer take their husband's family name. For alphabetizing, see 15.92.

8.13 **Russian names.** Russian family names, as well as patronymics (the name preceding the family name and derived from the name of the father), sometimes take different endings for male and female members of the family. For example, Vladimir Lenin's real name was Vladimir Ilyich Ulyanov (given name, patronymic, family name); his sister Maria was Maria Ilyinichna Ulyanova. In Russian sources (and, by extension, their English translations), often only the given name and patronymic are used; in such instances the patronymic should not be confused either for a middle name or for the family name.

8.14 **Hungarian names.** In Hungarian practice, the family name precedes the given name—for example, Molnár Ferenc, Kodály Zoltán. In English contexts, however, such names are usually inverted—Ferenc Molnár, Zoltán Kodály. In some cases, the family name includes an initial—for example, É. Kiss Katalin. When such a name is inverted for English contexts (i.e., to become Katalin É. Kiss), the initial should not be confused for a middle initial. When such a name is inverted, as for an index, it is properly listed under the initial (see 15.86).

8.15 **Arabic names.** Surnames of Arabic origin (which are strictly surnames rather than family names) are often prefixed by such elements as *Abu*, *Abd*, *Ibn*, *Al*, or *El*. Since these are integral parts of a name, just as *Mc* or *Fitz* forms a part of certain names, they should usually not be dropped when the surname is used alone. Some names, however, may be better known without the prefix (as in the last two examples); if in doubt, check against a reliable resource. Capitalization of such elements varies widely, but terms joined with a hyphen can usually be lowercased. See also 11.86, 11.87, 15.83.

Syed Abu Zafar Nadvi; Abu Zafar Nadvi
Abdul Aziz Ibn Saud; Ibn Saud

Tawfiq al-Hakim; al-Hakim
*but*
Anwar el-Sadat; Sadat
Nawal El Saadawi; Saadawi

Names of rulers of older times are often shortened to the first part of the name rather than the second. This practice is sometimes also followed for modern names; consult *Britannica* or another reliable resource (and see 8.24 for an example).

Harun al-Rashid; Harun (al-Rashid, "Rightly Guided," was Harun's *laqab*, a descriptive name he took on his accession to the caliphate)

8.16 **Chinese names.** In Chinese usage, the family name precedes the given name. This practice should be followed except for people whose names are known to follow Western order in English contexts. For use of the Pinyin and Wade-Giles systems of transliteration, see 11.89–99.

Chiang Kai-shek; Chiang (Wade-Giles)
Mao Tse-tung; Mao (Wade-Giles)
Li Bai; Li (Pinyin)
Du Fu; Du (Pinyin)
Yu Xuanji; Yu (Pinyin)
*but*
Laura Cha Shih May-lung; Laura Cha; Cha
Anthony Yu; Yu
Tang Tsou; Tsou

8.17 **Japanese names.** In Japanese usage, the family name precedes the given name. Japanese name order is frequently westernized, however, by authors writing in English or by people with Japanese names who live in the West.

Yoshida Shigeru; Yoshida
Kanda Nobuo; Kanda
Yosano Akiko; Yosano
*but*
Akira Kurosawa; Kurosawa
Shinzō Abe; Abe
Chiaki Mukai; Mukai

8.18 **Korean names.** In Korean usage, the family name precedes the given name, and this is how it is usually presented even in English-language contexts. People with Korean names who live in the West, however, often invert this order.

Kim Dae-jung; Kim
Oh Jung-hee; Oh
*but*
Chang-rae Lee; Lee

8.19 **Other Asian names.** In some Asian countries, people are usually known by their given name rather than by a surname or family name. The Indonesian writer Pramoedya Ananta Toer, for example, is referred to in short form as Pramoedya (not as Toer). For further examples, see 15.84, 15.88, 15.93, 15.94. If in doubt, use the full form of a name in all references or consult either an expert or the usage in a reputable source that discusses the person in question.

## TITLES AND OFFICES

8.20 **Titles and offices — the general rule.** Civil, military, religious, and professional titles are capitalized when they immediately precede a personal name and are thus used as part of the name (traditionally replacing the title holder's first name). In formal prose and other generic text, titles are normally lowercased when following a name or used in place of a name (but see 8.21). For abbreviated forms, see 10.13–24.

Abraham Lincoln, president of the United States (*or* President Abraham Lincoln of the United States); President Lincoln; the president
General Bradley; the general
Cardinal Newman; the cardinal
Governors Ige and Brown; the governors

Although a full name may be used with a capitalized title (e.g., President Abraham Lincoln)—and though it is perfectly correct to do so—some writers choose to avoid using the title before a full name in formal prose, especially with civil, corporate, and academic titles (see 8.23, 8.28, 8.29). (For titles used in apposition to a name, see 8.22.) Note also that once a title has been given, it need not be repeated each time a person's name is mentioned.

Elizabeth Warren, senator from Massachusetts (*or* Senator Elizabeth Warren of Massachusetts); Senator Warren; Warren; the senator

8.21 **Exceptions to the general rule for titles and offices.** In promotional or ceremonial contexts such as a displayed list of donors in the front matter of a book or a list of corporate officers in an annual report, titles are usually capitalized even when following a personal name. Exceptions may also be called for in other contexts for reasons of courtesy or diplomacy.

Maria Martinez, Director of International Sales

A title used alone, in place of a personal name, is capitalized only in such contexts as a toast or a formal introduction, or when used in direct address (see also 6.57, 8.37).

Ladies and Gentlemen, the Prime Minister.
I would have done it, Captain, but the ship was sinking.
Thank you, Mr. President.
*but*
We thanked the prime minister for her time.

8.22 **Titles used in apposition.** Unless it is separated from the name by a comma, a formal title used in apposition to a name should be capitalized when it precedes the name. (A title used in apposition is normally preceded by an adjective or an article that modifies or otherwise limits the title. See also 5.26.) This departure from the advice in previous editions aligns with common usage (and with 8.20) and will aid clarity in most instances.

the Empress Elisabeth of Austria
German Chancellor Olaf Scholz
the Argentinian-born Pope Francis
former President Carter
former Presidents Reagan and Ford
then–Secretary of State Hillary Clinton (with an en dash; see 6.86)
*but*
a meeting with the German chancellor, Olaf Scholz
the novelist Virginia Woolf (not a formal title; see also 8.31)

8.23 **Civil titles.** Much of the usage below is contradicted by the official literature typically generated by political offices, where capitalization of a title in any position is the norm (see 8.21). In formal prose, however, civil titles are capitalized only when used before a name (except as noted). See also 10.15.

the president; George Washington, first president of the United States; President Washington; the presidency; presidential; the Washington administration; Washington; Ferdinand Romualdez Marcos Jr., president of the Philippines; President Marcos; Marcos

the vice president; John Adams, vice president of the United States; Vice President Adams; vice-presidential duties

the secretary of state; Antony Blinken, secretary of state; Secretary of State Blinken *or* Secretary Blinken

the secretary of the treasury; Janet Yellen, secretary of the treasury; Treasury Secretary Janet Yellen *or* Secretary Yellen

the senator; the senator from New York; New York Senator Kirsten E. Gillibrand (see 8.22); Senator Gillibrand; Senators Gillibrand and Schumer; Raphael G. Warnock, Democrat from Georgia (*or* D-GA)

the representative; the congressman; the congresswoman; Robin Kelly, representative from Illinois *or* congresswoman from Illinois; Illinois Congresswoman Robin Kelly; Congresswoman Kelly *or* Rep. Robin Kelly (D-IL); Dan Crenshaw, representative from Texas; Congressman Crenshaw, Republican from Texas (*or* R-TX); the congressman *or* the representative; Representatives Kelly and Crenshaw

the Speaker; Mike Johnson, Speaker of the House of Representatives; Speaker Johnson (*Speaker* is best capitalized in all contexts to avoid conflation with generic speakers)

the chief justice; John G. Roberts Jr., chief justice of the United States; Chief Justice Roberts (see also 8.65)

the associate justice; Elena Kagan, associate justice; Justice Kagan; Justices Kagan and Sotomayor

the chief judge; Timothy C. Evans, chief judge of the Cook County Circuit Court; Judge Evans

the ambassador; Jane Hartley, ambassador to the Court of St. James's *or* ambassador to the United Kingdom; Ambassador Hartley

the governor; Gretchen Whitmer, governor of the state of Michigan; Governor Whitmer

the mayor; Brandon Johnson, mayor of Chicago; Mayor Johnson

the state senator; Sandra R. Williams, Ohio state senator; the Honorable Sandra R. Williams (*or* Senator Williams)

the state representative (same pattern as state senator)

the governor general of Canada; the Right Honourable Mary Simon

the minister of finance (*or* finance minister); Nirmala Sitharaman, finance minister of India; Sitharaman

the prime minister; the Right Honourable Pierre Elliott Trudeau, former prime minister of Canada; Rishi Sunak, the British prime minister

the premier (of a Canadian province); the Honourable Heather Stefanson

the member of Parliament (UK and Canada); Jane Doe, member of Parliament, *or, more commonly,* Jane Doe, MP; Jane Doe, the member for West Hamage
the chief whip; Pemmy Majodina, chief whip of the African National Congress; Majodina
the foreign secretary (UK); the foreign minister (other nations); the British foreign secretary; the German foreign minister
the chancellor; Olaf Scholz, chancellor of Germany; Chancellor Scholz
the chancellor of the exchequer (UK); Jeremy Hunt; Chancellor Hunt
the Lord Privy Seal (UK; always capitalized)

For use of *the Honorable* and similar terms of respect, see 8.34, 10.20.

8.24 **Titles of sovereigns and other rulers.** Most titles of sovereigns and other rulers are lowercased when used alone. See also 8.33.

King Abdullah II; the king of Jordan
King Charles; Charles III; the king (in a British Commonwealth context, the King)
the Holy Roman emperor
Nero, emperor of Rome; the Roman emperor
Hamad bin Isa Al Khalifa, king of Bahrain; King Hamad
the shah of Iran
the sharif of Mecca
the paramount chief of Basutoland
Wilhelm II, emperor of Germany; Kaiser Wilhelm II; the kaiser
the führer (Adolf Hitler)
Il Duce (used only of Benito Mussolini; both *i* and *d* capitalized)

8.25 **Military titles.** As is the case with civil titles, military titles are routinely capitalized in the literature of the organization or government with which they are associated. Nonetheless, in formal prose, most such titles are capitalized only when used as part of a person's name. Occasional exceptions may be made if ambiguity threatens. See also 10.15.

the general; General Ulysses S. Grant, commander in chief of the Union army; General Grant; the commander in chief
the general of the army; Omar N. Bradley, general of the army; General Bradley
the admiral; Chester W. Nimitz, fleet admiral; Admiral Nimitz, commander in chief of the Pacific Fleet
the chairman; General Charles Q. Brown Jr., chairman of the Joint Chiefs of Staff; General Brown
the captain; Captain Dominique Jackson, company commander
the sergeant; Sergeant Ajay Patel; a noncommissioned officer (NCO)

the warrant officer; Warrant Officer Lydia Valdez
the chief petty officer; Chief Petty Officer Tannenbaum
the private; Private T. C. Alhambra
the British general; General Sir Guy Carleton, British commander in New York City; General Carleton

For abbreviations, often used when a title precedes a name and appropriate in material in which many military titles appear, see 10.17.

8.26 **Quasi-military titles.** Titles and ranks used in organizations such as the police, the merchant marine, and the Salvation Army are treated the same way as military titles.

the chief of police; Frederick Day, Parkdale chief of police; Chief Day
the warden; Jane Simmons, warden of the state penitentiary; Warden Simmons

8.27 **Religious titles.** Religious titles are treated much like civil and military titles (see 8.23, 8.25).

the rabbi; Rabbi Avraham Yitzhak ha-Kohen Kuk; the rabbinate
the cantor *or* hazan; Deborah Bard, cantor; Cantor Bard
the sheikh; Sheikh Ibrahim el-Zakzaky
the imam; Imam Shamil
the ayatollah; Ayatollah Khomeini
the Dalai Lama (traditionally capitalized); *but* previous dalai lamas
the sadhu; the guru; the shaman
the pope; Pope Francis; the papacy; papal
the cardinal; John Cardinal Dew (in formal contexts) *or* Cardinal John Dew; Cardinal Dew; the sacred college of cardinals
the patriarch; Cyrillus Lucaris, patriarch of Constantinople; the patriarchate
the archbishop; the archbishop of Canterbury; Archbishop Welby
the bishop; the bishop of Toledo; Bishop Thomas; bishopric; diocese
the minister; the Reverend Shirley Stoops-Frantz
the rector; the Reverend James Williams (see also 8.34, 10.20)

8.28 **Corporate and organizational titles.** Titles of persons holding offices such as those listed below are rarely used as part of a name. If a short form is required, either the generic term or simply a personal name suffices.

the chief executive officer; Mary Barra, chief executive officer of General Motors; the CEO
the director; Christie Henry, director of Princeton University Press

the school superintendent; Janice Bayder, superintendent of Coriander Township High School District
the secretary-treasurer; Georgina Fido, secretary-treasurer of the Kenilworth Kennel Society

8.29 **Academic titles.** Academic titles generally follow the pattern for civil titles (see 8.23).

the professor; Françoise Meltzer, professor of comparative literature; Professor Meltzer
the chair; Michelle Kosch, chair of the Sage School of Philosophy at Cornell University; Professor Kosch (but see 8.31)
the provost; Katherine Baicker, provost of the University of Chicago; Baicker
the president; Paul Alivisatos, president of the University of Chicago; Alivisatos *or* President Alivisatos
the dean; Melina Hale, dean of the College at the University of Chicago (*the College* is an official division of the University of Chicago); Dean Hale
named professorships; Wendy Doniger, Mircea Eliade Distinguished Service Professor Emerita of the History of Religions in the Divinity School; Professor Doniger; William Chester Jordan, Dayton-Stockton Professor of History, Princeton University; Professor Jordan
the professor emeritus (masc.); the professor emerita (fem.); professors emeriti (masc. or masc. and fem.); professors emeritae (fem.); Professor Emerita Neugarten (note that *emeritus* and *emerita* are honorary designations and do not simply mean "retired")

8.30 **Other academic designations.** Terms denoting student status are lowercased.

freshman *or* first-year student
sophomore
junior
senior

Names of degrees, fellowships, and the like are lowercased when referred to generically. See also 10.23.

a master's degree; a doctorate; a fellowship; master of business administration (MBA)

8.31 **Descriptive titles.** When preceding a name, generic titles that describe a person's role or occupation—such as *philosopher* or *historian*—are normally lowercased. Such terms are not to be confused with formal titles like *president* and *queen* or academic and social titles like *professor* and *doctor* (all of which are usually capitalized before a name). Note that an initial *the* is often omitted (a usage that some consider to be less formal).

the historian Kevin M. Kruse *or* historian Kevin M. Kruse (*but not* historian Kruse)
*but*
Professor Kruse (see 8.29)

For the use of commas, which would be required when the name acts as a nonrestrictive appositive (e.g., "the panel's only historian, Kevin M. Kruse, spoke first"), see 6.30.

8.32 **Civic and academic honors.** Titles denoting civic or academic honors are capitalized when following a personal name. For awards, see 8.84; for abbreviations, see 10.24.

Roberta Bondar, Fellow of the Royal Society of Canada; the fellows

8.33 **Titles of nobility.** Unlike most of the titles mentioned in the previous paragraphs, titles of nobility do not denote offices (such as that of a president or an admiral). Whether inherited or conferred, they form an integral and, with rare exceptions, permanent part of a person's name and are therefore usually capitalized. The generic element in a title, however (duke, earl, etc.), is lowercased when used alone as a short form of the name. (In British usage, the generic term used alone remains capitalized in the case of royal dukes but not in the case of nonroyal dukes; in North American usage, such niceties may be disregarded.) For further advice, consult *The Times Style Guide: A Practical Guide to English Usage* (bibliog. 1.1) and, for a comprehensive listing, the latest edition of *Burke's Peerage and Baronetage* (bibliog. 4.1). See also 8.24.

the prince; Prince William; the Prince of Wales
the duke; the duchess; the Duke and Duchess of Windsor
the marquess; the Marquess of Bath; Lord Bath
the marchioness; the Marchioness of Bath; Lady Bath
the earl; the Earl of Shaftesbury; Lord Shaftesbury; Anthony Ashley Cooper, 7th (*or* seventh) Earl of Shaftesbury; previous earls of Shaftesbury
the countess (wife of an earl); the Countess of Shaftesbury; Lady Shaftesbury
the viscount; Viscount Eccles; Lord Eccles
Baroness Thatcher; Lady Thatcher

Dame Judi Dench; Dame Judi (*not* Dame Dench)
the baron; Lord Rutland
the baronet; the knight; Sir Paul McCartney; Sir Paul (*not* Sir McCartney)
Lady So-and-So [husband's last name] (wife of a marquess, earl, baron, or baronet)
Lady Olivia So-and-So (daughter of a duke, marquess, or earl); Lady Olivia
the Honourable Jessica So-and-So (daughter of a baron)
the duc de Guise (lowercased in accordance with French usage); François de Lorraine, duc de Guise
the count; Count Helmuth von Moltke *or* Graf Helmuth von Moltke; the Count of Toulouse *or* the comte de Toulouse

Note that marquesses, earls, viscounts, barons, and baronesses are addressed, and referred to after first mention, as Lord or Lady So-and-So, at least in British usage. The following entry, drawn from *Burke's Peerage and Baronetage*, illustrates the complexities of British noble nomenclature:

The 5th Marquess of Salisbury (Sir Robert Arthur James Gascoyne-Cecil, K.G., P.C.), Earl of Salisbury, Wilts; Viscount Cranborne, Dorset, and Baron Cecil of Essendon, Rutland; co-heir to the Barony of Ogle

8.34 **Honorifics.** Honorific titles and respectful forms of address are capitalized in any context. For the use of many such terms in formal correspondence, see "Forms of Address," a comprehensive listing at the back of the print edition of *Merriam-Webster's Collegiate Dictionary*. For abbreviations, see 10.20. See also 8.27.

the Honorable Angus Stanley King Jr. (US senator, member of Congress, etc.)
the Right Honourable Justin Trudeau (Canadian prime minister)
the First Gentleman; the First Lady
the Queen Mother
Pandit Nehru
Mahatma Gandhi
Her (His, Your) Majesty; His (Her, Your) Royal Highness
the Most Reverend Thomas Anthony Daly (Roman Catholic bishop)
Your (Her, His) Excellency
Mr. President; Madam President
Madam Speaker
Your Honor
*but*
sir, ma'am (see also 6.57)
my lord, my lady

## EPITHETS, KINSHIP NAMES, AND PERSONIFICATIONS

8.35 **Epithets (or nicknames) and bynames.** A descriptive or characterizing word or phrase used as part of, or instead of, a person's name is capitalized. A *the* used as part of such a name is not capitalized (except, e.g., at the beginning of a sentence; but see 8.6).

the Great Emancipator (Abraham Lincoln)
the Sun King (Louis XIV)
the Wizard of Menlo Park (Thomas Edison)
Stonewall Jackson
Old Hickory (Andrew Jackson)
the Young Pretender (Charles Edward Stuart)
the Great Commoner (William Jennings Bryan)
Catherine the Great
Babe Ruth
Magic Johnson
the Swedish Nightingale (Jenny Lind)
Ivan the Terrible
the People's Princess (Diana, Princess of Wales)

When used in addition to a name, an epithet is enclosed in quotation marks and placed either within or after the name. Parentheses are unnecessary.

George Herman "Babe" Ruth
Earvin "Magic" Johnson
Jenny Lind, "the Swedish Nightingale"
Ivan IV, "the Terrible"

8.36 **Epithets as names of characters.** In references to works of drama or fiction, epithets or generic titles used in place of names are normally capitalized.

John Barrymore performed brilliantly as Chief Executioner.
Alice encounters the Red Queen and the Mad Hatter.
Batman eluded the Joker.

8.37 **Kinship names and the like.** A kinship name is usually lowercased unless it is used as part of a personal name or in place of a personal name. This usage extends to certain words that express a similar type of relationship. Some editorial discretion will be required. For example, *mother* and *father* and *sister* and *brother* do not normally form part of a name (except in certain religious contexts), whereas *aunt* and *uncle* often do; thus, both *my sister Clarice* and *my Aunt Maud* could be considered correct, even though, because they are preceded by *my*, neither *sister Clarice* nor *Aunt Maud* is being used in place of a name in those phrases. See also 8.21.

my father and mother
the Brontë sisters
I told my mom that this wouldn't take long.
Please, Mom, this will only take a minute.
Our sister Clarice worked as an editor. (See also 6.31.)
Hi, Sister! (*Sister* refers to an actual sibling; cf. *brother* in the last example.)
Her aunt, Maud Ramirez, agreed to watch their dogs.
You can always count on Aunt Maud.
I can't wait to see my Aunt Maud's reaction. (See introductory text.)
I believe my grandmother's middle name was Marie.
Where is Grandpa Smith?
My cousin Fred was late to the party.
Will Cousin Trini be there?
I called my daughter's coach.
Ask Coach Wilson.
You can count on me, Coach.
*but*
You can say that again, brother. (The word *brother* is being used figuratively.)

Kinship terms used in connection with religious offices or callings are treated similarly.

The note referred to a certain Brother Thomas, one of the brothers from the Franciscan monastery.

When a job title is used in lieu of a name, it is capitalized only if it would also normally function as a title before a name.

Yes, Doctor, but will this hurt?
*but*
Hey, waiter, where's my order?

8.38 **Personifications.** The poetic device of giving abstractions the attributes of persons, and hence capitalizing them, is rare in today's writing. The use of capitals for such a purpose is best confined to quoted material.

"The Night is Mother of the Day, / The Winter of the Spring, / And ever upon old Decay / The greenest mosses cling." (John Greenleaf Whittier)
*but*
In springtime, nature is at its best.
It was a battle between head and heart; reason finally won.

## ETHNIC, SOCIOECONOMIC, AND OTHER GROUPS

8.39 **Ethnic, national, and regional groups and associated adjectives.** Names of ethnic and national and other regional groups are capitalized. Adjectives associated with these names are also capitalized. For hyphenation or its absence, see 8.40. For abbreviations, see 10.25.

Aboriginal peoples of Australia; Aboriginal Australians (*not* Aborigines); an Aboriginal person; Aboriginal Australians and Torres Strait Islanders
African Americans; an African American; African American culture (for *Black*, see text below)
American Indians; an American Indian (preferred to *Native American* by some who trace their roots to the Indigenous peoples of the Americas); Indian Country (of Native lands and communities in the United States)
Arab Americans; an Arab American; Arab American communities
Asian Americans; an Asian American; Asian American culture
the British people *or* the British; a British person *or, colloquially,* a Britisher, a Brit
Caribbean American; Caribbean American heritage
Chicanos; a Chicano; a Chicana
European Americans
First Peoples; First Nations (used in Canada when not referring to specific Indigenous groups by name)
French Canadians; French Canadian culture
Hispanics; a Hispanic person
the Hopi people *or* the Hopi; a Hopi person; Hopi customs (see also 7.10)
Indigenous peoples (referring to more than one group); the Indigenous peoples of the Caribbean; Indigenous cultures; Indigenous people; an Indigenous person (*but* peoples and cultures that are indigenous to the Americas)
Inuit (*pl. n.*; literally, "the people"); an Inuk (*sing. n.*); an Inuit teacher; Inuit sculpture
Irish Travellers (*or* Mincéirs); an Irish Traveller
Italian Americans; an Italian American neighborhood
Jews; a Jewish person *or* a Jew; Jewish ethnicity (see also 8.97)
Latinos; a Latino; a Latina; Latino immigration; Latinx *or* Latine (preferred by some as a gender-neutral alternative to *Latino* in any of its forms)

Métis; Métis history and culture
Native Hawaiians and other Pacific Islanders
Native Americans; Native American poetry; Native lands (see also *American Indians*, above)
New Zealanders; New Zealand immigration
Pacific Islanders; a Pacific Islander
Pygmy peoples; African Pygmies; a Mbuti Pygmy family
the Romani people *or* the Romani *or* Roma; a Romani person; the Romani language
*but*
people of color; writers of color

In the list above, the adjectives *Indigenous* and *Native*, though neither is derived from a place-name or related proper noun, are capitalized when referring to people. Similarly, the adjective *Black* is now usually capitalized to refer to people. Some writers and editors capitalize *White* also, on the principle that the capital letter in both instances signals a person rather than a color; others maintain that only *Black* refers to a meaningful (and often shared) cultural identity. The decision whether to capitalize either term (or the similar term *Brown*) is therefore best left up to the writer. Provided a writer's capitalization choices reflect conscious decisions, editors should limit any interventions to imposing consistency or, when appropriate, suggesting a more specific term. Note, however, that while many of the terms in the list above have long been accepted as both adjectives and nouns (e.g., Jewish, a Jew, Jews), it is usually best to avoid using *Black* and similar terms derived from common adjectives as nouns (i.e., refer to "a Black person" *or* "Black people," *not* "a Black" *or* "Blacks"). For some additional considerations, see 5.255–67.

8.40 **Compound nationalities.** Whether terms such as *African American, Italian American, Chinese American,* and others expressing a dual national or regional heritage should be spelled open or hyphenated has been the subject of some debate. But since the hyphen does not aid comprehension in such terms as those mentioned above, Chicago advises omitting it unless a particular author or publisher prefers otherwise. See also the table at 7.96, section 2, under *proper nouns and adjectives relating to geography or nationality*.

8.41 **Socioeconomic status.** Terms denoting socioeconomic status or class are lowercased. The list below shows some of the more commonly used terms.

the middle class; a middle-class neighborhood
the upper-middle class; an upper-middle-class family
the 1 percent
blue collar; blue-collar workers
the aristocracy
the proletariat
homeless people; people without housing; the unhoused (see also 5.255–67)

8.42 **Sexual orientation and gender identity or expression.** Terms that refer to individuals or groups according to sexual orientation or gender identity or expression are lowercased. Some common terms are listed below. For referring to people who do not use gender-specific pronouns, see 5.52.

lesbians; a lesbian; lesbian history
gay men; gay men and women; a gay man; gay rights
bisexual and pansexual people; a bisexual person
asexual people; an asexual person
nonbinary people; a nonbinary person
two-spirit people; a two-spirit person; she is two-spirit (but see text below)
cisgender men and women; a cisgender (*or* cis) man or woman
transgender men and women; a transgender (*or* trans) man or woman

Note that some authors prefer *Two-Spirit* (capital *T* and *S*) in line with other terms related to Indigenous identity. When in doubt, editors should query authors as to their preferred usage.

8.43 **Generation.** Terms denoting generations are usually capitalized when they include the word *generation*; otherwise, they are lowercased. This slight departure from previous editions of this manual accords with common usage. Because these terms are descriptive rather than scientific, they should generally be defined at first use.

the Lost Generation
the Silent Generation
Generation Jones
the Me Generation
the MTV Generation
Generation X, Generation Y, Generation Z (*or* Gen X, Y, and Z); a Gen Xer
Generation Alpha, Generation Beta, . . .
*but*
baby boomer(s); boomers; a baby boom
baby buster(s); a baby bust
millennial(s)

8.44 **Ability status or disability.** Terms describing groups or individuals according to abilities and disabilities are usually lowercased. For person-first versus identity-first language, see 5.261.

wheelchair users
people with autism; an autistic person *or* a person with autism
neurotypical people; a neurodivergent (*not* neurodiverse) person; neurodiversity
blind people (*or* persons); a blind person
deafness; a person who is deaf; *but* Deaf culture (see text below)

Writers often capitalize *deaf* when referring to people who identify themselves as members of the distinct linguistic and cultural group whose primary language is ASL (American Sign Language) or another signed language—the Deaf community—and lowercase it when referring to the audiological condition of deafness or as an all-inclusive way to refer to deaf people, including those who are hard of hearing or who lost their hearing after having acquired spoken-language skills. A similar distinction is made for the term *deafblind,* often capitalized as *DeafBlind.* See also 11.135.

## NAMES OF PLACES

8.45 **Names of places—additional resources.** For the spelling of place-names, start with the geographic listings in *Merriam-Webster* (see 7.1) or *Encyclopaedia Britannica* (bibliog. 4.3) or, for names not listed there, the United States Board on Geographic Names or one of the other resources listed in the bibliography (bibliog. 4.2). Since names of countries and cities often change, frequently updated online resources should be preferred over print for modern place-names. For the names of countries, the US Central Intelligence Agency's *World Factbook* is a good place to start (bibliog. 4.2). For historical works, writers and editors should attempt to use the form of names appropriate to the period under discussion.

### *Parts of the World*

8.46 **Continents, countries, cities, oceans, and such.** Entities that appear on maps are always capitalized, as are adjectives and nouns derived from them. An initial *the* as part of a name is lowercased in running text, except in the rare case of an initial *the* in the name of a city.

| | |
|---|---|
| Asia; Asian | the North Pole |
| Ireland; Irish | the Gambia |
| California; Californian | the Netherlands; Dutch |
| Chicago; Chicagoan | *but* |
| Atlantic Ocean; Atlantic | The Hague |
| South China Sea | |

8.47 **Points of the compass.** Compass points and terms derived from them are lowercased if they simply indicate direction or location. But see 8.48.

pointing toward the north; a north wind; a northern climate
to fly east; an eastward move; in the southwest of France; southwesterly

8.48 **Regions of the world and national and local regions.** Terms that denote regions of the world or of a particular country or state or other such entity are often capitalized, as are a few of the adjectives and nouns derived from such terms. The following examples illustrate not only the principles sketched in 8.1 but also variations based on context and observed usage. For terms not included here or for which no suitable analogy can be made, consult *Merriam-Webster* or an encyclopedia or other reliable source. If an otherwise generic term is not listed or discussed there (either capitalized or, for lowercase dictionary entries, with the indication *capitalized* next to the applicable subentry), opt for lowercase. Note that capitalized exceptions based on specific regional, political, or historical contexts are inevitable (a few that are generally applicable are included below) and that an author's strong preference should usually be respected. See also 8.47.

the Alps; the Swiss Alps; the Australian Alps; an Alpine village (if in the European or Australian Alps); Alpine skiing; *but* alpine pastures in the Rockies (see also 8.55)

Antarctica; the Antarctic Circle; the Antarctic continent

the Arctic; the Arctic Circle; Arctic waters; a mass of Arctic air (*but* lowercased when used metaphorically, as in "an arctic stare"; see 8.62)

Central America, Central American countries; central Asia; central Illinois; central France; central Europe (*but* Central Europe when referring to the political division of World War I)

the continental United States; the continent of Europe (*but* on the Continent, to denote mainland Europe); Continental cuisine (*but* continental breakfast); the Continental Divide (United States)

the East, Eastern, an Easterner (referring to the eastern part of the United States or other country as a national region); the Eastern Seaboard (*or* Atlantic Seaboard), East Coast (referring to the Eastern United States); eastern Massachusetts (*but* East Tennessee [one of three Grand Divisions of Tennessee]); the East, the Far East, Eastern (referring to the Orient and Asian culture); the Middle East (*or, formerly more common,* the Near East), Middle Eastern (referring to Iran, Iraq, etc.); the Eastern Hemisphere; eastern Europe (*but* Eastern Europe when referring to the post–World War II division of Europe); east, eastern, eastward, to the east (directions)

the equator; equatorial climate; an equatorial current; the North Equatorial Current; the Pacific Equatorial Countercurrent; Equatorial Guinea (formerly Spanish Guinea); the forty-second parallel north (of the equator)

the Great Plains; the northern plains; the plains (*but* Plains Indians)

the Midwest, Midwestern, a Midwesterner (as of the United States); the middle of Texas (*but* Middle Tennessee)

the North, Northern, a Northerner (of a national region); northern Ohio (*but* Northern California); North Africa, North African countries, in northern Africa; North America, North American, the North American continent; the North Atlantic, a northern Atlantic route; the Northern Hemisphere; the Far North; north, northern, northward, to the north (directions)

the Northeast, the Northwest, Northwestern, Northeastern, a Northwesterner, a Northeasterner (as of the United States); the Pacific Northwest; the Northwest Passage; northwest Illinois; northeast, northeastern, to the northeast (directions)

the poles; the North Pole; the North Polar ice cap; the South Pole; polar regions (*see also* Antarctica; the Arctic)

the South, Southern, a Southerner (of a national region); the Deep South; southern Minnesota (*but* Southern California); the South of France (region); Southeast Asia; South Africa, South African (referring to the Republic of South Africa); southern Africa (referring to the southern part of the continent); south, southern, southward, to the south (directions)

the Southeast, the Southwest, Southeastern, Southwestern, a Southeasterner, a Southwesterner (as of the United States); southeast, southeastern, to the southeast (directions)

the tropics, tropical; the Tropic of Cancer; the Neotropics, Neotropical (of the New World biogeographic region); the subtropics, subtropical

the Upper Peninsula (of Michigan); the upper reaches of the Thames; upstate; upstate New York

the West, Western, a Westerner (of a national region); the West Coast; western Arizona (*but* West Tennessee); the West, Western (referring to the culture of the Occident, or Europe and the Western Hemisphere; *but* westernize); west, western, westward, to the west (directions)

8.49 **Popular place-names.** Popular names of places are usually capitalized. Quotation marks are not needed. Some of the following examples may be used of more than one place. None should be used in contexts where they will not be readily understood. See also 8.35.

Back Bay
the Badger State
the Badlands
the Bay Area, the Bay (Northern California)
the Beltway
the Bible Belt
the Big Island
the Cape
City of Light
the Delta
the East End
the Eastern Shore
the Eternal City
the Fertile Crescent
the Five Towns (Long Island)
the Gaza Strip
the Gulf
the Holy City
the Jewish Quarter
the Lake District
the Left Bank
the Loop (Chicago)
Midtown (Manhattan)
the Old World
the Panhandle
the Promised Land
the Rust Belt
Silicon Valley
Skid Row
the South Seas
the South Side
the Sunbelt
the Twin Cities
the Upper West Side
the Village (Greenwich Village)
the West End
the Wild West
the Windy City

Certain terms considered political rather than geographic need not be capitalized. Some editorial discretion is advisable, however. In reference to Soviet-era global politics, for example, the terms *Iron Curtain* and *Third World* might be suitably capitalized; as generic concepts or used metaphorically, they would be lowercased (though *developing nations* would be preferred over *third world* except in direct quotations or, as here, when the term itself is under discussion).

8.50 **Urban areas.** Generic terms used for parts of urban areas are not normally capitalized.

the business district
the inner city
the metropolitan area; the greater Chicago metropolitan area; Chicagoland
the tristate area
*but*
Greater London (an official administrative region)

On the other hand, a work that treats a specific local culture may choose to favor an established local usage (e.g., Greater Boston).

8.51 **Real versus metaphorical names.** *Mecca* is capitalized when referring to the Islamic holy city, as is *Utopia* when referring to Thomas More's imaginary country. Both are lowercased when used metaphorically. See also 8.62.

Stratford-upon-Avon is a mecca for Shakespeare enthusiasts.
She is trying to create a utopia for her children.

## *Political Divisions*

8.52 **Political divisions — capitalization.** Words denoting political divisions—from *empire*, *republic*, and *state* down to *ward* and *precinct*—are capitalized when they follow a name and are used as an accepted part of the name. When preceding the name, such terms are usually capitalized in names of countries but lowercased in entities below the national level (but see 8.53). Used alone, they are usually lowercased, though reasonable exceptions based on specific regional, political, or historical contexts should be respected. See also 9.48.

the Ottoman Empire; the empire (*but* the Empire style of early nineteenth-century France)
the Commonwealth of Nations; the British Commonwealth; Commonwealth nations; the Commonwealth (*but* a commonwealth)
the United States; the republic; the Union (Civil War era); the Confederacy (Civil War era)
the United Kingdom; Great Britain; Britain (*not* the kingdom)
the Russian Federation (formerly the Union of Soviet Socialist Republics; the Soviet Union); Russia; the federation
the Republic of South Africa (formerly the Union of South Africa); South Africa; the republic
the Fifth Republic (France)
the Republic of Indonesia; the republic
the Republic of Lithuania; the republic
the Federal Democratic Republic of Ethiopia; the republic; the Amhara Region (a national regional state); the region
the Commonwealth of Australia; the commonwealth; the state of New South Wales; the Australian Capital Territory
the Commonwealth of Puerto Rico; Puerto Rico's commonwealth status
the State of Washington (the governmental entity; see 8.53); the state of Washington *or* Washington state (in general references to the state, to distinguish it from Washington, DC); the state

the New England states
the province of Ontario
Jiangxi Province
Massachusetts Bay Colony; the colony at Massachusetts Bay
the British colonies; the thirteen colonies; colonial America
the Indiana Territory; the territory of Indiana
the Northwest Territory; the Old Northwest
the Western Reserve
Lake County; the county of Lake; the county; County Kildare
New York City; the city of New York
the City (the old city of London, now the financial district, always capitalized)
Shields Township; the township
the Eleventh Congressional District; the congressional district
the Fifth Ward; the ward
the Sixth Precinct; the precinct

A generic term that is capitalized as part of the name of an official body remains capitalized when it is used in the plural to refer to two or more names and applies to both.

Lake and Cook Counties
the Republics of Indonesia and South Africa

8.53 **Governmental entities.** In contexts where a specific governmental body rather than the place is meant, the words *state*, *city*, and the like are usually capitalized when used as part of the full name of the body. See also 8.52.

She works for the Village of Forest Park.
That is a City of Chicago ordinance.
The State of California enacted several new laws targeting emissions.
*but*
Residents of the village of Forest Park enjoy easy access to the city of Chicago.

## *Topographical Divisions*

8.54 **Mountains, rivers, and the like.** Names of mountains, rivers, oceans, islands, and so forth are capitalized. The generic term (*mountain, river*, etc.) is also capitalized when used as part of the name. In the plural, it is capitalized when it is part of a single name (Hawaiian Islands) and when it is used with two or more names, whether the generic term comes first (e.g., Mounts Washington and Rainier) or the generic term comes second and applies to two or more names (e.g., the Pacific and Atlantic Oceans).

Walden Pond
Silver Lake
Lake Michigan; Lakes Michigan and Erie; the Great Lakes
the Illinois River; the Chicago River; the Illinois and Chicago Rivers
the River Thames
the Nile River Valley; the Nile Valley; the Nile Delta; the Mississippi River Valley; the Mississippi Delta (but see 8.55); the Nile; the Mississippi; the delta; *but* the Delta (as a region rather than as a geographic feature)
the Bering Strait
the Mediterranean Sea; the Mediterranean
the Pacific Ocean; the Pacific and Atlantic Oceans
the Great Barrier Reef
the Hawaiian Islands; Hawaii; *but* the island of Hawaii (the Big Island)
the Windward Islands; the Windwards
the Iberian Peninsula
Cape Verde
the Black Forest
Stone Mountain
Mount Washington; Mount Rainier; Mounts Washington and Rainier
the Rocky Mountains; the Rockies (see also 8.48)
Death Valley; the Valley of the Kings
the Continental Divide
the Horn of Africa; the Horn (to avoid confusion with a different kind of horn)
the Indian subcontinent (a descriptive rather than proper geographic name)

8.55 **Descriptive terms for geographic entities.** When a generic term is used descriptively rather than as a proper part of a name, or when used alone, it is lowercased.

the Amazon basin
along the Pacific coast (*but* the West Coast; see 8.48)
the California desert
the Hudson River valley

8.56 **Non-English terms for geographic entities.** When a generic term from a language other than English forms part of a geographic name, the equivalent English term should not be included. See also 11.5.

the Rio Grande (*not* the Rio Grande River)
Denali (*not* Mount Denali)
Fujiyama (*not* Mount Fujiyama)
Mauna Loa (*not* Mount Mauna Loa)
the Sierra Nevada (*not* the Sierra Nevada Mountains)

## *Public Places and Major Structures*

8.57 **Thoroughfares and the like.** The names of streets, avenues, squares, parks, and so forth are capitalized. The generic term is lowercased when used alone but capitalized when used as part of a name or as part of two or more names (as in the third and eleventh examples below).

Black Lives Matter Plaza; the plaza
Broadway (Manhattan)
Fifty-Fifth Street; Fifty-Seventh and Fifty-Fifth Streets
Hyde Park Boulevard; the boulevard
Interstate 80; I-80; an interstate highway; the interstate
the Ishtar Gate; the gate
Jackson Park; the park
London Bridge; the bridge
the Mall (in London)
Park Lane
Pennsylvania Avenue; Pennsylvania and New York Avenues; both avenues
Piccadilly Circus
the Spanish Steps; the steps
Tiananmen Square; the square
US Route 66; Routes 1 and 2; a state route

See also 9.52–54.

8.58 **Buildings and monuments.** The names of buildings and monuments are generally capitalized. The generic term is usually lowercased when used alone but capitalized when used as part of a name or as part of two or more names (as in the fifth example below).

the Babri Mosque; the mosque
the Berlin Wall; the wall
Buckingham Fountain; the fountain
the Capitol (where the US Congress meets, *as distinct from* the capital city)
the Chrysler Building; the building; the Empire State and Chrysler Buildings

the Houses of Parliament; Parliament (*but* a parliament)
the Leaning Tower of Pisa; the tower
the Martin Luther King Jr. Memorial; the memorial
the Pyramids (*but* the Egyptian pyramids)
Shedd Aquarium; the aquarium
the Stone of Scone; the stone
Symphony Center; the center
Tribune Tower; the tower
the Washington Monument; the monument
Westminster Abbey; the abbey
the White House

Though major works of art are generally italicized (see 8.200), some massive works of sculpture are regarded primarily as monuments and therefore not italicized.

the Statue of Liberty; the statue
Mount Rushmore National Memorial; Mount Rushmore; the memorial
the Colossus of Rhodes; the Colossus (a shortened form rather than a generic term)

8.59 **Rooms, offices, and such.** Official names of rooms, offices, and the like are capitalized.

the Empire Room (*but* room 421)
the Amelia Earhart Suite (*but* suite 219)
the Lincoln Bedroom
the Oval Office
the West Wing of the White House

8.60 **Non-English names for places and structures.** Non-English names of thoroughfares and buildings are not italicized and may be preceded by English *the* if the definite article would appear in the original language. See also 11.5.

the Champs-Élysées
the Bibliothèque Nationale (see 11.29)
the Bois de Boulogne
Unter den Linden (never preceded by *the*)
the Marktstrasse
the Piazza delle Terme

## WORDS DERIVED FROM PROPER NOUNS

8.61 **Adjectives derived from personal names.** Adjectives derived from the names of people (usually last names) are normally capitalized. Those in common use may be found in *Merriam-Webster* (e.g., Aristotelian, Jamesian, Machiavellian, Shakespearean). If not in the dictionary, adjectives can sometimes be coined by adding the suffix *-ian* (to a name ending in a consonant) or *an* (to a name ending in *e* or *i*)—or, failing these, *-esque*. As with Foucault and Shaw, the final consonant sometimes undergoes a transformation as an aid to pronunciation. A first name may occasionally be added for clarity. If a name does not seem to lend itself to any such coinage, it is best avoided. See also 8.62, 8.80.

Austen; Austenian
Baudelaire; Baudelairean
Bayes; Bayesian
Dickens; Dickensian
Elizabeth I; Elizabethan
Foucault; Foucauldian
Friedan; Friedanesque *or* Betty Friedanesque
Jordan; Jordanesque *or* Michael Jordanesque
Kafka; Kafkaesque
Kahlo; Kahloian
Marx; Marxist
Mendel; Mendelian
Rabelais; Rabelaisian
Sartre; Sartrean
Shaw; Shavian
Wollstonecraft; Wollstonecraftian

8.62 **Words derived from proper nouns.** Personal, national, and geographic names, and words derived from them, are often lowercased when used in a nonliteral sense or when they enter common usage. For example, *diesel engine*, named for Rudolf Diesel, generally gets a lowercase *d*. However, more than a few such terms retain their capital letters, so it is important to check a dictionary before applying lowercase. This shift from advice in previous editions of this manual is intended to align more closely with the entries in *Merriam-Webster* and, by extension, with common usage. For example, though the cheese known as *Gruyère* (lowercased in previous editions of this manual) is not always from the district in Switzerland (the name may apply to a style of cheese as well as its origins), a capital *G* is commonly retained, signaling a close association with both the name and the region. Likewise for *Swiss cheese* and *Emmentaler* (also both formerly lowercase). Some terms, like *french fries*, are far enough removed from their literal meaning (the *french* in "french fries" has little to do with France) that they may be safely lowercased; on the other hand, *French dressing* and *French windows*, though not necessarily from France, are more likely to merit capitalization. When in doubt, check *Merriam-Webster*; a term listed there in lowercase (even if it carries the label "often capitalized") can usually remain lowercase. See also 8.80.

ampere (see also 10.55)
anglicize
Arabic numerals (e.g., 1, 2, 3)
arctics (boots); an arctic stare (*but* the Arctic region; see 8.48)
bohemian (unless literally from Bohemia)
Bordeaux
Brie
brussels sprouts
Bunsen burner
buffalo wings (named for Buffalo, NY, but usually not capitalized)
Burgundy (the French wine and region); burgundy (as a style or color)
Champagne (the French sparkling wine); a glass of champagne (informal); champagne (as a style or color)
cheddar (*but* West Country Farmhouse Cheddar)
china (porcelain)
curaçao
Delphic (*but* delphically)
diesel engine
Dutch oven
epicure
frankfurter
French dressing
french fries
French windows
Gruyère
Herculean (of Hercules); herculean (used nonliterally)
Homeric
india ink
Italian dressing
italicize; italic type (see also "roman type")
jeremiad
joule (see also 10.55)
Lombardy poplar

manila envelope
morocco leather
ottoman (the furniture or fabric)
pasteurize
petri dish
Pharisaic (of Pharisees); pharisaic, pharisaical (used nonliterally)
Philistine (of Philistia); philistine, philistinism (used nonliterally)
plaster of paris
Platonic (of Plato); platonic (used nonliterally)
quixotic
Roman numerals (e.g., I, II, III)
roman type (see also "italic type")
Russian dressing
Scotch whisky, Scotch (a product of Scotland); scotch (informally, for the style of drink)
Stilton cheese
Swiss cheese
timothy grass
venetian blinds
venturi tube
vulcanize
wiener

## NAMES OF ORGANIZATIONS

### *Governmental Bodies*

8.63 **Legislative and deliberative bodies.** The full names of legislative and deliberative bodies, departments, bureaus, and offices are capitalized (but see 8.66). Adjectives derived from them are usually lowercased, as are many of the generic names for such bodies when used alone (as on subsequent mentions). For generic names used alone but not listed here, opt for lowercase. For administrative bodies, see 8.64; for judicial bodies, see 8.65. See also 11.5.

the United Nations General Assembly; the UN General Assembly; the assembly
the League of Nations; the league
the United Nations Security Council; the Security Council; the council
the United States Congress; the US Congress; the 119th Congress; Congress; 119th Cong.; congressional (see also 9.47)
the United States Senate; the Senate; senatorial; the upper house of Congress
the House of Representatives; the House; the lower house of Congress

the Electoral College
the Committee on Foreign Affairs; the Foreign Affairs Committee; the committee
the Illinois General Assembly; the assembly; the Illinois legislature; the state senate
the Chicago City Council; the city council
the British Parliament (*or* UK Parliament); Parliament; an early parliament; parliamentary; the House of Commons; the Commons; the House of Lords; the Lords
the Crown (the British monarchy); Crown lands
the Privy Council (*but* a Privy Counsellor)
the Parliament of Canada; Parliament; the Senate (upper house); the House of Commons (lower house)
the Legislative Assembly of British Columbia; the National Assembly of Quebec *or* Assemblée nationale du Québec (in French usage)
the Oireachtas (Irish parliament); Seanad Éireann (Irish upper house); Dáil Éireann (Irish lower house)
the Assemblée nationale (in French usage) *or* the National Assembly (present-day France); the (French) Senate; the parliamentary system; the Parlement de Paris (historical)
the States General *or* Estates General (France and Netherlands, historical)
the Cortes Generales; the Cortes (Spain); Cortes Españolas (Franco era)
the Cámara de Diputados (the lower house of Mexico's congress)
the Bundestag (German parliament); the Bundesrat (German upper house); the Reichstag (imperial Germany)
the House of People's Representatives; the House of Federation; the Council of Ministers (Ethiopia)
the Dewan Perwakilan Rakyat *or* the House of Representatives; the Majelis Permusyawaratan Rakyat *or* People's Consultative Assembly (Indonesia)
the European Parliament; the Parliament

8.64 **Administrative bodies.** The full names of administrative bodies are capitalized. Adjectives derived from them are usually lowercased, as are many of the generic names for such bodies when used alone; however, exceptions are made for terms that are likely to be ambiguous if lowercased (e.g., *Interior*, as short for *Department of the Interior*). See also 8.63.

the United States Census Bureau; census forms; the census of 2000
the United States Copyright Office; the office
the Centers for Disease Control and Prevention; the CDC (the abbreviation did not change when "and Prevention" was added to the name)
the Department of Homeland Security; Homeland Security

the Department of the Interior; the Interior
the Department of Justice; the Justice Department; the DOJ
the Department of State; the State Department; the department; departmental
the Department of the Treasury; the Treasury
the Eunice Kennedy Shriver National Institute of Child Health and Human Development; the NICHD
the European Centre for Disease Prevention and Control (note the spelling of *Centre*)
the Federal Bureau of Investigation; the bureau; the FBI; FBI agents
the Federal Reserve System; the Federal Reserve Board; the Federal Reserve
the United States Foreign Service; Foreign Service Officer; officer in the Foreign Service
the National Institutes of Health; the NIH; the National Institute of Mental Health; the NIMH
the Occupational Safety and Health Administration; OSHA
the Office of Human Resources; Human Resources
the Peace Corps
the United States Postal Service; the Postal Service; the post office
the United States Customs and Border Protection; CBP; Border Patrol (a division of CBP); Border Patrol agents
the Illinois State Board of Education; the board of education
the Ithaca City School District; the school district; the district

**8.65** **Judicial bodies.** The full name of a court, often including a place-name, is capitalized. Subsequent references to a court (or district court, supreme court, etc.) are lowercased, except for the phrase "Supreme Court" at the national level.

the United States (*or* US) Supreme Court; the Supreme Court; *but* the court
the United States Court of Appeals for the Seventh Circuit; the court of appeals
the Arizona Supreme Court; the supreme court; the supreme courts of Arizona and New Mexico
the District Court for the Southern District of New York; the district court
the Court of Common Pleas (Ohio); the court
the Circuit Court of Lake County, Family Division (Illinois); family court
the Supreme Court of Canada; the Supreme Court; the court
the Birmingham Crown Court; Newton Abbot Magistrates' Court
the Federal Supreme Court (Ethiopia)

States, counties, and cities vary in the way they name their courts. For example, *court of appeals* in New York State and Maryland is equivalent to *supreme court* in other states; and such terms as *district court, circuit court*, *superior court*, and *court of common pleas* are used for similar court systems in different states. Generic names should therefore be used only after the full name or jurisdiction has been stated.

8.66 **Government entities that are lowercased.** Certain generic terms associated with governmental bodies are lowercased. Compare 8.52.

administration; the Carter administration
brain trust
cabinet (*but* the Kitchen Cabinet in the Jackson administration)
city hall (the municipal government and the building)
civil service
court (a royal court)
executive, legislative, or judicial branch
federal; the federal government; federal agencies
government
monarchy
parlement (French; *but* the Parlement of Paris)
parliament, parliamentary (*but* Parliament, usually not preceded by *the*, in the United Kingdom)
state; church and state; state powers

## *Political and Economic Organizations and Movements*

8.67 **Organizations, parties, alliances, and so forth.** Official names of national and international organizations, alliances, and political movements and parties are capitalized (e.g., "the Labor Party in Israel"). Words like *party*, *union*, and *movement* are capitalized when they are part of the name of an organization. Terms identifying formal members of or adherents to such groups are also usually capitalized (e.g., "a Socialist"; "a Republican"). Names of the systems of thought and references to the adherents to such systems, however, are often lowercased (e.g., "an eighteenth-century precursor of socialism"; "a communist at heart"). Nonliteral or metaphorical references are also lowercased (e.g., "fascist parenting techniques"; "nazi tendencies"). For consistency, however—as in a work about communism in which the philosophy and its adherents, the political party, and party members and adherents are discussed—capitalizing the philosophy, together with the organization and its adherents, in both noun and adjective forms, will prevent editorial headaches.

the African National Congress party (*party* is not part of the official name); the ANC
Arab Socialist Ba'ath Party; the Ba'ath Party; the party; Ba'athists (see also 11.84)

Bahujan Samaj Party; the BSP
Bolshevik(s); the Bolshevik (*or* Bolshevist) movement; bolshevism *or* Bolshevism (see text above)
Chartist; Chartism
the Communist Party (*but* communist parties); the party; Communist(s); Communist countries; communism *or* Communism (see text above)
the Democratic Party; the party; Democrat(s) (party members or adherents); democracy; democratic nations
the Entente Cordiale (signed 1904); the Entente; *but* an entente cordiale
the Ethiopian Somali Democratic League; the league; the party
the European Union; the EU; the Common Market; *but* a common market
the Fascist Party; Fascist(s); fascism *or* Fascism (see text above)
the Federalist Party; Federalist(s) (United States, historical); federalism *or* Federalism (see text above)
the Free-Soil Party; Free-Soiler(s)
the General Agreement on Tariffs and Trade; GATT
the Green Party; the party; Green(s); the Green movement
the Hanseatic League; Hansa; a Hanseatic city
the Holy Alliance
the Know-Nothing Party; Know-Nothing(s)
the Labour Party; Labourite(s) (members of the British party)
the League of Arab States; the Arab League; the league
the Libertarian Party; Libertarian(s); libertarianism *or* Libertarianism (see text above)
Loyalist(s) (American Revolution; Spanish Civil War)
Marxism-Leninism; Marxist-Leninist(s)
the National Socialist Party; National Socialism; the Nazi Party; Nazi(s); Nazism
the North American Free Trade Agreement; NAFTA
the North Atlantic Treaty Organization; NATO
the Organisation for Economic Co-operation and Development; the OECD; the organization
the Popular Front; the Front; *but* a popular front
the Populist Party; Populist(s); populism *or* Populism (see text above)
the Progressive Party; Progressive movement; Progressive(s); progressivism *or* Progressivism (see text above)
the Quadruple Alliance; the alliance
the Rashtriya Janata Dal; the RJD (National People's Party)
the Republican Party; the party; the GOP (Grand Old Party); Republican(s) (party members or adherents); Republicanism (Republican Party principles) *or* republicanism (republican principles generally); a republican form of government
the Schengen Area; the area
the Social Democratic Party; the party; Social Democrat(s)

the Socialist Party (*but* socialist parties); the party; Socialist(s) (party members or adherents); socialism *or* Socialism (see text above)
the United Democratic Movement; the movement
the World Health Organization; WHO

8.68 **Adherents of unofficial political groups and movements.** Names for adherents of political groups or movements other than recognized parties are usually lowercased.

anarchist(s)
centrist(s)
independent(s)
moderate(s)
mugwump(s)
opposition (*but* the Opposition, in British and Canadian contexts, referring to the party out of power)
*but*
the Left; members of the left wing; left-winger(s); on the left; the far left; the radical left
the Right; members of the right wing; right-winger(s); on the right; the far right; the radical right
the Tea Party; Tea Partiers (modeled on names for established parties)

## *Institutions and Companies*

8.69 **Institutions and companies — capitalization.** The full names of institutions, groups, and companies and the names of their departments, and often the shortened forms of such names (e.g., the Art Institute), are capitalized. A *the* preceding a name, even when part of the official title, is lowercased in running text. Such generic terms as *company* and *university* are usually lowercased when used alone (though they are routinely capitalized in promotional materials, business documents, and the like). Note that *centre* and other non-US spellings are generally preserved in an American context when used as part of an official name; a period, however, may be added to an abbreviation (as in *St.* for *St*).

the University of Chicago; the university; the University of Chicago and Harvard University; Northwestern and Princeton Universities; the University of Wisconsin–Madison (see also 6.87)
the Department of History; the department; the Law School
the University of Chicago Press; the press
the Board of Trustees of the University of Chicago; the board of trustees; the board

the Art Institute of Chicago; the Art Institute
the Beach Boys; the Beatles; the Grateful Dead, the Dead; the Who (*but* Tha Eastsidaz; see also 8.6)
Captain Beefheart and His Magic Band; the band
the Cleveland Orchestra; the orchestra
the General Foods Corporation; General Foods; the corporation
the Green Bay Packers; the Packers
the Hudson's Bay Company; the company
the Illinois Central Railroad; the Illinois Central; the railroad
the Library of Congress; the library
Lincoln Center
the Manuscripts Division of the library
the Museum of Modern Art; MoMA; the museum
the National Theatre (London)
the New School (see also 8.70)
the New York Stock Exchange; the stock exchange
the Shell Centre (London headquarters of the petroleum company)
Skidmore, Owings & Merrill; SOM; the architectural firm (see also 10.29)
the Smithsonian Institution; the Smithsonian
St. Martin-in-the-Fields (*but* "St" [no period] in UK usage)
Miguel Juarez Middle School; the middle school

8.70 **Corporate names with unusual capitalization.** Corporate names that appear in all lowercase in logotype and other promotional settings can often be capitalized in the usual way. A copyright or "About Us" statement on a corporate website can be helpful in determining a usage that might be suitable for regular text. Words that would normally be lowercase in a title can usually be lowercased (see 8.160). Spellings that begin lowercase but include a capital letter are usually appropriate for running text, even at the beginning of a sentence, as are names with additional internal capitals (see 8.155). A preference for all uppercase should be respected. If a company appears to prefer all lowercase, even in running text, an initial capital can be applied as a matter of editorial expediency.

Adidas (*not* adidas)
Amazon (*not* amazon)
Intel (*not* intel)
*but*
GlaxoSmithKline
HarperCollins
the RAND Corporation
eBay

## *Associations*

8.71 **Associations, unions, and the like.** The full names of associations, societies, unions, meetings, and conferences, and often the shortened forms of such names, are capitalized. A *the* preceding a name, even when part of the official title, is lowercased in running text. Such generic terms as *society* and *union* are usually lowercased when used alone.

the Congress of Industrial Organizations; CIO; the union
Girl Scouts of the United States of America; a Girl Scout; a Scout
the Independent Order of Odd Fellows; IOOF; an Odd Fellow
Industrial Workers of the World; IWW; the Wobblies
the International Olympic Committee; the IOC; the committee
the League of Women Voters; the league
the National Conference for Community and Justice; the conference
the National Organization for Women; NOW; the organization
the New-York Historical Society (the hyphen is part of the official name of the society); the society
the 136th Annual Meeting of the American Historical Association; the annual meeting of the association
the Quadrangle Club; the club
the Textile Workers Union of America; the union

On the other hand, a substantive title given to a single meeting, conference, speech, or discussion is enclosed in quotation marks. For lecture series, see 8.88.

"Wikipedia's Enduring, Nuanced Perspective on Truth" (the title of a TED Talk by Katherine Maher presented at a TED conference in Monterey, CA, in July 2021)

# HISTORICAL AND CULTURAL TERMS

## *Periods*

8.72 **Numerical designations for periods.** A numerical designation for a period is usually lowercased; however, certain periods may be treated as proper nouns (in which both the numerical designation and the term for the period are capitalized) to avoid any confusion with the generic meaning of the same term (see also 8.52). For the use of numerals, see 9.35, 9.47.

the twenty-first century
the nineteen hundreds
the nineties
the quattrocento
the second millennium BCE
*but*
the Eighteenth Dynasty (Egypt)

8.73 **Descriptive designations for periods.** A descriptive designation of a period is usually lowercased, except for proper names or to avoid ambiguity with a generic term. For traditionally capitalized forms, see 8.74.

ancient Greece
the antebellum period
antiquity
the baroque period (see also 8.80)
the colonial period
a golden age
the Hellenistic period
imperial Rome
modern history
the Romantic period (see also 8.80)
the Shang dynasty (considered an era rather than a political division; see 8.52, 8.72)
the Victorian era

8.74 **Traditional period names.** Some names of periods are capitalized, either by tradition or to avoid ambiguity. See also 8.76.

the Augustan Age
the Common Era
the Counter-Reformation
the Dark Ages
the Enlightenment
the Gay Nineties
the Gilded Age
the Grand Siècle
the High Middle Ages (*but* the early Middle Ages, the late Middle Ages)
the High Renaissance
the Jazz Age
the Mauve Decade
the Middle Ages (*but* the medieval era)
the Old Kingdom (ancient Egypt)

the Old Regime (*but* the ancien régime)
the Progressive Era
the Reformation
the Renaissance
the Restoration
the Roaring Twenties

8.75 **Cultural periods.** Names of prehistoric cultural periods are usually capitalized. For geological terms, see 8.135–37.

| | |
|---|---|
| the Bronze Age | the Iron Age |
| the Ice Age | the Stone Age |

Similar terms for modern periods are often lowercased (but see 8.74).

| | |
|---|---|
| the age of reason | the information age |
| the age of steam *or* the steam age | the nuclear age |

### *Events*

8.76 **Historical events and programs.** Names of many major historical events and programs are conventionally capitalized. Others, more recent or known by their generic descriptions, are often lowercased but may be capitalized to prevent ambiguity. If in doubt, opt for lowercase. For wars and battles, see 8.114–15; for religious events, 8.109; for acts and treaties, 8.81.

the Arab Spring
Black Lives Matter
Boston Tea Party
the Boxer Rebellion
the California Gold Rush; the Gold Rush (*but* a gold rush)
the Cold War (*but* a cold war, used generically)
the Cultural Revolution
the Great Chicago Fire; the Chicago fire; the fire of 1871
the Great Depression; the Depression
the Great Fire of London; the Great Fire
the Great Plague; the Plague (*but* plague [the disease])
(President Johnson's) Great Society
the Industrial Revolution
the Long March

the May 18 Democratic Uprising (*or* the Gwangju Uprising)
Me Too *or* #MeToo (see also 7.86); the Me Too movement
the Middle Passage
the New Deal
Occupy Wall Street; the Occupy movement
Prohibition
Reconstruction
the Reign of Terror; the Terror
the South Sea Bubble
the War on Poverty
*but*
the baby boom
the Black September attacks
the civil rights movement
the COVID-19 pandemic
the crash of 1929
the Dreyfus affair
the Moroccan crises
the Tiananmen Square protests
the war on terror

**8.77** **Speeches.** Titles of a select few speeches are traditionally capitalized. Others are usually lowercased (but see 8.190).

Washington's Farewell Address
the Gettysburg Address
the annual State of the Union address
Franklin Roosevelt's second inaugural address
the Checkers speech
Martin Luther King Jr.'s "I Have a Dream" speech

**8.78** **Meteorological and other natural phenomena.** Named hurricanes and other tropical cyclones are capitalized, as are many other named meteorological phenomena. If in doubt, consult a dictionary or encyclopedia. Natural phenomena identified generically by a place-name or a year are usually lowercased.

Cyclone Becky; the 2007 cyclone
Hurricane Katrina; the 2005 hurricane
El Niño
the Northridge earthquake of 1994
the Arctic polar vortex

Use the pronoun *it*, not *he* or *she*, when referring to named storms, hurricanes, and the like (notwithstanding the practice of using first names to refer to such events).

8.79 **Sporting events.** The full names of major sporting events are capitalized.

the Kentucky Derby; the derby
the NBA Finals; the finals
the Olympic Games; the Olympics; the Winter Olympics
the World Cup

## *Cultural Movements and Styles*

8.80 **Movements and styles — capitalization.** Nouns and adjectives designating cultural styles, movements, and schools (artistic, architectural, musical, and so forth) and their adherents are capitalized if derived from proper nouns. (Words such as *school* and *movement* remain lowercased.) Others may be lowercased, though a few (e.g., *Beat, Cynic, Scholastic, New Critic*) are usually capitalized to distinguish them from the generic words used in everyday speech. Moreover, many of the terms lowercased below may appropriately be capitalized in certain works if done so consistently—especially those that, like *abstract expressionism, art deco, art nouveau, baroque*, and many of the other terms in the list, include the label "often capitalized" in *Merriam-Webster*. (But if one such term is capitalized—e.g., *impressionism* in a work about art—similar terms must also be capitalized.) For religious movements, see 8.98. See also 8.61.

abstract expressionism
Aristotelian
art deco
art nouveau
baroque
Beat movement; the Beats (*but* beatnik)
Beaux-Arts (derived from École des Beaux-Arts)
British Invasion
camp
Cartesian
Chicago school (of architecture, of economics, of literary criticism)
classicism, classical
conceptualism
cubism
Cynicism; Cynic
Dadaism; Dada
deconstruction
Doric
Epicurean (see text below)
existentialism
fauvism
formalism
Gothic (*but* gothic fiction)
Gregorian chant
Hellenism

Hudson River school
humanism
idealism
imagism
impressionism
Keynesianism
mannerism
minimalism
miracle play
modernism
mysticism; mystic
naturalism
neoclassicism; neoclassical
Neoplatonism; Neoplatonic
New Criticism; New Critic
nominalism
op art
Peripatetic (see text below)
philosophe (French)
Platonism
pop art
postimpressionism
postmodernism
Pre-Raphaelite
Reaganomics
realism
rococo
Romanesque
Romanticism; Romantic
Scholasticism; Scholastic; Schoolmen
scientific rationalism
the silent era; silent films
Sophist (see text below)
Stoicism; Stoic (see text below)
structuralism
Sturm und Drang (*but* storm and stress)
surrealism
symbolism
theater of the absurd
transcendentalism

Some words that are capitalized when used in reference to a school of thought are lowercased when used metaphorically.

epicurean tastes
peripatetic families
she's a sophist, not a logician
a stoic attitude

## *Acts, Treaties, and Government Programs*

8.81 **Formal names of acts, treaties, and so forth.** Formal or accepted titles of pacts, plans, policies, treaties, acts, programs, and similar documents or agreements are capitalized. Incomplete or generic forms are usually lowercased. For citing the published text of a bill or law, see 14.183, 14.184.

Article VI (of the US Constitution); the article (see also 9.30)
the Articles of Confederation
the Bill of Rights
the Brady Bill; the Brady Handgun Violence Prevention Act; the Brady Act; *but* the Brady law
the Constitution of the United States; the United States (*or* US) Constitution; the

Constitution (usually capitalized in reference to the US Constitution); *but* a constitutional amendment
the Illinois Constitution; the constitution
the Constitution Act, 1982 (Canada)
the Corn Laws (Great Britain)
the Declaration of Independence
the due process clause
the Equal Rights Amendment (usually capitalized though not ratified); ERA; *but* an equal rights amendment
the Family and Medical Leave Act of 1993; FMLA; the 1993 act
the Fifteenth Amendment (to the US Constitution); the Smith Amendment; the amendment
the Food Stamp Act of 1964; food stamps
the Smoot–Hawley (*or* Hawley–Smoot) Tariff Act (see also 6.85); the tariff act
Head Start
impeachment; the first and second articles of impeachment
the Kyoto Protocol; the protocol
the Marshall Plan
the Mayflower Compact; the compact
Medicare; Medicaid
the Monroe Doctrine; the doctrine
the Munich Agreement (1938); Munich; the agreement
the New Economic Policy; NEP (Soviet Union)
the Open Door policy
the Paris Agreement
the Peace of Utrecht
the Reform Bills; the Reform Bill of 1832 (Great Britain)
the Social Security Act; Social Security (*or, generically,* social security); Social Security number
Temporary Assistance for Needy Families; TANF
Title VII (see also 9.30)
Treaty for the Renunciation of War, *known as* the Pact of Paris *or* the Kellogg–Briand Pact (see also 6.85); the pact
the Treaty of Versailles; the treaty
the Treaty on European Union (official name); the Maastricht treaty (informal name)
the Wilmot Proviso

8.82 **Descriptive terms for pending legislation.** Informal, purely descriptive references to pending legislation are lowercased.

The anti-injunction bill was introduced on Tuesday. (See also the table at 7.96, section 4.)

## *Legal Cases*

8.83 **Legal cases mentioned in text.** The names of legal cases are italicized when mentioned in text. The abbreviation *v.* (versus) occasionally appears in roman, but Chicago recommends italics. In footnotes, legal dictionaries, and contexts where numerous legal cases appear, case names are sometimes set in roman. For legal citation style, see 14.170–207.

*Bloomfield Village Drain Dist. v. Keefe*
*Miranda v. Arizona*

In discussion, a case name may be shortened.

the *Miranda* case (or simply *Miranda*)

## *Awards*

8.84 **Capitalization for names of awards and prizes.** Names of awards and prizes are capitalized, but some generic terms used with the names are lowercased. For military awards, see 8.116.

the 2024 Nobel Prize in Physiology or Medicine; a Nobel Prize winner; a Nobel Prize–winning physiologist (see 6.86); a Nobel Peace Prize; the Nobel Prize in Literature
the 2024 Pulitzer Prize for Commentary (*but* a Pulitzer in journalism)
an Academy Award; the Academy Award for Best Picture; an Oscar
the Audie Awards; the Audies; the Audie Award for Fantasy; an Audie
an Emmy Award for Outstanding Supporting Actor in a Comedy Series; she has three Emmys
a Webby Award; the Webbys; the Webby Award for Activism; a Webby
the Presidential Medal of Freedom
a Guggenheim Fellowship (*but* a Guggenheim grant)
an International Music Scholarship
National Merit Scholarship awards; Merit Scholarships; Merit Scholar

## *Oaths and Pledges*

8.85 **Formal oaths and pledges.** Unofficial or descriptive names of formal oaths and pledges are usually lowercased, but official or accepted titles are capitalized.

the oath of citizenship
the Hippocratic oath
the presidential oath of office
marriage vows
*but*
the Oath of Allegiance (for US citizenship)
the Pledge of Allegiance

### *Academic Subjects, Courses of Study, and Lecture Series*

8.86 **Academic subjects.** Academic subjects are not capitalized unless they form part of a department name or an official course name (see 8.87) or are themselves proper nouns (e.g., English, Latin).

She has published widely in the history of religions.
They have a wide variety of courses in gender studies.
She is pursuing graduate studies in physics.
He is majoring in comparative literature.
*but*
Jones is chair of the Committee on Comparative Literature.

8.87 **Courses of study.** Official names of courses of study are capitalized.

I am signing up for Archaeology 101.
A popular course at the Graham School of General Studies is Basic Manuscript Editing.
*but*
His ballroom dancing classes have failed to civilize him.

8.88 **Lectures.** Names of lecture series are capitalized. Titles for individual lectures are capitalized and usually enclosed in quotation marks. See also 8.71.

This year's Robinson Memorial Lectures were devoted to the nursing profession. The first lecture, "How Nightingale Got Her Way," was a sellout.

## CALENDAR AND TIME DESIGNATIONS

8.89 **Days of the week, months, and seasons.** Names of days and months are capitalized. The four seasons are lowercased (except when used to denote an issue of a journal; see 14.70). For centuries and decades, see 8.72.

| | | |
|---|---|---|
| Tuesday | spring | the vernal (*or* spring) equinox |
| November | fall | the winter solstice |

8.90 **Holidays.** The names of secular and religious holidays or officially designated days or seasons are capitalized.

All Fools' Day
Black History Month
Christmas Day
D-Day
Diwali
Earth Day
Election Day
Father's Day
Flag Day
the Fourth of July, the Fourth
Good Friday
Halloween
Hanukkah
Holy Week
Inauguration Day
Independence Day
Indigenous Peoples' Day
Juneteenth
Kwanzaa
Labor Day
Lent
Lincoln's Birthday
Martin Luther King Jr. Day
Memorial Day
Mother's Day
National Poetry Month
New Year's Day
New Year's Eve
Nowruz
Passover
Presidents' Day
Ramadan
Remembrance Day (Commonwealth)
Rosh Hashanah
Saint Patrick's Day
Thanksgiving Day
Veterans Day
Yom Kippur
Yuletide
*but*
a bank holiday

8.91 **Time and time zones.** When spelled out, official designations of time and time zones are generally capitalized. This departure from advice in previous editions aligns with common usage. In shortened references, the word *time* is usually lowercased, as are generic references to *standard time* and the like. See also 9.39–42, 10.46.

Hawaii-Aleutian Standard Time (HST); Hawaii-Aleutian Daylight Time (HDT)
Alaska Standard Time (AKST); Alaska Daylight Time (AKDT); Alaska time
Pacific Standard Time (PST); Pacific time
Mountain Standard Time (MST); Mountain time
Central Standard Time (CST); Central time
Eastern Standard Time (EST); Eastern Daylight Time (EDT); Eastern time; nine o'clock Eastern
Atlantic Standard Time (AST); Atlantic time
Newfoundland Daylight Time (NDT)

Greenwich Mean Time (GMT); British Summer Time (BST)
Coordinated Universal Time (UTC)
*but*
standard time (ST), daylight saving time (DST), daylight time; summer time

## RELIGIOUS NAMES AND TERMS

### *Deities and Revered Persons*

8.92 **Deities.** Names of deities, whether in monotheistic or polytheistic religions, are capitalized. Generic references to gods and the like are lowercased.

| | | |
|---|---|---|
| Allah | Jehovah | Waheguru |
| Astarte | Kali | Yahweh |
| Freyja | Mithra | *but* |
| God | Satan | a devil, the devil (Satan and others) |
| Itzamna | Serapis | a god, gods; the Greek god of war (Ares) |

Some writers prefer to use lowercase for the word *god* in any expression that might be taken to be profane. Others follow a pious convention of not fully spelling out the name of a deity (e.g., *G-d*, with a hyphen; but see 6.99). These conventions should be respected when it is practical to do so.

8.93 **Alternative names.** Alternative or descriptive names for God as supreme being are capitalized. See also 8.94.

Adonai
the Almighty
the Deity
the Holy Ghost *or* the Holy Spirit *or* the Paraclete
the Lord
the Merciful
Providence
the Supreme Being
the Trinity

8.94 **Prophets and the like.** Designations of prophets, apostles, saints, and other revered persons are often capitalized.

the Buddha
the prophet Isaiah

Jesus; Christ; the Good Shepherd; the Son (*or* son) of man
John the Baptist
the Messiah
Muhammad; the Prophet
Saint John; the Beloved Apostle
Tenskwatawa; the Shawnee Prophet
the Virgin Mary; the Blessed Virgin; Mother of God
*but*
the apostles
the patriarchs
the psalmist

8.95 **Platonic ideas.** Words for transcendent ideas in the Platonic sense, especially when used in a religious context, are often capitalized. See also 7.54.

Good; Beauty; Truth; the One

8.96 **Pronouns referring to religious figures.** Pronouns referring to God or Jesus are not capitalized unless a particular author or publisher prefers otherwise. (Note that they are lowercased in most English translations of the Bible.)

They prayed to God that he would deliver them.
Jesus and his disciples

## *Religious Groups*

8.97 **Major religions.** Names of major religions are capitalized, as are their adherents and adjectives derived from them.

Buddhism; Buddhists; a Buddhist
Christianity; Christians; a Christian; Christendom (see also 8.99)
Confucianism; Confucians; a Confucian
Hinduism; Hindus; a Hindu
Islam; Islamic; Muslims; a Muslim
Judaism; Jews; a Jew; Jewry; Jewish
Shinto *or* Shintoism; Shintoists; a Shinto priest
Taoism; Taoists; a Taoist; Taoistic
*but*
atheism; atheists; an atheist; atheistic
agnosticism; agnostics; an agnostic

8.98 **Denominations, sects, orders, and religious movements.** Like the names of major religions, names of denominations, communions, sects, orders, and religious movements are capitalized, as are their adherents and adjectives derived from them. See also 8.100.

the Amish; Amish communities
Anglicanism; the Anglican Communion (*see also* Episcopal Church)
Baptists; a Baptist church; the Baptist General Convention; the Southern Baptist Convention
Catholicism (*see* Roman Catholicism)
Christian Science; Church of Christ, Scientist; Christian Scientist
the Church of England (*but* an Anglican church)
the Church of Ireland
Community of Christ
Conservative Judaism; a Conservative Jew
Dissenter (lowercased when used in a nonsectarian context)
Druidism; Druid (sometimes lowercased)
Eastern Orthodox churches; the Eastern Church (*but* an Eastern Orthodox church)
the Episcopal Church; an Episcopal church; an Episcopalian
the Episcopal Church of Scotland
Essenes; an Essene
Gnosticism; Gnostic
Hasidism; Hasid (singular); Hasidim (plural); Hasidic
Jehovah's Witnesses
Jesuit(s); the Society of Jesus; Jesuitic(al) (lowercased when used pejoratively)
Methodism; the United Methodist Church (*but* a United Methodist church); Wesleyan
Mormonism; Mormon; the Church of Jesus Christ of Latter-day Saints (where lowercase *day* follows church preference; cf. 8.162)
Nonconformism; Nonconformist (lowercased when used in a nonsectarian context)
Old Catholics; an Old Catholic church
the Order of Preachers; the Dominican order; a Dominican
Orthodox Judaism; an Orthodox Jew
Orthodoxy; the (Greek, Serbian, etc.) Orthodox Church (*but* a Greek Orthodox church)
Protestantism; Protestant (lowercased when used in a nonsectarian context)
Puritanism; Puritan (lowercased when used in a nonsectarian context)
Quakerism; Quaker; the Religious Society of Friends; a Friend
Reform Judaism; a Reform Jew
Roman Catholicism; the Roman Catholic Church (*but* a Roman Catholic church)
Satanism; Satanist

Seventh-day Adventist (following church preference; cf. 8.162); Adventist; Adventism
Shiism; Shia; Shiite
Sufism; Sufi
Sunnism; Sunni; Sunnite
Theosophy; Theosophist; the Theosophical Society
Vedanta
Wicca; Wiccan
Zen; Zen Buddhism

8.99 **"Church" as institution.** When used to refer to the institution of religion or of a particular religion, *church* is usually lowercased unless a particular author or publisher prefers otherwise.

church and state
the early church
the church in the twenty-first century
the church fathers

*Church* is capitalized when part of the formal name of a denomination (e.g., the United Methodist Church; see other examples in 8.98) or congregation (e.g., the Church of St. Thomas the Apostle).

8.100 **Generic versus religious terms.** Many terms that are lowercased when used generically, such as *animism*, *fundamentalism*, or *spiritualism*, may be capitalized when used as the name of a specific religion or a sect.

a popular medium in turn-of-the-century Spiritualist circles
*but*
liberal versus fundamentalist Christians

8.101 **Religious jurisdictions.** The names of official divisions within organized religions are capitalized. The generic terms used alone are lowercased.

the Archdiocese of Chicago; the archdiocese
the Eastern Diocese of the Armenian Church
the Fifty-Seventh Street Meeting; the (Quaker) meeting
the Holy See
the Missouri Synod; the synod

8.102 **Places of worship.** The names of the buildings in which religious congregations meet are capitalized. The generic terms used alone are lowercased.

Babri Mosque; the mosque
Bethany Evangelical Lutheran Church; the church
Temple Emanuel; the temple; the synagogue
Nichiren Buddhist Temple; the temple

8.103 **Councils, synods, and the like.** The accepted names of historic councils and the official names of modern counterparts are capitalized.

the Council of Chalcedon (*or* the Fourth Ecumenical Council)
the General Convention (Episcopal)
the Second Vatican Council; Vatican II
the Synod of Whitby

## *Religious Writings*

8.104 **Scriptures.** Names of scriptures and other highly revered early works are capitalized but not usually italicized (except when used in the title of a published work). Note that *biblical* is commonly lowercased in both literal and figurative uses, but some authors may prefer capitalization when the term refers specifically to the Bible.

the Bhagavad Gita (*or* Bhagavad Gītā)
the Bible (*but* biblical [see text above])
the Book of Common Prayer
the Dead Sea Scrolls
the Hebrew Bible (*or* Tanakh)
the Kama Sutra
the Mahabharata (*or* Mahābhārata)
the Mishnah; Mishnaic
the Qur'an; Qur'anic (*or* Quran; Quranic *or* Koran; Koranic)
Sunna (*or* Sunnah)
the Talmud; Talmudic
the Tao Te Ching
Tripitaka
the Upanishads
the Vedas; Vedic
*but*
sutra(s)

8.105 **Other names and versions for bibles.** Other names and versions of the Hebrew and Christian Bibles are usually capitalized but not italicized.

the Authorized Version *or* the King James Version
the Breeches (*or* Geneva) Bible
Codex Sinaiticus
Complutensian Polyglot Bible
the Douay (*or* Douay-Rheims) Version
the Holy Bible
Holy Writ (but lowercased when used figuratively)
the New English Bible
the New Jerusalem Bible
the New Revised Standard Version
the Peshitta
the Psalter (*but* a psalter)
the Scripture *or* Scriptures (the books of the Bible); *but* Bible scriptures (see also below)
the Septuagint
the Vulgate
*but*
scripture(s); scriptural (of sacred writings in general)

8.106 **Books of the Bible.** The names of books of the Bible are capitalized but never italicized. The word *book* is usually lowercased, and the words *gospel* and *epistle* are usually capitalized. But in a work in which all three terms are used with some frequency, they may all be treated alike, either lowercased or capitalized. See also 9.28, 10.50–54.

Genesis; the book of Genesis
Job; the book of Job
2 Chronicles; Second Chronicles; the second book of Chronicles
Psalms (*but* a psalm)
John; the Gospel According to John (see also 8.161)
Acts; the Acts of the Apostles
1 Corinthians; the First Epistle to the Corinthians

8.107 **Sections of the Bible.** Names of sections of the Bible are usually capitalized but not italicized.

the Hebrew scriptures *or* the Old Testament
the Christian scriptures *or* the New Testament
the Apocrypha; Apocryphal (*or, generically,* apocryphal)
the Epistles; the pastoral Epistles
the Gospels; the synoptic Gospels
the Pentateuch *or* the Torah; Pentateuchal
Hagiographa *or* Ketuvim; hagiographic

8.108 **Prayers, creeds, and such.** Named prayers, canticles, creeds, and such, as well as scriptural terms of special importance, are usually capitalized. Parables and miracles are usually lowercased.

the Decalogue; the Ten Commandments; the first commandment
Kaddish; to say Kaddish
the Lord's Prayer; the Our Father
Luther's Ninety-Five Theses
the Nicene Creed; the creed
Salat al-Fajr
the Sermon on the Mount
the Shema
*but*
the doxology
the miracle of the loaves and fishes
the parable of the prodigal son
the star of Bethlehem

## *Religious Events, Concepts, Services, and Objects*

8.109 **Religious events and concepts.** Religious events and concepts of major theological importance are often capitalized. Used generically, such terms are lowercased.

the Creation
the Crucifixion
the Diaspora
the Exodus
the Fall
the Hegira
the Second Coming
*but*
Most religions have creation myths.
For the Romans, crucifixion was a common form of execution.

Doctrines and principles are usually lowercased.

atonement
bhakti
dharma
original sin
resurrection; *but* the Resurrection (of Christ)

8.110 **Heaven, hell, and so on.** Terms for divine dwelling places, ideal states, places of divine punishment, and the like are usually lowercased (though they are often capitalized in a purely religious context). See also 8.51.

| | |
|---|---|
| heaven | purgatory |
| hell | *but* |
| limbo | Eden |
| nirvana | Elysium |
| outer darkness | Hades |
| paradise | Olympus |
| the pearly gates | |

8.111 **Services and rites.** Names of services and rites are usually lowercased (though they may be capitalized in strictly religious contexts; if in doubt, consult *Merriam-Webster*).

| | | |
|---|---|---|
| baptism | confirmation | the seder |
| bar mitzvah | morning prayer; matins | the sun dance |
| bat mitzvah | puja | vespers |

Terms denoting the Eucharistic sacrament, however, are traditionally capitalized, though certain terms may be lowercased in nonreligious contexts or when used generically.

the Eucharist
Holy Communion
High Mass; Low Mass; attend Mass; *but* an afternoon mass

8.112 **Objects.** Objects of religious use or significance are usually lowercased, especially in nonreligious contexts.

| | | |
|---|---|---|
| altar | mandala | sanctuary |
| ark | mezuzah | stations of the cross |
| chalice and paten | rosary | |
| kumkum | sacred pipe | |

## MILITARY TERMS

### *Forces and Troops*

8.113 **Armies, battalions, and such.** Titles of armies, navies, air forces, fleets, battalions, companies, corps, and so forth are capitalized. Unofficial but well-known names, such as *Green Berets* and *SEALs*, are also capitalized. Words such as *army* and *navy* are usually lowercased when standing alone, when used collectively in the plural, or when not part of an official title. However, many of the lowercased terms below are routinely capitalized in official or promotional contexts and by military organizations that use the terms in their work (see also 8.20). Also note that in a text focusing primarily on the US military, terms such as *Army*, *Navy*, and *Air Force* are usually capitalized. When referring to non-US militaries, such terms are often capitalized when they follow a country designation, particularly when both the official and the common terms are used in the text to prevent confusion (e.g., *Luftwaffe*, or *German Air Force*; but *air force* when used alone). See also 9.49.

the Allies (World Wars I and II); the Allied forces
American Expeditionary Force; the AEF
Army Corps of Engineers; the corps
Army of Northern Virginia; the army
Army of the Potomac
Army Special Forces
the Axis powers (World War II)
Canadian Army (a branch of the Canadian Forces)
Canadian Forces *or* Canadian Armed Forces
the Central powers (World War I)
Combined Chiefs of Staff (World War II)
Confederate army (American Civil War)
Continental navy (American Revolution)
Eighth Air Force; the air force
Fifth Army; the army
First Battalion, 178th Infantry; the battalion; the 178th
French Foreign Legion
Green Berets
Joint Chiefs of Staff
the Luftwaffe; the German air force
National Guard
Navy SEALs
Pacific Fleet (US, World War II)
Red Army (Russian, World War II); Russian army
the Resistance; the French Resistance; a resistance movement
Rough Riders
Royal Air Force; RAF; British air force
Royal Canadian Air Force (a branch of the Canadian Forces)
Royal Canadian Mounted Police; the Mounties; a Mountie
Royal Canadian Navy (a branch of the Canadian Forces)

Royal Navy; the British navy
Royal Scots Fusiliers; the fusiliers
Seventh Fleet; the fleet
Thirty-Third Infantry Division; the Thirty-Third Division; the division
Union army (American Civil War)
United States (*or* US) Army; the army
United States Army Signal Corps; the Signal Corps *or* the signal corps
United States Coast Guard; the Coast Guard *or* the coast guard
United States Marine Corps; the Marine Corps *or* the marine corps; the US Marines; a marine
United States Navy; the navy

## *Wars, Revolutions, Battles, and Campaigns*

**8.114** **Wars and revolutions.** Names of most major wars and revolutions are capitalized. The generic terms are usually lowercased when used alone. More recent, unresolved conflicts can usually be lowercased.

American Civil War; the War Between the States
American Revolution; American War of Independence; the revolution (sometimes capitalized); the Revolutionary War
Crusades; the Sixth Crusade; a crusader
First Balkan War; Second Balkan War; the Balkan Wars
French Revolution; the Revolution of 1789; the Revolution (usually capitalized to distinguish the Revolution of 1789 from the revolutions in 1830 and 1848); revolutionary France
Iran-Iraq War
Iraq War
Korean War; the war
Mexican Revolution; the revolution
Napoleonic Wars
Norman Conquest; the conquest of England
Opium Wars
Persian Gulf War *or* Gulf War
the revolution(s) of 1848
Russian Revolution; the revolution
Second Boer War *or* South African War
Seven Years' War
Shays's Rebellion (see also 7.17)
Sioux Wars; the Great Sioux War (*or* the Black Hills War)
Six-Day War; the June War; the Third (*or* 1967) Arab-Israeli War; the Setback (an-Naksa); *among other names*

South Sudanese Civil War (*but* the civil war in South Sudan)
Spanish-American War
Spanish Civil War
Vietnam War
War of 1812
Whiskey Rebellion
World War I; the First World War; the Great War; the war
World War II; the Second World War; World Wars I and II; the First and Second World Wars; the two world wars
*but*
the 2022 Russian invasion of Ukraine; the war in Ukraine

8.115 **Battles and campaigns.** The names of major battles and campaigns are usually capitalized. (Some of the examples below, lowercased in previous editions, have been capitalized for this edition to align with common usage.) In other, more generic descriptions, only proper names are capitalized. For names not included here, consult an encyclopedia.

Battle of Britain
Battle of Bunker Hill; Bunker Hill; the battle
Battle of the Bulge (*or* Battle of the Ardennes)
Battle of the Little Bighorn
Battle of Vimy Ridge
the Blitz
the European Theater of Operations; ETO
the Mexican Border War (*or* Border Campaign)
Operation Devil Siphon
Third Battle of Ypres (*or* Battle of Passchendaele)
Vicksburg Campaign
Western Front (World War I)
*but*
the battle for the Aleutian Islands (World War II)

## *Military Awards*

8.116 **Medals and awards.** Specific names of medals and awards are capitalized. For civil awards, see 8.84.

Croix de Guerre
Distinguished Flying Cross; DFC
Distinguished Service Order; DSO

Medal of Honor (US congressional award); the medal
Purple Heart
Silver Star
Victoria Cross; VC

## NAMES OF SHIPS AND OTHER VEHICLES

8.117 **Ships and other named vessels.** The names of ships and other vessels are capitalized; a specific name like *Phoenix* is also italicized (as in the first set of examples below). Note that when such abbreviations as USS (United States ship) or HMS (His [or Her] Majesty's ship) precede a name (where they are *not* italicized), the word *ship* or other vessel type should not be used. For names not included here, consult an encyclopedia or other reliable resource. For spacecraft, NASA's website can be helpful in determining capitalization (but not necessarily italics). For military vessels, Eric Wertheim's *The Naval Institute Guide to Combat Fleets of the World* (bibliog. 5) provides much useful information.

*Eagle* (lunar module for the Apollo 11 mission)
Mars Global Surveyor; Mars Polar Lander; the *Phoenix* Mars lander; *Phoenix*; the *Phoenix* lander; the *Perseverance* Mars rover; *Perseverance*
the space shuttle *Discovery*; the space shuttle
the *Spirit of St. Louis*
HMS *Frolic*; the British ship *Frolic*
SS *United States*; the *United States*
USS *SC-530*; the US ship *SC-530*
*but*
Sputnik 1 (the satellite)

Every US Navy ship is assigned a hull number (according to a system formally implemented in 1920), consisting of a combination of letters (indicating the type of ship) and a serial number. Where necessary to avoid confusion between vessels of the same name—in a work on naval history, for example—the numbers should be included at first mention. Smaller ships such as landing craft and submarine chasers are individually numbered but not named.

USS *Enterprise* (CVN-65) was already on its way to the Red Sea.

8.118 **Other vehicle names.** Names of makes and classes of aircraft, models of automobiles and other vehicles, names of trains or train runs, and names of space programs are capitalized but not italicized.

| | |
|---|---|
| Acela Express | Ford F-150 Lightning |
| Boeing 787 Dreamliner | Metroliner |
| Comac ARJ21 Xiangfeng | Project Apollo |
| Concorde | Subaru Impreza |

8.119 **Pronouns referring to vessels.** When a pronoun is used to refer to a vessel, the neuter *it* or *its* (rather than *she* or *her*) is preferred. See also 5.46, 8.78.

## SCIENTIFIC TERMINOLOGY

### *Scientific Names of Plants and Animals*

8.120 **Scientific style—additional resources.** The following paragraphs offer only general guidelines. Writers or editors requiring detailed guidance should consult *The CSE Manual* (bibliog. 1.1). The ultimate authorities are the *International Code of Nomenclature for Algae, Fungi, and Plants* (*ICN*), whose guidelines are followed in the botanical examples below, and the *International Code of Zoological Nomenclature* (*ICZN*) (see bibliog. 5). Note that some fields, such as virology, have slightly different rules. Writers and editors should try to follow the standards established within those fields.

8.121 **Genus and specific epithet.** Whether in lists or in running text, the Latin names of species of plants and animals are italicized. Each *binomial* contains a genus name (or *generic name*), which is capitalized, and a species name (also called *specific name* or *specific epithet*), which is lowercased (even if it is a proper adjective). Do not confuse these names with phyla, orders, and such, which are not italicized; see 8.127.

The Pleistocene saber-toothed cats all belonged to the genus *Smilodon*.
Many species names, such as *Rosa caroliniana* and *Styrax californica*, reflect the locale of the first specimens described.
The pike, *Esox lucius*, is valued for food as well as sport.
For the grass snake *Natrix natrix*, longevity in captivity is ten years.
Certain lizard taxa, such as *Basiliscus* and *Crotaphytus*, are bipedal specialists.

8.122 **Abbreviation of genus name.** After first use, the genus name may be abbreviated to a single capital letter. If two or more species of the same genus are listed together, the abbreviation may be doubled (to indicate the plural) before the first species, though repeating the abbreviation with each species is more common. But if species of different genera beginning with the same letter are discussed in the same context, abbreviations may not be appropriate.

Two methods allow us to estimate the maximum speeds obtained by *Callisaurus draconoides* in the field. Irschick and Jayne (1998) found that stride durations of both *C. draconoides* and *Uma scoparia* do not change dramatically after the fifth stride during accelerations from a standstill.

The "quaking" of the aspen, *Populus tremuloides*, is due to the construction of the petiole; an analogous phenomenon has been noted in the cottonwood, *P. deltoides*.

Among popular species of the genus *Cyclamen* are *CC. coum, hederifolium,* and *persicum* . . . [or, more commonly, *C. coum, C. hederifolium,* and *C. persicum* . . .]

Studies of *Corylus avellana* and *Corokia cotoneaster* . . . ; in further studies it was noted that *Corylus avellana* and *Corokia cotoneaster* . . .

8.123 **Subspecies and varieties.** A subspecific zoological name or epithet, when used, follows the binomial species name and is also italicized. If the two names are the same, the first one may be abbreviated.

*Noctilio labialis labialis* (or *Noctilio l. labialis*)
*Trogon collaris puella*

In horticultural usage, the abbreviations "subsp." (or "ssp."), "var.," and "f." (none of them italicized) are inserted before the subspecific epithet or variety or form name. See also 8.124.

*Buxus microphylla* var. *japonica*
*Hydrangea anomala* subsp. *petiolaris*
*Rhododendron arboreum* f. *album*

8.124 **Unspecified species and varieties.** The abbreviations "sp." and "var.," when used without a following element, indicate that the species or variety is unknown or unspecified. The plural "spp." is used to refer to a group of species. The abbreviations are *not* italicized.

*Rhododendron* spp.
*Rosa rugosa* var.
*Viola* sp.

8.125 **Author names.** The name of the person who proposed a specific epithet is sometimes added, often abbreviated, and never italicized. A capital *L.* stands for Linnaeus; *Mill.* stands for Miller.

*Diaemus youngi cypselinus* Thomas
*Euchistenes hartii* (Thomas)
*Felis leo* Scop.
*Molossus coibensis* J. A. Allen
*Quercus alba* L.
*Linaria spuria* (L.) Mill.

The parentheses in the second example above, from zoology, mean that Thomas originally described the species *E. hartii* but referred it to a different genus. In botanical usage, the name of the person who referred it to the new genus is added after the parentheses, as in the last example.

8.126 **Plant hybrids.** The crossing of two species is indicated by a multiplication sign (×; *not* the letter *x*) between the two species names, with space on each side. Many older primary plant hybrids are indicated by a multiplication sign immediately before the specific epithet of the hybrid, with space only before it.

*Magnolia denudata* × *M. liliiflora* (crossing of species)
*Magnolia* ×*soulangeana* (hybrid name)

8.127 **Higher divisions.** Divisions higher than genus—phylum, class, order, and family—are capitalized but *not* italicized. (The terms *order*, *family*, and so on are not capitalized.) Intermediate groupings are treated similarly.

Chordata (phylum)
Chondrichthyes (class)
Monotremata (order)
Ruminantia (suborder)
Hominidae (family)
Felinae (subfamily)
Selachii (term used of various groups of cartilaginous fishes)
The new species *Gleichenia glauca* provides further details about the history of Gleicheniaceae.

8.128 **English derivatives.** English words derived from the taxonomic system are lowercased and treated as ordinary words.

carnivore(s) (from the order Carnivora)
hominid(s) (from the family Hominidae)
irid(s) (from the family Iridaceae)
feline(s) (from subfamily Felinae)
astilbe(s) (from the genus *Astilbe*)
mastodon(s) (from the genus *Mastodon*)

## *Vernacular Names of Plants and Animals*

8.129 **Plants and animals—additional resources.** For the correct capitalization and spelling of common names of plants and animals, consult a dictionary or the authoritative guides to nomenclature, the *ICN* and the *ICZN*, mentioned in 8.120. In general, Chicago recommends capitalizing only proper nouns and adjectives, as in the following examples, which conform to the entries in *Merriam-Webster*:

Dutchman's-breeches
jack-in-the-pulpit
mayapple
Cooper's hawk
rhesus monkey
Rocky Mountain sheep

8.130 **Domestic animals and horticultural categories.** Either a dictionary or the guides to nomenclature *ICZN* and *ICN* should be consulted for the proper spelling of breeds of domestic animals and broad horticultural categories.

German shorthaired pointer
golden retriever
Hereford
Maine coon *or* coon cat
Thoroughbred horse (*but* purebred dog)
Rhode Island Red
boysenberry
rambler rose

Note that the names of breeds of domestic animals, including otherwise generic terms, are generally capitalized by professional organizations like the American Kennel Club and the Cat Fanciers' Association (e.g., Golden Retriever and Maine Coon). When in doubt, follow the first-listed capitalization in *Merriam-Webster* or another standard reference.

8.131 **Horticultural cultivars.** Many horticultural cultivars (cultivated varieties) have fanciful names that must be respected since they may be registered trademarks.

the Peace rose
a Queen of the Market aster

In some horticultural publications, such names are enclosed in single quotation marks; any following punctuation is placed *after* the closing quotation mark. If the English name follows the Latin name, there is no intervening punctuation. For examples of this usage, consult any issue of the magazine *Horticulture* (bibliog. 5).

The hybrid *Agastache* 'Apricot Sunrise', best grown in zone 6, mingles with sheaves of cape fuchsia (*Phygelius* 'Salmon Leap').

## *Genetic Terms*

8.132 **Genetic nomenclature — additional resources.** Only the most basic guidelines can be offered here. Writers or editors working in the field of genetics should consult the *AMA Manual of Style* or *The CSE Manual* (both in bibliog. 1.1) and online databases including the HGNC (HUGO Gene Nomenclature Committee) database of human gene names and the Mouse Genome Database (both in bibliog. 5).

8.133 **Genes.** Names of genes, or gene symbols, including any Arabic numerals that form a part of such symbols, are usually italicized. (Italicization helps differentiate genes from entities with similar names.) Symbols for genes contain no Greek characters or Roman numerals. Human gene symbols are set in full capitals, as are the gene symbols for other primates. Mouse and rat gene symbols are usually spelled with an initial capital. Gene nomenclature systems for other organisms (yeast, fruit flies, nematodes, plants, fish) vary. Symbols for proteins, also called gene products and often derived from the symbols of the corresponding genes, are set in roman type.

*Human genes*
*BRCA1*
*GPC3*
*IGH@* (the symbol @ indicates a family or cluster)
*SNRPN*

*Mouse genes*
*Cmv1*
*Fgf12*
*Rom1*
*Wnt1*
*NLP3* (gene symbol); NLP3p (encoded protein; note *p* suffix)
*GIF* (gene symbol); GIF (gastric intrinsic factor)

Only a very few gene symbols contain hyphens.

*HLA-DRB1*, for human leukocyte antigen D-related β chain 1

8.134 **Enzymes.** Enzyme names consist of a string of italic and roman characters. The first three letters, which represent the name of the organism (usually a bacterium) from which the enzyme has been isolated, are italicized. The Roman numeral that follows represents the series number. Sometimes an upper- or lowercase Latin letter or an Arabic numeral (or both), representing the strain of bacterium, intervenes between the name and series number.

*Ava*I *Bam*HI *Cla*I *Eco*RI *Hin*dIII *Sau*3AI

## *Geological Terms*

8.135 **Geological terms — additional resources.** The following paragraphs offer only the most general guidelines. Writers or editors working in geological studies should consult US Geological Survey, *Suggestions to Authors of the Reports of the United States Geological Survey*, and *The CSE Manual* (both listed in bibliog. 1.1).

8.136 **Formal versus generic geological terms.** Formal geological terms are capitalized in both noun and adjective forms; terms used generically are not. The generic terms *Eon*, *Era*, and the like are capitalized when they immediately follow a formal name (a departure from previous editions that aligns with common usage) but are often omitted. Eons are divided into eras, eras into periods, periods into epochs, and epochs into stages. The term *ice age* is best lowercased in scientific contexts because of the uncertainty surrounding any formal use of the term (cf. *Little Ice Age*); but see 8.75.

the Archean (*or* the Archean Eon); the eon
the Mesoproterozoic (*or* the Mesoproterozoic Era)
the Tertiary Period of the Cenozoic Era
the Paleocene (*or* the Paleocene Epoch)
the Pleistocene-Holocene boundary (*boundary* is descriptive)
the second interglacial stage *or* II interglacial
the Illinoian Glacial Stage *or* the Illinoian glaciation

The modifiers *early*, *middle*, and *late* are capitalized when used formally but lowercased when used informally.

| | |
|---|---|
| Early Archean | *but* |
| Middle Cambrian | early Middle Cambrian |
| Late Quaternary | in late Pleistocene times |

8.137 **Stratigraphy.** Formal stratigraphic names are capitalized. For prehistoric cultural terms, see 8.75.

| | |
|---|---|
| Fleur de Lys Supergroup | Niobrara Member |
| Ramey Ridge Complex | Morrison Formation |

## *Astronomical Terms*

8.138 **Astronomical terms—additional resources.** The following paragraphs offer only the most general guidelines. Writers or editors working in astronomy or astrophysics should consult *The CSE Manual* (bibliog. 1.1) and the website of the International Astronomical Union.

8.139 **Celestial bodies.** The names of galaxies, constellations, stars, planets, and such are capitalized. For *earth*, *sun*, and *moon*, see 8.141, 8.142.

Aldebaran
Alpha Centauri *or* α Centauri
the Big Dipper *or* Ursa Major *or* the Great Bear
Cassiopeia's Chair
the Crab Nebula
85 Pegasi
Halley's Comet (*or* Comet Halley)
the Magellanic Clouds
the Milky Way
the North Star *or* Polaris, polestar
Saturn
*but*
the solar system

8.140 **Catalog names for celestial objects.** Celestial objects listed in well-known catalogs are designated by the catalog name, often abbreviated, and a number.

Bond 619    Lalande 5761    Lynds 1251 *or* L1251    NGC 6165

8.141 **"Earth."** In nontechnical contexts, the word *earth*, in the sense of our planet, is usually lowercased when preceded by *the* or in such idioms as "down to earth" or "move heaven and earth." When used as the proper name of our planet, especially in context with other planets, it is capitalized and *the* is usually omitted.

Some still believe the earth is flat.
The gender accorded to the moon, the sun, and the earth varies in different mythologies.
Where on earth have you been?
The astronauts have returned successfully to Earth.
Does Mars, like Earth, have an atmosphere?

8.142 **"Sun" and "moon."** The words *sun* and *moon* are usually lowercased in nontechnical contexts and always lowercased in the plural.

The moon circles the earth, as the earth circles the sun.
Some planets have several moons.

Some publications in the fields of astronomy and related sciences, however, routinely capitalize these words when used as proper nouns. (See also 8.139.)

8.143 **Descriptive terms.** Merely descriptive terms applied to celestial objects or phenomena are not capitalized.

aurora borealis *or* northern lights
gegenschein
interstellar dust
the rings of Saturn

## *Medical Terms*

8.144 **Medical terms — additional resources.** The following paragraphs offer only the most general guidelines. Medical writers or editors should consult the *AMA Manual of Style* or *The CSE Manual* (both in bibliog. 1.1).

8.145 **Diseases, procedures, and such.** Names of diseases, syndromes, diagnostic procedures, anatomical parts, and the like are lowercased, except for proper names forming part of the term. Acronyms and initialisms are capitalized.

acquired immunodeficiency syndrome *or* AIDS
Alzheimer disease (see below)
computed tomography *or* CT
coronavirus disease 2019 *or* COVID-19

Down syndrome (see below)
finger–nose test (*or* finger-to-nose test; see also 6.83)
islets of Langerhans
non-Hodgkin lymphoma (see below)
severe acute respiratory syndrome *or* SARS
ultrasound; ultrasonography

The possessive forms *Alzheimer's*, *Down's*, *Hodgkin's*, and the like, though less common in medical literature, may be preferred in a general context. For x-rays and radiation, see 8.152.

8.146 **Infections.** Names of infectious organisms are treated like other specific names (see 8.120–28). Common forms of such names and the names of conditions based on such names are neither italicized nor capitalized, except in the case of a proper noun.

Microorganisms of the genus *Streptococcus* are present in the blood of persons with streptococcal infection.
The larvae of *Trichinella spiralis* are responsible for the disease trichinosis.
The Ebola virus (which refers to the species *Zaire ebolavirus*) derives its name from the Ebola River.
The coronaviruses that cause SARS and COVID-19 belong to the genus *Betacoronavirus*.

8.147 **Drugs.** Generic names of drugs, which should be used wherever possible in preference to brand names, are lowercased. Brand names must be capitalized; they are often enclosed in parentheses after the first use of the generic name. For guidance, consult the *AMA Manual of Style* and *The CSE Manual* (both in bibliog. 1.1) and the *USP Dictionary of USAN and International Drug Names* (bibliog. 3.3). For brand names and trademarks, see 8.154.

The patient takes weekly injections of interferon beta-1a (Avonex) to control their multiple sclerosis.

## *Physical and Chemical Terms*

8.148 **Physical and chemical terms—additional resources.** The following paragraphs offer only the most general guidelines for nontechnical editors. Writers or editors working in physics should consult the online resources for authors and researchers from the American Institute of

Physics (bibliog. 1.1) or, among other journals, *Physical Review Letters* (bibliog. 5); those working in chemistry should consult the *ACS Guide to Scholarly Communication* (bibliog. 1.1).

8.149 **Laws and theories.** Though usage varies widely, Chicago recommends that names of laws, theories, and the like be lowercased, except for proper names attached to them. However, capitalization may be applied in certain cases to follow common usage or to avoid ambiguity.

Avogadro's hypothesis (*or* Avogadro's law)
Boyle's law
(Einstein's) general theory of relativity
Newton's first law
*but*
the Big Bang theory

8.150 **Chemical names and symbols.** Names of chemical elements and compounds are lowercased when spelled out. Symbols, however, are capitalized and set without periods; the number of atoms in a molecule appears as a subscript. For a list of symbols for the elements, including atomic numbers, see 10.69.

| | |
|---|---|
| ozone; $O_3$ | sulfuric acid; $H_2SO_4$ |
| sodium chloride; NaCl | tungsten carbide; WC |

8.151 **Mass number.** In formal chemical literature, the mass number appears as a superscript to the left of the symbol. In work intended for a general audience, however, it may follow the symbol, after a hyphen, in full size.

$^{14}C$ (formal style); C-14 *or* carbon-14 (informal style)
$^{238}U$ (formal style); U-238 *or* uranium-238 (informal style)

8.152 **Radiations.** Terms for electromagnetic radiations may be spelled as follows:

β-ray (noun or adjective) *or* beta ray (in nonscientific contexts, noun or adjective)
γ-ray (noun or adjective) *or* gamma ray (in nonscientific contexts, noun or adjective)
x-ray (noun, verb, or adjective)
cosmic ray (noun); cosmic-ray (adjective)
ultraviolet ray (noun); ultraviolet-ray (adjective)

Note that the verb *x-ray*, though acceptable in a general context, is not normally used in scholarly medical literature, where writers would more likely speak of obtaining an x-ray image, or a radiograph, of something, or of subjecting something to x-ray analysis.

8.153 **Metric units.** Although the spellings *meter*, *liter*, and so on are widely used in the United States, some American business, government, and professional organizations have adopted the European spellings (*metre*, *litre*, etc.). Chicago's publications show a preference for the traditional American spellings. For abbreviations used in the International System of Units, see 10.57–65.

## BRAND NAMES AND TRADEMARKS

8.154 **Trademarks.** The advice in this section is intended for those who need to mention a trademarked name in text; it is not intended to guide usage by trademark holders themselves. Brand names that are trademarks—often so indicated in dictionaries—should be capitalized if they must be used. A better choice is to substitute a generic term when available. Although the symbols ® and ™ (for registered and unregistered trademarks, respectively) often accompany trademark names on product packaging and in promotional material, there is no legal requirement to use these symbols, and they should be omitted wherever possible. (If one of these symbols must be used at the end of a product name, it should appear before any period, comma, or other mark of punctuation.) Note also that some companies encourage the use of both the proper and the generic term in reference to their products ("Kleenex facial tissue," not just "Kleenex") and discourage turning product names into verbs, but these restrictions, while they may be followed in corporate documentation, are not legally binding. (*Merriam-Webster*, it should be noted, includes entries for lowercase verbs *google*, *photoshop*, and *xerox*.) See also 8.156.

Bufferin; buffered aspirin
Coca-Cola; Coke; cola; soda
Google; search engine; search
Jacuzzi; whirlpool bath
Kleenex; (facial) tissue
Levi's; jeans
Photoshop; image-editing software
Ping-Pong; table tennis
Post-it Note; sticky note
Pyrex; heat-resistant glassware
Scotch tape; adhesive tape
Scrabble
Sharpie; permanent marker
Vaseline; petroleum jelly
Xerox; photocopier; copy
Zoom; videoconference

Authors of fiction and other creative genres are free to use trademarked names in their work provided they take care not to use a name in a way that could be considered defamatory (see also 4.77). Though such names can occasionally be lowercased as a matter of creative license or for the sake of authenticity (e.g., in a fictionalized text-message exchange), capitalization is the best choice for most contexts. More information about registered trademarks can be found on the websites of the US Patent and Trademark Office and the International Trademark Association.

8.155 **Brand names or trademarks with an initial lowercase letter.** Brand names or trademarks spelled with a lowercase initial letter followed by a capital letter need not be capitalized at the beginning of a sentence or heading; the existing capital letter is sufficient to signal that these are proper nouns. Likewise, names that begin with a capital letter and include additional capitals in the middle of the word should be left unchanged. (In either scenario, such capital letters are sometimes referred to as intercaps or midcaps.) Chicago draws the line, however, at names in all lowercase; in order to signal that such a term is in fact a proper noun, an initial capital should be applied even mid-sentence (as for *Mini* in the last example below; see also 8.70, 8.156).

iTunes is both an app and a media service.
Does your iPhone have an AccuWeather app?
PowerPoint has become virtually synonymous with presentation software.
*but*
The Mac Mini is a good solution for cluttered workspaces.

In text that is set in all capitals, such distinctions are usually overridden (e.g., POWERPOINT); with a mix of capitals and small capitals, they are preserved (e.g., IPHONE).

## SOFTWARE AND DEVICES

8.156 **Names for applications, operating systems, and devices.** References to specific applications (also called programs or apps) and the operating systems and devices they run on are set in roman type without quotation marks (but see 8.192); capitalization can usually reflect the usage displayed by the software or the device itself. If in doubt, consult a help menu or a user's guide. Occasionally, an apparent preference for lowercase can be overridden (as in the first example below; see also 8.155). Generic references can be treated as ordinary text.

macOS Monterey; Mac Mini (contrary to corporate usage); Mac
Windows 11; HP desktop computer; notebook computer; PC
Microsoft Word; Apple Pages for macOS; LibreOffice Writer; Google Docs; word-processing program; word processor
iOS 16; iPhone; the Maps app for iOS 16; the Ring/Silent switch
Apple Watch; an Android watch; a smartwatch
Firefox; a browser; the Firefox app for Android
the Messenger app for Android; Apple's Messages app; a messaging app
Kindle; the Kindle app for Apple devices; Android's Kindle app
The iPhone's Clock app includes a stopwatch, a countdown timer, and an alarm.
Does your phone have a clock app?
I prefer *The New Yorker*'s iPhone app to the printed magazine.
Use your word-processing program to track changes and insert comments.

For typographic conventions for the names of particular keys, menus, commands, and the like, see 7.81–86.

## TITLES OF WORKS

8.157 **Treatment of titles in text and notes — overview.** The guidelines in this section (8.157–204) apply primarily to titles as they are mentioned or cited in text or notes. They apply to titles of books, journals, newspapers, and websites as well as to shorter works (stories, poems, articles, etc.), divisions of longer works (parts, chapters, sections), unpublished works (dissertations, lectures, etc.), plays and films, radio and television programs, musical works, and artworks. For details on citing titles in bibliographies and reference lists, see chapters 13 and 14. For the treatment of titles in languages other than English, see 11.8–12.

### *Capitalization, Punctuation, and Italics*

8.158 **Capitalization of titles of works — general principles.** Titles of works mentioned or cited in text or notes or listed in a bibliography are usually capitalized in headline style, or what this manual now prefers to call title case (see 8.160). For aesthetic purposes, titles appearing on the cover or title page of a book or at the head of an article or chapter may deviate from Chicago's rules for the capitalization of titles, but when mentioned or cited, such titles are adjusted to conform to Chicago style. For capitalization of non-English titles, see 11.8. For the use of quotation marks versus italics, see 8.164.

8.159 **Principles and examples of sentence case.** In sentence case, only the first word in a title, the first word in a subtitle, and any words that would normally be capitalized are capitalized—as in a sentence. This style or some variant of it is commonly used in library catalogs, in many news headlines, and in the reference lists of some journals, and it is the style recommended for most titles from other languages (see 11.8). Sentence case may also be used for subheads (see 2.22), where it can be helpful in works that feature longer headings or headings that include terms (such as species names) that require their own internal capitalization (but note that the specific epithet remains lowercase in title case; see 8.160, rule 7).

Science periodicals in nineteenth-century Britain: Constructing scientific communities
Crossing *Magnolia denudata* with *M. liliiflora* to create a new hybrid: A success story

Note, however, that title case, not sentence case, is usually applied to an English-language title or heading mentioned in the text regardless of how it is styled in the source itself or in the sources that mention or cite it (e.g., "The essays collected in the book *Science Periodicals in Nineteenth-Century Britain* . . ."; see also 8.164).

8.160 **Principles of title case.** The conventions of title case (or what previous editions of this manual referred to as headline style) are governed mainly by emphasis and grammar. The following rules, though occasionally arbitrary, are intended primarily to facilitate the consistent styling of titles mentioned or cited in text and notes. Note that Chicago now recommends capitalizing prepositions of five letters or more (see rule 3).

1. Capitalize the first and last words in titles and subtitles (but see rule 7) and all other major words (nouns, pronouns, verbs, adjectives, adverbs, and some conjunctions—but see rule 4).
2. Lowercase the articles *the*, *a*, and *an*.
3. Lowercase prepositions of fewer than five letters, except when they are used adverbially or adjectivally (*up* in *Look Up*, *down* in *Turn Down*, *on* in *The On Button*, *to* in *Come To*, etc.) or when they compose part of a Latin expression used adjectivally or adverbially (*De Facto*, *In Vitro*, etc.). In rare cases, a shorter preposition may be capitalized when paired with a longer preposition (*for* in *For and Against*). Note that the five-letter rule includes abbreviations (e.g., *Versus* would be capitalized, but *vs.* would not be).
4. Lowercase the common coordinating conjunctions *and*, *but*, *for*, *or*, and *nor*.

5. Lowercase *to* not only as a preposition (rule 3) but also as part of an infinitive (*to Run*, *to Hide*, etc.) and lowercase *as* in any grammatical function.
6. Lowercase the part of a proper name that would be lowercased in text, such as *de* or *von*.
7. Lowercase the second part of a species name, such as *fulvescens* in *Acipenser fulvescens*, even if it is the last word in a title or subtitle (and including the abbreviations "sp." and "spp." used in place of the second part of the name; see 8.124).

For examples, see 8.161. For hyphenated compounds in titles, see 8.162. Note that the rules of title case also generally apply to the names of organizations and companies and the like (as covered elsewhere in this chapter).

8.161 **Examples of title case.** The following examples illustrate the numbered rules in 8.160. All of them demonstrate the first rule; the numbers in parentheses refer to rules 2–7.

Mnemonics That Work Are Better Than Rules That Do Not
Singing While You Work
A Little Learning Is a Dangerous Thing (2)
Four Theories Concerning the Gospel According to Matthew (2, 3)
"The Trouble with Tribbles": Much Ado About Nothing? (3)
The Case For and Against AI (3)
Writing Under a Deadline and Without an Editor (2, 3, 4)
Taking Down Names, Spelling Them Out, and Typing Them Up (3, 4)
Tired but Happy (4)
The Editor as Anonymous Assistant (5)
From *Homo erectus* to *Homo sapiens*: A Brief History (3, 7)
Defenders of da Vinci Fail the Test: The Name Is Leonardo (2, 3, 6)
Sitting on the Floor in an Empty Room (2, 3), *but* Turn On, Tune In, and Enjoy (3, 4)
Ten Hectares per Capita, *but* Landownership and Per Capita Income (3)
Progress in In Vitro Fertilization (3)

8.162 **Hyphenated compounds in title case.** The following rules apply to hyphenated terms appearing in a title capitalized in title case. Note that Chicago now recommends capitalizing the second element in a hyphenated compound formed with a prefix (rule 2), a departure from previous editions. For rules of hyphenation, see 7.87–96.

1. Always capitalize the first element.
2. Capitalize any subsequent elements unless they are articles, prepositions of

fewer than five letters, coordinating conjunctions (*and*, *but*, *for*, *or*, *nor*), or such modifiers as *flat* or *sharp* following musical key symbols. This rule now also extends to subsequent elements in hyphenated compounds formed with prefixes (*anti-*, *pre-*, etc.).

3. Capitalize the second element in a hyphenated spelled-out number (*twenty-one* or *twenty-first*, etc.) or hyphenated simple fraction (*two-thirds* in *two-thirds majority*).

The examples that follow demonstrate the numbered rules (all the examples demonstrate the first rule; the numbers in parentheses refer to rules 2 and 3).

Under-the-Counter Transactions and Out-of-Fashion Initiatives (2)
Bed-and-Breakfast Options in Upstate New York (2)
Record-Breaking Borrowings from Medium-Sized Libraries (2)
Cross-Stitching for Beginners (2)
A History of the Chicago Lying-In Hospital (2; "In" functions as an adverb, not a preposition)
The E-flat Concerto (2)
Self-Sustaining Reactions (2)
Anti-Intellectual Pursuits (2)
Does Pre-Authorization Save Time? (2)
Why Drones Are the Future of E-Commerce (2)
A Two-Thirds Majority of Non-English-Speaking Representatives (2, 3)
Ninety-Fifth Avenue Blues (3)
Atari's Twenty-First-Century Adherents (3)

Under another, simplified practice that is not recommended by Chicago, only the first element and any subsequent element that is a proper noun or adjective are capitalized.

8.163 **Titles containing quotations.** When a direct quotation of a sentence or an independent clause is used as a title, title case may be imposed, even for longer quotations. See also 13.96.

"I Will Not Allow Books to Prove Anything": Establishing Truth in Fiction

8.164 **Italics versus quotation marks for titles.** The choice of italics or quotation marks for a title of a work cited in text or notes is determined by the type of work. Titles of books and periodicals are italicized (see 8.170); titles of articles, chapters, and other shorter works are set in roman and enclosed in quotation marks (see 8.179).

Many editors use *The Chicago Manual of Style.*
Refer to the article titled "A Comparison of MLA and APA Style."

For treatment of book series and editions, see 8.178; for poems and plays, see 8.183–86; for fairy tales and nursery rhymes, see 8.187; for pamphlets and forms, see 8.188–89; for unpublished works, see 8.190; for movies, television, radio, and podcasts, see 8.191; for video games, see 8.192; for websites and blogs, see 8.193–94; for musical works, see 8.195–99; for works of art and exhibitions, see 8.200–204. For titles from other languages, see 11.8–12.

8.165 **When italics are not an option.** When there is no option for italics (as on certain social media platforms), titles that would otherwise be italicized may be distinguished by capitalization alone. Note that any initial *The* that would be part of the italicized title remains capitalized (e.g., The Chicago Manual of Style; The New York Times; *but* the Los Angeles Times). See also 8.172.

8.166 **Subtitle capitalization.** A subtitle, whether in title case or sentence case, always begins with a capital letter. Although on a title page or in a chapter heading a subtitle is often distinguished from a title by a different typeface alone, when referred to it is separated from the title by a colon. When an em dash rather than a colon is used, the first word following the em dash is usually lowercased. See also 13.92.

Manuals of Style: Guidelines, Not Strangleholds (title case)
Tapetum character states: Analytical keys (sentence case)
*but*
Chicago—a Metropolitan Smorgasbord

8.167 **Permissible changes to titles.** When a title is referred to in text or notes or listed in a bibliography or reference list, its original spelling (including non-Latin letters such as π or γ) and hyphenation should be preserved, regardless of the style used in the surrounding text. The following changes, however, are permissible:

- Capitalization may be changed to title case (8.160) or sentence case (8.159), as applicable.
- If the title and subtitle on a title page are distinguished by typeface alone, a colon must be added when referring to the full title (unless the main title ends in a question mark or exclamation point; see 13.98).
- Any comma omitted from the end of a line on a title page for aesthetic reasons

should be restored, including a comma omitted before a date that appears on a line by itself at the end of a title or subtitle. (Serial commas should be added only if they are used in the work itself; see 6.19.)

- A dash in the original should be retained but should be changed if needed to a Chicago-style em dash with no space on either side (see 6.91); however, a semicolon or a period between title and subtitle may usually be changed to a colon. (For two subtitles in the original, see 13.92.) See also 8.166, 14.90.
- A hyphen in a number or other range may be changed to an en dash (see 6.83), as may a hyphen next to an open compound (as described in 6.86).
- Quotation marks may be adjusted as described in 12.7, item 1.
- As a matter of editorial discretion, an ampersand (&) may be changed to *and*, or, more rarely, a numeral may be spelled out (see also 13.90).

For older titles, see 13.99. For titles within titles, see 8.175, 8.179. For double titles connected by *or*, see 8.169. For permissible changes to punctuation in non-English titles, see 11.9.

8.168 **Titles in relation to surrounding text.** A title, which is considered to be a singular noun, always takes a singular verb. Moreover, any punctuation that is part of the title should not affect the punctuation of the surrounding text (with the exception of a sentence-ending period, which should be omitted after a title ending in a question mark or exclamation point; see 6.133). See also 6.30, 6.134, 8.176.

*The Waves* is not a typical novel. (singular verb in spite of plural in title)
Her role in *Play It Again, Sam* confirmed her stature. (no comma after *Sam*)
Three stories she never mentioned were "Are You a Doctor?," "The Library of Babel," and "The Diamond as Big as the Ritz." (comma after first title in spite of the question mark)

8.169 **Double titles connected by "or."** Old-fashioned double titles (or titles and subtitles) connected by *or* have traditionally been punctuated in a variety of ways. When referring to such titles, prefer the punctuation on the title page or at the head of the original source. In the absence of such punctuation (e.g., when the title is distinguished from the subtitle by typography alone), or when the source is not available to consult, prefer the simpler form shown in the first example below (see also 8.167). See also 13.93.

*The Tempest, or The Enchanted Island* (the play by William Shakespeare)
*but*
*Moby-Dick; or, The Whale* (the novel by Herman Melville)

## *Books and Periodicals*

8.170 **Treatment of book and periodical titles.** When mentioned in text, notes, or bibliography, the titles and subtitles of books and periodicals are italicized and capitalized in title case (see 8.160), though some publications may require sentence case for reference lists (see 8.159). A book title cited in full in the notes or bibliography may be shortened in text (e.g., a subtitle may be omitted). For short titles in notes, see 13.33.

8.171 **An initial "a," "an," or "the" in book titles.** An initial *a*, *an*, or *the* may be dropped from a book title in running text if it does not fit the surrounding syntax. When in doubt, or if the article seems indispensable, it should be retained.

Fielding, in his introduction to *The History of Tom Jones, a Foundling*, announces himself as a professional author.
Fielding's *History of Tom Jones* . . .
That dreadful *Old Curiosity Shop* character, Quilp . . .
*but*
In *The Old Curiosity Shop*, Dickens . . .
In L'Amour's *The Quick and the Dead* . . .

8.172 **An initial "the" in periodical titles.** When newspapers and other periodicals are mentioned in running text, an initial *The* that appears on the masthead or cover or is otherwise considered part of the official title is usually capitalized and italicized along with the title of the publication. This departure from advice in previous editions of this manual is intended to reflect the usage of the publications themselves and to make periodical titles more consistent with the titles of books and other titles set off by italics. (In source citations and index entries, an initial *The* in the title of a periodical may be omitted; see 14.69, 14.91, 15.56, 15.57.) In the examples below, an initial *The* is included on the masthead or cover of all but the *Los Angeles Times*, the *Chicago Tribune*, and the *Journal of Labor Economics* (an article never appears with *Forbes* or *Harper's Magazine*). If there is any doubt about whether the article belongs with the name of the publication, treat it as part of the surrounding text.

I prefer the paper editions of *The Washington Post* and *The New York Times*.
I read the *Los Angeles Times* during the week and the *Chicago Tribune* on Sundays.
She reads the *Journal of Labor Economics* at work and *The American Naturalist* at home.
Do you get your information from *The Wall Street Journal* or from *Forbes*?
*The New Yorker*'s cartoons have nothing to do with the surrounding text.

I read *Harper's Magazine* mainly for its puzzles.
Have you read *The Week* this week?
I saw it in *The Times.* (referring to the British publication; see text below)

As with book titles, use of the definite article may depend on the syntax of the surrounding text (see 8.171). In the third example below, note how the article (*the*) belongs to the word that follows the title (*reporter's*).

I'm a *New Yorker* fan for the cartoons alone.
Her *Wall Street Journal* subscription expired last month.
The letter objected to the *Washington Post* reporter's sources.

When the title of a periodical is shortened (as on subsequent mentions), any initial *the* is treated as part of the surrounding text.

The *Times* bought Wordle in 2022. (for *The New York Times* but not *The Times* UK)
We subscribe to the *Post.* (for *The Washington Post* or similar title with *Post*)

Because it may govern the inflection of the following word, non-English titles retain the article in the original language—but only if it is an official part of the title (see also 11.30).

We read *Le Monde* and *Die Zeit* while traveling in Europe.
*but*
Did you see the review in the *Frankfurter Allgemeine*?

In source citations, initial articles are retained in non-English titles (see 14.91, 14.92).

8.173 **"Magazine" and other descriptive terms.** A word like *magazine, journal,* or *review* should be italicized only when it forms part of the official title of a particular periodical. When such a word functions as an added descriptive term, it is treated as part of the surrounding text. See also 8.172.

I read it both in *Time* magazine and in *The Wall Street Journal.*
The archives included copies of *Ebony* and *Life* magazines from the 1950s.
*but*
His article was reprinted in *The New York Times Magazine.*

8.174 **Periodical titles in awards, buildings, and so forth.** When the title of a newspaper or periodical is part of the name of a building, organization, prize, or the like, it is not italicized.

the Los Angeles Times Book Prize
Chicago Defender Charities
Tribune Tower

8.175 **Italicized terms and titles within titles.** Any term within an italicized title that would itself be italicized in running text—such as a word used as a word, a word from another language, a genus name, or the name of a ship—should remain in italics rather than being set in roman type (or *reverse italics*). This departure from advice in previous editions is intended to make it clearer where such a title begins and ends. See also 8.117, 8.121, 8.167, 13.97.

*Y Is for Yesterday* (the novel by Sue Grafton)
*The Big E: The Story of the USS Enterprise* (the book by Edward P. Stafford)
*not*
*The Big E: The Story of the USS* Enterprise

A title of a work within another title, however, should be enclosed in quotation marks (even if it appears in italics on the title page). See also 13.96.

*Live from New York: An Uncensored History of "Saturday Night Live"*

8.176 **Title not interchangeable with subject.** The title of a work should not be used to stand for the subject of a work.

Dostoevsky wrote a book about crime and punishment. (*not* . . . about *Crime and Punishment*)
Edward Wasiolek's book on Dostoevsky's *Crime and Punishment* is titled *"Crime and Punishment" and the Critics*. (See also 8.175.)
In their book *The Craft of Translation*, Biguenet and Schulte . . . (*not* In their book on *The Craft of Translation*, Biguenet and Schulte . . .)

8.177 **Titles of multivolume works.** Titles of multivolume books are treated in the same manner as titles of single-volume works, as are named titles of individual volumes. The word *volume* may be abbreviated in parentheses and notes; it is capitalized (and never abbreviated) only if part of the title. For treatment of multivolume works in bibliographies and reference lists, see 14.18–24. See also 8.178.

*The Day of the Scorpion*, volume 2 of *The Raj Quartet*
*Art in an Age of Counterrevolution, 1815–1848* (vol. 3, *A Social History of Modern Art*)
the fourth volume of the landmark eleventh edition of *Encyclopaedia Britannica*

8.178 **Titles of series and editions.** Some books are published as part of a titled (and sometimes numbered) series or edition. Such titles are capitalized but not italicized. The words *series* and *edition* are capitalized only if part of the title. See also 14.25–28.

the Loeb Classical Library
a Modern Library edition
Late Editions: Cultural Studies for the End of the Century
the Crime and Justice series
a book in the Heritage of Sociology Series

Some books, on the other hand, belong to a series named after a title or character or other name in that series (often informally). In such cases, italicize the series title if it is based on the title of one of the books in the series, or if the books have been published together under the series title. But use roman for the series title if it is based on the name of a character or place or another such element in the series. (A similar approach may be used for movies and other works in a series; see 8.191.)

*Twilight*, the first novel in Stephanie Meyer's *Twilight* series
*Prince Caspian*, the second book in C. S. Lewis's *The Chronicles of Narnia*
*The Fellowship of the Ring*, the first novel in the *Lord of the Rings* series (see also 8.171)
*but*
*Beezus and Ramona*, the first book in the Ramona series
*The Other Wind*, the final novel in the Earthsea series
*Akata Witch*, the first novel in the Nsibidi Scripts series by Nnedi Okorafor
the Harry Potter books

Numbered or named editions of a specific publication (as in a cited source) are usually not part of a title and are set in roman and lowercase (if in doubt, consult a library catalog). See also 14.15.

*Black's Law Dictionary*, 10th ed.
Kuhn, *The Structure of Scientific Revolutions*, 50th anniversary ed.
*but*
Hayek, *The Constitution of Liberty: The Definitive Edition*

## *Articles in Periodicals and Parts of Books*

8.179 **Articles, stories, chapters, and so on.** Titles of articles and features in periodicals, chapter titles and titles of other individual sections in books, and titles of short stories and essays are set in roman type and enclosed in quotation marks.

Claire Curtis's article "Remainders of the American Century" appeared in the journal *American Political Thought*.
In chapter 3 of *The Footnote*, "How the Historian Found His Muse," Anthony Grafton explores the role of footnotes in reconstructing the past.
"Sweat," a story by Zora Neale Hurston, was first published in 1926.

Book titles and other normally italicized terms remain italicized within an article title. A term quoted in the original title is enclosed in single quotation marks (since it is already within double quotation marks). See also 13.96.

The article "Schiller's 'Ode to Joy' in Beethoven's Ninth Symphony" received unexpected attention.
Neuberger's "Sergei Eisenstein's *Ivan the Terrible* as History" calls the filmmaker's approach to history "serious and nuanced."

Titles of regular departments or columns in periodicals are set in roman with no quotation marks (see also 14.88, 14.93). An initial *the* belonging to such a title is lowercased in the middle of a sentence (cf. 8.172).

In the opening piece for the Talk of the Town, Steve Coll investigates . . .

8.180 **Collected works.** When two or more works originally published as separate books are included in a single volume, often as part of an author's collected works, they are best italicized rather than placed in quotation marks.

Baldwin's *If Beale Street Could Talk*, included in the collection *Later Novels*, . . .

8.181 **Terms like "foreword," "preface," and so on.** Such generic terms as *foreword*, *preface*, *acknowledgments*, *introduction*, *appendix*, *bibliography*, *glossary*, and *index*, whether used in cross-references or in reference to another work, are lowercased and set in roman type.

The author states in her preface that . . .
For further documentation, see the appendix.
Full details are given in the bibliography.
The book contains a glossary, a subject index, and an index of names.

8.182 **Numbered chapters, parts, and so on.** The words *chapter*, *part*, *appendix*, *table*, *figure*, and the like are lowercased and spelled out in text (though sometimes abbreviated in parenthetical references). Numbers can usually be given in Arabic numerals, regardless of how they appear in the original. (Subject to editorial discretion, an exception is sometimes made for references within a work to other parts of the same work numbered with Roman numerals; for other exceptions, see 9.28, 9.30.) If letters are used, they may be upper- or lowercase (following the original) and are sometimes put in parentheses. See also 3.9, 3.51.

This matter is discussed in chapters 4 and 5.
The Latin text appears in appendix B.
The range is presented numerically in table 4.2 and diagrammed in figure 4.1.
These connections are illustrated in table A3.
Turn to section 5(a) for further examples.

## *Poems and Plays*

8.183 **Titles of poems.** Titles of most poems are set in roman type and enclosed in quotation marks. A very long poetic work, especially one constituting a book, is italicized and not enclosed in quotation marks.

Langston Hughes's poem "I, Too" in his 1926 collection *The Weary Blues*
Dante's *Inferno*
Eliot's *The Waste Land*
*but*
Shakespeare's sonnets; Sonnet 18 (see also 8.184)

8.184 **Poems referred to by first line.** Poems referred to by first line rather than by title are capitalized in sentence case, even if the first word is lowercased in the original, but any words capitalized in the original should remain capitalized. See also 8.159, 15.144.

E. E. Cummings, in "My father moved through dooms of love," . . . ("my" is lowercased in the original)
"Shall I compare thee to a Summer's day?" (Sonnet 18; see also 8.183)

8.185 **Titles of plays.** Titles of plays, regardless of the length of the play, are italicized.

Shaw's *Arms and the Man*, in volume 2 of his *Plays: Pleasant and Unpleasant*

8.186 **Divisions of plays or poems.** Words denoting parts of long poems or acts and scenes of plays are usually lowercased and neither italicized nor enclosed in quotation marks. Numbers are Arabic, regardless of the original.

canto 2    stanza 5    act 3, scene 2

## *Fairy Tales and Nursery Rhymes*

8.187 **Titles of folktales, fables, nursery rhymes, and the like.** Folktales, fables, fairy tales, nursery rhymes, and the like are usually treated in the manner of shorter poems and set in roman type and enclosed in quotation marks. But italics should be used to refer to fairy tales published as books, plays, and the like.

"Aladdin" is arguably the most well-known tale in *A Thousand and One Nights*.
"Rumpelstiltskin" originally appeared in the Grimm brothers' *Children's and Household Tales*.
Everybody knows at least one verse of "Jack and Jill."
*Ella Enchanted* is a retelling by Gail Carson Levine of "Cinderella."
The opera *Hansel and Gretel* (*Hänsel und Gretel*) is based on the fairy tale of the same name.

## *Pamphlets, Reports, and Forms*

8.188 **Titles of pamphlets and reports.** Titles of pamphlets, reports, and similar freestanding publications are, like books, italicized when mentioned or cited in text or notes (see also 8.170, 14.117).

Paine's *Common Sense*, first published anonymously . . .
*E-Stats 2020: Measuring the Electronic Economy*, a report on e-commerce published by the US Census Bureau, . . .

8.189 **Titles of forms and standards.** Government, departmental, and other titled or numbered forms can usually be capitalized according to the usage in the form itself; wording should follow the usage in the document itself but may be shortened if necessary. Standards mentioned in the text can usually be treated similarly (but see 14.159).

Form 1040-ES, Estimated Tax for Individuals (*or* 1040-ES)
DHS TRIP Traveler Inquiry Form (*or* DHS TRIP)
United States Census 2020; the Census (*but* a census form)
the Unicode Collation Algorithm
the XML standard; XML 1.1, 2nd ed.

## *Unpublished Works*

8.190 **Titles of unpublished works.** Titles of unpublished works—theses, dissertations, manuscripts in collections, unpublished transcripts of speeches, and so on—are set in roman type, capitalized as titles, and enclosed in quotation marks. Titles of manuscript collections take no quotation marks. The title of a not-yet-published book that is under contract may be italicized, but the word *forthcoming* (or *in press* or some other equivalent term), in parentheses, must follow the title. For speeches, see 8.77.

In a master's thesis, "Charles Valentin Alkan and His Pianoforte Works," . . .
"A Canal Boat Journey, 1857," an anonymous manuscript in the Library of Congress Manuscripts Division, describes . . .
Letters and other material may be found in the Collis P. Huntington Papers at the George Arents Library of Syracuse University.
Gianfranco's *Fourth Millennium* (forthcoming) continues this line of research.

## *Movies, Television, Radio, and Podcasts*

8.191 **Titles for movies, television, radio, and podcasts.** Titles of movies (or films) and movie series and of television, radio, and podcast programs and series are italicized. A single episode in a television, radio, or podcast series is set in roman and enclosed in quotation marks. Sequels should be numbered as in the source itself; if in doubt, prefer Arabic numerals (see also 9.45). The names of networks, channels, streaming services, and the like are set in roman.

*Black Panther*, a film produced by Marvel Studios
*The Godfather, Part II* (see also 9.45)
*The Hunger Games*; *The Hunger Games: Mockingjay—Part 1*; the *Hunger Games* film series
*Dr. No*; the James Bond franchise (see also 8.178)
*Sesame Street* on PBS
*The Ten O'Clock News*, WGBH's long-running program
"The Alibi," the first episode in the podcast *Serial*, a *This American Life* spin-off
"How to Pay for College," an episode in the series *How to College*, on YouTube's CrashCourse channel
*We Fix Space Junk*, a podcast from Battle Bird Productions
*Performance Today*, hosted by Fred Child and produced by American Public Media; broadcast by Minnesota Public Radio and others and also available as a podcast

"Thirsty Bird," the first episode in the second season of the Netflix series *Orange Is the New Black*
Season 5, episode 4, of the *Masterpiece* series *Downton Abbey*, originally broadcast on ITV (UK) and PBS (US) and also available from Amazon Video
*but*
the ten o'clock news

## *Video Games*

8.192 **Titles of video games.** Though video games are technically software applications, or apps (see 8.156), they may be treated like movies, a usage that recognizes the narrative and audiovisual similarities between the two art forms. Older video games—despite being technically simpler than the majority of today's apps—are treated in the same way. (Note that this usage does not apply to other types of games, which are set in roman rather than italics and capitalized only if trademarked: e.g., Monopoly *but* poker.) See also 8.191.

*Pong*
*Ms. Pac-Man*
*Tetris*
*Angry Birds*; the *Angry Birds* app
Nintendo's *Mario Bros.*; *Mario Kart Wii*; *Mario Kart 8 Deluxe* for Nintendo Switch
*The Legend of Zelda: Breath of the Wild* for the Wii U
*Call of Duty*; *Call of Duty 2*; *Call of Duty: Black Ops Cold War*; the *Call of Duty* series
*The Sims 4*; *The Sims*, a series that debuted in 2000
*Pokémon GO*

## *Websites and Blogs*

8.193 **Titles of websites and web pages.** Titles of websites mentioned or cited in text or notes are normally set in roman, title case, without quotation marks. An initial *The* should be lowercased except at the beginning of a sentence. Titled sections, pages, and special features on a website are normally placed in quotation marks; however, generic titles such as *Help*, *Settings*, and the like can often be set without quotation marks (when in doubt, use quotation marks). Titles of the types of works discussed elsewhere in this chapter (i.e., books, journals, etc.) are usually treated the same whether they are published in print or online. An exception may be made for Wikipedia, which is usually treated as a website rather than as an encyclopedia and set in roman. On the other hand, a news site or blog would normally be treated as a periodical and set in italics (see 8.194). When in doubt, use title case without quotation marks or italics. See also 14.103–7.

Project Gutenberg; Jane Austen's *Emma*, available as an audiobook from Project Gutenberg
the Internet Movie Database; IMDb (note lowercase *b*); IMDb's page for *Live and Let Die*; "Roger Moore (I)"; the page for early Bond portrayer Roger Moore
Google; Google Maps; Google Maps Help
Facebook; Twitter *or* X; Instagram; the Facebook app (see 8.156)
Wikipedia; Wikipedia's "Let It Be" entry; Wikipedia's entry on the Beatles' album *Let It Be*
*but*
*The Chicago Manual of Style Online*; the Q&A at *CMOS Online*; "New Questions and Answers"
*Britannica*; the online version of *Encyclopaedia Britannica*
the *Oxford English Dictionary*; the *OED Online*
*The Onion* (see 8.172)

If a website either does not have a formal title or does not have a title that distinguishes it as a website, it can usually be identified according to the entity responsible for the site along with a description of the site and, in some cases, a short form of the URL. For example, https://www.apple.com/ might be referred to in running text as Apple.com.

The website for Apple Inc.; Apple.com
Microsoft's website; Microsoft.com
the website for the University of Chicago Press, Journals Division; the University of Chicago Press Journals website

8.194 **News sites and blogs.** Titles of news websites and blogs, like the titles of newspapers and other periodicals (see 8.164), are usually italicized. An initial *the* belonging to the title is usually italicized and capitalized along with the title (see also 8.172). Titles of articles and blog posts should be placed in quotation marks (untitled posts may be referred to by date). See also 14.103–7.

*Vox*; *Politico*; *Breitbart News*; *The Intercept*; *HuffPost* (news sites)
*Wasted Food*; "Food Waste Stump Speech," in *Wasted Food*, a blog by Jonathan Bloom
*HuffPost*; "The Best and Worst Hot Dogs at the Grocery Store, Ranked by Nutritionists," by Krissy Brady, in the Life section at *HuffPost*
*The Wall Street Journal*'s website; *WSJ.com*; the *WSJ* app

"Billie Eilish Pauses London Show over Fan Safety," by Mark Savage, an article published on *BBC News*
*but*
articles published online by Fox News, CNN, and the BBC

As the last example above illustrates, the name of a news channel or company is not the same thing as the title of a news site. When in doubt, put the name in roman type. For television, radio, and podcasts, see 8.191.

## *Musical Works*

8.195 **Musical works — additional resources.** The following paragraphs are intended only as general guidance for citing musical works. Writers or editors working with highly musicological material should consult D. Kern Holoman, *Writing About Music* (bibliog. 1.1). For a more general reference work, consult *The New Grove Dictionary of Music and Musicians* and the other Grove musical dictionaries, available from Oxford Music Online (bibliog. 4.1). For typographic conventions used in musicology, see 7.75–80.

8.196 **Operas, songs, and the like.** Titles of operas, oratorios, tone poems, and other long musical compositions are italicized and given standard title capitalization. Titles of songs and other shorter musical compositions are set in roman and enclosed in quotation marks, capitalized in the same way as poems (see 8.183, 8.184). The names of dances can usually be lowercased except for names derived from proper nouns (as in the last example below).

"La vendetta, oh, la vendetta" from *The Marriage of Figaro*
the "Anvil Chorus" from Verdi's *Il Trovatore*
Handel's *Messiah*
*Rhapsody in Blue*
*Finlandia*
"All You Need Is Love" (a song by the Beatles)
"So What" (a composition by Miles Davis)
"The Star-Spangled Banner"
"Oh, What a Beautiful Mornin'" from *Oklahoma!*
"Wohin?" from *Die schöne Müllerin*
the cueca; the fandango; the twist (dances); *but* the Charleston

8.197 **Instrumental works.** Many instrumental works are known by their generic names—*symphony, quartet, nocturne*, and so on—and often a number or key or both. Such names are capitalized but not italicized. A descriptive title, however, is usually italicized if referring to a full work, set in roman and in quotation marks if referring to a section of a work. The abbreviation *no.* (number; plural *nos.*) is set in roman and usually capitalized (a departure from previous editions that aligns with music-industry usage), whereas the words *sharp* and *flat* are usually lowercased (see also 8.162). Some publishers lowercase *major* and *minor* also, but Chicago prefers to capitalize these for consistency with its title-case recommendations in 8.160. (For letters indicating keys, see 7.76.)

B-flat Nocturne; Chopin's nocturnes
the Menuetto from the First Symphony; the third movement
Concerto No. 2 for Piano and Orchestra; the second movement, Allegro appassionato, from Brahms's Second Piano Concerto; two piano concertos
Bartók's Concerto for Orchestra (or *Concerto for Orchestra*)
Bach's Mass in B Minor *or* B Minor Mass (no hyphen; see also 7.76)
Hungarian Rhapsody No. 12; the Twelfth Hungarian Rhapsody
Charles Ives's Piano Sonata No. 2 (*Concord, Mass., 1840–60*); the *Concord* Sonata
Symphony No. 6 in F Major (*Pastoral*); the Sixth Symphony; the *Pastoral* Symphony; the *Pastoral*
Air with Variations ("The Harmonious Blacksmith") from Handel's Suite No. 5 in E
Elliott Carter's String Quartet No. 5 and his *Figment* for cello
Augusta Read Thomas's Triple Concerto (*Night's Midsummer Blaze*)

8.198 **Opus numbers.** The abbreviation *op.* (opus; plural *opp.* or *opera*) is set in roman and usually lowercased (as is *no.* when it follows an opus number rather than appearing within the main part of the title). An abbreviation designating a catalog of a particular composer's works is always capitalized (e.g., BWV [Bach-Werke-Verzeichnis]; D. [Deutsch] for Schubert; K. [Köchel] for Mozart; WoO [Werke ohne Opuszahl], assigned by scholars to certain unnumbered works). When *op.* or a catalog number is used restrictively (see 6.32), no comma precedes it.

Sonata in E-flat, op. 31, no. 3; Sonata op. 31
Fantasia in C Minor, K. 475; Fantasia K. 475

8.199 **Recordings.** The official title of an album (and sometimes a title under which it has come to be known) is italicized; the name of the performer or ensemble is set in roman. Individual items on the album—songs, movements, and the like—are treated as illustrated in the paragraphs above. See also 14.163.

On *The Art of the Trumpet*, the New York Trumpet Ensemble plays . . .
The single "Revolution" should not be confused with "Revolution 1," an earlier take of the song that appeared on *The Beatles* (a.k.a. *The White Album*).
Miles Davis's *Kind of Blue* is one of the most influential jazz records ever made.
His Majestie's Clerkes' *Hear My Prayer: Choral Music of the English Romantics* includes Vaughan Williams's Mass in G Minor.

## *Works of Art and Exhibitions*

8.200 **Paintings, photographs, statues, and such.** Titles of paintings, drawings, photographs, statues, and other works of art—including titles for series of such works—are italicized, whether the titles are original, added by someone other than the artist, or translated. The names of works of antiquity (whose creators are often unknown) are usually set in roman. See also 8.58.

Rothko's *Orange Yellow Orange*
Leonardo da Vinci's *Mona Lisa* and *The Last Supper*
*North Dome*, one of Ansel Adams's photographs of Kings River Canyon
Hogarth's series of drawings *The Rake's Progress*
*His Airness*, a digital portrait of Michael Jordan by Vakseen (Otha Davis III) sold as an NFT (nonfungible token)
Michelangelo's *David*
the Winged Victory
the Venus de Milo

8.201 **Maps.** Maps can often be referred to in text with generic descriptive titles. If a map is known by a formal title rather than a generic description, use italics. See also 11.11.

a fifteenth-century reconstruction of Ptolemy's world map (ca. AD 150)
the *Yu ji tu* (Map of the tracks of Yu), from 1136
the *Tabula Hungariae*, Lázár's map of Hungary
Arno Peters's projection of the world map; the Peters projection map
Google Maps, satellite view of metropolitan Los Angeles

Maps as illustrations require captions and credit lines as discussed in chapter 3. To cite a map included in a book, see 14.57. To cite a standalone map, see 14.135.

8.202 **Cartoons.** Titles of regularly appearing cartoons or comic strips are italicized.

*The Far Side* *Doonesbury* *Rudy Park* *Rhymes with Orange*

8.203 **Memes.** Titles of memes are usually capitalized in title case and set in roman without quotation marks. An exception may be made for memes known in the form of longer quotations (in which quotation marks may be added) or by reference to the title of a film or other work (in which italics may be used).

Grumpy Cat
Ermahgerd Girl
the Distracted Boyfriend meme
the Facepalm meme featuring Patrick Stewart
*but*
"I Will Find You and I Will Kill You" (*or* the *Taken* meme)

8.204 **Exhibitions and such.** Titles of world's fairs and other large-scale exhibitions and fairs are capitalized but not italicized. Smaller exhibitions (e.g., at museums) and the titles of exhibition catalogs (often one and the same) are italicized.

the Great Exhibition of the Works of All Nations; the Great Exhibition of 1851; London's Crystal Palace Exhibition; the exhibition
the World's Columbian Exposition
the Century-of-Progress Expositions (included more than one fair)
the New York World's Fair
*but*
*Jean-Michel Basquiat: King Pleasure*, an exhibition featuring the Brooklyn-born artist, opened in April.
We saw the exhibition *Ansel Adams at 100* when visiting the Museum of Modern Art.
We decided to buy the catalog *Ansel Adams at 100*, by John Szarkowski.

# 9 Numbers

## OVERVIEW

9.1 **Overview and additional resources.** This chapter summarizes some of the conventions Chicago observes in handling numbers, especially in making the choice between spelling them out and using numerals. Such a choice should be governed by various factors, including whether the number is large or small, whether it is an approximation or an exact quantity, what kind of entity it stands for, and what context it appears in. Sometimes the goal of consistency must give way to readability (e.g., at the beginning of a sentence; see 9.5). The guidelines in this chapter apply mainly to general works and to scholarly works in the humanities and social sciences, where numeric quantities are relatively infrequent. But even in scientific and other technical contexts, numerals can never totally replace spelled-out numbers. For a more detailed treatment of numbers in technical contexts, consult *The CSE Manual* (bibliog. 1.1). See also 9.14–19. For numerals versus words in fictional dialogue and other forms of direct discourse, see 12.51.

## NUMERALS VERSUS WORDS

### *General Principles*

9.2 **Chicago's general rule — zero through one hundred.** In nontechnical contexts, Chicago advises spelling out whole numbers from zero through one hundred and certain round multiples of those numbers (see 9.4).

Thirty-two children from eleven families were packed into eight vintage Beetles.
Many people think that seventy is too young to retire.
The property is held on a ninety-nine-year lease.
According to a recent appraisal, my house is 103 years old.
The three new parking lots will provide space for 540 more cars.
The population of our village now stands at 5,893.

Most of the rest of this chapter deals with exceptions and special cases. For hyphens used with spelled-out numbers, see 7.96, section 1. For some additional considerations, consult the index, under *numbers*. For numerals in quoted speech and dialogue, see 12.51. For an alternative rule, see 9.3.

9.3 **An alternative rule — zero through nine.** Many publications, including those in scientific or journalistic contexts, follow the simple rule of spelling out only single-digit numbers and using numerals for all others (but see 9.7). Most of the exceptions to the general rule (9.2) also apply to this alternative rule. Round multiples of hundreds, thousands, and hundred thousands, however, are typically expressed as numerals when the alternative rule is in force (cf. 9.4).

9.4 **Hundreds, thousands, and hundred thousands.** The whole numbers one through one hundred followed by *hundred, thousand,* or *hundred thousand* are usually spelled out (except in the sciences or with monetary amounts)—whether used exactly or as approximations. See also 9.9, 9.26.

> Most provincial theaters were designed to accommodate large audiences—from about seven hundred spectators in a small city like Lorient to as many as two thousand in Lyon and Marseille.
> A millennium is a period of one thousand years.
> The population of our city is more than two hundred thousand.
> Some forty-seven thousand persons attended the fair.
> *but*
> The official attendance at this year's fair was 47,122.

In a context with many large numbers—especially if round numbers occur alongside numerals that are not round—it may be best to opt for numerals for all such numbers. See also 9.7.

9.5 **Number beginning a sentence.** When a number begins a sentence, it is almost always spelled out, a convention intended to help readers identify a new sentence (particularly when numerals are presented using old-style figures, some of which have the appearance of lowercase letters). To avoid awkwardness, a sentence can often be recast. In the first example below, some writers prefer the form *one hundred and ten*; Chicago's preference is to omit *and* (a preference that extends to spelled-out years—e.g., *two thousand twenty-four*; but see below).

> One hundred ten candidates were accepted.
> *or*
> In all, 110 candidates were accepted.

If a number beginning a sentence is followed by another number of the same category, spell out only the first or reword.

> One hundred eighty of the 214 candidates had law degrees; the remaining 34 were doctoral candidates in fish immunology.
> *or, better,*
> Of the 214 candidates, 180 had law degrees; the remaining 34 were doctoral candidates in fish immunology.

There are a few exceptions to this rule. Years, which are almost always expressed as numerals and which can be unwieldy when spelled out, may begin a sentence if necessary (a departure from previous editions of this manual, which advised spelling them out when rewording was not possible). It is usually preferable, however, to reword. See also 9.31.

1937 was marked, among other things, by the publication of the eleventh edition of Bartlett's *Familiar Quotations*.
*or, better,*
The year 1937 . . .

A sentence may also begin with a term that includes a combination of letters and numerals (e.g., *401(k)*, *3D*, and *7-Eleven*).

3D imagery has come a long way since the stereoscopes of the nineteenth century.

9.6 **Ordinals.** The general and alternative rules apply to ordinal as well as cardinal numbers. Note that Chicago prefers, for example, *122nd* and *123rd* (with an *n* and an *r*) over *122d* and *123d*. The latter, however, are common especially in legal style (see 14.170–207). The letters in ordinal numbers should *not* appear as superscripts (e.g., 122nd, *not* 122$^{\text{nd}}$).

Gwen stole second base in the top half of the first inning.
The restaurant on the forty-fifth floor has a splendid view of the city.
She found herself in 125th position out of 360.
The 122nd and 123rd days of the strike were marked by a rash of defections.
The ten thousandth child to be born at Mercy Hospital was named Mercy.
*or, following the alternative rule,*
The restaurant on the 45th floor has a splendid view of the city.

In the expression "*n*th degree," Chicago style is to italicize the *n* (see also 7.67). And note that the ordinal ending for zero is *th* (zeroth).

9.7 **Consistency and flexibility.** Where many numbers occur within a paragraph or a series of paragraphs, maintain consistency in the immediate context. If according to a given rule you must use numerals for one of the numbers in a given category, use them for all in that category. (An exception may be made at the beginning of a sentence; see 9.5.) In the same sentence or paragraph, however, items in one category may be given as numerals and items in another spelled out. According to the general rule, in the first example below, the numerals 50, 3, and 4 would normally be spelled out (see 9.2); in the second and third examples,

30,000 and 2,000, respectively, would normally be spelled out (see 9.4; see also 9.9). According to the alternative rule, in the fourth and fifth examples, 9 and 1, respectively, would normally be spelled out (see 9.3).

*General rule*

A mixture of buildings—one of 103 stories, five of more than 50, and a dozen of only 3 or 4—has been suggested for the area.

In the second half of the nineteenth century, Chicago's population exploded, from just under 30,000 in 1850 to nearly 1.7 million by 1900.

Between 1,950 and 2,000 people attended the concert.

*Alternative rule*

Though most of the test subjects were between 13 and 18, two were 11 and one was 9.

The movie lasted 1 hour and 36 minutes, a typical length for a romantic comedy.

An exception to either rule may also be made to avoid a thickly clustered group of spelled-out numbers, regardless of category, or for a specific category of numbers in a work as a whole to make the text more readable. If, for example, a work includes many mentions of ages, centuries, or editions, these may be expressed with numerals throughout (e.g., "3 years old"; "11th and 12th centuries"; "the 18th edition"; see also 9.6, 9.34). Exceptions like these may also be appropriate in documents where space is limited. Editors should note such exceptions on a style sheet (see 2.61). For numerals in quoted speech and dialogue, see 12.51.

9.8 **When numerals are always used.** There are some contexts that almost always call for numerals rather than spelled-out numbers regardless of which rule is being followed. The examples listed here are not meant to be exhaustive. Additional details and examples can be found throughout this chapter and in chapter 10. For abbreviated units of measure, see 9.18, 10.55–76. For percentages, see 9.20. For numbered parts of a document, see 9.28–30. For decimal fractions, which are expressed with numerals regardless of context, see 9.21. For some additional contexts that usually require numerals, see 9.14.

*With abbreviated units of measure*

3 lb.

3 mph

10 km

72 dpi

4,000 rpm (see also 9.4)

*Before the word "percent"*
3 percent; a 3 percent raise (but see 9.20)

*For the parts of a document*
page 2; pages 3–9; p. 2; pp. 3–9
part 5; pt. 5
chapter 1; chap. 1
note 3; notes 1–5; n. 2; nn. 3–9 (but see 14.56)
section 3; sec. 3; § 3
paragraph 5; para. 5; ¶ 5
line 7; lines 12–18
figure 9; fig. 9
equation 4; eq. 4
column 2, row 3; col. 2; cols. 3–7
box 3
act 3; scene 4
vol. 3; vols. 3–7
issue 7; issue no. 7; no. 7
example 5
question 10
rule 6
Title IX (see also 9.30)

*With symbols*
$3 (*or* three dollars; see 9.22); $1,000 (see also 9.26)
8% (*or* 8 percent; see 9.20)
5° (*or* 5 degrees; see 9.18)

*In numbers for streets, rooms, and other places*
Highway 1
1427 E. 60th St.
room 9
suite 7A

*In dates*
June 1, 1941
May 5; the 5th of May

*For grades and other levels*
grade 3 (*but* third grade)
level 6

*In clothing sizes*
32-inch waist
size 12 dress

*In certain expressions indicating degree or severity*
type 1 or type 2 diabetes
stage IV (*or* 4) lung cancer (see also 9.67–69)
a Category 5 hurricane

*In scores and vote tallies*
a 34–3 victory over the Steelers
a Supreme Court vote of 6 to 3 (*or* 6–3)

## *Large Numbers*

9.9 **Millions, billions, and so forth.** Whole numbers used in combination with *million, billion,* and so forth are either spelled out or expressed as numerals according to the general rule (see 9.2). See also 9.4. For monetary amounts, see 9.22–27; for the use of superscripts in scientific contexts, see 9.10.

The city had grown from three million in 1960 to fourteen million in 1990.
The survey was administered to more than half of the city's 220 million inhabitants.
The population of the United States recently surpassed three hundred million.

To express fractional quantities in the millions or more, a mixture of numerals and spelled-out numbers is used. In the second example below, the number fourteen is expressed as a numeral for the sake of consistency (see 9.7).

By the end of the fourteenth century, the population of Britain had probably reached 2.3 million.
According to some scientists, the universe is between 13.5 and 14 billion years old.

Note that *billion* in some countries (including, until recently, Great Britain) means a million million (a trillion in American usage), not, as in American usage, a thousand million; in this alternate system, the prefix *bi-* indicates twelve zeros (rather than the American nine), or twice the number of zeros in one million. Likewise, *trillion* indicates eighteen zeros (rather than the American twelve), *quadrillion* twenty-four (rather than the American fifteen), and so on. Editors working with material by writers who may not be familiar with English usage for these terms may need to query how they are used. See 5.254, under *billion; trillion.*

9.10 **Powers of ten.** Large round numbers may be expressed in powers of ten, especially in scientific writing. This system is known as scientific notation. For further examples, consult *The CSE Manual* (bibliog. 1.1).

| | |
|---|---|
| $10^2 = 100$ | $10^9 = 1{,}000{,}000{,}000$ |
| $10^3 = 1{,}000$ | $10^{12} = 1{,}000{,}000{,}000{,}000$ |
| $10^6 = 1{,}000{,}000$ | $5.34 \times 10^8 = 534{,}000{,}000$ |

Inversely, very small numbers may be expressed in negative powers of ten.

| | |
|---|---|
| $10^{-2} = 0.01$ | $10^{-9} = 0.000000001$ |
| $10^{-3} = 0.001$ | $10^{-12} = 0.000000000001$ |
| $10^{-6} = 0.000001$ | $5.34 \times 10^{-8} = 0.0000000534$ |

9.11 **"Mega-," "giga-," "tera-," and so forth.** According to the International System of Units (*Système international d'unités*, abbreviated internationally as SI), very large quantities may be indicated in some contexts by the use of the prefixes *mega-* (million), *giga-* (billion), *tera-* (trillion), and so on, as part of the unit of measure. Inversely, very small numbers may be expressed by *milli-* (thousandth), *micro-* (millionth), *nano-* (billionth), and so on. These expressions are often formed with symbols (e.g., *M*, for *mega-*, as in MB, *megabytes*). In astrophysical contexts, the abbreviations *Myr* and *Gyr*, standing for megayear (one million years) and gigayear (one billion years), are sometimes used. See also 9.10. For a complete list of SI prefixes, see 10.62. See also 9.12.

3 terahertz = $3 \times 10^{12}$ hertz    7 Gyr = $7 \times 10^9$ years

9.12 **Binary systems.** Bases other than ten are common especially in computing, where numbers are usually expressed with bases that are powers of two (e.g., binary, octal, or hexadecimal). When such numbers are used, the base if other than ten should be indicated. Abbreviations *b* (binary), *o* (octal), and *h* (hexadecimal) may precede the number with no intervening space. Alternatively, the base can be expressed as a subscript. In the following example, the four-digit base-ten number is expressed without a comma, following SI usage (but see 9.58):

b11110010001 = 1937    *or*    $11110010001_2 = 1937_{10}$

Note that terms such as *megabyte*, when used as binary multiples, are approximations—a megabyte was originally equal to 1,048,576 (or $2^{10} \times 2^{10}$) bytes. Current SI usage dictates that such prefixes refer to positive powers of ten (where a megabyte is equal to 1,000,000 bytes). If binary multiples must be referred to, the first two letters of the prefix plus *bi* should be used (*kibibyte, mebibyte, gibibyte*, etc.).

9.13 **Use of "dex."** The term *dex* is sometimes used in scientific notation as shorthand for *decimal exponent*.

Errors of 3 dex (i.e., $10^3$) can lead to dangerous misconceptions.

## *Physical Quantities*

9.14 **Physical quantities in general contexts.** In nontechnical material, physical quantities such as distances, lengths, areas, and so on are usually treated according to the general rule (see 9.2). See also 9.16.

Within fifteen minutes the temperature dropped twenty degrees.
The train approached at seventy-five miles an hour.
Some students live more than fifteen kilometers from the school.
Three-by-five-inch index cards are now seldom used in index preparation.
She is five feet nine (*or, more colloquially,* five foot nine *or* five nine).

It is occasionally acceptable to depart from the general rule for certain types of quantities that are commonly (or more conveniently) expressed as numerals. It may also be appropriate in some cases to express an exact quantity as a numeral. Such departures, subject to editorial discretion, must be consistently applied for like quantities across a work. See also 9.7, 9.8. For the absence of the hyphen in the second example below, see 7.96, section 2, under *noun + numeral or enumerator*.

a 40-watt bulb
a size 14 dress
a 32-inch inseam
a fuel efficiency of 80 miles per gallon (or 3 liters per 100 kilometers)
a right angle is defined as an angle of 90 degrees
freezing point is exactly 32 degrees Fahrenheit, or 0 degrees Celsius

9.15 **Simple fractions.** Simple fractions are spelled out. For the sake of readability and to lend an appearance of consistency, they are hyphenated in noun, adjective, and adverb forms. An exception is made in the rare event that individual parts of a fractional quantity are emphasized (as in the last example below). See also 7.96, section 1, under *fractions, simple*. For decimal fractions, see 9.21.

She has read three-fourths of the book.
Four-fifths of the students are boycotting the class.
I do not want all of your material; two-thirds is quite enough.
A two-thirds majority is required.
*but*
We divided the cake into four quarters; I took three quarters, and my brother one.

9.16 **Whole numbers plus fractions.** Quantities consisting of whole numbers and simple fractions may be spelled out if short but are often better expressed in numerals (especially if a symbol for the fraction is available, as in the examples here). For decimal fractions, see 9.21. For fractions in mathematical text, see 9.17. See also 9.19, 10.74.

We walked for three and one-quarter (*or* three and a quarter) miles.
I need 6⅞ yards of the silk fabric.
Lester is exactly 3 feet, 5¼ inches tall.
Letters are usually printed on 8½″ × 11″ paper.

9.17 **Fractions in mathematical contexts.** Fractions in mathematical contexts are usually set in running text with a slash to separate the numerator and denominator; for example, 1/2, 2/3, 1/10, 97/100, $\pi/2$, 11/5, $a/b$. Some common numerical fractions may instead be set as case fractions, which are text-sized fractions with a horizontal bar rather than a slash: $\frac{1}{2}$, $\frac{2}{3}$, $\frac{1}{10}$. (These are not to be confused with the Unicode symbols for common [or vulgar] fractions in 9.16.) Fractions should be enclosed in parentheses if they are followed by a mathematical symbol or expression, as in $(a/b)x$. For simple algebraic fractions in text, the slash should be used rather than the horizontal fraction bar; for example, $(ax + b)/(cx + d)$, not $\frac{ax+b}{cx+d}$. Slashes should also be used for fractions in a numerator or denominator (whether in the text or in a displayed expression), as well as in an exponent that expresses a radical: $(b - d)^{1/2}$ (for the square root of $[b - d]$). Note that a slash connects only the two groups of symbols immediately adjacent to it; thus, $a + b/c$ is not the same as $(a + b)/c$. In displayed mathematical expressions, all fractions should be set with a horizontal bar unless they are part of a numerator or denominator or in a subscript or superscript. For spaces relative to plus signs and the like, see 6.130. For treatment of variables, see 7.73.

9.18 **Numbers with abbreviations and symbols.** If an abbreviation or a symbol is used for the unit of measure, the quantity is always expressed by a numeral. Such usage is standard in mathematical, statistical, technical, and scientific text, where physical quantities and units of time are expressed in numerals, whether whole numbers or fractions, and almost always followed by an abbreviated form of the unit (see also 10.55–76). Note that hyphens are never used between the numeral and the abbreviation or symbol, even when they are in adjectival form (see 7.96, section 1, under *number + abbreviation*). In the last example below (which can express feet and inches or minutes and seconds), note the use of symbols for prime and double prime, which are *not* equivalent to the apostrophe and quotation mark. A space is normally used between the numeral and the unit of measure, except in a few cases—for example, with degree, percent, and prime symbols (but see 10.64). See also 7.44.

| | |
|---|---|
| 50 km (kilometers); a 50 km race | 240 V (volts) |
| 21 ha (hectares) | 10°C, 10.5°C |
| 4.5 L (liters) | 3′6″ |
| 85 g (grams) | |

A unit of measurement used *without* a numeral should always be spelled out, even in scientific contexts.

We took the measurements in kilojoules (*not* kJ).

9.19 **Units for repeated quantities.** For expressions including two or more quantities, the abbreviation or symbol is repeated if it is closed up to the number but not if it is separated. See also 10.55. For the use of spaces with SI units and abbreviations or symbols, see 10.64.

35%–50%   3°C–7°C   6¾″ × 9″   2 × 5 cm

## *Percentages and Decimal Fractions*

9.20 **Percentages.** Except at the beginning of a sentence, percentages are usually expressed in numerals. In nontechnical contexts, the word *percent* is generally used; in scientific and statistical copy, the symbol % is more common. Note that *less* rather than *fewer* may be used with percentages, as in the first example below (a departure from previous editions of this manual; see also 5.254, under *less; fewer*). See also 7.96, section 1, under *number + percent*.

Less than 3 percent of the employees used public transportation.
With 90–95 percent of the work complete, we can relax.
A 75 percent likelihood of winning is worth the effort.
Her five-year certificate of deposit carries an interest rate of 5.9 percent.
Only 20% of the ants were observed to react to the stimulus.

The treatment resulted in a 20%–25% increase in reports of night blindness. (See also 9.19.)

*but*

Thirty-nine percent identified the "Big Bang" as the origin of the universe; 48 percent said they believed in human evolution. (See also 9.7.)

Note that *percent*, an adverb, is not interchangeable with the noun *percentage* (1 percent is a very small percentage). Note also that no space appears between the numeral and the symbol % (see also 10.64).

9.21 **Decimal fractions and use of the zero.** Large or complex fractions are expressed as numeric decimal fractions (cf. 9.15). When a quantity equals less than 1.00, a zero normally appears before the decimal point as an aid to readability, particularly in scientific contexts and especially if quantities greater than 1.00 appear in the same context. Note that a unit of measure with a quantity of less than one is generally treated as if it were plural (see 10.59, 10.73). See also 9.57, 9.60.

a mean of 0.73

the ratio 0.85

In Cyprus, there were 0.96 females for every male in the general population; in the sixty-five-and-over age group, the number was 1.30.

In contexts where decimal quantities must be 1.00 or less, as in probabilities, batting averages, and the like, or between −1.00 and 1.00, as in correlation coefficients, a zero is typically omitted before the decimal point. For zeros with decimal points in tables, see 3.73.

$p < .05$

$R = .10$

Ty Cobb's career batting average was .366 or .367, depending on the source.

By a similar token, the zero is routinely omitted from firearm calibers expressed as fractions of an inch (see also 10.64).

They found and confiscated a .38 police special and a .22-caliber single-shot rifle.

## *Money*

9.22 **Words versus monetary symbols and numerals.** Isolated references to amounts of money are spelled out for whole numbers of one hundred or less, in accordance with the general principle presented in 9.2. See also 9.3.

seventy-five cents = 75¢ fifteen dollars = $15 seventy-five pounds = £75

Whole amounts expressed numerically should include zeros and a decimal point only when they appear in the same context with fractional amounts (see also 9.21). Note the singular verb in the second example below.

Children can ride for seventy-five cents.
The eighty-three dollars was quickly spent.
The instructor charged €125 per lesson.
Prices ranged from $0.95 up to $10.00.

For larger amounts, see 9.26.

9.23 **Non-US currencies using the dollar symbol.** In contexts where the symbol $ may refer to non-US currencies, these currencies should be clearly identified.

three hundred Canadian dollars = C$300 *or* Can$300
$749 in New Zealand dollars = NZ$749
If you subtract A$15.69 from US$25.00, . . .
ninety-eight Mexican pesos = Mex$98

In more formal usage, the International Organization for Standardization's three-letter currency codes (e.g., USD for United States dollars, CAD for Canadian dollars, NZD for New Zealand dollars, AUD for Australian dollars, and MXN for Mexican pesos) may be more appropriate. See also 9.25. For a complete list, consult ISO 4217, available from ISO .org. See also *The CSE Manual* or the *GPO Style Manual* from the US Government Publishing Office (bibliog. 1.1). Where the context makes clear what currency is meant, the dollar sign alone is enough.

9.24 **British currency.** The basic unit of British currency is the pound, or pound sterling, for which the symbol is £. (The three-letter currency code defined by the International Organization for Standardization is GBP; see also 9.25.) One-hundredth of a pound is a penny (plural *pence*), abbreviated as *p* (no period).

fifteen pounds = £15 fifty pence = 50p £4.75, £5.00, and £5.25

Until the decimalization of British currency in 1971, the pound was divided into shillings (s.) and pence (d.).

Ten pounds, fifteen shillings, and sixpence = £10 15s. 6d.
twopence halfpenny = 2½d.

9.25 **Other currencies.** Most other currencies are handled the same way as US currency, with a decimal point between the main unit and subunits (e.g., EUR 10.75). When letters rather than symbols are used, a space separates the letter(s) from the numeral.

forty euros (*or, in European Union documents,* 40 euro) = €40 (*or* EUR 40)
95 (euro) cents (*or, in European Union documents,* 95 cent)
725 yen = ¥725 (*or* JPY 725)
100 yuan renminbi (*or* 100 yuan) = ¥100 *or* RMB 100 (*or* CNY 100)
65.50 Swiss francs = Fr. 65.50 (*or* CHF 65.50)
12.5 bitcoins = ₿12.5 *or* BTC 12.5 (*or* XBT 12.5)

Before adoption of the euro, monetary symbols included *F* (French franc), *DM* (deutsche mark), and *Lit* (Italian lira), among others. The International Organization for Standardization defines three-letter codes (including EUR) for most countries; these may be more appropriate in formal or technical contexts. See also 9.23.

9.26 **Large monetary amounts.** Sums of money of more than one hundred dollars are normally expressed by numerals or, for numbers of a million or more, by a mixture of numerals and spelled-out numbers, even for whole numbers (cf. 9.4, 9.9).

An offer of $1,000 once seemed high; we eventually agreed to pay more than fifteen times that amount.
Most of the homes that went into foreclosure were valued at more than $95,000.
She signed a ten-year, $250 million contract.
The military requested an additional $7.3 billion.
The marquess sold his ancestral home for £25 million.

In certain financial contexts, thousands are sometimes represented by *K*.

Three-bedroom condominiums are priced at $350K.

9.27 **Currency with dates.** In contexts where the value of a currency in any particular year is relevant to the discussion, the date may be inserted in parentheses, without intervening space, after the currency symbol. When letters alone are used, spaces intervene before and after the parentheses (see also 9.23, 9.25).

| | |
|---|---|
| US$(1992)2.47 | *but* |
| £(2002)15,050 | USD (1992) 2.47 |

## *Numbered Divisions in Books and Other Documents*

9.28 **Page numbers, chapter numbers, and so forth.** Numbers referring to pages, chapters, parts, volumes, and other divisions of a book, as well as numbers referring to illustrations or tables, are set as numerals. Pages of the front matter are usually in lowercase Roman numerals; those for the rest of the book are in Arabic numerals (see 1.5–9). For the use of en dashes with number ranges, see 6.83. For style in source citations, see chapters 13 and 14. See also 8.182.

The preface will be found on pages vii–xiv and the introduction on pages 1–35.
See part 3, especially chapters 9 and 10, for further discussion; see also volume 2, table 15 and figures 7–9.
Upon completion of step 3, on page 37, the reader is asked to consult appendix B, table 7.

Biblical references are given in numerals only; chapter and verse are separated by a colon with no space following it. For abbreviations, see 10.50–54.

| | |
|---|---|
| Acts 27:1 | 2 Corinthians 11:29–30 |
| Exodus 20:3–17 | Gen. 47:12 |
| Psalm 121; Psalms 146–50 | |

9.29 **Volume, issue, and page numbers for periodicals.** References to volumes, issues, and pages of a journal are usually made, in that order, with Arabic numerals; the words *volume* and *page* are usually omitted. See also 14.63–102.

The article appeared in *Modern Philology* 119, no. 4 (2022): 555–79.

9.30 **Numbered divisions in legal instruments.** Arabic or Roman numerals are commonly used to distinguish divisions within legal instruments and other documents. When in doubt about a reference to a legal document, prefer Arabic numerals or, if possible, consult the document itself for guidance. A mixture of Arabic and Roman numerals sometimes distinguishes smaller from larger divisions. For legal style in source citations, see 14.170–207.

They have filed for Chapter 11 protection from creditors.
Proposition 20 will be voted on next week.
A search of Title IX (of the Education Amendments of 1972) turns up no mention of athletics.
Do you have a 401(k)?
In paragraph 14(vi) of the bylaws, . . .
According to the Constitution of the United States, article 2, section 4 (*or* Article II, Section 4), . . .
*but*
the Fifth Amendment (*or* Amendment V)

## *Dates*

9.31 **The year used alone.** Years are generally expressed as numerals. A year at the beginning of a sentence need not be spelled out (a departure from previous editions of this manual), though rewording is usually the better option (see 9.5). For eras, see 9.36.

We all know what happened in 1776.
Records for solar eclipses go back at least as far as 3000 BCE.
2020 was a good year for clairvoyants.
*or, better,*
The year 2020 was a good one for clairvoyants.

9.32 **The year abbreviated.** In informal contexts, the first two digits of a particular year are often replaced by an apostrophe (not an opening single quotation mark). See also 6.125.

the spirit of ’76 (*not* ‘76)    the class of ’06

9.33 **Month and day.** When specific dates are expressed, cardinal numbers are used, although these may be pronounced as ordinals (see 9.6). For the month-day-year date form versus the day-month-year form, see 9.37; see also 6.41.

October 4, 2022, was a sad day for country music fans.
The manuscript is due no later than April 11.

*Watchmaker's Digest* (11 November 2024) praised the new model's precision.
*not*
October 4th, 2022, . . .

When a day is mentioned either without the month or (in the month-day-year form) ahead of the month, the number is presented as an ordinal and need not be spelled out (a departure from previous editions of this manual). In the last example below, "June 5" is usually preferred in formal prose.

On November 5, McManus declared victory. By the 25th, most of his supporters had deserted him.
The hearing was scheduled for the 5th of June (*or* June 5).

9.34 **Centuries.** Particular centuries referred to as such are spelled out as ordinals according to the general rule and lowercased (see also 9.6); when an entire century is expressed as a numeral (as in the fourth example below), it is followed by an *s* without an apostrophe (see 7.15). Either the spelled-out or the numeral form may be used, though consistency should be maintained across similar contexts (i.e., the choice should not be applied randomly). For the use of the singular versus the plural in the second and third examples, see 7.8.

the twenty-first century
the eighth and ninth centuries
from the ninth to the eleventh century
*but*
the 1800s and 1900s (the nineteenth and twentieth centuries; see also 9.35)

Note that expressions such as "turn of the twenty-first century" are potentially ambiguous; prefer "turn of the century," and only where the context makes the period absolutely clear.

9.35 **Decades.** Decades are either expressed in numerals or spelled out (as long as the century is clear) and lowercased. Chicago calls for no apostrophe to appear between the year and the *s* (see 7.15). For the apostrophe at the beginning of the two-digit form, see 6.125, 9.32.

the 1940s and 1950s (*or* the 1940s and '50s); the '40s
*or*
the forties and fifties

Note that the first decade of any century cannot be treated in the same way as other decades. Though it commonly appears in journalism and may be clear from the immediate context, "the 2000s" could easily be taken to refer not to a decade but to the whole of the twenty-first century (likewise for the 1900s, the 1800s, etc.). Some writers refer to the first decade as "the aughts," a term best suited to casual prose. As for the second decade, "the teens" may be used in casual prose, but in formal contexts either "the second decade" or numerals (e.g., "2010s") should be preferred. Once context has been established, first and second decades may be expressed in two-digit form.

the first decade of the twenty-first century (*or* the years 2000–2009); the '00s
the second decade of the twenty-first century *or* the 2010s (*or* the years 2010–19); the '10s

Note that some consider the first decade of, for example, the twenty-first century to consist of the years 2001–10; the second, 2011–20; and so on. Chicago defers to the preference of its authors in this matter. See also 8.72, 9.66.

9.36 **Eras.** Era designations, at least in the Western world, are usually expressed in one of two ways: either CE ("of the Common Era") and BCE ("before the Common Era"), or AD (*anno Domini*, "in the year of the Lord") and BC ("before Christ"). Other forms include AH (*anno Hegirae*, "in the year of [Muhammad's] Hegira," or *anno Hebraico*, "in the Hebrew year"); AUC (*ab urbe condita*, "from the founding of the city [Rome]"); and—for archaeological purposes—BP ("before the present"). Note that the Latin abbreviations AD and AH precede the year number, whereas the others follow it. (All abbreviations follow a spelled-out century, as in "the third century AD.") Choice of the era designation depends on tradition, academic discipline, or personal preference. These abbreviations often appear in small capitals, sometimes with periods following each letter. For consistency with the guidelines in chapter 10, Chicago recommends full capitals and no periods; see also 10.43.

Herod Antipas (21 BCE–39 CE) was tetrarch of Galilee from 4 BCE until his death.
Britain was invaded successfully in 55 BC and AD 1066.
The First Dynasty appears to have lasted from 4400 BP to 4250 BP in radiocarbon years.
Mubarak published his survey at Cairo in 1886 (AH 1306).
The campsite seems to have been in use by about 13,500 BP.
Rome, from its founding in the eighth century BCE, . . .

Note that the second half of a pair of inclusive dates used with BCE or BC, where the higher number comes first, should be given in full to avoid confusion (e.g., "350–345 BCE"). See also 9.66.

9.37 **All-numeral dates and other brief forms.** For practical reasons, all-numeral styles of writing dates (e.g., 5/10/99 or 5.10.99) should not be used in formal writing (except with certain dates that may be known that way: e.g., 9/11, for September 11, 2001). Whereas in American usage the first numeral refers to the month and the second to the day, in much of the rest of the world it is the other way around. When quoting letters or other material dated, say, 5/10/03, a writer must first ascertain and then make it clear to readers whether May 10 or October 5 is meant (not to mention 1903 or 2003). In text, therefore, the full date should always be spelled out (see 9.33). In source citations and tables, if numerous dates occur, months may be abbreviated, and the day-month-year form, requiring no punctuation, may be neater (e.g., 5 Oct 2003). See also 10.44. For ISO style, see 9.38.

9.38 **ISO style for dates.** The International Organization for Standardization (ISO) recommends an all-numeral style consisting of year-month-day (i.e., from largest component to smallest), hyphenated. The year is given in full, and the month or day, if one digit only, is preceded by a zero. Thus July 14, 2025, would appear as 2025-07-14. Among other advantages, this style allows dates to be sorted correctly in an electronic spreadsheet and other applications. See also 9.42.

## *Time of Day*

9.39 **Numerals versus words for time of day.** Times of day in even, half, and quarter hours are usually spelled out in text. With *o'clock*, the number is always spelled out. In the third example below, the *a* before *quarter* is optional.

Her day begins at five o'clock in the morning.
The meeting continued until half past three.
He left the office at a quarter of four (*or* a quarter to four).
We will resume at ten thirty.
Cinderella almost forgot that she should leave the ball before midnight. (See also 9.40.)

Numerals are used when exact times are emphasized. Numerals are also normally used when "a.m." or "p.m." is specified, though words may also be acceptable if used consistently (e.g., in fictional dialogue; see 12.51). Note that Chicago prefers lowercase a.m. (*ante meridiem*) and p.m. (*post meridiem*), though small capitals (with or without periods) and all capitals (usually without periods) are also widely used and will be preferred by some publishers. (Note that the abbreviations *a.m.* and *p.m.* should not be used with *morning*, *afternoon*, *evening*, *night*, or *o'clock*.)

The first train leaves at 5:22 a.m. and the last at 11:00 p.m.
She caught the 6:20 p.m. flight.
Please attend a meeting in Grand Rapids, Michigan, on December 5 at 10:30 a.m. (EST).
We stayed up talking until 2 a.m. (*or* two a.m.).

For more on time zones, see 10.47.

9.40 **Noon and midnight.** Except in the twenty-four-hour system (see 9.41), numbers should never be used to express noon or midnight (except, informally, in an expression like *twelve o'clock at night*). Although noon can be expressed as 12:00 m. (m. = *meridies*), very few use that form. And though many people would consider 12:00 p.m. and 12:00 a.m. to refer to noon and midnight, respectively—an assumption reinforced by electronic calendars—both of those forms are illogical and potentially ambiguous (12:00 p.m. would mean both exactly midday and after midday, and though "a.m." means *before* midday, midnight is not only twelve hours before the next midday but twelve hours after the last). In the second example below, note the double date for clarity.

The meeting began at 9:45 a.m. and was adjourned by noon.
Rodriguez was born at midnight, August 21–22.

9.41 **The twenty-four-hour system.** In the twenty-four-hour system of expressing time (used in military and scientific contexts and considered regular usage in many countries outside the United States, English-speaking Canada, and several other regions that still use the twelve-hour system), four digits always appear, often with no punctuation between hours and minutes. In settings where *hours* is not used, or where the time may be confused with a year, a colon may be used (as in the twelve-hour system). See also 9.42.

12:00 = noon
00:00 *or* 24:00 = midnight (24:00 generally refers to the end of a given day)
00:01 = 12:01 a.m.

14:38 = 2:38 p.m.
At 1500 hours (*or* 1500h) we started off on our mission.
General quarters sounded at 0415.

9.42 **ISO style for time of day.** The International Organization for Standardization (ISO) recommends the twenty-four-hour system (see 9.41), with or without colons, with the addition of seconds following minutes; fractions of a second follow a period. To avoid ambiguity, colons should be used between hours and minutes and between minutes and seconds in running text and similar contexts. This format may be preceded by an ISO-style date (see 9.38). (Note that when the time of day is spelled out, a comma between minutes and seconds denotes *and*; cf. 6.41.)

09:27:08.6 = 27 minutes, 8.6 seconds after 9:00 a.m.
2025-07-14 16:09:41.3 = July 14, 2025, at 9 minutes, 41.3 seconds after 4:00 p.m.

## *Numbers with Proper Names and Titles*

9.43 **Numerals for monarchs, popes, and so forth.** Sovereigns, emperors, popes, and Orthodox patriarchs with the same name are differentiated by numerals, traditionally Roman.

Elizabeth I; Elizabeth II
Innocent II; Innocent III

In continental European practice, the numeral is sometimes followed by a period (e.g., Wilhelm II.) or a superscript (e.g., François I$^{er}$) indicating that the number is an ordinal. In an English context, the Roman numeral alone should appear. See also 11.30.

9.44 **Numerals with personal names.** Some personal names are followed by a Roman numeral or an Arabic ordinal numeral. No punctuation precedes the numeral unless the name is inverted (as in an index entry). For *Jr.*, see 6.46.

Adlai E. Stevenson III
Michael F. Johnson 2nd
*but*
Stevenson, Adlai E., III

9.45 **Numbers for sequels.** Numerals are often used to designate the sequel to a novel or a movie or to differentiate two chapter titles dealing with the same subject matter. When quoting such titles, follow the usage—Roman or Arabic (or spelled out)—reflected in the source itself. (For the use of *sic*, see 12.72.)

*The Godfather*; *The Godfather, Part II*; *The Godfather, Part III*
*Jaws*; *Jaws 2*; *Jaws 3-D*
*Star Wars*; *Star Wars: Episode IV—A New Hope*; *Episode I—The Phantom Menace* (but see 8.166)
*Dumb and Dumber To* [*sic*]
chapter 9, "Alligator Studies in the Everglades—I"
chapter 10, "Alligator Studies in the Everglades—II"

9.46 **Vehicle and vessel numbers.** Boats and the like differentiated by a number usually take a Roman numeral, spacecraft an Arabic numeral. See also 8.117–19.

*Bluebird III* (boat)    *Voyager 2* (spacecraft)

9.47 **Numbers for successive governments.** Ordinal numbers designating successive dynasties, governments, and other governing bodies are spelled out if one hundred or less (but see 9.3). See also 8.52, 8.63, 8.72.

| | |
|---|---|
| Eighteenth Dynasty | Second International |
| Fifth Republic | Ninety-Seventh United States Congress |
| Second Continental Congress | 117th Congress |

9.48 **Numbered political and judicial divisions.** Ordinal numbers designating political or judicial divisions are spelled out if one hundred or less (but see 9.3). See also 8.52.

Fifth Ward    Twelfth Congressional District    Tenth Circuit    101st Precinct

9.49 **Numbered military units.** Ordinal numbers designating military units can often be spelled out if one hundred or less according to Chicago's general rule (but see 9.3).

| | |
|---|---|
| Fifth Army | First Corps Support Command |
| Fourth Infantry Division | 101st Airborne Division |

Note, however, that the various branches of militaries in the United States and elsewhere have routinely used their own numbering conventions that depend on the military branch and the era (e.g., 3rd Battalion, 5th Marine Division; Seventh Fleet; I Corps). For the appropriate numerical designations, consult official historical and contemporary sources for the military in question. See also 8.113.

9.50 **Numbered places of worship.** Ordinal numbers that are part of the names of places of worship are spelled out if one hundred or less (but see 9.3).

Fourth Presbyterian Church
Twenty-First Church of Christ, Scientist

9.51 **Unions and lodges.** Numbers designating local branches of labor unions and fraternal lodges are usually expressed in Arabic numerals after the name. Commas can usually be omitted.

Chicago Typographical Union No. 16
American Legion Post 21
United Auto Workers Local 890

## *Addresses and Thoroughfares*

9.52 **Numbered highways.** State, federal, and interstate highways are designated by Arabic numerals. Names for state routes vary from state to state. See also 8.57.

US Route 41 (*or* US 41)
Interstate 90 (*or* I-90)
Illinois Route 50 (*or* Illinois 50; IL 50); Route 50
M6 motorway (England)

9.53 **Numbered streets.** Names of numbered streets, avenues, and so forth are usually spelled out if one hundred or less (but see 9.3). For the use of *N*, *E*, *SW*, and the like, see 10.39. See also 8.57.

First Avenue    Ninety-Fifth Street    122nd Street

9.54 **Building and apartment numbers.** Building numbers, in Arabic numerals, precede the street name. Arabic numbers are also generally used for suites, rooms, and the like. For preferred forms of mailing addresses, consult the applicable postal service; for readability and to conform to the style of the surrounding text, however, usage may differ slightly from what might be appropriate for a mailing label or the like. See also 6.42, 10.39.

They lived in Oak Park, at 1155 South Euclid Avenue, for almost ten years.
She now lives in unit 114A, 150 Ninth Avenue, with an unrivaled view of the city.
Our office is at 1427 East Sixtieth Street, Chicago, Illinois.
Please mail a copy of the German-language edition to 1427 E. 60th St., Chicago, IL 60637.
The office is located on the third floor, room 317.

## PLURALS AND PUNCTUATION OF NUMBERS

9.55 **Plural numbers.** Spelled-out numbers form their plurals as other nouns do (see 7.5).

The contestants were in their twenties and thirties.
The family was at sixes and sevens.

Numerals form their plurals by adding *s*. No apostrophe is needed (see also 7.15).

Among the scores were two 240s and three 238s.
Jazz forms that were developed in the 1920s became popular in the 1930s.

9.56 **Comma between digits.** In a style followed in most general contexts in the United States and most other English-speaking parts of the world, for numerals of one thousand or more, commas are used between groups of three digits, counting from the right. Commas are *not* used for digits to the right of the decimal marker.

1,512 32,987 4,000,500 *but* 0.32987

Nor are commas used in page numbers, line numbers (e.g., in poetry and plays), addresses, or years (though years of five digits or more do include the comma). See also 9.36.

Punctuation conventions can be found on page 1535 of the tenth edition.
Our business office is at 11030 South Langley Avenue.
Human artifacts dating from between 35,000 BP and 5000 BP have been found there.

In scientific writing, commas are often omitted from four-digit numbers. See also 9.58.

9.57 **The decimal marker.** According to the predominant usage in the United States and elsewhere, where commas are used between groups of three digits for numerals of one thousand or more (see 9.56), a period is used as the decimal marker (and called a decimal point).

33,333.33

In many other countries, including France (and French-speaking Canada), Germany, Italy, and Russia, the decimal marker is represented by a comma. Where this is the case, a thin, fixed space, not a comma, separates groups of three digits. (In electronic publications, a narrow nonbreaking space may be used; see 6.129.)

33 333,33

This practice reflects SI usage, which allows either the comma or the decimal point as a decimal marker (see 9.58). English-speaking Canadians increasingly follow SI usage, using spaces rather than commas to separate groups of digits (while retaining the decimal point). In US publications, US style should be followed, except in direct quotations and except where SI style is required. See also 10.64.

9.58 **Space between digits (SI number style).** In the International System of Units (SI units), thin, fixed spaces rather than commas are normally used to mark off groups of three digits, both to the left and to the right of the decimal marker. (In electronic publications, a narrow nonbreaking space may be used; see 6.129.) No space is used for groups of only four digits either to the left or to the right of the decimal marker (except in table columns that also include numbers having five or more digits, where it is needed for alignment). To mark the decimal, either a decimal point or a comma may be used, according to what is customary in a given context or region (the examples that follow show the decimal point). See also 9.56, 9.57.

3 426 869
0.000 007
2501.4865 (*or* 2 501.486 5)

For more on SI units, see Ambler Thompson and Barry N. Taylor, *Guide for the Use of the International System of Units (SI)*, and *The International System of Units (SI)*, a brochure published in English and French by the Bureau International des Poids et Mesures (see bibliog. 2.4).

9.59 **Telephone numbers.** In the United States and Canada, telephone numbers consist of the prefix 1 (also called the trunk prefix), an area code (also called the trunk code), and a seven-digit number consisting of a three-digit exchange prefix followed by a four-digit line number. When written, the seven-digit number is conventionally separated by a hyphen; to signal that it may be optional for local calls, the area code is often placed in parentheses. The prefix 1, the same for all numbers (and not always necessary to place a call), can usually be omitted. (Its appearance with toll-free numbers beginning with 800 and the like is customary but not mandatory.) An extension follows the number, separated by a comma. In the examples that follow, consecutive digits are represented by lowercase *x*'s to avoid suggesting real numbers.

(xxx) xxx-xxxx *or* (1-xxx) xxx-xxxx
(xxx) xxx-xxxx, ext. xxxx

An alternative style, which recognizes the increasing need to use the area code even for local calls, drops the parentheses. Either style is acceptable, as long as it is used consistently. (On the other hand, the use of periods or other punctuation as separators in place of hyphens is generally not recommended.)

xxx-xxx-xxxx *or* 1-xxx-xxx-xxxx

For international numbers, use spaces rather than hyphens as separators. A plus symbol, which stands in for the international prefix (e.g., 011 for international calls from the United States or Canada), is placed immediately before the country code (e.g., 52 for Mexico, 66 for Thailand, or 44 for the United Kingdom) with no intervening space. Because their meaning may not be clear, parentheses should not be used for international numbers (e.g., to enclose a national access code that is not needed for international calls).

+52 55 xxxx xxxx (for a number in Mexico City, Mexico)
+66 2 xxx xxxx (for a number in Bangkok, Thailand)
+44 20 xxxx xxxx (for a number in London, UK)
*not*
+44 (0) 20 xxxx xxxx

If the international prefix must be expressed, it precedes the country code and is separated from it by a space (e.g., for a call initiated from the United States or Canada, 011 44 20 . . .). A US or Canadian number written for an international audience follows a similar pattern (the country code for both is 1).

+1 607 xxx xxxx (for a number in New York State)

Spaces or hyphens as separators are the norm within most countries; however, the use of parentheses and number groupings varies widely, not only across countries but also within countries, and for landline versus mobile numbers. For more guidance, consult the latest standard from the International Telecommunication Union (bibliog. 5) or, for more specific advice, a local or international directory.

**9.60** **Ratios.** Ratios composed of whole numbers may generally be expressed using *to* and spelled out in ordinary text according to one of the rules stated at 9.2 and 9.3. In contexts where numerals are preferred, a colon may be used as a shorthand for *to*, with no space on either side.

a three-to-one ratio
a 13-to-2 ratio (see 9.3; see also 9.7)
*or*
a 13:2 ratio

In some contexts, ratios may be expressed as decimal fractions, in the manner of percentages (see 9.21).

**9.61** **Numbered lists and outline style.** For the use of numerals (Arabic and Roman) and letters to distinguish items in lists, see 6.138–43.

## INCLUSIVE NUMBERS

**9.62** **The en dash for inclusive numbers.** An en dash used between two numbers implies *up to and including*, or *through*.

Please refer to pages 75–110.
Here are the figures for 2000–2009.
Campers were divided into age groups 5–7, 8–10, 11–13, and 14–16.

The en dash should not be used if *from* or *between* is used before the first of a pair of numbers; instead, *from* should be followed by *to* or *through* (or *until*), and *between* should be followed by *and*.

from 75 to 110 (*not* from 75–110)
from 1898 to 1903
from January 1, 1898, through December 31, 1903
between about 150 and 200

Inclusive spelled-out numbers should be joined by *to,* not by an en dash.

participants aged forty-five to forty-nine years
sixty-to-seventy-year-olds

For more on the use of the en dash, see 6.82–90. See also 7.96, section 1, under *age terms*.

9.63 **Abbreviating, or condensing, inclusive numbers.** Inclusive numbers are abbreviated according to the principles illustrated below (the examples show page numbers, which do not require commas). This system, used by Chicago in essentially this form since the first edition of this manual, is efficient and unambiguous. See also 9.62, 9.64, 14.47.

| *First number* | *Second number* | *Examples* |
|---|---|---|
| Less than 100 | Use all digits | 3–10<br>71–72<br>96–117 |
| 100 or multiples of 100 | Use all digits | 100–104<br>1100–1113 |
| 101 through 109,<br>201 through 209, etc. | Use changed part only | 101–8<br>808–33<br>1103–4 |
| 110 through 199,<br>210 through 299, etc. | Use two digits unless more are needed to include all changed parts | 321–28<br>498–532<br>1087–89<br>1496–500<br>11564–615<br>12991–3001 |

To avoid ambiguity, inclusive Roman numerals are always given in full.

xxv–xxviii    cvi–cix

9.64 **Alternative systems for inclusive numbers.** A foolproof system is to give the full form of numbers everywhere (e.g., 234–235, 25039–25041). Another practice, more economical, is to include in the second number only the changed part of the first (e.g., 234–5, 25000–1). Chicago, however, prefers the system presented in 9.63.

9.65 **Inclusive numbers with commas.** When inclusive numbers with commas are abbreviated, and only numbers in the hundreds place and below change, the rules described in 9.63 should apply. If a change extends to the thousands place or beyond, it is best to repeat all digits.

6,000–6,018
12,473–79
1,247,689–710
1,247,689–1,248,125

9.66 **Inclusive years.** Inclusive years may be abbreviated following the pattern illustrated in 9.63. When the century changes, however, or when the sequence is BCE, BC, or BP (diminishing numbers), all digits must be presented. See also 9.36.

1897–1901
the war of 1914–18
fiscal year 2024–25 (*or* 2024/25; see 6.114); FY 2024–25
the winter of 2000–2001
in 1504–5
327–321 BCE (seven years, inclusively)
327–21 BCE (307 years, inclusively)
115 BC–AD 10
15,000–14,000 BP

In book titles it is customary but not obligatory to repeat all digits; when a title is mentioned or cited, the form of the original should be respected (see also 8.167).

## ROMAN NUMERALS

9.67 **Roman numerals — general principles.** Table 9.1 shows the formation of Roman numerals with their Arabic equivalents. (Note that Chicago now capitalizes *Roman* and *Arabic* in this context to align with common usage. See also 8.62.) The general principle is that a smaller letter before a larger one subtracts from its value, and a smaller letter after a larger one adds to it; a bar over a letter multiplies its value by one thousand. Roman numerals may also be written in lowercase letters (i, ii, iii, iv,

TABLE 9.1. Roman and Arabic numerals

| Arabic | Roman | Arabic | Roman | Arabic | Roman |
|---|---|---|---|---|---|
| 1 | I | 17 | XVII | 200 | CC |
| 2 | II | 18 | XVIII | 300 | CCC |
| 3 | III | 19 | XIX | 400 | CD |
| 4 | IV | 20 | XX | 500 | D |
| 5 | V | 21 | XXI | 600 | DC |
| 6 | VI | 22 | XXII | 700 | DCC |
| 7 | VII | 23 | XXIII | 800 | DCCC |
| 8 | VIII | 24 | XXIV | 900 | CM |
| 9 | IX | 30 | XXX | 1,000 | M |
| 10 | X | 40 | XL | 2,000 | MM |
| 11 | XI | 50 | L | 3,000 | MMM |
| 12 | XII | 60 | LX | 4,000 | $\mathrm{M}\overline{\mathrm{V}}$ |
| 13 | XIII | 70 | LXX | 5,000 | $\overline{\mathrm{V}}$ |
| 14 | XIV | 80 | LXXX | 10,000 | $\overline{\mathrm{X}}$ |
| 15 | XV | 90 | XC | 100,000 | $\overline{\mathrm{C}}$ |
| 16 | XVI | 100 | C | 1,000,000 | $\overline{\mathrm{M}}$ |

etc.). In older sources, a final *i* was often made like a *j* (vij, viij), and sometimes a *v* appeared as a *u* (uj); citations to Roman numeral page numbers in older works should follow the original usage.

9.68 **The advent of subtrahends (back counters).** The use of subtrahends (back counters) was introduced during the Renaissance. Note that IIII, not IV, still appears on some clock faces. The Romans would have expressed the year 1999, for example, as MDCCCCLXXXXVIIII. A more modern form, approved by the US government and accepted (if reluctantly) by classical scholars, is MCMXCIX (*not* MIM, considered a barbarism).

9.69 **Chicago's preference for Arabic rather than Roman numerals.** Chicago uses Arabic numerals in many situations where Roman numerals were formerly common, as in references to volume numbers of books or journals or chapters of books (see 9.29). Most of the exceptions are treated elsewhere, as follows: For the use of Roman numerals in the front matter of books, see 1.4, 1.7, 9.28; in legal instruments, 9.30; with the names of monarchs, prelates, and such, 9.43; with personal names, 9.44; in titles of sequels, 9.45; with names of certain vessels, 9.46; and in outline style, 6.143.

# 10 Abbreviations

## OVERVIEW

10.1 **Abbreviations — additional resources.** This chapter provides guidance for using abbreviations and symbols in general and scholarly writing. It also offers some guidance in technical work, especially for the generalist editor confronted with unfamiliar scientific and mathematical terms. For abbreviations not listed here, Chicago recommends *Merriam-Webster* (see 7.1) and the multivolume *Acronyms, Initialisms & Abbreviations Dictionary* (bibliog. 4.7). Authors and editors of technical material will need to refer to more specialized manuals, starting with *The CSE Manual* (bibliog. 1.1).

10.2 **Acronyms, initialisms, contractions.** The word *acronym* refers to terms based on the initial letters of their various elements and read as single words (AIDS, laser, NASA, scuba); *initialism* refers to terms read as a series of letters (IRS, NBA, XML); and *contraction* refers to abbreviations that include the first and last letters of the full word (Mr., amt.). (For the type of contractions normally formed with apostrophes, see 7.30.) These definitions are not perfect. For example, sometimes a letter in an initialism is derived not, as the term might imply, from an initial letter but rather from an initial sound (as the *X* in XML, for *extensible markup language*) or from the repetition of a letter (e.g., the 3 in W3C, for World Wide Web Consortium). Furthermore, an acronym and an initialism are occasionally combined (JPEG), and the line between initialism and acronym is not always clear (FAQ, which can be pronounced either as a word or as a series of letters). In this chapter the umbrella term *abbreviation* will be used for all three, as well as for shortened (i.e., abbreviated) forms (ibid., vol., prof., etc.), except where greater specificity is required. (Occasionally, a *symbol* abbreviates a term, as in © for *copyright*. Note, however, that abbreviations for units are often referred to as symbols in SI usage; see 10.57–65.)

10.3 **When to use abbreviations.** Outside science and technology, abbreviations and symbols are most appropriate in tabular matter, notes, bibliographies, and parenthetical references. A number of expressions are almost always abbreviated, even in regular prose, and may be used without first spelling them out. Many of these will be listed as main entries with pronunciation (often labeled as nouns rather than as abbreviations) in the latest edition of *Merriam-Webster* (e.g., ATM, DIY, DNA, GPS, HMO, HTML, IQ, JPEG, laser, Ms., NASA). Others, though in more or less common use (CGI, FDA, HVAC, MLA), should generally be spelled out at first occurrence—at least in formal text—as a courtesy to those readers who might not easily recognize them. The use of less familiar abbreviations should be limited to terms that occur frequently enough to warrant abbreviation—roughly five times or more within an article or chapter—and the terms must be spelled out on their first occurrence. (Note that some abbreviations will benefit from being spelled out anew in each chapter or other major division where they occur, subject to editorial discretion.) The abbreviation usually follows immediately, in parentheses, but it may be introduced in other ways (see examples below). Such an abbreviation should not be offered only once, never to be used again, except as an alternative form that may be better known to some readers.

Among recent recommendations of the Federal Aviation Administration (FAA) are . . .

According to the weak law of large numbers (WLLN) . . .

The US Food and Drug Administration was established in 1906. Since its inception, the FDA has . . .

The benefits of ERISA (Employee Retirement Income Security Act) are familiar to many.

The debate over genetically modified organisms, or GMOs, is by no means limited to the United States.

Writers and editors should monitor the number of different abbreviations used in a document; readers trying to keep track of a large number of abbreviations, especially unfamiliar ones, will benefit from a list of abbreviations (see 1.49, 2.27). In a work with few abbreviations and no list, when an abbreviation reappears after a long interval in which it is not used, it may be helpful to repeat the spelled-out name as a reminder. For rules concerning the plural form of various abbreviations, see 7.15. For abbreviations preceded by *a*, *an*, or *the*, see 7.33, 10.10. For abbreviations in charts or tables, see 3.46, 3.63, 3.82.

10.4 **Periods with abbreviations.** In using periods with abbreviations, Chicago recommends the following general guidelines in nontechnical settings. For the use of space between elements, see 10.5.

1. Use periods with abbreviations that end in a lowercase letter: p. (page), vol., e.g., i.e., etc., a.k.a., a.m., p.m., Ms., Dr., et al. (*et* is not an abbreviation; *al.* is). An exception may be made for the few academic degrees that end in a lowercase letter (e.g., DLitt, DMin); see 10.23 and rule 3.
2. Use periods for initials standing for given names: E. B. White; do not use periods for an entire name replaced by initials: JFK.

3. Use no periods with abbreviations that include two or more capital letters, even if the abbreviation also includes lowercase letters: VP, CEO, MA, MD, PhD, UK, US, NY, IL (but see rule 4).
4. In publications using traditional state abbreviations, use periods to abbreviate *United States* and its states and territories: U.S., N.Y., Ill. Note, however, that Chicago recommends using the two-letter postal codes (and therefore *US*) wherever abbreviations are used; see 10.32. For Canadian provinces and territories, see 10.33. See also 14.175.

Note that the British and the French (among others) omit periods from contractions (Dr, assn, Mme). Note also that a slash is occasionally used instead of periods (as in *c/o* or *n/a*) but more often denotes *per* (see 6.116). Units of measure in nontechnical settings are usually spelled out. In scientific usage, periods are generally omitted for abbreviated units of measure and other technical terms (see 10.55–76).

10.5 **Abbreviations and spaces.** No space is left between the letters of initialisms and acronyms, whether lowercase or in capitals. Space is usually left between abbreviated words, unless an abbreviated word is used in combination with a single-letter abbreviation. For personal names, see 10.14.

| | | |
|---|---|---|
| RN | Gov. Gen. | *but* |
| C-SPAN | Mng. Ed. | S.Dak. (but see 10.32) |
| YMCA | Dist. Atty. | S.Sgt. |

10.6 **Capitals versus lowercase for acronyms and initialisms.** Acronyms and initialisms tend to appear in all capital letters, even when they are not derived from proper nouns (ASAP, NATO, HIV, VP, LCD, LOL). But especially in British usage, it is common to spell acronyms (which are pronounced as words) with an initial capital, whether or not they are derived from proper nouns (Nafta, Unicef, Sars, Covid-19). Chicago generally prefers the all-capital form (NAFTA, UNICEF, SARS, COVID-19), unless the term is listed otherwise in *Merriam-Webster*—as is the case for certain acronyms that have become lowercase through frequent use (laser, scuba). In the sciences, it is common to encounter abbreviations with a mix of lowercase and capital letters or in all lowercase (mRNA, IgG, bp, SARS-CoV-2); where such forms are considered standard, they should be followed. And in fiction and other creative genres, some authors may prefer lowercase (or sometimes an initial capital) for acronyms and initialisms that are frequently used that way in social media and similar contexts, regardless of how they may be listed in dictionaries and other sources (e.g., lol, covid *or* Covid). See also 8.145, 8.146, 10.78.

10.7 **Capitals versus lowercase for spelled-out acronyms and initialisms.** The words in a spelled-out version of an acronym or initialism are capitalized only if they would normally be capitalized (as in the name of an organization or a trademark or other proper noun); otherwise, they should be lowercased, even when they appear alongside the abbreviated form.

North American Free Trade Agreement (NAFTA)
KFC (Kentucky Fried Chicken)
severe acute respiratory syndrome (SARS)
OCD (obsessive-compulsive disorder)
TGIF (thank God it's Friday; see also 8.92)

10.8 **Italic versus roman type for abbreviations.** Chicago italicizes abbreviations only if they stand for a term that would be italicized if spelled out—the title of a book or periodical, for example. Common Latin abbreviations are set in roman (see also 7.57).

*OED* (*Oxford English Dictionary*)
*JAMA* (*Journal of the American Medical Association*)
ibid. etc. e.g. i.e.

10.9 **Small versus full-size capitals for acronyms and initialisms.** Some publishers specify small capitals rather than full-size capitals for acronyms and initialisms (e.g., NASA rather than NASA). Though such usage may be considered desirable for a work that includes many acronyms and initialisms, Chicago does not generally recommend it. If small capitals must be used, the decision of what to mark should be made by the editor, who should apply small capitals on the final manuscript (e.g., via the small-caps font style in a word-processing program). In general, small capitals should be limited to acronyms or initialisms mentioned in running text. Avoid applying small capitals to such items as two-letter postal codes in notes or bibliographies or to Roman numerals (e.g., following a personal name). It should be noted that small capitals are not treated in the same way across all software applications and markup systems; small capitals should therefore be checked after conversion for publication to make sure they have not reverted to lowercase or full capitals (see also 2.86–88). See also 10.43, 10.46. For the use of small capitals for emphasis, see 7.54.

10.10 **"A," "an," or "the" preceding an abbreviation.** When an abbreviation follows an indefinite article, the choice of *a* or *an* is determined by the way the abbreviation would be read aloud. Acronyms are read as words and are rarely preceded by *a, an,* or *the* ("member nations of NATO"), except when used adjectivally ("a NATO initiative"; "the NATO meeting"). See 10.2; see also 7.33.

an HMO
a UFO
a NATO member
a LOOM parade
an AA meeting
a AA battery (pronounced *double A*)
an NAACP convention
an NBA coach
an HIV test
an MS symptom (a symptom of multiple sclerosis)
*but*
a MS by . . . (would be read as *a manuscript by . . .*)

Initialisms, which are read as a series of letters, are often preceded by a definite article ("member nations of the EU"). Whether to include the article may depend on established usage. For example, one would refer to the NBA and the NAACP, on the one hand, but to W3C, PBS, and NATO, on the other—though all these organizations include the definite article in spelled-out form. If no established usage can be determined, use the definite article if it would be used with the spelled-out form. Some terms, such as DIY (do it yourself), do not ordinarily require a definite article in spelled-out form and therefore do not require one as an initialism.

10.11 **Abbreviations beginning a sentence.** Unlike numerals, which ordinarily should not begin a sentence (see 9.5), an abbreviation can begin a sentence without being spelled out. (Mathematical symbols, however, should not usually begin a sentence; see 10.71.)

NASA was created in response to the launch of Sputnik 1.
Rep. Robin Kelly was elected to her first term in 2013.

10.12 **Abbreviations containing ampersands.** No space is left on either side of an ampersand used within an initialism. See also 10.29.

R&D Texas A&M

## PEOPLE AND ORGANIZATIONS

### *Personal Names, Titles, and Degrees*

**10.13** **Abbreviations for personal names.** Normally, abbreviations should not be used for given names. A signature, however, should be transcribed as the person wrote it.

Benj. Franklin    Geo. D. Fuller    Ch. Virolleaud

**10.14** **Initials in personal names.** Initials standing for given names are followed by a period and a space. A period is normally used even if the middle initial does not stand for a name (as in Harry S. Truman). Stage names and the like may be styled differently; when in doubt, follow the usage of the bearer (as far as it can be determined).

Roger W. Shugg
P. D. James
M. F. K. Fisher
*but*
LL Cool J (a stage name)

If an entire name is abbreviated, spaces and periods can usually be omitted.

FDR (Franklin Delano Roosevelt)
MJ (Michael Jordan)
JLo (Jennifer Lopez)
*but*
*J.Lo* (the title of Lopez's 2001 album)

**10.15** **Abbreviating titles before names.** Many civil or military titles preceding a full name may be abbreviated. When preceding a surname alone, however, they should be spelled out. See also 8.20.

Rep. Lauren Underwood; Representative Underwood (*not* Rep. Underwood)
Sen. Kirsten E. Gillibrand; Senator Gillibrand
Vice Adm. Sara A. Joyner; Vice Admiral Joyner

**10.16** **Abbreviations for civil titles.** The following abbreviations, among others, may precede a full name where space is tight:

| | | | |
|---|---|---|---|
| Ald. | Atty. Gen. | Insp. Gen. | Prof. |
| Assoc. Prof. | Fr. (father) | Judge Adv. Gen. | Sr. (sister) |
| Asst. Prof. | Gov. | Pres. | Supt. |

10.17 **Abbreviations for military titles.** The US military omits periods in the official abbreviated forms of its ranks. The abbreviations for a given title may vary across branches. The army, for example, uses *SSG* for *staff sergeant*; the air force and marines prefer *SSgt*. (In the examples below, such variants are not presented.) In general contexts, however, including military history, traditional abbreviations—which tend not to vary across the armed forces—are preferred. The following very selective list merely illustrates the difference between military usage and traditional forms. Where no traditional abbreviation is appropriate before a name, use the full form.

| | | | |
|---|---|---|---|
| ADM | Adm. | 2LT | 2nd Lt. |
| A1C | Airman First Class | LG | Lt. Gen. |
| BG | Brig. Gen. | LTC | Lt. Col. |
| CDR | Cmdr. | MAJ | Maj. |
| COL | Col. | MG | Maj. Gen. |
| CPT | Capt. | MSG | M.Sgt. (master sergeant) |
| CWO | Chief Warrant Officer | PO | Petty Officer |
| GEN | Gen. | SGT | Sgt. |
| LT | Lt. | SSG | S.Sgt. (staff sergeant) |
| 1LT | 1st Lt. | WO | Warrant Officer |

For the latest official forms of rank insignia, consult the website of the US Department of Defense. In addition, there are many reference books containing more detailed lists of abbreviations and terms, some of which are published regularly. See, for example, Tim Zurick, *Army Dictionary and Desk Reference* (bibliog. 5). For Canadian military ranks and abbreviations, start with the website of the Department of National Defence and the Canadian Armed Forces. For the United Kingdom, consult the websites of the various forces. See also 8.113.

10.18 **Abbreviations for social titles.** Social titles are always abbreviated, whether preceding the full name or the surname only. The spelled-out forms *Mister* or *Doctor* might be used without a name—as in direct address (see also 8.21).

| | | |
|---|---|---|
| Ms. | Mr. | *but* |
| Mrs. | Mx. | Thank you, Doctor. |
| Messrs. | Dr. Jekyll | |

Social titles are routinely omitted in most prose, though a handful of periodicals still use them. When an academic degree or professional designation follows a name, such titles are always omitted.

Jennifer James, MD (*not* Dr. Jennifer James, MD)

Similarly, the now somewhat archaic abbreviation *Esq.* (Esquire) is used only after a full name and never when *Mr.*, *Dr.*, or the like precedes the name.

10.19 **Abbreviations for French social titles.** Note the presence or absence of periods after the following abbreviations for French social titles (which can be used with either a full name or a surname only). *Mme* and *Mlle* are considered contractions (see 10.2) and therefore do not take a period. This usage should be observed when such forms appear untranslated in English-language settings.

M.    MM.    Mme    Mlle

When *Monsieur*, *Messieurs*, *Madame*, or *Mademoiselle* is used without a name, in direct address, it is spelled out (and, in French usage, generally lowercased).

10.20 **Abbreviations for "Reverend" and "Honorable."** The abbreviations *Rev.* and *Hon.* are traditionally used before a full name when *the* does not precede the title. With *the*, such titles should be spelled out.

Rev. Sam Portaro; the Reverend Sam Portaro
Hon. Henry M. Brown; the Honorable Henry M. Brown

With a last name only, such titles are normally omitted. The construction "Reverend So-and-So," however, is common, especially in informal prose or speech.

Rev. Jane Schaefer; Schaefer (*or* Reverend Schaefer)
the Honorable Patricia Birkholz; Birkholz

10.21 **Abbreviations for "Junior," "Senior," and the like.** The abbreviations *Jr.* and *Sr.*, as well as Roman or Arabic numerals such as *III* or *3rd* after a person's name, are part of the name and so are retained in connection with any titles or honorifics. Note that these abbreviations are used only with the full name, never with the surname only. See also 6.46, 9.44.

Jordan Balfence Jr. spoke first. After Mr. Balfence relinquished the podium, . . .
Zayd Zephyr III, MBA, spoke last. In closing, Mr. Zephyr reiterated . . .

In some contexts—for example, a biography that includes frequent mentions of a father and son who share the same name—it may be appropriate to use *Jr.* or *Sr.* or the like with a first name alone.

Henry Jr., in his later years (and despite the publication of *The Golden Bowl* and other masterpieces), was never again to enjoy the kind of wealth that Henry Sr. had once taught him to take for granted.

10.22 **Abbreviations for the names of saints.** The word *Saint* is often abbreviated (*St.*, pl. *SS.*) before the name of a Christian saint; it should normally be spelled out in formal prose but need not be if space is at a premium. The choice of one or the other should be implemented consistently.

Saint (*or* St.) Teresa
Saints (*or* SS.) Francis of Paola and Francis of Sales

When *Saint* or *St.* forms part of a personal name, the bearer's usage is followed. See also 10.35.

Augustus Saint-Gaudens    Muriel St. Clare Byrne

10.23 **Abbreviations for academic degrees.** Chicago recommends omitting periods in abbreviations of academic degrees (BA, DDS, etc.) unless they are required for reasons of tradition or consistency with, for example, a journal's established style. In the following list of some of the more common degrees, periods are shown only where uncertainty might arise as to their placement. Spelled-out terms, often capitalized in institutional settings (and on business cards and other promotional items), should be lowercased in normal prose. See also 8.30.

| | |
|---|---|
| AB | artium baccalaureus (bachelor of arts) |
| AM | artium magister (master of arts) |
| BA | bachelor of arts |
| BD | bachelor of divinity |
| BFA | bachelor of fine arts |
| BM | bachelor of music |
| BPharm | bachelor of pharmacy |
| BS | bachelor of science |
| DB | divinitatis baccalaureus (bachelor of divinity) |

| | |
|---|---|
| DD | divinitatis doctor (doctor of divinity) |
| DDS | doctor of dental surgery |
| DLitt *or* DLit | doctor litterarum (doctor of letters; doctor of literature) |
| DMD | dentariae medicinae doctor (doctor of dental medicine) |
| DMin | doctor of ministry |
| DO | doctor of osteopathy *or* osteopathic physician |
| DVM | doctor of veterinary medicine |
| EdM | educationis magister (master of education) |
| JD | juris doctor (doctor of law) |
| LHD | litterarum humaniorum doctor (doctor of humanities) |
| LittD | litterarum doctor (doctor of letters) |
| LLB (LL.B.) | legum baccalaureus (bachelor of laws) |
| LLD (LL.D.) | legum doctor (doctor of laws) |
| LLM (LL.M.) | legum magister (master of laws) |
| MA | master of arts |
| MAT | master of arts in teaching |
| MBA | master of business administration |
| MD | medicinae doctor (doctor of medicine) |
| MDiv | master of divinity |
| MFA | master of fine arts |
| MS | master of science |
| MSN | master of science in nursing |
| MSW | master of social welfare *or* master of social work |
| PharmD | doctor of pharmacy |
| PhB | philosophiae baccalaureus (bachelor of philosophy) |
| PhD | philosophiae doctor (doctor of philosophy) |
| PsyD | doctor of psychology |
| SB | scientiae baccalaureus (bachelor of science) |
| SM | scientiae magister (master of science) |
| STB | sacrae theologiae baccalaureus (bachelor of sacred theology) |

These designations are set off by commas when they follow a personal name (see also 6.17).

Ariel Z. Lee, JD, attended the University of Chicago Law School.

10.24 **Abbreviations for professional, religious, and other designations.** Abbreviations for many other designations, professional and otherwise, follow the pattern of academic degrees (see 10.23), for which Chicago recommends dispensing with periods. Spelled-out terms, often capitalized in institutional settings, are lowercase unless they designate the proper name of an organization.

| | |
|---|---|
| CNM | certified nurse midwife |
| FAIA | fellow of the American Institute of Architects |
| FRS | fellow of the Royal Society |
| JP | justice of the peace |
| LAc | licensed acupuncturist |
| LPN | licensed practical nurse |
| MP | member of Parliament |
| OFM | Order of Friars Minor |
| OP | Ordo Praedicatorum (Order of Preachers) |
| RN | registered nurse |
| SJ | Society of Jesus |

These designations, like academic degrees, are set off by commas when they follow a personal name.

Jean Smith, LPN, will be working on the second floor.

## *Abbreviations Related to Identity*

10.25 **Abbreviations related to race and ethnicity.** Acronyms and initialisms related to race and ethnicity are usually capitalized. Their spelled-out forms are lowercased except for any terms that would otherwise be capitalized. Because such terms are frequently contested and subject to change, their use is generally best left to the author, though editors can help by querying any inconsistencies or other potential problems. In the case of an abbreviation that is likely to be unfamiliar to readers, consider spelling it out first. See also 8.39, 10.3.

AAPI (Asian American and Pacific Islander); APIDA (Asian Pacific Islander Desi American)
BIPOC (*usually* Black, Indigenous, and people of color)
POC (people [*or* person] of color)

10.26 **Abbreviations related to gender identity and sexual orientation.** Acronyms and initialisms related to gender identity and sexual orientation are usually capitalized. Their spelled-out forms are lowercased except for any terms that would otherwise be capitalized. The choice of such abbreviations and how to style them is ultimately up to the author, though editors should query any inconsistencies or other potential problems. See also 8.42.

LGBT; LGBTQ; LGBTQIA+ (lesbian, gay, bisexual, transgender, queer/questioning, intersex, and asexual/aromantic/agender)
AFAB (assigned female at birth); AMAB (assigned male at birth)
*but*
ace (asexual); aro (aromantic)

10.27 **Abbreviations related to health and disability status.** Acronyms and initialisms related to health and disability status are usually capitalized. Spelled-out forms are lowercased except for any terms that would otherwise be capitalized. See also 5.255–67.

ADD (attention deficit disorder); ADHD (attention deficit hyperactivity disorder)
ID (intellectual disabilities); IDD (intellectual and developmental disabilities)
OCD (obsessive-compulsive disorder)
PTSD (post-traumatic stress disorder)
*but*
AD (Alzheimer's disease; see also 8.145)

## *Companies and Other Organizations*

10.28 **Commonly used generic abbreviations for firms and companies.** All of the abbreviations in the following list may be found in *Merriam-Webster* and other standard dictionaries. Use periods, or not, according to the recommendations in 10.4. See also 10.77.

Assoc.
Bros.
Co.
Corp.
Inc.
LLC (limited liability company)
LLP (limited liability partnership)
LP (limited partnership)
Ltd.
Mfg.
PLC (public limited company)
RR (railroad)
Rwy. *or* Ry. (railway)

In certain languages other than English, periods are omitted from abbreviations if they are contractions (see 10.2).

Cía (Sp. *compañía*)     Cie (Fr. *compagnie*)

10.29 **Abbreviations and ampersands in company names.** Abbreviations and ampersands are appropriate in notes, bibliographies, tabular matter, and the like. See also 14.33, 14.34.

Ginn & Co.  JPMorgan Chase & Co.  Moss Bros.  RAND Corp.

In running text, company names are best given in their full forms. It should be noted, however, that some full forms include ampersands and abbreviations. If in doubt, especially with reference to contemporary firms, look up the company name at a corporate website or other authoritative source. Such elements as *Inc.*, *& Co.*, and *LLC* may be omitted unless relevant to the context.

Johnson & Johnson was founded in 1886.
JPMorgan Chase operates in more than sixty countries.
AT&T Corporation was once known as the American Telephone and Telegraph Company.

Abbreviations for companies and other organizations that use initialisms as described in 10.4, rule 3, generally appear without periods; the occasional exception may be made in the case of a clear and established preference (as in the band name R.E.M.). See also 10.12.

10.30 **Abbreviations for media companies.** Abbreviations for media companies often take the form of call letters used for broadcasting. These are always capitalized and do not take periods.

ABC  CBS  HBO  KFTV  MTV  NBC  TBS  WFMT  WTTW

10.31 **Abbreviations for associations and the like.** Both in running text (preferably after being spelled out on first occurrence) and in tabular matter, notes, and so forth, the names of many agencies and organizations, governmental and otherwise, are commonly abbreviated. Whether acronyms or initialisms (see 10.2), such abbreviations appear in full capitals and without periods. For *a*, *an*, or *the* with abbreviations, see 10.10.

| | | |
|---|---|---|
| AAUP | EU (European Union) | OPEC |
| AFL-CIO | HMO (*pl.* HMOs) | WHO |
| EPA | OECD | WTO (*formerly* GATT) |

## GEOGRAPHIC TERMS

10.32 **Abbreviations for US states and territories.** In running text, the names of states, territories, and possessions of the United States should always be spelled out when standing alone and preferably (except for DC) when following the name of a city: for example, "Lake Bluff, Illinois, was incorporated in 1895." In bibliographies, tabular matter, lists, and mailing addresses, they are usually abbreviated. In all such contexts, Chicago prefers the two-letter postal codes to the conventional abbreviations. Note that if traditional abbreviations must be used, some terms may not be subject to abbreviation. See also 10.4.

| | | | |
|---|---|---|---|
| AK | Alaska *or* Alas. | MP | Northern Mariana Islands |
| AL | Ala. | MS | Miss. |
| AR | Ark. | MT | Mont. |
| AS | American Samoa | NC | N.C. |
| AZ | Ariz. | ND | N.Dak. |
| CA | Calif. | NE | Neb. *or* Nebr. |
| CO | Colo. | NH | N.H. |
| CT | Conn. | NJ | N.J. |
| DC | D.C. | NM | N.Mex. |
| DE | Del. | NV | Nev. |
| FL | Fla. | NY | N.Y. |
| FM | Federated States of Micronesia | OH | Ohio |
| | | OK | Okla. |
| GA | Ga. | OR | Ore. *or* Oreg. |
| GU | Guam | PA | Pa. |
| HI | Hawaii | PR | P.R. *or* Puerto Rico |
| IA | Iowa | PW | Palau |
| ID | Idaho | RI | R.I. |
| IL | Ill. | SC | S.C. |
| IN | Ind. | SD | S.Dak. |
| KS | Kans. | TN | Tenn. |
| KY | Ky. | TX | Tex. |
| LA | La. | UT | Utah |
| MA | Mass. | VA | Va. |
| MD | Md. | VI | V.I. *or* Virgin Islands |
| ME | Maine | VT | Vt. |
| MH | Marshall Islands | WA | Wash. |
| MI | Mich. | WI | Wis. *or* Wisc. |
| MN | Minn. | WV | W.Va. |
| MO | Mo. | WY | Wyo. |

10.33 **Abbreviations for Canadian provinces and territories.** Canadian provinces and territories are normally spelled out in text (e.g., "Kingston, Ontario, is worth a visit") but may be abbreviated in bibliographies and the like—using the two-letter postal abbreviations, which have the advantage of applying to both the English and French forms.

AB Alberta
BC British Columbia *or* Colombie-Britannique
MB Manitoba
NB New Brunswick *or* Nouveau-Brunswick
NL Newfoundland and Labrador *or* Terre-Neuve-et-Labrador
NS Nova Scotia *or* Nouvelle-Écosse
NT Northwest Territories *or* Territoires du Nord-Ouest
NU Nunavut
ON Ontario
PE Prince Edward Island *or* Île-du-Prince-Édouard
QC Quebec *or* Québec
SK Saskatchewan
YT Yukon

Note that the province of Yukon (formerly Yukon Territory) is often referred to as "the Yukon" (with an initial *the*); whether to include the article is usually best left to the author, though editors should query any inconsistencies. An initial *the* is always included in references to the Northwest Territories. See also 8.46.

10.34 **Comma with city plus state abbreviation.** When following the name of a city, the names of states, provinces, and territories are enclosed in commas, whether they are spelled out (as in running text) or abbreviated (as in tabular matter or lists). In an exception to the rule, no comma appears between the postal code and a zip code. See also 6.17, 6.42.

Bedford, PA, and Jamestown, NY
*but*
Send the package to J. Sprocket, 3359 Fob Dr., Quartz, IL 60000.

Note that the US Postal Service writes "ZIP Code" (*ZIP* stands for "Zone Improvement Plan"); some styles specify "ZIP code" (lowercase *c*). However, all-lowercase "zip code"—the first-listed spelling in *Merriam-Webster*—is appropriate in most contexts.

10.35 **Abbreviations for place-names with "Fort," "Mount," and "Saint."** Generic terms as elements of geographic names are usually spelled out in formal prose (and in mailing addresses) but can be abbreviated where space is at a premium or to reflect predominant usage (as in the last two examples below). *San* and *Santa* (e.g., San Diego, Santa Barbara) are never abbreviated. For French place-names with *Saint*, see 11.28.

| | |
|---|---|
| Fort (Ft.) Myers | Saint (St.) Louis (*usually* St. Louis) |
| Mount (Mt.) Airy | Saint (St.) Paul (*usually* St. Paul) |
| Port (Pt.) Arthur | |

## *Names of Countries*

10.36 **Abbreviating country names.** Names of countries are usually spelled out in text but may be abbreviated in tabular matter, lists, and the like. Use discretion in forming the abbreviations; for tables, make sure they are defined in a note to the table if there is any possibility of confusion (see 3.77–81). The examples below reflect entries in standard dictionaries (all are listed in *Merriam-Webster*, with the exception of *Swed.*, which is listed in Dictionary.com, among other sources).

Fr. Ger. Isr. It. Neth. Russ. Sp. Swed.

Certain initialisms, on the other hand, may be appropriate in regular text, especially after the full form has been established (see 10.2, 10.3). For more on *US*, see 10.37.

UAE (United Arab Emirates)
US
UK
GDR (the former German Democratic Republic, or East Germany) *or* DDR (Deutsche Demokratische Republik)
FRG (the former Federal Republic of Germany) *or* BRD (Bundesrepublik Deutschland)
USSR (the former Union of Soviet Socialist Republics)

In certain technical applications, it may be advisable to use either the two-letter or three-letter standard abbreviations based on the English names of countries as defined by the International Organization for Standardization (ISO 3166-1, alpha-2 and alpha-3, respectively). For these lists, consult ISO.org.

10.37 **"US" versus "United States."** Where necessary, initialisms for country names can be used in running text according to the guidelines set forth in 10.3 (see also 10.36). Traditionally, *United States* has been spelled out as a noun, with *US* reserved for the adjective form (where the abbreviation is preferred) and for tabular matter and the like. Chicago now permits the use of *US* as a noun, subject to editorial discretion and provided the meaning is clear from context.

US dollars
US involvement in China
China's involvement in the United States
*or*
China's involvement in the US

See also 10.4.

## *Addresses*

10.38 **Mailing addresses — postal versus standard abbreviations.** Standard abbreviations preferred by the US Postal Service (first column) are in all caps and do not use periods; these forms are most appropriate for mailing addresses. In tabular matter and the like, Chicago prefers the form of abbreviations presented in the second column. For those not listed here, consult a dictionary. For standard postal abbreviations, consult the USPS or other regional postal service. In running text, spell out rather than abbreviate. See also 10.39.

| | | | |
|---|---|---|---|
| AVE | Ave. | PO BOX | PO Box |
| BLDG | Bldg. | RD | Rd. |
| CT | Ct. | RM | Rm. |
| DR | Dr. | RTE | Rte. |
| EXPY | Expy. | SQ | Sq. |
| HWY | Hwy. | ST | St. |
| LN | Ln. | STE | Ste. (*or* Suite) |
| PKWY | Pkwy. | TER | Ter. (*or* Terr.) |
| PL | Pl. | | |

10.39 **Abbreviations for compass points in mailing addresses.** Single-letter compass points accompanying a street name are normally followed by a period; two-letter compass points are not. (The US Postal Service does not use periods for either; see 10.38; see also 10.4.) Note that when used in an address, the abbreviations *NE*, *NW*, *SE*, and *SW* remain abbreviated even in running text (there is no comma before them when they follow a street name). The *N* in the third example below is a street name and not a compass point.

1060 E. Prospect Ave. (*or, in running text,* 1060 East Prospect Avenue)
456 NW Lane St. (*or, in running text,* 456 NW Lane Street)
I stayed in a building on N Street SW, close to the city center.

A compass point that is the name (or part of the name) of a street or a place-name must never be abbreviated (e.g., South Ave., Northwest Hwy., South Shore Dr., West Bend, East Orange). For the use of numerals in addresses, see 9.53, 9.54.

## *Compass Points, Latitude, and Longitude*

10.40 **Abbreviations for compass points.** Points of the compass may be abbreviated as follows, without periods (but see 10.39). In formal, nontechnical text, however, these terms are usually spelled out.

N, E, S, W, NE, SE, SW, NW, NNE, ENE, ESE, etc.
N by NE, NE by N, NE by E, etc.

10.41 **Abbreviations for "latitude" and "longitude."** In nontechnical contexts, the words *latitude* and *longitude* are never abbreviated in running text or when standing alone.

longitude 90° west
the polar latitudes

Global positioning coordinates are expressed in a variety of ways (though latitude is always given first). Some systems use a minus sign (or hyphen) to indicate south or west. Others use decimal minutes. The following three coordinates are equivalent. The comma is often omitted.

36 25.217, −44 23.017
N 36°25′13″, W 44°23′01″
N 36 25.217, W 44 23.017

In technical work, the abbreviations *lat* and *long*, usually without periods, may be used when part of a coordinate. They can sometimes be dropped, since the compass point identifies the coordinate.

lat 42°15′09″ N, long 89°17′45″ W
lat 45°16′17″ S, long 116°40′18″ E
The chart showed shoal water at 19°29′59″ N, 107°45′36″ W.

Note that primes (′) and double primes (″), *not* apostrophes or quotation marks, are used for minutes and seconds of angular measure, respectively. For greater detail, consult *The CSE Manual* (bibliog. 1.1).

## DESIGNATIONS OF TIME

10.42 **Other discussions related to time.** For units of time (seconds, minutes, etc.), see 10.76. For numerical designations of dates and times of day, see 9.32, 9.35, 9.37, 9.39–42.

10.43 **Abbreviations for chronological eras.** The following abbreviations are used in running text and elsewhere to designate chronological eras. Although these have traditionally appeared in small capitals (with or without periods), Chicago recommends full capitals (without periods), in keeping with the general guidelines in this chapter (see 10.4; see also 10.9). The first four precede the year number; the others follow it. See also 9.36.

| | |
|---|---|
| AD | *anno Domini* (in the year of the Lord) |
| AH | *anno Hegirae* (in the year of the Hegira); *anno Hebraico* (in the Hebrew year) |
| AM | *anno mundi* (in the year of the world) (not to be confused with *ante meridiem*; see 10.46) |
| AS | *anno salutis* (in the year of salvation) |
| AUC | *ab urbe condita* (from the founding of the city [Rome, in 753 BCE]) |
| BC | before Christ |
| BCE | before the Common Era |
| BP | before the present |
| CE | Common Era |
| KYA | thousand years ago |
| MYA | million years ago |
| YBP | years before the present |

10.44 **Abbreviations for months.** Where space restrictions require that the names of months be abbreviated, one of the following systems is often used. The second and third, which take no periods, are used respectively in computer systems and indexes of periodical literature. In formal prose, Chicago prefers the first.

| | | | | | |
|---|---|---|---|---|---|
| Jan. | Jan | Ja | July | Jul | Jl |
| Feb. | Feb | F | Aug. | Aug | Ag |
| Mar. | Mar | Mr | Sept. | Sep | S |
| Apr. | Apr | Ap | Oct. | Oct | O |
| May | May | My | Nov. | Nov | N |
| June | Jun | Je | Dec. | Dec | D |

10.45 **Abbreviations for days of the week.** Where space restrictions require that days of the week be abbreviated, one of the following systems is often used. The second (common in computer code) and third use no periods. In formal prose, Chicago recommends the first.

| | | | | | |
|---|---|---|---|---|---|
| Sun. | Sun | Su | Thurs. | Thu | Th |
| Mon. | Mon | M | Fri. | Fri | F |
| Tues. | Tue | Tu | Sat. | Sat | Sa |
| Wed. | Wed | W | | | |

**10.46** **Abbreviations for time of day.** The following abbreviations are used in text and elsewhere to indicate time of day. Chicago prefers lowercase and periods for *a.m.* and *p.m.*, though small capitals (with or without periods) and all capitals (usually without periods) are also widely used and will be preferred by some publishers. For further explanation and examples, see 9.39, 9.41. See also 10.4. For time zones, see 10.47.

| | |
|---|---|
| a.m. | *ante meridiem* (before noon) |
| m. | *meridies* (noon [rarely used]) |
| p.m. | *post meridiem* (after noon) |

The abbreviations *a.m.* and *p.m.* should not be used with *morning, afternoon, evening, night*, or *o'clock*. (See also 7.96, section 1, under *time*.)

10:30 a.m. *or* ten thirty in the morning
11:00 p.m. *or* eleven o'clock at night

**10.47** **Abbreviations for time zones.** Abbreviations for time zones, where needed, are usually given in parentheses following the time—for example, 4:45 p.m. (CST). (For *a.m.* and *p.m.*, see 10.46.) In a departure from previous editions, time zones are capitalized when spelled out in full (see 8.91).

| | |
|---|---|
| GMT | Greenwich Mean Time |
| BST | British Summer Time |
| NDT | Newfoundland Daylight Time |
| AST | Atlantic Standard Time |
| EST | Eastern Standard Time |
| EDT | Eastern Daylight Time |
| CST | Central Standard Time |
| CDT | Central Daylight Time |
| MST | Mountain Standard Time |
| MDT | Mountain Daylight Time |
| PST | Pacific Standard Time |
| PDT | Pacific Daylight Time |

| | |
|---|---|
| AKST | Alaska Standard Time |
| AKDT | Alaska Daylight Time |
| HST | Hawaii-Aleutian Standard Time |
| HDT | Hawaii-Aleutian Daylight Time |

It should be noted that Greenwich Mean Time has long been superseded by the nearly identical Coordinated Universal Time (UTC) as the basis of international time. (The International Astronomical Union adopted the name Universal Time, or UT, for Greenwich Mean Time in 1928.) References to GMT, however, remain widespread not only in the United Kingdom but also in the United States and Canada and elsewhere.

## SCHOLARLY ABBREVIATIONS

10.48 **Scholarly abbreviations.** Scholarly abbreviations and symbols such as those listed in this section are typically found in bibliographic references, glossaries, and other scholarly apparatus. Some of them are no longer widely used and are listed here mainly as an aid to interpreting older texts. In formal prose, Chicago prefers to confine such abbreviations to parentheses or notes. Some can stand for several terms; only the terms likely to be encountered in scholarly works (mainly in the humanities) and serious nonfiction are included here. The choice between different abbreviations for one term (e.g., *L.* and *Lat.* for *Latin*) depends on the writer's preference, context, readership, and other factors; if in doubt, choose the longer form. Note that Latin abbreviations are normally set in roman. Note also that *ab*, *ad*, *et*, and other Latin terms that are complete words take no periods. See also 7.57, 10.4. For terms used more commonly in science and technology, see 10.55.

| | |
|---|---|
| abbr. | abbreviated, abbreviation |
| ab init. | *ab initio*, from the beginning |
| abl. | ablative |
| abr. | abridged, abridgment |
| acc. | accusative |
| act. | active |
| add. | addendum |
| ad inf. | *ad infinitum* |
| ad init. | *ad initium*, at the beginning |
| ad int. | *ad interim*, in the intervening time |
| adj. | adjective |
| ad lib. | *ad libitum*, at will (often used without a period) |

| | |
|---|---|
| ad loc. | *ad locum*, at the place |
| adv. | adverb |
| aet. *or* aetat. | *aetatis*, aged |
| AFr. | Anglo-French |
| AN | Anglo-Norman |
| anon. | anonymous (see 13.81) |
| app. | appendix |
| arch. | archaic |
| art. | article |
| AS | Anglo-Saxon |
| b. | born; brother |
| Bd. | *Band* (Ger.), volume |
| bib. | Bible, biblical |
| bibl. | *bibliotheca*, library |
| bibliog. | bibliography, -er, -ical |
| biog. | biography, -er, -ical |
| biol. | biology, -ist, -ical |
| bk. | book |
| c. | century; chapter (in law citations) |
| c. *or* cop. | copyright (see 10.49) |
| ca. *or* c. | *circa*, about, approximately (*ca.* preferred for greater clarity) |
| Cantab. | *Cantabrigiensis*, of Cambridge |
| cet. par. | *ceteris paribus*, other things being equal |
| cf. | *confer*, compare ("see, by way of comparison"; should not be used when *see* alone is meant) |
| chap. *or* ch. | chapter |
| col. | color (best spelled out); column |
| colloq. | colloquial, -ly, -ism |
| comp. | compiler (*pl.* comps.), compiled by |
| compar. | comparative |
| con. | *contra*, against |
| conj. | conjunction; conjugation |
| cons. | consonant |
| constr. | construction |
| cont. | continued |
| contr. | contraction |
| corr. | corrected |
| cp. | compare (rarely used; *cf.* is far more common) |
| d. | died; daughter |
| Dan. | Danish |
| dat. | dative |
| def. | definite; definition |

| | |
|---|---|
| dept. | department |
| deriv. | derivative |
| d. h. | *das heißt* (or *das heisst*), namely (used only in German text; note the space between initials) |
| d. i. | *das ist*, that is (used only in German text; note the space between initials) |
| dial. | dialect |
| dict. | dictionary |
| dim. | diminutive |
| diss. | dissertation |
| dist. | district |
| div. | division; divorced |
| do. | ditto |
| dram. pers. | *dramatis personae* |
| Dr. u. Vrl. | *Druck und Verlag*, printer and publisher |
| DV | *Deo volente*, God willing; Douay Version (see 10.54) |
| ea. | each |
| ed. | editor (*pl.* eds.), edition, edited by (never add *by* after *ed.*: either "ed. Jane Doe" or "edited by Jane Doe"; use *eds.* only after, never before, the names of two or more editors; see examples throughout chapters 13 and 14) |
| EE | Early English |
| e.g. | *exempli gratia*, for example (not to be confused with *i.e.*; see also 6.54) |
| ellipt. | elliptical, -ly |
| ency. *or* encyc. | encyclopedia |
| eng. | engineer, -ing |
| Eng. | English |
| engr. | engraved, -ing |
| enl. | enlarged |
| eq. | equation (*pl.* eqq. *or* eqs.; see also 10.49) |
| esp. | especially |
| et al. | *et alii* (or *et alia*), and others (normally used of persons; no period after *et*) |
| etc. | *et cetera*, and so forth (normally used of things) |
| et seq. | *et sequentes*, and the following |
| ex. | example (*pl.* exx. *or* exs.) |
| exh. cat. | exhibition catalog |
| f. *or* fem. | feminine; female |
| f. | *für* (Ger.), for; and the following one (see 14.48) |
| fasc. | fascicle |
| ff. | and the following ones (see 14.48) |
| fig. | figure |

| | |
|---|---|
| fl. | *floruit*, flourished (used with a date to indicate the productive years of a historical figure whose birth and death dates are unknown) |
| fol. | folio |
| Fr. | French |
| fr. | from |
| frag. | fragment |
| fut. | future |
| f.v. | *folio verso*, on the back of the page |
| Gael. | Gaelic |
| gen. | genitive; genus |
| geog. | geography, -er, -ical |
| geol. | geology, -ist, -ical |
| geom. | geometry, -ical |
| Ger. *or* G. | German |
| ger. | gerund |
| Gk. | Greek |
| hist. | history, -ian, -ical |
| HQ | headquarters |
| ibid. | *ibidem*, in the same place (see 13.37) |
| id. | *idem*, the same (see 13.38) |
| i.e. | *id est*, that is (not to be confused with *e.g.*; see also 6.54) |
| IE | Indo-European |
| ill. | illustrated, -ion, -or |
| imp. *or* imper. | imperative |
| incl. | including |
| indef. | indefinite |
| indic. | indicative |
| inf. | *infra*, below (best spelled out) |
| infin. | infinitive |
| in pr. | *in principio*, in the beginning |
| inst. | instant (this month); institute, -ion |
| instr. | instrumental |
| interj. | interjection |
| intrans. | intransitive |
| introd. *or* intro. | introduction |
| irreg. | irregular |
| It. | Italian |
| L. | Latin; left (in stage directions) |
| l. | left; line (*pl.* ll., but best spelled out to avoid confusion with numerals 1 and 11) |
| lang. | language |
| Lat. *or* L. | Latin |

| | |
|---|---|
| lit. | literally |
| loc. | locative |
| loc. cit. | *loco citato*, in the place cited (best avoided; see 13.39) |
| loq. | *loquitur*, speaks (used to identify the speaker of a quoted passage) |
| m. | male; married; measure (*pl.* mm.) |
| m. *or* masc. | masculine |
| marg. | margin, -al |
| math. | mathematics, mathematical |
| MHG | Middle High German |
| mimeo. | mimeograph, -ed |
| misc. | miscellaneous |
| MM | Maelzel's metronome |
| m.m. | *mutatis mutandis*, necessary changes being made |
| Mod.E. | Modern English |
| MS (*pl.* MSS) | *manuscriptum* (pl. *manuscripta*), manuscript |
| mus. | museum; music, -al |
| n. | *natus*, born; note, footnote (*pl.* nn.); noun |
| nat. | national; natural |
| NB, n.b. | *nota bene*, take careful note (capitals are illogical but often used for emphasis) |
| n.d. | no date; not determined |
| neg. | negative |
| neut. | neuter |
| no. (*pl.* nos.) | number |
| nom. | nominative |
| non obs. | *non obstante*, notwithstanding |
| non seq. | *non sequitur*, it does not follow |
| n.p. | no place; no publisher; no page |
| n.s. | new series |
| NS | New Style (dates) |
| ob. | *obiit*, died |
| obs. | obsolete |
| occas. | occasional, -ly |
| OE | Old English |
| OFr. | Old French |
| OHG | Old High German |
| ON | Old Norse |
| op. cit. | *opere citato*, in the work cited (best avoided; see 13.39) |
| o.s. | old series |
| OS | Old Style (dates) |
| Oxon. | *Oxoniensis*, of Oxford |

| | |
|---|---|
| p. | page (*pl.* pp.); past (*also* pa.) |
| para. *or* par. | paragraph (see 10.49) |
| pass. | passive |
| pa. t. | past tense |
| path. | pathology, -ist, -ical |
| perf. | perfect |
| perh. | perhaps |
| pers. | person, -al |
| pers. comm. | personal communication |
| pl. | plate (best avoided; see 3.9); plural |
| posth. | posthumous, -ly |
| p.p. | past participle |
| ppl. | participle |
| PPS | *post postscriptum*, a later postscript |
| prep. | preposition |
| pres. | present |
| pron. | pronoun |
| pro tem. | *pro tempore*, for the time being (often used without a period) |
| prox. | *proximo*, next month |
| PS | *postscriptum*, postscript |
| pt. | part |
| pub. | publication, publisher, published by |
| QED | *quod erat demonstrandum*, which was to be demonstrated |
| quar. *or* quart. | quarter, -ly |
| q.v. | *quod vide*, which see (used only in a cross-reference *after* the term referred to; cf. *s.v.*) |
| R. | *rex*, king; *regina*, queen; right (in stage directions) |
| r. | right; recto; reigned |
| refl. | reflexive |
| repr. | reprint, -ed |
| rev. | review; revised, revised by, revision (never add *by* after *rev.*: either "rev. Jane Doe" or "revised by Jane Doe") |
| RIP | *requiescat in pace*, may that person rest in peace |
| s. | son; substantive, substantival |
| s.a. | *sine anno*, without year; *sub anno*, under the year |
| sc. | scene; *scilicet*, namely; *sculpsit*, carved by |
| Sc. *or* Scot. | Scottish |
| s.d. | *sine die*, without setting a day for reconvening; stage direction |
| sd. | sound |
| sec. | section (see 10.49); *secundum*, according to |
| ser. | series |

| | |
|---|---|
| s.h. | speech heading |
| sing. *or* sg. | singular |
| s.l. | *sine loco*, without place (of publication) |
| s.n. | *sine nomine*, without name (of publisher) |
| sociol. | sociology, -ist, -ical |
| Sp. | Spanish |
| s.p. | speech prefix |
| st. | stanza |
| subj. | subject, -ive; subjunctive |
| subst. *or* s. | substantive, substantival |
| sup. | *supra*, above |
| superl. | superlative |
| supp. *or* suppl. | supplement |
| s.v. (*pl.* s.vv.) | *sub verbo*, *sub voce*, under the word (used in a cross-reference *before* the term referred to; cf. *q.v.*; see also 14.130) |
| syn. | synonym, -ous |
| t. | *tome* (Fr.), *tomo* (Sp.), volume |
| techn. | technical, -ly |
| theol. | theology, -ian, -ical |
| t.p. | title page |
| trans. | translated by, translator(s) (never add *by* after *trans.*: either "trans. Jane Doe" or "translated by Jane Doe"); transitive |
| treas. | treasurer |
| TS | typescript |
| ult. | *ultimatus*, ultimate, last; *ultimo*, last month |
| univ. | university |
| usw. | *und so weiter*, and so forth (equivalent to *etc.*; used only in German text) |
| ut sup. | *ut supra*, as above |
| v. | verse (*pl.* vv.); verso; versus; *vide*, see |
| v. *or* vb. | verb |
| v.i. | *verbum intransitivum*, intransitive verb; *vide infra*, see below |
| viz. | *videlicet*, namely |
| voc. | vocative |
| vol. | volume |
| vs. *or* v. | versus (in legal contexts use *v.*) |
| v.t. | *verbum transitivum*, transitive verb |
| yr. | year; your |

10.49 **A few scholarly symbols.** The symbols below often appear in bibliographies and other scholarly apparatus rather than their equivalent abbreviations (see 10.48).

| | |
|---|---|
| © | copyright |
| = | equals, the same as (for examples, see 10.52) |
| ¶ (*pl.* ¶¶) | paragraph |
| § (*pl.* §§) | section |

## BIBLICAL ABBREVIATIONS

**10.50** **Biblical abbreviations — an overview.** In running text, books of the Bible are generally spelled out. See also 9.28.

The opening chapters of Ephesians constitute a sermon on love.
Jeremiah, chapters 42–44, records the flight of the Jews to Egypt.
According to Genesis 1:27, God created man in his own image.

In parenthetical citations or in notes, or where many such references appear in the text, abbreviations are appropriate.

My concordance lists five instances of the word *nourish*: Gen. 47:12, Ruth 4:15, Isa. 44:14, Acts 7:21, and 1 Tim. 4:6.

For authoritative guidance in many biblical areas not covered here, consult *The SBL Handbook of Style* (bibliog. 1.1). For citing scriptural references in notes and bibliographies, see 14.138–41.

**10.51** **Abbreviations for the Old Testament.** These are the traditional abbreviations and commonly used shorter forms for books of the Old Testament. (Note that the shorter forms have no periods.) The listing is alphabetical, both for easier reference and because the order varies slightly in different versions of the Bible. Alternative names for the same books are indicated by an equals sign (see 10.49). For the New Testament, see 10.53.

| | |
|---|---|
| Amos *or* Am | Amos |
| 1 Chron. *or* 1 Chr | 1 Chronicles |
| 2 Chron. *or* 2 Chr | 2 Chronicles |
| Dan. *or* Dn | Daniel |
| Deut. *or* Dt | Deuteronomy |
| Eccles. *or* Eccl | Ecclesiastes |
| Esther *or* Est | Esther |
| Exod. *or* Ex | Exodus |
| Ezek. *or* Ez | Ezekiel |

| | |
|---|---|
| Ezra *or* Ezr | Ezra |
| Gen. *or* Gn | Genesis |
| Hab. *or* Hb | Habakkuk |
| Hag. *or* Hg | Haggai |
| Hosea *or* Hos | Hosea |
| Isa. *or* Is | Isaiah |
| Jer. *or* Jer | Jeremiah |
| Job *or* Jb | Job |
| Joel *or* Jl | Joel |
| Jon. *or* Jon | Jonah |
| Josh. *or* Jo | Joshua |
| Judg. *or* Jgs | Judges |
| 1 Kings *or* 1 Kgs | 1 Kings |
| 2 Kings *or* 2 Kgs | 2 Kings |
| Lam. *or* Lam | Lamentations |
| Lev. *or* Lv | Leviticus |
| Mal. *or* Mal | Malachi |
| Mic. *or* Mi | Micah |
| Nah. *or* Na | Nahum |
| Neh. *or* Neh | Nehemiah |
| Num. *or* Nm | Numbers |
| Obad. *or* Ob | Obadiah |
| Prov. *or* Prv | Proverbs |
| Ps. (*pl.* Pss.) *or* Ps (*pl.* Pss) | Psalms |
| Ruth *or* Ru | Ruth |
| 1 Sam. *or* 1 Sm | 1 Samuel |
| 2 Sam. *or* 2 Sm | 2 Samuel |
| Song of Sol. *or* Sg | Song of Solomon (= Song of Songs) |
| Zech. *or* Zec | Zechariah |
| Zeph. *or* Zep | Zephaniah |

10.52 **Abbreviations for the Apocrypha.** The books of the Apocrypha are accepted in Roman Catholic versions of the Bible, though not in Jewish and Protestant versions. Some are not complete in themselves but are continuations of books listed in 10.51. These are the traditional abbreviations and commonly used shorter forms. (Note that the shorter forms have no periods.) Alternative names for the same books are indicated by an equals sign (see 10.49). Where no abbreviation is given, the full form should be used.

| | |
|---|---|
| Bar. *or* Bar | Baruch |
| Ecclus. | Ecclesiasticus (= Sirach) |
| 1 Esd. | 1 Esdras |

| | |
|---|---|
| 2 Esd. | 2 Esdras |
| Jth. *or* Jdt | Judith |
| 1 Macc. *or* 1 Mc | 1 Maccabees |
| 2 Macc. *or* 2 Mc | 2 Maccabees |
| Pr. of Man. | Prayer of Manasses (= Manasseh) |
| Sir. *or* Sir | Sirach (= Ecclesiasticus) |
| Sus. | Susanna |
| Tob. *or* Tb | Tobit |
| Ws | Wisdom (= Wisdom of Solomon) |
| Wisd. of Sol. | Wisdom of Solomon (= Wisdom) |

**10.53** **Abbreviations for the New Testament.** These are the traditional abbreviations and commonly used shorter forms for books of the New Testament. (Note that the shorter forms have no periods.) The listing is alphabetical, both for easier reference and because the order varies slightly in different versions of the Bible. Alternative names for the same books are indicated by an equals sign (see 10.49). For the Old Testament, see 10.51.

| | |
|---|---|
| Acts | Acts of the Apostles |
| Apoc. | Apocalypse (= Revelation) |
| Col. *or* Col | Colossians |
| 1 Cor. *or* 1 Cor | 1 Corinthians |
| 2 Cor. *or* 2 Cor | 2 Corinthians |
| Eph. *or* Eph | Ephesians |
| Gal. *or* Gal | Galatians |
| Heb. *or* Heb | Hebrews |
| James *or* Jas | James |
| John *or* Jn | John (Gospel) |
| 1 John *or* 1 Jn | 1 John (Epistle) |
| 2 John *or* 2 Jn | 2 John (Epistle) |
| 3 John *or* 3 Jn | 3 John (Epistle) |
| Jude | Jude |
| Luke *or* Lk | Luke |
| Mark *or* Mk | Mark |
| Matt. *or* Mt | Matthew |
| 1 Pet. *or* 1 Pt | 1 Peter |
| 2 Pet. *or* 2 Pt | 2 Peter |
| Phil. *or* Phil | Philippians |
| Philem. *or* Phlm | Philemon |
| Rev. *or* Rv | Revelation (= Apocalypse) |
| Rom. *or* Rom | Romans |
| 1 Thess. *or* 1 Thes | 1 Thessalonians |

| | |
|---|---|
| 2 Thess. *or* 2 Thes | 2 Thessalonians |
| 1 Tim. *or* 1 Tm | 1 Timothy |
| 2 Tim. *or* 2 Tm | 2 Timothy |
| Titus *or* Ti | Titus |

10.54 **Abbreviations for versions and sections of the Bible.** Versions and sections of the Bible are usually abbreviated in the form of initialisms, especially when they consist of more than one word.

| | |
|---|---|
| Apoc. | Apocrypha |
| ARV | American Revised Version |
| ASV | American Standard Version |
| AT | American Translation |
| AV | Authorized (King James) Version |
| CEV | Contemporary English Version |
| DV | Douay Version |
| ERV | English Revised Version |
| EV | English version(s) |
| HB | Hebrew Bible |
| JB | Jerusalem Bible |
| LXX | Septuagint |
| MT | Masoretic Text |
| NAB | New American Bible |
| NEB | New English Bible |
| NIV | New International Version |
| NJB | New Jerusalem Bible |
| NRSV | New Revised Standard Version |
| NT | New Testament |
| OT | Old Testament |
| RSV | Revised Standard Version |
| RV | Revised Version |
| Syr. | Syriac |
| Vulg. | Vulgate |
| WEB | World English Bible |

## TECHNOLOGY AND SCIENCE

10.55 **Miscellaneous technical abbreviations.** The following list, which cannot aim to be comprehensive, includes some abbreviations used in various branches of the physical and biological sciences and in technical writing. Some, such as *PC* and *DVD*, are also in wide general use. Abbreviations used in highly specialized areas have generally been omitted, as have most adjectival forms. Many of the abbreviations for units are identical to or compatible with those used in the International System of Units, or SI (see 10.57–65). Periods are omitted in any context (compare 10.4). The capitalization given below, based largely on current usage, sometimes departs from the listings in *Merriam-Webster* (see 7.1). Spelled-out forms are lowercased except for any proper nouns (including trademarks and the names of formal protocols; see also 7.85). Note that the first letter of an abbreviation derived from a proper name (e.g., A [ampere], V, Wb, and the *C* in °C) is usually capitalized (though the spelled-out term is lowercased—unless, like Celsius, it forms a unit name with another term, as in "degree[s] Celsius"), as are the prefix letters for *mega-* (M), *giga-* (G), *tera-* (T), and so on (see 10.62). Plurals do not add an *s* (10 A, 5 ha). With few exceptions (mainly abbreviations with degree symbols), a space usually appears between a numeral and an abbreviation (22 m *but* 36°C); see also 10.64. For units with repeated quantities, see 9.19. For statistical abbreviations, see 10.56. For traditional US units of measure, see 10.72–76. See also 9.18.

| | |
|---|---|
| A | ampere; adenine (in genetic code) |
| Å | angstrom |
| ac | alternating current |
| AF | audio frequency |
| Ah | ampere-hour |
| AM | amplitude modulation |
| ASCII | American Standard Code for Information Interchange |
| atm | atmosphere, -ic |
| av *or* avdp | avoirdupois |
| bar | bar (no abbreviation) |
| BD | Blu-ray Disc |
| Bé *or* °Bé | degree Baumé |
| bhp | brake horsepower |
| BMI | body mass index |
| bp | boiling point; base pair |
| bps | bits per second |
| Bps | bytes per second |
| Bq | becquerel |
| Btu | British thermal unit |
| C | coulomb; cytosine (in genetic code) |
| °C | degree Celsius |
| cal | calorie |

| | |
|---|---|
| Cal | kilocalorie (in nonscientific contexts; *see also* kcal) |
| cc | cubic centimeter (in clinical contexts; *see also* $cm^3$) |
| cd | candela |
| CD | compact disc |
| cgs | centimeter-gram-second system (SI) |
| Ci | curie |
| cm | centimeter |
| cM | centimorgan |
| $cm^3$ | cubic centimeter (in scientific contexts; *see also* cc) |
| cp | candlepower |
| CP | chemically pure |
| cps *or* c/s | cycles per second |
| CPU | central processing unit |
| cu | cubic |
| d | day; deuteron |
| Da | dalton |
| dB | decibel |
| dc | direct current |
| DNS | domain name system |
| DOI | digital object identifier (DOI is a registered trademark, but the spelled-out form may be lowercased) |
| DOS | disk operating system |
| dpi | dots per inch |
| DVD | digital versatile (*or* video) disc |
| dyn | dyne |
| emf | electromotive force |
| erg | erg (no abbreviation) |
| eV | electron volt |
| F | farad |
| °F | degree Fahrenheit |
| FM | frequency modulation |
| fp | freezing point |
| fps | frames per second; feet per second |
| FTP | File Transfer Protocol |
| g | gram; gas |
| G | guanine (in genetic code) |
| Gb | gigabit |
| GB | gigabyte |
| Gbps | gigabits per second |
| GeV | $10^9$ electron volts |
| GIF | graphics interchange format |
| GIS | geographic information system |

| | |
|---|---|
| GPS | Global Positioning System (the system originally developed by the US government); *but* a global positioning system |
| Gy | gigayear (but see 9.11); gray (joule per kilogram) |
| H | henry (*pl.* henries) |
| h | hour; helion |
| ha | hectare |
| hp | horsepower |
| HTML | hypertext markup language |
| HTTP | Hypertext Transfer Protocol |
| HTTPS | Hypertext Transfer Protocol Secure |
| Hz | hertz |
| IP | Internet Protocol |
| IR | infrared |
| IU | international unit |
| J | joule |
| JPEG | *from* Joint Photographic Experts Group (file format) |
| K | kelvin (no degree symbol); kilobyte (in commercial contexts) |
| kat | katal |
| kb | kilobar (*also abbreviated* kbar [SI]); kilobase (DNA, RNA) |
| kb *or* kbit | kilobit |
| KB | kilobyte (KB is typically used for binary units and kB for decimal units; *see also* K) |
| Kbps | kilobits per second (esp. in commercial contexts; *also* kbps) |
| kc | kilocycle |
| kcal | kilocalorie (in scientific contexts; *see also* Cal) |
| KE | kinetic energy |
| kg | kilogram |
| kHz | kilohertz |
| kJ | kilojoule |
| km | kilometer |
| kmh *or* km/h *or* kmph | kilometers per hour (km/h, with a slash, is SI style) |
| kn | knot (nautical mph) |
| kW | kilowatt |
| kWh | kilowatt-hour |
| L | liter (capitalized to avoid confusion with numeral 1) |
| LLM | large language model |
| lm | lumen |
| lx | lux |
| m | meter |

| | |
|---|---|
| M | molar; metal |
| Mb | megabase; megabit |
| MB | megabyte |
| Mbps | megabits per second |
| Mc | megacycle |
| mCi | millicurie |
| MeV | megaelectron volt |
| mg | milligram |
| MIDI | musical instrument digital interface |
| mks | meter-kilogram-second system (SI) |
| mL | milliliter |
| mol | mole |
| mp | melting point |
| MPEG | *from* Moving Pictures Experts Group (file format) |
| mpg | miles per gallon |
| mph | miles per hour |
| MP3 | *from* MPEG-1 Audio Layer 3 (file format) |
| MP4 | *from* MPEG-4 Part 14 (file format) |
| ms | millisecond |
| N | newton; number (often italic; see also 10.56) |
| neg | negative |
| nm | nanometer; nautical mile |
| Ω | ohm |
| OCR | optical character recognition |
| OS | operating system |
| Pa | pascal |
| pc | parsec |
| PC | personal computer |
| PDF | portable document format |
| PE | potential energy |
| pF | picofarad |
| pH | negative log of hydrogen ion concentration (measure of acidity) |
| PNG | *from* portable network graphics (file format) |
| pos | positive |
| ppb | parts per billion |
| ppm | parts per million |
| ppt | parts per trillion; precipitate |
| R | electrical resistance |
| °R | degree Réaumur |
| rad | radian |
| RAM | random-access memory |
| RF | radio frequency |

| | |
|---|---|
| ROM | read-only memory |
| rpm *or* r/min | revolutions per minute |
| s | second |
| S | siemens |
| satnav | satellite navigation |
| SGML | standard generalized markup language |
| soln | solution |
| sp gr | specific gravity |
| sq | square |
| sr | steradian |
| std | standard |
| STP | standard temperature and pressure |
| Sv | sievert |
| t | metric ton ($10^3$ kg); triton (nucleus of tritium) |
| T | tesla; thymine (in genetic code) |
| Tb | terabit |
| TB | terabyte |
| Tbps | terabits per second |
| TCP/IP | Transmission-Control Protocol/Internet Protocol |
| temp | temperature |
| U | uracil (in genetic code) |
| UCS | universal character set |
| URI | uniform resource identifier |
| URL | uniform resource locator |
| USB | universal serial bus |
| UV | ultraviolet |
| V | volt |
| VoIP | Voice over Internet Protocol |
| W | watt |
| Wb | weber |
| wt | weight |
| w/v | weight per volume |
| w/w | weight per weight |
| XML | extensible markup language |
| y | year |
| Z | atomic number (often italic) |

**10.56** **Statistical abbreviations.** The following abbreviations are used in statistical material, especially in tables. They are sometimes italicized.

| | |
|---|---|
| ANCOVA | analysis of covariance |
| ANOVA | analysis of variance |
| CI | confidence interval |

| | |
|---|---|
| CL | confidence limit |
| CLT | central limit theorem |
| df, DF, *or* dof | degrees of freedom |
| GLM | generalized linear model |
| HR | hazard ratio |
| IQR | interquartile range |
| LS | least squares |
| MLE | maximum likelihood estimate |
| MS | mean square |
| $N$ | number (of population or sample) |
| $n$ | number (of sample or subsample) |
| ns | not (statistically) significant |
| OLS | ordinary least squares |
| OR | odds ratio |
| $p$ | probability |
| $r$ | bivariate correlation coefficient |
| $R$ | multivariate correlation coefficient |
| $R^2$ | coefficient of determination |
| RMS | root mean square |
| sd *or* SD | standard deviation |
| se *or* SE | standard error |
| sem *or* SEM | standard error of the mean |
| SS | sum of squares |
| SSE | error sum of squares |
| SST | total sum of squares |
| WLLN | weak law of large numbers |
| $\overline{x}$ or $\overline{X}$ | mean value |
| $\chi^2$ | chi-square distribution |

## *The International System of Units*

10.57 **SI units — overview.** The International System of Units (*Système international d'unités*, abbreviated internationally as SI) is an expanded version of the metric system. It is in general use among the world's scientists and in many other areas. The following paragraphs discuss only the basics. For the latest official guidelines, consult *The International System of Units*, a brochure published in French and English by the Bureau International des Poids et Mesures and available online. For further guidance, see Ambler Thompson and Barry N. Taylor, *Guide for the Use of the International System of Units* (bibliog. 2.4); and *The CSE Manual* (bibliog. 1.1).

10.58 **SI units — form.** No periods are used after any of the SI symbols for units, and the same symbols are used for both the singular and the plural. Most symbols are lowercased; exceptions are those that stand for units derived from proper names (e.g., A, for *ampere*) and those that must be distinguished from similar lowercased forms. All units are lowercased in their spelled-out form except for terms like Celsius (which follows the word "degree" in its unit name; see also 10.55). See also 10.59.

10.59 **Plurals for SI units.** Though abbreviations for SI units are the same for plural and singular forms, the noun forms for such units would generally be written out or pronounced in the plural (e.g., 3 m = three meters; *but* a three-meter span). The only exception is for a quantity of exactly 1; for quantities such as 0.5 m or 1.6 m, the unit would generally be read as if it were plural (zero point five meters; one point six meters; *but* a zero-point-five-meter span). See also 9.21, 10.73.

10.60 **SI base units.** There are seven fundamental, or base, SI units. Note that although *weight* and *mass* are usually measured in the same units, they are not interchangeable. Weight is a force due to gravity that depends on an object's mass. Note also that no degree sign is used with the symbol K. See also 10.61.

| *Quantity* | *Unit* | *Symbol* |
|---|---|---|
| length | meter | m |
| mass | kilogram | kg |
| time | second | s |
| electric current | ampere | A |
| thermodynamic temperature | kelvin | K |
| amount of substance | mole | mol |
| luminous intensity | candela | cd |

Not to be confused with the symbols for base *units* are the corresponding symbols for base *quantities*. These symbols, which represent variable quantities, appear in italic type (e.g., *l*, length; *m*, mass; *t*, time).

10.61 **Kilogram versus gram as SI base unit.** Although for historical reasons the kilogram rather than the gram was chosen as the base unit, prefixes are applied to the term *gram*—megagram (Mg), milligram (mg), nanogram (ng), and so forth. See also 10.62.

10.62 **SI prefixes.** Prefixes, representing a power of ten, are added to the name of a base unit, a derived unit, or an accepted non-SI unit (see 10.63,

10.65) to allow notation of very large or very small numerical values. The units so formed are called multiples and submultiples of SI units. For example, a kilometer, or km, is equal to a thousand meters (or $10^3$ m), and a millisecond, or ms, is equal to one-thousandth of a second (or $10^{-3}$ s). The following prefixes, with their symbols, are used in the international system. Note that in three cases the final vowel of an SI prefix is omitted: kΩ, kilohm (*not* kiloohm); MΩ, megohm (*not* megaohm); ha, hectare (*not* hectoare).

| *Factor* | *Prefix* | *Symbol* | *Factor* | *Prefix* | *Symbol* |
|---|---|---|---|---|---|
| $10^{24}$ | yotta | Y | $10^{-1}$ | deci | d |
| $10^{21}$ | zetta | Z | $10^{-2}$ | centi | c |
| $10^{18}$ | exa | E | $10^{-3}$ | milli | m |
| $10^{15}$ | peta | P | $10^{-6}$ | micro | µ |
| $10^{12}$ | tera | T | $10^{-9}$ | nano | n |
| $10^{9}$ | giga | G | $10^{-12}$ | pico | p |
| $10^{6}$ | mega | M | $10^{-15}$ | femto | f |
| $10^{3}$ | kilo | k | $10^{-18}$ | atto | a |
| $10^{2}$ | hecto | h | $10^{-21}$ | zepto | z |
| $10^{1}$ | deka | da | $10^{-24}$ | yocto | y |

These prefixes should not be used to indicate powers of two (as in the field of electrical technology, or computing). If binary multiples must be used, the first two letters of the SI prefixes must be followed by *bi*, to form *kibi-* (Ki), *mebi-* (Mi), *gibi-* (Gi), *tebi-* (Ti), *pebi-* (Pi), and *exbi-* (Ei). See also 9.12.

10.63 **Units derived from SI base units.** Derived units are expressed algebraically in terms of base units or other derived units.

| *Derived unit* | *In terms of SI base units* |
|---|---|
| square meter | $m^2$ |
| cubic meter | $m^3$ |
| meter per second | m/s |
| meter per second squared | $m/s^2$ |
| kilogram per cubic meter | $kg/m^3$ |

Certain derived units have special names and symbols. Several of the most common—hertz (Hz), volt (V), watt (W), and so forth—are listed in 10.55. These are used in algebraic expressions to denote further derived units. A few are listed below. Note the symbol for newton meter; either a nonbreaking space (preferably the narrow no-break space defined by

Unicode as U+202F) or a dot operator (U+22C5) may be used between the unit symbols. See also 6.129, 11.2.

| *Derived unit* | *Symbol* | *In terms of SI base units* |
|---|---|---|
| joule per kelvin | J/K | $m^2\ kg\ s^{-2}\ K^{-1}$ |
| newton meter | N m *or* N·m | $m^2\ kg\ s^{-2}$ |
| newton per meter | N/m | $kg\ s^{-2}$ |

A derived unit can often be expressed in different ways. For example, the weber may be expressed either as Wb or, in another context, in terms of the volt second (V s *or* V·s).

10.64 **SI units and abbreviations — spacing.** Only numbers between 0.1 and 1,000 should be used to express the quantity of any SI unit. Thus 12,000 meters is expressed as 12 km (not 12 000 m), and 0.003 cubic centimeters as 3 $mm^3$ (not 0.003 $cm^3$). (For the use of spaces rather than commas between groups of digits in SI units, see 9.58.) In SI usage as in general usage, a space usually appears between the numeral and any abbreviation or symbol. Contrary to general usage, however, SI usage also stipulates a space before a percentage sign (%) and before a degree symbol used for temperature (compare the advice in the introduction to the table at 10.55). In expressions of degrees, minutes, and seconds, SI usage shows (but does not stipulate) a space between quantities. Many publications do not observe these exceptions, and Chicago does not require them in its publications.

| *SI style* | *Chicago style* |
|---|---|
| 22 °C | 22°C |
| 22° 14′ 33″ | 22°14′33″ |
| 0.5 % | 0.5% (see also 9.20) |

Note that in the context of firearms, many writers elide the space between the numeral and the unit of measure in expressions of caliber and related dimensions used as modifiers before a noun (e.g., a 9mm Luger). This style is acceptable if followed consistently. See also 9.21.

10.65 **Non-SI units accepted for use.** Certain widely used units such as liter (L, capitalized to avoid confusion with the numeral 1), metric ton (t), and hour (h) are not officially part of the international system but are accepted for use within the system.

## *Astronomy*

10.66 **Astronomical abbreviations — additional resources.** Astronomers and astrophysicists employ the International System of Units (see 10.57–65) supplemented with special terminology and abbreviations. The paragraphs in this section offer a minimum of examples for the generalist. Additional guidelines may be found at the website of the International Astronomical Union.

10.67 **Celestial coordinates.** Right ascension, abbreviated RA or α, is given in hours, minutes, and seconds (abbreviations set as superscripts) of sidereal time. Declination, abbreviated δ, is given in degrees, minutes, and seconds (using the degree symbol, prime, and double prime) of arc north (marked with a plus sign or left unmarked) or south (marked with a minus sign) of the celestial equator. Note the abbreviations (set as superscripts) and symbols used. See also 10.41, 10.64.

$14^h6^m7^s$ $-49°8'22''$

Decimal fractions of the basic units are indicated as shown.

$14^h6^m7^s.2$ $+34°.26$

10.68 **Some other astronomical abbreviations.** A few of the more commonly used astronomical abbreviations are listed here. A more extensive list is available in *The CSE Manual* (bibliog. 1.1).

| | |
|---|---|
| AU *or* ua | astronomical unit (mean Earth–Sun distance) |
| lt-yr | light-year ($9.46 \times 10^{12}$ km) |
| pc | parsec (parallax second: $3.084 \times 10^{13}$ km) |
| kpc | kiloparsec ($10^3$ pc) |
| Mpc | megaparsec ($10^6$ pc) |
| UT | Universal Time (see also 10.47) |

## *Chemical Elements*

10.69 **Naming conventions for chemical elements.** The International Union of Pure and Applied Chemistry (IUPAC) is the recognized body that formally approves element names. Each element bears a number (reflecting the number of protons in its nucleus) as well as a name—as in "element 106," also known as seaborgium. This number is an important identifier in cases where formal names are in dispute; between 1995 and

1997, for example, the American Chemical Society and IUPAC adopted different names for some of the same elements. The differences were reconciled, and the list that follows reflects names and symbols approved by IUPAC. Names for undiscovered or unconfirmed elements are provisionally assigned using Latin for the digits of their atomic number (e.g., *ununoctium*, one-one-eight, for element 118, which was confirmed in 2015 and named *oganesson* the following year). The elements in the following list are arranged in alphabetical order by common name. If the symbol is based on a term other than the common name—for example, Sb (*stibium*) for antimony—the term is added in parentheses. Although the names of elements are always lowercased, the symbols all have an initial capital. No periods are used. In specialized works, the abbreviations commonly appear in text as well as in tables, notes, and so forth. See also 8.150, 8.151.

| *Atomic number* | *Symbol* | *Name* |
|---|---|---|
| 89 | Ac | actinium |
| 13 | Al | aluminum (US), aluminium (IUPAC) |
| 95 | Am | americium |
| 51 | Sb | antimony (*stibium*) |
| 18 | Ar | argon |
| 33 | As | arsenic |
| 85 | At | astatine |
| 56 | Ba | barium |
| 97 | Bk | berkelium |
| 4 | Be | beryllium |
| 83 | Bi | bismuth |
| 107 | Bh | bohrium |
| 5 | B | boron |
| 35 | Br | bromine |
| 48 | Cd | cadmium |
| 20 | Ca | calcium |
| 98 | Cf | californium |
| 6 | C | carbon |
| 58 | Ce | cerium |
| 55 | Cs | cesium (US), caesium (IUPAC) |
| 17 | Cl | chlorine |
| 24 | Cr | chromium |
| 27 | Co | cobalt |
| 112 | Cn | copernicium |
| 29 | Cu | copper |
| 96 | Cm | curium |
| 110 | Ds | darmstadtium |

| *Atomic number* | *Symbol* | *Name* |
|---|---|---|
| 105 | Db | dubnium |
| 66 | Dy | dysprosium |
| 99 | Es | einsteinium |
| 68 | Er | erbium |
| 63 | Eu | europium |
| 100 | Fm | fermium |
| 114 | Fl | flerovium |
| 9 | F | fluorine |
| 87 | Fr | francium |
| 64 | Gd | gadolinium |
| 31 | Ga | gallium |
| 32 | Ge | germanium |
| 79 | Au | gold (*aurum*) |
| 72 | Hf | hafnium |
| 108 | Hs | hassium |
| 2 | He | helium |
| 67 | Ho | holmium |
| 1 | H | hydrogen |
| 49 | In | indium |
| 53 | I | iodine |
| 77 | Ir | iridium |
| 26 | Fe | iron (*ferrum*) |
| 36 | Kr | krypton |
| 57 | La | lanthanum |
| 103 | Lr | lawrencium |
| 82 | Pb | lead (*plumbum*) |
| 3 | Li | lithium |
| 116 | Lv | livermorium |
| 71 | Lu | lutetium |
| 12 | Mg | magnesium |
| 25 | Mn | manganese |
| 109 | Mt | meitnerium |
| 101 | Md | mendelevium |
| 80 | Hg | mercury (*hydrargyrum*) |
| 42 | Mo | molybdenum |
| 115 | Mc | moscovium |
| 60 | Nd | neodymium |
| 10 | Ne | neon |
| 93 | Np | neptunium |
| 28 | Ni | nickel |
| 113 | Nh | nihonium |
| 41 | Nb | niobium |

| *Atomic number* | *Symbol* | *Name* |
|---|---|---|
| 7 | N | nitrogen |
| 102 | No | nobelium |
| 118 | Og | oganesson |
| 76 | Os | osmium |
| 8 | O | oxygen |
| 46 | Pd | palladium |
| 15 | P | phosphorus |
| 78 | Pt | platinum |
| 94 | Pu | plutonium |
| 84 | Po | polonium |
| 19 | K | potassium (*kalium*) |
| 59 | Pr | praseodymium |
| 61 | Pm | promethium |
| 91 | Pa | protactinium |
| 88 | Ra | radium |
| 86 | Rn | radon |
| 75 | Re | rhenium |
| 45 | Rh | rhodium |
| 111 | Rg | roentgenium |
| 37 | Rb | rubidium |
| 44 | Ru | ruthenium |
| 104 | Rf | rutherfordium |
| 62 | Sm | samarium |
| 21 | Sc | scandium |
| 106 | Sg | seaborgium |
| 34 | Se | selenium |
| 14 | Si | silicon |
| 47 | Ag | silver (*argentum*) |
| 11 | Na | sodium (*natrium*) |
| 38 | Sr | strontium |
| 16 | S | sulfur |
| 73 | Ta | tantalum |
| 43 | Tc | technetium |
| 52 | Te | tellurium |
| 117 | Ts | tennessine |
| 65 | Tb | terbium |
| 81 | Tl | thallium |
| 90 | Th | thorium |
| 69 | Tm | thulium |
| 50 | Sn | tin (*stannum*) |
| 22 | Ti | titanium |
| 74 | W | tungsten (*wolfram*) |

| *Atomic number* | *Symbol* | *Name* |
|---|---|---|
| 92 | U | uranium |
| 23 | V | vanadium |
| 54 | Xe | xenon |
| 70 | Yb | ytterbium |
| 39 | Y | yttrium |
| 30 | Zn | zinc |
| 40 | Zr | zirconium |

## *Symbols for Math*

10.70 **Common mathematical signs and symbols.** Mathematical expressions are communicated using signs and symbols, including letters and numbers. Some of the standard mathematical characters, including code points for Unicode (see 11.2), are listed below. Also included are the commands for producing each character in LaTeX, a document markup and preparation system in wide use among STEM authors and accepted by many publishers. For more information, consult the LaTeX website. Manuscripts that include only the occasional in-line or displayed expression are usually prepared using a word processor's equation editor. Note that when there is an asterisk or other generic character similar to one of the symbols listed below, the mathematical version should be preferred because it encodes the correct spacing between symbols (see also 6.130).

| SIGN/SYMBOL | NAME | UNICODE | LATEX |
|---|---|---|---|
| *Operations* | | | |
| + | Plus sign | 002B | + |
| − | Minus sign | 2212 | - |
| × | Multiplication sign | 00D7 | \times |
| · | Dot operator (multiplication) | 22C5 | \cdot |
| ÷ | Division sign | 00F7 | \div |
| / | Division slash | 2215 | / *or* \slash |
| ∘ | Ring operator (composition) | 2218 | \circ |
| ∪ | Union | 222A | \cup |
| ∩ | Intersection | 2229 | \cap |
| ± | Plus or minus | 00B1 | \pm |
| ∓ | Minus or plus | 2213 | \mp |
| ∗ | Asterisk operator (convolution) | 2217 | \ast |
| ⊛ | Circled asterisk operator (convolution) | 229B | \circledast |

| SIGN/SYMBOL | NAME | UNICODE | LATEX |
|---|---|---|---|
| ⊕ | Circled plus (direct sum, various) | 2295 | \oplus |
| ⊖ | Circled minus (various) | 2296 | \ominus |
| ⊗ | Circled times (various) | 2297 | \otimes |
| ⊙ | Circled dot operator (various) | 2299 | \odot |
| ∶ | Ratio | 2236 | : |
| ∐ | Coproduct or amalgamation | 2210 | \amalg |
| *Relations* | | | |
| = | Equals sign | 003D | = |
| ≠ | Not equal to | 2260 | \neq |
| ≈ | Almost equal to, asymptotic to | 2248 | \approx |
| ≅ | Approximately equal to, isomorphic to | 2245 | \cong |
| < | Less than | 003C | < |
| ≪ | Much less than | 226A | \ll |
| > | Greater than | 003E | > |
| ≫ | Much greater than | 226B | \gg |
| ≤ | Less than or equal to | 2264 | \leq |
| ≥ | Greater than or equal to | 2265 | \geq |
| ≡ | Identical to, congruent to | 2261 | \equiv |
| ≢ | Not identical to, not congruent to | 2262 | \nequiv |
| ∣ | Divides, divisible by | 2223 | \divides |
| ∼ | Tilde operator (similar to, asymptotically equal to) | 223C | \sim |
| ≔ | Colon equals (assignment) | 2254 | \coloneqq |
| ∈ | Element of | 2208 | \in |
| ∉ | Not an element of | 2209 | \notin |
| ⊂ | Subset of | 2282 | \subset |
| ⊆ | Subset of or equal to | 2286 | \subseteq |
| ⊃ | Superset of | 2283 | \supset |
| ⊇ | Superset of or equal to | 2287 | \supseteq |
| ∝ | Proportional to | 221D | \propto |
| ≐ | Approaches the limit, definition | 2250 | \doteq |
| → | Tends to, maps to | 2192 | \rightarrow |
| ← | Maps from | 2190 | \leftarrow |
| ↦ | Maps to | 21A6 | \mapsto |
| ↪ | Maps into | 21AA | \hookrightarrow |
| ↩ | Maps into | 21A9 | \hookleftarrow |
| *Operators* | | | |
| ∑ | Summation | 2211 | \sum |
| ∏ | Product | 220F | \prod |
| ∫ | Integral | 222B | \int |
| ∮ | Contour integral | 222E | \oint |

| SIGN/SYMBOL | NAME | UNICODE | LATEX |
|---|---|---|---|
| *Logic* | | | |
| ∧ | And, conjunction | 2227 | \wedge |
| ∨ | Or, disjunction | 2228 | \vee |
| ¬ | Not sign (negation) | 00AC | \neg |
| ⇒ | Implies | 21D2 | \implies |
| → | Implies | 2192 | \rightarrow |
| ⇔ | If and only if | 21D4 | \iff |
| ↔ | If and only if | 2194 | \leftrightarrow |
| ∃ | There exists (existential quantifier) | 2203 | \exists |
| ∀ | For all (universal quantifier) | 2200 | \forall |
| ⊦ | Assertion | 22A6 | \vdash |
| ∴ | Hence, therefore | 2234 | \therefore |
| ∵ | Because | 2235 | \because |
| *Radial units* | | | |
| ′ | Minute (prime) | 2032 | \prime |
| ″ | Second (double prime) | 2033 | \second |
| ° | Degree | 00B0 | \degree |
| *Constants* | | | |
| *π* | Pi (≈3.14159265) | 03C0 | \pi |
| *e* | Base of natural logarithms (≈2.71828183) | 0065 | e |
| *Geometry* | | | |
| ⊥ | Perpendicular to (up tack) | 22A5 | \perp |
| ∥ | Parallel to | 2225 | \parallel |
| ∦ | Not parallel to | 2226 | \nparallel |
| ∠ | Angle | 2220 | \angle |
| ∢ | Spherical angle | 2222 | \sphericalangle |
| ≚ | Equiangular to | 225A | \veedoublebar |
| *Miscellaneous* | | | |
| *i* | Square root of −1 | 0069 | i |
| ′ | Prime | 2032 | \prime |
| ″ | Double prime | 2033 | \second |
| ‴ | Triple prime | 2034 | \third |
| √ | Square root, radical | 221A | \sqrt |
| ∛ | Cube root | 221B | \sqrt[3] |
| ! | Factorial | 0021 | ! |
| ‼ | Double factorial | 203C | !! |
| ∅ | Empty set, null set | 2205 | \varnothing *or* \emptyset |
| ∞ | Infinity | 221E | \infty |
| ∂ | Partial differential | 2202 | \partial |
| ∆ | Increment, Laplace operator | 2206 | \triangle |
| ∇ | Nabla, del; also Laplace operator (with superscript 2) | 2207 | \nabla |
| □ | d'Alembert operator (white square) | 25A1 | \square |

10.71 **Sentence beginning with a mathematical symbol.** Unlike acronyms and initialisms in nonmathematical contexts (see 10.11), mathematical symbols should not begin a sentence, especially if the preceding sentence ended with a symbol, since it may be difficult to tell where one sentence ends and another begins. If a sentence starting with a symbol cannot easily be rephrased, the appropriate term for the symbol can be inserted in apposition at the beginning of the sentence.

Assume that $x \in S$. The set $S$ is countable.
*not*
Assume that $x \in S$. $S$ is countable.

If the sentences are closely related, a semicolon may be used to connect them:

A function $f$ is even if $f(-x) = f(x)$; $f$ is odd if $f(-x) = -f(x)$.

Mathematical symbols in adjacent mathematical expressions should be separated by words or punctuation (or both):

Suppose that $a = bq + r$, where $0 \le r < b$.

For spaces next to mathematical signs for operations and relations, see 6.130. For the use of italics for variables, see 7.73.

## *US Measure*

10.72 **Periods with abbreviations of US measure.** In the rare instances in which abbreviations for US units of measure are used in scientific copy, they are usually set without periods; in nonscientific contexts, periods are customary. See also 10.4.

10.73 **Plural forms for abbreviations of US measure.** Abbreviations of US units of measure, like their scientific counterparts, are identical in the singular and the plural (but see 10.76).

10 yd.    5 lb.    8 sq. mi.

Note that the unit of measure in an expression such as 0.5 yd. or 1.5 yd. used as a noun is generally pronounced as if it were plural (i.e., point five yards; one point five yards; *but* a point-five-yard increment); the singular is reserved for measures of exactly one. See also 10.59.

10.74 **US abbreviations for length, area, and volume.** In the following examples, note that the proper symbols for foot and inch are prime (′) and double prime (″), *not* single (’) and double (”) quotation marks:

| *Length* | | *Area* | | *Volume* | |
|---|---|---|---|---|---|
| in. *or* ″ | inch | sq. in. | square inch | cu. in. | cubic inch |
| ft. *or* ′ | foot | sq. ft. | square foot | cu. ft. | cubic foot |
| yd. | yard | sq. yd. | square yard | cu. yd. | cubic yard |
| rd. | rod | sq. rd. | square rod | | |
| mi. | mile | sq. mi. | square mile | | |

As in expressions of latitude and longitude (see 10.41), there is no space in such expressions as the following (for a height or length of *6 ft., 1 in.*):

6′1″

Exponents are sometimes used with abbreviations to designate area or volume, but only when no ambiguity can occur.

425 $ft.^2$ (= 425 sq. ft. *not* 425 ft. by 425 ft.)  638 $ft.^3$ (= 638 cu. ft.)

10.75 **US abbreviations for weight and capacity.** The US system comprises three systems of weight and mass: avoirdupois (the common system), troy (used mainly by jewelers), and apothecaries’ measure. Although confusion is unlikely, an abbreviation can, if necessary, be referred to the appropriate system thus: lb. av., lb. t., lb. ap. Also, the systems of capacity measure used in the United States and the British Commonwealth differ (an American pint being more than three ounces smaller than a British pint, for example), but the same abbreviations are used.

| *Weight or mass* | | *Dry measure* | |
|---|---|---|---|
| gr. | grain | pt. | pint |
| s. | scruple | qt. | quart |
| dr. | dram | pk. | peck |
| dwt. | pennyweight | bu. | bushel |
| oz. | ounce | | |
| lb. *or* # | pound | | |
| cwt. | hundredweight | | |
| tn. | ton | | |

| | |
|---|---|
| *Liquid measure* | |
| min. *or* ♏ | minim |
| fl. dr. *or* f. ʒ | fluid dram |
| fl. oz. *or* f. ℥ | fluid ounce |
| gi. | gill |
| pt. | pint |
| qt. | quart |
| gal. | gallon |
| bbl. | barrel |

As with length and so forth, abbreviations do not change in the plural.

12 gal.   3 pt.

10.76 **US and general abbreviations for time.** The following abbreviations, though not limited to the US system of measure, are used mainly in nontechnical contexts:

| | |
|---|---|
| sec. | second |
| min. | minute |
| h. *or* hr. | hour |
| d. *or* day | day |
| wk. | week |
| mo. | month |
| yr. | year |

In nontechnical writing, the plurals of these abbreviations, unlike those of length, area, weight, and the like, are often formed by adding an *s*.

5 secs.   12 hrs. *or* 12 h.   15 yrs.

## COMMERCIAL AND SOCIAL ABBREVIATIONS

10.77 **Commercial abbreviations—some examples.** As for many other abbreviations in nonscientific contexts, periods for abbreviations of commercial terms are normally used in lowercased forms (see 10.4). See also 10.48–49, 10.72–76. For company names, see 10.28.

| | |
|---|---|
| acct. | account, -ant |
| agt. | agent |
| a.k.a. | also known as |
| amt. | amount |

| | |
|---|---|
| AP | amounts payable |
| APR | annual percentage rate |
| AR | amounts receivable |
| ASAP | as soon as possible |
| att. | attached, -ment |
| attn. | attention |
| a.v. *or* AV | ad valorem |
| bal. | balance |
| bbl. | barrel(s) |
| bcc | blind carbon copy *or* blind copy, -ies |
| bdl. *or* bdle. | bundle |
| bl. | bale(s) |
| BS | bill of sale |
| bu. | bushel(s) |
| c. *or* ct. | cent |
| cc | carbon copy *or* copy, -ies |
| c.l. *or* CL | carload |
| c/o | in care of |
| COD | cash on delivery |
| COGS | cost of goods sold |
| COLA | cost-of-living adjustment |
| CPI | consumer price index |
| CPM | cost per thousand (*mille*) |
| cr. | credit, -or |
| ctn. | carton |
| cttee. *or* comm. | committee |
| DEI | diversity, equity, and inclusion |
| d/b/a | doing business as |
| dis. | discount |
| dist. | district |
| distr. | distributor, -ion |
| DJIA | Dow Jones Industrial Average |
| doz. | dozen |
| dr. | debtor |
| dstn. | destination |
| ea. | each |
| EEO | equal employment opportunity |
| EOE | equal opportunity employer |
| EOM | end of month |
| exec. | executive |
| f.a.s. *or* FAS | free alongside ship |
| f.o.b. *or* FOB | free on board |
| FY | fiscal year |

| | |
|---|---|
| GAAP | generally accepted accounting principles |
| GL | general ledger |
| GM | general manager; genetically modified |
| gro. | gross |
| inst. | instant (this month) |
| inv. | invoice |
| IPO | initial public offering |
| JIT | just in time |
| LBO | leveraged buyout |
| LCL | less-than-carload lot |
| LIFO | last in, first out |
| M and A *or* M&A | mergers and acquisitions |
| mdse. | merchandise |
| mfg. | manufacturing |
| mfr. | manufacturer |
| mgmt. | management |
| mgr. | manager |
| MO | mail order; money order |
| msg. | message |
| mtg. | meeting |
| mtge. | mortgage |
| NA *or* n/a | not applicable; not available |
| NGO | nongovernmental organization |
| nt. wt. | net weight |
| OJT | on-the-job training |
| OS | operating system; out of stock |
| OTC | over the counter |
| P and H *or* P&H | postage and handling |
| pd. | paid |
| pkg. | package |
| POE | port of embarkation; port of entry |
| POP | point of purchase |
| POS | point of sale; point of service |
| PP | parcel post |
| ppd. | postpaid; prepaid |
| pr. | pair |
| QA | quality assurance |
| Q&A | question and answer |
| QC | quality control |
| qtr. | quarter |
| qty. | quantity |
| ® | registered trademark (see 8.154) |
| recd. *or* rec'd | received |

| | |
|---|---|
| S and H *or* S&H | shipping and handling |
| SM | unregistered service mark |
| std. | standard |
| TBA | to be announced |
| TBD | to be determined |
| ™ | unregistered trademark (see 8.154) |
| treas. | treasurer, -y |
| ult. | ultimo (last month) |
| VAT | value-added tax |
| whsle. | wholesale |

10.78 **Social abbreviations and emojis.** Acronyms and initialisms used in texting and on social media platforms are frequently lowercased in actual usage (see 10.6). In fiction and other creative contexts, the choice of all caps or lowercase (or, at the beginning of a sentence, an initial cap) is generally up to the author, though editors can help ensure consistency.

IMHO *or* imho (in my humble opinion)
LOL *or* lol (laughing out loud)
TL;DR *or* tl;dr (too long; didn't read)
TTYL *or* ttyl (talk to you later)

The use of emojis is also generally up to the author. Editors can help ensure consistency relative to punctuation and spacing (see 6.137). They can also verify that each emoji is rendered as a special character rather than as an image. If an author has used images in the manuscript, these should each be replaced with the corresponding Unicode character; where no such character is available, the emoji may have to be presented as art (see also 2.19). (It should be noted, however, that the appearance of a given emoji may depend on a user's operating system and may be subject to periodic design updates; if the precise historical rendering of a given emoji is required for any reason, an in-line image accompanied by alt text may be used instead. See also 3.28.) Emojipedia .org provides a searchable catalog of emojis with Unicode names and code points; a few of these are listed below. See also 11.2.

| | | |
|---|---|---|
| 😊 | smiling face with smiling eyes | U+1F60A |
| 🔥 | fire | U+1F525 |
| 🙏 | person with folded hands | U+1F64F |

# 11 Languages Other than English

## OVERVIEW

11.1 **Scope and organization.** This chapter provides guidelines for presenting text from languages other than English in English-language contexts. These guidelines are general: Authors or editors working with languages in which they are not expert should seek additional guidance from someone who is. More than two dozen languages are covered, with those languages that commonly appear and those that present complex problems being considered most fully. The chapter begins with the treatment of words and phrases, titles of works, and quotations, the principles of which apply to most of the languages discussed (see 11.3–19). It then addresses languages using the Latin alphabet, transliterated (or romanized) languages, classical Greek, Old English and Middle English, and American Sign Language. Individual languages or groups of languages are presented in alphabetical order within their particular sections. (For the treatment of personal names, see 8.3–19.)

11.2 **Unicode.** Many of the letters and symbols required by the world's languages are included in a widely used standard for character encoding called Unicode. The Unicode standard (published by the Unicode Consortium; bibliog. 2.8) is widely supported by modern operating systems and browsers and many other applications (including word processors) and is required by such standards as XML and EPUB. Unicode assigns a unique identifying hexadecimal number (or code point) and description to tens of thousands of characters. Even fonts with Unicode character mapping, however, typically support only a subset of the Unicode character set. For this reason, it is desirable to determine at the outset which characters will be needed for a publication. Table 11.1 lists special characters, with Unicode numbers and abbreviated descriptions, needed for each of the languages treated in this chapter that use the Latin alphabet. Table 11.2 lists special characters that may be needed for certain transliterated languages. For Russian (Cyrillic) and Greek characters, see tables 11.3, 11.4, and 11.5. Unicode numbers mentioned in text should be prefixed by U+ (e.g., U+00E0 for *à*).

## GENERAL PRINCIPLES

### *Words and Phrases from Other Languages*

11.3 **Non-English words and phrases in an English context.** In works intended primarily for an English-speaking readership, isolated words and phrases from another language are traditionally signaled by italics, especially if they are not listed in a standard English-language dictionary like *Merriam-Webster* (see 7.1) or are likely to be unfamiliar to readers (see also 7.56). This convention is intended to alert readers that such terms would not normally be found in English and can help prevent a non-English word from being misread as an error. Note that this rule does not necessarily apply to non-English words and phrases used by a multilingual author or speaker (as in fictional narrative and dialogue); see 11.4. (For proper nouns, see 11.5.) If an unfamiliar word or phrase becomes familiar through repeated use throughout a work, it need be italicized only on its first occurrence. If it appears only rarely, however, italics may be retained.

The *grève du zèle* is not a true strike but a nitpicking obeying of work rules.
She preferred to think of it optimistically as a *sueño reparador*—rather than, as in English, a sleep that was merely restful.
Obligatory service duty in the Assyrian military organization—known as the *ilku* tax—was imposed on all subjects of the empire, including those in vassal kingdoms.

Unless the term appears in a standard English-language dictionary and is being used as such, observe the capitalization conventions of the original language. In the following examples, the German word for *computer* (which is the same as the English word) is capitalized because it is a noun, and the French adjective *française* is lowercase even though it would be capitalized in English (as "French"). See also 11.20.

In German, a computer is a *Computer*. In French, it is an *ordinateur*. In Spanish, one refers to a *computadora* or an *ordenador*, depending on region or context.
We were prepared to learn the nuances of *la langue française*.

The plurals of non-English words should be formed as in the original language (see also 7.12).

We were sent off with some beautiful *Blumen* (not *Blumes* [italic ess] and not *Blume*s [roman ess]).

An entire sentence or a passage of two or more sentences in another language is usually set in roman and, unless it is set as a block quotation or extract (see 12.9–29), enclosed in quotation marks (see 11.13).

11.4 **Italics in multilingual narratives and dialogue.** Non-English words and phrases that would be familiar to a particular author, narrator, or speaker do not necessarily require italics even if they might be unfamiliar to readers (cf. 11.3). Especially in fiction and related genres, using regular text for words from other languages can help establish a narrator's or character's authenticity. Whether (and when) to use italics in such contexts is ultimately up to the author; editors can help by imposing consistency but should query before making any substantial changes. Note how the Spanish *Mamá* (Mom), *estoy bien* (I'm good), and *hamaca* (hammock), italicized as words in this sentence, are all in roman in the following excerpt from *Of Women and Salt*, a novel by Gabriela Garcia (Flatiron Books, 2021). By drawing attention to the switch from English to Spanish and back, italics would risk making the dialogue seem less realistic.

"Mamá?" . . .

"Estoy bien," she said. "Just faint from the walk. You know I am less and less capable."

"That isn't true."

María Isabel helped Aurelia steady herself with one hand to the wall.

"Mamá." María Isabel touched Aurelia's forehead with the back of her hand, which gave off such a stench of tobacco juice that her mother winced. "Stay out in the breeze and rest in the hamaca, won't you? I'll prepare lunch."

11.5 **Non-English proper nouns in an English context.** With the exception of titles of books and the like, proper nouns from other languages are generally *not* italicized, even on first mention (cf. 11.3). This usage extends to named places and structures, institutions and companies, brand names, and other categories as discussed in chapter 8. (For titles of works, see 11.8–12.) Capitalization should follow predominant usage in the original language. In some cases, this may entail observing a preference for capitalization that runs counter to the conventions for generic text. If the editor is unfamiliar with the language, an expert, or the author, should be consulted; when in doubt, opt for sentence case (see 8.159). See also 11.20. An initial *the* may be used if the definite article would appear in the original language.

She won the Premio Nadal for her second novel, *Viento del norte*.
Mexico City's Ángel de la Independencia is known familiarly as "El Ángel."
The Real Academia Española was founded in 1713.
The French national library is known as the Bibliothèque Nationale. (See 11.29.)
Leghorn—in Italian, Livorno—is a port in Tuscany.
Arashiyama (Mount Arashi) shares its name with the district on the outskirts of Kyoto.
The illustrated book *Unter den Linden Ecke Charlottenstraße*, as its title suggests,

explores the history of the building complex at the intersection of Unter den Linden and Charlottenstraße.

Original (or transliterated) names of proper nouns presented as glosses should not be italicized (but see 11.6).

The number of cases adjudicated by the Supreme People's Court of the People's Republic of China (Zhonghua renmin gongheguo zuigao renmin fayuan) has increased sharply.

**11.6** **Translations of terms from other languages.** A translation following a word, phrase, or title from another language is enclosed in parentheses or quotation marks (or both, as when the parentheses include explanatory text). See also 6.102, 11.3, 11.5, 11.11, 13.101.

The word she wanted was *pécher* (to sin), not *pêcher* (to fish).

The Prakrit word *majjao*, "the tomcat," may be a dialect version of either of two Sanskrit words: *madjaro*, "my lover," or *marjaro*, "the cat" (from the verb *mrij*, "to wash," because the cat constantly washes itself).

A group of German expressionists known as Die Brücke (The Bridge) were influential in the decade leading up to the First World War.

Leonardo Fioravanti's *Compendio de i secreti rationali* (Compendium of rational secrets) became a bestseller.

If a non-English word other than a proper noun is presented as a parenthetical gloss, it should be presented in italics as in running text (but see 11.5).

He said that to fish (*pêcher*) was to sin (*pécher*).

For quotations from other languages, see 11.13–19.

**11.7** **Language tags.** In works published in electronic formats, language tags can make the text more accessible to those who rely on text-to-speech applications. This can be done in HTML by applying tags with "lang" attributes to the relevant text, as in the excerpt below, which features a line of dialogue from the *Of Women and Salt* example reproduced in paragraph 11.4. The tag `<html lang="en">` in the second line specifies English as the language for the document as a whole, using the two-letter ISO 639 language code (see the list from the US Library of Congress, among other sources); the `<span lang="es">` tag in the sixth line switches the text to Spanish for the phrase "Estoy bien" (the ellipsis dots stand in for the rest of the document, not shown here). Responsibility for adding such tags usually falls to the publisher (who in turn may delegate this task to a copyeditor); authors, however, can help by highlighting or otherwise identifying non-English words, phrases, and excerpts in their manuscripts (e.g., using a word-processing style defined for that purpose; see also 2.87).

```
<!DOCTYPE html>

<html lang="en">

. . .

<body>

. . .

    <p>“<span lang="es">Estoy bien</span>,” she said.
    “Just faint from the walk. You know I am less and
    less capable.”</p>

. . .

</body>

</html>
```

## *Titles of Works from Other Languages*

11.8 **Capitalization of titles from other languages.** For titles of works from other languages, whether these appear in text, notes, or bibliographies, Chicago recommends a simple rule: Capitalize only the words that would be capitalized in normal prose, including the first word of the title and subtitle and all proper nouns and other terms that would be capitalized under the conventions of the original language. That is, use *sentence case* (see 8.159). This rule applies equally to titles using the Latin alphabet and to transliterated titles. For examples, see 13.100. For special considerations related to German capitalization, see 11.42. For variations in French, see 11.30.

11.9 **Punctuation of titles from other languages.** When a non-English title is included in an English-language context, the following changes are permissible: A period (or, more rarely, a semicolon) between title and subtitle may be changed to a colon (and the first word of the subtitle may be capitalized); guillemets (« ») or other non-English styles for quotation marks may be changed to regular quotation marks (“ ” or ‘ ’); and any space between a word and a mark of punctuation that follows may be eliminated. Commas should not be inserted (even in a series or before dates) or deleted, nor should any other mark of punctuation be added or deleted. See also 8.167.

11.10 **Italic versus roman type for titles from other languages.** Titles of works in languages that use the Latin alphabet (including transliterated titles) are set in italic or roman type according to the principles set forth in 8.157–204—for example, books and periodicals in italic; poems and other short works in roman.

Stendhal’s *Le rouge et le noir* was required reading in my senior year.
We picked up a copy of the *Neue Zürcher Zeitung* to read on the train.
She published her article in the *Annales de démographie historique*.
Strains of the German carol “Es ist ein’ Ros’ entsprungen” reached our ears.
Miguel Hernández’s poem “Casida del sediento” has been translated as “Lament of the Thirsting Man.”

11.11 **Non-English titles with English translation.** When the title of a work in another language is mentioned in text, an English gloss may follow in parentheses (see 6.102). If the translation has not been published, the English should be capitalized in sentence case (as in the first example below; see 8.159) and should appear neither in italics nor within quotation marks. A published translation, however, is capitalized in title case (as in the second and third examples; see 8.160) and appears in italics or quotation marks depending on the type of work (see 8.157–204). Some editorial discretion may be required, especially if the translation is incorporated into running text (as in the third example). For translations of non-English titles in notes and bibliographies, see 13.101. See also 11.12.

Leonardo Fioravanti’s *Compendio de i secreti rationali* (Compendium of rational secrets) became a bestseller.
Proust’s *À la recherche du temps perdu* (*Remembrance of Things Past*) was the subject of her dissertation.
*but*
*La ciudad y los perros*, which literally means “the city and the dogs,” was published in English under the title *The Time of the Hero*.

11.12 **Original-language title of work versus translation.** Readership and context will determine whether to use the original or the translated title of a non-English work mentioned in running text. In a general work, titles that are widely known in their English translation could be cited in English first, with the original following in parentheses; in some cases, the original can be omitted entirely. Some authors prefer to cite all non-English titles in an English form, whether or not they have appeared in English translation. As long as the documentation clarifies what has been published in English and what has not, translated titles standing in for the original may be capitalized in title case and treated like other English-language titles (see 8.160, 8.164). See also 11.11.

"The West" in the title of the Chinese classic *Journey to the West* (*Xī yóu jì*) refers mainly to the Indian subcontinent.

Molière's comedy *The Miser* may have drawn on an obscure late-medieval French treatise, *The Evils of Greed*, recently discovered in an abandoned château.

## *Quotations from Other Languages*

11.13 **Typographic style of quotations from other languages.** Quotations from a language other than English that are incorporated into an English text are normally treated like quotations in English, set in roman type and run in or set off as block quotations according to their length. (For a complete discussion of quotations, see chapter 12.) They are punctuated as in the original except that quotation marks can usually replace guillemets (or their equivalents), and punctuation relative to quotation marks and spacing relative to punctuation are adjusted to conform to the surrounding text (see 11.21). For isolated words and phrases, see 11.3. For excerpts from the original language following an English translation, see 11.14.

The narrator's "treinta o cuarenta molinos de viento" become Quixote's "treinta, o pocos más, desaforados gigantes," a numerical correspondence that lets the reader trust, at the very least, the hero's basic grasp of reality.

If em dashes rather than quotation marks are used for dialogue in the original (see 11.34, 11.54, 11.71, 11.110), they should be retained in a block quotation but may be replaced by quotation marks if only a phrase or sentence is quoted in running text.

11.14 **Translations relative to quotations.** A translation may follow the original in parentheses—or, as in 11.15, the original may follow a translation. Quotation marks need not be repeated for the parenthetical translation (or parenthetical original, as the case may be); any internal quotation marks, however, should be included (as in the second example below). See also 6.102, 11.6. If a long sentence or more than one sentence appears in parentheses or brackets, as in the second example, closing punctuation of the original and the translation should remain distinct.

A line from Goethe, "Wer nie sein Brot mit Tränen aß" (Who never ate his bread with tears), comes to mind.

À vrai dire, Abélard n'avoue pas un tel rationalisme: "je ne veux pas être si philosophe, écrit-il, que je résiste à Paul, ni si aristotélicien que je me sépare du Christ." (As a matter of fact, Abelard admits no such rationalism. "I do not wish to be so much of a philosopher," he writes, "that I resist Paul, nor so much of an Aristotelian that I separate myself from Christ.")

Whether to provide translations of quoted passages depends on the linguistic abilities of the intended audience. For example, in a work to be read by classicists, Latin or Greek sources may be quoted freely in the original. Or in a literary study of, say, Goethe, quotations from Goethe's work may be given in the original German only. For a wider readership, translations should be furnished.

11.15 **Source of quotation plus translation.** When both a source and a translation are required in text, the source may be placed in parentheses, with the original (or translation, as the case may be) following, separated by a semicolon. The following example quotes a thirteenth-century author writing in Middle Dutch. See also 12.79–80.

Hadewijch insists that the most perfect faith is "unfaith," which endlessly stokes desire and endlessly demands love from God. "Unfaith never allows desire to rest in any faith but always distrusts her, [feeling] that she is not loved enough" (letter 8:39; Ende ontrowe en laet gegherten niewers ghedueren in gheenre trowen, sine mestrout hare altoes, datse niet ghenoech ghemint en es).

If adding a translation or the original in text creates too much clutter, it may be placed in a note, in which case it is enclosed in quotation marks but not in parentheses or brackets. If the parenthetical passage in the second example in 11.14 were to appear in text without the French, as either a run-in or a block quotation, a note could read as follows:

1. "À vrai dire, Abélard n'avoue pas un tel rationalisme: 'je ne veux pas être si philosophe, écrit-il, que je résiste à Paul, ni si aristotélicien que je me sépare du Christ.'"

See also 12.30.

11.16 **Crediting the translation of a quoted passage.** When quoting a passage from a language that requires a translation, authors should use a published English translation if one is available and give credit to the source of that translation, including the title of the translation, the translator's name, relevant bibliographic details, and page number (see 13.101). Authors providing their own translations should so state, in parentheses following the translation, in a note, or in the prefatory material—for example, "my translation" or "Unless otherwise noted, all translations are my own." If an individual other than the author provided the translations, that person should be credited in a similar manner, but by name. If the source is a machine translation, that service should be credited—for example, "Translations generated by DeepL and edited by the author." See also 11.11.

11.17 **Adjusting translated quotations.** An author using a published translation may occasionally need to adjust a word or two; "translation modified" or some such wording must then be added in parentheses or in a note (see also 12.73). In addition, it is recommended that such modifications be indicated by square brackets (see 12.70, 12.71). These devices should be used sparingly. If a published translation is unsuitable for the author's purpose, it should be abandoned and all quoted passages newly translated. Machine translations may be edited without the use of square brackets, though authors should note whether any changes were made (see 11.16).

11.18 **Editing translated quotations.** Quotations from published translations can be modified only with respect to the permissible changes described in 12.7. In new translations furnished by the author, however (including an author's edited version of a machine translation), capitalization, punctuation, spelling, and idiom may be adjusted for consistency with the surrounding text.

11.19 **Avoiding retranslation.** Never should a passage from a work originally published in English (or any other language, for that matter) be retranslated from a version that has been translated into another language. For example, an author quoting from a German study of Blackstone's *Commentaries* that quotes from Blackstone in German must track down the original Blackstone passages in English and reproduce them. If unable to locate the original, the author must resort to paraphrase.

## LANGUAGES USING THE LATIN ALPHABET

11.20 **Capitalization—English versus other languages.** Capitalization is applied to more classes of words in English than in any other Western language (but see 8.1). Most of the other languages discussed in this chapter follow a simpler set of rules. Except where stated to the contrary, the language in question is assumed to lowercase all adjectives (except those used as proper nouns), all pronouns, months, and days of the week. In addition, capitals are used more sparingly than in English for names of offices, institutions, and so on. Translated terms, however, are subject to Chicago's recommendations for capitalization of names and terms (see chapter 8). For personal names, see 8.3–19.

11.21 **Punctuation—original-language versus English context.** The remarks in this chapter related to punctuation point out the more obvious departures from what is familiar to readers of English. For the purposes of illustration, quotation marks in the style of the original language have been preserved in the examples; however, spacing relative to these and other punctuation marks has been adjusted to conform to the typographic style of this manual. In quotations from other languages (and in translations), regular English-style quotation marks can usually replace the guillemets or whatever is used in the original (with the placement of periods and commas adjusted as needed; see 6.9–11). Dashes used to mark dialogue, however, should be preserved in block quotations presented in the original language. See 11.13. Another exception is the punctuation at the beginning of Spanish questions and exclamations (see 11.69), which should be preserved for quotations in Spanish (but omitted when the passage is translated).

11.22 **Word division for languages other than English.** Though conventions for dividing words at the ends of lines vary widely, the following general rules apply to non-English languages as well as to English: (1) Single-syllable words should never be broken. (2) No words should be broken after one letter, nor should a single letter be carried over to another line (see also 7.37). (3) Hyphenated words and closed compounds should be broken at the hyphen or between elements, if at all possible. See also 7.40; for proper nouns, see 7.42. Specific rules for some of the languages covered in this chapter appear in the relevant sections below.

11.23 **Special characters in the Latin alphabet.** Words, phrases, or titles from another language that occur in an English-language work must include any special characters that appear in the original language. Those languages that use the Latin alphabet may include letters with accents and other diacritical marks, ligatures, and, in some cases, alphabetical forms that do not normally occur in English. Table 11.1 lists the special characters that might be required for each language treated in this section. Most authors will have access to Unicode-compliant software (see 11.2) and will therefore be able to reproduce each of these characters without the addition of any specialized fonts. Authors should nonetheless supply a list of special characters used within a manuscript (see 2.19) to ensure the correct conversion to a particular font required for publication or, for electronic projects, to ensure compatibility across operating systems and devices. If type is to be reproduced from an author's hard copy, marginal clarifications may be needed for handwritten accents or special characters. In either case, use table 11.1 to correctly identify the character by name and Unicode number (e.g., for *Đ* or *đ*, indicate "D with stroke [U+0110]" or "d with stroke [U+0111]"). For diacritical marks used in transliteration, see 11.81.

11.24 **International Phonetic Alphabet (IPA).** Phonetic symbols using IPA notation are based on the Latin alphabet and are defined for Unicode (see 11.2). For the latest version of the IPA alphabet, consult the website of the International Phonetic Association. For additional information on the subject of phonetics, including treatment of other systems of notation, consult Geoffrey K. Pullum and William A. Ladusaw, *Phonetic Symbol Guide* (bibliog. 5).

## *African Languages*

11.25 **African capitalization and punctuation.** Most African languages—with the exception, most notably, of Arabic (see 11.83–88)—use the Latin alphabet and follow English capitalization and punctuation. The most widespread of these is Swahili, spoken by many different ethnic groups in eastern and central Africa. Hausa, Fulfulde, Yoruba, Igbo, Wolof, and Bambara are also spoken by millions, largely in western Africa; the same is true for Kikongo (or Kongo) and Lingala in the Congo-Zaire region and of Amharic and Somali in the Horn of Africa region. Amharic and other Ethiopian Semitic languages such as Tigrinya use the Geʻez alphabet, not covered here. Xhosa and other "click" languages spoken in southern Africa do not follow English capitalization. The names of African languages themselves vary widely from ethnic group to ethnic

TABLE 11.1. Special characters (and Unicode numbers) for languages using the Latin alphabet

| Character (and Unicode number) | Description | Languages that use it |
|---|---|---|
| „ (201E), " (201C) | double low-9 quotation mark, left double quotation mark | German |
| « (00AB), » (00BB) | double angle quotation marks (guillemets) | French, German (reversed), Italian, Spanish |
| ' (2018) | 'okina (represented by a left single quotation mark) | Hawaiian |
| ' (2019) | glottal stop and consonant marker (represented by an apostrophe) | Navajo |
| À (00C0), à (00E0) | A/a with grave | French, Italian, Portuguese |
| Á (00C1), á (00E1) | A/a with acute | Czech, Hungarian, Icelandic, Navajo, Portuguese, Spanish |
| Â (00C2), â (00E2) | A/a with circumflex | French, Moldovan, Portuguese, Romanian, Turkish |
| Ã (00C3), ã (00E3) | A/a with tilde | Portuguese |
| Ä (00C4), ä (00E4) | A/a with diaeresis | Finnish, German, Swedish, Turkmen |
| Å (00C5), å (00E5) | A/a with ring above | Finnish, Danish, Norwegian, Swedish |
| Ā (0100), ā (0101) | A/a with macron | Hawaiian, Latin |
| Ă (0102), ă (0103) | A/a with breve | Latin, Moldovan, Romanian |
| Ą (0104), ą (0105) | A/a with ogonek | Navajo, Polish |
| Ą́ (0104+0301), ą́ (0105+0301) | A/a with ogonek and combining acute | Navajo |
| Æ (00C6), æ (00E6) | ligature Æ/æ | Danish, Icelandic, Norwegian, Old English and Middle English |
| Ɓ (0181), ɓ (0253) | B/b with hook | Hausa |
| Ç (00C7), ç (00E7) | C/c with cedilla | Albanian, Azeri, French, Portuguese, Turkish, Turkmen |
| Ć (0106), ć (0107) | C/c with acute | Bosnian, Croatian, Montenegrin, Polish, Serbian |
| Č (010C), č (010D) | C/c with caron (haček) | Bosnian, Croatian, Czech, Montenegrin, Serbian |
| Ð (00D0), ð (00F0) | eth | Icelandic, Old English and Middle English |
| Ď (010E), ď (010F) | D/d with caron (haček) | Czech |
| Đ (0110), đ (0111) | D/d with stroke | Bosnian, Croatian, Montenegrin, Serbian |
| Ɗ (018A), ɗ (0257) | D/d with hook | Hausa |
| È (00C8), è (00E8) | E/e with grave | French, Italian, Portuguese |
| É (00C9), é (00E9) | E/e with acute | Czech, French, Hungarian, Icelandic, Italian, Navajo, Portuguese, Spanish |
| Ê (00CA), ê (00EA) | E/e with circumflex | French, Portuguese |
| Ë (00CB), ë (00EB) | E/e with diaeresis | Albanian, French |
| Ē (0112), ē (0113) | E/e with macron | Hawaiian, Latin |

*(continued)*

TABLE 11.1 (*continued*)

| Character (and Unicode number) | Description | Languages that use it |
|---|---|---|
| Ĕ (0114), ĕ (0115) | E/e with breve | Latin |
| Ě (011A), ě (011B) | E/e with caron (haček) | Czech |
| Ę (0118), ę (0119) | E/e with ogonek | Navajo, Polish |
| Ę́ (0118+0301), ę́ (0119+0301) | E/e with ogonek and combining acute | Navajo |
| Ȝ (021C), ȝ (021D) | yogh | Old English and Middle English |
| Ə (018F), ə (0259) | schwa | Azeri |
| Ğ (011E), ğ (011F) | G/g with breve | Azeri, Turkish |
| Ì (00CC), ì (00EC) | I/i with grave | Italian, Portuguese |
| Í (00CD), í (00ED) | I/i with acute | Czech, Hungarian, Icelandic, Navajo, Portuguese, Spanish |
| Î (00CE), î (00EE) | I/i with circumflex | French, Moldovan, Romanian, Turkish |
| Ï (00CF), ï (00EF) | I/i with diaeresis | French, Portuguese |
| Ī (012A), ī (012B) | I/i with macron | Hawaiian, Latin |
| Ĭ (012C), ĭ (012D) | I/i with breve | Latin |
| Į (012E), į (012F) | I/i with ogonek | Navajo |
| Į́ (012E+0301), į́ (012F+0301) | I/i with ogonek and combining acute | Navajo |
| İ (0130) | I with dot above | Azeri, Turkish |
| ı (0131) | dotless i | Azeri, Turkish |
| Ƙ (0198), ƙ (0199) | K/k with hook | Hausa |
| Ł (0141), ł (0142) | L/l with stroke | Navajo, Polish |
| Ñ (00D1), ñ (00F1) | N/n with tilde | Spanish |
| Ń (0143), ń (0144) | N/n with acute | Navajo, Polish |
| Ň (0147), ň (0148) | N/n with caron (haček) | Czech, Turkmen |
| Ò (00D2), ò (00F2) | O/o with grave | Italian, Portuguese |
| Ó (00D3), ó (00F3) | O/o with acute | Czech, Hungarian, Icelandic, Navajo, Polish, Portuguese, Spanish |
| Ô (00D4), ô (00F4) | O/o with circumflex | French, Portuguese |
| Õ (00D5), õ (00F5) | O/o with tilde | Portuguese |
| Ö (00D6), ö (00F6) | O/o with diaeresis | Azeri, Finnish, German, Hungarian, Icelandic, Swedish, Turkish, Turkmen |
| Ø (00D8), ø (00F8) | O/o with stroke | Danish, Norwegian |
| Ō (014C), ō (014D) | O/o with macron | Hawaiian, Latin |
| Ŏ (014E), ŏ (014F) | O/o with breve | Latin |
| Ǫ (01EA), ǫ (01EB) | O/o with ogonek | Navajo |
| Ǫ́ (01EA+0301), ǫ́ (01EB+0301) | O/o with ogonek and combining acute | Navajo |
| Ő (0150), ő (0151) | O/o with double acute | Hungarian |
| Œ (0152), œ (0153) | ligature Œ/œ | French |
| Ř (0158), ř (0159) | R/r with caron (haček) | Czech |
| Ś (015A), ś (015B) | S/s with acute | Montenegrin, Polish |

TABLE 11.1 *(continued)*

| Character (and Unicode number) | Description | Languages that use it |
|---|---|---|
| Ş (015E), ş (015F) | S/s with cedilla | Azeri, Turkish, Turkmen |
| Ș (0218), ș (0219) | S/s with comma below | Moldovan, Romanian |
| Š (0160), š (0161) | S/s with caron (haček) | Bosnian, Croatian, Czech, Montenegrin, Serbian |
| ẞ (1E9E), ß (00DF) | sharp S/s (eszett) | German |
| Ț (021A), ț (021B) | T/t with comma below | Moldovan, Romanian |
| Ť (0164), ť (0165) | T/t with caron (haček) | Czech |
| Þ (00DE), þ (00FE) | thorn | Icelandic, Old English and Middle English |
| Ù (00D9), ù (00F9) | U/u with grave | French, Italian, Portuguese |
| Ú (00DA), ú (00FA) | U/u with acute | Czech, Hungarian, Icelandic, Portuguese, Spanish |
| Û (00DB), û (00FB) | U/u with circumflex | French, Turkish |
| Ü (00DC), ü (00FC) | U/u with diaeresis | Azeri, French, German, Hungarian, Portuguese, Spanish, Turkish, Turkmen |
| Ů (016E), ů (016F) | U/u with ring above | Czech |
| Ū (016A), ū (016B) | U/u with macron | Hawaiian, Latin |
| Ŭ (016C), ŭ (016D) | U/u with breve | Latin |
| Ű (0170), ű (0171) | U/u with double acute | Hungarian |
| Ý (00DD), ý (00FD) | Y/y with acute | Czech, Icelandic, Turkmen |
| Ƴ (01B3), ƴ (01B4) | Y/y with hook | Hausa |
| Ź (0179), ź (017A) | Z/z with acute | Montenegrin, Polish |
| Ż (017B), ż (017C) | Z/z with dot above | Polish |
| Ž (017D), ž (017E) | Z/z with caron (haček) | Bosnian, Croatian, Czech, Montenegrin, Serbian, Turkmen |

group and from region to region. It is now standard practice to capitalize the names of African languages in the conventional way—for example, Kiswahili rather than KiSwahili or KISwahili. Xhosa speakers refer to and spell their language "isiXhosa" but "Isixhosa" (sometimes "Isizhosa") is also found in English-language publications.

11.26 **African special characters.** Swahili uses no additional letters or diacritics. Among the more than two thousand other African languages, however, many rely on diacritics and phonetic symbols to stand for sounds that cannot be represented by letters or combinations of letters. Hausa, which is spoken by millions of people across western Africa, requires the following special characters (see also table 11.1):

Ɓɓ, Ɗɗ, Ƙƙ, Ƴƴ

In Nigeria, both the upper- and the lowercase *y* with a "hook" are represented instead with an apostrophe (*'Y'y*). Additional diacritics, too numerous to be listed here, may be needed in other African languages. Languages such as French, Portuguese, and Arabic that are used in Africa are addressed in separate sections in this chapter.

## *French*

11.27 **French — additional resources.** As is the case with many languages, there is considerable variation in French publications with respect to capitalization and punctuation. For excellent advice, with frequent reference to the Académie Française and numerous examples from literature, consult the latest edition of *Le bon usage,* known to many by the name of its original editor, Maurice Grevisse (bibliog. 5). Further guidance may be had at the website of the Académie Française.

11.28 **French capitalization.** In a French context, generic words denoting roadways, squares, and the like are lowercased, whether used alone or with a specific name as part of an address. Only the proper name is capitalized. For usage in an English context, where certain generic terms may also be capitalized, see 11.29.

le boulevard Saint-Germain    la place de l'Opéra    13, rue des Beaux-Arts

In most geographic names, the generic word is lowercased and the modifying word capitalized.

la mer Rouge    le pic du Midi

Names of buildings are usually capitalized.

l'Hôtel des Invalides    le Palais du Louvre

In names of organizations and institutions, only the first substantive and any preceding modifier are capitalized, but not the preceding article (except at the beginning of a sentence).

l'Académie française (but see 11.29)
la Bibliothèque nationale de France (but see 11.29)
la Légion d'honneur
le Grand Théâtre de Québec

In hyphenated names, both elements are capitalized.

la Comédie-Française    la Haute-Loire

Names of religious groups are usually lowercased.

un chrétien    des juifs

In names of saints, the word *saint* is lowercased. But when a saint's name is used as part of a place-name or the name of a church or other institution, *saint* is capitalized and hyphenated to the following element.

le supplice de saint Pierre    *but*    l'église de Saint-Pierre

Adjectives formed from proper nouns are usually lowercased.

une imagination baudelairienne

See also 11.20.

11.29 **French capitalization in an English context.** As an aid to legibility, many of the types of proper nouns discussed in 11.28 can be capitalized in title case in an English context, subject to editorial discretion (see also 8.160). This usage should be reserved for the names of organizations and other proper nouns that are being retained in French (often preceded by *the*) rather than translated into English. When in doubt, use sentence case.

the Boulevard Saint-Germain
the Académie Française
the Bibliothèque Nationale de France
*but*
the Legion of Honor (Légion d'honneur)

11.30 **Titles of French works.** French publications vary in the way they capitalize titles of works. In general, Chicago recommends sentence case (see 8.159), the rule followed by Grevisse, *Le bon usage* (see 11.8, 11.27). Note that a superscript ordinal letter should remain in the superior position, as in the sixth example below (cf. 13.90). An exception may be made for the French newspaper *Le Monde*, which always appears thus.

*L'Apollon de Bellac: Pièce en un acte*
*L'assommoir*
*L'exil et le royaume*
*Les Rougon-Macquart*
*Le père Goriot*
*Paris au XX*$^{e}$ *siècle*
but
*Le Monde*

According to an alternative practice advocated by the Académie Française and others (and exemplified by the title *Le Monde*), for titles beginning with a definite article (*Le*, *La*, *L'*, *Les*), the article and the first substantive (noun or noun form) and any intervening modifier are capitalized (e.g., *La Grande Illusion*). Titles that begin with a modifier are treated in the same way, with the modifier and first substantive capitalized (e.g., *Mauvais Sang*); any other titles, including those beginning with an indefinite article (*Un*, *Une*) are capitalized in sentence case (e.g., "Un cœur simple"). This style, if adopted for French titles, should be used consistently. For punctuation in titles, see 11.9.

11.31 **Spacing with French punctuation.** In French typeset material, thin spaces generally occur before colons, semicolons, question marks, and exclamation points; between guillemets (« ») and the text they enclose (see 11.32); and after an em dash used to introduce dialogue (see 11.34). In electronic documents, nonbreaking spaces can be used to avoid stranding a mark at the beginning of a line or, in the case of an opening guillemet, at the end (see 6.129). In an English context, the typographic conventions of the publication as a whole can be observed, and such spacing need not be duplicated. (If for any reason French spacing is required, however, it must be followed consistently and according to French practice for all marks.) See also 11.21.

11.32 **French use of guillemets.** For quotation marks, the French use guillemets (« »), often with a thin space (or, especially in electronic documents, a regular nonbreaking space; see 6.129) to separate the guillemets from the quoted matter. If such guillemets are retained in an English context, as for a quotation in French (but see 11.21), they can usually be spaced like regular quotation marks, as in the examples below (see also 11.31). Such tags as *écrit-il* or *dit-elle* are often inserted within the quoted matter without additional guillemets. Only punctuation belonging to the quoted matter is placed within the closing guillemets; other punctuation follows them.

«Mission accomplie?» a-t-il demandé.

En ce sens, «avec» signifie «au moyen de».

À vrai dire, Abélard n'avoue pas un tel rationalisme: «je ne veux pas être si philosophe, écrit-il, que je résiste à Paul, ni si aristotélicien que je me sépare du Christ».

As in English (see 12.32), when a quotation (other than a block quotation) continues for more than one paragraph, opening guillemets appear at the beginning of each additional paragraph; closing guillemets appear only at the end of the last paragraph. See also 11.33.

11.33 **Quotation marks in French.** For quotations within quotations, double (or sometimes single) quotation marks are used. Formerly, additional guillemets were used, with opening guillemets repeated on each runover line. (Note that when guillemets are used, if the two quotations end simultaneously, only one set of closing guillemets appears.) See also 11.32.

> «Comment peux-tu dire, "Montre-nous le père"?»

Regular quotation marks are sometimes seen in French contexts in lieu of guillemets—especially in email correspondence and other electronic settings. This usage is considered informal.

11.34 **French dialogue.** In dialogue, guillemets are often replaced by em dashes. In French publications, the dash is usually followed by a thin space; in English publications, the space is not necessary (see 11.31). Such dashes are used before each successive speech but are not repeated at the end of a speech. To set off a quotation within a speech, guillemets may be used. See also 11.32.

> —Vous viendrez aussitôt que possible? a-t-il demandé.
> —Tout de suite.
> —Bien. Bonne chance!

> —Tu connais sans doute la parole «De l'abondance du cœur la bouche parle».
> —Non, je ne la connais pas.

11.35 **French ellipses.** The French often use an ellipsis to indicate an interruption or break in thought. An ellipsis is also sometimes used in lieu of *and so forth*. In French practice, an ellipsis consists of three unspaced dots closed up to the word they follow (*like* this... *rather than* this . . .); in English contexts, they may be spaced in the manner recommended elsewhere in this manual (see 12.59–69) and shown in the examples below. See also 11.21.

> «Ce n'est pas que je n'aime plus l'Algérie . . . mon Dieu! un ciel! des arbres! . . . et le reste! . . . Toutefois, sept ans de discipline . . .»

To indicate omissions, the French use unspaced ellipses enclosed in brackets, with thin spaces between the brackets and the dots. In English contexts, spaced periods may be used (but with no space between the brackets and the periods they enclose; see 12.67).

«Oh, dit-elle avec un mépris écrasant, des changements intellectuels! [. . .]»
Les deux amis se réunissaient souvent chez Luc [. . .].

11.36 **French word division — vowels.** In French, a word is divided after a vowel wherever possible. One-letter syllables at the ends or beginnings of lines should be avoided (see 11.22).

ache-ter (*not* a-cheter)    in-di-vi-si-bi-li-té    tri-age

Two or more vowels forming a single sound, or diphthong, are never broken.

écri-vain    fouet-ter    Gau-guin    éloi-gner    vieux

11.37 **French word division — consonants.** A division is normally made between two adjacent consonants, whether the same or different.

| | | |
|---|---|---|
| der-riè-re | Mal-raux | *but* |
| feuil-le-ter | ob-jet | qua-tre |
| ba-lan-cer | par-ler | ta-bleau |

Groups of three adjacent consonants are normally divided after the first.

es-prit    res-plen-dir

11.38 **French words containing apostrophes.** Division should never be made immediately after an apostrophe.

jus-qu'au
au-jour-d'hui

11.39 **French words best left undivided.** Since there are as many syllables in French as there are vowels or diphthongs (even if some are unsounded except in poetry), the French break words that appear to English speakers to be of only one syllable (e.g., *fui-te*, *guer-re*, *sor-tent*). French practice also permits division after one letter (e.g., *é-tait*). In English-language publications, however, such breaks should be avoided, since they may confuse readers not fluent in French. Words of four or fewer letters should in any case be left undivided. See also 7.37.

11.40 **French accents and ligatures.** French employs the following special characters (see also table 11.1):

À à, Â â, Ç ç, É é, È è, Ê ê, Ë ë, Î î, Ï ï, Ô ô, Œ œ, Ù ù, Û û, Ü ü

Although French publishers have often omitted accents on capital letters (especially *A*) and may set the ligature *Œ* as two separate letters (*OE*), all the special characters needed for French—including capitalized forms—are widely available, and they should be retained wherever needed in English-language contexts. This practice, advocated by the Académie Française, is especially helpful to readers who may not be familiar with French typographic usage.

## *German*

11.41 **The new German orthography.** The new rules for German orthography (including spelling and capitalization) adopted in 1998 and made mandatory for schools and public documents in 2005 (subject to certain revisions) have been controversial. Some publications have continued to follow traditional rules, or a combination of house style and traditional rules, whereas others have adopted the new rules. Some book publishers honor the preference of their authors and, by a similar token, do not update spelling when reprinting older works. Material quoted from German should therefore reflect the spelling in the source. For principles and details of the new orthography, consult the latest edition of *Duden: Die deutsche Rechtschreibung* (bibliog. 5). The recommendations and examples in this section reflect the new orthography.

11.42 **German capitalization.** In German, all nouns and words used as nouns are capitalized, whether in ordinary sentences or in titles of works (see 11.8).

| | |
|---|---|
| ein Haus | Deutsch (the German language) |
| die Weltanschauung | eine Deutsche (a German woman) |
| das Sein | etwas Schönes |

Adjectives derived from proper names are generally lowercased. Exceptions include invariable adjectives ending in *er* (often referring to a city or region) and adjectives that themselves are part of a proper name. For further exceptions, consult *Duden* (see 11.41).

die deutsche Literatur
nordamerikanische Sprachen
die platonischen Dialoge
*but*
eine berühmte Berliner Straße
der Nahe Osten
der Deutsch-Französische Krieg

The pronouns *Sie, Ihr,* and *Ihnen,* as polite second-person forms, are capitalized. As third-person pronouns they are lowercased. The familiar second-person forms *du, dich, dein, ihr, euch,* and so on—once routinely capitalized—are now lowercased.

11.43 **German apostrophes.** An apostrophe is used to denote the colloquial omission of *e.*

wie geht's  was gibt's  hab' ich

Although an apostrophe rarely appears before a genitive *s,* an apostrophe is used to denote the omission of the *s* after proper names ending in an *s* sound (*ce, s, ss, ß, tz, x,* or *z*) or in a silent *s, x,* or *z.*

Alice' Geburtstag  Cixous' Theaterstücke
Jaspers' Philosophie  Leibniz' Meinung

11.44 **German quotation marks.** In German, quotation marks (called *Anführungszeichen* or, more commonly, *Gänsefüßchen*—literally, goose feet) usually take the form of reversed guillemets (» «); split-level inverted quotation marks („ “); or, in Switzerland, regular guillemets (« »). (Single versions of these marks—› ‹ and ‚ ‘ and ‹ ›—may be used for quotations within quotations.) Other punctuation is placed outside the closing quotation marks unless it belongs to the quoted matter.

*Eros* bedeutet für sie primär »zusammen-sein mit« und nicht »anschauen«.
Denn: „An die Pferde“, hieß es: „Aufgesessen!“

11.45 **German word division—vowels.** In German, division is made after a vowel wherever possible. See also 11.22.

Fa-brik  hü-ten  Bu-ße

Two vowels forming a single sound, or diphthong, are never broken.

| | |
|---|---|
| Lau-ne | blei-ben |

Further, a break should never be made after a single vowel at the beginning or end of a word (*aber*, *Ofen*, *Treue*).

11.46 **German word division — consonants.** Two or more adjacent consonants, whether the same or different, are divided before the last one unless they belong to different parts of a compound (see also 11.22).

| | |
|---|---|
| klir-ren | Meis-ter |
| Was-ser | *but* |
| Verwand-te | Morgen-stern |

The consonant combinations *ch*, *ck*, *ph*, *sch*, and *th* are not divided unless they belong to separate syllables. (Until the 1998 spelling change, *st* was subject to this rule. The combination *ck*, on the other hand, used to be changed at the end of a line to *kk* and divided between the *k*'s.)

| | |
|---|---|
| Mäd-chen | *but* |
| Zu-cker | Klapp-hut |
| Philo-so-phie | Häus-chen |
| rau-schen | |

11.47 **German word division — compounds.** Compound words should be divided between their component elements whenever possible (see also 11.22).

| | |
|---|---|
| Meeres-ufer | Rasier-apparat |
| mit-einander | Tür-angel |

11.48 **German special characters.** For setting German in roman type (the old Gothic or Fraktur type having long been out of use), the eszett, or sharp *s* (*ß*), and three umlauted vowels are needed (see also table 11.1).

Ä ä, Ö ö, ẞ ß, Ü ü

Although umlauted vowels are occasionally represented by omitting the accent and adding an *e* (*ae*, *Oe*, etc.), the availability of umlauted characters in text-editing software makes such a practice unnecessary. The eszett (*ß*), also widely available, must not be confused with, or replaced by, the Greek beta (β); the capital form (*ẞ*, U+1E9E) was officially adopted in 2017. In the new spelling these are replaced by *ss* (or *SS* in an all-caps context) in certain words. Consult a German dictionary published after 1998. In German-speaking areas of Switzerland, the eszett is rarely used.

## *Indigenous Languages*

11.49 **Additional resources for Indigenous languages.** Writers and editors working with Indigenous languages should have a knowledge of the languages in question or rely on someone who does. Capitalization can be especially important in works by or about Indigenous peoples. For words and phrases written in an Indigenous language, English-style capitalization may be appropriate (i.e., for proper nouns and the like); however, editors should defer to an author's usage preferences whenever possible (see also 11.52). It should be noted that in English, many terms that might be lowercase in other contexts are capitalized in reference to Indigenous peoples and cultures. For example, *Elder, Longhouse* (the institution but not the structure), and *Oral Tradition* are frequently capitalized, as are many other such terms. See Gregory Younging's *Elements of Indigenous Style* (bibliog. 1.1), which provides a good overview of such editorial matters. (For terms like *Indigenous*, see 8.39.) In addition to capitalization, the use of accents and other diacritical marks can be important, especially when writing the names of Indigenous people and places. For example, use of the macron to indicate vowel length in place-names in te reo Māori (the Māori language) has become more or less standard in recent years (as in the city name Whangārei). For Indigenous writing systems, the Canadian government hosts an Indigenous languages web page that provides links to related resources. These and many other online resources in North America, Australasia, and throughout the world are supported by language professionals and others who promote Indigenous languages and cultures.

11.50 **Indigenous writing systems.** Among the most widely spoken languages in the Americas are the Tupian languages in South America; the Quechuan languages in South America; the Aymaran languages in South America; the Arawakan languages in South America, Central America, and the Caribbean; the Mayan languages in Mexico and northern Central America; the Oto-Manguean languages in Mexico; the Uto-Aztecan languages in the Western United States and Mexico; the Na-Dené languages in North America, which include the Athabascan, Haida, and Tlingit languages; the Algonquian languages in North America; and the Inuit languages in northern Alaska, Canada, and Greenland. Except for certain languages of Mesoamerica (notably the writing system of the Maya), there is no archaeological evidence of written Indigenous languages in the Americas or elsewhere before the sixteenth century. Since then, many Indigenous writing systems have been developed based on the Latin alphabet, and many Indigenous language communities use more than one writing system. For example, the Tohono O'odham language in the US

Southwest and Northern Mexico has officially adopted the Alvarez–Hale system (in which, for example, long vowels are written with the vowel letter followed by a colon), but significant works have also been published in the Saxton system (in which long vowels are written with the vowel followed by an *h*). Neighboring communities such as the Akimel O'odham (also known as the Pima) that speak mutually intelligible and related varieties use slightly different systems. All are derived from the Latin alphabet, but orthographic conventions vary (e.g., one group uses *w* where another uses *v*). Authors and editors should become familiar with community norms and variations in writing systems as they decide which conventions are appropriate for a given work. It is also important to note that Indigenous languages may not have standard spellings for words. Different communities may adopt different approaches to spelling, and they may not match the English-based view of "correct" and "incorrect" spellings of words. Also, not all orthographies based on the Latin alphabet use an upper- and lowercase distinction. For example, in the community orthography of the Coeur d'Alene Tribe in the Pacific Northwest, there are no uppercase letters, and any capitalization in writing is considered a typographical error.

11.51 **Navajo (Diné Bizaad).** Among the more widely used Indigenous writing systems is the one developed for Navajo (or Diné Bizaad, "the people's language"), an Athabascan language primarily spoken today by Navajo people (or Diné, "the people") in Arizona and New Mexico and the most widely used of the Na-Dené languages. Written Navajo uses a modified Latin alphabet that employs many accented and doubled vowels and two-letter consonants, as follows (see also table 11.1, which includes the uppercase forms):

a, á, ą, ą́, aa, áá, ąą, ą́ą́, b, ch, ch', d, dl, dz, e, é, ę, ę́, ee, éé, ęę, ę́ę́, g, gh, h, hw, i, í, į, į́, ii, íí, įį, į́į́, j, k, k', kw, l, ł, m, n, ń, o, ó, ǫ, ǫ́, oo, óó, ǫǫ, ǫ́ǫ́, s, sh, t, t', tł, tł', ts, ts', w, x, y, z, zh

Single and double vowels are short and long, respectively. Acute accents are added to vowels as tone markers. Single and double accents mark high tones (e.g., *á*, *áá*); on doubled vowels, a single accent marks a rising tone (*aá*) or a falling tone (*áa*). An ogonek (or hook) added to a vowel (with or without an acute accent) marks a nasal sound. An *l* with stroke (*ł*) represents a type of voiceless consonant; additional consonant sounds are marked by the apostrophes in *ch'*, *k'*, *t'*, *tł'*, and *ts'*. Apostrophes also mark glottal stops. (A modifier letter apostrophe, U+02BC, may be used to differentiate this mark from the common mark of punctuation; in most fonts the two glyphs are identical in appearance.

Compare 11.77, under "Hawaiian.") Many other Indigenous languages are similarly written using modified Latin alphabets. Others, notably the Inuit language Inuktitut (spoken primarily in northern Canada), use syllabaries (a system of characters each of which represents a syllable), some of which have been developed or are being developed for Unicode (see 11.2). See also 11.50.

11.52 **Indigenous language authorities.** In works by or about Indigenous peoples in the Americas and Australia, among other areas, the accepted authority on language presentation, usage, spelling, and the like is usually not the individual writer (particularly if the writer is not a member of the community) but rather the applicable nation, tribe, or other governmental entity. In North America many Indigenous, First Nations, and Native American governments have language and culture departments that make determinations about standards of language use and naming. Authors and editors should make every effort to abide by these authorities' specifications whenever possible. The legal and policy environments surrounding these matters are changing, and it is important that authors and editors work to understand the needs, rights, and regulations of the communities involved. Authors and editors who are members of these communities may need to approach such matters in ways different from those of outsiders, and authorial and editorial practices should reflect the various needs, preferences, and rights applicable to the specific situation. See also 14.136–37.

## *Italian*

11.53 **Italian capitalization.** In Italian, a title preceding a proper name is normally lowercased.

il commendatore Ugo Emiliano
la signora Rossi

In commercial correspondence, the formal second-person pronouns are capitalized in both their nominative forms, *Lei* (singular) and *Voi* (plural), and their objective forms, *La* (accusative singular), *Le* (dative singular), and *Vi* (accusative and dative plural). The older singular and plural forms *Ella* (*Le, La*) and *Loro* (*Loro, Loro*) are handled the same way. These pronouns are capitalized even in combined forms.

Posso pregarLa di farmi una cortesia?
Vorrei darLe una spiegazione.

See also 11.8, 11.20. For a fuller treatment of this and other matters of style, consult Roberto Lesina, *Il nuovo manuale di stile* (bibliog. 5).

11.54 **Italian quotations and dialogue.** Italian uses guillemets (« ») to denote quoted matter, but usually without the space between guillemets and quoted text that appears in many French publications. Regular quotation marks (double or single) are also frequently used in Italian—sometimes as scare quotes (see 7.60) in the same text in which guillemets are used for quotations. Note that periods and commas are correctly placed *after* the closing guillemet or quotation mark.

«Cosa pensi del fatto che io possa diventare "un qualcosa di imperial regio"? Questo non è proprio possibile».

In dialogue, em dashes are sometimes used, as in French. The dash is used before each successive speech. Unlike in French, however, another dash is used at the end of the speech if other matter follows in the same paragraph. The spaces that typically surround the dashes in Italian texts need not be used in English contexts (see 11.21).

—Avremo la neve,—annunziò la vecchia.
—E domani?—chiese Alfredo, voltandosi di scatto dalla finestra.

11.55 **Italian apostrophes.** An apostrophe is used to indicate the omission of one or more letters. A space should appear after an apostrophe that follows a vowel; after an apostrophe that follows a consonant, however, *no* space should appear.

po' duro    de' malevoli    l'onda    all'aura

11.56 **Italian ellipses.** Italian, like French (see 11.35), uses ellipses to indicate interruptions or breaks in thought. To indicate omitted material, the dots are enclosed in brackets. Though Italian typography usually calls for unspaced dots, in English publications Chicago recommends spaced periods wherever ellipses occur (see 12.59–69). See also 11.21.

Voglio . . . quattro milioni.
Davvero? [. . .] Non ci avevo pensato.

11.57 **Italian word division—vowels.** In Italian, division is made after a vowel wherever possible. One-letter syllables at the ends or beginnings of lines should be avoided (see 11.22).

acro-po-li (*not* a-cropoli)   mi-se-ra-bi-le   ta-vo-li-no

Consecutive vowels are rarely divided, and two vowels forming a single sound, or diphthong, are never divided.

miei   pia-ga   Gio-van-ni   Giu-sep-pe   pau-sa   gio-iel-lo

11.58 **Italian word division — consonants.** Certain consonant groups must never be broken: *ch*, *gh*, *gli*, *gn*, *qu*, *sc*, and *r* or *l* preceded by any consonant other than itself.

| | | | |
|---|---|---|---|
| ac-qua rio | la-ghi | pa-dre | ri-flet-te-re |
| fi-glio | na-sce | rau-che | so-gna-re |

Three groups of consonants, however, may be divided: double consonants; the group *cqu*; and any group beginning with *l*, *m*, *n*, or *r*.

| | | | |
|---|---|---|---|
| bab-bo | ac-qua | cam-po | den-tro |
| af-fre-schi | cal-do | com-pra | par-te |

11.59 **Italian word division — words containing apostrophes.** Division should never be made immediately after an apostrophe (but see 11.55).

dal-l'accusa   del-l'or-ga-no   quel-l'uomo   un'ar-te   l'i-dea

11.60 **Italian special characters.** In Italian, the following special characters are required (see also table 11.1):

À à, È è, É é, Ì ì, Ò ò, Ù ù

Although the grave accent on capitalized vowels is sometimes dropped, in stressed final syllables it must be retained to avoid confusion.

CANTÒ (he sang)   CANTO (I sing)   PAPÀ (daddy)   PAPA (pope)

Especially in older works, an apostrophe is sometimes seen with a capital letter in place of the accent on a stressed final (or single) vowel. In direct quotations, such usage should be retained.

E' (it is)   E (and)   PAPA' (daddy)

## *Latin*

11.61 **Latin capitalization — titles of works.** Titles of ancient and medieval Latin works should usually be capitalized in sentence case—that is, only the first word in the title and subtitle, proper nouns, and proper adjectives are capitalized (see 8.159).

*De bello Gallico* *De viris illustribus* *Cur Deus homo?*

Renaissance and modern works or works in English with Latin titles, on the other hand, can usually be capitalized in title case (see 8.160). (If there is any doubt about the era to which the title belongs, opt for sentence case.)

*Novum Organum* *Religio Medici*

See also 11.8.

11.62 **Latin word division — syllables.** A Latin word has as many syllables as it has vowels or diphthongs (*ae*, *au*, *ei*, *eu*, *oe*, *ui*, and, in archaic Latin, *ai*, *oi*, *ou*) and should be divided between syllables (see also 11.22).

na-tu-ra cae-li-co-la in-no-cu-us

11.63 **Latin word division — single consonants.** When a single consonant occurs between two vowels, the word is divided before the consonant unless it is an *x*. Note that *i* and *u* sometimes act as consonants (and, when they do, are sometimes written as *j* and *v*).

Cae-sar me-ri-di-es in-iu-ri-or (*or* in-ju-ri-or) *but* lex-is

11.64 **Latin word division — multiple consonants.** When two or more consonants come together, the word is divided before the last consonant, except for the combinations noted below.

om-nis cunc-tus

The combinations *ch*, *gu*, *ph*, *qu*, and *th* are treated as single consonants and thus never separated.

co-phi-nus lin-gua ae-qua-lis

The following consonant groups are never broken: *bl, br, chl, chr, cl, cr, dl, dr, gl, gr, phl, phr, pl, pr, thl, thr, tl,* and *tr.*

pan-chres-tus li-bris ex-em-pla pa-tris

11.65 **Latin word division — compounds.** Compound words are divided between parts; within each part the rules detailed elsewhere in this section apply. The commonest type of compound word begins with a preposition or a prefix (e.g., *ab-, ad-, in-, re[d]-*).

ab-rum-po ad-est red-eo trans-igo

11.66 **Latin special characters.** Latin requires no special characters for setting ordinary copy. Elementary texts, however, usually mark the long vowels with a macron and, occasionally, the short vowels with a breve, as follows. (See also table 11.1.)

Ā ā, Ă ă, Ē ē, Ĕ ĕ, Ī ī, Ĭ ĭ, Ō ō, Ŏ ŏ, Ū ū, Ŭ ŭ

## *Spanish*

11.67 **Spanish — additional resources.** There is considerable variation in Spanish-language publications throughout the world with respect to capitalization, punctuation, and other matters. For further guidance, consult the extensive resources available from the Real Academia Española, including such essential guides as the *Diccionario panhispánico de dudas* and the *Ortografía de la lengua española* (bibliog. 5).

11.68 **Spanish capitalization.** In Spanish, a title preceding a proper name is normally lowercased. When abbreviated, however, titles are capitalized.

| | |
|---|---|
| el señor Jaime López | *but* |
| la señora Lucía Moyado de Barba | el Sr. López |
| doña Perfecta | |

Nouns as well as adjectives denoting membership in nations are lowercased, but names of countries are capitalized.

los mexicanos la lengua española Inglaterra

Names of organizations and institutions, historical events, buildings, streets, and the like are usually capitalized (see also 8.160).

Real Academia Española
Universidad Nacional Autónoma de México
Plaza del Dos de Mayo

See also 11.5, 11.8, 11.20.

**11.69** **Spanish question marks and exclamation points.** A question or an exclamation in Spanish is preceded by an inverted question mark or exclamation point and followed by a regular mark.

¿Qué pasa, amigo? ¡Olvídalo en ese caso!

If a vocative or dependent construction precedes a question or exclamation, it is written as follows:

Amigo, ¿qué pasa? En ese caso, ¡olvídalo!

Because the opening marks are integral to Spanish punctuation, they should be retained even when Spanish is being quoted in an English context (see 11.21).

**11.70** **Spanish guillemets and quotation marks.** Spanish traditionally uses guillemets (« ») as quotation marks. Only punctuation belonging to the quoted matter is placed within the closing guillemets; other punctuation follows them. Within a quotation, em dashes may be used to set off words identifying the speaker. In Spanish publications, the opening dash is usually *preceded* by a space; the closing dash is then *followed* by a space unless immediately followed by punctuation. In English contexts, such spaces need not be used (see also 11.21). (For quotations within quotations, regular quotation marks are used, as in French; see 11.33.)

«Vino el negocio a tanto—comenta Suárez—, que ya andaban muchos tomados por el diablo».

In lexical studies, it is typical to see single quotation marks used for glosses, with no punctuation preceding the gloss (cf. 11.6).

Muchos adverbios se forman añadiendo *-ly* al adjetivo: *courteous* 'cortés', *courteously* 'cortésmente', *bold* 'atrevido', *boldly* 'atrevidamente'.

Increasingly, Spanish-language publications use regular quotation marks rather than guillemets for all quotations. Where this is the case, the rules for punctuation marks relative to the quotation marks are the same as they are for guillemets (but see 11.13).

11.71 **Spanish dialogue.** In dialogue, an em dash (or, less frequently, a guillemet) introduces each successive speech. Any other matter that follows the quoted speech in the same paragraph is generally preceded by a dash or a comma. See also 11.70.

—Esto es el arca de Noé, afirmó el estanciero.
—¿Por qué estas aquí todavía?—preguntó Juana alarmada.

11.72 **Spanish ellipses.** In Spanish, as in French (see 11.35), ellipses are used to indicate interruptions or breaks in thought. In Spanish publications, these dots are generally unspaced; in English contexts, they may be spaced as recommended elsewhere in this manual (see 12.59–69). To indicate omitted material, the dots are enclosed in brackets. See also 11.21.

Hemos comenzado la vida juntos . . . quizá la terminaremos juntos también . . .

La personalidad más importante del siglo XIX es Domingo Faustino Sarmiento [. . .], llamado el hombre representante del intelecto sudamericano. [. . .] El gaucho [. . .] servía de tema para poemas, novelas, cuentos y dramas.

11.73 **Spanish word division — vowels.** In Spanish, division is made after a vowel whenever possible. See also 11.22.

ca-ra-co-les    mu-jer    re-cla-mo    se-ño-ri-ta

Two or more vowels that form a single syllable (a diphthong or a triphthong) may not be divided.

cam-bias    fue-go    miau    tie-ne    viu-da

If adjacent vowels belong to separate syllables, however, they are divided between syllables.

ba-úl    cre-er    pa-ís    te-a-tro

11.74 **Spanish word division — consonants.** If two adjacent consonants form a combination that would generally not occur at the beginning of a Spanish word, the break is made between them.

| | | |
|---|---|---|
| ac-cio-nis-ta | al-cal-de | efec-to |
| ad-ver-ten-cia | an-cho | is-leño |

The consonant groups *bl*, *br*, *cl*, *cr*, *dr*, *fl*, *fr*, *gl*, *gr*, *pl*, *pr*, and *tr*—all pairs that can occur at the beginning of Spanish words—are inseparable (unless each belongs to a different element of a compound, as in *sub-lu-nar*; see 11.22, 11.75).

| | | | |
|---|---|---|---|
| ci-fra | li-bro | no-ble | re-gla |
| co-pla | ma-dre | pa-tria | se-cre-to |
| im-po-si-ble | ne-gro | re-fle-jo | te-cla |
| le-pra | | | |

Groups of three consonants not ending with one of the inseparable pairs listed above always have an *s* in the middle. They are divided after the *s*.

| | | | | |
|---|---|---|---|---|
| cons-pi-rar | cons-ta | ins-tan-te | obs-cu-ro | obs-tan-te |

Spanish *ch* and *ll* were long considered single characters, alphabetized as such, and never divided. The Spanish Royal Academy has now declared that these combinations are to be alphabetized as two-letter groups, and new publications have adopted this convention. Along with *rr*, however, they still cannot be divided, since they represent single sounds. For details, consult Real Academia Española, *Ortografía de la lengua española* (bibliog. 5).

| | |
|---|---|
| ci-ga-rri-llo | mu-cha-cho |

11.75 **Dividing Spanish compounds.** Compound words are often but not always divided between their component parts.

| | | | |
|---|---|---|---|
| des-igual | mal-es-tar | semi-es-fe-ra | sub-lu-nar |
| in-útil | trans-al-pi-no | bien-aven-tu-ra-do | sub-ra-yar |

*but*

no-so-tros (no longer considered a compound by Spanish speakers)

11.76 **Spanish special characters.** Spanish employs the following special characters (see also table 11.1):

Á á, É é, Í í, Ñ ñ, Ó ó, Ú ú, Ü ü

## *Other Languages Using the Latin Alphabet*

11.77 **Special considerations for other languages using the Latin alphabet.** In addition to the languages covered elsewhere in this section, there are dozens of other languages that use the Latin alphabet. Special considerations for a number of them are listed below. For the special characters required for each of these languages, see table 11.1. See also 11.8, 11.20.

**Albanian.** Since 1972, Albanian has had a single, unified orthography, based on a standard originally adopted in 1909. Writers and editors working with older texts may need to take historical context into account and determine whether a spelling is conditioned by the specific time when it was used or whether it is preferable to follow the current norm.

**Croatian and Bosnian.** The former Serbo-Croatian language used both Latin and Cyrillic alphabets. The modern Bosnian and Croatian standard languages use only the Latin version of those same alphabets. Although the substitution of *dj* for *đ* is sometimes seen (e.g., in informal correspondence), standard orthographic practice in all the successor languages of Serbo-Croatian distinguishes these two consistently. See also Serbian and Montenegrin.

**Czech**, a Slavic language written in the Latin alphabet, uses many diacritical marks to indicate sounds not represented by this alphabet, as shown in table 11.1. Note that the lowercase *d* and *t* with caron (the single glyphs *ď* and *ť*, respectively) are often seen with an apostrophe instead.

**Danish.** The polite second-person pronouns *De*, *Dem*, and *Deres* (increasingly rare, and not to be confused with the third-person pronouns *de*, *dem*, and *deres*) and the familiar *I* are capitalized in Danish. Until the middle of the twentieth century, common nouns were capitalized, as in German.

**Dutch.** For the capitalization of particles with personal names, see 8.11. Proper adjectives (as well as nouns) are capitalized as in English. When a word beginning with the diphthong *ij* is capitalized, both letters are capitals: *IJsland* (Iceland). When a single letter begins a sentence, it is lowercased, but the next word is capitalized: *'k Heb niet . . .*

**Finnish.** Because Swedish is the second official language in Finland, the Finnish alphabet taught in schools and the standard keyboard used in Finland include the Swedish *a* with ring above (see table 11.1).

**Hawaiian.** The Hawaiian alphabet was developed in the nineteenth century from the Latin alphabet. In addition to the five vowels with macrons listed in table 11.1, Hawaiian uses the *ʻokina*, a glottal stop represented by a left single quotation mark (U+2018)—for example, in the place-name *Hawai'i* (commonly spelled *Hawaii*). (To differentiate the *'okina* from the common mark of punctuation, some authors and publishers will prefer to use a modifier letter turned comma, U+02BB, instead of a left single quotation mark; in most fonts the two glyphs are identical in appearance.) See also 6.123, 11.49–52.

**Hungarian** uses a wide variety of accented vowels, as shown in table 11.1.

**Icelandic** includes the consonants *Ð ð* (eth) and *Þ þ* (thorn), which were also used in Old and Middle English (see 11.132–34). (The eth, which never begins a word in Icelandic, is capitalized only in contexts where all capitals are used.) In addition to featuring an acute-accented version of each regular vowel (including *Ý ý*), Icelandic includes the vowels *Æ æ* and *Ö ö*.

**Norwegian.** The polite second-person pronouns *De*, *Dem*, and *Deres* (increasingly rare, and not to be confused with the third-person pronouns *de*, *dem*, and *deres*) are capitalized in Norwegian. Until the middle of the twentieth century, common nouns were capitalized, as in German.

**Polish.** In formal address the second-person plural pronoun *Państwo* (you) is capitalized, as are related forms: *Czekam na Twój przyjazd* (I await your arrival); *Pozdrawiam Cię!* (Greetings to you!). Division of Polish words is similar to that of transliterated Russian (see 11.107–17). Division normally follows syllabic structure (e.g., *kom-pli-ka-cja*; *sta-ro-pol-ski*). Note that the conjunction *i* (and) should never appear at the end of a line but must be carried over to the beginning of the next.

**Portuguese.** Titles and nouns or adjectives denoting nationality are capitalized as in Spanish (see 11.68). Accented capitals, sometimes dropped in Portuguese running text, should always be used when Portuguese is presented in an English context.

**Romanian and Moldovan** are now both written using the same Latin orthography. Note that *Ș ș* and *Ț ț*—Latin *S s* and *T t* with comma below—often appear instead with a cedilla, though the comma is correct. *Â â* and *Î î* represent identical sounds but have different etymological origins. The use of *Â â* has been restricted, eliminated, and reinstated in whole or in part during various orthographic reforms. Writers and editors, therefore, should take care to determine whether a spelling is conditioned by the specific time when it was used or whether it is preferable to follow the current norm.

**Serbian and Montenegrin.** The former Serbo-Croatian language used both Latin and Cyrillic alphabets. In the modern Montenegrin standard language, versions of both of those alphabets are official. In the modern Serbian standard language, a version of the Cyrillic alphabet is official, though the Latin alphabet is also used, as regulated by law. Note that although the substitution of *dj* for *đ* is sometimes seen (e.g., in informal correspondence), standard orthographic practice in all the successor languages of Serbo-Croatian distinguishes these two consistently. In addition to the Latin letters needed for Serbian, two extra letters are required for Montenegrin: *Śś* and *Źź* (see table 11.1). See also Croatian and Bosnian.

**Swedish.** In Swedish, the second-person pronouns *Ni* and *Er*, traditionally capitalized in correspondence, are now lowercased in all contexts.

**Turkish and Azeri.** Modern Turkish has undergone a number of orthographic reforms since the original change to the Latin alphabet in 1928. Differences in the spellings of a name or word can therefore depend on the time period. Writers and editors should take care to determine whether a spelling is conditioned by the specific time when it was used or whether it is preferable to follow the current norm. In Turkish, as in English, the names of months and days of the week are capitalized. The Azeri (Azerbaijani) standard alphabet in use since 1992 is identical to the Turkish alphabet except for the presence of *Əə*, *Qq*, and *Xx* (lacking in Turkish), and the absence of vowels with circumflex. Conventions for capitalization and spelling are similar to those for Turkish. Note that in both languages, the letter *i* retains its dot when capitalized (*İ*) and should not be confused with the dotless *ı*, a separate letter that requires a special character for lowercase (see table 11.1).

**Turkmen and Uzbek.** Turkmenistan has successfully transitioned from a Cyrillic to a Latin alphabet. In Uzbekistan the transition is still ongoing. Uzbek requires no special characters aside from the left single quotation mark in the letters *O'o'* and *G'g'* (not shown in table 11.1).

## LANGUAGES USUALLY TRANSLITERATED (OR ROMANIZED)

11.78 **Transliteration.** In nonspecialized works it is customary to transliterate—that is, convert to the Latin alphabet, or romanize—words or phrases from languages that do not use the Latin alphabet. For discussion and illustration of scores of alphabets, see Peter T. Daniels and William Bright, eds., *The World's Writing Systems* (bibliog. 5). For alphabetic conversion, the most comprehensive resource is the Library of Congress publication *ALA-LC Romanization Tables* (bibliog. 5), available online. Do not attempt to transliterate from a language unfamiliar to you. Note that the recommendations elsewhere in this chapter related to capitalization (11.20), punctuation (11.21), and word division (11.22) for languages that use the Latin alphabet apply equally to transliterated text.

11.79 **Character sets for non-Latin alphabets.** Modern word-processing software readily allows users to enter words in many non-Latin alphabets. For a given alphabet, there may be a variety of non-Unicode character sets available as specialized fonts, but authors who want to include such copy should choose a font that includes the required Unicode characters (see 11.2), in consultation with their publisher. See also 2.19.

11.80 **Proofreading copy in non-Latin alphabets—a warning.** Anyone unfamiliar with a language that uses a non-Latin alphabet should exercise extreme caution in proofreading even single words set in that alphabet. Grave errors can occur when similar characters are mistaken for each other. If in doubt, editors should query the author; it may be advisable to consult the Unicode number and description (see 11.2) when referring to a given character or diacritical mark.

11.81 **Diacritics—specialized versus general contexts.** Nearly all systems of transliteration require diacritics—including, in the languages discussed below, macrons, underdots, and overdots, to name just a few. Except in linguistic studies or other highly specialized works, a system using as few diacritics as are needed to aid pronunciation is easier on readers, publisher, and author. Most readers of a nonspecialized work on Hindu mythology, for example, will be more comfortable with Shiva than Śiva or with Vishnu than Viṣṇu, though many specialists would want to differentiate the *Sh* in Shiva from the *sh* in Vishnu as distinct Sanskrit letters. For nonspecialized works, the transliterated forms without diacritics that are listed in *Merriam-Webster* (see 7.1) are usually preferred by readers and authors alike.

11.82 **Italics versus roman for transliterated terms.** Transliterated terms (other than proper names) that have not become part of the English language are italicized (but see 11.4). If used throughout a work, a transliterated term may be italicized on first appearance and then set in roman. Words listed in the dictionary are usually set in roman. See also 11.3–7.

The preacher pointed out the distinction between agape and eros.
*but*
Once the Greek words *erōs* and *agapē* had been absorbed into the English language, it became unnecessary to italicize them or to use the macrons.

## *Arabic*

11.83 **Arabic transliteration.** There is no universally accepted form for transliterating Arabic. One very detailed system may be found in the *ALA-LC Romanization Tables* (bibliog. 5). Another system is followed by the *International Journal of Middle East Studies* (bibliog. 5). Having selected a system, an author should stick to it with as few exceptions as possible. Some of the examples in this section feature the hamza (ʾ) and the ʿayn (ʿ) (see 11.84); others feature letters with underdots and macrons. These and other special characters used in transliteration from Arabic are included in table 11.2. (A table featuring the Arabic alphabet may be found under the entry for "alphabet" in *Merriam-Webster* [see 7.1], among other sources.)

11.84 **The hamza and the ʿayn.** The hamza (ʾ) and the ʿayn (ʿ) frequently appear in transliterated Arabic words and names. Writers using hamzas or ʿayns must on every occurrence make it clear, by coding or by careful instructions to the editor or typesetter, which of the two marks is intended. It should be noted that the Arabic characters are not the same as the ones used for transliteration; see table 11.2 for the preferred Unicode characters for hamza and ʿayn in transliteration. The hamza is sometimes represented—especially in nonspecialized works—by an apostrophe (as in Qur'an), and the ʿayn by a single opening quotation mark (as in 'ayn). (Since an ʿayn often occurs at the beginning of a word, a quotation mark must be used with caution.) Most transliteration systems drop the hamza when it occurs at the beginning of a word (anzala *not* ʾanzala). See also 6.123, 6.125.

11.85 **Arabic spelling.** Isolated references in text to well-known persons or places should employ the forms familiar to English-speaking readers.

Avicenna (*not* Ibn Sina)
Damascus (*not* Dimashq)
Mecca (*not* Makka *or* Makkah)

11.86 **The Arabic definite article.** Though there is considerable variation across publications, Chicago recommends joining the Arabic definite article, *al*, to a noun with a hyphen. (An exception may be made for a personal name that is better known without the hyphen; see 8.15.)

al-Islam    al-Nafud    Bahr al-Safi    al-Qaeda (*or* al-Qaida)

In speech the sound of the *l* in *al* is assimilated into the sounds *d*, *n*, *r*, *s*, *sh*, *t*, and *z*. Where rendering the *sound* of the Arabic is impor-

TABLE 11.2. Special characters (and Unicode numbers) for transliterated Arabic, Hebrew, Japanese, and South Asian languages

| Character (and Unicode number) | Description | Languages that use it |
|---|---|---|
| ʹ (02B9) | modifier letter prime (see 11.101) | Arabic, Hebrew |
| ʿ (02BF) | ʿayn *or* ʿayin (modifier letter left half ring) | Arabic, Hebrew |
| ʾ (02BE) | alif (hamza) *or* ʾalef (modifier letter right half ring) | Arabic, Hebrew |
| Ā (0100), ā (0101) | A/a with macron | Arabic, Hebrew, Japanese, South Asian languages |
| Ǎ (01CD), ǎ (01CE) | A/a with caron (haček) | Hebrew |
| Á (00C1), á (00E1) | A/a with acute | Arabic |
| Ḍ (1E0C), ḍ (1E0D) | D/d with dot below | Arabic, South Asian languages |
| Ē (0112), ē (0113) | E/e with macron | Hebrew, Japanese, South Asian languages |
| Ě (011A), ě (011B) | E/e with caron (haček) | Hebrew |
| ə (0259) | small schwa | Hebrew |
| Ḥ (1E24), ḥ (1E25) | H/h with dot below | Arabic, Hebrew, South Asian languages |
| Ī (012A), ī (012B) | I/i with macron | Arabic, Hebrew, Japanese, South Asian languages |
| Ḳ (1E32), ḳ (1E33) | K/k with dot below | Arabic, Hebrew |
| Ḷ (1E36), ḷ (1E37) | L/l with dot below[1] | South Asian languages |
| Ḹ (1E38), ḹ (1E39) | L/l with dot below and macron | South Asian languages |
| Ṁ (1E40), ṁ (1E41) | M/m with dot above | South Asian languages |
| Ṃ (1E42), ṃ (1E43) | M/m with dot below | South Asian languages |
| Ñ (00D1), ñ (00F1) | N/n with tilde | South Asian languages |
| N̄ (004E+0304), n̄ (006E+0304) | N/n with macron (combining character) | South Asian languages |
| Ṅ (1E44), ṅ (1E45) | N/n with dot above | South Asian languages |
| Ṇ (1E46), ṇ (1E47) | N/n with dot below | South Asian languages |
| Ō (014C), ō (014D) | O/o with macron | Hebrew, Japanese, South Asian languages |
| Ǒ (01D1), ǒ (01D2) | O/o with caron (haček) | Hebrew |
| Ṛ (1E5A), ṛ (1E5B) | R/r with dot below[2] | South Asian languages |
| Ṝ (1E5C), ṝ (1E5D) | R/r with dot below and macron | South Asian languages |
| Ś (015A), ś (015B) | S/s with acute | Hebrew, South Asian languages |
| Š (0160), š (0161) | S/s with caron (haček) | Hebrew |
| Ṣ (1E62), ṣ (1E63) | S/s with dot below | Arabic, South Asian languages |
| Ṭ (1E6C), ṭ (1E6D) | T/t with dot below | Arabic, Hebrew, South Asian languages |
| Ū (016A), ū (016B) | U/u with macron | Arabic, Hebrew, Japanese, South Asian languages |
| Ṿ (1E7E), ṿ (1E7F) | V/v with dot below | Hebrew |
| Ẏ (1E8E), ẏ (1E8F) | Y/y with dot above | South Asian languages |
| Ẓ (1E92), ẓ (1E93) | Z/z with dot below | Arabic |

[1] Variations of L/l with a combining ring below (U+0325) rather than a dot below may also be required.

[2] As with L/l, R/r variations may require a combining ring below (U+0325) rather than a dot.

tant (for example, when transliterating poetry), the assimilations are often shown, as in the examples below. In most other situations, the article-noun combination is written without indication of the elision, as above.

an-Nafud
Bahr as-Safi

Some authors drop the *a* in *al* and replace it with an apostrophe when it occurs after a long syllable (Abū 'l-Muhallab). Some also drop the *a* when it occurs connected with a particle (wa 'l-layl). Others do not replace the dropped *a* with anything (Abū l Muhallab; wa l-layl).

11.87 **Arabic capitalization.** Since the Arabic alphabet does not distinguish between capital and lowercase letter forms, practice in capitalizing transliterated Arabic varies widely. Chicago recommends the practice outlined in 11.8: Capitalize only the first word and any proper nouns. This practice applies to titles of works as well as to names of journals and organizations. Note that *al-* (with a hyphen), unlike *the*, may remain lowercase at the beginning of a title; the word to which it is joined is capitalized (as in the second example below). See also 11.11.

ʿAbd al-Raḥmān al-Jabartī, *ʿAjāʾib al-āthār fī al-tarājim wa al-akhbār* (The marvelous remains in biography and history)
Jabrā Ibrāhīm Jabrā, *al-Baḥth ʿan Walīd Masʿūd* (In search of Walid Masoud)
Avicenna's *Kitāb al-shifāʾ*, known in English as *The Book of Healing*

For citing and alphabetizing Arabic personal names, see 8.15, 15.83.

11.88 **Arabic word division.** Breaking transliterated Arabic words or names at the ends of lines should be avoided wherever possible. If necessary, a break may be made after *al* or *Ibn*. A break may be made after two letters if the second has an underdot (e.g., *iṭ-bāq*). Breaks must never be made between the digraphs *dh*, *gh*, *kh*, *sh*, or *th* unless both letters have underdots. Nor should breaks be made before or after a hamza. Aside from these niceties, the rules governing English word division may be followed (see 7.36–48). It should be noted, however, that untransliterated (or unromanized) Arabic is read from right to left; if a line break occurs within an untransliterated Arabic phrase, the words must still be read right to left on each line. For an example of this in Hebrew, see 11.105.

## *Chinese, Japanese, and Korean*

11.89 **Chinese romanization.** The Hanyu Pinyin romanization system, introduced in the 1950s, has largely supplanted both the Wade-Giles system and the place-name spellings of the *Postal Atlas of China* (last updated in the 1930s), making Pinyin the standard system for romanizing Chinese. Representing sounds of Chinese more explicitly, Pinyin has been widely accepted as the system for teaching Chinese as a second language. As of 2000, the Library of Congress issued new romanization guidelines reflecting the conversion of its entire online catalog records for the Chinese collections in the Library of Congress and almost all North American research libraries to comply with Pinyin, with slight modifications. Although a few authors, long familiar with Wade-Giles or other older systems (or Tongyong Pinyin, a more recent system still used by some in Taiwan), have not switched to Pinyin in their writings, Chicago joins librarians in urging that Pinyin now be used in all writing about China or the Chinese language. (In some contexts it may be helpful to the reader to add the Wade-Giles spelling of a name or term in parentheses following the first use of the Pinyin spelling.) The *ALA-LC Romanization Tables* (bibliog. 5) available online from the Library of Congress should be used with caution by anyone unfamiliar with Chinese.

11.90 **Exceptions to Pinyin.** Even where Pinyin is adopted, certain place-names, personal names, and other proper nouns long familiar in their older forms may be presented that way in English texts. Or, for greater consistency, the old spelling may be added in parentheses after the Pinyin version. If in doubt, consult the latest edition of *Merriam-Webster* (see 7.1); names not listed there in older forms should be presented in Pinyin. Editors who wish to alter spellings should do so in consultation with the author.

11.91 **Apostrophes, hyphens, and tone marks in Chinese romanization.** Pinyin spellings often differ markedly from Wade-Giles and other older spellings. Personal names are usually spelled without apostrophes or hyphens, but an apostrophe is sometimes used when syllables are run together (as in Xi'an to distinguish it from Xian), even in contexts where tone marks are used (e.g., Xī'ān). The Pinyin romanization system of the Library of Congress does not include tone marks, nor are they included in many English-language publications. However, tone marks may be appropriate in certain contexts (e.g., textbooks for learning Chinese).

11.92 **Some common Chinese names.** Some names frequently encountered are listed below.

| DYNASTIES | | PERSONAL NAMES | |
|---|---|---|---|
| *Wade-Giles* | *Pinyin* | *Wade-Giles* | *Pinyin* |
| Chou | Zhou | Fang Li-chih | Fang Lizhi |
| Ch'in | Qin | Hua Kuo-feng | Hua Guofeng |
| Ch'ing | Qing | Lin Piao | Lin Biao |
| Sung | Song | Lu Hsün | Lu Xun |
| T'ang | Tang | Mao Tse-tung | Mao Zedong |
| Yüan | Yuan | Teng Hsiao-p'ing | Deng Xiaoping |

The names Sun Yat-sen and Chiang Kai-shek, among many others, usually retain the old spellings.

| GEOGRAPHIC NAMES | | |
|---|---|---|
| *Wade-Giles* | *Postal atlas* | *Pinyin* |
| Kuang-tung | Kwangtung | Guangdong |
| Pei-ching (Pei-p'ing) | Peking (Peiping) | Beijing |
| Shang-hai | Shanghai | Shanghai |
| Su-chou | Soochow | Suzhou |
| Ta-lien | Dairen | Dalian |

11.93 **Japanese romanization.** The Japanese language in its usual written form is a mixture of Chinese characters (called *kanji* in Japanese) and two *kana* syllabaries. (A syllabary is a series of written characters, each used to represent a syllable.) Since romanized Japanese, *rōmaji*, was introduced into Japan in the sixteenth century, a number of systems of romanization have been developed. The one in most common use since the early part of the Meiji period (1868–1912) is the modified Hepburn (or *hyōjun*) system. This system is used in Oxford's *Pocket Kenkyusha Japanese Dictionary* (bibliog. 3.2) and most other Japanese–English dictionaries (and is the basis of the Japanese romanization tables from the Library of Congress); outside Japan it is also used almost exclusively, notably in Asian collections in libraries throughout the world.

11.94 **Modified Hepburn system.** In the modified Hepburn system, an apostrophe is placed after a syllabic *n* that is followed by a vowel or *y*: *Gen'e, San'yo*. A macron is used over a long vowel (usually an *o* or a *u*, though some systems allow for macrons over *a*, *i*, and *e*) in all Japanese words except well-known place-names (e.g., Tokyo, Hokkaido, Kobe) and words such as *shogun* and *daimyo* that have entered the English language and are thus not normally italicized. (When the pronunciation of such names or words is important to readers, macrons may be used: Tōkyō, Hokkaidō, Kōbe, shōgun, daimyō.) Hyphens should be used as needed: *Meiji jidai-shi* (or *jidaishi*) *no shinkenkyū*. *Shinjuku-ku no meisho.*

11.95 **Korean romanization.** The modern Korean language is written using *Hangul* (한글), an alphabetic syllabary first developed in the fifteenth century. The modern form of Hangul, which consists of nineteen consonants and ten vowels (as defined by the National Institute of Korean Language), displaced the traditional system of writing Korean words using Chinese characters (*Hanja*), which remained in wide use into the twentieth century. There are several systems of romanization used for Korean. The McCune–Reischauer system, introduced in the 1930s, was replaced in 2000 by the current system, Revised Romanization, as the official system of romanization in South Korea. McCune–Reischauer, however, in addition to being found in older sources, is also used as the basis of the Korean romanization table from the US Library of Congress and is the most widely used system in North America. A version of McCune–Reischauer is used as the official system in North Korea. Both the Revised Romanization and McCune–Reischauer systems are based primarily on spoken pronunciation and thus do not closely reflect written Korean. Another system, known as Yale romanization and introduced in the 1940s, is preferred by many linguists for its fidelity to Korean orthography.

11.96 **Revised Romanization of Korean versus McCune–Reischauer.** The system known as Revised Romanization represents modern Korean pronunciation using Latin letters with no diacritics or apostrophes. Hyphens are often inserted between two combined syllables to clarify pronunciation, as in the word *jung-ang* (중앙, "center/central"); however, this type of hyphen is rarely used in place-names, as can be seen in the name of the Jungang railway line. Hyphens are commonly used between syllables in Korean given names, as in Chang Wang-rok (장왕록), the name of the South Korean writer, whose given name would be strictly romanized as Wangrok (see also 8.18). Hyphens are also used before *do* (province), *si* (city), and the like in a place-name, as in the name Uijeongbu-si (의정부시; literally "Uijeongbu City"). The McCune–Reischauer system uses apostrophes to distinguish aspirated consonants *ch'*, *k'*, *p'*, and *t'* from their unaspirated counterparts, and a breve distinguishes rounded from unrounded vowels, as in *ŏ* (ㅓ) and *ŭ* (ㅡ). In the Revised Romanization system, by contrast, rounded vowels are represented by adding an *e* before the vowel, as in the city name Seoul, which is romanized as *Sŏul* in the McCune–Reischauer system.

11.97 **Chinese, Japanese, and Korean — capitalization and italics.** Although capital letters do not exist in Chinese, Japanese, or Korean, they are introduced in romanized versions of these languages where they would normally be used in English (see chapter 8). Personal names and place-names are capitalized. In hyphenated names, only the first element is capitalized in romanized Chinese, though both elements may be capitalized in Japanese (and are sometimes capitalized in Korean). Common nouns and other words used in an English sentence are lowercased and italicized (see 11.3, 11.6). Names of institutions, schools of thought, religions, job titles and other official titles, and so forth are capitalized if set in roman, lowercased if set in italics.

Donglin Academy; the Donglin movement
Buddhism, Taoism, feng shui [see 7.56], and other forms . . .
Under the Ming dynasty the postal service was administered by the Board of War (*bingbu*) through a central office in Beijing (*huitong guan*).
The heirs of the Seiyūkai and Minseitō are the Liberal and Progressive Parties of Japan.
It was Shōgun Ieyasu (the *shōgun* were military governors in Japan until 1868) who said . . . (note that *shōgun* is both singular and plural)
According to Park, *Repeatedly Recited Stories of the East* (*Tongp'ae naksong*) and other vernacular stories (*yadam*) probably did not originate from oral storytelling.

11.98 **Titles of Chinese, Japanese, and Korean works.** As in English, titles of books and periodicals are italicized, and titles of articles are set in roman and enclosed in quotation marks (see 8.157–204). The first word of a romanized title is always capitalized, as are many proper nouns (especially in Japanese and Korean).

Chen Shiqi, *Mingdai guan shougongye de yanjiu* [Studies on government-operated handicrafts during the Ming dynasty], . . .
Hua Linfu, "Qingdai yilai Sanxia diqu shuihan zaihai de chubu yanjiu" [A preliminary study of floods and droughts in the Three Gorges region since the Qing dynasty], *Zhongguo shehui kexue* 1 (1999): 168–79.
Okamoto Yoshitomo, *Jūrokuseiki Nichi-Ō kōtsūshi no kenkyū* [Study of the interchange between Japan and Europe during the sixteenth century], . . .
Akiyama Kenzō, "Gores wa Ryūkyūjin de aru" [The Gores are Ryūkyūans], *Shigaku zasshi* . . .
Cho Nam-joo, *82 nyeonsaeng Gim Jiyeong* [Kim Ji-young, born 1982], . . .

11.99 **Inclusion of Chinese, Japanese, and Korean characters.** Chinese, Japanese, and Korean characters, immediately following the romanized version of the item they represent, are sometimes necessary to help readers identify references cited or terms used. They are largely confined to bibliographies and glossaries. Where needed in running text, they may be enclosed in parentheses (but need not be). The advent of

Unicode has made it easier for authors to include words in non-Latin alphabets in their manuscripts, but publishers need to be alerted of the need for special characters in case particular fonts are needed for publication (see 11.2).

Harootunian, Harry, and Sakai Naoki. "Nihon kenkyū to bunka kenkyū" 日本研究と文化研究. *Shisō* 思想 7 (July 1997): 4–53.

Hua Linfu 華林甫. "Qingdai yilai Sanxia diqu shuihan zaihai de chubu yanjiu" 清代以來三峽地區水旱災害的初步研究 [A preliminary study of floods and droughts in the Three Gorges region since the Qing dynasty]. *Zhongguo shehui kexue* 中國社會科學 1 (1999): 168–79.

That year the first assembly of the national Diet was held and the Imperial Rescript on Education (*kyōiku chokugo* 教育勅語) was issued.

This study explores paratextual changes in the translations of *Kobal* 고발, a novel by the North Korean writer known only by the pseudonym Bandi 반디 (often cited as Pandi).

## *Hebrew*

11.100 **Hebrew transliteration systems.** There are several acceptable romanization systems for Hebrew, including the one in the *ALA-LC Romanization Tables* (see bibliog. 5). Any such system may be used, but it is the author's responsibility to use it consistently in a given work. (A table featuring the Hebrew alphabet may be found under the entry for "alphabet" in *Merriam-Webster* [see 7.1], among other sources.)

11.101 **Diacritics in transliterated Hebrew.** In transliterated Hebrew, the following accents and characters are sometimes needed (though usually only in specialist materials): underdots (Ḥ ḥ, Ḳ ḳ, Ṭ ṭ, Ṿ ṿ); macrons (Ā ā, Ē ē, Ī ī, Ō ō, Ū ū); acute accents (Ś ś); hačeks, or carons (Ǎ ǎ, Ě ě, Ǒ ǒ, Š š); and superscript schwa (ᵊ). The ʾalef and the ʿayin may be represented in the same way as the Arabic hamza and ʿayn (see 11.84 and table 11.2). In some systems, a prime may also be needed (to separate two distinct consonant sounds that might be mistaken for a digraph).

11.102 **Hebrew prefixes.** In Hebrew, several prepositions, conjunctions, and articles appear as prefixes. Some authors use apostrophes or hyphens after these prefixes in romanized text, and some do not. (In Hebrew no such marker is used.) Either approach is acceptable if used consistently.

11.103 **Hebrew capitalization and italics.** The Hebrew alphabet has no capital letters, and there is no universally used system for capitalizing romanized Hebrew. Writers may follow normal English usage—capitalizing proper names, book titles, and so forth (see 11.8, 11.20). Some writers eschew capitalization altogether. As always, the author must ensure internal consistency. For italics in romanized Hebrew, the normal English usage may also be followed (see 11.10).

11.104 **Hebrew word division.** For romanized Hebrew, or Hebrew words incorporated into English, the principles set forth in 7.36–48 may be followed. When a double consonant occurs at the point of division, one consonant goes with each division.

Rosh Ha-shana
Yom Kip-pur

11.105 **Unromanized Hebrew phrases.** Hebrew is read from right to left. In English sentences that contain an unromanized Hebrew phrase, the Hebrew order is maintained within the sentence. (Modern operating systems can usually handle a mix of left-right and right-left input in the same context.)

The first phrase in Lamentations is איכה ישבה בדד (How she sits in solitude!).

If a line break occurs within a Hebrew phrase, the words must still be read right to left on each line. Thus, if the Hebrew phrase in the example above had to be broken, the Hebrew words would appear to be in a different order.

The first phrase in Lamentations is איכה ישבה
בדד (How she sits in solitude!).
*or*
The first phrase in Lamentations is איכה
ישבה בדד (How she sits in solitude!).

As a safeguard, the author should highlight all the words in Hebrew phrases and furnish detailed instructions on how to implement line breaks.

11.106 **A note on Hebrew vowels.** Most Hebrew vowels are not letters; they are marks attached to the letters, most of which are consonants. In Hebrew texts the vowel marks (as well as dots that modify the pronunciation of consonants) rarely appear. Among texts in which the marks do appear are prayer books, printed Bibles, and poetry.

## *Russian*

11.107 **Russian transliteration.** Of the many systems for transliterating Russian, the most important are summarized in table 11.3. Journals of Slavic studies generally prefer a "linguistic" system that makes free use of diacritics and ligatures. In works intended for a general audience, however, diacritics and ligatures should be avoided. For general use, Chicago recommends the system of the United States Board on Geographic Names. Regardless of the system followed, the spellings for names listed in *Merriam-Webster* (see 7.1) should prevail.

| | | |
|---|---|---|
| Catherine the Great | Dnieper River | Nizhniy (*or* Nizhni) Novgorod |
| Chekhov | Moscow | Tchaikovsky |

11.108 **Russian capitalization.** Capitalization conventions in Cyrillic are much like those of French and should be preserved in transliteration. Pronouns, days of the week, months, and most proper adjectives are lowercased. Geographic designations are capitalized when they apply to formal institutions or political units but otherwise lowercased.

| | |
|---|---|
| Tverskaya guberniya | Moskovskiy universitet |
| tverskoye zemstvo | russkiy kompozitor |

11.109 **Titles of Russian works.** Only the first word and any proper nouns are capitalized in titles.

N. A. Kurakin, *Lenin i Trotskiy*

O. I. Skorokhodova, *Kak ya vosprinimayu i predstavlyayu okruzhayushchiy mir* [How I perceive and imagine the external world]

Note that in the original Cyrillic, titles are set in ordinary type; the Cyrillic *kursiv* is used more sparingly than our italic and never for book titles. In transliterations, however, italic should be used.

11.110 **Russian quotations and dialogue.** Russian generally resembles French in its use of guillemets (« ») for dialogue and quoted material and of dashes for dialogue (see 11.32, 11.34).

«Bozhe, bozhe, bozhe!» govorit Boris.

| | |
|---|---|
| —S kem ya rabotayu? | —Kak my rabotayem? |
| —S tovarishchem. | —S interesom. |

TABLE 11.3. Russian alphabet (and Unicode numbers) and romanization

| **Basic Russian (Cyrillic) alphabet (and Unicode numbers)** | | | | |
|---|---|---|---|---|
| **Upright** | **Cursive**[1] | **US Board on Geographic Names** | **Library of Congress** | **Linguistic system**[2] |
| А (0410), а (0430) | *А, а* | a | | |
| Б (0411), б (0431) | *Б, б* | b | | |
| В (0412), в (0432) | *В, в* | v | | |
| Г (0413), г (0433) | *Г, г* | g | | |
| Д (0414), д (0434) | *Д, д* | d | | |
| Е (0415), е (0435) | *Е, е* | ye,[3] e | e | e |
| Ё (0401), ё[4] (0451) | *Ё, ё* | yë,[3] ë (00EB) | ë | e, ë |
| Ж (0416), ж (0436) | *Ж, ж* | zh | | ž |
| З (0417), з (0437) | *З, з* | z | | |
| И (0418), и (0438) | *И, и* | i | | |
| Й (0419), й (0439) | *Й, й* | y | ĭ (012D) | j |
| К (041A), к (043A) | *К, к* | k | | |
| Л (041B), л (043B) | *Л, л* | l | | |
| М (041C), м (043C) | *М, м* | m | | |
| Н (041D), н (043D) | *Н, н* | n | | |
| О (041E), о (043E) | *О, о* | o | | |
| П (041F), п (043F) | *П, п* | p | | |
| Р (0420), р (0440) | *Р, р* | r | | |
| С (0421), с (0441) | *С, с* | s | | |
| Т (0422), т (0442) | *Т, т* | t | | |
| У (0423), у (0443) | *У, у* | u | | |
| Ф (0424), ф (0444) | *Ф, ф* | f | | |
| Х (0425), х (0445) | *Х, х* | kh | | x |
| Ц (0426), ц (0446) | *Ц, ц* | ts | t͡s[5] | c |
| Ч (0427), ч (0447) | *Ч, ч* | ch | | č |
| Ш (0428), ш (0448) | *Ш, ш* | sh | | š |
| Щ (0429), щ (0449) | *Щ, щ* | shch | | šč |
| Ъ (042A), ъ[6] (044A) | *Ъ, ъ* | ” (201D)[7] | ʺ (02BA)[8] | ʺ (02BA)[8] |
| Ы (042B), ы[6] (044B) | *Ы, ы* | y | | |
| Ь (042C), ь[6] (044C) | *Ь, ь* | ’ (2019)[9] | ʹ (02B9)[10] | ʹ (02B9)[10] |
| Э (042D), э (044D) | *Э, э* | e | ė (0117) | è (00E8) |
| Ю (042E), ю (044E) | *Ю, ю* | yu | i͡u[5] | ju |
| Я (042F), я (044F) | *Я, я* | ya | i͡a[5] | ja |

NOTE: The Library of Congress and linguistic systems employ the same characters as the US Board system except where noted.

[1] The Unicode numbers are the same for the upright and cursive characters; the differences in appearance depend on the italic version of a given typeface.

[2] The term *linguistic* describes a system generally preferred by journals of Slavic studies (see 11.107).

[3] Initially and after a vowel or ъ or ь.

[4] Not considered a separate letter; usually represented in Russian by *е*.

[5] Character tie, sometimes omitted, may be produced by using the combining double inverted breve (U+0361).

[6] Does not occur initially. [7] Right double quotation mark.

[8] Modifier letter double prime (hard sign). [9] Right single quotation mark.

[10] Modifier letter prime (soft sign).

To set off a quotation within a speech, guillemets may be used, as in French. For an example, see 11.34.

11.111 **Russian ellipses.** Ellipses are used as in French (see 11.35) to indicate interruptions or breaks in thought.

Ya . . . vy . . . my tol'ko chto priyekhali.

In Russian, an exclamation point or a question mark often takes the place of one of the dots; this convention may be regularized to three dots in English publications.

Mitya! . . . Gde vy byli? . . .

11.112 **Russian uses of the dash.** A dash is sometimes inserted, with a space on either side, between subject and complement when the equivalent of *is* or *are* is omitted.

Moskva — stolitsa Rossii.

Similarly, a dash, preceded and followed by a space, is used in place of a verb omitted because it would be identical to the preceding verb.

Ivan i Sonya poyedut v Moskvu poyezdom, Lev i Lyuba — avtobusom.

11.113 **Russian word division — general.** Transliterated Russian should be divided according to the rules governing word division in the Cyrillic original. The guidelines in this section are adapted from the transliteration system of the United States Board on Geographic Names.

11.114 **Combinations not to be divided in Cyrillic transliteration.** Combinations representing single Cyrillic letters—*ch*, *kh*, *sh*, *shch*, *ts*, *ya*, *ye*, *yë*, *yu*, *zh*—should never be divided, nor should combinations of a vowel plus short *i* (or yod, transliterated *y*): *ay*, *ey*, *yey*, and so on.

11.115 **Division between Russian consonants.** Words may be divided between single consonants or between a consonant and a consonant combination.

ubor-ku chudes-nym mol-cha sred-stvo mor-skoy

The following consonant combinations are not normally divided: *bl*, *br*, *dr*, *dv*, *fl*, *fr*, *gl*, *gr*, *kl*, *kr*, *ml*, *pl*, *pr*, *sk*, *skr*, *skv*, *st*, *str*, *stv*, *tr*, *tv*, *vl*, *vr*, *zhd*. They may, however, be divided if they fall across the boundary of a prefix and a root or other such units (e.g., ob-lech', ras-kol).

11.116 **Division of Russian words after prefixes or between parts.** Words may be divided after a prefix, but generally the prefix itself should not be divided.

bes-poryadok  pere-stroyka  za-dat'  pred-lozhit'  pro-vesti  obo-gnat'

Compound words should be divided between parts.

radio-priyëmnik  gor-sovet  kino-teatr

11.117 **Division of Russian words after vowel or diphthong.** Words may be divided after a vowel or a diphthong before a single (Cyrillic) consonant.

Si-bir'  voy-na  Gorba-chev  da-zhe

Division after a vowel may also be made before a consonant combination.

puteshe-stvennik  khi-trit'  pro-stak  ru-brika

## *South Asian Languages*

11.118 **South Asian special characters.** Transliteration of the principal South Asian languages may require the following special characters (see also table 11.2):

Ā ā, Ḍ ḍ, Ē ē, Ḥ ḥ, Ī ī, Ḷ ḷ, Ḹ ḹ, Ṁ ṁ, Ṃ ṃ, Ṇ ṇ, Ṅ ṅ, N̄ n̄, Ñ ñ, Ō ō, Ṛ ṛ, Ṝ ṝ, Ṣ ṣ, Ś ś, Ṭ ṭ, Ū ū, Ẏ ẏ

Many writers using South Asian languages, however, employ a simplified style that does not use diacritics at all—for example, substituting *sh* for various *s*'s and ignoring subscript dots for dental consonants (e.g., *Shiva* rather than *Śiva* and *Vishnu* rather than *Viṣṇu*) and omitting macrons altogether (*apsara* rather than *apsarā*).

11.119 **South Asian capitalization.** South Asian writing systems do not distinguish between capital and lowercase letters. Transliterated text, however, may be capitalized according to the usual conventions in English for proper nouns and the like. For titles of works, use sentence case (see 11.8).

Amrita Pritam's works include the novel *The Thirteenth Sun* (*Terhawāraṃ sūraja*) and the autobiographical *Shadows of Words* (*Aksharoṃ ke sāye*).

Some authors prefer title case for transliterated titles (see 8.160), particularly if using a simplified transliterated style (e.g., *Aksharon kay Saayee*, in which the Hindi *kay* [a postpositional "of," transliterated as *ke* above] remains lowercase); others capitalize each word. Editors encountering either style may query any apparent inconsistencies but should otherwise follow the author's lead.

## CLASSICAL GREEK

11.120 **Transliterating Greek.** Isolated Greek words and phrases in works not focusing on ancient Greece are usually transliterated. Table 11.4 shows the Greek alphabet (with Unicode numbers) and corresponding letters of the Latin alphabet. In transliteration, all Greek accents are omitted. The macron is used to distinguish the long vowels eta (*ē*) and omega (*ō*) from the short vowels epsilon (*e*) and omicron (*o*). The iota subscript is transliterated by an *i* on the line, following the vowel it is associated with (ἀνθρώπῳ, *anthrōpōi*). The rough breathing is transliterated by *h*, which precedes a vowel or diphthong and follows the letter *r* (as in the English word *rhythm*). The smooth breathing is ignored, since it represents merely the absence of the *h* sound. If a diaeresis appears in the Greek, it also appears in transliteration. Transliterated Greek words or phrases are usually italicized unless the same words occur frequently, in which case they may be italicized at first mention and then set in roman.

11.121 **Typesetting Greek.** Authors who need to present Greek should use a Unicode font (see 11.2). Publishers need to make sure that a Greek font is available for publication; Greek may need to be set in a slightly different size to make it visually match the surrounding type. Greek is normally not set in italics (but see 7.73). Extra white space must occasionally be added where more than one diacritic appears over a vowel.

### *Breathings and Accents*

11.122 **Greek breathing marks.** When Greek is set in the Greek alphabet, every initial vowel or diphthong or rho must be marked with a breathing, either rough (῾, dasia) or smooth (᾿, psili). The breathing mark is placed over the initial lowercase vowel (or the second vowel of a diphthong).

TABLE 11.4. Greek alphabet (and Unicode numbers) and romanization

| Name of letter | Greek alphabet (and Unicode numbers) | Transliteration |
|---|---|---|
| alpha | Α (0391), α (03B1) | a |
| beta | Β (0392), β (03B2) | b |
| gamma | Γ (0393), γ[1] (03B3) | g |
| delta | Δ (0394), δ[2] (03B4) | d |
| epsilon | Ε (0395), ε (03B5) | e |
| zeta | Ζ (0396), ζ (03B6) | z |
| eta | Η (0397), η (03B7) | ē (0113) |
| theta | Θ (0398), θ[3] (03B8) | th |
| iota | Ι (0399), ι (03B9) | i |
| kappa | Κ (039A), κ (03BA) | k |
| lambda | Λ (039B), λ (03BB) | l |
| mu | Μ (039C), μ (03BC) | m |
| nu | Ν (039D), ν (03BD) | n |
| xi | Ξ (039E), ξ (03BE) | x |
| omicron | Ο (039F), ο (03BF) | o |
| pi | Π (03A0), π (03C0) | p |
| rho | Ρ (03A1), ρ (03C1) | r; *initially,* rh; *double,* rrh |
| sigma | Σ (03A3), σ (03C3), ς[4] (03C2) | s |
| tau | Τ (03A4), τ (03C4) | t |
| upsilon | Υ (03A5), υ (03C5) | u; *often* y, *exc. after* a, e, ē, i |
| phi | Φ (03A6), φ[5] (03C6) | ph |
| chi | Χ (03A7), χ (03C7) | kh, ch |
| psi | Ψ (03A8), ψ (03C8) | ps |
| omega | Ω (03A9), ω (03C9) | ō (014D) |

[1] Note that γγ becomes ng, and γκ becomes nk.
[2] Sometimes incorrectly appears as ∂ (U+2202, partial differential).
[3] Also ϑ (U+03D1).
[4] Final letter.
[5] Also ϕ (U+03D5).

It is positioned to the left of capital letters. Note that a single quotation mark cannot function as a breathing because it is the wrong size and does not sit close enough to the letter.

αὖτε ἕτεραι Ἕλλην ἥβη Ἶρις ὑπέχω ὠκύς ῥᾴδιος

11.123 **Greek accent marks.** There are three Greek accent marks: acute, or oxia (´); circumflex, or perispomeni (῀), which in some texts may look like an inverted breve (̑); and grave, or varia (`). Accents in Greek occur only over vowels. The circumflex occurs only on the two final syllables of a word. The grave accent occurs only on the last syllable. Like breathings, accents are placed over lowercase vowels, over the second vowel of a diphthong, and to the left of capital vowels. A diaeresis is used to indicate that two successive vowels do not form a diphthong but are voiced separately (as in French *naïf*).

11.124 **Unaccented Greek words.** With two exceptions, all Greek words are marked with accents—usually one, occasionally two (see below). The first exception is a group of monosyllabic words called proclitics, which are closely connected with the words following them. The proclitics are the forms of the definite article ὁ, ἡ, οἱ, αἱ; the prepositions εἰς, ἐν, ἐκ (ἐξ); the conjunctions εἰ, ὡς; and the adverb οὐ (οὐκ, οὐχ). The second exception is a group called enclitics, short words pronounced as if part of the word preceding them. Enclitics usually lose their accents (Ἀρταξερξῆς τε), and in certain circumstances the word preceding them gains a second accent (φοβεῖταί τις).

11.125 **Greek vowels.** Vowels complete with breathing marks and accents, in all combinations, are an integral part of every Greek font used in publishing. Each font, for example, should be able to provide, for lowercase eta, η, ή, ῆ, ὴ, ἠ, ἡ, ἤ, ἥ, ἢ, ἣ, ἦ, ἧ, and, for uppercase eta,H, Ἠ, Ἡ, Ἤ, Ἥ, Ἢ, Ἣ, Ἦ, Ἧ. Additional symbols are needed for scholarly works treating ancient manuscripts or papyri. Consult the latest Unicode character charts for Greek alphabets.

## *Punctuation and Numbers*

11.126 **Greek punctuation.** In Greek the period and comma are the same as in English; the colon and semicolon are both represented by a raised dot called an ano teleia (·), defined for Unicode as U+0387 but often represented by a middle dot, U+00B7; the question mark is represented by a semicolon. The apostrophe, or coronis (which resembles a smooth breathing mark), is used as an elision mark when the final vowel of one word is elided before a second word beginning with a vowel. In English texts, quoted words or passages in the Greek alphabet, of whatever length, should not be enclosed in quotation marks.

11.127 **Greek numbers.** Numbers, when not written out, are represented in ordinary Greek text by the letters of the alphabet, supplemented by three additional, obsolete Greek letters—stigma, koppa, and sampi: ϛʹ = 6, ϙʹ = 90, ϡʹ = 900. The diacritical mark resembling a prime (and defined for Unicode as the Greek numeral sign, U+0374) distinguishes the letters as numerals and is added to such a letter standing alone or to the last sign in a series. For example, ριαʹ means 111. For thousands, the foregoing letters are used with a different diacritical mark (the Greek

TABLE 11.5. Greek numerals

| | | | | | | | |
|---|---|---|---|---|---|---|---|
| 1 | α' | 13 | ιγ' | 30 | λ' | 600 | χ' |
| 2 | β' | 14 | ιδ' | 40 | μ' | 700 | ψ' |
| 3 | γ' | 15 | ιε' | 50 | ν' | 800 | ω' |
| 4 | δ' | 16 | ις' | 60 | ξ' | 900 | ϡ'[3] |
| 5 | ε' | 17 | ιζ' | 70 | ο' | 1,000 | ͵α |
| 6 | ϛ'[1] | 18 | ιη' | 80 | π' | 2,000 | ͵β |
| 7 | ζ' | 19 | ιθ' | 90 | ϙ'[2] | 3,000 | ͵γ |
| 8 | η' | 20 | κ' | 100 | ρ' | 4,000 | ͵δ |
| 9 | θ' | 21 | κα' | 200 | σ' | 10,000 | ͵ι |
| 10 | ι' | 22 | κβ' | 300 | τ' | 100,000 | ͵ρ |
| 11 | ια' | 23 | κγ' | 400 | υ' | | |
| 12 | ιβ' | 24 | κδ' | 500 | φ' | | |

[1] Stigma (U+03DB); also represented with digamma (U+03DD): ϝ'.
[2] Archaic koppa (U+03D9); also represented with koppa (U+03DF): ϟ'.
[3] Sampi (U+03E1); formerly disigma (double sigma).

lower numeral sign, U+0375): ͵α = 1,000, ͵αρια' = 1,111, ͵βσκβ' = 2,222. See table 11.5.

## *Word Division*

11.128 **Greek word division — consecutive vowels.** Diphthongs (αι, αυ, ει, ευ, ηυ, οι, ου, υι, ωυ) are never divided. But two consecutive vowels that do not form a diphthong are divided.

θε-ά-ο-μαι    υἱ-ός    παύ-ε-τε    νε-ώς

11.129 **Greek word division — single consonants.** When a single consonant occurs between two vowels, the word is divided before the consonant.

φω-νή    κε-φα-λίς    μέ-γα    δέ-δω-κεν    μή-τηρ

11.130 **Greek word division — two or more consonants.** If a consonant is doubled, or if a mute is followed by its corresponding aspirate (πφ, βφ, κχ, γχ, τθ, δθ), the word is divided after the first consonant.

θά-λασ-σα    συγ-χαί-ρω

If the combination of two or more consonants begins with a liquid (λ, ρ) or a nasal (μ, ν), division is made after the liquid or nasal.

ἔμ-προ-σθεν    (*but before* μν: μέ-μνημαι)

All other combinations of two or more consonants *follow* the division.

| | | | |
|---|---|---|---|
| πρᾶ-γμα | τέ-χνη | βα-θμός | αἰ-σχρός |
| βι-βλί-ον | δά-κτυ-λος | σκῆ-πτρον | βά-κτρον |

11.131 **Greek word division — compounds.** Compound words are divided between parts; within each part the rules detailed elsewhere in this section apply. The commonest type of compound word begins with a preposition or a prefix.

| | | | |
|---|---|---|---|
| ἀμφ- | ἀφ- | ὑπ- | ἐξ-έβαλον |
| ἀν- | ἐφ- | ὑφ- | καθ-ίστημι |
| ἀπ- | κατ- | | δύσ-μορφος |

## OLD ENGLISH AND MIDDLE ENGLISH

11.132 **Special characters in Old and Middle English.** Several Old English or Middle English letters not used in Modern English occur in both lowercase and capital forms (see also table 11.1).

| | |
|---|---|
| Ð ð | edh or eth |
| Þ þ | thorn |

Both edh and thorn represent voiced or unvoiced *th*, as in *them* or *three*.

| | |
|---|---|
| Ȝ ȝ | Yogh; occurs in Old English representing *g* as in *good*, *y* as in *year*, or *gh* as in *light* and *thought*. Yogh sometimes occurs in Middle English representing *y* as in *year* and *gh* as in *light* and *thought*, but normally not *g* as in *good*. |
| Æ æ | Ligature; should *not* be printed as two letters in Old English names and text (Ælfric). |

Authors should use the correct Unicode characters for the ligature and for edh, thorn, and yogh, and should provide their publisher with a list of these and any other special characters (see 11.2). For the long *s* (ſ), see 12.7.

11.133 **Ampersand and wynn.** In Old English and Middle English texts the Tironian *et*, or ⁊ (U+204A, a symbol that resembles the numeral seven), may be found for *and*, but the modern ampersand may be substituted for this. In Old English texts Ƿ or ƿ (wynn) is found for *w*; the modern *w* is often substituted for this.

11.134 **Old English vowels.** Modern editors of Old English sometimes distinguish between long and short vowels and diphthongs by means of a macron over the long versions (e.g., *ā, ǣ, ē, ēa, ēo, ī, īo, ō, ū, ȳ*). Note that, with the exception of the *æ* ligature, diphthongs are usually marked with a macron over only the first vowel.

## AMERICAN SIGN LANGUAGE (ASL)

11.135 **Signed languages.** The visual-gestural and tactile languages used by deaf and deafblind people in different parts of the world are called signed languages. Signed languages are quite different from spoken languages (although there may be regional effects of language contact), and a particular signed language may or may not share the same national or geographic boundaries as spoken languages in the same locations. The individual, lexical elements of these languages are known as signs. Deafblind people use tactile forms of signed languages, in addition to Protactile, an emerging language that further orients the user toward touch and contact with the body.

11.136 **Components of signs.** Signs have five major articulatory components—handshape, location, orientation, movement, and (in some cases) distinctive nonmanual signals.

11.137 **Writing ASL.** Formal systems for writing signed languages exist; however, none has been adopted for widespread use by deaf signers. This section offers an overview of some of the most frequently employed conventions for written transcription of signing. For additional resources, see Charlotte Baker-Shenk and Dennis Cokely, *American Sign Language: A Teacher's Resource Text on Grammar and Culture*; and Clayton Valli, Ceil Lucas, Kristin J. Mulrooney, and Miako Villanueva, *Linguistics of American Sign Language: An Introduction* (bibliog. 5).

11.138 **Glosses in ASL.** The written-language transcription of a sign is called a *gloss*. Glosses are words from the spoken language written in small capital letters: WOMAN, SCHOOL, CAT. (Alternatively, regular capital letters may be used.) When two or more written words are used to gloss a single sign, the glosses are separated by hyphens. The translation is enclosed in double quotation marks.

The sign for "a car drove by" is written as VEHICLE-DRIVE-BY.

One obvious limitation of the use of glosses from the spoken/written language to represent signs is that there is not always a one-to-one correspondence between the words or signs in any two languages.

11.139 **Compound signs.** Some combinations of signs have taken on a meaning separate from the meaning of the individual signs. Various typographical conventions are used to indicate these compounds, including a "close-up" mark or a plus sign. Depending on the transcription system, the sign for "parents" might be glossed as follows:

MOTHER⁀FATHER *or* MOTHER+FATHER

11.140 **Fingerspelling.** For proper nouns and other words borrowed from the spoken language, the signer may fingerspell the word, using the handshapes from a manual alphabet. (There are numerous fingerspelling alphabets used by different signed languages, among them the American Manual Alphabet.) Fingerspelled words may be transcribed in any of the following ways:

fs-JOHN *or* J-O-H-N *or* j-o-h-n

11.141 **Lexicalized signs.** Over time, some fingerspelled words have taken on the quality of distinct signs, either by omission of some of the individual letter signs or by a change in the orientation or movement of the letter signs. These lexicalized signs are represented by the "pound" symbol (#): #WHAT, #BACK, #DO.

11.142 **Handshapes.** Most of the handshapes of American Sign Language are described by the corresponding alphabetic or numerical handshape or a variation thereof. For example, APPLE is made with an X handshape; CREATE is made with a 4 handshape; ANY is made with an Open A handshape; YELL is made with a Bent 5 handshape. Handshapes without a clear relative in the fingerspelling or number system are labeled idiosyncratically according to the transcription system in use. For example, SARCASTIC is made with the HORNS handshape; AIRPLANE is made with the ILY handshape. Handshapes for signed languages that do not use the American Manual Alphabet are often described in relation to the ASL handshapes.

11.143 **Transcriptions of signed sentences.** Signed sentences are written as a sequence of glosses, often with the spoken/written-language translation underneath in italics or quotation marks or both. (For examples, see 11.144, 11.145.) Punctuation is generally omitted from sentence transcriptions (though not from the translations). Some writers, however, add question marks and exclamation points, and a comma may be used to indicate a short pause in the sentence.

11.144 **Pronouns, possessives, and reference.** Pronouns are commonly transcribed either as IX (since these are frequently produced with the "index" finger) or as PRO. Either of these is followed by indication of person and sometimes number. A similar convention is used with the possessive marker, sometimes glossed as POSS. There are varying conventions about how to indicate person and number. Thus, a third-person-singular pronoun in ASL (equivalent to English "he," "she," or "it") might be glossed as $\text{IX}_{3\text{p}}$, IX-3p, or PRO.3. A second-person-plural pronoun could be glossed as $\text{IX}_{2\text{p-pl}}$. Subscript indices are often used to show signs articulated in the same location or to indicate coreferential noun phrases. The following example indicates that *he* and *his* refer back to the same person:

$\text{IX}_{3\text{p}i}$ LOSE $\text{POSS}_{3\text{p}i}$ HOUSE
*He lost his house.*

11.145 **Nonmanual signals.** Nonmanual gestures may be labeled based on anatomical behavior or grammatical interpretive function. These gestures, indicated by various abbreviations and terms, are typeset in a smaller font followed by a half-point rule above the ASL sentence. For example, the label *whq* is commonly used to refer to the facial expression that marks questions involving "who," "what," "when," "where," "how," or "why." This expression consists of a cluster of features that include furrowed brows and slightly squinted eyes. In the example below, *whq* occurs over the entire question (i.e., the expression is articulated simultaneously with all of the manual signs over which the line extends). In the same example, the label *t* indicates a topic marker that occurs simultaneously with the sign YESTERDAY. Correct alignment is critical to an accurate transcription.

__________*t* _______________*whq*
YESTERDAY, fs-JOHN SEE WHO
*Whom did John see yesterday?*

# 12 Quotations and Dialogue

## OVERVIEW

12.1 **Scope of this chapter — and where else to look.** This chapter offers recommendations for incorporating words quoted from other sources in text and for presenting speech and other forms of dialogue, as in fiction and other creative genres. For the use of quotation marks for purposes other than direct quotation, see the discussions throughout 7.49–86. For quotation marks with titles of works, see the discussions in 8.157–204. For citing the sources of quotations, discussed only peripherally here, see chapters 13 and 14. For formatting block quotations in a manuscript, see 2.23, 2.24; for the manuscript editor's responsibilities regarding quoted material, see 2.67. For quotation marks in relation to surrounding text and punctuation, see 6.6, 6.9–11. For quotations of material from languages other than English, see 11.13–19.

12.2 **Quotations and modern scholarship.** Scholarship has always depended at least in part on the words and ideas of others. Incorporating those words and ideas is central to the act of writing and publishing. The choice between quoting, on the one hand, and merely copying, on the other, can mean the difference between properly acknowledging and crediting the ideas of others and falsely representing them as your own, thus making the conventions outlined in this chapter and in chapters 13 and 14 essential to modern scholarship. These conventions extend beyond scholarship to encompass journalism and other categories of nonfiction.

12.3 **Giving credit and seeking permission.** Whether quoting, paraphrasing, or using others' words or ideas to advance their own arguments, authors should give explicit credit to the source of those words or ideas. This credit often takes the form of a formal citation incorporated into a note or parenthetical reference. For a full discussion of source citations, see chapters 13 and 14. In addition, written permission may be needed, especially for direct quotations, as follows: for more than a line or two of a poem or a song lyric in copyright; for prose quotations of, say, more than three paragraphs or for many short passages from a work in copyright; or for any excerpt from certain unpublished materials (letters, email messages, interviews, and so forth). For more information about permissions, consult chapter 4, especially 4.79–98.

12.4 **When to paraphrase rather than quote.** Authors drawing on the work of others to illustrate their arguments should first decide whether direct quotation or paraphrase will be more effective. Too many quotations with too little commentary can pose a distraction, and readers may choose to skip over long or frequent quotations. In some cases, authors who notice an error in a passage they wish to quote should paraphrase the original, eliminating the error. For "silent correction," see 12.7 (item 6); for *sic*, see 12.72. At their discretion, authors may also paraphrase to avoid reproducing outdated or offensive language verbatim (see also 6.99).

12.5 **When quotation and attribution is unnecessary.** Commonly known or readily verifiable facts can be stated without quotation or attribution unless the wording is taken directly from another source. Authors, of course, must be absolutely sure of any unattributed facts, and editors should flag anything that seems suspicious (see 12.6). Likewise, proverbs and other familiar expressions can usually be reproduced without quotation or attribution. Of the following statements, only the last—a direct quotation—requires quotation marks and attribution (as well as a source citation, either in the text or in a note; see 12.75–83).

Until July 20, 1969, no one had set foot on the moon.
The chemical symbol for gold, Au, derives from the Latin word *aurum*.
Ithaca, New York, is located at the southern end of Cayuga Lake.
No one can convince the young that practice makes perfect.
If reading maketh a full man, Henry is half empty.
*but*
It was Shakespeare's contemporary Francis Bacon who wrote that "reading maketh a ful man, conference a ready man, and writing an exact man."

For the treatment of unconventional spellings in quoted material (as in the quotation from Bacon), see 12.7, item 6.

12.6 **Ensuring accuracy of quotations.** It is impossible to overemphasize the importance of meticulous accuracy in quoting from the works of others. Authors should check every direct quotation against the original or, if the original is unavailable, against a careful transcription of the passage. This should be done *before* the manuscript is submitted to the publisher. Manuscript editors can help by spot-checking quotations against available resources to get an idea of how accurate the transcriptions are and by querying any apparent errors; they may not, however, have ready access to an author's sources, nor is it typically assumed to be an editor's responsibility to confirm the accuracy of quotations. Moreover, it takes far less time for authors to accurately transcribe quotations during the writing stage than for authors or editors to go back to the original sources once a work is submitted for publication. See also 2.38, 2.141.

## PERMISSIBLE CHANGES TO QUOTATIONS

12.7 **Permissible changes to punctuation, capitalization, and spelling.** Although in a direct quotation the wording of the source should be reproduced exactly, the following changes are generally permissible to make a passage fit into the syntax and typography of the surrounding text. See also 12.8.

1. Single quotation marks may be changed to double, and double to single (see 12.30); punctuation relative to quotation marks should be adjusted accordingly (see 6.9). "Smart" quotation marks and apostrophes may be imposed (see 6.123, 6.125), and guillemets and other types of quotation marks from languages other than English may be changed to regular double or single quotation marks (see 11.13).
2. En dashes or hyphens used as em dashes may be changed to em dashes, with any space before or after the dash or hyphen eliminated as needed (see 6.91–98). Hyphens may be changed to en dashes in number ranges or other contexts where an en dash may be appropriate (for use of the en dash, see 6.82–90).
3. The initial letter may be changed to a capital or a lowercase letter as needed to conform to the syntax of the surrounding text (see 12.18–21).
4. At the end of the quotation, a period or other mark of punctuation in the original may be omitted or changed to a period or comma as required by the surrounding text; a question mark or exclamation point may be retained if it continues to apply to the word or words as quoted. For punctuation with ellipses, see 12.59–69.
5. Original note reference marks (and the notes to which they refer) may be omitted unless omission would affect the meaning of the quotation. If an original note is included, the quotation may best be set off as a block quotation (see 12.9), with the note in smaller type at the end, or the note may be summarized in the accompanying text. Note references added to a quotation must be distinguished from any note references in the original (see also 13.54). On the other hand, parenthetical text references in the original should be retained; if a parenthetical text reference is added to the original, it must be placed in square brackets (see 12.70–74).
6. Obvious typographic errors may be corrected silently (without comment or *sic*; see 12.72), unless the passage quoted is from an older work or a manuscript or other unpublished source where idiosyncrasies of spelling are generally preserved. If spelling, capitalization, and punctuation are modernized or altered for clarity, readers must be so informed in a note, in a preface, or elsewhere.
7. In quoting from early printed documents, the archaic long *s* (ſ, Unicode

character U+017F), used to represent a lowercase *s* at the beginning or in the middle but never at the end of a word ("Such goodneſs of your juſtice, that our ſoul . . ."), may be changed to a modern *s*. Similarly, a title like *Vanitie and Vncertaintie* may be changed to *Vanitie and Uncertaintie*, but writers or editors without a strong background in classical or Renaissance studies should generally be wary of changing *u* to *v* or *i* to *j* (or vice versa). See also 11.63, 11.132–34.

12.8 **Permissible changes to typography and layout.** The following elements of typography and layout may be changed to assimilate a quotation to the surrounding text (see also 12.7):

1. The typeface or font should be changed to agree with the surrounding text.
2. Words in full capitals in the original may be set in small caps, if that is the preferred style for the surrounding text. (See also 10.9.)
3. In drama or dialogue, names of speakers may be moved from a centered position to flush left.
4. Underlined words in a quoted manuscript may be printed as italics, unless the underlining itself is considered integral to the source or otherwise worthy of reproducing.
5. In quoting correspondence, such matters as paragraph indents and the position of the salutation and signature may be adjusted.

For paragraph indents in block quotations, see 12.22. For reproducing poetry extracts, see 12.25–29. For permissible changes to titles of books, articles, poems, and other works, see 8.167.

## QUOTATIONS IN RELATION TO TEXT

### *Run In or Set Off*

12.9 **Run-in and block quotations defined.** Quoted text may be either run in to the surrounding text and enclosed in quotation marks, "like this," or set off as a block quotation, or extract. Block quotations, which are not enclosed in quotation marks, always start a new line. They are further distinguished from the surrounding text by being indented (from the left and sometimes from the right) or set in smaller type or a different font from the text. These matters are normally decided by the publisher's designer or by journal style. Authors preparing block quotations in their manuscripts can simply indent them from the left margin (see 2.23, 2.24). See also 12.22–24. For poetry, see 12.25–29. Fictional dialogue is usually run in to the text of the surrounding narrative (sometimes without quotation marks), though block quotations may be used for various purposes; for details and examples, see 12.39–53.

12.10 **Choosing between run-in and block quotations.** In deciding whether to run in or set off a quotation, length is usually the deciding factor. In general, a short quotation, especially one that is not a full sentence, should be run in. A hundred words or more can generally be set off as a block quotation. Other criteria apply, however. A quotation of two or more paragraphs is best set off (see 12.22–24), as are quoted correspondence (if salutations, signatures, and such are included), lists (see 2.25), and any material that requires special formatting. If many quotations of varying length occur close together, running them all in may make for easier reading. But where quotations are being compared or otherwise used as entities in themselves, it may be better to set them all as block quotations, however short. For setting off poetry, see 12.25–29.

## *Assimilation into the Surrounding Text*

12.11 **Logical and grammatical assimilation of quoted text.** In incorporating fragmentary quotations into a text, phrase the surrounding sentence in such a way that the quoted words fit into it logically and grammatically—as if there were no quotation marks—and quoting only as much of the original as is necessary. For the incorporation of full sentences (as in the last part of the example below), see 12.13–17.

> The narrator's constant references to "malicious code and obsolete data" detract from a more fundamental issue—that we are dumping "the burden of human history" onto computer hard drives. It is this vision of the future that is most alarming: "If (when?) we run out of sources of electricity," she asks, "will we forget who we are?"

12.12 **Integrating tenses and pronouns from quoted text.** In quoting verbatim, writers need to integrate tenses and pronouns into the new context.

> [*Original*] Mr. Moll took particular pains to say to you, gentlemen, that these eleven people here are guilty of murder; he calls this a cold-blooded, deliberate and premeditated murder.

> [*As quoted*] According to Darrow, Moll had told the jury that the eleven defendants were "guilty of murder" and had described the murder as "cold-blooded, deliberate and premeditated."

Occasional adjustments to the original may be bracketed. This device should be used sparingly, however (see also 12.71).

Roosevelt was frank about her own activism, writing as late as 1952 that she'd spent "many years of [her] life in opposition."

## *Quotations and Punctuation*

**12.13** **Punctuation relative to closing quotation marks.** For a full discussion of the use of periods, commas, and other marks of punctuation relative to closing quotation marks, see 6.9–11. See also 12.7, item 4. For examples of fictional dialogue and other forms of direct discourse, see 12.39–53. The rest of this section is primarily concerned with punctuation relative to the beginning of quoted material.

**12.14** **Comma to introduce a quotation.** When it is simply a matter of identifying a speaker or writer, a comma is used after *said, replied, asked, wrote,* and similar verbs to introduce a quotation. (When used with quoted speech, such identifiers are usually referred to as dialogue or speaker tags; see also 12.41.) Such usage is more traditional than logical, recognizing the syntactical independence of the quoted material from the surrounding text (even as the surrounding text often becomes dependent on the quoted material). A colon, though never wrong in such instances, should be used sparingly (see 12.16).

Garrett replied, "I hope you are not referring to me."

Fish writes, "What [the students] did was move the words out of a context (the faculty club door) in which they had a literal and obvious meaning into another context (my classroom) in which the meaning was no less obvious and literal and yet was different."

When the sentence is inverted and the quotation comes first (a common arrangement), a comma is usually required at the end of the quotation unless the quotation ends with a question mark or an exclamation point. See also 6.9, 6.10.

"I hope you are not referring to me," Garrett replied.

When the quotation is interrupted, two commas are required.

"I hope," Garrett replied, "you are not referring to me."

When the quotation is subordinated to or otherwise integrated into the surrounding text, no comma is needed (see also 12.15, 12.19).

> Fish observed that "what [the students] did was . . ."

See also 6.43, 6.45.

12.15 **No comma to introduce a quotation.** Many writers mistakenly use a comma to introduce any direct quotation, regardless of its relationship to the surrounding text. But when a quotation introduced mid-sentence forms a syntactical part of the surrounding sentence, no comma or other mark of punctuation is needed to introduce it, though punctuation may be required for other reasons. Note that the comma in the last example below is required by the convention described in 12.14.

> Donovan made a slight bow and said he was "very glad."

> One of the protesters scrawled "Long live opera!" in huge red letters.

> According to one observer, Miles Davis's recordings were "a central contribution to the idea of jazz as the main source of innovation in mid-twentieth-century American music."

> She said she would "prefer not to comment."

> *but*

> Miles Davis's recordings—"a central contribution to the idea of jazz as the main source of innovation in mid-twentieth-century American music"—have never gone out of style.

> She said that she would, in short, "prefer not to comment."

> She said, "I prefer not to comment."

See also 6.44.

12.16 **Colon to introduce a quotation.** When a quotation is introduced by an independent clause (i.e., a grammatically complete sentence), a colon should normally be used (but see 12.17). Such introductions may include a formal introductory phrase such as *the following* or *as follows* (see also 6.68).

The role of the author has been variously described. Henry Fielding, at the beginning of his *History of Tom Jones,* defines it as follows: "An author ought to consider himself, not as a gentleman who gives a private or eleemosynary treat, but rather as one who keeps a public ordinary, at which all persons are welcome for their money."

Faraday's conclusion was alarming: "Without significant intervention, your home town will have gone the way of Atlantis by century's end."

A colon may also be used in place of a comma to introduce a quotation. Such a colon, never wrong, should be used consistently—for example, to introduce quotations of more than one sentence or, occasionally, to add emphasis. See also 12.14.

Garrett replied: "I hope you are not referring to me. Because if you are . . ."

12.17 **Period rather than colon to introduce a block quotation.** Unless introduced by *as follows* or other wording that requires a colon (see 6.68), a block quotation may be preceded by a period rather than a colon. Such usage should be applied consistently. See also 12.22–24.

A paradigmatic case is "crunch time"—the days and hours before a game, a new level, or an important update is released.

> When crunch time is called, people bring their sleeping bags and stay for five days to finish the release. You cannot leave the office; you cannot go home. We order pizza and work all the time. If there are people who want to go home and look after their kids, they face negative sentiments.

## *Initial Capital or Lowercase Letter*

12.18 **Changing capitalization to suit syntax — an overview.** Aside from proper nouns and some of the words derived from them (see 8.1), most words are normally lowercased unless they begin a sentence (or, often, a line of poetry). To suit this requirement, the first word in a quoted passage must often be adjusted to conform to the surrounding text. In most types of works, this adjustment may be done silently, as such capitalization does not normally affect the significance of the quoted matter, which is assumed to have been taken from another context (see 12.7, item 3). In some types of works, however, it may be obligatory to indicate the change by bracketing the initial quoted letter; for examples of this practice, appropriate to legal writing and some types of textual commentary, see 12.21.

12.19 **Initial capital or lowercase — run-in quotations.** When a quotation introduced mid-sentence forms a syntactical part of the sentence (see also 12.15), it begins with a lowercase letter even if the original begins with a capital.

Benjamin Franklin admonishes us to "plough deep while sluggards sleep."

With another aphorism he reminded his readers that "experience keeps a dear school, but fools will learn in no other"—an observation as true today as then.

When the quotation has a more remote syntactic relation to the rest of the sentence, the initial letter remains capitalized.

As Franklin advised, "Plough deep while sluggards sleep."

His aphorism "Experience keeps a dear school, but fools will learn in no other" is a cogent warning to people of all ages. (See also 6.44.)

On the other hand, for a quotation that is only a part of a sentence in the original but forms a complete sentence as quoted, a lowercase letter may be changed to a capital if appropriate. In the example that follows, "those" begins mid-sentence in the original (see 12.20).

Aristotle put it this way: "Those who are eminent in virtue usually do not stir up insurrections, always a minority."

*but*

Aristotle believed that "those who are eminent in virtue usually do not stir up insurrections, always a minority."

12.20 **Initial capital or lowercase — block quotations.** The consideration of whether to lowercase a capital letter beginning a block quotation is exactly the same as it is for run-in quotations (see 12.19): The initial letter of a block quotation that is capitalized in the original may be lowercased if the syntax demands it. In the following example, the quotation from Aristotle in the Jowett translation (Modern Library) begins in the original with a capital letter and a paragraph indent. See also 12.22.

In discussing the reasons for political disturbances, Aristotle observes that

> revolutions also break out when opposite parties, e.g. the rich and the people, are equally balanced, and there is little or no middle class; for, if either party were manifestly superior, the other would not risk an attack upon them. And, for this reason, those who are eminent in virtue usually do not stir up insurrections, always a minority. Such are the beginnings and causes of the disturbances and revolutions to which every form of government is liable. (*Politics* 5.4)

On the other hand, the capital should be retained—or a lowercase letter should be changed to a capital—if the syntax requires it. See also 12.16.

In discussing the reasons for political disturbances, Aristotle makes the following observations:

> Revolutions also break out when opposite parties, e.g. the rich and the people, are equally balanced, and there is little or no middle class; . . .

12.21 **Brackets to indicate a change in capitalization.** In some legal writing, close textual analysis or commentary, and other contexts, it is considered obligatory to indicate any change in capitalization by brackets. Although this practice is unnecessary in most writing, in contexts where it is considered appropriate it should be employed consistently throughout a work. For the use of brackets in reviews and blurbs, see 12.38.

According to article 6, section 6, she is given the power "[t]o extend or renew any existing indebtedness."

"[R]eal estates may be conveyed by lease and release, or bargain and sale," according to section 2 of the Northwest Ordinance.

Let us compare Aristotle's contention that "[i]nferiors revolt in order that they may be equal, and equals that they may be superior" (*Politics* 5.2), with his later observation that "[r]evolutions also break out when opposite parties, e.g. the rich and the people, are equally balanced" (5.4).

Note that the brackets above signal changes to capitalization that are required by syntax alone, according to the principles outlined in 12.19. Brackets should *not* be used simply to adjust capitalization to match usage in the surrounding text. For example, in a document that capitalizes *Black* to refer to race, lowercase *black* would be retained in quoted text from a source that uses lowercase (except as required by syntax). If the stylistic discrepancy is relevant, it may be noted in parentheses or elsewhere (see also 8.39, 12.73).

According to Du Bois, the musical epigraphs "echo . . . black souls in the dark past" (viii; *black* is spelled with a lowercase *b* in the source).

## *Block Quotations*

12.22 **Block quotations of more than one paragraph.** Quoted material of more than a paragraph, even if very brief, is best set off as a block quotation. (For a less desirable alternative, see 12.32.) A multiparagraph block quotation should generally reflect the paragraph breaks of the original, with one notable exception: The first quoted paragraph should begin flush left, even if the original text has a first-line paragraph indent. Subsequent paragraphs in the quotation should be indicated either by first-line paragraph indents or (less desirably) by extra line space between the paragraphs (see also 12.24). The following example, from Jane Austen's *Pride and Prejudice*, includes four full paragraphs:

He began to wish to know more of her, and as a step towards conversing with her himself, attended to her conversation with others. His doing so drew her notice. It was at Sir William Lucas's, where a large party were assembled.

"What does Mr. Darcy mean," said she to Charlotte, "by listening to my conversation with Colonel Forster?"

"That is a question which Mr. Darcy only can answer."

"But if he does it any more I shall certainly let him know that I see what he is about. He has a very satirical eye, and if I do not begin by being impertinent myself, I shall soon grow afraid of him."

If the first part of the opening paragraph were to be omitted, it would still begin flush left. For ellipses at the beginning of paragraphs, see 12.65.

12.23 **Block quotations beginning in text.** A long quotation may begin with a few words run in to the text. This device should be used only when text intervenes between the quoted matter in the text and its continuation.

"There is no safe trusting to dictionaries and definitions," observed Charles Lamb.

> We should more willingly fall in with this popular language, if we did not find *brutality* sometimes awkwardly coupled with *valour* in the same

> vocabulary. The comic writers . . . have contributed not a little to mislead us upon this point. To see a hectoring fellow exposed and beaten upon the stage, has something in it wonderfully diverting. ("Popular Fallacies," *Essays of Elia*, 277)

"In short," says Crane, summarizing Gordon's philosophy,

> there has been "almost a continual improvement" in all branches of human knowledge; . . .

A permissible alternative is to set off the entire quotation, enclosing the intervening words of text in brackets.

> There is no safe trusting to dictionaries and definitions [observed Charles Lamb]. We should more willingly . . .

12.24 **Text following a block quotation or extract.** If the text following a block quotation or extract (whether prose or poetry) is a continuation of the paragraph that introduces the quotation or extract, it begins flush left. If, on the other hand, the resuming text constitutes a new paragraph, it receives a paragraph indent. The decision in each case is usually made by the author or, failing that, may be left to the editor (see 2.23, 2.24). In works where each new paragraph is to appear flush left, distinguished only by extra line space, such a distinction may have to be ignored (or it can be signaled by imposing more line space before new paragraphs than before continued text).

## *Poetry Extracts*

12.25 **Setting off poetry.** In a published work, two or more lines of verse are best set off as an extract. (In a note, set off three or more; see 13.41.) A poetry extract, if isolated, is often visually centered on the page between the left and right margins (usually relative to the longest line), but if two or more stanzas of the same poem appear on the same page, a uniform indent from the left may work better (see 12.26). A half line to a full line of space should appear between stanzas. Within each piece or stanza, the indentation pattern of the original should be reproduced (but indents should be distinguished from runover lines; see 12.27). For placement of the source, see 12.82. For advice on formatting poetry extracts in a manuscript, see 2.24.

Sure there was wine
Before my sighs did drie it: there was corn
Before my tears did drown it.
Is the yeare onely lost to me?
Have I no bayes to crown it?
No flowers, no garlands gay? all blasted?
All wasted?
(George Herbert, "The Collar")

If the quotation does not begin with a full line, space approximating the omitted part should be left.

there was corn
Before my tears did drown it.

For text that follows an extract, see 12.24.

12.26 **Uniform indents for poetry.** Where all or most poetry extracts consist of blank verse (as in studies of Shakespeare) or are very long, uniform indents from the left margin usually work best (e.g., a left indent that matches the one, if any, used for prose extracts).

I have full cause of weeping, but this heart
Shall break into a hundred thousand flaws
Or ere I'll weep. O Fool! I shall go mad.

12.27 **Long lines and runovers in poetry.** Runover lines (the remainder of lines too long to appear as a single line) are usually indented one em from the line above, as in the following quotation from Walt Whitman's "Song of Myself":

My tongue, every atom of my blood, form'd from this
    soil, this air,
Born here of parents born here from parents the same,
    and their parents the same,
I, now thirty-seven years old in perfect health begin,
Hoping to cease not till death.

Runover lines, although indented, should be distinct from new lines deliberately indented by the poet (as in the Herbert poem quoted in 12.25). Generally, a unique and uniform indent for runovers will be enough to accomplish this. See also 2.24.

12.28 **Quotation marks in poems.** Quotation marks at the start of a line can usually be aligned with the other lines in the excerpt.

He holds him with his skinny hand.
"There was a ship," quoth he.
"Hold off! unhand me, grey-beard loon!"
Eftsoons his hand dropt he.

Some publishers prefer instead to place quotation marks at the start of a line of poetry outside the alignment of the poem, with lines left-aligned as if the quotation marks were not there. This practice, not followed by Chicago, may be impractical in certain electronic publication formats.

12.29 **Run-in poetry quotations.** If space or context in the text or in a note requires that two or more lines be run in, the lines are separated by a slash, with one space on either side (in printed works, a thin space to an en space).

Andrew Marvell's praise of John Milton, "Thou has not missed one thought that could be fit, / And all that was improper does omit" ("On *Paradise Lost*"), might well serve as our motto.

For running in more than one stanza (to be avoided if at all possible), see 12.33.

## QUOTATION MARKS

### *Double or Single Quotation Marks*

12.30 **Quotations and "quotes within quotes."** Quoted words, phrases, and sentences run in to the text are enclosed in double quotation marks. Single quotation marks enclose quotations within quotations; double marks, quotations within these; and so on. (The practice in the United Kingdom and elsewhere is often the reverse: Single marks are used first, then double, and so on.) When the material quoted consists entirely of a quotation within a quotation, only one set of quotation marks need be employed (usually double quotation marks), though an exception may be made in quoted dialogue (see 12.46).

"Don't be absurd!" said Henry. "To say that 'I mean what I say' is the same as 'I say what I mean' is to be as confused as Alice at the Mad Hatter's tea party. You remember what the Hatter said to her: 'Not the same thing a bit! Why you might just as well say that "I see what I eat" is the same thing as "I eat what I see"!' "

Note carefully not only the placement of the single and double closing quotation marks but also that of the exclamation points in relation to those marks in the example above. Exclamation points, like question marks, are placed just within the set of quotation marks ending the element to which such terminal punctuation belongs. See also 6.9–11.

12.31 **Quotation marks in block quotations.** Although material set off as a block quotation is not enclosed in quotation marks, quoted matter *within* the block quotation is enclosed in double quotation marks—in other words, treated as it would be in otherwise unquoted text (see 12.30). An author or editor who changes a run-in quotation to a block quotation must delete the opening and closing quotation marks and change any internal ones. The following examples illustrate the same material first in run-in form and then as a block quotation:

The narrator then breaks in: "Imagine Bart's surprise, dear reader, when Emma turned to him and said, contemptuously, 'What "promise"?' "

The narrator then breaks in:

> Imagine Bart's surprise, dear reader, when Emma turned to him and said, contemptuously, "What 'promise'?"

Similarly, converting a block quotation to a run-in quotation requires adding and altering quotation marks. For interpolations that include quoted matter, see 12.74.

## *Run-In Quotations of More than One Paragraph*

12.32 **Quotation marks across paragraphs.** Quoted material of more than one paragraph should be presented as a block quotation if at all possible (see 12.10). If for some reason such a passage must be run in to the surrounding text, a quotation mark is needed at the beginning of the quotation and at the beginning of *each* new paragraph but at the end of only the *final* paragraph. (Note that each successive paragraph must begin on a new line, as in the original.) The same practice is followed in dialogue when one speaker's remarks extend over more than one paragraph; for examples, see 12.45.

12.33 **Quoting more than one stanza of poetry.** A poetry quotation that spans more than one stanza should be presented as an extract, if at all possible (see 12.25). If it must be run in to the text (set off by opening and closing quotation marks), two slashes (//), with a space before and after, should appear between stanzas. For the use of the slash between run-in lines of poetry, see 12.29.

12.34 **Quoting letters in their entirety.** A letter quoted in its entirety should be set off as a block quotation. In the undesirable event that it must be run in, it should carry an opening quotation mark before the first line (including the salutation) and before each new paragraph (each of which must begin on a new line, as in the original). A closing quotation mark appears only after the last line (often the signature). See also 12.32.

## *Quotation Marks Omitted*

12.35 **Epigraphs.** Quotation marks are not used around epigraphs (quotations used as ornaments preceding a text, usually to set the tone for what follows, rather than as illustration or documentation); quotation marks in the original, however, should be retained as needed. Like block quotations, epigraphs receive a distinctive typographic treatment—often being set in a smaller typeface and indented from the right or left, and sometimes italicized. Treatment of sources, which are usually set on a separate line, also varies, though more than one epigraph used in the same work should receive consistent treatment. For more on sources, see 12.81–83. See also 1.41. For permissions relative to epigraphs, see 4.91.

It is a truth universally acknowledged, that a single man in possession of a good fortune, must be in want of a wife.
    Jane Austen, *Pride and Prejudice*

Hold fast to dreams
For if dreams die
Life is a broken-winged bird
That cannot fly.
—Langston Hughes, "Dreams"

"Tommy," I said, quite sternly. "There's mud all over your shirt."
Kazuo Ishiguro, *Never Let Me Go*

If the source must be run in to the quoted text rather than placed on a new line, and the source is preceded by an em dash, no space precedes the em dash; alternatively, parentheses may be used for the source.

Cogito, ergo sum.—Descartes *or* Cogito, ergo sum. (Descartes)

12.36 **Decorative initials ("drop caps" and raised initials).** When the first word of a chapter or section opens with a large raised or dropped initial letter, and this letter belongs to the beginning of a run-in quotation, the opening quotation mark is often omitted.

OF THE MAKING OF MANY BOOKS there is no end," declared an ancient Hebrew sage, who had himself magnificently aggravated the situation he was decrying.

If the opening quotation mark is included, it should appear in the same size and with the same vertical alignment as the regular text.

12.37 **Maxims, questions, and the like.** Maxims, mottoes, rules, and other familiar expressions, sometimes enclosed in quotation marks, are discussed in 6.44 and 7.65. Questions that do not require quotation marks are discussed in 6.45 and 6.73. For dialogue without quotation marks, see 12.48.

12.38 **Publicity reviews and blurbs.** Brief endorsements of no more than a few sentences presented either in the front of a book or on the cover (and often included on the publisher's website and other promotional materials) may be formatted in the manner of epigraphs (see 12.35). (Such endorsements will generally consist either of excerpts from published reviews or of blurbs from individuals; blurbs are solicited by the author or publisher and are different from published reviews.) Unlike epigraphs, however, quoted endorsements are often placed in quotation marks, usually at the discretion of the publisher or book designer (and especially if the quoted text shares a line with the source). To suggest fidelity to the original, many publishers add brackets to signal changes to capitalization; such brackets are, however, unnecessary and arguably distracting (see also 12.21). See also 1.17.

From the original review:

The author has achieved a magnificent, once-in-a-generation feat. Not since *On the Origin of Species* has the landscape of an entire field been altered by the publication of a single book. Environmentalists will be citing this extraordinary opus for decades to come, if not longer. (Joni C. Reviewer, *Science First*)

As adjusted for cover copy and elsewhere:

A magnificent, once-in-a-generation feat. . . . Environmentalists will be citing this extraordinary opus for decades to come.
—Joni C. Reviewer, *Science First*

*or*

"A magnificent, once-in-a-generation feat. . . . Environmentalists will be citing this extraordinary opus for decades to come."
—Joni C. Reviewer, *Science First*

*or*

"Magnificent."—Joni C. Reviewer, *Science First*

*but not*

"[M]agnificent."—Joni C. Reviewer, *Science First*

Some publishers, drawing on the enthusiasm of a particularly positive review, add exclamation points that are not in the original ("Magnificent!"). This practice is best avoided unless prior approval has been obtained from the reviewer. For the use of ellipses to signal omissions, see 12.59–69.

## DIALOGUE AND OTHER FORMS OF DIRECT DISCOURSE

12.39 **Fictional dialogue versus other forms of direct quotation.** The advice in this section draws mainly on conventions for fiction, including novels and short stories. These conventions, however, overlap with the conventions for quoting the words of others in any context or genre, from scholarly prose to works with a more conversational tone. In any context the goal is the same: to differentiate the words of a narrator from the words of others, whether those other words have been quoted from a research paper or consist of the imagined dialogue of a fictional character. Writers and editors should therefore review this section in the context of the other sections in this chapter.

12.40 **Quotation marks for dialogue.** Dialogue—including speech and other forms of direct discourse—is traditionally enclosed in quotation marks. A change in speaker is usually indicated by a new paragraph, as in the following excerpt from the title story of Jhumpa Lahiri's *Interpreter of Maladies* (Houghton Mifflin, 1999):

> "I look forward to it, actually," Mr. Kapasi said as they continued on their way. "The Sun Temple is one of my favorite places. In that way it is a reward for me. I give tours on Fridays and Saturdays only. I have another job during the week."
>
> "Oh? Where?" Mr. Das asked.
>
> "I work in a doctor's office."
>
> "You're a doctor?"
>
> "I am not a doctor. I work with one. As an interpreter."
>
> "What does a doctor need an interpreter for?"
>
> "He has a number of Gujarati patients. My father was Gujarati, but many people do not speak Gujarati in this area, including the doctor. And so the doctor asked me to work in his office, interpreting what the patients say."
>
> "Interesting. I've never heard of anything like that," Mr. Das said.
>
> Mr. Kapasi shrugged. "It is a job like any other."
>
> "But so romantic," Mrs. Das said dreamily, breaking her extended silence.

Compare this example with the example in 12.48.

12.41 **Speaker tags.** The words that identify the speaker of dialogue—often referred to as speaker tags or dialogue tags—are traditionally separated from the speech by a comma or other punctuation. (Note that when a speech ends in a question mark or exclamation point, a comma or period is omitted; see also 6.133, 6.134.) The following variations, among others, may be used:

> "We're late," Ava said, "so hurry up."
> "What time is it?" her friend asked. "I don't have a watch."
> "Look at your phone." Ava was getting impatient. "Or don't you have one?"
> *or*
> "Look at your phone"—Ava was getting impatient—"or don't you have one?"

When a speaker tag introduces a quotation, it is followed by a comma (or, less often, a colon; see also 6.43, 6.69).

Ava said, "We're late."

Speaker tags are often inverted, a variation that is usually best avoided with pronouns.

"Are we late?" asked Ava.
*but usually not*
"Are we late?" asked she.

Speaker tags are normally limited to *said*, *asked*, *replied*, *answered*, and other verbs that can plausibly describe a physical act of speech or utterance of some kind. (Past-tense verbs are shown here; speaker tags using the present and other tenses are punctuated in the same way.) Some authors also use verbs such as *sighed* or *laughed* that do not necessarily suggest literal speech; editors may query such usage but should ultimately defer to the author. In general, however, avoid verbs that would not apply to speech or utterance of any kind.

"We're late," she said.
*not*
"We're late," she frowned.

Instead, *frowned* and other such action words can be incorporated in other ways. Note that when an action alone follows quoted speech, it usually begins a new sentence.

"We're late," she said, frowning.
*or*
"We're late." She was frowning.

**12.42** **Interrupted speech.** To show an interruption to quoted speech or dialogue, an em dash is normally used (see also 6.93). As with question marks and exclamation points, which take the place of commas and periods at the end of quoted speech (see 6.133, 6.134), the dash alone signals the end of the speech.

"Don't inter—" The egg came out of nowhere, striking the teacher on the forehead.

"Why do you always—"
"Always what?"

"Did I ever tell you about the—" he began, but nobody was listening.

Normally, the dash belongs to the interrupted speaker and is placed inside the quotation marks. But when the narrator intervenes in the middle of a speech, the dashes are placed outside the quotation marks, even if the speaker's words are themselves interrupted.

> "Don't you dare"—Cassandra paused for a moment to glare at Ralph—"interrupt me."

For faltering speech and incomplete thoughts, which are signaled by ellipses, see 12.43. For speakers interrupting themselves, see 12.44.

12.43 **Faltering speech and incomplete thoughts.** Faltering or fragmented speech or speech that pauses or trails off—as in dialogue or, less often, narrative text—is usually represented by an ellipsis (see also 12.59). The ellipsis may stand alone, or it may be preceded or followed by a question mark or exclamation point; however, in fiction and other creative genres, the convention is to *not* use an additional period at the end of a complete sentence (see the third example below; cf. 12.62). In the fourth example, note the absence of a comma before the closing quotation mark (a departure from previous editions intended to align with common usage in fiction).

> "I . . . I . . . that is, we . . . yes, *we* have made an awful blunder!"
> "The ship . . . oh my God! . . . it's sinking!" cried Henrietta.
> I thought back to my previous life . . . It no longer seemed real.
> "But . . . but . . ." said Tom.
> "Stop looking at me . . . !" It was at once a threat and an invitation.
> "Have you no scruples . . . ?" The question hung in the air.

For the use of ellipses to indicate editorial omissions—which are styled the same but with additional considerations relative to the punctuation of adjacent text—see 12.59–69. For interrupted speech, which is signaled by dashes, see 12.42.

12.44 **Stuttering and the like.** Stuttering is usually indicated by hyphens, whether for an initial sound or an entire word or phrase. Repetition involving the first word in a sentence may be lowercased unless the word is a proper noun. The choice, however, is arbitrary; unless a publisher specifies otherwise, editors should impose consistency but otherwise defer to an author's capitalization.

> "W-when do we start?" I asked. "I c-ca-ca-can't find my n-notes."
> "W-w-will you t-t-talk to K-Karima? What-what about Ph-Phoebe?"

*or, less commonly,*
"W-W-Will you t-t-talk to K-Karima?"

Interruptions or abrupt changes in thought are usually indicated by em dashes (see 12.42). When speakers interrupt themselves, em dashes may be used without observing the usual limit of two per sentence, as in ordinary prose (see 6.91).

"The sky's the limit—Vegas—Miami—wherever you want—and it won't cost you a cent."

12.45 **Dialogue across multiple paragraphs.** If the quoted words of one speaker occupy more than a paragraph (as for a particularly long speech), opening quotation marks are needed at the beginning of each new paragraph, with a closing quotation mark placed at the end of only the *final* paragraph. The example below, intended to show only how quotation marks would be applied, would typically feature longer paragraphs.

"This is the first paragraph of quoted speech," says a speaker. "This is a continuation of that speech.

"This is the second paragraph of the same speech by the same speaker. The speech continues.

"This is the end of the speech."

If such a passage consists of a quotation within a quotation that runs across more than one paragraph, a single quotation mark appears at the beginning and end of the interior quotation, and both double and single marks appear before each new paragraph belonging to the interior quotation.

"This is the first paragraph of quoted speech that quotes another speaker, who says: 'This is the beginning of a speech within a speech. This speech within a speech continues.

" 'This is the second paragraph of the speech within a speech. The speech within a speech continues.

" 'This is the end of both speeches.' "

For single quotation marks next to double, see 6.11.

12.46 **Quotations within dialogue.** Quoted words within dialogue that is itself enclosed in quotation marks are enclosed in single quotation marks. This usage applies even when a quoted section of dialogue consists entirely of another quotation.

"What did the law clerk say?" he asked.
"He said, 'I would prefer not to,'" I replied.
"'I would prefer not to'?" he asked. "What's that from?"
"'Bartleby, the Scrivener,'" I replied. "It's a famous story."

Note how nested single quotation marks are used even when the quoted text takes up the entire line of dialogue in double quotation marks (as at the beginning of the third and fourth examples above). This usage, intended to make it clear in the context of dialogue precisely which words belong to the speaker, does not normally apply in narrative text and other contexts outside of dialogue. In the following example, Bartleby's response, presented as quoted dialogue in Herman Melville's published story (and in single quotation marks in the example above), requires only double quotation marks when offered as a quotation in ordinary narrative prose (see also 12.30).

Melville's "Bartleby, the Scrivener" is perhaps best known for its protagonist's neurasthenic response to his boss: "I would prefer not to."

12.47 **Single-word speech.** Words such as *yes*, *no*, *where*, *how*, and *why*, when used singly, are not enclosed in quotation marks except as quoted dialogue. See also 6.73.

Ezra always answered yes; he could never say no to a friend.
Please stop asking why.
*but*
"Yes," he replied weakly.
Again she repeated, "Why?"

12.48 **Alternatives to quotation marks for dialogue.** Some authors present dialogue without quotation marks, a usage that has been around for centuries. (Such an approach removes a layer of artifice between the reader and the narrator, though at the expense of clarity.) Sometimes the dialogue is presented in the manner of drama, with speakers' names followed by a colon (or, less often, a period; see 12.54 for examples). More commonly, quotation marks are simply omitted, as in the following passage from Alice Walker's *The Color Purple* (Harcourt Brace Jovanovich, 1982):

Miss Celie! say Sofia. Shock.

Girl, I'm bless, I say to Sofia. God know what I mean.

Us sit round the kitchen table and light up. I show 'em how to suck in they wind. Harpo git strangle. Sofia choke.

> Pretty soon Sofia say, That funny, I never heard that humming before.
> What humming? Harpo ast.
> Listen, she say.
> Us git real quiet and listen. Sure enough, us hear ummmmmmmm.

In that passage, each speaker gets a new paragraph, as in quoted dialogue (see 12.40), and the punctuation relative to speaker tags is also the same as for quoted dialogue (see 12.41). Another alternative is to use em dashes to mark each new speech (usually in successive paragraphs), an approach modeled on publications in French and other languages; for examples, see 11.34, 11.54, 11.71, 11.110. Finally, some works dispense not only with quotation marks but also with conventional paragraph changes for new speakers, relying on a combination of punctuation, capitalization, and context instead.

12.49 **Unspoken discourse.** Thought, imagined dialogue, and other internal discourse (also called interior discourse) may be enclosed in quotation marks or not, according to the context or the writer's preference. When quotation marks are not used, italics may be applied, as in the second example below; this approach, though common, is usually best suited to works that feature mainly shorter passages of internal discourse (at most a sentence or two here and there). If a thought begins mid-sentence, it normally begins with a capital letter (as in the third example). See also 6.45.

> "I don't care if we have offended Morgenstern," thought Vera. "Besides," she told herself, "they're all fools."

> *Why,* he wondered, *did we choose this route?*

> She thought, If there isn't an app for that, I'll need to program it myself.

12.50 **Formatting text messages and the like as dialogue.** In most contexts, text messages may be rendered in quotation marks, particularly if the words are run in to the text. More than a few such messages, however, are best given a different typographical treatment to distinguish them from ordinary speech or dialogue. As with unspoken discourse, italics can be effective for messages that are run in to the narrative (see also 12.49). For conversations, speakers may be identified in parentheses rather than using conventional speaker tags, and italics may be used for the messages themselves. Instead of using ordinary paragraphs (as for dialogue), conversations are best presented as a series of individual block quotations, indented uniformly from the left margin (see 12.9).

(me) *Are they here yet?*
(him) *Yes.*
(me) *Give me a sec. I'll be right there.*

As a matter of authenticity, authors may prefer to punctuate and style such exchanges creatively (e.g., omitting question marks and periods at the ends of questions and statements, not using conventional capitalization, etc.); editors should query before making any changes. Others may expect conversations to be presented graphically (e.g., using staggered indents for incoming and outgoing texts and applying colors and graphics that identify each speaker). Publishers can help by presenting a range of options that may depend on publication format; editors will help by enforcing a consistent treatment.

12.51 **Numerals and abbreviations in quoted speech and dialogue.** In quoting directly from spoken sources (e.g., interviews, speeches, or dialogue from a film or a play), or when writing dialogue for a drama or a work of fiction, numbers that might otherwise be rendered as numerals can often be spelled out. This practice requires editorial discretion. Spelling out numbers clarifies how they are spoken, but some numbers will be more intelligible as numerals. Years, for example, can usually be rendered as numerals, as can brand names that include numerals. Exact times other than full, quarter, and half hours can also be rendered as numerals, as can days of the month. It can also make sense to use numerals that correspond to actual numerals, as in street addresses and room numbers or numbers on signs. And for dialogue that includes more than a few large numbers, it may be more practical to use numerals. When in doubt, choose the form that would be most recognizable. See also 9.2, 9.7.

Jarred's answer was a mix of rage and humiliation: "For the last time, I do not have seven hundred thirty-seven dollars and eleven cents! I don't even have a quarter for the parking meter, for that matter."

Like most proofreaders, she is a perfectionist. "I'm never happy with a mere ninety-nine and forty-four one-hundredths percent."

"You're so healthy I bet you live to be a hundred and ten."

"Set your alarm for four a.m."

*but*

"Do you prefer shopping at 7-Eleven or Circle K?"

"I didn't get around to reading *Nineteen Eighty-Four* until 1985," he finally admitted.

"My mobile number is 555-0133."

"I'm at 30 Crescent Lane, in apartment 3B."

"He was last seen on January the 5th at 2:25 p.m." (But see 9.33.)

Similarly, abbreviations that are always known in abbreviated form or that would be less intelligible when spelled out may remain abbreviated in quoted speech and dialogue. These include social titles used before a name, brand names that include abbreviations, and abbreviations pronounced as abbreviations, among others.

The man at the front desk called out to me: "Dr. Jayabalan will see you now."

"He works for AT&T Inc."

12.52 **Parentheses in dialogue.** Though once common in quoted dialogue, parentheses are best avoided in that context lest they be mistaken for the narrator's or author's words rather than the speaker's. Instead, use dashes (or incorporate the words into the narrative). For the use of square brackets for clarifications within quoted matter, see 12.71.

"I know it's early—my watch says 11:35—but can we please have lunch now?"
*not*
"I know it's early (my watch says 11:35), but can we please have lunch now?"

12.53 **Indirect discourse.** Indirect discourse, which paraphrases dialogue, takes no quotation marks. See also 6.45.

Tom told Huck they had to do it that way because the books said so.
Very well, you say, but is there no choice?

## DRAMA, DISCUSSIONS AND INTERVIEWS, AND FIELD NOTES

12.54 **Drama.** In plays, the speaker's name is usually set in a font distinct from the dialogue—caps and small caps, for example, or all small caps. The dialogue is not enclosed in quotation marks and is usually set with hanging indents (a style often used for bibliographies and indexes and illustrated below, using lines drawn from a classic sixteenth-century play by Nicholas Udall; see also 2.14).

R. ROISTER DOISTER. Except I have her to my wife, I shall run mad.
M. MERYGREEKE. Nay, "unwise" perhaps, but I warrant you for "mad."

Stage directions are usually italicized, as in the following example from Oscar Wilde's *The Importance of Being Earnest*:

ALGERNON. That is quite a different matter. She is my aunt. (*Takes plate from below.*) Have some bread and butter. The bread and butter is for Gwendolen. Gwendolen is devoted to bread and butter.
JACK, *advancing to table and helping himself.* And very good bread and butter it is too.

12.55 **Shared lines and runover lines in verse drama.** In quoted excerpts from drama in verse, a single line of verse shared between two speakers in a play should be presented such that the second line continues where the first has left off (as in the example below, from Shakespeare's *Hamlet*, where the line begun by Barnardo is finished by Marcellus). Runover lines may be indicated as in poetry, by an indent of one em or more from the line above (see also 12.27).

BARNARDO.
  It would be spoke to.
MARCELLUS.                Speak to it, Horatio.
HORATIO.
  What art thou that usurp'st this time of night,
  Together with that fair and warlike form
  In which the majesty of buried Denmark
  Did sometimes march? By heaven, I charge thee,
    speak.

12.56 **Discussions and interviews.** The transcription of a discussion or an interview is treated in much the same way as drama (see 12.54). Interjections such as "laughter" are italicized and enclosed in brackets (rather than parentheses, as in drama; see also 12.70–74). Paragraph indents are usually preferred to hanging indents (though hanging indents, which allow easier identification of the speaker, may work better if several speakers' names appear and the comments are relatively brief). Although speakers' names are usually followed by a period, a colon may be used instead. To save space, names may be abbreviated after their first appearance.

> INTERVIEWER. You weren't thinking that this technology would be something you could use to connect to the Office of Tibet in New York or to different Tibet support groups in Europe?
>
> RESPONDENT. No. Nobody seemed to have anything to do with GreenNet in the Tibet world at that time. That came much later. That's not really right. I specifically wasn't interested in connecting to the community of Tibet martyrs and fellow sufferers [*laughs*] and the emotional pathological there-but-for-the-grace-of-God-go-I people.

An author's previously unpublished transcriptions of interviews or discussions can usually be edited for such matters as capitalization, spelling, and minor grammatical slips or elisions (see also 12.57). If an author has imposed more significant alterations, these should be explained in a note, a preface, or elsewhere. See also 4.81. Previously published transcriptions should be quoted as they appear in the original source.

12.57 **Interviews transcribed by authors.** As with case studies and field notes (see 12.58), an author's transcriptions of oral interviews that they conducted personally (like those that commonly appear in ethnographies) should be edited for consistency in spelling, capitalization, punctuation, treatment of numbers, and so forth. If the transcriptions have also been translated by the author into English, a note should explain that the author both transcribed and translated them. Two additional caveats: Regarding spelling, editors should take care not to correct an author's representations of an individual's particular way of speaking, such as dropped consonants (e.g., *goin'*). (Authors, however, should use caution, transcribing speech patterns only to the extent they are relevant to the material at hand.) Regarding punctuation, editors should take care not to make any changes that would risk altering the meaning, tone, or pacing of the response (as approximated by the author). Editors can help by documenting the author's choices in a style sheet (see 2.61).

12.58 **Case studies and ethnographic field notes.** An author's transcriptions of unpublished ethnographic field notes or material from case studies (the author's own or those of a colleague or assistant) pose a special case. Unlike quotations from published sources or transcriptions of interviews, such material need not be presented verbatim—whether presented as quotations or woven into the text. Rather, it should be edited for consistency—with related material and with the surrounding text—in matters of spelling, capitalization, punctuation, treatment of numbers, and so forth. And even if the author is in possession of signed releases, any otherwise anonymous subjects or informants should generally be presented under pseudonyms; a note should be appended to the text to indicate that this is the case. Although modifications intended to maintain participants' anonymity are acceptable, authors must take care to ensure that any changes do not lead to misrepresentation. Editors should query authors if it is not clear that appropriate provisions have been made. See also 4.81.

## ELLIPSES

12.59 **Ellipses defined.** An *ellipsis* is a series of three dots used to signal the omission of a word, phrase, line, paragraph, or more from a quoted passage. Such omissions are made of material that is considered irrelevant to the discussion at hand (or, occasionally, to adjust for the grammar of the surrounding text). Chicago style is to use three spaced periods (but see 12.62) rather than another device such as asterisks. These dots (which are sometimes referred to as suspension points) may also be used to indicate faltering speech or incomplete thoughts (see 12.43). The dots in an ellipsis must always appear together on the same line (through the use of nonbreaking spaces; see 6.129), along with any punctuation that immediately follows; if an ellipsis appears at the beginning of a new line, any punctuation that immediately precedes it (including a period) will appear at the end of the line above. Some publishers use an ellipsis character instead of spaced periods; see 12.68 for more details. For bracketed ellipses, see 12.67.

12.60 **Danger of skewing meaning with ellipses.** Since quotations from another source have been separated from their original context, particular care needs to be exercised when eliding text to ensure that the sense of the original is not lost or misrepresented. A deletion must not result in a statement alien to the original material. And in general, ellipses should not be used to join two statements that are far apart in the original. Accuracy of sense and emphasis must accompany accuracy of transcription.

12.61 **When not to use an ellipsis.** Ellipses are normally *not* used (1) before the first word of a quotation, even if the beginning of the original sentence has been omitted; or (2) after the last word of a quotation, even if the end of the original sentence has been omitted, unless the sentence as quoted is deliberately incomplete (see 12.64).

12.62 **Ellipses with periods.** A period is added *before* an ellipsis to indicate the omission of the end of a sentence, unless the sentence is deliberately incomplete (see 12.64). Similarly, a period at the end of a sentence in the original is retained before an ellipsis indicating the omission of material immediately following the period. (A period in an abbreviation such as *etc.* is also retained before an ellipsis, whether or not it ends a sentence.) What precedes and, normally, what follows the four dots should be grammatically complete sentences as quoted, even if part of either sentence has been omitted. A complete passage from Emerson's essay "Politics" reads:

> The spirit of our American radicalism is destructive and aimless: it is not loving; it has no ulterior and divine ends; but is destructive only out of hatred and selfishness. On the other side, the conservative party, composed of the most moderate, able, and cultivated part of the population, is timid, and merely defensive of property. It vindicates no right, it aspires to no real good, it brands no crime, it proposes no generous policy, it does not build, nor write, nor cherish the arts, nor foster religion, nor establish schools, nor encourage science, nor emancipate the slave, nor befriend the poor, or the Indian, or the immigrant. From neither party, when in power, has the world any benefit to expect in science, art, or humanity, at all commensurate with the resources of the nation.

The passage might be shortened as follows:

> The spirit of our American radicalism is destructive and aimless. . . . On the other side, the conservative party . . . is timid, and merely defensive of property. . . . It does not build, nor write, nor cherish the arts, nor foster religion, nor establish schools.

Note that the first word after an ellipsis is capitalized if it begins a new grammatical sentence. Some types of works require that such changes to capitalization be bracketed; see 12.21. See also 12.67.

12.63 **Ellipses with other punctuation.** Other punctuation appearing in the original text—a comma, a colon, a semicolon, a question mark, or an exclamation point—may precede or follow an ellipsis (except when a period precedes the ellipsis; see 12.62). Whether to include the additional mark of punctuation depends on whether keeping it aids comprehension or is required for the grammar of the sentence. Placement of the other punctuation depends on whether the omission precedes or follows the mark; when the omission precedes it, a nonbreaking space should be used between the ellipsis and the mark of punctuation to prevent the mark from carrying over to the beginning of a new line (see 12.59). Note that this before-or-after distinction is usually *not* made with periods, where—without the aid of brackets (see 12.67)—it is likely to go unnoticed (see 12.62). The examples below are from Emerson's "Politics," Shelley's preface to *Adonais*, and Darwin's *On the Origin of Species*, respectively.

> It does not build, . . . nor cherish the arts, nor foster religion.

> As to *Endymion*, was it a poem . . . to be treated contemptuously by those who had celebrated, with various degrees of complacency and panegyric, *Paris*, and *Woman*, and *A Syrian Tale* . . . ? Are these the men who . . . presumed to draw a parallel between the Rev. Mr. Milman and Lord Byron?

> When a species . . . increases inordinately in numbers in a small tract, epidemics . . . often ensue: and here we have a limiting check independent of the struggle for life. But even some of these so-called epidemics appear to be due to parasitic worms . . . : and here comes in a sort of struggle between the parasite and its prey.

12.64 **Ellipses at the ends of deliberately incomplete sentences.** An ellipsis alone (i.e., three dots with no additional period) is used at the end of a quoted sentence that is deliberately left grammatically incomplete.

> Everyone knows that the Declaration of Independence begins with the words "When, in the course of human events . . ." But how many people can recite more than the first few lines of the document?

> Have you had a chance to look at the example beginning "The spirit of our American radicalism . . ."?

Note that no space intervenes between a final ellipsis dot and a closing quotation mark.

12.65 **Ellipses for the omission of whole or partial paragraphs.** The omission of one or more paragraphs within a quotation is indicated by a period followed by an ellipsis at the end of the paragraph preceding the omitted part (see also 12.62). (If that paragraph ends with an incomplete sentence, only the three-dot ellipsis is used; see 12.64.) If the first part of a paragraph is omitted within a quotation, a paragraph indent and an ellipsis appear before the first quoted word. It is thus possible to use an ellipsis both at the end of one paragraph and at the beginning of the next, as illustrated in the following excerpt from Alexander Pope's "Letter to a Noble Lord":

> I should be obliged indeed to lessen this respect, if all the nobility . . . are but so many hereditary fools, if the privilege of lords be to want brains, if noblemen can hardly write or read. . . .
>
> Were it the mere excess of your Lordship's wit, that carried you thus triumphantly over all the bounds of decency, I might consider your Lordship on your Pegasus, as a sprightly hunter on a mettled horse. . . .
>
> . . . Unrivalled as you are, in making a figure, and in making a speech, methinks, my Lord, you may well give up the poor talent of making a distich.

**12.66** **Ellipses in poetry and verse drama.** Omission of the end of a line of verse is indicated by a period followed by an ellipsis if what precedes them is a complete grammatical sentence (see 12.62); otherwise, only the three-dot ellipsis is used (as in the Poe example; see also 12.64). The omission of a full line or of several consecutive lines within a quoted poem or drama in verse is indicated by one line of widely spaced dots approximately the length of the line above (or of the missing line, if that is determinable). See also 12.25–29.

> Type of the antique Rome! Rich reliquary
> Of lofty contemplation . . .
> (Edgar Allan Poe, "The Coliseum")

> She would dwell on such dead themes, not as one who remembers,
> But rather as one who sees.
> . . . . . . . . . . . . . . . . . . . .
> Past things retold were to her as things existent,
> Things present but as a tale.
> (Thomas Hardy, "One We Knew")

> This royal throne of kings, this sceptred isle,
> . . . . . . . . . . . . . . . . . . . . . . . . . . . .
> This blessed plot, this earth, this realm, this England.
> (*Richard II*, 2.1.40–50)

12.67 **Bracketed ellipses.** Especially in languages that make liberal use of ellipses for faltering speech or incomplete thoughts, it is a common practice to bracket ellipses that are inserted to indicate an omission in quoted text (see, e.g., 11.35; see also 11.21). In an English context where ellipses are needed for a quotation that includes ellipses in the original text, the latter may be explained at each instance in a note (e.g., "ellipsis in original"; see also 12.73); for more than a few such instances, authors may choose instead to bracket their own ellipses, but only after explaining such a decision in a note, a preface, or elsewhere. The rules for bracketed ellipses are the same as the rules outlined in the rest of this section, with one exception—a period is placed before or after the ellipsis depending on its placement in the original. Compare the passage that follows to the passages in 12.62.

> The spirit of our American radicalism is destructive and aimless [. . .]. On the other side, the conservative party [. . .] is timid, and merely defensive of property. [. . .] It does not build, nor write, nor cherish the arts, nor foster religion, nor establish schools.

Note that a space appears before an opening bracket; a space appears after a closing bracket except when a period, comma, or other mark of punctuation follows. Within brackets, the sequence is bracket-period-space-period-space-period-bracket. Nonbreaking spaces are needed only for the two spaces between the periods within the brackets (see also 6.129). Bracketed ellipses may also be used in source citations to shorten very long titles; see 13.99.

12.68 **Spaced periods versus the ellipsis character.** A Chicago-style ellipsis consists of three spaced periods . . . like that. To prevent these periods from breaking at the end of a line, nonbreaking spaces must be applied before and after the middle period; additionally, a nonbreaking space is required between the third period and any comma, semicolon, question mark, or exclamation point that follows . . . , like that. (This must be done prior to publication and is usually the responsibility of the publisher or typesetter.) Some publishers instead use the horizontal ellipsis character (…), defined for Unicode as U+2026. This character, which has the advantage of not breaking over a line, may also be preferred by some authors when they are preparing their manuscripts (alternatively, three unspaced periods, which will also stay together, may be used, provided only one type of ellipsis appears throughout a document). A space should be used before and after an unspaced ellipsis … like that, except when the ellipsis is followed by a comma or other mark of punctuation …, like that. Copyeditors imposing Chicago style will replace these characters with Chicago-style spaced periods, adding nonbreaking spaces as needed. See also 6.129, 11.2.

12.69 **Ellipses in mathematical expressions.** Two kinds of ellipses are used in mathematical expressions. In elided operations and relations, the ellipsis is centered vertically to align with the operation or relation sign.

$$x_1 + x_2 + \cdots + x_n$$

In an elided list or the like (where the terms are separated by commas), the ellipsis should be on the baseline (as in ordinary text), and commas should come after each term in the list and after the ellipsis dots if the list has a final term.

$x_1, x_2, \ldots, x_n$

*not*

$x_1, x_2, \ldots x_n$

## INTERPOLATIONS AND CLARIFICATIONS

12.70 **Missing or illegible words.** In reproducing or quoting from a document in which certain words are missing or illegible, an author may use ellipses (see 12.59–69), a bracketed comment or guess (sometimes followed by a question mark), or both. If ellipses alone are used (useful for a passage with more than a few lacunae), their function as a stand-in for missing or illegible words must be explained in the text or in a note. If a bracketed gloss comes from a different source, the source must be cited in a note or elsewhere. See also 6.105.

> If you will assure me of your . . . [illegible], I shall dedicate my life to your endeavor.

> She marched out the door, headed for the [president's?] office.

A 2-em dash (see 6.99), sometimes in combination with an interpolated guess, may also be used for missing material. As with ellipses, this device should be used consistently and should be explained (in prefatory material or a note).

> I have great marvel that ye will so soon incline to every man his device and [counsel and ——] specially in matters of small impor[tance ——] yea, and as [it is] reported [unto me——] causes as meseemeth th[a——] nothing to [——]ne gentlewomen.

12.71 **Bracketed clarifications.** Insertions may be made in quoted material to clarify an ambiguity, to provide a missing word or letters (see 12.70), to correct an error, or, in a translation, to give the original word or phrase where the English fails to convey the exact sense. They must never be used in a way that changes or misrepresents the meaning of the original text or otherwise amounts to misquoting the source. Such interpolations, which should be kept to a minimum lest they irritate or distract readers, are enclosed in brackets (never in parentheses). See also 6.105, 12.12.

Marcellus, doubtless in anxious suspense, asks Barnardo, "What, has this thing [the ghost of Hamlet's father] appear'd again tonight?"

"Well," said she, "if Mr. L[owell] won't go, then neither will I."

Saha once remarked of Nehru that "his position in this country can be described by a phrase which Americans use with respect to Abraham Lincoln [read: George Washington], 'first in war, first in peace.'"

12.72 **"Sic."** Literally meaning "so," "thus," "in this manner," and traditionally set in italics, *sic* may be inserted in brackets following a word misspelled or wrongly used in the original. This device should be used only when it is necessary to call attention to such a mistake, as for a spelling that readers might otherwise assume is an error in the transcription rather than the original. And it should only be used when paraphrase or silent correction is inappropriate (see 12.4, 12.7, item 6).

In September 1862, J. W. Chaffin, president of the Miami Conference of Wesleyan Methodist Connection, urged Lincoln that "the confiscation law past [*sic*] at the last session of Congress should be faithfully executed" and that "to neglect this national righteousness" would prove "disastrous to the American people."

*Sic* should *not* be used merely to call attention to unconventional spellings, which should be explained (if at all) in a note or in prefatory material. Similarly, where material with many errors and variant spellings (such as a collection of informal letters) is reproduced as written, a prefatory comment or a note to that effect will make a succession of *sic*s unnecessary.

12.73 **"Italics added."** An author wishing to call particular attention to a word or phrase in quoted material may italicize it but must tell readers what has been done, by means of such formulas as "italics mine," "italics added," "emphasis added," or "emphasis mine." Occasionally it may be important to point out that italics in a quotation were indeed in the original. Here the usual phrase is "italics in the original" or, for example, "De Quincey's italics." This information appears either in parentheses following the quotation or in a source note to the quotation. If there are italics in the original of the passage quoted, the information is best enclosed in brackets and placed directly after the added italics. Consistency in method throughout a work is essential.

> You have watched the conduct of Ireland in the difficult circumstances of the last nine months, and that conduct I do not hesitate to risk saying on your behalf has evoked in every breast a responsive voice of sympathy, and an increased conviction that we may deal freely *and yet deal prudently* with our fellow-subjects beyond the Channel. Such is your conviction. (William Ewart Gladstone, October 1891; italics added)

> In reality not one didactic poet has ever yet attempted to use any parts or processes of the particular art which he made his theme, unless in so far as they seemed susceptible of poetic treatment, and only *because* they seemed so. Look at the poem of *Cyder* by Philips, of the *Fleece* by Dyer, or (which is a still weightier example) at the *Georgics* of Virgil,—does any of these poets show the least anxiety for the *correctness of your principles* [my italics], or the delicacy of your manipulations, in the worshipful arts they affect to teach? (Thomas De Quincey, "Essay on Pope")

12.74 **Interpolations requiring quotation marks.** Occasionally a bracketed or parenthetical interpolation that includes quotation marks appears in material already enclosed in quotation marks. In such cases, the double/single rule (see 12.30) does not apply; the quotation marks within the brackets may remain double.

> "Do you mean that a double-headed calf ["two-headed calf" in an earlier version] has greater value than two normal calves? That a freak of nature, even though it cannot survive, is to be more highly treasured for its rarity than run-of-the-mill creatures are for their potential use?"

## ATTRIBUTING QUOTATIONS IN TEXT

12.75 **Use of parentheses with in-text citations.** If the source of a direct quotation is not given in a note, it is usually placed in the text in parentheses. Although the source normally follows a quotation, it may come earlier if it fits more smoothly into the introductory text (as in the second example in 12.76). The examples in this section focus on full and short forms of parenthetical citation that may be needed in shorter works with no notes or bibliography or to provide in-text citations to a frequently quoted work. The advice in this section on placement relative to surrounding text is intended to supplement the system of notes and bibliography covered in chapters 13 and 14. These forms may also be appropriate for works that mention sources but are not required to formally cite them or for contexts that do not merit a formal citation (see 13.5). For author-date references, see 13.102–4.

12.76 **Full in-text citation.** An entire source may be given in parentheses immediately following a run-in quotation (as in the first example below), or some of the data may be worked into the text (as in the second example), with details confined to parentheses. See also 6.107. For more on the proper form for full citations, see chapter 13. For run-in versus block quotations, see 12.9. See also 12.79–80; compare 12.81.

"If an astronaut falls into a black hole, its mass will increase, but eventually the energy equivalent of that extra mass will be returned to the universe in the form of radiation. Thus, in a sense, the astronaut will be 'recycled'" (Stephen W. Hawking, *A Brief History of Time: From the Big Bang to Black Holes* [Bantam Books, 1988], 112).

In her foreword to the University of Chicago Press's 2022 reissue of *Deep South*, first published by Chicago in 1941, Isabel Wilkerson traces anthropologist Allison Davis's journey with his white coauthors to Natchez, Mississippi, where, "in the depths of the Jim Crow caste system . . . they would find their every move dictated by the very phenomenon that they were studying" (xiv).

12.77 **Shortened citations or "ibid." with subsequent in-text citations.** If a second passage from the same source is quoted close to the first and there is no intervening quotation from a different source, the author's name or *ibid.* (set in roman) may be used in the second parenthetical reference (e.g., "Hawking, 114" *or* "ibid., 114"). Chicago recommends repetition of the author's name as being the less ambiguous option, though *ibid.* may be appropriate if used consistently. Avoid overusing either form: For more than the occasional repeated reference to the same source—as in an extended discussion of a work of fiction—a parenthetical page number alone is usually a better option. Whichever form is used, if a quotation from another source has intervened, a shortened reference that includes the title in addition to the author may be necessary unless the title is mentioned in the text or would otherwise be clear from the context (e.g., "Hawking, *Brief History of Time*, 114"). For more on shortened citations, see 13.32–39; for the use of shortened citations versus *ibid.* in notes, see 13.37.

12.78 **Frequent reference to a single source cited in a note.** In a work containing notes, the full citation of a source may be given in a note at first mention, with subsequent citations made parenthetically in the text. This method is especially suited to literary studies that use frequent quotations from a single source (and may be appropriate whenever the usual method of repeating a short form of the citation in the notes threatens to become unduly repetitious). In a study of *Much Ado About Nothing*, for example, the note would list the edition and include wording such as "Text references are to act, scene, and line of this edition." A parenthetical reference to act 3, scene 4, lines 46–47, would then appear as in the example below. In references to a work of fiction, page numbers alone may be given.

> "Ye light o' love with your heels! then, if your husband have stables enough, you'll see he shall lack no barns," says Beatrice (3.4.46–47).

Where a number of such sources (or different editions of a single source) are used in the same work, the title (or edition) may need to be indicated in the parenthetical references; it may be advisable to devise an abbreviation for each and to include a list of the abbreviations at the beginning or end of the work (see 13.63, 13.64). See also 13.51, 14.146, 14.153.

## *Sources Following Run-In Quotations*

12.79 **Punctuation following source of run-in quotation.** After a run-in quotation, the source is usually given after the closing quotation mark, followed by the rest of the surrounding sentence (including any comma, semicolon, colon, or dash; but see 12.80) or the final punctuation of that sentence.

> With his "Nothing will come of nothing; speak again" (1.1.92), Lear tries to draw from his youngest daughter an expression of filial devotion.

> It has been more than a century since Henry Adams said: "Fifty years ago, science took for granted that the rate of acceleration could not last. The world forgets quickly, but even today the habit remains of founding statistics on the faith that consumption will continue nearly stationary" (*Education*, 493).

Has it been more than a century since Henry Adams observed that "fifty years ago, science took for granted that the rate of acceleration could not last" (*Education*, 493)?

A parenthetical reference need not immediately follow the quotation as long as it is clear what it belongs to. For examples, see 12.76 (second example), 12.78. See also 13.120.

12.80 **Punctuation preceding source of run-in quotation.** When a quotation comes at the end of a sentence and is itself a question or an exclamation, that punctuation is retained within the quotation marks, and a period is still added after the closing parentheses. (Compare the third example in 12.79.)

And finally, in the frenzy of grief that kills him, Lear rails, "Why should a dog, a horse, a rat, have life, / And thou no breath at all?" (5.3.306–7).

## *Sources Following Block Quotations and Poetry Extracts*

12.81 **Parenthetical source following a block quotation.** The source of a block quotation is given in parentheses at the end of the quotation and in the same type size. The opening parenthesis appears *after* the final punctuation mark of the quoted material. No period either precedes or follows the closing parenthesis. See also 6.107, 13.120.

If you happen to be fishing, and you get a strike, and whatever it is starts off with the preliminaries of a vigorous fight; and by and by, looking down over the side through the glassy water, you see a rosy golden gleam, the mere specter of a fish, shining below in the clear depths; and when you look again a sort of glory of golden light flashes and dazzles as it circles nearer beneath and around and under the boat; . . . and you land a slim and graceful and impossibly beautiful three-foot goldfish, whose fierce and vivid yellow is touched around the edges with a violent red—when all these things happen to you, fortunate but bewildered fisherman, then you may know you have been fishing in the Galapagos Islands and have taken a Golden Grouper. (Gifford Pinchot, *To the South Seas* [John Winston, 1930], 123)

Shortened references are treated in the same way as full ones. If a qualifier such as *line*, *vol.*, or *p.* is required at the beginning of the shortened reference (a *p.* may often be omitted, especially with repeated references), it should be lowercased as with sources to run-in quotations.

At last the fish came into sight—at first a mere gleam in the water, and then his full side. This was not even a distant cousin to the fish I thought I was fighting, but something else again entirely. (p. 142) *or* (142)

12.82 **Parenthetical citations with poetry extracts.** In order not to interfere with a poem's layout and overall presentation, parenthetical citations following poetry extracts are dropped to the line below the last line of the quotation. They may be centered on the last letter of the longest line of the quotation or set flush with the left margin of the poem; an additional line space may be added. Other positions are also possible (as in the examples in 12.25 and 12.83), as long as consistency and clarity are preserved.

Now more than ever seems it rich to die,
To cease upon the midnight with no pain,
While thou art pouring forth thy soul abroad
    In such an ecstasy!
(Keats, "Ode to a Nightingale," stanza 6)

12.83 **Shortened references to poetry extracts.** Shortened references to poetry are treated the same way as full ones. A quotation from Edmund Spenser's *The Faerie Queene*, once the reader knows that reference is to book, canto, and stanza, might appear as follows:

Who will not mercie unto others shew,
How can he mercy ever hope to have?
(6.1.42)

# III

# Source Citations and Indexes

# 13 Source Citations: Overview

## INTRODUCTION TO SOURCE CITATIONS

13.1 **The purpose of source citations.** Ethics, copyright laws, and courtesy to readers require authors to identify the sources of direct quotations or paraphrases and of any facts or opinions not generally known or easily checked (see 12.1–6). Conventions for citing sources vary according to scholarly discipline, the preferences of publishers and authors, and the needs of a particular work. Regardless of the convention being followed, source citations must always provide sufficient information either to lead readers directly to the sources consulted or, for materials that may not be readily available, to enable readers to positively identify them, regardless of whether the sources are published or unpublished or in printed or electronic form.

13.2 **Chicago-style source citations.** Chicago-style source citations come in two varieties:

1. **Notes and bibliography.** This system uses numbers in the text that correspond to numbered footnotes or endnotes. Sources cited in the notes may also be listed together in a separate bibliography at the end of the work.
2. **Author-date.** Instead of note numbers and notes, this system uses parenthetical references in the text that correspond directly to a list of sources at the end of the work.

Sources in both systems are treated the same in terms of capitalization, punctuation, and other stylistic considerations. The main difference between the two is in the use of numbered notes in one and parenthetical text references in the other. Because notes allow space for unusual types of sources as well as for commentary on the sources cited, the notes and bibliography system is preferred by many writers in literature, history, and the arts. It is also treated as the default system for source citations in this manual and for the examples in chapter 14. The author-date system, which credits researchers by name directly in the text while at the same time emphasizing the date of each source, is preferred for many publications in the sciences and social sciences but may be adapted for any work, sometimes with the addition of footnotes or endnotes. For journals, the choice between systems is likely to have been made long ago; anyone writing for a journal should consult that journal's instructions for authors (and see 13.3). This chapter gives a detailed overview of the two systems. For notes and bibliography, start with 13.18–20; for author-date, start with 13.102–4. For styling the names of authors in either system, see 13.74–86; for titles of works, see 13.87–101.

13.3 **Other systems of source citation.** Among other well-known systems are those of the Modern Language Association (MLA) and the American Psychological Association (APA), both of which use parenthetical citations in the text that correspond to a list of sources. The system used by the American Medical Association (AMA) features a numbered list of references cited in the text by reference number. Guidelines and examples for these three systems are to be found in the manuals of those associations. *The CSE Manual*, published by the Council of Science Editors in cooperation with the University of Chicago Press, uses a system of numbered references like AMA's while also providing useful overviews of other systems that are common in the sciences (see bibliog. 1.1 for these and other style manuals). Many journals and other serials either follow one of these styles or have their own, often based on or similar to the systems described here and in 13.2. For legal and public documents, Chicago recommends *The Bluebook*, published by the Harvard Law Review Association; see 14.170–207.

13.4 **Flexibility and consistency.** As long as a consistent style is maintained within any one work, logical and defensible variations on Chicago-style source citations are acceptable if agreed to by author and publisher. Such flexibility, however, is rarely possible in journal publication, which calls for adherence to the established style of the journal in question. See also 13.3.

13.5 **Mentioning versus citing.** Footnotes and bibliographies and related systems of citation emerged as a way for scholars to credit the work of others while providing a road map to the ideas that informed their own research. Such citations are expected in most types of academic writing, whether published or not. But in works without an academic focus, formal citations are rarely needed. For example, if an author were to mention the eighteenth edition of *The Chicago Manual of Style*—exactly like that—in a blog post or other nonacademic work, a more formal citation in a note or bibliography would be unnecessary. Most news writing and other types of journalism rely on such mentions rather than on formal citations. Even if your work *does* have an academic focus, you should consider carefully for each source you consult whether it merits a formal citation. Sources that are merely tangential to your own work may deserve to be mentioned in the text but rarely require a fuller citation in a note or bibliography. The same goes for certain types of informal or nonliterary sources that, unlike books and other formally published works, do not lend themselves to formal citation. In general, readers are better served by a disciplined, focused approach to source citations than by one that treats citations as a repository for every scrap of information consulted during the course of research and writing.

## *URLs and Other Identifiers*

13.6 **Uniform resource locators (URLs).** For sources consulted online, authors should record a URL (e.g., https://www.chicagomanualofstyle.org/) as the final element in a citation that includes all the components described throughout this chapter and in chapter 14. Whether the URL is retained for publication may depend on whether readers will need the URL to locate or assess the source. Journal publishers will often create links to sources cited in their articles automatically, whether a URL is provided or not (a process that is facilitated by accurate citation data). Book and journal publishers may retain URLs in citations of sources that would be difficult to locate without one but not in citations of journal articles, books, and other formally published sources that would be easy to find online from a title and other basic details alone. For many readers, a URL, which is designed to be read by a computer, will be less helpful—even as a hyperlink—than a link to the cited source from its title or other reader-friendly (and preferably unique) component of the citation (using the same URL as the link target).

**Bibliography entry in manuscript (with DOI-based URL):**

Hui, Andrew. "Dreams of the Universal Library." *Critical Inquiry* 48, no. 3 (2022): 522–48. https://doi.org/10.1086/718629.

**Published version (linked title instead of URL):**

Hui, Andrew. "Dreams of the Universal Library." *Critical Inquiry* 48, no. 3 (2022): 522–48.

Regardless of how they will be used in the published version of a work, the URLs in the examples in this chapter and in chapter 14 are intended mainly to show how *authors* should include them in the source citations in their manuscripts. For DOIs, see 13.7. For permalinks, see 13.8. For dividing URLs at the end of a line, see 7.47.

13.7 **Digital object identifiers (DOIs).** A DOI is a unique identifier that can be used to form the basis of a permanent URL. A DOI-based URL consists of https://doi.org/ followed by a DOI, which in turn consists of a prefix (e.g., 10.1086) assigned by a DOI registration agency such as Crossref and a suffix assigned by the publisher. For example, https://doi.org/10

.1086/718629 identifies the article "Dreams of the Universal Library," by Andrew Hui, which was published in the Spring 2022 issue of *Critical Inquiry*. This URL will, at a minimum, redirect the user to a page with information that identifies the content and includes up-to-date information about its location or availability (from the publisher or other content owner). Though DOIs are often still listed with a source in the form "DOI:" followed by the prefix and suffix, authors should avoid this deprecated usage in their own citations and instead append the DOI's prefix and suffix to https://doi.org/ to form a URL as described above. Examples are included throughout the section on journals (14.67–86) and at 14.60 and 14.132.

13.8 **Permalinks and the like.** The URL for a source citation can often be copied directly from a browser's address bar. But many sources offer another, more reliable, URL, typically near the top of the document (and sometimes from a "cite" or "share" button). A DOI, if there is one, is always preferable (see 13.7). If no DOI is listed, a URL identified as a persistent link, permalink, stable URL, or the like can be used instead. As with any URL, these should first be tested to make sure they lead where intended. Note that if the URL is excessively long or points to a library or commercial database that requires a subscription, it may be easier to list the name of the website or database instead (see 13.9, 13.10).

13.9 **Editing long URLs.** A very long URL—one that runs to as much as a line or more of text, especially if it includes long strings of punctuation or other syntax intended mainly for computers—can often be shortened simply by finding a better version of the link. A DOI or other stable identifier, if available, should always be preferred (see 13.7, 13.8). In the absence of a DOI or the like, it may still be possible to find a better URL, often by finding another way to link to the source. For example, a search for the 1913 novel *Pollyanna* in the Google Books database may yield a URL that looks like this:

https://books.google.com/books?id=bF81AAAAMAAJ&pg=PA226#v=onepage&q&f=false

That URL, the result of a search for a specific passage, points to a corresponding page in the book (p. 226). The URL for the main page for the book looks like this (and should be preferred, assuming a page reference is included as part of the full citation):

https://books.google.com/books?id=bF81AAAAMAAJ

Alternatively, it is usually acceptable for books and other formally published sources to record the URL for the home page (e.g., https://books.google.com/) or the name of the database (e.g., Google Books). Copyeditors should be able to double-check the cited source at Google Books or the like based on the full facts of publication. Whether or not a URL is included in the published citation (see 13.6), readers should likewise be able to find the source in the relevant database. See also 13.10. For dividing URLs at the end of a line, see 7.47.

13.10 **Library and other bibliographic databases.** For a source consulted via a library or other commercial bibliographic database and available only through a subscription or library account, it may be best to name the database in lieu of recording a URL (see also 13.9). Even a URL recommended for such a source (see 13.8) may lead a nonsubscriber to a log-on page with no information about the source itself. If in doubt, test the URL while logged out of the library or database; a URL that leads to information about the source, if not full access to it, is safe to use. A URL based on a DOI, which is supposed to direct readers to information about a source even when they do not have full access to it, should be preferred where available (see 13.7). For more information and examples, see 14.60 (books), 14.72 (journals), and 14.113 (theses and dissertations).

13.11 **Link-shortening services.** In their manuscripts, authors should record URLs as described elsewhere in this section and in the examples throughout chapters 13 and 14 rather than creating shortened versions via a third-party service such as TinyURL, Bitly, or shortDOI. Short URLs obscure domain names and other details that may be important to copyeditors and others assessing an author's source citations. Publishers, however, may choose in specific cases to use short URLs in the published version of a work; in addition to taking up less space, some types of short URLs can be redirected if a source moves to a new location.

13.12 **URLs in relation to surrounding text.** URLs are unique strings that contain no spaces. In references, URLs should be presented in full, beginning with the protocol (usually *https* or *http*). Even if it follows a period, the first letter of the protocol (i.e., the *h*) remains lowercase. (In running text, avoid beginning a sentence with a URL.) The capitalization of the remaining components varies; because some resource identifiers are case sensitive, they should not be edited for style. If a URL ends with a slash (/), retain the slash (see also 6.120). Any period or comma or other mark of punctuation that would follow a URL if it were an ordinary word should be retained. This approach, though it may result in the occasional cut-and-paste error, will prevent editorial headaches (see also 6.8).

## *Keeping Track of Your Research*

13.13 **Citation management tools.** It is rarely necessary for authors to create a source citation from scratch; even sources that are available only in print are usually listed in library catalogs and other online resources. From there, data about author and title and other relevant details can be copied and pasted or, depending on the available tools (some of which now make use of AI), extracted in one or more citation styles. Full-featured citation management applications such as EndNote and Zotero rely on such online data to help writers build libraries of source data that can be used to place citations directly into their manuscripts according to any number of styles (including Chicago). The results, however, are only as good as the data behind the citations. A few caveats:

- Double-check your data. As you build your library of source data, check each field against the actual source as soon as you acquire the data for it. Make sure authors' names, titles of works, publication dates, and so forth are accurate and that they are entered in the appropriate fields. Check also for missing or redundant data. (It is okay, however, to collect more data than you will use in your citations.) You will need to do this whether you entered the data yourself or exported the citation from a library catalog or other resource.
- Double-check your citations. Once a citation has been inserted in your manuscript, review it to make sure it is formatted according to the examples and recommendations in this chapter and chapter 14. Things to look for include errant punctuation or capitalization and missing or superfluous data. Enter any corrections in the citation management application (or adjust its settings, as applicable) and double-check the results in the manuscript.
- Make sure your citations are backed up. Some applications back up your data automatically. It is generally a good idea also to keep local copies as an additional safeguard. Such backups will not only protect your ongoing research but could also prove helpful in the event your manuscript must be resubmitted for any reason.

Citation management tools work best for citing published books and journal articles and other common publication formats. The variety of sources typically cited in a scholarly work, on the other hand, usually precludes an acceptable result from software alone. Authors are therefore strongly encouraged to review their citations for consistency, accuracy, and completeness before submitting their final manuscripts (editors, in turn, should be aware of how the software works so they can help identify any potential glitches). Note also that your publisher may require that such citations be presented as ordinary text, stripped of any of the underlying codes such as fields or hyperlinks used in creating or organizing them. Authors should double-check the results of this conversion to ordinary text but are advised also to save a backup copy of the penultimate version of the manuscript, with codes intact, in case the citations need to be regenerated for any reason. See also 2.26.

13.14 **Citing the right version.** In many cases the contents of the same publication published in different media (e.g., ebook and print) are intended to be identical. Moreover, publishers are encouraged to note explicitly any differences between the two (see 1.87). In practice, because there is always the potential for differences, intentional or otherwise, authors should note which version they consulted. Chicago recommends including a URL to indicate that a work was consulted online. For practical purposes, alternate electronic formats offered by a single publisher from the same URL—for example, PDF and HTML versions of the journal article mentioned in 13.7—do *not* need to be indicated in the citation. Moreover, a DOI-based URL technically points to each medium in which a work is published. (Though a print source may list a DOI, authors need not record it as part of their research unless their publisher or discipline requires it.) For items designed to be read using a particular application or device, however, the format or device should be specified.

13.15 **Access dates.** An access date—that is, the self-reported date on which an author consulted a source online—is of limited value: Previous versions may be unavailable to readers; authors typically consult a source any number of times over the course of days or months; and the accuracy of such dates, once recorded, cannot readily be verified by editors or publishers. Chicago therefore does not require access dates in its published citations of electronic sources unless no date of publication or revision can be determined from the source (see also 13.16). However, some publishers *do* require access dates (and students are typically required to record them); authors should therefore check with their publishers early on, and it never hurts to record dates of access during research, a task that citation management tools can help with (see 13.13). For examples, see 14.73, 14.104, and 14.131.

13.16 **"Last modified" and other revision dates.** Some electronic documents list a date indicating the last time the document was modified or revised.

There are no accepted standards for this practice, and for formally published sources a date of publication is generally more important. A revision date should be included, however, if it is presented as the de facto date of publication or is otherwise the only available date. Such dates may be particularly useful for citing wikis and other frequently updated works. For examples, see 14.104, 14.131, and 14.132.

**13.17** **Preserving a permanent record.** As part of their research—and in addition to recording accurate and complete source citations as described in this chapter and in chapter 14—authors are strongly encouraged to keep a copy of any source that is not formally published. Such a copy can prove valuable not only during research and writing but also in the event of any challenges to the research or data after publication. Such a source might include a social media post, a page from a corporate website, or a specific version of an article on a news site reporting an ongoing crisis—anything that might be difficult to track down at a later date in exactly the form in which it was consulted. (Examples of sources that would *not* be subject to this recommendation would include an article in a contemporary journal or magazine or any book cataloged by the Library of Congress or other national registry.) Copies may be kept in the form of printouts or as screen captures (the latter of which can be saved with the help of citation management software). Another option is to use a link-archiving service such as Perma.cc from Harvard University's Library Innovation Lab or the Save Page Now feature from the Internet Archive's Wayback Machine. For examples of how to cite archived content, see 14.104.

## NOTES AND BIBLIOGRAPHY: BASIC FORMAT

**13.18** **Notes and bibliography — an overview.** In the system favored by many writers in the humanities, bibliographic citations are provided in notes, preferably supplemented by a bibliography. The notes, whether footnotes or endnotes, are usually numbered and correspond to superscript note reference numbers in the text (but see 13.56, 13.57).

> According to science journalist Erica Gies, plans for future water infrastructure must include the restoration of natural ecologies, or what Gies refers to as "Slow Water": "The natural systems we are destroying could be our salvation."[1]

Notes are styled much like ordinary sentences, with authors' names in normal order and the elements separated by commas and parentheses and (depending on source type) other sentence punctuation.

1. Erica Gies, *Water Always Wins: Thriving in an Age of Drought and Deluge* (University of Chicago Press, 2022), 8, 27.

If the bibliography includes all works cited in the notes, a shortened form can be used in the notes because readers can consult the bibliography for publication details and other information. In works with no bibliography or only a selected list, full details must be given in a note at first mention of any work cited; subsequent citations need only include a short form.

2. Gies, *Water Always Wins*, 209–10.

In bibliographies, where entries are listed alphabetically, the name of the first-listed author is inverted, and the main elements are separated by periods.

Gies, Erica. *Water Always Wins: Thriving in an Age of Drought and Deluge*. University of Chicago Press, 2022.

For a detailed discussion of notes, see 13.27–64. For shortened references, see 13.32–39. For a detailed discussion of bibliographies, see 13.65–73.

13.19 **Abbreviations in notes versus bibliographies.** In a note, such terms as *editor* (sing. *ed.*, pl. *eds.*) *edited by* (*ed.*), *translator* (*trans.*, sing. and pl.), *translated by* (*trans.*), *volume* (sing. *vol.*, pl. *vols.*), and *edition* (sing. *ed.*, pl. *eds.*) are abbreviated. In a bibliography entry, noun forms such as *editor*, *translator*, *volume*, and *edition* are abbreviated (as in a note), but verb forms such as *edited by* and *translated by* are spelled out. Examples of these differences may be found throughout chapter 14.

13.20 **Page numbers and other locators.** In notes, where reference is usually to a particular passage in a book or journal article, only the page number or numbers pertaining to that passage are given. Multiple page numbers may include a range (separated by an en dash, as in the second example below) or separate locations (separated by a comma, as in the first example under 13.18).

1. Baihui Duan and Rebekah Clements, "Fighting for Forests: Protection and Exploitation of Kŏje Island Timber During the East Asian War of 1592–1598," *Environmental History* 27, no. 3 (2022): 422.

2. Duan and Clements, "Fighting for Forests," 431–32.

In bibliographies, no page numbers are given for books; for easier location of journal articles, the beginning and ending page numbers of the entire article are given.

Duan, Baihui, and Rebekah Clements. "Fighting for Forests: Protection and Exploitation of Kŏje Island Timber During the East Asian War of 1592–1598." *Environmental History* 27, no. 3 (2022): 415–40.

Sources consulted in electronic formats will not always include page numbers. When that is the case, it may be appropriate in a note to include a chapter or paragraph number (if available), a section heading, or a descriptive phrase that follows the organizational divisions of the work. In citations especially of shorter electronic works presented as a single, searchable document, such locators are often unnecessary. See also 14.59, 14.71.

## NOTES AND BIBLIOGRAPHY: EXAMPLES AND VARIATIONS

13.21 **Notes and bibliography — introduction to examples and variations.** The examples in this section provide an overview of the notes and bibliography style, featuring books and journal articles as models. Each example includes a numbered note and a corresponding bibliography entry. Each example also includes a shortened form of the note, suitable for subsequent citations of a source already cited in full; in practice, in works that include a bibliography that lists in full all sources cited, it is acceptable to use the shortened form in the notes even at first mention. For advice on constructing short forms for notes, see 13.32–39. For many more examples, see chapter 14.

13.22 **Book with single author or editor.** For a book with a single author, invert the name in the bibliography but not in the notes. Punctuate and capitalize as shown. Note the shortened form in the second note. Note also that page numbers are included in a note but not in a bibliography entry. The first note cites two consecutive pages; the second note cites two nonconsecutive pages. See also 14.47.

1. Charles Yu, *Interior Chinatown* (Pantheon Books, 2020), 95–96.
2. Yu, *Interior Chinatown*, 101, 103.

Yu, Charles. *Interior Chinatown*. Pantheon Books, 2020.

A book with an editor in place of an author includes the abbreviation *ed.* (*editor*; for more than one editor, use *eds.*). Note that the shortened form does not include *ed.*

1. Agnes Callard, ed., *On Anger* (Boston Review, 2020), 7.
2. Callard, *On Anger*, 9–10.

Callard, Agnes, ed. *On Anger*. Boston Review, 2020.

Note also that Chicago now omits the place of publication in most source citations for books (see 14.30).

13.23 **Book with multiple authors or editors.** For a book with two authors or editors, only the first-listed name is inverted in the bibliography entry. Both authors are listed in a note, whether full or shortened.

1. Terry Greene Sterling and Jude Joffe-Block, *Driving While Brown: Sheriff Joe Arpaio Versus the Latino Resistance* (University of California Press, 2021), 110.
2. Sterling and Joffe-Block, *Driving While Brown*, 205–6.

Sterling, Terry Greene, and Jude Joffe-Block. *Driving While Brown: Sheriff Joe Arpaio Versus the Latino Resistance*. University of California Press, 2021.

In a note that cites a book with more than two authors or editors (in previous editions it was more than three), list only the first author or editor, followed by "et al." (Latin for "and others"). In the bibliography, list up to six authors; if there are more than six, list only the first three, followed by "et al." (In a work with no bibliography, list up to six authors in the first, full citation in a note—as in a bibliography entry.)

1. Katie Aubrecht et al., eds., *The Aging–Disability Nexus* (UBC Press, 2020), 44.
2. Aubrecht et al., *Aging–Disability Nexus*, 49–50.

Aubrecht, Katie, Christine Kelly, and Carla Rice, eds. *The Aging–Disability Nexus*. UBC Press, 2020.

13.24 **Book with author plus editor or translator.** In a book with an editor or translator in addition to the author, *ed.* or *trans.* in the note becomes *Edited by* or *Translated by* in the bibliography entry. See also 14.6.

1. Gabriel García Márquez, *Love in the Time of Cholera*, trans. Edith Grossman (Alfred A. Knopf, 1988), 242–55.
2. García Márquez, *Cholera*, 33.

García Márquez, Gabriel. *Love in the Time of Cholera*. Translated by Edith Grossman. Alfred A. Knopf, 1988.

13.25 **Chapter in an edited book.** When citing a chapter or similar part of an edited book, include the chapter author; the chapter title, in quotation marks; and the editor. Precede the title of the book with *in*. Note that it is no longer necessary to record a page range for the chapter in the bibliography entry (a departure from previous editions of this manual). See also 14.8–14.

1. Glenn Gould, "Streisand as Schwarzkopf," in *The Glenn Gould Reader*, ed. Tim Page (Vintage Books, 1984), 310.
2. Gould, "Streisand as Schwarzkopf," 309.

Gould, Glenn. "Streisand as Schwarzkopf." In *The Glenn Gould Reader*, edited by Tim Page. Vintage Books, 1984.

13.26 **Journal article.** Citations of journals typically include the volume and issue number and year of publication. The volume number follows the italicized journal title in roman and with no intervening punctuation. A specific page reference is included in the notes; the page range for an article is included in the bibliography. In the full citation, page numbers are preceded by a colon. A month or season of publication can usually be omitted (but see 14.70). For the URL in the following example, which authors should record for articles consulted online, see 13.6, 13.7.

1. Hyeyoung Kwon, "Inclusion Work: Children of Immigrants Claiming Membership in Everyday Life," *American Journal of Sociology* 127, no. 6 (2022): 1824, https://doi.org/10.1086/720277.
2. Kwon, "Inclusion Work," 1830.

Kwon, Hyeyoung. "Inclusion Work: Children of Immigrants Claiming Membership in Everyday Life." *American Journal of Sociology* 127, no. 6 (2022): 1818–59. https://doi.org/10.1086/720277.

## NOTES

### *Note Numbers*

13.27 **Numbers in text versus numbers in notes.** Note reference numbers in text are set as superscript numbers. In the notes themselves, they are normally full size, not raised, and followed by a period. (In manuscripts, superscript numbers in both places—the typical default setting in the note-making feature of a word processor—are perfectly acceptable.)

"Crushed thirty feet upwards, the waters flashed for an instant like heaps of fountains, then brokenly sank in a shower of flakes, leaving the circling surface creamed like new milk round the marble trunk of the whale."[1]

1. Herman Melville, *Moby-Dick; or, The Whale* (New York, 1851), 627.

If a symbol rather than a number is used (see 13.28), the symbol appears as a superscript in the text but not in the note, where it is *not* followed by a period but may be followed by a space, as long as this is done consistently. (In some typefaces, symbols may become difficult to read as superscripts; in such cases, they may be set on the line, full size, in the text as well as the notes.) See also 14.31.

13.28 **Sequencing of note numbers and symbols.** Notes, whether footnotes or endnotes, should be numbered consecutively, beginning with 1, throughout each article and for each new chapter—not throughout an entire book unless the text has no internal divisions. Where only a handful of footnotes appear in an entire book or, perhaps, just one in an article, symbols may be used instead of numbers (see also 13.27). Usually an asterisk is enough, but if more than one note is needed on the same page, the sequence is * † ‡. For using a combination of numbers and symbols for two sets of notes, see 13.52–54. For notes to tables and other nontextual matter, which are usually handled independently of the notes to the text, see 3.77–81.

13.29 **Placement of note number.** A note number should generally be placed at the end of a sentence or at the end of a clause. The number normally follows a quotation (whether it is run in to the text or set as an extract). Relative to other punctuation, the number follows any punctuation mark except for the dash, which it precedes.

"Good fiction is made of that which is real," wrote Ralph Ellison, "and reality is difficult to come by."[1]

It was the hour of "national paths" toward socialism;[9] but that expression, which turned out to be temporary, was more an incantation than a discovery.

The bias was apparent in the Shotwell series[3]—and it must be remembered that Shotwell was a student of Robinson's.

Though a note number normally follows a closing parenthesis, it may on rare occasion be more appropriate to place the number inside the closing parenthesis—if, for example, the note applies to a specific term within the parentheses.

(In an earlier book he had said quite the opposite.)[2]

Men and their unions, as they entered industrial work, negotiated two things: Young women would be laid off once they married (the commonly acknowledged "marriage bar"[1]), and men would be paid a "family wage."

13.30 **Note numbers with chapter and article titles and subheads.** In books, a note number should never appear within or at the end of a chapter title. A note that applies to an entire chapter should be unnumbered and is preferably placed at the foot of the first page of the chapter, preceding any numbered notes (see 13.55–59). (In the case of an electronic format that does not support footnotes as such, an unnumbered note might appear immediately after, or be linked from, the chapter title.) Some journal publishers place an asterisk at the end of the article title for notes that apply to an article as a whole and reserve numbered references for other notes. Note references appearing with a subhead within a book chapter or an article should be numbered along with the rest of the notes, though some editors will prefer to move such references into the text that follows the subhead.

13.31 **Multiple citations and multiple note references.** More than one note reference should never appear in the same place (such as[5,6]); however, a single note can contain more than one citation or comment (see 13.61). Nor can a note number reappear out of sequence; the substance of a note that applies to more than one location must be repeated under a new note number. To avoid such repetition, especially for a longer discursive note, a cross-reference may be used—though these must be checked carefully before publication. (See also 13.32–39.)

18. See note 3 above.

Some systems of numbered references used by publications in the sciences not only allow multiple reference numbers in the same location but also allow numbers to reappear out of sequence for repeated notes; for more details, consult *The CSE Manual* (bibliog. 1.1).

## *Shortened Citations*

13.32 **When to use shortened citations.** To reduce the bulk of documentation in works that use footnotes or endnotes, citations of sources already given in full—either in a previous note or in a bibliography that provides complete bibliographic data—should be shortened whenever possible. In a work without a bibliography, it is preferable to repeat the full citation the first time it appears in each new chapter; though not mandatory, this approach may also be used in a work that includes a bibliography, since it saves readers the trouble of shuttling back and forth between notes and bibliography for every reference. The short form, as distinct from an abbreviation, should include enough information to remind readers of the full title or to lead them to the appropriate entry in the bibliography. (Some short forms are not covered here. For citing different chapters in the same work, see 14.10; for letters, see 14.13; for legal citations, see 14.176. Other short forms may be patterned on the examples in this section.)

13.33 **Basic structure of the short form.** The most common short form consists of the last name of the author and the main title of the work cited, usually shortened if more than four words, as in examples 4–6 below. For more on authors' names, see 13.35. For more on short titles, see 13.36. For more on journal articles, see 14.84.

1. Heather Hendershot, *When the News Broke: Chicago 1968 and the Polarizing of America* (University of Chicago Press, 2022), 149.
2. Marco Cavarzere, "History, Politics, and Fiction in Seventeenth-Century Italy: The Case of Baroque Novels," *History of Humanities* 7, no. 1 (2022): 39–40.
3. Tsugumi (Mimi) Okabe, "Starving Beauties? *Instabae*, Diet Food, and Japanese Girl Culture," in *Food Instagram: Identity, Influence, and Negotiation*, ed. Emily J. H. Contois and Zenia Kish (University of Illinois Press, 2022), 50.
4. Hendershot, *When the News Broke*, 165–66.
5. Cavarzere, "Seventeenth-Century Italy," 42.
6. Okabe, "Starving Beauties?," 55.

13.34 **Cross-reference to full citation.** When references to a particular source are far apart, readers encountering the short form may be helped by a cross-reference to the original note—especially in the absence of a full bibliography. These cross-references must be checked carefully before the work is published.

1. Miller, *Quest*, 81 (see chap. 1, n. 4).

It may be better simply to repeat the full details for a source at its first appearance in the notes to each new chapter, an approach recommended by Chicago especially for works that lack a full bibliography.

13.35 **Short form for authors' names.** Only the last name of the author, or of the editor or translator if given first in the full reference, is needed in the short form. Full names or initials are included only when authors with the same last name must be distinguished from one another. Such abbreviations as *ed.* or *trans.* following a name in the full reference are omitted in subsequent references. If a work has two authors, list both; for more than two, list only the first, followed by *et al.* (see also 13.23).

1. Stephen King and Peter Straub, *The Talisman* (Viking, 1984), 321.
2. Janka Kascakova et al., eds. *Katherine Mansfield: International Approaches* (Routledge, 2021), 44.
3. King and Straub, *Talisman*, 433.
4. Kascakova et al., *Katherine Mansfield*, 101.

13.36 **Short form for titles of works.** The short title contains the key word or words from the main title. An initial *A* or *The* is usually omitted from longer titles but may be retained if the title is short. The order of the words should not be changed (for example, *Daily Notes of a Trip Around the World* should be shortened not to *World Trip* but to *Daily Notes* or *Around the World*). Titles of four words or fewer are seldom shortened. The short title is italicized or set in roman and quotation marks according to the way the full title appears.

*The War Journal of Major Damon "Rocky" Gause*
(Short title) *War Journal*

"A Brief Account of the Reconstruction of Aristotle's *Protrepticus*"
(Short title) "Aristotle's *Protrepticus*"

*Kriegstagebuch des Oberkommandos der Wehrmacht, 1940–1945*
(Short title) *Kriegstagebuch*

In short titles in languages other than English, no word should be omitted that governs the case ending of a word included in the short title. If in doubt, ask someone who knows the language.

13.37 **Shortened citations versus "ibid."** The abbreviation *ibid.* (from *ibidem*, "in the same place") usually refers to a single work cited in the note immediately preceding. However, because *ibid.* can obscure the identity of a source, Chicago recommends instead using shortened citations as described elsewhere in this section. Shortened citations generally take up less than a line, meaning that *ibid.* saves no space, and in electronic formats that link to one note at a time, *ibid.* risks confusing the reader. In the following examples, shortened citations are used for the first reference, as in a work with a full bibliography (see 13.32). The shortened forms preferred by Chicago are followed by the same examples using *ibid.* Note that *ibid.* is appropriate only when it refers to the last item cited; where this is not the case, a shortened citation must be used. Note also that with the shortened form, a page reference must be repeated even if it is the same as the last-cited location (as in note 3); with *ibid.*, an identical page location is not repeated. The word *ibid.*, italicized here only because it is a word used as a word (see 7.66), is capitalized at the beginning of a note and followed by a period.

| | | |
|---|---|---|
| 1. Carson, *Silent Spring*, 3. | | |
| 2. Carson, *Silent Spring*, 18. | *or* | 2. Ibid., 18. |
| 3. Carson, *Silent Spring*, 18. | *or* | 3. Ibid. |
| 4. Carson, *Silent Spring*, 24–26. | *or* | 4. Ibid., 24–26. |
| 5. Carson, *The Sea Around Us*, 401–2. | | |
| 6. Carson, *The Sea Around Us*, 433. | *or* | 6. Ibid., 433. |
| 7. Darwin, *Origin of Species*, 37–38. | | |
| 8. Carson, *The Sea Around Us*, 403. | | |
| 9. Darwin, *Origin of Species*, 152. | | |
| 10. Darwin, *Origin of Species*, 201–2. | *or* | 10. Ibid., 201–2. |
| 11. Carson, *Silent Spring*, 240; *The Sea Around Us*, 32. | | |
| 12. Carson, *The Sea Around Us*, 33. | | |

To avoid repetition, an author or title alone may be used in successive citations, though the fuller form is usually preferred (which form to use may depend on whether the author or title has been mentioned in the text).

1. Carson, *Silent Spring*, 18.
2. Carson, 18.

*or*

2. *Silent Spring*, 18

An author-only reference (or *ibid.*) is often the best choice within one note in successive references to the same work.

3. Morris Birkbeck, "The Illinois Prairies and Settlers," in *Prairie State: Impressions of Illinois, 1673–1967, by Travelers and Other Observers*, ed. Paul M. Angle (University of Chicago Press, 1968), 62. "The soil of the Big-prairie, which is of no great extent notwithstanding its name, is a rich, cool sand; that is to say, one of the most desirable description" (Birkbeck, 63 [*or* ibid., 63]).

To avoid a succession of repeated notes for the same works, author-only versions of notes 2–4, 6, and 8–10 in the first set of examples above might instead be placed parenthetically in the text in place of the note references, but only if the works under discussion are clear from the text (see also 12.77).

13.38 **"Idem."** When several works by the same person are cited successively in the same note, *idem* ("the same," sometimes abbreviated to *id.*) has sometimes been used in place of the author's name. The term is rarely used anymore except in legal references, where the abbreviation *id.* is used in place of *ibid.* (see 14.176). Chicago discourages the use of both *idem* and *ibid.*, recommending instead the shortened forms described in 13.33. See also 13.37.

13.39 **"Op. cit." and "loc. cit."** *Op. cit.* (*opere citato*, "in the work cited") and *loc. cit.* (*loco citato*, "in the place cited"), used with an author's last name and standing in place of a previously cited title, have rightly fallen into disuse. Consider a reader's frustration on meeting, for example, "Wells, op. cit., 10" in note 95 and having to search back to note 2 for the full source or, worse still, finding that *two* works by Wells have been cited. Chicago disallows both *op. cit.* and *loc. cit.* and instead uses the short-title form described in 13.36.

## *Commentary and Quotations in Notes*

13.40 **Citations plus commentary in a note.** When a note contains not only the source of a fact or quotation in the text but related substantive material as well, the source comes first. A period usually separates the citation from the commentary. Such comments as "emphasis mine" are usually put in parentheses. See also 12.73.

1. Shakespeare, *Julius Caesar*, act 3, sc. 1. Caesar's claim of constancy should be taken with a grain of salt.

2. Little, "Norms of Collegiality," 330 (my italics).

13.41 **Quotation within a note.** When a note includes a quotation, the source normally follows the terminal punctuation of the quotation. The entire source need not be put in parentheses, which involves changing existing parentheses to brackets (see 6.107) and creating unnecessary clutter.

1. One estimate of the size of the reading public at this time was that of Sydney Smith: "Readers are fourfold in number compared with what they were before the beginning of the French war. . . . There are four or five hundred thousand readers more than there were thirty years ago, among the lower orders." *Letters*, ed. Nowell C. Smith (Oxford University Press, 1953), 1:341, 343.

Long quotations should be set off as extracts in notes as they would be in text (see 12.10). In notes, more than three lines of poetry should be set off (but see 12.25; see also 12.29).

13.42 **Substantive notes.** Substantive, or discursive, notes may merely amplify the text and include no sources. Such notes may augment any system of source citation, including the author-date system (see 13.128). When a source is needed, it is treated as in the example in 13.41 or, if brief and already cited in full, may appear parenthetically, as in the following example:

1. Ernst Cassirer takes important notice of this in *Language and Myth* (59–62) and offers a searching analysis of man's regard for things on which his power of inspirited action may crucially depend.

13.43 **Paragraphing within long notes.** To avoid page makeup problems, very long footnotes should be avoided (see 13.47). No such bar exists for endnotes, however, and very long endnotes should be broken into multiple paragraphs as an aid to reading. Authors and editors should first consider, however, whether such a note would be more effective if shortened or at least partially incorporated into the text. See also 13.48.

13.44 **Footnotes that break across pages in a printed work.** When a footnote begins on one page and continues on the next, the break should be made in mid-sentence lest readers miss the end of the note; a short rule appears above the continued part (see fig. 13.1). This advice applies only to the published form of a work (and is something that is generally imposed at the typesetting stage). At the manuscript stage, authors and editors should let the note-making feature in their word-processing software determine any such breaks.

HOMBERG'S LEGACY 395

the broadening scope of his investigations of combustion and the role of gaseous substances in chemical transformations, Lavoisier would later conduct a series of experiments with Homberg's pyrophorus, and present a memoir on this topic in the same year that he presented his more widely cited papers on respiration, the burning of phosphorus, and combustion in general.[162] Notably, Lavoisier's so-called balance-sheet method for comparing starting and ending weights of reacting substances, which emerged as crucial for such combustion experiments, actually represents a *return* to the evidentiary power of weight determinations that was fundamental to Homberg's own theory of combustion and calcination contained within his comprehensive "light as sulphur" theory.[163]

This chapter has followed the fate of several of Homberg's ideas and interests through much of the eighteenth century and down to the time of Lavoisier. Throughout this period, Homberg's experiments with the Tschirnhaus lens apparatus continued to fascinate. Newton built his own apparatus to repeat them, Hartsoeker endeavored to refute them, Geoffroy and Neumann explored them, and finally, after a hiatus of nearly sixty years, a group of academicians reerected Homberg's apparatus along the banks of the Seine and reinvestigated them, thereby guiding Lavoisier to the crucial experiments that led to his oxygen theory of combustion. Homberg's comprehensive theory of chymistry, emulated and extended by several younger chymists during and shortly after Homberg's life, had several of its aspects revived within a new framework by Macquer in the 1770s. As for the Batavian chymist's dogged pursuit of metallic transmutation, it too persisted in various guises in the work of a broad roster of later academicians down at least to the 1760s, despite carefully constructed images to the contrary.

---

lens was so great that it would have shattered the glass bell jar. It is more plausible that Lavoisier dismounted and used only the small secondary lens, which on its own would have provided sufficient heat for the experiments he carried out.

162. Antoine-Laurent Lavoisier, "Expériences sur la combinaison de l'alun avec les matières charbonneuses," *MARS* (1777): 363–72.

163. This statement is *not* to imply that Homberg was the originator of the method; William Newman and I showed that a very similar method was employed in chrysopoetic processes pursued by George Starkey in the 1650s, and that weight measurements were likewise crucial for Van Helmont. Homberg read both of these carefully; see *Alchemy Tried in the Fire* (University of Chicago Press, 2004), especially 71–91, 120–25, 296–314. A similar use of the problem of "missing weight" as a probe of chemical reactions appears even in the work of the fourteenth-century John of Rupescissa; see Principe, *Secrets of Alchemy*, 65–66.

FIGURE 13.1. A page of text with footnotes; the first note is continued from the previous page (with a short rule above it). See 13.44.

13.45 **"See" and "cf."** Notes are often used to invite readers to consult further resources. When doing so, authors should keep in mind the distinction between *see* and *cf.*, using *cf.* only to mean "compare" or "see, by way of comparison." Neither term is italicized in notes (though *see* is italicized in indexes; see 15.22).

1. For further discussion of this problem, see Jones, *Conflict*, 49.
2. Others disagree with my position; cf. Fisher and Ury, *Getting to Yes*, 101–3.

## *Footnotes Versus Endnotes*

13.46 **Footnotes and endnotes — an overview.** As their name suggests, footnotes appear at the foot of a page. In a journal, endnotes appear at the end of an article; in a book, at the end of a chapter or, more commonly, at the back of the book. In multiauthor books, where the notes may differ in kind and length, and where chapters may be offered separately, they are usually placed at the end of the chapter to which they pertain. (The decision of where to place the notes is generally made by the publisher.) In electronic formats, notes are often linked to the text, and the distinction between footnotes and endnotes may not apply. At the manuscript stage, authors can work with whichever form seems most convenient, though notes should be inserted with a word processor's note-making function to facilitate automatic renumbering when notes are added or deleted (see also 2.26). For footnotes to tables, see 2.36, 3.77–81. For notes in previously published material, see 2.50.

13.47 **Footnotes — pros and cons.** Readers of printed works usually prefer footnotes for ease of reference. This is especially true where the notes are closely integrated into the text and make interesting reading, or if immediate knowledge of the sources is essential to readers. The limiting factor in printed works is page makeup—it can be difficult or impossible to fit a close succession of long footnotes onto the pages they pertain to, especially in an illustrated work (a basic requirement for all footnotes is that they at least begin on the page on which they are referenced). There is also the matter of appearance; a page consisting almost exclusively of footnotes is daunting for many readers. For some remedies, see 13.60–64. On the other hand, certain information that appears in the text can often be omitted from a footnote but must appear in an endnote; for example, an author's name mentioned in the text need not be repeated in a corresponding footnote citing a work by that same author (cf. 13.51).

13.48 **Endnotes — pros and cons.** Endnotes, which pose no page makeup challenges beyond those of ordinary text, obviate many of the disadvantages of footnotes in printed works (see 13.47). Because of this flexibility, and because pages free of footnotes are less intimidating to many readers, publishers' marketing and sales staff may recommend endnotes in books directed to general as well as scholarly or professional readers. Nonetheless, because general readers may be disappointed to find a third or more of a book devoted to endnotes, authors still need to aim for a healthy balance between text and notes (i.e., by resisting the temptation to include an excessive number of discursive notes). The main problem with endnotes is that of finding a particular note. This difficulty (not always encountered in electronic texts, where text and notes may be linked) can be ameliorated by informative running heads (see 13.50).

13.49 **Endnote placement.** Endnotes to each chapter of a book are often best grouped in the end matter, following the text and any appendixes and preceding the bibliography if there is one (see 1.4). The main heading is simply "Notes," and the group of notes to each chapter is introduced by a subhead bearing the chapter number or title or both (see fig. 13.2). In a book that has a different author for each chapter, or whose chapters may be offered separately, endnotes normally appear at the end of each chapter. In a journal, they appear at the end of each article. In the latter two cases, a subhead "Notes" usually appears between text and notes (see fig. 13.3).

13.50 **Running heads for endnotes.** Where endnotes are gathered at the back of a printed book and occupy more than two or three pages, running heads (both verso and recto) showing the page numbers to which the notes pertain are a boon to readers (see 1.15). (In electronic formats without fixed pages, such running heads will not apply; instead, the notes may be linked to the text as an aid to navigation.) To determine what page numbers to use in the running head for a particular page of notes, find the numbers of the first and last notes beginning on that page (disregarding a runover from a previous page) and locate the references to these notes in the main text. The numbers of the first and last pages on which these references appear in text are the numbers to use in the running head: for example, "Notes to Pages 123–125." The last number is *not* abbreviated; compare 9.63. (If, as occasionally happens, only one note appears on a page, use the singular: e.g., "Note to Page 23.") Because these running heads can be completed only when the pagination for the published version is in place (usually on the first set of page proofs), the corrections are considered "alterations" (see 2.140), and the cost may be

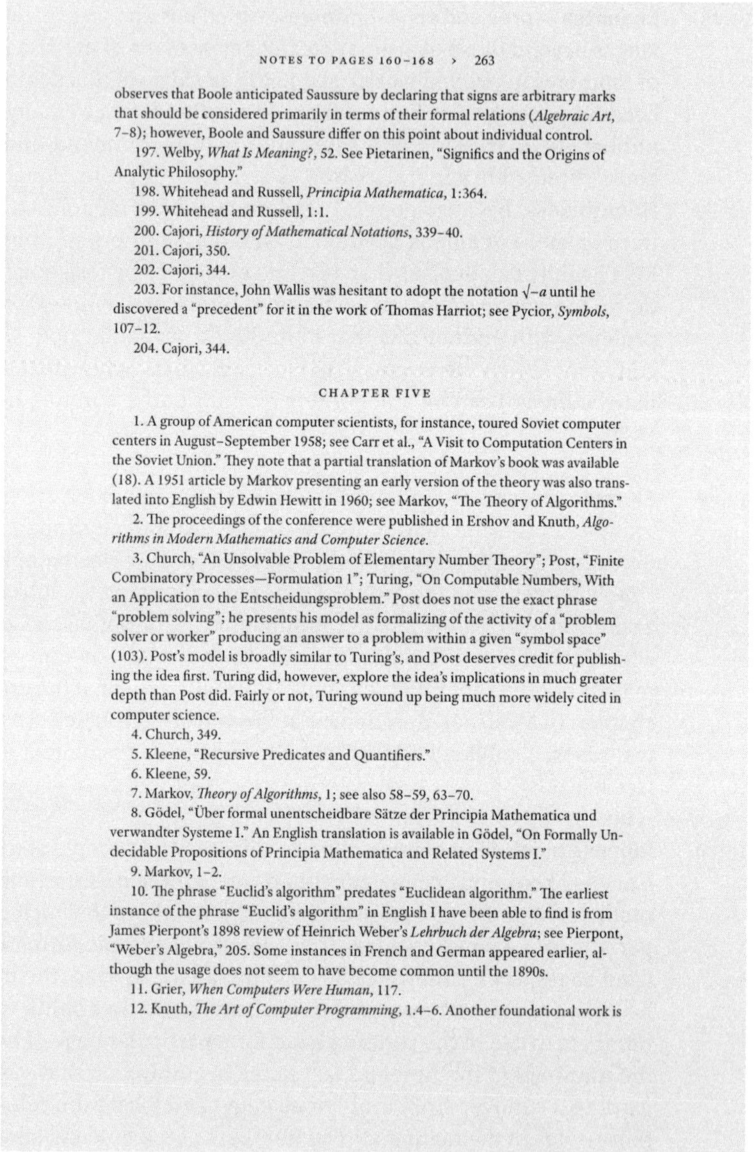

NOTES TO PAGES 160–168 › 263

observes that Boole anticipated Saussure by declaring that signs are arbitrary marks that should be considered primarily in terms of their formal relations (*Algebraic Art*, 7–8); however, Boole and Saussure differ on this point about individual control.

197. Welby, *What Is Meaning?*, 52. See Pietarinen, "Significs and the Origins of Analytic Philosophy."

198. Whitehead and Russell, *Principia Mathematica*, 1:364.

199. Whitehead and Russell, 1:1.

200. Cajori, *History of Mathematical Notations*, 339–40.

201. Cajori, 350.

202. Cajori, 344.

203. For instance, John Wallis was hesitant to adopt the notation $\sqrt{-a}$ until he discovered a "precedent" for it in the work of Thomas Harriot; see Pycior, *Symbols*, 107–12.

204. Cajori, 344.

CHAPTER FIVE

1. A group of American computer scientists, for instance, toured Soviet computer centers in August–September 1958; see Carr et al., "A Visit to Computation Centers in the Soviet Union." They note that a partial translation of Markov's book was available (18). A 1951 article by Markov presenting an early version of the theory was also translated into English by Edwin Hewitt in 1960; see Markov, "The Theory of Algorithms."

2. The proceedings of the conference were published in Ershov and Knuth, *Algorithms in Modern Mathematics and Computer Science*.

3. Church, "An Unsolvable Problem of Elementary Number Theory"; Post, "Finite Combinatory Processes—Formulation 1"; Turing, "On Computable Numbers, With an Application to the Entscheidungsproblem." Post does not use the exact phrase "problem solving"; he presents his model as formalizing of the activity of a "problem solver or worker" producing an answer to a problem within a given "symbol space" (103). Post's model is broadly similar to Turing's, and Post deserves credit for publishing the idea first. Turing did, however, explore the idea's implications in much greater depth than Post did. Fairly or not, Turing wound up being much more widely cited in computer science.

4. Church, 349.

5. Kleene, "Recursive Predicates and Quantifiers."

6. Kleene, 59.

7. Markov, *Theory of Algorithms*, 1; see also 58–59, 63–70.

8. Gödel, "Über formal unentscheidbare Sätze der Principia Mathematica und verwandter Systeme I." An English translation is available in Gödel, "On Formally Undecidable Propositions of Principia Mathematica and Related Systems I."

9. Markov, 1–2.

10. The phrase "Euclid's algorithm" predates "Euclidean algorithm." The earliest instance of the phrase "Euclid's algorithm" in English I have been able to find is from James Pierpont's 1898 review of Heinrich Weber's *Lehrbuch der Algebra*; see Pierpont, "Weber's Algebra," 205. Some instances in French and German appeared earlier, although the usage does not seem to have become common until the 1890s.

11. Grier, *When Computers Were Human*, 117.

12. Knuth, *The Art of Computer Programming*, 1.4–6. Another foundational work is

FIGURE 13.2. A page of endnotes, with a subhead introducing the notes to a new chapter and a running head showing the text pages on which the notes are referenced. The shortened citations shown here correspond to full citation data in a separate bibliography. See 13.49, 13.50.

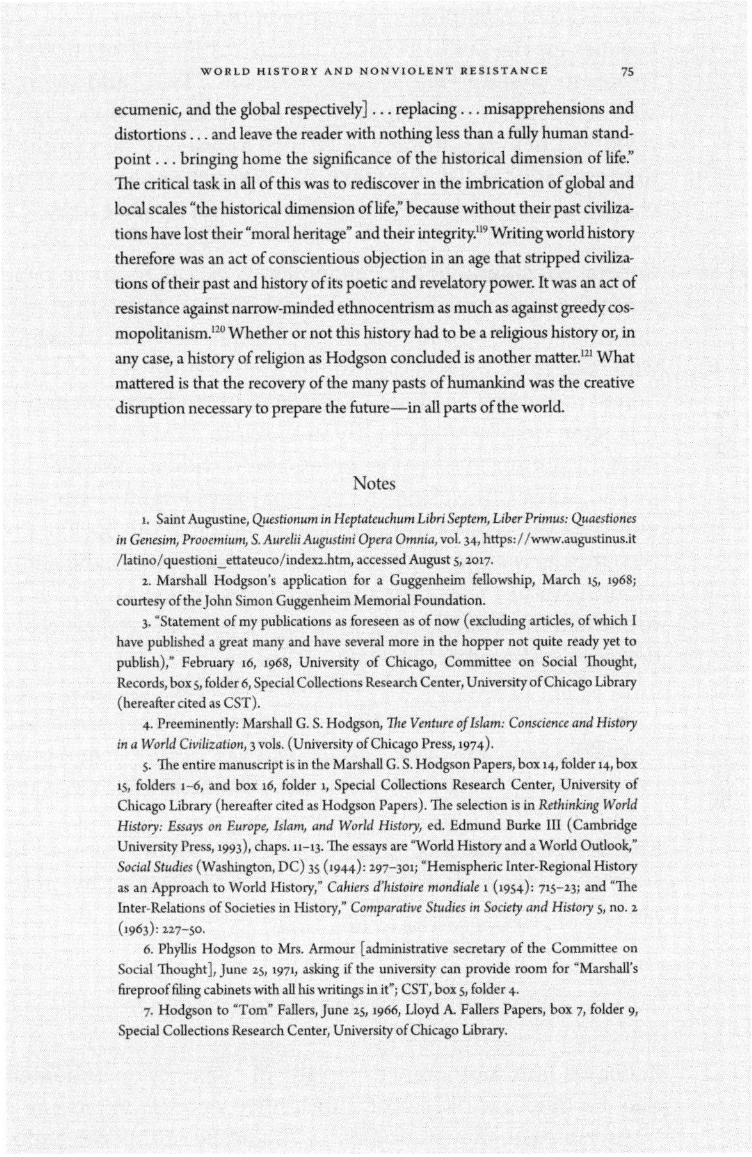

WORLD HISTORY AND NONVIOLENT RESISTANCE 75

ecumenic, and the global respectively] . . . replacing . . . misapprehensions and distortions . . . and leave the reader with nothing less than a fully human standpoint . . . bringing home the significance of the historical dimension of life." The critical task in all of this was to rediscover in the imbrication of global and local scales "the historical dimension of life," because without their past civilizations have lost their "moral heritage" and their integrity.[119] Writing world history therefore was an act of conscientious objection in an age that stripped civilizations of their past and history of its poetic and revelatory power. It was an act of resistance against narrow-minded ethnocentrism as much as against greedy cosmopolitanism.[120] Whether or not this history had to be a religious history or, in any case, a history of religion as Hodgson concluded is another matter.[121] What mattered is that the recovery of the many pasts of humankind was the creative disruption necessary to prepare the future—in all parts of the world.

Notes

1. Saint Augustine, *Questionum in Heptateuchum Libri Septem, Liber Primus: Quaestiones in Genesim, Prooemium, S. Aurelii Augustini Opera Omnia*, vol. 34, https://www.augustinus.it/latino/questioni_ettateuco/index2.htm, accessed August 5, 2017.

2. Marshall Hodgson's application for a Guggenheim fellowship, March 15, 1968; courtesy of the John Simon Guggenheim Memorial Foundation.

3. "Statement of my publications as foreseen as of now (excluding articles, of which I have published a great many and have several more in the hopper not quite ready yet to publish)," February 16, 1968, University of Chicago, Committee on Social Thought, Records, box 5, folder 6, Special Collections Research Center, University of Chicago Library (hereafter cited as CST).

4. Preeminently: Marshall G. S. Hodgson, *The Venture of Islam: Conscience and History in a World Civilization*, 3 vols. (University of Chicago Press, 1974).

5. The entire manuscript is in the Marshall G. S. Hodgson Papers, box 14, folder 14, box 15, folders 1–6, and box 16, folder 1, Special Collections Research Center, University of Chicago Library (hereafter cited as Hodgson Papers). The selection is in *Rethinking World History: Essays on Europe, Islam, and World History*, ed. Edmund Burke III (Cambridge University Press, 1993), chaps. 11–13. The essays are "World History and a World Outlook," *Social Studies* (Washington, DC) 35 (1944): 297–301; "Hemispheric Inter-Regional History as an Approach to World History," *Cahiers d'histoire mondiale* 1 (1954): 715–23; and "The Inter-Relations of Societies in History," *Comparative Studies in Society and History* 5, no. 2 (1963): 227–50.

6. Phyllis Hodgson to Mrs. Armour [administrative secretary of the Committee on Social Thought], June 25, 1971, asking if the university can provide room for "Marshall's fireproof filing cabinets with all his writings in it"; CST, box 5, folder 4.

7. Hodgson to "Tom" Fallers, June 25, 1966, Lloyd A. Fallers Papers, box 7, folder 9, Special Collections Research Center, University of Chicago Library.

FIGURE 13.3. Chapter endnotes (first page of notes only), prefaced by the subhead "Notes." See 13.49.

charged to the publisher. (Another option, less useful for readers but cheaper for the publisher, is to include running heads that simply read "Notes to Chapter One," "Notes to Chapter Two," and so on; however, since readers are often unaware of the number of the chapter they are reading, chapter numbers must also appear in the running heads of the text itself, as listed under 1.12.) When notes appear at the ends of chapters, note-related running heads are rarely necessary.

13.51 **Special considerations for endnotes.** Whereas footnote citations, because they appear so close to the text, can omit certain elements mentioned in the text, omitting them in endnotes risks irritating readers, who have to go back and forth. For example, an author or a title mentioned in the text need not be repeated in the footnote citation, though it is often helpful to do so. In an endnote, however, the author (or at least the author's last name, unless it is obvious) and title should be repeated, since at least some readers may have forgotten whether the note number was 93 or 94 by the time they find it at the back of the work. It is particularly annoying to arrive at the right place in the endnotes only to find another *ibid.* (see also 13.37). Such frustration can be further prevented by consolidating some of the endnote references, using the devices illustrated in the examples below.

1. This and the preceding four quotations are all from *Hamlet*, act 1, sc. 4.
2. Ellen Jovin, *Rebel with a Clause: Tales and Tips from a Roving Grammarian* (Mariner Books, 2022). Further citations of this work are given in the text.

The device in the second example above should be used only if the source is clear from the text, without reference to the endnotes. See also 12.78.

## *Two Sets of Notes*

13.52 **Endnotes plus footnotes.** Especially in a heavily documented work, it may be helpful to separate substantive notes from source citations. In such a case, the citation notes should be numbered and appear as endnotes. The substantive notes, indicated by asterisks and other symbols, appear as footnotes. (This dual arrangement, though more work to produce, is almost always beneficial for readers, who might otherwise turn to the endnotes hoping for substantive commentary only to find a source citation.) The first footnote on each printed page is referenced by an asterisk. If more than one footnote begins on a page, the sequence of symbols is * † ‡. Should more than three such notes appear on the same page, the symbols are doubled for the fourth to the sixth notes: ** †† ‡‡. (In reflowable electronic formats where notes are linked from their references in the text and there is no distinction between footnotes and endnotes, such a system may need to be adapted.) See also 3.80, 13.27.

13.53 **Footnotes plus author-date citations.** The rather cumbersome practice described in 13.52 may be avoided by the use of author-date citations for sources (see 13.102–4) and numbered footnotes or endnotes for substantive comments (see 13.128). Moreover, numbered notes can themselves contain parenthetical author-date citations when necessary, adding to the flexibility of such a system.

13.54 **Editor's or translator's notes plus author's notes.** In an edited or translated work that includes notes by the original author, any additional notes furnished by the editor or translator must be distinguished from the others. Most commonly, the added notes are interspersed and consecutively numbered with the original notes but distinguished from them either by appending "—Ed." or "—Trans." to the end of the note (following the period or other final punctuation, usually with no intervening space) or by enclosing the entire note, except the number, in square brackets. (An editor's or translator's comment can also be added as needed in square brackets within an original note; see 6.105.)

> 1. Millicent Cliff was Norton Westermont's first cousin, although to the very last she denied it.—Ed.

*or*

> 2. [The original reads *gesungen*; presumably *gesunken* is meant.]

Alternatively, if there are only a few added notes, these can be referenced by asterisks and other symbols and appear as footnotes; the original notes, numbered, then appear below them, as footnotes (see fig. 13.4), or are treated as endnotes (see 13.52). Separate sets of footnotes, however, can be difficult to implement in print and should therefore be considered only as a last resort.

## *Special Types of Notes*

13.55 **Unnumbered notes.** Footnotes without numbers or symbols always precede any numbered notes on the same page. They most often appear on the opening page of a chapter or other main division of a work. In

Each county has a court of justice,[10] a sheriff to execute the decrees of tribunals, a prison to hold criminals.

There are needs that are felt in a nearly equal manner by all the townships of the county; it was natural that a central authority be charged with providing for them. In Massachusetts this authority resides in the hands of a certain number of magistrates whom the governor of the state designates with the advice[11] of his council.[12]

The administrators of the county have only a limited and exceptional power that applies only to a very few cases that are foreseen in advance. The state and the township suffice in the ordinary course of things. These administrators do nothing but prepare the budget of the county; the legislature votes it.[13] There is no assembly that directly or indirectly represents the county.

The county therefore has, to tell the truth, no political existence.

In most of the American constitutions one remarks a double tendency that brings legislators to divide executive power and concentrate legislative power. The New England township by itself has a principle of existence that they do not strip from it; but one would have to create that life fictitiously in the county, and the utility of doing so has not been felt: all the townships united have only one single representation, the state, center of all national* powers; outside township and national action one can say that there are only individual forces.

*Here "national" refers to the states.
10. See the law of February 14, 1821, *Laws of Massachusetts,* 1:551 [2:551–56].
11. See the law of February 20, 1819, *Laws of Massachusetts,* 2:494.
12. The governor's council is an elected body.
13. See the law of November 2, 1791 [November 2, 1781], *Laws of Massachusetts,* 1:61.

FIGURE 13.4. Translator's footnote referenced by an asterisk, followed by author's numbered footnotes. At the foot of the page, notes referenced by symbols always precede numbered notes, regardless of the order in which the symbols and numbers appear in the text. See 13.54.

a work with endnotes in which an unnumbered footnote is not an option, an unnumbered endnote—to be used with caution in book-length works, where readers are likely to miss it—should appear immediately before note 1 to the relevant chapter. An example of such a note would be a note applying to a book epigraph (see 1.41), which would precede the endnotes to the first chapter and appear under a heading "Epigraph." Notes to chapter epigraphs can be handled similarly. Source notes, biographical notes, and other notes pertaining to an entire chapter or section—which often appear as unnumbered footnotes—are treated in 13.58 and 13.59. In the case of an electronic format that does not support footnotes as such, an unnumbered note might appear immediately after, or be linked from, the element to which it pertains.

13.56 **Notes keyed to line numbers.** In certain types of works—for example, classic editions of works in verse—notes are keyed to line numbers instead of note numbers. In preparing such works, authors may use the note feature in their word processor as described in 2.26. If the line numbers will be the same regardless of format (as in verse), they may be added at the manuscript stage; if not (as in ordinary prose), they must be added to the typeset version for publication. (Note numbers will also be removed or hidden at that stage.) Such notes may be presented as footnotes or endnotes; for an example with footnotes, see figure 13.5. For notes keyed to page numbers, see 13.57.

13.57 **Notes keyed to page numbers.** In books intended for a general audience, it may be desirable to suppress note numbers in the text. (Numbered notes may be off-putting or distracting for readers unaccustomed to academic texts.) Any notes may then be keyed to the text by page number, usually followed by the word or phrase being annotated. Such notes, which are generally presented as endnotes, are usually applied by the publisher; unless instructed otherwise, authors should insert numbered notes in their manuscripts as described in 2.26. Ideally, the author will highlight the key phrases in the text, the copyeditor will double-check them (and make any needed adjustments in consultation with the author), and the typesetter will then remove or hide the note numbers and the highlighting and add the page references and key phrases to create the endnotes. (Because of the extra time involved in producing unnumbered notes, the publisher's approval may be needed in advance.) The phrases, which should be short and meaningful, can usually be chosen from the sentence that introduces the quotation or other content that contains the note number.

Author's manuscript (text and numbered footnote):

Speaking "as a citizen," McConnell suggested that the verdict resulted from "a probable objection of some of the jurors to the death penalty on circumstantial evidence. . . . You will probably find that Mr. Culver was not the only man upon the jury who was opposed to the hanging of the three principal defendants."[33]

[33] Quoted in *Chicago Daily News*, "Four Men Guilty," Dec. 16, 1889.

Published version (text and endnote keyed to page number in book):

Speaking "as a citizen," McConnell suggested that the verdict resulted from "a probable objection of some of the jurors to the death penalty on circumstantial

O sweete soule Phillis w'haue liu'd and lou'd for a great while,
(If that a man may keepe any mortal ioy for a great while)
Like louing Turtles and Turtledoues for a great while:
One loue, one liking, one sence, one soule for a great while,
Therfore one deaths wound, one graue, one funeral only
Should haue ioyned in one both loue and louer Amintas.
  O good God what a griefe is this that death to remember?
For such grace, gesture, face, feature, beautie, behauiour,
Neuer afore was seene, is neuer againe to be lookt for.
O frowning fortune, ô death and desteny dismal:
Thus be the poplar trees that spred their tops to the heauens,
Of their flouring leaues despoil'd in an houre, in a moment:
Thus be the sweete violets that gaue such grace to the garden,
Of their purpled roabe despoyld in an houre, in a moment.
  O how oft did I roare and crie with an horrible howling,
When for want of breath Phillis lay feintily gasping?
O how oft did I wish that Phœbus would fro my Phillis
Driue this feuer away: or send his sonne from Olympus,
Who, when lady Venus by a chaunce was prickt with a
    bramble,
Healed her hand with his oyles, and fine knacks kept for a
    purpose.
Or that I could perceiue Podalyrius order in healing,
Or that I could obtaine Medæas exquisite ointments,
And baths most precious, which old men freshly renewed.
Or that I were as wise, as was that craftie Prometheus,
Who made pictures liue with fire that he stole from Olympus.
Thus did I cal and crie, but no body came to Amintas,
Then did I raile and raue, but nought did I get by my railing, [$C_4^v$]
Whilst that I cald and cry'd, and rag'd, and rau'd as a mad
    man,

45 for] *omit* C E
49 Therfore] Thefore A
58 roabe] roabes B C D E
59 roare and crie] cry, and roare D
62 this] that D
64 his] *omit* E purpose.] purpose: C E; purpose? D
70 Amintas,] Amintas. C E; Amintas: D

FIGURE 13.5. Footnotes keyed to line numbers—a device best used with verse. (With prose, the notes cannot be numbered until the text has been typeset.) See 13.56.

evidence. . . . You will probably find that Mr. Culver was not the only man upon the jury who was opposed to the hanging of the three principal defendants."

188 **Speaking "as a citizen"**: Quoted in *Chicago Daily News*, "Four Men Guilty," Dec. 16, 1889.

The annotated word or phrase in the endnotes may be distinguished from the annotation typographically (e.g., with boldface) and separated from it by a colon or other punctuation. Quotation marks, if used at all, should be reserved for words that are themselves direct quotations in the text. If there is more than one note on a page, the page numbers in the endnotes may be differentiated using the abbreviation *n* (e.g., 188n1, 188n2) but need not be (see also 14.56). See figure 13.6. In electronic formats, the annotated word or phrase may be linked directly to its appearance in the main text.

**13.58** **Source notes for previously published material.** In anthologies and other collections of previously published material, or in largely new publications that contain one or more previously published chapters, the source of each reprinted piece may be given in an unnumbered footnote on the first printed page of the chapter, preceding any numbered footnotes. If the other notes are endnotes, the source note should remain a footnote if possible (and some copyright holders may request such a placement). (In certain electronic formats that do not support footnotes as such, a source note may need to be linked from, or appear immediately after, the chapter title.) For material still in copyright, the note should include the original title, publisher or journal, publication date, page numbers or other locators, and—very important—mention of permission from the copyright owner to reprint. It may also include a copyright notice if requested. Some permissions grantors demand particular language in the source note. For exercising discretion versus acceding literally to the grantor's request, see 3.33, which deals with illustrations but applies equally to text. In many cases, wording can be adjusted for consistency as long as proper credit is given. The following examples show various acceptable forms. See also 4.106.

Reprinted with permission from Steven Shapin, *The Scientific Revolution* (University of Chicago Press, 1996), 15–64.

If an article or chapter is reprinted under a different title:

Originally published as "Manet in His Generation: The Face of Painting in the 1860s," *Critical Inquiry* 19, no. 1 (1992): 22–69, © 1992 by The University of Chicago. All rights reserved. Reprinted by permission.

If an article or chapter has been revised:

Originally published in a slightly different form in *The Metropolis in Modern Life*, ed. Robert Moore Fisher (Doubleday, 1955), 125–48. Reprinted by permission of the author and the publisher.

266 || NOTES

P. O'Sullivan is left to himself he will tell the whole truth about his contract with Dr. Cronin. It is not believed that O'Sullivan actually participated in the murder. He was merely an accomplice before the fact." *Chicago Tribune*, "Explaining That Ice Contract," Dec. 18, 1889.

186n6 ***Irish American papers generally praised the verdict:*** *Chicago Citizen*, "The Cronin Verdict," Dec. 21, 1889; *Chicago Herald*, "What Is Said in New York," Dec. 17, 1889.

187n1 ***The London* Times*, still smarting:*** *Times* (London), "The Cronin Murder Trial," Dec. 17, 1889.

187n2 ***Another London paper:*** Quoted in *New York Times*, "English View of It," "Dissatisfied with the Result," Dec. 17, 1889; *Chicago Herald*, "Press Opinion of the Verdict," Dec. 17, 1889.

187n3 ***The London* Graphic*:*** London *Graphic*, Dec. 23, 1889 quoted in *Chicago Tribune*, Jan. 10, 1890.

188 ***Speaking "as a citizen":*** Quoted in *Chicago Daily News*, "Four Men Guilty," Dec. 16, 1889. McConnell may have been pleased that no death sentences were passed, for he had been part of the clemency movement that followed the Haymarket trial. Later, however, he conceded that "the hanging of these men did do away with the hysteria which had pervaded the body of the people." He concluded, "And, aside from the injustice of such an occurrence, perhaps it did not matter who was hanged provided the public was satisfied." McConnell, "The Chicago Bomb Case," *Harper's Monthly* (1934), quoted in Carl Smith, *Urban Disorder and the Shape of Belief: The Great Chicago Fire, the Haymarket Bomb, and the Model Town of Pullman* (University of Chicago Press, 1995), 344n46.

190n1 ***Culver, a devout Methodist:*** *Chicago Daily Inter Ocean*, "Juryman Culver," Dec. 17, 1889; *Chicago Tribune*, "Juror Culver," Dec. 17, 1889; "Cronin Jurors Explain," Dec. 29, 1889.

190n2 ***The newspapers had little interest:*** *Chicago Daily Inter Ocean*, "Through Pat Grant's Eyes," Dec. 17, 1889; *New York Times*, "The Cronin Verdict," Dec. 18, 1889.

190n3 ***Kunze was released:*** Louis Epstean put up Kunze's $5,000 bail and paid him £100 a week for a season of ten weeks to appear at the Stanhope and Epstean Dime Museum. *Chicago Times*, "Motion for a New Trial," Dec. 17, 1889; *Los Angeles Herald*, "He Will Pose as a Dime Museum Freak," Jan. 19, 1890. In 1900 Kunze was arrested in Milwaukee and later returned to Joliet Prison—he had been convicted of swindling and had skipped town while on parole.

190n4 ***Coughlin, Burke, and O'Sullivan were handcuffed:*** *Chicago Citizen*, "The Cronin Prisoners," Jan. 18, 1890; *Chicago Tribune*, "They Start for Joliet Prison," Jan. 15, 1890; Bailie, *Cronin Case*, 425.

CHAPTER TEN

191n1 ***Looking back on the events:*** John Devoy, "The Story of Clan na Gael," *Gaelic American* (New York), Jan. 31, 1925.

191n2 ***The reputation of the Chicago police:*** Michael Whalen (Coughlin's partner) had been suspended from the force when Coughlin was arrested, but was later cleared of any involvement. However, in his trial testimony Whalen said that despite his innocence he was formally discharged from the force on August 31, 1889. Others dismissed included Detective Michael J. Crowe, Patrol Sergeant John Stift, and Patrolmen Michael Ahern, Daniel Cunningham, and Redmond McDonald. Cunningham, a long-serving detective, had given information to the defense. Ahern spent much of his time criticizing the prosecution while neglecting his patrol duty. *Chicago Times*, "Whalen Also Suspended," May 26, 1889; Testimony of Michael Whalen, *People of the State of Illinois v. Coughlin et al.*, Supreme Court of Illinois, Illinois State Archives, 7:2617–29; *Chicago*

FIGURE 13.6. Endnotes keyed to page numbers, with key phrases in bold and italics. Though unnumbered in the text, notes that share the same page have been numbered in the endnotes to facilitate reference to individual notes. See 13.57, 14.56.

If a work is in the public domain (such as government publications):

Reprinted from Ambler Thompson and Barry N. Taylor, *Guide for the Use of the International System of Units (SI)* (National Institute of Standards and Technology, 2008), 38–39.

13.59 **Biographical notes and acknowledgments.** In journals or multiauthor works, a brief biographical note on the author or authors may appear as an unnumbered note on the first page of each article or chapter. Alternatively, some publications put such notes at the end of the article or chapter (an approach that is sometimes also used for electronic formats that do not support the placement of unnumbered footnotes). Such identifying notes are unnecessary when the work includes a list of contributors with their affiliations. (See also 1.71, 1.75.)

William Germano is the author of several books, including *Getting It Published: A Guide for Scholars and Anyone Else Serious About Serious Books* and *From Dissertation to Book,* both also published by the University of Chicago Press.

Similarly, special acknowledgments may be given in an unnumbered note, sometimes appended to the biographical information.

I would like to thank Anita Chan, Jonathan Unger, Ben Hillman, and three reviewers for their valuable comments and suggestions on my manuscript.

Cathy J. Cohen is the David and Mary Winton Green Distinguished Service Professor at the University of Chicago. She would like to thank . . .

## *Remedies for Excessive Annotation*

13.60 **Avoiding overlong notes.** Lengthy, discursive notes—especially footnotes, which in printed formats cannot be used if they are too long (or too numerous)—should be reduced or integrated into the text (see 13.47). Notes presented as endnotes can generally accommodate lengthier commentary, but this should be limited in a judicious manner (see 13.48). Complicated tabular material, lists, and other entities not part of the text should be put in an appendix rather than in the notes (see 1.66). A parenthetical note in the text might read, for example, "For a list of institutions involved, see appendix A."

13.61 **Several citations in one note.** The number of note references in a sentence or a paragraph can sometimes be reduced by grouping several citations in a single note. The citations are separated by semicolons and must appear in the same order as the text material (whether works, quotations, or whatever) to which they pertain. Take care to avoid any ambiguity as to what is documenting what.

Text:

Only when we gather the work of several scholars—Walter Sutton's explications of some of Whitman's shorter poems; Paul Fussell Jr.'s careful study of structure in "Cradle"; Stanley K. Coffman Jr.'s close readings of "Crossing Brooklyn Ferry" and "Passage to India"; and the attempts of Thomas J. Rountree and John Lovell, dealing with "Song of Myself" and "Passage to India," respectively, to elucidate the strategy in "indirection"—do we begin to get a sense of both the extent and the specificity of Whitman's forms.[1]

Note:

1. Sutton, "The Analysis of Free Verse Form, Illustrated by a Reading of Whitman," *Journal of Aesthetics and Art Criticism* 18, no. 2 (December 1959): 241–54; Fussell, "Whitman's Curious Warble: Reminiscence and Reconciliation," in *The Presence of Walt Whitman*, ed. R. W. B. Lewis (Columbia University Press, 1962); Coffman, "'Crossing Brooklyn Ferry': A Note on the Catalogue Technique in Whitman's Poetry," *Modern Philology* 51, no. 4 (May 1954): 225–32; Coffman, "Form and Meaning in Whitman's 'Passage to India,'" *PMLA* 70, no. 3 (June 1955): 337–49; Rountree, "Whitman's Indirect Expression and Its Application to 'Song of Myself,'" *PMLA* 73, no. 5 (December 1958): 549–55; and Lovell, "Appreciating Whitman: 'Passage to India,'" *Modern Language Quarterly* 21, no. 2 (June 1960): 131–41.

In the example above, authors' given names are omitted in the note because they appear in the text. For inclusion of names in endnotes versus footnotes, see 13.51.

13.62 **Citing sources in the text rather than in the notes.** Another way to reduce the number of notes is to cite sources (usually in parentheses) in the text. This approach can work well for a string of consecutive citations that refer to the same source (with or without the use of *ibid.*; see 13.37). For discussion and examples, see 12.75–83.

13.63 **Abbreviations for frequently cited works.** If necessary, a frequently mentioned work may be cited either parenthetically in text or in subsequent notes by means of an abbreviation, with the full citation provided in a note at first mention. (This practice is more helpful with footnotes than with endnotes.) See also 12.78, 13.32–39, 13.64.

1. François Furet, *The Passing of an Illusion: The Idea of Communism in the Twentieth Century*, trans. Deborah Furet (University of Chicago Press, 1999), 368 (hereafter cited in text as *PI*).

(Subsequent text references) "In this sense, the Second World War completed what the First had begun—the domination of the great political religions over European public opinion," writes Furet (*PI*, 360). But he goes on to argue . . .

An abbreviated title differs from a short title (see 13.36) in that words may be abbreviated and the word order changed. In the following example, the author's name need not be repeated unless it is relevant to the citation.

2. Nathaniel B. Shurtleff, ed., *Records of the Governor and Company of the Massachusetts Bay in New England (1628–86)*, 5 vols. (Boston, 1853–54), 1:126 (hereafter cited as *Mass. Records*).
3. *Mass. Records*, 2:330.

13.64 **List of abbreviations.** Where many abbreviations of titles, manuscript collections, personal names, or other entities are used in a work—say, ten or more—they are best listed alphabetically in a separate section. In a book, the list may appear in the front matter (if footnotes are used) or in the end matter preceding the endnotes (if these are used). It is usually headed "Abbreviations" and should be included in the table of contents (see 1.4, 1.49). Where only a few abbreviations are used, these are occasionally listed as the first section of the endnotes (see fig. 13.7) or at the head of the bibliography. Titles that are italicized in the notes or bibliography should be italicized in their abbreviated form in the list of abbreviations and elsewhere.

## BIBLIOGRAPHIES

### *Overview*

13.65 **Relationship of bibliographies to notes.** Although not all annotated works require a bibliography, since full details can be given in the notes, an alphabetical bibliography serves a number of purposes. Specifically, a full bibliography that includes all the sources cited in the text, in addi-

## Notes

In citing works in the notes, short titles have generally been used. Works frequently cited have been identified by the following abbreviations:

| | |
|---|---|
| Ac. Sc. | Archives de l'Académie des sciences. |
| *A.P.* | *Archives parlementaires de 1787 à 1860, première série (1787 à 1799)*. Edited by M. J. Mavidal and M. E. Laurent. 2nd ed. 82 vols. Paris, 1879–1913. |
| Best. | Theodore Besterman, ed. *Voltaire's Correspondence.* 107 vols. Geneva, 1953–65. |
| B. Inst. | Bibliothèque de l'Institut de France. |
| B.N., nouv. acqu. | Bibliothèque nationale. Fonds français, nouvelles acquisitions. |
| *Corresp. inéd.* | Charles Henry, ed. *Correspondance inédite de Condorcet et de Turgot (1770–1779)*. Paris, 1883. |
| *HMAS* | *Histoire de l'Académie royale des sciences. Avec les mémoires de mathématique et de physique . . . tirés des registres de cette académie (1699–1790)*. 92 vols. Paris, 1702–97. Each volume comprises two separately paginated parts, referred to as *Hist.* and *Mém.*, respectively. |
| *Inéd. Lespinasse* | Charles Henry, ed. *Lettres inédites de Mlle de Lespinasse.* Paris, 1887. |
| *O.C.* | A. Condorcet-O'Connor and F. Arago, eds. *Oeuvres de Condorcet.* 12 vols. Paris, 1847–49. |

Preface

1. Peter Gay, *The Enlightenment: An Interpretation,* 2 vols. (New York, 1966–69), 2:319. I have suggested some criticisms of Gay's treatment of this theme in a review of the second volume of his work, *American Historical Review* 85 (1970): 1410–14.

2. Georges Gusdorf, *Introduction aux sciences humaines: Essai critique sur leurs origines et leur développement* (Strasbourg, 1960), 105–331.

FIGURE 13.7. A short list of abbreviations preceding endnotes. See 13.64.

tion to providing an overview of the sources and therefore an indication of the scope of an author's research, can serve as a convenient key to shortened forms of the notes (see 13.18, 13.32).

13.66 **Format and placement of bibliography.** A bibliography arranged in a single alphabetical list is the most common and usually the most reader-friendly form for a work with or without notes to the text. All sources to be included—books, articles, dissertations, and so on—are alphabetically arranged in a single list by the last names of the authors (or, if no author or editor is given, by the title or, failing that, by a descriptive phrase). A bibliography is normally placed at the end of the work, preceding the index. In a multiauthor book or a textbook (or in a book with chapters that might be sold individually), each chapter may be followed by a brief bibliography. For an illustration, see figure 13.8.

# Bibliography

Adams, Jake. "Historic *Stuber acropora* Photograph Documents 25 Years of Stony Coral Reefing." Reef Builders, News, January 5, 2011. https://reefuilders.com/2011/01/05/historic-stuber-acropora-photograph-documents-25-years-stony-coral-reefing/.

Adey, Walter H. "The Microcosm: A New Tool for Reef Research." *Coral Reefs* 1, no. 3 (1983): 193–201.

Adey, Walter H., and Karen Loveland. *Dynamic Aquaria: Building Living Ecosystems*. Academic Press, 1998.

Aeby, Greta S., Blake Ushijima, Justin E. Campbell, et al. "Pathogenesis of a Tissue Loss Disease Affecting Multiple Species of Corals Along the Florida Reef Tract." *Frontiers in Marine Science* 6 (2019): 678.

Allen, David. "23 Tastes and Crazes." In *Cultures of Natural History*, edited by N. Jardine, J. A. Secord, and E. C. Spary, 394–407. Cambridge University Press, 1996.

Allen, John, and Mark Nelson. "Overview and Design Biospherics and Biosphere 2, Mission One (1991–1993)." *Ecological Engineering* 13, nos. 1–4 (1999): 15–29.

Allmon, Warren D. "The Evolution of Accuracy in Natural History Illustration: Reversal of Printed Illustrations of Snails and Crabs in Pre-Linnaean Works Suggests Indifference to Morphological Detail." *Archives of Natural History* 34, no. 1 (2007): 174–91.

Anderson, Katharine. "Coral Jewelry." *Victorian Review* 34, no. 1 (2008): 47–52.

Andon, Alex. "Jellyfish Tank by Jellyfish Art." Kickstarter.com. https://www.kickstarter.com/projects/jellyfishart/jellyfish%ADaquarium/description (accessed May 17, 2017; no longer posted).

Armstrong, Isobel. *Victorian Glassworlds: Glass Culture and the Imagination 1830–1880*. Oxford University Press, 2008.

Baensch, Frank, and Clyde S. Tamaru. "Spawning and Development of Larvae and Juveniles of the Rare Blue Mauritius Angelfish, *Centropyge debelius* (1988), in the Hatchery." *Journal of the World Aquaculture Society* 40, no. 4 (2009): 425–39.

FIGURE 13.8. The first page of a bibliography for a book. See 13.66.

For the arrangement of entries, see 13.69–71. For division into sections, see 13.67.

13.67 **Dividing a bibliography into sections.** A bibliography may occasionally be divided into sections—but only if doing so would make the reader's job significantly easier. It may be appropriate to subdivide a bibliography (1) when it includes manuscript sources, archival collections, or other materials that do not fit into a straight alphabetical list; (2) when readers need to see at a glance the distinction between different kinds of works—for example, in a study of one writer, between works by the writer and those about the writer; or (3) when the bibliography is intended primarily as a guide to further reading (as in this manual). When divisions are necessary, a headnote should appear at the beginning of the bibliography, and each section should be introduced by an explanatory subhead (see fig. 13.9). No source should be listed in more than one section. For alphabetizing, see 13.69–71.

13.68 **Kinds of bibliographies.** Though Chicago generally recommends a full bibliography for book-length works, any of the bibliography categories listed here may be suited to a particular type of work. For author-date reference lists, see 13.111–14.

1. **Full bibliography.** A full bibliography includes all substantial works cited, whether in text or in notes, other than personal communications (see 14.111) and excluding works that are mentioned in the text but not relied on (see 13.5). Some particularly relevant works the author has consulted may also be listed, even if not mentioned in the text. The usual heading is Bibliography, though Works Cited or Literature Cited may be used if no additional works are included.
2. **Selected bibliography.** If, for whatever reason, the author does not wish to list all works cited, the title must so indicate: Selected Bibliography may be used (and is preferred over Select Bibliography) or, if the list is quite short, Suggested Readings or Further Readings. A headnote should explain the principles of selection. See figure 13.9.
3. **Annotated bibliography.** Generally more convenient for readers than a bibliographic essay (see next item) is an annotated bibliography. Annotations may simply follow the publication details (sometimes in brackets if only a few entries are annotated), or they may start a new line (and are often indented from the left margin). See figure 13.10.
4. **Bibliographic essay.** Less formal than an annotated bibliography is a bibliographic essay, in which the author treats the literature discursively. Because works treated in this way are not alphabetized, subject divisions may be made freely (see 13.67). Such an essay may be particularly suited to

## Selected Bibliography

This bibliography lists the chief writings and archival collections referenced in this book. It is not an exhaustive list of the sources consulted. The survey of government reports and archival collections is meant to introduce those who wish to pursue regional history to the range of repositories and government publications that preserve the history of greater New York. The selected bibliography of published scholarship is intended to serve as an introduction to the principal scholarship in the fields of urban and suburban history, the history of planning, and environmental history related to New York City and its coastal setting.

*Archival Collections*

Archives Center, National Museum of American History, Washington, DC
 Edward J. Orth Memorial Archives of the New York World's Fair
 Special Collections, World's Fairs Collection
 World's Expositions 1851–1965
Division of Home and Community Life, Smithsonian Museum of American History, Washington, DC

. . . . . . . . . . . . . . . . . . . . . . . . .

*Secondary Sources*

Archer, Jack H., Donald L. Connors, and Kenneth Laurence. *The Public Trust Doctrine and the Management of America's Coasts*. University of Massachusetts Press, 1994.
Aron, Cindy. *Working at Play: A History of Vacations in the United States*. Oxford University Press, 1999.
Ballon, Hilary, and Kenneth Jackson, eds. *Robert Moses and the Modern City: The Transformation of New York*. W. W. Norton, 2008.
Baxandall, Rosalyn, and Elizabeth Ewen. *Picture Windows: How the Suburbs Happened*. Basic Books, 2000.
Beckert, Sven. *The Monied Metropolis: New York City and the Consolidation of the American Bourgeoisie, 1850–1896*. Cambridge University Press, 2001.

FIGURE 13.9. The opening page of a bibliography divided into sections, with an author's note explaining the principle of selection. See 13.67, 13.68.

certain types of archival sources that do not easily lend themselves to an alphabetical list. It may be included in addition to a bibliography, in which case it should come first. If works discussed in the essay are listed in the bibliography, they may be given in shortened form (as in notes). If there is no bibliography, the essay must include full facts of publication, whether or not the titles also appear in the notes. For an illustration, see figure 13.11.

5. **List of works by one author.** A list of works by one author, usually titled Published Works [of Author's Name] or Writings [of Author's Name], is most often arranged chronologically. If several titles are listed for each year, the dates may appear as subheads.

14

# *Annotated Bibliography of Further Reading*

*The following is a partial list of the anthologies of poetry and the handbooks, articles, and books about poetry and prosody that I have found useful in writing, teaching, and thinking about poetry. After each entry I have added a brief description of its most appealing features. You will notice a preference for the work of poets about poetry. Poets who are articulate about the craft of verse are among the best expositors.*[1]

## I. Anthologies

Allen, Donald M., ed. *The New American Poetry.* Grove Press, 1960.

> Concentrates on the postwar period from 1945 to 1960 and presents the work of poets who identified themselves with antiformalist movements or waves, often associated with fugitive publications and little magazines (*Yugen, Neon, Kulchur, Big Table,* etc.): The most prominent groups were the Black Mountain school (Olson, Duncan) and the experimental city poets from New York (like Frank O'Hara, LeRoi Jones, and Gilbert Sorrentino) and San Francisco (the "Beats" Kerouac, Corso, Ginsberg). John Ashbery, James Schuyler, Denise Levertov, and Gary Snyder are also represented. An anthology that awakened many readers and would-be writers to another sort of pos-

1. W. H. Auden is exemplary, even in his eccentricity. (See my discussion of some of the many volumes edited by him.) Another poet, F. T. Prince, has looked closely at Milton's prosody in a way that sheds light on prosody in general; see *The Italian Element in Milton's Verse* (1954). Poets John Frederick Nims and J. V. Cunningham are also acute when they write about verse; and I have already mentioned Charles O. Hartman and Timothy Steele in connection with meter and rhythm (see chapter 8 on accentual-syllabic meter).

**483**

FIGURE 13.10. Part of the first section of an annotated bibliography. See 13.68.

*Bibliographic Essay*

Mark Silk's groundbreaking 1984 article "Notes on the Judeo-Christian Tradition in America" and the corresponding chapter in his book *Spiritual Politics: Religion and America Since World War II* (1988) inaugurated the serious historical study of Judeo-Christian formulations and laid out a chronological frame that has proven remarkably durable in the face of the information revolution that has taken place since the 1990s: Judeo-Christian formulations of American democracy and national identity emerged in the late 1930s and then spread widely during World War II, persisting throughout the 1950s and 1960s, before increasingly coming under fire in the 1970s. According to Silk, the "Judeo-Christian tradition," constructed during World War II, became enshrined in national lore during the early Cold War years and played a decisive role in the civil rights movement of the 1950s and 1960s as well. Silk also called attention to the diversity and ambiguity of the meanings assigned to the Judeo-Christian discourse and the lingering opposition to the very use of the concept in certain quarters.

Subsequent scholars, often drawing on Silk's work, have emphasized that liberal campaigns for tolerance, targeting both fascism abroad and anti-Semitism at home, drove Judeo-Christianity's rise to prominence as a descriptor of American democracy and national identity. A classic example is Martin E. Marty's 1986 *Christian Century* article, "A Judeo-Christian Looks at the Judeo-Christian Tradition." There, Marty wrote that the term's orientation had changed markedly in the 1970s and 1980s, when Judeo-Christian discourse became a tool for the promotion of the Christian right's conservative agenda. The earlier uses, he assumed, had been thoroughly liberal and inclusive by contrast.

FIGURE 13.11. The first page of a bibliographic essay. See 13.68.

## *Arrangement of Entries*

13.69 **Alphabetical order for bibliography entries.** The rules for alphabetizing index entries (see 15.64–101) apply also to a bibliography, with the modifications described in this section. As it does for index entries, Chicago now recommends the word-by-word system but will accept the letter-by-letter system. Under the word-by-word system, an entry for "Fernán Gómez, Fernando" would precede an entry for "Fernández, Angelines"; under the letter-by-letter system, the opposite order would prevail. Note that word processors, though they can provide a significant head start, will generally not produce a perfectly sorted list for either system. In addition to correcting any software-based errors and variations, authors may need to make adjustments for any entries beginning with a numeral or a mark of punctuation, including a 3-em dash (see 13.72).

13.70 **Alphabetical order for titles by the same author.** In the notes and bibliography system (as opposed to author-date; see 13.112), titles by the same author are normally listed alphabetically. (When the entry includes a chapter or article title before its associated book or periodical title, the first title determines alphabetical order.) An initial *the*, *a*, or *an* is ignored in the alphabetizing (as in the first Squire entry below). Note that *all* works by the same person (or by the same persons in the same order)—whether that person is editor, author, translator, or compiler—appear together, regardless of the added abbreviation. For the use of the 3-em dash for repeated names, see 13.72–73.

Judt, Tony. *A Grand Illusion? An Essay on Europe*. Hill and Wang, 1996.

Judt, Tony. *Reappraisals: Reflections on the Forgotten Twentieth Century*. Penguin Press, 2008.

Judt, Tony, ed. *Resistance and Revolution in Mediterranean Europe, 1939–1948*. Routledge, 1989.

Marty, Martin E., and R. Scott Appleby, eds. *Fundamentalisms Comprehended*. University of Chicago Press, 1995.

Marty, Martin E., and R. Scott Appleby. *The Glory and the Power: The Fundamentalist Challenge to the Modern World*. Beacon Press, 1992.

Monmonier, Mark. *Coast Lines: How Mapmakers Frame the World and Chart Environmental Change*. University of Chicago Press, 2008.

Monmonier, Mark. *How to Lie with Maps*. 3rd ed. University of Chicago Press, 2018.

Mulvany, Nancy C., ed. *Indexing, Providing Access to Information—Looking Back, Looking Ahead: Proceedings of the 25th Annual Meeting of the American Society of Indexers*. American Society of Indexers, 1993.

Mulvany, Nancy C. *Indexing Books*. 2nd ed. University of Chicago Press, 2005.

Mulvany, Nancy C. "Software Tools for Indexing: What We Need." *Indexer* 17 (October 1990): 108–13.
Squire, Larry R. "The Hippocampus and the Neuropsychology of Memory." In *Neurobiology of the Hippocampus*, edited by W. Seifert. Oxford University Press, 1983.
Squire, Larry R. *Memory and Brain*. Oxford University Press, 1987.

Note that a bibliography of works by a single author (Writings of Author Name) is usually arranged chronologically (with alphabetical order imposed for two or more titles published in any one year). See also 13.72.

13.71 **Arrangement of bibliography entries with more than one author.** A single-author entry precedes a multiauthor entry beginning with the same name. Only the name of the first author is inverted.

Kogan, Herman. *The First Century: The Chicago Bar Association, 1874–1974*. Rand McNally, 1974.
Kogan, Herman, and Lloyd Wendt. *Chicago: A Pictorial History*. Dutton, 1958.

Successive entries by two or more authors in which only the first author's name is the same are alphabetized according to the coauthors' last names (regardless of the number of coauthors).

Brooks, Daniel R., and Deborah A. McLennan. *The Nature of Diversity: An Evolutionary Voyage of Discovery*. University of Chicago Press, 2002.
Brooks, Daniel R., and E. O. Wiley. *Evolution as Entropy*. 2nd ed. University of Chicago Press, 1988.

Successive entries by two or more authors with the same last name are ordered by the first-listed authors' first names (such that a work by "Smith, Jane, and Ann Smith" would follow one by "Smith, Ann, and Jane Smith").

## *The 3-Em Dash for Repeated Names in a Bibliography*

13.72 **The 3-em dash—reasons to avoid.** Chicago no longer recommends using the 3-em dash to stand in for the same author(s) in consecutive bibliography entries, preferring instead a repetition of authors' names as shown in the previous section (13.69–71). Although the 3-em dash can show readers at a glance which successive works are by the same author(s), the practice effectively hides authors' names and can obscure entries from bibliographic databases and from readers using electronic formats, especially those who rely on assistive technology. See also 6.100.

13.73 **Using the 3-em dash for repeated names in a bibliography.** Though this manual now recommends repeating authors' names rather than using 3-em dashes (see 13.72), the following guidelines and examples may be followed by publishers and others who do use them. The 3-em dash stands in for the same two or more authors (including editors, translators, etc.) as in the previous entry, provided they are credited in the work in the same order and no author appears for one source but not for the other. Alphabetization is by title of work; abbreviations such as *ed.* and *trans.*, which must always be included, do not influence the order of entries (and note that each of the works listed below that do *not* include such an abbreviation are authored rather than edited works). Compare the following list to the entries in 13.70.

Judt, Tony. *A Grand Illusion? An Essay on Europe*. Hill and Wang, 1996.

———. *Reappraisals: Reflections on the Forgotten Twentieth Century*. Penguin Press, 2008.

———, ed. *Resistance and Revolution in Mediterranean Europe, 1939–1948*. Routledge, 1989.

Marty, Martin E., and R. Scott Appleby, eds. *Fundamentalisms Comprehended*. University of Chicago Press, 1995.

———. *The Glory and the Power: The Fundamentalist Challenge to the Modern World*. Beacon Press, 1992.

Monmonier, Mark. *Coast Lines: How Mapmakers Frame the World and Chart Environmental Change*. University of Chicago Press, 2008.

———. *How to Lie with Maps*. 3rd ed. University of Chicago Press, 2018.

Mulvany, Nancy C., ed. *Indexing, Providing Access to Information—Looking Back, Looking Ahead: Proceedings of the 25th Annual Meeting of the American Society of Indexers*. American Society of Indexers, 1993.

———. *Indexing Books*. 2nd ed. University of Chicago Press, 2005.

———. "Software Tools for Indexing: What We Need." *Indexer* 17 (October 1990): 108–13.

Squire, Larry R. "The Hippocampus and the Neuropsychology of Memory." In *Neurobiology of the Hippocampus*, edited by W. Seifert. Oxford University Press, 1983.

———. *Memory and Brain*. Oxford University Press, 1987.

A 3-em dash cannot be used for some authors but not others.

Brooks, Daniel R., and Deborah A. McLennan. *The Nature of Diversity: An Evolutionary Voyage of Discovery*. University of Chicago Press, 2002.

Brooks, Daniel R., and E. O. Wiley. *Evolution as Entropy*. 2nd ed. University of Chicago Press, 1988.

*not*

Brooks, Daniel R., and Deborah A. McLennan. *The Nature of Diversity: An Evolutionary Voyage of Discovery*. University of Chicago Press, 2002.

———, and E. O. Wiley. *Evolution as Entropy*. 2nd ed. University of Chicago Press, 1988.

If the authors are identical but listed in a different order, they must be repeated.

Monmonier, Mark, and George A. Schnell. *Map Appreciation*. Prentice Hall, 1988.

Schnell, George A., and Mark Monmonier. *The Study of Population: Elements, Patterns, Processes*. Charles E. Merrill, 1983.

*not*

Monmonier, Mark, and George A. Schnell. *Map Appreciation* . . .

———. *The Study of Population* . . .

Institutional or corporate authors are handled in the same way as personal authors.

Modern Language Association. *MLA Handbook*. 9th ed. Modern Language Association of America, 2021.

———. *MLA Style Manual and Guide to Scholarly Publishing*. 3rd ed. Modern Language Association of America, 2008.

## AUTHOR'S NAME

13.74 **Author's name — overview and related discussions.** This section, on the correct form for the name of the author in Chicago-style source citations, applies to most of the source types covered in chapter 14. (The examples in this section mainly show books and journal articles.) For personal names in index entries, which are inverted in the same manner as in bibliographies and reference lists, see 15.79–95.

13.75 **Form of author's name.** Authors' names are normally given as they appear with the source itself—that is, on the title page of a book or other stand-alone work or at the head of a journal article or the like. Certain adjustments, however, may be made to assist correct identification. First names may be given in full in place of initials (but see 13.76). If an author's given name appears in one cited work and initials in another (e.g., "Mary L. Jones" versus "M. L. Jones"), the same form, preferably the fuller one, should be used in references to that author for both works. To help differentiate similar names, middle initials may be given where known. Degrees and affiliations following names on a title page are omitted. Names that follow Eastern order (family name first) rather than Western order (family name last) should not be inverted in a bibliography or reference list; when in doubt about a particular author's name, check with the author or the author's listing at a publisher's website, among other sources. See also the paragraphs in chapter 15 on names in Chinese (15.85), Hungarian (15.86), Japanese (15.89), Korean (15.90), and other languages that do not follow Western order for personal names.

13.76 **Authors preferring initials.** Full names should not be supplied for authors who always use initials—for example, W. E. B. Du Bois, T. S. Eliot, M. F. K. Fisher, O. Henry (pseud.), P. D. James, C. S. Lewis, J. D. Salinger, H. G. Wells. Note that space is added between initials. (Exceptions may be made for special cases like H.D.—the pen name for Hilda Doolittle.) In some instances, a cross-reference may be appropriate (see 13.83). See also 10.14. Very rarely, a portion of an author's given name omitted in the source is supplied in brackets in a bibliography entry. This practice should be limited to authors who may be known by both forms: for example, R. S. Crane may be listed as R[onald] S. Crane.

13.77 **One author.** In a note, the author's name is given in the normal order. In a bibliography, where names are arranged alphabetically, it is usually inverted (last name first; but see 13.75). See also 13.21.

1. David Shields, *The Very Last Interview* (New York Review Books, 2022), 49.
2. Wendy Hui Kyong Chun, "On Hypo-Real Models or Global Climate Change: A Challenge for the Humanities," *Critical Inquiry* 41, no. 3 (2015): 677.
3. Laine Nooney, *The Apple II Age: How the Computer Became Personal* (University of Chicago Press, 2023), 201.
4. Shields, *Very Last Interview*, 100–101.
5. Chun, "Hypo-Real Models," 681.
6. Nooney, *The Apple II Age*, 210–11.

Chun, Wendy Hui Kyong. "On Hypo-Real Models or Global Climate Change: A Challenge for the Humanities." *Critical Inquiry* 41, no. 3 (2015): 675–703.
Nooney, Laine. *The Apple II Age: How the Computer Became Personal*. University of Chicago Press, 2023.
Shields, David. *The Very Last Interview*. New York Review Books, 2022.

13.78 **Two or more authors (or editors).** Two authors (or editors) of the same work are listed in the order in which they appear with the source. In a bibliography, only the first author's name is inverted, and a comma must appear both before and after the first author's given name or initials. Use the conjunction *and* (not an ampersand).

1. Ichiro Kishimi and Fumitake Koga, *The Courage to Be Disliked: The Japanese Phenomenon That Shows You How to Change Your Life and Achieve Real Happiness* (Atria Books, 2018), 257.

2. Kishimi and Koga, *Courage to Be Disliked*, 259.

Kishimi, Ichiro, and Fumitake Koga. *The Courage to Be Disliked: The Japanese Phenomenon That Shows You How to Change Your Life and Achieve Real Happiness.* Atria Books, 2018.

For works by or edited by three to six persons (in previous editions it was two to ten), all names are usually given in the bibliography. Word order and punctuation are the same as for two authors. In a note, only the name of the first author is included, followed by *et al.* with no intervening comma.

3. Beatriz Williams et al., *All the Ways We Said Goodbye: A Novel of the Ritz Paris* (William Morrow, 2021), 301–2.

4. Williams et al., *All the Ways*, 392.

Williams, Beatriz, Lauren Willig, and Karen White. *All the Ways We Said Goodbye: A Novel of the Ritz Paris*. William Morrow, 2021.

For works with more than six authors—more common in the natural sciences—Chicago recommends listing the first three in the bibliography, followed by *et al.* (in the notes, only the first would be listed). This departure from the advice in previous editions of this manual favors brevity while recognizing that an author whose name is hidden behind *et al.* in a source citation still receives cited-by credit in bibliographic databases thanks to the cited source's author metadata (see also 1.84; 1.101). In a work with no bibliography, list up to six authors in the first, full citation in a note—as in a bibliography entry.

13.79 **Two or more authors (or editors) with same family name.** When two or more authors (or editors) share the same family name (and are credited as such in the source), the name is repeated (even if the family name is not repeated in the source itself).

1. Lee Child and Andrew Child, *The Sentinel* (Delacorte Press, 2020), 128.
2. Child and Child, *The Sentinel*, 129–30.

13.80 **Author's name in title.** When the name of the author appears in the title or subtitle of a cited work (such as an autobiography), the note citation may begin with the title (i.e., assuming the authorship is clear either from the title or in the text). The bibliography entry, however, should begin with the author's name, even though it is repeated in the title. See also 14.5.

1. *The Critical Writings of Oscar Wilde: An Annotated Selection*, ed. Nicholas Frankel (Harvard University Press, 2022), 200–201.
2. *Critical Writings of Oscar Wilde*, 215.

Wilde, Oscar. *The Critical Writings of Oscar Wilde: An Annotated Selection*. Edited by Nicholas Frankel. Harvard University Press, 2022.

13.81 **No listed author (anonymous works).** If the author or editor is unknown, the note or bibliography entry should normally begin with the title. An initial article is ignored in alphabetizing. (For pseudonyms, see 13.82.)

1. *A True and Sincere Declaration of the Purpose and Ends of the Plantation Begun in Virginia, of the Degrees Which It Hath Received, and Means by Which It Hath Been Advanced* (London, 1610).
2. *Stanze in lode della donna brutta* (Florence, 1547).

*Stanze in lode della donna brutta*. Florence, 1547.
*A True and Sincere Declaration of the Purpose and Ends of the Plantation Begun in Virginia, of the Degrees Which It Hath Received, and Means by Which It Hath Been Advanced*. London, 1610.

Although the use of *Anonymous* is generally to be avoided for works with no attribution, it may stand in place of the author's name in a bibliography in which several anonymous works need to be grouped. Either *Anonymous* or *Anon.* may be used; when repeated, these do not necessarily imply the same anonymous author. (For 3-em dashes, see 13.72–73.)

Anonymous. *Stanze in lode della donna brutta*. Florence, 1547.
Anonymous. *A True and Sincere Declaration . . .*

If, on the other hand, a work is explicitly attributed to "Anonymous" (e.g., on the title page or at the head of the work), it should be cited accordingly.

Anonymous. "Down with the Robots." *The Stranger* (Seattle, WA), May 31, 2022.

If the authorship is known or guessed at but was omitted on the title page, the name is included in brackets (with a question mark for cases of uncertainty). (Note that in the Hawkes example below, both New York and Tea Party are hyphenated in the original source. For the city of publication, however, the modern spelling has been used. See also 14.30–31.)

1. [Samuel Horsley], *On the Prosodies of the Greek and Latin Languages* (London, 1796).

2. [James Hawkes?], *A Retrospect of the Boston Tea-Party, with a Memoir of George R. T. Hewes*, by a Citizen of New-York (New York, 1834).

[Hawkes, James?]. *A Retrospect of the Boston Tea-Party, with a Memoir of George R. T. Hewes*. By a Citizen of New-York. New York, 1834.

[Horsley, Samuel]. *On the Prosodies of the Greek and Latin Languages*. London, 1796.

13.82 **Pseudonyms.** If a work is attributed to an invented or descriptive name, and the author's real name is not known, *pseud.* (roman, in brackets) may follow the name, especially if it might not be immediately clear to readers that the name is false (as in the first two examples below). (An initial *The* or *A* or *An* may be omitted. In a text citation, or in a shortened form in a note, *pseud.* is usually omitted.)

AK Muckraker [pseud.]. "Palin Is Back at Work." *Mudflats: Tiptoeing Through the Muck of Alaskan Politics*, December 5, 2008. https://mudflats.wordpress.com/2008/12/05/palin-is-back-at-work/.

Centinel [pseud.]. Letters. In *The Complete Anti-Federalist*, edited by Herbert J. Storing. University of Chicago Press, 1981.

Cotton Manufacturer. *An Inquiry into the Causes of the Present Long-Continued Depression in the Cotton Trade, with Suggestions for Its Improvement*. Bury, UK, 1869.

A widely used pseudonym is generally treated as if it were the author's real name.

Eliot, George. *Middlemarch*. Norton Critical Editions. Norton, 1977.

Twain, Mark. *The Prince and the Pauper: A Tale for Young People of All Ages*. Boston, 1882.

The real name, if relevant, may follow the pseudonym in brackets. See also 13.83.

hooks, bell [Gloria Jean Watkins]. *Writing Beyond Race: Living Theory and Practice*. Routledge, 2013.

Jay-Z [Shawn Carter]. *Decoded*. Spiegel & Grau, 2010.

Stendhal [Marie-Henri Beyle]. *The Charterhouse of Parma*. Translated by C. K. Scott Moncrieff. Boni and Liveright, 1925.

If the author's real name is better known than the pseudonym, the real name should be used. If needed, the pseudonym may be included in brackets, followed by *pseud.*

Brontë, Charlotte. *Jane Eyre*. London, 1847.

*or*

Brontë, Charlotte [Currer Bell, pseud.]. *Jane Eyre*. London, 1847.

For examples of screen names, see 14.105 and 14.106.

13.83 **Cross-references for pseudonyms.** In some cases, a cross-reference from a real name to a pseudonym, or vice versa, may be desired. Italicize words like *See*.

Carter, Shawn. *See* Jay-Z.

If a bibliography includes two or more works published by the same author but under different pseudonyms, all may be listed under the real name followed by the appropriate pseudonym in brackets, with cross-references under the pseudonyms (see also 13.72–73). Alternatively, they may be listed under the pseudonyms, with a cross-reference at the real name to each pseudonym.

Ashe, Gordon. *See* Creasey, John.

Creasey, John [Gordon Ashe, pseud.]. *A Blast of Trumpets*. Holt, Rinehart and Winston, 1975.

Creasey, John [Anthony Morton, pseud.]. *Hide the Baron*. Walker, 1978.

Creasey, John [Jeremy York, pseud.]. *Death to My Killer*. Macmillan, 1966.

Morton, Anthony. *See* Creasey, John.

York, Jeremy. *See* Creasey, John.

*or*

Ashe, Gordon [John Creasey]. *A Blast of Trumpets*. Holt, Rinehart and Winston, 1975.

Creasey, John. *See* Ashe, Gordon; Morton, Anthony; York, Jeremy.

13.84 **Alternative real names.** When a writer has published under different forms of their name, each work should be listed under the name that appears with the work—unless the difference is merely the use of initials versus full names (see 13.75). Cross-references are occasionally used from one form of the name to the other (and are listed after the other titles by that same author).

Doniger, Wendy. *The Bedtrick: Tales of Sex and Masquerade*. University of Chicago Press, 2000.
Doniger, Wendy. *See also* O'Flaherty, Wendy Doniger.

If a person discussed in the text publishes under a name not used in the text, a cross-reference may be useful.

Overstone, Lord. *See* Loyd, Samuel Jones.

In rare cases, whether to cite an alternative form of a name will require editorial discretion—for example, when citing a work by an author who no longer wants to be known by an earlier name (as in the case of a deadname). In such cases, it may be best to cite under the current form of the name only, regardless of how the work was originally published.

13.85 **Authors known by a given name.** Authors generally known only by their given names (i.e., and not by any surname) or by a mononym (other than a mononymous pseudonym) are listed and alphabetized by those names. Such titles as "King" or "Saint" or identifiers by place (e.g., "of Hippo" or "of England") are omitted, as are any alternative or fuller versions of the name, unless needed for reasons of disambiguation.

Augustine. *On Christian Doctrine*. Translated by D. W. Robertson Jr. Bobbs-Merrill, 1958.
Elizabeth I. *Collected Works*. Edited by Leah S. Marcus, Janel Mueller, and Mary Beth Rose. University of Chicago Press, 2000.
Virgil. *The Aeneid*. Translated by Robert Fitzgerald. Vintage Books, 1990.

For pseudonyms, see 13.82. See also 14.146.

13.86 **Organization as author.** If a publication issued by an organization, association, or corporation carries no personal author's name on the title page, the organization is listed as author in a bibliography, even if it is also given as publisher. (But cf. 13.81.)

International Organization for Standardization. *Information and Documentation—Rules for the Abbreviation of Title Words and Titles of Publications*. ISO 4:1997.

University of Chicago Press. *The Chicago Manual of Style*. 18th ed. University of Chicago Press, 2024.

## TITLE OF WORK

13.87 **Additional discussion of titles.** This section discusses the correct form for a title of a work in source citations and applies to most of the resource types covered in chapter 14. The examples in this chapter mainly show titles of books (in italics) and journal articles (in quotation marks). For a detailed discussion of titles of works in terms of capitalization, punctuation, wording, and relationship to surrounding text, see 8.157–204. Most of the advice there applies equally to source citations.

13.88 **Italics versus quotation marks for titles of cited works.** In source citations as in running text, italics are used for the titles of books and journals. Italics are also used for the titles of newspapers and blogs, movies and video games, paintings, and other types of works. Quotation marks are generally reserved for the titles of subsections of larger works—including chapter and article titles and the titles of poems in a collection. For some types of works—for example, a book series or a website—neither italics nor quotation marks are used. For titles within titles, see 13.96. The examples below cite an article in a journal (first example) and a book (second example). For books, see 14.2–62; for journals, see 14.67–86. Other types of sources are treated in chapter 14.

He, Dongjin, Yuwei Jiang, and Gerald J. Gorn. "Hiding in the Crowd: Secrecy Compels Consumer Conformity." *Journal of Consumer Research* 48, no. 6 (2022): 1032–49.

Cole, Teju. *Black Paper: Writing in a Dark Time*. University of Chicago Press, 2021.

13.89 **Capitalization of titles of cited works.** As in running text, English-language titles of works are capitalized in title case (also called headline style) in source citations. In title case, the first and last words of title and subtitle and all other major words are capitalized. For a more detailed definition and many more examples, see 8.160. For hyphenated compounds in title case, see 8.162.

*Quiet: The Power of Introverts in a World That Can't Stop Talking*
"Shooting an Elephant"

For titles in other languages, which are usually capitalized in sentence case, see 13.100.

13.90 **Some permissible changes to titles of cited works.** The spelling, hyphenation, and punctuation in the original title should be preserved, with the following exceptions: Words in full capitals on the original title page (except for initialisms or acronyms) should be set in upper- and lowercase; title case should be applied (but see 13.100); and, subject to editorial discretion, an ampersand may be changed to *and*. Numbers should remain spelled out or given as numerals according to the original (*Twelfth Century* or *12th Century*) unless there is a good reason to make them consistent (but *12$^{th}$* may be changed to *12th*). In some cases, punctuation separating the main title from a subtitle may be added or adjusted (see 13.91, 13.92, 13.93). For more on permissible changes to titles, including the addition of colons and commas, see 8.167. For older titles, see 13.99.

13.91 **Subtitles in cited works and the use of the colon.** A colon is used to separate the main title from the subtitle (even if no colon appears in the source itself). A space follows the colon. In italicized titles, the colon is also italicized. The subtitle, like the title, always begins with a capital letter. Note that the generic subtitle "A Novel" can usually be omitted, even if it appears on the title page. See also 8.166, 8.167.

Wirth, Eileen. *The Women Who Built Omaha: A Bold and Remarkable History*. University of Nebraska Press, 2022.

Although in European bibliographic style a period often separates title from subtitle, English-language publications need not follow that convention for non-English titles. See also 13.100.

*Fausts Himmelfahrt: Zur letzten Szene der Tragödie*

13.92 **Two subtitles in a cited work.** If, as occasionally happens, there are two subtitles in the original (an awkward contingency), a colon normally precedes the first and a semicolon the second. The second subtitle also begins with a capital.

Sereny, Gitta. *Cries Unheard: Why Children Kill; The Story of Mary Bell*. Metropolitan Books / Henry Holt, 1999.

Note that an em dash is usually considered part of a title or subtitle.

Silver, Nate. *The Signal and the Noise: Why So Many Predictions Fail—but Some Don't*. Penguin Books, 2015.

13.93 **Use of "or" with double titles.** Old-fashioned double titles (or titles and subtitles) connected by *or* have traditionally been separated by a semicolon (or sometimes a colon), with a comma following *or*, or more simply by a single comma preceding *or*. (Various other combinations have also been used.) When referring to such titles, prefer the punctuation on the title page or at the head of the original source. In the absence of such punctuation (e.g., when the title is distinguished from the subtitle by typography alone), or when the original source is not available to consult, use the simpler form shown in the first example below. The second example preserves the usage on the original title page of the American edition of Melville's classic novel (and assumes that the original American edition, or a later edition that preserves such punctuation, was in fact consulted). The third example (of a modern film) preserves the colon of the original title sequence but adds a comma to separate the main title from the secondary title (distinguished only graphically in the original). In all cases, the first word of the subtitle (following *or*) should be capitalized. See also 13.89, 13.90.

*The Tempest, or The Enchanted Island*
but
*Moby-Dick; or, The Whale*
*Dr. Strangelove, or: How I Learned to Stop Worrying and Love the Bomb*

13.94 **"And other stories" and such.** When the title of a book ends with *and other stories* or *and other poems* or the like, place the main title (of the story, poem, essay, or whatever) in quotation marks as described in 13.96. No comma follows the main title unless one appears on the title page of the source. (Previous editions of this manual recommended adding a comma before *and* but no quotation marks for the main title.)

1. Norman Maclean, *"A River Runs Through It" and Other Stories* (University of Chicago Press, 1976), 104.

2. Lane DeGregory, *"The Girl in the Window" and Other True Tales* (University of Chicago Press, 2023), 195.

13.95 **Dates in titles of cited works.** When not introduced by a preposition (e.g., "from 1920 to 1945"), dates in a title or subtitle are set off by commas, even if differentiated only by type style or a new line on the title page or at the head of the work. If a colon has been used in the original, however, it should be retained (but see 13.92). (Note that commas should *not* be added to non-English titles before dates; see 11.9.)

Overy, Richard. *Blood and Ruins: The Last Imperial War, 1931–1945*. Viking, 2022.

13.96 **Quoted titles and other terms within cited titles of works.** The title of a book or other work appearing within an italicized title is enclosed in quotation marks, even if it would normally appear in italics when not enclosed in another title.

1. Franck Boulègue, *The Return of "Twin Peaks": Squaring the Circle* (Intellect, 2021).

2. Roland McHugh, *Annotations to "Finnegans Wake"* (Johns Hopkins University Press, 1980).

Quotation marks within an italicized title do not, of course, always denote another title.

3. Henry Louis Gates Jr., ed., *"Race," Writing, and Difference* (University of Chicago Press, 1986).

A term normally quoted is enclosed in single quotation marks when it appears within a title in quotation marks (see 12.30; see also 6.11). Retain both double and single quotation marks, if any, in short citations. See also 8.167, 8.179.

4. Judith Lewis, "'Tis a Misfortune to Be a Great Ladie': Maternal Mortality in the British Aristocracy, 1558–1959," *Journal of British Studies* 37, no. 1 (1998): 28–29.

5. Lewis, "'Tis a Misfortune,'" 32.

Lewis, Judith. "'Tis a Misfortune to Be a Great Ladie': Maternal Mortality in the British Aristocracy, 1558–1959." *Journal of British Studies* 37, no. 1 (1998): 26–53.

13.97 **Italicized titles and other terms within cited titles of works.** When terms normally italicized in running text, such as species names or the names of ships, appear within an italicized title, they may remain in italics rather than being set in roman; this departure from previous editions is intended to make cited titles more legible (see also 8.175). Note that the second part of a binomial species name remains lowercase in a title (see 8.160).

Zimmer, Carl. *Microcosm: E. coli and the New Science of Life*. Vintage Books, 2009.

Italicized terms (including titles of works) within an article or a chapter title or any other title set in roman type remain in italics. For the capitalization of non-English titles (as in the example from *Modern Philology*), see 13.100; for species names, see 8.160.

1. Gang Zhou et al., "Induction of Maggot Antimicrobial Peptides and Treatment Effect in *Salmonella pullorum*–Infected Chickens," *Journal of Applied Poultry Research* 23, no. 3 (2014): 380.

2. Bécquer Seguín, "Carl Schmitt's *Don Quixote*," *Critical Inquiry* 48, no. 4 (2022): 777.

3. Jacob Sider Jost, "Bergotte's Other Patch of Yellow: A Fragment of Heraclitus in Proust's *La prisonnière*," *Modern Philology* 112, no. 4 (2015): 714.

4. Zhou et al., "*Salmonella pullorum*–Infected Chickens," 381.

5. Seguín, "Carl Schmitt's *Don Quixote*," 779.

6. Sider Jost, "Proust's *La prisonnière*," 717–18.

13.98 **Question marks or exclamation points in titles of cited works.** When a main title ends with a question mark or an exclamation point, no colon is added before any subtitle. When the question mark or exclamation point is followed by a closing quotation mark, however, retain a colon before the subtitle (see fifth and sixth examples below). Any punctuation other than a period required by the surrounding text, note, or bibliography entry should be retained (as in example notes 3, 7–8, and 11–12; see also 6.134). In a shortened title, a question mark or exclamation point that would not make sense out of context may be dropped (as in example note 10).

1. Yogi Berra, *What Time Is It? You Mean Now? Advice for Life from the Zennest Master of Them All*, with Dave Kaplan (Simon & Schuster, 2002), 63.

2. Alison Oram, *Her Husband Was a Woman! Women's Gender-Crossing in Modern British Popular Culture* (Routledge, 2007), 183.

3. Michael Tessler et al., "Diversity and Distribution of Stream Bryophytes: Does pH Matter?," *Freshwater Science* 33, no. 3 (2014): 778.

4. Hyunkuk Cho, "Does Particulate Matter Affect Cognitive Performance? Evidence from the City of Seoul," *American Journal of Health Economics* 8, no. 3 (2022): 303.

5. Edward Buscombe, *"Injuns!": Native Americans in the Movies* (Reaktion, 2006), 12.

6. Daniel Bertrand Monk, "'Welcome to Crisis!': Notes for a Pictorial History of the Pictorial Histories of the Arab Israeli War of June 1967," *Grey Room*, no. 7 (Spring 2002): 139.

7. Berra, *What Time Is It?*, 55–56.
8. Oram, *Her Husband Was a Woman!*, 184.
9. Tessler et al., "Diversity and Distribution," 780.
10. Cho, "Particulate Matter," 337.
11. Buscombe, *"Injuns!,"* 114–15.
12. Monk, "'Welcome to Crisis!,'" 140.

When a title ending with a question mark or an exclamation point would normally be followed by a period, the period is omitted (see also 6.133).

Hornby, Nick. *Vous descendez?* Translated by Nicolas Richard. Paris: Plon, 2005.
Tessler, Michael, Kam M. Truhn, Meghan Bliss-Moreau, and John D. Wehr. "Diversity and Distribution of Stream Bryophytes: Does pH Matter?" *Freshwater Science* 33, no. 3 (2014): 778–87.

13.99 **Older titles and very long titles.** Titles of works published in the eighteenth century or earlier may retain their original punctuation, spelling, and capitalization (except for whole words in capital letters, which should be given an initial capital only). Very long titles may be shortened in a bibliography or a note; indicate such omissions by the use of bracketed ellipses. The brackets signal that the ellipsis has been supplied by the author and is not part of the original title (see also 12.67). At the end of a title, the bracketed ellipsis should be followed by a period.

Escalante, Bernardino. *A Discourse of the Navigation which the Portugales doe make to the Realmes and Provinces of the East Partes of the Worlde* [. . .]. Translated by John Frampton. London, 1579.
Ray, John. *Observations Topographical, Moral, and Physiological; Made in a Journey Through part of the Low-Countries, Germany, Italy, and France: with A Catalogue of Plants not Native of England* [. . .] *Whereunto is added A brief Account of Francis Willughby, Esq., his Voyage through a great part of Spain*. London, 1673.

13.100 **Non-English titles of cited works.** Sentence case is strongly recommended for non-English titles (see 8.159). Capitalize the first word of a title or subtitle and any word that would be capitalized in the original language (e.g., *Wahrheit*, *Sowjetunion*, and *Inquisición* in examples 2 and 3 below and *Gâtine*, *Société*, and *l'Ouest* in example 7). Writers or editors unfamiliar with the usage of the language concerned, however, should not attempt to alter capitalization without expert help (in a pinch, a library-catalog entry may prove helpful). See also 14.30.

1. Danielle Maisonneuve et al., *Les relations publiques dans une société en mouvance* (Presses de l'Université du Québec, 1998).

2. Gabriele Krone-Schmalz, *In Wahrheit sind wir stärker: Frauenalltag in der Sowjetunion* (Fischer Taschenbuch Verlag, 1992).

3. Daniel Muñoz Sempere, *La Inquisición española como tema literario: Política, historia y ficción en la crisis del antiguo régimen* (Tamesis, 2008).

4. G. Martellotti et al., *La letteratura italiana: Storia e testi*, vol. 7 (Riccardo Ricciardi, 1955).

5. Ljiljana Piletić Stojanović, ed., *Gutfreund i češki kubizam* (Muzej savremene umetnosti, 1971).

6. Dinda L. Gorlée, "¡Eureka! La traducción como un descubrimiento pragmático," *Anuario filosófico* 29, no. 3 (1996): 1403.

7. Marcel Garaud, "Recherches sur les défrichements dans la Gâtine poitevine aux XI^e^ et XII^e^ siècles," *Bulletin de la Société des antiquaires de l'Ouest*, 4th ser., 9 (1967): 11–28.

Note that, with non-English journal titles (as with any title in a language other than English), an initial definite article (*Le*, *Der*, etc.) should be retained, since it may govern the inflection of the following word (see also 8.172). (An initial *Le* or the like, unlike *A*, *An*, or *The*, would be counted in alphabetization by title; see also 13.70.) Months and the equivalents of such abbreviations as *no.* or *pt.* are usually given in English (but see 14.4). For a full discussion of non-English titles of works, see 11.8–12.

13.101 **Translated titles of cited works.** If an English translation of a title is needed, it follows the original title and is enclosed in brackets, without italics or quotation marks. It is capitalized in sentence case regardless of the bibliographic style followed. (In running text, parentheses are used instead of brackets; see 11.11.)

1. Henryk Wereszycki, *Koniec sojuszu trzech cesarzy* [The end of the Three Emperors' League] (PWN, 1977); includes a summary in German.

2. W. Kern, "Waar verzamelde Pigafetta zijn Maleise woorden?" [Where did Pigafetta collect his Malaysian words?], *Tijdschrift voor Indische taal-, land- en volkenkunde* 78 (1938): 272.

Kern, W. "Waar verzamelde Pigafetta zijn Maleise woorden?" [Where did Pigafetta collect his Malaysian words?]. *Tijdschrift voor Indische taal-, land- en volkenkunde* 78 (1938): 271–73.

Pirumova, Natalia Mikhailovna. *Zemskoe liberal'noe dvizhenie: Sotsial'nye korni i evoliutsiia do nachala XX veka* [The zemstvo liberal movement: Its social roots and evolution to the beginning of the twentieth century]. Izdatel'stvo "Nauka," 1977.

If a title is given only in English translation, however, the original language must be specified.

3. Natalia Mikhailovna Pirumova, *The Zemstvo Liberal Movement: Its Social Roots and Evolution to the Beginning of the Twentieth Century* [in Russian] (Izdatel'stvo "Nauka," 1977).

Chu Ching and Long Zhi. "The Vicissitudes of the Giant Panda, *Ailuropoda melanoleuca* (David)." [In Chinese.] *Acta Zoologica Sinica* 29, no. 1 (1983): 93–104.

A published translation is normally treated as illustrated in 14.6 or 14.82. If, for some reason, both the original and the translation need to be cited, both may be listed. For books, either of the following forms may be used, depending on whether the original or the translation is of greater interest to readers:

Ogawa, Yoko. *The Memory Police*. Translated by Stephen Snyder. Vintage Books, 2020. Originally published as *Hisoyaka na kesshō* (Kodansha, 1994).

*or*

Ogawa, Yoko. *Hisoyaka na kesshō*. Kodansha, 1994. Translated by Stephen Snyder as *The Memory Police* (Vintage Books, 2020).

For other types of sources, adapt the relevant example as needed.

## AUTHOR-DATE: BASIC FORMAT

13.102 **The author-date system — overview.** Chicago's author-date system is a variation on the notes and bibliography system and is used by many in the sciences and social sciences (see also 13.2). Rather than using numbered notes, sources are cited in the text, usually in parentheses, by the author's last (family) name and the year of publication. Full details appear in a corresponding reference list—usually titled "References" or "Works Cited"—which differs from a standard bibliography in one way: The year of publication appears immediately after the author's name (see fig. 13.12). This arrangement makes it easy to follow a text citation to the corresponding full source in the reference list.

Text citations:

Like many other cultural fields, the video game industry is one that rewards novelty, especially when it is packaged in terms that are recognizable to con-

The Birth Lottery of History

turning almost on a dime, in violent crime, incarceration, policing, and, recently, widespread protests against police brutality. Adolescence and young adulthood are turbulent times when such social change matters greatly. In the past two decades, "deaths of despair" from suicide, drug overdose, and alcoholism have also risen dramatically (Case and Deaton 2020), and more recently the COVID-19 pandemic has upended many aspects of everyday life, such as the nature of work. Coming of age and beyond has been transformed for successive birth cohorts differentially experiencing these relatively short-term but nonetheless substantial historical changes, imparting enduring consequences over the life course that will in turn spur new transformations.

REFERENCES

Achenbach, Thomas M. 1997. *Manual of the Young Adult Self-Report and Young Adult Behavior Checklist.* University of Vermont, Department of Psychiatry.

Alexander, Michelle. 2012. *The New Jim Crow: Mass Incarceration in the Age of Colorblindness.* New Press.

Alwin, Duane F., Ronald L. Cohen, and Theodore M. Newcomb. 1991. *Political Attitudes over the Life Span: The Bennington Women After Fifty Years.* University of Wisconsin Press.

Anderson, Elijah. 1990. *Streetwise: Race, Class, and Change in an Urban Community.* University of Chicago Press.

Anderson, Elijah. 2000. *Code of the Street: Decency, Violence, and the Moral Life of the Inner City.* W. W. Norton.

Baumer, Eric, Kelsey Cundiff, and Liying Luo. 2021. "The Contemporary Transformation of American Youth: An Analysis of Change in the Prevalence of Delinquency, 1991–2015." *Criminology* 59:109–36. https://doi.org/10.1111/1745-9125.12264.

Baumer, Eric, María B. Vélez, and Richard Rosenfeld. 2018. "Bringing Crime Trends Back into Criminology: A Critical Assessment of the Literature and a Blueprint for Future Inquiry." *Annual Review of Criminology* 1:39–61.

Bersani, Bianca E., and Elaine Eggleston Doherty. 2018. "Desistance from Offending in the Twenty-First Century." *Annual Review of Criminology* 1:311–34.

Blumstein, Alfred, Jacqueline Cohen, Jeffrey Roth, and Christy Visher, eds. 1986. *Criminal Careers and Career Criminals.* National Academy Press.

Brame, Robert, Michael G. Turner, Raymond Paternoster, and Shawn Bushway. 2012. "Cumulative Prevalence of Arrest from Ages 8 to 23 in a National Sample." *Pediatrics* 129:21–27.

Case, Anne, and Angus Deaton. 2020. *Deaths of Despair and the Future of Capitalism.* Princeton University Press.

Chaskin, Robert J., and Mark L. Joseph. 2015. *Integrating the Inner City: The Promise and Perils of Mixed-Income Public Housing Transformations.* University of Chicago Press.

Chen, Feinian, Yang Yang, and Guangya Liu. 2010. "Social Change and Socioeconomic Disparities in Health over the Life Course in China: A Cohort Analysis." *American Sociological Review* 75:26–150.

Chetty, Raj, and Nathaniel Hendren. 2018. "The Impacts of Neighborhoods on Intergenerational Mobility I: Childhood Exposure Effects." *Quarterly Journal of Economics* 133:1107–62.

1173

FIGURE 13.12. Part of a reference list for a journal article in the social sciences. See 13.102.

sumers and critics (Lampel et al. 2000; Hutter 2011). . . . But the forefront of the industry finds continuous experimentation with the singular challenge of video gaming: how to create a convincing form of narrative storytelling that is nonetheless animated, perhaps uniquely so, by the actions of the users (Bissell 2011).

Reference list entries:

Bissell, Tom. 2011. *Extra Lives: Why Video Games Matter*. Vintage Books.
Hutter, Michael. 2011. "Infinite Surprises: On the Stabilization of Value in the Creative Industries." In *The Worth of Goods: Valuation and Pricing in the Economy*, edited by Jens Beckert and Patrick Aspers. Oxford University Press.
Lampel, Joseph, Theresa Lant, and Jamal Shamsie. 2000. "Balancing Act: Learning from Organizing Practices in Cultural Industries." *Organization Science* 11 (3): 263–69.

For more examples of text citations and reference list entries, see 13.105–10. For a detailed discussion of reference lists, see 13.111–14. For text citations, see 13.115–28.

13.103 **Abbreviations in author-date citations.** In a reference list (as in a bibliography), noun forms such as *editor*, *translator*, *volume*, and *edition* are abbreviated, but verb forms such as *edited by* and *translated by* are spelled out (see also 13.19). In a text citation, all such terms are omitted.

13.104 **Page numbers in author-date citations.** Parenthetical text citations (like numbered notes) may include references to specific page numbers (for examples, see 13.117). A reference list entry (like an entry in a bibliography) includes the beginning and ending page numbers for a journal article (see 13.110) but omits most other page numbers (including for a chapter in a book; see 13.109).

## AUTHOR-DATE: EXAMPLES AND VARIATIONS

13.105 **Author-date references — introduction to examples and variations.** The examples in this section provide an overview of the author-date system, featuring books and journal articles as models. Each example includes a reference list entry and a corresponding text citation. For the sake of consistency, text citations are presented in parentheses, though they do not always appear that way in practice (see 13.122). For many more examples organized by type of source, see chapter 14, starting with 14.1, which shows how to adapt notes and bibliography citations to the author-date system.

13.106 **Author-date — book with single author or editor.** To cite a book with a single author in the author-date system, invert the name in the reference list; in the text, include only the last name. Punctuate and capitalize as shown. To cite a specific passage, a page number or range is included in a text citation, separated from the year by a comma (a comma is also used between nonconsecutive page references). Page numbers are not included in a reference list (even if the entry is for a chapter; see 13.109). See also 9.62–66.

Yu, Charles. 2020. *Interior Chinatown*. Pantheon Books.

(Yu 2020, 95–96)
(Yu 2020, 101, 103)

A book with an editor in place of an author includes the abbreviation *ed.* (*editor*; for more than one editor, use *eds.*). Note that the text citation does not include *ed.*

Callard, Agnes, ed. 2020. *On Anger*. Boston Review.

(Callard 2020, 7)

13.107 **Author-date — book with multiple authors.** For a book with two authors, only the first-listed name is inverted in the reference list. Both last names are included in the text.

Sterling, Terry Greene, and Jude Joffe-Block. 2021. *Driving While Brown: Sheriff Joe Arpaio Versus the Latino Resistance*. University of California Press.

(Sterling and Joffe-Block 2021, 110)

For a book with more than two authors or editors, list up to six authors in the reference list; if there are more than six, list only the first three, followed by "et al." In the text, list only the first author, followed by "et al."

Aubrecht, Katie, Christine Kelly, and Carla Rice, eds. 2020. *The Aging–Disability Nexus*. UBC Press.

(Aubrecht et al. 2020, 44)

13.108 **Author-date — book with author plus editor or translator.** In the reference list, do not abbreviate *Edited by* or *Translated by*. See also 14.6.

García Márquez, Gabriel. 1988. *Love in the Time of Cholera*. Translated by Edith Grossman. Alfred A. Knopf.

(García Márquez 1988, 242–55)

13.109 **Author-date — chapter in an edited book.** In citations of a chapter or similar part of an edited book, include the chapter author; the chapter title, in quotation marks; and the editor. Precede the title of the book with *In*. But note that it is no longer necessary to record a page range for the chapter in the reference list entry (a departure from previous editions of this manual). See also 14.8–14.

Gould, Glenn. 1984. "Streisand as Schwarzkopf." In *The Glenn Gould Reader*, edited by Tim Page. Vintage Books.

(Gould 1984, 310)

13.110 **Author-date — journal article.** Citations of journal articles typically include the volume and issue number and date of publication. The volume number follows the italicized journal title in roman and with no intervening punctuation; the issue number follows in parentheses unless a month or season of publication is included (see 14.70). A specific page reference is included in the text; the page range for an article is included in the reference list, preceded by a colon. For the URL in the following example, which authors should record for articles consulted online, see 13.6 and 13.7.

Kwon, Hyeyoung. 2022. "Inclusion Work: Children of Immigrants Claiming Membership in Everyday Life." *American Journal of Sociology* 127 (6): 1818–59. https://doi.org/10.1086/720277.

(Kwon 2022, 1824)

## AUTHOR-DATE REFERENCE LISTS

13.111 **Function and placement of author-date reference lists.** In the author-date system, the reference list is the prime vehicle for documentation. The text citations (see 13.115–28) are merely pointers to the sources in the reference list. A reference list, like a bibliography (see 13.66), is normally titled "References" or "Works Cited" and placed at the end of a work, preceding the index, if there is one. In a multiauthor book or a textbook (or in a book with chapters that might be sold individually), each chapter is usually followed by its own reference list. Journal articles are always treated this way.

13.112 **Alphabetical arrangement of reference list entries.** Reference lists, like bibliographies, are arranged alphabetically, with one difference: Multiple sources by the same author are arranged chronologically (in ascending order from oldest to newest) rather than alphabetically by title (but see 13.114). Compare the following list to the entries in 13.70. (For use of the 3-em dash for repeated names, see 13.113.)

Judt, Tony, ed. 1989. *Resistance and Revolution in Mediterranean Europe, 1939–1948*. Routledge.

Judt, Tony. 1996. *A Grand Illusion? An Essay on Europe*. Hill and Wang.

Judt, Tony. 2008. *Reappraisals: Reflections on the Forgotten Twentieth Century*. Penguin Press.

Marty, Martin E., and R. Scott Appleby. 1992. *The Glory and the Power: The Fundamentalist Challenge to the Modern World*. Beacon Press.

Marty, Martin E., and R. Scott Appleby, eds. 1995. *Fundamentalisms Comprehended*. University of Chicago Press.

Monmonier, Mark. 2008. *Coast Lines: How Mapmakers Frame the World and Chart Environmental Change*. University of Chicago Press.

Monmonier, Mark. 2018. *How to Lie with Maps*. 3rd ed. University of Chicago Press.

Mulvany, Nancy C. 1990. "Software Tools for Indexing: What We Need." *Indexer* 17 (October): 108–13.

Mulvany, Nancy C., ed. 1993. *Indexing, Providing Access to Information—Looking Back, Looking Ahead: Proceedings of the 25th Annual Meeting of the American Society of Indexers*. American Society of Indexers.

Mulvany, Nancy C. 2005. *Indexing Books*. 2nd ed. University of Chicago Press.

Squire, Larry R. 1983. "The Hippocampus and the Neuropsychology of Memory." In *Neurobiology of the Hippocampus*, edited by W. Seifert. Oxford University Press.

Squire, Larry R. 1987. *Memory and Brain*. Oxford University Press.

Note that, as in a bibliography, a single-author entry in a reference list precedes a multiauthor entry beginning with the same name, and successive entries by two or more authors in which only the first author's name is the same are alphabetized according to the coauthors' last names (regardless of how many coauthors there are). See 13.71 for examples.

13.113 **The 3-em dash for repeated names in a reference list.** Chicago now recommends repeating the names in a reference list for successive works by the same author(s), as shown in 13.112. Authors or publishers who need to use the 3-em dash may apply it as shown for the notes and bibliography system in 13.73, but using chronological order rather than alphabetical order by title. Note that in the following examples, Judt is the editor of the first work but the author of the second and third (the 3-em dash cannot stand in for *ed.*).

Judt, Tony, ed. 1989. *Resistance and Revolution in Mediterranean Europe, 1939–1948*. Routledge.
———. 1996. *A Grand Illusion? An Essay on Europe*. Hill and Wang.
———. 2008. *Reappraisals: Reflections on the Forgotten Twentieth Century*. Penguin Press.

13.114 **Reference list entries with same author(s), same year.** Two or more works by the same author in the same year must be differentiated by the addition of *a*, *b*, and so forth (regardless of whether they were authored, edited, compiled, or translated) and are listed alphabetically by title (see also 13.70). Text citations consist of author and year plus letter.

Fogel, Robert William. 2004a. *The Escape from Hunger and Premature Death, 1700–2100: Europe, America, and the Third World*. Cambridge University Press.
Fogel, Robert William. 2004b. "Technophysio Evolution and the Measurement of Economic Growth." *Journal of Evolutionary Economics* 14, no. 2 (June): 217–21.

(Fogel 2004b, 218)
(Fogel 2004a, 45–46)

When works by the same two or more authors list their names in a different order, then *a*, *b*, and so forth cannot be used. For undated works cited with "n.d." or "forthcoming," use a hyphen (n.d.-a, n.d.-b; forthcoming-a, forthcoming-b); see also 14.44, 14.45. See also 13.112.

## AUTHOR-DATE TEXT CITATIONS

13.115 **Agreement of author-date text citations and reference list entries.** For each author-date citation in the text, there must be a corresponding entry in the reference list under the same name and date. It is the author's responsibility to ensure such agreement as well as the accuracy of the reference (see 2.37). Among other things, specific page references to a journal article, when given in a text citation, must fall within the range of pages given for the article in the reference list entry. It is then up to manuscript editors to cross-check text citations and reference lists and rectify or query any discrepancies or omissions (see 2.69).

13.116 **Author-date text citations — basic form.** An author-date citation in running text or at the end of a block quotation usually consists of the last (family) name of the author, followed by the year of publication of the work in question. In this context, *author* may refer not only to one or more authors or an institution but also to one or more editors, translators, or compilers. No punctuation appears between author and date. Abbreviations such as *ed.* or *trans.* are omitted. See also 13.117.

Text citations:

(Ma 2022)
(Braverman and Johnson 2020)

References:

Ma, Shaoling. 2022. "Big Earths of China: Remotely Sensing Xinjiang Along the Belt and Road." *Critical Inquiry* 49 (1): 77–101.
Braverman, Irus, and Elizabeth R. Johnson, eds. 2020. *Blue Legalities: The Life and Laws of the Sea*. Duke University Press.

To refer to two or more sources in the same text citation, separate the sources with semicolons (but see 13.124).

(Ma 2022; Braverman and Johnson 2020)

Where two or more works by different authors with the same last name are listed in a reference list, the text citation must include an initial (or two initials or a given name if necessary).

Text citations:

(A. Miller 2020)
(D. Miller 2022)

References:

Miller, Angela. 2020. . . .
Miller, Daniel. 2022. . . .

13.117 **Page numbers and other locators in author-date text citations.** When a specific page, section, equation, or other division of the work is cited, it follows the date, preceded by a comma. When a volume as a whole is referred to, without a page number, *vol.* is used. For volume plus page, only a colon is needed. The *n* in the Fischer and Siple example below indicates "note" (see 14.56). The last example shows one strategy for citing a specific location (e.g., a section heading) in a work that contains no page or section numbers or other numerical signposts—the case for some electronic formats (see 14.59).

(Piaget 1980, 74)
(LaFree 2010, 413, 417–18)
(Claussen 2015, para. 2.15) *or* (Claussen 2015, ¶ 2.15)
(Johnson 1979, sec. 24) *or* (Johnson 1979, § 24)
(Fowler and Hoyle 1965, eq. 87)
(Hsu 2017, chap. 4)
(García 1987, vol. 2)
(García 1987, 2:345)
(Barnes 1998, 2:354–55, 3:29)
(Fischer and Siple 1990, 212n3)
(Hellman 2017, under "The Battleground")

Some journals omit page numbers in citations of other journal articles except when citing a direct quotation or a paraphrase.

13.118 **Additional material in author-date text citations.** The parentheses that enclose a text citation may also include a comment, separated from the citation by a semicolon (see also 13.124).

(Mandolan 2024; *t*-tests are used here)

13.119 **Author-date citations in relation to surrounding text.** Except at the end of block quotations (see 13.120), author-date citations are usually placed just before a mark of punctuation though need not be if the sentence would otherwise not require it. See also 13.122.

Recent literature has examined long-run price drifts following initial public offerings (Ritter 1991; Loughran and Ritter 1995), stock splits (Ikenberry et al. 1996), seasoned equity offerings (Loughran and Ritter 1995), and equity repurchases (Ikenberry et al. 1995).

*but*

There is evidence, for example, that the negative outcomes associated with family structure instability are more pronounced for young children as compared with older children (Sigle-Rushton and McLanahan 2004) and for boys as compared with girls (Cooper et al. 2011).

Where the author's name appears in the text, it need not be repeated in the parenthetical citation. Note that the date should immediately follow the author's name, even if the name is used in the possessive. This usage serves the logic and economy of the author-date style. (For a reference to a person rather than the work, it may be appropriate to include the given name on first mention.)

> Fiorina et al. (2005) and Fischer and Hout (2006) reach more or less the same conclusions. In contrast, Abramowitz and Saunders (2005) suggest that the mass public is deeply divided between red states and blue states and between churchgoers and secular voters.

> Tufte's (2001) excellent book on chart design warns against a common error.

13.120 **Author-date text citations in relation to direct quotations.** Although a source citation normally follows a direct quotation, it may precede the quotation—especially if such a placement allows the date to appear with the author's name.

> As Edward Tufte points out, "A graphical element may carry data information and also perform a design function usually left to non-data-ink" (2001, 139).

*or*

> As Edward Tufte (2001, 139) points out, "A graphical element may carry data information and also perform a design function usually left to non-data-ink."

When the source of a block quotation is given in parentheses at the end of the quotation, the opening parenthesis appears *after* the final punctuation mark of the quoted material. No period either precedes or follows the closing parenthesis.

> If you happen to be fishing, and you get a strike, and whatever it is starts off with the preliminaries of a vigorous fight; and by and by, looking down over the side through the glassy water, you see a rosy golden gleam, the mere specter of a fish, shining below in the clear depths; and when you look again a sort of glory of golden light flashes and dazzles as it circles nearer beneath and around and under the boat; . . . and you land a slim and graceful and impossibly beautiful three-foot goldfish, whose fierce and vivid yellow is touched around the edges with a violent red—when all these things happen to you, fortunate but bewildered fisherman, then you may know you have been fishing in the Galapagos Islands and have taken a Golden Grouper. (Pinchot 1930, 123)

See also 12.81–83.

**13.121** **Consecutive author-date citations to the same source.** When the same page (or page range) in the same source is cited more than once in one paragraph, the parenthetical citation can be placed after the last reference or at the end of the paragraph (but preceding the final period). When referring to different pages in the same source, however, include a full parenthetical citation at the first reference; subsequent citations need only include page numbers.

> Complexion figures prominently in Morgan's descriptions. When Jasper compliments his mother's choice of car (a twelve-cylinder Mediterranean roadster with leather and wood-grained interior), "his cheeks blotch indignantly, painted by jealousy and rage" (Chaston 2000, 47). On the other hand, his mother's mask never changes, her "even-tanned good looks" (56), "burnished visage" (101), and "air-brushed confidence" (211) providing the foil to the drama in her midst.

**13.122** **Syntactic considerations with author-date text citations.** An author-date citation is a form of bibliographic shorthand that corresponds to a fully cited work; it does not refer to a person. Note how, in the examples in 13.119 and 13.120, the wording distinguishes between authors and works. A locution such as "in Smith 1999," though technically proper, is usually best avoided except as part of a parenthetical citation. To help readers identify the source citation, prefer "in Smith (1999)" or, for example, "in Smith's (1999) study." Note that square brackets should be used in parenthetical text references that require additional parentheses, as in the second example below (see 6.107).

> There are at least three works that satisfy the criteria outlined in Smith's (1999) study (see Rowen 2006; Bettelthorp 2004a; Choi 2008).

> These processes have, in turn, affected the way many Latin Americans are treated in the United States (see, e.g., Haviland [2003, 767] on how US courts disregard the existence of Indigenous languages and "reluctantly" make allowance only for Spanish in translation services).

**13.123** **Author-date text citations of works with more than two authors.** For more than two authors (in previous editions it was more than three), only the name of the first author is used, followed by *et al.* (and others). Note that *et al.* is not italicized in text citations.

> (Schonen et al. 2024)
> According to the data collected by Schonen et al. (2024), . . .

If a reference list includes another work of the same date that would also be abbreviated as "Schonen et al." but whose coauthors are different persons or listed in a different order, the text citations must distinguish between them. In such cases, the first two authors (or as many as needed to distinguish the references) should be cited, followed by *et al.*

(Schonen, Baker, et al. 2024)
(Schonen, Brooks, et al. 2024)

Alternatively, a shortened title, enclosed in commas, may be added. In the following examples, *et al.* refers to different coauthors, so *a*, *b*, and so on cannot be used (see 13.114):

(Schonen et al., "Tilting at Windmills," 2024)
(Schonen et al., "Gasoline Farmers," 2024)

Had the examples above been published in different years, no such adjustments would be necessary (see also 13.124). For treatment of multiple authors in a reference list, see 13.107.

13.124 **Multiple author-date text references.** Two or more references in a single parenthetical citation are separated by semicolons. The order in which they are given may depend on what is being cited, and in what order, or it may reflect the relative importance of the items cited. If neither criterion applies, alphabetical or chronological order may be appropriate. Unless the order is prescribed by a particular journal style, the decision is the author's.

(Armstrong and Malacinski 1989; Beigl 1989; Pickett and White 1985)

Additional works by the same author(s) are cited by date only, separated by commas except where page numbers are required. This applies also to multiple works by the same author followed by "et al."—whether the coauthors are the same or not (see also 13.123).

(Whittaker 1967, 1975; Wiens 1989a, 1989b)
(Wong 1999, 328; 2000, 475; García 1998, 67)
(Schonen et al. 2023, 2024)

Additional references prefaced by "see also" follow any other references (see also 13.118).

(Guest et al. 2006; see also Stolle et al. 2008; Rahn et al. 2009)

13.125 **Author-date text citations with title rather than author.** If the author, editor, translator, or the like for a work is unknown, the reference list entry begins with the title. An initial article is ignored in alphabetizing. Text citations then refer to the title. A short form may be used (up to the first four words, not including an initial article), but it must include the first word (other than an initial article). See also 13.81.

*Stanze in lode della donna brutta*. 1547. Florence.

*A True and Sincere Declaration of the Purpose and Ends of the Plantation Begun in Virginia, of the Degrees Which It Hath Received, and Means by Which It Hath Been Advanced*. 1610. London.

(*Stanze in lode della donna brutta* 1547) *or* (*Stanze* 1547)

(*True and Sincere Declaration* 1610)

13.126 **Author-date text citations with pseudonyms.** Pseudonyms are indicated in reference lists in exactly the same manner as they are in bibliographies (see 13.82). Text citations should refer to the first-listed name and will omit the indication *pseud.*

Centinel [pseud.]. 1981. Letters. In *The Complete Anti-Federalist*, edited by Herbert J. Storing. University of Chicago Press.

(Centinel 1981)

13.127 **Author-date text citations with organization as author.** To facilitate shorter parenthetical text citations, an organization listed as author may be cited in the text using an abbreviation, in which case the entry must be alphabetized under that abbreviation (rather than the spelled-out name) in the reference list. See also 13.86.

ISO (International Organization for Standardization). 1997. *Information and Documentation—Rules for the Abbreviation of Title Words and Titles of Publications*. ISO 4.

(ISO 1997)

13.128 **Author-date system with notes.** Where footnotes or endnotes are used to supplement the author-date system, source citations within notes are treated in the same way as in text (see fig. 13.13). Such notes should be reserved for substantive commentary and should not be taken as permission to move parenthetical text citations into the notes.

We thus consider structurally constrained agentic action as central to decisions at the intersection of crime and employment, and particularly regarding the decision to apply based on the presence of CRQs or BCSs.[2] That is, seemingly agentic actions and calculations surrounding job seeking are structurally patterned by status distinctions while also fundamentally bounded by, and linked to, structural contexts. Those who believe they can surmount obstacles and status-based barriers may perceive their ability to get a job as higher than someone lacking this orientation, looking past the CRQ or inevitable background check and potentially using the stigma management strategies noted above (Harding 2003; Halushka 2016; Augustine 2019; Goodman 2020). Conversely, repeated rejections in the labor market may cause

[2] The concept of agency being bound, constrained, or restricted by structural conditions goes by many names within sociological subfields, such as *bounded rationality* in criminology (Cornish and Clarke 1986), *bounded agency* in life course studies (Staff and Mortimer 2007), and *constrained choices* in medical sociology (Bird and Rieker 2008).

FIGURE 13.13. A sample of text with both parenthetical text citations and a footnote. See 13.128.

1. James Wilson has noted that "no politician ever lost votes by denouncing the bureaucracy" (1989, 235). Yet little is actually ever done to bring major reforms to the system.

For the use of notes with legal-style citations, see 14.172. For more on footnotes and endnotes, see 13.27–64.

# 14 Source Citations: Examples

## OVERVIEW

**14.1** **Notes and bibliography as the default citation system for this chapter.** To reduce repetition, most of the examples in this chapter are based on the notes and bibliography system, Chicago's oldest and most flexible system of source citation. Those using the stylistically similar author-date system should be able to adapt these examples simply by reordering the elements. In the examples below, note especially the placement of the year of publication in a bibliography entry relative to its placement in a reference list entry.

Notes and bibliography (full note, shortened note, and bibliography entry):

1. Sarah Thankam Mathews, *All This Could Be Different* (Viking, 2022), 33.
2. Mathews, *All This*, 114–15.

Mathews, Sarah Thankam. *All This Could Be Different*. Viking, 2022.

Author-date (reference list entry and corresponding parenthetical text references):

Mathews, Sarah Thankam. 2022. *All This Could Be Different*. Viking.

(Mathews 2022, 33)
(Mathews 2022, 114–15)

Where a conversion to author-date format may not be straightforward, an example or clarification has been provided. Look for the boldface words **Author-date** at the end of a numbered section. Full details for both systems are covered in chapter 13. For a quick review, see the examples and variations in 13.21–26 (for notes and bibliography) and 13.105–10 (author-date).

## BOOKS

**14.2** **Elements to include when citing a book.** The elements listed below are included, where applicable, in full notes and bibliography entries. The order in which they appear may vary slightly according to type of book, and certain elements are sometimes omitted; such variation will be noted and illustrated in the course of this section.

1. Author: full name of author(s) or editor(s) or, if no author or editor is listed, name of institution standing in their place; see also 13.74–86
2. Title: full title of the book, including subtitle if there is one; see also 13.87–101
3. Edition, if not the first (a first edition is assumed by the absence of an edition statement)
4. Editor, compiler, or translator, if any, if listed on title page in addition to author
5. Volume: total number of volumes if multivolume work is referred to as a whole; individual number if single volume of multivolume work is cited, and title of individual volume if applicable
6. Series title if applicable, and volume number within series if series is numbered
7. Facts of publication: publisher and date (city of publication is no longer required)
8. Page number(s) (as for a specific citation in a note)
9. For books consulted online, a URL or persistent identifier; for other types of electronic books, the name of the application or format (see also 13.6–12)

14.3 **Form of author's name and title of book in source citations.** An author's name and the title of a book should generally be cited according to how each appears on the title page. In a bibliography entry, the first-listed author's name is normally inverted.

1. Ada Ferrer, *Cuba: An American History* (Scribner, 2021), 437.
2. Ferrer, *Cuba*, 440–41.

Ferrer, Ada. *Cuba: An American History*. Scribner, 2021.

For additional considerations related to authors' names and titles of works, see 13.74–86 (names) and 13.87–101 (titles).

14.4 **Non-English bibliographic terms and abbreviations.** When citing a book published in a language other than English, terms used for *volume*, *edition*, and so on may be translated—but only if the author or editor has a firm grasp of bibliographic terms in the other language. It is often wiser to leave them in the original. "Ausgabe in einem Band," for example, may be rendered as "one-volume edition" or simply left untranslated. Moreover, abbreviations such as "Bd." and "t." (German and French/Spanish equivalents of *vol.*, respectively) that are likely to have been recorded that way in a library catalog may best be left in that form. If in doubt, check the listing at a bibliographic database such as the US Library of Congress or OCLC's WorldCat or via the online catalog at a university or other large library.

## *Editors, Translators, Compilers, or Cowriters*

14.5 **Editor in place of author.** When no author appears on the title page, a work is listed by the name(s) of the editor(s), compiler(s), or translator(s). In full note citations and in bibliographies, the abbreviation *ed.* or *eds.*, *comp.* or *comps.*, or *trans.* follows the name, preceded by a comma. In shortened note citations, the abbreviation is omitted.

1. Marc Stein, ed., *The Stonewall Riots: A Documentary History* (New York University Press, 2019), 89.
2. Ibram X. Kendi and Keisha N. Blain, eds., *Four Hundred Souls: A Community History of African America, 1619–2019* (One World, 2021), xiv.
3. Rosemary Gray, comp., *London: An Illustrated Literary Companion* (Macmillan Collector's Library, 2017), 33.
4. Theodore Silverstein, trans., *Sir Gawain and the Green Knight* (University of Chicago Press, 1974), 34.
5. Stein, *Stonewall Riots*, 92.
6. Kendi and Blain, *Four Hundred Souls*, xx–xxi.
7. Gray, *London*, 54–56.
8. Silverstein, *Sir Gawain*, 38.

Gray, Rosemary, comp. *London: An Illustrated Literary Companion*. Macmillan Collector's Library, 2017.
Kendi, Ibram X., and Keisha N. Blain, eds. *Four Hundred Souls: A Community History of African America, 1619–2019*. One World, 2021.
Silverstein, Theodore, trans. *Sir Gawain and the Green Knight*. University of Chicago Press, 1974.
Stein, Marc, ed. *The Stonewall Riots: A Documentary History*. New York University Press, 2019.

Certain well-known reference works may be listed by title rather than by editor; for an example, see 14.130.

**Author-date.** Abbreviations such as *ed.*, *trans.*, and *comp.* are included in reference list entries but omitted from text citations.

Stein, Marc, ed. 2019. *The Stonewall Riots: A Documentary History*. New York University Press.

(Stein 2019, 89)
*not*
(Stein ed. 2019, 89)

14.6 **Editor or translator in addition to author.** The edited, compiled, or translated work of one author is normally listed with the author's name appearing first and the name(s) of the editor(s), compiler(s), or translator(s) appearing after the title, preceded by *edited by* or *ed.*, *compiled by* or *comp.*, or *translated by* or *trans.* Note that the plural forms *eds.* and *comps.* are never used in this position. Note also that *edited by* and the like are usually spelled out in bibliographies but abbreviated in notes. If a translator as well as an editor is listed, the names should appear in the same order as on the title page of the original. When the title page carries such phrases as "Edited with an Introduction and Notes by" or "Translated with a Foreword by," the bibliographic or note reference can usually be simplified to "Edited by" or "Translated by." See also 13.101, 14.9. An illustrator of a children's book or textbook or the like can be cited similarly to an editor or translator (as in the Guite example below).

1. Yves Bonnefoy, *New and Selected Poems*, ed. John Naughton and Anthony Rudolf (University of Chicago Press, 1995).

2. Rigoberta Menchú, *Crossing Borders*, trans. and ed. Ann Wright (Verso, 1998).

3. Liu Xinwu, *The Wedding Party*, trans. Jeremy Tiang (Amazon Crossing, 2021).

4. Theodor W. Adorno and Walter Benjamin, *The Complete Correspondence, 1928–1940*, ed. Henri Lonitz, trans. Nicholas Walker (Harvard University Press, 2001).

5. Mercy Vungthianmuang Guite, *Lengtonghoih: The Girl Who Wanted the Brightest Star*, art dir. Richard Khuptong, ill. Tanya Gupta (Seagull Books, 2022).

Adorno, Theodor W., and Walter Benjamin. *The Complete Correspondence, 1928–1940*. Edited by Henri Lonitz. Translated by Nicholas Walker. Harvard University Press, 2001.

Bonnefoy, Yves. *New and Selected Poems*. Edited by John Naughton and Anthony Rudolf. University of Chicago Press, 1995.

Guite, Mercy Vungthianmuang. *Lengtonghoih: The Girl Who Wanted the Brightest Star*. Art direction by Richard Khuptong. Illustrated by Tanya Gupta. Seagull Books, 2022.

Liu Xinwu. *The Wedding Party*. Translated by Jeremy Tiang. Amazon Crossing, 2021.

Menchú, Rigoberta. *Crossing Borders*. Translated and edited by Ann Wright. Verso, 1998.

Occasionally, when an editor or a translator is more important to a discussion than the original author, a book may be listed under the editor's name.

Eliot, T. S., ed. *Literary Essays*. By Ezra Pound. New Directions, 1954.

14.7 **Other contributors listed on the title page.** The title page may list the names of people other than an author, editor, compiler, or translator. Such names may be included in a full note or a bibliography entry if they are considered to be a significant factor in a reader's assessment of the book. For ghostwritten books, *with* is usually sufficient. For other contributions, descriptions should accurately convey the information on the title page. Authors of forewords or introductions to books by other authors may be included if they are considered sufficiently important to mention.

Conway, Tim. *What's So Funny? My Hilarious Life*. With Jane Scovell and with a foreword by Carol Burnett. Howard Books, 2013.

Crow, Martin M., and Clair C. Olson, eds. *Chaucer Life-Records*. From materials compiled by John M. Manly and Edith Rickert, with the assistance of Lilian J. Redstone et al. Oxford University Press, 1966.

Cullen, John B. *Old Times in the Faulkner Country*. In collaboration with Floyd C. Watkins. University of North Carolina Press, 1961.

Derrida, Jacques. *Heidegger: The Question of Being and History*. Edited by Thomas Dutoit with the assistance of Marguerite Derrida. Translated by Geoffrey Bennington. University of Chicago Press, 2016.

Hayek, F. A. *The Road to Serfdom*. With a new introduction by Milton Friedman. University of Chicago Press, 1994.

La Guma, Alex. *Culture and Liberation: Exile Writings, 1966–1985*. Edited and introduced by Christopher J. Lee and with a foreword by Albie Sachs. Seagull Books, 2022.

Prather, Marla. *Alexander Calder, 1898–1976*. With contributions by Arnauld Pierre and Alexander S. C. Rower. Yale University Press, 1998.

Rembert, Winfred. *Chasing Me to My Grave: An Artist's Memoir of the Jim Crow South*. As told to Erin I. Kelly. Bloomsbury Publishing, 2021.

For specific citation of a foreword or an introduction, see 14.12.

## *Chapters or Other Parts of a Book*

14.8 **Chapter in a single-author book.** When a specific chapter (or other titled part of a book) is cited in the notes, the author's name is followed by the title of the chapter (or other part), followed by *in*, followed by the title of the book. The chapter title is enclosed in quotation marks. The chapter number (if any) may be included in the note (as when the reference is to the chapter as a whole); however, the page range for the chapter is no longer required in the bibliography entry (a departure from previous editions of this manual). In the bibliography, either the chapter or the book may be listed first. For a multiauthor work, see 14.9. See also 14.52.

1. Alison Richard, "Human Footprints," in *The Sloth Lemur's Song: Madagascar from the Deep Past to the Uncertain Present* (University of Chicago Press, 2022), 148.

2. Kelefa Sanneh, "Hip-Hop," chap. 5 in *Major Labels: A History of Popular Music in Seven Genres* (Penguin Press, 2021).

3. Sanneh, "Hip-Hop," 301.

Richard, Alison. "Human Footprints." In *The Sloth Lemur's Song: Madagascar from the Deep Past to the Uncertain Present*. University of Chicago Press, 2022.

Sanneh, Kelefa. "Hip-Hop." Chap. 5 in *Major Labels: A History of Popular Music in Seven Genres*. Penguin Press, 2021.

*or*

Sanneh, Kelefa. *Major Labels: A History of Popular Music in Seven Genres*. Penguin Press, 2021. See esp. chap. 5, "Hip-Hop."

For chapters originally published as articles in a journal, see 14.80.

14.9 **Contribution to a multiauthor book.** When one contribution to a multiauthor book is cited, the contributor's name comes first, followed by the title of the contribution in roman, followed by *in* (also roman), followed by the title of the book in italics, followed by the name(s) of the editor(s). In a bibliography entry, the inclusive page numbers are no longer required (a departure from previous editions of this manual). In notes and bibliographies, the contribution title is enclosed in quotation marks. For several contributions to the same book, see 14.10.

1. Ruth A. Miller, "Posthuman," in *Critical Terms for the Study of Gender*, ed. Catharine R. Stimpson and Gilbert Herdt (University of Chicago Press, 2014), 325.

Ellet, Elizabeth F. L. "By Rail and Stage to Galena." In *Prairie State: Impressions of Illinois, 1673–1967, by Travelers and Other Observers*, edited by Paul M. Angle. University of Chicago Press, 1968.

14.10 **Several contributions to the same multiauthor book.** If two or more contributions to the same multiauthor book are cited, the book itself, as well as the specific contributions, may be listed in the bibliography. The entries for the individual contributions may then cross-refer to the book's editor, thus avoiding clutter. In notes, details of the book may be given the first time it is mentioned, with subsequent references in shortened form (see also 13.34).

1. William H. Keating, "Fort Dearborn and Chicago," in *Prairie State: Impressions of Illinois, 1673–1967, by Travelers and Other Observers*, ed. Paul M. Angle (University of Chicago Press, 1968), 84–85.

2. Sara Clarke Lippincott, "Chicago," in Angle, *Prairie State*, 363.

Draper, Joan E. "Paris by the Lake: Sources of Burnham's Plan of Chicago." In Zukowsky, *Chicago Architecture*.

Harrington, Elaine. "International Influences on Henry Hobson Richardson's Glessner House." In Zukowsky, *Chicago Architecture*.

Zukowsky, John, ed. *Chicago Architecture, 1872–1922: Birth of a Metropolis*. Prestel-Verlag in association with the Art Institute of Chicago, 1987.

**Author-date.** In a reference list, individual components of a multiauthor work should *not* be listed separately and then cross-referenced to the work as a whole (a departure from advice in previous editions that recognizes the difficulty of cross-linking references in electronic journals and similar publications). Instead, list only the multiauthor work as a whole. Components can then be mentioned in the text and cited to the collection.

Zukowsky, John, ed. 1987. *Chicago Architecture, 1872–1922: Birth of a Metropolis*. Prestel-Verlag in association with the Art Institute of Chicago.

In her essay "Paris by the Lake: Sources of Burnham's Plan of Chicago" (Zukowsky 1987), Joan E. Draper traces . . .

14.11 **Book-length work within a book.** If the cited part of a book would normally be italicized if published alone, it too may be italicized rather than placed in quotation marks. See also 8.164, 8.185.

1. Thomas Bernhard, *A Party for Boris*, in *Histrionics: Three Plays*, trans. Peter Jansen and Kenneth Northcott (University of Chicago Press, 1990).

Baldwin, James. *If Beale Street Could Talk*. In *James Baldwin: Later Novels*, edited by Darryl Pinckney. Library of America, 2015.

14.12 **Introductions, prefaces, afterwords, and the like.** If the reference is to a generic title such as *introduction*, *foreword*, *preface*, or *afterword*, that term (lowercased unless following a period) is added before the title of the book (see also 8.181). If the author of the introduction or other part is someone other than the main author of a book, that author comes first, and the author of the book follows the title. In a bibliography entry, the page number range for the cited part is no longer required (a departure from previous editions of this manual). Note that if the author of the introduction or other part is also the editor of the book, the full names should be repeated for each role (rather than using surnames alone), as in the Mansfield and Winthrop example below.

1. Toni Morrison, foreword to *Song of Solomon* (Vintage International, 2004).

2. Christopher Hitchens, introduction to *Civilization and Its Discontents*, by Sigmund Freud, trans. and ed. James Strachey (W. W. Norton, 2010).

Mansfield, Harvey C., and Delba Winthrop. Introduction to *Democracy in America*, by Alexis de Tocqueville. Translated and edited by Harvey C. Mansfield and Delba Winthrop. University of Chicago Press, 2000.

Wilkerson, Isabel. Foreword to *Deep South: A Social Anthropological Study of Caste and Class*, 2nd ed., by Allison Davis, Burleigh B. Gardner, and Mary R. Gardner. University of Chicago Press, 2022.

For including information about a foreword or other contribution to a book cited as a whole, see 14.7. See also 8.181.

14.13 **Letters in published collections.** A reference to a letter (or memorandum or similar communication) in a published collection begins with the names of the sender and the recipient, in that order, followed by a date and sometimes the place where the communication was prepared. Words such as *letter*, *postcard*, *email*, and the like are usually unnecessary, but other forms, such as reports or memorandums, should be specified. The title of the collection is given in the usual form for a book. If not clear in the text or otherwise, a short form for the collection may be needed if correspondents differ from those listed in the first full citation (as shown in note 4). For unpublished communications, see 14.111; see also 14.126.

1. Adams to Charles Milnes Gaskell, Baden, September 22, 1867, in *Letters of Henry Adams, 1858–1891*, ed. Worthington Chauncey Ford (Houghton Mifflin, 1930), 133–34.

2. White to Harold Ross, memorandum, May 2, 1946, in *Letters of E. B. White*, ed. Dorothy Lobrano Guth (Harper & Row, 1976), 273.

3. Adams to Gaskell, London, March 30, 1868, 141.

4. Adams to John Hay, Washington, October 26, 1884, in Adams, *Letters*, 361.

Adams, Henry. *Letters of Henry Adams, 1858–1891*. Edited by Worthington Chauncey Ford. Houghton Mifflin, 1930.

White, E. B. *Letters of E. B. White*. Edited by Dorothy Lobrano Guth. Harper & Row, 1976.

When it is necessary to include a single letter in a bibliography, it is listed under the writer's name only.

Jackson, Paulina. Paulina Jackson to John Pepys Junior, October 3, 1676. In *The Letters of Samuel Pepys and His Family Circle*, edited by Helen Truesdell Heath, no. 42. Clarendon Press, 1955.

**Author-date.** In the author-date system, letters in published collections should be cited by the date of the collection. The dates of individual correspondence should be incorporated into the text.

Adams, Henry. 1930. *Letters of Henry Adams, 1858–1891*. Edited by Worthington Chauncey Ford. Houghton Mifflin.

White, E. B. 1976. *Letters of E. B. White*. Edited by Dorothy Lobrano Guth. Harper & Row.

In a letter to Charles Milnes Gaskell from London, March 30, 1868 (Adams 1930, 141), Adams wrote . . .

White (1976, 273) sent Ross an interoffice memo on May 2, 1946, pointing out that . . .

14.14 **Online-only supplement to a book.** To cite an online-only supplement or enhancement to a book, include a title or a description of the content and a URL (see 13.6) in addition to the publication details for the book. Specify file format if applicable. For databases, see 14.157.

1. Kevin Vallier, "Accommodating Radicals in a System of Trust" (PDF), online appendix to *Trust in a Polarized Age* (Oxford University Press, 2020), https://global.oup.com/us/companion.websites/fdscontent/uscompanion/us/static/companion.websites/9780190887223/Appendix_B.pdf.

## *Edition*

14.15 **Editions other than the first.** When an edition other than the first is cited, the number or description of the edition follows the title. An edition number usually appears on a book's title page and is repeated, along with the date of the edition, on the copyright page. Such wording as *Second Edition, Revised and Enlarged* is abbreviated in notes and bibliographies simply as *2nd ed.*; *Revised Edition* (with no number) is abbreviated as *rev. ed.* Other terms are similarly abbreviated. (Any information about volumes follows the edition number; for an example, see 14.130.) For the use of the word *edition* and Chicago's preferences, see 1.28. For inclusion of the original date of an older work cited in a modern edition, see 14.16.

1. Amy Einsohn and Marilyn Schwartz, *The Copyeditor's Handbook: A Guide for Book Publishing and Corporate Communications*, 4th ed. (University of California Press, 2019), 401–2.

2. Rickie Solinger, *Pregnancy and Power: A History of Reproductive Politics in the United States*, rev. ed. (New York University Press, 2019), 99.

3. Jane Austen, *Emma*, annotated ed., ed. Bharat Tandon (Belknap Press of Harvard University Press, 2012), 14–15. All subsequent citations refer to this edition.

Garner, Bryan A. *Garner's Modern English Usage*. 5th ed. Oxford University Press, 2022.

Shakespeare, William. *The Complete Works*. 2nd ed. Edited by Stanley Wells, Gary Taylor, John Jowett, and William Montgomery. Clarendon Press, 2005.

14.16 **Reprint editions and modern editions.** Books may be reissued in paperback by the original publisher or in paper or hardcover by another company. Normally, these may be cited without reference to the original edition. But if the original publication details—particularly the date—are relevant, they may be included. If page numbers are mentioned, specify the edition cited unless pagination is the same. The original publication details can usually be listed first; in a bibliography entry, however, these may be given after the details for the later edition. Modern editions of Greek, Latin, and medieval classics are discussed in 14.142–52; modern editions of English classics in 14.153–54; ebook formats in 14.58–62.

1. Ralph Ellison, *Invisible Man* (Random House, 1952; repr., Vintage Books, 1995), 242–43. Citations refer to the Vintage Books edition.

2. Ralph Waldo Emerson, *Nature* (Boston, 1836; facsimile ed., Beacon Press, 1985).

Ellison, Ralph. *Invisible Man*. Random House, 1952. Reprint, Vintage Books, 1995.

*or*

Ellison, Ralph. *Invisible Man*. Vintage Books, 1995. Originally published in 1952 by Random House.

Emerson, Ralph Waldo. *Nature*. Boston, 1836. Facsimile of the first edition, with an introduction by Jaroslav Pelikan. Beacon Press, 1985.

Fitzgerald, F. Scott. *The Great Gatsby*. Scribner, 1925. Reprinted with preface and notes by Matthew J. Bruccoli. Collier Books, 1992.

National Reconnaissance Office. *The KH-4B Camera System*. National Photographic Interpretation Center, 1968. Now declassified and available at https://www.nro.gov/Portals/65/documents/foia/CAL-Records/Cabinet5/DrawerB/5%20B%200063.pdf.

Schweitzer, Albert. *J. S. Bach*. Translated by Ernest Newman. 2 vols. Breitkopf and Härtel, 1911. Reprint, Dover, 1966.

**Author-date.** In the author-date system, an original publication date may be added as shown below. Information about the earlier edition may be added but need not be. Note that parentheses in the reference list become square brackets in the text citation.

Ellison, Ralph. (1952) 1995. *Invisible Man*. Random House. Reprint, Vintage Books.

*or*

Ellison, Ralph. (1952) 1995. *Invisible Man*. Vintage Books.

(Ellison [1952] 1995, 242–43)

14.17 **Microform editions.** Works consulted in microform editions (i.e., copies of printed matter reproduced for storage at a smaller size, usually on film, and read using a specialized viewer) should be cited according to the format of the original publication (e.g., book, newspaper article, or dissertation). Specify the format (e.g., microfiche or microfilm) after the facts of publication. In the first example below, the page number refers to the printed text; the other locator indicates the fiche (i.e., sheet) and frame numbers, and the letter indicates the row. Such locators will vary according to the resource.

1. Beatrice Farwell, *French Popular Lithographic Imagery, 1815–1870*, vol. 12, *Lithography in Art and Commerce* (University of Chicago Press, 1997), microfiche, p. 67, 3C12.

Tauber, Abraham. "Spelling Reform in the United States." PhD diss., Columbia University, 1958. Microfilm.

## *Multivolume Works*

14.18 **Volume numbers and page numbers.** In source citations, volume numbers are always given in Arabic numerals, even if in the original work they appear in Roman numerals or are spelled out. If the volume number is immediately followed by a page number, the abbreviation *vol.* is omitted and a colon separates the volume number from the page number with no intervening space. See the examples throughout this section. See also 14.74.

14.19 **Citing a multivolume work as a whole.** When a multivolume work is cited as a whole, the total number of volumes is given after the title of the work and any edition number (or, if an editor as well as an author is mentioned, after the editor's name). If the volumes have been published over several years, the dates of the first and last volumes are given, separated by an en dash (see 9.66). See also 13.80.

1. *The Complete Works of Aristotle: The Revised Oxford Translation*, ed. Jonathan Barnes, 2 vols., Bollingen Series (Princeton University Press, 1984).

Byrne, Muriel St. Clare, ed. *The Lisle Letters*. 6 vols. University of Chicago Press, 1981.

Grene, David, and Richmond Lattimore, eds. *The Complete Greek Tragedies*. 3rd ed. Edited by Mark Griffith and Glenn W. Most. 9 vols. (unnumbered). University of Chicago Press, 2013.

James, Henry. *The Complete Tales of Henry James*. Edited by Leon Edel. 12 vols. Rupert Hart-Davis, 1962–64.

14.20 **Citing a particular volume in a note.** If a particular volume of a multivolume work is cited, the volume number and the individual volume title, if there is one, are given in addition to the general title. If volumes have been published in different years, only the date of the cited volume is given.

1. Muriel St. Clare Byrne, ed., *The Lisle Letters* (University of Chicago Press, 1981), 4:243.

2. *The Complete Tales of Henry James*, ed. Leon Edel, vol. 5, *1883–1884* (Rupert Hart-Davis, 1963), 32–33.

3. Byrne, *Lisle Letters*, 4:245.

4. *Complete Tales of Henry James*, 5:34.

The different treatment of the volume numbers in the examples above is prescribed by logic: All six volumes of the Byrne work appeared in 1981 under the same title, whereas volume 5 of the James tales carries an additional title with a publication date not shared by all volumes in the set. The shortened form, however, need not refer to the title of the individual volume. Information about the total number of volumes (as in a work without a corresponding bibliography) may be added as follows:

1. Muriel St. Clare Byrne, ed., *The Lisle Letters*, 6 vols. . . .
2. *The Complete Tales of Henry James*, ed. Leon Edel, vol. 5 of 12, . . .

See also 14.24.

14.21 **Citing a particular volume in a bibliography.** If only one volume of a multivolume work is of interest to readers, it may be listed alone in a bibliography in either of the following ways:

Carson, Clayborne, ed. *The Papers of Martin Luther King, Jr.* Vol. 7, *To Save the Soul of America, January 1961–August 1962*, edited by Tenisha Armstrong. University of California Press, 2014.

*or*

Armstrong, Tenisha, ed. *To Save the Soul of America, January 1961–August 1962*. Vol. 7 of *The Papers of Martin Luther King, Jr.*, edited by Clayborne Carson. University of California Press, 1992–.

If they are different, the editor(s) for the series as a whole and for the individual volume should both be listed (as in the examples above; see also 14.24). The publication date (or date range; see 14.19) should normally correspond to the last-mentioned title. See also 14.23, 14.43.

**Author-date.** In the author-date system, the individual volume normally comes first in the reference list entry. If the publication date of the collection is different from the publication date of the individual volume, both should be listed.

Armstrong, Tenisha, ed. 2014. *To Save the Soul of America, January 1961–August 1962*. Vol. 7 of *The Papers of Martin Luther King, Jr.*, edited by Clayborne Carson. University of California Press, 1992–.

(Armstrong 2014, 85)

14.22 **Chapters and other parts of individual volumes.** Specific parts of individual volumes of multivolume books are cited in the same way as parts of single-volume books (see 14.8–14). If the individual volume has no title of its own, the volume number precedes any page number(s) in a note (e.g., "3:181"; see 14.20).

1. Chen Jian, "China and the Cold War After Mao," in *The Cambridge History of the Cold War*, ed. Melvyn P. Leffler and Odd Arne Westad, vol. 3, *Endings* (Cambridge University Press, 2010), 181.

2. Unpublished letter to the editor of the *Afro-American* (Washington, DC), in *The Papers of Martin Luther King, Jr.*, ed. Clayborne Carson, vol. 7, *To Save the Soul of America, January 1961–August 1962*, ed. Tenisha Armstrong (University of California Press, 2014), 169–71.

Chen Jian. "China and the Cold War After Mao." In *Endings*, vol. 3 of *The Cambridge History of the Cold War*, edited by Melvyn P. Leffler and Odd Arne Westad. Cambridge University Press, 2010.

See also 14.9, 14.24, 15.85.

14.23 **One volume in two or more books.** Occasionally, if it is very long, a single volume of a multivolume work may be published as two or more physical books. The reference must then include book as well as volume number.

1. Donald F. Lach, *Asia in the Making of Europe*, vol. 2, *A Century of Wonder*, bk. 3, *The Scholarly Disciplines* (University of Chicago Press, 1977), 351.

Harley, J. B., and David Woodward, eds. *The History of Cartography*. Vol. 2, bk. 2, *Cartography in the Traditional East and Southeast Asian Societies*. University of Chicago Press, 1994.

*or*

Harley, J. B., and David Woodward, eds. *Cartography in the Traditional East and Southeast Asian Societies*. Vol. 2, bk. 2, of *The History of Cartography*. University of Chicago Press, 1987–.

14.24 **Authors and editors of multivolume works.** Some multivolume works have both a general editor and individual editors or authors for each volume (and, as in the third example below, additional editors for new editions). When individual volumes are cited, the name of the editor(s) follows that part for which they are responsible.

1. *The Cambridge History of America and the World*, ed. Mark Philip Bradley, vol. 3, *1900–1945*, ed. Brooke L. Blower and Andrew Preston (Cambridge University Press, 2021).

2. *The Variorum Edition of the Poetry of John Donne*, ed. Gary A. Stringer, vol. 6, *The "Anniversaries" and the "Epicedes and Obsequies,"* ed. Gary A. Stringer and Ted-Larry Pebworth (Indiana University Press, 1995).

3. *Orestes*, trans. William Arrowsmith, in *Euripides IV*, unnumbered vol. 6 of *The Complete Greek Tragedies*, ed. David Grene and Richmond Lattimore, 3rd ed., ed. Mark Griffith and Glenn W. Most (University of Chicago Press, 2013).

Note the different capitalization and punctuation of *edited by* in the following alternative versions, analogous to the treatment of a chapter in a multiauthor book (see 14.9). (Certain multivolume works may, for bibliographic purposes, more conveniently be treated as series; see 14.26.)

Donne, John. *The Variorum Edition of the Poetry of John Donne*. Edited by Gary A. Stringer and Jeffrey S. Johnson. Vol. 6, *"The Anniversaries" and the "Epicedes and Obsequies,"* edited by Gary A. Stringer and Ted-Larry Pebworth. Indiana University Press, 1995.

*or*

Donne, John. *The "Anniversaries" and the "Epicedes and Obsequies."* Edited by Gary A. Stringer and Ted-Larry Pebworth. Vol. 6 of *The Variorum Edition of the Poetry of John Donne*, edited by Gary A. Stringer and Jeffrey S. Johnson. Indiana University Press, 1995–2022.

Bradley, Mark Philip, ed. *The Cambridge History of America and the World*. Vol. 3, *1900–1945*, edited by Brooke L. Blower and Andrew Preston. Cambridge University Press, 2021.

*or*

Blower, Brooke L., and Andrew Preston, eds. *The Cambridge History of America and the World*, vol. 3, *1900–1945*. Series editor Mark Philip Bradley. Cambridge University Press, 2021.

## *Series*

14.25 **Series titles, numbers, and editors.** Including a series title in a citation often helps readers decide whether to pursue a reference. But if books belonging to a series can be located without the series title, it may be omitted to save space (especially in a footnote). If the series title is included, it is capitalized in title case, but it is neither italicized nor put in quotation marks or parentheses. Some series are numbered; many are not. The number (if any) follows the series title with no intervening comma unless *vol.* or *no.* is used. These abbreviations may be omitted, however, unless both are needed in a single reference (see third example below) or unless a series editor or other notation intervenes (see 14.26, third example). For a non-English series title, use sentence case (see 11.8 and second example below).

1. Duane Esarey and Kjersti E. Emerson, eds., *Palos Village: An Early Seventeenth-Century Ancestral Ho-Chunk Occupation in the Chicago Area*, Studies in Archaeology 14 (Illinois State Archaeological Survey, 2021).

Devésa, Jean-Michel, ed. *L'édition africaine et la fabrique de la littérature*. L'un et l'autre en français. Presses Universitaires de Limoges, 2022.

Wauchope, Robert. *A Tentative Sequence of Pre-Classic Ceramics in Middle America*. Middle American Research Records, vol. 1, no. 14. Tulane University, 1950.

The name of the series editor is usually omitted. When included, it follows the series title.

Allen, Judith A. *The Feminism of Charlotte Perkins Gilman: Sexualities, Histories, Progressivism*. Women in Culture and Society, edited by Catharine R. Stimpson. University of Chicago Press, 2009.

14.26 **Series or multivolume work?** Certain types of series may lend themselves to being cited as a whole. In such cases, the series may be treated as a multivolume work, with the title of the series in italics.

Boyer, John W., and Julius Kirshner, eds. *Readings in Western Civilization*. 9 vols. University of Chicago Press, 1986–87.

Grene, David, and Richmond Lattimore, eds. *The Complete Greek Tragedies*. 3rd ed., edited by Mark Griffith and Glenn W. Most. 9 vols. (unnumbered). University of Chicago Press, 2013.

Usually, however, it is preferable to cite individual titles in the series, as described in 14.25; the series title then appears in roman.

Cochrane, Eric, Charles M. Gray, and Mark A. Kishlansky, eds. *Early Modern Europe: Crisis of Authority*. Readings in Western Civilization, edited by John W. Boyer and Julius Kirshner, vol. 6. University of Chicago Press, 1987.

Euripides. *Orestes*. Translated by William Arrowsmith. In *Euripides IV*, edited by David Grene and Richmond Lattimore. 3rd ed., edited by Mark Griffith and Glenn W. Most. The Complete Greek Tragedies. University of Chicago Press, 2013.

14.27 **Multivolume work within a series.** If a book within a series consists of more than one volume, the number of volumes or the volume number (if reference is to a particular volume) follows the book title.

Ferrer Benimeli, José Antonio. *Masonería, iglesia e ilustración*. Vol. 1, *Las bases de un conflicto (1700–1739)*. Vol. 2, *Inquisición: Procesos históricos (1739–1750)*. Publicaciones de la Fundación Universitaria Española, Monografías 17. Madrid, 1976.

14.28 **"Old series" and "new series."** Some numbered series have gone on so long that, as with certain long-lived journals, numbering has started over again, preceded by *n.s.* (new series), *2nd ser.* (second series), or some similar notation, usually enclosed in commas. (A change of publisher may also be the occasion for a change in series designation.) Books in the old series may be identified by *o.s.*, *1st ser.*, or whatever complements the notation for the new series.

1. C. R. Boxer, ed. *South China in the Sixteenth Century*, Hakluyt Society Publications, 2nd ser., vol. 106 (Hakluyt, 1953).

Palmatary, Helen C. *The Pottery of Marajó Island, Brazil*. Transactions of the American Philosophical Society, n.s., vol. 39, pt. 3 (1949). American Philosophical Society, 1950.

## *Facts of Publication*

**14.29** **Publisher and date.** The facts of publication for books include the publisher and the date (year). (Note that a city of publication is no longer required; see 14.30.) These elements are put in parentheses in a note but not in a bibliography. In a note or a bibliography, the date follows the publisher, preceded by a comma. See also 13.21.

1. Virginia Woolf, *To the Lighthouse* (Hogarth Press, 1927).

Coates, Ta-Nehisi. *The Water Dancer*. One World, 2019.

### PLACE OF PUBLICATION

**14.30** **Place of publication.** In line with emerging practice, Chicago no longer requires a place of publication for books published since 1900 (see also 14.31). If for any reason a place is included (authors should resist doing so, but the occasional reference may benefit from readers knowing its place of origin), use the first-listed city on the title page or, if no city is listed there, refer to the copyright page and cite the city where the publisher's main editorial offices are located. City names are followed by a colon.

Joyce, James. *Ulysses*. Paris: Shakespeare and Company, 1922.

If the city of publication may be unknown to readers or may be confused with another city of the same name, add the abbreviation of the state, province, or (if relevant) country (e.g., Ithaca, NY). City names in languages other than English can usually be recorded as they appear in the source; for contemporary publications, however, a commonly used English name may be used instead (e.g., Mexico City for Ciudad de México or Rome for Roma).

14.31 **Place and date only, for books published before 1900.** For books published before 1900, the city of publication is typically of greater interest than the name of the publisher (often a long-defunct printer); it is therefore usually preferable to omit publishers' names and instead include only a place and date of publication. A comma follows the place. See also 14.30.

1. Oliver Goldsmith, *The Vicar of Wakefield* (Salisbury, 1766).

Cervantes Saavedra, Miguel de. *El ingenioso hidalgo Don Quixote de la Mancha.* 2 vols. Madrid, 1605–15.

If for any reason the publisher is included, retain the city of publication, followed by a colon.

Austen, Jane [as "A Lady"]. *Sense and Sensibility*. London: T. Egerton, 1811.

## PUBLISHER'S NAME

14.32 **Preferred form of publisher's name.** The publisher's name may be given either in full (e.g., as printed on the title page of the book) or in a somewhat abbreviated form. The shorter forms are preferred in most bibliographies (see 14.33). The form should, however, reflect the publisher's name at the date of publication, not the current name if the name has changed. Most publishers' names at the time of publication can be double-checked through any number of reputable sources, including the catalogs of the Library of Congress and WorldCat in addition to those of university and other large library systems. For reprint and other editions, see 14.15–17.

14.33 **Abbreviations and omissible parts of a publisher's name.** In notes and bibliography entries, an initial *The* is omitted from a publisher's name, as are such abbreviations as *Inc., Ltd.,* or *S.A.* following a name. *Co., & Co., Publishing Co.,* and the like are also omitted, even if *Company* is spelled out. (An exception may be made for Shakespeare and Company, the famous bookstore that published books by James Joyce and others.) Such corporate features of a publisher's name—often subject to many changes over the years—are far less important in leading a reader to the source consulted than the publication date, and attempting to include them will invariably lead to inconsistencies. A given name or initials preceding a family name, however, may be retained, as may terms such as *Sons*, *Brothers*, and so forth. *Books* is usually retained (Basic Books, Riverhead Books). The word *Press* can sometimes be omitted (for example, Pergamon Press and Ecco Press can be abbreviated to Pergamon and Ecco, but Free Press and New Press—whose names might be confusing without *Press*—must be given in full). *Press* should not be omitted from the name of a university press because the university itself may issue publications independent of its press. The word *University* may be abbreviated to *Univ.* if done consistently.

Houghton Mifflin *not* Houghton Mifflin Co.
Little, Brown *not* Little, Brown & Co.
Macmillan *not* Macmillan Publishing Co.
W. W. Norton *not* W. W. Norton & Company

Note that there is no comma in Houghton Mifflin, but there is one in Little, Brown. Likewise, Harcourt, Brace has a comma, but Harcourt Brace Jovanovich does not. If in doubt, consult one of the sources mentioned in 14.32.

14.34 **"And" or ampersand in publisher's name.** An *and* or *&* in a publisher's name should usually be recorded as it is rendered on the title page. If, however, a publisher's name appears with an *and* in some sources but an *&* in others, it is permissible to make the name consistent throughout a bibliography and anywhere else the publisher's name is mentioned. If the publisher's name is not in English, the equivalent of *and* must be used unless an ampersand is used instead.

Duncker und Humblot *or* Duncker & Humblot
Harper and Row *or* Harper & Row

In publisher names that form a series, the serial comma is usually omitted before an ampersand but not before *and* (see also 6.21). An exception may be made for Farrar, Straus and Giroux, which is generally so written (i.e., with an *and* but not with a serial comma).

14.35 **Non-English publishers' names.** No part of a publisher's name in a language other than English should be translated. (This recommendation applies even if a city name—no longer required for most sources—has been included in its English form; see 14.30.)

Fondo de Cultura Económica, 2019
Aufbau-Verlag, 2022
Presses Universitaires de France, 2024

Note that abbreviations corresponding to *Inc.* or *Ltd.* (German *GmbH*, for example) are omitted (see 14.33). Capitalization of a publisher's name should follow the source unless the name appears in full capitals there; in that case, it should be capitalized in title case. If in doubt about the correct capitalization, consult one of the sources mentioned in 14.32.

14.36 **Self-published or privately published books.** Books published independently by the author, like traditionally published books, should be cited according to information on the title page or copyright page or otherwise known. Unless the book has been published under a publisher or imprint name (in which case it can be cited like other books), "published by the author" can stand in for the publisher's name. (Because "author" is more logical than "self" in this context, Chicago now prefers this phrase in source citations over the term "self-published.") The name of any self-publishing platform or distributor such as Amazon is usually omitted, as is any listed place of publication (see also 14.30). For ebooks, name the format consulted (see also 14.58).

1. Jamie McGuire, *Sins of the Immortal: A Novella*, Providence Series 5 (pub. by author, 2021), Kindle.

Hammel, Sara. *The Strong Ones: How a Band of Civilian Women Made Their Mark on the Army*. Published by the author, 2021.

For books published by the author before 1900, like other such books, it is usually preferable to list a place of publication in lieu of other publication details (see also 14.31); however, such wording as "printed by the author" may be added to the end of the reference if desired.

Whitman, Walt. *Leaves of Grass*. Brooklyn, 1855. Printed by the author.

14.37 **Parent companies, imprints, and such.** When a parent company's name appears on the title page in addition to the publisher's name or imprint, it is usually sufficient to cite the imprint (but see 14.38). For example, a 2021 edition of *The Interpreters*, a novel by Wole Soyinka that was first published by British publisher André Deutsch in 1965, bears the following information at the bottom of the title page:

VINTAGE INTERNATIONAL
*Vintage Books*
*A Division of Penguin Random House LLC*
*New York*

The first-listed name is often the imprint, as it is here (Vintage International). The copyright page begins with the line "First Vintage International edition, 2021," which helps to confirm this. The work can therefore be cited as follows:

Soyinka, Wole. *The Interpreters*. Vintage International, 2021.

If it is not clear which name is the imprint, consult one of the sources mentioned in 14.32; if it is still not clear, cite the first-listed name.

**14.38** **Special academic imprints and joint imprints.** Some academic publishers issue certain books through a special publishing division or under a special imprint or as part of a publishing consortium (or joint imprint). Because the name of a university carries extra weight in assessing a source, it is usually best to include both names in the citation (cf. 14.37). Either specify the imprint or follow the wording on the title page. If the arrangement is not clear from the title page or copyright page, consult one of the resources mentioned in 14.32; if still in doubt, cite under the name of the university or comparable academic institution.

Early, Mary Frances. *The Quiet Trailblazer: My Journey as the First Black Graduate of the University of Georgia*. Mary Frances Early College of Education and the University of Georgia Libraries, 2021.

Gates, Henry Louis, Jr., and Andrew S. Curran, eds. *Who's Black and Why? A Hidden Chapter from the Eighteenth-Century Invention of Race*. Belknap Press of Harvard University Press, 2022.

Sanders, David. *Bread of the Moment: Poems*. Swallow Press / Ohio University Press, 2021.

**14.39** **Copublication.** When books are published simultaneously (or almost so) by two publishers, usually in different countries, only one publisher need be listed—the one that is more relevant to the users of the citation. For example, if a book copublished by a British and an American publisher is listed in the bibliography of an American publication, only the American publication details need be given. If both publishers are listed on the title page, however, both may be included, separated by a semicolon. (Occasionally, the dates of publication will be different; in such cases, record both.) For reprints, see 14.16.

Ikehara-Tsukayama, Hugo C., and Juan Carlos Vargas Ruiz, eds. *Global Perspectives on Landscapes of Warfare*. University Press of Colorado; Editorial de la Universidad del Magdalena, 2022.

Some copublications occur between a publisher and another institution such as a library or a museum. These can usually be handled in the same way. For exhibition catalogs, see 14.134.

14.40 **Distributed books.** For a book published by one company and distributed by another, the name on the title page should be used. Since distribution agreements are sometimes impermanent, the distributor's name is best omitted unless it appears together with the publisher's name on the title page, as it does in the Henry Adams book cited below. (In a note, such information can usually be omitted.)

Adams, Henry. *The Education of Henry Adams: A Centennial Version*. Edited by Edward Chalfant and Conrad Edick Wright. Massachusetts Historical Society, 2007. Distributed by the University of Virginia Press.

Wording on the title page such as "Published by arrangement with . . . ," if it is of particular interest, may be included in a similar manner. For books distributed by a retail self-publishing platform, see 14.36.

## DATE OF PUBLICATION

14.41 **Publication date — general.** For books, only the year, not the month or day, is included in the publication date. The date is found on the title page or, more commonly, on the copyright page. It is usually the same as the copyright date. If two or more copyright dates appear in a book, the first being those of earlier editions or versions, the most recent indicates the publication date. Chicago's books normally carry both copyright date and publication date on the copyright page. For any edition other than the first, both the edition and the date of that edition must be included in a listing (see 14.15–17).

1. *The Chicago Manual of Style*, 18th ed. (University of Chicago Press, 2024), 6.60; cf. 17th ed. (2017), 6.56.

Turabian, Kate L. *A Manual for Writers of Research Papers, Theses, and Dissertations*. 9th ed. Revised by Wayne C. Booth, Gregory G. Colomb, Joseph M. Williams, Joseph Bizup, William T. FitzGerald, and the University of Chicago Press Editorial Staff. University of Chicago Press, 2018.

14.42 **New impressions and renewal of copyright.** The publication date must not be confused with the date of a subsequent printing or a renewal of copyright. Such statements on the copyright page as "53rd impression" or "Copyright renewed 1980" should be disregarded. For new editions as opposed to new impressions, see 1.28; for reprints, see 14.16.

14.43 **Multivolume works published over more than one year.** When an entire multivolume, multiyear work is cited, the range of dates is given (see 6.83). If the work has not yet been completed, the date of the first volume is followed by an en dash, with no space between the en dash and the punctuation that follows (see also 6.84). See also 9.66. If a single volume is cited, only the date of that volume need appear. See also 14.18–24.

1. *The Collected Works of F. A. Hayek*, ed. Bruce Caldwell, vol. 19, *Law, Legislation, and Liberty: A New Statement of the Liberal Principles of Justice and Political Economy*, ed. Jeremy Shearmur (University of Chicago Press, 2021).

Hayek, F. A. *Law, Legislation, and Liberty: A New Statement of the Liberal Principles of Justice and Political Economy*. Edited by Jeremy Shearmur. Vol. 19 of *The Collected Works of F. A. Hayek*, edited by Bruce Caldwell. University of Chicago Press, 1988–.

Tillich, Paul. *Systematic Theology*. 3 vols. University of Chicago Press, 1951–63.

**Author-date.** When a multivolume, multiyear work is included as an entry in the reference list (as in the Tillich example below), the range of dates follows the author's name. The corresponding text citation should include a volume number with any references to specific page numbers or to cite a specific volume (see also 13.117).

Tillich, Paul. 1951–63. *Systematic Theology*. 3 vols. University of Chicago Press.

(Tillich 1951–63, 1:133)
(Tillich 1951–63, vol. 2)

14.44 **No date of publication.** When the publication date of a printed work cannot be ascertained, the abbreviation *n.d.* takes the place of the year in the publication details. A guessed-at date may either be substituted (in brackets) or added.

Boston, n.d.
Edinburgh, [1750?] *or* Edinburgh, n.d., ca. 1750

A work for which no publisher, place (as for works published before 1900; see 14.31), or date can be determined or reasonably guessed at should be included in a bibliography only if accompanied by the location where a copy can be found (e.g., "Two copies in the Special Collections Department of the University of Chicago Library").

**Author-date.** Though it follows a period in the reference list, *n.d.* remains lowercase to avoid conflation with the author's name; in text citations, it is preceded by a comma. A guessed-at date in brackets remains in brackets in a text citation. See also 13.114, 14.104.

Smith, John. [1750?]. *Title of First Work . . .*
Smith, John. n.d. *Title of Second Work . . .*

(Smith [1750?])
(Smith, n.d.)

14.45 **Forthcoming publications.** When a book is under contract with a publisher and is already titled, but the date of publication is not yet known, *forthcoming* is used in place of the date. Although *in press* is sometimes used (strictly speaking for a printed work that has already been typeset and paginated), Chicago recommends the more inclusive term, which can also be used for any nonprint media or work under contract. If page numbers are available, they may be given. Books not under contract are treated as unpublished manuscripts (see 14.113–18).

1. Jane Q. Author, *Book Title* (Publisher, forthcoming).
2. John J. Writer, *Another Book Title* (Publisher, forthcoming), 345–46.

Contributor, Anna. "Contribution." In *Edited Volume*, edited by Ellen Editor. Publisher, forthcoming.

When a publication that cites a forthcoming title is reprinted, the citation need not be updated. For a revised edition, on the other hand, the citation can be updated to provide the final facts of publication, but only after direct quotations and other details have been checked for accuracy against the published source.

**Author-date.** Like *n.d.* (see 14.44), *forthcoming* can stand in place of the date in author-date references. The word is capitalized in a reference list but not in a text citation, where it is preceded by a comma. See also 13.114.

Faraday, Carry. Forthcoming. "Protean Photography." In *Seven Trips Beyond the Asteroid Belt*, edited by James Oring. Launch Press.

(Faraday, forthcoming)

## *Page, Volume, and Other Locating Information*

**14.46** **Arabic versus Roman numerals.** As the examples throughout this chapter suggest, Arabic numerals should be used wherever possible in source citations—for volumes, chapters, and other divisions—regardless of the way the numerals appear in the works cited, with the notable exception of pages numbered with Roman numerals in the original (usually lowercased, in the front matter of a book). Occasional exceptions are made, for example, in certain legal contexts (see 14.181).

1. See the article "Feathers," in *Johnson's Universal Cyclopaedia*, rev. ed. (New York, 1886), vol. 3.

2. Rainn Wilson, foreword to *Moving Foreword: Real Introductions to Totally Made-Up Books*, ed. Jon Chattman (BenBella, 2019), xvi–xvii.

Any number in a title of a work should generally be left as is (see also 13.90).

**14.47** **Citing a range of page numbers or other specific locators.** For Chicago's preferred style in expressing a range of consecutive pages, paragraphs, or similar numbered divisions, see 9.63. First and last numbers should be used rather than first number plus *ff.* (but see 14.48).

1. *The Chicago Manual of Style*, 18th ed. (University of Chicago Press, 2024), 14.46–57.

2. Sabine Hossenfelder, *Existential Physics: A Scientist's Guide to Life's Biggest Questions* (Viking, 2022), 170–71.

See the rest of this chapter for many more examples in context. References to nonconsecutive pages or other locations in the same work are separated by commas.

3. Hossenfelder, *Existential Physics*, 172, 174.

**Author-date.** Author-date text citations follow the same pattern. The reference list entry is provided in the example below for context. See also 13.117.

Hossenfelder, Sabine. 2022. *Existential Physics: A Scientist's Guide to Life's Biggest Questions*. Viking.

(Hossenfelder 2022, 170–71)
(Hossenfelder 2022, 172, 174)

14.48 **Page references with "ff." and "passim."** Only when referring to a section for which no final number can usefully be given should *ff.* ("and the following pages, paragraphs, etc.") be resorted to. Instead of the singular *f.*, the subsequent number should be used (e.g., "140–41" *not* "140f."). Similarly, *passim* ("here and there") is to be discouraged unless it follows a stated range of pages within which there are more than three or four precise references ("324–32 passim"). When used, *ff.* has no space between it and the preceding number and is followed by a period (e.g., "220ff."); *passim*, being a complete word, takes no period. Neither is italicized. (For *passim* in indexes, see 15.12.)

14.49 **Abbreviations for "page," "volume," and so on.** In source citations, the words *page*, *volume*, and the like are usually abbreviated and often simply omitted (see 14.50). The most commonly used abbreviations are *p.* (pl. *pp.*), *vol.*, *pt.*, *chap.*, *bk.*, *sec.*, *n.* (pl. *nn.*), *no.*, *app.*, and *fig.*; for these and others, see chapter 10, especially 10.48. Unless following a period, all are lowercased, and none is italicized (except in the rare case where it forms part of an italicized book title). All the abbreviations mentioned in this paragraph, except for *p.* and *n.*, form their plurals by adding *s*.

*A Passage to India*, chap. 2
*A Dance to the Music of Time*, 4 vols.

14.50 **When to omit "p." and "pp."** When a number or a range of numbers clearly denotes the pages in a book, *p.* or *pp.* may be omitted; the numbers alone, preceded by a comma, are sufficient. Where the presence of other numerals threatens ambiguity, *p.* or *pp.* may be added for clarity. (And if an author has used *p.* and *pp.* consistently throughout a work, there is no need to delete them.) See also 14.51, 14.55.

*Charlotte's Web*, 75–76
*but*
*Complete Poems of Michelangelo*, p. 89, lines 135–36

14.51 **When to omit "vol."** When a volume number is followed immediately by a page number, neither *vol.* nor *p.* or *pp.* is needed. The numbers alone are used, separated by a colon but no space. A comma usually precedes the volume number, except with periodicals (see 14.70) and certain types of classical references (see 14.142–52). For more on volume numbers, see 14.18–24. For citing a particular volume, with and without the abbreviation *vol.*, see 14.20.

*The Complete Tales of Henry James*, 10:122

**14.52** **Page and chapter numbers.** Page numbers, needed for specific references in notes and parenthetical text citations, are usually unnecessary in bibliographies (and no longer required for chapters; see 14.8). If the chapter or other section number is given in a note, page numbers may be omitted. The total page count of a book is not included in source citations. (Total page counts do, however, appear in headings to book reviews, catalog entries, and the like. For book review headings, see 1.107.)

1. Heather McGhee, "Ignoring the Canary," in *The Sum of Us: What Racism Costs Everyone and How We Can Prosper Together* (One World, 2022), 75.
2. Annette Gordon-Reed, *On Juneteenth* (Liveright, 2021), chap. 4.

**Author-date.** Page numbers are usually omitted from author-date reference lists (as from bibliographies). When a specific reference is needed in the text, a page or chapter number is preceded by a comma. See 13.117 for more examples.

(McGhee 2022, 75)
(Gordon-Reed 2021, chap. 4)

**14.53** **Signed signatures.** Some books printed before 1800 did not carry page numbers, but each signature (a group of consecutive pages) bore a letter, numeral, or other symbol (its "signature") to help the binder gather them in correct sequence. In citing pages in books of this kind, the signature symbol is given first, then the number of the leaf within the signature, and finally *r* (*recto*, the front of the leaf) or *v* (*verso*, the back of the leaf). Thus, for example, G6v identifies one page, G6r–7v a range of four pages.

**14.54** **Numbered leaves, or folios.** Some early books had leaf numbers rather than page numbers. Such leaves were typically numbered only on the front, or recto, side. A page citation therefore consists of the number on the leaf plus *r* (recto) or *v* (verso)—for example, 176r, 231v, or 232r–v. Such leaves are sometimes referred to as folios, a term that may be abbreviated in citations (e.g., fol. 176r [the front of a leaf], fol. 176r–v [the front and back of a leaf], fols. 176r–177v [the front and back of two consecutive leaves]). For books or parts of books with no discernible numbers, pages can sometimes be counted and the result placed in square brackets. See also 14.53, 14.123.

**14.55** **Line numbers.** The abbreviations *l.* (line) and *ll.* (lines) can too easily be confused with the numerals 1 and 11 and so should be avoided. *Line* or *lines* should be used or, where it has been made clear that reference is to lines, simply omitted (see 12.78).

1. Ogden Nash, "Song for Ditherers," lines 1–4.

14.56 **Citing numbered notes.** Notes are cited with the abbreviation *n* or *nn*. The usage recommended here is also used for indexes (see 15.34, 15.35, 15.36). If the note cited is the only footnote on a particular page or is an unnumbered footnote, the page number is followed by *n* alone.

1. Anthony Grafton, *The Footnote: A Curious History* (Harvard University Press, 1997), 72n, 80n.

If there are other notes on the same page as the note cited, a number must be added. In this case the page number is followed by *n* or (if two or more consecutive notes are cited) *nn*, followed by the note number (or numbers or, in rare cases, an asterisk or other symbol). No intervening space or punctuation is required.

2. Dwight Bolinger, *Language: The Loaded Weapon* (Longman, 1980), 192n23, 192n30, 199n14, 201nn16–17.
3. Richard Rorty, *Philosophical Papers* (Cambridge University Press, 1991), 1:15n29.

A note that spans two pages takes the form "10–11n5" (for note number five on pages 10 and 11). To avoid confusion when citing a note on a page with Roman numerals (as in the front matter of a book), add a space between the page number and *n* (e.g., "vii n3").

14.57 **Citing illustrations and tables.** The abbreviation *fig.* may be used for *figure*, but *table*, *map*, *plate*, and other illustration forms are spelled out. The page number, if given, precedes the illustration number, with a comma between them.

1. Rasmus Grønfeldt Winther, *When Maps Become the World* (University of Chicago Press, 2020), 76, table 3.1.
2. Winther, *Maps*, 228, fig. 8.3.

To cite art in collections and other stand-alone works, see 14.133–35.

## *Electronic Books*

14.58 **Downloadable ebook formats and audiobooks.** Many books are published both in print and as a downloadable file in one or more ebook formats. Ebook formats include EPUB, a standard that features reflowable text (though fixed layouts are also supported), and PDF, a standard for fixed-layout books. Because fixed-layout ebooks generally match any printed counterpart, including pagination, these do not need to be mentioned in a citation (but see 14.60). Reflowable formats, however, should be noted, as the potential for differences relative to print is greater. These include Apple Books and Amazon Kindle, proprietary formats based on EPUB. The following examples show how to list different versions of the same book in a bibliography, starting with the print version and followed by versions acquired from a variety of different sources, from Apple to Google, for use with their branded applications or devices.

Obama, Michelle. *Becoming*. Crown, 2018.
Obama, Michelle. *Becoming*. Crown, 2018. Apple Books.
Obama, Michelle. *Becoming*. Crown, 2018. Kindle.
Obama, Michelle. *Becoming*. Crown, 2018. Google Play Books.

In some cases, a book will be offered as either EPUB or PDF rather than in a proprietary application like one of the ones listed above. If EPUB, add that to the end of the citation.

Bashford, Alison. *The Huxleys: An Intimate History of Evolution*. University of Chicago Press, 2022. EPUB.

In a note, the format would follow any indication of a page or chapter number or other location (see also 14.59).

1. Alison Bashford, *The Huxleys: An Intimate History of Evolution* (University of Chicago Press, 2022), chap. 7, EPUB.

To cite an audiobook, include the name of the narrator(s). If a specific location is needed, a time stamp may be added to the note; in the bibliography, include the duration of the book.

1. Matt Cain, *The Secret Life of Albert Entwistle*, narrated by Simon Vance (Recorded Books, 2022), at 3 hr., 14 min.

Obama, Michelle. *Becoming*. Narrated by the author. Random House Audio, 2018. 19 hr., 4 min.

Many ebooks consist of a reissue of an earlier printed edition published before an ebook format was available (see also 1.25). Where that is the case, cite the book according to the original publication data (typically included in the title page and copyright information for the ebook), followed by information about the ebook. According to the copyright page, the Roy book cited below was originally published by Random House in 1997 and reprinted in paperback with a reading group guide by Random House Trade Paperbacks in 2008. The Kindle version features the 1997 title page but includes the 2008 copyright date and features the additional content of the paperback. These additional details can be omitted in most citations but are shown here as an option. See also 14.16.

Roy, Arundhati. *The God of Small Things*. Random House, 1997; repr., Random House Trade Paperbacks, 2008. Kindle.

*or, more simply,*

Roy, Arundhati. *The God of Small Things*. Random House, 2008. Kindle.

For self-published books, see 14.36.

14.59 **Page numbers in ebooks.** Many ebook formats feature reflowable text without fixed page numbers. Depending on the application and on the book itself, information about location within the book may vary according to user-defined text size, making any reference to such information unhelpful to others wishing to consult the same place in the text. Even when a book provides fixed location numbers, these may be helpful only to those who consult the same ebook format. It is therefore often best to cite a chapter number or a section heading or other such milepost in lieu of a number. (But if paragraphs are numbered, as in this manual, those can be cited.)

1. Michele Obama, *Becoming* (Crown, 2018), chap. 15, Apple Books.
2. Obama, *Becoming*, chap. 16.

Some ebooks feature page number data corresponding to a printed edition of the same work. Where this is the case, page numbers may be cited in the usual way. Bear in mind, however, that unless page breaks corresponding to the print edition are displayed in some way, such references may be off by a page. (If possible, check page numbers against the printed version.)

3. Ellen Jovin, *Rebel with a Clause: Tales and Tips from a Roving Grammarian* (Mariner Books, 2022), 195, Kindle.

14.60 **Books consulted online.** For a book consulted online through a website, add a URL to the end of the citation (but see below). If a DOI is available, use that as the basis of the URL (see also 13.6, 13.7). For freely available older books online, see 14.61.

1. Samhita Sunya, *Sirens of Modernity: World Cinema via Bombay* (University of California Press, 2022), 166–67, https://doi.org/10.1525/luminos.130.
3. Sunya, *Sirens of Modernity*, 201.

Sunya, Samhita. *Sirens of Modernity: World Cinema via Bombay*. University of California Press, 2022. https://doi.org/10.1525/luminos.130.

A suitable URL may not be available for books consulted via a commercial library database. Even suggested links listed with the source may work only for subscribers or those with access to a particular library. In such cases, an acceptable alternative is to list the name of the commercial database rather than the URL. Note, however, that this information is optional for books like the one in the example below (as is a URL); though it may be helpful to know that it was consulted via EBSCOhost, the book (like most formally published works) is easily located through Google and other channels from the author and title data alone.

Ferreras, Isabelle, Julie Battilana, and Dominique Méda, eds. *Democratize Work: The Case for Reorganizing the Economy*. Translated by Miranda Richmond Mouillot. University of Chicago Press, 2022. EBSCOhost.

14.61 **Freely available electronic editions of older works.** Books that have fallen out of copyright are often freely available online (see also 4.20–34). When possible, prefer scanned pages to reflowable text for the purposes of source citation. In the James examples below, the Project Gutenberg text is based on the 1909 New York edition of *The Ambassadors*—and is available in a number of reflowable formats, including HTML and EPUB. But the scanned pages from the Internet Archive of an actual copy of the 1909 edition (published in two volumes) are preferable. Not only is the scanned version more authoritative (in part because the original title and copyright pages are included), but it also facilitates citations to fixed page numbers (see 14.59; see also 14.20).

1. Henry James, *The Ambassadors* (1909; Project Gutenberg, 2022), bk. 6, chap. 1, https://www.gutenberg.org/ebooks/432.

*or, better,*

2. Henry James, *The Ambassadors*, 2 vols. (Charles Scribner's Sons, 1909), 1:243, https://archive.org/details/ambassadors01jameiala.

The Melville examples below further demonstrate the importance of finding and citing the publication details for the original source. The citations are for the same passage of text (see 13.27)—first, as it appears in a scanned copy of the first American edition, and next, as it appears in a similarly prepared copy of the first British edition (published in three volumes under a different title). The URL gives interested readers a chance to consult the same resources, but the citation does not depend on it (because the originals have been sufficiently identified). See also 14.31.

3. Herman Melville, *Moby-Dick; or, The Whale* (New York, 1851), 627, https://melville.electroniclibrary.org/moby-dick-side-by-side.

4. Herman Melville, *The Whale*, 3 vols. (London, 1851), 3:302, https://melville.electroniclibrary.org/moby-dick-side-by-side.

A bibliography entry would not include page references.

Melville, Herman. *Moby-Dick; or, The Whale*. New York, 1851. https://melville.electroniclibrary.org/moby-dick-side-by-side.

See also 13.9, 14.16.

14.62 **Books on CD-ROM and other fixed media.** To cite a book on CD-ROM or other fixed media, indicate the medium after the full facts of publication, including any page or other locator information in a note. For audiobooks, use the form shown in 14.58, adding the medium to the end of the citation.

1. *The Chicago Manual of Style*, 15th ed. (University of Chicago Press, 2003), 1.4, CD-ROM.

Hicks, Rodney J. *Nuclear Medicine: From the Center of Our Universe*. ICE T Multimedia, 1996. CD-ROM.

## PERIODICALS

14.63 **"Periodicals" defined.** In this manual, *periodical* refers to scholarly and professional journals, popular magazines, and newspapers. Periodicals are frequently consulted online, and many of the examples in this section show a URL in addition to the information that would be required whether the content is consulted in print or online. For examples and additional considerations, consult the sections for specific types of periodicals. See also 13.6–12.

14.64 **Information to be included.** Citations of periodicals require some or all of the following data:

1. Full name(s) of author(s)
2. Title and subtitle of article or column
3. Title of periodical
4. Issue information (volume, issue number, date)
5. Page reference (where appropriate)
6. For periodicals consulted online, a URL or, in some cases, the name of the database used to consult the resource (see 13.6–12)

Indispensable for newspapers and most magazines is the specific date (month, day, and year). For journals, the volume, issue number, and year are usually cited.

14.65 **Journals versus magazines.** A *journal* is a scholarly or professional periodical available mainly by subscription (e.g., *The Library Quarterly*, *The New England Journal of Medicine*). Journals are normally cited by volume and date (see 14.70). A *magazine* is a weekly or monthly (or sometimes daily) periodical—professionally produced, sometimes specialized, but more accessible to general readers—that is available in individual issues at libraries, bookstores, or newsstands or offered online, with or without a subscription (e.g., *Scientific American*, *The New Yorker*). Magazines are normally cited by date alone (see 14.20). If in doubt whether a particular periodical is better treated as a journal or as a magazine, use journal form if the volume number is easily located, magazine form if it is not. These definitions, developed decades ago when printed editions were the norm, still generally apply.

14.66 **Basic structure of a periodical citation.** In notes, commas appear between author; title of article (in quotation marks); title of magazine, newspaper, or journal (in italics); and, for sources consulted online, URL or database name. In bibliographies, periods replace these commas. Note that *in* is *not* used between the article title and the periodical title. (*In* is used only with chapters or other parts of books; see 14.8, 14.9.) Punctuation relative to any volume and issue number and for dates and page numbers depends on periodical type. In bibliography entries, the first and last pages of a journal article are given (for inclusive numbers, see 9.63). In notes and text citations, only specific pages need be cited. In some electronic formats, page numbers will be unavailable (see 13.20). For examples, see 14.67–86 (journals), 14.87–88 (magazines), and 14.89–98 (newspapers).

## *Journals*

14.67 **Journal article — author's name.** Authors' names are normally given as they appear at the heads of their articles. Adjustments can be made, however, as indicated in 13.75. For the treatment of two or more authors, see 13.78. For additional considerations related to names of authors, see 13.74–86.

14.68 **Journal article — title.** Titles of articles are set in roman (except for individual words or phrases that require italics, such as species names or book titles; see 13.97); they are usually capitalized in title case and put in quotation marks. As with a book, title and subtitle are separated by a colon. For shortened forms of article titles (as in subsequent citations in a note), see 14.84. For additional considerations related to titles of works, see 13.87–101.

14.69 **Title of journal.** Titles of journals are italicized and capitalized in title case. They are usually given in full. An initial *The*, which this manual now recommends retaining in running text when it is part of the journal's name (see 8.172), may be omitted in source citations as a matter of editorial expediency (as in the examples in this chapter). Non-English titles always retain an initial article belonging to the name (e.g., *Der Spiegel*). See also 8.172. Occasionally an initialism, such as *PMLA*, is the official title and is never spelled out. In some disciplines, especially in science and medicine, journal titles are routinely abbreviated (e.g., *Plant Syst Evol*), unless they consist of only one word (e.g., *Science*, *Mind*). Chicago recommends giving titles in full unless a particular publisher or discipline requires otherwise.

14.70 **Journal volume, issue, and date.** Most journal citations include volume number, issue number, and year. The volume number, set in roman, follows the title without intervening punctuation. Arabic numerals are used even if the journal itself uses Roman numerals. The issue number follows the volume number, separated by a comma and preceded by *no.* The issue number should be recorded even if pagination is continuous across issues in each volume. The year appears in parentheses after the volume and issue data. A month or season need not be included in addition to the year for journals that include both a volume and an issue number.

1. Stefan Riedener and Philipp Schwind, "The Point of Promises," *Ethics* 132, no. 3 (2022): 625, https://doi.org/10.1086/718080.
2. Riedener and Schwind, "Promises," 630–31.

Riedener, Stefan, and Philipp Schwind. "The Point of Promises." *Ethics* 132, no. 3 (2022): 621–43. https://doi.org/10.1086/718080.

Where more than one issue number is included, follow the usage in the journal itself, using either plural *nos.* or singular *no.* (always lowercase) and separating the digits by a slash or an en dash (see 6.83).

3. Lina Perkins Wilder, "'My Exion Is Entered': Anatomy, Costume, and Theatrical Knowledge in *2 Henry IV*," *Renaissance Drama* 41, nos. 1–2 (2013): 60, https://doi.org/10.1086/673907.

When a journal is published in numbered issues with no volume number, a comma follows the journal title. In such cases, it can be helpful to include a month or a season in addition to the year. Note that seasons, lowercased in running text, are capitalized in source citations.

4. J. M. Beattie, "The Pattern of Crime in England, 1660–1800," *Past and Present*, no. 62 (February 1974): 52, https://www.jstor.org/stable/650463.

Li, Jie. "The Hot Noise of Open-Air Cinema." *Grey Room*, no. 81 (Fall 2020): 6–35. https://doi.org/10.1162/grey_a_00307.

The month or season can also be helpful when citing an article in a journal published in numbered volumes with no issue numbers.

5. Tan Zhao, "Professionalizing China's Rural Cadres," *China Journal* 89 (January 2023): 48, https://doi.org/10.1086/722215.

When neither a volume nor an issue number is available, treat the resource like a magazine (see 14.87).

**Author-date.** Because the year of publication follows the author's name in author-date reference lists, the issue number usually appears in parentheses.

Riedener, Stefan, and Philipp Schwind. 2022. "The Point of Promises." *Ethics* 132 (3): 621–43. https://doi.org/10.1086/718080.

If the journal is published in numbered issues with no volume number, a comma precedes the issue number, and a month or season, if the source includes one, is included in parentheses.

Beattie, J. M. 1974. "The Pattern of Crime in England, 1660–1800." *Past and Present*, no. 62 (February): 47–95. https://www.jstor.org/stable/650463.
Li, Jie. 2020. "The Hot Noise of Open-Air Cinema." *Grey Room*, no. 81 (Fall): 6–35. https://doi.org/10.1162/grey_a_00307.

If no month or season is available, the issue number is followed by a comma rather than a colon.

. . . *Past and Present*, no. 62, 47–95. . . .

In the case of a numbered volume with no issue number, any month or season is listed in parentheses.

Zhao, Tan. 2023. "Professionalizing China's Rural Cadres." *China Journal* 89 (January): 45–69. https://doi.org/10.1086/722215.

If no month or season is available, the page number follows the colon with no intervening space.

. . . *China Journal* 89:45–69. . . .

14.71 **Journal page references.** In citing a particular passage in a journal article, only the page or pages concerned are given. In references to the article as a whole (as in a bibliography or reference list), first and last pages are given.

1. Esteban M. Aucejo et al., "Teachers and the Gender Gap in Reading Achievement," *Journal of Human Capital* 16, no. 3 (2022): 375–76, https://doi.org/10.1086/719731.
2. Aucejo et al., "Teachers," 380.

Aucejo, Esteban M., Jane Cooley Fruehwirth, Sean Kelly, and Zachary Mozenter. "Teachers and the Gender Gap in Reading Achievement." *Journal of Human Capital* 16, no. 3 (2022): 372–403. https://doi.org/10.1086/719731.

To facilitate online publication schedules, some journals have adopted a continuous publishing model in which each article is assigned a unique ID and is considered final the moment it is published online; any subsequent print version is reproduced without any changes. Articles that include a PDF version are all paginated starting at 1 and can be cited in the notes accordingly. In a note, cited page numbers precede the article ID (e0263069 in the example below). In a bibliography, do not include the page range for an article published in this way.

3. Amiel A. Dror et al., "Pre-Infection 25-Hydroxyvitamin D3 Levels and Association with Severity of COVID-19 Illness," *PLOS ONE* 17, no. 2 (2022): 4–5, e0263069.
4. Dror et al., "Pre-Infection," 7.

Dror, Amiel A., Nicole Morozov, Amani Daoud, et al. "Pre-Infection 25-Hydroxyvitamin D3 Levels and Association with Severity of COVID-19 Illness." *PLOS ONE* 17, no. 2 (2022): e0263069. https://doi.org/10.1371/journal.pone.0263069.

Most journals published online provide page numbers. Where this is not the case, another type of locator such as a subheading may become appropriate in a note. None, however, is required. See also 13.20.

5. Shelly Jamison, "I(nternet) Do(mains): The New Rules of Selection," *Culture Critique* 3, no. 5 (2009), under "Park Avenue Revisited."

14.72 **URLs for journal articles.** Authors should generally record a URL for sources consulted online, as shown in many of the examples in this section. A URL based on a DOI (appended to https://doi.org/), if it is available, is preferable to the URL that appears in a browser's address bar when viewing the article (or the abstract). In the absence of a DOI, choose the form of the URL offered along with the article, if any. (If an article was consulted in print, there is no need to include a URL.)

1. Frank P. Whitney, "The Six-Year High School in Cleveland," *School Review* 37, no. 4 (1929): 268, https://www.jstor.org/stable/1078814.

Sarkar, Debapriya. "The Utopian Hypothesis." *English Literary Renaissance* 52, no. 3 (2022): 371–84. https://doi.org/10.1086/721062.

Sometimes a URL for a source consulted in a subscription database (as through a library) will be very long or otherwise unsuitable. In such cases, it may be preferable to list the name of the database rather than a URL (see also 13.10).

Hebert, B. T. "The Island of Bolsö: A Study of Norwegian Life." *Sociological Review* 17, no. 4 (1925): 307–13. EBSCOhost.

*instead of*

Hebert, B. T. "The Island of Bolsö: A Study of Norwegian Life." *Sociological Review* 17, no. 4 (1925): 307–13. https://search.ebscohost.com/login.aspx?direct=true&db=edb&AN=13630952&site=eds-live&scope=site.

14.73 **Access dates for journal articles.** Access dates are not required by Chicago in citations of formally published electronic sources, for the reasons discussed in 13.15. Some publishers and some disciplines, however, may require them. When they are included, they should immediately precede the URL (or database information), separated from the surrounding citation by commas in a note and periods in a bibliography entry.

1. Heather M. Arterburn and Robert F. McMahon, "Population and Reproductive Dynamics of Zebra Mussels (*Dreissena polymorpha*) in Warm, Low-Latitude North American Waters," *Biological Bulletin* 242, no. 3 (2022): 211, accessed September 1, 2024, https://doi.org/10.1086/720151.

2. Arterburn and McMahon, "Zebra Mussels," 211–12.

Arterburn, Heather M., and Robert F. McMahon. "Population and Reproductive Dynamics of Zebra Mussels (*Dreissena polymorpha*) in Warm, Low-Latitude North American Waters." *Biological Bulletin* 242, no. 3 (2022): 207–21. Accessed September 1, 2024. https://doi.org/10.1086/720151.

14.74 **Article page numbers in relation to volume or issue numbers.** When page numbers immediately follow a volume number, separated only by a colon (as in a shortened citation; see 14.84), no space follows the colon. But when parenthetical information intervenes, a space follows the colon. (This rule applies to other types of volumes as well; see, e.g., 14.18.)

*Social Networks* 14:213–29
*Critical Inquiry* 1, no. 3 (1975): 479–96

When, as occasionally happens, the page number follows an issue number, a comma—not a colon—should be used (see also 14.70).

*Diogenes*, no. 25, 84–117

14.75 **Ahead-of-print and forthcoming articles.** Many journals publish articles online ahead of a print issue. (These ahead-of-print articles are not to be confused with preprints; see 14.76.) For such an article, use the posted publication date; include volume and issue information only if these are available (page numbers may also be unavailable). Copyeditors should check such a citation and update it with volume and issue information if it has become available before editing must be completed.

1. Ryan Mullan et al., "An Investigation into the Mechanism Mediating Counterillumination in Myctophid Fishes (Myctophidae)," *Biological Bulletin*, ahead of print, April 5, 2023, https://doi.org/10.1086/724803.
2. Mullan et al., "Investigation."

Mullan, Ryan, Alex D. Davis, Tracey T. Sutton, and Sönke Johnsen. "An Investigation into the Mechanism Mediating Counterillumination in Myctophid Fishes (Myctophidae)." *Biological Bulletin*, ahead of print, April 5, 2023. https://doi.org/10.1086/724803.

Some journals post articles that have been accepted for publication (and in some cases assigned a DOI) but not yet copyedited and otherwise prepared for publication. In this case, use *forthcoming* instead of *ahead of print* (and note the different placement of the date). (Note that some publishers refer to these articles as "preprints," but that term should be reserved in source citations for articles posted to a preprint server; see 14.76.) If the published version of such an article becomes available in time to update the citation, any related information in the text must be checked for accuracy.

1. Marc K. Chan et al., "The Effect of Job Search Requirements on Family Welfare Receipt," *Journal of Labor Economics*, accepted January 6, 2023, forthcoming, https://doi.org/10.1086/724157.

If an article has been accepted for publication but not yet made available, *forthcoming* stands in place of the year. (Note that any article not yet accepted should be treated as an unpublished manuscript; see 14.114.)

1. Margaret Smith, "Article Title," *Journal Title* 98 (forthcoming).

Smith, Margaret. "Article Title." *Journal Title* 98 (forthcoming).

**Author-date.** To cite an ahead-of-print article posted online in author-date style, move the year to follow the author's name in the reference list entry and cite as follows.

Mullan, Ryan, Alex D. Davis, Tracey T. Sutton, and Sönke Johnsen. 2023. "An Investigation into the Mechanism Mediating Counterillumination in Myctophid Fishes (Myctophidae)." *Biological Bulletin*, ahead of print, April 5. https://doi.org/10.1086/724803.

(Mullan et al. 2023)

To cite a forthcoming article in a reference list, place *forthcoming* after the name of the author (where it is capitalized); in the parenthetical text reference, it is preceded by a comma and lowercased.

Smith, Margaret. Forthcoming. "Article Title." *Journal Title* 98.

(Smith, forthcoming)

14.76 **Journal article preprints.** Preprints are cited much like published journal articles, except "preprint," followed by the name of the preprint server, takes the place of information about a journal issue. See also 1.122. Articles not posted to a preprint server are best treated as unpublished manuscripts (see 14.114).

1. Holt Bodish and Robert DeYeso III, "Obstructing Reducible Surgeries: Slice Genus and Thickness Bounds," preprint, arXiv, September 4, 2022, https://doi.org/10.48550/arXiv.2209.01672.

Fiallo, Kathy, and Alexia Galati. "The Influence of Auditory Processing Difficulties on Perceptual Learning." Preprint, PsyArXiv, September 4, 2022. https://doi.org/10.31234/osf.io/p723u.

14.77 **Journal special issues.** A journal issue devoted to a single theme is known as a special issue. It carries the normal volume and issue number. Such an issue may have an editor and a title of its own. An article within the issue is cited as in the first example below; a special issue as a whole may be cited as in the second example.

1. Arne Kaijser, "Driving on Wood: The Swedish Transition to Wood Gas During World War Two," in "Historicizing Renewables," ed. Ute Hasenöhrl and Patrick Kupper, special issue, *History and Technology* 37, no. 4 (2021): 471, https://doi.org/10.1080/07341512.2022.2033387.

Hasenöhrl, Ute, and Patrick Kupper, eds. "Historicizing Renewables." Special issue, *History and Technology* 37, no. 4 (2021).

14.78 **Journal supplements.** A journal supplement, unlike a special issue (see 14.77), is numbered separately from the regular issues of the journal. Like a special issue, however, it may have a title and editor of its own.

Yeh, Rihan. "*La Racha*: Speed and Violence in Tijuana." In "Qualia and Ontology: Language, Semiotics, and Materiality," ed. Lily Chumley. Supplement, *Signs and Society* 5, no. S1 (2017): S53–S76. https://doi.org/10.1086/690088.

The issue as a whole may be cited under the name of the supplement's editor.

Chumley, Lily, ed. "Qualia and Ontology: Language, Semiotics, and Materiality." Supplement, *Signs and Society* 5, no. S1 (2017).

14.79 **Articles published in installments.** Articles published in parts over two or more issues may be listed separately or in the same entry, depending on whether the part or the whole is cited.

1. George C. Brown, ed., "A Swedish Traveler in Early Wisconsin: The Observations of Fredrika Bremer," pt. 1, *Wisconsin Magazine of History* 61, no. 4 (1978): 312.

2. Brown, "Swedish Traveler," pt. 2, *Wisconsin Magazine of History* 62, no. 1 (1978): 50.

Brown, George C., ed. "A Swedish Traveler in Early Wisconsin: The Observations of Fredrika Bremer." Pts. 1 and 2. *Wisconsin Magazine of History* 61, no. 4 (1978): 300–318; 62, no. 1 (1978): 41–56.

14.80 **Article appearing in two publications.** Chapters in books have sometimes begun their lives as journal articles, or vice versa. Revisions are often made along the way. The version actually consulted should be cited in a note or text citation, but annotation such as the following, if of specific interest to readers, may follow the citation. See also 13.58.

Previously published as "Article Title," *Journal Title* 20, no. 3 (2023): 345–62.

A slightly revised version appears in *Book Title*, ed. E. Editor (Publisher, 2024).

14.81 **Place where journal is published.** If a journal might be confused with another with a similar title, or if it might not be known to the users of a bibliography, add the name of the place or institution where it is published in parentheses after the journal title. Note that the journal in the first example below is not divided into numbered issues.

1. Diane-Dinh Kim Luu, "Diethylstilbestrol and Media Coverage of the 'Morning After' Pill," *Lost in Thought: Undergraduate Research Journal* (Indiana University South Bend) 2 (1999): 65–70.

Garrett, Marvin P. "Language and Design in *Pippa Passes*." *Victorian Poetry* (West Virginia University) 13, no. 1 (1975): 47–60.

14.82 **Translated or edited article.** A translated or edited article follows essentially the same style as a translated or edited book (see 14.6).

1. Michael Houseman, "The Hierarchical Relation: A Particular Ideology or a General Model?," trans. Eléonore Rimbault, *HAU: Journal of Ethnographic Theory* 5, no. 1 (2015): 255, https://doi.org/10.14318/hau5.1.012.
2. Houseman, "Hierarchical Relation," 261–62.

Houseman, Michael. "The Hierarchical Relation: A Particular Ideology or a General Model?" Translated by Eléonore Rimbault. *HAU: Journal of Ethnographic Theory* 5, no. 1 (2015): 251–69. https://doi.org/10.14318/hau5.1.012.

14.83 **New series for journal volumes.** New series in journal volumes are identified by *n.s.* (new series), *2nd ser.*, and so forth, as they are for books (see 14.28).

1. "Letter of Jonathan Sewall," *Proceedings of the Massachusetts Historical Society*, 2nd ser., vol. 10 (January 1896): 414.

Kosambi, D. D. "Some Extant Versions of Bhartṛhari's Śatakas." *Journal of the Bombay Branch of the Royal Asiatic Society*, n.s., vol. 21 (1945): 17–32.

14.84 **Short titles for articles.** In subsequent references to journal articles, the author's last name and the main title of the article (often shortened) are most commonly used (as in many of the examples in this section). In the absence of a full bibliography, however, the journal title, volume number, and page number(s) may prove more helpful guides to the source.

1. Yubraj Acharya and Jiyoon Kim, "Targeting Using Differential Incentives: Evidence from a Field Experiment," *Economic Development and Cultural Change* 70, no. 2 (2022): 780, https://doi.org/10.1086/713883.
2. Acharya and Kim, "Targeting," 782.

*or*

3. Acharya and Kim, *Economic Development and Cultural Change* 70:782.

The page numbering for *Economic Development and Cultural Change* is continuous throughout a single volume. Where that is not the case, the short form should include the issue number (in parentheses) in addition to the volume number (i.e., "70 (2): 782").

14.85 **Abstracts.** Generally speaking, an abstract is not substantial enough to warrant a dedicated entry in a bibliography. Instead, mention the abstract in the text or include it in a note, in lieu of page numbers. In the bibliography, cite the article as a whole.

1. Talat Ahmad et al., "Tso Morari Eclogites, Eastern Ladakh: Isotopic and Elemental Constraints on Their Protolith, Genesis, and Tectonic Setting," *Journal of Geology* 130, no. 3 (2022): abstract.

Ahmad, Talat, Irfan Maqbool Bhat, Tsuyoshi Tanaka, et al. "Tso Morari Eclogites, Eastern Ladakh: Isotopic and Elemental Constraints on Their Protolith, Genesis, and Tectonic Setting." *Journal of Geology* 130, no. 3 (2022): 231–52. https://doi.org/10.1086/719333.

14.86 **Electronic supplements or enhancements to journal articles.** An online-only component of a journal article with a printed counterpart—including supplementary data or supporting information, sometimes also referred to as an enhancement—can often be cited in terms of the article (cf. 14.57). Include information about the component either in the text or in a note (in addition to the article citation). An independent dataset, on the other hand, should be cited as described in 14.157. For audiovisual materials, see 14.161–69.

In "Naraya No. 2," a Ghost Dance that was recorded in . . .[1]

1. Richard W. Stoffle et al., "Ghost Dancing the Grand Canyon: Southern Paiute Rock Art, Ceremony, and Cultural Landscapes," *Current Anthropology* 41, no. 1 (2000): MP3 audio file, https://doi.org/10.1086/300101.

2. Gaku Takimoto et al., "The Relationship Between Vector Species Richness and the Risk of Vector-Borne Infectious Diseases." *American Naturalist* 200, no. 3 (2022): appendix S4 (online only), https://doi.org/10.1086/720403.

## *Magazines*

14.87 **Basic citation format for magazine articles.** Many of the guidelines for citing journal articles apply to magazines also (and see 14.65). Titles of magazine articles, like the titles of journal articles, are capitalized in title case, set in roman, and placed in quotation marks (see 14.68). The title of the magazine itself is set in italics. An initial *The* that would be retained in running text (see 8.172) may be omitted in source citations as a matter of editorial expediency (as in example notes 1, 2, and 5 below). Weekly or monthly (or bimonthly) magazines, even if numbered by volume and issue, are usually cited by date only. While a specific page number may be cited in a note, the inclusive page numbers of an article may be omitted, since they are often widely separated by extraneous material. When page numbers are included, a comma rather than a colon separates them from the date of issue.

1. Susie Allen, "Eyes on the Story," *University of Chicago Magazine*, Summer 2022, 45.

2. Isaac Bashevis Singer, "A Pair," trans. Isaac Bashevis Singer and Blanche and Joseph Nevel, *New Yorker*, December 3, 1973, 48.

3. Mandy Walker, "Secrets to Stress-Free Flying," *Consumer Reports*, October 2016.

4. "Aviation," *Forbes*, July 1, 1928, 52.

To cite an article consulted online, authors should include the URL or, if no suitable URL is available, the name of the database (see also 14.72). Specific page numbers may not be available but may be cited if they are (see also 13.20).

5. Helen Lewis, "The Second Elizabethan Age Has Ended," *Atlantic*, September 8, 2022, https://www.theatlantic.com/ideas/archive/2022/09/queen-elizabeth-ii-death-british-royal-family-transition/671370/.

6. Merryle Stanley Rukeyser, "What We May Expect from Commercial Aviation," *Forbes*, July 1, 1927, 11, ArticlesPlus.

Like newspaper articles, magazine articles can often be cited in the text or in a note with no corresponding bibliography entry (see also 14.96). If included in a bibliography, they are listed under the name of the author; unsigned articles may be listed under the title of the publication.

Singer, Isaac Bashevis. "A Pair." Translated by Isaac Bashevis Singer and Blanche and Joseph Nevel. *New Yorker*, December 3, 1973.

*Forbes*. "Aviation." July 1, 1928.

**Author-date.** In an author-date reference list entry, the year of publication follows the author's name; the remainder of the date follows the title of the magazine.

Lewis, Helen. 2022. "The Second Elizabethan Age Has Ended." *Atlantic*, September 8. https://www.theatlantic.com/ideas/archive/2022/09/queen-elizabeth-ii-death-british-royal-family-transition/671370/.

(Lewis 2022)

An unsigned magazine article can usually be cited by the title of the magazine (see also 14.97).

*Forbes*. 1928. "Aviation." July 1.

(*Forbes* 1928)

14.88 **Magazine departments.** Titles of regular departments in a magazine are capitalized in title case but not put in quotation marks.

1. Rachel Levin, "The Adele of Audiobooks," Listen Up, *New Yorker*, August 1, 2022, https://www.newyorker.com/magazine/2022/08/01/the-adele-of-audiobooks.

2. Debra Klein, "Doing It All on Vacation," Focus on Travel, *Newsweek*, September 4, 2000.

Wallraff, Barbara. Word Fugitives. *Atlantic*, July/August 2008.

A department without a named author is best cited by the title of the magazine.

*Gourmet*. Kitchen Notebook. May 2000.

## *Newspapers and News Sites*

14.89 **Basic citation format for news articles.** The name of the author (if known) and the headline or column heading in a daily newspaper (or its online counterpart) are cited much like the corresponding elements in magazines (see 14.87–88). The month (often abbreviated), day, and year are the indispensable elements. A specific page number may be cited in a note but need not be. In a note or bibliographic entry, it may be useful to add "Final Edition," "Midwest Edition," or some such identifier (following the wording in the source). If the paper is published in several sections, the section number (e.g., sec. 1) or title (e.g., Opinion) may be given. To cite an article consulted online, include the URL or, if no suitable URL is available, the name of the database (see also 14.72).

1. *Philadelphia Inquirer*, editorial, July 30, 1990.

2. Mike Royko, "Next Time, Dan, Take Aim at Arnold," *Chicago Tribune*, September 23, 1992.

3. Céline Gounder and Elisabeth Rosenthal, "How Helpful Will the New COVID Booster Really Be?," Opinion, *Los Angeles Times*, September 9, 2022, https://www.latimes.com/opinion/story/2022-09-09/covid-boosters-cost-efficacy.

4. R. W. Apple Jr., "Nixon Tapes Must Be Kept 3 Years for Use in Court," *New York Times*, September 9, 1974, Late City Edition, p. 1, col. 7.

5. "Pushcarts Evolve to Trendy Kiosks," *Lake Forester* (Lake Forest, IL), March 23, 2000.

6. John Myers, "Invasive Faucet Snails Confirmed in Twin Ports Harbor," *Duluth (MN) News-Tribune*, September 26, 2014, EBSCOhost.

A newspaper article can often be cited in the text or in a note with no corresponding bibliography entry (see 14.96). If included in a bibliography, it is cited as follows (see also 14.97).

Apple, R. W., Jr. "Nixon Tapes Must Be Kept 3 Years for Use in Court." *New York Times*, September 9, 1974. Late City Edition.

Because news sites may update certain stories as they unfold, it may be appropriate to include a time stamp for an article that includes one. List the time as posted with the article; if the time zone is not included, it may need to be determined from context (e.g., EST in the example below). A copy of the article should be retained as cited (see 13.17). See also 10.46.

7. Jason Samenow, "Blizzard Warning: High Winds, About Two Feet of Snow Forecast for D.C. Area," *Washington Post*, January 21, 2016, 3:55 p.m. EST, https://www.washingtonpost.com/news/capital-weather-gang/wp/2016/01/21/blizzard-warning-high-winds-around-two-feet-of-snow-forecast-for-d-c-area/.

For blog posts, which are cited similarly to online news articles, see 14.103–7.

**Author-date.** In an author-date reference list, the year of publication follows the author's name; the month and day follow the title of the newspaper.

Apple, R. W., Jr. 1974. "Nixon Tapes Must Be Kept 3 Years for Use in Court." *New York Times*, September 9. Late City Edition.

(Apple 1974, p. 1, col. 7)

14.90 **Newspaper headlines.** Because headlines often consist of complete sentences, many newspapers put them in sentence case (see also 8.159). Chicago, however, recommends title case for cited headlines for the sake of consistency with other titles (see 8.160). If the title is divided by a period, convert the period to a colon; if the result is unwieldy, use only the first part of the title (or the part that makes the most sense as a main title; see also 13.90).

Headline in source:

California's heat wave fueling destructive fires. The worst is yet to come, officials fear

Citation:

5. Summer Lin and Jessica Garrison, "California's Heat Wave Fueling Destructive Fires: The Worst Is Yet to Come, Officials Fear," *Los Angeles Times*, September 9, 2022.

Headlines presented entirely in full capitals in the original are usually converted to upper- and lowercase in a citation (but see 7.54).

14.91 **Titles of newspapers.** An initial *The* that appears on the masthead, which this manual now recommends retaining in running text (see 8.172), may be omitted in source citations as a matter of editorial expediency (as in the examples in this section). A city name, if not part of the title of a local newspaper, may be added in parentheses after the title. The name of the state or province (as for Canada) may also be added if needed (usually in abbreviated form and in italics when in the middle of a title but roman when following the title). See also 10.32, 10.33.

| | |
|---|---|
| *Chicago Tribune* | *Oregonian* (Portland) |
| *Los Angeles Times* | *Ottawa (IL) Daily Times* |
| *Guardian* (Manchester) | *St. Paul (Alberta* or *AB) Journal* |
| *Record* (NJ) | *New York Times* |

For such well-known national papers as *The Wall Street Journal* or *The Christian Science Monitor*, no city name is added. In some cases, however, a newspaper will need to be identified by nation.

| | |
|---|---|
| *Globe and Mail* (Canada) | *Guardian* (UK edition) |
| *Times* (UK) | *Guardian* (US edition) |

14.92 **Non-English titles of newspapers.** Names of cities not part of the titles of newspapers published in languages other than English may be added in roman and parentheses after the title (see also 14.30). The equivalent of an initial *The* is retained (see also 13.100). Use title case for the name of the newspaper if the source itself does (in the masthead or elsewhere); otherwise, use sentence case (see 11.8). (Titles in all capitals should be rendered in sentence case.)

| | |
|---|---|
| *Al-Akhbar* (Beirut) | *Il Messaggero* (Rome) |
| *Al-Akhbar* (Cairo) | *La Crónica de Hoy* (Mexico City) |
| *El País* (Madrid) | *Mladá fronta dnes* (Prague) |
| *Frankfurter Zeitung* | *Wen Hui Bao* (Shanghai) |

14.93 **Regular columns or features.** Regular columns or features may carry headlines as well as column titles. Like the names of sections (see 14.89), these should appear in roman and be capitalized in title case but without quotation marks when they are included in a citation.

1. Elizabeth Chang, "Was This a Meet-Cute or Meet Creep?," Modern Love, *New York Times*, August 12, 2022, https://www.nytimes.com/2022/08/12/style/modern-love-meet-cute-living-in-library-basement.html.

Editorials and the like may be described generically.

2. "A Bricklayer Rebuilds His Life," editorial, *New York Times*, December 26, 2022, New York Edition, sec. A, p. 14.

14.94 **Letters to the editor and readers' comments.** Published letters to the editor, like editorials (see 14.93), are treated generically, usually without headlines.

1. John Q. Public, letter to the editor, *Los Angeles Times*, September 2, 2024.

Online readers' comments (including replies to comments) are usually mentioned in a text or in a note and cited to the relevant article. The identity of the commenter should use the wording on the site.

2. Judith (Reality), September 7, 2022, comment on Daniel Bergner, "Daring to Speak Up About Race in a Divided School District," *New York Times*, September 6, 2022, https://www.nytimes.com/2022/09/06/magazine/leland-michigan-race-school.html.

3. Joseph Katz (Hamburg, Germany), reply to comment by Judith on Bergner, "Daring to Speak Up."

14.95 **Weekend supplements, magazines, and the like.** Articles from Sunday supplements or other special sections are treated in the same way as magazine articles—that is, cited by date (see also 14.87).

1. Sarah Viren, "The Safe Space That Became a Viral Nightmare," *New York Times Magazine*, September 7, 2022, https://www.nytimes.com/2022/09/07/magazine/arizona-state-university-multicultural-center.html.

14.96 **Citing a newspaper article in text rather than in a bibliography.** Because they are typically brief and often ephemeral, newspaper articles are more commonly cited in notes or parenthetical references than in bibliographies. For example, no corresponding entry in a bibliography would be needed for the following citation:

The Green Bay Packers are the only publicly owned team in the NFL; to date, the Packers count more than half a million shareholders, most of them fans (Ken Belson, "How Much Do N.F.L. Teams Make? Packers Fans Paid to Find Out," *New York Times*, Aug. 12, 2022).

A bibliography entry, if required for any reason, would appear as follows:

Belson, Ken. "How Much Do N.F.L. Teams Make? Packers Fans Paid to Find Out." *New York Times*, August 12, 2022. https://www.nytimes.com/2022/08/12/sports/football/green-bay-packers-shareholders-fans.html.

14.97 **Unsigned newspaper articles.** Unsigned newspaper articles or features are best dealt with in text or notes. If a bibliography entry should be needed, the title of the newspaper stands in place of the author.

1. "In Texas, Ad Heats Up Race for Governor," *New York Times*, July 30, 2002.

*New York Times*. "In Texas, Ad Heats Up Race for Governor." July 30, 2002.

**Author-date.** An unsigned newspaper article can usually be cited by the title of the publication.

*New York Times*. 2002. "In Texas, Ad Heats Up Race for Governor." July 30.

(*New York Times* 2002)

14.98 **News services and news releases.** Names of news services, unlike titles of newspapers, are capitalized but not italicized.

Associated Press (AP)  United Press International (UPI)

1. Associated Press, "Liverpool Deals Man United Crushing Defeat," *Toronto Star*, March 6, 2023.

A news release (also called a press release) is treated similarly.

2. US Government Publishing Office, "GPO Director Names Yale Librarian as Superintendent of Documents," news release, September 8, 2022.

## *Reviews*

14.99 **Basic citation format for reviews.** To cite reviews of publications, performances, and the like, include the following elements:

1. Name of reviewer if the review is signed
2. Title of the review, if any
3. The words *review of*, followed by the name of the work reviewed and its author (or composer, or director, or whomever) or sponsor (network, studio, label, etc.) or both
4. Location and date (in the case of a performance)
5. The listing of the periodical in which the review appeared

If a review is included in a bibliography, it is alphabetized by the name of the reviewer or, if unattributed, by the title of the periodical (see 14.102).

14.100 **Book reviews.** Cite book reviews by author of the review and include book title and author(s), translator(s), and editor(s). Follow applicable guidelines for citing periodicals. If the review has a title, it may be included (in quotation marks).

1. Ben Ratliff, review of *The Mystery of Samba: Popular Music and National Identity in Brazil*, by Hermano Vianna, ed. and trans. John Charles Chasteen, *Lingua Franca* 9 (April 1999): B13–B14.

2. Jennifer Szalai, "In 'Strangers to Ourselves,' a Revelatory Account of Mental Illness," review of *Strangers to Ourselves: Unsettled Minds and the Stories That Make Us*, by Rachel Aviv, *New York Times*, September 7, 2022, https://www.nytimes.com/2022/09/07/books/rachel-aviv-strangers-to-ourselves.html.

Feng Dong. Review of *Two Studies of Friedrich Hölderlin*, by Werner Hamacher, edited by Peter Fenves and Julia Ng, translated by Julia Ng and Anthony

Curtis Adler. *Critical Inquiry* 48, no. 4 (2022): 810–11. https://doi.org/10.1086/719895.

**14.101** **Reviews of plays, movies, and the like.** Reviews of plays, movies, television shows, concerts, and the like may include the name of a director in addition to any author, producer, sponsor, or performer, as applicable. If the review has a title, it may be included (in quotation marks).

1. Naveen Kumar, review of *Happy Life,* by Kathy Ng, directed by Kat Yen, Walkerspace, New York, *New York Times,* July 29, 2022, https://www.nytimes.com/2022/07/29/theater/happy-life-review.html.

2. Doreen St. Félix, "How Many Generations of 'Katrina Babies' Are There?," review of *Katrina Babies,* dir. Edward Buckles Jr., HBO Max, *New Yorker,* September 5, 2022, https://www.newyorker.com/magazine/2022/09/12/how-many-generations-of-katrina-babies-are-there-untold.

3. Kumar, review of *Happy Life.*

4. St. Félix, review of *Katrina Babies.*

Tommasini, Anthony. Review of recital by Zhu Wang (piano), Zankel Hall, New York. *New York Times,* November 12, 2021. https://www.nytimes.com/2021/11/12/arts/music/young-concert-artists-zhu-wang.html.

**14.102** **Unsigned reviews.** Unsigned reviews are treated similarly to unsigned articles (see 14.97). If such a review must appear in the bibliography, it is listed under the title of the periodical.

1. Unsigned review of *Geschichten der romanischen und germanischen Völker,* by Leopold von Ranke, *Ergänzungsblätter zur Allgemeinen Literatur-Zeitung,* February 1828, nos. 23–24.

*Ergänzungsblätter zur Allgemeinen Literatur-Zeitung.* Unsigned review of *Geschichten der romanischen und germanischen Völker,* by Leopold von Ranke. February 1828, nos. 23–24.

## WEBSITES, BLOGS, AND SOCIAL MEDIA

**14.103** **Titles for websites, blogs, and social media.** Whether they are mentioned in the text or cited in notes or a bibliography, titles of websites are usually set in roman without quotation marks and capitalized in title case (see 8.160). Italics may be used, however, for the title of a website that shares its name with the title of a publication that is normally italicized or is in a category (e.g., a periodical or book) that would normally be italicized. (An exception is usually made for Wikipedia and other websites from the Wikimedia Commons, which are styled as websites rather than as reference works—though they are both.) Titled sections and pages of a website, like the titles of articles, can often be placed in quotation marks, though roman and title case alone (with no quotation marks) may be used for generic or descriptive titles. Blogs are treated like periodicals, their titles set in italics. The names of social media platforms like Facebook are treated like the names of other websites. If a website or web page does not have a title, a description may be used instead. For additional examples, see 8.193–94.

Google; Google Books; Google Scholar
Wikipedia; Wiktionary; Wikidata
*Vox*; *BBC*; a *Vox* news article; *but* a story published at BBC.com
*Britannica* (the website for *Encyclopaedia Britannica*)
*The Chicago Manual of Style Online*; *CMOS Online*; the Chicago Style Q&A; "New Questions and Answers"
*Merriam-Webster Dictionary*; *Merriam-Webster*; *but* Merriam-Webster.com
*CMOS Shop Talk*; the *Shop Talk* blog
YouTube; YouTube Music; the Music channel on YouTube
Facebook; Twitter *or* X; LinkedIn

14.104 **Citing web pages and websites.** Content from websites and web pages (aside from books, journal articles, and many of the other formally published sources that are discussed elsewhere in this chapter) can usually be cited in the text or in a note rather than in a bibliography. Include as much of the following as can be determined: the title or description of the specific page (if cited); the title or description of the site as a whole (see 14.103); the owner or sponsor of the site; and a URL. In the notes, the title will usually come first; in a bibliography entry, the source should be listed under the owner or sponsor of the site. Include a publication date or the date of the most recent update or revision (see also 13.16); if no such date can be determined, include an access date (see 13.15). For frequently updated resources, a time stamp may be included (as in the Wikipedia example, which records the time as it was listed with the entry; see also 9.41).

1. "Microsoft Privacy Statement," Microsoft, updated February 2023, https://privacy.microsoft.com/en-us/privacystatement.

2. "Privacy Policy," Privacy & Terms, Google, effective December 15, 2022, https://policies.google.com/privacy.

3. "Balkan Romani," Endangered Languages Project, First Peoples' Cultural Council and ELCat/ELP, University of Hawai'i at Mānoa, accessed October 1, 2022, https://www.endangeredlanguages.com/lang/5342.

4. "Wikipedia: Manual of Style," Wikimedia Foundation, last modified September 9, 2022, 21:35 (UTC), https://en.wikipedia.org/wiki/Wikipedia:Manual_of_Style.

5. "Land Acknowledgement," City of Chicago, accessed September 11, 2022, https://www.chicago.gov/city/en.html.

If a bibliography entry is needed, adapt the note form accordingly.

Microsoft Corporation. "Microsoft Privacy Statement." Updated February 2023. https://privacy.microsoft.com/en-us/privacystatement.

If a site or page ceases to exist before publication, or if the cited content has been modified or deleted, this information should be included in the text or note.

6. "Biography," on Pete Townshend's official website, accessed December 15, 2001, http://www.petetownshend.co.uk/petet_bio.html (site discontinued).

However, if a permanent, publicly available archive of the content has been saved using the Internet Archive's Wayback Machine or similar service (a strategy Chicago encourages for any source that is likely to change or become unavailable), the link for that version may be cited. If the original URL is not part of the archived link as in example note 7 below (which shows a page saved via the Wayback Machine), it should be included as in note 8 (which shows a Perma.cc record). See also 13.17.

7. "Academics," Howard University, archived October 19, 2023, at https://web.archive.org/web/20231019175606/https://howard.edu/academics.

*or*

8. "Academics," Howard University, https://howard.edu/academics, archived October 19, 2023, at https://perma.cc/W39H-X2SP.

**Author-date.** In author-date style, when there is no date of publication or revision for a website or web page—that is, when only an access date is used—record *n.d.* as the date of publication in the reference list entry and for the in-text citation. To avoid conflation with the name of the author, *n.d.* is always lowercase, and it is preceded by a comma in text citations (see also 14.44). For the use of abbreviations in author-date citations, see 13.127.

ELP (Endangered Languages Project). n.d. "Balkan Romani." First Peoples' Cultural Council and ELCat/ELP, University of Hawai'i at Mānoa. Accessed October 1, 2022. https://www.endangeredlanguages.com/lang/5342.

(ELP, n.d.)

14.105 **Citing blog posts and blogs.** Blog posts are cited like—and are frequently indistinguishable from—news articles (see 14.89–98). Citations include the author of the post; the title of the post, in quotation marks; the title of the blog, in italics (see 14.103); the date of the post; and a URL. Blogs that are part of a larger publication should also include the title of that publication; if it is not clear from the titles, the word *blog* may be added in parentheses after the title of the blog. Blog posts can often be cited in the text or notes rather than in a bibliography (see also 14.96). If a bibliography entry is needed, it should be listed under the author of the post.

1. Carol Saller, "Formatting Text Messages in Fiction," *CMOS Shop Talk*, March 10, 2020, https://cmosshoptalk.com/2020/03/10/formatting-text-messages-in-fiction/.

2. William Germano, "Futurist Shock," *Lingua Franca* (blog), *Chronicle of Higher Education*, February 15, 2017, https://www.chronicle.com/blogs/linguafranca/2017/02/15/futurist-shock/.

Germano, William. "Futurist Shock." *Lingua Franca* (blog). *Chronicle of Higher Education*, February 15, 2017. https://www.chronicle.com/blogs/linguafranca/2017/02/15/futurist-shock/.

Readers' comments (including replies to comments) are usually mentioned in text or in a note and cited to the relevant post. The identity of the commenter should use the wording on the site. The following examples assume the Germano post has been cited in full in a previous note.

3. Jim, February 16, 2017, comment on Germano, "Futurist Shock."

4. Stephanos C, February 21, 2017, reply to Jim on Germano, "Futurist Shock."

**Author-date.** In author-date style, comments on a blog post included in a reference list are cited in the text only and in terms of that entry.

Germano, William. 2017. "Futurist Shock." *Lingua Franca* (blog). *Chronicle of Higher Education*, February 15. https://www.chronicle.com/blogs/linguafranca/2017/02/15/futurist-shock/.

A comment on Germano (2017) by "Jim" (on February 16, 2017) revealed that . . .

**14.106** **Citing social media content.** Posts and comments shared on social media are usually mentioned or cited in the text or in a note, as illustrated in the examples that follow (see also 13.5). Because such content is typically brief and often informal, it is not usually listed in a bibliography. The following example gives sufficient information in the text. Note that Twitter content posted before the company's 2023 rebranding as X need not be updated to refer to the new name (though that information may be added parenthetically, as in the first note example below).

The day before images were officially made public, NASA tweeted an image of the James Webb telescope's "First Deep Field," which featured the galaxy cluster SMACS 0723. NASA called it "the deepest & sharpest infrared image of the early universe ever taken" (@NASAWebb, July 11, 2022, 6:22 p.m. EDT).

Citations in the notes should include enough text from the original post to identify it (up to 280 characters, including spaces, and retaining any emojis). Add a URL to the end of the citation.

1. NASA Webb Telescope (@NASAWebb), "👀 Sneak a peek at the deepest & sharpest infrared image of the early universe ever taken—all in a day's work for the Webb telescope. (Literally, capturing it took less than a day!)," Twitter (now X), July 11, 2022, https://twitter.com/NASAWebb/status/1546621080298835970.

Readers' comments (including replies to comments) are usually mentioned in the text in terms of the original post. Though a note is usually unnecessary, it may be styled as follows:

2. Chelsea E. Manning (@xychelsea), "do the stars have six points as an artifact because of the hexagonal mirrors?," reply to NASA Webb Telescope, July 11, 2022, https://twitter.com/xychelsea/status/1546633841649016832.

Facebook and other platforms may be treated similarly.

3. Chicago Manual of Style (@ChicagoManual), "Is the world ready for singular they? We thought so back in 1993," Facebook, April 17, 2015, https://www.facebook.com/ChicagoManual/posts/10152906193679151.

4. Pete Souza (@petesouza), "9/11 anniversaries from the past," series of seven Instagram photos, September 11, 2022, https://www.instagram.com/p/CiXjR5junw6.

Private content, including direct messages and posts on private accounts, is treated as personal communication (and cited as described in 14.111). Authors who rely on social media for data and other facts should first consider whether the same information is available in a published source; editors can help by querying questionable citations. Because social media content is subject to editing and deletion, authors are advised to retain a copy of anything they cite (see 13.17). If a deleted post must be cited, that fact should be added in parentheses at the end of the citation. See also 13.6–12, 14.104.

**Author-date.** Social media content can usually be cited entirely in the text as in the first example featuring NASA above. However, if needed for any reason (e.g., to facilitate multiple text references to the same thread), an author-date reference list entry may be styled as follows.

Chicago Manual of Style (@ChicagoManual). 2015. "Is the world ready for singular they? We thought so back in 1993." Facebook, April 17. https://www.facebook.com/ChicagoManual/posts/10152906193679151.

(Chicago Manual of Style 2015)

Comments are cited in the text in terms of the reference list entry.

Michele Truty agreed, saying that "we do need a gender-neutral pronoun" (April 17, 2015, comment on Chicago Manual of Style 2015).

14.107 **Electronic mailing lists and forums.** Content posted to electronic mailing lists or forums can be cited much like other types of social media (see 14.106). Include the name of the correspondent, the title of the subject or thread (in quotation marks and capitalized as in the original), the title of the list or forum (followed by *list* or *forum* or the like, if not part of the title), the title of any host site (see also 14.103), the date of the message or post, and a URL. (Posts on private forums or lists are cited like personal communications; see 14.111.)

1. John Powell, "Pattern matching," Grapevine digest mailing list archives, Electric Editors, April 23, 1998, https://www.electriceditors.net/grapevine/archives.php.

2. Caroline Braun, reply to "How did the 'cool kids' from high school turn out?," Quora, August 9, 2016, https://www.quora.com/How-did-the-cool-kids-from-high-school-turn-out/.

## INTERVIEWS AND PERSONAL COMMUNICATIONS

14.108 **Unpublished interviews.** Unpublished interviews are best cited in text or in notes, though they occasionally appear in bibliographies. Citations should include the names of both the person interviewed and the interviewer; brief identifying information, if appropriate; the place or date of the interview (or both, if known); and, if a transcript or recording is available, where it may be found. Permission to quote may be needed; see chapter 4.

1. Mfundishi Maasi (cofounder, Black Community Defense and Development), in discussion with the author, March 2013. Transcript available on request.

2. Benjamin Spock, interview by Milton J. E. Senn, November 20, 1974, interview 67A, transcript, Senn Oral History Collection, National Library of Medicine, Bethesda, MD.

3. Maasi, discussion; Spock, interview.

**14.109** **Unattributed interviews.** An interview with a person who prefers to remain anonymous or whose name the author does not wish to reveal may be cited in whatever form is appropriate in context. The absence of a name should be explained (e.g., "All interviews were conducted in confidentiality, and the names of interviewees are withheld by mutual agreement").

1. Interview with health-care worker, June 15, 2024.

**14.110** **Published or broadcast interviews.** An interview that has been published or broadcast or made available online can usually be treated like an article or other item in a periodical. Note, however, that interviews are usually cited under the name of the interviewee rather than the interviewer. Interviews consulted online should include a URL or database name and any other relevant information (see 13.6–12). See also 14.164, 14.167.

1. Lydia Davis, "The Art of Fiction No. 227," interview by Andrea Aguilar and Johanne Fronth-Nygren, *Paris Review*, no. 212 (Spring 2015): 172, EBSCOhost.

2. McGeorge Bundy, interview by Robert MacNeil, *MacNeil/Lehrer NewsHour*, PBS, February 7, 1990.

3. Bernie Sanders, interview by Cardi B, TEN Nail Bar, Detroit, MI, July 29, 2019, posted August 15, 2019, by Bernie Sanders, YouTube, https://youtu.be/p1ub TsrZFBU.

O, Karen [Karen Lee Orzolek]. "Karen O Has Found a More Joyful Kind of Wildness." Interview by Jia Tolentino. *New Yorker*, September 11, 2022. https://www.newyorker.com/culture/the-new-yorker-interview/karen-o -has-found-a-more-joyful-kind-of-wildness.

14.111 **Personal communications.** References to conversations (whether face-to-face or by telephone, video, or the like) and to letters, email or text messages, and direct or private messages shared through social media and received by the author are usually run in to the text or given in a note. They are rarely listed in a bibliography. Most such information can be referred to simply as a conversation, message, or the like; the medium may be mentioned if relevant.

In a conversation with the author on January 6, 2019, lobbyist John Q. Advocate admitted that . . .

Though inconclusive, a fifteen-second video shared with the author via Instagram by the subject's family did suggest minor neurocognitive disorder.

1. Jane E. Correspondent, email message to author, April 23, 2024.
2. Facebook direct message to author, April 30, 2017.

An email address or the like belonging to an individual should be omitted. Should it be needed in a specific context, it must be cited only with the permission of its owner. See also 12.3.

**Author-date.** In author-date style, personal communications are usually cited entirely in the text (but see 14.136–37). The term *personal communication* (or *pers. comm.*), or a more specific equivalent, is added after the name, following a comma. Though reference list entries are usually unneeded, each person cited must be fully identified elsewhere in the text. Unless it is mentioned in the text, a date should be added to the parenthetical citation, following a comma. The abbreviation *et al.* ("and others") should be avoided in such citations.

(John Smith, pers. comm.)
(Rudy Smith, text message to author, August 1, 2024)

14.112 **Citing AI-generated content.** Authors who have relied on content generated by a chatbot or similar AI tool must make it clear how the tool has been used (either in the text or in a preface or the like). Any specific content, whether quoted or paraphrased, should be cited where it occurs, either in the text or in a note. Like personal communications (see 14.111) and social media posts (see 14.106), chatbot conversations are not usually included in a bibliography or reference list (but see below). In the first three examples that follow, ChatGPT is the author of the content (though not in the traditional sense), and OpenAI is the publisher or developer. The URL points to a publicly archived copy of the conversation (see also 13.6, 13.17). Include the date the content was generated in addition to a version number. If the AI-generated text has been edited or adapted in any way, this fact should be acknowledged in the text or in the note (as in example note 2).

Cited in the text:

The following recipe for pizza dough was generated on December 9, 2023, by ChatGPT-3.5.

Cited in a note:

1. Text generated by ChatGPT-3.5, OpenAI, December 9, 2023, https://chat.openai.com/share/90b8137d-ff1c-4c0c-b123-2868623c4ae2.

A prompt, if not included in the text, may be added to the note. Multiple prompts (as in an extended conversation) may be summarized.

2. Response to "Explain how to make pizza dough from common household ingredients," ChatGPT-3.5, Open AI, December 9, 2023, edited for style and accuracy.

If for any reason an AI conversation is included in a bibliography or reference list, cite it under the name of the publisher or developer rather than the name of the tool and include a publicly available URL (see also 14.104).

Google. Response to "How many copyeditors does it take to fix a book-length manuscript?" Gemini 1.0, February 10, 2024. https://g.co/gemini/share/cccc26abdc19.

## PAPERS, CONTRACTS, AND REPORTS

14.113 **Theses and dissertations.** Titles of theses and dissertations appear in quotation marks—not in italics; otherwise, they are cited like books. The kind of thesis, the academic institution, and the date follow the title. Like the publication data for a book, these are enclosed in parentheses in a note but not in a bibliography. If the document was consulted online, include a URL or, for documents retrieved from a commercial database, the name of the database and, in parentheses, any identification number supplied or recommended by the database. For dissertations issued on microfilm, see 14.17. To cite an abstract (as in the notes), simply add the word "abstract" after the title (see also 14.85).

1. Ilya Vedrashko, "Advertising in Computer Games" (master's thesis, MIT, 2006), 59, https://hdl.handle.net/1721.1/39144.

2. Alison E. Stout, "Cats and Coronaviruses: One Health in the Age of COVID-19" (PhD diss., Cornell University, 2021), 39–40, ProQuest (28490261).

3. Vedrashko, "Advertising in Computer Games," 61–62.

Blajer de la Garza, Yuna. "A House Is Not a Home: Citizenship and Belonging in Contemporary Democracies." PhD diss., University of Chicago, 2019. ProQuest (13865986).

14.114 **Unpublished manuscripts.** Manuscripts housed in libraries and other archives are cited as described in 14.119–29. Unpublished manuscripts shared with the author but otherwise unavailable for others to consult may be mentioned in the text or in a note but are not usually included in a bibliography. Titles (if any) of unpublished manuscripts are placed in quotation marks. Parentheses (shown in previous editions of this manual) are no longer used to enclose information about the manuscript.

In an unpublished manuscript shared with the author, . . .[1]

1. Jess Smith, "Analyzing the Unknowable," unpublished manuscript, May 5, 2024.

14.115 **Papers or posters presented at meetings.** To cite a paper or poster presented at a meeting, add information about sponsorship, location (if applicable), and date of the meeting following the title. Such citations are normally limited to the text or a note. If the information is available online, include a URL. Parentheses (shown in previous editions of this manual) no longer enclose information about the presentation. For recorded lectures and talks, see 14.164, 14.167.

1. David G. Harper, "The Several Discoveries of the Ciliary Muscle," PowerPoint presentation, 25th Anniversary Meeting of the Cogan Ophthalmic History Society, Bethesda, MD, March 31, 2012.

2. Toby Lee, "Documentary Operationality: Beyond Representation," paper presented at the annual Society for Cinema and Media Studies conference (virtual), March 20, 2021.

A paper included in the published proceedings of a meeting may be treated like a chapter in a book (see 14.22). If published in a journal, it is treated as an article (see 14.67–86).

**14.116** **Working papers and the like.** Working papers and similar documents, sometimes produced in advance of publication on a particular topic, can be treated in much the same way as a dissertation or thesis (14.113). In the example cited below, the term *working paper* is part of a formal series title and therefore capitalized (see also 14.25–28).

1. Ernest Liu et al., "Judicial Independence, Local Protectionism, and Economic Integration: Evidence from China," Working Paper No. 2022-120 (Becker Friedman Institute for Economics, University of Chicago, August 30, 2022), 44–45.

2. Liu et al., "Judicial Independence," 71.

Liu, Ernest, Yi Lu, Wenwei Peng, and Shaoda Wang. "Judicial Independence, Local Protectionism, and Economic Integration: Evidence from China." Working Paper No. 2022-120. Becker Friedman Institute for Economics, University of Chicago, August 30, 2022.

**Author-date.** In author-date style, the year of publication follows the name of the author in the reference list, whereas a month and day (if any) follow the publication details.

Liu, Ernest, Yi Lu, Wenwei Peng, and Shaoda Wang. 2022. "Judicial Independence, Local Protectionism, and Economic Integration: Evidence from China." Working Paper No. 2022-120. Becker Friedman Institute for Economics, University of Chicago, August 30.

(Liu et al. 2022)

**14.117** **Pamphlets, reports, and the like.** Pamphlets, corporate reports, brochures, and other freestanding publications are treated similarly to books. Data on author and publisher may not fit the normal pattern, but sufficient information should be given to identify the document.

1. Hazel V. Clark, *Mesopotamia: Between Two Rivers* (Trumbull County [Ohio] Historical Society, 1957).

2. *Lifestyles in Retirement*, Library Series (TIAA-CREF, 1996).

3. *Starbucks Fiscal 2021 Annual Report* (Starbucks Corporation Form 10-K, 2022), https://investor.starbucks.com/financial-data/annual-reports/.

Material obtained through loose-leaf services can be handled similarly.

4. *Standard Federal Tax Reporter*, 1996 ed., vol. 4 (Commerce Clearing House, 1996), ¶ 2,620.

14.118 **Private contracts, wills, and such.** Private documents are occasionally cited in notes but rarely in bibliographies; in most cases, a mention in the text (or in a note) rather than a formal citation will be sufficient (e.g., "Marcy T. Feldspar, in her will dated January 20, 1976, directed . . ."). Capitalization is usually a matter of editorial discretion. For items in manuscript collections, see 14.119–29.

1. Samuel Henshaw, will dated June 5, 1806, proved July 5, 1809, no. 46, box 70, Hampshire County Registry of Probate, Northampton, MA.

## MANUSCRIPT COLLECTIONS

14.119 **Overview and additional resources.** The 1987 edition of the *Guide to Federal Records in the National Archives of the United States* offers the following advice: "The most convenient citation for archives is one similar to that used for personal papers and other historical manuscripts. Full identification of most unpublished material usually requires giving the title and date of the item, series title (if applicable), name of the collection, and name of the depository. Except for placing the cited item first [in a note], there is no general agreement on the sequence of the remaining elements in the citation. . . . Whatever sequence is adopted, however, should be used consistently throughout the same work" (761). A searchable, updated version of the *Guide*, which applies to federal records only, is available at the National Archives website. Its advice has been extended by the leaflet *Citing Records in the National Archives of the United States* (see bibliog. 4.5), which covers textual and nontextual records, including electronic records and digitized resources. Citations of collections consulted online (still a relative rarity for this type of material) will usually take the same form as citations of physical collections, aside from the addition of a URL or database name (see 13.6–12). This section offers general guidance on citing items in manuscript collections, including government collections and collections maintained by universities and other institutions. For examples featuring items from the US National Archives, see 14.193.

14.120 **Note forms versus bibliography entries.** In a note, the main element of a manuscript citation is usually a specific item (a letter, a memorandum, or whatever) and is thus cited first. In a bibliography, the main element is usually either the collection in which the specific item may be found, the author(s) of the items in the collection, or the depository for the collection. (Entries beginning with the name of the collection or the last name of the author—which sometimes overlap—tend to be easiest to locate in a bibliography.) For date style, see 14.122.

1. James Oglethorpe to the Trustees, 13 January 1733, Phillipps Collection of Egmont Manuscripts, 14200:13, University of Georgia Library.

2. Alvin Johnson, memorandum, 1937, file 36, Horace Kallen Papers, YIVO Institute for Jewish Research, New York.

3. Revere's Waste and Memoranda Book (vol. 1, 1761–83; vol. 2, 1783–97), Revere Family Papers, Massachusetts Historical Society, Boston.

Egmont Manuscripts. Phillipps Collection. University of Georgia Library.
Kallen, Horace. Papers. YIVO Institute for Jewish Research, New York.
Revere Family Papers. Massachusetts Historical Society, Boston.

Specific items are not included in a bibliography unless only one item from a collection is cited. For more examples, see 14.127, 14.128.

14.121 **Specific versus generic titles for manuscript collections.** In notes and bibliographies, quotation marks are used only for specific titles (e.g., "Concerning a Court of Arbitration") but not for generic names such as *report* or *minutes*. Generic names of this kind are capitalized if part of a formal heading that appears on (or sometimes with) the manuscript itself, lowercased if merely descriptive. Compare 14.127, example notes 7–10.

14.122 **Dates for manuscript collections.** Names of months may be spelled out or abbreviated, if done consistently (see 10.44). If there are many references to specific dates, as in a collection of letters or diaries, the day-month-year form (8 May 1945), used in some of the examples in this section, may improve readability, though the American month-day-year style used throughout this manual may be preferred instead (May 8, 1945). See also 6.41, 9.33.

14.123 **Folios, page numbers, and such for manuscript collections.** Older manuscripts are usually numbered by signatures only or by leaves (sometimes called folios) rather than by page (see 14.53, 14.54). More recent ones usually carry page numbers (and some older manuscripts have been paginated in the modern era); if needed, the abbreviations *p.* and *pp.* should be used to avoid ambiguity. Leaves introduced at the beginning or end of a manuscript when rebound (e.g., by a modern library or publisher) are not usually counted in the numbering. Some manuscript collections have identifying series or file numbers, which may be included in a citation.

14.124 **"Papers" and "manuscripts."** In titles of manuscript collections, the terms *papers* and *manuscripts* are synonymous. Both are acceptable, as are the abbreviations *MS* and (pl.) *MSS*. If it is necessary to distinguish a typescript or computer printout from a handwritten document, the abbreviation *TS* may be used. See also 10.48.

14.125 **Location of depositories.** The location (city and state) of such well-known depositories as major university libraries is rarely necessary (see examples in 14.127).

University of Chicago Library
Oberlin College Library

14.126 **Collections of letters and the like.** A note citation of a letter starts with the name of the letter writer, followed by *to*, followed by the name of the recipient. Given names may be omitted if the identities of sender and recipient are clear from the text. (Identifying material may be added if appropriate; see 14.108.) The word *letter* is usually omitted—that is, understood—but other forms of communication (telegram, memorandum) are specified. If such other forms occur frequently in the same collection, it may be helpful to specify letters also. For capitalization and the use of quotation marks, see 14.121. For date style, see 14.122. See also 14.13, 14.111, 14.129.

14.127 **Examples of note forms for manuscript collections.** See also 14.120, 14.121. For date style, see 14.122.

1. George Creel to Colonel House, 25 September 1918, Edward M. House Papers, Yale University Library.

2. James Oglethorpe to the Trustees, 13 January 1733, Phillipps Collection of Egmont Manuscripts, 14200:13, University of Georgia Library (hereafter cited as Egmont MSS).

3. Burton to Merriam, telegram, 26 January 1923, box 26, folder 17, Charles E. Merriam Papers, Special Collections Research Center, University of Chicago Library.

4. Minutes of the Committee for Improving the Condition of the Free Blacks, Pennsylvania Abolition Society, 1790–1803, Papers of the Pennsylvania Society for the Abolition of Slavery, Historical Society of Pennsylvania, Philadelphia (hereafter cited as Minutes, Pennsylvania Society).

5. Hiram Johnson to John Callan O'Laughlin, 13 and 16 July 1916, 28 November 1916, O'Laughlin Papers, Theodore Roosevelt Collection, Harvard College Library.

6. Memorandum by Alvin Johnson, 1937, file 36, Horace Kallen Papers, YIVO Institute for Jewish Research, New York.

7. Undated correspondence between French Strother and Edward Lowry, container 1-G/961 600, Herbert Hoover Presidential Library, West Branch, IA.

8. Memorandum, "Concerning a Court of Arbitration," n.d., Philander C. Knox Papers, Manuscripts Division, Library of Congress.

9. Joseph Purcell, "A Map of the Southern Indian District of North America" [ca. 1772], MS 228, Ayer Collection, Newberry Library, Chicago.

10. Louis Agassiz, report to the Committee of Overseers . . . [28 December 1859], Overseers Reports, Professional Series, vol. 2, Harvard University Archives.

11. Gilbert McMicken to Alexander Morris, 29 November 1881, Glasgow (Scotland), Document 1359, fol. 1r, Alexander Morris Papers, MG-12-84, Provincial Archives of Manitoba, Winnipeg.

12. Daily Expenses, July 1787, images 7–8, George Washington Papers, Series 5: Financial Papers, 1750–96, Library of Congress, Washington, DC, https://www.loc.gov/item/mgw500032/.

The content of subsequent citations of other items in a cited manuscript collection (short forms) will vary according to the proximity of the earlier notes, the use of abbreviations, and other factors. Absolute consistency may occasionally be sacrificed to readers' convenience.

13. R. S. Baker to House, 1 November 1919, House Papers.

14. Thomas Causton to Martha Causton, 12 March 1733, Egmont MSS, 14200:53.

15. Minutes, 15 April 1795, Pennsylvania Society.

**14.128** **Examples of bibliography entries for manuscript collections.** The style of the first six examples below is appropriate if more than one item from a collection is cited in the text or notes. Entries are usually listed under the name of the collection or under the author(s) of the items contained therein. See also 14.120.

Egmont Manuscripts. Phillipps Collection. University of Georgia Library.

Merriam, Charles E. Papers. Special Collections Research Center, University of Chicago Library.

Pennsylvania Society for the Abolition of Slavery. Papers. Historical Society of Pennsylvania, Philadelphia.

Strother, French, and Edward Lowry. Undated correspondence. Herbert Hoover Presidential Library, West Branch, IA.

Washington, George. Papers. Series 5: Financial Papers, 1750–96. Library of Con-

gress, Washington, DC. https://www.loc.gov/collections/george-washington-papers/.
Women's Organization for National Prohibition Reform. Papers. Alice Belin du Pont files, Pierre S. du Pont Papers. Eleutherian Mills Historical Library, Wilmington, DE.

If only one item from a collection has been mentioned in text or in a note and is considered important enough to include in a bibliography, the entry will begin with the item.

Dinkel, Joseph. Description of Louis Agassiz written at the request of Elizabeth Cary Agassiz, n.d. Louis Agassiz Papers. Houghton Library, Harvard University.

**Author-date.** When citing manuscript collections in author-date format, it is generally unnecessary to use *n.d.* (no date) in place of the date. Dates of individual items should be mentioned in the text, when applicable.

Egmont Manuscripts. Phillipps Collection. University of Georgia Library.
Kallen, Horace. Papers. YIVO Institute for Jewish Research, New York.

Oglethorpe wrote to the trustees on January 13, 1733 (Egmont Manuscripts), to say . . .

Alvin Johnson, in a memorandum prepared sometime in 1937 (Kallen Papers, file 36), observed that . . .

If only one item from a collection has been mentioned in the text, however, the entry may begin with the writer's name (if known). In such a case, the use of *n.d.* may be appropriate. See also 14.44.

Dinkel, Joseph. n.d. Description of Louis Agassiz written at the request of Elizabeth Cary Agassiz. Louis Agassiz Papers. Houghton Library, Harvard University.

(Dinkel, n.d.)

Alternatively, information about a manuscript collection may be cited in a note instead of in the reference list, in which case a parenthetical text reference would be unnecessary (see 13.128).

14.129 **Letters and the like in private collections.** Letters, memorandums, and such that have not been archived may be cited like other unpublished material. Information on the depository is replaced by such wording as "in the author's possession" or "private collection," and the location is not mentioned.

## SPECIAL TYPES OF REFERENCES

### *Reference Works*

14.130 **Reference works consulted in physical formats.** Well-known reference works, such as major dictionaries and encyclopedias, are normally cited in notes rather than in bibliographies. They are more likely than other types of books to be consulted online (see 14.131). If a physical edition is cited, specify the edition number (if not the first) and the date the volume or set was published. References to an alphabetically arranged work cite the item (not the volume or page number) in quotation marks. Though the word "under" may be added for clarity, this manual no longer recommends using the Latin abbreviation *s.v.* ("under the word"; plural *s.vv.*).

1. *Encyclopaedia Britannica*, 15th ed. (1980), under "salvation."
2. *Oxford English Dictionary*, 2nd ed. (CD-ROM, version 4.0, 2009), under "hoot(e)nanny, hootananny."
3. *Dictionary of American Biography* (1937), "Wadsworth, Jeremiah."

Most other reference works, however, are more appropriately listed with full publication details like any other book resource. (For examples of how to cite individual entries by author, see 14.132.)

4. *The Times Style and Usage Guide*, comp. Tim Austin (Times Books, 2003), under "police ranks," "postal addresses."
5. *MLA Handbook*, 9th ed. (Modern Language Association of America, 2020), 6.8.

*Diccionario de historia de Venezuela*. 2nd ed. 4 vols. Fundación Polar, 1997.

Garner, Bryan A. *Garner's Modern English Usage*. 5th ed. Oxford University Press, 2022.

14.131 **Reference works consulted online.** Online dictionaries and encyclopedias are normally cited in the notes rather than in bibliographies. Like their printed counterparts, they are usually cited under the title of the resource (see 14.130). For continually updated resources, an edition number will usually be unnecessary; instead, include a publication date or the date of the most recent update or revision (see also 13.16). If no such date can be determined, include an access date (see 13.15). Time stamps may be included for frequently updated resources (as in the Wikipedia example, which records the time as it was listed with the entry; see also 9.41). Include a URL as the last element of citation (see also 13.6–12). The facts of publication are often omitted, but signed entries may include the name of the author. Note that names in entries are not always inverted as in printed editions; follow the usage in the source (cf. example notes 1 and 2 below). For the use of italics versus roman in titles like Wikipedia, see 14.103. See also 14.104.

1. *Britannica*, "William Shakespeare," last updated April 19, 2023, https://www.britannica.com/biography/William-Shakespeare.

2. *Grove Music Online*, "Ellington, Duke [Edward Kennedy]," by Marcello Piras, October 16, 2013, https://doi.org/10.1093/gmo/9781561592630.article.A2249397.

3. Wikipedia, "Stevie Nicks," last modified September 9, 2022, 23:42 (UTC), https://en.wikipedia.org/wiki/Stevie_Nicks.

4. *Merriam-Webster Dictionary*, "footnote," accessed February 8, 2024, https://www.merriam-webster.com/dictionary/footnote.

14.132 **Citing individual reference entries by author.** For certain reference works—particularly those with substantial, authored entries—it may be appropriate to cite individual entries by author, much like contributions to a multiauthor book (see 14.9). Such citations may be included in a bibliography.

1. Dismas Masolo, "African Sage Philosophy," in *Stanford Encyclopedia of Philosophy* (Stanford University, 1997–), published February 14, 2006; last modified February 22, 2016, https://plato.stanford.edu/archives/spr2016/entries/african-sage/.

Isaacson, Melissa. "Bulls." In *Encyclopedia of Chicago*, edited by Janice L. Reiff, Ann Durkin Keating, and James R. Grossman. Chicago Historical Society, 2005. https://www.encyclopedia.chicagohistory.org/pages/184.html.

Masolo, Dismas. "African Sage Philosophy." In *Stanford Encyclopedia of Philosophy*. Stanford University, 1997–. Article published February 14, 2006; last modified February 22, 2016. https://plato.stanford.edu/archives/spr2016/entries/african-sage/.

Middleton, Richard. "Lennon, John Ono (1940–1980)." In *Oxford Dictionary of National Biography*. Oxford University Press, 2004. Last modified September 1, 2017. https://doi.org/10.1093/ref:odnb/31351.

## *Artwork and Illustrations*

**14.133** **Citing paintings, photographs, and sculpture.** Information about paintings, photographs, sculpture, and other works of art is usually presented in the text. If a more formal citation is needed (as in a note or a bibliography—or a separate section of a bibliography devoted to images; see also 13.67), list the name of the artist, a title (in italics) or a description, and a date of creation or completion, followed by information about the medium and the location of the work. To help readers locate the item, a museum accession number may be included; for works consulted online, add a URL.

1. Salvador Dalí, *The Persistence of Memory*, 1931, oil on canvas, 9½ × 13 in. (24.1 × 33 cm), Museum of Modern Art, New York, object no. 162.1934, https://www.moma.org/collection/works/79018.

2. Dorothea Lange, *Black Maria, Oakland*, 1957, printed 1965, gelatin silver print, 39.3 × 37 cm, Art Institute of Chicago, ref. no. 2013.1220, https://www.artic.edu/aic/collections/artwork/220174.

3. Rodney McMillian, *Untitled (the Great Society) I*, 2006, video, 15 min. 48 sec. loop, Art Institute of Chicago, ref. no. 2016.327, https://www.artic.edu/artworks/236624/untitled-the-great-society-i.

4. Steve McCurry, *Afghan Girl*, December 1984, photograph, *National Geographic*, cover, June 1985.

Picasso, Pablo. *Bull's Head*. Spring 1942. Bicycle saddle and handlebars, 33.5 × 43.5 × 19 cm. Musée Picasso Paris.

To cite a work of art included as a numbered illustration in another publication, see 14.57. To cite the text that accompanies a work of art at a museum (as on a wall), simply credit the museum in the text or in a note (e.g., "In the text accompanying Picasso's sculpture at the Musée Picasso . . ."). Finally, note that a citation is not the same as a caption or credit. For detailed information on captioning and crediting artwork and other types of illustrations (including advice on writing alternative text), see chapter 3.

**14.134** **Citing exhibition catalogs.** An exhibition catalog is often published as a book and treated as such. In the notes, the abbreviation "exh. cat." may be used (as in the first example below); however, if the nature of the source is clear in the text and included in a corresponding bibliography entry, it need not be specified in a note. See also 14.40.

1. Cemal Pulak, "The Uluburun Shipwreck and Late Bronze Age Trade," in *Beyond Babylon: Art, Trade, and Diplomacy in the Second Millennium B.C.*, exh. cat., ed. Joan Aruz, Kim Benzel, and Jean M. Evans (Metropolitan Museum of Art, 2008), 294.

2. Orianna Cacchione, *Zhang Peili: Record. Repeat.* (Art Institute of Chicago, 2017).

Cacchione, Orianna. *Zhang Peili: Record. Repeat.* With contributions by Pi Li, Robyn Farrell, and Katherine Grube. Art Institute of Chicago, 2017. Distributed by Yale University Press. Published in conjunction with an exhibition of the same title, organized by and presented at the Art Institute of Chicago, March 31–July 9, 2017.

*or, if space is tight,*

Cacchione, Orianna. *Zhang Peili: Record. Repeat.* Art Institute of Chicago, 2017. Distributed by Yale University Press. Exhibition catalog.

A brochure—the kind often available to visitors to an exhibition—may be treated similarly.

14.135 **Citing maps.** Information about maps is usually presented in the text. If a more formal citation is needed (as in a note or, rarely, a bibliography), list the cartographer (if known) and the title of the map (in italics) or a description (in roman), followed by the scale and size (if known) and publication details or location of the map (see also 8.201, 14.133). Undated maps consulted online should include an access or revision date (see also 13.15, 13.16).

1. Samuel de Champlain, cartographer, *Carte geographique de la Nouvelle Franse*, 1612, 43 × 76 cm, in *The History of Cartography*, vol. 3, *Cartography in the European Renaissance* (University of Chicago Press, 2007), fig. 51.3.

2. *Yu ji tu* [Map of the tracks of Yu], AD 1136, Forest of Stone Steles Museum, Xi'an, China, stone rubbing, 1933?, 84 × 82 cm, Library of Congress, https://www.loc.gov/item/gm71005080/.

3. Satellite view of Chicago, Google Maps, accessed May 5, 2024, https://www.google.com/maps/@41.7682665,-87.723154,114690m/data=!3m1!1e3.

US Geological Survey. *California: Yosemite Quadrangle*. 1909; repr., 1951. 30-minute series quadrangle, 1:125,000 scale. National Map, Historic Topographic Map Collection. https://www.usgs.gov/media/images/scan-1909-usgs-quadrangle-yosemite-california-area-include-el-capitan-usgs-historic.

See also 14.57.

## *Indigenous Sources*

14.136 **Citing secondary sources of Indigenous knowledge.** Secondary sources related to Indigenous peoples, cultures, and histories that consist of published books and articles and the like or other publicly available content can usually be cited according to the type of source as described elsewhere in this chapter; however, caution should be used, especially with older materials. Historically, many published works, particularly within the academy, have ignored Indigenous customary law, resulting in theft or inappropriate use of Indigenous information while devaluing, diminishing, and erasing Indigenous intellectual contributions. Acknowledging oral sources in citation is a step toward righting this historic injustice while supporting articles 13 and 31 of the United Nations Declaration on the Rights of Indigenous Peoples (UNDRIP, adopted in 2007). For more details, consult the latest edition of the *Publication Manual of the American Psychological Association* as well as Gregory Younging's *Elements of Indigenous Style* (bibliog. 1.1). See also 14.137.

14.137 **Citing Indigenous sources of knowledge directly.** Information acquired directly from an Indigenous person can often be cited as a form of personal communication. However, when the source of information is an Indigenous Elder or other Indigenous Knowledge Keeper, there are some additional requirements beyond those described in 14.111. These requirements will acknowledge the authority of the Traditional Knowledge and Oral Traditions passed down through Indigenous Knowledge Keepers, an authority that deserves the same level of respect typically given to scholarly sources outside of Indigenous communities. In a full note or bibliography entry, it is generally best to include the name of the Elder or Knowledge Keeper, the nation or community to which they belong, a brief description of the information or teaching they have shared, and the date of the interaction. In addition, a treaty territory and a city of residence may be included. These must be confirmed with the Elder or Knowledge Keeper, as must whether the information to be discussed and cited is suitable for publication or requires following additional protocol and obtaining additional permission in order to publish. The template for a bibliography entry below has been adapted from "More than Personal Communication: Templates for Citing Indigenous Elders and Knowledge Keepers," an article by Lorisia MacLeod (James Smith Cree Nation) in the journal *KULA* (bibliog. 1.3).

Last Name, First Name (Traditional Name [if applicable]). Nation/community. Treaty territory [if applicable]. Where they live [if applicable]. Topic/subject of communication. Interview, month, day, year.

This would be styled as a note as follows:

1. First Name Last Name (Traditional Name [if applicable]), nation/community, treaty territory [if applicable], where they live [if applicable], topic/subject of communication [if not mentioned in the text], interview [specify only if not clear from the text], month, day, year.

Note that some Elders and Knowledge Keepers will prefer to be listed under their Traditional Name rather than their legal name, sometimes without listing a legal name also. Whenever possible, confirm with the Elder or Knowledge Keeper. For additional considerations related to Indigenous languages and to conventions in English (including capitalization of terms like *Elder*), see 11.49–52.

**Author-date.** The bibliography entry above would be adapted to author-date style as follows:

Last Name, First Name (Traditional Name [if applicable]). Year. Nation/community. Treaty territory [if applicable]. Where they live [if applicable]. Topic/subject of communication. Interview, month, day.

(Last Name year)

## *Scriptural References*

14.138 **Biblical references — additional resource.** Any writer or editor working extensively with biblical material should consult the latest edition of *The SBL Handbook of Style* (bibliog. 1.1), which offers excellent advice and numerous abbreviations.

14.139 **Bible chapter and verse.** References to the Jewish or Christian scriptures usually appear in text citations or notes rather than in bibliographies. Parenthetical or note references to the Bible should include book (in roman and usually abbreviated), chapter, and verse—never a page number. A colon is used between chapter and verse. Note that the traditional abbreviations use periods but the shorter forms do not. For guidance on when to abbreviate and when not to, see 10.50. For full forms and abbreviations, see 10.51, 10.52, 10.53.

Traditional abbreviations:

1. 1 Thess. 4:11, 5:2–5, 5:14.
2. Heb. 13:8, 13:12.
3. Gen. 25:19–36:43.

Shorter abbreviations:

4. 2 Sm 11:1–17, 11:26–27; 1 Chr 10:13–14.
5. Jo 5:9–12; Mt 26:2–5.

14.140 **Versions of the Bible.** Since books and numbering are not identical in different versions, it is essential to identify which version is being cited. For a work intended for general readers, the version should be spelled out, at least on first occurrence. For specialists, abbreviations may be used throughout. For abbreviations of versions, see 10.54.

1. 2 Kings 11:8 (New Revised Standard Version).
2. 1 Cor. 6:1–10 (NRSV).

14.141 **Other sacred works.** References to the sacred and revered works of other religious traditions may, according to context, be treated in a manner similar to those of biblical or classical works. Citations of transliterated texts should indicate the name of the version or translator. The Koran (or Qur'an) is set in roman, and citations of its sections use Arabic numerals and colons (e.g., Koran 19:17–21). Such collective terms as the Vedas or the Upanishads are normally capitalized and set in roman, but particular parts are italicized (e.g., the *Rig Veda* or the *Brihadaranyaka Upanishad*). For authoritative usage, consult *History of Religions*, an international journal for comparative historical studies (bibliog. 5).

## *Classical Greek and Latin References*

14.142 **Where to cite classical references.** Classical primary source references are ordinarily given in text or notes. They are included in a bibliography only when the reference is to information or annotation supplied by a modern author (see 14.146, 14.151).

The eighty days of inactivity reported by Thucydides (8.44.4) for the Peloponnesian fleet at Rhodes, terminating before the end of Thucydides's winter (8.60.2–3), suggests . . .

14.143 **Identifying numbers in classical references.** The numbers identifying the various parts of classical works—books, sections, lines, and so on—remain the same in all editions, whether in the original language or in translation. (In poetry, line content may vary slightly from the original in some translations.) Arabic numerals are used. Where letters also are used, they are usually lowercased but may be capitalized if the source being cited uses capitals. Page numbers are omitted except in references to introductions, notes, and the like supplied by a modern editor or to specific translations. See also 14.145, 14.150.

1. Ovid, *Amores* 1.7.27.

2. Aristotle, *Metaphysics* 3.2.996b5–8; Plato, *Republic* 360e–361b.

14.144 **Abbreviations in classical references.** Abbreviations of authors' names as well as of works, collections, and so forth are used extensively in classical references. The most widely accepted standard for abbreviations is the list included in *The Oxford Classical Dictionary* (bibliog. 5). When abbreviations are used, these rather than *ibid.* should be used in succeeding references to the same work. (Abbreviations are best avoided when only two letters are omitted, and they must not be used when more than one writer could be meant—Hipponax or Hipparchus, Aristotle or Aristophanes.)

1. Thuc. 2.40.2–3.

2. Pindar, *Isthm.* 7.43–45.

14.145 **Punctuation in classical references.** Place a comma between the name of a classical author (abbreviated or not) and the title of a work. No punctuation intervenes, however, between title and identifying number (or between author and number when the author is standing in for the title). Numerical divisions are separated by periods with no space following each period. Commas are used between two or more references to the same source, semicolons between references to different sources, and en dashes between continuing numbers. If such abbreviations as *bk.* or *sec.* are needed for clarity, commas separate the different elements.

1. Aristophanes, *Frogs* 1019–30.

2. Cic., *Verr.* 1.3.21, 2.3.120; Caes., *B Gall.* 6.19; Tac., *Germ.* 10.2–3.

3. Hdt. 7.1.2.

4. Sappho, *Invocation to Aphrodite*, st. 1, lines 1–6.

14.146 **Citing specific editions of classical references.** Details of the edition used, along with translator (if any) and the facts of publication, should be either specified the first time a classical work is cited or given elsewhere in the scholarly apparatus. If several editions are used, the edition (or an abbreviation) should accompany each citation. Although many classicists will recognize a well-known edition merely from the last name of the editor or translator, a full citation, at least in the bibliography, should be furnished as a courtesy.

1. Epictetus, *Dissertationes*, ed. Heinrich Schenkl (Teubner, 1916).
2. Herodotus, *The History*, trans. David Grene (University of Chicago Press, 1987).
3. Solon (Edmonds's numbering) 36.20–27.

**14.147** **Titles of classical works and collections.** Titles of works and published collections are italicized whether given in full or abbreviated (see 14.144). Latin and transliterated Greek titles are capitalized in sentence case (see 8.159, 11.8, 11.61).

1. Cato's uses of *pater familias* in *Agr.* (2.1, 2.7, 3.1, 3.2) are exclusively in reference to estate management. For the *diligens pater familias* in Columella, see *Rust.* 1.1.3, 1.2.1, 5.6.37, 9.1.6, 12.21.6.
2. *Scholia graeca in Homeri Odysseam*, ed. Wilhelm Dindorf (Oxford, 1855; repr. 1962).
3. *Patrologiae cursus completus, series graeca* (Migne, 1857–66).

**14.148** **Superscripts in classical references.** In classical references, a superior (superscript) numeral is sometimes used immediately after the title of a work (or its abbreviation), and preceding any other punctuation, to indicate the number of the edition.

1. Stolz-Schmalz, *Lat. Gram.*$^{5}$ (rev. Leumann-Hoffmann; Munich, 1928), 390–91.
2. *Ausgewählte Komödien des T. M. Plautus*$^{2}$, vol. 2 (1883).

In former practice, the letters accompanying numerals in citations of classical works (see 14.143) sometimes appeared as superscripts (e.g., 3.2.996$^{b}$5–8).

**14.149** **Collections of inscriptions.** Arabic numerals are used in references to volumes in collections of inscriptions. Periods follow the volume and inscription numbers, and further subdivisions are treated as in other classical references.

1. *IG* 2$^{2}$.3274. [= *Inscriptiones graecae*, vol. 2, 2nd ed., inscription no. 3274]
2. *IG Rom.* 3.739.9–10. [*IG Rom.* = *Inscriptiones graecae ad res romanas pertinentes*]
3. *POxy.* 1485. [= *Oxyrhynchus papyri*, document no. 1485]

Some collections are cited only by the name of the editor. Since the editor's name here stands in place of a title, no comma is needed.

4. Dessau 6964.23–29. [= H. Dessau, ed., *Inscriptiones latinae selectae*]

14.150 **Fragments of classical texts.** Fragments of classical texts (some only recently discovered) are not uniformly numbered. They are published in collections, and the numbering is usually unique to a particular edition. Two numbers separated by a period usually indicate fragment and line. The editor's name, often abbreviated in subsequent references, must therefore follow the number.

1. Empedocles, frag. 115 Diels-Kranz.
2. Anacreon, frag. 2.10 Diehl.
3. Hesiod, frag. 239.1 Merkelbach and West.
4. Anacreon, frag. 5.2 D.
5. Hesiod, frag. 220 M.-W.

In citations of two or more editions of the same set of fragments, either parentheses or an equals sign may be used.

6. Pindar, frag. 133 Bergk (frag. 127 Bowra).

*or*

7. Pindar, frag. 133 Bergk = 127 Bowra.

14.151 **Modern editions of the classics.** When Greek, Latin, or medieval classics are cited by page number, the edition must be specified, and the normal rules for citing books are followed. See also 14.146.

1. Propertius, *Elegies*, ed. and trans. G. P. Goold, Loeb Classical Library 18 (Harvard University Press, 1990), 45.

Aristotle. *Complete Works of Aristotle: The Revised Oxford Translation*. Edited by Jonathan Barnes. 2 vols. Bollingen Series. Princeton University Press, 1984.

Maimonides. *The Code of Maimonides, Book 5: The Book of Holiness*. Edited by Leon Nemoy. Translated by Louis I. Rabinowitz and Philip Grossman. Yale University Press, 1965.

14.152 **Medieval references.** The form for classical references may equally well be applied to medieval works.

1. Augustine, *De civitate Dei* 20.2.
2. Augustine, *The City of God*, trans. John Healey (Dutton, 1931), 20.2.

3. *Beowulf*, lines 2401–7.
4. Abelard, *Epistle 17 to Heloïse* (Migne, *PL* 180.375c–378a).
5. *Sir Gawain and the Green Knight*, trans. Theodore Silverstein (University of Chicago Press, 1974), pt. 3, p. 57.

## *Classic English Poems and Plays*

14.153 **Citing editions of classic English poems and plays.** Classic English poems and plays can often be cited by book, canto, and stanza; stanza and line; act, scene, and line; or similar divisions. Publication facts can then be omitted. For frequently cited works—especially those of Shakespeare, where variations can occur in wording, line numbering, and even scene division—the edition is normally specified in the first note reference or in the bibliography. The edition must be mentioned if page numbers are cited (see 14.151).

1. Chaucer, "Wife of Bath's Prologue," *Canterbury Tales*, frag. 3, lines 105–14.
2. Spenser, *The Faerie Queene*, bk. 2, canto 8, st. 14.
3. Milton, *Paradise Lost*, bk. 1, lines 83–86.
4. *King Lear*, ed. David Bevington et al. (Bantam Books, 2005), 3.2.49–60. References are to act, scene, and line.

Dryden, John. *Dramatic Essays*. Everyman's Library. Dutton, 1912.
Shakespeare, William. *Hamlet*. Rev. ed. Edited by Ann Thompson and Neil Taylor. Arden Shakespeare, 3rd ser. Bloomsbury Arden Shakespeare, 2016.

14.154 **Short forms for citing classic English poems and plays.** A citation may be shortened by omitting *act*, *line*, and the like, as long as the system used has been explained. Arabic numerals are used, separated by periods. In immediately succeeding references, it is usually safer to repeat all the numbers. The author's name may be omitted if clear from the text. For citing sources in text, see 12.78.

1. Pope, *Rape of the Lock*, 3.28–29.
2. *Lear* (Bevington), 4.1.1–9, 4.1.18–24.
3. "Wife of Bath's Prologue," 115–16.

## *Musical Scores*

14.155 **Published scores.** Published musical scores are treated in much the same way as books.

1. Giuseppe Verdi, *Il corsaro* (*melodramma tragico* in three acts), libretto by Francesco Maria Piave, ed. Elizabeth Hudson, 2 vols., *The Works of Giuseppe Verdi*, ser. 1, *Operas* (University of Chicago Press; G. Ricordi, 1998).

Mozart, Wolfgang Amadeus. *Sonatas and Fantasies for the Piano*. Prepared from the autographs and earliest printed sources by Nathan Broder. Rev. ed. Theodore Presser, 1960.

Schubert, Franz. "Das Wandern (Wandering)," *Die schöne Müllerin (The Maid of the Mill)*. In *First Vocal Album* (for high voice). G. Schirmer, 1895.

In the last example above, the words and titles are given in both German and English in the score itself. See also 13.101.

14.156 **Unpublished scores.** Unpublished scores are treated in the same way as other unpublished material in manuscript collections (see 14.119–29).

1. Ralph Shapey, "Partita for Violin and Thirteen Players," score, 1966, Special Collections, Joseph Regenstein Library, University of Chicago.

## *Databases*

14.157 **Citing databases and datasets.** Whenever a claim depends on data, those data should be cited in such a way that readers can access and evaluate the same data for themselves. Data that can be found in a journal article or book or other published source can be described in the text or in a note and cited in reference to that source as detailed elsewhere in this chapter. Data available via an independent database, dataset, or other collection of files, however, can usually be cited directly, even when tied to another publication (as in the case of the Zou and Rudolf dataset below, which supports an article in *The American Naturalist*). The elements will vary depending on the repository (many of which offer suggested citations) but should include any title displayed with the data and, if not clear from the rest of the citation, an indication of the type of source (e.g., "dataset"). The examples below, designed for general use, may be adapted as needed. For additional guidance, refer to the Data Citation Synthesis Group's *Joint Declaration of Data Citation Principles* (bibliog. 5). Some journals also offer data citation guidelines for authors. See also 14.86.

1. Data for object Messier 31 (IRAS F00400+4059), NASA/IPAC Extragalactic Database, California Institute of Technology, accessed September 14, 2022, https://ned.ipac.caltech.edu/.

2. Data for *Homo sapiens* chromosome 15 clone RP11-322N14 map 15, low-pass

sequence sampling, accession no. AC087526.3, National Center for Biotechnology Information (US), accessed September 14, 2022, https://www.ncbi.nlm.nih.gov/nuccore/19683167.

MIT Election Data and Science Lab. "U.S. Senate Precinct-Level Returns 2020." Version 1.1. Harvard Dataverse, March 17, 2022. https://doi.org/10.7910/DVN/ER9XTV.

US Bureau of Labor Statistics. "Labor Force Statistics from the Current Population Survey." Dataset for 2020–22. BLS Data Labs. Accessed June 9, 2023. https://beta.bls.gov/dataViewer/view/timeseries/LNS12000000.

Zou, Heng-Xing, and Volker H. W. Rudolf. Data from "Priority Effects Determine How Dispersal Affects Biodiversity in Seasonal Metacommunities." Dryad dataset, February 9, 2023. https://doi.org/10.5061/dryad.sbcc2frb4.

For work that relies on many related datasets, listing only the database as a whole in the bibliography can reduce repetition and prevent the list from becoming too long.

National Center for Biotechnology Information (US). Nucleotide database. Accessed June 22, 2023. https://www.ncbi.nlm.nih.gov/nuccore/.

Datasets with their own DOIs, however, should normally be listed individually in a bibliography or reference list to facilitate citation tracking by publishers and others.

**Author-date.** In author-date format, only the year of publication (and not a month or day) follows the name of the author(s) (see also 14.89).

Zou, Heng-Xing, and Volker H. W. Rudolf. 2023. Data from "Priority Effects Determine How Dispersal Affects Biodiversity in Seasonal Metacommunities." Dryad dataset, February 9. https://doi.org/10.5061/dryad.sbcc2frb4.

(Zou and Rudolf 2023)

If there is no date of publication, specify *n.d.* (no date) in addition to an access date (see also 14.104). But if the cited data apply to a specific year (or years), use that information instead of *n.d.*

California Institute of Technology. n.d. Data for object Messier 31 (IRAS F00400+4059). NASA/IPAC Extragalactic Database. Accessed September 14, 2022. https://ned.ipac.caltech.edu/.

(California Institute of Technology, n.d.)

*but*

US Bureau of Labor Statistics. 2020–22. “Labor Force Statistics from the Current Population Survey.” BLS Data Labs. Accessed June 9, 2023. https://beta.bls.gov/dataViewer/view/timeseries/LNS12000000.

(US Bureau of Labor Statistics 2020–22)

## *Patents and Standards*

14.158 **Patents.** Patents are cited under the names of the creators, a description of the patent, and the year of filing. Include a URL for patents consulted online.

Iizuka, Masanori, and Hideki Tanaka. Cement admixture. US Patent 4,586,960, filed June 26, 1984, and issued May 6, 1986. https://patents.google.com/patent/US4586960A/.

**Author-date.** In author-date format, patents and other documents that include more than one date should repeat the year (in this case, the year of issue) to avoid ambiguity:

Iizuka, Masanori, and Hideki Tanaka. 1986. Cement admixture. US Patent 4,586,960, filed June 26, 1984, and issued May 6, 1986. https://patents.google.com/patent/US4586960A/.

14.159 **Standards.** Standards published by a specific industry group or by a national or international standards organization can usually be cited in the notes by title. In a bibliography entry, list under the name of the organization; if the organization and publisher are the same, an abbreviation may be used for the publisher data.

1. *Bibliographic References,* ANSI/NISO Z39.29-2005 (R2010), NISO, approved June 9, 2005; reaffirmed May 13, 2010, 3.2.2, https://www.niso.org/publications/ansi niso-z3929-2005-r2010.

2. *Extensible Markup Language (XML) 1.1,* 2nd ed., ed. Tim Bray et al., W3C, August 16, 2006, https://www.w3.org/TR/xml11/.

National Information Standards Organization. *Bibliographic References.* ANSI/NISO Z39.29-2005 (R2010). NISO. Approved June 9, 2005; reaffirmed May 13, 2010. https://groups.niso.org/higherlogic/ws/public/download/12969.

World Wide Web Consortium. *Extensible Markup Language (XML) 1.1.* 2nd ed. Edited by Tim Bray, Jean Paoli, C. M. Sperberg-McQueen, Eve Maler, François Yergeau, and John Cowan. W3C, August 16, 2006. https://www.w3.org/TR/xml11/.

## *Citations Taken from Secondary Sources*

14.160 **Citations taken from secondary sources.** To cite a source from a secondary source ("quoted in . . .") is generally to be discouraged, since authors are expected to have examined the works they cite. If an original source is unavailable, however, both the original and the secondary source must be listed.

1. Louis Zukofsky, "Sincerity and Objectification," *Poetry* 37 (February 1931): 269, quoted in Bonnie Costello, *Marianne Moore: Imaginary Possessions* (Harvard University Press, 1981), 78.

**Author-date.** In author-date format, mention the original author and date in the text but cite the secondary source in the reference list.

Costello, Bonnie. 1981. *Marianne Moore: Imaginary Possessions*. Harvard University Press.

In Louis Zukofsky's "Sincerity and Objectification," from the February 1931 issue of *Poetry* magazine (quoted in Costello 1981) . . .

## MULTIMEDIA

14.161 **Multimedia — elements of the citation.** Citations of multimedia content will vary depending on the type of source. The following elements are usually included:

1. The person or group or other entity responsible for creating or compiling the content
2. A title or description of the content
3. The name of the publisher or other entity responsible for making the content available
4. The date that the content was recorded or published
5. Information about the medium
6. For sources consulted online, a URL (see 13.6–12).

Other information that may help readers locate or assess the content may be added as needed. Consult the examples throughout this section.

14.162 **Discographies, filmographies, and the like.** Discographies, filmographies, and the like are specialized bibliographies that list (and sometimes annotate) materials such as audio recordings, video recordings, and multimedia packages. The examples in this section are modeled on notes and bibliography entries but would be appropriately presented as a separate list, either preceding the bibliography or as an appendix (see also 13.67). For advice on music discographies, consult Suzanne E. Thorin and Carole Franklin Vidali, *The Acquisition and Cataloging of Music and Sound Recordings* (bibliog. 5).

## *Recordings and Live Performances*

14.163 **Musical recordings.** For the typographic treatment of musical compositions in running text, see 8.195–99. Most of those guidelines apply also to cited sources, though titles of works may vary according to published version. A citation may begin with a title in a note; in a bibliography entry, list by author, performer, or other primary contributor. If the conductor or performer is the focus of the recording or is more relevant to the discussion than the composer or songwriter, either one may be listed first. Include either the date of the recording or a publication date, or both. If a date cannot be determined from the recording (a common problem with older recordings and with music files downloaded out of context), consult a library catalog or other resource. If no date can be found, use "n.d." (for *no date*). Recordings on LP or disc typically include acquisition numbers, which follow the name of the publisher with no intervening comma. For digital recordings other than compact discs, a streaming service or file format may be noted if relevant but is not required.

1. *The Fireside Treasury of Folk Songs*, vol. 1, orchestra and chorus dir. Mitch Miller, Golden Record A198:17A–B, 1958, 33⅓ rpm.

2. New York Trumpet Ensemble, with Edward Carroll (trumpet) and Edward Brewer (organ), *Art of the Trumpet*, recorded at the Madeira Festival, June 1–2, 1981, Vox/Turnabout PVT 7183, 1982, compact disc.

3. Richard Strauss, *Don Quixote*, with Emanuel Feuermann (violoncello) and the Philadelphia Orchestra, conducted by Eugene Ormandy, recorded February 24, 1940, Biddulph LAB 042, 1991, compact disc.

4. Billie Holiday, vocalist, "I'm a Fool to Want You," by Joel Herron, Frank Sinatra, and Jack Wolf, recorded February 20, 1958, with Ray Ellis, track 1 on *Lady in Satin*, Columbia CL 1157, 33⅓ rpm.

5. "Umbrella," featuring Jay-Z, MP3 audio, track 1 on Rihanna, *Good Girl Gone Bad*, Island Def Jam, 2007.

6. “Everything I Wanted,” by Billie Eilish and Finneas O’Connell, produced by Finneas O’Connell, Darkroom / Interscope Records, released as a single on November 13, 2019.

Eilish, Billie. *When We All Fall Asleep, Where Do We Go?* Produced by Finneas O’Connell. Darkroom / Interscope Records (US); Polydor Records (UK). Released March 29, 2019.

Mozart, Wolfgang Amadeus. *Don Giovanni*. Orchestra and Chorus of the Royal Opera House, Covent Garden. Sir Colin Davis. With Ingvar Wixell, Luigi Roni, Martina Arroyo, et al. Recorded May 1973. Philips 422 541-2, 1991, 3 compact discs.

Pink Floyd. *Atom Heart Mother*. Capitol CDP 7 46381 2, 1990, compact disc. Originally released in 1970.

Rubinstein, Artur, pianist. *The Chopin Collection*. Recorded 1946, 1958–67. RCA Victor / BMG 60822-2-RG, 1991, 11 compact discs.

Weingartner, Felix von, conductor. *150 Jahre Wiener Philharmoniker*. Recorded in 1936. Preiser Records PR90113 (mono), 1992, compact disc. Includes Beethoven’s Symphony No. 3 in E-flat Major and Symphony No. 8 in F Major.

Musical recordings are usually listed in a separate discography rather than in a bibliography. If included in a bibliography, they are best grouped under an appropriate subhead (see 13.67).

14.164 **Recorded readings, lectures, and the like.** Recordings of drama, prose or poetry readings, lectures, and the like are treated much the same as musical recordings (see 14.163). Facts of publication, where needed, follow the style for print media. For examples in video format, see 14.167.

1. Dylan Thomas, *Under Milk Wood*, performed by Dylan Thomas et al., Caedmon TC-2005, 1953, 33⅓ rpm, 2 LPs.

2. Harry S. Truman, “First Speech to Congress,” April 16, 1945, Miller Center of Public Affairs, University of Virginia, transcript and audio, 18:13, https://millercenter.org/the-presidency/presidential-speeches/april-16-1945-first-speech-congress.

3. Calvin Coolidge, “Law and Order,” recorded March 2, 1920, New York, in American Leaders Speak: Recordings from World War I, Library of Congress, copy of a 78 rpm disc, 4 min., 40 sec., https://lccn.loc.gov/2004650650.

4. Eleanor Roosevelt, “Is America Facing World Leadership?,” convocation speech, Ball State Teachers College, May 6, 1959, Muncie, IN, radio broadcast, reel-to-reel tape, MPEG copy, 1:12:49, https://dmr.bsu.edu/digital/collection/ElRoos/id/1.

Auden, W. H. *Selected Poems*. Read by the author. Spoken Arts 7137, 1991. Audiocassette.

14.165 **Video and film recordings.** Like sound recordings, video and film recordings are cited according to the nature of the material (television show, movie, etc.). Any facts relevant to identifying the item should be included. Indexed scenes are treated as chapters and cited by title or by number (as in example note 2 below). Ancillary material, such as critical commentary and interviews, is usually cited in terms of the related content. Note that in the *Monty Python* example, the citation is of material original to the 2001 edition, so the original release date of the film (1975) is omitted. See also 14.167.

1. *American Crime Story: The People v. O. J. Simpson*, episode 6, "Marcia, Marcia, Marcia," written by D. V. DeVincentis, directed by Ryan Murphy, featuring Sterling K. Brown, Kenneth Choi, and Sarah Paulson, aired March 8, 2016, on FX, https://www.amazon.com/dp/B01ARVPCOA/.

2. "Crop Duster Attack," *North by Northwest*, directed by Alfred Hitchcock (1959; Warner Home Video, 2000), DVD.

3. Louis J. Mihalyi, *Landscapes of Zambia, Central Africa* (Visual Education, 1975), 35 mm slides, 40 frames, 15 min.

4. *Star Trek*, season 2, episode 15, "The Trouble with Tribbles," written by David Gerrold, directed by Joseph Pevney, aired December 29, 1967, on NBC.

Bong Joon-ho, dir. *Parasite*. Barunson E&A, 2019. In Korean, with English subtitles by Darcy Paquet.

Cleese, John, Terry Gilliam, Eric Idle, Terry Jones, and Michael Palin. "Commentaries." Disc 2. *Monty Python and the Holy Grail*, special ed. DVD. Directed by Terry Gilliam and Terry Jones. Columbia Tristar Home Entertainment, 2001.

Cuarón, Alfonso, dir. *Gravity*. 2013; Warner Bros. Pictures, 2014. Blu-ray Disc, 1080p HD.

Handel, George Frideric. *Messiah*. Atlanta Symphony Orchestra and Chamber Chorus, Robert Shaw. Performed December 19, 1987. Video Artists International, 1988. Videocassette (VHS), 141 min.

Mayberry, Russ, dir. *The Brady Bunch*. Season 3, episode 10, "Her Sister's Shadow." Aired November 19, 1971, on ABC. https://www.paramountplus.com/shows/the_brady_bunch/.

14.166 **Live performances.** Live performances, unlike recordings, cannot be consulted as such by readers. For that reason, it is generally sufficient to mention details in the text or in the notes rather than in a bibliography. In addition to specifying the name and location of the venue and the date of the performance, include as much information as needed to identify the performance according to the guidelines outlined in 14.161.

For the use of italics and quotation marks and other considerations for titles of works, see 8.157–204.

In a performance of Michael R. Jackson's *A Strange Loop* at the Lyceum Theatre in New York on September 20, 2022, . . .

1. *A Strange Loop*, music and lyrics by Michael R. Jackson, dir. Stephen Brackett, chor. Raja Feather Kelly, Lyceum Theatre, New York, NY, September 20, 2022.

To cite a recording of a live performance, consult the relevant examples at 14.163, 14.164, and 14.165.

## *Videos, Podcasts, and Apps*

14.167 **Online videos.** Online videos are cited similarly to the recordings and live performances discussed in 14.163–66. Adapt the examples below to suit the content. If the material consists of a recording of a speech or other performance or a digitized copy of a source published in a different medium, include information about the original source. Whether to list the original or the copy first may depend on the information available and is usually up to the author. Copies of sources under copyright that have been posted without ties to any publisher or sponsor should be cited with caution; whenever possible, locate a better version of the source. For multimedia designed to run in a web browser, a file format does not need to be mentioned, though it may be specified for files offered as downloads. For the musical conventions illustrated in the Lang Lang example below (which have been updated for this edition), see 8.195–99. For photos, see 14.133. Note that Talks at Google, University of Chicago, and Amazon in example notes 2, 3, and 5 are the names of YouTube channels (see also 14.103).

1. A. E. Weed, *At the Foot of the Flatiron* (American Mutoscope and Biograph Co., 1903), 35 mm film, from Library of Congress, *The Life of a City: Early Films of New York, 1898–1906*, MPEG video, 2:19 at 15 fps, https://www.loc.gov/item/00694378.

2. "Lang Lang: *The Chopin Album*," interview by Jeff Spurgeon, October 15, 2012, posted October 18, 2012, by Talks at Google, YouTube, 54 min., 47 sec., featuring performances of Nocturne in E-flat Major, op. 55, no. 2; Etude in F Minor, op. 25, no. 2; Etude in E Major, op. 10, no. 3; and "Grande valse brillante" in E-flat Major, op. 18, https://youtu.be/1d8xv1HHKtI.

3. Eric Oliver, "Why So Many Americans Believe in So Many 'Crazy' Things," moderated by Andrew McCall, virtual lecture, February 23, 2022,

posted March 21, 2022, by University of Chicago, YouTube, https://youtu.be/hfq7AnCF5bg.

4. Vaitea Cowan, "How Green Hydrogen Could End the Fossil Fuel Era," TED Talk, Vancouver, BC, April 2022, 9 min., 15 sec., https://www.ted.com/talks/vaitea_cowan_how_green_hydrogen_could_end_the_fossil_fuel_era.

5. "Amazon's Big Game Commercial: Alexa's Body," advertisement, featuring Michael B. Jordan, directed by Wayne McClammy, created by Lucky Generals, posted February 2, 2021, by Amazon, YouTube, 1 min., https://youtu.be/xxNxqveseyI.

Brown, Evan. "The 10 Commandments of Typography." Infographic. DesignMantic, April 11, 2014. https://www.designmantic.com/blog/infographics/ten-commandments-of-typography/.

Laffin, Ben, ed. "(Re)Defining the American Dream." Produced by Emma Cott and Ben Laffin. *New York Times*, August 21, 2022. Video, 4 min., 15 sec. https://www.nytimes.com/video/us/politics/100000008465172/-re-defining-the-american-dream.html.

Lyiscott, Jamila. "3 Ways to Speak English." TED Talk, New York, NY, February 2014. 4 min., 16 sec. https://www.ted.com/talks/jamila_lyiscott_3_ways_to_speak_english.

To cite comments, adapt the recommendations for citing comments on blog posts or social media (see 14.105, 14.106).

4. Frithjof Meyer, comment on "Lang Lang," March 2015.

14.168 **Podcasts.** Podcasts, whether consulted online via a browser or via an app, are cited much like television episodes and series (see 14.165).

1. Lauren Ober, host, *The Loudest Girl in the World*, podcast, season 1, episode 2, "Goodbye, Routine; Hello, Meltdown!," Pushkin Industries, September 13, 2022, https://www.pushkin.fm/podcasts/loudest-girl-in-the-world.

2. Dexter Thomas Jr., host, *Authentic: The Story of Tablo*, produced by Stephanie Kariuki, VICE / iHeart Podcast Network, March 24, 2022, https://omny.fm/shows/authentic-the-story-of-tablo/6-jeong-ui-justice.

14.169 **Video games and other apps.** Video games and other software programs or apps can usually be cited in the text or notes with no corresponding bibliography entry. Include a version number and release date and, if applicable, the platform or operating system. If a bibliography entry is included (as in a separate section for games or software; see 13.67), list under the name of the publisher or developer. See also 8.192.

1. *Angry Birds Transformers*, v. 2.24.0, Rovio Entertainment, released June 28, 2023, Android 4.4 or later.

2. *Gran Tourismo 7* for PlayStation 4 and 5, Mojang Studios, Sony Interactive Entertainment, released March 4, 2022.

3. Microsoft Word for Microsoft 365 for Windows, v. 2306, build 16.0.16529.20226, released August 8, 2023.

Rovio Entertainment. *Angry Birds Transformers*. V. 2.24.0. Released June 28, 2023. Android 4.4 or later.

## LEGAL AND PUBLIC DOCUMENTS

**14.170** **Recommended stylebooks.** Citations in predominantly legal works generally follow one of two guides: (1) *The Bluebook: A Uniform System of Citation*, published by the Harvard Law Review Association; or (2) the *ALWD Guide to Legal Citation*, prepared by the Association of Legal Writing Directors and Carolyn V. Williams (see bibliog. 1.1). *The Bluebook* is the most widely used citation guide; its conventions predominate in law reviews. The *ALWD Guide* differs in some elements and aims to be somewhat simpler. Chicago recommends using one of these systems for citing legal and public documents—including cases, constitutions, statutes, and other government documents—even in works with predominantly nonlegal subject matter. This approach recognizes the ubiquity of these citation formats in legal publications, commercial databases, and government archives. Any editor working extensively with legal and public documents should have one of these manuals on hand. Most of the examples in this section are based on *The Bluebook* (exceptions are made for secondary sources and certain unpublished government documents; see 14.192, 14.193). *The Bluebook* and the *ALWD Guide* are used in the United States. For citation guides used in Canada, see 14.194; for those used in the United Kingdom, see 14.198.

**14.171** **Legal and public documents online.** *The Bluebook* includes specific guidelines for citing sources consulted online. In general, for citations of cases, constitutions, statutes, and like materials, print sources are preferred, but online versions authenticated by a government entity or otherwise considered to be the official version or an exact copy thereof (e.g., an unaltered PDF) can be treated as if they were print. (If a URL is required, it may be appended as the last element of the citation; see also 14.177.) Citations of sources consulted through commercial databases such as Westlaw or Lexis should include the database name and any applicable identification number (or, in the case of constitutions and statutes, information about the currency of the database). For examples, see 14.177. To cite books, articles in periodicals, and other types of nonlegal sources consulted online, Chicago's recommendations can usually be followed (see 13.6–12).

14.172 **Note form for legal-style citations.** Legal publications use notes for documentation and rarely include bibliographies. The examples in this section, based on the recommendations in *The Bluebook*, are accordingly given in note form only. Any work so cited need not be listed in a bibliography (but see 14.192).

**Author-date.** Any work using the author-date system that needs to do more than mention the occasional legal document should use supplementary footnotes or endnotes (see also 13.128). This advice does not extend to documents cited in secondary sources or published as freestanding works (see 14.192), since these are readily adapted to the author-date system (see 14.1). Works with only a handful of citations to legal documents may be able to limit these to the text, borrowing the note forms detailed in the rest of this section.

In *NLRB v. Somerville Construction Co.* (206 F.3d 752 (7th Cir. 2000)), the court ruled that . . .

In the *Congressional Record* for that day (168 Cong. Rec. S7012 (daily ed. Dec. 7, 2022)), Senator Durbin is quoted as saying that . . .

See also 14.175 and 14.187. For the use of parentheses within parentheses, see 6.103.

14.173 **Typefaces in legal-style citations.** Like Chicago and many other styles, *The Bluebook* recommends italics for emphasis and for uncommon terms from other languages. But in a major departure from nonlegal usage, *The Bluebook* specifies italics for titles of articles and chapters, certain introductory signals indicating a cross-reference (such as *See*), explanatory terms related to case history and the like (such as *aff'd*; see 14.179), and procedural phrases (such as *In re*). In addition, italics are used for case names in textual sentences, whether in the running text or in the notes, and for titles of books and other publications mentioned in textual sentences. Most other material, including case names in citations (but not their shortened forms), appears in roman. (See 14.177.) In another departure from nonlegal style, *The Bluebook* specifies caps and small caps for the names of constitutions, the titles of books and their authors, and the names of periodicals and websites when these appear in citations. For the sake of simplicity, the examples in this section that feature such sources use either regular upper- and lowercase letters (as for constitutions) or, for books and other nonlegal materials, Chicago-style italics or quotation marks (see 14.192). Though *Bluebook*-style citations to books, articles, and other types of secondary sources may be appropriate in works with predominantly legal subject matter, these are not covered here.

14.174 **Page numbers and other locators in legal-style citations.** In *Bluebook* style, for most sources the first page number is cited, following the name of the source and usually with no intervening punctuation; except in shortened citations, references to specific page numbers follow the first page number, separated by a comma. Some types of sources are cited by section (§) or paragraph (¶) or other number; references to specific pages within such sections follow a comma and *at* (in roman type). A comma plus *at* may also be used when needed for clarity (as before a page number consisting of Roman numerals or when a page number immediately follows a source name ending in an Arabic numeral).

14.175 **Abbreviations in legal-style citations.** *The Bluebook* specifies abbreviations for the names of reporters, cases, courts, and legislative documents, as well as journals and compilation services. It also includes guidelines for abbreviating certain terms commonly used in legal citations (some of which, like *ed.* and *vol.*, are the same in Chicago style). Most abbreviations in *The Bluebook* use either periods or apostrophes, but exceptions are made for organizations and other entities commonly referred to by their initials (such as NBC or FDA). (See 14.199 for another exception.) In citations (but not in running text), *Bluebook* style specifies *2d* and *3d* rather than *2nd* and *3rd* for ordinals and capitalizes abbreviations like *No.* and *Sess.* Works that otherwise follow Chicago style—which differs on some of these points (see, e.g., 10.4)—should, for legal citations, follow *Bluebook* style, as shown in the examples in this section. The following example cites a decision by the United States Court of Appeals for the Seventh Circuit, reported in volume 206 of the *Federal Reporter*, third series, beginning on page 752, with the citation specifically referring to footnote 1 on that page (see also 14.179).

1. NLRB v. Somerville Constr. Co., 206 F.3d 752, 752 n.1 (7th Cir. 2000).

In running text, most terms should be spelled out—including terms such as *chapter*, *part*, *article*, *section*, *paragraph*, and so forth (but, in case names, not *v.* or common abbreviations such as *Co.*, *Inc.*, or *Gov't*). For more specific recommendations, consult *The Bluebook*. See also 8.81, 8.83.

14.176 **Short forms for legal-style citations.** *The Bluebook* allows certain short forms for subsequent citations to the same source. Short forms include case names reduced to the name of only one party (usually the plaintiff or the nongovernmental party); statutes and legislative documents identified only by name or document and section numbers; treaties identified only by name (or sometimes a short form thereof); and the use of *id.* (in italics). Cases are the most readily shortened forms; examples are included in the section that treats them (14.177–80). Works that cite only a few legal documents may be better off using the full form for each citation. See also 13.32–39.

## *Cases and Court Decisions*

14.177 **Cases and court decisions — basic elements.** Full case names in citations, including the abbreviation *v.*, are set in roman in notes; short forms in subsequent citations are italicized (as are full case names mentioned in textual sentences; see example 3 below). Full citations include the volume number, abbreviated name, and (if applicable) ordinal series number of the reporter(s); the abbreviated name of the court (if not indicated by the reporter) and the date (together in parentheses); and other relevant information (see 14.180). A single page number designates the opening page of a decision; an additional number designates an actual page cited. In a shortened citation, *at* is used to cite a particular page (example 3); absence of *at* implies reference to the decision as a whole (example 4). See also 14.173, 14.176.

1. United States v. Christmas, 222 F.3d 141, 145 (4th Cir. 2000).
2. Profit Sharing Plan v. Mbank Dallas, N.A., 683 F. Supp. 592 (N.D. Tex. 1988).
3. *Christmas*, 222 F.3d at 145. The court also noted that under *United States v. Sokolow*, 490 U.S. 1, 7 (1989), police may briefly detain a person without probable cause if the officer believes criminal activity "may be afoot." *Christmas*, 222 F.3d at 143; *see also* Terry v. Ohio, 392 U.S. 1 (1968).
4. *Profit Sharing Plan*, 683 F. Supp. 592.

When citing a commercial electronic database, include the docket number, name of the database, and any identifying date and number supplied by the database. References to page or screen numbers are preceded by an asterisk. Short forms may include only the database identifier.

6. Oral Surgeons, P.C. v. Cincinnati Ins., No. 20-3211, 2021 U.S. App. LEXIS 19775 (8th Cir. July 2, 2021).
7. *In re* D.S., No. 13-0888, 2014 WL 1495489 (Iowa Ct. App. Apr. 16, 2014).
8. *Oral Surgeons*, 2021 U.S. App. LEXIS 19775, at *4.
9. *D.S.*, 2014 WL 1495489, at *1.

Though rarely used in *Bluebook*-style citations, a URL that points directly to an official source such as a government website may be added in certain instances (e.g., for a case that is otherwise unpublished); consult *The Bluebook* for guidance. See also 13.6, 14.171.

14.178 **United States Supreme Court decisions.** All Supreme Court decisions are published in the *United States Reports* (abbreviated "U.S.") and are preferably cited to that reporter. Cases not yet published therein may be cited to the *Supreme Court Reporter* (S. Ct.), which publishes decisions more quickly. Because the court's name is indicated by the reporter, it is not repeated before the date.

1. Citizens United v. Federal Election Comm'n, 558 U.S. 310 (2010).
2. Chiafalo v. Washington, 140 S. Ct. 2316 (2020).
3. *Citizens United*, 558 U.S. at 322.

14.179 **Lower federal-court decisions.** Lower federal-court decisions are usually cited to the *Federal Reporter* (F.) or to the *Federal Supplement* (F. Supp.). Relevant case history should be included.

1. United States v. Dennis, 183 F.2d 201 (2d Cir. 1950).
2. Locke v. Shore, 682 F. Supp. 2d 1283 (N.D. Fla. 2010), *aff'd*, 634 F.3d 1185 (11th Cir. 2011).
3. Eaton v. IBM Corp., 925 F. Supp. 487 (S.D. Tex. 1996).
4. *Dennis*, 183 F.2d at 202.
5. *Locke*, 682 F. Supp. 2d at 1292.

For the use of spaces relative to ordinals, see 14.180.

14.180 **State- and local-court decisions.** Decisions of state and local courts are cited much like federal-court decisions. If both the official and the commercial reporters are cited, they are separated by a comma. If the court's name is identified unambiguously by the reporter, it is not repeated before the date. If a case was decided in a lower court, the abbreviated court name appears before the date (as in example 4 below). Note that a space is used before an ordinal that follows an abbreviated reporter name consisting of two or more letters—"Cal. 2d" (*California Re-*

*ports*, second series)—but not with initialisms like "A." in "A.2d" (*Atlantic Reporter*, second series) or "N.Y.S." in "N.Y.S.2d" (*New York Supplement*, second series). Some state courts have adopted a public-domain citation format for more recent cases; consult *The Bluebook* for guidance.

1. Williams v. Davis, 27 Cal. 2d 746 (1946).
2. *Id.* at 747.
3. Henningsen v. Bloomfield Motors, Inc., 32 N.J. 358, 161 A.2d 69 (1960).
4. Kendig v. Kendig, 981 N.Y.S.2d 411 (App. Div. 2014).
5. *Williams*, 27 Cal. 2d 746.

If it is important to avoid *id.* (as in an electronic format where individual notes may be presented out of context), use a shortened citation form instead. The short form for note 2, above, would be "*Williams*, 27 Cal. 2d at 747." See also 13.37, 13.38.

## *Constitutions*

14.181 **Constitutions.** In citations to constitutions, the article and amendment numbers appear in Roman numerals; other subdivision numbers are in Arabic. (For nonlegal style see 9.30.) In *Bluebook* style the name of the constitution is capitalized; other abbreviations are lowercased.

1. U.S. Const. art. I, § 4, cl. 2.
2. U.S. Const. amend. XIV, § 2.
3. Ariz. Const. art. VII, § 5.
4. Ark. Const. of 1868, art. III, § 2 (superseded 1874).

## *Legislative and Executive Documents*

14.182 **Legislative documents — abbreviations.** Abbreviations for federal legislative documents include "Cong." (Congress), "H." (House), "S." (Senate), and other standard shorthand for such terms as *document*, *session*, and *resolution*. Unless it is not clear from the context, "U.S." may be omitted (and, for certain House and Senate documents and reports, the session number may be omitted; see *The Bluebook* for guidance). For lists of abbreviations and many examples, consult *The Bluebook*. See also 14.175.

14.183 **Laws and statutes.** Federal bills or joint resolutions that have been signed into law—"public laws," or statutes—are first published separately, as slip laws, and then collected in the annual bound volumes of the *United States Statutes at Large* (abbreviated in legal style as "Stat."), where they are referred to as session laws. Later they are incorporated into the *United States Code* (U.S.C.). For session laws, the year that a statute was passed should be included in parentheses at the end of the citation unless it is part of the name (as in the second example below); in citations to the federal code (third example), the year is normally omitted whether it appears in the name of the statute or not.

1. Patient Protection and Affordable Care Act, Pub. L. No. 111-148, 124 Stat. 119 (2010).
2. American Rescue Plan Act of 2021, Pub. L. No. 117-2, 135 Stat. 4.
3. Homeland Security Act of 2002, 6 U.S.C. § 101.

14.184 **Bills and resolutions.** Federal bills (proposed laws) and resolutions are published in pamphlet form (slip bills). In citations, bills or resolutions originating in the House of Representatives are abbreviated "H.R." or "H.R. Res.," and those originating in the Senate, "S." or "S. Res." The title of the bill (if there is one) is followed by the bill number, the number of the Congress, a section number (if relevant), and the year of publication in parentheses. A bill that has been enacted should normally be cited as a statute (see 14.183); if cited as a bill to show legislative history, "enacted" may be added in parentheses after the date.

1. Respect for Marriage Act, H.R. 8404, 117th Cong. (2022) (enacted).

14.185 **Hearings.** Records of testimony given before congressional committees are usually published with titles, which should be cited in full and set in italics. The relevant committee should be listed as part of the title. Include the number of the Congress, the page number cited (if any), the year in parentheses, and the speaker's name, title, and affiliation in parentheses.

1. *Homeland Security Act of 2002: Hearings on H.R. 5005, Day 3, Before the Select Comm. on Homeland Security*, 107th Cong. 203 (2002) (statement of David Walker, Comptroller General of the United States).

14.186 **Congressional reports and documents.** In *Bluebook* style, numbered reports and documents are cited by the number of the Congress, which is joined to the document number by a hyphen. House and Senate reports are abbreviated "H.R. Rep." or "S. Rep."; documents are abbreviated "H.R. Doc." or "S. Doc." A specific page reference, if needed, is added following a comma and *at*. The year of the report or document is placed in parentheses. Additional information (e.g., to indicate a conference report) follows the year, in parentheses. If not mentioned in text, a title and author (if any) may be included in the citation.

1. Select Comm. on Homeland Security, Homeland Security Act of 2002, H.R. Rep. No. 107-609, pt. 1 (2002).
2. H.R. Rep. No. 113-564, at 54 (2014) (Conf. Rep.).
3. S. Doc. No. 77-148, at 2–5 (1941).

14.187 **Congressional debates since 1873.** Since 1873, congressional debates have been published by the government in the *Congressional Record*. Daily issues are bound in paper biweekly and in permanent volumes (divided into parts) yearly. Since material may be added, deleted, or modified when the final volumes are prepared, pagination will vary among the different editions. Whenever possible, citation should be made to the permanent volumes. Note that, following *Bluebook* style, italics are not used for the name of the publication. The page number (preceded by "H" or "S," for House or Senate, in the daily edition) is followed by the date, which is placed in parentheses. If the identity of a speaker is necessary, include it in parentheses.

1. 147 Cong. Rec. 19000 (2001).
2. 168 Cong. Rec. S7012 (daily ed. Dec. 7, 2022) (statement of Sen. Durbin).

14.188 **Records of congressional debates before 1873.** Until 1873, congressional debates were privately printed in *Annals of the Congress of the United States* (covering the years 1789–1824; also known by other names), *Register of Debates* (1824–37), and *Congressional Globe* (1833–73, but usually cited starting with 1837). In citing the date, refer to the year of publication rather than the year in which the debate occurred. Note that the *Globe* is normally cited by number and session of Congress (and page number), whereas the *Annals* and *Debates* are cited by volume and page number. As with citations to the *Congressional Record*, the titles are abbreviated and not italicized.

1. Cong. Globe, 34th Cong., 3d Sess. 149 (1856).
2. 42 Annals of Cong. 1697 (1824).
3. 3 Reg. Deb. 388 (1829).

14.189 **State laws and municipal ordinances.** The titles of state codes (compilations) for laws and municipal ordinances are set in roman type. The publication date is included in parentheses, along with a name where necessary, to indicate the edition of the code being cited. Form of citation will vary by state. For an exhaustive treatment of state-by-state variations, consult *The Bluebook*.

1. Ohio Rev. Code Ann. § 2913.44 (West 2022).
2. Kentucky Campus Due Process Protection Act, Ky. Rev. Stat. Ann. § 164.370 (LexisNexis 2022).

**14.190** **Presidential documents.** Presidential proclamations, executive orders, vetoes, addresses, and the like are published in the *Weekly Compilation of Presidential Documents* (Weekly Comp. Pres. Doc.) and in the *Public Papers of the Presidents of the United States* (Pub. Papers). Proclamations and executive orders are also carried in the daily *Federal Register* (Fed. Reg.) and then published in title 3 of the *Code of Federal Regulations* (C.F.R.). Some executive orders and proclamations appear in the *United States Code*; include a citation if therein (as in example 3 below).

1. Proclamation No. 8099, 72 Fed. Reg. 1907 (Jan. 11, 2007).
2. Exec. Order No. 14028, 3 C.F.R. 556 (2021).
3. Exec. Order No. 13758, 3 C.F.R. 231 (2017), *reprinted as amended in* 10 U.S.C. § 1129 (2017).

For more examples, consult *The Bluebook*.

**14.191** **Treaties.** The texts of treaties signed before 1950 are published in *United States Statutes at Large*; many also appear in the *Treaty Series* (T.S.) or the *Executive Agreement Series* (E.A.S.), each of which assigns a number to a treaty covered. Those signed in 1950 and later appear in *United States Treaties and Other International Agreements* (U.S.T., 1950–) or the *Treaties and Other International Acts Series* (T.I.A.S., 1945–), which also assigns a number. Treaties involving more than two nations may be found in the *United Nations Treaty Series* (U.N.T.S., 1946–) or the *League of Nations Treaty Series* (L.N.T.S., 1920–46). These and other sources are listed in *The Bluebook*. Titles of treaties are set in roman type and capitalized in title case. Country names are generally abbreviated (see also 14.175). An exact date indicates the date of signing and is therefore preferable to a year alone, which may differ from the year the treaty was published in one of the works above. Page numbers are given where relevant.

1. Treaty Banning Nuclear Weapon Tests in the Atmosphere, in Outer Space and Under Water, U.K.-U.S.-U.S.S.R., Aug. 5, 1963, 14 U.S.T. 1313.
2. Agreement Concerning Civil Uses of Atomic Energy, U.S.–S. Kor., Feb. 3, 1956, T.I.A.S. No. 3490, at 161.

14.192 **Secondary sources and freestanding publications.** When citing secondary sources and other freestanding publications, Chicago rather than *Bluebook* style can usually be followed. Such materials include not just books and articles but also legislative documents, pamphlets, and reports. For subsequent citations or citations of individual documents, shortened forms may be devised as needed (as in example notes 2 and 4 below; see also 13.63). The following examples are not meant to be exhaustive. Those who are required to follow *Bluebook* style should consult that manual, whose recommendations differ.

1. *The Federalist Papers*, ed. Lawrence Goldman (Oxford University Press, 2008).

2. *Federalist*, no. 42 (James Madison).

3. *Journals of the Continental Congress, 1774–1789*, ed. Worthington C. Ford et al. (Washington, DC, 1904–37), 15:1341.

4. *JCC* 25:863.

5. *Public Papers of the Presidents of the United States: Herbert Hoover, 1929–1933*, 4 vols. (Washington, DC, 1974–77), 1:134.

6. Susan Dicklitch-Nelson and Indira Rahman, "Transgender Rights Are Human Rights: A Cross-National Comparison of Transgender Rights in 204 Countries," *Journal of Human Rights* 21, no. 5 (2022): 525–41.

7. *Median Gross Rent by Counties of the United States, 1970*, prepared by the Geography Division in cooperation with the Housing Division, Bureau of the Census (Washington, DC, 1975).

8. Ralph I. Straus, *Expanding Private Investment for Free World Economic Growth*, special report prepared at the request of the Department of State, April 1959, 12.

9. Illinois General Assembly, Law Revision Commission, *Report to the 80th General Assembly of the State of Illinois* (Chicago, 1977), 14–18.

Though the legal-style citations discussed elsewhere in this section are usually limited to the notes (see 14.172), the secondary sources or freestanding works discussed here may be included in a bibliography (see also 13.65).

Continental Congress. *Journals of the Continental Congress, 1774–1789*. Edited by Worthington C. Ford et al. 34 vols. Washington, DC, 1904–37.

14.193 **Unpublished documents in US archives.** For general guidelines and many examples that can be adapted to government documents, see 14.119–29. Most unpublished documents of the federal government are housed in the National Archives and Records Administration in Washington, DC, or in one of its branches. All, including films, photographs, and sound recordings as well as written materials, are cited by record group (RG) number. Record groups and their numbers are searchable at the National Archives website (see also bibliog. 4.5). In addition to a title or description for the document, a National Archives ID (NAID) for the specific item may be included as shown.

1. "Anti-Slavery Petition from Women of America," Feb. 27, 1849, NAID 7741397, Records of the US Senate, RG 46, National Archives, Washington, DC.

2. Population Schedule for Milwaukee County, Wisconsin, ED 72-383, Sixteenth Census of the United States, 1940, NAID 139237090, Records of the Bureau of the Census, RG 29, National Archives, Washington, DC.

## *Canada*

14.194 **Canadian reference works.** The major reference work for citing Canadian public documents and legal cases in a Canadian context is the *Canadian Guide to Uniform Legal Citation*, prepared by the McGill Law Journal (in English and French) and published by Carswell (see bibliog. 1.1). Also valuable are Philip Whitehead and Anne Matthewman, *Legal Writing and Research Manual* (bibliog. 5); the *Canadian Almanac and Directory*, published by Grey House (bibliog. 4.4); and Gerald L. Gall, F. Pearl Eliadis, and France Allard, *The Canadian Legal System* (bibliog. 5). Authors citing more than a few Canadian legal or public documents should consult one of these works. Additional resources may be found online through Lexum. For citing the occasional example in a US context, *The Bluebook* (see 14.170) provides some recommendations and examples.

14.195 **Canadian legal cases.** The following examples illustrate *Bluebook* style. The basic elements are similar to those used in US law citations; the date is enclosed in square brackets, followed by the volume number of the reporter (if applicable), the abbreviated name of the reporter, and the page number. Canadian Supreme Court cases since 1876 are cited to *Supreme Court Reports* (S.C.R.). Federal Court cases are cited to *Federal Courts Reports* (F.C., 1971–2003; F.C.R., 2004–) or *Exchequer Court Reports* (Ex. C.R., 1875–1971). Cases not found in any of these sources are cited to *Dominion Law Reports* (D.L.R.). Cite the year of the decision in parentheses if it is different from the reporter year. Add "Can." and the abbreviated court name in parentheses if not clear from the context. For citing other reporters, including those covering the provinces and territories, consult *The Bluebook.*

1. Egan v. Canada, [1995] 2 S.C.R. 513.
2. American Cyanamid Co. v. Novopharm Ltd., [1972] F.C. 739 (Can. C.A.).
3. Canada v. CBC/Radio-Canada (2012), [2014] 1 F.C.R. 142.

Since 1998, many cases have been assigned neutral citations to facilitate immediate publication online. A neutral citation should appear first, ahead of any parallel citation to an official reporter. In the following example, "SCC" (no periods) refers to the Supreme Court of Canada.

4. Fleming v. Ontario, 2019 SCC 45, [2019] 3 S.C.R. 519.

14.196 **Canadian statutes.** Federal statutes appeared through 1985 in the *Revised Statutes of Canada* (R.S.C.), a consolidation that was published every fifteen to thirty years; federal statutes enacted since then are cited as session laws in the annual *Statutes of Canada* (S.C.). Current consolidated federal statutes are also available online from the Justice Laws Consolidated Acts collection. Citation elements are similar to US statutes: the name of the act, the abbreviated name of the compilation, publication date, chapter number (in *R.S.C.*, the chapter number includes the initial letter of the name of the act), and section number if applicable. Add "Can." in parentheses if it is not clear from the context. Statutes for the provinces and territories are cited similarly; consult *The Bluebook* for guidance.

1. Companies' Creditors Arrangement Act, R.S.C. 1985, c. C-36, s. 5 (Can.).
2. Canada Elections Act, S.C. 2000, c. 9.

14.197 **Unpublished documents in Canadian archives.** Library and Archives Canada (LAC) houses the unpublished records of the federal government, both individually written and institutional, as well as historically significant documents from the private sector. The guide to the entire LAC collections is available online, as are the archives for each province and territory. For citing unpublished materials, see the guidelines and examples in 14.119–29.

## *United Kingdom*

14.198 **UK reference works.** The catalogs of the National Archives (the official archive for England, Wales, and the central UK government), available online, extend to the documents of the former Public Record Office, the Historical Manuscripts Commission, the Office of Public Sector Information, and His (or Her) Majesty's Stationery Office (HMSO), among others. The UK Parliament also makes its catalogs available online. Printed guides include the *Guide to the Contents of the Public Record Office* and Frank Rodgers, *A Guide to British Government Publications* (both in bibliog. 4.5). For citing UK legal and public documents in a US context, *The Bluebook* (see 14.170) provides an overview.

14.199 **Periods in UK legal citations.** In contemporary usage, periods are normally omitted from abbreviations in citations to legal cases and other types of legal and public documents from the United Kingdom, a difference from the predominant style in the United States (see 14.175). In this section, which mostly reflects *The Bluebook* (specifically, table T2.43), periods are omitted from initialisms that consist of two or more capital letters but retained in most other abbreviations (with the notable exception of "R"; see 14.200). For example, "HL" (House of Lords) has no periods, whereas "v." (contrary to British usage) does. When in doubt—and if no suitable citation is offered with the source—apply Chicago style as outlined in 10.4.

14.200 **UK legal cases.** In *Bluebook* style, the basic elements in citations to UK legal cases are similar to those used in US law citations (but see 14.199): the name of the case, in roman type (cases involving the Crown use the abbreviation "R" for Rex or Regina); the date, which is enclosed in parentheses when the volumes of the reporter are numbered cumulatively, or in square brackets when the year is essential to locating the case (either there is no volume number or the volumes for each year are numbered anew, not cumulatively); the abbreviated name of the reporter; and the opening page of the decision. If the court is not apparent from the name of the reporter, or if the jurisdiction is not clear from the context, include either or both, as necessary, in parentheses. Until 2005, the courts of highest appeal in the United Kingdom (except for criminal cases in Scotland) were the Appellate Committee of the House of Lords (HL) and the Judicial Committee of the Privy Council (PC). In 2005 the Supreme Court of the United Kingdom was established. In 2009 it assumed the appellate jurisdiction of the House of Lords and the devolution jurisdiction of the Judicial Committee of the Privy Council. Most cases are cited to the applicable report in the *Law Reports*, among these the Appeal Cases (AC), Queen's (King's) Bench (QB, KB; sometimes followed by a *D*, for *Division*), Chancery (Ch.), Family (Fam.), and Probate (P.) reports. For other reports applicable to cases dating back to AD 1094, consult *The Bluebook*.

1. R v. Dudley and Stephens, (1884) 14 QBD 273 (DC).
2. Regal (Hastings) Ltd. v. Gulliver, [1967] 2 AC 134 (HL) (appeal taken from Eng.).

Cases heard since 2001 are assigned a neutral citation to allow for immediate online publishing. A neutral citation should appear first, ahead of any parallel citation to an official reporter. In the following example, "UKSC" refers to the Supreme Court of the United Kingdom.

3. R (Miller) v. Secretary of State for Exiting the European Union [2017] UKSC 5, [2018] AC 61.

14.201 **UK parliamentary publications.** Parliamentary publications include all materials issued by both houses of Parliament, the House of Commons (HC) and the House of Lords (HL): journals of both houses (sometimes abbreviated *CJ* and *LJ*); votes and proceedings; debates; bills, reports, and papers; and statutes.

14.202 **UK statutes.** The Acts of Parliament are identified by title (in roman type), year (also include the regnal year for statutes enacted before 1963), and chapter number ("c." for chapter; Arabic numeral for national number, lowercase Roman numeral for local). Monarchs' names in regnal-year citations are abbreviated as follows: Ann., Car. (Charles), Edw., Eliz., Geo., Hen., Jac. (James), Phil. & M., Rich., Vict., Will., W. & M. The year precedes the name; the monarch's ordinal, if any, follows it (15 Geo. 6), both in Arabic numerals. An ampersand is used between regnal years and between names of dual monarchs (1 & 2 W. & M.). *The Bluebook* advises including the jurisdiction in parentheses if it is not clear from the context.

1. Act of Settlement 1701, 12 & 13 Will. 3, c. 2.
2. Consolidated Fund Act 1963, c. 1 (Eng.).
3. Manchester Corporation Act 1967, c. xl.

Early statutory material for the United Kingdom is compiled in *The Statutes of the Realm* (1235–1714) and *Acts and Ordinances of the Interregnum* (1642–60); additional material through 1806 has been published in various versions of *The Statutes at Large*. Later acts have been published as Public General Acts. For more information, see Legislation.gov.uk, a database of UK legislation published by the National Archives.

14.203 **Publication of UK parliamentary debates.** Before 1909, debates from both houses were published together; since then they have been published in separate series.

*Hansard Parliamentary Debates*, 1st series (1803–20)
*Hansard Parliamentary Debates*, 2d series (1820–30)

*Hansard Parliamentary Debates*, 3d series (1830–91)
*Parliamentary Debates*, 4th series (1892–1908)
*Parliamentary Debates*, Commons, 5th series (1909–81)
*Parliamentary Debates*, Commons, 6th series (1981–)
*Parliamentary Debates*, Lords, 5th series (1909–)

*The Bluebook* advises citing debates by applicable house of Parliament (HC Deb. or HL Deb.), date (in parentheses), volume number (in parentheses), and column number(s). If known, the series number may be added in parentheses before the date.

1. HC Deb. (3d ser.) (9 Aug. 1879) (249) cols. 611–27.
2. HL Deb. (4th ser.) (4 May 1893) (12) col. 12.
3. HC Deb. (5th ser.) (18 Jan. 1945) (407) cols. 425–46.
4. HL Deb. (5th ser.) (25 Jul. 1988) (500), cols. 82–83.

Parliamentary debates are searchable by series, volume, and column number at the Hansard website.

14.204 **UK command papers.** Command papers are so called because they originate outside Parliament and are ostensibly presented to Parliament "by command of Her [His] Majesty." The different abbreviations for "command" indicate the series and must not be altered. No *s* is added to the plural (Cmnd. 3834, 3835).

C. (1st series) (1833–69)
C. (2d series) (1870–99)
Cd. (1900–1918)
Cmd. (1919–56)
Cmnd. (1956–86)
Cm. (1986–2018)
CP (2019–)

A command paper may consist of a pamphlet or several volumes. If not clear from the context, the author of the report is included. Dates usually include just a year, and paper numbers are included as shown.

1. HM Treasury, The Basle Facility and the Sterling Area, 1968, Cmnd. 3787, at 15–16.

2. First Interim Report of the Committee on Currency and Foreign Exchanges After the War, 1918, Cd. 9182.

3. Review Body on Doctors' and Dentists' Remuneration, Thirteenth Report, 1983, Cmnd. 8878.

14.205 **Unpublished documents in UK archives.** The main depositories for unpublished government and other public documents in the United Kingdom are the National Archives and the British Library, both in London. Their catalogs are available online through their respective websites. (The British Library was until 1973 part of the British Museum.) References to document series at the National Archives (abbreviated "TNA"; the *T* stands for *The*) usually begin with letter abbreviations, such as C (Chancery), CO (Colonial Office), E (Exchequer), FO (Foreign Office), PROB (Probate), or SP (State Papers), followed by volume number, sub or part number(s), and, where relevant, folio or page number(s). Collections in the British Library (abbreviated "BL") are named and include Cotton (with subdivisions named after Roman emperors; e.g., Cotton MS Caligula D VII), Harley, King's (cited as Kings), Lansdowne, Music, Sloane, Royal, and Royal Music, as well as the catchall category Additional (Add. or Addit.). When in doubt, use the abbreviated reference format provided by the institution in addition to a title or description, date, and other relevant information. For additional guidance on citing items in manuscript collections, see 14.119–29.

1. Will of William Shakespeare, Gentleman of Stratford upon Avon, Warwickshire, after 22 June 1616, TNA, PROB 11/127/771, fol. 466r.

2. Hodgson to Halifax, 22 Feb. 1752, TNA, CO 137/48.

3. Clarendon to Lyons, 22 Apr. 1869, TNA, FO 27/1740.

4. Records and correspondence concerning England and France, 1518–1520, BL, Cotton MS Caligula D VII, fol. 21r–v.

5. John William Gerard de Brahm, "Report of the General Survey in the Southern District of North America," 1773–74?, BL, Kings MS 210–11, vol. 1, fol. 94.

6. Book of Hours, use of St. Omer, c. 1318–25, BL, Add. MS 36684, fol. 3r.

Additional documents for the United Kingdom and its devolved and local governments may be found in the county record offices throughout Britain and at the National Library of Wales, the National Records of Scotland, the Public Record Office of Northern Ireland, and the Parliamentary Archives, as well as in some university and college libraries.

## *International Entities*

14.206 **Intergovernmental bodies.** *The Bluebook* outlines the main reporters for international courts (such as the International Court of Justice), commissions, and tribunals. Also included are abbreviations for intergovernmental bodies such as the United Nations (and its principal organs), the European Union, and those devoted to specific areas such as human rights, trade, and health. The basic elements of citations to international law cases are similar to those used in US law citations (see 14.177–80); for examples, consult *The Bluebook*. (In addition to intergovernmental bodies, *The Bluebook* covers more than three dozen jurisdictions outside the United States.) For treaties, see 14.191.

14.207 **United Nations documents.** The United Nations makes many of its documents available online (in English)—including those published by the General Assembly and the Security Council and dating back to the first General Assembly in 1946. *The Bluebook* prefers the printed Official Records as the source for United Nations documents and provides citation guidance using standard abbreviations, including "G.A. Res." and "S.C. Res." (for resolutions of the General Assembly and Security Council, respectively).

1. G.A. Res. 217 (III) A, Universal Declaration of Human Rights (Dec. 10, 1948).

Alternatively, documents may be cited according to document number (or *symbol* in UN terminology) and other details as found in the Official Document System at the United Nations website. To cite a resolution found there, list the authorizing body, resolution number, document title or parenthetical description, document symbol, page number or other locator, and date, followed by a URL. For additional guidance on citing United Nations documents, consult *The Bluebook*. See also 13.6–12.

1. G.A. Res. 217 (III) A, Universal Declaration of Human Rights, A/RES/217(III), art. 6 (Dec. 10, 1948), https://undocs.org/en/A/RES/217(III).
2. S.C. Res. 2664 (on general issues related to sanctions), S/RES/2664, ¶ 5 (Dec. 9, 2022), https://undocs.org/en/S/RES/2664(2022).
3. A/RES/217(III), art. 17.

# 15 Indexes

## OVERVIEW

15.1 **The back-of-the-book index as model.** This chapter offers basic guidelines for preparing and editing an alphabetically arranged index that will appear at the end of a book-length work. Though the advice is modeled primarily on the requirements of a book with fixed page numbers (as in print or PDF) or other fixed locators (like the paragraph numbers in this manual), the principles should apply also to works that lack such mileposts (see 15.13). General principles of indexing are covered, as are the specifics of Chicago's preferred style in matters of typography, alphabetizing, and the like.

15.2 **Why index?** In this age of searchable text, the need for an index made with human input is sometimes questioned. But a good index can do what a plain search cannot: It gathers all the substantive terms and subjects of the work, sorts them alphabetically, provides cross-references to and from related terms, and includes specific page numbers or other locators or, for electronic formats, direct links to the text. This painstaking intellectual labor serves readers of any longer work, whether it is searchable or not. For searchable texts, an index provides insurance against fruitless queries and unintended results. For example, if the text reads, "In the 1960s, countries outside the sphere of US and Soviet influence played those two nations against each other," there should be an index entry for "Cold War." A search for that term may not pick this up. In a word, a good index makes the text more accessible.

15.3 **Who should index a work?** The ideal indexer sees the work as a whole, understands the emphasis of the various parts and their relation to the whole, and knows—or guesses—what readers of the particular work are likely to look for and what headings they will think of. The indexer should be widely read, scrupulous in handling detail, analytically minded, well acquainted with publishing practices, and capable of meeting almost impossible deadlines. Although authors know better than anyone else their subject matter and the audience to whom the work is addressed, not all can look at their work through the eyes of a potential reader. Nor do many authors have the technical skills, let alone the time, necessary to prepare a good index that meets the publisher's deadline. Some authors produce excellent indexes. Others would do better to enlist the aid of a professional indexer.

15.4 **The indexer and deadlines.** Most book indexes must be made between the time page proofs are issued and the time they are returned to the typesetter—usually from two to six weeks. (For an illustration of how indexing fits into the overall publishing process for books, see 2.2.) Authors preparing their own indexes will have to proofread as well as index the work in that short time span. Good indexing requires reflection; the indexer needs to stop frequently and decide whether the right choices have been made. A professional indexer, familiar with the publisher's requirements and equipped with specialized software and experience, may be better equipped for such reflection. For those few journals that still publish a volume index (see 1.119), the indexer may have several months to prepare a preliminary index, adding entries as new issues of the journal arrive. The final issue in the volume is typically indexed from page proofs, however, and the indexer may have as little as a week to work on the last issue and prepare the final draft of the index. In a similar manner, page proofs for textbooks and other very large works may arrive in sections over several months, and the index is usually due one to two weeks after the final proofs arrive.

15.5 **The role of software in indexing.** A concordance—or a complete list of terms (typically minus articles, prepositions, and other irrelevant elements) and their page locations or frequency of use—can be produced automatically. But a concordance is not the same as an index. Most indexes of the type described in this chapter are produced from scratch, typically from paginated page proofs, either electronic or hard copy, generated by a page-layout program. Word processors are typically used in entering and editing terms and locators in a separate document and can provide rudimentary help in the process of sorting entries and managing cross-references. Most professional indexers use dedicated indexing software, which provides shortcuts for creating and editing entries and automates formatting, allowing the indexer to focus on the creative analysis of the text. This type of software is an essential investment for a professional indexer and may be worth it for an author planning to index many books over time (see 15.113). See also 15.7, 15.13.

15.6 **Single versus multiple indexes.** A single, comprehensive index—one that includes concepts and names of persons and other subjects—is recommended for most works. Certain publications, however, such as lengthy scientific works that cite numerous authors of other studies, may include an index of named authors (see 15.38) in addition to a subject index. An anthology may include an author-and-title index, and a collection of poetry or hymns may have an index of first lines as well as an index of titles. It is generally an advantage if two or more indexes appearing in one work are visually distinct from one another so that users know immediately where they are. In a biological work, for example, the headings in the index of names will all be in roman type and will begin with capital letters, and there will be no subentries, whereas most of the headings in the general subject index will begin lowercase and many subentries will appear; and if there is a taxonomic index, many headings will be in italics. Separate running heads should be used, indicating the title of each index (e.g., Index of Names, Index of Subjects).

15.7 **Embedded indexes.** An embedded index consists of key terms anchored with underlying codes to particular points in the text of an electronic publication. These terms can facilitate a reader's queries to a search engine in much the same way that a good subject index gathers keywords under subject headings to increase the chances that a reader will be led only to the relevant areas of a text. For example, a search for the word "because" in a properly coded online encyclopedia might lead to those passages that discuss the Beatles' *Abbey Road* song "Because" rather than to every instance of the omnipresent conjunction. The principles of selection for embedded indexes are similar to those for traditional back-of-the-book indexes. Many journal publishers, especially in the sciences, rely on standard keyword vocabularies and have largely done away with traditional indexes. On the other hand, many book publishers anchor their back-of-the-book index entries to the electronic files that drive publication in print and other formats in order to facilitate hyperlinked indexes for ebook formats (see also 15.13).

15.8 **Resources for indexers.** For greatly expanded coverage of the present guidelines, along with alternative methods, consult the second edition of Nancy Mulvany's *Indexing Books* (bibliog. 2.5). Anyone likely to prepare a number of indexes should acquire that work. For further reference, see Hans H. Wellisch, *Indexing from A to Z*, and Linda K. Fetters, *Handbook of Indexing Techniques* (bibliog. 2.5).

## COMPONENTS OF AN INDEX

### *Main Headings, Subentries, and Locators*

15.9 **Main headings for index entries.** The main heading of an index entry is normally a noun or noun phrase—the name of a person, a place, an object, or an abstraction. In general, count nouns and count noun phrases should be plural rather than singular. An adjective alone should almost never constitute a heading; it should rather be paired with a noun to form a noun phrase. A noun phrase is sometimes inverted to allow the keyword—the word a reader is most likely to look under—to appear first. The heading is typically followed by page (or paragraph) numbers (see 15.12) and sometimes a cross-reference (see 15.15–23). For capitalization, see 15.11.

agricultural collectivization, 143–46, 198
Aron, Raymond, 312–14
Bloomsbury group, 269
Brest-Litovsk, Treaty of, 61, 76, 85
Cold War, 396–437
Communist Party (American), 425
Communist Party (British), 268
imperialism, American, 393, 403
police, Soviet secret. *See* Soviet secret police
prisoners of war, 93
war communism, 90, 95, 125
World War I, 34–61
Yalta conference, 348, 398

15.10 **Index subentries.** An entry that requires more than five or six locators (page or paragraph numbers) is usually broken up into subentries to spare readers unnecessary excursions. A subentry, like an entry, consists of a heading (usually referred to as a subheading), page references, and, rarely, cross-references. Subheadings often form a grammatical relationship with the main heading, whereby heading and subheading combine into a single phrase, as in the first example below. Other subheadings form divisions or units within the larger category of the heading, as in the second example. Both kinds can be used within one index. See also 15.126. For sub-subentries, see 15.27, 15.28.

capitalism: and American pro-Sovietism, 273, 274; bourgeoisie as symbol of, 4, 13; as creation of society, 7; Khrushchev on burying, 480; student protests against, 491, 493

Native American peoples: Chichimec, 67–68; Huastec, 154; Olmec, 140–41; Toltec, 128–36; Zapotec, 168–72

15.11 **Initial lowercase letters in main headings and subheadings.** The first word of a main heading is normally capitalized only if capitalized in text—a proper noun (as in the second example in 15.10), a genus name, the title of a work, and so on. Traditionally, all main headings in an index were capitalized. Chicago recommends this practice only where the subentries are so numerous that capitalized main headings make for easier navigation. Indexes in the sciences, however, should generally avoid initial capitals because the distinction between capitalized and lowercased terms in the text may be crucial. Subheadings are always lowercased unless the keyword is capitalized in text (like "Khrushchev" in the first example in 15.10 and all the subentries in the second example).

15.12 **Locators in indexes.** In a printed work or PDF, locators are usually page numbers, though they can also be paragraph numbers (as in this manual), section numbers, or the like. When discussion of a subject continues for more than a page, paragraph, or section, the first and last numbers (inclusive numbers) are given: 34–36 (if pages), 10.36–41 (if paragraphs), and so on (see 15.14). The abbreviations *ff.* and *et seq.* should never be used in an index. Scattered references to a subject over several pages or sections are usually indicated by separate locators (34, 35, 36; *or* 8.18, 8.20, 8.21). Though the term *passim* has often been used to indicate scattered references over a number of not necessarily sequential pages or sections (e.g., 78–88 passim), individual locators are preferred. For use of the en dash, see 6.83.

15.13 **Indexes for ebooks and other electronic formats.** At a minimum, indexes destined for ebook formats should be linked to the text. Page number data for a printed format can provide the basis of such links, and publishers are encouraged to include this data in their electronic publication formats. In formats with reflowable text, however, the actual place in the text may be several screens beyond the location of the first "page." For this reason, index entries are best linked directly to the passage of text to which they refer. (In works like this manual, links can be made directly to numbered paragraphs.) This approach, though it requires considerable intervention on the part of the publisher or indexer, produces a better experience for the reader. A detailed specification for ebook indexes is available from the World Wide Web Consortium, which maintains the EPUB standard.

15.14 **Inclusive numbers in indexes.** Publishers vary in their preferences for the form of inclusive numbers (also known as continuing numbers). Although the simplest and most foolproof system is to give the full form of numbers everywhere (e.g., 234–235), Chicago prefers its traditional system (presented below), which is efficient and unambiguous. The system is followed in all examples in this chapter. Whichever form is used in the text should be used in the index as well.

| *First number* | *Second number* | *Examples* |
|---|---|---|
| Less than 100 | Use all digits | 3–10<br>71–72<br>96–117 |

| | | |
|---|---|---|
| 100 or multiples of 100 | Use all digits | 100–104<br>1100–1113 |
| 101 through 109,<br>201 through 209, etc. | Use changed part only | 101–8<br>808–33<br>1103–4 |
| 110 through 199,<br>210 through 299, etc. | Use two digits unless more are needed to include all changed parts | 321–28<br>498–532<br>1087–89<br>1496–500<br>11564–615<br>12991–3001 |

Roman numerals are always given in full—for example, xxv–xxviii, cvi–cix. In an index that refers to section numbers, the same principles apply as for page numbers (e.g., 16.9–14, 16.141–45). For use of the en dash between numerals, see 6.83; see also 9.62.

## *Cross-References*

15.15 **Cross-references in indexes—general principles.** Cross-references are of two main kinds—*see* references and *see also* references. Each is treated differently according to whether it refers to a main heading or to a subheading. *See* and *see also* are set in italics (but see 15.22). In electronic publication formats, cross-references should link to the terms in the index to which they refer. Cross-references should be used with discretion; an overabundance, besides irritating the reader, may signal the need for consolidation of entries.

15.16 **"See" references and "double posting."** *See* references are used to direct readers from a term they initially looked up to the place in the index where the information they are seeking appears. They should never include locators. *See* references direct a reader from, for example, an informal term to a technical one, a pseudonym to a real name, an inverted term to a noninverted one. They are also used for variant spellings, synonyms, aliases, abbreviations, and so on. The choice of the term under which the full entry appears depends largely on where readers are most likely to look. *See* references should therefore be given only where the indexer believes many readers might otherwise miss the full entry. Further, the indexer and anyone editing an index must make certain that no *see* reference merely leads to another *see* reference. If, on the other hand, the entry to which the *see* reference refers is about the same length as the *see* reference itself, it is often more useful to omit the *see* reference and simply give the page numbers under both headings. Such duplication (or "double posting") will save readers a trip.

FBI (Federal Bureau of Investigation),
  145–48
Federal Bureau of Investigation,
  145–48
*rather than*
Federal Bureau of Investigation. *See*
  FBI

See also 15.54.

15.17 **"See" references following a main heading.** When a *see* reference follows a main heading, as it usually does, it is preceded by a period and *See* is capitalized. If two or more *see* references are needed, they are arranged in alphabetical order and separated by semicolons. They reflect the capitalization and word order of the main heading.

adolescence. *See* teenagers; youth
American Communist Party. *See*
  Communist Party (American)
baking soda. *See* sodium bicarbonate
Clemens, Samuel. *See* Twain, Mark
Den Haag ('s Gravenhage). *See* Hague,
  The
Lunt, Mrs. Alfred. *See* Fontanne, Lynn
Mormons. *See* Latter-day Saints,
  Church of Jesus Christ of
Roman Catholic Church. *See* Catholicism
The Hague. *See* Hague, The
Turwyn. *See* Terouenne
universities. *See* Harvard University;
  Princeton University; University of
  Chicago
Virgin Queen. *See* Elizabeth I
von Humboldt, Alexander. *See* Humboldt, Alexander von

15.18 **"See" references following a subheading.** When a *see* reference follows a subheading, it is put in parentheses and *see* is lowercased.

statistical material, 16, 17, 89; as online supplement (*see* supplements,
  online); proofreading, 183

This usage applies to both run-in and indented indexes, and to subsubentries. See 15.27, 15.28.

15.19 **"See" references to a subheading.** Most *see* references are to a main entry, as in the examples in 15.17. When a cross-reference directs readers to a subentry under another main heading, *see under* may be used.

lace making. *See under* Bruges
*Pride and Prejudice. See under* Austen,
  Jane

An alternative, to be used when a *see under* reference might fail to direct readers to the right spot, is to drop the word *under* and add the wording of the subheading, following a colon. (Although a comma is sometimes used, a colon is preferred.) The wording of the cross-reference must correspond to that of the relevant subheading so that readers can find it quickly.

lace making. *See* Bruges: lace making
*Pride and Prejudice. See* Austen, Jane:
  *Pride and Prejudice*

15.20 **"See also" references.** *See also* references direct readers to additional information elsewhere in the index, including related but nonsynonymous concepts. They can be used as an alternative to making the structure of an index more complex. *See also* references are placed at the end of an entry when *additional* information can be found in another entry. When planning *see also* references between related concepts, indexers should make sure the concepts are not actually synonyms that should be combined into one entry. Nor should a *see also* entry lead to an entry that does not list any page numbers not already included in the original entry. (*See also* entries are not the place to show relationships between terms.) In run-in indexes, they follow a period; in indented indexes, they appear on a separate line (see 15.26). *See* is capitalized, and both words are in italics. If the cross-reference is to a subentry under another main heading, the words *see also under* may be used. If two or more *see also* references are needed, they are arranged in alphabetical order and separated by semicolons. As with *see* references, *see also* references must never lead to a *see* reference.

copyright, 95–100. *See also* permission to reprint; source notes
Maya: art of, 236–43; cities of, 178;
  present day, 267. *See also under*
  Yucatán

If *see also under* does not work in a particular context—for example, when one of the *see also* references is to a main entry and another to a subentry—the word *under* should be dropped and the wording of the subentry added after a colon.

Maya: art of, 236–43; cities of, 178.
  *See also* Mexican art; Yucatán:
  Maya

When a *see also* reference comes at the end of a subentry—a rare occurrence, and somewhat distracting—it is put in parentheses and *see* is lowercased.

equality: as bourgeois ideal, 5–6,
  7; contractual quality, 13; in
  democracy's definition, 24 (*see also*
  democracy); League of the Rights
  of Man debate on, 234–35

15.21 **Correspondence between cross-references and headings.** All cross-referenced headings (and subheadings, if used) should generally be cited in full, with capitalization, inversion, and punctuation exactly as in the heading referred to. But a long heading may occasionally be shortened if no confusion results. For example, in an index with frequent references to Beethoven, "*See also* Beethoven, Ludwig van" could be shortened to "*See also* Beethoven" if done consistently.

15.22 **Italics for "see," "see also," and so forth.** The words *see*, *see under*, and *see also* are normally italicized. But if what follows (e.g., a book title or a word in another language) is in italics, the words are preferably set in roman to distinguish them from the rest of the cross-reference. This is not necessary when they follow italics.

Austen, Jane. See *Pride and Prejudice*
*but*
*Pride and Prejudice*. *See* Austen, Jane

15.23 **Generic cross-references.** Both *see* and *see also* references may include generic references; that is, they may refer to a type of heading rather than to several specific headings. The entire cross-reference is then set in italics.

public buildings. *See names of individual buildings*
sacred writings, 345–46, 390–401, 455–65. *See also specific titles*

When generic cross-references accompany specific cross-references, the former are placed last, even if out of alphabetical order. The conjunction *and* is normally used, following a semicolon (even if the generic cross-reference follows only one other cross-reference).

dogs, 35–42. *See also* American Kennel Club; shelters; *and individual breed names*

## *Run-In Versus Indented Indexes*

15.24 **Flush-and-hang formatting for indexes.** Indexes are generally formatted in flush-and-hang (or hanging-indent) style. The first line of each entry, the main heading, is set flush left, and any following lines are indented. When there are subentries, a choice must be made between run-in and indented styles (see 15.25, 15.26). In print publications (and electronic works modeled on the printed page), indexes are usually set in multiple columns. In manuscripts, however, columns should not be used (see 15.130).

15.25 **Run-in style for indexes.** In run-in style, the subentries follow the main entry and one another without starting a new line. They are separated by semicolons. If the main heading is immediately followed by subentries, it is separated from them by a colon (see first example below). If it is immediately followed by locators, these are preceded by a comma and followed by a semicolon (see second example). Further examples of run-in entries may be seen in 15.10, 15.20, 15.140.

coordinate systems: Cartesian, 14; distance within, 154–55; time dilation and, 108–14. *See also* inertial systems; moving systems

Sabba da Castiglione, Monsignor, 209, 337; on cosmetics, 190; on whether to marry, 210–11; on wives' proper behavior, 230–40, 350

Chicago and many other publishers generally prefer run-in style because it requires less space. It works best, however, when there is only one level of subentry (but see 15.27). For the examples above in indented style, see 15.26.

15.26 **Indented style for indexes.** In indented style (also known as stacked style), each subentry begins a new line and is indented (usually one em). No colon appears before the first subheading, and subentries are not separated by semicolons. Runover lines must therefore be further indented (usually two ems) to distinguish them clearly from subentries; whether runover lines belong to the main entry or to subentries, their indentation should be the same. (Indentation is always measured from the left margin, not from the first word in the line above.) *See also* cross-references belonging to the entry as a whole appear at the end of the list of subentries (as shown in the first example below). A *see* or *see also* reference belonging to a specific subentry is placed in parentheses at the end of the subentry, as in run-in indexes (see 15.18, 15.20). See also 15.23.

coordinate systems
  Cartesian, 14
  distance within, 154–55
  time dilation and, 108–14
  *See also* inertial systems; moving
    systems

Sabba da Castiglione, Monsignor,
    209, 337
  on cosmetics, 190
  on whether to marry, 210–11
  on wives' proper behavior, 230–40,
    350

Indented style is usually preferred in scientific works and reference works (such as this manual). It is particularly useful where sub-subentries are required (see 15.28).

15.27 **Sub-subentries in run-in indexes.** If more than a handful of sub-subentries are needed in an index, the indented format rather than the run-in type should be chosen. A very few, however, can be accommodated in a run-in index or, better, avoided by repeating a keyword (see example A below). If repetition will not work, subentries requiring sub-subentries can be indented, each starting a new line but preceded by an em dash flush with the margin; the sub-subentries are then run in (see example B). Em dashes are *not* used where only one level of subentry is needed.

Example A (run-in index: sub-subentries avoided)

Inuit: language, 18; pottery, 432–37;
  tradition of, in Alaska, 123; tradition of, in California, 127

Example B (run-in index: subentries requiring sub-subentries indented with em dash, sub-subentries run in)

Argos: cremation at, 302; and Danaos of Egypt, 108; Middle Helladic, 77; shaft graves at, 84
Arkadia, 4; Early Helladic, 26, 40; Mycenaean, 269, 306
armor and weapons
— attack weapons (general): Early Helladic and Cycladic, 33; Mycenaean, 225, 255, 258–60; from shaft graves, 89, 98–100; from tholos tombs, 128, 131, 133
— body armor: cuirass, 135–36, 147, 152, 244, 258, 260, 311; greaves, 135, 179, 260; helmets, 101, 135
— bow and arrow, 14, 99, 101, 166, 276
Asine: Early Helladic, 29, 36; Middle Helladic, 74; Mycenaean town and trade, 233, 258, 263; tombs at, 300

15.28 **Sub-subentries in indented indexes.** In an indented index, sub-subentries are best run in (see example A below). If, in a particular index, running them in makes the index hard to use, they have to be indented more deeply than the subentries (example B). When the first method is used, runover lines need not be indented more than the standard two ems, already a fairly deep indentation. When the second is used, runover lines have to be indented three ems, which may result in some very short lines. See also 15.141, 15.142.

Example A (indented index: run-in sub-subentries)

nutritional analysis of bamboo, 72–81
  digestible energy, 94–96, 213–14, 222
  inorganic constituents: minerals, 81, 83–85, 89; silica (*see* silica levels in bamboo); total ash, 73, 79, 80, 91, 269, 270
  methods used, 72–73
  organic constituents, 73–79, 269, 270; amino acids, 75–76, 86, 89; amino acids compared with other foods, 77; cellulose, 73, 78, 269, 270; crude protein, 73–75, 80, 89–91, 213, 269, 270; standard proximate analysis of, 78–80; vitamin C, 78, 79

Example B (indented index: sub-subentries indented)

nutritional analysis of bamboo, 72–81
  digestible energy, 94–96, 213–14, 222
  inorganic constituents
    minerals, 81, 83–85, 89
    silica (*see* silica levels in bamboo)
    total ash, 73, 79, 80, 91, 269, 270
  methods used, 72–73
  organic constituents, 73–79, 269, 270
    amino acids, 75–76, 86, 89
    amino acids compared with other foods, 77
    cellulose, 73, 78, 269, 270
    crude protein, 73–75, 80, 89–91, 213, 269, 270
    standard proximate analysis of, 78–80
    vitamin C, 78, 79

If sub-sub-subentries are required (which heaven forbid!), style B must be used, and they must be run in.

## GENERAL PRINCIPLES OF INDEXING

15.29 **Style and usage in the index relative to the work.** Each index is a tool for one particular work. By the time the index is prepared, the style used in the work has long been determined, and the index must reflect that style. If British spelling has been used throughout the text, it must be used in the index. Shakspere in the text calls for Shakspere in the index. Hernando Cortez should not be indexed as Cortés. Older geographic terms should not be altered to their present form (Constantinople to Istanbul, Siam to Thailand, etc.). The use of accents and other diacritical marks must be observed exactly as in the text (Schönberg *not* Schoenberg). Only in the rare instance in which readers might not find information sought should a cross-reference be given. Any terms italicized or enclosed in quotation marks in the text should be treated similarly in the index. If inclusive numbers are given in full in the text (see 15.14; see also 9.64), that style should be used in the index.

15.30 **Choosing indexing terms.** The wording for all headings should be concise and logical. As far as possible, terms should be chosen according to the author's usage. If, for example, the author of a philosophical work uses *essence* to mean *being*, the main entry should be under *essence*, possibly with a cross-reference from *being*. If the terms are used interchangeably, the indexer may either choose one (in this case a cross-reference is imperative) or list both (see 15.16). An indexer relatively unfamiliar with the subject matter may find it useful to ask the author for a brief list of terms that must appear in the index, though such terms will usually suggest themselves as the indexer proceeds through the proofs. Common sense is the best guide. See also 15.21.

15.31 **Terms that should not be indexed.** Although proper names are an important element in most indexes, there are times when they should be ignored. In a work on the history of the automobile in the United States, for example, an author might write, "After World War II small sports cars like the British MG, often owned by returning veterans, began to make their appearance in college towns like Northampton, Massachusetts, and Ann Arbor, Michigan." An indexer should resist the temptation to index these place-names; the two towns mentioned have nothing to do with the theme of the work. The MG sports car, on the other hand, should be indexed, given the subject of the work. Similarly, names or terms that occur in passing references and scene-setting elements that are not essential to the theme of a work need not be indexed. (An exception might be made if certain readers of a publication would be likely to look for their own names in the index. Occasional vanity entries are not forbidden.)

## WHAT PARTS OF A WORK TO INDEX

15.32 **Indexing the text, front matter, and back matter.** The entire text of a book, including substantive content in notes (see 15.33), should be indexed. Much of the front matter, however, is not indexable—title page, dedication, epigraphs, lists of illustrations and tables, and acknowledgments. A preface, or a foreword by someone other than the author of the work, may be indexed if it concerns the subject of the work and not simply how the work came to be written. Substantive material in an introduction, whether in the front matter or, more commonly, in the body of the work, is always indexed (for introduction versus preface, see 1.48). Appendixes should be indexed if they contain information that supplements the text, but not if they merely reproduce documents that are discussed in the text (the full text of a treaty, for example, or a questionnaire). Glossaries, bibliographies, and other such lists are usually not indexed.

15.33 **Indexing footnotes and endnotes.** Notes, whether footnotes or endnotes, should be indexed only if they continue or amplify discussion in the text (substantive notes). Notes that merely contain source citations documenting statements in the text (reference notes) need not be indexed. The same note may of course contain a mix of substantive, indexable content and source citations.

15.34 **Endnote locators in index entries.** Endnotes in printed works are referred to by page, the letter *n* (for *note*), and—extremely important—the note number, with no internal space (334n14). If two or more consecutive notes are referred to, two *n*'s and an en dash are used (e.g., 334nn14–16). Nonconsecutive notes on the same page are treated separately (334n14, 334n16, 334n19). If an index entry refers to numbered notes from more than one chapter that occur on the same page in the endnotes, it can be helpful to include the chapter number in parentheses after the note number, especially if two notes share the same number or where the notes might otherwise appear to be out of order.

birds, 334n2 (chap. 8), 334n2 (chap. 9), 335n9
cats, 212n18 (chap. 1), 212n2 (chap. 2), 218n25

15.35 **Footnote locators in index entries.** Footnotes in a printed work are generally referred to in the same way as endnotes. When a footnote is the only one on the page, however, the note number (or symbol, if numbers are not used) may be omitted (156n). Note numbers should never be omitted when several notes appear on the same page. (If symbols are used, use the symbol: e.g., 156n*, 173n*, 173n†.) If there is indexable material in a text passage and in a related footnote, only the page number need be given. But if the text and the footnote materials are not connected, both text and note should be cited (156, 156n, 278, 278n30).

15.36 **Indexing notes spanning more than one printed page.** For endnotes or footnotes that continue onto another page, normally only the first page number is given. But if the reference is specifically to a part of a note that appears on the second page, the second page number should be used. Referring to a succession of notes, however, may require inclusive page numbers (e.g., 234–35nn19–23).

15.37 **Indexing parenthetical text citations.** Documentation given as parenthetical author-date citations in text is not normally indexed unless the citation documents an otherwise unattributed statement in the text (see 15.33). Any author discussed in text should be indexed. In some fields it is customary to index every author *named* in the text; check with the publisher on the degree of inclusiveness required. In primarily legal works, parenthetical case citations are usually indexed. See also 15.38.

15.38 **Indexing authors' names for an author index.** Author indexes are more common in disciplines that use a variation of the author-date system (see 13.102). Since most authors are cited in text by last name and date only, full names must be sought in the reference list. Occasional discrepancies between text and reference list, not caught in editing, have to be sorted out or queried, adding to the time it takes to create an author index. Is L. W. Dinero, cited on page 345, the same person as Lauren Dinero, discussed on page 456? If so, should she be indexed as Dinero, Lauren W.? (Answer: Only if all or most authors are indexed with full first names—a situation that may be determined by the reference list.) Where a work by two or more authors is cited in text, the indexer must determine whether each author named requires a separate entry. Should Jones, Smith, and Black share one index entry, or should three entries appear? And what about Jones et al.? Chicago recommends the following procedure: Make separate entries for each author whose name appears in text. Do not index those unfortunates whose names are concealed under *et al.* in text.

| *Text citations* | *Index entries* |
|---|---|
| (Jones, Smith, and Black 1999) | Black, M. X., 366 |
| (Sánchez et al. 2001) | Cruz, M. M., 435 |
| (Sánchez, Cruz, et al. 2002) | Jones, E. J., 366 |
| | Sánchez, J. G., 435, 657 |
| | Smith, R. A., 366 |

**15.39** **Indexing illustrations, tables, charts, and such.** Illustrative matter may be indexed if it is of particular importance to the discussion, especially when such items are not listed in or after the table of contents. References to illustrations may be set in italics (or boldface, if preferred); a headnote should then be inserted at the beginning of the index (see 15.140 for an example). Such references usually follow in page order.

reptilian brain, 199, 201–3, *202*, 341,
*477*, 477–81

Alternatively, references to tables may be denoted by *t*, to figures by *f*, plates by *pl*, or whatever works (all set in roman, with no space following the page number). Add an appropriate headnote (e.g., "The letter *t* following a page number denotes a table"). If the number of an illustration is essential, it is safer to use *table*, *fig.*, and so on, with no comma following the page number.

authors and printers, 69, 208t, 209t,
210f
titi monkeys, 88 table 5, 89–90, 122–
25, 122 fig. 7

## INDEXING PROPER NAMES AND VARIANTS

**15.40** **Choosing between variant names.** When proper names appear in the text in more than one form, or in an incomplete form, the indexer must decide which form to use for the main entry and which for the cross-reference (if any) and occasionally must furnish identifying information not given in the text. Few indexes need to provide the kind of detail found in biographical or geographic dictionaries, though reference works of that kind will help in decision-making.

15.41 **Indexing familiar forms of personal names.** The full form of personal names should be indexed as they have become widely known. (Any variant spelling preferred in the text, however, must likewise be preferred in the index; see 15.29.) Note that brackets are used in the following examples to distinguish Chicago's editorial glosses from parenthetical tags such as those in some of the examples elsewhere in this section, which would actually appear in a published index.

Cervantes, Miguel de [*not* Cervantes Saavedra, Miguel de]
Fisher, M. F. K. [*not* Fisher, Mary Frances Kennedy]
London, Jack [*not* London, John Griffith]
Poe, Edgar Allan [*not* Poe, E. A., *or* Poe, Edgar A.]

But in a work devoted to, say, M. F. K. Fisher or Cervantes, the full form of the name should appear in the index.

15.42 **Indexing pseudonyms, stage names, and other alternative names.** Persons who have used pseudonyms or other professional names are usually listed under their real names (assuming both forms of the name appear in the indexed work). If the pseudonym has become a household word, however, it should be used as the main entry, with the real name in parentheses if it is relevant to the work; a cross-reference is seldom necessary. If there is any doubt about adding an alternative form of a name that does not appear in the text (particularly for a living person who is no longer known by that alternative form, as in the case of a deadname), it should be omitted.

Æ. *See* Russell, George William
Ouida. *See* Ramée, Marie Louise de la
Ramée, Marie Louise de la (pseud. Ouida)
Russell, George William (pseud. Æ)
*but*
Molière (Jean-Baptiste Poquelin)
Monroe, Marilyn (Norma Jean Baker)
Rihanna (Robyn Rihanna Fenty)
Twain, Mark (Samuel Langhorne Clemens)
Voltaire (François-Marie Arouet)

15.43 **Indexing persons with the same name.** Persons with the same name should be distinguished by a middle initial (if either has one) or by a parenthetical tag.

Campbell, James
Campbell, James B.
Field, David Dudley (clergyman)
Field, David Dudley (lawyer)
Pitt, William (the elder)
Pitt, William (the younger)

In works that include many persons with the same last name (often a family name), parenthetical identifications are useful. For example, in *Two Lucky People*, by Milton Friedman and Rose D. Friedman (University of Chicago Press, 1998), the following identifications appear:

Friedman, David (son of MF and RDF)
Friedman, Helen (sister of MF)
Friedman, Janet (daughter of MF and RDF)
Friedman, Milton (MF)
Friedman, Rose Director (RDF)
Friedman, Sarah Ethel Landau (mother of MF)

15.44 **Indexing married women's names.** A married woman who is known variously by her birth name or by her married name, depending on context, should be indexed by her birth name unless the married name is the more familiar. A married woman who uses both birth and married names together is usually indexed by her married name (unless the two names are hyphenated). Parenthetical clarifications or cross-references may be supplied as necessary.

Marinoff, Fania (married to Carl Van Vechten)
Sutherland, Joan (married to Richard Bonynge)
Van Vechten, Fania. *See* Marinoff, Fania
*but*
Besant, Annie (née Wood)
Browning, Elizabeth Barrett
Clinton, Hillary Rodham

15.45 **Indexing monarchs, popes, and the like.** Monarchs, popes, and others who are known by their official names, often including a Roman numeral, should be indexed under the official name. Identifying tags may be omitted or expanded as appropriate in a particular work.

Anne, Queen
Benedict XVI (pope)
Charles III (king)

15.46 **Indexing princes, dukes, and other titled persons.** Princes and princesses are usually indexed under their given names. Dukes, earls, and the like are indexed under the title. A cross-reference may be needed where a title differs from a family name.

Catherine, Princess of Wales
Cooper, Anthony Ashley. *See* Shaftesbury, 7th Earl of
Shaftesbury, 7th Earl of (Anthony Ashley Cooper)
William, Prince of Wales

Unless necessary for identification, the titles *Lord* and *Lady* are best omitted from an index, since their use with given names is far from simple. *Sir* and *Dame*, while easier to cope with, are also unnecessary in most indexes. Brackets are used here to denote Chicago's editorial glosses (see 15.41).

Churchill, Winston [*or* Churchill, Sir Winston]
Hess, Myra [*or* Hess, Dame Myra]
Thatcher, Margaret [even if referred to as Lady Thatcher in text]

But in a work dealing with the nobility, or a historical work such as *The Lisle Letters* (University of Chicago Press, 1981), from which the following examples are taken, titles may be an appropriate or needed element in index entries. The last two examples illustrate distinctions for which expert advice may be needed.

Arundell, Sir John
Audley, Thomas Lord
Grey, Lady Jane ["Lady Jane Grey" in text]
Whethill, Elizabeth (Muston), Lady ["Lady Whethill" in text]

15.47 **Clerical titles in index entries.** Like titles of nobility, such abbreviations as *Rev.* or *Msgr.* should be used only when necessary for identification (see 15.46).

Councell, George E. (rector of the Church of the Holy Spirit)
Cranmer, Thomas (archbishop of Canterbury)
Jaki, Rev. Stanley S.
Manniere, Msgr. Charles L.

15.48 **Academic titles and degrees in index entries.** Academic titles such as *Prof.* and *Dr.*, used before a name, are not retained in indexing, nor are abbreviations of degrees such as *PhD* or *MD*.

15.49 **"Jr.," "Sr.," "III," and the like in index entries.** Abbreviations such as *Jr.* are retained in indexing but are placed after the given name and preceded by a comma (see also 6.46).

King, Martin Luther, Jr.
Stevenson, Adlai E., III

15.50 **Indexing saints.** Saints are indexed under their given names unless another name is equally well or better known. Parenthetical identifications or cross-references (as well as discretion) may be needed. See also 15.82.

Aquinas. *See* Thomas Aquinas, Saint
Borromeo, Saint Charles
Catherine of Siena, Saint
Chrysostom, Saint John
Thomas, Saint (the apostle)
Thomas Aquinas, Saint

15.51 **Indexing persons whose full names are unknown.** Persons referred to in the work by first or last names only should be parenthetically identified if the full name is unavailable.

John (Smith's shipmate on *Stella*)
Thaxter (family physician)

15.52 **Indexing incomplete names or names alluded to in text.** Even if only an epithet or a shortened form of a name is used in the text, the index should give the full form.

| *Text* | *Index* |
|---|---|
| the lake | Michigan, Lake |
| the bay | San Francisco Bay |
| the Village | Greenwich Village |
| the Great Emancipator | Lincoln, Abraham |

15.53 **Indexing confusing names.** When the same name is used of more than one entity, identifying tags should be provided.

| | | |
|---|---|---|
| New York (city) | *or* | New York City |
| New York (state) | *or* | New York State |

15.54 **Indexing abbreviations.** Organizations that are widely known under their abbreviations should be indexed and alphabetized according to the abbreviations. Parenthetical glosses, cross-references, or both should be added if the abbreviations, however familiar to the indexer, may not be known to all readers of the particular work. Lesser-known organizations are better indexed under the full name, with a cross-reference from the abbreviation if it is used frequently in the work. See also 15.16.

EEC (European Economic Community)
MLA. *See* Modern Language Association
NATO

## INDEXING TITLES OF PUBLICATIONS AND OTHER WORKS

15.55 **Typographic treatment for indexed titles of works.** Titles of newspapers, books, journals, stories, poems, artwork, musical compositions, and such should be treated typographically as they appear in text—whether italicized, set in roman and enclosed in quotation marks, or simply capitalized (see also 8.157–204).

15.56 **Indexing newspaper titles.** English-language newspapers should be indexed as they are generally known, whether or not the city of publication appears on the masthead. The name is italicized, as in text. An initial *The* included in the text may be omitted as a matter of editorial expediency (see also 8.172, 15.59). If necessary, a city of publication may be added in parentheses following the title.

*Chicago Sun-Times*
*Christian Science Monitor*
*New York Times*
*Plain Dealer* (Cleveland)
*Times* (London)
*Wall Street Journal*

For newspapers published in languages other than English, any article (*Le*, *Die*, etc.) follows the name in a main index entry, separated by a comma (but see 15.60). The city of publication may be added parenthetically, following the title.

*Akhbar, Al-* (Cairo)
*Monde, Le* (Paris)
*Prensa, La* (Buenos Aires)
*Süddeutsche Zeitung, Die*

15.57 **Indexing magazine and journal titles.** Magazines and journals are indexed in the same way as newspapers (see 15.56). An initial *The* included in the text may be omitted as a matter of editorial expediency (see also 8.172, 15.59). The article is retained, however, following the name, for non-English titles (but see 15.60).

*JAMA* (*Journal of the American Medical Association*)
*New England Journal of Medicine*
*Spiegel, Der*
*Time* (magazine)

15.58 **Indexing authored titles of works.** A published work, a musical composition, or a piece of art that merits its own main entry should also be indexed under the name of its creator, often as a subentry. The main heading is followed by the creator's name in parentheses (except in an index in which all titles cited have the same creator).

*Look Homeward, Angel* (Wolfe), 34–37
Wolfe, Thomas: childhood, 6–8;
  early literary influences on, 7–10;
  *Look Homeward, Angel*, 34–37; and
  Maxwell Perkins, 30–41

Several works by a single creator are sometimes treated as subentries under a new main heading, following a main entry on the creator. This device is best employed when many works as well as many topics are listed. Separate main entries may also be included for the works.

Mozart, Wolfgang Amadeus, 49–51,
  55–56; early musical compositions
  of, 67–72, 74–80; to Italy with
  father, 85–92; Salzburg appointment, 93–95; in Vienna, 98–105

Mozart, Wolfgang Amadeus, works of:
  *La clemenza di Tito*, 114; *Don Gio-*
  *vanni*, 115; *Idomeneo*, 105–6; *Jupiter*
  Symphony, 107; *The Magic Flute*, 111–
  13; *The Marriage of Figaro*, 109–12

15.59 **Indexing English-language titles beginning with an article.** In titles beginning with *A*, *An*, or *The*, the article is traditionally placed at the end of the title, following a comma, when the title forms a main heading. (Note, however, that an initial *The* may be omitted from the title of a periodical; see 15.56, 15.57.) When such a title occurs as a subheading, it appears in its normal position in a run-in index, where inversion would be clumsy and unnecessary, but is inverted in an indented index for easier alphabetic scanning.

*Professor and the Madman, The* (Win-
  chester), 209–11
Winchester, Simon: *Pacific*, 190–95;
  *The Professor and the Madman*,
  209–11; *The River at the Center of the*
  *World*, 211–15

Winchester, Simon
  *Pacific*, 190–95
  *Professor and the Madman, The*,
    209–11
  *River at the Center of the World, The*,
    211–15

Subtitles in index entries and subentries are normally omitted (see 15.63). If the subtitle is retained for any reason, an initial article follows the main title in a main index entry or an indented subentry (but appears in its normal position in a run-in subentry).

*Vampire, His Kith and Kin, The: A Critical Edition*, 88–91

See also 15.64.

15.60 **Indexing non-English titles beginning with an article.** Since initial articles in non-English titles sometimes modify the following word, they are usually retained in an index. In publications intended for a general audience, especially those that mention only a few such titles, it is acceptable to list the titles in the index exactly as they appear in the text, without inversion and alphabetized according to the article.

*Eine kleine Nachtmusik* (Mozart), 23
*La bohème* (Puccini), 211

In a more specialized work, or any work intended for readers who are likely to be well versed in the languages of any non-English titles mentioned in the text, the titles may be inverted as they are in English (see 15.59). According to this practice, the articles follow the rest of the title in main entries but remain, as in English titles, in their normal position in run-in subentries. In both positions, the articles are ignored in alphabetizing.

*bohème, La* (Puccini), 211
*clemenza de Tito, La* (Mozart), 22
*kleine Nachtmusik, Eine* (Mozart), 23
Mozart, Wolfgang Amadeus: *La clemenza de Tito*, 22; *Eine kleine Nachtmusik*, 23
*trovatore, Il* (Verdi), 323
*but*
"Un deux trois" (Luboff), 47 [alphabetize under *U*]

An indexer unfamiliar with the language of a title should make sure that the article is indeed an article and not a number (see last example above). French *un* and *une* and German *ein* and *eine*, for example, can mean *one* as well as *a*. See also 11.8–12.

15.61 **Indexing titles beginning with a preposition.** Unlike articles, prepositions beginning a title always remain in their original position and are never dropped, whether in English or non-English titles—nor are they ignored in alphabetizing (but see 15.76).

*For Whom the Bell Tolls*
*Por quién doblan las campanas*

15.62 **Indexing titles ending with a question mark or exclamation point.** A question mark or exclamation point at the end of an indexed title should be followed by a comma wherever a comma is called for by the syntax of the heading. See also 6.134, 15.102.

Carver, Raymond, 23–27, 101, 143–44;
"Are You a Doctor?," 25; *Will You Please Be Quiet, Please?*, 25–27, 143.
*See also* Iowa Writers' Workshop

15.63 **Subtitles in index entries.** Subtitles of books or articles are omitted both in main headings and in subheadings unless essential for identification.

## ALPHABETIZING

15.64 **Alphabetizing main headings — the basic rule.** To exploit the virtues of alphabetizing and thus ease the way for readers, the first word in a main heading should always determine the location of the entry. This principle occasionally entails inversion of the main heading. Thus, for example, *A Tale of Two Cities* is inverted as *Tale of Two Cities, A* and alphabetized under *T*, where readers would be inclined to look first. See also 15.9, 15.59, 15.60. For subentries, see 15.76–78.

15.65 **Computerized sorting.** Few computerized sorting options—and none of the standard options available with ordinary word processors—will perfectly conform to either system of alphabetization as described here. Those using a word processor to create their index will need to edit the finished product for the glitches and inconsistencies that invariably remain. Note that word processors typically produce a version of the word-by-word system, which Chicago now prefers (see 15.66). Some dedicated indexing programs, on the other hand, have been specially programmed to sort according to either the word-by-word or letter-by-letter system in conformance with the detailed guidelines presented in this section. See also 15.113.

### *Letter by Letter or Word by Word?*

15.66 **Two systems of alphabetizing — an overview.** The two principal modes of alphabetizing—or sorting—indexes are the *letter-by-letter* and the *word-*

*by-word* systems. A choice between the two should be made before indexing begins, though occasionally an indexer will find, as indexing progresses, that a change from one to the other is appropriate. (Such a change would of course need to be applied to the entire index.) Dictionaries are arranged letter by letter, library catalogs word by word (though online catalogs can usually be sorted by other criteria, such as format, date, availability, or relevance to a search). In an index with many open compounds starting with the same word, the word-by-word system is generally easier for users. For that reason, and because word processors typically sort word by word, Chicago now prefers the word-by-word system (a departure from previous editions) but will not normally impose it on a well-prepared index that has been arranged letter by letter. Both systems have their advantages and disadvantages, and few users are confused by either. Most people simply scan an alphabetic block until they find what they are looking for. The indexer must understand both systems, however, and the following paragraphs offer guidelines for each. For a fuller discussion, consult Nancy Mulvany, *Indexing Books* (bibliog. 2.5).

15.67 **The letter-by-letter system.** In the letter-by-letter system, alphabetizing continues up to the first parenthesis or comma; it then starts again after the punctuation point. Spaces and all other punctuation marks are ignored. The order of precedence is one word, word followed by a parenthesis, word followed by a comma, then (ignoring spaces and other punctuation) word followed by a number, and word followed by letters.

15.68 **The word-by-word system.** In the word-by-word system, alphabetizing continues only up to the end of the first word (counting an abbreviation or a hyphenated compound as one word), using subsequent words only when additional headings begin with the same word. As in the letter-by-letter system, alphabetizing continues up to the first parenthesis or comma; it then starts again after the punctuation point. The order of precedence is one word, word followed by a parenthesis, word followed by a comma, word followed by a space, then (ignoring other punctuation) word followed by a number, and word followed by letters. The index to this manual, in accordance with Chicago's new preference, is arranged word by word.

15.69 **The two systems compared.** In both systems a parenthesis or comma (in that order) interrupts the alphabetizing, and other punctuation marks (hyphens, slashes, quotation marks, periods, etc.) are ignored. The columns below illustrate the similarities and differences between the systems.

| *Letter by letter* | *Word by word* |
|---|---|
| NEW (Neighbors Ever Watchful) | N. Ewing & Sons |
| NEW (Now End War) | NEW (Neighbors Ever Watchful) |
| New, Arthur | NEW (Now End War) |
| New, Zoe | New, Arthur |
| new-12 compound | New, Zoe |
| newborn | New Deal |
| newcomer | new economics |
| New Deal | New England |
| new economics | new math |
| newel | New Thorndale |
| New England | new town |
| "new-fangled notions" | New Year's Day |
| Newfoundland | new-12 compound |
| N. Ewing & Sons | newborn |
| newlyweds | newcomer |
| new math | newel |
| new/old continuum | "new-fangled notions" |
| news, lamentable | Newfoundland |
| *News, Networks, and the Arts* | newlyweds |
| newsboy | new/old continuum |
| news conference | news, lamentable |
| newsletter | *News, Networks, and the Arts* |
| *News of the World* (Queen) | news conference |
| news release | *News of the World* (Queen) |
| newt | news release |
| NEWT (Northern Estuary Wind Tunnel) | newsboy |
| New Thorndale | newsletter |
| new town | newt |
| New Year's Day | NEWT (Northern Estuary Wind Tunnel) |

## *General Rules of Alphabetizing*

15.70 **Alphabetizing items with the same name.** When a person, a place, and a thing have the same name, they are arranged in normal alphabetical order.

| | |
|---|---|
| hoe, garden | London, England |
| Hoe, Robert | London, Jack |

Common sense must be exercised. If Amy London and Carolyn Hoe were to appear in the same index as illustrated above, adjustments in the other entries would be needed.

garden hoe
hoe. *See* garden hoe
Hoe, Carolyn
Hoe, Robert
London (England)
London, Amy
London, Jack

15.71 **Alphabetizing initials versus spelled-out names.** Initials used in place of a given name come before any spelled-out name beginning with the same letter.

Oppenheimer, J. Robert
Oppenheimer, James N.
Oppenheimer, K. T.
Oppenheimer, Katharine S.

15.72 **Alphabetizing abbreviations.** Acronyms, initialisms, and most abbreviations are alphabetized as they appear, not according to their spelled-out versions, and are interspersed alphabetically among entries. See also 15.54, 15.82.

faculty clubs
FBI
Feely, John
LBJ. *See* Johnson, Lyndon B.
NATO
North Pole
NOW (National Organization for Women)

Two exceptions: An ampersand (&) may be treated as if spelled out, and an at sign (@), which normally can be treated like the letter *a*, may be ignored as part of a screen name.

15.73 **Alphabetizing headings beginning with numerals.** Isolated entries beginning with numerals are alphabetized as though spelled out. (For numerals occurring in the middle of a heading, see 15.69, 15.74.)

*1984* (Orwell) [*alphabetized as* nineteen eighty-four]
125th Street [*alphabetized as* one hundred twenty-fifth street]
10 Downing Street [*alphabetized as* ten downing street]

If many such entries occur in an index, they may be listed together in numerical order at the beginning of the index, before the *A*s.

15.74 **Alphabetizing similar headings containing numerals.** When two or more similar headings with numerals occur together, they are ordered numerically, regardless of how they would be spelled out.

Henry III
Henry IV
Henry V

L7
L44
L50

section 9
section 44
section 77

The *L* entries above would be placed at the beginning of the *L* section. See also 15.69.

15.75 **Alphabetizing accented letters.** Words beginning with or including accented letters are alphabetized as though they were unaccented. (Note that this rule is intended for English-language indexes that include some non-English words. The alphabetizing practices of other languages are not relevant in such instances.)

| | |
|---|---|
| Ubeda | Schoenberg |
| *Über den Gipfel* | Schomberg |
| Ubina | Schönborn |

This system, more than adequate for most English-language indexes, may need to be supplemented by more comprehensive systems for indexes that contain many terms in other languages. The Unicode Consortium has developed extensive specifications and recommendations for sorting (or collating) the characters used in many of the world's languages. For more information, refer to the latest version of the *Unicode Collation Algorithm*, published by the Unicode Consortium (bibliog. 5). See also 11.2.

## *Subentries*

15.76 **Alphabetical order of subentries.** Introductory articles, prepositions, and conjunctions are disregarded in alphabetizing subentries (but see 15.61), whether the subentries are run in or indented. To preserve the alphabetic logic of the keywords, avoid substantive introductory words at the beginnings of subheadings (e.g., "*relations* with," "*views* on").

Churchill, Winston: as anti-Fascist,
  369; on Curzon line, 348, 379; and
  de Gaulle, 544n4

In indented style, where alphabetizing functions more visually, it may be better to dispense with such introductory words or to invert the headings, amplifying them as needed. The subheadings from the first example could be edited for an indented index as follows:

Churchill, Winston
  anti-Fascism of, 369
  Curzon line, views on, 348, 379
  de Gaulle, relations with, 544n4

15.77 **Numerical order of subentries.** Occasional subentries demand numerical order even if others in the same index (but not the same entry) are alphabetized.

Daley, Richard J. (mayor): third term, 205; fourth term, 206–7
flora, alpine: at 1,000-meter level, 46, 130–35; at 1,500-meter level, 146–54; at 2,000-meter level, 49, 164–74

15.78 **Chronological order of subentries.** In a run-in index, the subentries for the subject of a biography may be arranged chronologically rather than alphabetically so as to provide a quick summary of the subject's career and to avoid, for example, a subheading "death of" near the beginning of the entry. This system should be used with caution, however, and only when the biographical and chronological logic is obvious from the subentries.

## *Personal Names*

15.79 **Indexing names with particles.** In alphabetizing family names containing particles, the indexer must consider the individual's personal preference (if known) as well as traditional and national usages. The biographical entries in Merriam-Webster's dictionaries (bibliog. 3.1) are authoritative for well-known persons long deceased; library catalogs and encyclopedias are far broader in scope. Cross-references are often advisable (see 15.17). Note the wide variations in the following list of actual names arranged alphabetically as they might appear in an index. See also 8.5, 15.83, 15.92.

Beauvoir, Simone de
Ben-Gurion, David
Costa, Uriel da
da Cunha, Euclides
D'Amato, Alfonse
de Gaulle, Charles
di Leonardo, Micaela
Keere, Pieter van den
La Fontaine, Jean de
Leonardo da Vinci
Medici, Lorenzo de'
Van Rensselaer, Stephen

Charles de Gaulle is a good example of the opportunity for occasional editorial discretion: *Merriam-Webster* and the Library of Congress, for example, list the French statesman under "Gaulle"; the entry in *American Heritage* is under "de Gaulle"—the usage normally preferred by Chicago.

15.80 **Indexing compound names.** Compound family names, with or without hyphens, are usually alphabetized according to the first element (but see 15.44). See also 8.7, 8.12, 15.91, 15.92.

Lloyd George, David
Mies van der Rohe, Ludwig
Sackville-West, Victoria
Teilhard de Chardin, Pierre

15.81 **Indexing names with "Mac," "Mc," or "O'."** Names beginning with *Mac* or *Mc* are alphabetized letter by letter, as they appear.

Macalister, Donald
MacAlister, Paul
Macauley, Catharine
Macmillan, Harold
Madison, James
McAllister, Ward
McAuley, Catherine
McMillan, Edwin M.

Names beginning with *O'* are alphabetized as if the apostrophe were missing.

Onassis, Aristotle
O'Neill, Eugene
Ongaro, Francesco dall'

15.82 **Indexing names with "Saint."** A family name in the form of a saint's name is alphabetized according to how the name is spelled, whether *Saint*, *San*, *St.*, or however. A cross-reference may be useful if *Saint* and *St.* are far apart in an index. See also 15.50, 15.101.

Sainte-Beuve, Charles-Augustin
Saint-Gaudens, Augustus
Saint-Saëns, Camille
San Martin, José de
St. Denis, Ruth
St. Laurent, Louis Stephen

15.83 **Indexing Arabic names.** Modern Arabic names consisting of one or more given names followed by a surname present no problem.

Himsi, Ahmad Hamid
Sadat, Anwar

Arabic surnames prefixed by *al* or *el* (the) are alphabetized under the element following the particle; the article is treated like *de* in many French names.

Hakim, Tawfiq al-
Jamal, Muhammad Hamid al-

Names beginning with *Abu*, *Abd*, and *Ibn*, elements as integral to the names as *Mc* or *Fitz*, are alphabetized under those elements.

Abu Zafar Nadvi, Syed
Ibn Saud, Abdul Aziz

Context and readership may suggest cross-references. For example, in an index to a work likely to have readers unfamiliar with Arabic names, a cross-reference may be useful (e.g., "al-Farabi. *See* Farabi, al-").

15.84 **Indexing Burmese names.** Burmese persons are usually known by a given name of one or more elements and should be indexed under the first element. If the name is preceded in text by a term of respect (*U*, *Daw*, etc.), that term either is omitted or follows in the index.

Aung San Suu Kyi [alphabetize under *A*]
Thant, U [alphabetize under *T*]

15.85 **Indexing Chinese names.** Chinese names should be indexed as spelled in the work, whether in the Pinyin or the Wade-Giles system. Cross-references are needed only if alternative forms are used in the text. Since the family name precedes the given name in Chinese usage, names are not inverted in the index, and no comma is used.

Li Bai [Pinyin; alphabetize under *L*]
Mao Tse-tung [Wade-Giles; alphabetize under *M*]

Persons of Chinese ancestry or origin who have adopted the Western practice of giving the family name last are indexed with inversion and a comma.

Kung, H. H. Tsou, Tang

Note that strict alphabetical order in an index that includes entries for multiple people who share the same family name can be modified if some of the names are inverted and others are not. For example, the following order would be preferred as an exception in both word-by-word and letter-by-letter order:

Li Jinghan
Li, Lillian
Liang Qichao
*not this (strict word by word):*
Li, Lillian
Li Jinghan
Liang Qichao
*and not this (strict letter by letter):*
Li, Lillian
Liang Qichao
Li Jinghan

Elsewhere in the same index, any name that is not inverted may be treated similarly for the sake of consistency.

15.86 **Indexing Hungarian names.** In Hungarian practice the family name precedes the given name—for example, Bartók Béla, Molnár Ferenc. In English contexts, however, such names are usually inverted; in an index they are therefore reinverted, with a comma added.

Bartók, Béla  Molnár, Ferenc

Family names beginning with an initial should be indexed under the initial (see also 8.14).

É. Kiss, Katalin

15.87 **Indexing Indian names.** Modern Indian names generally appear with the family name last and are indexed accordingly. As with all names, the personal preference of the individual as well as usage should be observed.

Gandhi, Mohandas Karamchand
Krishna Menon, V. K.
Narayan, R. K.

15.88 **Indexing Indonesian names.** Usage varies. Some Indonesians (especially Javanese) use only a single, given name. Others use more than one name; even though the given name comes first, these are often indexed like Chinese names, with no inversion or punctuation (see third and fourth examples below). Indonesians with Muslim names and certain others whose names may include a title or an honorific are indexed by the final element, with inversion. The indexer must therefore ascertain how a person's full name is referred to in text and which part of the name is used for a short reference.

Habibi, B. J.
Hatta, Mohammed
Marzuki Darusman
Pramoedya Ananta Toer
Suharto
Sukarno
Suryokusumo, Wiyono

15.89 **Indexing Japanese names.** In Japanese usage the family name precedes the given name; names are therefore not inverted in the index, and no comma is used. If the name is westernized, as it often is by authors writing in English, the family name comes last. The indexer must therefore make certain which practice is followed in the text so that the family name always appears first in the index.

Tajima Yumiko [alphabetize under *T*]
Yoshida Shigeru [alphabetize under *Y*]
*but*
Kurosawa, Noriaki [referred to in text as Noriaki Kurosawa]

15.90 **Indexing Korean names.** In Korean usage the family name precedes the given name, and this is how it is usually presented even in English-language contexts. Persons of Korean origin living in the West, however, often invert this order. The indexer must therefore make certain which practice is followed in the text so that the family name appears first, with or without inversion, in the index.

Kim Dae-jung [alphabetize under *K*]
Oh Jung-hee [alphabetize under *O*]
*but*
Lee, Chang-rae [referred to in text as Chang-rae Lee]

15.91 **Indexing Portuguese names.** Portuguese surnames, unlike Spanish surnames (see 15.92), are indexed by the last element. This does not include the designations *Filho* (son), *Neto* (grandson), and *Júnior*, which always follow the second family name.

Câmara Júnior, José Mattoso
Jucá Filho, Cândido
Martins, Luciana de Lima
Silva Neto, Serafim da
Vasconcellos, J. Leite de

Where both Portuguese and Spanish names appear in the same context, cross-references may be necessary.

15.92 **Indexing Spanish names.** In Spain and in some Latin American countries a double family name is often used, of which the first element is the father's family name and the second the mother's birth name (*her* father's family name). The two names are sometimes joined by *y* (and). Such compound names are alphabetized under the first element. Cross-references will often be needed, especially if the person is generally known under the second element or if the indexer is uncertain where to place the main entry. *Merriam-Webster* is a good guide for persons listed there. Where many Spanish names appear, an indexer not conversant with Spanish or Latin American culture should seek help.

García Lorca, Federico
Lorca, Federico García. *See* García Lorca, Federico
Ortega y Gasset, José
Sánchez Mendoza, Juana

When the particle *de* appears in a Spanish name, the family name, under which the person is indexed, may be either the preceding or the following name (depending in part on how a person is known). If it is not clear from the text and the name is not in *Merriam-Webster* or otherwise widely known, a cross-reference will be needed.

Balboa, Vasco Núñez de
Esquivel de Sánchez, María
Fernández de Navarrete, Juan
Fernández de Oviedo, Gonzalo

Traditionally, a married woman replaced her mother's family name with her husband's (first) family name, sometimes preceded by *de*. Her name should be alphabetized, however, by the first family name (her father's).

Mendoza de Peña, María Carmen [woman's name after marriage]
Mendoza Salinas, María Carmen [woman's name before marriage]
Peña Montalvo, Juan Alberto [husband's name]

In telephone directories and elsewhere, some women appear under the husband's family name, but this is not a recommended bibliographic or indexing practice. Many modern women in Spanish-speaking countries no longer take the husband's family name. See also 8.12.

15.93 **Indexing Thai names.** Although family names are used in Thailand, Thai persons are normally known by their given names, which come first, as in English names. The name is often alphabetized under the first name, but practice varies. Seek expert help.

Sarit Thanarat [*or* Thanarat, Sarit]
Sivaraksa, Sulak [*or* Sulak Sivaraksa]
Supachai Panitchpakdi

15.94 **Indexing Vietnamese names.** Vietnamese names consist of three elements, the family name being the first. Since Vietnamese persons are usually referred to by the last part of their given names (Premier Diem, General Giap), they are best indexed under that form.

Diem, Ngo Dinh [*cross-reference under* Ngo Dinh Diem]
Giap, Vo Nguyen [*cross-reference under* Vo Nguyen Giap]

15.95 **Indexing other Asian names.** Throughout Asia, many names derive from Arabic, Chinese, the European languages, and other languages, regardless of where the bearers of the names were born. In the Philippines, for example, names follow a Western order, giving precedence to the family name, though the names themselves may be derived from local languages. In some parts of Asia, titles denoting status form part of a name as it appears in written work and must be dealt with appropriately. When the standard reference works do not supply an answer, query the author.

## *Names of Organizations and Businesses*

15.96 **Omission of article in indexed names of organizations.** In indexing organizations whose names begin with *the* (which would be lowercased in running text), the article is omitted.

Beatles (band)    Unicode Consortium    University of Chicago

15.97 **Indexing personal names as corporate names.** When used as names of businesses or other organizations, full personal names are not inverted, and the corporate name is alphabetized under the first name or initials. An organization widely known by the family name, however, should be indexed under that name. In both instances, cross-references may be appropriate.

A. G. Edwards & Sons, Inc. [alphabetize under *A*]
Penney, J. C. *See* J. C. Penney Company, Inc.
Saphir, Kurt. *See* Kurt Saphir Pianos, Inc.
*but*
John G. Shedd Aquarium. *See* Shedd Aquarium

A personal name and the name of that person's company should be indexed separately.

J. S. Morgan & Company, 45–48. *See also* Morgan, Junius S.
Morgan, Junius S., 39, 42–44; J. S. Morgan & Company, 45–48

## *Names of Places*

15.98 **Indexing names beginning with "Mount," "Lake," and such.** Proper names of mountains, lakes, and so forth that begin with a generic name are usually inverted and alphabetized under the nongeneric name. If the generic term is from another language, however, it can usually be left as is. If inverted (as in an index with more than a few such entries), it may be helpful to explain the decision in a headnote—for example, "Names beginning with *Mauna* (Mountain) have been inverted, as in 'Kea, Mauna.'" For isolated instances, double posting under both forms may be the better option (see also 15.16). A name that has recently changed may include a cross-reference under the old form of the name; if the older form occurs in the text (as in a direct quotation), this fact should be mentioned in parentheses after the main entry.

Denali (*also as* Mount McKinley)
Geneva, Lake
Japan, Sea of
McKinley, Mount. *See* Denali
*but*
Loch Ness
Mauna Kea
Sierra Nevada

Names of cities or towns beginning with topographic elements, as well as islands known as "Isle of . . . ," are alphabetized under the first element.

Isle of Pines
Isle of Wight
Lake Geneva, WI
Mount Vernon, NY
Valley Forge

15.99 **Indexing names beginning with the definite article.** Aside from a very few cities such as The Hague (unless the Dutch form *Den Haag* is used; see 15.100) and The Dalles, where *The* is part of the formal name and thus capitalized, an initial *the* used informally with place-names is omitted in indexing. See also 8.46.

| | | |
|---|---|---|
| Bronx | Loop (Chicago's downtown) | Ozarks |
| Hague, The | Netherlands | Philippines |

15.100 **Indexing names beginning with non-English definite articles.** Names of places beginning with definite articles such as *El*, *Le*, *La*, and the like, whether in English- or non-English-speaking countries, are alphabetized according to the article.

| | |
|---|---|
| Den Haag | La Mancha |
| El Dorado | Le Havre |
| El Paso | Les Baux-de-Provence |
| La Crosse | Los Alamos |

15.101 **Indexing names of places beginning with "Saint."** Names of places beginning with *Saint*, *Sainte*, *St.*, or *Ste.* should be indexed as they appear in the text—that is, abbreviated only if abbreviated in text. Like personal names, they are alphabetized as they appear. Cross-references may be appropriate (e.g., "Saint. *See* St.," or vice versa). Note that French hyphenates place-names with *Saint*. See also 10.35, 11.28.

| | |
|---|---|
| Saint-Cloud (in France) | St. Louis |
| Sainte-Foy | St. Vincent Island |
| Saint-Luc | Ste. Genevieve |
| St. Cloud (in Florida) | |

## PUNCTUATING INDEXES: A SUMMARY

15.102 **Comma in index entries.** In both run-in and indented indexes, when a main heading is followed immediately by locators (usually page or paragraph numbers; see 15.12), a comma appears before the first locator. Commas appear between locators. Commas are also used when a heading is an inversion or when a main heading is qualified, without subentries. The second example below illustrates three uses of the comma. For the role of commas in alphabetizing, see 15.69.

lighthouses, early history of, 40–42
Sabba da Castiglione, Monsignor,
  209, 337; on cosmetics, 190, 195, 198

15.103 **Colon in index entries.** In a run-in index, when a main heading is followed immediately by subentries, a colon appears before the first subheading. In an indented index, no punctuation is used after the main heading. A colon is also used in a cross-reference to a subentry. See also 15.20.

Maya: art of, 236–43; cities of, 178.
  *See also* Yucatán: Maya

Maya
  art of, 236–43
  cities of, 178
  *See also* Yucatán: Maya

15.104 **Semicolon in index entries.** When subentries or sub-subentries are run in, they are separated by semicolons. Cross-references, if more than one, are also separated by semicolons.

astronomy: Galileo's works on, 20–21,
  22–23, 24; skills needed in, 548–49.
  *See also* Brahe, Tycho; comets;
  Flamsteed, John

15.105 **Period in index entries.** In a run-in index a period is used only before *See* (or *See under*) or *See also* (or *See also under*). In an indented index a period is used only before *See*. When a *see* or *see also* reference in parentheses follows a subheading or a subentry in either a run-in or an indented index, no period is used. No period follows the final word of any entry. For examples, see 15.17, 15.19, 15.20, 15.142.

15.106 **Parentheses in index headings.** Parentheses enclose identifying or supplementary information. For the role of parentheses in alphabetizing, see 15.69.

Charles I (king of England)
Charles I (king of Portugal)
*Of Human Bondage* (Maugham)

15.107 **Em dash in index entries.** For use of the em dash in run-in indexes that require occasional sub-subentries, see example B in 15.27.

15.108 **En dash in index entries.** The en dash is used for page ranges and all other inclusive locators (e.g., "dogs, 135–42"). For abbreviating inclusive numbers in indexes, see 15.14. See also 6.83, the index to this manual, and examples throughout this chapter.

## THE MECHANICS OF INDEXING

### *Before Indexing Begins: Tools and Decisions*

15.109 **Preliminary indexing work and when to begin.** Although some planning can be done at the manuscript stage, most indexes are prepared as soon as a work is in final, paginated form, or "page proofs." It is crucial, in fact, that indexing not begin until pagination is final. For indexes in which the locators are paragraph or section numbers rather than page numbers, however (or where entries will be linked to specific locations in the text for electronic formats), earlier iterations of the final or near-final manuscript can often be used to get a head start. Authors who are not preparing their own indexes may compile a list of important terms and preferred wordings for the indexer, but doing much more is likely to cause duplication or backtracking.

15.110 **Schedule for indexing.** Anyone making an index for the first time should know that the task is intensive and time-consuming. An index for a three-hundred-page book could take as much as three weeks' work or more. See also 15.4.

15.111 **Indexing from page proofs.** For a printed work, the indexer must have in hand a clean and complete set of proofs (usually showing final pagination) before beginning to index. A PDF version is generally more helpful than a printout because it can be used to search for specific terms (and can be printed out as needed; see also 15.114). For a journal volume, the work may begin when the first issue to be indexed has been paginated, and it may continue for several months, until page proofs for the final issue in the volume have been generated. For electronic formats, where index entries are linked to their location in the text, additional considerations may apply (see 15.13). See also 15.109, 15.116–24.

15.112 **Publisher's indexing preferences.** Before beginning work, the indexer should know the publisher's preferences in such matters as alphabetizing, run-in or indented style, inclusive numbers, handling of numeric headings, and the like (all matters dealt with in earlier sections of this chapter). For a journal volume index, the style is likely to be well established, and the indexer must follow that style. If the publisher requests an index of a particular length, the indexer should adjust the normal editing time accordingly. See also 15.130.

15.113 **Indexing tools.** The dedicated indexing programs used by many professional indexers automate such tasks as cross-referencing and the collation of entries and subentries and include special options for alphabetizing—for example, to exclude certain words or characters and to conform to either the letter-by-letter or word-by-word system (see 15.66). Such programs, however, tend to require more learning time than most authors can afford (see 15.4). Fortunately, an index can be prepared according to the guidelines in this chapter by simply entering terms and locators into a separate document using an ordinary word processor—though cross-references and alphabetizing, in particular, will need to be checked manually throughout the process (see 15.65; see also 15.5). For the latest information about tools for indexing, consult the website of the American Society for Indexing.

15.114 **Using the electronic files to index.** Publishers' policies vary as to whether they can agree to supply indexers with page proofs in electronic form. A searchable PDF file can be helpful in double-checking that additional instances of particular terms have not been overlooked. Some indexers may prefer also to annotate and refer to the PDF rather than a paper copy as they create the index. It should be noted, however, that an index cannot be automatically "generated" from a PDF file and that there is no substitute for rereading the whole work. See also 15.5, 15.118.

15.115 **Formatting index entries.** Consult with the publisher up front to determine whether a run-in or indented index is required (see 15.24–28) and whether there are any other specific requirements. Format the manuscript accordingly, using a flush-and-hang style (see 15.24). See also 15.130.

## *Marking Proofs and Preparing Entries*

15.116 **Beginning to highlight and enter terms.** After a perusal of the table of contents and the work as a whole, an indexer should begin highlighting terms to be used as main headings or subheadings. This is normally done by hand-marking a set of proofs (on either paper or PDF). Inexperienced indexers are advised to mark the proofs—at least in the early stages—with the same kind of detail as is illustrated in figure 15.1. (Marking up the proofs in this way is less important for experienced indexers, who typically enter terms into their indexing software as they are encountered in the text.) Most indexers prefer to mark one section (or chapter) at a time and—using a word processor or dedicated indexing software (see 15.113)—to enter and alphabetize the marked terms in that section before going on to the next section. The notes belonging to the section, even if endnotes, should be checked and, if necessary, indexed at the same time (see 15.33). As the indexer becomes more skilled in marking the proofs, less underlining and fewer marginal notes may suffice.

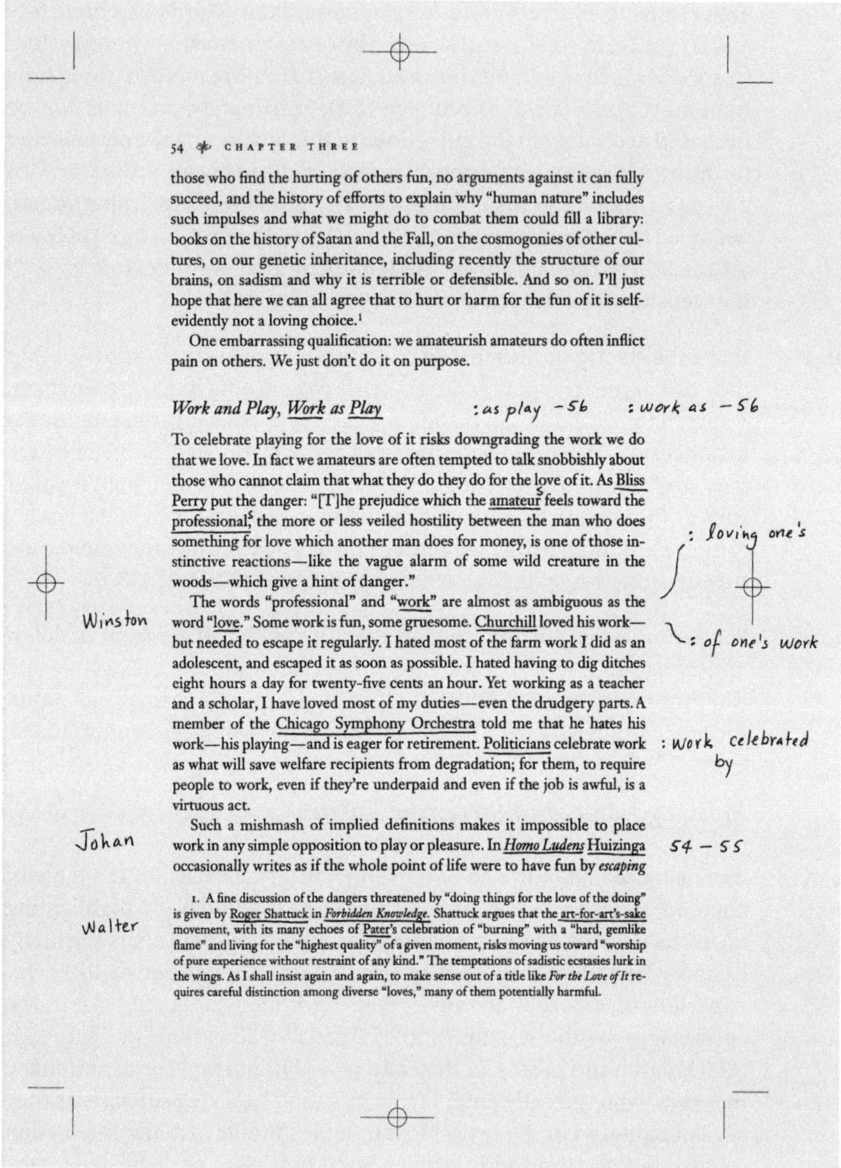

54 ❧ CHAPTER THREE

those who find the hurting of others fun, no arguments against it can fully succeed, and the history of efforts to explain why "human nature" includes such impulses and what we might do to combat them could fill a library: books on the history of Satan and the Fall, on the cosmogonies of other cultures, on our genetic inheritance, including recently the structure of our brains, on sadism and why it is terrible or defensible. And so on. I'll just hope that here we can all agree that to hurt or harm for the fun of it is self-evidently not a loving choice.[1]

One embarrassing qualification: we amateurish amateurs do often inflict pain on others. We just don't do it on purpose.

*Work and Play, Work as Play*

To celebrate playing for the love of it risks downgrading the work we do that we love. In fact we amateurs are often tempted to talk snobbishly about those who cannot claim that what they do they do for the love of it. As Bliss Perry put the danger: "[T]he prejudice which the amateur feels toward the professional, the more or less veiled hostility between the man who does something for love which another man does for money, is one of those instinctive reactions—like the vague alarm of some wild creature in the woods—which give a hint of danger."

The words "professional" and "work" are almost as ambiguous as the word "love." Some work is fun, some gruesome. Churchill loved his work—but needed to escape it regularly. I hated most of the farm work I did as an adolescent, and escaped it as soon as possible. I hated having to dig ditches eight hours a day for twenty-five cents an hour. Yet working as a teacher and a scholar, I have loved most of my duties—even the drudgery parts. A member of the Chicago Symphony Orchestra told me that he hates his work—his playing—and is eager for retirement. Politicians celebrate work as what will save welfare recipients from degradation; for them, to require people to work, even if they're underpaid and even if the job is awful, is a virtuous act.

Such a mishmash of implied definitions makes it impossible to place work in any simple opposition to play or pleasure. In *Homo Ludens* Huizinga occasionally writes as if the whole point of life were to have fun by *escaping*

1. A fine discussion of the dangers threatened by "doing things for the love of the doing" is given by Roger Shattuck in *Forbidden Knowledge.* Shattuck argues that the art-for-art's-sake movement, with its many echoes of Pater's celebration of "burning" with a "hard, gemlike flame" and living for the "highest quality" of a given moment, risks moving us toward "worship of pure experience without restraint of any kind." The temptations of sadistic ecstasies lurk in the wings. As I shall insist again and again, to make sense out of a title like *For the Love of It* requires careful distinction among diverse "loves," many of them potentially harmful.



FIGURE 15.1. Sample page of proof from Wayne Booth's *For the Love of It,* marked up for indexing. See 15.116–24.

15.117 **Deciding how many terms to mark.** The number of terms to mark on any one page obviously depends on the kind of work being indexed. As a very rough guide, an average of five references per text page in a book will yield a modest index (one-fiftieth the length of the text), whereas fifteen or more will yield a fairly long index (about one-twentieth the length of the text or more). If the publisher has budgeted for a strictly limited number of pages, the indexer should work accordingly. Remember that it is always easier to drop entries than to add them; err on the side of inclusiveness. See also 15.30, 15.31, 15.32–39, 15.112.

15.118 **How to mark index entries.** To visualize the method advocated here, suppose you are indexing a chapter from Wayne Booth's *For the Love of It* (University of Chicago Press, 1999), a consideration of work and play and work as play (see fig. 15.1). You have read through the chapter once and now have to go back and select headings and subheadings for indexing this particular section (of which only the first paragraphs are shown here). You decide that the whole section (pp. 54–56) will have to be indexed under both *work* and *play*, so you mark the section head as shown. (On the marked proofs, a colon separates a proposed principal heading from a proposed subheading.) Going down the page, you underline *Bliss Perry* (which will of course be inverted—Perry, Bliss—as a heading; similarly for the other personal names). You also underline *amateur* and *professional* (modifying them to the plural). In the second paragraph, you underline *work* and *love*, with proposed subheads, and *Churchill* (noting the first name in the margin). You decide to index *Chicago Symphony Orchestra*—which in another work might be tangential but here ties in with the book's major subtheme of musical performance and appreciation—and also mark *politicians*, with proposed subhead. You underline *Huizinga* (adding "Johan" in the margin) and the work *Homo Ludens*, which might also be a subheading under "Huizinga, Johan." Because the sentence spans two pages, you write "54–55" in the right margin. In the note, you mark two names (supplying a first name for Pater), one title, and one additional term (see also 15.33).

15.119 **Planning index subentries.** For each term marked, you should make an effort to write in a modification—a word or phrase that narrows the application of the heading, hence a potential subentry. Although some such modifications may eventually be dropped, they should be kept on hand in case they are needed. Otherwise you may end up with some headings that are followed by nothing but a long string of numbers, which makes for an all but useless index entry. The modifications can be altered and added to as the indexing proceeds.

15.120 **Recording inclusive numbers for index terms.** If a text discussion extends over more than one page, section, or paragraph, both beginning and ending numbers—which will depend on what locator system is being used (see 15.12)—must be recorded. See also 15.14.

15.121 **Typing and modifying index entries.** Most entries at this stage will include three elements: a heading, a modification (or provisional subentry), and a locator (page or paragraph number). While typing, you will probably modify some of the headings and add, delete, or alter subheadings and locators (a process that may at the same time entail changes to cross-references and to alphabetical order). After typing each entry, read it carefully against the page proofs—in particular, checking that the page numbers or other locators are correct. You are unlikely to have time to read your final index manuscript against the marked-up proofs, though you should certainly retain the proofs for reference until the work has been published. See also 15.115.

15.122 **Alphabetizing entries as part of the indexing process.** Many indexers alphabetize as they type; others let their software do it, intervening as necessary. By this time the indexer should have decided whether to use the letter-by-letter or the word-by-word system (see 15.66–69). If the system chosen proves unsatisfactory for the particular work as the index proceeds, a switch can be made if the publisher agrees. See also 15.65.

15.123 **Final check of indexed proofs.** After typing all the entries, read quickly through the marked-up proofs once again to see whether anything indexable has been omitted. You may find some unmarked items that seemed peripheral at the time but now, in the light of themes developed in later chapters, declare themselves to be significant. Or you may have missed major items. Now is the time to remedy all omissions.

15.124 **Noting errors during indexing.** Although not engaged to proofread, the indexer has to read carefully and usually finds a number of typographical errors and minor inconsistencies. If indexing a book (rather than a journal volume, most of which will already have been published), keep track of all such errors and send a list to the publisher (who will be very grateful) when, or before, submitting the index.

## *Editing and Refining the Entries*

15.125 **Refining the terms for main headings.** The assembled entries must now be edited to a coherent whole. You have to make a final choice among synonymous or closely related terms—*agriculture, farming,* or *crop raising; clothing, costume,* or *dress; life, existence,* or *being*—and, if you think necessary, prepare suitable cross-references to reflect those choices. It is possible that you have already made many of these editing decisions as you entered terms into the index, in which case editing the index will also involve finalizing and checking those decisions. For journals, the terms may have been established in the indexes for previous volumes and should be retained.

15.126 **Main entries versus subentries.** You also have to decide whether certain items are best treated as main entries or as subentries under another heading. Where will readers look first? In a work dealing with schools of various kinds, such terms as *kindergarten, elementary school, middle school,* and *public school* should constitute separate entries; in a work in which those terms appear but are not the primary subject matter, they may be better treated as subentries under *school.* An index with relatively few main entries but masses of subentries is unhelpful as a search tool. Furthermore, in an indented index an excessively long string of subentries may begin to look like a set of main entries, so that users lose their way alphabetically. Promote subentries to main entries and use the alphabet to its best advantage.

15.127 **When to furnish subentries.** Main headings unmodified by subentries should not be followed by more than five or six locators. If, for example, the draft index of a work on health care includes an entry like the first example below, it should be broken up into a number of subentries, such as those in the second example, to lead readers quickly to the information sought. The extra space needed is a small price to pay for their convenience.

hospitals, 17, 22, 23, 24, 25, 28, 29–31,
  33, 35, 36, 38, 42, 91–92, 94, 95, 96,
  98, 101, 111–14, 197
*becomes*
hospitals: administration of, 22, 96;
  and demand for patient services,
  23, 91–92; efficiency of, 17, 29–31,
  33, 111–14; finances of, 28, 33,
  36, 38, 42, 95, 112; and length of
  patient stay, 35, 94, 98, 101, 197;
  quality control in, 22–25, 31

15.128 **How to phrase subheadings.** Subheadings should be as concise and informative as possible and begin with a keyword likely to be sought. *A, an,* and *the* are omitted whenever possible. Example A below, *not* to be emulated, shows poorly worded and rambling subheadings. Example B shows greatly improved subentries that conserve space. Note the page references immediately following the main entry; when a main entry has one or more subentries, such undifferentiated locators should normally be reserved for definitive or extended discussions of the term (some indexers will prefer to add *defined* or a similar subhead). Example C adds sub-subentries, making for quicker reference but requiring more space (see 15.27, 15.28). For arrangement of subentries, see 15.76–78.

Example A (*not* to be emulated)

house renovation
  balancing heating system, 65
  building permit required, 7
  called "rehabbing," 8
  correcting overloaded electrical circuits, 136
  how wallboard is finished, 140–44
  installing ready-made fireplace, 191–205
  painting outside of house adds value, 11
  plumbing permit required, 7
  removing paint from doors and woodwork, 156–58
  repairing dripping faucets, 99–100
  replacing clogged water pipes, 125–28
  replacing old wiring, 129–34
  separate chimney required for fireplace, 192
  straightening sagging joists, 40–42
  termite damage to sills a problem, 25
  three ways to deal with broken plaster, 160–62
  violations of electrical code corrected, 135
  what is involved in, 5

Example B (improvement with fairly inclusive subentries)

house renovation, 5, 8
  electrical repairs, 129–34, 135, 136
  fireplace, installing, 191–205
  heating system, balancing, 65
  legal requirements, 7, 135, 192
  painting and decorating, 11, 156–58
  plaster repair, 160–62
  plumbing repairs, 99–100, 125–28
  structural problems, 25, 40–42
  wallboard, finishing, 140–44

Example C (improvement with sub-subentries)

house renovation, 5, 8
  electrical repairs: circuit overload, 136; code violations, 135; old wiring, 129–34
  heating system: balancing, 65; fireplace installation, 191–205
  legal requirements: electrical code, 135; permits, 7; separate chimney for fireplace, 192
  painting and decorating: painting exterior, 11; stripping woodwork, 156–58
  plumbing repairs: clogged water pipes, 125–28; dripping faucets, 99–100
  structural problems: sagging joists, 40–42; termite damage, 25
  wall and ceiling repairs: broken plaster, 160–62; wallboard, finishing, 140–44

If it looks as though an index is going to require a great many sub-subentries, the indexer should check with the publisher before proceeding.

15.129 **Checking cross-references against edited index headings.** As a final or near-final step in editing the index, make sure that all cross-references match the edited headings. And if two entries are double-posted (see 15.16), make sure they have identical locators. The following examples need their locators made consistent.

FBI (Federal Bureau of Investigation), 26, 98–99
Federal Bureau of Investigation (FBI), 98–99 [*add* 26 (or delete 26 from above)]

Churchill, Winston
  on Curzon Line, 45–46, 50, 100
Curzon Line
  Churchill on, 45–46, 100 [*add* 50 (or delete 50 from above)]

See also 15.15–23.

## *Submitting the Index*

15.130 **Index submission format.** Having carefully proofread the draft and checked alphabetical order and all cross-references, punctuation, and capitalization to ensure consistency—and having produced an index of the required length, if one has been specified—you will now send the final draft to the publisher. If the publisher requires a printout, allow margins of at least one inch both left and right, and leave the text unjustified. Do not format the index in columns. Use hard returns only at the end of each entry and, for an indented-style index (see 15.26), at the end of each subentry. Use single line spacing, and apply hanging indents using your software's indentation feature (see 15.24; see also 2.14). Do not impose end-of-line hyphenation (see 2.16). If there is more than one index, give each an appropriate title (Author Index, Subject Index, etc.) and save each in a separate file. To avert disaster, keep a copy of the final draft that you send to the publisher, as well as your marked-up proofs, until the work has been published. Send the publisher a list of any errors you have found (see 15.124).

# EDITING AN INDEX FOR PUBLICATION

15.131 **Evaluating an index.** Editing a well-prepared index, whether it has been created by a professional indexer or by the author, can be a pleasure.

Little work should be needed to get it ready for publication. A poorly prepared one, however, presents serious problems. As an editor, you cannot remake a really bad index. If an index cannot be repaired, you have two choices: Omit it or have a new one made by another indexer (at additional cost).

15.132 **Index-editing checklist.** Editing an index requires some or all of the following steps, not necessarily in the order given here. Note that it is not necessary to check every heading and every locator against the work—which would take forever—but it is necessary to read the index carefully and to refer to the latest version of the page proofs from time to time.

1. Check headings—in both the main entries and subentries—for alphabetical order.
2. Check the spelling, capitalization, and font (i.e., italics or roman) of each heading, consulting the page proofs if in doubt.
3. Check punctuation—commas, colons, semicolons, en dashes, etc.—for proper style and consistency (see 15.102–8).
4. Check cross-references to make sure they go somewhere and that headings match (see 15.21). Make sure they are needed; if only a few locators are involved, substitute these for the *see* reference (see 15.16). Ensure that the placement of all cross-references within entries is consistent.
5. Add cross-references you believe are necessary.
6. Check to make sure there are no false locators such as "193–93" or "12102" (and figure out whether these may be the product of a typo) and make sure the locators to each main heading and subheading are in ascending order.
7. Check subentries for consistency of order, whether alphabetical or chronological. See 15.76–78.
8. If some entries seem overanalyzed (many subentries with only one locator or, worse, with the same locator), try to combine some of them if it can be done without sacrificing their usefulness. If subheadings are more elaborately worded than necessary, try to simplify them.
9. If awkward or unnecessary sub-subentries appear, correct them by adding appropriate repeated subentries or by adjusting punctuation (see 15.27, 15.28).
10. Look for long strings of unanalyzed locators and break them up, if possible, with subentries (see 15.10, 15.128).
11. Evaluate the accuracy of locators by a random check of five to ten entries. If more than one error shows up, consult the author or the indexer; every locator may have to be rechecked.
12. If the index needs trimming, delete any entries (and cross-references thereto) that you know from your work on the book are trivial, such as references to persons or places used only as examples of something. But be

careful. You may offend someone or let yourself in for a lot of work. A handful of unnecessary entries, if they are very short, will not mar an otherwise good index. It may also make sense to eliminate some subentries (expanding the number of locators allowed without modifications; see also 15.127) rather than deleting access points. Finally, in some cases it may make sense to convert an indented index to run-in format.

15.133 **Instructions for typesetting the index.** At this stage the publisher will have prepared specifications for typesetting the index, and few further instructions are needed. To avoid problems, a brief note such as the following (for an indented index to a book) may be prefixed to the index manuscript after consulting the detailed specifications:

> Set two columns, flush and hang, ragged right; indent subentries one em; indent runovers two ems; preserve en dashes between continuing numbers; leave one line space between alphabetical blocks. Set headnote across both columns. See publisher's design specifications for size and measure.

For an example of a headnote, see 15.140.

## TYPOGRAPHICAL CONSIDERATIONS FOR INDEXES

15.134 **Type size and column width for indexes.** In print works, indexes are usually set in smaller type than the body of the work, often two sizes smaller. That is, if the body copy is set in ten-on-twelve-point type, and the extracts, bibliography, and appendixes in nine-on-eleven, the index will probably be set in eight-on-ten (with a blank line before each new alphabetic grouping). Indexes are usually set in two columns; with a line length of twenty-six picas (in a book with a trim size of six by nine inches), the index columns will each be twelve and a half picas wide, with a one-pica space between them. In large-format print works, however, the index may be set in three or more columns.

15.135 **Ragged right-hand margin for indexes.** For very short lines, such as those in an index, justifying the text usually results in either gaping word spaces or excessive hyphenation, making for difficult reading. Chicago therefore sets all indexes without justification ("ragged right").

15.136 **Indenting index entries.** All runover lines are indented, whether the subentries are run in or indented. In indexes with indented subentries (see 15.26), runover lines have to be indented more deeply than the subentries; all runovers, whether from a main entry or a subentry (or even a sub-subentry, should these too be indented), should be indented equally from the left margin. Thus, in an indented index the subentries may be indented one em, the sub-subentries two ems, and the runovers for all entries three ems. (For avoiding sub-subentries, see 15.27, 15.28.) All these matters, however, must be determined before type is set.

15.137 **Fixing bad breaks in indexes.** The final, typeset index should be checked for bad breaks. A line consisting of only one or two page numbers should not be left at the top of a column, for example. A single line at the end of an alphabetic section (followed by a blank line) should not head a column, nor should a single line at the beginning of an alphabetic section remain at the foot of a column. Blemishes like these are eliminated by rebreaking entries or transposing lines from one column to another, by adding to the white space between alphabetic sections, and sometimes by lengthening or shortening all columns on facing pages by one line.

15.138 **Adding "continued" lines in an index.** If an entry breaks at the foot of the last column on a right-hand page (a recto) and resumes at the top of the following left-hand page (a verso), the main heading should be repeated, followed by the word *continued* in parentheses, above the carried-over part of the index. (In an especially long or complex index it may make sense to add *continued* lines for every entry that breaks at the end of a column, as in the print edition of this manual.)

ingestive behavior (*continued*)
  network of causes underlying, 68;
    physiology of, 69–70, 86–87; in
    rat, 100; in starfish, 45, 52–62

In an indented index with indented sub-subentries, it may be necessary to repeat a subentry if the subentry has been broken.

house renovation (*continued*)
  structural problems (*continued*)
    termite damage, 25–27
    warped overhangs, 46–49

15.139 **Making typographic distinctions in index entries.** A complicated index can sometimes be made easier to read by using different type styles or fonts. If, for example, names of writers need to be distinguished from names of literary characters, one or the other might be set in caps and small caps. Page references to illustrations might be in italic type (see

15.39) and references to the principal treatment of a subject in boldface. If devices of this kind are used, a headnote to the index must furnish a key (see 15.140, 15.142).

## EXAMPLES OF INDEXES

15.140 **A run-in index with italicized references to figures and tables.** Run-in indexes are the most economical of the five formats exemplified in this section. Note the italic page references and the headnote explaining their use. Boldface could also be used for that purpose (see 15.142). For more examples and further discussion, see 15.25, 15.27, 15.102–8. See also 15.76, 15.139.

*Page numbers in italics refer to figures and tables.*

Abbot, George, 241–42
*ABC*, printing of, 164
abridgment: cases of, 246n161; as offense, 455–56, 607; of *Philosophical Transactions*, 579n83; restrictions on, 226, 227; works as, *302–3*, *316*, 316–17
*Abridgment* (Croke), *302–3*
*Abridgment* (Rolle), *316*, 316–17
absolutism: absence of in England, 48; arbitrary government and, 251–52, 252n182; Cromwell and, 273–74; Hobbes and, 308; patronage and, 24; property and, 253, 255; royal authorship of laws and, 312, 317, 336n29; royal prerogative and, 251, 253–54
Académie royale des sciences (France), 436, 491n91, 510, 554

If occasional sub-subentries are required in a run-in index, you may resort to the style illustrated in 15.27, example B, using em dashes.

15.141 **An indented index with run-in sub-subentries.** For further examples and discussion, see 15.28. See also 15.76.

American black bear
  compared with giant panda:
    activity, 216–17; habitat, 211–12; home range, 219; litter size, 221; movement patterns of males, 124–26, 219
  delayed implantation in, 191
  reproductive flexibility of, 221
  *See also* bears
amino acid content of bamboo, 75–76, 86, 89; compared with other foods, 77
artificial insemination, 179
*Ascaris schroederi*, 162
Asiatic black bear
  constructing sleeping nests, 140
  giant panda serologically close to, 228
  *See also* bears

15.142 **An indented index with indented sub-subentries and highlighted definitions.** Note the deep indentation for runover lines (see 15.136). A boldface page number indicates that the term is defined on that page (explained in a headnote at the beginning of the index). Italics could also be used for that purpose (see 15.140). For further discussion and examples, see 15.28. See also 15.76, 15.139.

*Page numbers for definitions are in boldface.*



If occasional sub-sub-subentries are essential (they should be avoided if at all possible), they must be run in to the sub-subentries in the same way as sub-subentries are run in at 15.28, example A.

15.143 **An index of first lines.** Unless all the poems, hymns, or songs indexed have very short lines, indexes of this kind are often set full measure (rather than in multiple columns) for easier reading. Note that lines beginning with *A*, *An*, or *The* are alphabetized under *A* or *T* (and are arranged below according to the word-by-word system; see 15.66).

The young Endymion sleeps Endymion's sleep, 316
There is no flock, however watched and tended, 107

15.144 **An index with authors, titles, and first lines combined.** To distinguish the elements, authors' names may be set in caps and small caps, titles of poems in italics, and first lines in roman type, sentence case, without quotation marks. If needed, a headnote to this effect could be furnished.

Cermak, it was, who entertained so great astonishment, 819
Certain she was that tigers fathered him, 724
CHESTERVILLE, NORA M., 212
Come, you whose loves are dead, 394
*Coming Homeward Out of Spain*, 73
Commemorate me before you leave me, Charlotte, 292
*Complaint of a Lover Rebuked*, 29
COMPTON, WILBER C., 96
Confound you, Marilyn, confound you, 459

In a general index, poem titles would be set in roman and enclosed in quotation marks, as in text or notes (see 8.183, 8.184).

# Glossary

This glossary focuses on key terms related to editing and publishing, including the typography, design, and production of works published in both print and electronic formats. Some of these terms are too specialized to be treated in the text of the *Manual* but are included here because they are directly related to the process of publishing; for terms not covered here that may be defined within the text of the *Manual*, consult the index.

**AA.** An abbreviation for *author's alteration*. See also **alteration**.

**academic publishing.** The publishing sector dedicated to books and journal articles by scholars writing either for other scholars (and their students) or for a more general readership (usually with the goal of informing that readership). Also called *scholarly publishing*.

**accessibility.** In publishing, accessibility refers to the attributes of a book or other document that make its content available to people with a range of disabilities and usable across different reading technologies, including assistive tools. Though *accessibility* can be associated with printed documents, the term most often applies to websites, ebooks, and other electronic formats. Accessible electronic publications include alternative text for images, strong color contrast, multiple options for navigation, and a logical, well-tagged structure, among other attributes. See also **alt text**.

**acquiring editor.** An editor who acquires new books for a publisher. See also **managing editor**; **production editor**.

**adhesive binding.** A method of binding that employs glue instead of stitching to hold the pages or signatures together and is widely used for journals and paperback books. Three types of adhesive binding are currently used: perfect binding, notch binding, and burst binding. Contrast **case binding**; **flexibinding**.

**alt text.** Short for *alternative text*. Alt text provides a brief description of an image in an online document or other electronic format for people with print disabilities. Alt text is intended to be read aloud by a text-to-speech application and may appear on the screen in place of any image that does not load (as on a web page for which images are not enabled). Alt text may also be rendered into braille and is helpful for readers with cognitive or learning disabilities who rely on other assistive technologies. Alt text, which is typically brief, is sometimes supplemented by a longer description. See also **accessibility**; **print disabilities.**

**alteration.** A change from the manuscript copy introduced in proof, as distinguished from a *correction* made to eliminate a typesetter's or printer's error. See also **AA**; **DA**; **EA**.

**app.** An abbreviation for *application*. Now commonly used to refer to any computer program, *app* can be used more narrowly to refer to an interactive version of a publication such as a dictionary or other reference work.

**Arabic numerals.** The familiar digits used in arithmetical computation. In many type fonts, Arabic numerals are available in two basic forms: *lining*, or *aligning* (1 2 3 4 5 6 7 8 9 0), and *old style* (1 2 3 4 5 6 7 8 9 0), abbreviated *OS* and characterized by ascenders and descenders. Another variation, *tabular*, consists of digits designed to each take up the same width, thus facilitating vertical alignment of the numerals in a table. Contrast **Roman numerals**.

**ARCs.** An abbreviation for *advanced reading copies*. ARCs are printed-and-bound versions of a book sent out ahead of publication to reviewers and booksellers for marketing purposes. They typically consist of bound sets of inexpensive laser printouts (of page or galley proofs) but may be more elaborately produced (as for an art book). Also called *bound galleys*.

**artwork.** Illustrative material (photographs, drawings, maps, and so forth) intended for reproduction.

**ascender.** The portion of a lowercase letter that extends above the *x-height*, as in *b* and *d*. Contrast **descender**; see also **Arabic numerals**.

**ASCII file.** See **plain-text file**.

**back margin.** The inner margin of a page; that is, the margin along the binding side of the page. See also **gutter**.

**back matter.** The components of a book or journal that follow the main text. These may include acknowledgments, appendixes, glossaries (like this one), endnotes, bibliographies, and indexes, among other components. Also known as *end matter*. Compare **front matter**.

**baseline.** In type, an imaginary common line that all letters without descenders and lining Arabic numerals rest on.

**beta reader.** A person invited by the author to review and give feedback on a manuscript before it is sent out to agents or publishers.

**beta testing.** The checking of a website or other application before it is released to the public. Such testing is ideally carried out under normal operating conditions by users who are not directly involved in developing the application.

**binding.** (1) A covering for the pages of a publication, using such materials as leather, cloth, and paper. (2) The process by which such a covering is attached. See also **adhesive binding**; **case binding**; **flexibinding**.

**BISAC subject codes.** A standard set of alphanumeric codes defined by the Book Industry Study Group and used to identify a book's subject or genre for libraries, booksellers, and publishers. For example, the code LAN028000 (under Language Arts & Disciplines) would be assigned to a style manual like this one and added to its metadata.

**bitmap.** A digital representation of an image consisting of an array of pixels, in rows and columns, that can be saved to a file. Each pixel in the grid of the bitmap contains information about the color value of its position, which is used, for example, to display an image on a monitor or print it to a page. Contrast **vector graphic**.

**blanket.** In offset printing, the resilient rubber covering of the blanket cylinder, which receives the ink impression from the plate cylinder and offsets it onto the paper.

**bleed.** To run an illustration or other ink coverage beyond the edge of a sheet of paper before it is trimmed. Also used as a noun, to refer to the area beyond the trim.

**block quotation.** Quoted material set off typographically from the text. Also called *extract*. Contrast **run in**.

**bluelines.** An abbreviation for *blueline proof*; also called *blues* or (in Europe and Asia) *ozalids*. A blueline is made by exposing the film negative of a book page to an arc light and projecting it onto light-sensitive paper. Though most printers no longer use film to print books, the term is still sometimes used to refer to the final proof produced from a typesetter's electronic files. See also **digital proof**.

**blurb.** A brief statement made in favor of a book, usually by a well-known or influential person or a person who is an expert in a particular field related to the book. Blurbs are typically used in marketing copy, as on the cover or first pages of a book or in promotional materials sent out or posted online by a publisher or author.

**boards.** Stiffening material used in binding to form the foundation of the cover; formerly wood, now generally a paper product such as binder's board (the finest quality), pasteboard (often used in case binding), or chipboard (low quality). Redboard is used for flexible bindings. The bare board is sheathed in (or sometimes affixed to) one of a variety of cover materials.

**body text.** The running text of a work, as distinguished from the display text used for chapter openings, subheads, and so forth.

**boldface.** Type that has a darker and heavier appearance than standard type (as in the entries in this glossary).

**bound galleys.** See **ARCs**.

**broadside.** Designed to be read or viewed normally when the publication is turned ninety degrees. In University of Chicago Press practice, the *left* side of a broadside table or illustration is at the *bottom* of the page. Because most publications are taller than they are wide, broadside images are usually landscape. See also **landscape**.

**bulk.** The thickness of paper measured in number of pages per inch; also used loosely to indicate the thickness of a publication, excluding the cover.

**burst binding.** A type of adhesive binding in which the untrimmed spine is perforated and force-fed with glue.

**callout.** An instruction in a manuscript specifying within the text the location of a figure or table. Callouts do not appear in the published work. Compare **text reference**.

**caps.** An abbreviation for *capital letters*. See also **small caps**.

**case.** (1) A hard cover or binding made by a case-making machine or by hand and usually printed, stamped, or labeled before being glued to the gathered endpapers that are attached to the signatures. A case that is covered entirely by one type of material is a one-piece case; a case in which the spine is covered by one type of material and the front and back cover boards by another (often in a different color) is a three-piece case. (2) The grammatical relationship between a noun or pronoun and other words in a sentence. For example, the pronoun *their* is said to be in the possessive case. (3) A term that refers to the capitalization of a letter, as in *uppercase* or *lowercase*. See also **sentence case**; **title case**.

**case binding.** A method of encasing a book in a rigid cover, or *case*. The gathered signatures can be Smyth sewn or side sewn together or adhesive-bound; endpapers are attached to the first and last signatures either with spine glue or through Smyth sewing; a hinge of heavy gauze (the *super*) is glued to the spine of the sewn signatures; and the case is secured to the book by being glued to the flaps of the super and to both endpapers. Contrast **adhesive binding**; **flexibinding**. See also **Smyth sewing**.

**casebound.** See **clothbound**.

**castoff.** An estimate of the space, or number of printed pages, that a manuscript will occupy when typeset.

**catchword.** In very old books, a word or part of a word printed below the last line of text to signal the word on the following page. Also called *catchphrase*.

**character.** A letter, numeral, symbol, or mark of punctuation.

**character count.** An approximate measure of the length of a manuscript made by multiplying the number of characters and spaces in an average line by the number of lines in the manuscript. The "character count" feature of many word-processing programs can provide a precise total.

**character encoding.** A set of machine-readable numbers—or *code points*—that correspond to a set of alphanumeric characters and symbols such that they can be interpreted by a computer. See also **Unicode**.

**character reference.** A plain-text placeholder defined for an SGML- or XML-based tag set and used to refer to a special character that is unavailable in a particular character encoding or from a particular input device such as a keyboard. For example, the character reference © represents the copyright symbol ©.

**cleanup.** (1) The process of preparing an electronic manuscript for copyediting by removing inconsistencies in formatting, spacing, dashes, quotation marks, italics, and the like. (2) The process of removing tracked changes and resolving and removing any remaining queries in a manuscript prior to typesetting. A production editor or a copyeditor may perform either or both of these tasks.

**clothbound.** Bound with a rigid cover, usually cloth wrapped around boards. Also known as *casebound*. Contrast **paperback**.

**CMYK.** An abbreviation for the basic colors used in process color printing—cyan (C), magenta (M), and yellow (Y), plus black (K)—to approximate all the colors in the spectrum. See also **RGB**.

**code.** See **tag**.

**colophon.** A statement, usually at the back of a publication (as in this manual), about the materials, processes, and individuals or companies involved in its preparation, production, and manufacturing. The term is also used to refer to a publisher's logo as it often appears on the title page and spine of a book. See also **imprint**.

**color printing.** See **process color printing**.

**color proof.** A form of proof used to check the accuracy of color reproduction before printing. Also called *prepress proof*.

**color separation.** (1) The analysis of color copy for reproduction in terms of the three process colors (plus black) to be used in printing; separation is achieved by shooting through filters or by electronic scanning. (2) A film negative or positive, or a digital file, so produced for preparation of the printing plate. See also **process color printing**.

**comp.** An abbreviation for *comprehensive layout*, as for a dust jacket, and also for *composition* or *compositor*.

**compositor.** See **typesetter**.

**computer-to-plate (CTP) technology.** A process in which print-ready electronic files are imposed directly onto offset printing plates, thus eliminating the need for an intermediate stage involving film.

**continuous tone.** An image, such as a photograph, with gradations of tone from dark to light, in contrast to an image formed of pure blacks and whites, such as a pen-and-ink drawing. See also **halftone**.

**contract proof.** An image proof that shows the tonal range, color, and quality that the printer is contractually obligated to match on press.

**copyediting.** The final editing stage on a manuscript before publication, performed by a *copyeditor*. Copyeditors pay attention to details both large and small, reading for style, grammar, consistency, and typographical errors. Copyeditors may also apply (or check) markup. Also called *manuscript editing*. Compare **developmental editing**; **line editing**. See also **markup**; **style**.

**cover.** The two hinged parts of a binding, front and back, and the center panel, or *spine*, that joins them; also the three surfaces making up the covers in this sense, when used to carry printed matter. See also **dust jacket**.

**crop.** To cut down an illustration, such as a photograph, to improve the appearance of the image by removing extraneous areas.

**CSS.** An abbreviation for *cascading style sheets*. A style sheet language used to define the presentation of a document marked up in HTML or another formal markup language.

**cyan.** A greenish blue, one of the three primary colors (plus black) used in process color printing. See also **CMYK**.

**DA.** An abbreviation for *designer's alteration*. See also **alteration**.

**descender.** The portion of a lowercase letter that extends below the baseline, as in *g* and *p*. Contrast **ascender**; see also **Arabic numerals**.

**designer.** In publishing, a designer is someone who specifies the typography and layout for a book, journal, website, or other publication, including the design of any covers and other promotional materials.

**developmental editing.** Editing that helps an author shape the content and substance of a work and how it should be organized. Developmental editing generally occurs before any line editing and prior to the copyediting stage. Compare **copyediting; line editing**.

**die.** See **stamping**.

**digital printing.** A type of printing in which the transfer of electronic images to paper is accomplished with ink-jet or laser printers. Contrast **offset printing**; see also **print on demand**.

**digital proof.** A type of proof generated directly from electronic files and typically output on a laser printer. See also **bluelines**.

**display type.** Type used for title pages, chapter openings, subheads, and so on, usually distinguished from the type used for body text by a different, often larger font. See also **body text**.

**DOI.** A trademarked abbreviation for *digital object identifier*, a unique alphanumeric string (e.g., 10.1086/597483) assigned to a publication or other unit of intellectual property. A DOI appended to https://doi.org/ provides a means of looking up the current location(s) of such an object on the internet. See also **ISBN; ISSN**.

**dots per inch (dpi).** See **resolution**.

**DRM.** An abbreviation for *digital rights management*. Refers to a system designed to protect copyrighted electronic works from unauthorized use, copying, or distribution.

**drop cap.** An uppercase character set in a type size larger than the text and "dropped," or nested, into lines of text, usually as the first character in the opening paragraph of a chapter or other section of text.

**drop folio.** See **folio**.

**DTD.** An abbreviation for *document type definition*. In a markup language based on SGML or XML, a set of rules about the structure of a document that dictate the relationships among different tags and allowable text or elements within specified tags. Also called *schema*. See also **tag**.

**dust jacket.** Also called *jacket*. A protective wrapping, usually made of paper, for a clothbound book; its *flaps*, which fold around the front and back covers, usually carry promotional copy (referred to as *flap copy*). See also **cover**.

**EA.** An abbreviation for *editor's alteration*. See also **alteration**.

**ebook.** An abbreviation for *electronic book*. See also **EPUB**.

**ECF.** An abbreviation for *elemental chlorine-free*. Refers to paper bleached with a chlorine derivative that releases hazardous substances, including dioxin, into the environment. Contrast **PCF**; **TCF**.

**edition.** (1) A publication in its original form, or any subsequent reissue of the publication in which its content is significantly revised. (2) More informally, a term used to refer to each format in which a publication appears (for example, a book published in both cloth and paperback bindings, or a journal published in both electronic and print forms). However, the designation *second edition* would not be applied to the secondary format, or to a second or subsequent *impression* of the publication, in the absence of significant content changes. See also **impression**; **reprint**.

**em.** A unit of type measurement equal to the point size of the type in question; for example, a six-point em is six points wide. See also **point**.

**em dash.** A short typographical rule measuring the width of an em.

**embossing.** Forming an image in relief (that is, a raised image) on a surface such as a case or a paper cover or dust jacket. If the process does not involve metallic leaf or ink, it is called *blind embossing*. See also **stamping**.

**en.** A unit of type measurement half the size of an em.

**en dash.** A short typographical rule measuring the width of an en.

**endpaper.** Either of two folded sheets of paper pasted or, rarely, sewn at the base to the first and last signatures of a book. Half of each sheet is then pasted to the inside of the front and back covers to secure the book within the covers; the free half is called a *flyleaf*. Sometimes endpapers feature printed text or illustrations. Also called *endsheets*.

**EPS.** An abbreviation for *encapsulated PostScript*. A file format used to encode graphics so they can be embedded in a larger file.

**EPUB.** An abbreviation for *electronic publication*. An international standard format for packaging and encoding content for distribution as a single file based on XHTML and CSS together with compatible formats and technologies. EPUB can be used as an open format for electronic books, or ebooks, or in conjunction with commercial products that employ systems of digital rights management. See also **CSS**; **DRM**; **XHTML**.

**extract.** See **block quotation**.

**fact-checking.** The process of checking factual statements in a book or other manuscript for accuracy and proper attribution. Copyeditors typically do some basic fact-checking as they edit, and news organizations may use dedicated fact-checkers. In book publishing, however, except for certain titles singled out in advance, the responsibility for fact-checking usually lies with the author rather than the publisher.

**fair use.** A legal principle that allows for limited quoting and related use of copyrighted works without permission, as in a book review or an academic paper. See paragraph 4.88 in this manual for more details.

**F&Gs.** See **folded-and-gathered signatures**.

**figure.** (1) An illustration printed with the text (hence also called a *text figure*), as distinguished from a plate, which is printed separately. More generally, *figure* is used to refer to any illustration in a published work, including charts (but not tables). (2) Another word for *numeral* or *digit* (referring to numbers).

**figure callout.** See **callout**.

**file.** A block of digital information with a unique name and location in a computer system or storage medium that can be accessed and manipulated by users of the system or by the system itself. Programs, documents, and images are all examples of data stored in files.

**file cleanup.** See **cleanup**.

**flaps.** See **dust jacket**.

**flexibinding.** Also called *limp binding*. A method of binding in which the pages or signatures are sewn together and a lightweight cover (sometimes with flaps) is then affixed, as in adhesive binding. The result is a publication that is lighter and less bulky than a casebound book but sturdier and more flexible than an adhesive-bound paperback. Contrast **adhesive binding**; **case binding**.

**flush.** Even, as with typeset margins. Lines that are set *flush left* are aligned vertically along the left-hand margin; lines set *flush right* are aligned along the right-hand margin. See also **justified**; **ragged right**.

**flush-and-hang style.** A copy-setting style in which the first line of each paragraph begins flush left and subsequent, or runover, lines are indented (as in this glossary). Also referred to as *hanging indent*.

**flyleaf.** See **endpaper**.

**folded-and-gathered signatures.** Abbreviated *F&Gs*; also called *folded-and-gathered sheets*. The collection of all printed signatures in a publication, folded into imposed page sequence and gathered for binding. See also **imposition**; **signature**.

**folio.** A page number, often placed at the outside of the running head at the top of the page. If it is placed consistently at the bottom of the page, the number is a *foot folio*; if it is placed at the bottom of the page on display pages only, it is a *drop folio*. The word *folio* is also sometimes used to refer to the page, or leaf, itself.

**font.** A complete assortment of a given size and style of type, usually including capitals, small capitals, and lowercase together with numerals, punctuation marks, ligatures, and the commonly used symbols and accents. The italic of a typeface is considered a part of the equipment of a font of type but is often spoken of as a separate font. Often used as a synonym for **typeface**.

**foot folio.** See **folio**.

**four-color process.** See **process color printing**.

**freelance editor.** A copyeditor who works independently, offering their services on a contract basis to one or more publishers or authors.

**front matter.** The components of a book that precede the main text and that are counted in the Roman numeral pagination preceding Arabic page 1. Most books include a half-title page, title page, copyright page, and table of contents. Other elements include dedications, epigraphs, lists of illustrations and tables, forewords, prefaces, and some types of introductions, among other components. Compare **back matter**.

**FTP.** An abbreviation for *File Transfer Protocol*. A protocol, or set of instructions and syntax, for moving files between computers on the internet.

**gallery.** A section of illustrations grouped on consecutive pages rather than scattered throughout the text. Also known as an *insert*.

**galley proof.** Proof showing typeset material but without final pagination. The term, an anachronism, once referred to the long, narrow columns of type, or "galleys," prepared by a printer before pages were composed, by hand. See also **page proof**.

**GIF.** An abbreviation for *graphics interchange format*. A file format for compressing and storing graphics as bitmaps for viewing on-screen. Because GIFs achieve compression by limiting the number of distinct colors in a file, they are best suited to images of line art or text or to low-resolution images where precise color fidelity is not crucial. Contrast **JPEG**; see also **PNG**.

**gutter.** The two inner margins (back margins) of facing pages of a book or journal.

**hairline rule.** A very thin rule—whose width is variously defined as one-quarter point, one-half point, or one-fifth of an em.

**hair space.** See **thin space**.

**halftone.** An image formed by breaking up a continuous-tone image, such as a photograph, into a pattern of dots of varying sizes. When printed, the dots, though clearly visible through a magnifying glass, merge to give an illusion of continuous tone to the naked eye.

**halftone screen.** A grid used in the halftone process to break an image up into dots. The fineness of the screen is denoted in terms of lines per inch, as in *a 133-line screen*.

**hanging indent.** See **flush-and-hang style**.

**hard copy.** A paper copy of text, artwork, or other material, as opposed to a copy that has been stored in digital form.

**hardcover.** A format for a printed book that includes a hard outer cover usually made of cardboard and wrapped in either paper or cloth glued to the cardboard. Compare **paperback**. See also **clothbound**.

**hardcover binding.** See **case binding.**

**head margin.** The top margin of a page.

**HTML.** An abbreviation for *hypertext markup language*. A specific set of tags used to describe the structure of hypertext documents that make up most web pages. Web browsers interpret these tags to display text and graphics. HTML is an application of SGML. See also **SGML.**

**HTTP.** An abbreviation for *Hypertext Transfer Protocol*. The protocol, or set of instructions and syntax, for exchanging web pages and related content on the internet and for enabling links between such content. HTTPS (the *S* stands for *Secure*) is a version of the protocol that adds support for encryption and related security mechanisms.

**hypertext.** The organization of digital information into associations connected by links. In a hypertext environment, objects such as text and images can contain links to other objects in the same file or in external files, which users can choose to follow. See also **HTML; HTTP.**

**imposition.** The process of arranging the pages for a printed book in such a manner that, when folded, they will appear in the correct order and sequence and in the correct orientation. See also **computer-to-plate (CTP) technology; folded-and-gathered signatures.**

**impression.** (1) The inked image on the paper created during a single cycle of a press; the speed of a sheet-fed printing press is given in terms of impressions per hour. (2) A single printing of a publication; that is, all the copies printed at a given time. See **edition; reprint.**

**imprint.** The name of a publisher or a division of a publisher, often as it appears on the title page of a book, sometimes together with a location and a date. See also **colophon.**

**in print.** Books that are *in print* are currently available for sale, either because physical copies of the book are available from the publisher or booksellers or because the book is available using print-on-demand technology. A book may also be said to be in print as long as an ebook version remains available, though this meaning is less common.

**indent.** To set a line of type so that it begins or ends inside the normal margin. In *paragraph* indentation the first line is indented from the left margin and the following lines are set full measure. In *hanging* indentation (also referred to as *flush and hang*) the first line is set full measure and the following lines are indented. See also **flush-and-hang style.**

**independent publisher.** A publisher not owned by a larger corporation. Also called *indie publisher*. Not to be confused with a self-published author, also known as an *indie author*. See also **self-publishing.**

**indexing.** The process of creating a list of key terms for a book, arranging them alphabetically, and keying them to specific pages or paragraph numbers (also known as *locators*). Indexing in this sense is the subject of chapter 15 of this manual. Indexing can also refer to the collection and processing of data to facilitate and optimize its retrieval by a search engine.

**insert.** See **gallery**.

**ISBN.** An abbreviation for *International Standard Book Number*. Publishers usually assign an ISBN to each book in each format (e.g., cloth, paperback, or ebook format) under a system maintained by the International ISBN Agency and administered in the United States by R. R. Bowker. The ISBN uniquely identifies the book, thus facilitating order fulfillment and inventory tracking. See also **DOI; ISSN**.

**ISSN.** An abbreviation for *International Standard Serial Number*. An ISSN is a unique eight-digit number that identifies a titled journal or other periodical through a database maintained by the ISSN International Centre. Books that are part of a monograph series may also be assigned an ISSN in addition to an ISBN. See also **DOI; ISBN**.

**issue.** Used primarily to refer to journals or other periodical publications, typically to indicate the publication's sequence within a larger volume. Although the issue is often designated by a numeral, other means of identification (such as a month or season) may be used instead of or in addition to issue number. See also **volume**.

**italic.** A slanted type style suggestive of cursive writing (*like this*). Contrast **roman**.

**jacket.** See **dust jacket**.

**JPEG.** An abbreviation derived from *Joint Photographic Experts Group*. A file format commonly used to compress and store bitmapped graphics that contain photographic and other continuous-tone images for viewing on-screen. Contrast **GIF; PNG**.

**justified.** Spaced out to a specified measure, as with printed lines, so that left and right margins are aligned. Contrast **ragged right**.

**kern.** The part of a letter that extends beyond the edge of the type body and overlaps the adjacent character, as the *j* in *adjacent* or the *T* in *To*.

**kerning.** The selective adjustment of space between particular characters (called *letterspacing*) to improve appearance or ease of reading.

**keywords.** Words and phrases that identify important concepts and names in a book or article. Together with title and other metadata, keywords increase a work's visibility to search engines. See also **metadata**.

**landscape.** Having a greater dimension in width than in length (or height), as with an image or a document. Contrast **portrait**; see also **broadside**.

**layout.** A designer's plan of how the published material, including illustrative content, should appear.

**leading.** Also called *line spacing*. The vertical space between lines of type, usually measured in points from baseline to baseline. This word, derived from the element *lead*, rhymes with "heading."

**letterspacing.** See **kerning**.

**ligature.** A single character formed by joining two characters, such as *œ*, *fi*, or *ff*. Older, more decorative forms (such as a *c* joined to a *t* by a loop) are known as *quaint characters*.

**line art.** Copy for reproduction that contains only solid blacks and whites, such as a pen-and-ink drawing. Contrast **continuous tone**.

**line editing.** A close edit that focuses on word choice, phrasing, and other matters of writing style. If line editing is needed, it is usually arranged for by the author rather than the publisher and precedes copyediting. Compare **copyediting**; **developmental editing**.

**line spacing.** See **leading**.

**lining numbers.** See under **Arabic numerals**.

**literary agent.** A person who represents authors and helps them to get published by negotiating on their behalf with publishers.

**lowercase.** The uncapitalized letters of a font. Contrast **uppercase**.

**macro.** From *macroinstruction*. A sequence of operations that is defined for reuse in a computer program. In word processing, a macro can be used to perform complex or repetitive tasks.

**main text.** The text of the chapters and other main parts of a book, excluding the front matter and the back matter. Compare **back matter**; **front matter**.

**makeup.** Arrangement of type lines and illustrations into page form.

**managing editor.** In book publishing, the head of a department that oversees production editors and copyeditors (including freelancers). See also **acquiring editor**; **production editor**.

**manuscript.** The name for a document in any of the stages of writing and editing. Now usually consisting of one or more word-processed files (or a printout thereof), manuscripts were once handwritten and, later, typewritten. See also **typescript**.

**manuscript editing.** See **copyediting**.

**margin.** The white space surrounding the printed area of a page, including the back, or gutter, margin; the head, or top, margin; the fore edge, or outside, margin; and the tail, foot, or bottom, margin. Contrast **type page**.

**markup.** (1) A sequence of characters, often called *tags* or *codes*, that indicate the logical structure of a manuscript or provide instructions for formatting it. (2) The insertion of such tags in an electronic manuscript; also, traditionally, pencil markup on a paper manuscript.

**MathML.** An application of XML for tagging mathematical expressions. MathML can be embedded in HTML to display math in web pages or ebooks.

**measure.** The length of the line (usually in picas) in which type is set. *Full measure* refers to copy set the full width of the type page. *Narrow measure* refers to a block of copy (such as a long quotation) indented from one or both margins to distinguish it from surrounding full-measure copy, or to copy set in short lines for multicolumn makeup.

**metadata.** A form of structured resource description; literally, data about data. The metadata for a given publication may include, among other things, copyright information, an ISBN or ISSN, volume and issue numbers, information about authors and other contributors, title of work, subject category or genre, publication date, keywords, and description. To facilitate sharing among publishers and booksellers and via library catalogs and search engines, metadata is usually recorded using a standard syntax based on a markup language such as XML.

**monograph.** A usually book-length work on an academic subject.

**notch binding.** A type of adhesive binding in which the untrimmed spine is notched and force-fed with glue.

**OCR.** An abbreviation for *optical character recognition*. A technology that converts images of text (as from a scan of a printed page) into character data that can be manipulated like any other digital text.

**offprint.** An article, chapter, or other excerpt from a larger work issued as a separate unit. When offered electronically, sometimes called *digital offprint*.

**offset printing.** Also called *offset lithography*. The most common type of printing for large print runs of books and journals. The pages to be printed are transferred through computer-to-plate technology to a thin, flexible metal plate, curved to fit one of the revolving cylinders of a printing press. The image on this plate is then transferred to, or *offset* onto, the paper by means of a rubber blanket on another cylinder. Contrast **digital printing**.

**old-style numbers.** See under **Arabic numerals**.

**opacity.** The measurement of transparency of paper. The higher a paper's opacity, the less tendency there is for text and images printed on one side of a sheet to show through to the other side.

**orphan.** The first line of a paragraph stranded at the bottom of a page or column. An orphan can be avoided by changes in wording or spacing to the text that precedes it. Contrast **widow**.

**out of print.** See **in print**.

**page proof.** Proof showing typeset material that has been paginated to reflect the placement of text, illustrations, and other design elements. Some publications may require one or more stages of *revised page proof* for checking corrections.

**paperback.** Bound with a cover stock rather than a cloth-and-board cover. Also called *paperbound*. Contrast **clothbound**.

**pattern matching.** In word processing, a find or find-and-replace operation that uses a formal syntax to find every instance of text matching a specified pattern and, conditionally, replace it with a different string. Such patterns are known in some contexts as *regular expressions*. See also **regular expression**.

**PCF.** An abbreviation for *process chlorine-free*. Refers to recycled papers bleached without using chlorine or chlorine derivatives beyond what may have been used originally to produce the recovered wastepaper. Contrast **ECF**; see also **TCF**.

**PDF.** An abbreviation for *portable document format*. An Adobe Systems file format—and now a formal, open standard (ISO 32000-1)—for stable, device-independent delivery of electronic documents. Preserving such elements as fonts, layout, and pagination, PDF is used not only as the basis for many printed publications but also as a format for electronic publications, including many journal articles and ebooks. See also **PostScript (PS)**.

**PE.** An abbreviation for *printer's error*. See also **printer's error (PE)**.

**peer review.** In scholarly publishing, a system whereby a manuscript is evaluated for suitability for publication by experts in the same field as the author.

**perfect binding.** A type of adhesive binding that involves mechanically roughening off about an eighth of an inch from the spine of the folded-and-gathered signatures. This treatment produces a surface of intermingled fibers to which an adhesive is applied, and a cover (usually paper) is wrapped around the pages. Note that the design of a perfect-bound book should account for the fact that part of the inside margin will be lost in the binding process.

**permission.** Formal consent granted to an author or publisher by an owner of copyrighted material to reproduce that material in the author's or publisher's work. For a full discussion of copyright and permissions, see chapter 4.

**pica.** A unit of type measurement equal to twelve points (approximately one-sixth of an inch).

**pixel.** See **resolution**.

**plain-text file.** An informal term for a file that contains data encoded using only letters, numerals, punctuation marks, spaces, returns, line breaks, and tabs with no additional formatting or special characters. Plain-text files are often referred to as ASCII files, although newer encoding schemes may be used, and other kinds of data (such as XML) can also be stored as plain-text files.

**plate.** (1) An image-bearing surface that, when inked, will produce one whole page or several pages of printed matter at a time. (2) A printed illustration, usually of high quality and produced on special paper, pasted or bound into a publication; when so printed, plates are numbered separately from other illustrations.

**PNG.** An abbreviation for *portable network graphics*. A file format for compressing and storing graphics as bitmaps for viewing on-screen and intended as an alternative to GIF. Contrast **JPEG**; see also **GIF**.

**point.** (1) The basic unit of type measurement—0.01384 (approximately one seventy-second) of an inch. (2) A unit used in measuring paper products employed in printing and binding—0.001 inches.

**portable document format.** See **PDF**.

**portrait.** Having a greater dimension in length (or height) than in width, as with an image or a document. Contrast **landscape**.

**PostScript (PS).** An Adobe Systems programming language used to describe pages (in terms of trim size, font, placement of graphics, and so forth) and to tell output devices how to render the data. Portable document format (PDF), a descendant of PostScript, is somewhat more flexible. See also **PDF**.

**prelims.** Short for *preliminary matter*. See **front matter**.

**prepress.** The processes undertaken by a printing firm between the receipt of the electronic files and any other materials from the publisher (or its typesetter) and the printing of the publication.

**prepress proof.** See **color proof**.

**preprint.** An article or part of a book that has been posted to a repository or preprint server but has not been formally published in a journal or book and has not been peer reviewed.

**press.** Either the organization that publishes books and other works (as in the University of Chicago *Press*) or, when used as a short form for *printing press*, an apparatus that makes printed copies of a work. A book that is in the process of being printed is said to be *in press*.

**press sheet.** Also called *printed sheet* or *running sheet*. In offset printing, a large sheet of paper that emerges from the press with pages printed on both sides, each from a single plate. The sheet must then be folded so that the pages fall into proper sequence. See also **signature**.

**presswork.** The actual printing of a publication, as distinguished from composition, which precedes it, and binding, which follows.

**print disabilities.** A general term for disabilities or impairments (usually visual, perceptual, or motor) that affect a person's ability to read printed publications and, by extension, other types of documents, both printed and electronic. See also **accessibility**.

**print on demand (POD).** An application of digital printing that allows one or more copies of a book or other publication to be printed and bound at the time it is ordered. See also **digital printing**.

**printer's error (PE).** An error made by the typesetter (or *compositor*), as distinguished from an *alteration* made in proof by the author, editor, or designer.

**printing.** See **impression** (sense 2).

**process color printing.** The halftone reproduction of full-color artwork or photographs using several plates (usually four), each printing a different color. Each plate is made with a halftone screen. *Process colors* are cyan, magenta, and yellow, plus black (CMYK). See also **halftone screen**.

**production editor.** In book publishing, an editor who oversees the conversion and typesetting of copyedited manuscripts (and sometimes the copyediting itself) as they are produced for publication. See also **acquiring editor**; **managing editor**.

**proof.** The printed or electronic copy made from electronic files, plates, negatives, or positives and used to examine and correct a work's text, illustrations, and design elements before final printing. A publication may involve several stages of proof; see **bluelines**; **color proof**; **digital proof**; **galley proof**; **page proof**.

**proofreading.** The process of checking the final text of a book or other work for errors (as on page proofs) before it is published.

**protocol.** A standard set of instructions and syntax that define the rules by which documents are shared between computers over a network. See also **FTP**; **HTTP**.

**PS.** See **PostScript (PS)**.

**ragged right.** Set with an uneven right-hand margin, as with printed lines. Contrast **justified**.

**recto.** The front side of a leaf; in a book or journal, a right-hand page. To *start recto* is to begin on a recto page, as a preface or an index normally does. Contrast **verso**.

**redline.** In word processing, a document in which changes (additions and deletions) are shown, or "tracked," by the application of text attributes such as strikethrough, underlining, boldface, or color. Often used as a verb: *to redline*. Also called *legal blackline*.

**regular expression.** A string of one or more characters that defines a pattern to be searched for in the text of a document. For example, the expression `advis[eo]r` might be used to find both "adviser" and "advisor" wherever they occur. In Microsoft Word, regular expressions are called *wildcards* and use a variation of the regular expressions that are more common in computing. Also referred to by the short forms *regex* and *regexp*.

**reprint.** A publication in its second or subsequent printing, or *impression*. A reprint may include corrections or new material or both and may be published in a format different from the original printing (for example, as a paperback rather than a clothbound book, or as an ebook). The extent of the changes usually determines whether the reprint is considered a new *edition* of the publication. See also **edition**; **impression**.

**resolution.** (1) The number of pixels per unit of measure used to form an image. In the United States, image resolution is calculated per inch; the more pixels per inch, the higher the quality of the image. (2) The number of actual dots per unit of measure at which an image or page is output, usually by a printer or an image-setting device. In the United States, output resolution is usually expressed per inch; the more dots per inch, the higher the quality of the output.

**RGB.** An abbreviation for the additive color model that uses red (R), green (G), and blue (B) pixels to render color images on displays for computers and other devices. RGB images are converted to CMYK for printing.

**roman.** The primary type style (like this), as distinguished from italic (*like this*). Also known as *regular text*.

**Roman numerals.** Numerals formed from traditional combinations of Roman letters, either capitals (I, II, III, IV, etc.) or lowercase (i, ii, iii, iv, etc.). Contrast **Arabic numerals**.

**run in.** (1) To merge a paragraph or line with the preceding one. (2) To set quoted matter continuously with text rather than setting it off as a block. Contrast **block quotation**.

**run-in subhead.** See **sidehead**.

**running head.** Copy set at the top of a page, often containing the title of the publication or chapter, chapter number, or other information. Such copy is sometimes placed at the bottom of the page, in which case it is referred to as a *running foot*.

**runover.** (1) The continuation of a heading, figure legend, or similar copy onto an additional line. (2) In flush-and-hang material, all lines after the first line of a particular item. (3) Text that is longer than intended, running onto another page, or reset material that is longer than the material it was meant to replace.

**saddle stitching.** Also called *saddle wiring*. A method of binding that involves inserting thread or staples through the folds of gathered sheets, as in pamphlets and magazines.

**sans serif.** A typeface with no serifs (like this). Contrast **serif**.

**scale.** To calculate (after cropping) the proportions and finish size of an illustration and the amount of reduction or enlargement needed to achieve this size. In electronic formats, illustrations and other elements are often scaled to adjust to a particular screen size or other parameters.

**scan.** To produce a digital bitmap of an image (text or graphics) using a device that senses alternating patterns of light and dark and of color. The resolution and scaling percentage of the desired output should be considered before the image is scanned.

**schema.** See **DTD**.

**scholarly publishing.** See **academic publishing**.

**screen.** A halftone screen; also the dot pattern in the printed image produced by such a screen.

**self-publishing.** The act of writing and publishing a book independently, without going through a traditional publisher. Self-published authors (also called *indie authors*) typically rely on one or more commercial distribution platforms designed for that purpose. See also **independent publisher**.

**sentence case.** Capitalized in the manner of a sentence, in which only the first word and any proper nouns or initialisms (among other exceptions) are capitalized. Usually used in reference to the title of a work or a headline capitalized in this manner. Compare **title case**.

**serif.** A short, light line projecting from the top or bottom of a main stroke of a letter; originally, in handwritten letters, a beginning or finishing stroke of the pen. Contrast **sans serif**.

**sewing.** The process of stitching signatures together as part of binding. See also **side sewing; Smyth sewing.**

**SGML.** An abbreviation for *standard generalized markup language*, an international standard for constructing sets of tags. SGML is not a specific set of tags but a system for defining *vocabularies of tags* (the names of the tags and what they mean) and using them to encode documents. See also **tag; XML.**

**sheet-fed press.** A printing press using paper in sheet form. Contrast **web-fed press.**

**side sewing.** In binding, a method of sewing that involves stitching the signatures from the side, close to the spine, before attaching the case. Libraries typically rebind books in this manner. A side-sewn book is more durable than a Smyth-sewn book but will not open flat. See also **Smyth sewing.**

**sidehead.** A subhead that (1) lies partly outside the margin of the text and is set on a line of its own; (2) lies wholly outside the text margin; or (3) begins a paragraph and is continuous with the text. A subhead of the third sort is sometimes called a *run-in sidehead* or *run-in subhead*. See also **run in.**

**signature.** A press sheet as folded, ready for binding. A signature is usually thirty-two pages but may be only sixteen, eight, or even four pages if the paper stock is very heavy, or sixty-four pages if the paper is thin enough to permit additional folding. The size of the press also affects the size of the signature. See also **folded-and-gathered signatures; press sheet.**

**small caps.** An abbreviation for *small capitals*. Capital letters set at the x-height of a font (LIKE THIS), usually for display.

**Smyth sewing.** A method of sewing that involves stitching the signatures individually through the fold before binding them. A Smyth-sewn book has the advantage of lying flat when open, unlike a side-sewn or perfect-bound book. See also **perfect binding; side sewing.**

**spec.** An abbreviation for *specification* (plural *specs* or *spex*)—as in *design specs*.

**spine.** The "back" of a bound publication; that is, the center panel of the binding, hinged on each side to the two covers, front and back, and visible when the book or other item is shelved. Typically the title of the publication is printed on the spine. Also called the *backbone*.

**spread.** Two facing pages, a verso and a recto.

**stamping.** Imprinting the spine of a case and sometimes the front cover with hard metal dies. Stamping may involve ink, foil, or other coloring material; if it does not, it is called *blind stamping*. See also **embossing.**

**STM publishing.** An abbreviation for *scientific, technical,* and *medical* publishing. A major sector of scholarly publishing that focuses on original research, much of it published in the form of peer-reviewed journal articles and, to a lesser extent, books. STM is often used interchangeably with the more common acronym STEM (for *science, technology, engineering,* and *medicine*).

**stub.** The left-hand column of a table. The individual stub entries are also known as *row headings*. See also **table.**

**style.** A particular set of rules for punctuation, capitalization, spelling, hyphenation, word usage, and related matters. Style is the central concern of copyeditors, whose job it is to impose or ensure a specific style (as in Chicago style) prior to publication.

**style sheet.** (1) A set of programming instructions that, in conjunction with a markup language such as HTML, determine how a document is presented on a screen, on a printed page, or in another medium such as speech. (2) A record of terms kept by a manuscript editor to document particular usages for a specific manuscript. See also **CSS**.

**subhead.** A heading, or title, for a section within a chapter or an article. Subheads are usually set in type differing in some way from that of the text; for example, in boldface, all capitals, caps and small caps, or upper- and lowercase italic. See also **sidehead**.

**subscript.** A small numeral, letter, fraction, or symbol that prints partly below the baseline, usually in mathematical material or chemical formulas.

**superscript.** A small numeral, letter, fraction, or symbol that prints partly above the x-height, often in mathematical or tabular material or to indicate a footnote or endnote.

**SVG (scalable vector graphics).** See **vector graphic**.

**table.** A more or less complex list presented as an array of vertical columns and horizontal rows.

**tag.** In SGML or XML and languages derived therefrom, a generic marker used to specify and (when paired) delimit an element in the structure of a document. The process of adding tags to a manuscript is known as *tagging* or *markup*. See also **markup**; **SGML**; **XML**.

**TCF.** An abbreviation for *totally chlorine-free*. Refers to paper bleached without using chlorine or chlorine derivatives. Contrast **ECF**; see also **PCF**.

**text reference.** A reference within the text to a numbered table or figure, as in "see table 11.1." The first text reference for a table or figure usually appears near the item to which it refers. Compare **callout**.

**thin space.** A very small space, defined as one-fifth (or sometimes one-sixth) of an em, added between characters. A similar space, known as a *hair space*, is even smaller than a thin space.

**thumbnail.** A miniature rendition of a page or an image. In electronic publications, a thumbnail is often used to indicate a link to a larger electronic object.

**TIFF.** An abbreviation for *tagged image file format*. A file format developed by Aldus and Microsoft and used to store bitmapped graphics, including scanned line art, halftones, and color images.

**title case.** A capitalization style according to which each major word in a title, heading, or the like begins with a capital letter. Minor words such as articles, coordinating conjunctions, and prepositions are usually lowercased, with further exceptions among these categories that vary according to publisher and style guide. Also called *headline style*. Compare **sentence case**.

**TOC.** An abbreviation for *table of contents*.

**trade publishing.** A category of book publishing aimed at the general reader as distinct from scholarly publishing and other types of publishing intended for specialized audiences.

**trim size.** The dimensions, usually in inches, of a full page in a printed publication, including the margins.

**type page.** The area of a typeset page occupied by the type image, from the running head to the last line of type on the page or the folio, whichever is lower, and from the inside margin to the outside margin, including any area occupied by sideheads.

**type styles.** See **boldface**; **italic**; **roman**.

**typeface.** A collection of fonts with common design or style characteristics. A typeface may include roman, italic, boldface, condensed, and other fonts. The various typefaces are designated by name: Baskerville, Caslon, and Times Roman, for example. See also **font**.

**typescript.** A term that formerly referred to the typewritten version of a manuscript marked up by a copyeditor and sent to a printer for typesetting. In British English, the term is synonymous with *manuscript* as defined above. See also **manuscript**.

**typesetter.** A person, firm, facility, or machine that prepares books, articles, or other documents for publication. The term has its origins in the composing—or "setting"—of individual pieces of type, by hand, and binding them together to make individual pages. Also called *compositor*.

**Unicode.** A system of character encoding developed by the Unicode Consortium and incorporated into the ISO standard for universal multiple-octet coded characters (ISO/IEC 10646). See also **character encoding**.

**university press.** A publishing house sponsored by or affiliated with a college or university. University presses usually publish scholarly monographs but may also publish reference works (like this manual), textbooks, and trade publications.

**unjustified.** See **ragged right**.

**uppercase.** The capital letters of a font. Contrast **lowercase**.

**URL.** An abbreviation for *uniform resource locator*, or the address used to locate a document on the internet (e.g., https://www.press.uchicago.edu/).

**vector graphic.** A digital representation of an image defined by shapes such as lines and curves rather than by pixels. Line art is typically created, edited, and scaled as a vector graphic. SVG (*scalable vector graphics*) is a standard format that defines vector graphics using XML syntax. Because SVG images are both searchable and resolution independent, they are a preferred format for websites and mobile devices. Contrast **bitmap**.

**verso.** The back side of a leaf; in a book or journal, a left-hand page. Contrast **recto**.

**volume.** Used to refer (a) to a book or a specific, usually numbered, book in a series or (b) to a series of issues of a journal or other periodical publication. See also **issue**.

**web-fed press.** A printing press using paper in roll form. Contrast **sheet-fed press**.

**website.** A collection of closely related and hyperlinked web pages maintained by an individual or organization.

**widow.** A short, paragraph-ending line appearing at the top of a page. Widows should be avoided when possible by changes in wording or spacing that either remove the line or lengthen it. Contrast **orphan**.

**wiki.** A website designed to allow visitors to edit and contribute content.

**wildcard.** See **regular expression**.

**x-height.** In type, a vertical dimension equal to the height of the lowercase letters (such as *x*) without ascenders or descenders.

**XHTML.** An application of XML for producing HTML that conforms to XML syntax. See also **EPUB**; **HTML**.

**XML.** An abbreviation for *extensible markup language*. A subset of the SGML standard, used for structuring documents and data on the internet and for publication in a variety of electronic formats. See also **SGML**.

**XSL.** An abbreviation for *extensible style sheet language*. A family of style sheet languages used to define the presentation of XML documents and their conversion, or transformation, into other formats such as HTML (using XSLT, extensible style sheet language transformations).

# Bibliography of Additional Resources

The works listed here offer a starting point for writers, editors, and others involved in publishing who would like more information about topics covered in this manual. The list includes all the works cited in the text as further resources along with other useful references. Although some make recommendations that diverge from those of this manual, they reflect the specific demands of different disciplines and the evolving traditions of writing, editing, and publishing. As with all reference sources, readers should carefully evaluate their suitability for a given purpose.

## 1 WRITING AND EDITING

### 1.1 *Style*

*ACS Guide to Scholarly Communication*. Edited by Gregory M. Banik, Grace Baysinger, Prashant Kamat, and Norbert Pienta. American Chemical Society, 2020. https://doi.org/10.1021/acsguide.

*ALWD Guide to Legal Citation*. 7th ed. Edited by the Association of Legal Writing Directors and Carolyn V. Williams. Aspen Publishing, 2021.

*AMA Manual of Style: A Guide for Authors and Editors*. 11th ed. Edited by Cheryl Iverson. Oxford University Press, 2020. https://doi.org/10.1093/jama/9780190246556.001.0001.

American Institute of Physics. Featured Resources for Researchers. Includes *AIP Style Manual*, 4th ed. (1990). AIP Publishing. https://publishing.aip.org/resources/researchers/.

*Apple Style Guide*. Apple. Continually updated. https://support.apple.com/guide/applestyleguide/.

*The Associated Press Stylebook*. Edited by Paula Froke, Anna Jo Bratton, Andale Gross, et al. Updated every two years in print and regularly online. Associated Press. https://www.apstylebook.com/.

*Audiovisual Citation: Learning on Screen Guidelines for Referencing Moving Image and Sound*. 2nd ed. Edited by Sergio Angelini and Hetty Malcolm-Smith. Learning on Screen, January 2018. https://learningonscreen.ac.uk/resources/guides/audiovisual-citation/.

*Australian Guide to Legal Citation*. 4th ed. Melbourne University Law Review Association, in collaboration with Melbourne Journal of International Law. Melbourne, 2018. https://www.mulr.com.au/aglc/AGLC4-2021-v1.pdf.

*The Bluebook: A Uniform System of Citation*. 21st ed. Harvard Law Review Association, 2020. https://www.legalbluebook.com/.

*Canadian Guide to Uniform Legal Citation*. 9th ed. In English and French. McGill Law Journal. Carswell, 2019.

Catholic News Service. *CNS Stylebook on Religion: Reference Guide and Usage Manual*. 4th ed. Catholic News Service, 2012.

Commonwealth of Australia. *Style Manual*. https://www.stylemanual.gov.au/.

*The CSE Manual: Scientific Style and Format for Authors, Editors, and Publishers*. 9th ed. Council of Science Editors in cooperation with the University of Chicago Press, 2024. https://www.csemanual.org/.

*Editing Canadian English*. 3rd ed. Editors' Association of Canada. Editors Canada, 2015.

Fogarty, Mignon. Grammar Girl. Quick and Dirty Tips. https://www.quickanddirtytips.com/grammar-girl/.

Garner, Bryan A. *The Redbook: A Manual on Legal Style*. 4th ed. West Academic Publishing, 2018.

Holoman, D. Kern. *Writing About Music: A Style Sheet*. 3rd ed. University of California Press, 2014.

International Organization for Standardization. *Information and Documentation—Guidelines for Bibliographic References and Citations to Information Resources*. 4th ed. ISO 690:2021. https://www.iso.org/standard/72642.html.

Lipson, Charles. *Cite Right: A Quick Guide to Citation Styles—MLA, APA, Chicago, the Sciences, Professions, and More*. 3rd ed. University of Chicago Press, 2018.

*The Maroonbook: The University of Chicago Law Review Legal Citation and Style Guide*. Vol. 89. Edited by Candice Yandam Riviere, Ryne M. Cannon, Kelly Gregg, Jasper Primack, Henry Walter, and Tyler M. Wood. University of Chicago, [2021]. https://lawreview.uchicago.edu/maroonbook.

*Microsoft Writing Style Guide*. Microsoft. Continually updated. https://learn.microsoft.com/en-us/style-guide/.

*MLA Handbook*. 9th ed. Modern Language Association of America, 2021.

*New Oxford Style Manual*. 3rd ed. Oxford University Press, 2016. Combines *New Hart's Rules* and *New Oxford Dictionary for Writers and Editors*.

*The New York Times Manual of Style and Usage*. 5th ed. By Allan M. Siegal and William G. Connolly. Revised and updated by Philip B. Corbett, Jill Taylor, Patrick LaForge, and Susan Wessling. Three Rivers Press, 2015.

*Publication Manual of the American Psychological Association*. 7th ed. APA, 2020.

*Religion Stylebook*. Religion Newswriters Association. Continually updated. https://religionstylebook.com/.

Sambuchino, Chuck. *Formatting and Submitting Your Manuscript*. Writer's Digest Books, 2009.

Sampsel, Laurie J. *Music Research: A Handbook*. 3rd ed. Oxford University Press, 2019.

*The SBL Handbook of Style: For Biblical Studies and Related Disciplines*. 2nd ed. Edited by Billie Jean Collins. SBL Press, 2014.

*Scientific Style and Format*. See *The CSE Manual*.

Strunk, William, Jr., and E. B. White. *The Elements of Style*. 4th ed. Allyn and Bacon, 2000.

*Style Manual for Political Science*. Rev. ed. American Political Science Association, 2018. https://connect.apsanet.org/stylemanual/.

*The Times Style Guide: A Practical Guide to English Usage*. 3rd ed. Edited by Ian Brunskill. London: Times Books, 2022.

Turabian, Kate L. *A Manual for Writers of Research Papers, Theses, and Dissertations: Chicago Style for Students and Researchers*. 9th ed. Revised by Wayne C. Booth, Gregory G. Colomb, Joseph M. Williams, Joseph Bizup, William T. FitzGerald, and the University of Chicago Press editorial staff. University of Chicago Press, 2018.

Turabian, Kate L. *Student's Guide to Writing College Papers*. 5th ed. Revised by Gregory G. Colomb, Joseph M. Williams, Joseph Bizup, William T. FitzGerald, and the University of Chicago Press editorial staff. University of Chicago Press, 2019.

US Geological Survey. *Suggestions to Authors of the Reports of the United States Geological Survey*. 7th ed. Revised and edited by Wallace R. Hansen. USGS Unnumbered Series, 1991. https://doi.org/10.3133/7000088.

US Government Publishing Office. *GPO Style Manual: An Official Guide to the Form and Style of Federal Government Publishing*. 31st ed. Washington, DC, 2016. https://www.govinfo.gov/gpo-style-manual.

*Words into Type*. 3rd ed. Based on studies by Marjorie E. Skillin, Robert M. Gay, and other authorities. Prentice Hall, 1974.

Younging, Gregory. Opaskwayak Cree Nation. *Elements of Indigenous Style: A Guide for Writing By and About Indigenous Peoples*. Brush, 2018.

## 1.2 *Grammar and Usage*

Aarts, Bas. *Oxford Modern English Grammar*. Oxford University Press, 2011.

Bernstein, Theodore M. *Miss Thistlebottom's Hobgoblins: The Careful Writer's Guide to the Taboos, Bugbears, and Outmoded Rules of English Usage*. Farrar, Straus and Giroux, 1971.

Casagrande, June. *The Joy of Syntax: A Simple Guide to All the Grammar You Know You Should Know*. Ten Speed Press, 2018.

Crystal, David. *Making Sense of Grammar*. Pearson Education, 2004.

Curme, George O. *A Grammar of the English Language*. 2 vols. D. C. Heath, 1935.

Dreyer, Benjamin. *Dreyer's English: An Utterly Correct Guide to Clarity and Style*. Random House, 2019.

*Fowler's Dictionary of Modern English Usage*. 4th ed. Edited by Jeremy Butterfield. Oxford University Press, 2015.

Garner, Bryan A. *The Chicago Guide to Grammar, Usage, and Punctuation*. University of Chicago Press, 2016.

Garner, Bryan A. *Garner's Modern English Usage*. 5th ed. Oxford University Press, 2022.

Garner, Bryan A., and David Foster Wallace. *Quack This Way: David Foster Wallace & Bryan A. Garner Talk Language and Writing*. RosePen Books, 2013.

Gowers, Ernest. *Plain Words: A Guide to the Use of English*. Revised and updated by Rebecca Gowers. Penguin Books, 2015.

Hale, Constance. *Sin and Syntax: How to Craft Wickedly Effective Prose*. Rev. ed. Three Rivers Press, 2013.

Huddleston, Rodney, and Geoffrey K. Pullum. *The Cambridge Grammar of the English Language*. Cambridge University Press, 2002. https://doi.org/10.1017/9781316423530.

Jovin, Ellen. *Rebel with a Clause: Tales and Tips from a Roving Grammarian*. Mariner Books, 2022.

O'Conner, Patricia T. *Woe Is I: The Grammarphobe's Guide to Better English in Plain English*. 4th ed. Riverhead Books, 2019.

*The Oxford Dictionary of English Grammar*. 2nd ed. Edited by Bas Aarts, Sylvia Chalker, and Edmund Weiner. Oxford University Press, 2014.

Stamper, Kory. *Word by Word: The Secret Life of Dictionaries*. Pantheon Books, 2017.

Trask, R. L. *Language: The Basics*. 2nd ed. Routledge, 1999.

Wallraff, Barbara. *Word Court: Wherein Verbal Virtue Is Rewarded, Crimes Against the Language Are Punished, and Poetic Justice Is Done*. Harcourt, 2000.

Wallraff, Barbara. *Your Own Words*. Counterpoint, 2004.

Walsh, Bill. *Lapsing into a Comma: A Curmudgeon's Guide to the Many Things That Can Go Wrong in Print—and How to Avoid Them*. Contemporary Books, 2000.

Williams, Joseph M., and Joseph Bizup. *Style: Lessons in Clarity and Grace*. 12th ed. Pearson, 2016.

## 1.3 *Research and Writing*

Abbott, Andrew. *Digital Paper: A Manual for Research and Writing with Library and Internet Materials*. University of Chicago Press, 2014.

Becker, Howard S. *Writing for Social Scientists: How to Start and Finish Your Thesis, Book, or Article*. 3rd ed. University of Chicago Press, 2020.

Belcher, Wendy Laura. *Writing Your Journal Article in 12 Weeks: A Guide to Academic Publishing Success*. 2nd ed. University of Chicago Press, 2019.

Bell, Susan. *The Artful Edit: On the Practice of Editing Yourself*. W. W. Norton, 2007.

Booth, Wayne C., Gregory G. Colomb, Joseph M. Williams, Joseph Bizup, and William T. FitzGerald. *The Craft of Research*. 5th ed. University of Chicago Press, 2024.

Gastel, Barbara, and Robert A. Day. *How to Write and Publish a Scientific Paper*. 9th ed. Greenwood, 2022.

Gerard, Philip. *The Art of Creative Research: A Field Guide for Writers*. University of Chicago Press, 2017.

Germano, William. *From Dissertation to Book*. 2nd ed. University of Chicago Press, 2013.

Germano, William. *On Revision: The Only Writing That Counts*. University of Chicago Press, 2021.

Ghodsee, Kristen. *From Notes to Narrative: Writing Ethnographies That Everyone Can Read*. University of Chicago Press, 2016.

Graff, Gerald, Cathy Birkenstein, and Russel Durst. *"They Say / I Say": The Moves That Matter in Academic Writing*. With Laura J. Panning Davis. 5th ed. W. W. Norton, 2021.

Greene, Anne E. *Writing Science in Plain English*. University of Chicago Press, 2013.

Harnby, Louise. *Editing Fiction at Sentence Level: A Guide for Beginning and Developing Writers*. Published by the author, 2020.

Hart, Jack. *Storycraft: The Complete Guide to Writing Narrative Nonfiction*. 2nd ed. University of Chicago Press, 2021.

Hart, Jack. *Wordcraft: The Complete Guide to Clear, Powerful Writing*. University of Chicago Press, 2021.

Jensen, Joli. *Write No Matter What: Advice for Academics*. University of Chicago Press, 2017.

Kidder, Tracy, and Richard Todd. *Good Prose: The Art of Nonfiction*. Random House, 2013.

Lamott, Anne. *Bird by Bird: Some Instructions on Writing and Life*. Anchor Books, 1995.

Lanham, Richard A. *Revising Prose*. 5th ed. Pearson Longman, 2007.

Lerner, Betsy. *The Forest for the Trees: An Editor's Advice to Writers*. Rev. ed. Riverhead Books, 2010.

Lipson, Charles. *How to Write a BA Thesis: A Practical Guide from Your First Ideas to Your Finished Paper*. 2nd ed. University of Chicago Press, 2018.

Luey, Beth, ed. *Revising Your Dissertation: Advice from Leading Editors*. Updated ed. University of California Press, 2007.

MacLeod, Lorisia. James Smith Cree Nation. "More than Personal Communication: Templates for Citing Indigenous Elders and Knowledge Keepers." *KULA: Knowledge Creation, Dissemination, and Preservation Studies* 5, no. 1 (2021). https://doi.org/10.18357/kula.135.

McCloskey, Deirdre Nansen. *Economical Writing: Thirty-Five Rules for Clear and Persuasive Prose*. 3rd ed. University of Chicago Press, 2019.

McMillan, Victoria E. *Writing Papers in the Biological Sciences*. Library consultant, Margaret Smith. 7th ed. Bedford / St. Martin's, 2021.

Miller, Jane E. *The Chicago Guide to Writing About Multivariate Analysis*. 2nd ed. University of Chicago Press, 2013.

Miller, Jane E. *The Chicago Guide to Writing About Numbers*. 2nd ed. University of Chicago Press, 2015.

Montgomery, Scott L. *The Chicago Guide to Communicating Science*. 2nd ed. University of Chicago Press, 2017.

Pinker, Steven. *The Sense of Style: The Thinking Person's Guide to Writing in the 21st Century*. Viking, 2014.

Pyne, Stephen J. *Voice and Vision: A Guide to Writing History and Other Serious Nonfiction*. Harvard University Press, 2009.

Stein, Arlene, and Jessie Daniels. *Going Public: A Guide for Social Scientists*. University of Chicago Press, 2017.

Sword, Helen. *Stylish Academic Writing*. Harvard University Press, 2012.

Sword, Helen. *The Writer's Diet: A Guide to Fit Prose*. University of Chicago Press, 2016.

Trimble, John R. *Writing with Style: Conversations on the Art of Writing*. 3rd ed. Pearson, 2010.

Zeiger, Mimi. *Essentials of Writing Biomedical Research Papers*. 2nd ed. McGraw-Hill, 2000.

Zinsser, William. *On Writing Well: The Classic Guide to Writing Nonfiction*. 30th anniversary ed. HarperCollins, 2006.

## 1.4 *Inclusive Language*

American Psychological Association. "Disability." APA Style. https://apastyle.apa.org/style-grammar-guidelines/bias-free-language/disability.

American Psychological Association. *Inclusive Language Guide*. 2nd ed. APA, 2023.

Baron, Dennis. *What's Your Pronoun? Beyond He and She*. Liveright, 2020.

"Bias-Free Language Guidelines." Chapter 5 in *Publication Manual of the American Psychological Association*, 7th ed. APA, 2020.

*GLAAD Media Reference Guide*. 11th ed. Continually updated. https://www.glaad.org/reference.

Gussine Wilkins, Ebonye. *Respectful Querying with NUANCE*. EFA Booklet. Editorial Freelancers Association Publications, 2020.

Kanigel, Rachele, ed. *The Diversity Style Guide*. Wiley-Blackwell, 2019. https://www.diversitystyleguide.com/.

Kapitan, Alex. "On 'Person-First Language': It's Time to Actually Put the Person First." *Radical Copyeditor*, July 3, 2017. https://radicalcopyeditor.com/2017/07/03/person-centered-language/.

Linguistic Society of America. "Guidelines for Inclusive Language." LSA, 2016. https://www.linguisticsociety.org/resource/guidelines-inclusive-language.

National Center on Disability and Journalism. *Disability Language Style Guide*. Walter Cronkite School of Journalism and Mass Communication, Arizona State University. https://ncdj.org/style-guide/.

Omar, Renée. *Editing for Sensitivity, Diversity, and Inclusion: A Guide for Professional Editors*. 2nd ed. Cambridge University Press, 2023.

"Principles of Inclusive Language." Chapter 3 in *MLA Handbook*, 9th ed. Modern Language Association of America, 2021.

Smith, Christen A., founder. Cite Black Women. https://www.citeblackwomen collective.org/.

*Style Guide*. Trans Journalists Association. https://transjournalists.org/style -guide/.

Wamsley, Laurel. "A Guide to Gender Identity Terms." *NPR News*, June 2, 2021. https://www.wbur.org/npr/996319297/gender-identity-pronouns-expression -guide-lgbtq.

Yin, Karen, ed. *Conscious Style Guide*. https://consciousstyleguide.com/.

Yin, Karen. *The Conscious Style Guide: A Flexible Approach to Language That Includes, Respects, and Empowers*. Little, Brown Spark, 2024.

## 2 PUBLISHING

### 2.1 *Manuscript Editing and Proofreading*

ACES: The Society for Editing (US). https://aceseditors.org/.

Anderson, Laura. *McGraw-Hill's Proofreading Handbook*. 2nd ed. McGraw-Hill, 2006.

Borel, Brooke. *The Chicago Guide to Fact-Checking*. 2nd ed. University of Chicago Press, 2023.

Bűky, Erika, Marilyn Schwartz, and Amy Einsohn. *The Copyeditor's Workbook: Exercises and Tips for Honing Your Editorial Judgment*. University of California Press, 2019.

Butcher, Judith, Caroline Drake, and Maureen Leach. *Butcher's Copy-Editing: The Cambridge Handbook for Editors, Copy-Editors, and Proofreaders*. 4th ed. Cambridge University Press, 2006. https://doi.org/10.1017/CBO9780511482106.

CIEP: Chartered Institute of Editing and Proofreading (UK). https://www.ciep .uk/.

Editors of Color Database. A project of *Conscious Style Guide*. https://editorsof color.com/.

EFA: Editorial Freelancers Association (US). https://www.the-efa.org/.

Einsohn, Amy, and Marilyn Schwartz. *The Copyeditor's Handbook: A Guide for Book Publishing and Corporate Communications*. 4th ed. University of California Press, 2019.

Judd, Karen. *Copyediting: A Practical Guide*. 3rd ed. Crisp Learning, 2001.

Norris, Mary. *Between You & Me: Confessions of a Comma Queen*. W. W. Norton, 2015.

Norton, Scott. *Developmental Editing: A Handbook for Freelancers, Authors, and Publishers*. 2nd ed. University of Chicago Press, 2023.

Saller, Carol Fisher. *The Subversive Copy Editor: Advice from Chicago (or, How to Negotiate Good Relationships with Your Writers, Your Colleagues, and Yourself)*. 2nd ed. University of Chicago Press, 2016.

Schneider, Amy J. *The Chicago Guide to Copyediting Fiction*. University of Chicago Press, 2023.

Stainton, Elsie Myers. *The Fine Art of Copyediting*. 2nd ed. Columbia University Press, 2002.

University of Chicago Press Editorial Staff. *But Can I Start a Sentence with "But"? Advice from the Chicago Style Q&A*. With a foreword by Carol Fisher Saller. University of Chicago Press, 2016.

## 2.2 *Illustrations*

Briscoe, Mary Helen. *Preparing Scientific Illustrations: A Guide to Better Posters, Presentations, and Publications*. 2nd ed. Springer-Verlag, 1996. https://doi.org/10.1007/978-1-4612-3986-4.

Frankel, Felice C. *The Visual Elements—Design: A Handbook for Communicating Science and Engineering*. University of Chicago Press, 2024.

Frankel, Felice C. *The Visual Elements—Photography: A Handbook for Communicating Science and Engineering*. University of Chicago Press, 2023.

Healy, Kieran. *Data Visualization: A Practical Introduction*. Princeton University Press, 2019.

Monmonier, Mark. *Mapping It Out: Expository Cartography for the Humanities and Social Sciences*. University of Chicago Press, 1993.

Ross, Ted. *The Art of Music Engraving and Processing: A Complete Manual, Reference, and Text Book on Preparing Music for Reproduction and Print*. Hansen Books, 1970.

Swan, Ann. *Botanical Portraits with Colored Pencils*. Barron's Educational Series, 2010.

Tufte, Edward R. *Envisioning Information*. Graphics Press, 1990.

Tufte, Edward R. *The Visual Display of Quantitative Information*. 2nd ed. Graphics Press, 2001.

Tufte, Edward R. *Visual Explanations: Images and Quantities, Evidence and Narrative*. Graphics Press, 1997.

Zweifel, Frances W. *A Handbook of Biological Illustration*. 2nd ed. University of Chicago Press, 1988.

## 2.3 *Rights and Permissions*

Aufderheide, Patricia, and Peter Jaszi. *Reclaiming Fair Use: How to Put Balance Back in Copyright*. 2nd ed. University of Chicago Press, 2018.

Bielstein, Susan M. *Permissions, a Survival Guide: Blunt Talk About Art as Intellectual Property*. University of Chicago Press, 2006.

Crews, Kenneth D. *Copyright and Your Dissertation or Thesis: Ownership, Fair Use, and Your Rights and Responsibilities*. ProQuest, 2013. https://pq-static-content.proquest.com/collateral/media2/documents/copyright_dissthesis_ownership.pdf.

Fischer, Mark A., E. Gabriel Perle, and John Taylor Williams. *Perle, Williams & Fischer on Publishing Law*. 4th ed. Wolters Kluwer, 2013. Annual loose-leaf updates.

Fishman, Stephen. *The Copyright Handbook: What Every Writer Needs to Know*. 14th ed. Nolo, 2021.

Goldstein, Paul. *Goldstein on Copyright*. 3rd ed. Wolters Kluwer, 2005. Loose-leaf updates.

Goldstein, Paul, and P. Bernt Hugenholtz. *International Copyright: Principles, Law, and Practice*. 4th ed. Oxford, 2019.

Kaufman, Roy S. *Publishing Forms and Contracts*. Oxford University Press, 2008.

Nimmer, Melville, and Paul Edward Gellner, eds. *International Copyright Law and Practice*. LexisNexis Matthew Bender, 2004. Loose-leaf updates.

Nimmer, Melville, Paul Marcus, David A. Myers, and David Nimmer. *Cases and Materials on Copyright and Other Aspects of Entertainment Litigation, Including Unfair Competition, Defamation, Privacy*. 8th ed. LexisNexis, 2012.

Nimmer, Melville, and David Nimmer. *Nimmer on Copyright*. Rev. ed. 11 vols. LexisNexis Matthew Bender, 2005. Loose-leaf updates.

Patry, William F. *The Fair Use Privilege in Copyright Law*. 2nd ed. Bureau of National Affairs, 1995.

Patry, William F. *Moral Panics and the Copyright Wars*. Oxford University Press, 2009.

Patry, William F. *Patry on Copyright*. 8 vols. Thomson/West, 2007–. Loose-leaf updates.

Strong, William S. *The Copyright Book: A Practical Guide*. 6th ed. MIT Press, 2014.

Suber, Peter. *Open Access*. MIT Press, 2012. https://cyber.law.harvard.edu/hoap/Open_Access_(the_book).

## 2.4 *Mathematics*

*Concise Dictionary of Mathematics*. Edited by Richard Earl and James Nicholson. 6th ed. Oxford University Press, 2021.

Gowers, Timothy, ed. *The Princeton Companion to Mathematics*. Princeton University Press, 2008.

Henderson, Lori. "Mathematics." Section 5.4.2 in *ACS Guide to Scholarly Communication*. ACS Publications, 2020. https://doi.org/10.1021/acsguide.50402.

Higham, Nicholas J. *Handbook of Writing for the Mathematical Sciences*. 3rd ed. Society for Industrial and Applied Mathematics, 2019.

Knuth, Donald E. *The TeXbook*. Illustrations by Duane Bibby. Addison-Wesley, 1986.

Lamport, Leslie. *LaTeX: A Document Preparation System; User's Guide and Reference Manual*. 2nd ed. Addison-Wesley, 1999.

The LaTeX Project. Includes LaTeX software and documentation. https://www.latex-project.org/.

Letourneau, Mary, and Jennifer Wright Sharp. *AMS Style Guide: Journals*. American Mathematical Society, 2017. https://www.ams.org/publications/authors/AMS-StyleGuide-online.pdf.

Mittelbach, Frank, and Michel Goossens. *The LaTeX Companion*. 2nd ed. Addison-Wesley, 2004.

Oetiker, Tobias, Hubert Partl, Irene Hyna, and Elisabeth Schlegl. *The Not So Short Guide to LaTeX 2ε*. Version 6.4, 2021. https://mirrors.rit.edu/CTAN/info/lshort/english/lshort.pdf.

Paulos, John Allen. *Innumeracy: Mathematical Illiteracy and Its Consequences*. Hill and Wang, 2001.

*SI Brochure: The International System of Units (SI)*. 9th ed. Bureau International des Poids et Mesures, 2019. https://www.bipm.org/en/publications/si-brochure.

Swanson, Ellen. *Mathematics into Type*. Updated edition by Arlene O'Sean and Antoinette Schleyer. American Mathematical Society, 1999. https://www.ams.org/arc/styleguide/mit-2.pdf.

Thompson, Ambler, and Barry N. Taylor. *Guide for the Use of the International System of Units (SI)*. National Institute of Standards and Technology, 2008. https://physics.nist.gov/cuu/pdf/sp811.pdf.

## 2.5 *Indexing*

Browne, Glenda, and Jon Jermey. *The Indexing Companion*. Cambridge University Press, 2007.

Cleveland, Donald B., and Ana D. Cleveland. *Introduction to Indexing and Abstracting*. 4th ed. Libraries Unlimited, 2013.

Fetters, Linda K. *Handbook of Indexing Techniques: A Guide for Beginning Indexers*. 5th ed. Information Today, 2013.

Mulvany, Nancy. *Indexing Books*. 2nd ed. University of Chicago Press, 2005.

Stauber, Do Mi. *Facing the Text: Content and Structure in Book Indexing*. Cedar Row Press, 2004.

Wellisch, Hans H. *Indexing from A to Z*. 2nd ed. H. W. Wilson, 1995.

## 2.6 *Design*

Berne, Debbie. *The Design of Books: An Explainer for Authors, Editors, Agents, and Other Curious Readers*. University of Chicago Press, 2024.

Borsuk, Amaranth. *The Book*. MIT Press, 2018.

Bringhurst, Robert. *The Elements of Typographic Style*. 4th ed. Hartley and Marks, 2013.

Craig, James, and Irene Korol Scala. *Designing with Type: The Essential Guide to Typography*. 5th ed. Watson-Guptill, 2006.

Dowding, Geoffrey. *Finer Points in the Spacing and Arrangement of Type*. Rev. ed. Hartley and Marks, 1995.

Duckett, Jon. *HTML and CSS: Design and Build Websites*. Wiley, 2011.

Felici, James. *The Complete Manual of Typography: A Guide to Setting Perfect Type*. 2nd ed. Adobe Press, 2011.

Gill, Eric. *An Essay on Typography*. 1931; repr., Penguin, 2013.

Hendel, Richard. *Aspects of Contemporary Book Design*. University of Iowa Press, 2013.

Hendel, Richard. *On Book Design*. Yale University Press, 1998.

Houston, Keith. *Shady Characters: The Secret Life of Punctuation, Symbols, and Other Typographical Marks*. W. W. Norton, 2013.

Johnston, Edward. *Writing and Illuminating and Lettering*. 1946; repr., Dover, 1995.

Lupton, Ellen. *Thinking with Type: A Critical Guide for Designers, Writers, Editors, and Students*. 3rd ed. Princeton Architectural Press, 2024.

Tschichold, Jan. *The New Typography*. New ed. Translated by Ruari McLean. With a foreword by Richard Hendel and an introduction by Robin Kinross. University of California Press, 2006.

## 2.7 *Accessibility*

"Alternative Text." WebAIM. https://webaim.org/techniques/alttext/.

DAISY Consortium. Accessible Publishing Knowledge Base. https://kb.daisy.org/publishing/docs/.

DAISY Consortium. Inclusive Publishing. https://inclusivepublishing.org/.

*EPUB Accessibility 1.1*. Edited by Matt Garrish, George Kerscher, Charles LaPierre, Gregorio Pellegrino, and Avneesh Singh. W3C Recommendation, May 25, 2023. https://www.w3.org/TR/epub-a11y-11/.

Gilbert, Regine M. *Inclusive Design for a Digital World: Designing with Accessibility in Mind*. Apress, 2019.

Orme, Richard, host. "Describing Images in Publications—Guidance, Best Practices and the Promise of Technology." Webinar, DAISY Consortium, June 17, 2020. https://daisy.org/news-events/articles/describing-images-in-publications-w/.

Rosen, Stephanie. Describing Visual Resources Toolkit: Describing Visual Resources for Accessibility in Arts & Humanities Publications. https://describingvisualresources.org/.

W3C Web Accessibility Initiative. World Wide Web Consortium. https://www.w3.org/WAI/.

## 2.8 *Production*

Berger, Sidney E. *Rare Books and Special Collections*. American Library Association, 2014.

*The Columbia Guide to Digital Publishing*. Edited by William E. Kasdorf. Columbia University Press, 2003.

Eckersley, Richard, Richard Angstadt, Charles M. Ellertson, Richard Hendel, Naomi B. Pascal, and Anita Walker Scott. *Glossary of Typesetting Terms*. University of Chicago Press, 1994.

*EPUB 3 Overview*. Edited by Matt Garrish and Ivan Herman. W3C Group Note. Continually updated. https://www.w3.org/TR/epub-overview-33/.

Friedl, Jeffrey E. F. *Mastering Regular Expressions*. 3rd ed. O'Reilly, 2006.

Glaister, Geoffrey Ashall. *Encyclopedia of the Book*. 2nd ed. Oak Knoll Press, 2001.

Johnson, Arthur W. *The Thames and Hudson Manual of Bookbinding*. Thames and Hudson, 1981.

Lee, Marshall. *Bookmaking: Editing, Design, Production*. 3rd ed. Norton, 2004.

National Information Standards Organization. *Journal Article Versions (JAV): Recommendations of the NISO/ALPSP JAV Technical Working Group*. Proposed standard NISO RP-8. In partnership with the Association of Learned and Professional Society Publishers. April 2008. https://doi.org/10.3789/niso-rp-8-2008.

*Pocket Pal: A Graphic Arts Production Handbook*. 21st ed. International Paper, 2020.

Register, Renée, and Thad McIlroy. *The Metadata Handbook: A Book Publisher's Guide to Creating and Distributing Metadata for Print and Ebooks*. 2nd ed. DataCurate, 2015.

Rogondino, Michael, and Pat Rogondino. *Process Color Manual: 24,000 CMYK Combinations for Design, Prepress, and Printing*. Chronicle Books, 2000.

*The Unicode Standard*. Unicode Consortium. Continually updated. https://www.unicode.org/versions/latest/.

World Wide Web Consortium. *Extensible Markup Language (XML) 1.1.* 2nd ed. Edited by Tim Bray, Jean Paoli, C. M. Sperberg-McQueen, Eve Maler, François Yergeau, and John Cowan. W3C Recommendation, August 16, 2006. https://www.w3.org/TR/xml11/.

XML.com. Textuality Services. https://www.xml.com/. *See also* World Wide Web Consortium, *Extensible Markup Language*.

## 2.9 *The Publishing Industry*

Brenner, Erin. *The Chicago Guide for Freelance Editors: How to Take Care of Your Business, Your Clients, and Yourself from Start-Up to Sustainability*. University of Chicago Press, 2024.

Eckstut, Arielle, and David Henry Sterry. *The Essential Guide to Getting Your Book Published*. Workman Publishing, 2015.

Friedman, Jane. *The Business of Being a Writer*. University of Chicago Press, 2018.

Germano, William. *Getting It Published: A Guide for Scholars and Anyone Else Serious About Serious Books*. 3rd ed. University of Chicago Press, 2016.

Ginna, Peter, ed. *What Editors Do: The Art, Craft, and Business of Book Editing*. University of Chicago Press, 2017.

Greco, Albert N. *The Book Publishing Industry*. 3rd ed. Routledge, 2013.

*ILMP (International Literary Market Place)*. Information Today. Published annually. Also available at https://books.infotoday.com/directories/ilmp.shtml.

*Journal of Electronic Publishing*. Published quarterly by Michigan Publishing, University of Michigan Library. https://journals.publishing.umich.edu/jep/.

*Journal of Scholarly Publishing*. Published quarterly by the University of Toronto Press. https://www.utpjournals.press/loi/jsp.

Kurowski, Travis, Wayne Miller, and Kevin Prufer, eds. *Literary Publishing in the Twenty-First Century*. Milkweed Editions, 2016.

Levine, Mark. *The Fine Print of Self-Publishing: A Primer on Contracts, Printing Costs, Royalties, Distribution, Ebooks, and Marketing*. 6th ed. North Loop Books, 2016.

*LMP (Literary Market Place)*. Information Today. Published annually. Also available at https://books.infotoday.com/directories/lmp.shtml.

Luey, Beth. *Handbook for Academic Authors*. 6th ed. Cambridge University Press, 2022.

Portwood-Stacer, Laura. *The Book Proposal Book: A Guide for Scholarly Authors*. Princeton University Press, 2021.

Rabiner, Susan, and Alfred Fortunato. *Thinking Like Your Editor: How to Write Great Serious Nonfiction—and Get It Published*. W. W. Norton, 2002.

Striphas, Ted. *The Late Age of Print: Everyday Book Culture from Consumerism to Control*. Columbia University Press, 2009.

Suzanne, Claudia. *This Business of Books: A Complete Overview of the Industry from Concept Through Sales*. 5th ed. Published by the author, 2016.

Thompson, John B. *Book Wars: The Digital Revolution in Publishing*. Polity, 2021.

Thompson, John B. *Merchants of Culture: The Publishing Business in the Twenty-First Century*. 2nd ed. Plume, 2012.

# 3 DICTIONARIES

## 3.1 *English Dictionaries*

*American Heritage Dictionary of the English Language*. 5th ed. 50th Anniversary Printing. Collins Reference, 2018. Also available at https://www.ahdictionary.com/.

Barber, Katherine, ed. *Canadian Oxford Dictionary*. 2nd ed. Oxford University Press, 2004. https://doi.org/10.1093/acref/9780195418163.001.0001.

*Concise Oxford English Dictionary*. 12th ed. Oxford University Press, 2011.

*Historical Thesaurus of English*. 2nd ed. University of Glasgow, 2020. https://ht.ac.uk/.

*Merriam-Webster Dictionary*. Continues *Merriam-Webster's Collegiate Dictionary*, 11th ed. (first published in 2003). Continually updated at https://www.merriam-webster.com/.

*Merriam-Webster Unabridged*. Continues *Webster's Third New International Dictionary of the English Language, Unabridged* (first published in 1961). Continually updated at https://unabridged.merriam-webster.com/.

*Merriam-Webster's Collegiate Thesaurus*. 2nd ed. Merriam-Webster, 2019.

Moore, Bruce, ed. *Australian Oxford Dictionary*. 2nd ed. Oxford University Press, 2004. https://doi.org/10.1093/acref/9780195517965.001.0001.

*New Oxford American Dictionary*. 3rd ed. Edited by Angus Stevenson and Christine A. Lindberg. Oxford University Press, 2010. https://doi.org/10.1093/acref/9780195392883.001.0001.

*Oxford English Dictionary*. Continues *Oxford English Dictionary*, 2nd ed., 20 vols. (first published in 1989). Continually updated at https://www.oed.com/.

*Random House Unabridged Dictionary*. 2nd ed. Random House Reference, 1994. Updated and expanded at https://www.dictionary.com/.

*Roget's II: The New Thesaurus*. 3rd ed. Houghton Mifflin, 1995; repr., 2009.

Sollars, Michael D. *Dictionary of Literary Characters*. 5 vols. Facts on File, 2010.

*Webster's New World College Dictionary*. 5th ed. Houghton Mifflin Harcourt, 2016.

*Webster's Third New International Dictionary of the English Language*. See *Merriam-Webster Unabridged*.

*Wiktionary: The Free Dictionary*. Wikimedia Foundation. https://www.wiktionary.org/.

## 3.2 *Bilingual Dictionaries*

*ABC Chinese–English Comprehensive Dictionary*. Edited by John DeFrancis. University of Hawai'i Press, 2003.

*Cassell's Italian Dictionary*. Compiled by Piero Rebora with the assistance of Francis M. Guercio and Arthur L. Hayward. John Wiley, 1994.

*Compact Oxford Italian Dictionary*. Edited by Pat Bulhosen, Francesca Logi, and Loredana Riu. Oxford University Press, 2013.

*Larousse Unabridged French Dictionary: French–English, English–French*. Edited by Faye Carney. Larousse, 2010.

*Minjung's Essence English–Korean Dictionary*. 11th ed. Hollym International, 2015.

*Oxford Arabic Dictionary: Arabic–English, English–Arabic*. Edited by Tressy Arts. Oxford University Press, 2014.

*Oxford German Dictionary: German–English, English–German*. 3rd ed. Edited by Werner Scholze-Stubenrecht, J. B. Sykes, M. Clark, and O. Thyen. Oxford University Press, 2008.

*Oxford Hindi–English Dictionary*. Edited by R. S. McGregor. Oxford University Press, 1993.

*Oxford Latin Dictionary*. 2nd ed. Edited by P. G. W. Glare. 2 vols. Oxford University Press, 2012.

*Oxford Russian Dictionary*. 4th ed. Edited by Marcus Wheeler, Boris Unbegaun, Paul Falla, and Della Thompson. Oxford University Press, 2007.

*Oxford Spanish Dictionary*. 4th ed. Edited by Beatriz Galimberti Jarman, Roy Russell, Nicholas Rollin, and Carol Styles Carvajal. Oxford University Press, 2008.

*Oxford-Hachette French Dictionary*. 4th ed. Edited by Marie-Hélène Corréard et al. Oxford University Press, 2007.

*Pocket Kenkyusha Japanese Dictionary*. New ed. Edited by Shigeru Takebayashi. Oxford University Press, 2007.

*The University of Chicago Spanish–English Dictionary*. 6th ed. Edited by David Pharies. University of Chicago Press, 2012.

## 3.3 *Medical and Scientific Dictionaries*

*A Dictionary of Biology*. 8th ed. Edited by Robert Hine. Oxford University Press, 2019. https://doi.org/10.1093/acref/9780198821489.001.0001.

*A Dictionary of Chemistry*. 8th ed. Edited by Jonathan Law and Richard Rennie. Oxford University Press, 2020. https://doi.org/10.1093/acref/9780198841227.001.0001.

*A Dictionary of Mechanical Engineering*. 2nd ed. Edited by Marcel Escudier and

Tony Atkins. Oxford University Press, 2019. https://doi.org/10.1093/acref/9780198832102.001.0001.

*A Dictionary of Physics*. 8th ed. Edited by Richard Rennie and Jonathan Law. Oxford University Press, 2020. https://doi.org/10.1093/acref/9780198821472.001.0001.

*Dorland's Illustrated Medical Dictionary*. 33rd ed. Elsevier, 2020. Also available at https://www.dorlandsonline.com/.

*Oxford Dictionary of Science*. 7th ed. Edited by Jonathan Law. Oxford University Press, 2017.

*Stedman's Medical Dictionary*. 28th ed. Lippincott Williams & Wilkins, 2006.

*USP Dictionary of USAN and International Drug Names*. US Pharmacopeial Convention. Revised annually. Available at https://www.usp.org/products/usp-dictionary.

## 4 GENERAL REFERENCE

### 4.1 *Biography*

*American Men and Women of Science*. 41st ed. K. Lee Lerner, adviser. Gale, 2023.

*American National Biography*. Oxford University Press, 2000–. https://www.anb.org/.

*Burke's Peerage and Baronetage*. 107th ed. Multiple vols. Burke's Peerage, 1826–. Also available, with additional related resources, at https://www.burkespeerage.com/.

*Canadian Who's Who*. Grey House Publishing Canada, 1910–. https://canadianwhoswho.ca/.

*Chambers Biographical Dictionary*. 9th ed. Chambers, 2011.

*Concise Dictionary of National Biography: From Earliest Times to 1985*. 3 vols. Oxford University Press, 1992.

*Dictionary of American Biography*. 11 vols. Scribner's, 1995. Supplements. Succeeded by *American National Biography*.

*Dictionary of Canadian Biography*. 14 vols. University of Toronto / Université Laval, 1966–. Supplements. Continued, with updates, at http://www.biographi.ca/.

*A Dictionary of Scientists*. Oxford University Press, 1999. Published online 2003. https://doi.org/10.1093/acref/9780192800862.001.0001.

*Grove Music Online*. See *The New Grove Dictionary of Music and Musicians*.

*The International Who's Who*. Europa/Routledge, 1935–. Published annually. Also available at https://www.worldwhoswho.com/.

*Marquis Who's Who*. Marquis Who's Who, 1898–. Continually updated. https://www.marquiswhoswho.com/.

*Merriam-Webster's Biographical Dictionary*. Merriam-Webster, 1995. Continued by the biographical entries in *Merriam-Webster Dictionary* and *Merriam-Webster Unabridged* (bibliog. 3.1).

*The New Grove Dictionary of Music and Musicians*. 2nd ed. 29 vols. Edited by Stanley Sadie. Grove, 2001. Continued, as *Grove Music Online*, at https://www.oxfordmusiconline.com/.

*The New York Times*. Obituaries. https://www.nytimes.com/section/obituaries/.

*Oxford Dictionary of National Biography*. 60 vols. Prepared under various editors. Oxford University Press, 1885–2004. Continued at https://www.oxforddnb.com/.

Thomson, David. *The New Biographical Dictionary of Film*. 6th ed. Knopf, 2014.

*Who's Who*. A&C Black, 1849–. Published annually. Also available at https://www.ukwhoswho.com/.

*Who's Who in America*. Marquis Who's Who, 1899–. Published biennially. See also *Marquis Who's Who*.

## 4.2 *Geography*

Canadian Geographical Names. Geographical Names Board of Canada, Natural Resources Canada. Continually updated. https://www.nrcan.gc.ca/maps-tools-and-publications/maps/geographical-names-canada/10786.

*Columbia Gazetteer of the World*. 2nd ed. Edited by Saul B. Cohen. Columbia University Press, 2008. Also available at http://www.columbiagazetteer.org/.

Everett-Heath, John. *Concise Oxford Dictionary of World Place Names*. 6th ed. Oxford, 2020. https://doi.org/10.1093/acref/9780191905636.001.0001.

Geographic Names Server (GNS). National Geospatial-Intelligence Agency. Continually updated. https://geonames.nga.mil/geonames/GNSHome/.

Getty Thesaurus of Geographic Names Online. Getty Research Institute. J. Paul Getty Trust. Continually updated. https://www.getty.edu/research/tools/vocabularies/tgn/.

Mayhew, Susan. *A Dictionary of Geography*. 5th ed. Oxford University Press, 2015. https://doi.org/10.1093/acref/9780199680856.001.0001.

*Merriam-Webster's Geographical Dictionary*. 3rd ed. Merriam-Webster, 1997. Continued by the geographic entries in *Merriam-Webster Dictionary* and *Merriam-Webster Unabridged* (bibliog. 3.1).

*Oxford Atlas of the World*. Oxford University Press, 1992–. Updated annually.

*The Times Comprehensive Atlas of the World*. 15th ed. Times Books UK, 2018.

United States Board on Geographic Names. US Department of the Interior and US Geological Survey. Continually updated. https://www.usgs.gov/us-board-on-geographic-names.

*The World Factbook*. Central Intelligence Agency (US). Continually updated. https://www.cia.gov/the-world-factbook/.

## 4.3 *Encyclopedias*

*The Canadian Encyclopedia*. Historica Canada. https://www.thecanadianencyclopedia.ca/.

*The New Encyclopaedia Britannica*. 15th ed. 32 vols. Encyclopaedia Britannica, 2010. Final print version. Continued online, as *Britannica*, at https://www.britannica.com/.

*Wikipedia: The Free Encyclopedia*. Wikimedia Foundation. https://www.wikipedia.org/.

## 4.4 *Almanacs and Yearbooks*

*Canadian Almanac and Directory*. Grey House Publishing Canada, 1847–. Published annually.

*The Europa World of Learning*. Europa/Routledge, 1947–. Published annually. Also available at https://www.worldoflearning.com/.

*Europa World Year Book*. Europa/Routledge, 1926–. Published annually. Also available at https://www.europaworld.com/.

*The Statesman's Yearbook*. Palgrave Macmillan, 1864–. Published annually. Also available at https://link.springer.com/referencework/10.1057/978-1-349-95972-3.

*Whitaker's Almanack*. J. Whitaker & Sons / Stationery Office / Bloomsbury / Rebellion, 1868–. Published annually.

*World Almanac and Book of Facts*. World Almanac Books, 1868–. Published annually.

## 4.5 *Guides to Public Documents*

*Catalog of U.S. Government Publications*. Government Publishing Office. https://catalog.gpo.gov/.

*Citing Records in the National Archives of the United States*. General Information Leaflet 17. National Archives and Records Administration, 2010. https://www.archives.gov/publications/general-info-leaflets/17-citing-records.html.

*Guide to the Contents of the Public Record Office* (UK). 3 vols. Her Majesty's Stationery Office, 1963–68.

*Guide to U.S. Government Publications*. Edited by Donna Batten. Formerly known as *Andriot*. Gale. Updated annually.

Rodgers, Frank. *A Guide to British Government Publications*. H. W. Wilson, 1980.

## 4.6 *Quotations and Trivia*

Bartlett, John. *Bartlett's Familiar Quotations: A Collection of Passages, Phrases, and Proverbs Traced to Their Sources in Ancient and Modern Literature*. 19th ed. Edited by Geoffrey O'Brien. Little, Brown, 2022.

*The Oxford Dictionary of Quotations*. 8th ed. Edited by Elizabeth Knowles. Oxford University Press, 2014. https://doi.org/10.1093/acref/9780199668700.001.0001.

Schott, Ben. *Schott's Original Miscellany*. Bloomsbury, 2003.

Shapiro, Fred R., ed. *The New Yale Book of Quotations*. With a foreword by Louis Menand. Yale University Press, 2021.

## 4.7 *Abbreviations*

Abbreviations.com. STANDS4 Network. Continually updated. https://www.abbreviations.com/.

*Acronyms, Initialisms & Abbreviations Dictionary: A Guide to Acronyms, Abbreviations, Contractions, Alphabetic Symbols, and Similar Condensed Appellations*. 55th ed. 11 vols. Gale, 2021.

Davis, Neil M. *Medical Abbreviations: 32,000 Conveniences at the Expense of Communication and Safety*. 16th ed. Neil M. Davis Associates, 2019.

*Department of Defense Dictionary of Military and Associated Terms*. US Joint Chiefs of Staff. Available at https://irp.fas.org/doddir/dod/dictionary.pdf.

*Dorland's Dictionary of Medical Acronyms and Abbreviations*. 7th ed. Elsevier, 2015.

International Organization for Standardization. *Information and Documentation—Rules for the Abbreviation of Title Words and Titles of Publications*. ISO 4:1997.

Molloy, Mike, founder. Acronym Finder. Continually updated. https://www.acronymfinder.com/.

Vance, Burt. *A Dictionary of Abbreviations*. Oxford University Press, 2011. https://doi.org/10.1093/acref/9780199698295.001.0001.

*Webster's Guide to Abbreviations*. Merriam-Webster, 1985. Continued by the entries for abbreviations in *Merriam-Webster Dictionary* and *Merriam-Webster Unabridged* (bibliog. 3.1).

# 5 MISCELLANEOUS WORKS CITED IN TEXT

*ALA-LC Romanization Tables: Transliteration Schemes for Non-Roman Scripts*. Approved by the Library of Congress and the American Library Association. https://www.loc.gov/catdir/cpso/roman.html.

Baker-Shenk, Charlotte, and Dennis Cokely. *American Sign Language: A Teacher's Resource Text on Grammar and Culture*. Gallaudet University Press, 1991.

Daniels, Peter T., and William Bright, eds. *The World's Writing Systems*. Oxford University Press, 1996.

Data Citation Synthesis Group. *Joint Declaration of Data Citation Principles*. Edited by M. Martone. FORCE11, 2014. https://doi.org/10.25490/a97f-egyk.

*Duden: Die deutsche Rechtschreibung*. 28th ed. 12 vols. Dudenverlag, 2020.

Gall, Gerald L., F. Pearl Eliadis, and France Allard. *The Canadian Legal System*. 5th ed. Carswell, 2004.

Grevisse, Maurice. *Le bon usage: Grammaire française*. 16th ed. Edited by André Goosse. De Boeck Supérieur, 2016. Also available at https://www.grevisse.fr/ouvrage/9782807300699-le-bon-usage.

HGNC. Database of human gene names. HUGO Gene Nomenclature Committee. https://www.genenames.org/.

*History of Religions*. Journal published quarterly by the University of Chicago Press. https://www.journals.uchicago.edu/toc/hr/current.

*Horticulture*. Magazine published six times a year by Active Interest Media. https://www.hortmag.com/.

*International Code of Nomenclature for Algae, Fungi, and Plants (Shenzhen Code)*. Prepared and edited by Nicholas J. Turland et al. Regnum Vegetabile 159. Koeltz Botanical Books, 2018. https://doi.org/10.12705/Code.2018.

*International Code of Zoological Nomenclature*. 4th ed. International Trust for Zoological Nomenclature, 1999. https://www.iczn.org/the-code/the-code-online/.

*International Journal of Middle East Studies*. Journal published quarterly by Cambridge University Press for the Middle East Studies Association of North America. https://www.cambridge.org/core/journals/international-journal-of-middle-east-studies.

International Telecommunication Union. *Notation for National and International Telephone Numbers, E-Mail Addresses and Web Addresses*. ITU-T Recommendation E.123, February 2, 2001. https://www.itu.int/rec/T-REC-E.123-200102-I/en.

Lesina, Roberto. *Il nuovo manuale di stile*. 2nd ed. Zanichelli, 2009.

Mouse Genome Database. Mouse Genome Informatics. https://www.informatics.jax.org/.

*The Oxford Classical Dictionary*. 4th ed. Edited by Simon Hornblower, Anthony Spawforth, and Esther Eidinow. Oxford University Press, 2012. https://doi.org/10.1093/acref/9780199545568.001.0001.

*Physical Review Letters*. Published weekly by the American Physical Society. https://journals.aps.org/prl/.

Pullum, Geoffrey K., and William A. Ladusaw. *Phonetic Symbol Guide*. 2nd ed. University of Chicago Press, 1996.

Real Academia Española and Asociación de Academias de la Lengua Española. *Diccionario panhispánico de dudas*. RAE/ASALE, 2005. Also available at https://www.rae.es/.

Real Academia Española and Asociación de Academias de la Lengua Española. *Ortografía de la lengua española*. RAE/ASALE, 2010. Also available at https://www.rae.es/.

Thorin, Suzanne E., and Carole Franklin Vidali. *The Acquisition and Cataloging of Music and Sound Recordings: A Glossary*. Music Library Association, 1984.

*Unicode Collation Algorithm*. Unicode Technical Standard No. 10. Edited by Ken Whistler and Markus Scherer. Unicode Consortium. Continually updated. https://www.unicode.org/reports/tr10/.

Valli, Clayton, Ceil Lucas, Kristin J. Mulrooney, and Miako Villanueva. *Linguistics of American Sign Language: An Introduction*. 5th ed. Gallaudet University Press, 2011.

Wertheim, Eric. *The Naval Institute Guide to Combat Fleets of the World: Their Ships, Aircraft, and Systems*. 16th ed. US Naval Institute Press, 2013.

Whitehead, Philip, and Anne Matthewman. *Legal Writing and Research Manual*. 8th ed. LexisNexis Canada, 2018.

Zurick, Tim. *Army Dictionary and Desk Reference*. 4th ed. Stackpole Books, 2010.

# Index

References are to paragraph numbers except where specified as table or figure (fig.).

*The Chicago Manual of Style*

Designed by Isaac Tobin
Typeset by Classic City Composition, Athens, Georgia
Book printed and bound by Sheridan Books, Chelsea, Michigan
Jacket printed by Phoenix Color, Hagerstown, Maryland

Composed in Frank Grießhammer's Source Serif; USWDS Public Sans (Dan Williams, Pablo Impallari, and Rodrigo Fuenzalida), and Isaac Tobin's Seamoss.
Printed on 50# Glatfelter Offset

DISTRIBUTED BY THE CHICAGO DISTRIBUTION CENTER